English Origins of
New England Families

From The New England Historical
and Genealogical Register

English Origins of
*N*EW *E*NGLAND *F*AMILIES

From The New England Historical
and Genealogical Register

Second Series

in Three Volumes

VOLUME II

Selected and Introduced by

GARY BOYD ROBERTS

Baltimore
GENEALOGICAL PUBLISHING CO., INC.
1985

Excerpted and reprinted from *The New England*
Historical and Genealogical Register ©
with added Table of Contents and Index, by
Genealogical Publishing Co., Inc., Baltimore, 1985.
Added matter copyright © 1985 by Genealogical Publishing Co., Inc.
Baltimore, Maryland. All Rights Reserved.
Library of Congress Catalogue Card Number 84-81872
International Standard Book Number, Volume II: 0-8063-1093-6
Set Number: 0-8063-1091-X
Made in the United States of America

Contents

―――――――――――

v

vii

ix

x

NOTES

xv

English Origins of
NEW ENGLAND FAMILIES

From The New England Historical
and Genealogical Register

THE ENGLISH ORIGIN OF
GEORGE GIDDINGS
OF IPSWICH, MASSACHUSETTS

*David L. Greene**

When Minot S. Giddings published his inadequate genealogy, *The Giddings Family. . .* (Hartford, Conn., 1882), nothing was known about the origin of the immigrant, George Giddings of Ipswich, Massachusetts, except that at the age of twenty-five he embarked in April 1635 on the *Planter* with his wife Jane, aged twenty, and various members of her family, all with certificates from the minister of St. Albans, Hertfordshire (John Camden Hotten, ed., *The Original Lists of Persons of Quality. . .* [London, 1874; reprint ed., Baltimore, 1976], 45; "Founders of New England," *Register,* 14 [1860]: 304).

In his posthumous *Topographical Dictionary of 2885 English Emigrants to New England . . .* (Elijah Ellsworth Brownell, ed., [Philadelphia, 1937], 1), Charles Edward Banks states that George Giddings came from Clapham, co. Bedford. The only reference given in Brownell's flawed edition of Colonel Banks's notes—many of which Banks intended only as clues for further research—is "Banks Mss.," probably those at the Library of Congress; Banks's source was almost certainly the St. Albans marriage bond for George Giddinge and Jane Lawrence, which states explicitly that he was from Clapham, co. Bedford. The bond is abstracted below. Apparently nothing further has been published on George Giddings's origin and ancestry.

In this article, we provide George Giddings's ancestry so far as it has been determined from Bedfordshire parish and probate records. Only those wills that clearly refer to his family are transcribed below, but I have examined all sixteenth- and early seventeenth-century Gidding(s), Purrier, and Tilbrooke wills now at the Bedfordshire Record Office. (In early records, the Giddings surname usually did not have the concluding "s.")

*I am indebted to Mrs. Lloyd R. Knauss of Poughkeepsie, New York, who supplied photocopies of the wills of Michael, Catharine, John, and Elizabeth Gidding, and for her kind permission for me to include them in this study; to Mr. John Dorrance Morrell of Brooklyn, New York, for information on the Giddings-Proctor problem and for permission to include the Proctor records he discovered in England; to Dr. Douglas G. Greene of Old Dominion University, Norfolk, Virginia, for providing some of the parish records cited in this paper; to Mr. Douglas Richardson of Bethany, Oklahoma, for reading a draft of this paper and for providing helpful comments; to Mr. Peter Walne, Archivist, Hertfordshire Record Office, County Hall, Hertford, England, for a xeroxed copy of George Giddings's marriage bond and for the marriage record of George "Goodwin" and Jane Lawrence; to Mrs. E. M. Blore of Northampton, England, for abstracting the Gidding, Phage, and Purrier records in the Clapham Manorial Court Rolls; and to Mr. C. J. Pickford, Assistant Archivist, Bedfordshire Record Office, County Hall, Bedford, England, for xeroxed copies of all the Bedfordshire wills cited in this paper except the four supplied by Mrs. Knauss.

The relationship between the Giddings of the Bedfordshire parishes of Clapham and Oakley and the Giddings of Odell and Turvey (both co. Bedford) has not yet been established. John Giddinge of Odell left a will in 1578 (Bedfordshire Record Office, ABP/R 19 f78), Oliver Giddinge of Turvey left one in 1593 (ABP/W 1593/42), and Roger Gydding of Turvey left one in 1600/1 (ABP/W 1600-1/76), all clearly of one family. Odell is about five miles from Turvey, and both parishes are perhaps six miles from Clapham. In addition, Ralph Purrier of Turvey left a will in 1599 mentioning, among others, Elizabeth Gidding, apparently of the Turvey family (ABP/W 1599/125). As we suggest below, it is at least possible that George Giddings's grandfather, Thomas Purrier, was of the Turvey Purriers. We should also mention William Parrier or Purrier of Olney, Buckinghamshire, who immigrated with his wife and children on the *Hopewell* in 1635. William Purrier went to Ipswich, as did George Giddings, and then moved to Salisbury, Massachusetts, and to Southold, Long Island (Hotten, *Original Lists,* 44; Banks, *Topographical Dict.,* 10; "Founders of New England," *Register,* 14 [1860]: 303; "Some Early New York Settlers from New England," *ibid.,* 55 [1901]: 378, 379). Olney is across the Buckinghamshire line from Bedfordshire and about nine miles from Clapham.

Clapham Church was originally a chapel attached to Oakley, and the two parishes have remained closely associated, so much so that in 1627 testimony was taken about whether they were one parish or two. Among parishes of medieval origin, Clapham is unusual in that it originally had no churchyard; its dead were buried at Oakley (*Victoria History of the County of Bedford,* 3 [1912]: 128, 131, 132). The surviving Clapham registers begin in 1696, but fortunately the earlier records from the Bishop's Transcripts have been published. Unless it is stated otherwise, all parish records cited below, including the Bishop's Transcripts for Clapham, are in volume 16 of F. G. Emmison's *Bedfordshire Parish Registers*; all wills cited are at the Bedfordshire Record Office; and the Clapham Manorial Rolls are in the Trevor Wingfield Collection, Bedfordshire Record Office (TW 738 to 755).

We begin this account of George Giddings's ancestry with his grandfather.

1. MICHAEL[1] GIDDING was born probably between 1550 and 1560; he was buried at Oakley, co. Bedford (recorded Clapham), 2 April 1615. His wife CATHARINE was buried at Oakley (recorded Clapham), 14 February 1625/6.

Michael Gidding died testate:*

---

*In transcribing the five wills included in this paper, I have lowered superscript letters to level, rendered the thorn as "th" rather than "y," and silently inserted a minimum of punctuation. Other insertions are in square brackets; they include the addition of letters to words that might be confusing otherwise (e.g., "on[e]"), the enlargement of abbreviations indicated in the original by a horizontal line over part of the word, and a few additions made for clarification.

In the name of god Amen: I michael Gyddyn of clapham in the county of Bedd husbandman being sicke in bodye but of sound minde & memory thankes be gyven unto almightye God doo ordeine & make this my last will & testament in manner & ~~following~~ [sic] forme following, that is to say ffirst I bequeath my soule to God almightye my maker, creator & redeemer trusting by the meryts, death & passion of Jesus christ and by noe other meanes to be saved, and my bodye to be buryed in Okelye churchyard at the discretion of my executors hereunder named. Also I will & bequeath to my sonn John Gyddyns twelve pence of lawful money of England. Also I gyve & bequeath unto Henrye Gyddyns my sonne xijd. Also I gyve & bequeath unto my sonne william Gyddyns o xijd. Also I gyve & bequeath unto Robert Gyddyngs my sonn o xijd. Also I gyve & bequeath unto my sonne James o xijd. Also I gyve & bequeath unto my daughter Jone Savage o xijd. Also I gyve & bequeath unto my daughter Elizabeth o xijd. Also I doo gyve & bequeath unto the three children of my sonn John eche of them iiijd. Also I doo gyve & bequeath unto the fyve children of my son Harrye everye of them iiijd. Also I doo gyve & bequeathe unto the too children of my sonne Robert eche of them o iiijd. Also I doo gyve & bequeath unto my sonn James his childe o iiijd. Also I doo gyve & bequeath unto the three children of my daughter Savage eche of them— iiijd. Also I gyve & bequeath unto my daughter Elizabeth the bedd & bedding whereupon she lyeth & thereunto doth belong; The rest of all my goods & chattles unbequeathed I doo gyve & bequeath them to Caterynne my welbeloved wife and to Richard Gyddyns my sonn whome I make my Executors of this my last will & testament. In witnes whereof I the said michael Gyddyns have hereunto sette my hand the thirtenth day of march in the yere of o[u]r Lord God 1614 [/5] and the twelf yere of the Reigne of o[u]r Sov[er]aigne Lord King James of England, ffrance & Ireland & of Scotland the xlviijth (ABP/W 1615/225).

Michael Gidding signed the will by mark; the witnesses were John ffortdor (?) and John Palmer. The will was proved 17 April 1615. Since he left his grandchildren and all but one of his children only token sums, Michael Gidding had probably provided for most of his family earlier and executed a will to insure that his wife and youngest son would receive whatever property remained at his death.

Catharine Gidding also died testate:

1626 [1625/6]

In they [sic] naime of god amen I cattron gidding of clappam being sick of bodi but perfit in memorie I bequeith my Soule to allmightie god Tristing [sic] in Jesus christ to be saved and I be queith my bodie to be buried in okele church yearde. Item I give and be queith to my Soun William gidding my feather bed and my chest and on[e] littel tabell and on[e] joyned stoule presentli after my deaseise. Item I give and be queith to my daughter Joune Sauidge my best goune and my best hattle[?] and my *presentli after my death* [italicized words interlined and misplaced] bedd, best peticout and on[e] bourde cloth to anna Sauadge the daughter of Joune Sauage which I give presentlie after my deaseise. Item I give unto elizabeth Sauidge on[e] joyned stoule. Item I give unto my Soune Robart gidding—xijd. Item my give unto my Soune Jaimes gidding—xijd. Item I give unto my daughter elizabeth gidding three shetes and too bolsters and too fether pillowes and on[e] couer lede and on[e] blancket and my cowe to be deleuered presentlie after my deaseise and on[e] petecote and my waring neck clothes. Item I

3

give unto elizabeth gidding the daughter of Richard gidding on[e] holone pelo beire. And all my other goodes unbequethed I give unto my Soune Richard gidding, all these gifts being discharged, whome I maike my whole exekttor wheirto I have set my hand the ninth of february (ABP/W 1625/124).

Catharine Gidding signed the will by mark; the witnesses were Ailes [Alice] Negus and Elizabeth Negus. The copy provided me has no date of probate.

Of the eight known children of Michael Gidding, John and Henry were dead by the date that Catharine Gidding wrote her will; she mentioned all the other children. Joan Gidding, who married William Savage on 21 May 1604, was the first of the children to marry. If we assume that she married at a somewhat younger age than her brothers, it is likely that Henry, who also married in 1604, was the oldest child; Joan may have been the second child. Since Catharine called Joan "my daughter," left Joan her best gown, and remembered two of Joan's children in her will (Elizabeth Savage, not specifically called Joan's child in Catharine Gidding's will, is identified as Joan's daughter in the will of Elizabeth Gidding), it seems almost certain that Catharine was Joan's mother, not stepmother, and probable that she was mother of all eight children of Michael Gidding.

Children, order uncertain:

2. i. HENRY[2].
   ii. JOAN, m. at Clapham, 21 May 1604, WILLIAM SAVADG [SAVAGE]. She is mentioned in the will of her mother (1625/6) and in the will of her sister Elizabeth (1630). Both documents mention Joan's daughters, *Anna* (or *Agnes*) and *Elizabeth*; the will of Elizabeth Gidding mentions Joan's three sons, not by name.
3. iii. JOHN.
   iv. ROBERT, dates unknown. Michael Gidding left iiijd (fourpence) to the two children (names not given) of his son Robert; he is mentioned in the will of his mother but not in that of his sister.
   v. WILLIAM, dates unknown. He is mentioned in the will of his father, at which time he apparently had no children. He is included in his mother's will, and his daughter (name not given) is mentioned in the will of Elizabeth Gidding.
   vi. JAMES, dates unknown. He and his child (name not given) are mentioned in the will of his father. He is mentioned in the will of his mother but not in that of his sister. "Jn," son of "Jas Gooddin," bp. at Clapham, 30 Nov. 1634; "Gidding" was sometimes misrecorded as "Goodwin" and its variants, but in this case, I suspect it is a different surname.
   vii. ELIZABETH, bur. at Oakley (recorded Clapham), 30 Dec. 1630, unm. She is mentioned in the wills of her father and mother. Her own brief will is helpful genealogically:
   In the name of God Amen the xxxth day of October A[n]no D[omi]ni 1630 I Elizabeth Gidding of clapham in the county of

4

Bedforde single woman (and in the dioces of lincolne) being sicke in body but whole in mind & of good & pfect remembrance thankes & praise be to almightie god, make & ordaine this my last will and testament, in ma[n]ner & forme following; first I co[m]mend my soule to Almightie god, my creator, redemer, sa[n]ctifier and pseruer [preserver], and my bodie to be buried in the church yard of okeley. Imprimis I give to my two cozens martha Gidding & Rebecca her sister v pounds apeice at my depture out of this life. Ite[m] I give to my brother Robert ffage his sonn Thomas iij pounds of current english money and my cow, at my depture. Item I give to my cozen catharin Gidding & Emm her sister xx shillings apeice at my deperture. Item I give to my sister Joan Savidg x shillings, to her daughter Agnis xx shillings & to her daughter Elizabeth x shillings. Ite[m] I give to my Brother Henry Gidding his iij sons videsint Georg, Robert & Joseph x shilling apeice, at my depture. Ite[m] I give to my sister Savidg her iij sonnes x shillings to be equaly divided amongst them at my depture. Ite[m] I give to my Brother Richard his iiij children xij [probably pence but not so indicated] a peice, at my depture. Ite[m] I give to my Brother williams daughter xijd. Ite[m] I give to my Brother ffage his maide Joan Shemers one shipp. Ite[m] I give to the poore people in clapham v shillings. Ite[m] all the rest of my goods unbequithed, my funerall discharged, I give to my brother ffagge. I make him full Executor. In witnesse where of I have here unto set my hand the day & yeare above written (signed by mark; witnesses were Thomas Chamberlaine and Margart [sic] Bucher; proved 10 Jan. 1630 [/1]) (ABP/W 1630-1/112).

Although Elizabeth Gidding refers to Robert Phage or Fage as "my brother," he was actually the second husband of her brother John's widow, Joan Purrier. Beyond doubt, Elizabeth lived with Robert and Joan (Purrier) (Gidding) Phage.

4.   viii. RICHARD.

2. HENRY[2] GIDDING (*Michael[1]*) was born [say 1580] and buried at Oakley (recorded Clapham), 18 March 1616 [/7]. He married at Oakley, 15 October 1604, ELIZABETH RUSSELL (the published transcript gives his last name as "Gidd[————]"). "Widow Gyddinge," with four acres and one cow, is included in the Clapham Manorial Rolls, 18 January 1620/1. Widow "Elyzabeuth Gydding" is mentioned in the will of Thomas Purrier (1622[/3?]), transcribed below, and she is probably the Elizabeth Gidding who married at Clapham, 22 January 1623 [/4], Henry Lane. A widow Gidding was buried (recorded Clapham) 21 April 1660, but she is probably the widow of Richard Gidding, who died in 1657.

Henry Gidding is mentioned in the will of his father Michael Gidding (1614 [/5]), and his children are mentioned in the will of his sister Elizabeth Gidding, dated 1630.

Children, baptized at Clapham, co. Bedford:

    i.   HENRY[3], bp. 11 Aug. 1605. Ch.: *Mary,* bp. at Clapham, 2 Feb. 1630 [/1].

ii. GEORGE, bp. 1 Nov. 1607. The possibility that he was the immigrant to Massachusetts is discussed below.
iii. KATHARINE, bp. 17 June 1610.
iv. EMME, bp. 5 Oct. 1612. Ch.: *Thomas,* illegitimate son of Emma Giddin, bp. at Bromham, co. Bedford, 5 Aug. 1637. Bromham is about two miles from Clapham.
v. ROBERT, bp. 28 Jan. 1614 [/5].
vi. JOSEPH (posthumous), bp. 7 Sept. 1617.

3. JOHN[2] GIDDING (*Michael*[1]) was born [say 1584] and buried at Oakley, 19 February 1619 [/20], recorded both at Oakley ("Jn Gitten of Clapham") and Clapham ("Jn Husband Joan Gittens"). He married at Clapham, 20 January 1607 [/8], JOAN PURRIER, baptized at Oakley, 1 May 1588, daughter of Thomas and Isabel (————) (Tilbrooke) Purrier. She married secondly at Clapham, 3 September 1620, Robert Phage or Fage.

John Gidding is mentioned in the will of his father Michael Gidding (1614 [/5]), and two of his children are mentioned in the will of his sister Elizabeth Gidding (1630).

He died testate:

In the name of God Amen I John Gidding of Clapham in the County of Bedd and in the dioces of Lincolne husbandman being somewhat weacke in body neverthelesse in good and pfect health and [sic] memory thancks be to almighty god doe ordayne, constitue [sic] and make this my last will and testament the 7th day of ffebruary Anno d[omi]ni 1619 [/20] in manner and forme following that is to say ffirst I bequeath my soule to almighty God my maker and redeemer and my body to be buryed in the Church yard of Ockley in the sayd County. And whaereas I am in debted unto sundry and diuers psons to the valeue or summe amounting to threescore and eighte pounds or thereaboutt, And for that it is my true intent and meaning as in consciencc it ought to be that my said debte should be well and truly payd, I will therefore that thirteene Acres and a halfe Arrable of my land with the appurtenances lying and being devidely by pcell in the feilds of Clapham aforesd shalbe soulde by my executrix hereafter named for the paying and dischardging of my debt aforesd according my true meaning. Item I will and bequeathe to Joane my wife my house with the appurtenances to have and to houlde to her and her assignes untill George Gidding my sonne shall accomplishe the full age of Twentyon[e] years and then to remayne to my sonne George Gidding and to his heres for ever, Which sd thirdene Acres and a halfe of land Arrable on[e] Acre lyeth at Stonehill and on[e] Acre and a halfe more at the same Stonehill and an other Acre and a halfe at Crosse peece. Item on[e] Acre in the Commonty furlong soe called, Twoe Acres in currene[?] feilde. Item twoe loame Acres more ther and alsoe twelve lands lying together at Bekpedan[?] on the fether side conteyning by estimation ffoure Acres & a halfe. Also I will that the sd Joune my wife shall have my house with the apptenances in Clapham aforesd wherein Thomas Purryar dweleth wth the [illegible] unto it to a [sic] have and to houlde unto the sd Joane my wife during her life and alsoe that shee the sd Joane shall have yearely every yeare during the life of the sd Thomas Purryar to be chosen by her or her assigne on[e] good Acre of Barley and halfe an Acre of wheate and a good Acre of Peays and Beans out of my land of Clapham aforesd during the life of the sd Thomas Purryar, and all my goods moveable and un-moveable Chattell of [sic] and househould stuff, my buriall expence dischardged, I freely give and bequeath to the sd Joane my wife for ever, whom I ordayne and make my sole executrix of this my last will and testament. In wittnes wherof I the said John gidding have heerunto sett my hand & seale the day and year aboue written (ABP/W 1620/125).

The will was signed by John Gidding; the witnesses were George Cox and Richard Giddings. The will was proved 3 April 1620. The Clapham Manorial Roll of 2 April 1623 states in Latin that "John Giddinge has died seized of a messuage and about 30 acres of land" and "that George Giddinge is his son & heir & of full age"—though George was only thirteen.

Although his will mentions no children except George, John Gidding had other surviving children, as proven by the will of his sister Elizabeth. Clearly, John Gidding expected his wife to provide for his daughters. He did not limit his wife's rights in his estate to her widowhood, as one would expect, and that suggests that he expected her to remarry and retain those rights. She did remarry seven months later, and it is hardly cynical to point out that the rights she had retained in her first husband's estate probably made it easier for a widow with four young children to acquire a new husband. Robert Phage, Joan (Purrier) Gidding's second husband, and Richard Gyddinge were on the Clapham Manorial Rolls, 18 January 1620/1 and 2 April 1623, with forty acres, six beasts, and forty-eight sheep. At Michaelmas 1627, the Clapham and Oakley Rolls include among the rents, "of the heyre of Michaell Gyddinge for the house & Land in the tenure of Robert Phage, o2li ijs vjd." Since Richard Gidding was Michael Gidding's heir, it seems that Robert Phage rented land from him.

Research into the Purriers has not established Joan (Purrier) Gidding's ancestry beyond her parentage. Sixteenth-century Purriers left wills in Cranfield and Turvey, both co. Bedford. "Jone" Purrier of Turvey, obviously a widow, left a will dated 28 August 1555, naming sons William, Thomas, John, and probably—the relationship is not stated—Robert; daughter Annes Edwards; various grandchildren; and others (ABP/W 1555/126). The name "Thomas" in the will may be significant, but is too common to suggest a pattern. Thomas Purrier, father of Joan Gidding, was probably born too late to be mentioned in a 1555 will. As mentioned earlier, Turvey is about six miles from Clapham; as is also mentioned above, the possibility of a connection with Buckinghamshire should not be overlooked.

Thomas Purrier married Isabel Tilbrooke at Oakley, 16 January 1586 [/7]. Isabel Purrier was buried (recorded at Clapham) 13 December 1621. There are no Tilbrooke entries at Clapham; the few entries for the name at Oakley include Joan, wife of John Tilbrooke, buried 12 May 1578; Catharine, daughter of John Tilbrooke, baptized 7 January 1579 [/80]; Mary, daughter of John Tilbrooke, baptized 13 May 1583; and John

Tilbrooke, buried 4 October 1586. John Tilbrooke's will, dated 25 March, 28 Elizabeth [1585/6] (proved 23 February 1586 [/7]), names wife Isabel, sons Lewis and John, and daughters Catharine and Mary, the daughters to receive their legacies at sixteen (ABP/W 1586-1587/144). Isabel Tilbrooke who married Thomas Purrier was undoubtedly his widow.

Thomas Purrier was included in the Clapham Manorial Roll, 18 January 1620/1, with seventeen acres of freehold land, two beasts, and twenty sheep; he is mentioned in the rolls, 1621-1627.

Thomas Purrier left a will that enables us fully to identify his daughter's first and second marriages. It is also a document of considerable human interest.

In the name of god amen the 22th of ffebruary Ano do[mini] 1622 [/3?]—I Thomas Purrier of Clapham in the County of Bedd[ford] husbandman beinge at this present sicke and weake of Body but yet of good and perfect memory thankes be to god doe ordayne & make this my last will and testament in manner and forme following. ffirst and Principally I comende my soule into the handes of Allmighty god that [sic] trustinge assuredly and belevinge to be saved by the only meritte & Passion of Christ Jesus my only savior and Redeemer And my body to the earth to be buryed at the discretion of my executors in the church yard of Okley. ffirst I give and bequeath to Thomas Candy a blinde poore man—iijs— And to wydow hather[?], wydow Elyzabeuth Gydding, wydow Randes, wydow meadowes—ijs a peace to be payd presently after my decease. It[em] I give and bequeath to my daughter Joane now wyfe of Robert Phage my best cowe, ij ewes &—ij—wether sheep called hoggesvilles, wich my will is that my daughter should have them at hur owne disposinge and that my executors shall have power to take them or the profittes that doe arise of them frome the husband of my daughter Joane if he doe not suffer her quietly to Inoye [sic] them and to have them leest and the profittes arisinge to hur only use and as as[?] hur mind is they should be bestowed. It[em] I give and bequeath to Thomas, mary, martha and Rebecca the Children of my daughter Joane aforsayd—xxs a peece to be sett and Increeassed to the benifitt of the sayd children untill the day of mariage or of lawfull age wich doe please god shall first come, wich money is to be Imployed at the discretion of my executors hearafter named; also I give to the sayd children every one of them a sheep, a sheot & a pewter dish. It[em] all the rest of my goods and chatteles whatsoever I give and bequeath to George Giddinge the sonne of my daughter Joane whome I doe make my executor and because he is under age I make his uncull Richard Gyddinge and my cozen Edward [corrected from Robert] Gayle of Okley as sole executors with him for the better bringinge of him up in learninge and other thinges needfull for him. And of this my last will and testament I doe ordayne John Colbey and John Becke overseers of the same and the sayde John Becke shall have for his paynes xijd [sic] ijs. And all other wills I doe deny and shalbe of noe effect. In wittnes heerof I the sayd Thomas Purrier have sett to my hand the day and yeare first above wrighten (ABP/W 1629/102).

Thomas Purrier signed by mark, as did two of the three witnesses, John Becke and Robert Phage. The third witness, John Colbey, wrote his signature, and it is clear that he was the scribe. The will was proved 28 April 1629.

8

Although in 1630 Elizabeth Gidding left most of her property to Robert Phage, in 1622 [/3?] Thomas Purrier did not trust him, and by making him one of the witnesses to his will, he made sure that his son-in-law knew what he thought of him. Purrier was also forestalling any claim that Phage might make that he was not cognizant of the terms of the will.

Children of John and Joan (Purrier) Gidding, baptized at Clapham, co. Bedford:

5. i. GEORGE³, bp. 24 Sept. 1609.
   ii. MARY, bp. 2 Feb. 1611 [/2]; Mary, dau. of Jane [sic] Giddin, bur. (recorded Clapham) 19 Oct. 1625. It is strange that Joan was called "Giddin" in this entry, since she had been married to Robert Phage since 1620, but there is no question that the record refers to John Gidding's daughter. She is mentioned in the will of her grandfather, Thomas Purrier.
   iii. MARTHA, bp. 14 Aug. 1614; mentioned in the wills of her grandfather and of her aunt. The suggestion that she married John Proctor of Ipswich, Mass., is disproven below (see Giddings-Proctor Addendum).
   iv. REBECCA, bp. 10 Oct. 1619; mentioned in the wills of her grandfather and of her aunt.

Children of Robert and Joan (Purrier) (Gidding) Phage, baptized at Clapham, co. Bedford (they are not Gidding descendants):

   v. THOMAS, bp. 18 Oct. 1621; mentioned in the wills of his grandfather, Thomas Purrier, and of Elizabeth Gidding.
   vi. WILLIAM, bp. 30 Oct. 1625, bur. (recorded Clapham) 31 Oct. 1625.

4. RICHARD² GIDDING (*Michael¹*) was born [say 1595]; he or possibly a younger man of the same name was buried (recorded at Clapham) 29 April 1657. He married at Clapham, 22 June 1620, MARY WHITMAN; she is probably the Widow Gidding buried (recorded Clapham) 21 April 1660.

Richard Gidding was the chief heir of his father and mother, and his children are mentioned (not by name) in the will of his sister. Thomas Purrier, who must have thought more highly of him than he did of his son-in-law, Robert Phage, made Richard Gidding an executor of his will and one of those responsible for rearing George Gidding. Although the Clapham Manorial Roll of 18 January 1620/1 mentions that "if Richard Giddinge shall goe & dwell out of this parish. . . then he maye lett his Commons to the Inhabitants within this Mannor & to no other," he apparently did not leave and is mentioned in the rolls to 1637.

Children:

   i. ELIZABETH³, bp. at Clapham, co. Bedford, 13 Dec. 1620.
   ii. MARY, bp. at Clapham, 1 Dec. 1622.

iii. SON [name torn off], bp. at Clapham, 27 Feb. 1624 [/5].
iv. CHILD, bp. not found, but b. 1626-1630, since four children are mentioned in the will of Elizabeth Gidding, 1630.
v. MICHAEL, bp. 14 Sept. 1634.

5. GEORGE[3] GIDDINGS (*John[2], Michael[1]*) was baptized at Clapham, co. Bedford, 24 September 1609, and died at Ipswich, Massachusetts, 1 June 1676 (*Vital Records of Ipswich, Massachusetts* [Salem, 1910], hereafter *Ipswich VRs*). He married at St. Albans, co. Hertford, 20 February 1633 [/4], JANE LAWRENCE, who was baptized at St. Albans, 18 December 1614, and died at Ipswich, 2 March 1680. She was a daughter of Thomas and Joan (Antrobus) Lawrence. (For her baptism, see William Brigg, *The Parish Registers of St. Albans Abbey, 1558-1689* [Harpenden, 1897], 49; her death is recorded in *Ipswich VRs*. Other significant sources include the Antrobus, Lawrence, and Tuttle sections of Mary Walton Ferris, *Dawes-Gates Ancestral Lines* [1943]; Donald Lines Jacobus and Edgar Francis Waterman, *Hale, House and Related Families. . .* [Hartford, Conn., 1952], 772, 773; Sir Reginald L. Antrobus, *Antrobus Pedigrees. . .* [London, 1929]; and Consuelo Furman, "St. Albans Origin of John Lawrence. . ." [rev. ed., 1955, typescript in the Society's library].)

There were two George Giddings baptized at Clapham at about the same period: one was baptized 1 November 1607, son of Henry and Elizabeth (Russell) Gidding, while the other was baptized 24 September 1609, son of John and Joan (Purrier) Gidding. The evidence for the conclusion that the immigrant was the George baptized in 1609 is circumstantial. "Geo. Giddins" is listed as twenty-five years old in the April 1635 passenger list, which fits the 1609 George, who would not have been twenty-six for several more months; the other George was fully two years older. Ages in depositions and passenger lists are often mere estimates by the recorder, and indeed the ages provided in later documents for George Giddings of Ipswich would fit either child. In this case, however, the ages for the Tuttle-Lawrence-Giddings group in the April 1635 list are reasonably accurate and were surely provided by one or more members of the party. The onomastic evidence also favors the 1609 George. George and Jane (Lawrence) Giddings had eight known children: Thomas, John, James, Samuel, Joseph, Rebecca, Abigail and Mary (the 1882 genealogy does not include two children in George Giddings's estate and adds two children he probably did not have). George, baptized in 1607, had a brother named Joseph, while George baptized in 1609, had sisters named Rebecca and Mary and a father named John. George and Jane Giddings gave their children names indicating Puritan sympathies (and hence did not name any child after themselves), but they named their first two sons, Thomas and John, obviously for the children's grandfathers, Thomas Lawrence and John Gidding, as well as for Thomas Purrier, George Giddings's grandfather and benefactor. In addition, the economic status of George Giddings of Ipswich is consistent with that of the 1609 George. George Gidding, baptized in 1609, was the principal heir of his father, who left thirty acres, and of his maternal grandfather, doubtless the reason that his aunt, Elizabeth Gidding, did not mention him in her will. John Gidding and Thomas Purrier called themselves husbandmen in their wills, while George Gidding when he married in 1633/4 felt confident enough to claim in his marriage bond a higher title, that of yeoman, though the 1635 passenger list again calls him husbandman. What little we know about the George Gidding baptized in 1607 suggests a different economic status, since his mother had only four acres and one cow in the 18 January 1620/1 Clapham Manorial Roll and was later included among those Thomas Purrier clearly considered poor widows eligible for charity in his will. George Giddings, the immigrant, married into a substantial family, transported three servants with him, was among the highest rate payers in Ipswich in 1664, and left an estate valued at over £1020. The circumstantial evidence—most clearly the onomastic, supported by George Giddings's age in the passenger list and his economic status—strongly favor the conclusion that the immigrant was the son of John and Joan (Purrier) Gidding.

George Giddings married Jane Lawrence at St. Albans, co. Hertford, some thirty miles from Clapham. His marriage bond is the key document establishing his origin. An abstract follows:

[In Latin] George Giddinge of Clapham, co. Bedd, yeoman, and John Tuttell [George's future stepfather-in-law] of St. Albans draper, are bound for £100. . . 20 Feb. 1633 [/4]. [In English] George Giddinge Batchelor & one Jane Lawrence of St. Albans maiden are licensed to be married together; therefore there shall not heerafter appeare any lawfull impedmt. . . And that the sd marriage be penty [presently?] solimized in the pish Church of St. Albans or St. Peters And that betweene the howers of eight & twelve of the clock in the forenoone. . . . (Hertfordshire Record Office, ref no ASA 22/1).

The marriage of George "Goodwin" and Jane Lawrence was performed the same day at the parish church of St. Peters, Borough of St. Albans, co. Hertford (St. Peters parish registers, Hertfordshire Record Office, ref no D/P93/1/1).

George Giddings and his wife Jane are in the April 1635 passenger lists of the *Planter*. Also on the lists are various connections of hers: her mother and stepfather, Joan (Antrobus) (Lawrence) Tuttle and John Tuttle; Joan Tuttle's mother, Joan (Arnold) Antrobus; John Tuttle's mother, Isabel (Wells) Tuttle, and his brothers, Richard and William Tuttle; and others (for these relationships, see Jacobus and Waterman, *Hale, House,* 771-773, and David L. Greene, "Origin of John Tuttle of Ipswich, Massachusetts," *The American Genealogist,* 54 [1978]: 167-175). For George Giddings's life in Ipswich, see Abraham Hammatt's *Early Inhabitants of Ipswich, Mass.* (Ipswich, 1880), 116, and Charles Henry Pope's *Pioneers of Massachusetts* (Boston, 1900), 186.

11

George Giddings died intestate; the records of his estate are abstracted in *Probate Records of Essex County,* 3(1920):63-65; some additional information is in *Records and Files of the Quarterly Courts of Essex County,* 9 volumes to date, 9(1975):440, 441.

Giddings-Proctor Addendum

Because of what seemed to be a possibility that John Proctor of Ipswich had married a sister of George Giddings, I undertook some investigation of the relationship, if any existed, between George Giddings and John Proctor, a problem that remains unsolved, at least so as I am aware. On 26 March 1667 in Ipswich Quarterly Court, "Gordge Giddeng," aged fifty-nine made a deposition, and John Prockter, Sr., aged seventy-five, deposed the same as "my brother Giddens" (Henry F. Waters, "Genealogical Gleanings in England," *Register,* 51 [1897]: 409; *Records and Files of the Quarterly Courts of Essex County,* 3[1913]: 396, 397). It is this relationship that is in question.

Proctor and Giddings were not, of course, full brothers, nor could they have been half brothers. For some time, it seemed likely that John Proctor's wife, Martha, was a sister of George Giddings. In the April 1635 passenger lists of the *Susan and Ellen,* John Proctor's wife, Martha, was aged twenty-eight and his children, John and Marie, were aged three and one respectively ("Founders of New England," *Register,* 14[1860]: 309; Hotten, *Original Lists,* 59); the will of John Procter, Sr., of Ipswich (dated 28 August 1672) mentions wife Martha and others (*Probate Records of Essex County,* 2 [1917]: 315, 316). George Giddings had a sister named Martha who could have married John Proctor, if her age was misstated in 1635, but this possibility has recently been upset by Mr. John Dorrance Morrell's discovery of the marriage of John Proctor. He expects to use this material elsewhere but has most graciously given me permission to mention it here as well. John Proctor married Martha Harper at Groton, co. Suffolk, 1 June 1630. Two children were baptized at Assington, co. Suffolk: John (baptized 9 October 1631) and Marie (baptized 17 October 1633). When this marriage occurred, Martha Gidding was not quite sixteen, and she was referred to as Martha Gidding in the will of her aunt three months later, a fact which precludes the unlikely possibility that—at the age of fifteen—she was a widow Harper. Martha Harper could not have been a full- or half-sister of George Giddings, and enough is known of the Lawrence and Tuttle families to negate the theory that John Proctor or his wife were half- or step-siblings of Jane (Lawrence) Giddings.

There seem three possible solutions to this problem. Mr. Morrell has suggested the possibility, which he considers unlikely, that Martha (Harper) Proctor died after 1635, and that John Proctor married as his second wife Martha Gidding(s). It is also possible that John Proctor and George Giddings had children that married; in the seventeenth century

Winifred Combe, but it does considerably more. It is no doubt a fictitious suit, and merely indicates that John and Winifred were selling their land to Nicholas Rossiter. Nicholas, in the Colket list, was a son of Edward, probably the oldest. He is thought to have been in America from about 1630 to 1635.* The transaction goes far to reinforce the conclusion that when Joseph Combe referred to Edward Rossiter as "brother" he meant brother-in-law, and that Edward was a brother of Winifred. It also gives an approximate date for the Gilbert departure for America; in spite of various traditions that include them in the passenger list of the *Mary and John*, I know of no evidence of their presence earlier than January 1635-6.† It gives us still another piece of information, to which I shall revert below; it shows that in 1635 Joan Combe was a still unmarried member of the Gilbert family.

Incorporating the above facts, we get the following outline for John Gilbert of Dorchester:

JOHN GILBERT, son of Giles and Joan (Pearce) Gilbert, was baptized 30 Aug. 1580 in Bridgwater, Somerset; died 1657 in Taunton, Mass. (will signed 6 April 1656, proved 3 June 1657). He married (1), 17 Jan. 1602-3, in Bridgwater, MARY STREET, bapt. 22 March 1578-9 in Taunton, Somerset; probably she who was buried 25 Oct. 1605, in Bridgwater; daughter of Nicholas Street. He married (2), in September 1606, perhaps in Bristol, ALICE HOPKINS, buried 25 April 1618 in Bridgwater; daughter of Thomas Hopkins of Bristol. He married (3), in or after 1620, WINIFRED (ROSSITER) COMBE, widow of Joseph Combe of Combe St. Nicholas, Somerset, and sister of Edward Rossiter of that place.

Children by first wife:

?. Twins MARY and JOAN, bapt. 4 Aug. 1603, Bridgwater; buried there 5 and 9 Aug. Parentage not stated, but they may have been daughters of John and Mary, born prematurely.
? MARY, bapt. 19 Aug. 1604, Bridgwater. Parentage not stated; if a daughter of John, she probably died young, as she could hardly have been the Mary listed below.

Children by second wife:

? ELIZABETH. The will of Emma Escott of Bridgwater, widow, dated 10 Nov. 1632, mentions "Elizabeth daughter of Mr. John Gilbert" (Somerset Wills, 2nd series, p. 96). Nothing further is known of her.
i. THOMAS, b. probably about 1612, perhaps in Trull, Somerset; d. about 1676, England.
ii. JOHN, b. about 1614, and probably the "Joan" bapt. 19 Aug. 1614, Bridgwater; prob. also the John who d. there 10 Feb. 1691.

Children by third wife:

iii. MARY. Mentioned in John's will as Mary Norcross. Her husband was probably Rev. Nathaniel Norcross, bapt. in 1619 in London; in America 1638 to about 1649-50; d. 10 Aug. 1662, London. If this identification is

*Colket, *idem.*
†Boston Record Commissioners, Fourth Report, pp. 14-15.

and earlier, parents of children who married sometimes called themselves brothers or sisters. It might be significant to mention here that the unidentified first wife of John Proctor, Jr., was a Martha who died at Ipswich, 13 June 1659 (Waters, "Genealogical Gleanings," *Register,* 51 [1897]: 409). George Giddings's estate records do not support such a tentative identification, though it is possible—but not probable—that children who had previously received their portions were not mentioned. The third possibility is that George Giddings and John Proctor were "brothers in the church" and that no other relationship existed between them. In seventeenth-century New England records, the terms "brother" and "sister" occur in the sense of a church relationship, but this usage is rare (see George E. McCracken, "Terms of Relationship in Colonial Times," *The American Genealogist,* 55 [1979]: 52).

David L. Greene is Professor of English and Chairman of the English Department at Piedmont College, Demorest, Georgia.

THE WIVES OF JOHN GILBERT
OF DORCHESTER, MASS.

By GEOFFREY GILBERT, of Victoria, B. C., Canada

John Gilbert of Bridgwater, Somerset, one of the original purchasers of Taunton, Mass., brought with him to Dorchester, in or about 1635, a wife Winifred, four sons, and a daughter. He was born in 1580, and in January 1602-3 he married Mary Street, both in Bridgwater. Mary has been considered the mother of the two older sons, Thomas and John, Jr., who were "well grown youths" in 1636. The two younger sons, Giles and Joseph, and probably the daughter Mary, have been assigned more or less doubtfully to Winifred. As to the identity of Winifred, the only clue has been a clause in John's will referring to his wife's grandchild Elizabeth———; the surname has been variously deciphered as Peaslee, Peslee, Peter, and Pester. This clause has been the basis for a guess that Peaslee or a variant was the name of Winifred's first husband, and she has appeared in some genealogies as "widow Peaslee", though obviously this would only be true if Elizabeth were the child of a son of Winifred, not of a daughter.

Somewhat later, restudies of the Bridgwater records suggested that there might be still another wife. A daughter Joan was born in 1614 to John and Alice Gilbert and Alice, wife of John Gilbert, died in 1618. It was not considered certain that these records related to John, the immigrant, but on the other hand evidence was uncovered that a John Gilbert, who later became mayor of Bridgwater, was born about 1614, and there is reason to suppose that the Joan of the 1614 baptism is really this John. If so, he is in all likelihood the second son of John, the immigrant, who is known to have returned permanently to England in 1645, after about ten years in America.

In the late 1920's, my father, Philip H. Gilbert, engaged an English genealogist, Mr. H. Tapley-Soper, of Exeter, to try to uncover further details about John Gilbert, Sr., and his antecedents. The Chancery Reports, neglected by earlier workers, yielded several pieces of information about John and his father Giles. One in particular, a suit brought against John in 1610 by one Valentine Babb, clears up the question of the second wife. It shows that John married Alice Hopkins, daughter of Thomas Hopkins of Bristol, in September 1606; a reference to Nicholas Street as John's father-in-law removes all doubt as to his identity. In all probability a Mary Gilbert who was buried in Bridgwater in October 1605 was John's first wife, and beyond any doubt the Alice who died in 1618 was the second. Alice must certainly have been the mother of the sons Thomas and John, Jr.

The Babb document reads in part as follows:

Chancery Proceedings C.2 James I, B.26-7.
26 April 1610. Complaint of Valentine Babb of Trull, co. Somerset, yeoman, that whereas one John Gilbert of Trull, gent., by virtue of the last will of Giles Gilbert his father deceased . . . . . was possessed of a lease . . . . . called Peasehay containing 80ac in Baudripp, co. Somerset . . . . . said John Gilbert about 29 Nov. last in consideration of £600 . . . . . did sell to orator said premises . . . . . Since then there hath been a paper book made embodying the contract, which paper book was made by one Nicholas Street, gent., fatherinlaw to Gilbert . . . . . Gilbert refused to . . . . . perform the covenants of the agreement.

15 June 1610. Answer of John Gilbert, gent. He . . . . . made an agreement with the complainant . . . . . but 3 years before the time of the agreement he, in consideration of a marriage then shortly after to be had between him & Alice his now wife, which was then very shortly after solemnized, by his writing indented between him & Thomas Hoptkins & William Hoptkins of city of Bristol, merchants, & Richard Winter, gent. of same city dated 1 Sept. 4 Jas.I.1606 conveyed his interest in the premises to them for the jointure of Alice now his wife being daughter of said Thomas Hoptkins, & at the time of the agreement he thought he would procure and get the good liking of Alice & her trustee to relinquish the same assurance . . . . . but cannot succeed . . . . . and as this was the case Gilbert was unable to sign the agreement.

Mr. Tapley-Soper also found two other documents which, taken together, definitely establish the identity of the third wife, Winifred. The first is the will of Joseph Combe of Combe St. Nicholas, Somerset, proved in April 1620. It mentions among others wife *Winifred*, daughter *Joan*, and "brother" Edward Rossiter. It has been printed in two collections of Somerset wills, and reprinted in an important article by Colket.*

The other document is as follows:

Feet of Fines, Somerset, Easter, 11 Charles I. 1635.

"Nicholas Rossiter gent. querent & John Gilbert gent. & Winifred his wife deforciant of a moiety of 15 ac of land & 8 ac of meadow in Combe St. Nicholas which John & Winifred granted to Nicholas to hold for life of Winifred & of *Joan Combe daughter of Winifred* & for the life of the longer liver of them".

This suit establishes the identity of Winifred Gilbert with widow

*Colket, Meredith B., Jr.; "Edward Rossiter, his Family, and Notes on his English Connections", *American Genealogist*, vol. 13, 1937, pp. 145-51.

correct, Mary was probably born in the early 1620's and married in the early 1640's.

   iv. GILES, b. perhaps about 1627 (apparently under military age of 16 in 1643); d. 8 Jan. 1717-18, Rehoboth, Mass.

   v. JOSEPH, b. perhaps about 1629; migrated from Taunton to North Carolina.

This paper is intended to be primarily factual, but I should like to end it on a note of conjecture regarding two Gilbert questions that still await an answer. One of these has already been implied. Now that we know who Winifred was, what are we to do about her granddaughter, Elizabeth Peaslee?

The other relates to Jane Rossiter, who married John's oldest son Thomas in Taunton on 23 March 1639-40. The ancient statement that she was a daughter of Hugh Rossiter has been shown by Colket to be baseless. The most probable alternative is that she was Hugh's widow.* If so, whose daughter was she?

I think that both birds can be killed with one stone. My evidence so far is circumstantial, but it is still coming in, and it makes at least a very plausible story. I hope to present it eventually, either in another paper in this journal or in the "John Gilbert Genealogy", of which I am at present a co-compiler. Meanwhile I should like to stake my claim to the "discovery", and invite rebuttal.

I believe that Jane Rossiter was the widow of Hugh, and that Hugh died in 1638 or 1639, leaving her with an infant daughter Elizabeth. She was also Hugh's first cousin. She was the daughter of Winifred Gilbert, and the stepdaughter of John Gilbert. She was stepsister of her second husband, Thomas Gilbert. Her maiden name was Joan Combe.

As for Elizabeth of the illegible surname, it should be pointed out that the illegibility must be blamed on the clerk who at an uncertain date transcribed the will into the Plymouth records. The will itself has perished. Instead of burdening Winifred with an unaccountable Pester relative (Pester is fully as logical a reading as Peaslee†) can we not assume that the clerk slipped, and that the word written by John was something like Roseter or Rocester? If so, the conjecture is just about set up. Winifred was a Rossiter herself, but the only way she could have had a Rossiter grandchild would be by marrying a daughter to a Rossiter. We have an available daughter in Joan (Jane is a mere variant), and an available Rossiter in Hugh. What more do we need?

What became of young Elizabeth? I think I know that, too. She makes one more brief appearance, in the Thomas Gilbert inventory.‡ She is referred to as "the daughter of Mr. Thomas Gilbert",

---

*Colket, idem.

†Plym. Col. Records, Wills, vol. 2, pp. 46-7. See also the printed version in The Mayflower Descendant, vol. 14, 1912, p. 114, which gives it as Pester.

‡Plym. Col. Records, Wills, vol. 3, pp. 78-9.

and perhaps she was, by adoption. Anyway, she did not share in the estate. She had married Thomas Starr, Jr., and died before 1677.

PEDIGREE (conjectural as to Joan Combe).

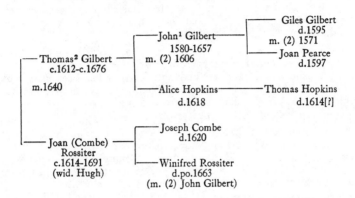

THE ROYAL DESCENT OF A NEW ENGLAND SETTLER

By G. ANDREWS MORIARTY, A.M., LL.B., of Newport, R. I.

OCCASIONAL perusals of the Genealogical Department of the *Boston Evening Transcript* and other publications have convinced the writer of this article that, in spite of the fact that "all men are created equal" and in spite of the good old American contempt for royalty and the "effete nobility of Europe," the American genealogical public have an exceedingly strong desire to deduce their descent by hook or by crook from the same "effete" royal and noble houses of Europe. Furthermore, an investigation of these claims usually shows that not one in twenty of such pedigrees can stand up under the searching test of modern scientific investigation. These lines are usually based upon the standard works of Dugdale and their derivatives, upon printed county histories, and upon the notoriously inaccurate so-called Visitation pedigrees of the sixteenth and seventeenth centuries edited by the Harleian Society; and, when these fail, the most wild and careless statements are relied upon.

Now Dugdale was a very great investigator. He was the first person who approached the subject of mediæval genealogy with anything like a scientific spirit; and, when we consider his difficulties, the scattered records, the total lack of calendars, and the lack of the splendid Rolls Series and the admirable publications now being produced by the Record Office, his achievements may be considered remarkable. But Dugdale suffered from these handicaps. His great work, the "Baronage," contains errors of fact and of omission into which he would never have fallen had he had the resources of the present day at his command. In fact, while Dugdale did for England what Savage did for New England, he suffered from the same handicaps; but, like him, in spite of his errors, his work remains a standard one, although, like Savage, he is now somewhat antiquated. From Dugdale's time until the latter half of the nineteenth century practically no original work was undertaken in the mediæval archives of England; the eighteenth-century writers were content to follow him and perpetuated all his errors; and it was not until the eminent English antiquary, J. Horace Round, arose that a new school was formed under his severe training. Of this new school and its methods of dealing with mediæval sources the American genealogist appears to be profoundly ignorant. While thoroughly modern in dealing with his own records, he is deplorably weak when it comes to earlier work which for the most part he does not understand. Nor is he usually equipped to read the writing or the language in which these records are written, much less to understand the series of shorthand symbols with which the mediæval clerk abbreviated his Latin and his Norman French.

The present article is written as an indicator, to point out the path in which those who desire to deal with mediæval genealogy in a serious manner must travel; and it is written solely to encourage such work. No statement will be made without citing the original document relied upon for it, so that the reader may judge for himself of the value of the evidence and decide whether the conclusions reached are justified. To prepare such a pedigree is no easy matter; and I especially wish to show those persons who write glibly of "royal descents" how much labor is involved if a careful pedigree is to be presented. *Tantæ molis erat Romanam condere gentem.*

In this article documents will be presented which prove the descent of Lucy de Morteyn, an ancestress of William Sargent of Malden in New England (cf. REGISTER, vol. 74, pp. 231–237, 267–283, and vol. 75, pp. 57–63, 129–142), from the royal Scottish house of Kenneth McAlpin and from the royal line of Egbert, through two ancient families of Norman origin, the Gobions of Northamptonshire and the Merlays of Northumberland; and a few brief notes will be added on the connection of the latter family with that of Stuteville or Estouteville.

GOBION

There can be no doubt that the origin of the Gobion or Gubion family must be sought upon the Breton-Norman border. In or about 1070 Wido (Guy) Gobio witnessed a charter of Geoffrey de Dinan as one of his knights (Morice, Hist. bret., Preuves, 1–439), and a William Gobio occurs in a charter of the same date (cf. The Norman People). The name does not occur in Domesday, and it seems most probable that the ancestor of this family was a Norman-Breton who arrived in England in the reign of Henry Beauclerc.

I. The first of the name of whom we have any record in England

19

was Hugh Gobion, who appears in the Pipe Roll of 31 Henry I (1130–31) as a landowner in Northampton vill, where he owned 10 silver marks for a plea. It is uncertain when he died, but he witnessed a charter of the first Simon de St. Liz (Reg. 11, B. ix).

II. His son and successor was also a Hugh Gobion. Mr. Farrer, in his "Honors and Knights' Fees," vol. 1, pp. 83–87, under Horton in the Honor of Wahull, thinks that he was the tenant of William de Ferrers in Yardley Gobion in 1166, but doubts whether he was the father of Richard Gobion and is not sure of his being the son of the first Hugh. He was clearly the tenant of William de Ferrers in the return of 1166, but he is equally clearly the son of the first Hugh and the father of the first Richard, as is proved by a charter of his grandson, Richard Gobion, son of Richard, made in King John's time, whereby King John grants to Richard Gobion all the lands that were his grandfather's, Hugh Gobion's, in the fields of Northampton, outside of the East Gate (E. 14, Cart. Antiquae*). This second Hugh was sheriff of Northamptonshire from 1161 to Michaelmas, 1164, when he was displaced and amerced £200 (Pipe Rolls, 7–11 Henry II). In 1166 Hugh's land in Northampton was taken into the King's hand for some offence (Pipe Roll, 12 Henry II, p. 64), and in 1168 Hugh's wife began to answer for the residue of her husband's debt (Pipe Roll, 14 Henry II, p. 50). In the return of William de Ferrers in 1166 it was stated that Hugh Gobion held one-third of a knights' fee (i.e., Yardley Gobion) of the Earl and had been enfeoffed by Earl Robert, father of William, of three parts of a fee of his demesne (Liber Niger, vol. 1, p. 221, and Baker's Northamptonshire, vol. 2, p. 227); and the fact that his son, Richard, appears in the Pipe Rolls as early as 1159 is accounted for by his holding the Bedfordshire estates of his wife, Beatrice, who was an heiress. Moreover, we find in entry in the Pipe Roll for 1175 stating that the sheriff owed £6. 13s. 4d. of the aid of the burgesses of Northampton for the marrying of the king's daughter, which sum remained due from the wife of Hugh Gobion (Pipe Roll, 21 Henry II, p. 41). As the first Hugh held lands in Northampton vill and as the entry obviously refers to the later Hugh, I am forced to the conclusion that they are father and son, since the Northampton land subsequently appears in the hands of Richard Gobion, the son of the second Hugh. Now it is clear that, although Hugh's Northampton land had been taken into the King's hand in 1166, he was alive in 13 Henry II (1166–67), when he paid in £39 on his fine (Pipe Roll, 13 Henry II, p. 115), and his wife, who begins to appear in the Pipe Roll for the following year, 1167–68 (Pipe Roll, 14 Henry II, p. 50), disappears after 21 Henry II (1174–75) (Pipe Roll, 21 Henry II, p. 41). We may conclude, therefore, that Hugh Gobion (I) held lands in Northampton vill in 1130 and was succeeded by a son Hugh, who received one-third of a knight's fee in Yardley Gobion from Robert, Earl Ferrers, which he was holding in the great return of 1166. The second Hugh died about 13 or 14 Henry II (1166–1168), and his wife died about 1175. They had certainly a son Richard

*I am indebted for this charter to my friend, G. Herbert Fowler, Esq., of the Bedfordshire Record Society.

Gobion and probably a son Simon, who appears in the Pipe Roll of 1179–80 (26 Henry II), when the sheriff rendered an account for 33s. 4d. profit of the land of Simon Gobion, when it was in the King's hand (Pipe Roll, 26 Henry II, p. 87). This Simon apparently founded a family in East Anglia, and the one-third fee held by the second Hugh in Yardley Gobion seems to have passed to a cadet of the family, as in the return of 1242–43 it was held by a Henry Gobion (Book of Fees, p. 934). Hugh Gobion (II) is perhaps the person referred to in the Close Roll under date of 21 August, 7 John (1205), where the land that was Hugh Gobin's in Oleron is mentioned (Rot. Litt. Claus., p. 47).

III. The eldest son and heir of Hugh Gobion (II) was Richard Gobion, who first appears in the Pipe Roll of 5 Henry II (1159), when he was pardoned 2 marks of the gift of his knights in Bedfordshire and Buckinghamshire and 65s. 4d. as a knight holding of Simon de Beauchamp (Farrer's Honors and Knights' Fees, vol. 1, p. 83, and Pipe Roll, 5 Henry II, p. 19). This entry shows him holding lands in Bedfordshire and Buckinghamshire in addition to those held by his father in Northampton vill, and in 1165 he accounted for 100 marks for the daughter of Hugh de Lucelles and her lands in Bedfordshire (Farrer's Honors and Knights' Fees, vol. 1, p. 84, and Pipe Roll, 11 Henry II, p. 23). The "Testa de Nevill" (p. 249) shows that the Gobions in the next century held two fees of the fee of Beauchamp of Bedford in Heigham Gobion, Streatley, Faldo, and Sharpenhoe, co. Beds (cf. Farrer's Honors and Knights' Fees, vol. 1, p. 84). This clearly shows that Richard Gobion had married before 1159 the daughter and heiress of Hugh de Lucelles, who appears as a donor to Woburn Abbey and who had died shortly before 1159 (ib.). This Hugh was in turn the son of Richard de Lucelles, who by his charter covenanted with the Abbot of Ramsey for the use of the water rising at Pekesdene (Pegsdon in Shillington), and he also agreed to obtain the confirmation of his lord, Simon de Pulchro Campo (Beauchamp) (1114–1130) (cf. Cart. Ram. (R. S., 79), vol. 1, p. 136). This Richard de Lucelles was in turn the son of William de Locels, who in the Domesday held Streatley cum Sharpenhoe and Heigham Gobion of Hugh de Beauchamp, the founder of the Barony of Beauchamp of Bedford (Farrer, op. cit., vol. 1, p. 84, and Victoria County Histories, Bedfordshire, vol. 1, p. 239, vol. 2, p. 344). This William de Locels came, evidently, from Loucelles, in the canton of Tilly-sur-Seulles and arrondissement of Caen (cf. Etienne Dupont, Recherches hist. et topog. sur les Compagnons de Guillaume le Conquérant, vol. 1, p. 48). In the Bedford Eyre for 1202 Muriel de Lucell and Isabel her wife [sic,? sister] gave the king a mark for a licence to agree with Beatrice Gobion by the pledge of Richard Gobion (Bedfordshire Hist. Rec. Soc., vol. 1, p. 195). In the return of 1166 Richard appears as a tenant of Simon de Beauchamp (Liber Rubeus, 320).

In addition to the Bedfordshire manors acquired by his marriage with Beatrice de Lucelles, Richard Gobion (III) also held in the great return one fee of Walter de Wahull (Liber Rubeus, 323). This fee is clearly Horton in Northamptonshire, which in the Domesday was held by Otbert of Walter the Fleming and passed with other of his property to his son Alulf de Merke, who held it at the time of the Northamptonshire survey of Simon de Wahull, the successor of Walter the Fleming (Farrer, *op. cit.*, vol. 1, pp. 83, 61–62). How Horton passed to Gobion from Alulf de Merke is not clear. But this Richard gave to the Abbey of St. James, Northampton, the church of Horton with the wood, etc. (*ib.*, vol. 1, p. 84). He appears to have died by 1182, when his wife accounted for him for the unpaid portion of a fine (Farrer, *loc. cit.*, and Pipe Roll, 28 Henry II, p. 118). In 1185 he was certainly dead, for then his relict Beatrice, aged 40 years, had dower in Northampton, and in Bedfordshire she had of her own inheritance lands worth £18 a year, in the fee of Simon de Beauchamp. At this date she had seven sons and six daughters (Rot. de Dominabus, p. 32; also Farrer, *loc. cit.*).

IV. The son and heir of Richard Gobion (III) was another Richard (IV), who in 1199 impleaded Alice, late wife of William Blundell, of a third part of 100s. of land in Northampton (Rot. Curiæ Regis, ii, 106, and Farrer, *loc. cit.*). In 1201 the sheriff accounted for 2s. of the farm of the land of Richard Gobion, outside the gate of Northampton (Rot. Cancel., 89, and Farrer, *op. cit.*, vol. 1, p. 85). That same year he paid 40s. to have seisin of 100s. of land in Northampton town and outside the gate, called Granga, by order of the King, whereof (as the King's justice and sheriff ascertains), his grandfather, Hugh Gobion, had been disseised by the then King (Farrer, *loc. cit.*, and Rot. Obl. Fin., 513, 515). In 17 John (1216) an order was given to the sheriff of Northamptonshire to give Robert Scutellarius the rent of Richard Gobion's land outside the East Gate of Northampton and of his lands in Bustardsley, etc. (Farrer, *loc. cit.*, and Rot. Litt. Claus., i, 245). That same year the lands of Richard Gobion in Leicestershire and Northamptonshire were given to Roger de Gaugy (Farrer, *loc. cit.*, and Rot. Litt. Claus., i, 247), but in the following year Richard Gobion received them back, having returned to his allegiance upon the death of King John (Rot. Litt. Claus., i, 318). On 20 April 1230 he, a member of the household of William de Vescy, had letters of protection upon going overseas with the royal forces (i.e., to Gascony) (Farrer, *loc. cit.*, and Pat. Rolls, 362).

Richard Gobion (IV) died, probably in Gascony, before 27 December 1230, when it was found that he held 2 carucates in the suburbs of Northampton of the King in chief for 2s. rent and his son and heir, Hugh Gobion, claimed to owe only 16s. 4d. for relief of the land by the custom of Northampton vill; he was to have livery of seisin if no relief was found due (Excerpt. e Rot. Fin., 1, 208, and Farrer, *loc. cit.*). This Richard Gobion (IV) married Agnes, daughter of Roger de Merlay by Alice, daughter of Roger and sister and coheiress of Anselm de Stuteville. De Merlay was a great Northern baron, and in this way the Gobions acquired their Yorkshire property. The proof of this marriage will presently appear in the account of their son, Hugh Gobion (VI).

V. Richard Gobion (IV) appears to have had a son, Richard (V), who gave lands, prior to his decease, to the monks at Newminster

22

(*vide infra*) and died very soon without issue, as in 1231 Katherine,* late wife of Richard Gobion, son and heir of Richard Gobion, was demanding dower in the lands in the suburbs of Northampton, in Harlestone, in Horton, in Heigham, and in Streatley (Farrer, *op. cit.*, vol. 1, p. 262, and Bracton's Note Book, no. 518). It also appears that there was a third son, William, whose widow, Floria, daughter of Hugh de Nevill, sued Hugh Gobion (VI) for dower rights (Farrer, *loc. cit.*, and Bracton, no. 517). The elder Richard was succeeded by his son, Hugh (VI), before 27 December 1230 (*vide supra*).

At this point, when the family's holdings were largely increased by the Northern lands that were received by Agnes de Merlay, as her *maritagium*, it seems well to sum up briefly the original holdings of the family. The lands in the suburbs of Northampton formed the original Gobion holding that Hugh (I) held in 1130. To this was added the fee of Horton, held of the Honor of Wahull, which Richard Gobion (III) was holding in 1166, but how it was acquired is not clear.† In addition to these Northamptonshire lands Richard Gobion (III) acquired Streatley cum Sharpenhoe, Heigham Gobion, and Faldo in Bedfordshire, by his marriage with Beatrice, daughter and coheiress of Hugh de Lucelles, who held of the Beauchamp Barony of Bedford.

VI. Richard Gobion (IV) was succeeded, as we have seen, in 1230 by his son and surviving heir, Hugh Gobion (VI). On 4 October 1232 Lescelina, widow of William de Bruchull, levied a fine with Hugh Gobion upon lands in Sharpenhoe, and she quitclaimed the surplus in the said lands and her rights in the lands that Agnes, widow of Richard de Lucell, held in dower in Sharpenhoe (*Bedfordshire Hist. Rec. Soc.*, vol. 5–6; Beds Feet of Fines, no. 345). Hugh Gubyon, son of Richard Gubyon, gave in Yeddingham (Yorks) to Yeddingham Priory, for the souls of his uncles, Roger and William de Merlay, and of his brother, Richard Gubyon, lands that he held of Roger de Merlay. This charter was witnessed by Roger de Merlay. (Farrer, *op. cit.*, vol. 1, p. 85, and Burton, Monast. Ebor., 286.) Prior to his decease his brother, Richard Gobion (V), gave the monks of Newminster 20s. rent in Shilvington, at the prayer of his uncle, William de Merlay, for the souls of Dame Alice de Stutevile, his grandmother, and Agnes de Merlay, his mother, for a pittance on his grandmother's anniversary, to wit, the Morrow of Peter and Paul, Apostles. This gift was confirmed by Hugh Gobion, brother of the said Richard, and by Roger de Merlay, their uncle (Newminster Cartul. (Surtees Soc.), 15–16, and Farrer, *loc. cit.*).

Mr. Farrer points out that Agnes de Merlay had received lands in Shilvington and Horsley in Northumberland for her *maritagium*. In addition to these we find her descendants holding other Merlay lands, namely, in Yeddingham, Brentingham, Cliff, Cave, and Burton in Yorkshire, which Hugh Gobion held of Roger de Merlay in 50 Henry III (1265) (Cal. Inq. Post Mortem, vol. 1, no. 636). They also held in Leicestershire the Merlay manor of Knaptoft. The only

---

*Mr. Fowler of the Bedfordshire Record Society believes her to have been a second wife of Richard Gobion (IV), but the Newminster grant shows that there was a son Richard (V).

†It is possible that Hugh Gobion (II) had married a daughter of Alulf de Merke and that she received Horton from her father.

one of these manors that we subsequently find the Gobions holding was Knaptoft, which at his death, in 1275, Hugh Gobion held of Robert de Somervill, husband of one of the daughters and coheiresses of Roger de Merlay and one of his heirs (Nichols's Leicestershire, vol. 4, p. 216). Of the above manors it may be here noted that Horsley in Northumberland had come to the Merlays as part of the *maritagium* of Juliana, the daughter of Gospatric, Earl of Dunbar, through whom their royal descent is deduced.

From the "Testa de Nevill" we learn that in 1242–43 Hugh Gobion, John de Shirinton, and Ralph Dayrel held a fee in Horton of Saher de Wahull (Testa, 26b; Farrer, *op. cit.*, vol. 1, p. 86), while in 1235–36 William Fitz Warin accounted to the aid in respect of one-half of a fee in Horton (Farrer, *loc. cit.*; Testa, 28b). It should be noted here that part of the Gobion holdings belonged to the one-half fee in Horton, parcel of three and one-half fees that the Foliots and their feoffees held in Horton of the Honor of Wahull (Farrer, *op. cit.*, vol. 1, pp. 86, 82). Hugh Gobion also held at this time one-half of a fee in Shilvington, Northumberland, of the Merlay barony (Testa, 383b).

Hugh Gobion (VI) espoused the cause of the Great Earl and was taken at Northampton in 1264 (Cal. Pat. Rolls, 359; Farrer, *op. cit.*, p. 86); and in 1268, after Evesham, his manor of Knaptoft, Leics., was given by the King to Hugh de Turbervill, but he subsequently recovered it (Cal. Miscell. Inq., i, 122; Farrer, *loc. cit.*). In 1271 Hugh Gobion and his wife Matilda were claiming a third of two watermills in Harrold, Beds (Abb. Plac., 180; Excerpta, ii, 542; Farrer, *loc. cit.*). He died in 1275, when his inquisition post mortem was taken. At his death he was holding 2 carucates in the suburbs of Northampton, the manor of Knaptoft, Leics., held of Robert de Somervill, who held of the Earl of Leicester's fee, and the manors of Heigham Gobion and Streatley, Beds, held of the Barony of Beauchamp (Cal. Inq., ii, 78; Farrer, *loc. cit.*). It should be noted that the Horton lands are not given among his holdings at his death, but they subsequently reappear in the hands of the family and are of the utmost importance to this article.

VII. The son and heir of Hugh (VI) was Richard (VII), aged 30 years and more at the time of the inquisition. This Richard held in the Feudal Aid of 1284 one and one-fifth fee in Heigham Gobion and a fee in Streatley and Sharpenhoe of the Barony of Hawnes (Feudal Aids, iv, 7). He died towards the end of the year 1300, holding in addition to the lands his father had held at his death a parcel of assart in Horton, held of the King, and one-tenth of a fee there (i.e., he held of the Honor of Wahull). His heirs were Hawise, wife of Ralph le Botiler, aged 18, and Elizabeth, aged 13 (Cal. Inq., iv, 17; Farrer, *loc. cit.*). With this Richard ended the male line of the eldest branch of the Gobions, and we pause here for a moment, leaving this family, to turn to that of Morteyn of Marston Morteyne and Tilsworth, co. Beds.

De Morteyn

In *The Genealogist*, N. S., vol. 38, pp. 194–203, I printed a full account of the family of Morteyn, with the citations relied upon to prove the pedigree, and I shall refer to this article in the following account.

John de Morteyn (I), son of John and Constance (de Merston) de Morteyn, was holding Tilsworth in Bedfordshire in the Feudal Aid of 1284 (Feudal Aids, i, 2). At this time his mother Constance was holding her inheritance of Merston (*ib.*); but by 1293 she was dead, and John de Morteyn held both Tilsworth and Merston (Cal. Chart. Rolls, p. 433). This John de Morteyn (I) died in 1296, and John (II), his son and heir, had married Joan, daughter of Richard de Rothwell (Dunstable Chronicle, Rolls Series, vol. 3, p. 408). On the Octaves of St. Michael, 2 Edward II (1308), a fine was levied between Stephen Brun of Rothwell and John de Morteyn, whereby the manor of Merston was settled on John for life, with remainder in tail to his son Thomas, remainder in tail to Edmund, brother of Thomas, and remainder in tail to John, brother of Edmund (Beds Fines, case 3, file 39, no. 24). Three weeks before Michaelmas, 6 Edward II (1312), John de Morteyn and his wife Joan levied a fine with William Broun of Rothwell for one-third of the manor of Tilsworth, etc., *which Henry de Sewell and his wife Joan hold in dower of the said Joan,* to revert on the death of Joan to John and Joan for life, with remainder in tail to Thomas, their son, remainder in tail to Edmund, and remainder to the right heirs of John de Morteyn (Beds Fines, case 3, file 41, no. 30). John de Morteyn (II) died in 1346 (Feudal Aids, i, 31, 117), and was succeeded by his son, Magister Edmund de Morteyn (III), D. C. L., canon of York and parson of Merston. In 1346 Edmund settled half of Tilsworth manor on his brother, John de Morteyn (IV), and his wife Catherine (Beds Fines, Mich., 20 Edward III, no. 8). This John (IV) died in 1362, leaving a son and heir, John (V), aged 20 years and more in 1366 (Inq. Post Mortem, Edward III, file 191, no. 54b). Master Edmund (III) died in 1366, leaving his nephew, the said John de Morteyn (V), as his heir (*ib.*). This John (V) married Elizabeth ———, and died in 1375. His heirs were Richard Chamberlain, son of Joan, sister of his father, John de Morteyn (IV), aged 60 years, and Thomas Giffard, son of Lucy, also sister of his father, John de Morteyn (IV), aged 30 years (Inq. Post Mortem, Richard II, file 16, no. 39). Elizabeth, his widow, was alive in 1428, holding Marston Morteyne (Feudal Aids, i, 36). The Thomas Giffard above mentioned was Sir Thomas Giffard of Twyford, Bucks, an ancestor of William Sargent of Malden in New England (cf. *The Genealogist*, N. S., vol. 38, p. 202, and Register, vol. 74, pp. 231–237, 267–283, and vol. 75, pp. 57–63, 129–142).

I have gone thus fully into both the families of Gobion and Morteyn, although Mr. Farrer's account of the former is fuller than the above and my own account of the Morteyns in *The Genealogist* is much fuller than the above brief account, because a complete picture of the situation is absolutely necessary in order to grasp the significance of what is to follow. In taking leave of Mr. Farrer's excellent account of the Gobions I cannot refrain from calling attention to his remarkable book, entitled "Honors and Knights' Fees," the first volume of which was published in London in 1923, which, so far as it extends, is indispensable to every student of English mediæval history, topography, and genealogy. The untimely death of Mr. Farrer, however, has made it necessary to discontinue the publication of this valuable work. I wish also to acknowledge herewith the helpful suggestions of my friend, G. Herbert Fowler, Litt.D., of the Old House, Aspley Guise, Beds, Secretary of the Bedfordshire Record Society, who generously placed at my disposal, during a recent visit at his house, his valuable Gobion notes, and who will undoubtedly print, in the near future, an exhaustive account of the Gobions, whose first known ancestor, Hugh, appears to have been a brother of Ralph, Abbot of St. Albans.

Having brought before the reader's mind the situation of these two families, it is necessary to return once more to the fee of Horton and its different proprietors. Mr. Farrer has shown that the original holding of Otbert, who held two hides of Walter the Fleming in the Domesday at Horton, was broken up into several parts. One part passed to the Foliot family and their feoffees (Farrer, *op. cit.*, vol. 1, p. 82), and the other part passed, as we have seen, to Richard Gobion (III), who held one knight's fee there in 1166 of Walter de Wahull. It is with this last tenement that we are concerned. We have seen that Hugh Gobion (VI) and two others held a fee in Horton of Saher de Wahull in 1242–43, but it does not appear among his lands at the time of his death in 1275. It does, however, appear among his son's lands at his death in 1300. We now turn to the great Aid of 1284, to see what had become of Horton in the meantime. There we learn that in 1284 *John de Morteyn* (I) and Lawrence de Preston held one-half of a fee in Horton of John de Wahull. John de Sherington held one carucate in Horton of John de Wahull, and Aubrey de Wytlebury held one carucate in Horton of Lawrence de Preston, and he of John de Wahull. (Feudal Aids, iv, 6.) We note that John de Sherington is apparently the successor in title of the John de Sherinton who was holding with Hugh Gobion (VI) and Ralph Dayrel in Horton in the "Testa" in 1242–43. Lawrence de Preston may be the successor of Ralph Dayrel, and Aubrey de Wytlebury is an undertenant and feoffee of Lawrence de Preston. In 1300 Sir Richard Gobion (VII) at his death held a parcel of assart in Horton and one-tenth of a fee there. Now in 1304 the inquisition post mortem of Thomas de Wahull was taken; and it appeared that John de Sheryngton held one-fourth of a fee in Horton of him, John de Wytlebury one-fourth of a fee, *and Ralph le Botiler, Henry de Sewelle, and the heirs of Richard Gobion one-half of a fee* (Cal. Inq. Post Mortem, iv, 141).

We now jump down almost a hundred years to the reign of Richard II. On 13 March, 5 Richard II (1382), Sir Richard Chamberlain made an indenture of quitclaim to Richard Reynes, son of Sir Thomas Reynes, of the manors of Merston, co. Bedford, and Horton, co. Northampton, with a condition of defeasance in case the manor of Tilsworth or any parcel thereof be recovered against Sir Richard, his heirs, assigns, or any tenant having his estate therein, by Elizabeth, who was the wife of John de Morteyn (V), Knight, the said Richard, son of Thomas, John Reynes, or any of their heirs male, or by John Morteyn of Dunnesby or any heir male of his body (Cal. Close Rolls, p. 117). This Sir Richard Chamberlain was cousin and one of the heirs of the last John de Morteyn (V) of Marston, and Elizabeth, was his widow, who will now presently appear in another document of great importance.

In Easter Term, 7 Henry V (1419), Philip le Botiler, chivaler, sued Elizabeth, widow of Sir John de Morteyn (V), for 8 acres and 100s. rent in Horton. He states that on the Octaves of Trinity, 4 Edward I [sic, II] (1311), Ralph le Botiler and his wife Hawise levied a fine as plaintiffs with Thomas Paynel and his wife Elizabeth, deforciants, for the manor of Heigham Gobion and 4 carucates of land, 24 acres of meadow, 84 acres of wood, and £7 rent in Strateleye, Wrast, Sheppenho, Westhay, Pollokeshull, and Faldo, co. Bedford, and 8 acres of wood and 100s. rent in Horton, co. Northampton, which Margery, who was the wife of Richard Gubyon, held for life; and that Thomas and Elizabeth granted the same, as of the inheritance of Elizabeth, to Ralph and Hawise. He then goes on to state his descent from Ralph and Hawise through John, Ralph, and Philip le Botiler, his father, and he says that Elizabeth, who was the wife of John Morteyn, chivaler, has entered upon the 8 acres of wood and 100s. rent in Horton and holds the same adversely to the fine. Elizabeth Morteyn disputes his claim to be the next heir, and says that Thomas de Reynes, chivaler, John Lovel, parson of Purlok, Richard Maydewel, parson of Clifton, and Nicholas, parson of Statherne (De Banco Rolls, no. 539, m. 409, 19 Richard II, shows that these persons were feoffees for John de Morteyn in a fine of 47 Edward III [1373-74]), were seised of the manor of Horton, whereof said wood and rent were a parcel; and by an indenture dated 1 May, 46 Edward I [sic, III] (1372), they granted the same, together with the manor of Tyllsworth, co. Beds, and Triffeld (i.e., Turville), co. Bucks, to Elizabeth for life, with remainder to Richard de Reynes in tail male, and with contingent remainders to John de Reynes, his brother, and John de Morteyn of Donesby in tail male, with remainder to the right heirs of John de Morteyn. She asks that the remainder men and the heirs of John de Morteyn, her husband, be joined. Philip le Botiler, in his replication, denies her need of them, and says that after the death of Margery, wife of Richard Gobion, John de Morteyn, chivaler, intruded upon the premises, took possession of the said wood and rent, and held them all his life, and that after his death Elizabeth did likewise, and that she has continued to hold them without any right until now, namely, 23 November, 6 Henry V [1418]. The case was adjourned without judgment. (De Banco Rolls, no. 633, m. 403, Easter, 7 Henry V.) It may be here observed that the case errs in saying that the last John de Morteyn and his wife Elizabeth intruded upon the premises after the death of Margery, widow of Richard Gobion. It must have been his grandfather, John de Morteyn (II).

The Feudal Aid for 1302 states that Ralph le Botiler and wife

Hawis and Thomas Paynel and wife Elizabeth hold a knight's fee in Heiham, Stratle, and Faldo, whence the Abbot of Woburn holds a hide for one-fourth of a fee. In 1346 Hawise le Botiler held the fee, and in 1428 Lawrence Cheyne and wife Elizabeth (Feudal Aids, i, 14, 33, 46). In the Nomina Villarum return of 1316 Ralph le Botiler held Horton vill; in 1346 a Hugh Gobion and Ralph Darrell held one-half of a fee in Horton of the fee of Wahull (this may be simply a copy of an earlier entry); and in 1428 ——— accounted for one-half of a fee in Horton which Hugo Gobion and Ralph Daryel once held of the fee of Wahull (Feudal Aids, iv, 26, 447, 42).

The evidence upon the most obscure and difficult and therefore the most important point in the whole pedigree being now all in, the time has arrived to analyze it and to deduce its import. In 1242–43 Hugh Gobion (VI), together with John de Shirinton and Ralph Dayrel, was holding a fee in Horton. This fee does not appear in the inquisition post mortem of Hugh Gobion in 1275. In 1284 John de Morteyn (I) and Lawrence de Preston were holding one-half of a fee there. In 1300 Sir Richard Gobion (VII) was holding a parcel of assart and one-tenth of a fee there. In 1304 Ralph le Botiler, Henry de Sewell, and the heirs of Richard Gobion (VII) (i.e., Hawise, wife of Ralph le Botiler, and Elizabeth, wife of Thomas Paynel) were holding the Gobion tenement in Horton, namely, one-half of a fee, and in 1316 Ralph le Botiler was holding it. We now note that John de Morteyn (I) died in 1296, leaving a widow Joan, who afterwards married Henry de Sewell. In 1373–74 John de Morteyn (V), the great-grandson of John and Joan, held a manor in Horton; and in 1419 the heirs of Ralph and Hawise (Gobion) le Botiler brought suit against Elizabeth, widow of John de Morteyn (V), to recover a parcel of land in Horton of which they claimed the Morteyns had disseised their family after the death of Margery, mother of Hawise and widow of Richard Gobion. The only conclusion to be drawn from this is that John de Morteyn (I) married Joan, the daughter of Hugh Gobion (VI), who died in 1275, that Joan received property in Horton as her *maritagium*, and that John de Morteyn (I) held it in 1284 *jure uxoris*. He died in 1296, and his widow afterwards married Henry de Sewell, who, in 1304, held Horton, *jure uxoris*, along with the Gobion heirs. Finally, we find it, in 1373–74, held by Sir John de Morteyn (V), the great-grandson of John (I) and Joan de Morteyn; and in 1419 the heirs of Hawise Gobion seek to recover 8 acres of wood and 100s. rent in Horton of Elizabeth de Morteyn, widow of Sir John (V), to whom the property had passed down from his great-grandmother.

The marriage of John de Morteyn (I) and Joan, daughter of Hugh Gobion (VI), is proved conclusively by the following copy of a charter, which was furnished to me, after this article was written, by my friend, Oswald Barron, Esq., F.S.A.:

"Ego Hugo Gubiene miles dedi Johi de Morteyne filio Johis de Morteine tota terra mea de Horton cū Johanna filia mea in libero maritagio." (British Museum, Addit. MSS., 5527, fo. 3, being a book of pedigrees compiled by an unknown author between 1595 and 1603 and containing copies of charters then extant. This grant was copied from Robert Chamberlayne's Book of Evidence, fo. 481.)

28

The marriage of Sir John de Morteyn (I) of Marston and Tilsworth to Joan, a daughter of Hugh Gobion (VI), being now proved, it remains to show the royal descent of the Gobions. It is derived through the marriage of Richard Gobion (IV) with Agnes de Merlay, a member of the Norman family of Merlay, one of the great baronial houses of the North Country.

DE MERLAY

The family of Merlay takes its name from Le Merlerault, formerly called Le Merle-Raoult or Raoul, the chief town of a canton of that name, lying between Argentan, in the arrondissement of Argentan, and Laigle, in the arrondissement of Mortagne, all these places being in the department of the Orne, in the old Normandy. (Dupont, Recherches hist. et topog. sur les Compagnons de Guillaume le Conquérant, vol. 1, p. 94.) M. Leopold Delisle mentions a certain Roger de Merle among the followers of Duke William in 1066, who is also cited by Dumoulin. The branch that remained in Normandy long figured among the local nobility of the province. In 1224 William de Merle was one of those assisting at the Court of the Exchequer at Caen. In 1295 Foulques de Merlay, chevalier, lord of Merle-Raoul, was associated with Jean, sieur d'Harcourt (of the great Norman house of Harcourt), admiral of France. In 1302 Foulques (III) de Merle was a marshal of France and one of the victors at Mons-en-Puel (Dict. de la Noblesse, vol. 13, p. 687).

Concerning the origin of the family Orderic Vitalis, the monk of St. Evroult-en-Ourche, in the first half of the twelfth century, has considerable to say:

"Giroie, son of Arnold le Gros of Courcerant [near Mortagne-sur-Orne], son of Abbo le Breton, was of a family that conferred many benefits upon the monks of St. Evroult. Giroie did great deeds in the time of Hugh the Great and King Robert. His sister Hildegarde had three sons and eleven daughters, whose posterity in the next generation were formidable in the wars in France, in England, and in Apulia. Giroie was to marry the daughter and heiress of Heugon, a Norman knight, and he gave him Montreuil and Echaufour, but she died before the marriage, and thereafter he received Heugon's lands from Duke Richard at Rouen. Giroie then married Gisela, sister of Turstin de Bastembourg, and had seven sons and four daughters. Of these, William de Giroie had Arnold d'Echaufour, whose son William was afterwards called in Apulia the Good Norman. Their daughter Emma married Robert de Meleraut (Merle), and had Rodolph (Ralph or Raoul) and William, who is the father of our neighbors Rodolph and Roger." (Orderic Vitalis, vol. 1, pp. 389–395.)

I. From this it would appear that Robert, and not Roger, was the father of the Northumbrian baron William, and that his wife was a niece of Turstin de Bastembourg.

"William de Merlay, with the consent of his wife and his sons, gave to the Durham monks Morewic with all that appertains to it, for the salvation of his soul and the soul of Menialde his wife and the souls of his sons Ralph, Gosfried, and Morello, and all his other sons. Witnessed by William de Merlay, Ralph his son, Gosfrid his son, Moreli his son, Robert, Anseri de Merlai, and Geoffrey de Cliftun. After the death of William, Ralph, his son and heir, came to Durham in the year 1129, in the month of September, one day after St. Cuthbert's, and confirmed the gift" in the presence of many witnesses [who are named, among them his son William]. (Reg. Durham, Dean and Chapter; Monast. Ang., vol. 1, p. 49.)

A charter in the Hallam MS. may also be a charter of his rather than of his grandson William. By this charter William de Merlai gave a carucate to the hospital at Morpeth for the souls of his father and mother and of his ancestors. Witnesses: Peter de Morepeth, Helia the priest, Gaufrid Parchier, Walter de Rochesboro, Aldret de Windegate, Reginald Fitz Wlfoe, Peter the janitor, and many others (Monast. Ang., vol. 1, p. 801b).

William appears to have been a tenant of Geoffrey, Bishop of Coustances. He died before September 1129, leaving William, Ralph, Gosfrid, Morello, and others, among them probably a Roger who is mentioned by Orderic Vitalis as a neighbor of the monks of St. Evroult. William appears in the Pipe Roll of 1130 as owing on his brother's lands in Northumberland (Pipe Roll, 31 Henry I, p. 36). Morellus de Merlay witnessed a charter of William de Albineio, the *pincerna* (butler) of Henry I, to the church at Wimundham in Norfolk (Monast. Ang., vol. 1, p. 339a).

II. Ralph de Merlay, the son and heir of William, was the founder of Newminster Abbey on the eighth day before the Nones of January 1138 (Monast. Ang., vol. 1, pp. 800–801; also Newminster Cartulary (Surtees Soc., 66), vol. 1, pp. 1–2, and original MS. of the foundation in the Arundel Coll., fo. 8b). The Newminster Cartulary states that five years after the foundation of Fountains Abbey Ralph de Merlay, with the consent of his wife and sons, built the Abbey for the health of himself, his wife, his sons, his lords, and all his antecessors, and for the souls of his father and mother and all his dead relatives and friends, and he endowed it with lands in Ritton, Witton, Wansbeck, and Ulgham (Newminster Cartulary, vol. 1, pp. 1–2). Dugdale in his "Baronage" says that he gave to the Abbey his lordship of Kytton and part of the woods of Wytton and the valley between Morpeth and Mitford. Roger de Merlay and his brother William confirmed the above gift of their father Ralph to Newminster (Newminster Cartulary, vol. 1, p. 2). This Ralph de Merlay and his wife Juliana also gave the grange of Hulwane to Newminster (Martyrology of Newminster, in Newminster Cartulary, vol. 1, p. 299). Ralph was dead by 1160, when his son William paid £10 for his fees and was quit (Pipe Roll, 7 Henry II, p. 23). William was dead, without issue, by the time of the great return of 1166, when his brother Roger was holding the barony (Liber Niger, p. 339). Besides William and Roger, Ralph had a son, Master Osbert (Newminster Cartulary, vol. 1, p. 299). Ralph de Merlay married, in the latter part of Henry I's reign, Juliana, daughter of Gospatric, Earl of Dunbar, as is shown by the Newminster Cartulary and other documents. A charter from the old rolls of William, Lord Howard of Naworth, is cited in the "Monasticon," which recites that King Henry [I] has given to Ralph de Merlay in marriage Juliana, daughter of the Earl Gospatric, and, by an agreement made between him and her father, he grants in frank marriage to her and her heirs Horsley, Stanton, Witton, Ritton, and Wyndgates. Witnesses: Patrick, son of ———, John Peverell of Baal-

30

campe, and Edgar, son of Earl Gospatric. And Edgar, son of Gospatric the Earl, confirmed to Juliana his sister the land which his father and her father, namely Earl Gospatric, gave her in frank marriage in Witton, Horsley, Stanton, Ritton, Windcgates, and Leverchilde (Monast. Ang., vol. 1, p. 801, and Newminster Cartulary, vol. 1, p. 269). It may here be noted that Ralph gave to the Newminster monks lands in Wytton and Ritton that were part of Juliana's *maritagium*. The Horsley land passed eventually, as we shall see, into the hands of the Gobions.

As the royal descent of the Gobions comes through Juliana of Dunbar, we must pause here in our account of the Merlays to consider her ancestry. Her father, Gospatric, Earl of Dunbar, first appears shortly after 1100. Henry I, soon after that date, granted to "Gospatric brother of Dolfin," lands between Wooler and Morpeth in Northumberland, which were confirmed to him at York about 1136. These were held in grand sergeanty of being inborwe and outborwe between England and Scotland, i.e., to give security to those persons passing between the two countries. He also received from the Abbot of St. Alban's, between 1097 and 1119, lands adjacent to Berwick and Eylingham. He was present in the Scottish Army at the Battle of Northallerton, and, as he was dead by 16 August 1139, he probably fell in that action (cf. The Scots Peerage, vol. 3, pp. 239–249, where the documents relied upon to prove this account are cited in the account of the earliest house of Dunbar). He was the son of Gospatric, Earl of Northumberland in 1067, who was deprived of his earldom in 1072 and fled to Scotland, where Malcolm granted him the lands at Dunbar. He married ———, "sister of Edmund," to whose lands her son Gospatric obtained right from Henry I. This Gospatric died shortly after he went to Scotland (*ib.*, vol. 3, p. 243). He was the son of Maldred or Malcolm, who married Ealdgith, daughter of Uchtred of Northumberland by Ælgifu, daughter of King Æthelred the Unready. Maldred was the son of Crinan, lay abbot of Dunkeld and seneschal of the Isles, who married Bethoc or Beatrice, daughter and heiress of Malcolm II, King of Scotland, who was slain in 1045 (Annals of Trighernac, 78).

The pedigree of Gospatric, Earl of Dunbar, is well known, and has already been carefully set forth in "The Scots Peerage" (article by Rev. John Anderson), vol. 3, pp. 239–279, so that I have not thought it necessary to go into it with the same fullness that I have used in the rest of the pedigree; but a passage from Symeon of Durham is important in this connection. As Symeon was a monk at Durham in 1083 and was an adult as early as 1073 and was living as late as 1104, his statements must be primary evidence with regard to the great families of his neighborhood.

"Osulf was succeeded by Walthof, Senior, who had a son Uchtred. He submitted by necessity to Knut, and was murdered by a Dane. Earl Uchtred had three sons, Aldred, Eadulf, and Cospatric. The two elder were Earls of Northumberland." (Cf. Symeon of Durham (Surtees Soc., 51), vol. 1, pp. 90–91.)

"Osulf being dead [i.e., Osulf II, Earl of Northumberland, who died in the autumn of 1067, the son of Eadulf, the son of Uchtred], Cospatricus, son

31

of Maldred, the son of Crinan, coming to King William with much money, bought the earldom of Northumberland. For from his mother's blood the honor of that county belonged to him; for he was son of Algitha, daughter of Uchtred the Earl, being the daughter that he had by Algiva, daughter of King Æthelred. This Algitha her father gave in marriage to Maldred, son of Crinan." (Symeon of Durham (Surtees Soc., 51), vol. 1, pp. 90–92.)

III. Having now shown the descent of Juliana de Dunbar from the royal houses of Scotland and England, we return once more to her son, Roger de Merlay. This Roger succeeded his brother, William, who died after 1161–62 and before 1164–65 (Pipe Roll, 8 Henry II, p. 10, and 11 Henry II, p. 28). In the latter year he returned his carta, as follows: Walter de Clinton held one fee and Reginold held two fees of the old feoffment. Roger de Merlay held one-fourth of a fee and Robert Fitz Peter one-third of a fee of the new feoffment, and he owes four knights' fees on his demesne (Liber Rubeus, p. 32). He married Alice de Stuteville, daughter of Roger, and died in 1188, when Earl Duncan of Fife gave 500 marks for the wardship of his son Roger (Pipe Roll, 34 Henry II, and Dugdale's Baronage, vol. 1, p. 570). There was also a son William, who, with his brother Roger, witnessed a charter of William Paris of Schotton to Richard, son of Richard de Plesseto, of lands in Shotton (Cart. Rid., 69, and Hodgson's Northumberland, part 2, vol. 2, p. 336). Agnes, the wife of Richard Gobion (IV), was the daughter of Roger de Merlay (III) and sister of Roger (IV) and William.

IV. This younger Roger de Merlay (IV) confirmed to Newminster Abbey the confirmation of his father Roger (III) of his grandfather's donation (Newminster Cartulary, vol. 1, pp. 2–3). He died in 1239, and was succeeded by his son Roger de Merlay (V) (cf. Hodgson's Northumberland, part 2, vol. 2, p. 375).

V. This last-named Roger died in 1265, leaving three daughters, Alice, Mary, wife of William de Greystock, and Isabel, wife of Robert de Somervill (Cal. Inq. Post Mortem, 1, no. 636). At his death Hugh Gobion was holding Jetingham, Brentingham, Clif, and Cave of him by service of a fee, and in Burton Hugh held five bovates of him by service of one-twentieth of a fee.

The Gobions also inherited Shilvington and Horsley from the Merlays, the latter, as we have seen, having been part of the *maritagium* of Juliana de Dunbar.

Roger de Merlay (V) held *in capite* Morpeth cum Tranewell (its member), Algham, Heppicotes, Shyluyngton, Twysill, Saltwyk, Dudder East and West, Clifton, Cauldwell, Stanyngton, Shotton, Blakeden, Wetslade North and South, Killyngworth, Benton, and Walker for four fees of the old feoffment. Ralph de Merlay held one-fourth of a fee of the new feoffment of him in Heppiscote, and Hugh Gobyon held Shiluynton of him for one-half a fee of the new feoffment. (Newminster Cartulary, vol. 1, p. 267; cf. Cal. Inq. Post Mortem, 1, nos. 636, 683, 775.)

An inquisition was taken in 1247 (writ dated 11 April, 31 Henry III) concerning the sergeanty in Northumberland of Earl Patrick. It states that the Lord King Henry, grandfather of the grandfather of the King that now is, and Earl Quaspatric gave to Raudulf de

Merlaco in frank marriage with Juliana, daughter of Quaspatric, Wytton, Wyndegate, Horsley, Stanton, Ritton, and Leverilcheld. Roger de Merlaco holds Wytton and Wyndegates, but in those are many feoffees. Walter, son of William and his wife Joanna, holds Stanton and Leverilcheld, and Hugh Gubion and William de Horseley hold Horseley. (Cf. Cal. Doc. Scotland, i, 1712.) The Gobion manor of Knaptoft was also a Merlay inheritance (cf. inq. post mortem of Hugh Gobion, writ of 3 Edward I, according to which he held Knaptoft of "Robert de Somervill, who married one of the heirs of Roger de Mereleye;" cf. Cal. Inq. Post Mortem, 2, no. 78).

DE STUTEVILLE

As the question of the ancestry of Alice de Stuteville, who married Roger de Merlay (III), offers some difficulties, I have deemed it best to treat this family separately, especially as the Merlays and their descendants, the Gobions, appear holding certain manors that formed part of the Stuteville inheritance.

The Norman family of Stuteville or Estuteville takes its name either from Estouteville-Ecalles, in the canton of Bouchy and arrondissement of Rouen, or from Estouteville-sur-Mer—probably the former. On the eve of the Conquest a knightly family of the name were the lords of the former parish (Dupont, Recherches, etc., vol. 1, p. 9).

I. The first known ancestor of this family was Robert d'Estouteville (I), who, as "le sire d'Estouteville," figures in the "Roman de Rou" of Wace as one of the victors at Hastings. This Robert, often called Robert Fronte-boef, witnessed a charter of Fulk, dean of Evereux, to St. Evroult-en-Ourche, whereby he gave to the monks, about 1089, the church of Guernanville (Orderic Vitalis, vol. 2, p. 187). He was governor, in 1085, of the castle of Ambrières, which he held against Geoffrey Martel, until relieved by Duke William. As Estouteville was a dependency of the fief of La Ferté-en-Brai, of which the Gourneys were lords, Robert probably came to England in the array of Hugh de Gourney, but strangely enough he does not appear as an English landowner in 1086. He is said to have married Jeanne de Tallebot, daughter of Hue, lord of Cleuville, by Marie de Meulan (Dict. de la Noblesse, vol. 7, p. 558). The Norman branch of the family, descending from his grandson, Robert, sieur de Cleuville, who died, according to the Fécamp Chronicle, in 1185, was long distinguished in Norman history. Henri d'Estouteville swore allegiance to Philip Augustus in 1205, upon the loss of Normandy, and was the ancestor of Jean II, sire d'Estouteville, the grand butler of France, who was taken at Harfleur by the English in 1415 and died a prisoner in England in 1436. He was the father of Louis d'Estouteville, one of the defenders of Mont St. Michel in 1417 and 1427. (Dict. de la Noblesse, vol. 7, pp. 558 et seq.)

II. Robert de Stouteville (I) died about 1090, and was succeeded by his son Robert (II). The father and son have been frequently confused. The second Robert was an adherent of Robert Courtheuse, and had command of his troops in the Pays de Caux. Taken prisoner at the Battle of Tinchebrai (1107), he was sent to England and died in captivity.

33

III. His son, Robert de Stuteville (III), was, like his father, an adherent of Robert Courtheuse. He was taken prisoner at the storming of Dives, and soon afterwards was freed by Henry I, but his lands in England were confiscated. He or his son Robert fought at the Battle of Northallerton in 3 Stephen (1138). He appears to have married the daughter of Hugh Fitz Baldric, the great Domesday tenant in Yorkshire, as the later members of the family are found holding many of Hugh's manors, among them Cottingham, Cowsby, and Boltby (cf. Domesday, vol. 1, folios 327b–328). His property appears to have been given to Nigel de Albini, the ancestor of the Mowbrays, and his son Robert (IV), who rose to favor with Henry II, by agreement received a partial restoration of the lands in question. This Robert (IV) appears in the return of 1166 as holding eight fees of Roger de Mowbray (Liber Niger, p. 309).

IV. The family were liberal benefactors of Rivaulx Abbey, and this Robert (IV) gave to the monks there for his soul and the souls of his grandfather Robert and his father and mother, Robert and Erneburga, and his own wife, Helwise, with the consent of his son William and his other sons, his lands in Honetona. Among the witnesses were John, Nicholas, Roger, and Bartholomew de Stuteville, who were evidently his sons (Rivaulx Cart. (Surtees Soc., 83), pp. 80–82). Odo de Boltby, with the consent of his lord, Robert de Stuteville, and Helwise his wife, and of Iveta, his own wife, and of his heirs Adam, John, and Jordan, gave lands at Boltby to Rivaulx, and among the witnesses were Robert de Stuteville and Walter Espec. This charter, therefore, may have been dated shortly before 1142, when Walter Espec died. (Rivaulx Cart., p. 45.) A title of the same abbey, now lost but extant in September 1640, shows that Robert granted to Rivaulx four carucates in Causby and one in Kepewyk (Rivaulx Cart., p. 267).

In the Gisburn Cartulary there is cited in a note the pedigree given by Baldwin de Wake regarding his liberties in Cottingham in the "Placita Quo Warranto," 7, 8, and 9 Edward I (1278–1281). Baldwin claimed certain rights in Cottingham, Buttercrambe, and its member Scraingham, all of them manors that Hugh, son of Baldric, had held in 1086, "because Robert Front de bos de Stutevile, his ancestor, came at the Conquest with William the Bastard and received the said manors [sic]. He was succeeded by his son Robert, whom Henry, son of King William, ejected from the said manors, but Henry Fitz Empress gave to Robert, his son, parts of Cottyngham and Buttercrambe as his right." This last Robert was succeeded by his son William, and his son Robert received confirmation from King John. (Gisburn Cart., vol. 2, p. 257 (Surtees Soc., 89), and Placita Quo Warranto, p. 198.) We should note here that several generations have been omitted in this pedigree, as was not uncommon in pedigrees entered in legal disputes.

The Yorkshire cartularies contain much information regarding Robert de Stuteville (IV) and his descendants, into which I will not now go as we are concerned with a younger son of Robert (III) called Osmund; but enough has been given to show the connection between Robert de Stuteville (IV) and the manors of Cottingham, Boltby, and Causby.

In 6 Edward III (1332) the King confirmed to Rivaulx Abbey lands at Causby which Osmund de Stuteville had given it, and its road made in the time of Osmund's father is mentioned and the gift of lands in Causby by Osmund's brother William (Rivaulx Cart., p. 290).

We now turn to the cartulary of Meaux or Melsa Abbey. Roger, son of Osmund of Kent, confirmed to the monks there the gift that his father made to them of the land and stone quarry at Brantyngham and the mill of Cotyngham. This confirmation was made in the time of Abbot Alexander (i.e., 1197–1210). (Melsa Cartulary (Surtees Soc.), vol. 1, p. 313.) In the time of Thomas III, Abbot (1183–1197), the gift of Osmund of Kent of the stone quarry is recorded (ib., vol. 1, p. 228). So we find Osmund de Stuteville giving to Rivaulx Abbey lands in Causby and Osmund of Kent giving to Melsa Abbey lands in Cottingham and Brantyngham. While I am not certain whether Osmund de Stuteville, the benefactor of Rivaulx, is identical with Osmund of Kent or a later Osmund, a descendant of his, I do expect to show that Osmund of Kent is the Osmund de Stuteville whose son was Roger de Stuteville. We now find him or a descendant of the same name holding land in Causby and Osmund of Kent holding the mill of Cotyngham and lands in Brantyngham, which latter manor will be traced into the hands of the Merlays. As to Osmund of Kent or Osmund de Stuteville, we may, I think, conclude that he was a younger son of Robert Stuteville (III), as both Cotyngham and Causby were manors of Hugh, son of Baldric, which we have already seen had passed to the Stutevilles, had been lost, and had been subsequently recovered by the family. As to Brantingham, it is a new manor, which had belonged to the Bruce fee and passed with a number of other Bruce manors into the hands of Osmund de Stuteville. In the return of 1166 he appears as holding one-half of a fee of Robert de Stuteville (Liber Niger, p. 321), and in the same *carta* of Robert de Stuteville we find Adam de Boltebi (i.e., the son of Odo de Boltby) holding one-half of a fee of Robert.

Osmund de Stuteville married Isabel, daughter of William Fitz Roger de Gressinghall, the *dapifer* of the Earl of Warenne, and widow of Beranger de Cressi. Isabel de Gressinghall, wife of Beranger Gressi, gave, with the consent of William de Hunterfield, to the monks of Castle Acre Priory, co. Norfolk, the homage of Hugo de Crec, etc., with his tenement in Weseham. Osmund de Stuteville, lord of the Honor of Gressinghall, with the consent of his wife Isabel and his heirs, confirmed all the prior gifts made to the monks of Castle Acre by Wimar, the seneschal of Gressinghall, and Roger his son, and by Walter, son of Wimar, and William, son of Roger, and Roger, son of William, and by Drogo, his brother, and by Beranger de Cressi. Roger, son of William, *dapifer*, gave to the monks of Castle Acre Lechesham Mill (Estlechesham) and lands in Weseham. Witnesses: Ælina, his mother, William, his brother, Walter, son of Wimar, and William, his son, and others named. Drogo, son of William, *dapifer* de Gressinghall, gave to the said monks the churches of Kemestune, Estlechesham, Dunham, etc. Roger, *dapifer* of the Earl of Warenne, gave for the souls of his brother Oddo and his father

William lands in Lechesham to Castle Acre Priory. Witnesses: Ralph and Baldwin de Frivill, Walter Fitz Wimar, Ralph, son of Osmund, William, son of Walter, and others named. (Cf. for these five charters Monast. Ang., vol. 1, pp. 627–628.)

After Osmund's death Isabel married William de Hunterfield, who, with his wife Isabel, levied a fine with William de Stuteville (i.e., son of Osmund) for her dower in the free tenements that were her husband's, Osmund de Stuteville's, in Brantingham, Riplingham, Newehald, Stiuelingflet, Newesum, Causby, Kipwic, and Nesse, and William gave to her all the lands in Causby, 29 September–27 October 1202 (York Fines (Surtees Soc., 94), p. 57). This is evidently a final concord. We may note here that Newsham and Brantingham were part of the Bruce fee. It is not easy to say just when Osmund de Stuteville died, but it is clear that he was dead before September 1202.

Osmund had with certainty two sons, William and Roger, and probably a son or grandson, Osmund, for in the Patent Roll of 18 John (1216) there is a safe conduct for those who come to the King's service through Osmund de Stutevile (Rot. Litt. Pat., 198), and in the Close Roll there is an order to the sheriff of Norfolk to give to Osmund de Stuteville the lands of William de Mandeville in that county, to be held during the King's pleasure (Rot. Litt. Claus., 256b).

William, son of Osmund de Stuteville, was a benefactor of Byland Abbey. Odo de Baylof and Agnes his wife gave by their charter 16 acres in Nesse to the monks of Byland, to wit, 10 acres of the fee of Robert de Stuteville and 6 acres of the fee of Robert de Gaunt. This grant was confirmed by Robert, son of William de Stuteville, and by William, son of Osmund de Stuteville. In the margin of the charter the monks have given a tabular pedigree of the confirming lords, as follows: "Robert de Stutevile avus Willelmi, Osmund de Stutevile filius Roberti, Willelmus filius Osmundi de Stutevile, Robertus filius Willelmi." (Cart. Byland Abbey, Egerton MS., 2823, fo. 79.) Nesse, as we have seen, was part of the fee of Osmund de Stuteville. William may have been the eldest son of Osmund, and he may be, although chronology does not make it likely, the William de Stouteville who was granted a yearly fair at his manor of Gressinghall on 8 May 1229 (Cal. Close Rolls, 174). We should also note at this point that in the Feudal Aid of 1284 Jordan Foliot (the eventual heir of William de Stuteville, son of Osmund) held Causby of the fee of Roger de Mowbray (Feudal Aids, vi, 53), and we also recall that de Mowbray was the heir of Nigel de Albini, to whom Henry I gave the forfeited estates of Robert de Stuteville after Tinchebrai.

Leaving now the family of William, we turn to his brother Roger, whose line we are following down into the Merlay family. This Roger de Stuteville was sheriff of Northumberland from 1169 (16 Henry II) to 1183 (Pipe Rolls, and Hutchinson's Northumberland, p. 451). He is frequently called Roger de Stuteville of Burton Agnes, a manor of the Bruce fee that he held. He appears frequently in the reign of Henry II as a witness to charters, etc., in Yorkshire of members of his family. He inherited from his father's fee Branting-ham, which, as we have seen, passed to his daughter Alice, who married Roger de Merlay (III), and appears in the inquisition post mortem of Roger de Merlay (V), 50 Henry III (1265), as being held at that time of him by Hugh Gobion, that is to say, this manor of Osmund de Stuteville, which was a part of the Bruce fee, passed with Alice, daughter of Roger, to the Merlays, as part of her in-heritance, and was carried as part of her *maritagium* by her daughter into the Gobion family. Roger de Stuteville was certainly dead by 1202 (Abb. Plac., p. 76). He had held Brentingham, Jetingham (Yeddingham), Burton, Clif, and Cave — all in Yorkshire, and these passed to his descendants. In 1265 (50 Henry III) Roger de Merlay (V) had held Burton; Hubert de St. Quintin held of him two and one-half fees, and Hugh Gobion held in Yeddingham, Brentingham, Clif, and Cave one fee of the said Roger.

At his death Roger de Stuteville left one son, Anselm, who died *s.p.* before 1202, and five daughters, Beatrice, wife of William de Colville, Agnes, wife of Hubert de St. Quintin, Alice, widow of Roger de Merlay (III), Gundred, and Isabel. Concerning these children and their holdings there is considerable information both in the public records and in the cartularies.

Fifteen days after Easter, 4 John (1203), a precept was issued to William de Colvill and Beatrice his wife that they permit the prior of Lewes to present to the church at Weston (co. Cambridge). William and Beatrice say that Osmund de Stuteville, who held it, gave it to a certain Roger in the time of King Henry, father of King John, and the right to the advowson descended from Osmund to Roger and from Roger to Anselm de Stuteville and from Anselm to Beatrice, as of right of heritage (Abb. Plac., p. 39). William de Colvill must have died soon after this, because a final concord was made on 3 December 1202 between William de Rocheford and Beatrice his wife and Hubert de St. Quintin regarding the manor of Brandes-burton. William and Beatrice renounced their rights in the vill and Hubert gave to William and Beatrice 18 bovates in Turkileby (Thir-kleby, Swine parish in Holderness), as the *maritagium* of Beatrice, and William and Beatrice renounced their rights to 6 carucates in Burton (York Fines (Surtees Soc., 94), p. 76).

Hubert de St. Quintin and Agnes his wife brought suit against Alice de Stuteville for 2 carucates, 40 acres, in Burton, as her share of a free tenement which was the property of Anselm de Stuteville, brother of Agnes and Alice. Alice in her answer states that there were five sisters of Anselm, and that his estate was divided between them on his death, and that the two daughters of Gundred, one of the sisters, have one-fifth in her purparty, and that she cannot answer without them. (Abb. Plac., p. 76, in an uncertain year of King John.)

Hubert de St. Quintin and Agnes his wife complain against the Countess of Albemarle for distraining them in their lands at Mapelton for failure of the homage and service and relief of Peter de Brus, chief lord of the said lands, to whom Alice de Stuteville did service for her lands and Hubert and Agnes hold of her, etc., October, 8 John (1206). (Abb. Plac., p. 52.)

William Ingram granted to Alice de Stuteville, sister of Anselm, a carucate in Yeddingham, which her father formerly held of him, for a carucate in Heslarton and 6½ carucates and 2½ bovates in Cave, Brantingham, Cliffe, and Hotham (Dods. MSS., vii, 217, and Gisburn Cart., vol. 2, p. 283).

Agnes de Stuteville gave a toft in Tirnom to Burlington Priory for the soul of her sister Isabel. Alice de Stuteville also gave to this priory a toft there, which was confirmed by Roger de Merlay; and in 1299 Sir William de St. Quintin gave to the Prior of Burlington a free road, etc., in Burton Agnes. (Burton's Monast. Ebor., pp. 219, 242.)

The above-cited documents, together with those previously cited under Gobion and Merlay, make it clear that Alice, wife of Roger de Merlay, was the daughter of Roger de Stuteville. She had lands in Yeddingham and Brantlingham, Burton and Cliff. Roger de Stuteville, her father, inherited Brantingham from his father, Osmund de Stuteville, and Osmund held in Cottingham and Causby; and, as these manors were part of the Fitz Baldric fee in 1086, Osmund must belong to the family that inherited the fee of Hugh, son of Baldric, or the Cottingham Stutevilles, and in that case he must be the son of Robert de Stuteville (III). Finally, care must be taken not to confuse Roger, son of Osmund, with his cousin Roger, son of John (the son of Robert de Stuteville III). (Cf. Cal. Rot. Chart., vol. 1, p. 206, and Dugdale's Warwickshire, vol. 1, p. 95.) It seems likely that Osmund married first a lady of the Bruce family, who was the mother of his son Roger.

This closes the account of the royal descent of Lucy de Morteyn, the wife of Sir John Giffard of Twyford. The whole pedigree is very clear, and offered no very great difficulties to a person familiar with such work, except at the point of the marriage of Sir John de Morteyn (I) and Joan Gobion; and on this point the charter found after this article was written and inserted above (p. 368) confirms absolutely the correctness of the conclusion at which the writer had already arrived, namely, that Joan, wife of Sir John de Morteyn, was a daughter of Hugh Gobion (VI). From Lucy de Morteyn to William Sargent, the emigrant to New England, the evidence of the descent has already been printed in the REGISTER, as stated in the last paragraph of the introduction to this article (*vide supra*, p. 359).

The sole object of the writer being to point out to the readers of the REGISTER how mediæval genealogy is worked out, he will feel himself amply repaid for the labor spent upon this article if it shall prove to be of any help to other investigators.

GODDARD.—A genealogy of the American family of Goddard was published in Worcester, 1833, by Wm. Austin Goddard, in which the account of the origin of the family seems to be not quite correct. The account as there given is from the manuscript of Edward Goddard, a grandson of the Edward first mentioned, who may have relied on tradition for some of his facts. It runs thus : " Edward Goddard, farmer, was born & lived in Norfolk co., England, was once very wealthy but afterwards much reduced by oppression during the Civil War. He being on the Parliament side, his house was beset & demolished by a company of cavaliers, who also plundered his substance. He escaped through their midst in disguise but died soon after. He was married to a Doyley & had children as follows, but not in order as to age,—William, John, Richard, Edward, James, Vincent, Benjamin, Thomas, Josias. These with three daughters arrived at the age of men & women." William, the seventh son, was the emigrant who came over in 1661, having had six children born in London, of whom three survived, born after 1653.

The account here given seems to identify this Edward not with any Goddard of Norfolk, but with an Edward Goddard of Inglesham, Wilts, who lived at the same time, and of whom we have an account in Burke's Commoners, and in a book lately published in England by Richard Jefferies, " Memoir of the Goddards of North Wilts," noticed in the last REGISTER. For this Edward Goddard of Inglesham, living at the same time as the Edward of the American genealogy, married a Priscilla D'Oyley and had children : John, James, Francis, Thomas, Edward, and three daughters, Priscilla, Martha and Elizabeth, according to both Burke and Jeffries; and according to Jeffries, also had Richard, William, Josiah, Benjamin, all of which names correspond to those of children in the other account, except Francis, who may have died young, it being stated in the American account that " all these children arrived at the age of men and women," and Vincent, whose name occurs in the family as given in the American book, but not in the English, but which is a name which occurs in other branches of the family. Jefferies gives this Edward as the ancestor of the American branch through William his seventh son.

The family of Goddard as thus given traces to Walter Godardville, who added the Norman termination -ville to his Saxon name Goddard, a termination which his descendants however dropped. He had lands in North Wilts, temp. Henry III., was made castellar of Devizes Castle 1231-2, and died 1273. The next we come to was John Godard de Poulton, near Marlborough, whom Jefferies calls his son, but who was more likely as Burke has it a descendant, as he lived nearly a hundred years later. This John Godard de Poulton was succeeded by a second John Godard de Poulton, who appears from 1386 to 1434, living in the reign of King John and the days of John of Gaunt, to whom there is a tradition that John of Gaunt gave a residence at Upham in Aldbourne. His son, Walter Godard de Cherhill, appears 1460, and was succeeded by his son, John Godard de Upham, a large landed proprietor, in the latter part of the fifteenth century, who was the founder of the family. He married Elizabeth, dau. of William Berenger, of Manningford Bruce, and died March 10, 1545. His eldest son, John, became the ancestor of the Goddards, of Cliffe Pypard, the senior branch of the family in Wilts. The second son, Thomas, married first, Anne, sister of Sir George Gifford, Buckingham, from whom descend the Goddards of Swindon, which manor Thomas Goddard bought in 1560. He was succeeded by Richard Goddard, of Swindon, who married Elizabeth, dau. of Thomas Walrond, of Albourne, who left with two other children, Thomas, his heir at Swindon, and Edward Goddard of Englesham. Thomas's family afterward died out, and Swindon passed to Ambrose Goddard, a descendant of Edward, of Englesham. This Edward, of Englesham, seems to be the one from whom the American family descends. He married Priscilla, the daughter (by Ursula, a sister of Sir Anthony Cope, Bart., of Hanwell, Oxon) of John D'Oyley of Chiselhampton, descended from the ancient family of D'Oyley, of Oxfordshire, who came over with the conqueror, were Barons of Hokenorton, and who built Oxford Castle and Osenay Abbey. Edward Goddard's second son, William, was a sufferer by the great fire of London, of which he was a citizen, and emigrated to America, settling at Boston in 1666. He married Elizabeth, dau. of Benjamin or William Miles, of London, and was ancestor of the American Goddards.

Harvard College.   E. R. WILLSON.

A TWELVE-YEAR HUNT
FOR
AN IMMIGRANT ANCESTOR

By LOUIS THORN GOLDING of Washington, D. C.

THIS is the story of a twelve-year hunt for an immigrant ancestor, that began in New Jersey, skipped to Westchester County, N. Y., Long Island, and Connecticut, leaped to the Province of New Brunswick, thence to Barbados, and from there to Bermuda, and finally spanning the Atlantic, reached London, where the problem was solved.

The hunt began in 1921, soon after the writer's election as a life member of the New England Historic Genealogical Society had stirred his latent curiosity as to his ancestry. As a boy in New Jersey, his father had told him that he believed the family came from Canada. None of his father's generation knew or seemed to care about family history more than a generation back, or wanted to talk about it; therefore, unsatisfied but silenced, he dropped the question. Later his interest was aroused by finding that persons of his name had been Loyalists in Massachusetts and had gone to the Province of New Brunswick early in the Revolutionary War. This seemed in accord with the statement of his father that the family came from Canada. He knew from an old family Bible that his great-grandfather and great-great-grandfather were buried in Westchester County, N. Y., but how they came to be there and where they came from he did not know, but he rather inclined to the theory that they were descended from or connected with the Massachusetts Loyalists of the name and had come to New York State after the Revolution.

This was all that he knew or thought that he knew for many years, when, having become a member of the Society, he determined to make some investigations. The outlook was not promising. His parents were long dead, as was also every member of his father's generation; his cousins had not as much information as he nor any particular interest; and there was a complete absence of any documentary or material evidence except the old Bible, published in 1802, and purchased that year by Joseph Golding, his great-grandfather. He began by procuring the services of a Boston genealogist, who, according to instructions, searched for a connection with the Golding family of Massachusetts. This gentleman soon found that he was on the wrong trail, and moved the search to Westchester County, with the result that he unearthed the will of Thomas Golding of Northcastle, who died in 1759, whose eldest son was named Joseph; but no will of Joseph could be found or anything to connect him with Abraham (great-great-grandfather), who died in 1810, or Joseph (great-grandfather), who died in 1813, except the latter name.

The writer then recalled that, when a boy in Perth Amboy, his father had shown him some letters, etc., left by his grandfather, referring to an inquiry as to possible property in New Brunswick. Where these papers were he did not know; they had been in an old secretary, used by his father but emptied of its contents after his father's death a dozen years before.

Wearing overalls, the writer made a most careful search of the old Golding house at Perth Amboy, then dismantled and awaiting the house wreckers. He crawled into odd corners and under the eaves, pulled up floors in garrets, and finally collected a great mass of old documents, receipted bills, letters, etc. Hours of examination finally brought to light the looked-for packet, yellowed with age, dated 1831, and containing a transcript of the will of Joseph Golding, son of Thomas of Northcastle, filed in Gagetown, N. B., in 1789, and mentioning his son Abraham, the writer's great-great-grandfather, who returned to Westchester County after his father's death and settled in Somers, where he died and was buried. This find linked up Thomas and Joseph and carried the search two generations back. Further search in Westchester County developed that Thomas had been one of the earliest settlers of the northeastern part of the county about 1720, and that he had been tax collector and constable and had owned a slave, but nothing more—nothing about his parentage. The hunt seemed to have come to an end. However, the writer was not convinced that Thomas was the immigrant. While there was nothing tangible to disprove it, all the surrounding circumstances indicated that Thomas had not come from England; nevertheless there seemed nothing more to do. The genealogist made his report and returned to Boston, and the matter rested until chance took a hand.

About a year later the writer happened upon a bound volume of the magazine of a New York historical society, and turning to the index found that one William Golding had witnessed a will in Brooklyn in 1686. Hope was revived, and another genealogist was retained, this time a New Yorker, a descendant of the early Dutch settlers. Then things began to happen. The William Golding lead was followed until he and all his family were eliminated. This search was most interesting and disclosed amusing details, including an account of the cure by the ducking stool of the scolding tongue of one of the Golding females during the period of Dutch control. When the William Golding clue had been eliminated, the search was pushed farther out on Long Island, and an Ephraim Golding was found to have bought land in Hempstead in 1688 and to have lived there until his death in 1707. His will named his wife Rebecca as executrix and Thomas as one of his sons. As Thomas of Northcastle had had a son named Ephraim, it was recognized that another generation had been added to the ancestral line.

Just here a discovery was made that much surprised the writer. It was revealed that the Joseph Golding who died in New Brunswick had been for many years an officer in the Provincial Militia of New York and had served with the Westchester County company in two campaigns of the French and Indian War. But he sided with King George in the troubles preceding the Revolution, and was imprisoned by the Westchester County patriots for his opposition. In 1776 he was granted a warrant by General Howe, raised a company, and as its captain served in the Queen's Rangers, with the British Army, until the Loyalist regiments were disbanded. The writer was a member of the Society of Sons of the Revolution, by virtue of the services of his father's mother's ancestors in Washington's army, and was president of his chapter. He had been early and deeply grounded in the patriotic spirit of these ancestors, and was startled and a trifle embarrassed to find himself descended from a despised "Tory." However, he consoled himself with the reflection that, although his ancestor's judgment of the right side of the quarrel had been poor, he had had the courage to draw his sword and fight for his convictions, a course which forced him to leave his native land and go to New Brunswick, and also cost him two farms in West- chester County and other property confiscated by the State of New York.

The discovery of Ephraim as a settler on Long Island in 1688 seemed promising, but not conclusive of his immigrant status. It must be learned who he was and whence he came. The search was pressed on Long Island, and the genealogist soon found a clue at Huntington. In 1673, so say the Huntington town records, "Thomas Skidmore gave unto his son-in-law John Golding, according to the custom of our English nation by turf and twig, a farm," etc.

Huntington is only about twenty miles from Hempstead, the dates did not conflict, and Ephraim's eldest son had been named John. It seemed likely that John of Huntington was Ephraim's father. Accordingly search for John's will was made, but none could be found. The records of his father-in-law Skidmore were also ex- amined in Fairfield and other Connecticut towns. Nothing definite was found, although John's name appeared in the tax lists of Hun- tington and in the records of various lawsuits. The last record, the transfer of his farm, appeared in 1686 and, coupled with the failure to find his will, seemed to indicate that he had removed from the neighborhood. Unfortunately the census report of Huntington for the year 1680, which had been stored with other Colonial records in the attic of the State Capitol at Albany, was destroyed when the top story of that building was burned some twenty years ago. With the loss of this positive evidence, for the report undoubtedly contained a full record of John and his family, strong efforts were made to find other evidence, but without result. Thus the matter stood for a year or two, while Westchester County, Connecticut, and Long Island records were combed. It seemed as though the search had ended inconclusively, and that John must be accepted as the probable immigrant ancestor. The genealogist was strongly of that opinion, and so stated in his final report. He based his opinion on the proximity and the dates, and, above all, leaned heavily, and, as it proved, too heavily, upon the circumstance that Ephraim had named his eldest son John (presumably after his father) and another son Thomas (presumably after his wife's father).

The writer was unsatisfied; it might be true that John was the immigrant, but he wanted proof. However, there seemed no other place in which to continue the search, and therefore the matter rested for a year or so, when chance again intervened.

One day the writer ran across Hotten's "Original Lists," and, as he always did with genealogical books, examined the index, and found the name of Golding. It seemed that one John Golding had gone to Barbados in 1631. Then the writer recalled that John of Huntington's wife was the sister of the wife of Thomas Higbie, "a ship captain and merchant trading to the West Indies." He speculated: perhaps John of Huntington was originally one of Higbie's sailors; perhaps he was a descendant of John of Barbados and had been shipped by Higbie when the latter visited that island, as was probable, because Barbados, in the third quarter of the seventeenth century, was very prosperous and the seat of a lucrative trade in sugar and rum. Perhaps, when the vessel returned to Long Island, Captain Higbie took John, who seems to have been a "likely" lad and a favorite with his father-in-law, home, and thus he met Grace Skidmore, Mrs. Higbie's sister, and married her. Very speculative and not promising, but perhaps worth a try, since there was nothing else in sight. Besides, in the genealogical section of the New York Public Library there was mention of the filing of the will of one Gideon Golding in Barbados in 1686. So, taking a long shot, he sent a summary of the problem to the United States consul at Bridgetown, Barbados, asking him to pass it on to someone there who engaged in genealogical research. However, before he could receive a report, the writer departed, with his wife and son, on the Cunarder *Tuscania* for a cruise in the West Indies, and in due season made a day's stop at Barbados. There he made the acquaintance of Mr. W. T. Fitzpatrick, a venerable old gentleman, the head verger of the Anglican cathedral in Bridgetown, to whom the consul had turned over the matter.

Mr. Fitzpatrick had already searched various records, and among the dozen or so entries referring to Goldings was one showing that Ephraim Golding had married, on 26 June 1687, Rebecca Gibbs. Since Ephraim of Hempstead left a widow named Rebecca, and the dates harmonized, it seemed pretty certain that he had been the bridegroom in this wedding in the Church of St. Michael at Bridgetown. There was also a transcript of the will of Gideon Golding, filed in 1686, in which he mentioned his brothers Arthur of London and

Percival of Bermuda, the latter having eight children. Here was another clue in the name *Percival*, for Ephraim had a grandson by that name, who was born in 1717, and there was record of another Percival, who died in 1818. This recurrence of the unusual name *Percival* among the descendants of Ephraim indicated at once the advisability of a search for the descendants of Percival of Bermuda, and accordingly the hunt was presently transferred to that delightful seagirt winter resort.

After some difficulty the writer secured the services of a lady in Bermuda, who promptly furnished interesting information. It appeared that there had been two Goldings in Bermuda in the seventeenth century—William, the clergyman, who came about 1630, and Percival, the schoolmaster, who came about 1637 and was living in 1680, but was described as "very aged." William died about 1650, leaving a will, in which he mentioned his "only son John." No will of Percival or John could be found, but a record of John's baptism in 1631 was found. Also it was found that Ephraim Golding was mentioned in Bermuda history as "among those who brought ashore treasure from the Spanish wreck" in January 1687 [1686/7]. Also it was discovered later that Ephraim was a passenger on the sloop *Experience,* which sailed from Bermuda for Barbados on 3 June 1687. Here was a clear chain of events that connected Ephraim with Bermuda. He was there in January 1687 [1686/7] getting "treasure" from the wreck, and, having received his share, sailed on 3 June 1687 for Barbados and married there 26 June 1687, Rebecca Gibbs, whom he must have known previously, probably in Bermuda, as the Gibbs family was at that time numerous and prominent there. The next year, in November, he is found in Hempstead, Long Island, well supplied with money, for he bought two farms and the rights of one of the proprietors, assumed a leading place in the town, and served on the grand jury.

Interesting and romantic as all this was, it threw no clear light upon Ephraim's parentage and did nothing to prove that he was the original immigrant. In fact, the theory of the New York genealogist that John of Huntington was the original immigrant and Ephraim's father was strengthened. John of Bermuda was of about the right age; and, if the writer's theory that John of Huntington came there in Captain Higbie's ship was sound, it was clear that he might have come from Bermuda as well as from Barbados.

The writer worked for a year or so on the theory that John of Bermuda and Huntington was the immigrant, and exhausted every source of information he could think of. He made a second visit to Barbados, and also went to Bermuda and New Brunswick in the hope of discovering something definite, but without results. It seemed as though the hunt had finally ended inconclusively with the question: "Was Ephraim or John the immigrant?"

The hunt had now been going on for nine years, and had led quite clearly and apparently finally to Bermuda. The recurrence of the name *Percival* seemed to indicate Ephraim's descent from the "aged" schoolmaster of that name, but there was no proof; and then there

44

was John of Huntington, who might well be Ephraim's father, but who seemed very likely to have been the "only son John" (baptized in 1631) of William, the clergyman. The writer speculated: perhaps William and Percival were brothers; this might possibly explain the survival of the latter name among Ephraim's descendants, even if he was John's son and not Percival's. This might also explain Ephraim's presence in Bermuda at the salvaging of the Spanish wreck; he might have gone there to see his relatives, and, being a sailor like his father, had taken a hand in a nautical enterprise. The brother theory seemed the only way out, and the writer was quite impressed with it and decided to see if search in England would not throw some light on the question.

The possibility of finding a clue in England had been in his mind since he had seen the first brief transcript of Gideon's will in Barbados a couple of years before. At that time he had been struck with the fact that Gideon had mentioned his brothers Arthur and Percival, for he recalled having encountered these names before.

Several years previously, in pursuance of his long interest in the struggle for Dutch independence, the writer had purchased a book called "The Fighting Veres," by Sir Clements Markham, an account of the two brothers who commanded the English troops in that long contest against Spain. Markham commenced his story with an account of the Vere family from which came the Earls of Oxford, holders of one of the oldest and proudest titles in England. In 1548 the sixteenth Earl of Oxford, cousin of Francis and Horace Vere (the Fighting Veres), married Margaret Golding, daughter of John Golding of the parish of St. Paul, Belchamp, co. Essex, an auditor of the exchequer for Henry VIII. Their son Edward, the seventeenth Earl, was, when about twelve years of age, placed under the tutelage of his mother's brother, the "learned Arthur Golding," his father being dead. Arthur Golding was a famous scholar of the Elizabethan Age, the friend and literary executor of Sir Philip Sidney, translator of the "Metamorphoses" of Ovid and other classics, and, as such, one of the sources of Shakespeare. He was also, oddly enough, translator of Calvin's sermons and many other religious works. The similarity of name had interested the writer, and probably caused him to remember that Markham in a footnote stated that Percival Golding had written a history of the Vere family in 1605. At the time he wondered if Percival were not the son of Arthur. Now these two names appeared again in Gideon's will, and it seemed highly probable that the brothers of Bermuda and Barbados were descended from or at least related to the Elizabethan scholar and author. That the connection appeared to be with the family of a distinquished man seemed to make it probable that the search in England would not be entirely in the dark and was worth trying. If it were discovered that William and Percival were brothers it would greatly strengthen the existing probability that John was Ephraim's father. Then, too, there was the possibility that some direct evidence of Ephraim's parentage might be found.

In June 1929, being in London, the writer called upon Maj. Alfred

Trego Butler, Windsor Herald of the College of Arms, and laid all the facts before him. Major Butler, impressed by the recurrence and conjunction of the names *Arthur* and *Percival,* decided that the English connection was with the Suffolk branch of the Golding family, and kindly undertook to superintend the necessary searches. For over two years the work went on, finally bringing to light the wills of Gideon's nephew and others of that and preceding generations in England, and clearly establishing the pedigree in the direct line through Percival, the author of the history of the Vere family, and his father, Arthur Golding, back as far as the fourteenth century. Still nothing definite had been found as to Ephraim's parentage.

Both American and English lines had now been traced to Bermuda, but the link there was yet to be found. Thus the matter stood until Major Butler asked for a full copy of Gideon's will, feeling that the two summaries which the writer had already obtained were unsatisfactory. Application was again made to the United States consul, this time requesting a complete certified copy of Gideon's will, exactly as written and spelled. In due season there came to hand eleven typewritten legal-cap pages, bearing the certificate of the Barbados official. It was a most interesting document, drawn with all the elaborate care and pompous phraseology popular at the time.

The testator, after making a number of other bequests, being himself childless, left to each of the eight children of his brother Percival in Bermuda, who were also children of his wife's sister, one thousand pounds of Muscovy sugar, *when they should come to Barbados to claim it.* This proved to be the long-looked-for proof by which Ephraim's father was determined to have been Percival, and the two lines were linked up in Bermuda. This explained the presence in Barbados, as indicated by the records, of five young Goldings. They had come to Barbados in a year or so after Gideon's death, to receive their rich sugar-planter uncle's bequest. That thousand pounds of Muscovy sugar, then the currency of Barbados, as tobacco was of Virginia, was probably equivalent to $1000 to-day—a tidy sum, which furnished dowries for Dorothy and Eliza, made it easier for Abraham to marry, and formed a comfortable addition to the fortune of Ephraim, already founded on his share of the "treasure from the Spanish wreck." All the children of Percival who were old enough seemed to have hurried to Barbados, as Uncle Gideon evidently intended; and all seemed to have embarked upon matrimony except William, the sea captain, who died.

Thus reconstructed out of the past, the Golding pedigree was laid by Major Butler before the examining committee of the College of Arms, and by them accepted and recorded.

The search in England had developed that the writer's "brother" theory was wrong. William and Percival were not brothers, although probably related, as in a collateral branch of the Goldings the name *William* was frequent. However, this did not entirely eliminate John of Huntington from the picture. The writer thinks that he was William's son, that Higbie brought him to Long Island, and that it was through him that Ephraim decided to go there after his marriage.

Ephraim had doubtless heard about it from John, whom he probably knew in Bermuda as a boy, or perhaps he had made a voyage there. At any rate, whether through John's influence or not, he did come to Long Island in 1688, and thus became the immigrant ancestor for whom the long search had been made.

This search had been most interesting, embracing as it did both hemispheres and the "islands of the sea." It furnished the writer with leisure occupation, took him on many journeys, and left with him as material souvenirs the sword carried by Capt. Joseph Golding in the French and Indian War and in the Revolution and a bound volume of the sermons of Calvin, translated by Arthur Golding and published by him in 1584. It also cleared up the mystery of the ignorance of his father's generation as to the family history. His father's mother's father and grandfather had been soldiers in Washington's army; hence a policy of silence as to the Loyalist Goldings, which finally resulted in burying the family history in oblivion.

A by-product of the hunt was the right to the arms of the Golding family of Cavendish (confirmed to them at the Heralds' Visitation of 1577), as set forth in the certificate of arms issued to the writer by Major Butler, Windsor Herald and genealogist of the Order of the Bath.

[The pedigree thus established by Mr. Golding's twelve-year hunt shows that Ephraim[1] Golding of Hempstead, Long Island, the immigrant ancestor of this Golding family in America, who bought land at Hempstead in 1688 and lived there until his death in 1707, was a son of Percival Golding of Bermuda, schoolmaster, who had come to Bermuda about 1637 and was living, "very aged," in 1680, and that Percival Golding of Bermuda was a son of Percival Golding of co. Suffolk and London, whose father was the illustrious Arthur Golding, one of the scholars of the Elizabethan Age, whose ancestry has been traced to the fourteenth century. From Ephraim[1] Golding of Hempstead the line of descent runs through Thomas[2] of Northcastle, Westchester Co., N. Y., who died in 1759, Joseph[3] of Northcastle, the Loyalist, whose will was filed at Gagetown, N. B., in 1789, Abraham,[4] 1748–1810, of Somers, Westchester Co., Joseph[5] of Somers, who died in 1813, Abraham,[6] who was born at Somers in 1805 and died at Perth Amboy, N. J., in 1847, and Isaac Thorn,[7] who was born at Perth Amboy in 1835 and died there in 1909, the father of the writer of this article.—EDITORS.]

THE GOOKIN FAMILY.

BY J. WINGATE THORNTON, ESQ., OF BOSTON.

In an extensive research among the county and other local histories of England, the name of Gookin has been nowhere found but in connection with the family of the County of Kent. The following pedigree is a literal copy, taken for the writer * from the original "visitation" in the *Herald's College* in London, and is the *only one* of the name on the records of that Institution.

ARNOLDUS GOKIN, = de Com. Cantii.

Tho. Gokin de Bekes,=.... filia et haeres borne in Com. Cantii. | de Durant.

Johes Gokin de = Katherina filia Ripple Court in | G. mi. Den. Com. Cantii. | de Kingstone.(‡)

Elizabetha nupta Tho. Long Aldermanus Cantii.

ARMS — *Quarterly. 1st, gules, a chevron ermine between 3 cocks or, 2 in chief, 1 in base.. Gookin. 2nd and 3rd, sable, a cross crosslet, ermine. 4th, or, a lion rampant, gules between 6 crosses fitchée.*
CREST — *On a mural crown, gules, a cock or, beaked and legged azure, combed and wattled gu.*†

Vincent Gokin, fil: 4th dux: filiam .... Wood.

Daniel Gokin filius tertius duxit Mariam filiam Rici Birde, Sacræ Theolog. Co. Esse.

Johannes Gokin = Anna, filia fil. 2ans juris pe- | Johes Brett. ritus.

Thomas Gokin de = Jana filia Richardi Ripple Cort. fil. et | Thurston de Chalhæres. | lock.

Thomas, filius secundus.

Johes Gokin, fil. et hæres de Ripple. | Richard Gookin of Ripple, living 1699.

Catharina nupt. Gms. Warren de Ripple predict.

Maria. Anna. Elizab. Margareta.

The omission in the pedigree of the descendants of *Daniel* and *Vincent*, the third and fourth sons of *"John Gokin of Ripple Court,"* who were both married in England, may be accounted for by the probable

---

* By Mr. H. G. Somerby. This pedigree is published in Berry's Kent Genealogies, p. 194.

† These arms were borne by Gov. Gookin, with no essential difference.

‡ She was of the 12th generation from " *Sir Allured Denne,* Knt., Seneschal of the Priory of Christ Church, Canterbury, and Escheator of the County of Kent, 19th Henry III., 1234, son of William Denne of East Kent, living in the time of King John, gr. son of Ralph de Dene, 20th William the Conqueror, Lord of Buckhurst, Sussex ; grandson of ROBERT DE DEN, or DE DENE, who held large estates in Sussex, Kent, and Normandy, in the time of Edward the Confessor." See Berry's Kent Genealogies.

ARMS. — Quarterly. 1st and 4th azure, three leopards' heads, (affronteé,) couped at the neck, or. 2nd and 3rd, ar. two flaunches sa. each charged with a leopard's head or.
CREST. — On a mount vert, a stag, lodged, ermine, attired or, resting the dexter fore foot upon a fleur-de-lis, erect, or.
The mother of Catharine Denne, who married Gokin, was Agnes, daughter of Nicholas Tufton, of Sussex, ancestor of the first *Earl of Thanet,* and died 1588, at Beaksbourne, Kent.

removal of *Vincent* and *Daniel* to the county of Cork in Ireland, and of *Daniel* from thence to Virginia, in the beginning of the seventeenth century, (the period when the pedigree closes,) of which there is the following evidence.

William Penn in a letter to his Colony, dated at London, 28th 7th mo., 1708, said, "Now, my dear friends, as to outward things I have sent a new Governor [Col. Charles Gookin] *of years* and experience ; of a quiet easy temper, that I hope will give offence to none, nor too easily put up with any if offered him, without hope of amendment, &c. He is sober, understandeth to command and obey, *and of what they call a good family, his grand father Sir Vincent Gookin, having been an early great planter in Ireland in King James the first and the first Charles' days."* *

In 1655-6, Henry Cromwell wrote to Secretary Thurloe. "I heare my Lord Broghill, William Johnson, *Vin. Gookin*, are chosen for Corke County and townes therein" — "for the parliament of this nation." Several letters from Sir Vincent to the Protector, and to Secretary Thurloe are preserved in "Thurloe's State Papers," some of them written in cipher.†

"*Master Daniel Gookin*" was the tenth in a list of 26 Patentees, to whom patents were granted in 1620, [18 James 1st] and who had "Vndertaken to transport great multitudes of people and cattle to Virginia."‡ The famous Capt. John Smith has chronicled Gookin's arrival in Virginia, and preserved his memory in the pages of his "Generall Historie."§

GOCKING'S PLANTATION.

In "1621 — The 22d of November arrived Master Gookin out of Ireland, with fiftie men *of his owne* and thirtie Passengers, exceedingly well furnished with all sorts of Provision and cattle and planted himself at Nupors-Newes, [Newport's-News, Virginia.] The cotten in a yeere grew so thick as one's arme, and so high as a man : here any-thing that is planted doth prosper so well as in no place better."

On the twenty-second of March, in the year following, the general massacre by the Savages, took place, when three hundred and forty-seven whites were slàin in various parts of the Colony — the entire population at that time being about four thousand. Then, says Captain Smith,

"This lamentable and so unexpected disaster, . . . drave them all to their wit's end. It was twenty or thirty daies ere they could resolve what to doe : but at last it was concluded all the petty Plantations should be abandoned, and drawne only to make good five or six places. Now for want of boats, it was impossible on such a sudden to

---

* The whole letter is printed in " Proud's Hist. of Pennsylvania," Vol. II, note on pages 4th and 5th. " His Majesty in Council, of the 8th of January, 1719-20, ordered " the petition of " Captain Charles Gookin, late Deputy-Governor of Pennsylvania," " setting forth his many years faithful service in the army, wherein he lost his rank, on account of being preferred to the Government of Penna. and for supporting the dignity whereof," &c. &c., praying for a grant of " Islands lying waste and uninhabited in the midst of Delaware River," &c., to be considered by the " Lords of Trade," who made a favorable Report at " Whitehall, Sept. 1721." It is singular that Penn should appoint an officer of the British Army, to be Governor of his Quaker Colony.
† See Vol. VI. pp. 19, 37, 327, 646.
‡ Purchas' Pilgrims, Vol. IV., p. 1785.
§ " The Generall Historie of Virginia, New England and the Summer Isles, from 1584 to 1626, by Capt. John Smith." London. 1627, folio, pp. 140, 150.

bring also their Cattle and many other things, which they had then in possession, all which for the most part at their departure, was burnt, ruined, and destroyed by the Salvages. Only *Master Gookins* at Nuport's-news would not obey the Commissioners' command in that, though he scarce had five and thirty of all sorts with him, yet he thought himself sufficient against what could happen, and so did, to his great credit, and the content of his Adventurers."

" Master *Gookins* at *Nuports*-Newes, hauing thirtie fiue of all sorts with him refused that order and made good his part against the Sauvages."*

This indication of Gookin's character renders it probable that he was one of those referred to by Sir William Keith, who having their own private gain more in view than any regular settlement of the Colony, went over and carried Stock and Servants along with them, separate from those of the Company, each designing to take land for himself as Capt. Newport had done, and others again who grasped not only at large Grants of Land, but even royalties and *particular Immunities within their own Manors which were truly inconsistent with, as well as independent of the Civil Power,* and consequently very destructive of that equality of Right and Good Order, that ought to be maintained in such a settlement.†

Among the records of the General Court of Virginia is an indenture made the 16th of November, A. D. 1626, " between John Thurlby merchant, Thomas Coe and William Streets, mariners, in the behalf of Daniel Gookinge of Carygoline in the county of Corke within the kingdome of Ireland esq^r of the one part and Richard Griffin late servant to the said Daniell Gooking, resident at Elizabeth City in Virginia, yeoman, of the other part," whereby the parties of the first part, "in the behalf of the said Daniel Gooking, as well for and in consideracon of the good and honnest service the said Daniel Gooking and his assignes have had and reced from the said Richard Griffen, as also for and in consideracon of the yearly rent and other conditions hereafter mentioned and expressed," " doe give, grant, assigne and confirme unto the said Richd Griffen his heires and assignes one hundred acres of land, being part of the land belonging to the lordshipp of the said Daniel Gooking, scituate and lyeth above Newport Newes at the place now called Maries Mount."

Among the records of the said General Court, there is also an indenture made the first day of February, A. D. 1630, "between Daniell Gooking of Newport Newes in Virginia, gent. of the one part and Thomas Addison late servant to the said Daniell his father of the other part," whereby "the said Daniell Gooking younger, in the behalfe of his father, as well for and in consideracon of the good and honnest service the said Daniel Gooking and his assignes have had and received from the said Thomas Addison, as alsoe for and in consideration of the yearly rent and other conditions hereafter mentioned and expressed, doe give, grant, assigne and confirme unto the s^d Thomas Addison his heires one fifty acres of land, being part of the land belonging to the lordshipp of the said Daniel Gooking, is scituate and leyeth above Newport Newes at a place there now called Maries Mount."

The following are extracts from the order book of the General Court of Virginia :

---

* Purchas' Pilgrims, Vol. IV., p. 1792.
† Keith's History of Virginia. London, 1728, 4to, p. 140.

50

"At a court holden at James Citty the nyne and twentyeth of June 1642. Present Sr William Berkeley kn^t Governo^r &c. Capt. John West Mr Rich. Kemp Capt. William Brocas Capt. Christ. Wormley Capt. Hum. Higginson. The comicon for the monethly court of Upp. Norfolke to be renewed and the com^rs to be as followeth: Capt. Daniell Gookin comander. M^r ffrancis Hough Capt. Tho. Burbage Mr John Hill Mr. Olliver Spry, Mr. Thomas Dew Mr Randall Crew Mr Robert Bennett Mr. Philip Bennett. The Capts. of trayned Bands to be as followeth: Capt. Daniell Gookin, Capt. Thomas Burbage."

"At a Quarter Court holden at James Citty the 22th of November 1642. Present Sr William Berkeley knight" &c. "Whereas Capt. John Gookin hath represented to the Board certayne Outrages and Robberyes comitted by the Indians belonging to Nanzemond in the county of the Lower Norfolke, The Court hath therefore ordered according to the request of the said Capt. John Gooking, That Authority be given to the Comander of the Upp. Norfolke either by Lre or Commicon to send to the Indian King of Nansimond that those Indians who have comitted the Outrages may be sent in to receive such condigne punishm^t as the nature of the offence may justly merritt, as alsoe to restore the goods stollen, which if he shall refuse to pforme that then the said Comander shall have power to apprehend any of the Indians they can and to keepe them in hold untill satisfaccon and restitucon be accordingly made."

There is also an order of court made the 20th of January, 1644, upon the petition of dame Elizabeth Harvey, substituting Richard Kemp, Esq., and Capt. William Peirce, as trustees in the place of "Capt. Samuell Mathews esq. George Ludlow esq. Capt. Daniell Gookin and Capt. Thomas Bernard," the former trustees under a feoffment made by the said dame Elizabeth for the use of Samuel Stevens, gent., her son by a former marriage.*

"A grant of 2500 acres in the Upper County of Norfolk, upon the North West of Nansemond River, issued to Daniel Gookius Esq. 29 Decr 1637: also a grant of 1400 acres on Rappahannock River, about thirty five miles upon the North side, issued to Capt. Daniel Gookin, 4th of November, 1642." †

It is probable that the Master Gookin mentioned in Smith's History of Virginia was the father of the Daniel Gookinge who made the deed of February, 1630, to Thomas Addison; that at the date of that deed the elder Daniel Gookin had returned to Ireland; and that the "Captain Daniel Gooking" mentioned in the various orders of the General Court was Daniel Gooking the younger. Capt. John Gookin may have been a brother to Daniel, Jr., and named for John Gokin of Ripple Court, his grandfather. Several grants of land were issued to John Gookin.

In 1642, our Puritan Colonists sent Missionaries to Episcopalian Virginia, which soon excited opposition there, and in the next year, 1643, the Assembly passed an Act, which not only forbade the New England Clergy "to teach or preach publicly or privately," but ordered also that "the Governor and Council do take care that ALL Non-conformists . . . shall be compelled to depart the Colonie with all conveniencie,"‡ so that

* The above extracts are certified by N. P. Howard, Esq., Clerk of the General Court of Virginia, Sept. 7, 1847.
† Letter from William W. Parker, Esq., first Clerk of "Virginia Land Office."
‡ "Hening's Statutes at Large," Vol. I., p. 227, communicated by the Rev. Henry Gookin Storer of Scarboro', Me., late of Virginia, a grandson of the late Hon. Daniel Gookin of North Hampton, N. H.

the removal to New England of some of the converts of the Missionaries may have been compulsory rather than from choice. Cotton Mather in his biography of Thompson, one of the Missionaries, recording his success there, says : •

> " A constellation of Great *Converts* there
> Shone round him, and his *Heavenly Glory* were,
> GOOKINS was one of these ; By Thompson's pains,
> CHRIST and NEW ENGLAND, a dear GOOKINS gains."*

Daniel Gookin here referred to is distinguished in the Annals of the Colony of Massachusetts. He came with his family probably, in the Ship which arrived at Boston, May 10th, 1644, and on " y⁰ 26th day of y⁰ 3d moneth," 1644, Captaine Daniell Gookin " was admitted to the 1st chh. in Boston, and on the 29th was honored with the freedom of the Colony, favors rarely conferred on persons of so short a residence, only six and nine days after his arrival, and probably intended as an acknowledgment of his kindness to the missionaries in Virginia,† and his distinction in that Colony.

About five months after, on the motion of Thomas Leverett, on the 12th, 8th, 1644, " Mrs. Mary Gookin, oʳ brother Captaine Gookin's wife " was also admitted to the same church, of which John Cotton was pastor.‡

Gov. Winthrop in a letter written at Boston " 14. (3) [16] 47 " says, " there came in this morning, a ship from Virginia with Capt. *Gookin* and some others. *She was bought by him [of] the Governor there.—* She came out ten days since."§ From this it appears that *Gookin* was a man of property, and perhaps engaged in commercial transactions, and it is not improbable that he may have engaged in other voyages to Virginia.— In an old paper, dated " March 28th, 1648," he is mentioned as " late of Virginia, Gent." and reference is made to a record " in Nansamond in Virginia."‖ In 1648, Captain Gookin removed to Cambridge, and from this time appears to have resided permanently in New England. " The 3d Day of y⁰ 7th Month 1648, our brother Captaine *Gookin* and oʳ Sister Mrs. *Mary Gookin* his wife, were according to their owne Desires wᵗʰ y⁰ Consent of y⁰ Church by their silence dismissed to y⁰ church at Cambridge and to have tres accordingly " from Mr. Cotton's church in Boston.‡ There, various offices of trust were conferred upon him. In 1649 and 1651, he was elected a representative of Cambridge, and in the last year was chosen Speaker of the House. In 1652 he was elected an Assistant, and re-elected continuously to 1686, a space of thirty-five years. In November, 1655, Cromwell had a favorite project of colonizing Jamaica, which England had recently acquired from Spain, by capture, with people from New England, and had " sent Commissioners and Instructions into New England to try what people might be drawn thence." " Long correspondences about it, and details, from assiduous Mr. Gookin, Chief of those Commissioners," are preserved in Thurloe.¶ The

---

* Magnalia, Book III., Ch. 17.
† Savage's Winthrop, Vol. II., p. 165, and First Church Records in Boston.
‡ First Church Records, Boston.
§ Savage's Winthrop, Vol. II., p. 353.
‖ Middlesex Court Records.
¶ " Letters and Speeches of Oliver Cromwell, by Thomas Carlyle "— Letter CXLIII, and note *—" Thurloe's State Papers," Vol. IV., pp. 6, 440, 449, Vol. V., p. 509, Vol. VI., p. 362.

scheme was unsuccessful, from "the unhealthfulness of the Island," and strong fears of continual invasions and disquiet from the Spaniards. Mr. Gookin in his letter, written at Boston, Jan. 21, 1655, informed Secretary Thurloe " that it pleased the Lord, two days since to land him safe in New England after ten weekes of an exercising passage from the Isle of Wight;" and that " it cannot yet be collected upon any grounds of certainty what will be the issue of my imploy." Govs. Endecott and Bellingham, in a letter to Cromwell of date Oct. 23ᵈ, 1656, acknowledged the receipt " by Capt. Gookin of his highness proposals for the removal of some of ours to Jamaica." The late date of this letter may indicate that Gookin had again been to England, after January, the date of his first letter. In 1656, he was appointed by the " General Court " superintendent of all the Indians who had submitted to the Government of Massachusetts; but he still faithfully urged Cromwell's plan, which he did not abandon as utterly hopeless until the summer of 1657, when he addressed a letter at " Cambridge in New England, June 20ᵗʰ, 1657," to Secretary Thurloe, which concludes as follows: " And now, right honourable, since my service for his highness in this place seems fully ended at present, I hope it may be no offense if *I return for England by the next shipps, respecting some particular ocasions of my owne left undone at my coming away;* and also to tender myself ready, (if called thereunto), with my poor mite to serve his renowned highness in the Lord, unto whome my hart stands firmely bent and devoted, as to him, whome the God of heaven hath eminently designed to doe great things for the honour of his great name, inlardgement of the Kingdome of his Christ, and good of his poore church; which the good Lord strengthen him and his helpers unto every day more and more; and when their work is finished receive him and them into the third heaven, to triumph in glory through eternitie — so he humbly and earnestly desires to pray, who is

His highnesse's
and your honour's servant,

Daniel: Gookin"

To prevent contentions and heresies, laws were passed abridging the liberty of the press, and for a time no printing was allowed in any town within the jurisdiction of Massachusetts except Cambridge. In 1662, Gen. Daniel Gookin and the Rev. Mr. Mitchell were appointed the first licensers of the printing press.*

Mr. Gookin's office of Indian Commissioner, enabled him to obtain a thorough knowledge of the Indian nations, and as the result of eighteen years of official observation, in 1674, Dec. 7ᵗʰ, " he dedicated his Historical Collections of the Indians in New England, of their several nations, numbers, customs, manners, religion and government, before the English planted there," to King Charles II.† In the work he says of his active and earnest associate, the Apostle Eliot, " the truth is, Mr. Eliot engaged in this great work of preaching unto the Indians upon a very pure and sincere account; for I being his neighbor and intimate friend, at the

* Hutchinson's History of Massachusetts Bay, pp. 257, '8. — Thomas' History of Printing in the United States, Vol. I., p. 207.
† First volume of the Massachusetts Historical Collections.

time when he first attempted the enterprise, he was pleased to communicate unto me his design and the motives that induced him thereunto."* In 1677, Dec. 18th, he dedicated to the Hon. Robert Boyle his "Historical Account of the doings and sufferings of the Christian Indians in New England, in the years 1675-6-7."†

King Philip's war had excited extreme jealousy toward the friendly Indians, and Gookin and Eliot, convinced of their innocence, by their unwavering friendship and fidelity to them, became very unpopular. Gookin was afraid to walk the streets.‡ Eliot records, in "1676, 2 month, 4th," Election Day, that "the people in their distemper left out Capt. Gookins, and put him off the Bench.§

The following incident also related by Eliot, exhibits the popular feeling. "1676, on the 7th day of the 2d month, Capt. Gookins, Mr. Danforth,|| Mr. Stoughton,¶ wr sent by the councill to order matters at Long Island, for the Indians planting there — yy called me wth ym — in or way thither, a great boat of about 14 tun, meeting us, turned hard upon us, (whethr wilfully or by negligence, God, he knoweth.)

"yn run the stern of or boat wr we 4 sat under water, or boat's saile, or something tangled wth the great boat and by God's mercy kept to it, my Cosin Jakob and Cosin Perrie, being forward in or boat quickly got up into the great Boat — I so sunk I drank in salt water twice and could not help it. God assisted my two cosins to deliver us all, and help us into the great boat, wch ws not far from the Castle, where we went ashore, dryed and refreshed, and yn went to the Island, p'formed or work, returned, praised be the Lord. Some thanked God, and some wished we had been drowned — Soone after [he] yt wished we had been drowned, was himself drowned about the same place wr we wr so wonderfully delivered"—"day 12th the Indians came off the Island — Capt. Gookins cars for them at Cambridg."**

"Gookin was a very Moses in those pious efforts on behalf of the Indians of which Eliot was the Aaron."†† — His friend Eliot in a letter to Robert Boyle calls him "a pillar in our Indian work."‡‡

Gookin by his inflexible integrity and earnest action, gradually regained the popular confidence, particularly by his bold and strong support of the charter against the machinations of the infamous Randolph, the evil genius of New England "who exhibited to the Lords of the Council, articles of high misdemeanor against him and others." He drew up a remonstrance against sending an agent to England, and as the paper is an important document, it may be published in a future number.

Gookin in "his old age" wrote "The History of New England," in eight Books, which he left in manuscript, and which is now supposed to be lost. In the close of the 3rd Book he gave "a brief account of the author's life, and the reasons inducing him to remove himself and family into New England."§§

* Chap. V.
† Second volume of the Transactions of the American Antiquarian Society.
‡ Baylies' "Memoir of Plymouth," Vol. II., Part 3, p. 64.
§ First Church Records, Roxbury. — Bliss's History of Rehoboth, pp. 101, '2.
|| Deputy-Governor of Massachusetts, President of Maine, &c. &c.
¶ Chief-Justice of the Province, Lieutenant-Governor, &c. &c.
** First Chh. Records, Roxbury.
†† MS. of the Rev. Samuel Sewall of Burlington, Ms.
‡‡ Birch's Life of Boyle, p. 437.
§§ Massachusetts Historical Collections, Vol. I., pp. 224, '5

In 1681, when about 70 years of age, he was appointed Major General of the Colony.*

Chief-Justice Samuel Sewall, in his journal of March 18, 168⁶⁄₇, says, "I go to Charlestown Lecture, and yⁿ wᵗʰ Capt. Hutchinson to see dying Major Gookin: He speaks to us, March 19, Saterday abᵗ 5 or 6 in yᵉ Morn. Major Daniel Gookin dies, a right good man — Tuesday, March 22, 1686-7, Major Gookin buried."

His resting-place, in the south-east corner of the old Cambridge burying-ground, is beneath a brick monument covered with a stone slab, bearing this inscription, thus:

> Here lyeth intered
> yᵉ body of MAJOR GENᴱᴸ
> DANIEL GOOKINGS, aged
> 75 yeares, who
> departed this life
> yᵉ 19ᵗʰ of March,
> 1686-7

Johnson, who was from the County of Kent, and who knew Gookin, terms him "a Kentish Soldier;" † and the following evidence from the correspondence of Gov. Charles Gookin, the grandson of Sir Vincent Gookin, with a grandson of Gen. Gookin, confirms the presumption of the General's descent from Daniel, the brother of Sir Vincent.

"Philadelphia, Nov. 28, 1709. I assure you that the account you gave me of that part of our family settled in America, was extremely satisfactory. . . The Spring will be a time of some leisure with me; I mean from the beginning of March to the last of April. I purpose, God willing, to pass one part of that time with you and others, our relations at Boston." And in another letter, dated "9ᵇʳ· 22d. 1710:" "By letters from Ireland I am informed two of our relatives are lately dead, viz. Robert Gookin, son of my uncle Robert, and Augustine Gookin, eldest son of my uncle Charles." "By the packet I have letters from the Proprietors, &c.

Dʳ Cossⁿ yʳ very affecᵗᵉ Kinsman
and Serv't
CHARLES GOOKIN.‡

---

* Hutchinson's History, pp. 331, 335.   ‡ MS. and p. 113 of the Register.
† "Wonder Working Providence," Ch. 26.

THE GOOKIN FAMILY.

[The following extracts may afford some reasonable conjecture respecting the name *Gookin.*

On page 221 of Harris' History of the County of Kent, folio, London, 1729, he says that "Nonington lies about the middle of the East part of Kent, about five miles Southward from *Sandwich,* in the Bailiwick of Eastry, Lath of St. Austin, East Division of the County. In the Deanery of Bridge and Diocese of Canterbury," and among the "Places of note there" he mentions "Fredville, in old writings called *Froidville* from its bleak and high situation. It was anciently belonging to the Family of COLKIN, or as commonly called *Cokin;* who probably built the seat here. The *Colkins* came originally from Canterbury where they had a Lane called Colkin's Lane; and were also Proprietors of *Worth-Gate* in that city. William Colkin who lived in King John's Reign [1199 — 1216] founded an Hospital near Eastbridge there, which bore his name and he was also a great Benefactor to those Hospitals of St. Nicholas, St. Katharine and St. Thomas of East Bridge. *John Colkin* died possessed of Fredville in the 10th year of King Edward III., [1336,] and his family held it till about the reign of King Edward II., [1307 — 1327,] and then it was sold to Thomas Charleton." In a list of the officers of the city of Canterbury, he mentions under the title *Ballivi* [the chief Magistrate of a corporation was originally denoted by that word] "*Willielmus Cockin,*" in 1250 and in 1267, and "*Edmundus Cokyn,*" in 1358. In the general index to the volume, but not citing any page, is the following — "*Gooking;* Gules, a Chevron between three Cocks, or."

Camden mentions "*Ashburn,* [in Derbyshire] a town where the family of *Cockains* have long flourished."* And Sylvanus Morgan gives "Argent, 3 cocks gules, Armed, Crested and Jelloped Sable," of *Cokain,* a family of dignity at ASHBORNE, "and in Kent County gives the name *Cakyn;* another author assigns the same arms to *Cockayn.* These variations in the etymology of the name, of *Colkin* to *Cokin,* and of *Gookin* to *Gokin,* and *Gocking,* changed with the pronunciation, as Capt. John Smith, who probably knew Daniel Gookin, of Va., 1621, personally, [see p. 346, Reg.] called him *Gockin,* and then *Gookin.* Harris distinctly mentions the change both of the pronunciation and writing, from *Colkin* to *Cokin;* and in his index as quoted we find Gooking, and while the name was written by the visiting Herald, *Gokin.* (See p. 345.) Burke, of the present day, writes it Gookin.† Some of the early New England chroniclers spell the name "Goggin." Thus we find the successive changes — *Colkin, Cockin, Cockayn, Cockyn, Cokain, Cokin, Gockin, Gokin, Gookin,* and others. This conjecture is strengthened by the affinity of the arms, for in Heraldry, coat armor distinguishes families with nearly, if not quite the certainty of surnames. Guillim calls "the cock the Knight among birds, being both of noble courage and prepared evermore to the battle; having his comb for an helmet, his sharp and hooked bill for a faucheon (falchion) or courtlax to flash and wound his enemies, and as a complete soldier armed cap-a-pie, he hath his legs armed with spurs, giving example to the valient soldier to expel danger by fight, and not by flight." The "Cokyn" and "Colkyn" and all subsequent changes were, no doubt, mere contrivances to get rid of the *un*euphoneous and objectionable title worn by the first soldier of the Family, whose vigilance and chivalric bravery in the rude days of old England set him down for a Cockin by name, with three cocks in his shield, thus winning the name and the insignia together. The instances in which armorial devices were borrowed from, or correspond with the names of the men for whom they were intended, are somewhat numerous. As the Bulkleys (that is the *Bullockleys*) have three *bullock's heads* in their arms, the Dobells (that is Doe-bells) have *three does and a bell* for theirs, and Earl Bellomont, Lord *Coote,* Gov. of Massts in 1699, had on his coat of arms, two or more *coots.*

In Hakluyt's Voyages, p. 183, the name *Godekin,* occurs thus: "About the feast of Easter, in the yeere of our Lord 1394, Henry van Pomeren — *Godekin,* Michael, Clays sheld, Hans Howfoote, Peter Hawfoote, and many others with them of Wismer and of Rostok being of the Society of the Hans, tooke by main force, a ship of New-Castle upon Tyne called Gasezere, sailing upon the sea toward Prussia, belonging to Roger de Thorneton, and others." In the subsequent narrative the name *Godekin* seems to be used as a *Christian* name and a *Surname* indiscriminately.]

The following paper, relating to political difficulties, is the one referred to in the former number, [p. 351.] Considerable inquiry has been made [1]

* *Britannia.* Fol. 491. London: 1695.   † "Burke's *Commoners.*"
[1] P. 54, this volume.

for it from time to time, unsuccessfully, and it is of great value in the history of that critical period:—

"Honored Gentlemen:— Haueing liberty by law [title Liberties common] to present in speech or writing any *necessary* motion, or information, *whereof* that meeting hath proper cognizance so it bee don in *conuenient* time, due order and Respective manner—I have chosen the latter way and hope I shall attend the qualifications as to time, order and manner.

It is much upon my hart to suggest to your prudent, pious, and serious consideration my poore thoughts touching the matters lyeing before you, which (to my weake understanding) is a case of great concernment, as to the weale or woe of thousands of the Lord's poore people in this wilderness yt for the testimony of Jesus transplanted themselves into this wilderness yn vnhabited ; and here purchasing ye right of the natives did sit downe in this vacuum, as it were, and who with great labour and sufferings, for many yeares conflicting with hard winters and hot summers haue possessed and left to yr posterity Those inheritances so rightfully alloted to ym According to the Law of God and man ; these considerations render the matter most momentous to me.

Your present work (as I vnderstand) is, to draw up instructions for An Agent or Agents to bee sent for England, in complyance with his ma'ties commands in his last letter, which requires vs to send Agents, within 3 months duly impoured to Answer a claime made by one Mr. Mason claiming title to a certaine tract of land within this jurisdiction, particularly between the riuers of Naumkeike [Salem] and Merimack, upon wh land many of our principal townes are seated, and many thousands of people interested and concerned who haue right to these lands by the Generall Court's grant, Indian Title, and yt impoured, and that for about fifty yeares, and without any claime made by Mr. Mason or his *predecessors*, and besides their title hath beene established by o'r law till possession, printed and published, when conuenient time was granted to enter ye claimes if any, and upon the pr'mises many sales and Alienations haue (doubtles) beene made ; and diuers of the first planters deceased, leaving their inheritances to ye quiet poss'ion of yr posterity ; All this notwithstanding by the Letters aforesaid (wch there is good ground to think hath beene procured and sent ouer more by the solicitation of our enimies yn any disposition in his moste excelent ma'tie (o'r gracious king) to quel so great disquiet and disturbance to his poore inocent and Loyal Subjects, inhabiting in this place, as is occasioned therby, in requiring us to send an Agent or Agents to Answer before him and unto Mr. Mason's claimes, on behalf of these proprietors called Ter tennants, and to abide by the termination y't shall be there giuen ; Could wee promise o'rselues, that the conclusion would bee in o'r fauor, which we have no assurance to expect, yet the scruple with me for sending at all as the case is circumstanced is not remoued, but remains vntouched.

1. Because this pr'cedent in conceding to send Agent or Agents for the tryalls and to Answer particular complaints and claymes in England before his ma'tie touching proprieties, [companies,] will (as I humbly conceue) have a tendency, if not certenly subuert and destroy the mayne nerves of o'r Government and Charter, lawes and liberties. Besides (as I apr'hend) it wil bereaue us of o'r liberties as Englishmen, (confirmed many times by magna charta, who are to bee tryed in all their concernes, ciuil, or criminal by 12 honest men of the neighbourhood, under oath and in his ma'ties Courts, before his sworn Judges and not before his ma'ties Royal person ;

surely o'r com'g 3 thousand miles under security of his ma'ties title, and by his good leave to plant this howling wilderness hath not deuested us of that native liberty w'h o'r countrymen injoy.   Now if Mr. Mason haue any claime to make, of any man within this jurisdiction, his ma'ties Courts heere established by charter are open to him : And hee may implead any man yt doth him wrong before ye Jury and sworne Judges ; according to law and pattent heretofore and lately confirmed by his Royal ma'tie as under his signet doth or may appeare.

2d. To send Agents not duly impoured as his ma'ties lt'r requires will probably offend and prouoake his ma'tie rather yn please him and give him occasion either to imprison o'r Agents, until they bee fully impoured or otherwise pass a finall Judgment in the case (if Agents bee there) though they stand mute and doe not plead to the case.   And on the other hand if Agents are sent duly impoured to Answer as the letter requires, yn let it bee considered whether wee doe not, at once, undoe ourselues and posterity, in being obliged to Respond any complaint or try any case, ciuill or criminal wch it shall please any person, that delights in giuing us trouble, is pleased to bring thither, the Greevous Burden and inconvienience whereof would bee intolerable.   I conceue, if one of the twaine must bee submitted to, It were much Better to desire yt A General Gouernor or Commission'rs might bee constituted here in the country to try all cases ciuil, criminal and military according to discretion, as was Attempted by the Commissioners Anno 1664, 1665.   But then God was pleased to influence his people with such a degree of virtue and courage, firmely to Adhere unto o'r charter and the Laws and Liberties thereby established ; and God of his grace and goodness was then pleased, upon our humble Adreses to o'r King, to incline his ma'ties Royall hart to accept of o'r Answer and not to give us further trouble, the consequence whereof was yt we have enjoyed o'r mercys 15 years longer, and who knows But it may bee so now, if wee make our humble Adreses and give o'r reasons for not sending Agents ; surely o'r God is the same, yesterday and to-day and for euer ; and our king is the same, inclining to fau'r the Righteous caus of his poore inocente and loyal subjects and I doubt not if wee make triall and follow our endea'r by faith and prair but God will appear for us, in mercy, & make a good Isue of this affayre.

The sending of Agents will contract a very great charge and expenses wch the poore people are very unable to stand under, considering the great diminishings yt wee haue had by warr, small pox, fires, sea loses, Blastings and other publicke loses, for my part, I see not how mony will be raised to defray this charge unles it bee borrowed upon interest of some particular man ; moreouer the country is yet in debt and pays interest for mony yearly ; especially to bee at so great cost for no other end (in probability) but to cut us short of o'r Liberties and priviledges as too late experience in o'r former Agent's Negotiation doth evidence.

Besides this matter of Mr. Mason's claims wee are required to send Agents to Attend the Regulation of o'r Government, &c., and to satisfy his ma'tie in Admitting freemen as is proposed in ye letter.   And to give an Acc't what incouragement is giuen to such persons as desire to worship God According to the way of the church of England.

Now to send Agents to Answer and attend these things, who sees not how grate a snare It may proue unto us, for Touching our Government wee are well contented with it and o'r charter and desire no change.   If there should bee any Lawes yt are Repugnant to ye Laws of England, (I know not any,) they may be repealed.

58

Concerning freemen's Admission, nothing is more cleare in the charter, yn this, that the Gouern'r and Company haue free liberty to admit whome they thinke meet.

As for any that desire to worship God According to the manner of the church of England, there is no law to pr'hibite or restraine ym neith'r is it meet to make any law to yt effect because it would bee repugnant to the law of England. But for this Gou'ment to declare or make a law to Encourage Any to practise yt worship here, may it not bee feared this would offend God, and bee condemning the doings and sufferings of o'rselues and fathers that first planted this country.

These things considered and many more I might Aleadge giue mee cause to desire your pardon that I cannot consent or iudge it expedient to send An Agent or Agents at this time as things are circumstanced.

Therefore I conceiue it is much the Best and safest course not to send any Agent at all and consequently the committe may forbeare to draw up Instruction for them but rather pr'sent to the court the difficulties in the case; and if you please, I am not unwilling that this paper bee pr'sented to the Honored Court to consider of.

And rather if you see meet to draw up and pr'sent to the Gen'll Court a humble and Argumentative Address to his Sacred ma'tie To pardon his poore yet Loyall people in this matter so destructive to the quiet and so inconsistent with their well being.

But to this it may be objected,

1 objection, that it is our duty to send Agents because the King commands it, otherwise we may be found Breakers of the fi'th command.

Answer—I humbly conceue wee ought to distinguish of o'r duty to Super'rs, sometimes possibly they may require vnlawful things as the Rulers of the Jewes did of the Apostles; Acts, 4: 18. 19.—in wch case [the] Holy Ghost tels us our duty in yt text. 2dly. Rulers may command things yt considered in their tendencies and circumstances and comixture with religion, may be of a morall nature and consequently unlawful and not to be allow'd in doing, But rather Runne the Hazard of Suffering, of which nature I humbly conceaue is the pr'sent cause, for if wee send agents as the letter requires wee doe destroy ourselues in our greatest concerns as I apr'-hend; now selfe preseruation, is a moral duty and not only Reason and Religion but nature, doth teach us this. Againe, if this Gouernment of ours bee of Chhts establishing and gift and a part of his purchase, as I iudge it is, will it not bee a moral end for us to bee Active in parting with it. I remember yt eminent Mr. Mitchell, now in heaven, in his publicke lecture (February 1660,) speaking of Cht's Kingly Gouernment upon a ciuil Acct, did Declare that this Gouernment setled in ye Massachus'ts according to pattent and laws was as hee said a specimen of that ciuil Gour'nt, that the lord Cht Jesus Design'd to establish in the whole world wherein such as are godly p'rsons, and vnder his Kingly Gouernment in his church should bee electers and elected to pouer. And therfore said hee who eu'r hee bee yt shall goe about to subuert or undermine this Gouernment, hee sets himselfe against Cht Jesus, and hee will (then) haue Cht for his enimy. Also Reverend Mr. Shepard in his booke of the ten Uirgins, 25 math. in ye 1 part, page 166, speaks to ye same purpose. These persons were burning and shineing lights in yr Generation and much of God's mynd did they know and speak.

Object. 2. But if wee send no Agents wee must expect sad consequences yrof such as putting us out of his ma'ties Allegeance, damning o'r patent, inhibiting trade, and such like.

Answer 1: Something hath been spoken aboue to this matter to wh I Refer.

2: I verily Belieue yt so gracious a prince as o'r king is will bee very slow to deale so seuerely against his poore loyall subjects yt Are not conscious wee haue shewed any disloyalty to him or his pr'desc'rs, nor have been unwilling to obey him in the lord. But when the case is so circumstanced yt we must be Accounted offenders or Ruine o'rselues; of 2 evels ye least is to be chosen.

3: But if it should bee soe yt wee must suffer in this case wee may have ground to hope yt God o'r father in Cht will support and comfort us in all o'r tribulations and in his due time deliuer vs. Much more might be s'd Touching the pr'my'es. But I have been too tedious And longer yn I intended for wch I crave yr pardon and humbly intreat a candid construction of this paper a coveringe of all the imperfections yr off: This case, as is aboue hinted, is very momentous and therefore I intreat you candidly to peruse what is s'd, if there bee little waight in it (as some may thinke) it is satisfactory to me, that I haue offered it to yr consideration, and yt I have in this great cause (before I goe hence and bee no more wch I must shortly expect) giuen my testimony and declared my judgment in this great concerne of Jesus Cht, To whome I commit all and yorselues also desiring him to be to you as hee is in himselfe, the mighty counsellor, King of Kings and Lord of Lords.

I remaine your most humble seruant
and His ma'ties most Loyal Subject,
DANIEL GOOKIN, Sen'r.
Cambridge, February 14, 1680.

These for the Hon'rable Symon Bradstreet Esq. Gouernour, and Thomas Danforth, Esq. Deputy Gouernor, and the Rest of the Honored Gent. of the Committee of the Generall Court appointed to draw up and prepare instructions for Agents to bee sent for England Sitting in Boston, pr'-sented."

General Gookin's Will shows the solemnity with which our fathers executed such instruments ; it contains a clear and full confession of the essentials of the faith of that time, and furnishes a glimpse at the domestic and social condition of the early days of New England.

" The will and testament of Daniel Gookin, Senior, living at Cambridge in New England, made and done this 13th day of August 1685, being through the Grace of God at the present writing hereof, of a perfect understanding and of a sound mind, although under some bodily infirmity at present, and considering also that I am through God's favor arrived to nearly seventy three years of age, and expecting daily when my change will come, I consider it my duty, incumbent upon me, to set my house in order and to dispose of that small estate (much more than I deserve) which God hath committed to my guardianship, for the prevention of any difference among my relations after my decease.

" In the first place, I commit my immortal soul, and the concerns thereof into the everlasting arms of the Infinite and Eternal God, the Father, the Son, and the Holy Ghost, three persons, yet but one essence, the only living and the true God ; I rely upon the free grace of God for my eternal salvation, through the merits, satisfaction and righteousness of Jesus Christ, the only begotten Son of the Father full of grace and truth, being also equal with the Father and Holy Spirit, one God, blessed forever, who for us men, and our salvation, in fullness of time, came from heaven, and took upon him the nature of man, being born of the blessed Virgin Mary, was conceived by the Holy Ghost, and He is God-man in one person, and is the great Mediator between God and man, and ever lives at the right hand of God, in the eternal heavens, making continued intercession for all the elect, for whom He shed his precious blood, to redeem them from sin and the wrath of God, which work of redemption, performed fully by Him is accepted by God, and I believe that by His righteousness, satisfaction and merits imputed to me by faith, and my sins and transgressions, being of God's free grace imputed to Him, I have good hope, through grace, that I am justified and accepted, and my sins pardoned, and in some measure begun to be sanctified by the Holy Ghost, and that after my death and resurrection, be perfectly glorified in the full enjoyment of God to all eternity, for my body which though naturally frail and corrupt, yet through grace, is made a temple of the Holy Ghost, and therefore my will is that it may be decently interred in the earth in Cambridge burying place near the dust of my wife but I desire no ostentation or much cost, to be expended at my funeral because it is a time of great tribulation * and my estate is little and weak.

" Secondly, touching my outward estate I dispose of it as follows, to my dearly beloved wife Hannah,† I give and bequeath to her all that estate real and personal that she was possessed of before her marriage. I give also unto her for the term of her life my dwelling-house, barn and out houses, orchards and gardens appertaining to it, and the use of three commons belonging to it, for wood and pasturage (my house lyes adjoining to the back-lane in Cambridge) to have and to hold the premises for her use and benefit during her natural life, provided she endeavor to keep both houses and fences in repair ; again I give unto my wife one cow, or the

* This " great tribulation " was originated by the demand of a " full submission and entire resignation of their Charter " to *Charles II.*, in the fall of 1683. " Some Wicked Men, whereof the Principal was one *Randolph*," were the Agents. The people, convinced that " they would act neither the part of *Good Christians*, nor of *True Englishmen*, if by any Act of theirs they should be Accessary to the *Plot* then managing to produce a *General Shipwreck of Liberties*," and to deprive them of the " Inheritance of their Fathers," and " truly believing that they should sin against the GOD of Heaven, if they Voted an affirmative," " the Country was preserved from a *Mean Compliance* with the *Vile Proposal*," Increase Mather made a " short and prudent speech in the Town House, Jan. 23, 1684 ; many of the Freemen fell into Tears, the Question was upon the Vote, carried in the Negative, *Nemine Contradicente*. And this act of Boston had a great influence upon all the Country."

The language of that time is given, as it affords the best idea of the degree and extent of their feeling of " tribulation." At the date of the Will, judgment had been entered against the Charter, in legal process, and the whole country was filled with alarm for the safety of their civil and religious liberties. The history of Sir Edmund Andros's administration fully justifies their apprehensions.

† She was his second wife — the eldest child of Edward Tyng, born 7 March, 1640, married Habijah, eldest son of Thomas Savage, 8 May, 1661 ; had Joseph, born 15 Aug., 1662, died early ; Thomas, born 17 August, 1664, who married, 5 Feb., 1691, Mehitable Hanwood, was Colonel of the Boston Regiment, and died 3 March, 1721 ; and twin daughters, Hannah and Mary, born 27 Aug., 1667. *Hannah* was the wife of Rev. *Nathaniel Gookin* in 1685, as appears by his father's will. *Mary* married Rev. Thomas Weld, first minister of Dunstable, grandson of Rev. Thomas Weld, of Roxbury, who had been one of the fiercest enemies of her grandmother's mother, Faith Hutchinson. Habijah Savage died in 1669, it is probable, for his inventory was taken 24 May of that year, and probably without much warning, for he left no will. The valuation was only £443. 17s. 1-2d. His father's will, made 28 June, 1675, at the moment of setting off in command of the forces in King Phillip's War, begun that week, and so judiciously made, that it was not altered in following years, gives £150 to Thomas, son of Habijah, £50 to each of the daughters, and £50 to Hannah, the *widow*, so that she was not married to Gookin, then. There is a deficiency in our Records, 1662 to 1689, so that the date of the marriage is lost. — *Hon. James Savage's MS. note.* See also pp. 83 and 328 of Vol. I. of the " *Register.*"

red heifer with a white face, also I give to her one brown ambling mare, I give to her my second bible, also I give and bequeath forever a piece of plate either a cup or tankard to be made new for her, marked $\frac{G}{D.H.}$, and household furniture.

" To my son Daniel Gookin, I give my silver tankard, my biggest carbine which he hath received already, my death's head gold ring, which I wear on my finger, my curtelax [a broad, curving sword, used by soldiers in the cavalry] and a silver spoon to my son Daniel, to be delivered to him, or in case of his death before me to his wife and son Daniel, three months after my death.

" Unto my son Samuel and his children forever, I give and bequeath the dwelling-house, outhouses, and barn yard, gardens and orchards where he now dwelleth and all to it belonging with two commons and although I changed this house with him for that which I now live in unto which house he built an addition and barn. I order that all the writings and deeds that I had of Mr. Ed. Collins for the said house and land be delivered to my son Samuel, moreover I give unto him my rapier and my buff belt with silver buckles, my pistols and holsters my fowling piece and one silver wine cup and half of my apparell, and to his three children each of them a silver spoon ;

" Unto my son Nathaniel Gookin, and his heirs my house where I live, orchard and gardens thereunto appertaining, with three cow commons and what belongs to them, to be possessed and enjoyed by him after my wife's decease, but in case my son Nathaniel should die without children and before his present wife Hannah, then my will is that the said houses and appurtenances be for her use during her life and after her decease to be for him or them unto whom my son Nathaniel shall dispose of them, provided it be to some of his relations by blood — also my silver cup called the Erench cup, and the biggest of the two other silver cups, and a silver wine cup, — I mention no bed and furniture here, because I gave him that at his marriage, also I give my blue couch, unless son Daniel desire it, being suitable to his bed, but if Daniel have it, he must allow Nathaniel full value of it, also my smallest carbine and a gold ring which I wear on my finger, &c., &c.

" Unto my daughter Batter I give a silver salt cellar, and another silver cup, the lesser of the two, &c., &c.

" I give to daughter Elizabeth [Eliot, Quincy,] one gold ring and to each of her children a silver spoon. I mention no more plate, bedding or other things because I gave her such things, at her first marriage, besides I have not been wanting to her having helped to breed up her son John Elliot for 17 yeares, at my house, and at College. I give to Mr. Hezekiah Usher and his wife —— ——, my good friends, to each a gold ring; to son [Edmund] Quincy a gold ring." All the rest of his Estate to be divided into six equal parts of which his " Eldest Son Daniel " had a double share. " Unto John Elliott my grandchild I give one sixth part, the reason of this bequest and not to my other grand children, is with respect to a benefit received from his grand-father Elliott, which he ordered me to give to John, of a greater value than a sixth part."

He made his " deare wife Hannah and three sons Daniel, Samuel and Nathaniel," executors. In a " Postscript," he gave to his " wife's son Thomas " [Savage] and " wife's two daughters, Hannah Gookin, and Mary Savage, a gold ring to each of them." " In my account book intitled Ledger, No. 1650, post 112, is expressed an account of my whole estate D^r. & C^r. according as I could arrive at it."

The will was proved before "the Hon. Joseph Dudley, Esq," on the 31 March, 1687, by Samuel Andrew, Senior, and Joseph Cooke.*

In the inventory† of his estate are mentioned 1 negro, £7, "land near Concord," "land and meadow at Marlboro."‡ The whole amounted to £323. 3s. 11d.

SIR FERDINANDO GORGES, KT.

The man who persevered so long, and against such adverse fortune, to colonize New England, has scarcely received from the historian notice proportionate to his sacrifices. Nor is it proposed here to do more than to bring into view a few additional materials for the biographer of Sir Ferdinando Gorges. It is a very common and it may be said perhaps a very natural error, for biographers to claim too much for their heroes. It has been recently asserted* that Sir Ferdinando was "the father of English colonization in America." We know of no process of reasoning by which to arrive at that conclusion. And according to some notions which have crept into our mind, we feel quite sure that, instead of calling Sir Ferdinando the father of colonization, we should call him at least the great-grandson of *that gentleman*. But we must waive discussion on that head, at present, as we are now to deal only with original papers.

The following pedigrees, from Heralds' Visitations in the British Museum, furnish the pedigree of Sir Ferdinando, and his relationship to others

----

* See Historical Magazine, vol. iii, 336.

* Suffolk Probate Records, liber. 11, folio 75.
† Recorded in Suf. Prob. Rec., liber. 9, folio 185.
‡ See in Lincoln's Hist. of Worcester, notices of his efficient agency in promoting the settlement of that town, and in Shattuck's Hist. of Concord of his labors there.

of the name. Lord Edward Gorges, it appears, was a first cousin to Edward Gorges, father of Sir Ferdinando. Robert Gorges, the son of Sir Ferdinando, had a commission as governor of New England, came here in 1623 with a colony, and settled at Weymouth; but returned in the course of the year. John, the other son, was father of Ferdinando Gorges, who published, in 1658, "America painted to the Life."

PEDIGREE OF GORGES.

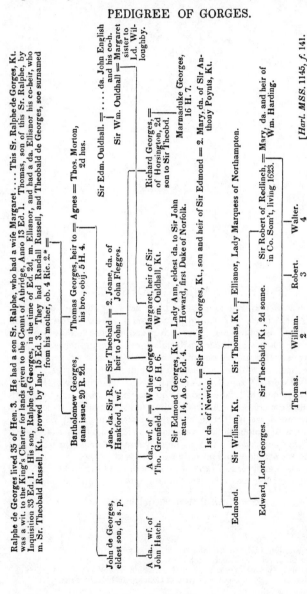

Sir Theobald Gorge, Kt. and Bart., 2 brother to
John George, sonnes of Tho. George,* sonne of Ralph

Walter Gorge = ... dau. and heire of Owld hale.

Sir Edm. Gorge, ward to Jo : Lo : Howard in the time of Edward 4th. = Ann, d. of the said John Lord Howard, Duke of Norfolk.

William Gorge. = ... da. of Sir .... Poynes. = Sir Edmond, Kt. = ... da. of Sir Jo. Newton, Kt., 2 wf.

Edmond Georg = ... da. of Sir John Walsh in Co. Glou.

William Gorge. Incolus Gorge. Sir Wm.

Sir Thomas, Kt. A dau. m. William Gorge. Robert. Edward = Cicely, d. of Hyones of Wc. Alice. Margt.

Sir Ferdinando Gorge, Kt., 2d sonne. = Sir Edward Gorge, Kt., living ao. 1623. = ... da. Sir George Speake, Kt. of the Bath.

Robert. John. Anne vx Ed. Tynt. Dorothy vx. Francis vx 1 Luterell, 2 Sir Edward Southcott. William 2. Thomas 3. Samuell 4. Sir Robert = Mary, d. Sir Marmaduke Dayrell. of Wraxall, living 1623. Dorothy vx Cary of Clovelly. Elizabeth vx Trenchard of Wilts. [*Harl. MSS.* 1445, *f.* 106.]

Sir William George of Wraxall, Kt. =

Robert Gorge of Batcombe in Co. Somersett, 2d son, = Ann, da. of .... Webb of Batcombe.

Henry of Batcombe, now living, 1623. = Barbara, da. of Tho. Baynard of Cullorne, in Co. Wilts. Margaret, wf. to Edward Kinnersley. 2 Ann, wf. to John Guyse. 3 Joyce, wf. to James Spencer. 4 Christian. wf. to Tho. Stephens. [*Harl. MSS.* 1141, 73 b.

Edward, 2d son. Mary, wife to John Moore. Thomas, son and heire, aetat. 5, annores, 1623. John, 2. Ann.

Signed HE: GORGS.

* Several generations are omitted here, if the preceding pedigree is correct. According to that pedigree this Thomas Gorges was the 3d gen. from one Ralph de Gorge and the 7th gen. from the earliest mentioned Ralph. Burke's "Extinct and Dormant Baronetcies," (1844) p. 221, has a pedigree of this family, which, except omitting Thomas, grandson of the first Ralph, agrees with Pedigree No. 1, in these early generations. There are discrepancies, however, in later ones.

SIR ARTHUR GORGES, Chelsea, knighted 1597, d. 1625. He built a house on this site [of Stanley House] for his own residence. As the Queen [Eliz.] passd by the faire new building, Sir Arthur Gorges presented her with a faire jewell. *Sidney papers*—Letter from Rowland White to Sir Robert Sidney, 15 Nov. 1599. Sir Arthur was the intimate friend of Spencer, who made a beautiful elegy on the first Lady Gorges, dau. of Viscount Bindon, who d. 1590, entitled *Daphnaida*, and her husband is meant by Alcyon. Sir Arthur's second wife was the Lady Elizabeth, dau. of Henry, Earl of Lincoln, by which marriage he became possessed of Sir Thomas More's house, which, in 1619, he conveyed to Lionel, Lord Cranfield. He left by his second wife six children, viz., Arthur,(1) first son and heir, a. then 24 (1625), Timoleon,(2) Egremont, (3) Carew,(4) Henry,(5) Elizabeth.—*Faulkner's Hist. Chelsea*, i. 56–7, 2 *vols.* 8°. 1829.

On the south side of the church at Chelsea—

> Here sleeps, and feels no presure of this stone,
> He that had all the Gorges Souls in one, &c.

The generous and worthy gentleman Arthur Gorges, Esq., eldest son of Sir Arthur Gorges, Kt. The last surviving Branch of the first Male Line of that Honourable Family.—*Strype's Stow*, ii. B. vi. p. 72.

In the chancel of the church of St. Michael near Exeter, parish of Hevitree, is this inscription to " Thomas Gorges of Hevitree, Esq., and Rose, his wife. He departed this life the 17th of October, 1670; and she the 14th day of April, 1671.

> The lovinge Turtell havinge mist her mate
> Beg'd she might enter ere they shut the gate
> Their dust lies whose soules to Heaven are gonne
> And waite till Angells rowle away the stone.
> *Jenkins's Hist. Exeter*, 441.

ARMS.—Gorges of Somersetshire bear—Argent a whirlpool azure. CREST—A greyhound's head erased argent collared gules. A Devonshire branch bore—Ermin a fesse between three fleurs-de-lis gules. Another—Ermin a fesse between three roses gules. CREST—An annulet, stoned azure. See Burke's *Heraldic Dictionary*.

GORGES AND ARCHDALE.

In a document published in the *Register*, vol. XIII, pp. 303–4, John Archdale calls Ferdinando Gorges, his brother. A friend has furnished us with an inscription from a mural tablet to the Gorges family in Ashley Church, copied from Hutchins's *History and Antiquities of Dorset*, III, 35, which explains the connection. There is a full pedigree of the Gorges family here which we shall use in another number.

" Near this place lieth the body of Ferdinando Gorges, late of Westminster, Esq., sometime Governor of the Province of Maine in New England. He was born at Loftas in Essex, grandson and heir to Sir Ferdinando Gorges, of Ashton-Phillips, in the county of Somerset, knight. He married Mary, the eldest daughter of Thomas Archdale, of Loaks, in Chipping Wycomb, in the county of Bucks, Esq. They were a very eminent example of virtue, and entirely happy in their mutual affection; and had many children, of whom only two survived their indulgent and tender parents. He was charitable and patient, courteous and beneficent, zealous and constant to the church, and a great admirer of learning. He is interred in the same grave in which Sir Theobald Gorges was buried Anno Domini 1647, second son of the Marchioness of Northampton and uncle to the Right Hon. Richard, Lord Gorges.—Obit, xxv Janu. Anno Domini 1718, æt. 89."

GORGES AND HARDING.

Communicated by JOHN WARD DEAN, A.M.

THE following genealogical statement prepared by Rev. Frederick Brown, of Nailsea, near Bristol, England, is printed from the original found among the papers presented to the New-England Historic, Genealogical Society by the sons of the late Rev. Abner Morse (*ante*, xix. 371). It was received by them subsequent to the death of their father. Mr. Brown, in a letter accompanying the manuscript dated June 26, 1865, and addressed to W. M. Harding of New-York city, writes: "The whole of the account of Sir Robert Gorges, I can verify from registers, wills and authentic documents. I am quite sure of my ground as to the Gorges family." He also states that he had been collecting materials concerning that family for fifteen years.

In 1861, Mr. Drake printed in the REGISTER (xv. 17-20) some pedigrees of the * Gorges family from Heralds' Visitations, with memoranda from other sources. The present paper gives some new facts concerning the relatives of Sir Ferdinando Gorges, the proprietor of the province of Maine. Mr. Drake's article showed that Sir Ferdinando was a cousin-nephew of Edward, Lord Gorges. This paper shows that he was also a brother-in-law. We would suggest whether Thomas Gorges, whom Sir Ferdinando called his "trusty and well-beloved cousin," when he placed him at the head of the government of the province of Maine in 1640, may not have been the Thomas Gorges, below, born in 1613, who married Margaret Pointz. This Thomas was his second cousin by blood and his nephew by marriage.[1]

The first wife of Sir Ferdinando Gorges, and the mother of all his children, was, it appears, Ann Bell. His second wife was Elizabeth, widow of Sir Hugh Smith, and daughter of Sir Thomas Gorges. Her mother, Eleanor, dowager Marchioness of Northampton, was, we presume, the third wife of William Parr, Marquess of Northampton, brother of Catharine Parr, queen of Henry VIII.

PEDIGREE.

SIR THOMAS GORGES = Marchioness of Northampton.
b. 1636, d. 1610; 5th son of Sir Edw. | Both buried in Salisbury Cathedral,
Gorges, of Wraxall, Somerset. | under a superb monument.

Edw. Lord Gorges.	Sir Theobald Gorges, of Ashley Wilts, m. Ann Poole.	Sir Robert Gorges, of Redlynch, m. Mary Harding.	Elizabeth, m. Sir Hugh Smyth. m. 2nd, Sir Ferdinando Gorges.	Frances, m. Sir T. Tyringham (Bucks).	Bridget, m. Sir R. Philips, of Montacute.

Sir Robert Gorges, 3d son.

In Records of Oxford.—"The King (James 1st) came to Oxford & was entertained at Magdalene College with speeches & Philosophical Disputations. Mr. W. Seymour, 2d son of Edwd. Lord Beauchamp and grandson of the Earl of Hertford, Respondent. Opposed by Charles sixth son of Earl of Worcester, Edwd Seymour eldest son of Lord Beauchamp, Mr. Robert Gorges son of Sir Thos. Gorges by March. of Northampton &c., all of whom gave his Highness so much satisfaction by the readiness of their wits that he gave them his hands to kiss."

He was knighted by James I., June 30, 1616.—Nichols's *Progresses of James I.*, vol. iii. p. 176.

He is described as of *Redlynch, Somerset*. He m. Mary, dau. of Will.

---

[1] It was this fact which led us in the July number (*ante*, p. 348) to say that Thomas Gorges, who came to New-England, was possibly a nephew of Sir Ferdinando.—ED.

*Pp. 63-66, this volume.

Harding.—*History of Surrey.* Manor of Cleygate, Surrey, was conveyed in 1567 to William Harding, of Wanborough (near Guildford, Surrey), who married Catharine, dau. of Sir John White, Alderman and afterwards Lord Mayor of London, 1563.

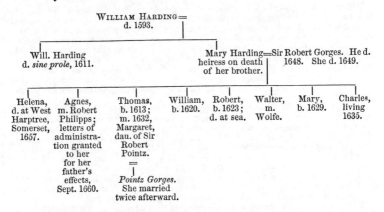

WILLIAM HARDING=
d. 1593.

Will. Harding
d. *sine prole*, 1611.

Mary Harding=Sir Robert Gorges. He d.
heiress on death | 1648. She d. 1649.
of her brother.

Helena,
d. at West
Harptree,
Somerset,
1657.

Agnes,
m. Robert
Philipps;
letters of
administra-
tion granted
to her
for her
father's
effects,
Sept. 1660.

Thomas,
b. 1613;
m. 1632,
Margaret,
dau. of Sir
Robert
Pointz.
=
Pointz Gorges.
She married
twice afterward.

William,
b. 1620.

Robert,
b. 1623;
d. at sea.

Walter,
m.
Wolfe.

Mary,
b. 1629.

Charles,
living
1635.

Sir Robert Gorges of Redlynch was present at the consecration of the Church of Wich Champflower [Huish Champflower], by Bishop Lake, July 18, 1624.— Collinson's *History of Somerset.*

He purchased the Manor of Olney, Bucks, of Sir John Rumsay and endowed the Vicarage, & 1642 conveyed the Advowson & Titles to Will: Johnson.—*History of Bucks.*

He was M.P. for Taunton 1625   } Browne Willis
      ditto   Ilchester, Somerset, 1628 } Notitia Parl:

He is frequently mentioned in the wills of his father and mother. Of the latter he was sole executor.

He settled the Manor of Redlynch on the wife of his eldest son.

At his death his affairs were much involved.

In the Registry of Wills, Doctors Commons, London, Letters of Adm. granted Feb. 1659 to Will Johnson, the principal Creditor to Sir Robert Gorges of Redlynch, Somerset, deceased.

2nd Letters of Adm: granted, Sept. 1660, to *Agnes Philipps*, natural & legitimate *daughter* of Sir Robert Gorges of Redlynch, deceased.

A very interesting, nuncupative will of Helena Gorges of West Harptree, Somerset, made June 11, 1657, daughter, unmarried, of Sir Robert Gorges.

1651. Administration granted to Elizabeth Buckland, wife of John Buckland of West Harptree, niece by the natural & legitimate sister of Lady Maria Gorges, widow, lately of West Harptree, deceased.

She was the widow of Sir Robert Gorges.

N.B. It is evident from the above entry that Mary Harding who married Sir Robert Gorges, had another sister, Elizabeth, who married John Buckland.

The Bucklands were a very ancient family of West Harptree. There are many entries of their names in the West Harptree Registers.

There are no monuments in Redlynch Church, nor is any burial ground attached. The present church was erected as late as 1740.

N. B. The Robert Gorges, who came to N. England, Sept. 1623, to begin a Plantation, was the son of Sir *Ferdinando Gorges* by *Ann Bell*. (Sir F. Gorges had no children by his second wife, Lady Elis. Smyth, who was the sister of Sir Robert Gorges.)   On Robert Gorges's death, the patents he had obtained from the Council of Plymouth descended to his brother John.

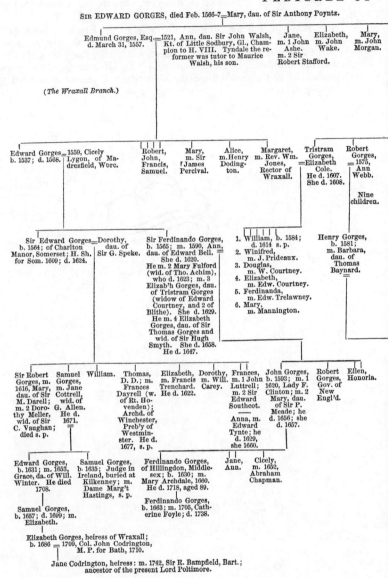

Sir EDWARD GORGES, died Feb. 1566-7═Mary, dau. of Sir Anthony Poyntz.

Edmund Gorges, Esq.═1521, Ann, dau. Sir John Walsh,   Jane,   Elizabeth,   Mary,
d. March 31, 1557.   Kt. of Little Sodbury, Gl., Cham-   m. 1 John   m. John   m. John
       pion to H. VIII. Tyndale the re-   Ashe.   Wake.   Morgan.
       former was tutor to Maurice   m. 2 Sir
       Walsh, his son.   Robert Stafford.

(*The Wraxall Branch.*)

Edward Gorges═1559, Cicely   Robert,   Mary,   Alice,   Margaret,   Tristram   Robert
b. 1537; d. 1568.   Lygon, of Ma-   John,   m. Sir   m.Henry   m. Rev. Wm.   Gorges,   Gorges,
     dresfield, Worc.   Francis,   ſ James   Doding-   Jones,   ═Elizabeth   ═ 1575,
       Samuel.   Percival.   ton.   Rector of   Cole.   Ann
          Wraxall.   He d. 1607.   Webb.
            She d. 1608.

               Nine
               children.

Sir Edward Gorges═Dorothy,   Sir Ferdinando Gorges,   1. William, b. 1584;   Henry Gorges,
b. 1564; of Charlton   dau. of   b. 1565; m. 1590, Ann,   d. 1614 s. p.   b. 1581;
Manor, Somerset; H. Sh.   Sir G. Speke.   dau. of Edward Bell. ═   2. Winifred,   m. Barbara,
for Som. 1609; d. 1624.   She d. 1620.   m. J. Prideaux.   dau. of
          He m. 2 Mary Fulford   3. Douglas,   Thomas
          (wid. of Tho. Achim),   m. W. Courtney.   Baynard.
          who d. 1623; m. 3   4. Elizabeth,   ═
          Elizab'h Gorges, dau.   m. Edw. Courtney.
          of Tristram Gorges   5. Ferdinanda,
          (widow of Edward   m. Edw. Trelawney.
          Courtney, and 2 of   6. Mary,
          Blithe). She d. 1629.   m. Mannington.
          He m. 4 Elizabeth
          Gorges, dau. of Sir
          Thomas Gorges and
          wid. of Sir Hugh
          Smyth. She d. 1658.
          He d. 1647.

Sir Robert   Samuel   William.   Thomas,   Elizabeth,   Dorothy,   Frances,   John Gorges,   Robert   Ellen,
Gorges, m.   Gorges,   D. D.; m.   m. Francis   m. Will.   Luttrell;   m. 1 John   Gorges,   Honoria.
1616, Mary,   m. Jane   Frances   Trenchard.   Carey.   m. 2 Sir   b. 1593; m. 1   Gov. of
dau. of Sir   Cottrell,   Dayrell (w.   He d. 1622.   Edward   1620, Lady F.   New
m. 2 Doro-   wid. of   of Rt. Ho-   Southcot.   Clinton; m. 2   Engl'd.
thy Meller,   G. Allen.   venden);   —   Mary, dau.
wid. of Sir   He d.   Archd. of   Anna, m.   of Sir P.
C. Vaughan;   1671.   Winchester,   Edward   Meade; he
died s. p.   ═   Preb'y of   Tynte; he   d. 1656; she
          Westmin-   d. 1629,   d. 1657.
          ster. He d.   she 1660.
          1677, s. p.

Edward Gorges,   Samuel Gorges,   Ferdinando Gorges,   Jane,   Cicely,
b. 1631; m. 1653,   b. 1635; Judge in   of Hillingdon, Middle-   Ann.   m. 1652,
Grace, da. of Will.   Ireland, buried at   sex; b. 1630; m.   Abraham
Winter. He died   Kilkenney; m.   Mary Archdale, 1660.   Chapman.
1708.   Dame Marg't   He d. 1718, aged 89.
      Hastings, s. p.
                     Ferdinando Gorges,
Samuel Gorges,   b. 1663; m. 1705, Cath-
b. 1657; d. 1699; m.   erine Foyle; d. 1738.
Elizabeth.

Elizabeth Gorges, heiress of Wraxall;
b. 1686 ═ 1709, Col. John Codrington,
       M. P. for Bath, 1710.

Jane Codrington, heiress: m. 1742, Sir R. Bampfield, Bart.;
    ancestor of the present Lord Poltimore.

GORGES.

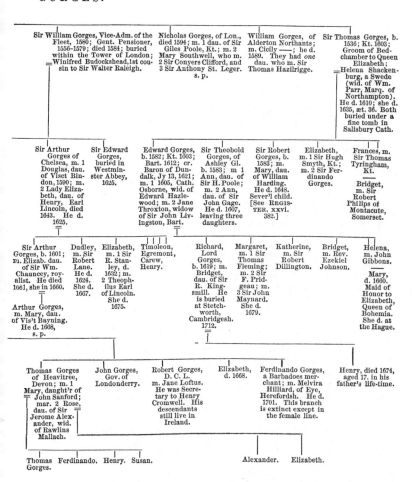

Sir William Gorges, Vice-Adm. of the Fleet, 1580; Gent. Pensioner, 1556–1579; died 1584; buried within the Tower of London; =Winifred Budockshead, 1st cousin to Sir Walter Raleigh.

Nicholas Gorges, of Lon., died 1594; m. 1 dau. of Sir Giles Poole, Kt.; m. 2 Mary Southwell, who m. 2 Sir Conyers Clifford, and 3 Sir Anthony St. Leger. s. p.

William Gorges, of Alderton Northants; m. Cicily ——; he d. 1589. They had one dau. who m. Sir Thomas Hazilrigge.

Sir Thomas Gorges, b. 1536; Kt. 1603; Groom of Bedchamber to Queen Elizabeth; =Helena Shackenburg, a Swede (wid. of Wm. Parr, Marq. of Northampton). He d. 1610; she d. 1635, æt. 36. Both buried under a fine tomb in Salisbury Cath.

Sir Arthur Gorges of Chelsea, m. 1 Douglas, dau. of Visct Bindon, 1590; m. 2 Lady Elizabeth, dau. of Henry, Earl Lincoln, died 1643. He d. 1625.

Sir Edward Gorges, buried in Westminster Abbey, 1625.

Edward Gorges, b. 1582; Kt. 1603; Bart. 1612; cr. Baron of Dundalk, Jy 13, 1621; m. 1 1605, Cath. Osborne, wid. of Edward Hazlewood; m. 2 Jane Throxton, widow of Sir John Livingston, Bart.

Sir Theobold Gorges, of Ashley Gl. b. 1583; m 1 Ann, dau. of Sir H. Poole; m. 2 Ann, dau. of Sir John Gage. He d. 1607, leaving three daughters.

Sir Robert Gorges, b. 1583; m. Mary, dau. of William Harding. He d. 1648. Sever'l child. [See REGISTER, xxvi. 382.]

Elizabeth, m. 1 Sir Hugh Smyth, Kt.; m. 2 Sir Ferdinando Gorges.

Frances, m. Sir Thomas Tyringham, Kt. ——
Bridget, m. Sir Robert Philips of Montacute, Somerset.

Sir Arthur Gorges, b. 1601; m. Elizab. dau. of Sir Wm. Chauncey, royalist. He died 1661, she in 1660.

Arthur Gorges, m. Mary, dau. of Vis't Bayning. He d. 1668, s. p.

Dudley, m. Sir Robert Lane. He d. 1624.

Elizabeth, m. 1 Sir R. Stanley, d. 1632; m. 2 Theophilus Earl of Lincoln. She d. 1675.

Timoleon, Egremont, Carew, Henry.

Richard, Lord Gorges, b. 1619; m. Bridget, dau. of Sir R. Kingsmill. He is buried at Stetchworth, Cambridgesh. 1712.

Margaret, m. 1 Sir Thomas Fleming; m. 2 Sir F. Pridgeau; m. 3 Sir John Maynard. She d. 1679.

Katherine, m. Sir Robert Dillington.

Bridget, m. Rev. Ezekiel Johnson.

Helena, m. John Gibbons. ——
Mary, d. 1660. Maid of Honor to Elizabeth, Queen of Bohemia. She d. at the Hague.

Thomas Gorges of Heavitree, Devon; m. 1 Mary, daught'r of John Sanford; mar. 2 Rose, dau. of Sir Jerome Alexander, wid. of Rawlins Mallach.

John Gorges, Gov. of Londonderry.

Robert Gorges, D. C. L. m. Jane Loftus. He was Secretary to Henry Cromwell. His descendants still live in Ireland.

Elizabeth, d. 1668.

Ferdinando Gorges, a Barbadoes merchant; m. Melvira Hilliard, of Eye, Herefordsh. He d. 1701. This branch is extinct except in the female line.

Henry, died 1674, aged 17. in his father's life-time.

Thomas Gorges. Ferdinando. Henry. Susan.

Alexander. Elizabeth.

THE GORGES FAMILY.

By the Rev. FREDERICK BROWN, of Beckenham, Kent, Eng.

[THERE has long been a desire among historical students to obtain fuller, more authentic and precise details of the personal history of Sir Ferdinando Gorges, the founder of the state of Maine, and his numerous and distinguished relatives, some of whom are connected with American as well as English history. We have now the pleasure of laying before the readers of the REGISTER, a communication from the Rev. Mr. Brown, of Fern Bank, Beckenham, Kent, formerly of Nailsea near Bristol, England, who, for more than twenty years, has been collecting materials relative to the Gorges family, and to whom several of our American writers have been indebted for important facts. He has already sufficient material—a great part gathered from wills, registers, and other unprinted sources—to prepare a good sized volume on the subject; and we hope he will be prevailed upon to do so. The present contribution is of course a very small part of his collections. It is a small part even of those relating to Sir Ferdinando Gorges and his descendants; for he has not attempted to give all the multifarious information derived from English and American printed books.

The tabular pedigree on the preceding pages and the following illustrative notes will show us the precise relationship of some of the actors in the colonization of New-England, concerning whom there has been some obscurity.

For other pedigrees and notices of the Gorges family, see the REGISTER, xv. 17–20 (where earlier generations will be found); xviii. 287; xxvi. 331–2; xxviii. 404–9. *   J. W. DEAN.]

Sir FERDINANDO[4] GORGES was the younger son of Edward Gorges, Esq., of Wraxall, Somerset, whose will, dated Aug. 10, 1568, was proved Sept. 17, 1568. The elder son was Sir Edward Gorges, of Wraxall, who married Dorothy, daughter of Sir George Speke, kt., and died at Wraxall, where he was buried Dec. 16, 1624. It is not certain that Sir Ferdinando Gorges was born at Wraxall; and the probability is that he was not, as the Wraxall Registers, which have been carefully kept, contain no record of his baptism. Moreover, his father, Edward Gorges, Esq., died at Clerkenwell, Aug. 29, 1568. His funeral certificate is in the College of Arms (i. 5, 161). The mother of Sir Ferdinando was Cicely, daughter of William Lygon, of Madresfield, Worcestershire, an ancestor of the present Earl of Beauchamp. She married, secondly, John Vivian, Esq.

Edward Gorges, in his will, bequeathed to his son Ferdinando, "a chayne of gold waying 23 oz.," 100£, and "his manor of Birdcombe, Wraxall, to have and to hold to him and his assigns for and during the term of xxiv years, if he so long shall live." As the elder brother of Sir Ferdinando, Edward Gorges, was baptized at Wraxall, Sept. 5, 1564, and their father died in 1568, the date of his birth may be between 1565 and 1567. His father speaks of "my little children."

It is generally thought that Sir Ferdinando Gorges was knighted in 1591,[1]

---

[1] In a "Journal of the Siege of Rouen," by Sir Thomas Coningsby, edited by John Gough Nichols, F.S.A., in the Camden Miscellany, vol. i. (Camden Society's Publications, vol. xxxix.) p. 27, under date of Oct. 8, 1591, it is recorded that "our lord generall.....made

*The first two are pp. 63-66, this volume.

and this date was communicated to me by Colonel Chester; but this does not agree with the fact that Sir Nicholas Gorges, his great uncle, whose will is dated Oct. 28, 1590 (proved 1594), bequeaths "to my nephew, Sir Ferdinando Gorges, my greatest guilt boll [i. e. bowl] with the cover." There is an interesting incident connected with Sir Ferdinando Gorges mentioned in the "Archæologia" of the Society of Antiquaries (vol. 35, part i.), entitled "New Materials for a Life of Sir Walter Raleigh by J. Payne Collier," read before the society, June 22, 1853.

I omit in my statement relative to Sir Ferdinando all the many references to him in his connection with the Earl of Essex's rebellion, his governorship of Plymouth, the civil war and the colonization of America, which are contained in the State Papers and other printed documents. See also Oldmixon's "History of the Stuarts," vol. i. p. 76; Seyer's "History of Bristol," vol. ii. pp. 309 and 404; Barrett's "History of Bristol," p. 414.

Sir Ferdinando's first wife was Ann Bell, daughter of Edward Bell, of Writtle, Essex. They were married at St. Margaret's, Westminster, Feb. 24, 1589-90. She was buried in St. Sepulchres, London, Aug. 6, 1620. William Gorges, of St. Budeaux, Devon, son of Tristram Gorges, Esq., in his will, June 20, 1614, bequeaths "a mourning cloke to Sir Ferdinando Gorges," and "mourning weeds to my Lady Ann Gorges."

Sir Ferdinando by Ann, his first wife, had four children, viz.:—

i. JOHN.
ii. ROBERT.
iii. ELLEN, } who died young.
iv. HONORIA, }

He married, secondly, Mary Fulford, daughter of Sir Thomas Fulford, and sister of Bridget Fulford, the wife of Arthur Champernown of Dartington, Devon. Mary Fulford was the widow of Thomas Achim, of Hall, Cornwall, whose will was proved 1619. She died 1623. "Admⁿ Aug. 1, 1623, of Dame Mary Achim alias Gorges, late of Plymouth, Devon, deceased, granted to her brother Sir Francis Fulford, kt., and John Berriman of kin to the deceased, Sir Ferdinando Gorges, kt., the husband of deceased renouncing."

It was through this marriage that Francis Champernown, the son of Arthur and Bridget Champernown, is called the nephew of Sir Ferdinando Gorges. Sir Ferdinando had no children by her.

He married thirdly, Elizabeth Gorges, one of the daughters of Tristram Gorges, son of Sir William Gorges, kt., of St. Budeaux, Devon, by Elizabeth daughter of Martyn Cole. He was her third husband. She married first, in 1614, Aug. 1, Edward Courtney, son of Sir Peter Courtney, of Landrake, Cornwall. (Her sister, Douglas Gorges, married, in 1615, William Courtney, brother of Edward.) They were the parents of Sir Peter Courtney,[1] of Trethurffe, kt. Elizabeth Courtney married secondly, ———— Blithe, of whom I know nothing. She died in 1629. Administration, March 19, 1628-9, of Dame Elizabeth Gorges, alias Blithe, alias Court-

24 knights." The editor (p. 71) as a note to this, prints from the Harleian MSS. 6063, art. 26, a list of "Knights made by Robert Erle of Essex before Roane, 1591," containing, however, only 22 names, of which "Sir Ferdinando Gorge" is the last. See REGISTER, xxviii. 405.   J. W. D.

[1] State Papers, 1629, June 15, Sir Will. Courtney to Secretary Dorchester. "Sir Ferdinando Gorges keeps possession of his (i. e. William Courtney's) nephew, Peter Courtney's estate, in spite of his Majesty's pleasure that Sir William should have the care both of his person & estate." Sir Ferdinando was the step-father of Peter Courtney.

ney deceased, while she lived of Ladocke, Cornwall. Commission granted to her husband, Sir Ferdinando Gorges. They had no issue.

Sir Ferdinando Gorges married fourthly, Elizabeth (Gorges) Smyth, third daughter of Sir Thomas Gorges, kt., by Helena Shackenburgh, the widow of William, Marquess of Northampton. She was baptized at St. Dunstan's in the West, London, June 4, 1578. She married first, Sir Hugh Smyth, kt., of Ashton Court, Somerset, who died in 1627, and had by him: 1. *Thomas Smyth*, the Royalist; 2. *Mary Smyth*, married Sir Thomas Smith, of Cheshire; 3. *Helena Smyth*, married Sir Francis Rogers, of Cannington, Somerset.

" Sir Ferdinando Gorges, of Kintbury, Devon, kt., and Madame Elizabeth Smyth de Long Ashton, Sept. 23, 1629." (Marriages at Wraxall, Somerset.)

They lived at Lower Court, called sometimes " Ashton Phillipps," Long Ashton, probably the dower house of his wife. She died about 1658. Her will is dated Sept. 13, 1657, and proved June 13, 1659. Thomas Smyth, in his will March 27, 1638, bequeaths 40s. for a ring " to Sir Ferdinando Gorges my father-in-law," *i. e.* his step-father.

Sir Ferdinando Gorges died at Long Ashton, and was buried there, May 14, 1647. The Registers of Long Ashton of that date are not extant. His will was in the Diocesan Registry of Wells, Somerset, but cannot now be found.

JOHN[5] GORGES, eldest son of Sir Ferdinando Gorges by Ann Bell, was born April 23, 1593.

1620, July 31. John Gorges, eldest son of Sir Ferdinando Gorges, kt., and the Lady Frances Fynes, daughter of the Earl of Lincoln. (Marriage Registers of St. James, Clerkenwell.) John Gorges married secondly, Mary daughter of Sir John Meade, of Wendon Loftus, Essex. She was buried at St. Margaret's, Westminster, Sept. 15, 1657. He was buried there, April 6, 1657. His will is dated March 5, 1656, proved June 1, 1657. He speaks of his wife, Mary Gorges ; his son, Ferdinando, to whom he bequeaths his Patent of the Province of Maine, in New-England, and all other Patents, maps and pictures. His children were :—

  i. FERDINANDO, of Ashley, Wilts.
  ii. JANE, bapt. July 24, 1632.
  iii. ANN, born May 2, bapt. May 12, 1635 ; buried Dec. 19, 1655.
     Her will, dated Dec. 8, was proved Dec. 21, 1655.
  iv. CICELY, bapt. Feb. 14, 1631. She married at St. Denis Backchurch, London, May 6, 1652, Mr. Abraham [son of Sir John] Chapman, of West Hampnet, Sussex. They had a son *John Chapman*, who is mentioned as his grandson in John Gorges's will.

ROBERT[5] GORGES, second son of Sir Ferdinando Gorges. Of him, little is known beyond the mention of his name in the patents of New-England. He probably died in 1624, or soon after his return to England.

FERDINANDO[6] GORGES, son of John Gorges, was born at Wendon Loftus, Essex, August 19, 1630. He is described in the Herald's Visitation as of Hillingdon, near Uxbridge, Middlesex. His name also occurs often in connection with the Province of Maine. He married at St. Bride's, London, May 22, 1660, Mary, daughter of Thomas Archdale,[1] of Loaks near

---

[1] John Archdale, son of Thomas Archdale, came to New-England, in 1664, as the agent of his brother-in-law, Ferdinando Gorges, and remained here about a year. Josselyn, in his " Voyages to New-England " (p. 272), states that he arrived with the King's Commissioners, and that he " brought to the colony in the province of Main, Mr. *F. Gorges.*

74

Chipping Wycomb, Bucks. He became possessed of the manor of Ashley, Wilts, which had formerly belonged to Sir Thomas Gorges. He was buried there in the tomb of Sir Theobald Gorges. He died Jan. 25, 1718, aged 89. " He was charitable and patient, courteous and beneficent, zealous and constant to the church, and a great admirer of learning." His children were :—

i. FERDINANDO, born 1663. He married Catherine Foyle, of Somerford, Wilts, niece of Fleming, of Stoneham, Hants. He was buried at Ashley, Feb. 20, 1738.[1] He had two sons who died young, Richard[7] and Ferdinando.[7]

ii. MARY, born 1661, buried August 29, 1689.

iii. THOMAS, of whom I know nothing further. It is recorded on the tomb of his father that only two of the children survived him.

iv. ELIZABETH, bapt. May 8, buried Sept. 22, 1669.

v. CECILIA, bapt. June 22, 1670.

vi. ANN, bapt. Jan. 9, 1671-2.

order from his Majesty *Charles* the Second, under his manual, and his Majestie's Letters to the *Massachusets* concerning the same, to be restored unto the quiet possession and enjoyment of the said province in *New-England* and the Government thereof, the which during the civil Wars in *England* the Massachusets colony had usurpt." But if Archdale arrived in July, 1664, in company with the King's Commissioners, he could not have brought the two documents named by Josselyn, for they are both dated June 11, 1664, whereas the commissioners sailed from England several weeks previous to that date. The royal letter to the inhabitants of Maine is printed in the Hutchinson Papers 385-8, Prince Society's edition ii. 110-12; and that to the governor and council of Massachusetts in the Records of Massachusetts, vol. iv. pt. ii. pp. 243-5. Archdale brought commissions to twelve persons as counsellors or magistrates. " On his arrival," says Williamson, " he visited every town in the Province, and granted commissions to Henry Josselyn, of Blackpoint, Robert Jordan, of Spurwick, Edward Rishworth, of Agamenticus, and Francis Neale, of Casco, who took upon themselves to rule." Josselyn, Archdale, Jordan and Rishworth, addressed a letter to the government of Massachusetts, requiring a surrender of the jurisdiction to the commissioners of Gorges; but Massachusetts refused to comply. The king's commissioners did not sustain Gorges. On the 23d of June, 1665, they issued an order instituting a new government for Maine, and forbidding the inhabitants to yield obedience either to the commissioners of Gorges or to the corporation of Massachusetts-Bay. This order is printed by Williamson (i. 416-17). Archdale probably left soon after; as he says, in a document dated Feb. 4, 1687-8, that he " was resident there for the space of a twelve month or thereabouts." (REGISTER, xiii. 304.)

He was afterward one of the proprietaries of Carolina, and was governor of the colony from 1695 to 1696. He had previously visited Carolina, for a letter written in 1686 from that colony by him to George Fox is printed in Hawks's History of North Carolina; but he was not a resident there in 1694 when he was appointed governor. After his return to England, he was elected, in 1698, a member of Parliament for Chipping Wycombe; but his conscience not allowing him to take the oath, he was not admitted to a seat. He published, in 1707, " A Description of the Province of Carolina." See REGISTER, xiii. 303-4 ; xviii. 287 ;—*Notes and Queries* (London, 1870), 5th S., vi. 382; Drake's *Dictionary of American Biography*, 32; Willis's *Portland*, 1st ed. i. 109-10; 2d ed. 157; Williamson's *Maine*, i. 403, 411, 414, 663; *Massachusetts Colony Records*, iv. pt. ii. 243-7; Josselyn's *Voyages*, 272; *Massachusetts Historical Collections*, 3d S., iii. 391; Folsom's *Saco and Biddeford*, 91.

J. W. D.

[1] Ashley, Wilts.—The last of the Gorges Family was Ferdinando Gorges, Esq., who died 1736 [sic], at the age of 76. He was succeeded by his cousin, John Beresford, Esq. Ashley was eventually sold, under the decrees of the court of chancery, to Sir Onesiphorus Paul. Mrs. Beresford died 1742.—*Beauties of Wilts, Britton*. I am not clear as to the date of the death of the last Ferdinando Gorges.

Pedigree of Gorges [*ante*, 42–7].* — The following additions and corrections to the article of the Rev. Frederick Brown, M.A., F.S.A., on the Gorges family have been furnished us by the author after examining the printed sheets sent to him :

Mary, the second wife of John[5] Gorges son of Sir Ferdinando, was the daughter of Sir *John* Meade, not *P.* Mead as printed on page 42. It is correctly printed on page 46.

William[5] Gorges son of Sir Edward (p. 42) was baptized at Wraxall, Feb. 2, 1605-6, and I believe is the same man who was *buried* at Wraxall, Feb. 9, 1658-9, as "Mr. William Gorges." He is described by Savage as returning to England, after 1636. Of Frances[5] Gorges, sister of the preceding, there is no record of baptism at Wraxall, but it is quite certain that she married John Luttrell, second son of Andrew Luttrell, Esq., of Hartland, Devon, before 1610, as among the Wraxall baptisms is that of "John Luttrell son of Mr. John Luttrell, Oct. 21, 1610." Her husband, John Luttrell's will, was proved March 26, 1616-17, and her own will, as Frances Southcott, widow, was proved Nov. 25, 1664.

Dudley[4] Gorges, daughter of Sir Arthur. This christian name is correct.—1619, Aug. 12, Married in Chelsea church, Sir Robert Lane and Mrs. Dudley Gorges, daughter of Sir Arthur Gorges.—1667, Aug. 24, Buried Dame Dudley Lane. His will was proved Oct. 2, 1624 ; her will, Sept. 17, 1667.

Douglas, daughter of Viscount Bindon and wife of Sir Arthur Gorges. Her baptism is on the register of Stratford le Bow church, Jan. 29, 1571-2.

Will of Ferdinando Gorges, Esqr. of Ashley, Wilts, Feb. 2, 1737. The Manor &c. of Ashley to my kinsman, John Beresford. My sister, Cecilia Kingham, commonly called Moody, widow. My cousin, Mary Horne, of Ashley, widow. My cousin Mary Williams, daughter of Mr. Wilson Williams of Aylesbury. Proved Feb. 20, 1738.

Ferdinando Gorges of Ashley was the last male descendant of Sir Ferdinando Gorges. I think that all the persons mentioned in his will were his kinsmen on his wife's side, except Cecilia, his sister, who was baptized at St. Margaret's, Westminster, June 22, 1670 ; but who her husband was, I know not.

John Beresford was buried at Ashley 1742.

*Pp. 70-75, this volume.

CONTRIBUTION TO A GORTON GENEALOGY.

By Elliot Stone, Esq., of Riverdale, New York City.

Although we know from Samuel Gorton's own words that he and his forefathers "for many generations" were born in the town of Gorton in Lancashire, the precise date of his birth does not seem to be anywhere stated. Savage says he was born about 1600, and Mr. J. O. Austin gives the year as 1592, stating that Gorton was forty-four years of age when he landed in Boston in 1637 with wife Elizabeth, son Samuel, and other children. In "Miscellanea Genealogica et Heraldica" for 1873 there is a long list of Gortons of Lancashire* which includes the following:

Feb. 12, 1592-3   Samuel son of Thomas Gorton bapt Colleg. Ch. Manchester.

1600 & odd.   Samuel Gorton, the founder of a religious sect in America, "was born early in the 17th century in the town of Gorton &c."

Oct. 2, 1601.   Samuel son of Adam Gorton bapt Colleg. Ch. ("probably the Samuel above referred to ").

1607.   Adam Gorton one of the two Constables of Droylsden near Manchester.

1629.   Adam Gorton of Droylsden, will proved at Chester.

Gorton and Droylsden were close to Manchester and tributary to the Collegiate Church. The second item is probably an extract from Sparks's American Biography, and the question is, which of the two Samuels baptized is our Gorton? If Mr. Austin is correct, he would seem to be the son of Thomas, but it may be observed that Adam had a son named Otywell and our Samuel had a grandson named Othniel, between which names there is sufficient resemblance to warrant a suspicion that the first has suffered in transcription. Perhaps some one may have an opportunity to examine the will of Adam Gorton proved at Chester in 1629.

In the same volume of "Miscellanea" there is a heraldic seal showing gules, ten billets or, a chief of the second: crest—a goat's head erased, ducally gorged, which was used by a Gorton in the 18th century. This coat is ascribed to Gorton, without a crest, in early editions of Burke, so it may be regarded as ancient, and probably that which Samuel Gorton had in mind when he said that his "ancestors were not unknown to the records of the heraldry of England."

The wills of Mrs. Mary Mayplett of London and Dr. John Maplett of Bath, discovered by Mr. Henry F. Waters and published in the Register

---

*Dr. Howard's Miscellanea Genealoc^{--- at} Heraldica, Vol. I, New Series, pp. 321-5; 378-9.

for 1890, p. 384, and 1892, p. 153, prove that Samuel Gorton's wife was Mary Maplett, whose parentage would seem to justify the statement that "she had been as tenderly nurtured as any man's wife in Plymouth." Judge Brayton in his "Defence of Gorton," and Mr. Austin, call the wife Elizabeth, and it has been suggested that two sets of children are rather indicated by Gorton's special bequest to his eldest son Samuel for helping "me bring up my family when my children were young"; but the third son, Benjamin, named a child Maplet, and if Gorton had lost a first wife in New England it would hardly have escaped notice. Mrs. Mayplett's will refers to her daughter Mary, wife of Samuel Gorton, in New England, and Dr. Maplett made bequests to his sister, Mrs. Mary Gorton of New England, and to each of her children. This Dr. Maplett was an eminent physician, and a long account of him can be found in Wood's Athenæ Oxoniensis, which states that he was "son of a father of both his names, a *sufficient shoemaker*, in the parish of St. Martin's le Grand in London." [What was a "sufficient" shoemaker?] Foster's Alumni Oxon. refers to him as John Maplett, son of John of London, city, gent., Christ Church College, matriculated 24 Feb. 163½, aged 20, D. Med., Principal Gloucester Hall, and the Dictionary of National Biography states that he seems to have had an uncle residing in Holland or the Low Countries, whom he visited. His monument is in St. Peter's Church, Bath, and the following reference thereto is made in "Monumental inscriptions at Bath from MSS. of Antony à Wood," in Miscellanea Genealogica et Heraldica, New series, Vol. 4, p. 58. "The ar'es (armes) over it are arg. three chevrons b. [blue], his epitaph ye may see at length in Mr. Thomas Guidot's book of ye Bath." It appears, therefore, that Mrs. Samuel Gorton was Mary, daughter of John Maplett, gent. of St. Martin's le Grand, London, and Mary, his wife, and that her family probably bore arms, although it must be added that the heraldic ordinaries do not mention them. In fact, Maplett must be a very uncommon name, for an extended search through tables of English names has revealed only the following other instances, which may therefore be of interest:

Rev. John Maplet, as to whom we learn from Newcourt's Repertorium, Cooper's Athenæ Cantabrigiensis, and Dict. Nat. Biog., that he was matriculated as sizar of Queen's Coll., Camb., in Dec. 1560, M.A. 1567, instituted to rectory of Great Lees in Essex, 26 Nov. 1568, which he exchanged for vicarage of Northall in Middlesex, where he was buried 7 Sept. 1592. He was author of "Argemonie or the pryncipall vertues of Stones," "A greene forest &c." and "The Diall of Destiny." He married a widow named Ellen Leap and had *John*, Thomas 1577, Margaret, Ellen 1576, and Mary 1581. In view of his residence close to London, might not his son John have been the father of Dr. John Maplett and Mrs. Gorton?

Le Neve in Fasti Anglicanæ mentions Edward Maplet, collated as Prebend of Carlisle, 4 March 168⁴₅, died 31 Aug. 1624. Lysons says he was also vicar of Addinghay in Cumberland.

The Register of Oxford University refers to Henry Maplet of Cumberland, clerici filius, matriculated Queen's Coll. 1619, aged 18, who was probably son of above Edward.

Hutchinson's History of Cumberland states that Christopher Richmond of Highhead Castle, who died in 1642, had first wife Ann, daughter of Thomas Mayplate of Salkeld.

From these few instances the name would seem to have been chiefly associated with Cumberland.

78

FAMILY CONNECTIONS OF BARTHOLOMEW GOSNOLD

By WARNER F. GOOKIN, B.D., of Oak Bluffs, Mass.

Bartholomew Gosnold died in Virginia on 22 Aug. 1607, aged about thirty-six. In the last six years of his life, he had opened the way to the settlement of New England by the discovery of Cape Cod, Martha's Vineyard, and the Elizabeth Islands in 1602,[1] and in the following years, had become "the first mover" of the venture that resulted in the settlement of Jamestown, Va., in 1607.[2] When he died, he left behind him in England a widow with six children under eleven years of age. The story of his marital connections gives a hint as to the position that Gosnold might have attained, had he lived to complete his work as the "projector" and chief leader of the Jamestown settlement.

Bartholomew's wife was Mary Golding, daughter of Robert Golding and Martha Judd.[3] The Parish register of the church in Latton, Essex, has these entries:

Marriages: 1571   Robert Goldinge to Martha Judd
            1595   Bart. Gosnolde to Mary Goldinge.[4]

The relationships suggested by these entries are confirmed by the will of Dame Mary Judd, "widdowe", of Latton, Essex, probated in the Prerogative Court of Canterbury, 19 Feb. 1602. No abstract of this will has as yet been printed. The writer obtained from Somerset House, London, photostats of its six large, closely written pages. Among the chief beneficiaries are "Mr. Robert Golding my sonne in law, and Martha his wife my daughter". Mention of Bartholomew's wife is made in the following words: "Item I give unto Marye Gosnoll my grandchild the hanging bedstead and bedd with all the furnyture in that chamber which is called my sonne Goldings chamber and all the household stuff in that chamber".

The will is an amazing document, bequeathing the furniture and the furnishings of the manorial hall, four or five parlors, and a dozen or so separately named chambers. The tapestries, bed linens and towels, table linens and napkins, add up to fantastic dozens. Some one hundred pieces of plate, silver, "parcel gilt", and "gilt", are mentioned for various beneficiaries. Dame Judd's personal jewelry, gold rings with precious stones and a gold chain, was divided between six favored daughters and granddaughters. A thousand pounds in cash (representing a present value of nearly twenty times as much) was to be distributed to relatives, servants, the clergy, and the poor.

Dame Judd, whose maiden name was Mary Mathew, had married successively three wealthy London merchants: first, Thomas Langton, by whom she was the mother of Jane Langton, who married John Barne, uncle of Sir Christopher Carleill and brother-in-law of

Sir Francis Walsingham, Secretary of State;[5] secondly, Sir Andrew Judd, one time Lord Mayor of London, whose name she retained;[6] and thirdly, James Alltham, who, on retiring from London, had purchased the manor in Latton, Essex, Dame Judd's home until her death. In her will, Dame Judd names also as her "sonnes" and daughters several children of Sir William Winter, Surveyor of the Navy, but owing to obvious confusions in the visitation pedigrees, it is impossible to state at the present time how this relationship was established. It may be that there was a fourth marriage at an advanced age to the Admiral, who was then a widower with adult children.

Martha was the only child of her mother's marriage to Sir Andrew Judd, but as the latter was a widower with children by his first marriage, Martha had an older half-sister, Alice Judd, who had died before Dame Judd made her will. Sir Andrew Judd was buried in St. Helen's Church, Bishopsgate, London.[7] A small painted wall-monument on the east wall of the "nun's quire", fortunately not injured in the bombings of London, has the following inscription:[8]

To Russia and Mussova ' To Spayne Gynney without fable
Traveled He by land and sea ' Both Mayor of London and Staple
The Commonwealth he norished ' So worthelie in all his daies
That ech state fullwell him loved ' To his perpetuall prayse.
Three wyves he had one was Mary ' Fower sons one mayde had he by her
Annys had none by him truly ' By Dame Mary had one daughter
Thus in the month of September ' A Thousand fyve Hundred fyftey
And eight died this worthie stapler ' Worshipynge his posteryte.

This inscription is fraught with significance for the America that was to be. The "mayde" of the first marriage was Alice Judd, who married the wealthy Sir Thomas Smith, known from his office of Collector as "Mr. Customer Smith". The third son of this marriage was Sir Thomas Smith, governor of the East India Company and the presiding Treasurer of the first Virginia Company of London, under which the expedition of 1606–7 that settled in Jamestown, Va., was sent out.[5] He is reputed to have been the wealthiest London merchant of his day. Sir Andrew Judd's other daughter, the child of his third marriage, was Martha Judd, who became the mother-in-law of Bartholomew Gosnold, the first to lead colonists to Massachusetts, and vice admiral of the fleet that succeeded in settling Virginia. This newly discovered fact, that Bartholomew Gosnold's mother-in-law was an aunt of the financier believed to be chiefly responsible for the organization of the London Company that operated under King James' charter of 1606, seemingly dispels much of the obscurity surrounding Gosnold's prominence in the expedition sent to Virginia under that charter.

Among Martha Golding's many bequests from her mother was one item that seems to have been given as a token of her paternity, — "one neaste of gilte gobletts, with a cover wch were Mr. Andrew Judds". Her mother also gave her a "sylver pillowe with my Armes on yt. my coche with the stonehorses thereto belonging and their furniture". Martha, with her husband Robert Golding, resided in

Bury St. Edmunds, Suffolk. This town, surrounding the ruins of a famous abbey, whose demolished walls furnished the stones for the building of two beautiful churches, early became the resort of gentry from the three nearby counties. A century after the Goldings' day, Daniel Defoe wrote of it, — "But the beauty of this town consists in the number of gentry who dwell in and near it, . . . the affluence and plenty they live in; . . . Here is no manufacturing, . . . the chief trade of the place depending upon the gentry who live there, or near it, and who cannot fail to cause trade enough by the expence of their families and equipages."[9]

The residence of Robert and Martha Golding in Bury is established by entries in the parish register of St. James, — a daughter, Martha, was baptized there on 21 Sept. 1580, and a son, John, was buried there on 7 Sept. 1592.[10] The burial of Robert Golding, armiger, is recorded in the same register under date of 1 March 1610. There is, however, no baptismal record in Bury of the two older children, Mary, who married Bartholomew Gosnold, and John, whose burial is recorded. It may be assumed, therefore, that the family lived elsewhere before 1580. The daughter, Martha, apparently also died early, as neither she, nor any other children except Bartholomew's wife, are mentioned in Martha Golding's will of 1614.

Robert Golding was presumably one of the numerous descendants of Robert Golding of Chelmsford, Essex, who died in 1470; but by which of several lines it has thus far been impossible to discover.[11] He may have been of fairly close kinship to the Gosnold family, as two sons of Robert Golding of Grays in Cavendish, Suffolk, married two of Bartholomew's great-aunts.

The career of this father-in-law of Bartholomew Gosnold may have been a notable one, if certain unrelated notices of Robert Golding all refer to the gentleman in question. One "of these names", as Venn quaintly puts it, was matriculated at Cambridge University, a pensioner from Christ's, in 1549.[12] He was admitted to the Inner Temple in 1556, and was subsequently called to the bench, appointed a Reader in 1578, and was Treasurer in 1589–91. These appointments imply that he was a lawyer of brilliance and wealth. Anthony Gosnold, Bartholomew's father, was a contemporary of this Robert Golding, as he was matriculated at Cambridge University in 1550, and admitted at Gray's Inn for the study of law in 1554.[12]

Robert Golding, Esq., appears in a Chancery Court case as the leading plaintiff in an action by the governors of the Free Grammar School at Bury St. Edmunds to recover certain properties for the School.[13] In 1596, a lawyer named Robert Golding acted with a lawyer named William Tyffin in settling the involved financial affairs of Arthur Golding of Little Birch, Suffolk, a well-known author and translator of Elizabeth's reign.[14] Arthur Golding was a son of John Golding of Belchamp Hall, Essex, cousin of the Goldings previously mentioned as great-uncles of Bartholomew Gosnold.

John Golding was also the father of Margaret Golding, Arthur Golding's older half-sister, who married the 16th Earl of Oxford and became the mother of Edward de Vere, 17th Earl of Oxford.

Still another mention of a Robert Golding occurs in connection with the Manor of Denney's in Coddenham, a village a few miles from the seat of Bartholomew's family in Otley. In 1599, Robert Golding and others bought the share in the Manor of Denney's inherited by Margaret, wife of Sir John Cutts, Knt., from her mother, daughter and coheir of Sir Thomas Lytton.[15] At this time another manor in Coddenham was owned by cousins of Bartholomew Gosnold, and three others were owned by Ralph Scrivener, whose second son, Matthew Scrivener,[16] sailed for Virginia in the first supply ship of 1607, to join the Gosnolds already there. Robert Golding's share of Denney's was later sold to Sir Edward Bacon, son of Sir Nicholas Bacon, Keeper of the Great Seal, both kinsmen of Dorothy Bacon Gosnold, Bartholomew's mother.

It is unfortunate that in none of these mentions of a Robert Golding, several of which place a gentleman of that name in the environment of Bartholomew Gosnold, is there direct evidence that we have in them information about Gosnold's father-in-law. No will has been found of the Robert Golding, armiger, who was buried at Bury St. Edmunds on 1 March 1610. Happily, it is otherwise with Martha Golding, daughter of Dame Mary Judd and grandmother of Bartholomew's children, as her will indubitably mentions these children.

Young Mary Golding, although her parents' home was in Bury St. Edmunds, went to her grandmother's palatial manor in Latton, Essex, for her marriage to Bartholomew Gosnold in 1595. Shortly thereafter, she and Bartholomew established their home in Bury St. Edmunds, as all of their children but one were baptized in Bury between the years 1597 and 1607. They may have made their home in the household of Mary's parents, the Goldings; Bartholomew's long absences at sea would make this seem likely.

The baptismal records of Bartholomew's children from the parish register of St. James' Church, Bury St. Edmunds, were first published in this country by Dr. Fulmer Mood, in THE NEW ENGLAND HISTORICAL AND GENEALOGICAL REGISTER, July 1929. The baptismal dates and names are as follows: (1) 24 April 1597, Martha; (2) 20 Oct. 1600, Robert; (3) 2 Aug. 1602, Susan; (4) 16 Dec. 1603, Bartholomew; (5) 11 Dec. 1605, Paul; (6) 5 Feb. 1606 (–07), Martha.[10] It will be noted that the first Martha must have died before the baptism of the second Martha in 1607. There is a burial record of a "Martha Gossnull gent." on 2 Dec. 1598, but the inference usually drawn that this records the death of an infant Martha seems to the writer by no means certain. There is the possibility that Martha Golding, baptized in 1580, the younger sister of Mary, married Bartholomew's younger brother Anthony and died shortly after marriage at the age of eighteen. There are no records, to be sure, to prove this possibility, although it is reasonably certain that Martha Golding, the daughter, had died before her mother, whose will of 1614 does not mention a daughter named Martha. The writer is reluctant to believe that Bartholomew would have named an island Martha's Vineyard in 1602, if his first born infant bearing that name had died four years previously. One wonders also, why the name Susan (of unknown origin) was used for the daughter born in 1602, if the name Martha was available at that time. The desire to perpetuate the grandmother's given name appears obvious, and one would expect that it would be used for the next daughter born after the death of the first Martha.

It will be noted also from these baptismal records that there is an interval of three and a half years between the births of the first and second child. Another daughter, named Mary, was born sometime within this interval, as the will of her step-father, to be described below, designates her as Bartholomew's oldest child. There is also the possibility that Bartholomew was away from home for a year or more beginning in 1597, which happens to be the year of the Azores expedition. If it is assumed that he was at sea at that time, then Mary was most likely born early in 1599, and baptized at some place where the records have not survived.

Martha Golding's will, dated in Bury St. Edmunds on 30 Nov. 1614, mentions no relatives except Bartholomew Gosnold's widow and children, the testator's daughter, and grandchildren. This will, recently discovered for the writer by Mr. L. H. Haydon Whitehead, record searcher of Long Melford, co. Suffolk, England, is here published in complete form for the first time.[17] Owing to the circumstance that it was impossible to remove for photostating the volume of the Archdeaconry of Sudbury probates in which it was recorded, Mr. Whitehead was fortunately able to have the original will itself photostated, which is here transcribed. Several abbreviations indicated by signs impossible to reproduce in print have been resolved.

"In the name of god amen the laste daye of November in the yeare of our |Lord god one thousande six hvndred and Fourtene I Martha Goldynge of Bury S Ede in the county of Sufk widowe being sicke in body yet of ye best mynde and memory (thanks be gyven to almighty god) doe ordayne and make this my psent laste will and Testament, revokinge all former wills by me heretofore made in manner and forme following, that is to saye: Firste I comend my soule into the merciful hands of almight god, my maker and redeemer and my body to be buryed in christian buryall at the discretion of my executrix hereunder named. Item my will and meaneinge is that my executrix and supviser hereunder named shall within one yeare right after my decease sell to the best advantage and benefytt that she can my gold cheyne and brasiletts and all the beddinge hangings, beste coverlett, quilte, and all the furnyture in my beste chamber, my turky carpet and the livery cupboard clothe suitable to yt, all my gilte and pcell gilte plate and all my damaske and diaper Lynnen lyeing together in one chiste. And the money thereof comeing (together with one hundred pounds wh lyeth by me in golde) my will and meaninge is shall be equally devyded amongst my grandchildren, that is to saye: Robt Gosnold, Bartholomew Gosnolde, Paule Gosnolde, Mary Gosnold, Susan Gosnold and Martha Gosnolde, pt and pt lyke. And to have the same as they shall attayne their severall ages of one and twenty yeares. Itm I give and bequeathe to the saide Mary Gosnold my grandchild sixe silver spoones and sixe gold buttons. Itm I give and bequeathe to the saide Susan Gosnold sixe silver spoones and sixe gold buttons. Itm I give and bequeathe to the saide Martha Gosnold sixe silver spoones and sixe golde buttons with a lytle Jewell. Itm I give and bequeathe to

John Anthony my servante Fourty shillings in money and a mourning cloake. Itm I give to Barbara Copsey my servante fyve shillings. Itm I give to John Eagle tenn shillings. All the reste of my goods and chattells as well moveable as ymmoveable of what nature or quality soev therewith of ready money, plate, Jewells, utensills and furnyture of householde whatsoever (not before gyven and bequeathed) I give and bequeath them to my loveing daughter Mary Gosnolde, widowe, whom I doe ordayne and make my sole executrix of this my last will and Testament. And I doe hereby nominate and appointe my servante Thomas Claydon to be superviser hereof, and doe give him for his paynes a mourneinge cloake. In witness whereof I the saide Martha Goldynge have to every leafe of this my laste will beinge in number two put to my hande and seale the daye and yeare first above wrytten.

"Subscribed sealed and published by the saide Martha Goldinge for her last will and Teastment in the presence of Willyam Partridge."

[Note: Martha's signature on both pages is an undecipherable scrawl beginning with M.]

Martha Golding was buried, according to the parish register of St. James, Bury St. Edmunds, on 7 Dec. 1614, a week after signing her will. Five months later, on 23 May 1615, her daughter Mary, Bartholomew Gosnold's widow, married Jasper Sharpe, gentleman, at Fornham St. Martin, a northern suburb of Bury.[18] Under the will of his father, an unusually wealthy yeoman, Jasper Sharpe had inherited a considerable fortune, and was still a man of large means when he made his own will in 1653. Both father and son owned property in Hessett, the seat of the Bacon family, and were quite likely kinsmen of the Robert Sharpe who married a sister of Sir Nicholas Bacon, Keeper of the Great Seal, and kinsman of Bartholomew Gosnold's mother, Dorothy Bacon of Hessett.[19]

In his will, Jasper Sharpe says of Bartholomew's children, "In my lifetime I have given all my wife's estate she brought to me at the time of our intermarriage to her six children and much more also, yet I give them a remembrance as follows".[20] As none of the boys appears in the list of the scholars of the Free Grammar School of Bury, it is to be inferred that the children enjoyed the luxury of private tutoring; and that otherwise the family lived on the most expensive scale. Some interesting facts about the lives of three of them who survived to maturity are matters of record.

Paul Gosnold, Bartholomew's third son, was matriculated at Cambridge University, a pensioner from Christ's, in 1621; B.A., 1624-5, and M.A., 1628. He was Vicar of Alciston, Sussex, in 1640, and Rector of Bradfield St. Clare, Suffolk, 1641-4. He was one of those sequestered, that is, deprived of his parish, by the Puritans.[21] He was tried by the Puritans on 17 Nov. 1643, and ejected on 22 March 1644. After the Restoration, an effort was made to secure a parish for him. The Calendar of the 1660 Volume for Church Preferments contains this paragraph.[22] "83. Paul Gosnold. For presentation to the Rectory of Fobbing, co. Essex, void by the death of Dr. Samson Johnson. Was the last man that was fetched out of bed by troopers in Suffolk and Norfolk for loyalty during the late troubles. Constantly vindicated monarchy, episcopacy, and liturgy, and cried down rebellion and schism, in almost every sermon; was often forced to fly, often imprisoned, and reduced to such poverty, that having sacrificed liberty to duty, he must now forfeit it for debt, unless aided. Annexing, 83 I, Certificate by John Rous, and two others, that Paul Gosnold, of Suffolk, minister, has suffered much for his loyalty". The sequel of this appeal to the King is unknown to the writer.

Martha Gosnold, Bartholomew's youngest daughter, born after he left England to go to his death in Virginia, married the Rev. John Blemell, either at Horringer or Bury on 20 Aug. 1633, the marriage for some reason being recorded in both parishes.[21] John Blemell had been matriculated at Christ's College, Cambridge, in 1619; B.A., 1623 and M.A., 1627. He was thus a contemporary of Paul Gosnold at Christ's College, taking his degrees a year before Paul. A friendship between the two students doubtless accounts for Martha Gosnold's marriage to John Blemell. John was a son of Thomas Blemell, a carpenter, of London, who married on 7 March 1604, in St. Olave, Old Jewry, Thomasine Neale, widow of William Neale. John's grammar school education had been at the Merchant Taylors' School in London.

After ordination, John Blemell served as curate at St. James in Bury St. Edmunds, and as assistant master at the Bury Grammar School. He apparently soon attained high standing. In the Calendar of State Papers, Domestic, under date of 23 Feb. 1640–1, appears this note.[23] "47. Certificate of John Blemell, curate of St. James', Bury St. Edmunds, Thomas Stephens, Headmaster, and John Hobman, undermaster, of the Grammar School, Bury St. Edmunds, to Bishop Montague of Norwich, that Paul Gosnold, M.A., has diligently studied, and made progress in theology, has lived soberly and piously, and has never, so far as we know, held anything which is not orthodox and conforms to the rights and ceremonies of the English Church in all particulars." [Latin, ½ pp.] This certificate was evidently written at the time of Paul Gosnold's appointment as rector of Bradfield St. Clare.

According to the Induction Book of the Archdeaconry of Sudbury, John Blemell was appointed Rector of Bradfield St. Clare in 1644, obviously to take the place of his brother-in-law, ejected by the Puritans. The presentation did not receive the approval of the "Suffolk Committee", who elected a Samuel Crossman to the rectorship. Evidently John Blemell did not submit gracefully to this decision, as according to the "Proceedings of the Committee for Plundered Ministers", Blemell was summoned on 14 July 1647 to answer charges brought against him by Crossman for disturbing him in the possession of Bradfield Rectory. Nothing more is known of his conduct under the Puritans, except that he appears in the register of St. James at Bury as having assisted at marriages in 1656 and 1657.

After the Restoration, the Rev. John Blemell was appointed rector of the ancient and important church, All Hallows the Great, Upper Thames Street, London.[24] The appointment was made on 27 Aug. 1662, and Blemell held the rectorship until his death on 1 Jan. 1665–6. This church is remembered as one that might have had the Rev. Richard Hakluyt as its rector if an expected vacancy had occurred. In 1600, the Privy Council recommended to the Archbishop of Canterbury that Hakluyt be rewarded for his notable services by appointment to this rectorship, "if by the decease of the incumbent it shall be void". The incumbent, however, recovered, and Hakluyt remained at Wetheringsett.[25] About a century ago, the parish of All Hallows the Great was united with that of St. Michael, Paternoster Row, and the church building was demolished.

John Blemell and his wife Martha Gosnold were the parents of eight children baptized in St. James, Bury St. Edmunds. One son, whose first name is not recorded, was matriculated at Christ's College, Cambridge, in 1651.[26]

Mary Gosnold, Bartholomew's oldest daughter, became the second wife of Richard Pepys, Esq., later knighted, and the stepmother of his six children.[27] Sir Richard Pepys was a cousin of the famous diarist, but apparently not on intimate terms with him. Sir Richard had a distinguished career as a jurist, enjoying the favor of the Puritans. In his last years Sir Richard was Lord Chief Justice of Ireland, dying in Dublin on 2 Jan. 1658-9. His wife, Mary Gosnold Pepys, died the next year.

The will of Jasper Sharpe, Mary Golding's second husband, was dated at Bury St. Edmunds on 5 Aug. 1653, and probated the following year.[20] Three of Bartholomew's children, then approaching fifty years of age, and the Blemell grandchildren, receive legacies. "To Martha the wife of John Blemill, clerk, one of my wifes daughters, 100 pounds". "To Jasper Blemill his son twenty pounds". Other step-grandchildren, John, Thomas, James, Mary, and Martha Blemill, receive ten pounds each. "To Paull Gosnold (clerk) one of my wives sons 100 pounds to be paid within a year after my wives decease. To Mary now the wife of Richard Pepis Esqre my wives eldest daughter a bed and bedding, stools and wrought chairs, after my wives decease, for her life, then to Martha Blemill and her heirs. To the said Mary and Martha my best carpets and cushions equally between them after their mothers decease". Some eight messuages, tenements and parcels of land are left to his wife Mary for her lifetime, then to revert to the heirs of the testator's nephew, Jasper Sharpe. The Sharpe relatives receive cash benefactions amounting to nearly two thousand pounds. The will ends as follows: "To the said Richard Pepys Esqre my son-in-law a gold ring with a saphire set therein, also two gilt tankards for his use during his and his wifes life time, then to Elizabeth and Judith his daughters. I forgive my wife Mary the 100 pounds I lent her. I nominate my executors the said Richard Pepys Esqre and John Blemill, clerk, my sons-in-law".

His wife Mary survived him by twelve years, dying in 1665, seventy years after her marriage to Bartholomew Gosnold. She must therefore have been about ninety at the time of her death. To the end, she retained Bartholomew's title. The record of her passing, in the St. James register, reads:

"1665, 23 October. Magistar Maria Sharpe vidua."

NOTES

[1] John Brereton, A Briefe and true Relation of the Discoverie of the North part of Virginia (London, 1602). Gabriel Archer, The Relation of Captaine Gosnols Voyage to the North part of Virginia, in Purchas His Pilgrims, vol. IV, pp. 1647 ff. Both Relations are available in modern reprints.

[2] John Smith, Map of Virginia, Part II, in E. Arber, Ed., Travels and Works of John Smith (New edition, Edinburgh, 1910), p. 89. In a note to his Pedigree of the Gosnold Family (British Museum Add. MS. 19,133), David Elisha Davy, summarizing this and other early sources, wrote: "In 1607, during the establishment of the Colony at Jamestown in Virginia, 50 men, one half of the colony, perished before autumn; among them Bartholomew Gosnold, the projector of the settlement, a man of rare merits, worthy of a perpetual memory in the plantation, whose influence had alone thus far preserved some degree of harmony in the Council."

[3] The assertion of J. H. Lea (THE REGISTER, vol. LVIII, p. 396), that Bartholomew Gosnold's wife was a Barrington is an error derived from D. E. Davy's Pedigree of the Gosnold Family, British Museum Add. MS. 19,133. The confusion perhaps arose from the fact that a cousin of Bartholomew married a widow Barrington.

[4] Communicated to the writer by Mr. Irvine Gray, of the County Archivist's office, County Hall, Chelmsford, co. Essex. Mr. Gray also supplied the reference for Dame Mary Judd's will, P. C. C. Montague 5, dated at Latton, Essex, 1602.

[5] See Alexander Brown, Genesis of the United States (Boston, 1890), vol. II, Brief Biographies, for accounts of Sir Thomas Smith (Smythe), Barne, Walsingham, William Winter, Carleill, and others mentioned in connection with the Virginia Colony.

[6] For an account of Sir Andrew Judd's marriages, see Fane Lambarde, Sir Andrew Judd, in Archaeologia Cantiana, vol. 43 (1931), pp. 99 ff. Lambarde was mistaken in saying of the daughter of Dame Mary mentioned in the inscription of the monument that "nothing more is heard of her". He was unaware, of course, of the Latton Parish Register entries, and of Dame Judd's will.

[7] The will of Sir Andrew Judd is dated 2 Sept. 1558. Proved 15 Oct. 1558, P. C. C. Noodes 58, duplicated, Welles 54. John Judd, his son and executor having died, a commission to administer was issued 6 March 1558-9 to "Thomas Smythe and Alice his wife natural and lawful daughter of Andrew Judd, Knt., deceased, . . . Dame Mary Judd the widow relict of said deceased renouncing execution" (she having been named executrix in the will).

[8] A description of this monument, sent to the writer by the Rev. Gorden Huelin, Hon. Archivist and Librarian, St. Michael, Paternoster Royal, was taken from the London County Council's Survey of London (London, 1924), vol. IX, The Parish of St. Helen, Bishopsgate (Part II). See also Note 24.

[9] Daniel Defoe, A Tour through England and Wales, 1724–26. Various editions, see index, Bury St. Edmunds.

[10] The parish registers of St. James Church, Bury St. Edmunds, for the years 1558 to 1800, were published as No. XVII of the Suffolk Green Books (Bury St. Edmunds, 1915–1916), 3 vols. All references to these registers in this article are taken from this work.

[11] Harleian Society, vol. xiv, p. 580. See also, Louis Thorn Golding, An Elizabethan Puritan, Arthur Golding the Translator . . . (New York, 1937), p. 13 and wills in the Appendix.

[12] J. Venn, Ed., Alumni Cantabrigienses (Cambridge, England, 1922), for all mentioned in this article as matriculated at Cambridge University. For Robert Golding, see also, Students Admitted to the Inner Temple, 1547–1660 (London, 1877). Under date, 1556, November.

[13] Calendars to the Proceedings in Chancery in the Reign of Queen Elizabeth, vol. I (London, 1827), p. 85. B. b. 14.

[14] L. T. Golding, An Elizabethan Puritan (cited above), p. 109.

[15] W. A. Copinger, Manors of Suffolk (Manchester, 1908), vol. II, pp. 282 ff., Coddenham.

[16] Walter C. Metcalfe, The Visitation of Suffolk (Exeter, 1882) Index, Scrivener.

[17] Will of Martha Golding, Bury St. Edmunds, 30 Nov. 1614, proved 26 March 1615, Arch. Sudbury, Steven 203.

[18] Boyd's Index of Marriages. Communicated to the writer by Mr. L. H. Haydon Whitehead, of Long Melford, England.

[19] Sir Nicholas Bacon served as the Overseer of the will of Dorothy (Bacon) Gosnold's grandfather, Thomas Bacon of Hessett, proved 1547, P. C. C. Allen 41, and of the will of her uncle, John Bacon of Bury St. Edmunds, proved 1559, P. C. C. Chaynay 16. In the latter will he is designated "Lord Keeper". Abstracts of these wills by J. H. Lea, THE REGISTER, vol. LVII, pp. 310, 311.

[20] Will of Jasper Sharpe, gentleman. Dated at Bury St. Edmunds, 5 August 1653, proved, —, 1654, P. C. C. Alchin 506. Abstract communicated to the writer by L. H. Haydon Whitehead, of Long Melford, co. Suffolk, England.

[21] R. Freeman Bullen, Sequestrations in Suffolk, in Suffolk Institute of Archeology Proceedings, vol. XIX, p. 47, Paul Gosnold; pp. 24–25, John Blemell.

[22] Calendar of State Papers, Domestic, Charles II, 1660–1 (London, 1860), vol. XII, p. 229. Volume for Church Preferments, all addressed to the King.

[23] Calendar State Papers, Domestic, 1640–41, vol. CCCCLXXVII, p. 470.

[24] There were seven churches in London named All Hallows. The writer is indebted to the Rev. P. B. Clayton, Rector of All Hallows by the Tower, now being rebuilt with American aid, and to the Rev. Gorden Huelin, Hon. Archivist and Librarian, St. Michael, Paternoster Royal, for the identification of All Hallows the Great, of which John Blemell was Rector.

[25] George Bruner Parks, Richard Hakluyt and the English Voyages (New York, 1928), p. 201.

[26] Free Grammar School, Bury St. Edmunds, Suffolk Green Books No. XIII (Bury St. Edmunds, 1908), p. 31.

[27] For an account of Sir Richard Pepys, see Dictionary of National Biography.

THE ANCESTRY OF BARTHOLOMEW GOSNOLD
The Gosnolds of Otley, Suffolk
By Warner F. Gookin, B.D., of Oak Bluffs, Mass.

In 1602, Bartholomew Gosnold's company, a group of prospective settlers who crossed the Atlantic in the *Concord*, built and occupied on one of the Elizabeth Islands, a "fort" large enough to shelter twenty traders and their stores. Although a shortage of provisions made it necessary to abandon the project, Gosnold may rightly be considered the first, though a transient, settler in New England. Two years after this venture, Gosnold is found in London, described as "the first mover" in getting a Virginia Company organized and chartered. His ultimate success in this endeavor among the merchants, gentry, and nobles who made possible the settlement at Jamestown, Va., in 1607, was unquestionably due in large measure to his background of ancient lineage, and his connections with the well-known families of Bacon, Naunton, Wingfield, Tallmache, and Windsor, together with his marriage into the family of the wealthiest of London merchants, Sir Andrew Judd and his grandson Sir Thomas Smith — all of which is set down in the following pages. Nothing of this picture of Bartholomew Gosnold's social standing has been known to our historians; hence he has been presented as an obscure adventurer of doubtful significance. Now he no longer stands alone, but emerges from the mists of uncertainty as a memorable representative of England's ruling classes, who gave his life in the founding of this nation.

The abbreviations set off in brackets refer to sources of information, more fully described at the end of this article. The dates of birth in italics are approximations based on probabilities.

The Arms of the Gosnold family are described in Appendix A.

Thomas Gosenell of Clopton, will dated 20 Dec. 1464, pr. 9 Feb. 1464/5, Arch. Suff., fo. 134. Abstr. by Lea, THE REGISTER, LVIII, 398. The only names decipherable were those of his wife, Isabell, and of his son, William. The testator may be a brother of John[1] below; the will is interesting because of its suggestion that the Gosnolds were originally seated in Clopton.

1. JOHN GOSNOLD, of Otley [Vis.], 18 Henry V (1440) [Davy]. Netherhall Manor in Otley passed into the possession of John Gosnold at an unascertained date following the death in 1454 of William Cressener, the previous owner and lord [Cop., III, 53].

Children [Vis.]:
    2. i.   JOHN, b. (perhaps) in *1470*.
       ii. EDMUND, conjectured to be the father of Edmund Gosnold of Bildeston, whose will is dated 18 Jan. 1539, pr. 14 Oct. 1540, Arch. Sudbury, 294 Poope. (*See* "Gosnolds of Bildeston", in preparation by the author.)
       iii. KATHERINE, m. WILLIAM GARDINER of Otley [Vis.].
       iv. ANNE, m. THOMAS CADGE of Ipswich [Vis.], or, WILLIAM CADY [Blois], or THOMAS CADY [Davy].

2. JOHN GOSNOLD, of Otley [Vis.], 10 Edward IV (1470) [Davy]. (Reckoning back from the date of his son William's degree at Cambridge, 1510/11, this undefined date of 1470 may possibly be the date of John's birth.) He married KATHERINE KEBELL [Vis.].

As the present Otley Hall, formerly known as Netherhall Manor, dates from the reign of Henry VII, 1485–1509 (see descriptions in Appendix B), it was presumably built by this John Gosnold, to replace an older manor house. In 1491, John Gosenoll fil. John Gosenoll de Ottley was Steward at Framsden [Davy NP], probably a sinecure office. From Davy, NM, fo. 308, citing "Lands etc. holden of the Honor of Clare", undated: — Robert Gosnold lately acquired from John his father one messuage, etc., in Otley and Clopton . . . John Gosnold holds other lands and tenements in Otley of le Overhall for rent of one capon. (Overhall was the other manor in Otley, owned for generations by the Nevill family, the Lords Abergavenny.) . . . The same John holds land acquired from William Wall (mentioned in his will below).

Will of John Gossenold in the Diocese Norwich. [Reference letter A — to be used hereafter to indicate the persons named in the will.] Dated, 26 Jan. 1510/11; pr. 17 Feb. 1511/12, P.C.C. 6 Fetiplace. Abstr. Lea, THE REGISTER, LVII, 96. To be buried in the church yard of St. Mary's at Otley. Benefactions to the High Altars at Otley, Swilland, and Helmingham, and to the Gray, White, and Black Friars at Ipswich. For making a steeple at Otley, 20 marks. Repair of the Chapel of St. Bottell in Burgh, and of the Church of St. Peter at Thorpe. To son Robert: the tenement the testator dwells in; lands in Otley, Helmingham, and Framesden. To son Edmond: the tenement Pakkerdes (Packards) and lands purchased of Thomas Edgar and of the executor of Margaret Gardiner, widow, in Clopton; lands purchased of William Fosdick, executor of Simon Shilby, and of William Wall. To son William: "I will that William Gosnold my son shall sing at Cambridge for my soul the space of three years and have 9 marks a year". To Sir John Clood, 20 s. Executors: Robert Gosnold his son, Thomas Baldry of Ipswich, and Robert Gardiner of Cretingham, the elder. To the executors: lands in Hemingstone, Burgh, and Swilland, to dispose of in alms. Witnesses: Lionell Talmage, Esq., Sir William Base, priest, Jeffry Hill of Bokking Ashe [Ashbocking], John Armiger, Sr., John Morse.

Children [Vis.]:

3. i. ROBERT [Will A], b. (probably) before 1490.
   ii. EDMUND [Will A], seated at Coddenham. (*See* "Gosnolds of Coddenham", in preparation by the author.)
   iii. WILLIAM [Will A], priest, twin to Edmund. Bachelor's degree at Cambridge (Civil Laws), 1510/11 [Venn]. To sing masses for his father [Will A]. Appointed to the church at Otley, 1514. [*Cat. of Beneficed Clergy of Suff.*, *1086–1550*, PSIA, XXII, p. 54.]
   iv. ALICE, m. (1) [Vis.] THOMAS MERRELL of Whepstead; m. (2) THOMAS WEBBE of Dedham; m. (3) JOHN BERIFFE of Bridgeley.
   v. MARGARET [Will A], m. [Vis.] WILLIAM CARDINALL of Wenham, co. Suffolk.
   vi. KATHERINE [Will A, not named in Vis.], not m. in 1511.

3. ROBERT GOSNOLD, the elder, Lord of the Manor of Netherhall, was apparently born shortly before 1490. He outlived his sons and was the patriarch of the family until his death in 1572, aged about 85, and the great-grandfather of eight children named in his will, including Bartholomew Gosnold. He married first, AGNES HILL, the daughter of John Hill of Ashbocking [Vis.], a parish three miles west of Otley. She was the mother of his children. He married secondly, ANN DOGGETT, daughter of Richard Doggett of Groton Lappage and widow of Thomas Bacon of Hessett [Vis. and Doggett Pedigree in Muskett, I, 344]. A marriage settlement, dated 10 Oct. 1547, mentioned in the will of Robert Gosnold below, followed shortly after the death of Thomas Bacon, whose will was proved 30 June 1547. There was no issue of this marriage. (See Appendix C.)

Two land transactions of Robert Gosnold are recorded. In 1553/4 he was party to a deed of land in Otley [Davy NM, citing deeds at Ipswich, 1811, No. 9]. In 1558, Edward Nevill, arm. (Lord Abergavenny, lord of the manor of Overhall in Otley), had licence to alienate to Robert Gosnold, sen. arm., and his son and heir Robert Gosnold, jun., the manor of Burwash in Witnesham. [Davy NP, citing Originalia MSS. index Br. Mus. vol. 8, fo. 21.]

Will of Robert Gosnolde the elder of Otteley, co. Suffolk, Esquir. (Reference letter B, for relatives named.) Dated 20 Oct. 1572, pr. 4 Feb. 1572/3, P.C.C. 6 Martyn. Abstr. by Lea, THE REGISTER, LVI, 402.) To be buried in the church at Ottelie. To his wife, Anne, all household stuff and plate, all ready money she hath of her own gathering, and 'all her jewells, with a pot of silver and 13 silver spoons with Apostles, and also 100 pounds by marriage settlement, dated 10 Oct. 1547. For a jointure, "my manor of Netherhall in Otteley" with other lands and tenements; reversion to his grandson Robert. Lands bequeathed: — To his grandson Robert, capital messuage in Otteley, with lands and tenements called Hawes, Lorkins, Bakers [Davy NM, citing, fo. 308, "Lands holden of the Honor of Clare" mentions "Baker of Clopton holds parcel of land called Knowles in Clopton"], Walles Meadows [purchased by his father from William Wall], Earles in Swyneland [the manor of Swilland, formerly owned by the Earl of Warwick], Brodemeadow, Cloddes with lands called Shribbes [probably the lands in his father's will mentioned as purchased of William Clood], said Shribbes being in the tenure of Thomas Pettawe [Pettoughe, in the Subsidy Return of 1568]. To his grandson

Anthony, Gardiner's with its lands [in Clopton, mentioned in his father's will as purchased of the executors of Margaret Gardiner, widow], meadows called Packard's and Reves, tenement Prattes and its lands, lands and tenements called the Falle, a reversionary right to Chamberlain's in Grundisburgh [alias Alfrydes Chantry in the will of Anthony's father, Robert Gosnold the younger, d. 1559]. To his grandsons, John and Richard, all of his lands and tenements in Ashefield, Cretingham, and Some [Soham]. Executors, his grandsons, Robert and Anthony. Overseer, Sir Robert Wingfield, Knight [son of Sir Anthony Wingfield, K. G., formerly a land owner in Grundisburgh, and a brother of Anthony Wingfield of Sibton, second husband of the testator's daughter-in-law, Katherine Blennerhassett]. Witnesses, Richard Ruben and Edward Gosse.

Will of Anne Gosnold of Otley, widow, late wife of Robert Gosnold, Esquire, deceased. 20 July, 1578, pr. ii Nov. 1578, Cons. Norwich, 140 Woodstock. Abstr. by Lea, REGISTER, LVIII, 311. (Reference letter, C, used hereafter for the numerous Gosnold and Bacon relatives named as the testator's own.) Bequests of gold coins, plate, and furniture. A Mrs. Naunton is named [presumably mother of her grandson's wife, Ursula Naunton]. Executors, her grandchildren, Elizabeth (Bacon) Coxall and Mary Bacon. Overseer: her grandchild, Anthony Gosnold, to whom is given her "ring with the death's head". Witnesses: John Coggeshall [alternate spelling of Coxall], John Threlkeld, Clerk, William Jollye [a servant], and others.

Children by first wife:

4. i. JOHN, s. & h. [Vis.], b. *circa 1512* [mentioned as deceased, Will B].
5. ii. ROBERT, 2nd s. [Vis.], b. *circa 1514* [mentioned as deceased, Will B.]
   iii. KATHERIN, b. before 1511 [Will A]; m. THOMAS GOLDING, Lord of the Manor of Poslingford Hall [Vis. and Cop. V, 279], and of Stonehouse in Clare [Cop. V, 201–2]. Four sons and six daughters [named in Vis. (Golding), pp. 93–4, and in Will below.]

Thomas Golding was a son of Robert Golding of Gray's, Cavendish, Suff. [Vis., pp. 93–4, and Harleian Soc., XIV, 580] and a first cousin of John Golding of Belchamp Hall, Essex, whose daughter Margaret married the 16th Earl of Oxford, and became the mother of Edward de Vere, 17th Earl of Oxford. [See, L. T. Golding, "An Elizabethan Puritan", printed by Richard R. Smith, New York, 1937.] His will, dated 14 Aug. 1575, pr. 4 Dec. 1575, P.C.C. 48 Pyckeryng. Abstr. by Lea, THE REGISTER, LVII, 219.

   iv. JONE [Vis.], Johan Bromley [*sic*] [Will B], b. after 1511 [not mentioned in Will A]; m. (1) JOHN GOLDING of Walter Belchamp, co. Essex, d. in 1551–2. [Vis. is in error in saying that he died *sans* issue; see Will, below.] He had four sons and three daughters by his wife Joan. She m. (2), after 1552, —— BRYMELEY. [Will of her son Robert, below.]

John Golding was a brother of Thomas Golding, above. His will, dated 10 Dec. 1551, pr. 30 Jan. 1551/2, P.C.C. 3 Powell, abstr. by L. H. Haydon Whitehead, communicated to the author, mentions purchases of lands in Framsden, Cretingham, and Soham from Robert Gosnold, Esq., names wife, Joan, and children Robert, John, Roger, Alice, Ursula, Katherine, and Thomasine, all under 21 except Robert, and names his brother Thomas and his brother-in-law Robert Gosnold as supervisors of the will. The will of his son, Robert Golding, of Walter Belchampe, Essex, dated 11 March, 1591/2, codicil same date, pr. 1 July, 1592, P.C.C. 61 Herrington, abstr. by Lea, THE REGISTER, LVII, 220, refers to his mother as Joane Brymeley.

   v. CRYSEN [Vis.], Christian Ryvett [Will B], b. after 1511 [not mentioned in Will A]; m. JAMES RYVETT of Mendlesham. She died a widow, about 1588, leaving five children and twenty-eight grandchildren, mentioned in her will below. "Rivett. This family is very ancient. . . . They were possessed of the manors of Ribost and Brandston, 5 Henry 7 (1490)" [Gipps].

The will of Christian Ryvett of Witnesham, widow, dated 2 Feb. 1587/8, pr. 2 Apr. 1589, Arch Suff. 1588/9, fo. 132. Abstr. by Lea, THE REGISTER, LVIII, 313. Children, named in her will:— (i.) Robert, father of four; (ii.) Rachel, m. Edmund Stiles, parents of six; (iii.) Alice, m. John Daynes, parents of three [see

"Gosnolds of Coddenham", in preparation]; (iv.) Margaret, m. Samuel Scrutton, parents of four; (v.) Mary, m. William Yorke, parents of eleven. [William Yorke, first cousin of Anthony Gosnold, father of Bartholomew, lived in Grundisburgh, and appears in land transactions there with his cousin; see Anthony Gosnold.] Will of Robert Revett of Witnesham, yeoman, dated 21 April, 1616, pr. 26 Sep. 1616, Arch. Suff. 1616, fo. 132. Abstr. by Lea, THE REGISTER, LVIII, 313. Will of William Yorke of Grundisborough, Suff., dated 20 May, 1599, pr. 15 Sep. 1599, Arch. Suff., Bk 37, fo. 449. Abstract by Miss Lilian J. Redstone communicated to the author. Supervisor of his will, Robert Rivet, his brother-in-law.

4. JOHN GOSNOLD, born about 1511, was the oldest son of Robert Gosnold the elder, and great-uncle of Bartholomew Gosnold. His early death about a year after the accession to the throne of the Catholic Queen Mary and at the time of the "humiliation of England" to Cardinal Pole, in 1554, when he was in his forty-fourth year, terminated a distinguished career as lawyer and Parliamentarian. He married KATERYN BLENNERHASSET, 5th daughter of Sir Thomas Blennerhasset of Frenze, co. Norfolk, and of his wife, Margaret Braham of Wetheringsett, co. Suffolk, and had no issue by her [Vis., pp. 7, 8, and 36]. Katherine Blennerhasset married secondly Anthony Wingfield, 4th son of Sir Anthony Wingfield, K.G.

John Gosnold was admitted to Gray's Inn in 1526, and was twice honored by appointment as Reader there, in 1542 and again in 1551. [Davy NP, citing Sir William Dugdale, Origines Juridiciales, etc., London, editions 1666, 1671, and 1680, — p. 293]. In the southern windows of the Hall of Gray's Inn appear the arms of Johannes Gosnold — Quarterly 1 and 4, Party per pale crenellé, or and b., 2 and 3, Arg. a fleur de lis, sa., charged with three plates (sic: Bezants) [ibid., p. 305]. Davy elsewhere identifies this quartering as that of the Person family. (There was a family of that name about 1600 in Boxford [Winthrop Papers, p. 43, note, otherwise Parson], but what remote Person heiress might have married into the Gosnold family in the fifteenth century is unknown. No other record of the arms has been found.) John Gosnold was a member of Parliament for Ipswich in 1547 and again in 1553 [Davy NP, citing "John Kirby, The Suffolk Traveller, 1732-4", (2nd ed., London, 1764)]. In 1549, and again in 1551, John Gosnold among others was on commissions to enquire into heretical errors [Davy NP, citing Thomas Rymer, Foedera Convocationis, pp. 181 and 250]. In 1550, it appears from the household accounts of the Lestranges of Hunstanton, that Mr. Gossenoldes was entertained with "the Deanes of Norwyche" at various inns, apparently en route to London [Davy, PSIA, vol. 25, pp. 558-9]. In 1552, Master Gosnolle, among others, was mentioned as a possible appointee to the office of Chief Justice of England [Davy, citing Machyn's Diary (Camden Society, 1848) for 4 and 5 Oct. (1552), p. 26]. In 1552, John Gosnold was appointed Solicitor General, and was one of those who signed the Engagement of the Council and others to maintain the succession as limited by the King (Edward VI): his name is last on the list. He also signs the Letters Patent for the Limitation of the Crown [Davy NP, citation indecipherable]. (This was in connection with Northumberland's plot to put Lady Jane Grey on the throne. Davy cites also, John Lord Campbell, "The Lives of the Lord Chancellors", etc. [2nd ed. London, John Murray, 1846], vol. 2, p. 34). Gosnold held sinecure stewardships, — in 1544, at Peasenhall, chief steward of the mews [Davy NP, citing Court Rolls], and in 1551, steward of the manor of Framlingham to the King [Davy NP, citing Robert Loder, "The History of Framlingham, Suff". (Woodbridge, 1799)]. In 1539 he was party to a deed [Davy NP, citing Deeds, Fressingfield, No. 53]. In 1544 he acquired from John Tyrell the manor Cardon Hall, in Witnesham [Cop., III, 122]. In 1550, Edward Warner, Knight, and John Gosnold, Esq., held lands in Clopton of the King, as of the Honour of Eye [Davy NM, citing No. 50, MS of Robt. Sparrow, tr. by L.J.R.]. Another document in identical wording, ascribes to Warner and Gosnold land in Grundisburgh [Davy NM, citing No. 24, Harl. MS. 1232, pp. 158, 159].

Will of John Gosnolde of Shryblande, co. Suffolk [perhaps Shribbes mentioned in the will of his father, Robert Gosnold the elder.] (Hereafter, Will D.) Will and codicil undated; pr. 7 Nov. 1554, P.C.C. 11 More. Abstr. Lea, THE REGISTER, LVII, 97. To his wife, Kateryn: lease of lands and tenements in the site of the late Abbey of Sibton, held of the Duke of Norfolk; if she declines, the lease is to go successively to his "brothers", Robert Gosnold, John Eyer [husband of his wife's sister Margaret], and John Blennerhasset [his brother-in-law]. If she resigns lands given for her jointure in Otley, Framsden, and Clopton, she is to have his moiety in the Manor of Layborne, co. Kent, held jointly with his father. To his father, to his uncle Edmund, and to his nephew Robert, his robes. To his nieces, daughters of his brother Robert, a share of 60 pounds at marriage, and in the codicil, the residue of the estate. Executors, John Eyer, John Blennerhasset, and Robert Gosnold, his brother. Witnesses, John Rouse, George Golding, Robert Marks, and William Gaseley.

5. ROBERT GOSNOLD the younger, born about 1512 or 1513, was the second son and heir apparent of Robert Gosnold the elder, Lord of the Manor of Otley, and became the grandfather of Bartholomew Gosnold. He married MARY VESEY, daughter of Robert Vesey of Hadley, clothier [Vis. and Muskett, I, 63]. She was the mother of his thirteen children, and died before her husband, who was about forty-eight years old when he died in 1559. His father, Robert Gosnold the elder, outlived him by some thirteen years, consequently the lordship of the manor of Netherhall, Otley, passed to Robert the younger's oldest son, Robert Gosnold III. (The last named likewise outlived his son and heir, so that the manor again passed to a grandson, Robert Gosnold V.) For the Vesey connection with the Winthrop family of Groton, and with the Bay Colony Governor, see Appendix D.

Will of Robert Gosnold the younger of Ottley, Suff. (Reference letter E for the relatives named, mentioned hereafter). Dated 26 Jan. 1558/9, pr. 27 Apr. 1559,

P.C.C. 2 Chaynvey. Abstr. by Lea, THE REGISTER, LVII, 98. To be buried in the churchyard at Otley, nigh unto his wife's grave. To his son Robert — the manor called Cardon Haulle [Witnesham] in tail male (Cop., III, 122); . . . "and a bed of mine which he hath in London." To his son Anthony — Chamberlain's, sometime called Alfrydes Chantry [Grundisburgh], after twenty-one years occupation by his brother, John. To his son, William — 200 pounds out of the testator's moiety in the manor of Layborne (Kent). To his son Edward — 100 pounds "as appointed in the will of my father Robert Gosnold, and a further 100 pounds at his age of 21." "To him that shall be the owner of the house I now dwell in", the residue of his term in Charefield, and the movables in his house. To his daughters [named as below], 50 pounds each at marriage or at 24, "viz. 30 pounds from myself and 20 pounds of the gift of Robert Vesey my father-in-law", to each. To his executors — his farm at Charefield Close for the upbringing of his children for ten years. Other beneficiaries — Robert Wythe, Robert Bonde, Thomas Dryver, Thomas Stamperd, and Thomas Chantnes. Executors, sons Robert and Anthony. Witnesses: Lyonell Morse, Sr., Wyllyam Armigerd, Robert Tovell.

Will of Robert Vesey of Hadleigh, co. Suffolk, clothier. [Hereafter, reference letter, F.] 11 Oct. 1559; pr. 7 May 1561, P.C.C. 16 Loftus. Abstr. in Muskett, "Suffolk Manorial Families", p. 58. Bequeathes lands in Leigham [Layham] and Royden. Bequests to Vesey sons and children, including Abram [who later married Mary Winthrop]. To John Smith, husband of his daughter Rose, and their children. To Anthony, John, and William, sons of Robert Gosnold, late of Ottley; to Judith, daughter of the said Robert, and to Alice Gosnold, "my maide". [His other eight Gosnold grandchildren are not named in this brief abstract. His daughter, Mary Vesey Gosnold, had died before the date of this will.]

Children:

6. i.   ROBERT, s. & h. [Vis. Wills B, C, D, E], b. *1533 to 1535*.
7. ii.   ANTHONY [Vis. Wills B, C, E, F], b. *1535 to 1537*.
    iii. JOHN [Vis. Wills B, C, E, F], b. *1537 to 1538*. He removed to Coddenham, married KATHERINE KINNELLMARCH, and had a son, Capt. Robert Gosnold. (See "Gosnolds of Coddenham", in preparation.)
    iv. WILLIAM [Vis. Wills B, E, F], b. *1540 to 1550*; d. without issue [Davy].
8. v.   EDWARD [Wills B, E], b. *1550 to 1556*.
    vi. ALICE [Vis. Wills E, F]. "Maid" in her grandfather Vesey's house [Will F].
    vii. KATHERINE [Vis. Will E]; m. ALEXANDER PRATT of Needham, at Coddenham, 28 May 1568 [Davy], 24 May 1568 [Coddenham P. R.].
    viii. DOROTHY [Vis. Will E, C ?], m., as his first wife, SIR JOHN GILBERT of Finborough Hall, Suff., son of Henry Gilbert, London goldsmith [Vis. p. 202, and Cop., VI, 173]. (Davy gives by error Anthony Calle as the husband of Dorothy. He may have been the husband of the Dorothy of the next generation.)

      There were three daughters of this marriage, co-heiresses (cousins of Bartholomew Gosnold): — (i.) Dorothy, m. (1) Sir William Forthe of Butley Abbey; m. (2) Gresham Parkin of Aldham; (ii.) Elizabeth, m. Sir Roger North of Mildenhall, Suff., son of Sir Henry North. (The latter, "taking early to arms was 23 Elizabeth [1583] in that expedition to Norembega under Sir Humphrey Gilbert . . ." [Collin's "Peerage of England", Brydges' ed., London, 1812, vol. IV, p. 463.]); (iii.) Ursula, m. Sir John Poley [associated with Capt. Robert Gosnold and Capt. Richard Saltonstall in coast defences at Ipswich, 1627. (State Papers, Dom. Charles I., vol. II, 1627–8, London, 1858, pp. 106 and 409.)]. For the Forth connections, see Appendix E.
    ix. MARY [Vis. Will E].
    x.   AGNES [Vis. Will E.], m. in 1572 [Boyd's Index] JOHN ROSSINGTON of Framlingham, Norwich M. L. (Davy gives by error — Rossington, as the husband of Mary, preceding.)
    xi. CECYLL (CICELY) [Vis. Wills B, E], m. THOMAS THORN, "Rector of Hemingstone"; who matriculated from Trinity, Cambridge, 1577 [Venn, Alumni Cantab., names other parishes, and cites Blomefield, Hist. of Norfolk, II, 195, and Vis. of Suff. 1664]. He was

buried at Hemingstone 9 Nov. 1630 [Davy's Pedigree]. Thomas
Thorne's will, dated at Hemingstone, Suff. 22 Apr. 1628, pr. P.C.C.
114 Scrope, mentions his wife, Sycely. Abstr. by Lea, THE
REGISTER, LVIII, 312. His son Oliver (cousin of Bartholomew),
"built a commodious house in Hemingstone". Davy's Notes,
cited in PSIA, XVII, 142.

xii. ANNE [Will E], not mentioned in the Visitation, may have died in
infancy.

xiii. JUDITH [Vis. Wills B, D, E], m. 29 Oct. 1578 HENRY RISE, at St.
George Tombland, Norwich. [? Norwich Gosnold Pedigree, not
confirmed.] He was admitted pensioner (age sixteen) at Caius,
29 April 1572. Son of William, b. at North Repps, Norfolk.
Matriculated 1572, B.A., 1575/6. Rector of Ovington, Norfolk,
1600–1603. Will proved Norwich, 1603 [Venn].

Note: The parish register of Framsden records a marriage of John
With to Mary Gosnold, 1565 [Boyd's Index]; and a burial of
Dorothy, daughter of Mr. Antony Gosnoll, 10 May, 1567 [re-
ported by L.H.H.W.]. It is impossible at the present time to
relate these entries to this pedigree.

6. Robert Gosnold III was probably born about 1534. He and
his two brothers, Anthony and John, were all matriculated
at Cambridge, "sizar from Jesus, Michs. 1550", the two
younger brothers being designated as "impubes" (immature).
Three years later, Robert Gosnold III was admitted to Gray's
Inn (1553), Anthony Gosnold's admission to the same Inn
for the study of law following in 1554. Robert Gosnold III
married URSULA NAUNTON, daughter of William Naunton of
Letheringham, and his wife, Elizabeth Wingfield (For the
Naunton connections, see Appendix E). "Mrs. Naunton" is
mentioned in the will of Ann Doggett Gosnold [Will C,
above]. She was Elizabeth Wingfield, daughter of Sir Anthony Wingfield, K.G., and his wife Elizabeth Vere, sister of
John de Vere, 14th Earl of Oxford, and granddaughter of the
12th Earl of Oxford. The children of Robert Gosnold III
(first cousins of Bartholomew Gosnold), were therefore descended from the ancient houses of Naunton, Wingfield, and
de Vere. The arms of Robert Gosnold III in the church at
Otley are impaled with those of Naunton [drawing by Davy,
Br. Mus. Add. MSS. 19186].

Robert Gosnold III at the time of his father's death, 1559
[Will E], maintained chambers in London, doubtless for the
practice of law. Until he became Lord of the Manor of
Netherhall on his grandfather's death in 1572, his residence
was perhaps at Earl's Hall, the Manor of Swilland, in which
he was living at the time he wrote his will in 1615. He became a Justice of the Peace for Suffolk in 1561 [Davy]. Numerous notes on his court appearances and land transactions
are recorded by Davy: as most of these were in collaboration
with his brother Anthony, they are reserved for a fuller treatment of Anthony's affairs than can be given in this genealogy.
About 1593, he bought a manor in Clopton later called Rous
Hall, which in 1600 he sold to Thomas Rous [Davy NM, fo.
123, 135, citing Court Rolls]. One of Davy's notes, citing

deeds in the Treasury of the Corporation of Ipswich, 1811, reads in the original as follows: "No. 17. 18 Oct. 40 Eliz. (1598). Robertus Gosnolde de Otley Suff. Armiger dominus manorii de Netherhall concedit Willelmo Smarte, Radulpho Scryvener, etc. licenciam alienare nativum tenementum in Otley." Ralph (Radulphus) Scrivener was the father of Matthew Scrivener, a second son, who followed Bartholomew Gosnold to Virginia in the "First Supply" ship. In 1599, a dispute between Robert Gosnold, Esq., and Lionel Talmache, Esq., as to meadows in Helmingham was adjudicated by Sir Anthony Wingfield of Letheringham [Ipswich Public Library, XI/5/77, reported by Miss L. J. Redstone.].

A portrait of Robert Gosnold III painted about 1610 shows him as an elderly gentleman of austere and commanding presence, with the Gosnold arms on the wall in the background. This portrait is identified in the Rev. E. Farrer's (MS) "Portraits in Suffolk Houses (East)", vol. A–H, p. 229, Ipswich Library, reported by Mr. Charles Partridge. The portrait has recently been returned to Otley Hall; an excellent photograph of it was sent to the author by Miss Hilda Clark, a descendant of the Norwich Gosnolds.

Robert Gosnold III lived to be eighty or over. Of his six children mentioned in his grandfather's will of 1572 (B), only two survived to be mentioned in his own will of 1615. Four others, born evidently after 1572, are known from his will, below, and other sources. In his latter years, after the death of his son and heir determined that Netherhall Manor was to pass to his grandson, he seems to have made a favorite of his son Anthony, who as Anthony Gosnold of Swilland founded a new branch of the family. There is obviously some bitterness over the loss of his two nephews, Bartholomew and Anthony, in his bequest to his grandson Anthony "now in Virginia, if he shall return. . . ."

Will of Robert Gosnold of Earlshall, Suff., Esq. Dated, 15 Aug. 13 Jac. I (1615, not 1616, as in Copinger and elsewhere), pr. 1 Nov. 1615, P.C.C. 101 Rudd. Abstr. by L(othrop) Withington, in the *Virginia Mag. of Hist. and Biog.*, July, 1906, pp. 87–88, correcting one by Lea, THE REGISTER, LVI, 405. (Hereafter, reference letter G). To be buried at Otley "near my wife". To his son John Gosnold, 500 pounds "which he owes me for buying his office at the court". To his son, Anthony Gosnold his house in Swillon [Swilland] called Eales [Earles or Earleshall, as above]. To his grandson, Robert Gosnold [succeeding him as Lord of the Manor of Netherhall] "all moveable goods in the house at Otely". "To Anthony Gosnold my grandchild now in Virginia, 100 pounds if he shall return within one year after my decease". To John Joanes "my house in Otely in occupation of Francis Butterhall". Executors, Son Anthony and Mr. Francis Cornwallis of Earleshall.

Children:
9. i.   ROBERT IV [Vis., Will B], *b. about 1560.*
   ii. (?) RICHARD [Will B, not in Davy].
10. iii. JOHN [Wills B, G, and Davy], b. in 1568 [Tablet in Otley Church].
    iv. EDMUND [Wills B, C, not in Davy].
    v.   ANTHONY [Davy; Will G; also mentioned, deceased, in the will of his brother Thomas, dated 1648], b. perhaps in 1582, if matriculated at Cambridge 1598 [Venn]; m. URSULA PRATT, daughter of Roger

97

Pratt [Vis. Suff., 1664–8 (Harl. Soc., 1910)]. Davy has a supplementary pedigree 'A' for the descendants of Anthony Gosnold of Swilland. Many of the wills collected by Lea, THE REGISTER, vols. LVI and LVII, relate to this branch of the family, and are too extensive for further description here.

vi. THOMAS [Davy, Will G], b. after Anthony above, m. a widow of —––— Barrington of Colchester, but had no issue by her. He is described as of Bentley, but dated his will at Stonham Aspall, 27 Sept. 1648, abstr. by Lea, THE REGISTER, LVII, 98.

vii. ELIZABETH [Wills B, G], oldest daughter, m. THOMAS KEENE, and had sons Henry and Thomas Keene [Will G]. [Davy gives "Mary m. Henry Keene of Thrandeston", either by error, or perhaps a younger daughter.]

viii. DOROTHY [Wills B, C; Davy confuses her with her aunt, Dorothy Gosnold, who married Sir John Gilbert]. She may have married Anthony Calle, named by Davy as her aunt's husband.

ix. ANN [Davy, and will of Thomas Gosnold, 1648], m. EDMOND WARNER, son of Francis Warner of Framlingham [Vis., Warner pedigree, p. 174].

x. URSULA, m. (1) FRANCIS PRATT, of Riston, Norf. [Davy, and Vis. Norf., 1664 (Harl. Soc., 1934)]; m. (2), as his second wife, THOMAS CUTLER of Sproughton [Davy, and Vis., Cutler Pedigree, p. 188].

7. ANTHONY GOSNOLD, father of Bartholomew, was a second son, and therefore had no rights in Netherhall Manor. He is known as "of Clopton and Grundisburgh" [Davy, and various documents]. He was matriculated at Cambridge University a "sizar from Jesus (College), Michaelmas [29 Sept.], 1550, impubes", that is, at the age of thirteen or fourteen, having passed a certain examination, he was exempted from the payment of all fees and charges. Four years later, he was admitted to Gray's Inn, London, for the study of law. About 1569 or 1570, he married DOROTHY BACON, daughter of George and Margaret Bacon of Hessett, and granddaughter of Thomas Bacon, whose third wife and widow, Ann, became the second wife of Robert Gosnold the elder, Anthony's grandfather (see Appendix C, The Bacons).

A considerable number of notes on the court appearances and land transactions of Anthony Gosnold and his older brother Robert III have recently been sent to the author by Miss Lilian J. Redstone, Suffolk County Archivist, of Woodbridge, Suffolk. These are too extensive for description here, and have been reserved for a later study of Bartholomew Gosnold's father. In brief, Anthony Gosnold seems to have undertaken in 1589, after an early residence in Clopton, to establish himself in manors in Burgh extending into Grundisburgh, doubtless that he might leave them to his two sons. The disappearance of his name from the records as of 1609 leads the writer to surmise that he died in that year, soon after the receipt of the news that he had lost his second son, as well as his first, in Virginia. Unfortunately, there is no will of his, and the parish records of the churches where he might have been buried are not extant. He is not mentioned in his brother's will of 1615, above.

98

Children:

11. i. BARTHOLOMEW, b. *circa 1571* [Wills B, C, and Davy].
    ii. ANTHONY, b. *between 1572 and 1578* [Will C]. Drowned in Virginia 7 Jan. 1609 [Part II of John Smith's Map of Virginia, in "Travels and Works of Captain John Smith", Edward Arber, ed., New Edition, Edinburgh, 1910, p. 143].
    iii. ELIZABETH [Will C], m. THOMAS TILNEY, of Shelley Hall, Suff. [Vis.; Tilney pedigree, p. 170; Copinger, VI, 81; Dict. Natl. Biog.]. The Tilneys were distant but recognized kinsmen of Queen Elizabeth.
    iv. MARGARET [Will C], probably m. ZACHARY NORMAN of Dunwich. Will of Zachary Norman of Dunwich, dated 30 Aug. 1624, pr. 20 Sept. 1624, Arch. Suffolk, 1624, orig. no. 65, abstr. by L. H. Haydon Whitehead communicated to the author, names wife Margaret, but no children or other relatives.

Note: Davy does not give the names of Anthony Gosnold's daughters, which are taken from the greatgrandmother's will, "C." Davy does give, however, the names of four sons-in-law, the above two, and two others, viz., Edmund Goldsmith and ―――― Bowtell of Ipswich. Any one of the three daughters following may have married either of these sons-in-law.

    v. DOROTHY [Will C].
    vi. ANN [Will C].
    vii MARY [Will C].
    viii. URSULA, b. apparently after the date of Will C, 1578. From the Grundisburgh P. R., transcript at the Ipswich Public Library: "1588. Ursula daughter of Anthony Gosnold was buryd the xth of Julye A° p'd."

8. EDWARD GOSNOLD, youngest son of Robert Gosnold the younger, is mentioned in the latter's will of 1559, but is unmarried and under twenty-four in his grandfather's will of 1572. He was probably born shortly after 1550. (Davy's identification of him as the Edmund Gosnold who married Catherine Clifton in Norfolk is impossible, as the will of Catherine's mother, proved 1558, mentions the marriage [Blomefield's History of Norfolk, vol. 7, p. 202]. The Edmund Gosnold of the Clifton marriage is said to be of Bildeston, Suff., which is undoubtedly correct.) This Edward of Otley is almost certainly the lad who scribbled "Edward Gosnold" in the MS. of the Canterbury Tales at Helmingham, while visiting the Talmache family there, one of a number of such scribblings. [Text of the Canterbury Tales, by J. M. Manly and Edith Rickert (Univ. of Chicago, 1940), noted by L. J. R.] The authors cited mention the gift of a gold ring by Lionel Talmache, who died in 1575, to "Master Gosnolde" of Otley, quoting British Museum Add. MS. 19151. There is no further mention of Edward Gosnold, but whether this is because he died early, or because of a dearth of sources at this point, is left to conjecture. An Edward Gosnold was buried at Campsey Ash, 1603, 6 Feb. [L.H.H.W.].

9. ROBERT GOSNOLD IV, the oldest son of Robert Gosnold III and his wife Ursula Naunton, was born about 1560. He is presumably the Robert Gosnold who was admitted to Gray's Inn in 1578. He married AMY FORTH, born in 1568, daughter of Robert Forth of Butley [Muskett, I, 118]. (See Appendix

D for the Forth connections.) Among the land conveyances, it appears that Robert Gosnold, jun., was party to a deed in 1586 [Davy NM, citing Deeds at Ipswich, 1811]. He did not succeed to the Lordship of Netherhall, as his father outlived him by nearly twenty years. The date of his death, about 1596, is inferred from the re-marriage of his widow on 14 Feb. 1597/8, to Edward Ward of Mendham [Davy, and Muskett, pedigrees cited]. The descent of the Manor of Netherhall to his son, Robert Gosnold V, and thereafter, will be found in Appendix F.

It may be well to insert at this point a mention of the second son of Robert Gosnold IV and his wife Amy Forth — Anthony Gosnold, who in 1606 accompanied to Virginia his deceased father's first cousin, Bartholomew Gosnold. He was aged about eighteen at the time the expedition sailed, and was known as "Anthony Gosnold the younger" of the Jamestown settlement. He did not return to England to claim the bequest of 100 pounds in his grandfather's will, 1615, conditional on his return within a year of the latter's decease. Having survived the fevers and the "starving time" that devastated the early colonists, he remained in Virginia for nearly sixteen years. On petition presented to the Virginia Company, 30 Oct. 1621, he was granted three shares of land, one of which was to be delivered to his brother Robert Gosnold and another to Roger Castle (brother-in-law of Ann Talmache, his brother's wife) ["Records of the Virginia Company" (Washington, 1906), p. 541]. After his return from Virginia, Anthony Gosnold married first, Margaret Risby, daughter of Robert Risby of Thorpe Morieux and widow of John Betts of Eye (Margaret's sister, Elizabeth Risby, married John Winthrop (1547–1613), uncle of the Massachusetts Bay Governor) [Davy, and Muskett, I, Risby Pedigree, p. 73]; and secondly, —— Barrington, of Colchester [Davy]. The date of his death is not known.

10. JOHN GOSNOLD, the third son of Robert Gosnold III and Ursula Naunton, was about two years older than his cousin Bartholomew. The intimacy of their fathers, and the reasonable certainty that in their youth, the two boys lived not more than two miles apart, indicates that they grew up as close companions. This is important, as in the years that Bartholomew was seeking support for the Virginia venture, 1604–1606, his cousin John was Gentleman Usher at court, in daily contact with visitors to the King, as well as with the King himself. The salient facts of John Gosnold's career are told on a tablet, still in place in the church at Otley.

"Here resteth interred the body of John Gosnold Esqr. 3d sonne of Robert Gosnold of Otley Esqr. and Ursula his Wife, borne of the right antient and worthy families of Naunton and Wingfield of Letheringham. He spent His tender yeares in good studies at Oxford and his talents were not hidden, his riper yeares he spent in Court where he served in the place of Gentleman Usher in ordinary the Maies of Q. Elizabeth and K. James 26 yeares and was after a gentleman of the privy chamber in ordinarie to K. Charles.

"He married Winifred ye daughter of Walter Windsor Esqr. and son of Williám Lo: Windsor and of margarett his Wife daughter of Sr. Geffery Poole Knight sonne of Sr. Richard Poole Kt. and the Lady Margarett Countesse of Salisbury his Wife, daughter of the right noble Prince George Duke of Clarence Brother to K. Edward the fourth of England, &c.

"He departed this Life the 17th of February Anno Dni 1628 aged 60 years, who had issue by his said Wife 5 sonnes and 3 daughters, to whose memory his sadd Wife caused this inscription to be erected." [As transcribed on the Norwich Pedigree chart, and by Davy, NM.]

The escutcheon of John Gosnold and his wife of royal descent displayed on the walls of the church, has sixteen Windsor quarterings on the sinister side, a brave array of color as Davy reproduced it in his Notes. The position at court was doubtless secured through the influence of this well-connected lady, together with the five hundred pounds provided by John's father for the purchase of the office [Will G] according to the custom of the time. For his faithful service to King James and himself, King Charles in 1623 ordered the payment of a royal grant to John Gosnold [State Papers, Dom., vol. II, 1623-1625 (London, 1859), p. 109]. The marriage had issue [Davy], but nothing of significance is known of John Gosnold's children. (For the Windsor connections, see Appendix E.)

The will of John Gosnold of Oteley, Suff., Esquier, dated 27 Jan. 1627/8, pr. 10 June 1629, P.C.C. 55 Ridley; abstr. by Lea, THE REGISTER, LVI, 406. To his wife, Wynnefred Winsor, his messuage and freehold lands in Otley, and his lease of the lands of the manor of Overhall in Otley, with remainder to his son and heir Robert. Two other sons, John and Ralph, are under 21; a daughter Mary is unmarried.

One hundred and eight pounds, eighteen shillings, eleven pence, "and also ten pounds more", is owed to him by his "brother", Sir William Winsor. Witnesses, Robert Tovill, William Drane, Richard Harte, clerk.

The will of Sir Robert Naunton, (see art. D.N.B., and will in H. F. Waters, "Genealogical Gleanings in England," 1901, ii, 1088), mentions Winifred Gosnold, widow, and her daughter, Mary Gosnold, as his "cousins".

11. BARTHOLOMEW GOSNOLD, son and heir of Anthony Gosnold of Clopton and Grundisburgh, was born in 1571 [reckoned from the date of his matriculation at Cambridge, 1587, and the mention of his name in the will of his grandfather, 1572]. There is no record of a degree at Cambridge, but the following shows an intention to study law at the Middle Temple. "1592, Feb. 9, Mr. Bartholomew Gosnold, late of New Inn, gent., son and heir apparent of Antony Gosnold of Grunsbrowgh [Grundisburgh], Suffolk, gent., generally: fine, 20 s. Bound with Messrs. John Ethell and Thomas Eliott." [Middle Temple Records, ed. by Charles Henry Hopwood, K. C., London, 1904, vol. I.] Nothing is known of any connection with the sureties named, except that Eliott was matriculated at Cambridge two years after Bartholomew Gosnold. The writer is of the opinion, based on a considerable amount of circumstantial evidence, that through his father Anthony, Bartholomew Gosnold came early in life under the influence

of the great geographer, the Rev. Richard Hakluyt, who in 1590 became rector of Wetheringsett, fifteen miles from Otley, by the appointment of Lady Dorothy Stafford. Davy's Notes to the Gosnold Pedigree contain long condensations of primary and secondary sources on the activities of Bartholomew Gosnold. Davy's one serious error was in naming Bartholomew's wife. She was not "—— Barrington", but MARY GOLDING, daughter of Robert Golding and his wife Martha Judd. Martha Judd was the daughter of Sir Andrew Judd, one time Lord Mayor of London, and his third wife, Dame Mary (Mathew) Judd. By his first marriage, Sir Andrew Judd was the grandfather of Sir Thomas Smith (Smythe), founder of the East India Company and first Treasurer of the Virginia Company of London. Bartholomew's wife was therefore a first cousin, and his mother-in-law an aunt, of this fabulously wealthy London merchant and adventurer. [For references, see the articles mentioned below.]

For the basic sources, consult the article on Bartholomew Gosnold by Fulmer Mood in the "Dictionary of American Biography". For more recent information, the writer suggests his articles — Who Was Bartholomew Gosnold? in the *William and Mary Quarterly*, July, 1949; The Family Connections of Bartholomew Gosnold, in THE REGISTER, January, 1950; and The First Leaders at Jamestown, in the *Virginia Magazine of History and Biography*, April, 1950.

Bartholomew Gosnold was about thirty-six years old when he died in Virginia on Aug. 22, 1607.

One of the most arresting of Davy's condensations is the following, based on Howes' (Stowe's) Annales, Smith's Generall History, and G. Percy, in "Purchas His Pilgrims".

"In 1607, during the establishment of the Colony at Jamestown in Virginia, 50 men, one half of the colony, perished before autumn; among them Bartholomew Gosnold, the projector of the settlement, a man of rare merits, worthy of a perpetual memory in the plantation, whose influence had alone thus far preserved some degree of harmony in the council."

APPENDIX A
The Gosnold Arms

The coat of arms borne by the Gosnolds is Per pale crenellé or and azure. The crest is a bull's head affronté, couped at the neck, per pale or and azure. (Davy uses the term guardant for affronté.) The Motto: *Ferendo et feriendo*.

It is interesting to note that in the portrait of Robert Gosnold III the crest is a bull's head affronté erased, instead of couped, and that in the arms (Visitation of Suffolk, 1664-68, Harl. Soc., 1910, p. 148) confirmed to Henry Gosnold of Ipswich, a grandson of Robert III through Anthony of Swilland, the crest is a ram's head affronté, couped at the neck, per pale or and azure, as in the arms, which have a mullet for difference.

The bull's head, couped, again appears in the arms confirmed to the Buckinghamshire Gosnolds (who derive from the Suffolk family), but the colors of both arms and crest are given as or and vert (Visitation, 1664, Harl. Soc., 1909, p. 65), though Davy speaks of them as still or and azure.

In Metcalfe's edition of the earlier Suffolk Visitations, and in that for 1664-68, the Gosnold arms are shown quartered with Argent, a fleur de lis sable charged with three bezants, with no name assigned to the coat. Davy (Add. MSS. 19086, fo. 315), in his Otley Church Notes, assigns these arms to Person, but describes the same arms as occurring at Otley Hall in quite different colors: Argent, a fleur de lis gules, on each leaf a plate. (Contributed by F. A. F.)

APPENDIX B

A Description of Netherhall Manor, later known as Otley Hall, by David Elisha Davy, October 27, 1829

"OTLEY HALL" has considerable remains of antiquity about it; it was inclosed by a moat, part of which still remains, and not far from it is another moated space, but not of such large dimensions; the latter may perhaps have been the site of a more ancient residence.

The Hall of the old house is now the keeping room [family sitting-room] of the present occupier; it is large and lofty and has a window which takes up nearly the whole of one side; this window with the glass in it appears of the same date with the building, for upon the quarries [panes] are the following inscriptions:

1. "Rob. Gosnold, Nemo mortalium omnibus horis sapit."
2. "Will. Gosnold."
3. "Henry Wyngfeild."
4. "God made man with the power of his hand, And made him ruler both of sea & land. Tho. Wythe."
5. "A wall and glasse, paper for an asse. R. I." [Robert Ingolde]

At right angles to the Hall is a building now used as a cart-shed, on the walls of which have been paintings now nearly defaced; over each of these were two Latin lines explanatory of the subject of them; but these are all now illegible, except one, which is as follows, and was probably over the representation of Curtius, throwing himself into the gulph in the Forum.

Curtius in vastum sive telluris hiatum
Conjicit, ut Patriae cedat acerba (lues).

There were at least two other inscriptions of the same kind.

On a bracket in the hall [two ornate initials, apparently] A.G.

Above stairs is a large room, now divided, which was handsomely painted on the stucco; the following arms still remain:

1. Gosnold, quartering Person. Arg. a fleur de lis, gu. On each leaf a plate.
2. Naunton. Sa. 3 martlets arg. 2 and 1.

(From Davy's Notes, Manors, Otley, Carlford Hundred, fo. 310, No. 38. British Museum Add. MS. 19086.)

Excerpts from an Account of Otley, May 16, 1925
By Mr. Charles Partridge, M.A., F.S.A., of Stowmarket, Suffolk Antiquarian

The name Otley stands for Ota's lea or meadow, . . . home of an Anglo-Saxon settler. Suffolk genealogists know Otley best as the home for centuries of the Gosnold family. . . . Their old manor, Otley Hall, remains an architectural gem of Henry the Seventh's reign, (1485–1509). The present owner-occupier, Mrs. Arthur Sherston, . . . shows visitors the linen-fold panelling and moulded beams of this ancient moated house, and the charming garden she has created about it. Of course it has its traditions and mysteries — somewhere under its roof is buried a "glass table" of necromantic powers, and there is a huge unexplored chimney base; and to an upper chamber, on whose walls are painted with Elizabethan art the arms of Gosnold and Naunton, there hangs the tale of a bridal feast prepared for a bride who came not. . . .

(Printed in the *East Anglian Daily Times*, Ipswich, under the pen-name "Silly Suffolk.")

APPENDIX C

The Gosnolds' Connection with the Bacons of Hessett

Canon William Cooke (*Materials for a History of Hassett*, in PSIA, V, 48ff.) proves that the second wife of Thomas Bacon was Anne Rouse, dau. of Henry Rouse of Dennington, but he is mistaken in assuming that she was the "Ann" of Thomas Bacon's will, his widow who married Robert Gosnold. The Ann of the will is a third wife, Ann Doggett. Her will, "C", above, names along with Thomas Bacon's offspring, her own Doggett relatives, Alice More, and Alice Edgar [see

Muskett, Doggett Pedigree, I, 344]. The will of Edmund, oldest son of Thomas Bacon, pr. 1553, P.C.C. 20 Taske, abstr. by Lea, THE REGISTER, LVII, 312, provides for the continuance of his father's annuity to his step-mother, Ann Gosnold. In Ann Gosnold's will, C, the children of George and Margaret Bacon — John, Robert, Edward, Thomas, Dorothy, Elizabeth, Mary, and Ann — are called her grandchildren, but whether George was her own son or a step-son cannot be determined; she ignores the "step" relationship in naming the Gosnold grandchildren as her own. The will of George Bacon of Hedgesett (Hessett), dated 6 Oct. 1569, pr. 28 Nov. 1569, P.C.C. 24 Sheffield, abstr. by Lea, THE REGISTER, LVII, 312, mentions Ann Gosnold as his wife's "mother", i.e., mother-in-law, and names Anthony Gosnold as an executor. The will of George Bacon's widow, Margaret, dated 18 March 1573/4, pr. 11 June 1574, Arch. Sudbury, 1574–78, fo. 34, abstr. by Lea, THE REGISTER, LVII, 312, has bequests to her daughter Dorothy Gosnold, and "to everyone of her children", the latter to be paid into the hands of Anthony Gosnold, gent., their father, until they come of age. It is important to note that in the wills of Thomas Bacon, pr. 1547, and of his son John, pr. 1559, abstracts by Lea, THE REGISTER, LVIII, 310–311, Nicholas Bacon as "attorney" in 1547, and as "the Rt. Honourable, Lord Keeper of the great seal of England" in 1559, appears as the Overseer of the wills, indicating an honored and presumably close relationship. These were the wills of the grandfather and of an uncle of Dorothy Bacon, Bartholomew Gosnold's mother.

APPENDIX D

The Vesey and Forth Connections with the Winthrops of Groton

A nephew of Bartholomew Gosnold's grandmother, Mary Vesey, named Abraham Vesey, son of her brother Lawrence, married Mary Winthrop, sister of Adam Winthrop, who in his Diary [*Winthrop Papers*, Massachusetts Historical Society, 1929], frequently mentions Abraham and Mary as his "brother" and sister Vesey. Mary Winthrop thus became by marriage a first cousin of Anthony Gosnold, Bartholomew's father; and a daughter of the marriage, Amy Vesey, Bartholomew's second cousin, was at the same time a first cousin of Gov. John Winthrop of the Massachusetts Bay colony. There is no evidence that the Puritan governor recognized the connection with a family noted for its adherence to episcopacy; but it would be strange indeed, in view of the close-knit manorial social structure of Suffolk in that period, if he did not know that the first to show the way to New England was a kinsman of his aunt [see Vesey pedigree in Muskett, Vesey of Holton, Pedigree A, page 63].

The Forth family, like the Vesey, was seated at Hadleigh, not far from Groton. William Forth of Hadleigh, who bought Butley Abbey, and died in 1559, had two sons of interest to us. His oldest son, Robert Forth of Butley, was the father of Sir William Forth, who married Dorothy Gilbert of Finborough, and of a daughter Amy, who married Robert Gosnold IV of Otley. Both Dorothy Gilbert and Robert Gosnold IV were first cousins of Bartholomew Gosnold. The sixth son of William Forth of Hadleigh (died in 1559), was John Forth of Great Stambridge, whose only daughter and heiress became the first wife (died in 1615) of John Winthrop, later Governor of the Massachusetts Bay colony. Thus two of Bartholomew's cousins were married to first cousins of John Winthrop's wife. The third son of William Forth of Hadleigh, William Forth, junior, had a grandson John Forth, who married Mary, a daughter of Harbottle Wingfield of Crofield near Coddenham. Harbottle Wingfield was a second cousin of John Gosnold, the Gentleman Usher, and a brother-in-law of Matthew Scrivener, who followed the Gosnolds to Virginia. [Muskett, I, Forth pedigrees, pp. 119–120].

APPENDIX E

The Wingfield, Naunton, and Windsor Connections

Ursula Naunton, wife of Robert Gosnold III, as the granddaughter of Sir Anthony Wingfield, K. G., and his wife Elizabeth Vere, sister of the 14th Earl of Oxford, brought to her husband as "cousins" the numerous and important sons and grandsons of the illustrious Knight of the Garter. The relationship between the two families seems to have been close from the early days of the Gosnolds in

Otley; Sir Robert Wingfield, son of Sir Anthony, was called in as the overseer of the will of Robert Gosnold the elder. Harbottle Wingfield of the fourth generation (a second cousin of Ursula Naunton's son, John Gosnold, the Gentleman Usher), married Elizabeth Scrivener, a sister of Matthew Scrivener, of the Jamestown colony. The latter's sudden appearance at Jamestown and his immediate appointment to the Council have not hitherto been seen by historians as the result of his connection with the Gosnolds in Suffolk.

Another unsuspected relationship is discovered by noting that Dorothy Vere, sister of Elizabeth, married John Nevill, Lord Latimer, and became the grandmother of Katherine Nevill, who married Henry (Percy), Duke of Northumberland. Katherine Nevill and Ursula Naunton were, therefore, second cousins by their common descent from Sir George de Vere, a relationship that would not have been forgotten in that age by Katherine's son, George Percy, and Ursula's nephew, Bartholomew Gosnold, when they met together for the great adventure to Virginia.

The relationships brought into the picture by the marriage of John Gosnold, the Gentleman Usher, to Winifred Windsor, are too manifold for more than a brief sampling here. Her mother, Margaret Pole, who married Walter Windsor, was a granddaughter of Sir Richard Pole, K.G., and therefore a first cousin of many highly placed persons. Among them was Lady Dorothy Stafford, for forty years an intimate of Queen Elizabeth, who employed Anthony Gosnold, Bartholomew's father, as attorney, and who appointed the Rev. Richard Hakluyt as Rector of Wetheringsett. Dame Stafford's daughter-in-law, Douglas Howard, wife of Sir Edward Stafford, ambassador at Paris, was a sister of the Lord High Admiral. Another "cousin" of John Gosnold's wife was Sir Francis Barrington, who married Joan, daughter of "the Golden Knight of Huntingdonshire". She was a sister of Sir Oliver Cromwell of the first Virginia Council in London, for which Bartholomew had sought patrons. Scores of other doors may thus have been opened to the "first mover" of the Virginia plantation of 1607 by his cousin's wife, the lady of royal descent.

Appendix F
The Last Lords of Netherhall Manor, Otley

The succession, after the death of Robert Gosnold IV, was as follows: Robert Gosnold V, son of Robert Gosnold IV and Amy Forth, was born about 1587, matriculated at Cambridge 1603, married Ann Talmache at Helmingham 20 Feb. 1609, and became Lord of the Manor of Netherhall on his grandfather's death in 1615. He died between 8 Feb. 1632/3, when he gave consent to his son's marriage at the age of 22, and 20 Aug. 1635, when his wife, Ann Talmache, re-married, Samuel Blennerhassett of Loudham. (Venn confuses Robert Gosnold V with his son below.) Robert Gosnold VI, son of Robert Gosnold V and Ann Talmache, was born in 1611, baptized 2 May 1611 at Helmingham. By licence of 8 Feb. 1632/3, he married Dorothy Jeggon, aged 17, only daughter of the late Bishop of Norwich, with the consent of her mother, Dame Dorothy Cornwallis. He succeeded as Lord of the Manor of Netherhall about 1634. He became a Colonel in the Loyalist forces fighting for Charles I, "but sunk with the Royal Cause, and at last was forced to compound for his estate, for acting according to the Laws of God and of man, with those who first trampled upon both, and then murdered their Sovereign". (Gipps.) He died about 1658 (will pr. 25 May 1658), leaving the impoverished estate to his son, Robert VII. (The main sources for the last years of the Gosnolds of Otley are Davy, the Norwich Pedigree, and various wills printed by Lea in abstracts in THE REGISTER, vols. LVI-LVII.) A painstaking and detailed study of these years by Mr. Charles Partridge of Stowmarket, Suffolk, a well-known antiquarian, was printed in the *East Anglian Daily Times* (Ipswich), Jan. 16, Feb. 6, 20, and Mar. 6, 1926, under the title, "The Last Gosnold Squire of Otley". A set of galley-proof clippings of these articles, sent to the writer by Mr. Partridge, will be preserved in the Dukes County Historical Society collection, Edgartown, Mass.

ABBREVIATIONS AND REFERENCES
Vis. The Visitation of Suffolk, 1561, 1577, 1612. By Walter C. Metcalfe (Exeter, 1882).
Davy. The Pedigree of the Gosnold Family, British Museum Add. MS. 19133, in Collection of Pedigrees of Suffolk Families, etc., by David Elisha Davy (d. in 1851), British Museum Add. MSS., 43 volumes, numbered 19114-19156, arranged alphabetically. (The writer has used

a transcript of the Gosnold Pedigree, which he obtained from London. Where Davy's datum coincides with that of the Visitation above, only the Vis. reference has been used.)

Davy NP. Davy's Notes to the above Pedigree. Six pages of the MS. 19133, of which the writer obtained photostats.

Davy NM. Davy's Notes to the Manors of Suffolk. Carlford Hundred, Add. MS. 19086. The items from this source were selected and reported to the writer by Miss Lilian J. Redstone, County Archivist, of Woodbridge, Suffolk.

Blois. Suffolk Families (Genealogies), by Sir F. Blois, British Museum Add. MS., a transcript sent to the writer without MS. number. Incomplete, and erratic in the spelling of names.

Norwich Gosnold Pedigree, a printed pedigree bearing dates from 1440 down to 1927, of which the Virginia Historical Society had a damaged copy without any legend of origin. It has been identified as one printed by Mr. George Clark, husband of Jane Elizabeth Gosnold, of Norwich, shortly before his death in 1937. Copies were obtained from his daughter, and are now available at the Virginia Historical Society, the New England Historic Genealogical Society, the College of William and Mary, the American Antiquarian Society, the Dukes County Historical Society (Edgartown, Mass.), and the Library of Congress. The earlier part of the pedigree follows faithfully Davy's in the British Museum, with a few emendations.

Muskett. Suffolk Manorial Families, by Joseph James Muskett, 3 vols. (Exeter, 1900–08).

Lea, THE REGISTER. Genealogical Gleanings among the English Archives, by J. Henry Lea, in THE REGISTER, vol. LVI, p. 402 (October, 1902), continued in vols. LVII and LVIII. A collection of Gosnold and related wills, only a few of which were useful for this study.

Boyd. Boyd's Marriage Index, an extensive MS. work compiled from the available Parish Registers. The Gosnold entries in the section for Suffolk were abstracted for the writer by Miss Dorothy M. White, Chief Librarian, Central Library, Ipswich.

Matriculations at Cambridge University are from J. Venn's Alumni Cantabrigienses (Cambridge, 1922). Some admissions to Gray's Inn are given by Venn; others are from The Register of Admissions to Gray's Inn, 1521–1889, Joseph Foster, ed. (London, 1889).

Cop. (Copinger). Manors of Suffolk: "Notes on their History and Devolution", by W. A. Copinger, 7 vols. (London, 1905–1911).

PSIA. Proceedings of the Suffolk Institute of Archaeology. Contains:
Gipps, Sir Richard. Antiquitates Suffolkaienses . . . an account of the ancient families of Suffolk, vol. VIII, pp. 124 ff.
Cooke, Canon William. Materials for a History of Hessett, vol. IV, 301 ff.; vol. V, 1 ff. and vol. VI, 85.

Visitation of Norfolk, 1664. A. W. H. Clarke and A. Campling, eds. (Harleian Soc., 1934).

Blomefield's Norfolk. An Essay toward a Topographical History of the County of Norfolk, by Francis Blomefield. 5 vols. (Fersfield, etc., 1739–75), with 6 additional vols. by Blomefield and Charles Parkin.

The author is deeply indebted to those mentioned in the text and others who have sent to him in his remote island home the transcriptions, photostats, and microfilms of the original sources on which this study is based.

GRAY AND COYTMORE.

Communicated by WILLIAM S. APPLETON, A.M., of Boston.

I. THOMAS GRAY.

LONG and careful researches have been made by myself, and for me by the late Horatio G. Somerby, into the ancestry of Parnel Gray, wife of Increase Nowell, and into all the connections of her mother Katharine Coytmore, who came to this country a widow. I luckily found at the Principal Registry of Probate, London, the wills of both her husbands, who died in England, which are here printed. The register of Harwich, in Essex, has been examined, and contains so many Grays that there has been trouble in arranging the line of descent. It seems, however, to begin with THOMAS[1] GRAY, who had a son THOMAS[2] GRAY who was father of RICHARD[3] GRAY and JOHN[3] GRAY. RICHARD[3] GRAY, by wife Susan had THOMAS[4] GRAY, baptized at Harwich, August 18, 1572; and died in 1602, leaving widow Josuan, who married secondly, November 2, 1603, Christopher Johns.

THOMAS[4] GRAY, born in 1572, married Katharine, daughter and coheiress of Robert Miles,* of Sutton, in Suffolk, and died at Harwich, in 1607, buried May 7. Children:

 i. SUSAN, baptized at Harwich, January 31, 1593.
 ii. THOMAS, baptized at Harwich, May 4, 1595; was of Wapping, mariner; died in 1627.
 iii. ROBERT, baptized at Harwich, October 8, 1598; buried November 27, 1598.
 iv. PARNEL, born about 1602; married —— Parker, who died before 1626, leaving a daughter, and she married secondly, Increase Nowell, and died at Charlestown, March 25, 1687; he died Nov. 1, 1655.
 v. KATHARINE, born about 1604; married Thomas Graves; d. at Charlestown, February 21, 1682; he had the title of Admiral, and d. July 31, 1653.

II. ROWLAND COYTMORE.

Katharine, widow of Thomas Gray, of Harwich, married there December 23, 1610, ROWLAND COYTMORE, of Wapping, widower. He was undoubtedly of Welsh descent, a member, I presume, of the family of Coetmor,

---

* Alice, the other daughter and coheiress of Robert Miles, married Thomas Wiseman of Canfield in Essex, and was mother of William, created a Baronet August 29, 1628, ancestor of the present Sir William Wiseman, Baronet.

whose genealogy may be read in Volume II. of the "Heraldic Visitations of Wales," &c., 1846. We find there a Rowland of about 1600, who had a sister Alis, wife of Hugh ab John Wyn, which Alis is almost certainly the same as Elizabeth, mother of Hugh Hughs, alias Gwyn, named later Be this as it may, we find Rowland Coitmore as a grantee in the second charter of Virginia, May 23, 1609. He lived at Wapping, and had a first wife Dorothy Harris. He died in 1626, and his widow came to New England in 1636 or 1637, settling at Charlestown, where she was admitted to the church in 1638, and died Nov. 28, 1659, an aged widow. Children :

   i.   THOMAS, b. —— ; married at Wapping, June 24, 1635, Martha, dau. of Captain William Rainsborough ; was a sea-captain ; came to Charlestown, Mass., in 1636 ; member of the Artillery Company of Boston, 1639 ; admitted to the Church of Charlestown, February 16, 1640 ; freeman of the Colony of Massachusetts, May 13, 1640 ; Deputy to the General Court, 1640 and 1641 ; was lost by shipwreck, December 27, 1644,* on the coast of Cales, i. e. Spain, not Wales, as has been written. He had three children : 1. Katharine, b. and d. at Wapping in 1636 ; 2. Thomas, b. at Charlestown in 1642, died young ; 3. William, b. and d. at Charlestown in 1644. His widow married secondly in December, 1647, Governor John Winthrop, who died March 26, 1649, and she married thirdly, March 10, 1652, John Coggan, of Boston, who died in 1658.

   ii. ELIZABETH, b. —— ; married William Tyng, who died at Boston, January 18, 1653.

Thomas Gray.

In the name of God Amen, The xvi[th] day of August in the yeare of the Raigne of our soveraigne Lord James by the grace of God of England Scotland Fraunce and Ireland Kinge defendo[r] of the faith &c that is to saye of England Fraunce and Ireland the foureth And of Scotlande the fortye And in the yere of our Lorde God one thousand six hundred and sixe I Thomas Gray of the Borrough of Harwich in the County of Essex and Diocesse of London being somewhat weake in body but in good and pfect remembraunce thancks be given to almightie God therefore, Callinge to my mind the instabilitye of this mortall life, and intending to dispose of such landes tenements hereditaments and other substance after my decease wherewith it hath pleased almightie God of his goodnesse to endowe me in this world do make ordeyne and declare this my last will and Testament in manner and forme following that is to saie. First I doe yeild and bequeath my soule into the hands of almightie God, hoping through the merritts death and passion of our Lorde and saviour Christe Jesus to have full pardon and remission of all my synnes, and my body to be commytted to christian buriall at the discreĉon of my Executrix. Item I doe give bequeath and devise unto Katherine my wife All my moyetie parte and purparte of all and singuler those messuags lands tenements and hereditaments whatsoever with all and singuler their appurtennĉs aswell free as bonde or coppihoulde or custymary tennte scituate lieinge and beinge in Sutton in the Countie of Suff. which late were of Robert Miles late of Sutton Yeoman deceased father of the said Katherine my wife, th'othe[r] moyetie part or purparte whereof one Thomas Wyseman Esquire my brother in law now houldeth, To have and to hould my saide moyetie parte and purparte of all and singuler the saide messuags lands Tennements and heriditaments with all and singuler th'appurtennĉs unto the saide Katherine

---

* On his will he used a seal with the arms of Coytmore of Coytmore, Carnarvon, viz. : Gules, a chevron between three stags' heads cabossed Argent, a crescent for difference.

my wife and her assignes for and during the time and terme of her naturall
life, And after the decease of the saide Katherine my wife I doe give will
and bequeath my said moyetie parte or purparte of all and singuler the said
messuags lands tenements and heriditaments with th'appurtenncs unto
Thomas Gray my sonne To have and to hould to the said Thomas Gray
and to the heires of his bodie lawfullie begotten. And if it shall happen
the saide Thomas Gray my sonne to die withoute heires of his bodie lawfully begotten, Then I will ordeyne and devise by these presents That my
saide moyetie parte or purparte of all and singuler the saide messuags lands
tenements and hereditaments with th'appurtenncs shall whollie remaine and
be unto Suzan Gray Parnell Gray and Katherine Gray my daughters and
to the heires of their bodies lawfulie begotten. And if it shall happy my
saide daughters to die without heires of their bodies lawfully begotten,
Then I will and ordeyne that all and singuler the p'misses before willed and
devised shall whollie remaine to the saide Katherine my wife and her heires
for ever. Provided alwayes that if the saide Katherine my wief at any tyme
hereafter shall thinke meet and convenient for the better good proffitt and
advancement of her selfe and of my saide children to make sale of my saide
moyetie parte and purparte of all the said messuags lands tenements
hereditaments and other the p'misses with thappurtenncs either for and
towards the purchasinge buyenge of thother moyetie parte or purparte of
the saide messuags lands tenements and heriditaments with thappurtenncs which the saide Thomas Wiseman my brother in law doe nowe hould
or of any other lands and tenements whatsoever, Then my full true intent
and meaning is, And I doe will ordeyne and devise by these p'nts that my
saide moyetie parte or purparte of all and singuler the saide messuags lands
tennements and heriditaments with appurtenncs shall be sould by my
saide wife to and for the best proffitt and advantage that may be had for the
same, And the money arisinge growinge and cominge of for and uppon the
sale thereof to be used bestowed imployed and disposed for and towards the
purchasing and buyenge either of the saide other moyetie parte or purparte
of the saide messuags lands tennements and heriditaments which the saide
Thomas Wiseman nowe houldeth at of any other lands or Tennements whatsoever, w[ch] saide lands Tennements and heriditaments to be purchased and
bought as aforesaid I will and ordaine by these p'nts to be assured and conveyed by good and lawfull writings surrenders assurannes and conveyannes
in the law accordinge to the nature of the tenure of the p'misses in manner
and forme followinge, That is to saie, to the saide Katherine my wife and
her assignes for and during the terme of her naturall life, And after her
decease to the saide Thomas Gray my sonne and to the heires of his bodie
lawfullie begotten, And for defaulte and wante of such heires to the said Suzan Gray Parnell Gray and Katherine Gray my saide daughters and to
their heires of their bodies lawfullie begotten, And for want of such heires
to remaine to the next heires of the said Katherine my wife for ever. And
I doe further will and ordaine by these p'nts That the said Katherine my
wife before she doe make anie sale of the saide moyetie parte or purparte of the saide lands tennements and heriditaments shall become
bounden to my Supvisor hereafter named in this my last will and Testament in one writinge obligatory in the somme of One Thowsand poundes of
lawfull English money with condicōn thereuppon to be indorsed for the
true pforminge accomplishing and fulfilling of all things especified and conteyned in this my last will and Testament of her parte to be done accomplished and fulfilled according to the true intent purporte and plaine mean-

109

inge of the same. And if the saide Katherine my wife shall nott become bounden or refuse to become bounden in manner (and) forme aforesaide, Then my will and true intent is, and I doe will and ordaine by these p^rnts That any such bargaine and sale to be made as aforesaide of my saide moyetie parte or purparte of the said messuags lands tennements and hereditaments with th'appurtenncs or of any or every parte or pcell thereof to be utterly voide and of none effect to all intents and purposes and she utterly disabled to make any such sale thereof, And that my former guifts and devises above made of the same and of every parte and pcell thereof to my saide wife and children shall stande and remaine in their full force and effect, Anie thinge in these p^rnts conteyned to the contrary notwithstandinge.

Item I do give and bequeath unto the saide Suzan Gray my daughter the somme of one hundreth pounds of lawfull English money to be paide to her by my Executrix when she shall accomplish her full age of xviij^en yeres (if she shall happen to live so longe). Item I doe give and bequeath unto the saide Parnell Gray my daughter the like somme of one hundreth poundes of like English money to be paide her by my Executrix at her full age of xviij^en yeres (if she shall happen to live so longe.) Item I give and bequeath unto the saide Katherine Gray my daughter the like somme of one hundreth pounds of like English money to be paide unto her by my saide Executrix at her full age of eightene yeres (if she the saide Katherine shall happen to live so long.) The residue of my goodes and Chattells plate money Jewells moveables utensills and household stufe unbequeathed I doe whollie give and bequeath unto the saide Katherine my wife towards the payment of my saide legacies and discharging of my debts, which saide Katherine my wife I doe ordeyne constitute and make my sole Executrix of this my last Will and Testament. And I further constitute and ordaine Hugh Branham clerke to be the Supvisor of the same, giving and bequeathinge unto him for his paines and labour the somme of thre poundes.

In witnesse whereof I the saide Thomas Gray have to ev'y sheete of pap of this my last will and Testament conteyning in all six sheets of paper putt to my handes the day and yere above written.   Thomas Gray.

These being witnesses hereunto.
Anthony Branham.   Richard Reynolds.   John Moore his marke.
Proved at London 29 June 1607.

Rowland Coytmore.

In the name of God Amen The fiveth daye of June Anno Dñi one thousand sixe hundred twentie sixe And in the second yeare of the Raigne of our Soveraigne lord Charles by the grace of God King of England Scotland Fraunce and Ireland defendo^r of the faith etc. I Rowland Coytemore of Wapping in the Countie of Midd. marriner being in good and perfect health and memory laud and praise bee given to God for the same doe make and declare this my last Will and testament in manner and forme followinge that is to saie First and principally above all earthly thinges I commend my soule to the allmightie God my maker and creator and to his Sonne Christ Jesus my Saviour and Redeemer, hopeing and stedfastly assuring myselfe that thorough the meritts bitter death and passion wch my Savio^r suffered for mee to bee one of Gods elect in heaven there to receave life everlasting. My body I comend to the earth wherof it was made and as touching and concerning the disposicon of all and singuler such worldly goods and substance wch God hath endued we w^thall I give and bequeath the same as followeth vizt.

110

Item I give & bequeath unto my loveing Sonne Thomas Coytmore and to his heires and assignes for ever All that my messuage or Tenement and all my lands hereditaments and appteñncs thereunto belonging aswell freehold as Coppyhold Scituate lying and being in the mannor of Milton in the parish of Prittlewell als Pricklewell in the countie of Essex now in the tenure and occupation of John Greene together wth fower kedles* lying and being at Southend in the aforesaid mannor now in the tenure and occupaĉón of —— Crips.

Item I give and bequeath unto my said sonne Thomas Coytemore and to his heires and assignes for ever All that my farme and Coppyhold land wth th'appurteñncs thereunto belonging conteyning forty and fower acres or thereabouts scituate lying and being in the parish of great Bursted in the Countie of Essex all wch said coppyhold land before by mee given and beqeathed unto my said Sonne Thomas Coytemore I have according to the custome of the said Manno^r surrendred to the lymitaĉón and use of this my last will and testament Provided allwaies and never the lesse my mind will and mening is that my wife Katherin Coytemore shall have and enjoy to her owne use and behoofe the aforesaid messuag or tenement Kedles Farme and coppyhold lands wth th'appteñncs thereunto belonging before by mee given and bequeathed unto my said Sonne Thomas Coytemore And shall have receave and take the rents issues profitts and benefitts thereof untill my said Sonne shall accomplish his age of one and twentie yeares But neverthelesse upon condiĉón that my said wife Katherin Coytemore shall satisfy and paie out of the Rents of the said messuage or tent. Keddles Farme and coppyhold lands wth theire appurtenances (as the same shall grow due and payable) unto my daughter Elizabeth Coytemore the some of threescore pounds of lawfull money of England when she shall accomplish the age of one and twentie yeares or bee married wch which shall first happen.

Item my will mind and meaning is that my said daughter Elizabeth Coytemore before she receave the said some of threescore pounds shall give sufficient bond and put in sufficient suretie to repay the said some of threescore pounds unto my said wife if my said Sonne Thomas shall happen to depart this life before he shall accomplish his full age of one and twentie yeares For then and in such case my said Sonne Thomas Coytmore dying my mind and will is that my said daughter Elizabeth shall have and enjoy to the onely proper use and behoofe of her and her heires and assignes for ever all that my foresaid messuag or tenement, Keddles Farme and Coppyhold land wth thappteñncs thereunto belonging aswell scituate lying and being in the parish of Prittlewell als Pricklewell as in the pish of great Bursted aforesaid before by mee geven and bequeathed to my said Sonne Thomas Coytemore.

Item I give and bequeath unto my said daughter Elizabeth Coytmore and to her heires and assignes for ever All that my messuage or Tenement and backside wth thappurteñncs thereunto belonging aswell freehold as coppyhold commonly called and knowne by the signe of the blew boare scituate and being in the towne or parish of Retchford in the Countie of Essex aforesaid now in the tenure and occupaĉón of William Ashwell als Hare Which said messuage or tenement and backside wth the appurtenances or such pte thereof as is Coppyhold I have according to the custome of the said Manno^r surrendred in the hands of the Lord to the lymitaĉón and use of this my last will & testament.

* Kedles or Kidells are weirs to catch fish.

Item my will is that my Executrix hereunder named shall sell the said messuag or tenem^t wth the appurtenances thereunto belonging to the use profitt and behoofe of my said daughter Elizabeth my said Executrix putting in good securitie to my Overseers to buy wth the said money that she shall receave for the same as good or better purchase for my said daughter and to the use of her and her heires onely forever. Provided allwaies and my will is That if it happen my said daughter Elizabeth to dye or decease out of this p^{r}nte life before she shall accomplish the age of one and twentie yeares or bee married That then the said messuag or tenement Backside and premisses called and knowne by the signe of the blew boare aforesaid soe to her bequeathed or such other purchase as shalbe purchased for the same shall descend come and remaine unto my aforesaid Sonne Thomas Coytmore and to his heires and assignes for ever.

Item my mind and meaninge is that my said wife Katherin Coytmore shall alsoe have and enjoy the aforesaid messuag or tenement Backside and appurteñncs before by mee given and bequeathed unto my said daughter Elizabeth and shall have receave and take the rents issues profitts and benefitts thereof untill my said daughter Elizabeth shall accomplish her age of one and twentie yeares or bee married (wch of either of the said tymes shall first happen to come or bee) for and towards the maintenance appelling and well bringing up of my said daughter according as shall seeme fitting and to the likeing of my Overseers.

Item I give and bequeath unto my Sonne in lawe Thomas Gray and to his heires and assignes for ever All those my two coppyhold Tenements wth their appurteñncs scituate lying and being wthin the parish of Rederith als Rederiff in the countie of Surrey now in the severall tenures and occupañons of Francis Welbey and John Moore the wch coppyhold tenements I have according to the custome of the said mannō surrendred into the hands of the Lord to the lymitañon and use of this my last will and testament.

Item my mind is that if it shall happen the aforesaid somē of threescore pounds shall not bee satisfied and paid unto my said daughter Elizabeth Coytemore before my said sonne Thomas Coytemore shall accomplish his age of one and twentie yeares That then my said Sonne shall satisfie and paie the same And if he refuse to paie then I doe recall from my said Sonne All my freehold land before to him bequeathed and doe give and bequeath the same unto my Executrix hereunder named to bee sold by her for the payment of the said somē of fowerscore pounds unto my said daughter Elizabeth as aforesaid.

Item my will is that if it shall happen all my Children and Childrens children to dye or decease out of this p^{r}te life before mee or before they shall accomplish theire severall ages of one and twentie yeares or bee married then all my foresaid lands shall remayne come & bee unto my kinsman Hugh Hughs als Gwyn my Sister Elizabeths Sonne.

Item I give and bequeath unto my Grandson William Ball the sonne of William Ball* the somē of fortie shillings and unto the aforesaid Hugh Hughes als Gwyn three pounds and unto my daughter in lawe daughter Dorothy Lamberton† fortie shillings to bee paid unto them severally wthin one yeare after my decease if they shalbe liveing.

Item I give and bequeath unto the poore of Wapping three pounds and to the poore of the upper hamlett of Whitechapple the somē of fortie shillings to bee paid to them severally wthin one month after my decease.

* He probably married a daughter of Rowland Coytmore by his first wife.
† She may have been daughter of Susan, the eldest daughter of Thomas Gray, otherwise only mentioned in his will.

Item I give and bequeath unto the M^rs of the Trynoty house for theire poore the some of ten pounds to bee paid w^thin one yeare after my decease.

Item the rest and Residue of all and singuler my goods chattells leases shipping and all other things and substance whatsoever to mee belonging and not bequeathed I doe give and bequeath unto my foresaid wife Katherin Coytemore Whom I doe nominate my full and sole Executrix of this my last will and testament and gardian unto my aforesaid children. And I doe nominate and appoint my Sonnes in law Thomas Gray and William Rainsborough* of Wapping aforesaid marrin^rs overseers hereof entreating them to be carefull in seeing the same performed and I doe give to each of them forty shillings a peece for theire paines to bee taken therein.

In witnes whereof I have hereunto sett my hand and seale the daie and yeare first above written. ROWLAND COYTEMORE.

Read signed sealed and as the last will and testament of the said Rowland Coytemore published and delivered in the presents of Raph Bower Pub. Scr. John Wheatley ser^t to the said Scr.

Proved at London 24 November 1626.

---

* Judith, wife, probably second, of Capt. William Rainsborough, may have been a dau. of Rowland Coytmore by his first wife.

SARA, FIRST WIFE OF EDMUND GREENLEAF
(1588-1663)

By Mrs. DOROTHY GREENLEAF BOYNTON, of Elkhart, Ind.

Edmund Greenleaf, the original ancestor of the Greenleaf family in America, is known to have come from Ipswich, Suffolk, where the registers of St. Mary's at the Tower and St. Margaret's record the baptism of his children between 1613 and 1631. Numerous efforts have been made to determine Edmund's ancestry without success, although bits of information have been found but all is speculation so far, for example see J. Gardner Bartlett's note in THE REGISTER, vol. 69, p. 358-359, October 1915. Thirty years before this William Sumner Appleton, in an article "The Greenleaf Ancestry" pointed out that the will of Edmund, dated 25 Dec. 1668, made a bequest to his eldest son's son James when actually no such grandson could be found (*ibid.,* vol. 38, p. 299-301, July 1884; see also p. 322 in the same volume for detail about Edmund's second wife).

In the obituary of Charles C. Beaman of Boston in THE REGISTER, vol. 38, p. 100, January 1884, it is definitely stated that Edmund's wife was named Sarah Dole. James Edward Greenleaf's *Genealogy of the Greenleaf Family,* 1896 (p. 71-74, 190), continues this claim and gives information on the Dole family.

With the help of Mr. T. Woodard of Laughton, co. Essex, I have attempted to solve the question of Edmund's parentage. Mr. Woodard reports that not all Ipswich parish records are available and that some are known to be copies from older registers which means that errors and omissions are quite possible. In our search some few additional facts have been turned up but nothing conclusive. However, a real step toward the solution of the Greenleaf puzzle can be reported because definite proof of the parentage of Sarah, the mother of his children, has been found.

The author by chance saw in the Essex volumes of the Boyd Marriage Index an entry, "Moor Sar and Edm Greenleaf Langford" (Women's Volume, p. 33, copy in Salt Lake City). The time, 1611, was about right, the names are right and seemed to explain the Cousin Thomas Moor, the overseer of Edmund's will.

To be absolutely sure Mr. Woodard was employed to look for proof. This he found in the will of Samuel More of the Parish of Much Totham, co. Essex, dated 24 Dec. 1615 and proved by his brother Francis More the 2nd of February following. A transcription of the will follows:

In the name of God Amen the 24th day of December in the year of our Lord god 1615. I Samuell More late of Much Totham in the county of Essex husbandman being poor of body but of good and perfect remembrance (thanks be given unto allmighty god) Do make and ordayn my last will and testament in manner and forme following:

First I commend my soule into the hands of god my creator hoping through the . . . merits of Jesus Christ my Blessed savior that att the generall resurrection both body and soule shall be rejoined together and made perteker of his everlasting kingdom: I bequeath my body unto the earth from which it first came to be buried in decent Christian burial att the Discretion of my Executor.

Item I give to the poor of Much Birch at the time of my . . . six shillings eight pence to be payd at the discretion of the minister and brothers:

Item I give unto my sister Sara the wife of Edmund Grinleaf of Ipswich in the county of Suffolk a flockbed one bolster two pillows.

Item I give unto her two children John and Enoch either of them ten pounds of lawful english money . . . sayd summe my will is shall be paid by my executor to Edmond Grinleaf their father for their use and he enter bond unto my sayd executor for the true payment thereof and . . . from me when they shall come to the several ages of one and twenty years:

Item I give to Anna Hewster my Aunt twenty shillings to buy her a gold ring to be worn by her for my sake.

Item I give unto my father Enoch More of Haverill the like summe of twenty shillings:

Item I give unto Enoch more my brother and to my two sisters Merry and Judith to each of them six shillings eight pence.

All the residue of my goods and shattells unto him as well moveables and imoveables I give unto Francis More my brother whom I nominate and ordayn my sole Executor: And lastly I do . . . Nicholas More of Mauldon my Uncle to be supervisor unto this my will unto whom I give for his payment twenty shillings: In witness whereof I have hereto set my hand the Day and Year above written

Samuell More
His mark

In presence of
Robert Ham (?)
Edward ——— (maybe Bailer or Kailer)
John Hewster
Arthur Gaywood (Bishop of London Commissory in Essex, Essex Record Office, Chelmsford).

Reference to the parish registers of Maldon, co. Essex (to be found in the old library attached to the medieval tower of St. Peter's church) gives a few of the vital statistics of the family, though they have to be used in conjunction with the existing wills, two of which are those of Nicholas and Willamin Moore, the paternal grandparents of Sara (More) Greenleaf. Nicholas Moore, according to the parish records of St. Peter's, was living in that parish when his son Enoch was baptised, 19 Jan. 1560-1, but by 17 Sept. 1570, when Nicholas the Younger was baptised, the family was in All Saints parish. No other baptisms of their children are recorded though there were sons Samuel, Thomas and Edward, and daughters Anna and Phillip, according to the various wills.

Marriages [Moor-Moore]
  1585 Enoch and Catherine 23 November
  1605-6 Edward and Elizabeth Burton 6 February
  1612 Thomas and Bridget Lufkin 31 May [Recorded as Bridget Lusk in St. Peter's]
  1618 Phillip and William Harrington 31 August

Burials [Moor-Moore]
    1593 Catherine 11 October
    1594 Nicholas 8 October
    1606 Willamin 20 July
    1617 Bridget 12 September
    1619 Edward 6 November
    1622-3 Elizabeth 9 February
    1624 Thomas 19 September
    1646 Nicholas 30 May

Baptisms [Moor-Moore]
  (St. Peter's)
    1560-1 Enoch Jan. 19
  (All Saints)
    1570 Nicholas the Younger 17 September
    1588 Sara daughter of Enoch 13 December
    1590 Anne daughter of Thomas 8 May
    1591 Samuel son of Enoch 20 April
    1591 Nicholas son of Thomas 6 October
    1592 Francis son of Enoch 2 September
    1594 Felice daughter of Thomas 4 July
    1622 Edward son of Nicholas 14 July

As is apparent from the above records the parents of Sara were married in All Saints parish 23 Nov. 1585. Sara herself was baptised there 13 Dec. 1588, probably not far inside the curious triangular tower to be seen in Maldon today. Her mother died in that parish a little more than a month after the birth of Sara's brother Francis and was buried 11 Oct. 1593. At some time, perhaps after his father's death in 1594, Enoch Moore moved to Haverhill, co. Suffolk. By 1599, according to a fragmentary record found in the Withington material (Essex Institute, Salem, Mass.), Enoch had married again for the baptism of daughters Mary and Jane occurred in Haverhill. This scrap may have come from the Bishop's transcripts and could be an indication that other bits of information will in time turn up even though the Haverhill parish records are said not to have survived.

It would appear that the daughter Jane did not live because the will of Samuel of Much Totham, given above, speaks of only sisters Merry and Judith in addition to Sara. It tells us, however, that Samuel had a brother Enoch, that Enoch, Sr., was still living in Haverhill in 1615 and Francis was the brother he chose as his main heir.

One of the most important facts given in Samuel's will is that Sara and Edmund had in 1615 two sons, John and Enoch. The list of children baptised in Ipswich does not include John, the first born, nor was he baptised in Langford or Maldon, the parish records of which have been examined. The second son Enoch was baptised 1 Dec. 1613 at St. Mary's le Tour in Ipswich. Then Edmund and Sara moved to St. Margaret's parish, where we find the following Greenleaf entries:

Baptisms
    1615-6 Samuel son of Edmund and Sarah 8 January
    1617-8 Enoch son of Edmund and Sarah 20 March

1620-1 Sara daughter of Edmund and Sarah 26 March
1621-2 Elizabeth daughter of Edmund and Sarah 16 January
1624 Nathaniel son of Edmund and Sarah 27 June
1626 Judith daughter of Edmund and Sarah 29 September
1628 Stephen son of Edmund and Sarah 10 August
1631 Daniel son of Edmund and Sarah 14 August

Burials

1617 Enoch son of Edmund and Sarah 12 September
1616-7 Samuel son of Edmund and Sara 5 March
1633 Nathaniel son of Edmund and Sara 24 July

The naming of John, the first born son, in the will of his uncle, Samuel More, who, as far as we can know, survived baby-hood, explains the bequest of Edmund Greenleaf to a grandson James, his eldest son's son. One cannot help surmising that John Greenleaf, the silk dyer of St. Andrews Undershof, London, who married Hester Hoste, daughter of James Host of Stepney, 18 May 1636, in St. Augustine's church near Paul's Gate in London, may have been that eldest son and elected to remain in England when the rest of the family migrated. For him the usual pattern would be to name a son James. It might also be that the John Greenleaf who married in Braintree, Mass., whom nobody has been able to place might be another grandson though it is granted that actual proof is needed. Also curiously an Edmund Grenelif, a mariner, in the City of Tangier, made a will, dated 10 April 1670, in which he left a dwelling in the parish of Stepney to his wife, if she was living—it was proved 21 Jan. 1670-1 by Hannah Greneleafe, the widow (see James Edward Greenleaf, *op. cit.*, p. 499, under "Enoch Greenleaf;" also p. 472, the account of John of Braintree; the will of Edmund of Tangier is filed in London).

Returning to the history of Sara (More) Greenleaf, is seems apparent that she came from a family of considerable substance; possibly a search of the town records of Maldon would reveal interesting information. The wills of her grandparents, Nicholas and Willamin Moore and their younger sons Nicholas and Edward as well as the latter's wife, are all to be found in Chelmsford, the shire town of Essex.

The oldest will so far found is that of Nicholas Moore, written by his son Samuel as clerk, 18 Aug. 1590, and proved in Chelmsford by Samuel as attorney for his mother, 22 Oct. 1594. Enoch and Nicholas the Younger were the witnesses.

In the name of god amen Anno 1590 the 18th daye of August in the 32nd yere of the Reigne of Soverigne Lady Elizabeth by the grace of god of England France and Ireland Queene Defender of the Faith I Nicholas Moore of Maldon in the County of Essex and ... diocesse Sick of body but of sound and perfect memory god be thanked doe ordayne and make this my ... last will and testament in manner and forme folowinge

First I bequeath my soule into the hands of almight god my creator and Redeemer and my body to the earth in sure hope of Resurrection with the Just through my Lord and Savior Christ Jesus

Item I give and bequeath unto Willamin my wife my notage [?] or tenament situated in Maldon aforesaid in the street called ffulbridge street now in the tenure and occupation of Thomas Moore my son and of his assignes, to have and to hold the same to her and her heirs forever

Item I give and bequeath unto her my said wife my lease and tenure of . . . that I have in the house that I now dwell in To have and to hold the same unto her and her assignes payinge the rent and discharging the covenant in the same lease specified.

Lastly I give and bequeath unto the said Willamin my wife all and singular my other moveables good debts Stock of leather . . . Tallow oile and all other my chattles and Implements of household in hand I make and ordain my sole executrix revokinge all . . . wills whatsoever In witness whereof I have to this . . . set my hand and seale the Daye and Year above written

Signum hefi [i.e. the mark of]
Nicholas Moore

In the . . . of Enoch Moore
    Nicholas Moore the Younger Et
    mei Samueila Moore Script

Then in 1603 the following will was written for Willamin, his widow:

In the name of god Amen the thirtieth daye of August in the year of our Lorde James by the grace of god now kinge of Englande I willamin Moore of the parish of all Saints in maldon in the county of Essex Wyddow being now very weaken bodye by reason of my great age and years whereby I am put in remembrance that my time and end approacheth and cometh on a pace, do therefore make publishe and declare this my last will and testament in writing in manner and forme following:

First I commend my Soule into the hands of almighty god the Father the sonne and the holy ghost assuredly believing that all my Sinnes of gods great mercy in Jesus christ are doomed and done away And my bodie I comytt to christian buryall at the discretion of the executor of this my last will and testament here under named

Item I will and give unto my sonne nicholas Moore my tenement with the appertances situated and being in or near agenst Fulbridge street in the parish of Saint Peter in maldon aforesaid now in the tenure and occupation of [?] hybberd wyddow or her assigns to have and to hold the said tenement with appertances unto the said nicholas his heirs and assigns forever.

Item I give and bequeath unto the said nicholas a hall bedstead standing in the chamber over the hall of the messauge in which I now dwell and a downe bed now being thereon and other the bedding and furniture thereunto belonging in all things fully furnished and a . . . chest in the same chamber with all the linen in the same chest

And it is in my minde and will that if in future the said nicholas (after my death) to marrye or to settle and occupe (by himself) the trade of a shoemaker that then the executor of this my testament shall immediately thereupon pay and deliver to him the said nicholas (as my gift) ten pounds of lawful money of england.

Item I give and bequeath unto Sara Moore the daughter of my sonne Enoch Moore Five pounds of lawful english money to be payd her by my executor at her age of 21 years or day of marriage which shall first happen

Then I will and give to be paid by my executor uppon my buryall unto my sonnes Samuel Enoch and Thomas Moore and to my daughters Anne and Phillip to everyone of the same my children (in token of a friendly remembrance) Five shillings a piece and no more for that my said daughters and ye one of my said sonnes last named have had already their full portions

All the rest of my goods moveable household stuff and implements of household and whatsoever ellse I have or may dispose of that is testamentary I give fully and wholly unto Edward Moore my Sonne whome I do make constitute and ordain sole and only executor of this my last will and testament and him do appoint and require to pay my funerall and debts and the legacies of this my testa-

118

ment In witness whereof I have hereunto put my Seale subscribed my name the day and year first above written

In the prive of George Purcas [?]   the marke of
Thomas Chesse the writer hereof   Willamin Moore widdow

The above will was proved in 1606. It indicates that Willamin and her husband must have had quite a little property since five of their children had already had their portions. One wonders also whether Sara had not made her home with her grandmother as she is the only grandchild mentioned, although both Thomas and Enoch had other children. Sara had been about six when her mother died and fifteen when her grandmother's will was drawn and past seventeen when Willamin actually died. In July 1611 Sara was still in the Maldon area as Langford and its church of St. Giles in which she and Edmund were married is practically a part of Maldon today.

Edward Moore's will was drawn up 30 April 1617 and was proved 10 Dec. 1619, about a month after his burial. His will provided carefully for his wife thus giving us a pretty good picture of the kind of home in which the Moores evidently lived and some idea as to where their property was located. Searching in those areas might take us back further in time. One might surmise that the brother Samuel had died since he is not mentioned. The mother's will was written in 1603. The will follows:

In the name of god amen the Thirtieth day of April in the yere of our Lord one Thousand Six hundred and seventeen and in the ffifteenth yere of the reigne of our Soveringne Lord James by the grace of god now king of England I Edward Moore of the parish of All Saints in maldon in the county of Essex shoomaker being weeke in body yet of sound and perfect memory (thanks be god) knowing that all men are subject to mortality do therefore make publize and declare this my last will and testament in writing in manner and form folowing

First and principally I commend my Soule into the hands of almighty god (that blessed trinity) the father the sonne and the holy ghost assuredly believing by faith in my Lord and Savior Jesus Christ of god's great mercy in him that all my synnes are freely forgiven and that eternal life in the heavens is reserved for me after the end of this mortall life. And my body I comytt to christian Buryall at the discretion and appointment of Elizabeth my well beloved wife and of the executor of this my last will and testament hereinafter named.

And as touching my Lands and possessions and other things of this life my minde and will is thereof as followeth:

First I give unto the sayd Elizabeth my wife all the movable goods household stuff and Implements of household and bedding which she had before my intermarraige with her (Excepting the linen brass and pewter which I had with her)

Item I give to the sayd Elizabeth my wife all the wearing apparell linen and rayment and also a featherbed a feather bowlster a great joined chest ... with a drawer which now standeth in the chamber over the Buttery And I give unto the said Elizabeth one half of all the linen brass and pewter whatsoever whereof I am now possessed Excepting only the brass pannies now used for my trade for stuffing [?] or currying of Leather to be indifferently divided and set out unto her by my brother Thomas Moore and my Brother-in-law John Hewster or the survivor of them with all convenient speede next after my death and also I give unto the said Elizabeth five pounds of lawful money of England to be payd unto her by my said Executor within one month next after my death

Item I give unto the said Elizabeth one of my two drawing tables (to be taken at her choice) my settall in the hall and two reasonable loads of wood

Item my minde and will is that the said Elizabeth my wife shall have and enjoy for and during the time of her naturall life if she so longe for time to life solo and unmarryed and not other wife the use and occupation of the great chamber over the shopp of my now dwelling house with convenient room and place in my yarde or backside for laying and bestowing of her wood and also a piece of my garden (of twenty ffeet square) and also the joint or common use and benefitt (with the tenant or dweller in my dwelling house for the time being) of one chamber therein called the storyers chamber hanging and drying of the linen with free accesse ingresse egresse and regresse by and through my said dwelling house unto and from the said chamber's yard and garden and any of them at all times and from time to time without any lett or molestation whatsoever.

Item I give and will to be payd unto the sayd Elizabeth by my said executor or his assignes after my death yearly every year during the time of her natural life (at the messuage in which I dwell one early sume of Five pounds of lawful money of England at the ffour usual ffeasts and times of payment in the year by equal portyons for and in full compensation and satisfaction of the estate jointure dower or things which to her shall or may arrive or grow after my death of in and to or out of my lands and tenaments whatsoever either freeholds or copyholds which I am now seized or shall be seized at my death or an estate of inheritance (the first payment thereof to begin and to be made at first one of the said ffeasts which shall first happen and come next after my death)

Item I will and do devise and give unto my Brother Nicholas Moore his heirs and assigns forever those two tenements (customary or copyhold to the manor of Bradwell juxta Mare in the said county of Essex) whereof one is called Reeves containing by estimation ten acres of land and that which is called ffeldmans containing by estimation eight acres of land with their appertances and all my estate reversion [?] and remaynder of and in the said tenements and lands after the death of the said Elizabeth my wife

Item I devise will and give unto my sayd Brother Nicholas Moore his heir and assignes forever the said messuage (in which I dwell) situated and being in the said parish of All Saints in maldon aforesaid with the edifice [?] buildings yards backsides gardens and orchards ways and easments to the sayd messuage belonging or now used and other appertances.

Item I will and do give unto the said Nicholas Moore my Brother one messauge and six acres of land with the appertances called Myllers late in the tenure and occupation of Robert Sooke in the said county of Essex to have and to hold to the sayd Nicholas Moore his heirs and assignes forever according to the custom of the said manor

Item I give and bequeath unto Francis Moore the sonne of my Brother Enoche Moore ten pounds of lawful english money to be payd to him by my sayd Executor within one yere next after my decease (over and besides the ten pounds which I am to pay him for and out of the rent and profitts of a certain shop situated in the sayd parish of all Saints near unto the ffish stalls)

Item I give unto Nicholas Moore and Phillip Moore the sonne and daughter of my Brother Thomas Moore to either of them ten pounds a piece of like money to be payd within one year next after my decease by my said Executor

And I give unto my said Brothers Enoch and Thomas Moore to either of them tenne shillings a piece and to my Sister Phillip ffive Shillings of lawful english money as a small remembrance of my Love and goodwill to them

Item I give to the poor of All Saints parish in maldon aforsaid Six shillings and eight pence to be payd to the overseers of the said poore within three months next after my death

All the rest of my goods chattles movables household stuff and implements of household wares shop stuff ready money and debts and whatsoever ellse I have or may dispose that is testamentary I do give fully and wholly unto the said Nicholas Moore my brother which said Nicholas I do make and constitute sole and only Executor of this my last will and testament and I require and charge him duly and truly to pay my funerall charges and debts and the legacies and portions of money by this testament bequeathed provided always and nevertheless my minde and full meaning and will is that if at the time of my decease there shall be a surrender in force to the use of my will of and concerning my said coppyhold lands and tenements holden of the manor of Walton aforsaid that then the said Nicholas Moore my Brother after my decease and before probate of this my testament shall become bounden by Deede obligatory sufficient in the . . . unto the said Elizabeth my wife in the Some of Thirty Pounds of lawful money of England with condition theron for the sure payment of the said yearly Some of ffive Pounds by the year to the said Elizabeth yearly during her life in the manner and order and according to the effect and purpose afore declared in this my will; But if no sure Surrender shall from time to be at my death of the said copyhold lands and tenements last mentioned for the use of my will that then the said gift of ffive Pounds a year to my wife yearly during her life shall be voided and of no effect (any thinge afore in this my will confirmed to the contrary in any wise not withstanding). In witness whereof I the said Edward Moore to this my last will and testament have put my seale and subscribed my name the day and year first above written in the presence of the persons herein-under named Joseph Walker John Dandy and Thomas Chese [? Chase, one of Enoch's daughters married the apothecary Thomas Chese of Boston] Edward Moore.

Elizabeth, the widow of Edward Moore, had her will drawn 18 Jan. 1622, giving the property that was hers to distribute to her children of her first marriage, a son William Burton and a daughter Elizabeth, then the wife of a John Merrill, with two sons John and William. From the Greenleaf-Moore point of view this will has little of interest.

Nicholas Moore the Younger left a will, also available in Chelmsford, dated 21 April 1646 and probated 23 June. Like his brothers he could sign his name at least indicating reasonable education for the time. His property went to his widow Margaret except for a silver wine bowl as he said his son, Edward, had had his share already though likely as an only child he would in the end get the rest just as he got the Bradwell juxta Mare property after his Aunt Elizabeth's death as his Uncle Edward had directed.

Unfortunately no wills have been found for either Samuel, who seems to have gotten special education, Thomas, or Sarah's father Enoch, though perhaps through related families some more information may yet be garnered.

Of special interest, however, is Sarah's brother Francis who appears in two of the wills. It seems reasonable to think that he was the father of Cousin Thomas Moore, the mariner of Boston, who Edmund years later, on this side of the Atlantic made overseer of his will.

Francis Moore, Jr., of Cambridge, Mass., called Thomas Moore of Boston his brother in his will, probated 23 Feb. 1689. Francis, if his recorded age at death was correct, was born about 1620. Thomas who was reported to have died at 66 on 5 Jan. 1689-90 would have been born about 1623 (see Lucius R. Page's *History of Cambridge, Genealogical Register Supplement and Index by Mary Isabella Gozzaldi*, 1930, p. 517, reference 611).

The father of these men, Francis Moore, Sr., according to Savage's *Dictionary*, became a freeman in Cambridge 22 May 1639. His wife Katherine died in 1648, after having several children born in Cambridge. The family names Francis, Samuel, Thomas, John, Anne and Sarah fit remarkably with the family in Maldon, co. Essex. The only problem is that his age 85 at death 20 Aug. 1671 given in the Cambridge record and Savage, does not jibe with the baptismal date, All Saints, Maldon, which is 1593 instead of 1586. However, it must be remembered that elderly people did (and do) make mistakes in recalling their age. Note that the birth of the first child at 27, Francis, Jr., would be much more reasonable than at 34 if the earlier date is to be taken as correct.

While there are quite a few court records about the marine experiences of Thomas Moore, the Boston mariner, thus far the writer has found no clear connection with the Greenleafs even though a number of business associates appear in both family records. Only one possible evidence has turned up and that in the Suffolk Superior Court Records which show that a Thomas Moore, in July 1675, was bound for the appeal of John and Thomas Wells, carpenters, in a case brought by Timothy Batts. John Wells was the husband of Mary Greenleaf, possibly one of Enoch's daughters. While there is nothing conclusive about this other evidence may still be found. Samuel Moore, one of the brothers, was in the Barbadoes. We know Edmund had trading ventures in the West Indies involving his Hill stepson (see his will) so records in that area may give further evidence. A further search for a record of the marriage of Francis, Sr., and Katherine might be informative.

In any case the discovery of this Moore material gives more substance to the story of Edmund Greenleaf, the identity of his wife Sara, and adds to our knowledge of his descendants and progenitors.

MILES GREENWOOD, of Greenwood, in Yorkshire, Weaver, admitted a citizen of Norwich, May 3, 1627.

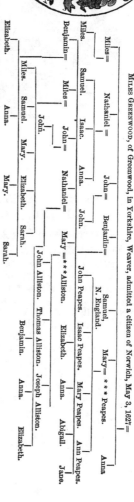

Norwich, Septemb. 25, 1723. The foregoing is a Genealogical Table of yᵉ Family of Greenwood in this Place. Miles Greenwood came very Yong from Yorkshire. And as I find it in yᵉ Public Records of this City, was an apprentice with Josiah Robbs, Worsted Weaver, and admitted a Citizen May 3, 1627. The Arms I took from an Ancient Seal of His.

"The original of the above, written within circles, is in a volume of miscellaneous pedigrees in the College of Arms, lettered on the back J.P.I." H. G. Somerby, London, Apr. 2, 1864.

The above arms are the same as those cut upon the family tomb in the Copps Hill burial ground, Boston, for the engraving of which we are indebted to the politeness of WM. H. WHITMORE, A.M., of Boston, and correspond to the armorial bearings of the Greenwoods of Norwich, towards the close of the sixteenth century, namely:—argent, a fesse sable, between three spur-rowels in chief and three ducks in base, all of the second. In the above pedigree Miles Greenwood has been represented as coming originally from Greenwood (Lee) Yorkshire, but by the Records of St. Peters of Mancroft, &c., it would appear that his father, Miles Greenwood, a citizen of Norwich, married Anne Scath, Oct. 21, 1599, and that Miles (above mentioned) was baptized at St. Peters, Sept. 1, 1600, and died in 1658, leaving a widow Abigaell and several children. Of these latter, Nathaniel, bapt. at St. Michael at Plea, Aug. 23, 1631, came to Boston, N. E., before 1654, and established himself as a shipwright; here all his children were born, with perhaps the exception of Isaac, who was probably born during a visit of his father to England, about 1665, whence he returned, bringing with him his brother Samuel, his nephew Benjamin, and some female relatives. The son Isaac Greenwood, a graduate of Harvard College, 1685, died in England, 1701, and was, it is supposed, the namesake of an uncle Isaac Peapes, or Pepys, of Norwich.

The family, though doubtless descended from the same stock as the Greenwoods of Greenwood-Lee, co. York (there located since 1154) was probably more immediately connected with a branch which has settled in Heversham parish, co. Westmoreland, with whom the christian name of Miles frequently occurs. The first of the family-name I have met with in Norfolk, is Richard Grinwode, Rouge-Croix pursuivant under Richard III., and continued in that office for upwards of ten years by Henry VII., and who was also, "Bailiff off Richmond Fee in the Countie of Noffolke." The arms of the De Lattre family of Picardy, Flanders, Artois and Champaigne, differ but in coloring from those of the Greenwoods of Norwich. (*Vide* Livre d'Or, 4me livre, p. 270.)

NEW YORK, JAN. 13, 1868.

ISAAC J. GREENWOOD.

123

GREGORYS OF LEICESTERSHIRE AND NOTTINGHAM, ENGLAND, AND OF CONNECTICUT.

[Communicated by Isaac J. Greenwood, Esq., of New-York.]

From Nichols's Hist. of Leicester, Throsby's Town of Nottingham, &c., we gather the following information respecting the Gregory family located in those parts of England.

The Gregorys of Asfordby, co. Leic., according to the Visitation of 1619, bore arms, *Or* two bars, in chief a lion passant azure; and were descended from :—

John[1] Gregory, lord of the manors of Freseley and Asfordby, who m. Maud, dau. of Sir Roger Moton, knt. of Peckleton, co. Leic. These manors were probably the same as Frisby and Asorby, which on Camden's maps, 1610, are located on either side of the Wreke, facing each other. He had children—
  1. Richard[2] (see further). 2. Nicholas,[2] father of Adam.[3] 3. Walter,[2] father of Richard.[3] 4. Alice, m. Hugh, son of Stephen Erdwick.

Richard[2] Gregory of Fresely and Asfordby, died at a very advanced age in 1292, and had

Sir Francis,[3] liv. 1240, father of

Ralph,[4] son and heir, liv. 1262, father of

Ralph,[4] son and heir, liv. 1262, father of

1. Thomas[5] (see further). 2. William,[5] m. Alice, dau. and heir of Robert de Cawley, lord of Cawley, co. Warwick, and had issue Thomas[6] of Harpole, co. Northampton; over two centuries later Sir Edmund Gregory was rector of Harpole 1531, vicar of Watford 1535, and was buried at the former place 6 Ap. 1543. Francis Gregory died 9 Oct., 1610, leaving a son of the same name, aged 15, heir to an estate at Harpole; in 1554 Valentine Gregory was patron of St. Andrews, Harleston, co. Northamp., and among the incumbents were Marc. Gregory, clericus, 8 Mar. 1562, and Thomas Gregory, buried 22 Dec. 1602, &c. 3. Henry,[5] killed in the Scotch war, had sons Henry[6] and Gregory.[6]

Thomas[5] of Asfordby, educated at Cambridge, a learned clerk, liv. 1328, m. Isabel, dau. and heir of Richard Segrave, and lady of the manor of Cately. Among his children were

Francis[6] Gregory, D.D., a canon of St. Mary de Pratis at Leicester, and—

John[6] of Asfordby, whose gt. gt. grandson

William[10] Gregory, Esq., of Asfordby, m. Helen, sister and heir of John Malyn of Tuxford, co. Nott.; his eldest son

Thomas,[11] was cousin and heir of Will. Dymock of Eiton, co. Nott.; he m. Elizabeth, dau. of Christopher Wade, merchant, and mayor of Coventry; liv. 38 H. VIII. (1546–7) and died 16 Eliz. (1573–4); sons, 1. Arthur[12] (see further). 2. Henry.[12] 3. Christopher.[12] 4. Edmund.[12]

Arthur,[12] lord of Styvichall, near Coventry, co. Warwick, aged 34 at time of father's decease, 16 Eliz., m. Jane, dau. of John Ferrers, son of Sir Humphrey Ferrers of Tamworth, and died 1 Dec. 1604 (2 Jac.), aged about 65; sons, 1. Thomas,[13] ob. s. p.; 2. John,[13] aged 25 at father's decease, liv. 1656; 3. Robert.[13]

John Gregory, mayor of Nottingham, 15 Eliz. (1571), and 29 Eliz. (1586).

Will. Gregory, g't., one of the two burgesses for the town of Nottingham, in the parliament held at Westminster 43 Eliz. (1601).

Will. Gregory, g't., sometime town-clerk of Nott., by will 11 Jac. (1613), gave 11 small tenements, with the appurtenances, called the White Rents, situate at Hundgate and within said town, for poor aged people to dwell in rent free, and 40s. yearly forever towards the reparation of said tenements. His arms in St. Peter's church, and formerly in the old Town Hall, were *Or*, two bars, and a lion pass. in chief azure.

Marmaduke Gregory, mayor of Nottingham, 12 and 18 Jac. (1614 and 1620).

William Gregory, mayor of Nottingham, 8 and 15 Chas. (1632 and 1639).

Deering's Hist. of Nottingham, 1751, gives the following pedigree of the Gregorys of that town:

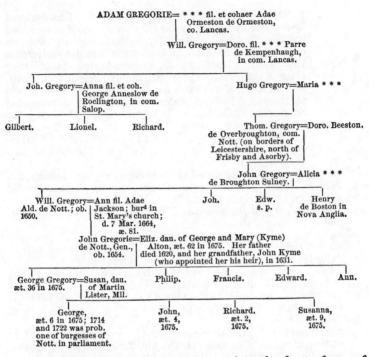

ADAM GREGORIE= * * * fil. et cohaer Adae
Ormeston de Ormeston,
co. Lancas.

Will. Gregory=Doro. fil. * * * Parre
de Kempenhaugh,
in com. Lancas.

Joh. Gregory=Anna fil. et coh.   Hugo Gregory=Maria * * *
George Anneslow de
Roclington, in com.
Salop.

Gilbert.   Lionel.   Richard.   Thom. Gregory=Doro. Beeston.
de Overbroughton, com.
Nott. (on borders of
Leicestershire, north of
Frisby and Asorby).

John Gregory=Alicia * * *
de Broughton Sulney. |

Will. Gregory=Ann fil. Adae   Joh.   Edw.   Henry
Ald. de Nott.; ob. | Jackson; bur⁴ in   s. p.   de Boston in
1650.   St. Mary's church;   Nova Anglia.
d. 7 Mar. 1664,
æ. 81.

John Gregorie=Eliz. dau. of George and Mary (Kyme)
de Nott., Gen., | Alton, æt. 62 in 1675. Her father
ob. 1654.   died 1620, and her grandfather, John Kyme
(who appointed her his heir), in 1631.

George Gregory=Susan, dau.   Philip.   Francis.   Edward.   Ann.
æt. 36 in 1675. | of Martin
Lister, Mil.

George,   John,   Richard.   Susanna,
æt. 6 in 1675; 1714   æt. 4,   æt. 2,   æt. 9,
and 1722 was prob.   1675.   1675.   1675.
one of burgesses of
Nott. in parliament.

According to an inscription on stone set into the front of one of
four tenements in Barkergate, Nottingham, William Gregory, gent., by
will 1650 left 12d. a week for ever, to be raised out of the rents of
these houses, and to be given in bread every Sunday, to twelve poor
people of the parish of St. Mary's, and to this amount his son John
added by will, in 1654, an additional 12d. a week. The arms of this
latter John Gregory, as they occur in St. Peter's church, are as follows : Gregory,[1] quartering Ormeston or Urmeston, viz. 1st and 4th,
Party per pale argent and azure, 2 lions rampant endorsed, counter-
changed. 2nd and 3rd, Sable, a chevron between three spear-heads
all within a bordure, argent. This coat is empaled with that of Alton
quartering Kyme, viz. : 1st and 4th, *Or*, on a chief vert, a lion passant of the field ; 2nd and 3rd, Gules, a chevron between ten cross-
crosslets *or*.

But in 1662, George Gregory (son of John), then in his 23d year,
not being able to show sufficient proof of his descent from the Highhurst Gregorys, received from Wm. Dugdale, Norroy, the following
new grant of arms : Gules, on a chevron betw. ten crosses crosslet *or*,
three crosses crosslet of the first, in relation to his descent from the
ancient family of Kyme, founded by Simon de Kyme, Lord of Keste-
ven, co. Linc., temp. Stephen. The crest granted at the same time
(a garb *or*, banded gules) was doubtless in reference to the family es-

[1] Arms of Gregory of Highhurst, co. Lancas., and of Wm. Gregory, Sheriff of London,
1436; Mayor, 1451.

tate which had been acquired by his grandfather William Gregory, principally by grazing. The Gregorys of Lenton, co. Nott., still bear the arms last referred to.

The Henry Gregory, of Boston, N. E., whom we find mentioned in the foregoing pedigree, was at Springfield 1639, and removed in a few years to Stratford, Ct. Savage says that he probably died soon after, as a distribution of his estate was ordered 19 June, 1655, his eldest son John being appointed administrator, and to receive double portion, and that no other children are mentioned ; though perhaps Judah Gregory, of Springfield, who m. 1643, Sarah, dau. of Henry Burt, was another son. John Gregory, of New-Haven, and afterwards of Norwalk, Ct., was possibly the administrator above referred to ; he had Joseph, bapt. 26 July, 1646 ; Thomas, 19 Mch, 1648 ; his other children and their issue are mentioned by Savage, and by Hall in his history of Norwalk ; of his daus. two m. into the family of Thomas Benedict, of Southold, L. I., and afterwards of Norwalk, who came out at the age of 22 about 1639, and was said to be the only son of Wm. Benedict, of Nottinghamshire.

ENGLISH ANCESTRY OF MR. THOMAS GREGSON
OF NEW HAVEN

By PAUL W. PRINDLE, F.A.S.G. of Darien, Conn.

Ancestry and Descendants of Amaziah Hall and Betsy Baldwin, by Edith B. Sumner (1954) shows on page 77 the emigrant, Mr. Thomas Gregson of New Haven, to have been baptized at Duffield, Derbyshire, 14 July 1611, son of Henry and Edith (Allestree) Gregson, grandson of Thomas and Ann (Merry) Gregson, and great-grandson of Thomas and Ann (Twiford) Gregson. This claimed English ancestry is rather optimistically based on *The Publications of The Harleian Society,* 37:216, and THE REGISTER, 46:151-3.

In reviewing the Hall-Baldwin book in *The American Genealogist,* 32:255-6, Donald Lines Jacobus wrote, with his customary perspicacity, "It is proved Thomas Gregson came from the Derbyshire family, but he would seem to be an older man than the Thomas baptized at Duffield, Derbyshire, 14 July 1611, and may have been an older cousin."

During a visit to England in 1966-7, I was able to add considerably to the record of this family now available in print, and to determine to my own satisfaction the identity of Thomas' father and paternal grandparents. Copies (minor punctuation added) of abstracts of wills and of a church register are given below, followed by family groupings in genealogical form and comments on the alleged ancestry of the first Gregson to appear in the Derbyshire records.

ORIGINAL GREGSON WILLS FOUND AT THE
COUNTY ARCHIVIST'S OFFICE, LICHFIELD, STAFFORDSHIRE

The 27 Jan. 1583 will of Thomas Gregson of Thurvaston, Derbyshire, proved 28 Feb. 1585/6. Thurvaston, with Osleston, constitutes a township in the parish of Sutton-on-the-Hill, union of Burton-upon-Trent, hundred of Appletree, south division of co. of Derby, 7¾ miles west by north of Derby (Samuel Lewis, *A Topographical Dictionary of England,* 1844). Because this is the will of the earliest proven ancestor of Thomas Gregson of New Haven, it is reproduced here in full.

In the name of the father and of the Sonne and of the holy ghost, Amen. In the year of our lorde 1583, the xxvij th day of Januarye I, Thomas Gregson of Over thurvaston in the p'she of Sutton-in-the-field, set in the Countye of Derbye, yeoman; Sicke in bodye but yet of sounde and p'ferte memorye, ordayne and make my last will and Testamente in mann' and forme followinge. First, I bequeath my Soule to the holy, blessed and glorious Trinitie, the father, the Sonne and the holy ghost, one trewe and ev'lastinge god, beleevinge stedfastlie to be saved by the passion, deathe and resurrectione of Jhesus christe and by none other means. Secondlie, I bequeathe my bodye to the earthe from whence ytt came, there to rest untill the gen'all resurrectione, belevinge assuredlie that I shall receave ytt agayne, a glorified bodye, and so forev' after shall dwell [with] both god and his chosen worlde, without ende. Thirdlie, concerninge my temporall landes and goods. First, I will and devyse the occupation

128

and comoditie of all the whole farme that I now dwell in, both all the appurtenances thereto belonginge, to Elizabeth my wiffe for three whole yeares next come after the date here of yf she keepe her selfe widowe. And yf she marrye agayne, then I will that she shall have the third p'te of my landes and goods and goe her waye. And after the foresayd three yeares be expired, yf she kepe her selfe widowe still, I will and devyse unto her the occupation of the one halfe of the farme that I now dwell in, with the appurtenances thereof, until such tyme as the lease that Richarde Gregorye hath of my house and landes in Overthurvaston aforesayd be expired, And the other halfe to remayne to John my sonne. And after that the sayd Lease that Richarde Gregorye hathe as is aforesayd be expired, I will and devyse unto the sayd John my Sonne all the whole lease of my farme that I now dwell in, w'th all the appurtenances thereto belonginge. Allso, I will and devyse unto the sayd John my sonne, at his entringe upon halfe my farme as is aforesayd, halfe my husbandrye geare, as wagnes, ploughes, yockes, teames and such lyke things, and the other half thereof to remayne to Gregorye my sonne. Also, I will and devyse unto the sayd John my sonne, and to the heyres males of his body lawfully begotten, for'er, all my lande in Oslaston and Thurvaston aforesayd w'ch I purchased of Richarde Pomfrett, of John Cooke and of Edward yoman, and he to enter upon the same immediatlie after my decease; and also, foure landes lyinge in Crople feilde that did belonge to Sheerehall [Sherrow Hall, alias Sheryhall, Sharrowhall, etc. is located within Oleston and Thurvaston, Appletree Hundred, Derbyshire (Kenneth Cameron, *The Placenames of Derbyshire*, 1959).] and one hundrethe markes in current money. Allso, I will and devyse my house and landes in Overthurvaston aforesayd, now in tenure and occupation of Richarde Gregorye aforesayd, to Elizabeth my wiffe for the tearme of fyve yeares next ensouinge after that the sayd Richarde Gregorye's Lease shalbe expyred, Paying yearlie during the sayd tearme of fyve yeares unto Will'm my Sonne the Sume of xxiij s. iiij d. And after the sayd fyve yeares be expyred, I will and devyse the forresayd house and landes, w'th all theyr appurtenances, nowe in tenure and occupation of Richarde Gregorye as is aforesayd, unto Gregorye my Sonne and to the heyres male of his bodye lawfully begotten, for'er, payinge yearlie unto William my Sonne duringe the tearme of the naturall lyffe of the sayd William the some of xxiij s. iiij d. All these thinges before rehearsed, I will and devyse unto Gregorye my sonne conditionallie; that is to wytt: that yf the sayd Gregorye shall and does marrye and take a wiffe by the advise and consente of his owne mother and of his owne bretherne, Thomas Gregson and Will'm Gregson, then the sayd Gregorye my sonne shall have and enjoye all things whatsoe' I have before in this my last will bequeathed, willed and devised unto him, in mann' and forme before mentioned. Butt yf he, the sayd Gregorye, shall or doe marrye or take a wiffe against theyr myndes and w thout theyr consente, w'ch they shall have instanse to dislike of, then I will and devise in makinge of this my last will and testamente that he, the sayd Gregorye my Sonne, for his disobedience shown towardes those whom I leave to be his tutors and overseers in my steede, shall have nothinge yt all that w'ch is before mensioned, but onlye one hundreth shillings in money, and goe whither he will, anythinge in this p'sente will beforesayd to the contrarye not withstandinge. Allso, I geve free libertye by this my last will unto Elizabeth my wiffe, besides whatsoe' I have geven her in this my last will and testament, to take the thirde p'te of all my landes duringe her lyffe, except [what] she of her owne good will doe geve ytt [to] my children. Allso, I bequeathe to Thomas my Sonne my best horse. Also, to Ellyn my daughter a yoke of oxen the w'ch she hath in her possession allreadye. To my three daughters, Margerye, Agnes and Anne, eche one of them, a Sylver Spoone. Also, to Charles my Sonne xx s. in money. Also, to enye one of my children's children, an Ewe sheepe. To enye one of my godchildren, xij d. To Isabell Carver's sonne Thomas, a payre of hoose, a dublett, a jerkyn and a hatt. Also, to certayne p'sones being in my wage towardes Lecester, w'ch are still unpayde, xxiij s. iiij d. Amongst them, to wytt: to Lecester, iij s. iiij d.; to Bristone, iij s. iiij d.; to Bowthorpe, iij s. iiij d.; to Swarston, iij s. iiij d.; to Twyforde and Steenson, iij s. iiij d. betwixt them; to Barrowe, iij s. iiij d.; to lytle Walton, iij s. iiij d. Allso, towardes the restoration of the p'ishe church of Sutton afore sayd, x d; to the poore of the p'ishe of Sutton, x d. Towardes the mending of the highe wayes w'thin the Lordshippe of Thurvaston and Oslaston aforesayd, x d. To enye of my servants, xij d. All the residewe of my land and leases and of all my goodes and chattells, moveable and unmoveable, nott before or after in this will bequeathed, my debtes payde and my fun'all discharged. I geve and bequeathe them whollye to Elizabeth my wiffe, trustinge that she wilbe good to my children w'th good discrec'on. Allso, I ordayne and make the sayd Elizabeth my wiffe my sole and full Executrix of this, my last will and testamente. Allso, I ordayne and make John Merye of Barton parke and Thomas Gregson my sonne and Henry Clerke my pastor, myne ov'seers to see that this my last will and testamente be trulie executed and fulfilled accordinge to the true meaning thereof. And for theyr paynes takinge therein, I bequeathe to enye one of them vj s. viij d. And thus I end, remitting my selfe whollye to the m'cye of allmightye god, whom I beseache to graunte unto me trewe and hartye repentance, p'fecte pacience in all myne afflicc'ons, and a lyvelie and constante faithe in Jesus Christe, and continuance in the same unto the ende and in the end. Amen.

Wyttnesses to this p'sente will is John Merye aforesayde, Henrye clerke aforesayd, Thomas Gregson, Will'm harryson, with others.

Copied by J. Weston, Reg'rar.

Abstract of the 18 July 1584 will of Elizabeth Gregson, proved 24 July 1584.

I, Elizabeth Gregson, Wydow, late wyfe of Thom's gregson, latelye deceased, of Thurvaston in ye p'ysshe of Sutton in ye fyeld, w'hin contye of Darbye . . . . unto Gregorye my sone ye sume of one hundrethe poundse of lawfull englisshe mooneye, ye w'ch he shall receive at ye handes of Thom's gregson, Wyll'm gregson, John gregson, and Thom's goddarde when he, ye said Gregorye, hath xxi yeares of age; the w'ch sume of one h'ndreth poundes beinge nowe in ye hands of one Mr. Ilsleye . . . . these four to receive the same from Mr. Isleye [sic] and to give to Gregorye a byll of their hands, sealed for ye sure payme't thereof . . . . at ye xxj yere of his age . . . . unto ye said Gregorye my sonne, eyghtene poundes in currant mooneye yt Robt. Glossoppe . . . ou'th me. Also [to Gregory, a bed and various items of bedding, cloth, furniture and household fixtures] . . . . I bequeath unto Charles my sone, fourtye shylly'ge in currant mooneye. also I bequeath to ye rest of my sones: Thom's, a colt and twelve pou's in mooney. . . . Also, I bequeath [various household items and a colt] to John my sone . . . . to Joane his wyfe . . . . unto lytle John gregson my nephew, one lytle sylver spone. . . . unto Margerye my sone Will'm's wyfe . . . . unto my iij sones Wyll'm, John a'd Gregorye, and to Elyn harryson my daughter, vj li. vj s. viij d. yt my sone John oweth me. . . . to be equallye devyded amongest they . . . . to my doughter margerye goddarde, iiij li. x s. . . . . to my doughter Agnes Kynge, xiij li. x s. . . . to my doughter Anne borrowes, iiij li x s. . . . . to my daughter El'yn harryson, iiij li. x s. [and various household furnishings and clothing to each of her daughters] . . . . unto Jane harryson my nece [various household items] . . . . to ye p'rish church of sutto', vi s. viij d., to ye poore of ye p'rish of sutto' aforsaid, vi s. viij d., to evry one of my godchyldren, vi d. . . . . unto Gregorye my sone afore named, ye rent of ye farme now in the occupacyo' of Rycharde gregorye . . . . a'd said leasse once beinge ended, I wyll a'd devyse yt ye said Gregorye shall enter upo' ye wholle farme, and enjoye yt as hys own free land forever, payinge yerelye unto Wyll'm my sone so much mooney as is appoy'ted in hys father's wyll. Also, I ordey'e and make ye said Gregorye my sone my sole a'd full executor . . . . Also my sones Tho's Gregson, Wyll'm Gregson, a'd John Gregson and my sone-in-law, Tho's goddarde, my overseers.

[Witnesses:] Henrye Clarke, vycar of sutton aforesaid, John goddard, w'th others.

Abstract of the 12 July 1589 will of William Gregson of Crich, a township and extensive parish in Derbyshire, four miles west by south of Alfreton (J. H. F. Brabner, ed., *Comprehensive Gazetteer of*

England and Wales, 1897). Crich is about six miles north-northeast of Turnditch.

In the name of god, Ame', ye xij th daye of July in the xxx th yeare of the reyne of our sovereyne Ladie, Elizabeth . . . . I, Will'm Gregson of Crych in the comitie of Darby . . . . unto Robert walker, tow yos; unto John hursthous, tow yos; unto Richard Gregson, tow yos; unto Thomas Redfort, tow yos. Also, I give unto William gregson in respect of sume money yt I owe unto him, one cubbord; & unto Thomas Redfort, one foulden booard. Also, the resedue of my goods I geve unto my wyfe, & the use of the third p'te of my farme during her lyfe naturall. And I ordayne & make my said wyfe, Jone Gregson, my tru & lawful executrix, And my S'nne Will'm overser to see that this, my last will, be p'formed, as the[y] will answer to the contrarie att the Dredfull daye of Judgmet.
Witnesses: Robert Redfort, John Redfort, Rychard Masse, & Others.

Abstract of the 28 Feb. 1600 will of Alice Gregson, proved 5 July 1604.

The Laste of february, one thousand and syx hundryth, and In the three and fortyth yere of the raigne of our sovraigne Lady Elizabeth . . . I, ales grygson of Sherowe halle In the County of Derby, widdow . . . . my wyll is . . . . yt my sonne henry ma'ch hymselfe in maryage to the lyckynge and w'th the consent of Mr. Lawrance wryght of [Sudeson?] and Mr. arthur Lathbury of [Loone?] and James Draper of [Celand?]; and do well and truly pay unto eche of his three brothers forty marks of Curant Englyshe mony . . . . that is to say, to francis, twenty marks, and to thomas and RyChard grygson, other of them, twenty nobles a pece; and if that my sonne henry refuse to be ruled or advysed, or wyll not taCk the counsell of the afore namyd Mr. Wryght, Mr. Lathbury and James Drap', then my will and mynde [is] that he shall pay unto his 3 brethren afore said, frances, thomas & rychard, to every of them, thyrty poundes a pece of good and lyCke mony aforesaid, w'hin one yere after his maryage as aforesaid. ffurther my wyll is that my sonne henry shall mack unto his brother thomas grygson, and to his heyres for ever, a good and p'fct assuerance in the law of the house in Burton-upon-Trent, and yf my sonne henry refuse . . . . he shall pay unto his brother thomas grygson, in Current Englyshe mony, the some of thre score pounds, to be payd unto the said thomas, his brother, w'in two yers after the aforesaid henry is come to the age of one and twenty yeres. Item, I gyve and bequath unto my sonne henry grygson . . . . the bedstead in the p'lor, the sealinge in p'lor and all the glas in the wyndoes; allso . . . . eyght poundes a yere . . . . untyll he doth come to the age of one and twenty yeres . . . . unto my daughter Maria, the porthon left by her father's wyll . . . . unto my daughter martha, thyrty pounds of Lawful Englyshe mony, whereof my wyll is that she shall have in household stufe to the valey of twenty poundes, and the rest in ready mony to mack up the thyrty pounds. . . . unto my daughter Martha, my wearynge apparel, both of my lynyn and woly. Allso, my wyll is that Martha, my daughter, shallbe w'th her brother hyll untyll such tyme as she shalbe maryed, and to have her porsion w'hin one yere next after my dyeathe . . . . unto thomas, frances & Rychard, my sonnes, theyre porcyons left them by thyr father's wyll. allso, my wyll is that this, my sayd lyvynge, shallbe set forth towardes the bringing up of thomas, franCes & RyChard grygson, my sunes and to the paying of them theyr porChons . . . . unto my mother mery, in money, the some of ten shillynges; and to an hyll, my daughter, in mony, other ten shillynge; and to mary yeare, my daughter, other ten shyllinges. Item, I gyve unto every chyld that I am grandmother unto, fyve shyllynges a peCe. And I gyve unto the pore of the p'she of suton, wheare I am a parishioner, in mony, three shyllynge, foure pence. Item, I gyve unto the church in mony, three shylynges, foure pence. Allso, yf my sonne hill wyllbe Content to be one of my exeCutors . . . I gyve unto hyme for his paynes therein to be taCken, the some of fower pounds; but if he refuses to taCk upon hym to be my executor, then my wyll and mynd is that he shall have but fyve shillings in money. and I Constystute, make and ordayne my

131

lovynge frynds, my sonne-In-Law, Larance hyll and my sonne henry gregson my executors . . . . and I gyve unto eche of them for theyre panes therein to be taCken, fouer pounds a peCe of Lawfull Englysh mony. allso, my wyll is that all that . . . . doth aryse owte of my lyvynge shallbe equally devyded to and amonge thomas, frances and RyChard grygson, my sonnes. allso, I do desyer James Draper, my brother-in-Law, and grygory yearye, my sonne-In-Law, to be ove'sers of this, my last will and testament, and I gyve unto them for theyre paynes thereunto betaken, five shillings a peCe of Currant Englishe mony . . . .

[Witnesses:] James Drap', ffrances Lathburye.

Abstract of the 27 Aug. 1670 will of George Gregson Sr. of Turnditch, proved 22 Sept. 1670. Turnditch (All Saints) is a chapelry in the parish of Duffield, union of Belper, hundred of Appletree, south division of the county of Derby (Lewis, *op. cit.*). Turnditch is about six miles north-northeast of Thurvaston.

George Gregson the elder of Turnditch, in the County of Derby, gen. . . . . unto my Loveinge wife, all my Jewells, plate, Chaines, bracelets, rings And one-halfe of my household goods whatsoever, to make use of duringe her naturall life. Item, after the decease of my said wife I give & bequeath all my said Jewells [etc.] and one-halfe of my said household goods to my two daughters, Mary & Anne Gregson, equally to be devided betwixt them . . . & . . . . Thirty pounds apeece, to be paid unto them by my Exec'tor hereafter named w'thin Eighteene months next after my decease . . . . and . . . . ffive pounds apeece yearely & evy yeare untill they shall attaine theire sev'all & respective ages of one & twenty yeares. Item, I give unto my eldest Sonne, George Gregson, the longe table standinge in the Hall, w'th all the benches thereunto belonginge, & all my latin bookes & Doctor hamonds Comentary upon the new testament. Item, I give, devise & bequeath unto my second Sonne, Phillipp Gregson, all those my lands, tenements & herediments in Windley now in the possession of Richard Woodhouse or of his assignes . . . . Item, I give all my Sonns & Sonns-in-lawe, And all my daughters & daughters-in-lawe, Tenne Shillings apeece to buy them mourneinge rings. It'm, I give to all & eny of my Grandchildren, two shillings, six pence a peece to buy them gloves. It'm, I give & bequeath unto my said sonne Phillipp Gregson, all the rest & residue of my p'sonall estate of what kinde, nature or Condition fo'ever, not before herein devised, he payinge my debts, legacies & funerall expenses. And I doe hereby nominate & appoint my said Sonne Phillipp to be Sole Executor of this, my last Will & testam't. . . . In witnes whereof I have hereunto put my hand & seale this Twenty seventh day of August in the two & twentieth yeare of the rayne of or Sov'aigne Lord, Charles the second, by the grace of God of England, Scotland, ffrance & Ireland, kinge, defender of the faith. Annoque dm. 1670.

[Signed:] G. Gregson [*without* seal]

[Witnessess:] Geo. Gregson Jun.; W. Turner; Eliz: Lee; Jane Harrison

---

Gregson Wills Probated at the Prerogarive Court of Canterbury

(Registers seen in 1967 at Somerset House, London, but moved in 1970 to the Public Record Office)

The 30 July 1539 will of Mr. Edward Gregson, parson of Fladbury, proved 1 July 1540 (P.C.C. 8 Alenger). Fladbury is a parish and village three miles northwest of Evesham, Worcestershire.

30 July a thousand fyve hundreth and nyne and thyrty, I, Maister Edward Gregeson, p'sonne of ffladburye in the Dioc. of Worcester, make this my testament and last will . . . to be buried in the channcell of the churche of ffladburye . . . to Thomas Charneley, my s'v'nt, twenty shillings . . . to Margaret Lewes, my S'v'nt, twenty shillings . . . to Margaret Cowp' [Cooper?], my S'v'nt, twenty shillings, provyded alwais that if it happen the said Thomas, Margaret and Margaret, or any of them, do depart and go from my S'v'ce before my departure out of this present lif, that then I will that any of the said bequests to the said Thomas, Margaret and to any one that dep'tithe of them, shalbe as no bequest, and shall stand in none effect; and I will that my executor shall in no wise stand charged with the same. It'm, I bequeath and give unto Mr. Rauff Aynesworth, fellowe of peter house in Cambrydge, my Chalice, a paire of vestments and a boke, the which one Sr. Richard Kendall, prest, hath in his kepying, the which saith masse for my father and mother in the p'yshe Church of preston in Amoundornes in Lanc. It'm, I bequeath ten pounds to poore folkes, the which shalbe Distributed by the Discretion of my Executor. Item, I bequeath unto Kateryn Currer vj £., xxij s., iiij d. which is and shalbe in the Custodye of Laurence Aynesworthe unto she be mariede, and if it happen the said Kateryne to dye, dep'te this p'nt lif before she be maried or if it happen the said kateryne to myskarye and do not kepe herself a good woman unto she be maried, as is before said, That then I will this bequest to be as voide and of none effect, And then I give and bequeith the said Some of vj £., xiij s., iiij d. unto the said Laurence Aynesworth and John Aynesworth his brother, to be divided equally betwixt them. The Resydue of all and singular, my goods . . . I bequeith and give to John Aynesworth, Late my S'v'nt, whom I do constitute, ordeyne and make by these p'nts my full and sole executor. In wytnes whereof to this p'nt will I have subscribed my name and sett my Seale the day and yere above namyd. Teste, Raduphe Aynesworthe, Clico; Joh'e Browne of per'she; Will'm harryson de Cadyaok. p'me, Edwardi Gregson

---

The 20 Oct. 1595 will of Thomas Gregson of Sherrow Hall, proved 30 Dec. 1595 (long religious preamble omitted) (P.C.C. 74 Scott).

In the name of God the ffather, the sonne and the hole ghoste, Amen. The twentethe Day of october, Anno dm. 1595. I, Thomas Gregsonne of Sherehall in the Countie of Darbie . . . . ffirst, I give and bequeathe to Alice my wief, the use and occupation of all my landes, makinge no voluntarie wast, to bringe upp my children at the schoole till such time as my heire come to th'age of one & twentie yeares, and then yt my said heire to have and enioye the'one half of the Sherehall, with th'appurtenace, and his mother th'other. Also, I give and bequeathe unto my sonne heirre Gregsonne my bible, the best bed I have, excepte one with the furniture thereto belongeinge, the Longe table and frame standinge in the hall. Also, I give unto Thomas Gregsonne my sonne, one house situate and beinge in Burton-uppon-trent, with th'appurtence', which house I bought of Anthony Gilbert. And also I give to the said Thomas my sonne, one hundrethe markes of currant englishe money, to be paid unto him by my executors when he shall come to the age of 23th yeares. Also, I give and bequeathe to ffranncis my sonne, one hundrethe marks of currant money of England, to be paid unto him by my Executors when he shall come to the'age of 24th yeares. Also, I give and bequeathe to Mary Gregsonne & Martha, my daughters, either of them, one hundrethe poundes of usuall englishe money, to be paid by my Executors to them and either of them when they shall come to th'age of 21th yeares [if] they wilbe ruled and counselled in matchinge themselves in marriage by there mother, my brother henry mery, John Gregsonn, Thomas Goddard or any two of them, my wief thereunto yeildinge her consent. But if they or either of them will not be ruled by these, their foresaide frendes, Then my will is that they and either of them shall have but five poundes a peece, and provide for themselves as they thinke good; and the rest of their porcons to be equally devided among the rest of my children. Also, my will is that my sonne Henry Gregsonn, when he shall to the age of one and twentie yeares as is beforesaid, over and besides the one half of Sherehall with th'appurtenice', shall have the

use and occupacon of all my Landes, meadowes and pastures, with th'appurtennce' which I have purchased, situate, lyinge and beinge in the parrishe of
Sutton, till such time as my sonne Richard come to the age of 21th years, and
then the said Henrye, my sonne, shall pay unto the said Richard Gregsonne my
sonne, the sume of one hundrethe poundes of Lawfull Englishe money, and soe
keepe the saide landes to himself and his heires for ever, if he will. But and if
he will not pay unto my sonne Richard the some before specified when he shall
come to the age of 21th, or within one year after, Then my will is that my sonne
Richard shall have and enioye the landes, meadowes & pastures, with their appurtennce' before mencoed, to himself and his heirs for ever, which I purchased
within the parrishe of Sutton. But if any of my Children doe dye before they
come to the severall ages before menco'ed, Then my will is that theire porc'ons
so dyinge, shall remaine th'one half to my wief, Alice Gregsonn, and th'other
half to be equallie distributed amonge the rest of my Children liveinge. Also, I
give and bequeath to Lawrence Hill, my sonne, one spurr Royall, and to my
daughter, his wife, six silver spones. And to Henrie Hill, their sonne, one silver
spone. Also, I give unto ffranncis Pegge, one twinter heiffer with a calf, to be
deliverd to my brother henrie Mery to the said ffranncis, his use, at may day
nexte. Also, I give and bequeathe to maister Weawall, my pastor, tenn shillings.
To the Churche, six shillings, eighte pence. to the poore in the parrishe, six
shillings, Eight pence. Also, I doe give twentie shillings to be bestowede in mend-
inge the highe waies about hardlowe hill before midsomer nexte. Also, I give and
bequeath to all my godchildren and servants, twelve pence apeece. And of this,
my last will and testament, I doe ordaine and make Alice Gregsonn, my wief,
and Richard Gregsonne, my sonne, my true and lawfull executors, to see this my
will, and everie parte and percell thereof, to be fathfully and truly accomplished
accordinge to the true meaninge thereof. And I do revooke and call back all will
or wills heretofore by me made, from the begininge of my lief at any time till
the present day of the date hereof. Also, I doe desire maister henrie Meery,
maister Thomas Goddard, John Gregsonne and Gregory Gregsonn, my brethren, to be the overseers of this, my last will and testament.

By me, Thomani Gregson.

Theis beinge witnesses: Robert Wawall, Cler., Lawrence hill.

Condensation of the 20 Jan., 4 James (1607) will of John Gregson
of Thurvaston, proved 1 June 1607 (P.C.C. 56 Huddlestone).

John Gregson the elder of Over Thurvaston in the Countie of Derbye, yeoman . . . . to be buried in the parish church of Sutton at the discrecon of my
Executrix . . . . unto John Gregson my sonne, that my farme in Oslaston, with
all th'appurten'nces, to enter uppon it at th'annunciacon of the virgin Marie
next following the date hereof; and if he die without have' males of his bodie
lawfully begotten, the same farme to come to Richard Gregson my sonne, and the
heire males of his bodie lawfully be gotten; And for wante thereof, to come to
Thomas Gregson my sonne [etc.] . . . . to Edward Gregson my sonne [etc.] . . . .
And for wante thereof, to return to the lawful heires of John Gregson for ever.
Alsoe, if my saide sonne John Gregson doe marry with the likinge and consent
of Joane Gregson, his mother, then I give unto him all my landes I have purchased
of whomever, to enter uppon them at the said daie of his marriage, except onely
a close called by the name of ffistlio close, which I give unto Joane Gregson my
wief during her naturall life, and harlowe meadowe and swansneth, which I
give unto Edward Gregson my sonne; But with this Proviso: that if my saide
sonne John Gregson will pay or cause to be paid unto my sonne Edward, when
he cometh to the age of full seaventene yeres, One hundreth pounds of curraunt
English money, to be putt forth to the use of the saide Edward, soe that he
maye receive both the stock and increase when he commeth to the age of fower
and Twentie yeres, That then my saide sonne John Gregson shall have the
two p'cells of groundes. . . to him and the heire males of his bodie lawfully
begotten for ever. Also, I give unto Joane Gregson my wief all the lands my
father Gregson gave me for and during her naturall life, And after her death

134

the same lands to returne to John Gregson, my sonne, and the heire males of his bodie lawfully begotten; then all the lands before specified, the ffarme in Oslaston onelie excepted, to come to Robert Grigson my sonne, and the heire males [etc.] . . . to Will'm Grigson my sonne [etc.] . . . . to Richard gregson my sonne [etc.] . . . . to Thomas Gregson my sonne [etc.] . . . . to Edward Gregson my sonne [etc.]; And for want of heire males of the saide Edward lawfullie begotten, then to return to the right heires of the saide John Gregson. Also, I give unto Robert, William, Richard and Thomas Gregson, my sonnes, every of them, One hundreth poundes to be paide unto them by my Executrix when they come to the age of fower and twentie yeres. Also, if Anne, Elizabeth and Anne [sic] Gregson, my daughters, doe marrie with the consent and likinge of Joane Gregson my wief, Then I give to every one of them One hundreth poundes, to be paide by my Executrix at the dayes of their marriages. But if they will not be ruled by her in their choices, then shall they have but five pounds a peece, and no more. And which soever of my children dye, their porcons unpaide, the porcons of them soe dyenge shall be equallie devided amonge the reste. Also, I give unto Joane Gregson my wife, the lease of that farme in Thurvaston wherein I now dwell, duringe her naturall Life. And if she die before that every childe have their porcons paide, my will is that she pass the saide lease in truste to any frende she liketh for and during the space of Tenne yeres after her death for the payment of those porcons then unpaid; And then the Revercon of the saide lease to return to John Gregson my sonne, and his heires. Also, I give to the parish church of Sutton, x s. To the poore of the same parish, x s. To Mr. Waywall, x s. To every one of my godchildren, vij d. To the mending of the high wayes in the towneshippes of Thurvaston and Oslaston, x s. All the rest of my goodes, moveable and unmoveable whatsoever, my debts, legacies and funerall expenses discharged, I give to Joane Gregson my wief, whom I make my sole and onely Executrix, to see this my last will and Testament faithfullie p'formed accordinge to my true intente and meaninge therein. And I make my brother Gregorie Gregson and my cosen [i.e., nephew] Henrie Gregson, and Mr. James Drax the Overseers of the same.

Signum Johannis Gregson

[Witnesses:] Edward Neale (his marke), Thomas Trobshawe, Henrie Harrison (his marke).

Abstract of the 16 Dec. 1623 will of Gregory Gregson of Thurlaston proved 1 March 1623/4 (P.C.C. 24 Byrde). Thurlaston is a parish in the union of Blaby, hundred of Sparkenhoe, some six miles west-southwest of the city of Leicester. Thurlaston, Leicestershire, is, accordingly, about 25 miles southeast of Thurvaston, Derbyshire.

I, Gregorie Gregson of rough Bracker Holme [?] in the parish of Thurlston and County of Leicester, yeoman . . . unto Elizabeth my wife, the yearlie interest and increase of one hundred and fortie pounds which is now in sundrie men's hands . . . . during all the term of her naturall life if she continue widowe, but if she marry againe, then but the one-halfe of the said interest and increase, namely, seaven pounds a year; And the other seaven pounds a year to bee yearlie devided amongst all my children equally, My sonne Edward onlie excepted, and hee to have noe parte thereof. And to him I give one silver spoone for his portion. Item, for my stock of one hundred and fortie pounds, I will that it shall be devided thus: To my daughter Pricscilla I give six pounds, thirtene shillings, fowre pence . . . . to my sonne James, thirtie pounds . . . . to my daughter Dorothie, twentie six pounds, six shillings, eight pence . . . . to my daughter Elizabeth, xxvi li., vi s., viij d. All which to bee paid . . . . by my Executors within six monthes next after my wive's decease. And if it shall please god that anie of my said children shall departe this life before the time that the said portions shall become due, That then my will is that theire portions, soe deceased, shalbe equallie devided amongst the rest of my children then living, my sonne Edward still excepted. And I doe give to John Samon, the writer of this my will, iij s.,

iiij d. All the rest of my goods . . . I give to Elizabeth my wife, James my sonne, and Dorothie and Elizabeth my daughters, equally to be devided amongst them. And doe make Elizabeth my wife and James my sonne my full Executors. And doe entreate my cozen John Latham, and my sonne Edward Gregson, to be overseers to see this my will performed. In Witnes hereof I, the said Gregory Gregson . . . . have hereto put my hand the sixtenth daie of December, Anno Dni. 1623.
Witnessed by me, John Samon, Curate.

The undated will of Richard Gregson of London, proved 31 Aug. 1640 (P.C.C. 116 Coventry). Although an abstract of this will appears in THE REGISTER, 46:151, a somewhat more generous abstract is here given in order to have in one place all known wills relating to the Gregson family of Derbyshire.

My body to be buried in the church of sainte Augustins, St. Austin's Gate, as neare and as conveniently as I may unto the bons of my deceased wife, who hath been formerly buryed in the same church, without pomp or ostentacon, and soe without mourninge cloth or stuffe or like; and for other things concerning my buriall, I leave it to the discretion of my executor . . . to Ephraim Udall of this parrishe, 40 s. . . . . unto my father-in-lawe, Mr. Nich. Hurt, and unto Mrs. Dorothy his wife, and to my deare and loving brother, Mr. Henry Gregson, and unto Edith his wife, To Mr. William Dickins, Mr. John Goddard, Mr. Robert Lewis and Mr. Thomas Haford, to every severall person thus named, twenty shillings a peece. I will and bequeath to George Gregson that lyveth in Paternoster Roe, five pounds, and for the residue of the money that hee shall pay it in to my executors att yeare and yeares after the tyme of my decease. Item, I give and bequeath to my servant, Ann Hill, all the money that she oweth mee; if it fall out uppon accompte twenty shillings, that it shalbee made upp twenty shillinges . . . . to Mary Arnold, my now nurse, tenn s. . . . . unto my kinsman Thomas Gregson, my nowe partner, and to his wife Mary, and to Mr. Thomas Howrne, twenty shillings a piece; and to Thomas Gregson in new England, twenty shillinges . . . . unto Nicho., my eldest sonne, what soever shalbee recovered of Roger Stephens and George Burtun or from either of their estates, lands or chattells belonginge to either of them. Item, the remainder of my estate, whether Jewells, plate, lease or leases, with all manner of household stuffe, shalbee equally devided unto my aforesaid sonne Nicholas, John, Thomas, Anne, and Elizabeth, equall shares part and part alike. My mind and will beinge that first, all my inst' debtts, whether they bee my own personall debtts or debtts by mee oweinge in partnershipp, my true and reall debtts being first payd. It., I will and bequeathe unto my now partner, Thomas Gregson, fiftye pounds in full satisfaccon of what money hee doth pretend hee hath lent unto my cosen, Thomas Gregson in Newe England, and unto mee, Richard Gregson, his naturall unckle. It., I will and bequeathe unto my cosen, Richard Gregson of Bristol, one Judgement confessed by one Samuel Oldfeild unto Thomas Gregson, which the said Thomas assigned to me. It., I will and bequeathe unto the said Richard Gregson of Bristol, one deed or Indenture made over and assigned by one Roger Clisant, Vintner of the said Citty of Bristoll . . . . I doe make and ordeine by this, my last will and testament, my deare and loving sonne Nicholas Gregson, my sole executor . . . . I doe heereby earnestly intreate these, my loving kindred and friends heereafter named, as my father-in-lawe, Mr. Nicho. Hurt; my brother-in-lawe, Mr. Rogert Hurt; my naturall brother, Mr. Henry Gregson; Mr. John Goddard, Citizen and Grocer of London; first cosen, Mr. William Dickens, gent.; Mr. Robert Lewise, Citizen and Grocer of London; and Mr. William Baker, an Attorny att the King's Ma'ties Courte at Westminster; to whome I bequeath twenty shillinges, that they and every of them would bee pleased to councell and advise and to assiste my foresaid named executor. This, my last will and testament, is written uppon wone-halfe sheete of paper and two whole sheets, with my name subscribed, w'th my hand and seale sett too att the side or foote of theis three peeses of paper, with my owne hand and seale, without anye [witnesses] subscribed, but onely Marye Arnold, my nowe nurse keeper.

Witnessed by mee, Mary Arnold (her marke).

Richard Gregson

GREGSON WILLS PROVED IN THE
BISHOP OF LONDON'S COMMISSARY COURT

Abstracted by the English genealogist,
Jo-Ann (Mrs. John) Buch of Colchester, Essex

The original 29 Aug. 1565 will of Robert Grigson of the Citie of London, Habourdasher, proved 19 Sept. 1565 (Ref., 15/233v., 1565).

He desired to be buried in the church called "Christes Church in the Citie of London," and made bequests to his father, John Grigson, £5. 40 shillings each to his elder brother John and his brothers Will(ia)m, Thom(a)s and Edward; 40 shillings to his sister Catharine and another 40 shillings to Alice, his wife's sister; 40 shillings to the poor; 10 shillings to his "boye" Edward (no doubt his apprentice), "to contynue his diligent service to his M[ist]r[es]s"; 10 shillings to Peter Grigge, "boocher", and a like amount to John Dowrishe, "Scolemaster"; 5 shillings to R[ichar]d Carter's wife; and to John Harrison, Brewer, and Rich[ard] Carter, baker, to each of them, "a bowe and shaftes." The testator also aquitted John Amourton of a debt of 18 chillings and Rich[ard] Carter of 5 shillings. Executrix, wife Margaret; witnesses: John Harrison [signed by mark], Richard Carter and Johannes Dourish.

The 25 Jan. 1663/4 will (registered copy) of Thomas Gregson of Wapping, co. Middlesex, citizen and draper of London, proved 11 July 1664 (Ref., 20/120, 1664).

He provided that "At my funeral onely a sprigg of Rosemary shall be given to them that are invited to see my corps interred." He forgave "unto son-in-law Edward Moore of parish of Stebenheath alias Stepney in the said co. of Middlesex, Mariner, and unto my daughter Mary his wife—all such sums of money as she doth owe unto me. All such bonds and Bills and writings as are now in my hands belonging unto him. . . to be delivered unto him by my executrix suddenly after my decease." To William Brasse of parish of Stebenheath otherwise Stepney, Tincker, and Hanna his wife, "Who pretendeth to be the daughter of my now wife," twelve pence each. To son Thomas Gregson and to daughter Edith Gregson, twelve pence each. To friends Edward Wallis of parish of Stebenheath, Gent., and William Tomlinson of Wapping, Citizen and Draper of London, whom he made overseers of his will, five shillings each, to buy them gloves "as a remembrance of my love." He gave to his wife, Mary Gregson, his executrix, the remainder of all his estate during her life, after which the residue was to be devided equally between his sons Henry Gregson and Philip Gregson; if "either depart this life before the age of 21 years or day of marriage, his part to survivor for ever." Witnesses, Thomas Guy and James (Mallard, Scribe?).

ST. MICHAEL OLD ANGELS,
SUTTON-ON THE-HILL, DERBYSHIRE

Entries taken by the author from the church register from its beginning in 1567 through 1618. Entries from 5 March 1597/8 to 3 June 1598, and from 1618 to January 1623 are omitted in the register.

Gegerie Gregson, fil. Thom. Gregson, Bapt. 4 July 1567.
Thom. Goddard and Margerie Gregson married 29 June 1574.
Eliz. Gregson, fil. Thom. Gregson, Bapt. 20 Feb. 1574/5.
Willia' Gregson and Margerie Rowe maried 5 May 1576.
Marie Gregson, fil. Thomas. gregson, bapt. 2 March 1577/8.
Thomas Kinge and Agnes gregsone maried 6 July 1579.
Martha Gregson, fil. Thom. Gregson, bapt. 12 Feb. 1580/1.
Willia' Burrowe and Anne gregson maried 26 Julie 1582.
Henrie Gregson, fil. Thoma. Gregson, bapt. 27 March 1583.
John Gregson, fil. Johan's Gregsone, bapt. 2 June 1583.
Elizab. Gregson, fil. Thom. gregson, buried 11 Jan. 1583/4.
Thomas Gregson, senior buried 23 Aprill 1584.
Elizab. Gregson, widowe, buried 24 July 1584.
Thomas Gregson, fil. Thom. Gregson, bapt. 9 May 1585.
Robt. Gregson, fil. Johan's Gregson, bapt. 23 July 1585.
ffrancis Gregson, fil. Thom. Gregson, bapt. 29 June 1586.
Anne Gregson, fil. Johan's Gregson, bapt. 29 Feb. 1587/8.
Edward Gregson, fil. Gregorii Gregson, bapt. 25 June 1589.
Willia' Gregson, fil. Johan's Gregson, bapt. 25 June 1589 [sic].
Arthure Gregson, fil. Thom. Gregson, bapt. 24 Feb. 1590/1.
Priscilla Gregson, fil. Gregorij Gregson, bapt. 23 Apr. 1592.
Arthure Gregson, fil. Thom. Gregson, buried 14 Oct. 1592.
Elizabeth Gregson, fil. Johan' Gregson, bapt. 23 Dec. 1593.
Lawrance hill and Ann Gregsone married 22 May 1594.
Susanna Gregson, fil. Thom. Gregson, bapt. 13 Sept. 1594.
The same Susanna Gregson buried 14 Sep. 1594.
Joseph Gregson, fil. Gregorii Gregson, bapt. 29 Jan. 1594/5.
Thomas Gregson, yeoman, buried at London 21 Dec. 1595.
Richard Gregson, fil. Johan's Gregson, bapt. 8 Aug. 1596.
Marie Gregson, fil. Gregorii Gregson, bapt. 12 June 1597.
Gregorie heire and Marie Gregsonne married 13 Nov. 1597.
Anne Gregson, fil. Johan's Gregson, bapt. 11 Feb. 1598/9.
Thomas Gregson, fil. Gregorie Gregson, bapt. 13 Jan. 1599/1600.
Widow Gregson buried the 19 April 1601.
James Gregson, fil. Joh'is Gregson and Joanna his wife, bapt. 19 July 1601.
James Gregson, fil. Joh'is Gregson, buried 23 Sep. 1601.
James Grigson, fil. Gregorij Grigson et Eliza., bapt. 26 Jan. 1602/3.
Dorothie Gregson, daughter of Gregorij Gregson et Eliz., bapt. 22 Apr. 1605.
Phillip Gregson, son of Henry Gregson and Millisant his wife, bapt. 28 June 1605.
Edward Gregson, son of John Gregson, bapt. 25 Dec. 1605.
George Gregson, son of Henrici Gregson and Idith his wife, bapt. 5 Nov. 1606.
John gregson buried 22 Jan. 1606/7.
Alice Gregson, daughter of Henrici Gregson and Ideth, bapt. 30 Apr. 1609.
Willia' Cockera' and Anne Gregson married 4 June 1610.
Catheren Gregson, fil. Joh. Gregson and Marie his wife, bapt. 4 June 1610.
Willa' Gregson, fil. Edwardi Gregson et Margerie his wife, bapt. 25 May 1614.

ENGLISH ANCESTRY OF MR. THOMAS GREGSON OF NEW HAVEN

By Paul. W. Prindle, F.A.S.G., of Darien, Conn.

The Gregson Family of Derbyshire and London

As noted below, it is believed that the ancestry of Thomas Gregson of New Haven, Conn., can be traced, with reasonable confidence, to the Thomas Gregson of Thurvaston, Derbyshire, whose will was dated 27 Jan. 1583. According to an entry in the register of St. Michael Old Angels, Sutton-on-the-Hill, Derbyshire, his son Thomas was buried in London 21 Dec. 1595, which ties this Derbyshire family to the London Gregsons. There were, however, other early Gregsons living in Derbyshire and in London, or whose wills were probated at Canterbury, to whom the above Thomas may have been related.

The following family group may be reconstructed from the 1565 will of Robert "Grigson", haberdasher, of London:

JOHN GREGSON SR., living in 1565, who had children:

    i.   JOHN JR., living in 1565 and older than his brother Robert.

    ii.   ROBERT, London haberdasher, maker of the 1565 will and apparently childless. His wife Margaret had a sister Alice.

    iii. WILLIAM, perhaps the one of that name who lived in Crich, Derbyshire, and whose will of 1589 named wife Joan and son William. He made a minor bequest to an unidentified Richard Gregson.

    iv. THOMAS, possibly the Thomas Gregson of Thurvaston, Derbyshire, whose will was drawn in 1583.

    v.   EDWARD.

    vi. CATHARINE.

Another early Gregson was Edward, parson of Fladbury, Leicestershire, who, surely unmarried, made his will on 30 July 1539. Masses for his parents were said in the parish church in Preston, Lancastershire. He may have been an uncle, perhaps an older brother, of the John Gregson Sr. above. It should be noted that a William Harryson of Cadayack witnessed this Edward's will in 1539. The 1565 will of Robert Grigson was witnessed by a John Harrison; a William Harrison witnessed the 1583 will of Thomas[1] Gregson, whose daughter Ellen, as shown by the 1584 will of his widow, married a Harryson, perhaps this William; a Henrie Harrison was a witness to the 1607 will of John[2] Gregson; and, many years later, a Jane Harrison witnessed the 1670 will of George[4] Gregson Sr. It might also be noted that John Gregson Sr. (above) named a son Edward; and that John[2] Gregson did likewise.

The Robert "Grigson" of London, maker of the 1565 will, called himself a "habourdasher", a trade closely allied to that of "draper", the occupation, according to Percival Boyd in his Citizens of London collection at The Society of Genealogists, London, of Richard Gregson (Boyd's No. 15393; No. 7 infra); Gregory Gregson (No. 38005; son of James, No. 9); John Gregson and James Gregson (No. 38005; sons of James and putative grandsons of James Gregson, No. 9); Thomas Gregson of Stepney (No. 38006; No. 12), and Thomas Gregson of St. Botolph Aldergate (No. 49229; son of Gregory Gregson, No. 4), all members of the Derbyshire and London Gregsons. These extremely tenuous relationships tend to tie the Derbyshire and London Gregsons to Robert "Grigson" of London and to the Gregsons of Preston, Lancastershire. There were many Gregson families in the Preston and Whalley areas of Lancastershire in the sixteenth and seventeenth centuries, and claims have been made that Thomas[1] Gregson came originally from that section of England. A comparison of given names lends some support to the theory that Thomas[1] Gregson was the Thomas, son of John Gregson Sr. above. John Gregson Sr. gave the names John, Robert, William, Thomas and Edward to his sons. Thomas[1] Gregson named sons John, William and Thomas; and John[2] Gregson gave the names John, Robert, William, Thomas and Edward to his sons, precisely the same names as those used by John Gregson Sr. These are all common names, however; consequently, one should be reluctant to attach too much significance to their repetition. In this account, therefore, the parentage of Thomas[1] Gregson is considered to be unproven, and our genealogical account of the Derbyshire family will begin with him.

The Gregson genealogical compilation which follows is not claimed to be complete. It is based primarily on the wills and parish register records rendered above, and on published records. No investigation of chancery and other legal actions, inquisitions, post mortems, deeds, manor rolls or subsidy and tax returns has been attempted.

1. THOMAS[1] GREGSON, the earliest ancestor claimed herein for the emigrant Thomas Gregson of New Haven, is that Thomas of the 27 Jan. 1583 will.

An account "found among the papers of John Milnes, Esq." shows Thomas Gregory [sic, should be Gregson] as having married ANN TWIFORD, "daughter and heir of Wil'm Twiford of Sherrow Hall." It was through this marriage that the Gregson family came into possession of Sherrow Hall. Thomas and Ann are shown as having four sons: (1) Thomas Gregson, married Ann [sic, she was Alice, as shown by his and her wills, infra], daughter of Henry Merry Esq. of Barton Blount; (2) John Gregson; (3) William Gregson, and (4) Gregory Gregson (The Publications of the Harleian Society, 37:216-7).

Thomas must have married, secondly, ELIZABETH ——, referred to in his will.

Thomas Gregson bequeathed the major part of his property to son John, and a substantial part to minor son Gregory who was, no doubt, living with Elizabeth. The will pointedly refers to Gregory's "owne mother" [Elizabeth] and to "his owne brethrene, Thomas Gregson and Will'm Gregson." Elizabeth's 18 July 1584 will styles all of Thomas' children as "my sonnes" or "my daughters". After making bequests to son John and his wife Joane, Elizabeth left "unto lytle John Gregson, my nephew, one lytle sylver spone"; and after a bequest to daughter Ellen Harryson, Elizabeth left various household effects "unto Jane harryson, my nece."

Anthony J. Camp, B.A., Director of Research of The Society of Genealogists, London, was asked if, at that time and place, the terms "nephew" and "niece" could have the present day meaning of "grandson" and "granddaughter". Mr. Camp said there was a remote possibility of such usage, but felt there was a far greater probability that the terms then signified "step-grandson" and "step-granddaughter". John and Ellen, parents of the two children, are therefore considered identified as children of Thomas by his first wife, and Ann is placed in the same category by reason of her given name. Based on the phraseology of Thomas' will, sons Thomas, William and Gregory are treated as Elizabeth's "owne" children, and the remaining children are arbitrarily assigned to the second marriage.

Thomas Gregson was buried at Sutton-on-the-Hill 23 April 1584, and his widow Elizabeth, 24 July 1584.

Children of Thomas[1] Gregson and first wife, Ann Twyford:

2. i. JOHN[2].
   ii. ELLEN, mar. —— HARRISON and had a daughter, Jane, all mentioned in her mother's will, which gave Ellen £6-1-8 and left various household items to Ellen and Jane. A William "harryson" was a witness to Thomas' will, which left Ellen a yoke of oxen, "w'ch she hath in her possessione allreadye." He may have been Ellen's husband.
   iii. ANNE, called Anne Borrowes [Burroughs] in Elizabeth's will, which gave her £4-10-0 and various household articles. Anne mar. WILLIAM BURROWE at Sutton-on-the-Hill, 26 July 1582. In his will, her father gave her a silver spoon.

Children of Thomas[1] Gregson and second wife, Elizabeth:

3. iv. THOMAS.
   v. WILLIAM, mar. MARJORIE ROWE on 5 May 1576, recorded in the register of St. Michael Old Angels, Sutton-on-the-Hill. No record of any will, administration or children of this couple has been found, and they are presumed to have died childless. His father's will made special provision for William. He was to receive the sum of 23 s., 4 d. yearly "duringe the tearme of the naturall lyffe of the sayd William", a form of bequest sometimes used to provide for persons not fully capable of providing for themselves. Nevertheless, perhaps to spare his feelings, his mother in her will, while confirming this annuity to be paid to William and leaving him £1-11-8 in money, made him, with his brothers Thomas and John and their brother-in-law Thomas Goddard, trustees of £100 left to their brother Gregory during his minority, and also made all four of them overseers of her will. Elizabeth also made a bequest to William's wife, "Margerye".
   vi. CHARLES. He was left 20 s. by the will of his father, and 40 s. by his mother, very modest bequests in comparison to those made to his brothers. No records of marriage, will or administration found. It is assumed he left no descendants.
   vii. MARGERY, mar. THOMAS GODDARD at Sutton-on-the-Hill, 29 June 1574. He was of Beeby, co. Leicester, son of John Goddard of Crosson of that county, and grandson of William Goddard of Berks (*The Visitation of London*—Cheap Ward, *Harleian, idem*, 15:319). Margery was left a silver spoon by the will of her father, and £4-10 and a portion of brass and pewter utensils by that of her mother, who made by her son-in-law, Thomas Goddard, one of the four overseers of her will. John Goddard, presumably his father, was one of the two witnesses. "Maister Thomas Goddard" was designated by Thomas[2] Gregson as one of his four "brethern" to oversee his 1595 will. Margery was incorrectly called "Margaret, daughter of John Gregson of Thurvaston" in *Harleian, idem*, 2:190. She and Thomas Goddard had at least two children: 1. *William Goddard* of Crosson, b. 1583. 2. *John Goddard,*

b. 1591. "Mr. John Goddard, Citizen and Grocer of London," was named as one of the seven "loving kindred and friends" requested by Richard[3] Gregson [No. 7] to be overseers of his will, proved 1640, and left 20 shillings. John Goddard married Dorothy, dau. of Nicholas Pendlebury of London, "descended out of Lancash'r by Mary his wife," and had a son Thomas Goddard, who d. inf. (*ibid.*, 15:319).

viii. AGNES, mar. 6 July 1579 at Sutton-on-the-Hill, THOMAS KINGE. She was given a silver spoon by the will of her father. Elizabeth left her daughter Agnes Kynge xiij li., x s., and a share of her wearing apparel and household effects.

4. ix. GREGORY.

2. JOHN[2] GREGSON (*Thomas[1]*), doubtless the eldest son of Thomas Gregson by first wife Ann Twyford, was the eventual devisee by his father's will to "the whole lease of my farme that I now dwell in [in Over Thurvaston] w'th all the appurtenances thereto belonginge"; plus "all my lande in Oslaston and Thurvaston aforesayd, w'ch I purchased of Richard Pomfret, of John Cooke, and of Edward yoman"; and four parcels of land "that did belonge to Sheerehall, and one hundrethe marks in currant money."

He was named as one of the four overseers of the will of his brother Thomas[2] Gregson.

John Gregson married JOAN ——, and was buried 22 Jan. 1606/7 at Sutton-on-the-Hill. His 20 Jan., 4 James (1607) will was proved 1 June 1607. It provided that, "if Anne, Elizabeth and Anne [*sic*] Gregson, my daughters, doe marrie with the consent and liking of Joan Gregson my wief, Then I give to every one of them One hundred pounds. . . ." Because John then had two surviving unmarried daughters named Anne Gregson, it would be reasonable to believe that he had given the name Anne to a daughter by each of two marriages, and that his second marriage had taken place during the four and one-half years between the baptisms of William in 1589 and Elizabeth in 1593. But that is not possible, for Elizabeth, widow of Thomas[1] Gregson, made a bequest in her 1585 will " to John my sonne . . . to Joane his wyfe. . . ." Since both Anne Gregsons were born *after* 1584, it is evident that they were both children of Joan, named to perpetuate the name of John's mother. This was not an uncommon occurrence, although generally those so named were half rather than full sisters (*The American Genealogist*, 36:158-9; 37:62-3). There remains the possibility, of course, that John *did* marry twice, each of his wives having been named Joan.

In his will, John left the lands he had inherited from his father to his wife during her life, then conditionally and successively to his sons, obviously named in the order of their births. Doubtless following the principle of primogeniture, John passed the bulk of his lands to his eldest son, John Jr., with other holdings going to Edward, youngest son, who would be expected to live longest with his widowed mother. In addition to the considerable holdings of lands bequeathed by John in his will, he gave £700 in money to his children other than John, Jr., and Edward, a very considerable amount for that time. John's brother Gregory and nephew Henry [No. 6] were named as overseers of his will. The Henri Harrison who, by his mark, subscribed as a witness to John's will, was presumably related to the Harrison who married John's sister Ellen.

John was one of the four overseers of his stepmother's will, which left him £1-11-8 in money, "a colt, a fether bedde, a'd my brazen mortar." Joane, his wife, was given "a kettell, a paire of canvas shetes, and vij peuter dysshes yt goo aboute in ye house".

John Gregson and wife Joan had ten children, all unmarried at the date of their father's will (baptisms and burials having been recorded in the register of St. Michael Old Angels, Sutton-on-the- Hill):

i. JOHN[3], bapt. 2 June 1583; mar. MARIE ——. He was called "lytle John Gregson, my nephew" [i.e. step-grandson] by Elizabeth, widow of Thomas[1] Gregson, in her will, and left "one lytle sylver spone." On 4 June 1610, John Gregson and Marie, his wife, baptized a daughter Catherine. "A true & p'fecte Inventorie of all the goods, Chatles and rattes of John Gregson of Overthurvaston, yeoman, decease, [was] praysed the five and twentith day of Aprill . . . in the year of our Lord god 1620, by Thomas Stidman, James Walker, Thomas Hopkins."

ii. ROBERT, bapt. 23 July 1585; left £100 in father's 1607 will.
iii. ANNE, bapt. 29 Feb. 1587; received bequest of £100 from her father; mar. 4 June 1610 at Sutton-on-the-Hill, WILLIAM COCKERAL.
iv. WILLIAM, bapt. 25 June 1589; left £100 in will of father.
v. ELIZABETH, bapt. 23 Dec. 1593; left £100 in will of father.
vi. RICHARD, bapt. 8 Aug. 1596, and left £100 in will of father. He was not the Richard Gregson whose will was proved at Coventry 31 Aug. 1640, for that Richard made a bequest "to my deare and loving brother, Mr. Henry Gregson and unto Edith his wife. . . ."
5. vii. THOMAS, evidently bapt. during the 5 March 1597/8 to 3 June 1598 hiatus in the church register.
viii. ANNE [Jr.], bapt. 11 Feb. 1598/9. She was also left a bequest of £100 in the 1607 will of her father.
ix. JAMES, recorded as son of "Joh'is and Joanna his wife," was bapt. 19 July 1601 and bur. 23 Sept. 1601.
x. EDWARD, bapt. 25 Dec. 1605. He was left Hardlowe Meadow and Swansneth by his father's will of 1607. No further record seen.

3. THOMAS[2] GREGSON (*Thomas[1]*) was one of the three overseers under the terms of his father's will, and one of its witnesses. He, with his brother William and their mother Elizabeth, were to pass on the desirability of any marriage his brother Gregory might contemplate. Thomas[1] Gregson bequeathed his best horse to this son Thomas, but no devise of real estate was included in the will. Since this Thomas lived at Sherrow Hall and disposed of it in his will, it is evident he had received the property from his father before the 1583 drafting of the latter's will. Doubtless, Sherrow Hall was given to Thomas at the time of his marriage.

Thomas was named one of the four overseers of his mother's will, and left a colt and £12. He presumably married somewhat earlier than his elder brother John, for Thomas' firstborn was baptized in 1574/5, and John's in 1583, less than one year before their father's death. It is possible that John had contracted an earlier marriage, but the fact that the bulk of his father's lands passed to him by will rather than by deed rather negates that theory.

The register of St. Michael Old Angels in Sutton-on-the-Hill records the 21 Dec. 1595 burial in London of Thomas Gregson, yeoman.

His 20 Oct. 1595 will was proved 30 Dec. 1595 in the Prerogative Court of Canterbury and is reproduced above. In it, Thomas named "my brother henrie Mery" and made him one of the four overseers. Henry was Thomas' brother-in-law, for Thomas had married ALICE MERRY [see account of Thomas[1]]. The 31 Oct. 1599 will of "Symon Merry of Barton p'he in the County of Derby" is to be seen at the County Archivist's Office, Lichfield, Staffordshire. It mentions, among others, "John Merrye, the sonne of my brother Henry Merry . . . Henry Merry the younger . . . the rest of my brother Henry, his children . . . my brother John . . . Agnis, my mother . . my brother Drap' [Draper] . . . ."

Widow Alice (Merry) Gregson was buried at Sutton-on-the-Hill on 19 April 1601. In her 1600 will she named "James Draper, my brother-in-law," and he signed as a witness. There can be little doubt that Alice, Simon, Henry and John were siblings. A John Merye of Barton Park was one of the overseers and witnesses of the will of Thomas[1] Gregson. Presumably he was Alice's brother or uncle. It has not been determined how they were related to "Henry Merrie, Esq., sonne of Sir Henry Merry, knt., late whilst he lived of the p'ish of Barton Blount, Deceased", quoted from the 11 Aug. 1636 administration of Sir Henry, recorded at Lichfield. One of Sir Henry's daughters, Marie, was in her minority in 1636, so Sir Henry was probably of a later generation than Alice, Henry, Simon and John.

Thomas Gregson and wife Alice Merry had ten children (records from the register of St. Michael Old Angels, Sutton-on-the-Hill, Derbyshire):

    i.   ANN[3], mar. LAWRENCE HILL, 22 May 1594 at Sutton-on-the-Hill, and had son, *Henry Hill*, who was left one silver spoon in Thomas' will. Ann was left six silver spoons by her father, and 10 s. by her mother. Lawrence was given one spur royal by his father-in-law, witnessed the latter's will, and was named a co-executor of Alice's will.

    ii.   ELIZABETH, bapt. 20 Feb. 1574/5; bur. 11 Jan. 1583/4.

    iii. MARIE, bapt. 2 March 1577/8; mar. GREGORIE HEIRE [or Yeare], 13 Nov. 1597. Her father left "Mary" £100; her mother made a bequest to Mary of 10 s., and "unto my daughter Maria, the porthon left by her father's Wyll." Alice designated "grygory yearye, my sonne-In-Law," as one of the two overseers of her will.

    iv. MARTHA, bapt. 12 Feb. 1580/1. Her father gave her £100, and her mother, £30 worth of household goods and money, and her wearing apparel, "both of lynyn and woly"; she to live "w'th her brother hyll [brother-in-law Lawrence Hill] untyll such tyme as she shalbe maryed."

6. v.   HENRY, bapt. 27 March 1583.

    vi. THOMAS, bapt. 9 May 1585. He was legatee in his father's will of 100 marks and "one house situate and beinge in Burton-uppon-trent, with th'appurtence', which house I bought of Anthony Gilbert." In her will, Alice directed her son Henry to pay Thomas 40 nobles, and to see that Thomas received this house, or otherwise to pay him three score pounds more. No further reference to this Thomas has been identified. Since he was a brother, not a cousin, of the Richard Gregson whose will was proved in 1640, this Thomas could not have been the Thomas of New Haven; and since he was a brother of Richard, not a nephew, he could not have been Richard's partner.

    vii. FRANCIS, bapt. 29 June 1586. Francis was given a bequest of 100 marks in his father's will, and Alice in her will directed her son Henry to

pay 40 marks to Francis.
7. viii. RICHARD, baptismal record not found.
   ix. ARTHURE, bapt. 24 Feb. 1590/91; bur. 14 Oct. 1592.
   x. SUSANNA, bapt. 13 Sept. 1594; bur. 14 Sept. 1594.

4. GREGORY[2] GREGSON (*Thomas*[1]) was baptized 4 July 1567 at St. Michael Old Angels, Sutton-on-the-Hill, Derbyshire, and married ELIZABETH ———. He was named as one of the four overseers of the 1595 will of his brother Thomas.

In his 1583 will, Thomas Gregson left to his son Gregory "halfe my husbandry geare, as wagnes, ploughes, yockes, teames and such like things", and his house and lands in Over Thurvaston, then under lease to Richard Gregory, to take effect five years after the expiration of the lease. Gregory was to pay 23 s., 4 d. annually to his brother William during the latter's lifetime. Both these bequests were made conditionally. If Gregory did not "take a wiffe by the advise and consente of his owne mother and of his owne bretherne, Thomas Gregson and Will'm Gregson . . . he, the sayd Gregorye my sonne . . . shall have . . . onlye one hundrethe shillings in money, and goe wither he will. . . ."A year and a half later, Gregory's mother Elizabeth made her will, evidencing much more confidence in him than did his father, for she made Gregory her sole executor (although he was then only 17 years of age), and left him "eyghtene poundes in currant mooney yt Robt. Glossoppe . . . ou'th me"; £1-11-8 "yt my sone John oweth me, one hundrethe poundse of lawful englisshe mooneye . . . when he, ye said Gregorye, hath xxi yeares of age"; various household articles, and "ye rent of ye farme now in the occupacyo' of Rycharde gregorye."

The 16 Dec. 1623 will of "Gregorie Gregson of rough Bracker Holmes in the parish of Thurlston and County Leicester, yeoman," was proved 1 March 1623/4 (P.C.C. 24 Byrde), naming wife Elizabeth; sons Edward and James; daughters Priscilla, Dorothy and Elizabeth; and cousin John Latham.

Gregory and Elizabeth had eight known children, baptisms from the register of St. Michael Old Angels:

    i.   ELIZABETH[3], named in her father's will and given £26-6-8. She was probably the Elizabeth Grexson who mar. the widower THOMAS BAGNALL, citizen and draper, of London, at St. Nicholas Acons on 1 May 1610. She d. 15 April 1630, and he d. 21 Feb. 1653, both being bur. at St. Nicholas Acons (*Citizens of London, op. cit.*, No. 1011).

8. ii.   EDWARD, bapt. 25 June 1589.
    iii. PRISCILLA, bapt. 23 April 1592; she was left £6-13-4 in her father's will.
    iv. JOSEPH, bapt. 29 Jan. 1594/5; not mentioned in his father's will. The *Calendar of Wills and Administrations* of the Bishop of London's Commissary Court shows a 1619/20 entry (No. 33), not investigated, for a Joseph Gregson.
    v.   MARIE, bapt. 12 June 1597; not mentioned in her father's will.
    vi. THOMAS, bapt. 13 Jan. 1599/1600. Percival Boyd in his *Citizens of London* (No. 49229) calls him Thomas Gregson of St. Botolph Aldersgate, son of Gregory Gregson, yeoman, of Purbeston [i.e., Thurlaston, Leicestershire], citizen and draper, apprenticed 14 June 1615 to Henry Gerye and freed 16 July 1623. He paid Quarterage (quarterly dues) to the Worshipful Company of Drapers from 1624 to 1656. The only child Boyd gives to this Thomas is Matthew, b. 5 July 1635. Boyd (No. 38006) also attributes this same Matthew, but with a ques-

tion mark, to Thomas[4] Gregson [No. 12], who had been freed from his apprenticeship in 1634. Since it seems more probable that Matthew was son of a Thomas freed from apprenticeship in 1634 rather than son of a Thomas freed in 1623, particularly when the latter Thomas is given no other children by Boyd, Matthew is treated herein as a son of Thomas[4] Gregson [No. 12]. We also know that Thomas[4] was living after Matthew was freed from his apprenticeship *to his father* in 1658, whereas the latest record we have of this Thomas being alive is in 1656.

9. vii. JAMES, bapt. 26 Jan. 1602/3.

   viii. DOROTHY, bapt. 22 April 1605; her father left her £26-6-8 in his will and made her one of four residuary legatees.

ENGLISH ANCESTRY OF MR. THOMAS GREGSON
OF NEW HAVEN

By PAUL W. PRINDLE, F.A.S.G., of Darien, Conn.

5. THOMAS[3] GREGSON (*John[2], Thomas[1]*) was undoubtedly baptized at St. Michael Old Angels, Sutton-on-the-Hill, Derbyshire, during the hiatus of 5 March to 3 June 1598 in the church register entries. He was lost at sea in 1645/6, and an inventory of his estate was taken 2 Nov. 1647.

He married in England soon before 1630, JANE ——, who died at New Haven, 4 June 1702, "aged and weak".

Thomas Gregson's father by will devised certain of his lands to son John and, by successive contingent devolutions, to other living sons: Robert, William, Richard, Thomas and Edward, obviously named in the order of their births, placing Thomas as born after Richard and before Edward.

In the spring of 1637 a group of London merchants had formed a company to establish a successful commercial settlement in the New World. On 26 June of that year "Mr. John Davenport, Mr. Samuel Eaton, Theophilus Eaton and Edward Hopkins, Esquires, Mr. Thomas Gregson and many others of good characters and fortunes, arrived at Boston" (Benjamin Trumbull, *A Complete History of Connecticut*, 1898 ed., 1:70). Mr. Davenport became the influential minister of the New Haven Colony, Theophilus Eaton, its first governor, and Thomas Gregson, its first treasurer. Edward Hopkins was later to be the governor of the Connecticut Colony. Mr. Trumbull continued:

> The reputations and good estates of the principal gentlemen of this company made the people of the Massachusetts [Bay Colony] exceedingly desirous of their settlement in that commonwealth. Great pains were taken, not only by particular persons and towns, but by the general court, to fix them in the colony. Charlestowne made them large offers, and Newbury proposed to give up the whole town to them. The general court offered them any place which they should choose. But they were determined to plant a distinct colony.

After an exploratory trip in the fall of 1637, the company sailed from Boston on 30 March 1638 and settled at Quinnipiac, site of the present city of New Haven, founding the New Haven Colony. Rights to the land were purchased from the Indian sachem Momauguin in exchange for various utensils and articles of clothing, assurances of protection from the Pequot and Mohawk Indians, and a sufficient quantity of land to plant on. This land was on the east side of the harbor, between the water and the Saybrook fort, and was the site of the present East Haven.

The influential merchants soon induced the colony to undertake the first of three attempts to establish a trading post at the mouth of the Delaware River. The major losses incurred in the first effort almost impoverished the New Haven Colony. In an endeavor to recoup that and other losses, the colony tried a new venture, the shipment of goods directly to Old England. To undertake this project a vessel was built for a newly formed company. This company was called The Ship Fellowship, and many of the townspeople subscribed to its stock. The vessel was chartered for the London voyage by an association called The Company of Merchants of New Haven, composed of Governor Theophilus Eaton, Deputy Governor Stephen Goodyear, Mr. Richard Malbon and Mr. Thomas Gregson (Edward E. Atwater, *History of The Colony of New Haven*, 1881, p. 208). An account given many years later by the Rev. James Pierpont stated that the ship was built in Rhode Island, but a 1651 entry in *New Haven Town Records* (1:63) implies she was constructed in New Haven:

> Mr. Goodyeare desired the Court would remitt a fine of 40 s. a good whille sinc laid upon Jno. Harriman for drawing wine w'thout order. he acknowledgeth the Justice of the Court in so proceeding, but desires their favour to remit it. The Court, considering the usefullness of Jno. Harriman to ye Towne in keeping the Ordinary, and that it was but a remnant of wine that was left when ye ship fellowship was finished, did remitt it to him.

Although there is an implication here that the vessel was named *Fellowship*, the reference may have been to the company rather than to the ship. In any event, historians have considered the name of the vessel to be unknown and have called it only "The Great Shippe", as it was generally referred to in contemporary records.

In January 1645/6 the ship was loaded with cargo by the impatient townspeople. They were unwilling to await more auspicious weather, and the journey began that month. Later in the year John Winthrop, governor of the Massachusetts Bay Colony, wrote in his diary (THE REGISTER, 33:237):

> There fell a sad affliction upon the country this year, though it more particularly concerned New Haven and those parts. A small ship of about 100 tons set out from New Haven in the middle of the eleventh month last (the harbor there being so frozen, as they were forced to hew her through the ice near three miles). She was laden with pease and some wheat, all in bulk, with about 200 West India hides, and store of beaver, and plate, so as it was estimated in all at 5,000 pounds. There were in her about seventy persons, whereof divers were of very precious account, as Mr. Grigson, one of their magistrates, the wife of Mr. Goodyear, another of their magistrates (a right godly woman), Captain Turner, Mr. Lambertson, master of the ship, and some seven or eight others, members of the church there. The ship never went voyage before, and was very crank-sided, so as it was conceived, she was overset in a great tempest, which happened soon after she put to sea, for she was never heard of after.

Tradition has it that five months after "The Great Shippe" sailed, a remarkable apparition was observed in New Haven harbor by a multitude. Many years later the Rev. Cotton Mather asked the then New Haven minister, the Rev. James Pierpont, about the alleged miracle. Pierpont's undated response is given in Atwater's *History* (*op. cit.*, pp. 540-41):

> Reverend and Dear Sir,—In compliance with your desires I now give you the relation of that apparition of a ship in the air, which I have received from the most credible, judicious, and curious surviving observers of it . . . In June next ensuing, a great thunder-storm arose out of the north-west; after which (the hemisphere being serene), about an hour before sunset, a ship of like dimensions with the aforesaid, with her canvas and colors abroad (though the wind northerly) appeared in the air coming up from our harbor's mouth, which lies southward from the town, seemingly with her sails filled under a fresh gale, holding her

course north, and continuing under observation, sailing against the wind for the space of half an hour.

Many were drawn to behold this great work of God; yea, the very children cried out, "There's a brave ship." At length, crowding up as far as there is usually water sufficient for such a vessel, and so near some of the spectators, as that they imagined a man might hurl a stone on board her, her main-top seemed to be blown off, but left hanging in the shrouds; then her mizzen-top; then all her masting seemed blown away by the board; quickly after the hulk brought to a careen, she overset and so vanished into a smoky cloud, which in some time dissipated, leaving, as everywhere else, a clear air. The admiring spectators could distinguish the several colors of each part, the principal rigging, and such proportions, as caused not only the generality of persons to say, "This was the mould of their ship, and this was her tragic end"; but Mr. Davenport also in public declared to this effect, that God had condescended, for the quieting of their afflicted spirits, this extraordinary account of his sovereign disposal of those for whom so many fervent prayers were made continually.

In 1858, some 212 years after the event, Henry Wadsworth Longfellow commemorated the tragedy with his poem, "The Phantom Ship".

The large investments lost in this ship and in the three Delaware ventures discouraged the New Haven Colony from further attempting major commercial projects. Considering their situation unsatisfactory for farming, the colony explored the possibility of moving elsewhere. An invitation came from Jamaica, in the West Indies, and negotiations were actually entered into to remove the colony to "Galloway" [i.e. Galway], Ireland. These came to naught, however, and eventually the New Haven inhabitants prospered as farmers (Trumbull, *op. cit.*, 1:129).

Among the distinguished passengers on "The Great Shippe" was Mr. Thomas Gregson, on his way to England as agent for the New Haven Colony to obtain from Parliament a much desired charter. The Connecticut Colony, seated at Hartford, claimed that the New Haven Colony fell within its jurisdiction, and New Haven was eager to prove otherwise. At a General Court sitting 11 Nov. 1644 at New Haven, it was resolved:

> Whereas the Gen'rll Court for this jurisdictio' did see cause to putt forth their best endevors to procure a Pattent fro' the Parliament, as judging itt a fitt season now for thatt end, and therefore desired Mr. Gregson to undertake the voyage and business and agreed to furnish him with £ 200 in this jurisdictio' of which, in proportio' to the other plantations, Newhaven is to pay £ 110 in good marchantable beaver, itt was thereupon ordered thatt the said £ 110 shalbe procured at the charge of the town's treasury . . .

Years later, when the jurisdictional dispute was warmer than ever, the New Haven Colony in February of 1663 sent to the Connecticut Colony a long account of their views of the matter, item six of which recited:

> That in the yeare 1644 the gen'll court for Newhaven Colonie . . . agreed unanimously to send to England for a Pattent, & in ye yeare 1645 com'itted the p'cureing of it to Mr. Grigson, one of our magistrates, who entered upon his voyage in January yt year from Newhaven, furnished with some beaver in order thereunto, as we suppose, but by the providence of God, the ship & all the passengers & goods were lost at sea in their passage toward England, to o'r great [loss] & the frustration of yt designe for yt time; after which the troubles in England put a stop to o'r p'ceedings therein . . . .

149

The "troubles in England" were, of course, the overthrowing of Charles I and the establishment of the Commonwealth under Oliver Cromwell.

Thus ended the brief but distinguished services of Mr. Gregson to the New Haven Colony. Record of his service first entered in the minutes of the General Court is found under date of 23 Oct. 1640:

> Itt is ordered that Mr. Gregson shall be Truck ma[ste]r of this town for this yeare ensueing, to truck [i.e. barter] w'th the Indians for venison, so as he may afforde to sell to the planters thatt have need att 3 ob. a pound, all together, good and bad, one w'th another.
>
> Itt is ordered thatt no Englishman thatt kills venison shall sell the fattest for above 3 d. a pound, and the leane att 2 d. ob.

The abbreviation "ob." stands for obolus, a rarely used word representing one halfpenny.

At a Court of Elections held the following May, Mr. Gregson was chosen to be the "treasurer, to receive the yearely rates and keep accounts of all disbursements upon all necessary occasions for the como[n] affayres of the towne." He was elected to the same office in 1642. At the October 1640 Court of Elections Mr. Gregson was named as a deputy and was reelected to that post for each of the sessions of the General Court held from 1640 through April of 1643. In October 1643 he was chosen as a magistrate, and in October of 1646 was again named to that office. Seemingly, despite the apparition of the previous June, the town had hopes that the passengers of "The Great Shippe" might return. At the October 1643 meeting Mr. Gregson was honored by being named, with the governor, as the first commissioners for the New Haven Colony to the newly formed United Colonies of New England.

Encroachment by the Dutch and an expectation of the various Indian tribes uniting to drive the Englishmen out of New England had caused the several colonies to consider in 1638 some form of union as a matter of self-preservation. Territorial disputes between them and their unequal sizes, however, delayed fruition of the union (Trumbull, *op. cit.*, 1:98). At a town meeting at New Haven, 6 April 1643:

> Itt was ordered thatt Mr. Eaton and Mr. Gregson, as commissioners for this jurisdictio' of Newhaven, shall goe w'th other comissioners of other plantatio's into the Bay of Massacuetts to treate about a Gen'rll combinatio' for all the plantations in New England, and to conclude and determine the same, as in their wisdome they shall see cause, for the exalting of Christ's ends and advanceing the publique good in all the plantations.

The minutes of the town meeting of 6 July 1643 note:

> Mr. Eaton [the Governor] and Mr. Gregson, lately sent from this Court as comissioners w'th full power to treate, and if itt might be, to conclude a combination or confoederation w'th the Gen'rll Court for the Massachusetts, and w'th the commissioners for New Plymouth and Connectecutt, did this day acquaint the Court w'th the issue and successe of thatt treaty. The articles agreed and concluded att Boston, the 19th of May, 1643, were now read and . . . Lastly, the said Mr. Eaton and Mr. Gregson were by this Court chosen and invested with full power (according to the tenner and true meaning of the said Articles), as com'issioners for this jurisdectio' in the meeting for this confoederatio' to be held att Boston, the 7th of September next.

The Articles of Confederation adopted at that meeting, sometimes called the New England Confederation, created the United Colonies of New England. They formed the first "constitution" to be written in the New World. Some of its features were embodied in the Constitution of the United States of America, drafted some 144 years later. The 1643 document begins with the words:

Articles of Confederatio' betwixt the Plantations under the Governm't of the Massachusetts, the Plantations under the Govrnt. of Newplymouth, the Plantations under the Govrmt. of Conecticutt, and the Govermt. of Newhaven w'th the Plantatio's in combinatio' w'th itt.

Whereas we all came into these p'ts of America w'th one and the same end 'and ayme, namely, to advance the Kingdome of o'r Lord Jesus Christ, and to enjoy the libertyes of the Gospell in purity w'th peace . . . .

One of the first acts of the confederation is described in the minutes of the Commissioners of the United Colonies (THE REGISTER, 28:44), under date of 19 Sept. 1643:

Upon information and complaynt made by Mr. Eaton and Mr. Gregson to the comissioners of sondry injuries and outrages they have received both from the Dutch and Sweads, both at Delaware Bay and elsewhere, the p'ticulers w'th their proofs being duly considered. It was agreed and ordered That a l're be written to the Sweadish Gov'nor expressing the p'ticulers and requireing satisfaction, w'ch l're is to be underwritten by John Winthrop, Esqr., as Govnr. of the Massachusetts and President of the Commissioners for the united Colonies of New-England.

Mr. Gregson was one of the 111 subscribers on 4 June 1639 to the Fundamental Agreement of the New Haven Colony, and was also one of the 183 men to take the oath of fidelity to that colony on 1 July 1644.

In 1641 Thomas Gregson was granted an attachment on goods of Mr. Trowbridge to satisfy a debt of £ 20. Two years later, on the tax list, Mr. Gregson was shown heading a household of six persons and having a taxable estate appraised at £ 600, including 45 acres of land in the first division, nine in the neck, 33 in the meadow, and 133 in the second division. Since the parents had some six children surviving at that date, it appears two of them were living elsewhere. As is shown below, their son Richard was in 1640 called of Bristol, England, doubtless living with relatives or attending school.

The minutes of a court sitting 1 Nov. 1643 record that "Robert Lea, for comeing to tray'ing w'th his gun charged w'th shott, co_ _rary to order, and carelessly discharging itt against Mr. Gregso' his home, to the great danger of the lives of divers persons who were in the chamber when the shott came through the window, was fined 20 s. to the towne, and to repaire the window w'ch was broken by the said shott."

In the 1645 layout of the second division of commonage, it was ordered that "Mr. Gregson shall have the upland for his second devission on the east side of the harbour, by t'ıe meddow called the solitary cove." He thus became the first white settler of what is now East Haven. It seems doubtful that the Gregson family ever lived on the farm at Solitary Cove. They had a fine residence in New Haven proper. Ezra Stiles, president of Yale College, "records the tradition that Gregson's house was one of four which excelled in stateliness all other houses erected in New Haven by the first generation of its inhabitants; the three which he groups with Gregson's belonging respectively to Mr. Theophilus Eaton (the governor), Mr. John Davenport (the minister) and Mr. Isaac Allerton" the erstwhile business manager of Plymouth Colony. Mr. Gregson's house in the Gregson Quarter stood "where the glebe building now is . . . Next west of Mr. Gregson lived Stephen Goodyear, another of the London merchants originally associated together for the commencement of a plantation in New England" (Atwater, *op. cit.,* p. 135). Of the eight "quarters" surrounding the sequestered central market or square, the south-center one was called Gregson's Quarter. It lay south of the Herefordshire Quarter and was bounded on the east by the road to Milford (*ibid.,* pp. 76, 105).

The town requested Mr. Gregson in 1640 to appraise the goods of George Spencer. Stephen Goodyear and Thomas Grgeson were appointed by the town in August 1642 to determine the amount of damages involved in a lawsuit, and three months later, to settle a dispute between two proprietors. In 1643 and 1645 Mr. Gregson and Mr. Malbon were called upon to settle such disputes out of court.

Hope for the safety of "The Great Shippe" having long since been abandoned, the inventory of the estate of Mr. Thomas Gregson, deceased, was taken 2 Nov. 1647 by Matthew Gilbert and Richard Miles, delivered to the court on 7 Dec. 1647 and recorded in New Haven Probate Records, 1:12. Real estate, consisting of dwelling house and home lot, the little house and barn, and meadow acreage, was appraised at £ 246:00:00; personal estate was valued at £ 225:19:06; and claims against others, including "an adventure in the *Susan* to Barbadoes," £ 18:07:00; resulting in a gross estate of £ 490:06:06. Indebtedness to others, principally Stephen Goodyear, amounted to £ 126:03:02, reducing the estate to a net value of £ 364:03:04. Distribution was not made until 2 April 1716 to daughters Phebe Russell and to the heirs of his only son Richard and of his daughters Anna Daniel, Susanna Crittenden, Rebecca Bowers and Sarah Whitehead (*ibid.,* 4:397).

In the reassignment of the meeting house seats made 10 March 1646, "Mrs. Grigson" and three other women were placed in seat number two of "the weomens seates, in the midle", just behind the empty seat reserved exclusively for the excommunicated wife of Governor Theophilus Eaton. Mrs. Gregson was also assigned to seat number two in the 1656 and 1662 revisions of meeting house seating.

At a court sitting 6 Feb. 1648 at New Haven, Mrs. Gregson and 17 others were each fined "12 d. for not bringing their waights & measures to be tryed upon the day appoynted".

Early colonial records contain many accounts of the difficulties the proprietors had with their servants, i.e. apprentices. Of interest here is a trial held 5 Feb. 1649/50 (*New Haven Town Records,* 1:3 ff.):

Richard Fido, servant to Mr. Gibbard, and Nicolas Sloper, servant to M'ris Gregson, were called before the Court & told that they stand charged w'th sundrie miscariages, as theft, lying, disorderly night meetings, drinking sacke, strong watter, and having ther feasts in the night, w'th goods stollen from ther Governors or others; w'ch upon Examination they have confessed, and deserved to be kept in prison, but they were left to the dispose of ther Master and Mistris, w'ch might have bine and Ingagment upon them to have made them keep from such sinnfull courses; but notw'thstanding they have since runn away, and that upon the Saboth, stolle sundrie things, and brought great disturbanc upon the Saboth, the Magistrats being necessitated to send men after them, the charge whereof they must beare, though the men tooke them not; but God sent Indians after them, who tooke them and brought them backe by force. they were now wished to speake and make a true, full and free confession of the severall miscariages of this nature, w'ch they know by themselves or others.

The account of the trial runs on for more than ten printed pages, involving a number of others, including Captive, an Indian servant of Mr. Richard Malbon, Thomas Meekes and his wife, and their servant, James Clements. All were found guilty, the Meekes of receiving stolen goods and of fraternizing with other men's servants "in ye night when ther Governers were in bed, to drinke strong water", etc. The sentences for Mrs. Gregson's apprentice reads:

For Nicolas Sloper, who hath robbed his M'ris and gon on in such a tract and course of stealing, w'th the same agravations and w'th hardness of heart, adding many lyes to his theft, the sentenc of the Court is that, for the things he hath stole, first and second time, he make treble restitution, and paye halfe the charge in pursuing them and taking them, and ye charge of ye prison; and if he be not able to paye he must be sould for his theft, for that is ye law of God [See Exodus 22:3]; and for the sinn of stealing a second time after conviction, for his running away and for sundrie lyes told, that he be whipped, & to continew in prison till the Lecture day [i.e. Wednesday] next weeke, when he is to receive his correction.

Mrs. Gregson complained in 1653 that the bounds of her land at Solitary Cove were not defined in the town's original grant. The court ordered "that the Townsmen shall goe and set out ye bounds of it, w'th due respect to M'ris Gregsons conveniency and also the Townes, both in refferenc to high wayes and any other consideration".

According to a footnote in *New Haven Town Records* (1:8), Mrs. Jane Gregson resided on the southwest corner of Church and Chapel Streets.

The third division of commonage on the western side of New Haven was made in 1680. "Mrs. Greckson" received 116 acres. She was listed as heading a household of four persons and having a taxable estate assessed at £ 500. In the fifth division, made in 1711, "Mrs. grexons Lott" was 12 acres in size. Since she was not living then, the reference was to her estate. In the minutes of a town meeting held 20 Sept. 1720, these 12 acres are referred to as belonging to "Mrs. Grizson and Danll". Anna, daughter of Jane Gregson and widow of Stephen Daniel, was intended. The second division of the Sequestered Land took place in 1713, "Mr. grixons Lott" being four acres in size. In the minutes of a meeting held that year the grant is referred to as "Mrs. Jane grixsons Lott". Both she and her husband had long been deceased, the lot being granted to their heirs.

Jane, widow of Mr. Gregson, died 4 June 1702. Her will, dated 5 Feb. 1691/2, called her aged and weak. She requested "to be buried by her executrix and dear relatives". She left to her "daughter, Anna Daniel, my house and homelot and the remainder of my upland not yet disposed of at my farm in the east side of New Haven harbor, unless some of the children of my son Richard Gregson in England come over," in which event such children were to have the farm. Also, "my meadow at my said farm for life, then to her daughter . . . also to my daughter, Anna Daniel, 6 or 7 acres of meadow near Westfield, for life, then to those of the children that need it most." Finally, "daughter Daniel to have all moveables in the house, and be executrix."

Mrs. Gregson left to her "daughter Mary in England, 30 acres of my Third Division near Sperries farm". To "grandchild Ruth Frisbie of Branford, 14 acres of my East Side farm" [Ruth was the daughter of Rebecca Bowers and wife of John Frisbie]; "also 15 acres of said farm to daughter Susanna Crittenden". To "daughter Phebe, 9 acres of Third Division . . . grandchild Elizabeth Winston, 8 acres of meadow and 10 acres of the Third Division". [She was a daughter of Anna Daniels and the wife of John Winston]. To "grandchild Johanna Thompson, 9 acres of the Third Division and 5 acres in the Quarter by the west lane, after my daughter Daniels decease." [Johanna, daughter of Anna Daniel, was the wife of William Thompson.] To "grandchild Rebecca Thompson, 6 acres meadow at Westfield (so called) now in her possession, and 10 acres of Third Division". [She was a sister of Joanna Thompson and the wife of John Thompson.] To "great-grandchild Elizabeth Glover that now lives with me, 9 acres on the Neck." [Elizabeth was a daughter of John and Joanna (Daniel) Glover and granddaughter of Stephen and Anna (Gregson) Daniel.] To "the four children of my daughter Whitehead, 6 acres of Third Division each". Witnesses to the will were William Peck and John Jones.

A verbal codicil was made a short time after the will was drawn, giving her daughter Anna Daniel a life interest in three acres of meadow at the South End and three acres at the west side, to go after Anna's death to her daughter Joanna and children; and three acres of meadow at the South End were to go to Jane's daughter, Susanna Crittenden. The sole witness to the codicil was Hannah Falconer. The three witnesses were sworn in at the Probate Court 30 July 1702 (THE REGISTER, 46:152).

An inventory of Jane Gregson's estate was taken 4 Aug. 1702 by Thomas Tuttle and Nathaniel Boykin. Her house and homelot were appraised at £ 80; the meadow on the West Side Cove, £ 24; meadow on the East Side, £ 30; land on the East Side not yet taken up, £ 15, and Third Division Land, £ 27. The total estate, including personal property, was valued at £ 198. Distribution was ordered to Mrs. Ruth Frisby alias Hoadly, Joanna Thompson, Mrs. Susanna Crittenden and Mrs. Mary Wyke (*ibid.*, 46:152).

Thomas and Jane (——) Gregson had eight children. Unless otherwise noted, their records have been taken from *Families of Ancient New Haven* by Donald Lines Jacobus:

10. i.   RICHARD[4], b. in England ca. 1630.
    ii. ANNA, b. ca. 1632 in England; d. 3 May 1709 at New Haven; mar. STEPHEN DANIEL at New Haven in 1651.
    iii. REBECCA, b. ca. 1635; d. bef. Jan. 1685; mar. the Rev. JOHN BOWERS, b. ca. 1629; d. 14 June 1687 at Derby, Conn., son of George and Barbara Bowers. John mar. (2) Bridget Thompson, dau. of Anthony; she d.

19 May 1720 at Derby (Edward S. Frisbie, *The Frisbee-Frisbie Genealogy*, p. 27).

iv. SUSANNA, b. ca. 1637; d. 8 Sept. 1712 at Guilford, Conn.; mar. at New Haven 13 May 1661, ABRAHAM CRITTENDEN JR., who d. 25 Sept. 1694, son of Abraham and Mary Crittenden of Guilford.

v. MARY, bapt. 26 Jan. 1639/40 at First Congregational Society, New Haven. In the probate record of her mother's estate, she was called Mary Wyke, living in England.

vi. PHEBE, bapt. 15 Oct. 1643 at New Haven; d. 19 Sept. 1730; mar. (1) at New Haven in 1673, the Rev. JOHN WHITING, b. ca. 1635; d. 8 Sept. 1689 at Hartford, son of William and Susanna Whiting and widower of Sybil Collins, who d. 3 June 1672, dau. of Edward and Martha Collins; Phebe mar. (2) 1692, as his third wife, the Rev. JOHN RUSSELL, d. at Hadley 10 Dec. 1692, ae. 66 years, son of John Russell of Cambridge, Wethersfield and Hadley. The Rev. Mr. Russell mar. (1) Mary Talcott, who d. between 1655 and 1660, dau .of "The Worshipful Mr. John Talcott" and his wife, Dorothy Mott of Hartford; mar. (2) Rebecca Newberry, d. 21 Nov. 1688, ae. 57 years, at Hadley, dau. of Thomas and Jane Newberry of Windsor, Conn. (S. V. Talcott, *Talcott Pedigree in England and America*, 1876, pp. 30-31; J. Gardner Bartlett, *Newberry Genealogy*, 1914, p. 46).

vii. ABIGAIL, bapt. 23 Feb. 1644/5 at New Haven; d.y.

viii. SARAH, b. ca. 1646; d. in 1697; mar. (1) at New Haven 12 Dec. 1667, JOHN GILBERT, bapt. there in April 1644, son of Matthew and Jane (Baker) Gilbert; d. there 26 Nov. 1673; she mar. (2) at New Haven 9 May 1676, Capt. SAMUEL WHITEHEAD, who d. there in September 1690.

ENGLISH ANCESTRY OF MR. THOMAS GREGSON OF NEW HAVEN

By PAUL W. PRINDLE, F.A.S.G., of Darien, Conn.

6. HENRY³ GREGSON (*Thomas²*, *Thomas¹*) was baptized 27 March 1583 at St. Michael Old Angels, Sutton-on-the-Hill, Derbyshire. As shown in the register of that church, he was married twice. His first wife was MILLISANT ——, whose son Phillip was baptized 28 June 1605. On 5 Nov. 1606 "Henrici Gregson and Idith his wife" baptized a son George, subsequently called Henry's eldest son and heir, so both Millisant and Phillip must have died soon after Phillip's baptism.

The second wife "Ideth" was EDITH ALLESTREE, daughter of George Allestree. On 5 July 1588, and again on 20 July 1588, this George "Alestrye" and six other tenants of Duffield attended at Nottingham to place their grievances before Mr. Edward Stanhope, the representative of Queen Elizabeth, and to propose remedies (*Derby Archaeological Journal*, 25:213). The Derby Public Library, Derbyshire, has a manuscript, "Pedigrees and Biographies of Allestree Family," compiled by F. Williamson, Esq., Fellow, Royal Historical Society, which states that George Allestree, gent., dead in 1635, married Ideth and had Ideth, daughter and heiress, who married Henry Gregson of Turnditch, gent., living in 1635 (Box 57, parcel No. 222).

Additional data of the Allestree family are given in *The Genealogist*, n.s., 32:169, which provides an abstract of the 30 Oct. 1630 will, proved in London 28 Jan. 1630/31, of Thomas Allestree the elder, gent., of Alvaston, co. Derby:

> ... John Allestrie, my fifth son, had by the wills of Roger Harrison & Alice Harrison of Alvaston, deceased, £50 which I have not yet paid him; my executors must pay him when he is 21 years of age & I give him in addition £70 ... John Osborne of Derby & Henry Gregson of Turnditch, gent., together with my brothers, Richard Allestrie & Robert Allestrie, overseers.

This additional Harrison tie-in to the Gregson family should be noted.

The 1595 will of Henry's father, Thomas, left to Henry, his "sonne heire Gregsonne", one-half of Sherrow Hall, with the appurtenances, and

> [M]y bible, the best bed I have, except one with the furniture thereto belongeinge, the Longe table and frame standinge in the hall ... the use and occupacon of all my Landes, meadowes and pastures, with th'appurtennce' which I have purchased, situate, lyinge and beinge in the parrishe of Sutton, till such time as my sonne Richard come to the age of 21th years, and then the said Henrye, my sonne, shall pay unto the said Richard Gregsonne my sonne, the sume of one hundrethe poundes of Lawfull Englishe money, and soe keep the saide landes to himself and his heires for ever, if he will [otherwise, Richard to receive these Sutton lands] ...

In her will made in 1600, Henry's mother directed him "to ma'ch hymselfe in maryage to the lyckynge and w'th the consent of Mr. Lawrence wryght ... Mr. arthur Lathbury ... and James Draper";

made him a co-executor with his brother-in-law, Lawrence Hill, each to receive four pounds for his trouble; and gave him "the bedstead in the p'lor, the sealinge in p'lor and all the glass in the wyndoes; allso . . . eyght poundes a yeare . . . until he doth come to the age of one and twenty yeres. . . ."

A grant from the bailiffs and burgesses to Henry Gregson and Edith, his wife, of Turnditch, daughter and heiress of George Allestree of Turnditch, yeoman, dated 17 Jan. 1622, gave the right to "inclose and being inclosed in severalty henceforth keepe at all tyme and tymes of the year" the piece of meadow in the Parcel Meadow, containing about three acres, "being the inheritance of the said Edith, the bailiffs quitclaiming all their rights, interest Edith; and the bailiffs hereby quit clam all their rights, interest and title of common of pasture in the same. To hold by service of 10 shillings yearly." Witnesses were George Gregson and Francis Bingley (*Calendar of Ancient Records, Borough of Derby*, p. 33).

The will of Henry's brother Richard, proved in 1640, bequeathed "to my deare and loving brother, Mr. Henry Gregson, and unto Edith his wife . . . twenty shillings a peece" and named "my naturall brother Mr. Henry Gregson" and six other "loving kindred and friends . . . to councell and advise and to assiste my foresaid named executor."

On 2 May 1651 Henry Gregson of Turnditch leased sequestered estates of John Merry of Brisingcote (*i.e.*, Brislingcote, near Burton-on-Trent) at Kniveton and Brisingcote for £98 a year (*Derby Archaeological Journal*, 13:158).

In "Familiae Minorum Gentium" (*The Publications of The Harleian Society*, 37:215-17), a pedigree of the Gregson family is given, showing Thomas and Alicia (Merry) Gregson to have had a son "Hendricus Gregson of Sherrow-hall and of Turnditch, jure ux., aged 12 years and 354 days at his father's death, 18 December, 38 Elizabeth (1595). He was Escheator of Derbyshire 12 Charles I." His wife is shown as "Editha, fil. and her., George Allestree de Turnditch hall in parish of Duffield." The stated age of Henry yields a computed birthdate of 29 Dec. 1582, in conformity with his date of baptism. The pedigree omits Henry's first marriage and the baptism of his son Phillip, and fails to show the baptisms at St. Michael Old Angels, Sutton-on-the-Hill, of George and Alice, but provides baptism records at the parish church, Duffield, for the last four children.

Children of Henry Gregson, first by wife Millisant; the rest by wife Edith:

    i.   PHILLIP[4], bapt. 28 June 1605 at St. Michael Old Angels; d.y., for "Familiae Minorum Gentium" calls his brother George their father's eldest son and heir.

11. ii. GEORGE, bapt. 5 Nov. 1606.

    iii. ALICE, bapt. 30 April 1609; mar. 5 July 1632, WILLIAM MILNES of Chesterfield, gent., at the parish church in Duffield.

12. iv. THOMAS, bapt. 14 July 1611.

    v. VINCENT, bapt. 14 Feb. 1613 at Duffield.

    vi. RICHARD, bapt. there 9 May 1619.

    vii. HENRY, bapt. 27 Oct. 1621 at Duffield; residing at Wapping, London, in 1663.

?viii. MARTHA; pedigree No. 1055 of The Jackson Collection, Sheffield Reference Library, gives Henry Gregson this daughter, who mar. RICHARD POLE of Dalbury Lees, co. Derby, gent.

7. RICHARD[3] GREGSON (*Thomas[2]*, *Thomas[1]*) was undoubtedly baptized during the 1587 to 1590 gap in the baptismal register of St. Michael Old Angels, for he was the last named son (and to receive 20 nobles) in the 1600 will of his mother. He was also the last named son in the 1595 will of his father, who provided that Richard, when 21 years of age, was to receive from his brother Henry "all my Landes, meadowes and pastures, with th'appurtennce' which I have purchased, situate, lyinge and beinge in the parrishe of Sutton" or, at Henry's election, "the sume of one hundrethe poundes of Lawful Englishe money." Richard and his mother were made co-executors of the will.

He married —— HURT.

Percival Boyd, in his *Citizens of London* (v.c. 15393), states that Richard Gregson of All Hollows Bread Street, draper, in 1638 paid rent of £36 in St. Augustine Parish. Richard died 21 Aug. 1640 (THE REGISTER, 46:151).

The undated will of Richard Gregson, draper, proved 31 Aug. 1640 by his son Nicholas, provided that he be buried in the church of St. Augustine, St. Austin's Gate, London "as neare and as conveniently as I may unto the bons of my deceased wife who hath beene formerly buryed in the same church." He made a bequest "unto my father-in-lawe, Mr. Nich. Hurt and unto Mrs. Dorothy, his wife" and another "to my deare and loving brother, Mr. Henry Gregson, and unto Edith, his wife", and named "my naturall brother, Mr. Henry Gregson" to be one of the seven overseers of his will, which identifies this Richard as the son of Thomas[2] Gregson. This will is also the key to the identification of Thomas Gregson of New Haven, to whom 20 shillings were left, and who was referred to as "my cosen Thomas Gregson in Newe England."

Richard Gregson and his wife, a daughter of Nicholas and Dorothy Hurt, had five children (Boyd, *op. cit.*), who were to share equally in the residue of his estate:

    i.   NICHOLAS[4], bapt. 6 Jan. 1619; sole executor of his father's will; merchant tailor and citizen of London; warden in 1677; d. in 1693 and was bur. at Hackney, co. Middlesex (*ibid.*, v.c. 45423).

    ii. JOHN, bapt. 11 Feb. 1620; may have been the John Grigson, cooper, of St. Michael Barrishaw, who mar. at Stepney 15 Oct. 1646, ANNE MORGAN (*ibid.*, v.c. 41900).

    iii. THOMAS, named as a son in the will of his father, to share equally with his brothers and sisters in the residue of his father's estate. He was not mentioned in Boyd's record.

    iv. ANNE, bapt. 17 Nov. 1622; she appears to have been the Anne Gregson of Turnditch, living in 1680, who mar., as his second wife, JOHN MANWARING, D.D., record of Stoke upon Trent, co. Stafford ("Staffordshire Pedigrees, 1664-1700" in *Harleian Society, op. cit.*, 63:165).

    v. ELIZABETH; mar. THOMAS SMITH of Hanley, co. Stafford, aged 38 in 1663, and had five children: 1. *Nicholas*. 2. *John*, aged 5 in 1663. 3. *Damaris*. 4. *Elizabeth*. 5. *Dorothy*. Thomas was son of Thomas Smith of Hanley (aged 30 in 1614 and died in 1653) and his wife, Dorothy Young, and grandson of John Smith of Newcastle under Lyme, co.

Stafford. He was twice mayor of that city and represented a younger branch of Smith of Hough, Knt. John Smith mar. Alice, dau. of Humfrey Weston of Maidley, Staffordshire (*ibid.*, 63:209).

8. EDWARD³ GREGSON (*Gregory²*, *Thomas¹*) was baptized 25 June 1589 at St. Michael Old Angels, Sutton-on-the-Hill, Derbyshire.
He married MARGERIE ――.
Gregory had presumably given Edward his portion prior to making his will in 1624, for Edward was left only one silver spoon, but was made co-executor of the will.
Edward and his wife had two known children:

    i.   WILLIAM⁴, bapt. 25 May 1614 at St. Michael Old Angels, surely the William Gregson who had son: 1. *Gregory*, bapt. 19 Oct. 1645 at All Saints, Derby, Derbyshire.
    ii. HENRY, bapt. 4 July 1617 at All Saints, Derby.

9. JAMES³ GREGSON (*Gregory²*, *Thomas¹*) was baptized 26 Jan. 1602/3 at St. Michael Old Angels, Sutton-on-the-Hill, Derbyshire.
With his mother he was co-executor of his father's will, which left him £30 and made him one of the residuary legatees.
In his *Citizens of London* (v.c. 38005), Percival Boyd calls him "James Gregson, Yeo., of Thurlestone, Leics.," *i.e.*, Thurlaston, Leicestershire, where his father's will was drawn in 1623. No further record of this James Gregson has been found. Boyd gives him a son, and implies another:

    i.   GREGORY⁴, was freed from apprenticeship 12 May 1652 by John Andrews; served as city crier and appears on the 1696 Association Oath Roll (*ibid.*, v.c. 38005); he d. 13 Nov. 1709 and was bur. at St. Olave, Silver Street. His will was presumably proved 1710 at the Bishop of London's Commissary Court, but a thorough search of some 250 loose wills for that year proved fruitless.*
    ii. JAMES, putative son. In abstract v.c. 38005 Boyd shows the will of the above Gregory as mentioning his kinsmen John Gregson, draper; James Gregson, draper, and May Gregson, all three being children of a James Gregson. Since no record has been found of a James Gregson whose children might be considered kinsmen of Gregory, it is tentatively assumed here that James³ Gregson had such a son, named after himself.

10. RICHARD⁴ GREGSON (*Thomas³*, *John²*, *Thomas¹*) was born in England about 1630. He appears to have been left there, perhaps for the purpose of being educated, when his family sailed to the New World. As shown below, he was living at Bristol, England, in 1640. By March of 1656, however, Richard was residing in New Haven, for he was then assigned seat number five of the cross seats at the upper end of the meeting house (*New Haven Town Records*, I:271). He was back in England by 1692 when his mother drew her will.
Confirmation of the identity of Thomas³ Gregson of New Haven

――――――――――
* An abstract of the missing will, as given by Boyd, shows wife May; five children, unnamed; three kinsmen, children of James Gregson: John Gregson and James Gregson, both drapers and members of the guild, and May Gregson; granddaughter Mary Faulconer, who was to receive "£5 if she do not marry Philip Planner', and John Benson of St. Alphage, carpenter and guild member, his wife Elizabeth and her four children. Witnesses, Susah Philpot and S. Beaumont, scrivener.

is provided by two documents, each involving this son Richard. The first is the will of the London draper, Richard³ Gregson (No. 7), proved 31 Aug. 1640 in the Prerogative Court of Canterbury (116 Coventry). He referred to "my cosen, Thomas Gregson in Newe England" (*i.e.*, Thomas³ Gregson (No. 5), the testator's first cousin), and bequeathed "unto my cosen [*i.e.*, first cousin once removed] Richard Gregson of Bristol, one Judgement confessed by one Samuel Oldfeild unto Thomas Gregson, which the said Thomas assigned to me." As will now be shown, the Richard Gregson of Bristol was this man.

The second document is a deed dated 26 March 1736 and recorded in New Haven Land Records (X:520), by which "William Grigson of the City of London, Gent., son and heir of William Grigson, late of the same place, Gent., deceased, who was the only surviving son and heir of Richard Grigson, formerly of New Haven, in New England, but lately of the City of Bristol, deceased, which said Richard was the only son and heir of Thomas Grigson, late of New Haven aforesaid, deceased . . . out of his piety towards God and out of his zeal for the protestant religion and the Church of England, as by law established," conveyed in trust to the Rev. Jonathan Arnold of New Haven "a minister of the Church of England [and] a missionary from the Honorable Society in England for Propagating the Gospel in Foreign Parts", land in New Haven to be used for the erection of a church edifice and parsonage. This same land had earlier been distributed, in the settlement of the estate of Thomas³ Gregson, to the "heirs of Richard, the oldest and only son of the deceased, 1 Acres 3/4 and 24 rods of the Home lot, north part" (New Haven Probate Records, IV:397-8).

As noted above, Richard Gregson had one surviving son:

    i.   WILLIAM⁵, called "William Grigson . . . Gent." He d. bef. 26 March 1736, leaving a son and heir: 1. *William Jr.*, grantor of the New Haven property described above; he styled himself "William Grigson of the City of London, Gent."

11. GEORGE⁴ GREGSON (*Henry³, Thomas², Thomas¹*) was baptized 5 Nov. 1606 at St. Michael Old Angels, Sutton-on-the-Hill, Derbyshire.

On 19 Aug. 1634, George married at North Darley, ALICE MILNES, daughter of Richard Milnes, merchant of Chesterfield, co. Derby, and his wife, Dorothy, daughter of John Woodward. George Gregson of Turnditch, Gent., was called eldest son and heir of Henry, and was recorded as aged 26 (*sic*) in 1634 and 66 (*sic*) in 1663. He was buried at Duffield 2 Sept. 1670, as was Alice, four days later (*Harleian, op. cit.,* 37:215-17).

He was doubtless the "George Gregson that lyveth in Paternoster Roe" to whom his uncle Richard Gregson in his will left "five pounds, and for the residue of the money that hee shall pay it to my executors att yeare and yeares after the tyme of my decease".

The 27 Aug. 1670 will of "George Gregson the elder of Turnditch in the County of Derby, gen." devises to his "Loveinge" but unnamed wife; his two minor daughters, Mary and Anne Gregson; his eldest son, George Gregson; "second Sonne, Phillip Gregson . . . all my Sonns & Sonns-in-lawe And all my daughters & daughters-in-law, Tenne Shillings apeece to buy them mourneing rings . . . [and] all & eny of my Grandchildren, two shillings, six pence a peice to buy them gloves." The will was witnessed by George Gregson Jr., W. Turner, Elizabeth Lee and Jane Harrison. The last was perhaps daughter of Ellen (Gregson) Harrison, sister of George's grandfather, Thomas.

Known children of George and Alice (Milnes) Gregson (there were perhaps other sons, and certainly more than one married daughter):

13. i. GEORGE⁵.
   ii. PHILLIP, "second Sonne", to receive "all those my lands, tenements & hereditments in Windley"; executor and residuary legatee in his father's will.
   iii. MARY, a minor in 1670; under the terms of their father's will, she and her sister Anne were to receive, equally, after the death of their mother, "all my Jewells, plate, Chaines, bracelets, rings", one-half of his household goods, "Thirty pounds apeece . . . and . . . ffive pounds apeece yearely & evy yeare untill they shall attaine theire sev'all & respective ages of one & twenty yeares".
   iv. ANNE, a minor in 1670.
14. v. HENRY, not mentioned in his father's will.

12. THOMAS⁴ GREGSON (Henry³, Thomas², Thomas¹) was baptized 14 July 1611 at the parish church in Duffield, Derbyshire. He was doubtless the one referred to in the will, proved in 1640, of Richard³ Gregson (No. 7) as "my kinsman Thomas Gregson, my nowe partner, and to his wife Mary . . . twenty shillings a piece . . . I will and bequeathe unto my now partner, Thomas Gregson, fiftye pounds in full satisfaction of what money hee doth pretend hee hath lent unto my cosen, Thomas Gregson in Newe England, and unto mee, Richard Gregson, his natural unckle".

He married MARY ———.

In his Citizens of London (No. 38006), Percival Boyd notes that Thomas Gregson of Stepney was a citizen and draper, freed from apprenticeship 31 July 1634 by redemption; a woolen draper, St. Paul's Churchyard, Wapping. In 1638 he paid rent of £12 in St. Augustine and paid a poll tax in 1641 in Watling Street.

The 25 Jan. 1663/4 will of Thomas Gregson of Wapping, co. Middlesex, citizen and woolen draper, was proved 11 July 1664 in the Bishop of London's Commissary Court. It provided that "At my funeral onely a sprigg of Rosemary shall be given to them that are invited to see my corps interred"; gave his wife Mary a life interest in his residuary estate and named her his executrix; made bequests to four of his children; and devised rather obscurely to William Brasse, tinker, of the parish of Stebenheath otherwise Stepney, and Hanna his wife, "who pretendeth to be the daughter of my now wife," twelve pence each.

The fact that this Thomas Gregson gave the names Henry and Edith to two of his children and that Richard³ Gregson styled himself Thomas' "natural unckle" confirms the assumption that this Thomas was indeed the son of Henry and Edith (Allestree) Gregson.

Thomas Gregson and wife Mary had one putative and five known children:

?i.   MATTHEW[5], b. 5 July 1635; not mentioned in Thomas' will; he attended the Merchant Taylor's School in 1646 and 1647, and was apprenticed to his father in 1651, being freed in 1658. Boyd (*op. cit.*, No. 38006) enters him, with a question mark, as a son of this Thomas and also as a son of Thomas[3], son of Gregory. See the latter's section for reasons indicating this Thomas rather than the other as the father of Matthew. As a first-born child of Thomas, and aged 29 when Thomas drew his will, he may well have received his portion and thus been omitted from the named legatees.

ii.   MARY; mar. in 1658 at St. George, Southwark, EDWARD MOORE of the parish of Stebenheath alias Stepney. In his will, Thomas forgave all such sums as this daughter owed him.

iii.   THOMAS; received twelve pence in the will of his father.

iv.   EDITH; also left twelve pence by her father.

v.   HENRY; he, with brother Philip, was a residuary legatee in the will.

vi.   PHILIP; an equal residuary legatee with brother Henry.

13. GEORGE[5] GREGSON (*George*[4], *Henry*[3], *Thomas*[2], *Thomas*[1]) was called "eldest Sonne" in his father's will and left "the longe table standinge in the Hall, w'th all the benches thereunto belonginge, & all my latin bookes & Doctor hammonds Commentary upon the new testament". This was a very minor bequest, and we must assume his father had previously given this eldest son substantial property. Although a minor legatee, George Gregson Jr. signed the will as a witness.

A pedigree entitled "Gregson of Turnditch", prepared from the Wolleys Manuscript Collection for a Mr. Ince, may be seen at the Sheffield Reference Library. It gives the following account of descendants of George Gregson Jr.

George Gregson of Turnditch, attorney at law, married ELIZABETH BEIGHTON, daughter of Thomas of Wicksworth. Elizabeth died 24 Aug. 1712 and was buried at Duffield. Their children were:

i.   GEORGE[6] of Derby, attorney at law; d. 17 Oct. 1716 and was bur. at Duffield; mar. MARY BUXTON, dau. and co-heir of John Buxton, and had three children: 1. *Elizabeth*, mar. Henry Noton of Dalbury, co. Derby. 2. *Anne*, d. 8 Sept. 1749, ae. 30; mar. John Wall of Wensley, Derbyshire, who d. 19 Nov. 1782, ae. 89; had sons George Wall and John Wall. 3. *Robert* of Turnditch, Gent., who mar., as her first husband, Jane Rogers, dau. of Jos'h. Rogers; their only son, George Gregson, d. unmar. 25 April 1752, ae. 25, so this branch of the Gregson family became extinct in the male line.

ii.   ELIZABETH; mar. —— HAYNE of Shottle, parish of Duffield, co. Derby; a widow when she signed an agreement 10 July 1741.

iii.   MARY of Ashbourn, co. Derby, widow of ELLIS FARNSWORTH, clerk, in 1741 when she, with her sister Elizabeth as devisees of their sister Orphana, deeded land in consideration of receiving £222:10:00.

iv.   ORPHANA of Shottle, co. Derby, spinster; sole executrix under her mother's will; left her estate to sisters Elizabeth and Mary.

v.   FRANCIS; no further record.

vi.   HENRY of Turnditch and Higham, attorney at law and author of *Account of Duchy of Lancastershire;* mar. TROTH SHERBROOKE, dau. and heiress of Thomas of Higham; two children: 1. *Mary*, d. unmar. 2. *Thomas*, a lieutenant in the army, killed 1740 at Carthagena in America; mar. Jane Rogers, widow of his cousin Robert Gregson, and had one child, Thomas, who d. 1 Nov. 1738 as an infant, this branch of the family thus becoming extinct; Jane, widow of Robert Gregson and Thomas Gregson, mar. (3) the Rev. Lawrence Bourne of Dronfield.

14. HENRY[5] GREGSON (*George*[4], *Henry*[3], *Thomas*[2], *Thomas*[1]) was not mentioned by name in his father's will, presumably having received his portion of his father's estate prior to the drawing of that instrument. *The Visitation of Derbyshire—1662* by William Dugdale (p. 27) calls him aged 25 in 1662, son of George of "Townedich" and grandson of Henry of "Sharrowhall". His arms are given as Argent, a saltire Gules, a canton chequy Or and Azure. Crest: a dexter hand holding a forest bill.

Magna Britannia by Daniel and Samuel Lysons (1817, 5:clx) gives the following account of "Gregson of Turnditch":

> This family had been for three generations at Turnditch in 1662, when Henry Gregson, its representative, was twenty-five years of age. They had been for two generations of Sherowhall in this county [Derby] in consequence of a match with the heiress of Twyford. This family is supposed to be extinct.
> Arms: Argent, a saltier, Gules; a canton, checky, Or and Azure.
> Crest: A cubit arm, erect, vested, Arg., charged with three bends wavy, Sable, holding in the hand, Proper, a battle-axe, Sable, the blade, Or.

This account appears in general to be correct. Henry[3] Gregson (No. 6) acquired property in Turnditch through his marriage to Edith Allestree, his son George and grandson Henry subsequently owning it. If, as appears probable, Thomas[1] Gregson acquired Sherrow Hall through his marriage to Ann, daughter and heiress of William Twyford of Sherrow Hall, and since Thomas[2] Gregson by his will devised Sherrow Hall to his son Henry, the Lysons were correct in stating that the Gregsons "had been for two [prior] generations of Sherowhall".

CHARTER OF GOSPATRIC II, EARL OF DUNBAR, TO THE MONKS OF DURHAM, BEFORE 1138

(From the original in the Durham Cathedral Library)

THE ORIGIN OF THE
FAMILIES OF GREYSTOKE AND DUNBAR

By S. H. LEE WASHINGTON, M.A., of Cambridge, Mass.

As the poet Horace reminds us, there were brave men before Agamemnon; and, similarly, in the less martial annals of genealogy there were notable forerunners of Professor Freeman and Dr. J. H. Round. But such earlier figures as Eyton, Stapleton, and Surtees were to a large extent isolated phenomena; and it was not until Round [1] and Freeman [2] published their monumental essays in England in the latter part of the nineteenth century that the reawakening of interest in this subject really began. As G. Andrews Moriarty, Esq., remarked, in a pregnant comment in the REGISTER more than fifteen years ago, "Of this new school and its methods of dealing with mediaeval sources the American genealogist appears to be profoundly ignorant. While thoroughly modern in dealing with his own records, he is deplorably weak when it comes to earlier work which for the most part he does not understand." (*Ibid.*, vol. 79, p. 359). The truth of this *dictum* becomes apparent from the perusal of any American genealogical compilation which attempts to trace a pedigree in England back of the sixteenth and seventeenth centuries—the ground which Colonel Chester and Henry F. Waters covered so well. Wild and unsupported statements are relied on, and even wilder conjectures hazarded, reminding one forcibly of a remark once made by that eminent historian, Bishop Stubbs, that "Everyone who didn't cross on the *Mayflower* seems to have come over with the Conqueror's ships!" In part, such a state of affairs can be attributed to the unfamiliarity—inevitable under the circumstances—of the American genealogist with the latest views and researches of his brethren across the Atlantic. But even more is it due to the fact that in England itself, despite Freeman's bitter tirades and Round's scathing criticism, many of the same genealogical errors and absurdities are still being annually repeated thirty or forty years after they had originally been exposed. For instance, so long ago as 1901 Round (*Studies in Peerage and Family History,*) exploded the cherished beliefs regarding the founders of the illustrious families of Feilding, Howard, and Wake: yet in the current (1942) edition of Burke's *Peerage*, the Feildings (Earls of Denbigh) continue to deduce descent from the imperial house of Hapsburg, and the Howards (Dukes of Norfolk) and the Wakes (baronets of Courteenhall) alike claim the blood of the "magnificent Duke Oslac" and of the renowned Hereward. Nor, for the most part, does one find oneself in any happier *milieu* when dealing with those families that have es-

---

[1] Cf. J. H. Round, *Studies in Peerage and Family History* (1901) and *Peerage and Pedigree* (2 vols. 1910). A further collection of papers was published in book form after the author's death (see *Family Origins*, ed. William Page [1930]).

[2] See E. A. Freeman, "Pedigrees and Pedigree-Makers" in the *Contemporary Review*, vol. XXX, pp. 11–41.

caped the critics' scorn. Thus, it is hard to resist a smile upon reading that the name of Sewallis, the Doomsday ancestor of the Shirleys (Earls Ferrers), "argues him to be of the old English stock"; for this unusual Christian name "argues", on the contrary, that Sewallis (or Sewall) was of direct Germanic origin (*vide* Forssner, *Continental-Germanic Personal Names in England*, p. 223). No less fantastic is the alleged descent of the Borrowes, baronets, of Gilltown from Hubert de Burgh, Henry III's great Justiciar (who, incidentally, was himself totally unconnected—as so frequently stated—with the Burkes of Ireland). Moreover, the claim now made by Lord St. Davids to be sprung from the Emperor Maximus is irresistibly reminiscent of those mythical progenitors of the Lytes and the Coultharts, 'Leitus' and 'Coulthartus', [3] and of the Royalist squire who fell at the battle of Naseby and whose epitaph proclaimed him "the twenty-fourth titular Earl Cox"! Indeed, one can anticipate, with a certain cynical satisfaction, the contents of future editions of Burke's *Peerage* and *Landed Gentry*,—editions in which Hereward the Wake will be perpetually jostling Duke Oslac and the Emperor Maximus, and in which the unfortunate Sewallis (despite the possible handicap of a slight German accent) will still be vainly arguing his claims as "one of the old English stock."

As regards the families with which this present paper is concerned, —namely, those of Greystoke and Dunbar,—we are confronted with typical examples of great feudal houses that have been *par excellence* the sport of the pedigree-maker. The early Earls of Dunbar have been adopted, though entirely without supporting proofs, as the ancestors of the Nevilles; while their original connection with the Northumbrian barony of Beanley, with its unique tenure of serving as keeper of the March between England and Scotland, has never so far been properly unravelled. Moreover, in the case of the Greystokes, zealous local historians have transformed a certain Sigulf, the founder of the race, who lived at the beginning of the twelfth century, into "Lyulph, a Saxon nobleman" and "a descendant of the ancient Northumbrian kings". Indeed when the Earl of Arundel (who had inherited Greystoke Castle) built a summer house in the eighteenth century within the park of Greystoke on the shores of Lake Ullswater, "as a retreat from the noise and bustle of state to the enjoyments of rural ease and peace", as the chronicle of the day described it,[4] he was but following the genealogical conceptions of his time when he christened the new edifice "Lyulph's Tower". Not content with this, it has further been claimed that Lake Ullswater itself took its name from Lyulph, or L'Ulf, "the Wolf" [*sic*]! [5] Even Dr. Round did not hesitate to identify Sigulf with Lyulp, and

---

[3] For 'Leitus', *vide* Round's *Studies in Peerage and Family History*, pp. X–XI, and the late Sir Henry Maxwell-Lyte's "The Lytes of Lytescary" in *Trans. Somerset Arch. Soc.*, vol. XXXVIII, pp. 3–101. The late Mr. Oswald Barron exposed the fictitious Coulthart pedigree in "The Bonny House of Coulthart", *The Ancestor*, no. IV, pp. 61–80.

[4] See Clarke, *Survey of the Lakes* (ed. 1789), p. 27.

[5] So careful an authority as the late Mr. Hodgson Hinde, the historian of Northumberland, boldly suggested a mistake in the text when he found Symeon of Durham alluding to Sigulf of Greystokes son, Forne of Greystoke, as the son Sig' (Symeon Dunelm. [Surtees Soc.] pt. l, p. 116), and actually explained that this should be Lig [i.e. Ligulf, or "Lyulph" and not Sig' as written!

to deduce the Greystokes from Liulf son of Eduff of Bamburgh, of the stock of Earl Aldred (cf. Round, *Geoffrey de Mandeville*, p. 434). Yet the names Sigulf and Lyulph, or Ligulf, are clearly distinct; nor is there any valid reason for supposing the Greystokes to be connected with Lyulph at all. On the contrary, the writer will endeavour to clear up the mystery of the Greystokes' origin by presenting evidence that their ancestor, Sigulf, was the son of Forne, the King's Thegn (probably the son of another Sigulf, living *circa* 1030), who held Nunburholme, co. Yorks., in chief at the date of the Doomsday Survey. It should be added that the early Greystokes were ancestors, through the d'Eyncourts, of the Stricklands of Sizergh (who inherited from them lands at Yanwath, c. Westmorland), and hence also of the Washingtons of Virginia and the Carletons of Rowley, Mass.: whilst the first two Earls of the house of Dunbar, were likewise progenitors of the Stricklands,[6] as well as of the Massachusetts emigrant, William Sargent.[7] The writer hopes that the story of their origin will thus prove of interest not merely as a study of two great English houses but as providing an example of the difficulties, both in the matter of records and of their interpretation, with which the modern student of genealogy has perforce to contend.

The Greystokes, who were summoned to Parliament as barons by writ in the reign of Edward II, long remained among the chief rulers of the Border. Unlike the majority of feudal magnates, they were of native English blood,—their lordship of Greystoke, co. Cumberland, being one of those northern baronies that had continued even after the Norman invasion to be held by its original pre-Conquest tenure. Besides their great Cumbrian fief, which owed simply a fixed rent of £4 and "cornage" services, the lords of Greystoke in 1166 also held 3⅓ fees *in capite* in Yorkshire and Northumberland (*Red Book* [Rec. Com.], p. 434; *Pipe Roll*, 14 Henry II, p. 89); and their ancestor, Forne son of Sigulf of Greystoke, was a trusted minister of the Crown in Yorks. during the second part of the reign of Henry I (*Early Yorks. Charters*, ed. Farrer, vol. II, pp. 505–6). Indeed, Edith, Forne's daughter, is memorable as having been one of King Henry's mistresses and the mother by him of Robert fitz Edith (or fitz Roy), who was at the siege of Winchester in 1141 (cf. Round, *Geoffrey de Mandeville*, pp. 94, 434). The antiquary Leland has preserved the legend of the "chattering magpies" whose clatter so disturbed the fair Edith that, believing they were conveying to her some supernatural warning about her licentious life, she hastily founded the abbey of Oseney as atonement for her sins! Forne son of Sigulf of Greystoke was one of the witnesses to Earl Ranulf 'le Meschin's' foundation charter of the priory of Wetheral (Prescott, *Reg. Wetherhal*, p. 4); and *circa* 1120 he attested a grant made by Alexander, King of Scots, to the priory of Scone (*Symeon Dunelm.* [Surtees Soc.], vol. II, p. 261; Lawrie, *Early Scottish*

---

[6] Cf. the writer's papers on "The Early History of the Stricklands of Sizergh" in the REGISTER, vol. XCVI, pp. 99–126 and 307–320.

[7] See Mr. G. Andrews Moriarty's masterly article, "The Royal Descent of a New England Settler," in the REGISTER, vol. LXXIX, pp. 358–378. (Pp. 18-38, this volume.)

Charters, p. 30). Until the famous charter of Earl Gospatric was discovered at Lowther Castle,[8] it had been believed that Forne and the other tenants-in-chief in Cumberland had been enfeoffed of their estates by Henry I. But it is now evident that King Henry had simply confirmed them in possession of their fiefs, all of which were held by "cornage" (the names of the lords themselves show them all to have been of native descent), and that Forne's father, Sigulf, must have been lord of Greystoke prior to the conquest of Cumberland by William Rufus.

Reference has already been made to the wild theory (which even Dr. Round accepted) that identifies Sigulf with Lyulph or Ligulf, an alleged descendant of the ancient kings of Northumbria. The present writer ventures to present another, and more reasonable, solution to the problem of Sigulf's origin, although the fact that Cumberland and the other Border counties were excluded from Doomsday Book makes it extremely difficult to trace the Greystoke pedigree at such an early period. However, among the Yorkshire lands held by Sigulf of Greystoke's son Forne *temp*. Henry I was the manor of Nunburholme in the East Riding (*Early Yorks. Charters*, ed. Farrer, vol. II, p. 509). Now "Brurham", *i.e.* Nunburholme, was in 1086 in the possession of Forne, the King's Thegn: and it seems to the writer extremely likely that we have here the grandfather of Forne of Greystoke (son of Sigulf), who flourished *circa* 1120–30. The Doomsday Forne had succeeded three Yorkshire thegns, Morcar, Turuet, and Turchill, the joint holders of Nunburholme *temp*. Edward the Confessor; and it is necessary to distinguish him from the Forne who in 1086 held Skirpenbeck, Yorks., where his successor was an Ulf "Fornesson" (cf. *Cal. Charter Rolls*, 1300–26, p. 114).[9]

The later Forne, son of Sigulf, died in 1130–1 (*Pipe Roll*, 31 Henry I, p. 25); whereupon King Henry I confirmed to his son and successor, Ivo son of Forne, the lands in Yorkshire, Cumberland, Northumberland, and Westmorland that his father had held in chief (*Early Yorkshire Charters*, ed. Farrer, vol. II, pp. 509–510). This Ivo, lord of Greystoke, was among the northern magnates who supported David, King of Scots, and his son, Earl Henry during the Scottish occupation of the Border counties in the reign of Stephen. In conjunction with his wife, Agnes, he granted a carucate and two messuages in Stainton, in the parish of Dacre, co. Cumb., to the church of St. Mary, Carlisle; and Henry son of Robert son of Ivo later recovered his right to the advowson of Dacre church against Ranulf son of Walter (de Greystoke), Ivo's grandson (Dugdale, *Monasticon*, vol. VI, p. 144; *V.C.H. Cumb.*, vol. I, p. 358). Ivo died in 1156, shortly after the accession of Henry II, when Cumberland and the other northern

---

[8] See Canon Wilson's article, "An English Letter of Gospatric" in the *Scottish Historical Review* for October, 1903; also *The Ancestor*, no. VI, pp. 121–134.

[9] It seems very possible that Forne of Nunburholme (? and of Greystoke) was the son of yet another Sigulf, living apparently about 1030, who is named by Earl Gospatric in his charter preserved at Lowther Castle (which was issued before 1074 and addressed to his "men of Cumbria") as one of the Cumbrian magnates "in Eadred's days" [this was Aldred, or Eadred, Earl of Northumberland 1018–38]. The Sigulf of Gospatric's charter has been erroneously identified by historians with Sigulf, father of Forne who flourished *temp*. Henry I.

shires were recovered from the Scottish Crown: and in the Pipe Roll of 1157 there is an entry stating that Henry d'Oyley (his nephew and the son of his sister Edith, the king's mistress) [10] was pardoned 20s. "Danegeld" in Yorks., apparently in respect of the Greystoke fee in that county, which may indicate a favour obtained by d'Oyley for Walter, Ivo's heir (*Pipe Roll*, 2 Henry II, p. 127).

Ivo himself was the father of a daughter Alice de Greystoke who married Edgar of Dunbar, the son of Gospatric II, Earl Dunbar, by whom she had a daughter Agnes, wife of Anselm le Fleming, who became the ancestress of the d'Eyncourts and the Stricklands of Sizergh. [11] Alice's brother Walter son of Ivo, the heir of the Greystoke family, apparently only survived until 1162; since in the Pipe Roll of 1162–3 the sheriff of Northumberland accounted for one mark for a knight's fee held by Walter son of Ivo (de Greystoke) in that county, while the sheriff of Yorkshire similarly accounted for one mark for a knight's fee held by Ranulf son of Walter (son of Ivo) and showed the king's writ excusing the payment of one mark to Henry d'Oyley,—this being, no doubt, the knight's fee which the latter held in Huggate and Millington, Yorks., of the Greystoke barony (*Pipe Roll*, 8 Henry II, p. 11; *Early Yorkshire Charters*, ed. Farrer, vol. II, p. 506). This would seem to indicate that Walter son of Ivo had died during the fiscal year, and that the sheriff of Northumberland had neglected to alter his account in conformity with the event. Walter's son Ranulf (died *circa* 1190), [12] the next lord of Greystoke, left an heir William (died 1209) who married Helewise de Stuteville, the relict of William II de Lancaster, lord of Kendal, and of Hugh de Morville, by whom he became the father of a son Thomas, the ancestor of the Lords Greystoke (cf. Clay, *Extinct and Dormant Peerages of the Northern Counties*, pp. 94–5). Ranulf's daughter Alice married Hugh fitz Henry, lord of Ravensworth, co. Yorks. (Gale, *Reg. hon. de Richmund*, Appendix, pp. 57–8), and had *inter alia* a daughter Ada, the wife of Michael III le Fleming of Aldingham.

We must next consider the question of the lands granted by Ivo son of Forne to his daughter Alice de Greystoke (the ancestress of the d'Eyncourts and Stricklands) in marriage with Edgar of Dunbar. These possessions, as we learn from Walter son of Ivo's confirmation to his sister and her husband, consisted of Knock Salcock and Yanwath, co. Westmorland; Blencowe, co. Cumberland; Caistron, Trewhitt, Great and Little Tosson, and Flotterton, all in the parish of Rothbury, co. Northumberland; and Ulnetby and Thornton-juxta-Tees (now known as Thornton Hall), in the parish of Coniscliffe, co. Durham (*Newminster Chartul.* [Surtees Soc.], p. 117).

[10] Edith had been married by Henry I to Robert d'Oyley, and *circa* 1145, as his widow, granted land in Huggate to St. Peter's, York (*Early Yorks. Charters*, ed. Farrer, vol. II, p. 510). Henry d'Oyley, the son of Robert and Edith, held a knight's fee at Huggate and Millington, Yorks., under the lords of Greystoke, which passed at his death in 1164 to his nephew Arnulf de Mandeville (*Red Book* [Rec. Com.], p. 434).

[11] Cf. the REGISTER, vol. XCVI, p. 320.

[12] Ranulf's mother (the wife of Walter son of Ivo) was named Beatrice (*Early Yorks. Charters*, ed. Farrer, vol. II, p. 515); and he himself married Amabel, who after his death espoused Roger fitz Hugh (de Balliol), lord of Cowpen, Northumb. (*Rot. Litt. Claus.* [Rec. Com.], vol. I, p. 174; *Chartul. Brinkburn*, pp. 159–60).

Dr. Farrer threw doubts on the authenticity of Ivo's enfeoffment, on the grounds that "Little more than Caistron descended in the line of Edgar [the husband of Ivo's daughter, Alice] and his son Patrick" (cf. Farrer, *Early Yorks. Charters*, vol. II, pp. 506, 512): but a closer examination proves such objections to be baseless. For it seems certain from the Northumberland records that not only Caistron, but Trewhitt, the two Tossons, Flotterton, and the Coniscliffe property as well, were held by Alice and Edgar and their immediate posterity (*vide infra*); while evidence as to Alice and Edgar's tenure of the Westmorland estates is afforded by a grant which they made of half the manor of Yanwath to their daughter Agnes and her husband Anselm le Fleming, whose descendants, the d'Eyncourts and Stricklands, inherited lands there (Rydal Hall MSS.; and *vide* REGISTER, vol. XCVI, p. 320). In the thirteenth and fourteenth centuries the Greystokes held Yanwath and their other Westmorland possessions (Brampton, Dufton, and Bolton) under the Cliffords, lords of Appelby (*Trans. Cumb. and West. Antiq. Soc.*, New Series, vol. VIII, p. 281); but these estates were held of the Crown *in capite* prior to King John's grant of the barony of Appelby to Hugh de Morville.[13] Like the Greystokes' Northumbrian domains (Caistron, Trewhitt, etc.), the above properties owed "cornage" services, and from ancient times they must have been attached to the Greystoke fief.[14] Evidently the holdings in the parish of Coniscliffe, co. Durham, formed part of the Greystoke possessions held by knight's service. Walter son of Ivo had one knight's fee in Northumberland at his death in 1162 (*vide ante*). This was undoubtedly the manor of Coniscliffe, afterwards held as one fee by the Greystokes of the bishops of Durham (Surtees, *Hist. Durham*, vol. I, Appendix, p. 128). Coniscliffe is in the wapentake of Sadberge, which was puchased of King Richard I by Hugh du Puiset, Bishop of Durham in 1189: but before that date it was not included in the county of Durham, being in a district that was still regarded as lying in the county of Northumberland. Originally, Coniscliffe would appear to have belonged to the lords of Bolam; since soon after his accession Henry II confirmed Walter son of Ivo in his tenure of Coniscliffe, which the Greystokes had apparently acquired at some previous date from the Bolams in exchange for the three Northumbrian townships of Aydon, Thornburgh, and Little Whittington in the parish of Corbridge (Dugdale, *Monasticon*, vol. III, p. 313). The Greystokes' tenure of Coniscliffe would account for one out of the three and a third knights'

[13] Cf. King Henry I's confirmation of the Greystoke fief to Ivo son of Forne in 1131 (*supra*).

[14] At the end of the twelfth century the manor of Brampton, co. Westmorland, was held of the Greystoke fief by Ranulf de "Brankestone" [Brampton], who may have been a younger son of Ranulf son of Walter of Greystoke, who died 1190. For it is suggestive that in 1202 Theobald de Scotton granted (as trustee) to Alexander, son of Ranulf de "Brankestone", one bovate in Coniscliffe and half a carucate in Thornton, co. Durham (*Yorks. Fines* [Yorks. Rec. Soc.], no. 196): and about the same date a settlement of the manor of Brampton, co. Westd., with land at Coniscliffe, co. Durham, and Caistron, co. Northumb., was made on the marriage of Alexander (son of Ranulf) de Brampton and his wife Margery, sister of William and aunt of another Ranulf de Brampton, who was presumably a cousin (cf. *Newminster Chartul.* [Surtees Soc.], pp. 133–5). Alexander and Margery had a daughter Elizabeth, who received land in Caistron as her marriage portion, and married Henry de Roddam, the ancestor of the Roddams of Roddam, co. Northumberland (*vide Northumb. Co. Hist.*, vol. XV, p. 391).

170

fees that they held in 1166 (*supra*, p. 4), the remaining two and a third fees comprehending Huggate, Nunburholme, and the other estates in the county of York.

In Yorkshire, also, the lords of Greystoke had possessed from early times an extensive fief in the Honour of Richmond (cf. *V.C.H. Yorks.* [North Riding], vol. II, pp. 120–3). The lands in question consisted of Mickleton, Lonton, Thringarth, and Crossthwaite in the parish of Romalkirk: and William son of Thomas de Greystoke, when summoned to prove his right to free chase at Crossthwaite *temp.* Edward I, alleged, with pardonable exaggeration, that his ancestors had held it "ever since the Conquest" (*Plac. de Quo Waranto* [Rec. Com.], p. 192). According to a fifteenth century genealogy of the Fitzhughs, lords of Ravensworth, preserved in the Cotton Library, Ranulf son of Walter de Greystoke before 1190 granted *toute Mikelton et les demesnes ovec le service de Guidon de Bovencourt* [*i.e.* Rimbeaucourt] *et les services de Lonton et Thirngarth ovec la forest de Loun et franc chase* to Henry fitz Hervey, lord of Ravensworth, in marriage with Alice his daughter (Gale, *Reg. hon de Richmund*, Appendix, pp. 57–8). In 1235 Ranulf fitz Henry of Ravensworth had a Final Concord regarding Crossthwaite (which had originally been included in Thringarth) with Thomas son of William de Greystoke (*Yorks. Fines* [Yorks. Rec. Soc.]): and a generation later (1262), Henry fitz Ranulf of Ravensworth was confirmed by William son of Thomas de Greystoke in his possession of the manors of Mickleton, Thringarth, and Lonton (*ibid.*). All of these lands had belonged at the time of Doomsday to Bodin, the younger brother of Alan the Red, Earl of Richmond and Count of Penthièvre in Brittany; and the writer suggests that they had been brought to the Greystokes by marriage with a daughter of Bodin's family. It is noteworthy that Bodin's fief in 1086 comprised not only the lands afterwards held by the lords of Ravensworth, but also all those later included in the fee of the Fitzalans, lords of Bedale. According to the fifteenth century genealogy already referred to, Bodin gave the Ravensworth half of his fief in his old age to his brother Bardulf and thereupon, in company with another brother Ribaud, the 1st lord of Middleham, retired to the Abbey of St. Mary, York: and Bardulf, at Bodin's request, subsequently granted to the Abbey the church of Patrick Brompton with a carucate of land and the church of Ravensworth with a carucate of land in pure alms (Gale, *Reg. hon. de Richmund*, Appendix, p. 57). The truth of this assertion, as regards the gifts of Bardulf, is precisely verified by the confirmation charter later issued to St. Mary's, York., by Henry II (cf. Farrer's *Early Yorks. Charters*, ed. Clay, vol. V, p. 199). Ribaud and Bardulf are described as "brothers of the Count" in a grant made by Count Alan the Red, while Bodin is called "brother" of Bardulf in a charter of Odo the Chamberlain (*ibid.*, pp. 178, 199). The Ravensworth lands were inherited by Bardulf's son Acaris, who flourished 1125–40, and whose grandson was Henry fitz Hervey, from whom the Lords Fitzhugh were descended. However, the second half of Bodin's fief, *i.e.* the lordship of Bedale, was not inherited by Bardulf, but passed after Bodin's death to Scolland, the Earl of Richmond's *dapifer*. There seems no doubt, from the evidences printed by Mr. Clay in the latest volume of his edition of Farrer's *Early Yorkshire Charters* (*ibid.*, vol. V, pp. 199–202), that this Scolland was the ancestor in the male line of the Fitzalans of Bedale, hitherto credited with deriving from Brian, a younger son of Alan of Penthièvre, 4th Earl of Richmond, three quarters of a century afterwards. Scolland's origin is not referred to in any existing document; but it may be inferred that he was either Bodin's son or son-in-law,—more probably the latter. We may therefore conclude that Bodin had partitioned his fief between his brother Bardulf, who received the Ravensworth share, and his only daughter and her husband Scolland, who received the Bedale portion. Towards the end of the twelfth century, as we have seen, Henry fitz Hervey—Bardulf's great-grandson —regained some of the original land (Mickleton, Thringarth, etc.) in marriage with a daughter of Ranulf son of Walter, lord of Greystoke, who presumably himself derived from either Bardulf or Bodin on the distaff side. It may perhaps be hazarded that this connection of the Greystokes with Bodin's family had actually arisen through Ivo son of Forne, who was at all events associated with the Honour of Richmond (*Early Yorks. Charters*, ed. Farrer, vol. II, pp. 505–6), and whose wife Agnes (the mother of the Alice de Greystoke who married Edgar of Dunbar) may well have been a daughter either of Acaris son of Bardulf or of Scolland of Bedale.[15]

In conclusion, we must consider the ancestry of Edgar of Dunbar, the husband of Alice de Greystoke (the heiress of Yanwath) and the father of Agnes de Dunbar, wife of Anselm le Fleming, from whom the d'Eyncourts and Stricklands traced descent. For Edgar was a scion of the illustrious Scottish house of Dunbar which, boasting a great Celtic origin, derived in the male line from the family of the kings of Scotland and in the female line from the royal stock of Wessex.

The founder of the race, Maldred, lord of the land of Carlisle and of Allerdale in Cumberland *circa* 1045–50, was the younger brother of Duncan I, King of Scots, slain in 1040 by Macbeth (*Scots Peerage*, ed. Paul, vol. III, pp. 239–41; also *Scottish Hist. Rev.* for October, 1903). Maldred's wife Edith was the daughter of Uctred, Earl of Northumbria (murdered in 1016 while on his way south to do homage to King Canute), by his third wife Edith (Aelfgifu), daughter of King Ethelred of England (the Unready) and half-sister of Edward the Confessor. Gospatric, the son and successor of Maldred and Edith and a "noble youth" (*Lives Edw. the Confessor* [Rolls Ser.], ed. Luard, p. 411), accompanied Aldred, the new Archbishop of York, to Rome in 1061, along with his kinsman Earl Tostig, the brother of King Harold (*ibid.*). He inherited from his father, Maldred, the lordships of Allerdale and Carlisle (his charter at Lowther

---

[15] Bardulf and his brothers Bodin (the presumed father-in-law of Scolland) and Ribaud (of Middleham) are usually called natural brothers of Count Alan the Red, the 1st Earl of Richmond; but there seems no reason to doubt their legitimacy. They were sons of Eudes, Count of Penthièvre, of a younger branch of the ducal house of Brittany.

Castle, to which reference has already been made, specifies "all things that are mine in Alnerdale"): and at Christmas 1067, after King William's conquest of the North, he compounded with that monarch for a large sum of money in order to be recognized as Earl of Northumberland,—having an hereditary claim (through his maternal grandfather, Earl Uctred) to the earldom, which was just then vacant on account of the murder of his mother's nephew, Earl Osulf. But his relationship to the old English royal house inevitably made him an object of suspicion to the Norman conquerors: he was implicated in the rebellion of Earls Edwin and Morcar in 1068, and in 1072 was deprived of his earldom and retired to Scotland to the court of his cousin, King Malcolm III. It is generally stated that the latter then "created" him Earl of Dunbar, in recompense for the lost earldom of Northumberland (cf. *Scots Peerage, loc. cit.*). But Dunbar, *i.e.* Lothian, was simply the northern half of the ancient earldom of Northumbria, which had been wrested in 1018 from Earl Edulf 'Cutel' (the brother and successor of Earl Uctred) by King Malcolm II, Gospatric's great-grandfather on his father's side: and it may be suggested that Gospatric himself, instead of being granted Dunbar (Lothian) afresh after 1072, had merely inherited it from his father Maldred.[16] According to Hoveden, he died in 1074 and was buried at Norham (*Chron. Roger de Hovenden*, ed. Stubbs, vol. I, p. 59): and his second son Dolfin became lord of Carlisle, whilst his third son Waldeve (or Waltheof) was lord of Allerdale.[17] (Both Allerdale and Carlisle remained under Scottish rule until the conquest of Cumbria by William Rufus in 1092.)

Meanwhile, his eldest son, Gospatric II, succeeded to the earldom of Dunbar: and, although neither the latter nor any of his descendants ever regained the earldom of Northumberland, Gospatric II subsequently received a charter of the Northumbrian barony of Beanley from Henry I, which, as we shall see, he had probably inherited from his wife's brother. King Henry's charter assured to him, as "(Earl) Gospatric brother of Dolfin", all the land [unspecified] previously held in chief by his (Gospatric's) "Uncle" Edmund, who must have been a brother of Gospatric I. The charter further stipulated that the grantee was to have "the land of Winnoc", viz., Beanley with the appurtenant manors of Brandon, Branton, Titlington, Hedgley, and Harehope, co. Northumberland, "with all the men and goods which were on that land when the King gave the aforesaid manor to Hamo" (cf. *Priory of Hexham*, vol. I, p. xiii).[18] Other Northumbrian property is also mentioned in a second charter to the Earl issued in 1135–6 by King Stephen, which recites the terms

---

[16] Lothian was actually regained under William Rufus (cf. Moore, *Lands of the Scottish Kings in England*, pp. XI and 2), and probably continued to be ruled as part of Northumberland until the cession of the northern counties to Scotland in the reign of Stephen.

[17] Historians have invariably reversed the order of Gospatric's children, having been misled by the order in which they are mentioned by Symeon (*Symeon Dunelm.*, vol. II, pp. 199-200). But the confirmations issued to Gospatric II by Henry I and Stephen clearly show that the latter was his father's heir,—which thus obviates the difficulty as to the reason why Gospatric II should have inherited his father's earldom.

[18] Who Hamo was is unknown. He might perhaps have been a son of Winnoc who died without issue, or else have gained a temporary interest in Beanley through marriage with Winnoc's widow.

of the earlier grant and adds that King Henry gave him, in addition, the service of Liulf son of Uctred [of Ilderton] for Roddam, Horseley, and the three Middletons, as well as that of a certain Gospatic [doubtless a kinsman] for Long Witton, Nether Witton, Ritton, Stanton, and Windegate (*ibid*.).[19] King Stephen's charter (which, as has been said, recapitulates the previous charter issued by Henry I) is well known and has been several times reprinted (*vide Northumb. Co. Hist.*, vol. VII, pp. 30–1); since Beanley and its dependant manors (therein specified) represented the 'baronia de Benelegh', which was held by the subsequent Earls of Dunbar in grand serjeanty of being 'inborwe' and 'outborwe' between the kingdoms of England and Scotland. This unique and interesting service was that of acting as insurety and outsurety for the peaceful intentions of all those passing across the Border, who had first to obtain the master of Beanley's permission to do so,—a position that corresponded closely to the later office of Lord Warden of the Marches.

But the full significance of the grants issued by Kings Henry and Stephen to Gospatric II have not hitherto been realized. For the manors of Bewick and Eglingham, co. Northumb., which were held of the abbey of St. Albans, can be shown to have passed from Winnoc to Gospatric II and thence to his son Edgar (the husband of Alice de Greystoke); and there can be no doubt that this is the same Winnoc who preceded Gospatric II in the lordship of Beanley. A series of charters, preserved in the chartulary of Tynemouth priory (cf. *Northumb. Co. Hist.*, vol. VII, pp. 31–2), reveal that, soon after Henry I's accession in 1101, Winnoc made an agreement with Richard (d'Aubigny), Abbot of St. Albans, regarding his tenure of Bewick and Eglingham, which had previously been held under the abbey by a certain Arkil Morel: and a precisely similar agreement was afterwards made with the same Abbot Richard before 1119 by Gospatric II and his younger son, Adam. Moreover, yet another agreement was made, 1119–46, between Gospatric II's son, Edgar, and Abbot Richard's successor, Abbot Geoffrey de Gorham. These various confirmations support the conclusion that Gospatric II became possessed of Bewick and Eglingham, as well as of the barony of Beanley, as successor to Winnoc; and very possibly Gospatric's wife, who was named Sybil (*Liber Vitae* [Surtees Soc.], p. 102; *Liber de Calchou* [Bannatyne Club], p. 234), was Winnoc's sister and heiress. Indeed, the contemporary case of Cumberland warns us of the danger of misconstruing Henry I's "grants" of baronies to native owners as grants *de novo*, instead of merely as confirmations of existing titles: and certainly in the instance of Beanley we must conclude that King Henry's charter did no more than *confirm* Gospatric's right to the barony upon Winnoc's death. It should also be observed that Winnoc was the successor at Bewick and Eglingham of Arkil Morel, who was doubtless his predecessor at Beanley also. Berwick and Eglingham are described as 'the land of Arkil Morel' in

---

[19] Part of these additional lands were held by knight service; and Earl Gospatric III is recorded as having held six knights' fees in Northumberland in 1161 (*Pipe Roll*, 11 Henry II, p. 30).

the St. Albans charters, above quoted: and Arkil Morel himself can be none other than the personage of that name who was the lieutenant of Robert de Mowbray, the Norman Earl of Northumberland, in his rebellion against William Rufus in 1095. According to the *Anglo-Saxon Chronicle* (ed. Thorpe, vol. I, p. 360), Arkil Morel had been the "gossip" (foster brother) of King Malcolm III: but, despite his native descent, he could evidently boast a Norman grandfather *ex parte materna*, since the chronicler Orderic expressly informs us that he was the "nephew" (presumably sister's son) of Earl Robert de Mowbray (*Ordericus Vitalis*, cols. 620, 623). The *Anglo-Saxon Chronicle* adds that it was he who slew King Malcolm with an arrow beneath the walls of Alnwick castle during the Scottish invasion of 1093: and two years later (1095), when his master Earl Robert rebelled against Rufus, he and the Earl's wife, Maude, were besieged in the fortress of Bamburgh by the Red King's army. He is further described as being the Earl's steward, or *dapifer;* but after Earl Robert's death and the suppression of the rebellion he made his peace with Rufus and became the means by which many of the Earl's followers were brought to justice (*Anglo Saxon Chron., ibid.*, p. 362). Orderic says that he died shortly afterwards, during a journey to the Continent (*Ordericus Vitalis*, cols. 624–5); whereupon Winnoc succeeded to his estates. It may not be too fantastic to suppose that Arkil Morel was the father of Winnoc, as well as of Sybil, the wife of Gospatric II, Earl of Dunbar.

This second Earl Gospatric, although a great subject both of the kings of Scotland and of England, left comparatively little impress on the history of his time. He supported his cousin King David of Scots in the wars of the reign of Stephen, and was slain at the battle of the Standard, 23 August 1138 (Twysden, *Decem Scriptores*, col. 1027). Two of his sisters made alliances that deserve mention, viz., Gunnilda, who married Orm son of Ketel, lord of Workington, co. Cumb. (Prescott, *Reg. Wetherhal*, p. 384); and Ethreda, who married her kinsman Duncan II, King of Scots, and was the mother of the well-known William fitz Duncan, lord of Coupland and Skipton. For from Gunnilda and her husband, Orm, descended the ancient family of Curwen, whose representative is still the owner of Workington Hall; while Ethreda was the ancestress, in the female line, of the powerful Cumbrian houses of Lucy and Dacre. Christian de Dacre, the great-great-great-granddaughter of Ethreda's son and heir, William fitz Duncan, became the wife of John de Washington of Warton, younger son of Robert de Washington and Joan de Strickland; and this Christian's mother, Isabel wife of Sir Edmund de Dacre, was a direct descendant of Earl Gospatric II's niece, Uctreda of Dunbar, by the latter's first marriage with Ranulf de Lindsay (cf. the REGISTER, vol. XCVI, pp. 93–4).[20] A younger brother of Earl Gospatric II is stated to have been the Uctred whose son Dolfin "son of Uctred" held Staindrop of the prior of Durham in 1131, and was the paternal ancestor of the historic family of Neville. However, no

[20] Uctreda's second husband was William de Esseby, for whom see the REGISTER, vol. XCVI, p. 319.

proof of such an affiliation between the Earl and Uctred, the father of Dolfin, is forthcoming; and the names of Dolfin and Uctred are much too common in the North in the eleventh and twelfth centuries to warrant any assumption of relationship. The Nevilles, and their present representative the Marquess of Abergavenny, must be content with a mere descent from Uctred and with a later pedigree with which, in the words of the late Mr. Oswald Barron, "no other in the peerage books may be matched".

But we must pass on to Earl Gospatric II's son, Edgar. He was apparently the second child of Gospatric and Sybil (being thus next brother to the heir, Gospatric III, who succeeded as Earl of Dunbar at his father's death in 1138), and inherited a considerable share of his family's Northumbrian estates, including the manors of Bewick and Eglingham.[21] Moreover, his marriage to Alice de Greystoke, already described, still further increased his possessions. He is often mentioned in the annals of the day, and on account of his bravery in battle received the nickname of Unnithing, "the dauntless" (cf. *Newminster Chartul.* [Surtees Soc.], p. 301; and *Pipe Roll*, 20 Henry II, p. 107). Richard of Hexham calls him *nothus* ("bastard"): but this must have been merely an opprobrious term, for Edgar was certainly not illegitimate,[22] and Richard of Hexham clearly had reason to dislike him, since he goes on to say that during the Scottish invasion of 1138 Edgar and other "miscreants" plundered certain vills in Northumberland belonging to Hexham priory (*vide Priory of Hexham*, vol. I, p. 95). To one of Edgar's charters to Tynemouth a very fine impression of his seal is attached, the device consisting of a winged monster with a lion's head reversed and griffin's paws, and the legend: *Hoc est sigillum Edgari filii Gospatricii Comitis* (see Gibson, *Mon. of Tynemouth*, vol. I, p. 50). Edgar joined with King William the Lion and the other northern magnates in the revolt of the "young Henry" against Henry II in 1174, and forfeited all his paternal possessions (Bewick, Eglingham, etc.) as a consequence (*Abbrev. Placit.* [Rec. Com.], pp. 67–8; Curia Regis Roll, 11 John, no. 21, m. 9 d.; *Northumb. Co. Hist.*, vol. VII, p. 39). But the lands of his wife Alice de Greystoke,—Caistron, Flotterton, Ulnetby, etc.,—were retained and inherited in turn by his sons Alexander and Gospatric; while the property at Yanwath was settled, as has been mentioned, upon his daughter Agnes (ancestress of the Stricklands) and her husband, Anselm le Fleming (cf. REGISTER, vol. XCVI, p. 320).

Edgar and Alice's second son, Gospatric (or Patric), became his parent's eventual heir, and was father of a son John, who assumed the surname of "de Kestern", *i.e.* Caistron, from his possession of the (Greystoke) manor of Caistron on the river Coquet above Rothbury (*Northumb. Co. Hist.*, vol. XV, pp. 390–2). The latter's son and grandson, John II and John III de Caistron, granted Caistron about the middle of the thirteenth century to the abbey of New-

---

[21] He was also given the three Middletons, Horsley, etc.

[22] In John of Hexham's chronicle he is simply described as *filius Comitis* (*Priory of Hexham*, vol. I, p. 121).

minster (*ibid.*).[23] The third John de Caistron appears to have married Agnes, one of the sisters and co-heirs of Ranulf de Haughton (of Haughton, co. Northumb.), and to have left an only daughter and heiress, Joan de Dunbar, *alias* de Caistron, who carried the remaining Greystoke manors (Trewhitt, Great and Little Tosson, and Flotterton) in marriage to Richard de Chartenay of Hepple (*Northumb. and Durham Deeds* [Newcastle Rec. Soc.], pp. 169–70, and 245; *Northumb. Co. Hist.*, vol. XV, pp. 382, 396–7, 399, and 404).

From Edgar's elder brother, Gospatric III, descended the subsequent Earls of Dunbar, lords of Beanley, who, both as the holders of vast estates and as a branch of the ancient royal line, continued to rank as the greatest family in Scotland until the fifteenth century, when their power was finally undermined by the rise of the house of Douglas.

From Edgar's sister Juliana, wife of Ranulf de Merlay, derived the Merlays, Gobions, Morteynes, and Giffords of Twyford, Bucks., a descendant of whom, Margaret Gifford, married in the sixteenth century Hugh Sargent of Courteenhalls, Northanton., and was ancestress of the emigrant William Sargent of New England.

---

[23] Shortly after 1154, John III de "Kestern" quitclaimed the service of William de Somerville in Ulnetby (in Coniscliffe, co. Durham) to the overlord, William son of Thomas de Greystoke (*Newminster Chartul.* [Surtees Soc.], p. 147).

THE ENGLISH HOME AND ANCESTRY
OF
JOHN GROSVENOR OF ROXBURY, MASS.

By DANIEL KENT, B.A., of Worcester, Mass.

IN the old burying ground at the corner of Washington and Eustis Streets in Roxbury (now a part of Boston), Mass., on the right of the entrance gate and not far distant, near the wall on the Eustis Street side, stands a dark slate stone in a good state of preservation, on which is inscribed:

> Here Lyeth Buried ye Body of : Iohn Grosuenor who Decd Septem ye 27th in ye 49 Year of his Age   1691

On this stone is cut a coat of arms, the garb in the dexter quartering and the crest, a talbot statant on a wreath, pointing apparently to a connection with the ancient Grosvenor family of co. Chester, England.*

The family tradition that John Grosvenor of Roxbury, Mass., came from Chester, where he married Esther Clarke, an heiress, has been accepted as an established fact. Most published genealogical sketches of him state that he was a son of Sir Richard Grosvenor, Bart.; but this cannot be true, as Sir Richard, the first baronet, who died 14 Sept. 1645, left only one surviving son, Sir Richard, the second baronet. This second Sir Richard, who died 31 Jan. 1664/5, had five sons, of whom all except Roger, the eldest, died unmarried.

* The well-known family of the Grosvenors, of which the Duke of Westminster, of Eton Hall, co. Chester, is at present the most prominent member, claims descent from Norman lords who in the tenth century held a barony at Venables in the Duchy of Normandy, about thirty miles from Rouen, on the road to Paris.   Hugh Lupus came into England with the Conqueror and was made Count Palatine of Chester.   With him, it is said, came his nephew, the ancestor of the later Grosvenors, Gilbert le Veneur (the Huntsman), who, with others of the family, received large estates in Cheshire. The appellation *le Veneur* was taken from the office of huntsman (in Latin *venator*) to the Dukes of Normandy, which was hereditary in this family before the Norman Conquest of England.   The name *Grosvenor*, which, according to Ormerod, the historian of Cheshire, is not found before 1260, is said to be derived from the title *le Grand Veneur*, which appears in various forms, such as *le Graunt Venur, Grauntvenour, le Gros Venour, le Grosvenour, le Gravenor*, and finally *Grosvenor*.   Pedigrees of the various branches of the family may be found in the English Visitations, and much information is given in Ormerod's History of Cheshire.   The Grosvenor arms were: Azure, a garb or.   Various signs for difference distinguished the various branches of the family.

The writer of this article has made an exhaustive search of the Grosvenor records in England. Having become convinced, by research and by correspondence with the Duke of Westminster, the Rector of Eton Hall, co. Chester, and the Secretary of the Lancashire and Cheshire Historical Society, that John Grosvenor, the immigrant ancestor of the family in New England, did not come directly from the Chester family, he turned his attention to the branches of this family scattered throughout England. Guided by the coat of arms on the gravestone at Roxbury, he decided that John Grosvenor must have come from Shropshire; and his labors were rewarded by finding in St. Leonard's Church, at Bridgnorth, Shropshire, the record of John Grosvenor's baptism. At the College of Arms in London he found a pedigree of the Grosvenors of Bridgnorth, certified in 1663 by Leicester Grosvenor, the eldest brother of John of Roxbury, which was respited "to make proofe of the Descent from the Grosvenours of Eton in Cheshire," but "nothing [was] done therein." This pedigree, a copy of which is given in this article, enabled the writer to go back to the grandfather of John of Roxbury; and the wills of the grandfather and father of the immigrant, abstracts of which are given below, as well as entries in the registers of the parish of St. Leonard, Bridgnorth, confirm the line given in the pedigree. The writer has not succeeded in determining the connection of the Grosvenors of Bridgnorth with the Chester family; but that John Grosvenor of Roxbury was descended from that family there can be little doubt.

The English records relating to the Grosvenors of Bridgnorth follow.

The Will of WILLIAM GRAVENOR of Bridgnorth within the countie of Salop, gent., 28 December 1599. Whereas I have one daughter, whose name is Margery Gravenor, I do appointe that the rent, proffitt, and commoditie, whatsoever shall arise of and for my great meadow above the Fryers dissolued neare Bridgnorth and the litle close called the Hose, shall remaine to my saide daughter Margerie for the terme of six yeares nexte after the decease of my mother in lawe Anne Dovie, to be a stock maintenance or marriage good for my saide daughter; yet upon condition that my said daughter be ruled and placed in marriage at the good likeinge of my wife, her mother, and if [sic, ? of] my sone & heire and of other my frendes; or ells otherwise, if she be unrulye and obstinate, the same to remaine to my wife and my heire. I will that my tableboarde uppon a frame shall remaine to my sonne and heire William Grauenor. To my sister Joice Grauenor the tenement in Lessley Street which Fraunces Farelam dwelleth in and the backside thereunto belonging, To have the same during her naturall life, payeng therefore during her saide life to my heires and assignes 3s. 4d. yerelie at our Ladie daie and Michaelmas, keping reparations thereof and mayneteyninge it also tennauntable. My wife Ursula shall have the bringing up of my two children, my son and my daughter; and she shall bring up my sonne to be a scholler, if he prove to be apt; if nott, to learne to write and reade, and set him to some good occupation. And my wife shall haue also the third parte after my sonne shall come to his age for her joynture (as the lawe doth appointe), and untill my heire come to age, my wife to haue the whole proffitt of my landes towards her owne maintenaunce and for the rearinge of my children. All my landes, tenementes, and hereditaments I give to my sonne William Gravenor, to his heires and assignes foreuer. If my saide sonne die without issue of his body

179

lawfully begotten, then my saide landes, Tenementes, and hereditaments to remaine to my saide daughter Margerie and to her issue. And for wante of issue of her bodie lawfully begotten, to remaine to the right and nexte heires in bloude of me, the saide William Grauenor. All my wearing apparrell I give to Roger Grauenor of Coventry, being my brother. All the rest of my goodes I leaue to the discretion of my wife. I appoint my saide wife and my sonne William Grauenor executors of this my last will and testamente. Debts which I owe, videlicet, to John Steenton £5. 10s., to master Patchet 50s., to Thomas Minshew 29s., to Mr. Pevis 12s. or thereaboute. Thomas Hoorde, Esquier, oweth me £15, parcell of the purchase of my meadow. Mr. Staunton oweth me 6s. 8d. Witnesses: Richarde Blackwey, Clerke, Richard Dovie, and William Kinge. Proved 22 November 1604 by John Davis, husband of Ursula Davis alias Gravenor, relect of the said deceased and one of the executors named in the will, with power reserved to the other executor. (P.C.C., Harte, 88.)

The Will of WILLIAM GRAVENER the elder of Bridgenorth in the County of Salopp, gent., 27 May 1652. To bee buried in the parish Church of St Leonards in Bridgenorth, neere unto the place where my father was buried. To Susanna, my wife, the moity or one halfe of all that my messuage wherein I now dwell called and knowne by the name of the Fryers, and the Moity or one halfe of the garden thereunto adioyneing and belonging, scituate in or neere Bridgnorth aforesaid, in the said County of Salop, dureing the Terme of her naturall life. And after her decease I give the same to Lester Gravenor, sonne and heire appearent of mee the said William Gravener, and his heires for ever. And the other Moity of the said Messuage, and alsoe All the Lands, meadows, Leasows, and Passures to the said Messuage belonging or in any wise app'teyneing, scituate in or near Bridgenorth aforesaid, and alsoe all other the Messuages, lands, Tenemts, and hereditamts of mee, the said William Gravener, scituate within the town and Lib'ties of Bridgenorth aforesaid and in Ouldbury in the said County of Salop, I give to the said Lester Gravener and his heires forever. And alsoe I give to him All my goods, Cattells, and Chattells whatsoever, upon Condition that the said Leister Gravener or his heires shall wth in twoe yeares next after my decease pay and discharge all such Debts wch I doe owe or shall owe at the tyme of my decease, and also wth in two yeares next after my decease pay To my daughter Susanna Gravener £40 of lawfull money of England, To my Daughter Grace Gravener £40 of like money, To my Daughter Jane Gravener £40 of like money, To my Daughter Mary Harrison £5, To my Daughter Lettice Levinge £5, To her daughter Lettice Levinge £5, To John Eddowes £5, To my sonne Jerrard Gravenor the sume of threscore poundes, and to my sonne John Gravenor the sume of threscore poundes of lawfull money of England. Provided allwaies that if my sonne Lester Gravener or his heires shall make defaulte of paymt of my sayd debts or of the said other severall somes of money limitted to bee payd as aforesaid, then the guifts and bequests made by mee to the said Lester Gravener and his heires shall be utterly voyd; and then I give and bequeath all my said Messuages, lands, Tenemts, and p'misses before mentioned (except the said Moity of the said Messuage and garden called the Fryers, which I give to the said Susanna, my wife, for the Terme of her naturall life) to the said Susanna Gravener, my Daughter, Grace Gravener, Jane Gravener, Gerrard Gravener, William Gravener, and John Gravener, their Executors, Administrators, and assignes, from and immediately after my decease, for and dureing the full end and Terms of Fowerscore and Nyneteene yeares then next following. And I give to them all my goods, cattells, and Chattells for ye payinge of my said debts and for payment of the severall Somes of money before limitted to bee payd to them, the said Susanna, my daughter, Grace, Jane, Gerard, William

Gravener, and John Gravener, my sonnes, and to the said Mary Harrison, Lettice Leving and her Daughter Lettice Leving, and John Eddowes. Provided allways I give to the s^d Susanna, my wife, the one halfe of my househould goods and implements of househould, anything before mentioned to the Contrary in any wise notw^th standing. Executors: Thomas Leving and Edward Harrison, gent., my sonne in lawes, and I give to them £4 for their paynes, to be equally devided betwene them. Witnesses: Thomas Tyther, Robert Ranolds, Thomas Llawe, W. barter. Proved 12 September 1653 by the executors named in the will. (P. C. C., Brent, 366.)

GROSVENOR ENTRIES IN THE REGISTERS OF THE PARISH OF ST. LEONARD, BRIDGNORTH, CO. SALOP, 1551–1708*

Baptisms

1593 W^m sonne of Wm Gravener Gent the xviii of Dec^r.
1596 Margaret ye daughter of Willm Gravener gent. xvi^h of Maye
1634 William the sonne of William Gravenor gen the xvii^h daie of Aprill
1636 Jane the daughter of William Gra'venor gent and Susanna his wife the xxvi day of July
1640 John the sonne of William Gravenor and Susanna his wife ye second day of January [1640/1]
1655 Christopher son of Mr Leicester Grosvenor and Ellenor his wife ye 8 August
1662 William, son of Mr Leicester Grosvenor and Ellenor his wife, March ye 19th [1662/3] [sic]
1663 William son of Mr Leicester Grosvenor and Ellenor his wife ye 20 September
1666 Eastwicke, the sonne of Mr Leicester Grosvenor and Ellenor his wife, ye 4th of March [1666/7]

Marriages

1590 Wm Gravener & Ursula Blunt the xvi^th of November
1592 Wm Peat & Johoane Gravener the xxvi^th of June
1593 Hugh Gravener & Joane Streete the xi^th day of December
1600 John Davies & Ursula Gravenor the iv^th of June
1624 Willm Gravenor & Anne Baskerfield the xxviii^h day of November
1630 Richard Phillips and Margere Gravenor the second day of June
1641 John Wood and Lettice Gravenour the 19th of October

Burials

1583 Margaret Gravenor ye v^th of October
1589 William Gravęner Hon^le Gen. xxx Octobr
1599 Willm Gravonor the xvii^th day of January [1599/1600]
1613 Barbara Gravenor the xviii^th day of Marche [1613/14]
1652 William Gravenor Gent. the xxi of June
1655 Christopher Grosvenor son of Leicester Grosvenor Gent. 17 September
1655 Leycester Grosvenor son of Leicester Grosvenor Gent. 24 September
1667 Mrs Susanna Grosvenor the 20 day of June
1669 Eastwicke, the sonne of Leicester Grosvenor gent. the 18th March [1669/70]
1670 Richard Grosvenor 25th of April
1671 Gerald Grosvenor June the 27th
1672 William Grosvenor 3 Feb. [1672/3]
1690 Leicester Grosvenor Gent. 14 May
1708 Mrs. Eleanor Grosvenor 26 November

* From 1551 to 1642 all Grosvenor entries found in these registers are given; but from 1642 to 1708 only those Grosvenor entries are given which are known to refer to the immediate relatives of John Grosvenor, the immigrant to New England.

FROM THE RECORDS OF THE COLLEGE OF ARMS, LONDON

Grosvenour of Bridgnorth

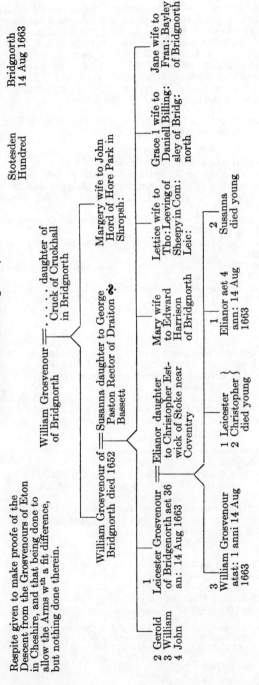

Respite given to make proofe of the Descent from the Grosvenours of Eton in Cheshire, and that being done to allow the Arms wᵗʰ a fit difference, but nothing done therein.

Stotesden Hundred

Bridgnorth 14 Aug 1663

William Grosvenour of Bridgnorth = ... daughter of Cruck of Cruckhall in Bridgnorth

Margery wife to John Hord of Hore Park in Shropsh:

William Grosvenour of Bridgnorth died 1652 = Susanna daughter to George Paston Rector of Draiton Bassett

1 Leicester Grosvenour of Bridgenorth aet 36 an: 14 Aug 1663 = Elianor daughter to Christopher Estwick of Stoke near Coventry

Mary wife to Edward Harrison of Bridgnorth

Lettice wife to Tho: Leeving of Sheepy in Com: Leic:

Grace 1 wife to Daniell Billing: sley of Bridg: north

Jane wife to Fran: Bayley of Bridgnorth

2 Gerold
3 William
4 John

3 William Grosvenour ætat: 1 anni 14 Aug 1663

1 Leicester
2 Christopher } died young

1 Elianor aet 4 ann: 14 Aug 1663

2 Susanna died young

Certified by Mʳ Leicester Grosvenour

From the foregoing and a few other English records and from various New England sources the following Grosvenor* pedigree has been compiled:

1. —— GROSVENOR.†
   Children (order of births unknown):
   2. i. WILLIAM.
      ii. ROGER, of Coventry, co. Warwick, living in 1599, when he was mentioned in the will of his brother William.
      iii. JOYCE, living in 1599, when she was mentioned in the will of her brother William.

2. WILLIAM GROSVENOR, of Bridgnorth, co. Salop, Gent., the testator of 1599, was buried in the parish of St. Leonard, Bridgnorth, 17 Jan. 1599/1600.‡ He married in that parish, 16 Nov. 1590, URSULA BLUNT,§ who married secondly, in the same parish, 4 June 1600, John Davies (or Davis) and was living, as the wife of John Davis, 22 Nov. 1604, when her second husband proved the will of her first husband.
   Children, baptized in the parish of St. Leonard, Bridgnorth:
   3. i. WILLIAM, bapt. 18 Dec. 1593.

* In the early records this surname often appears in the forms *Gravener* and *Gravenor*.
† Perhaps the William Gravener, "Honʳˡᵉ Gen.," who was buried in the parish of St. Leonard, Bridgnorth, co. Salop, 30 Oct. 1589, was identical with No. 1 of this pedigree; and the Margaret Gravenor who was buried in that parish 5 Oct. 1583 may have been his wife. The Barbara Gravenor who was buried in the same parish 18 Mar. 1613/14 was perhaps a sister of the William who was buried there in 1589. In the same parish William Peat and Johoane Gravener were married 26 June 1592, and Hugh Gravener and Joane Streete were married 11 Dec. 1593; but the connection of these Graveners with the family described in this article is unknown.
‡ The Church of St. Leonard, founded in the tenth or eleventh centuries, stands in a close near High Street, Bridgnorth, which is surrounded by buildings of Elizabethan or Jacobean date. Its fine old stained glass and its tombs were destroyed during the siege of Bridgnorth by Cromwell in 1646. But in more recent years the church has been restored, and is worthy of the ancient town that it adorns. The original church was built mainly in the style of the thirteenth century, though its handsome tower, of salmon-red sandstone, is of a somewhat later style. A fine open-timbered roof was brought to light during the restoration. The nave is remarkable for its exceptional width, and in this respect the church is exceeded by no other parish church in England and by only three cathedrals.
§ In the pedigree entered by Leicester Grosvenor, her grandson, in 1663, the wife of William Grosvenor (2) is called "daughter of Cruck of Cruckhall in Bridgnorth." The marriage record in the registers of the parish of St. Leonard, Bridgnorth, calls her "Ursula Blunt." In 1404 Sir Nicholas Blunt or Blount, who had been involved in a plot for the restoration of King Richard II, changed his name to Croke, in order to escape punishment from Henry IV; and his descendants appear sometimes under the name of Croke or Cruke and sometimes under the name of Blunt or Blount. In the registers of the parish of St. Leonard both names are found for this family. Members of the Blount family played important parts in English history. Sir Walter Blount, a supporter of John of Gaunt, Duke of Lancaster, and of his son, King Henry IV, was slain by Archibald, Earl of Douglas, at the Battle of Shrewsbury, 23 July 1403. He is a prominent character in Shakspere's King Henry IV, Part I. He married Donna Sancha de Ayála, a Spanish lady of high rank, and in the reign of Edward IV their grandson became the first Baron Mountjoy and was Lord High Treasurer of England. William Blount, the fourth Baron Mountjoy, a grandson of the first Baron Mountjoy, was a patron and friend of Erasmus. Mrs. Anne (Marbury) Hutchinson, so famous in the early history of New England, was a descendant of Sir Walter Blount and his wife, Donna Sancha de Ayála, and several New England families may trace their ancestry, through the Marbury family, to this Shaksperean knight and his Spanish consort. For the Blount family see pedigrees in various English Visitations, articles in the Dictionary of National Biography, and Sir Alexander Croke's Genealogical History of the Croke Family, surnamed Le Blount.

183

ii. MARGARET (or MARGERY), bapt. 16 May 1596; m. JOHN HORD of Hord Park, co. Salop.*

3. WILLIAM GROSVENOR (*William*), of Bridgnorth, co. Salop, Gent., the testator of 1652, was baptized in the parish of St. Leonard, Bridgnorth, 18 Dec. 1593, and was buried in the same parish 21 June 1652. He married, probably about 1625, SUSANNA PASTON,† who was buried in the parish of St. Leonard, Bridgnorth, 20 June 1667, daughter of Rev. George, Rector of Drayton-Bassett, co. Stafford, who was buried 10 Jan. 1629/30. William Grosvenor's messuage at Bridgnorth was called "The Friars," and was near the site of the present carpet works in the lower town of Bridgnorth.‡ He was a churchwarden of St. Leonard's Church in 1635, and was a Royalist in the Civil War.

Children:§

  i. SUSANNA, b. probably abt. 1626; living unm. 27 May 1652, when she was mentioned in her father's will; not mentioned in the pedigree of 1663.

4. ii. LEICESTER, eldest son, b. abt. 1627.

  iii. MARY, b. probably abt. 1628; living 27 May 1652, when she was mentioned in her father's will; m. before that date EDWARD HARRISON of Bridgnorth.

  iv. LETTICE, b. probably abt. 1630; d. in 1690, aged 60; m. before 27 May 1652, when she was mentioned, with her dau. *Lettice*, in her father's will, THOMAS LEVINGE of Sheepy, co. Leicester.‖

  v. GERALD (or GERRARD), second son, b. probably abt. 1631; bur. in the parish of St. Leonard, Bridgnorth, 27 June 1671.

  vi. GRACE, b. probably abt. 1632; m. after 27 May 1652 DANIEL BILLINGSLEY of Bridgnorth.

  vii. WILLIAM, third son, bapt. in the parish of St. Leonard, Bridgnorth, 17 Apr. 1634; bur. in the same parish 3 Feb. 1672/3.

  viii. JANE, bapt. in the parish of St. Leonard, Bridgnorth, 26 July 1636; m. after 27 May 1652 FRANCIS BAYLEY of Bridgnorth.

5. ix. JOHN, fourth son, bapt. in the parish of St. Leonard, Bridgnorth, 2 Jan. 1640/1; probably the emigrant to New England.¶

* Perhaps she had been married previously to her marriage to John Hord, for the marriage of Richard Phillips and Margere Gravenor, 2 June 1630, is recorded in the registers of the parish of St. Leonard, Bridgnorth.

† Perhaps she was his second wife, for the marriage of a William Gravenor and Anne Baskerfield, 28 Nov. 1624, is recorded in the registers of the parish of St. Leonard, Bridgnorth.

‡ The name of the messuage may have been derived from the priory of the Grey Friars that existed in Bridgnorth before the dissolution of the monasteries in the reign of Henry VIII.

§ The names of the children of William Grosvenor are given in what seems to be the most probable order. The order of births of the four sons is given in the pedigree entered in 1663, and Leicester, the eldest son, is said in this pedigree to have been 36 years old at that time. The baptisms of the sons William and John and the daughter Jane are recorded in the registers of the parish of St. Leonard, Bridgnorth. In his will of 1652 William Grosvenor apparently mentions first his unmarried daughters in the order of their births and then his married daughters in the order of their births. The pedigree of 1663 gives the daughters (except Susanna, who does not appear there) in this order: Mary, Lettice, Grace, Jane.

‖ If this Lettice Grosvenor was born about 1630, she was, of course, too young to have been the Lettice Gravenour whose marriage to John Wood, 19 Oct. 1641, is recorded in the registers of St. Leonard's, Bridgnorth.

¶ Since the gravestone of John Grosvenor of Roxbury, Mass., states that he died 27 Sept. 1691, in his 49th year, and since the John Grosvenor who was baptized at Bridgnorth 2 Jan. 1640/1 would have been in his 51st year in Sept. 1691, it is possible that the John who was baptized 2 Jan. 1640/1 died in infancy, and that another son was born about two years later, who was named John and became the emigrant to New England. It is more likely, however, that the gravestone at Roxbury gives the

4. LEICESTER GROSVENOR (*William, William*), of The Friars, Bridgnorth, co. Salop, Gent., eldest son of his father, was born about 1627 (since in the pedigree entered by him in 1663 he declared that he was 36 years of age on 14 Aug. 1663), and was buried in the parish of St. Leonard, Bridgnorth, 14 May 1690. Administration on his estate was granted, 7 Oct. 1690, to Eleanor, his widow. He married, probably about 1652, ELEANOR EASTWICKE (or ESTWICKE), who was buried in the parish of St. Leonard, Bridgnorth, 26 Nov. 1708, eldest daughter of Christopher and Eleanor (Walden) of Stoke, co. Warwick, Eleanor Walden being daughter of Isaac of Coventry, co. Warwick. In 1663 he entered a pedigree of his family that went back as far as his grandfather, William Grosvenor; but this pedigree was respited in order that descent from the Grosvenors of Eton, co. Chester, might be proved, and nothing further was done in the matter. When Leicester Grosvenor died in 1690, all his sons and all his brothers except John were dead; and therefore his only surviving brother, John Grosvenor, then residing in New England, became the head of this branch of the Grosvenor family.

Children:

i. LEICESTER, d. young; bur. in the parish of St. Leonard, Bridgnorth, 24 Sept. 1655.

ii. CHRISTOPHER, bapt. in the parish of St. Leonard, Bridgnorth, 8 Aug. 1655; bur. in the same parish 17 Sept. 1655.

iii. ELEANOR, b. abt. 1658, since she was 4 years of age on 14 Aug. 1663.

iv. SUSANNA, d. young before 14 Aug. 1663.

v. WILLIAM, bapt. in the parish of St. Leonard, Bridgnorth, 19 Mar. 1662/3 [*sic*, ? 1661/2]; probably d. between 14 Aug. and 20 Sept. 1663.

vi. WILLIAM, bapt. in the parish of St. Leonard, Bridgnorth, 20 Sept. 1663; d. before 14 May 1690.

vii. EASTWICKE, bapt. in the parish of St. Leonard, Bridgnorth, 4 Mar. 1666/7; bur. in the same parish 18 Mar. 1669/70.

5. JOHN GROSVENOR (*William, William*), of Roxbury, Mass., tanner, baptized in the parish of St. Leonard, Bridgnorth, co. Salop, 2 Jan. 1640/1, emigrated to New England probably about 1670, a few years after the death of his mother, and settled at Roxbury, Mass., where he died 27 Sept. 1691, being then, according to his gravestone, in the 49th year of his age.* He married, probably about 1672, HESTER (or ESTHER) CLARKE, born, probably at Watertown, Mass., about 1651, died at Pomfret, Conn., 15 June 1738, aged about 87 years,† daughter of Hugh and Elizabeth.‡

age at death incorrectly. There can be no doubt that John Grosvenor of Roxbury was a son of William and Susanna (Paston) Grosvenor of Bridgnorth.

* *Vide supra*, p. 137, footnote.

† On her gravestone in the Wappaquian Burial Ground, at the foot of Prospect Hill, Pomfret, Conn., is the following inscription: "Here lyes yᵉ Body of Mʳˢ Esther Grosvenor yᵉ Widow of Mʳ John Grosvenor Died June 15ᵗʰ 1738 Aged About 87 years." In the same cemetery are many other gravestones bearing inscriptions to members of the Grosvenor family.

‡ Hugh Clarke was at Watertown, Mass., as early as 1641, and lived there until about 1660, when he removed to Roxbury, Mass. He was freeman 30 May 1660, and died at Roxbury 20 July 1693, aged 80. His wife Elizabeth died 11 Dec. 1692.

On 14 Mar. 1672 [1672/3] John Grosvener was one of the witnesses to a deed in Roxbury.* The Roxbury records show that on 13th, 2 mo., 1673, Esther Gravener was excommunicated, but that on 2d, 9 mo., 1673, she was reconciled to the church and solemnly owned the covenant. On 28 Jan. 1684 [1684/5] John Grosvenor's father-in-law, Hugh Clarke of Roxbury, confirmed to him by deed a grant made about 1672 of the land on which John Grosvenor's house stood and the land on which his tanyard and tan house stood, a portion of the deed reading as follows:

"Know Yee that the said Hugh Clarke Sometime past about twelve or thirteene Yeares agoe or thereabout for and in consideration of a part of my Daughter Hester Graveners portion and many other good and considerable Considerations: Hath . . . granted and given possession and . . . by these presents Doth . . . grant . . . and confirme unto John Gravener my Sonne in Law, and Hester Gravener his wife, two Small peices of Land, the one peice of Land is that Land whereon John Graveners dwelling House now Standeth being in Roxbury, and as it is now fenced from the land of Hugh Clarke, and abutting on the Highway Leadeing from Stony River towards Muddy River Southerly, and upon the Land of Hugh Clarke or his Successors West North, and Southeasterly. And the other Smal peice of Land lyeing neerer to the Now dwelling house of sd Hugh Clarke whereon John Gravenors Tanyard and Tan house standeth being in Roxbury and as it is now fenced from the Land of Hugh Clark or his assignes, and abutting upon the Highway leadeing from the Mill at Stony River Towards Muddy River Southerly, and upon the Land of Hugh Clarke Southwest and easterly with all and Singular the appurtenances and priviledges thereunto belonging." (Suffolk Deeds, lib. 13, fo. 328.)†

Drake in his "Town of Roxbury" (p. 323) says that John Grosvenor's dwelling house and four acres of orchard and pasture were on the northeasterly corner of the present Tremont and Parker Streets. He was the first person to carry on the trade of a tanner in Roxbury, a town later noted for its tanneries. In the seventeenth century, along the valley of the River Severn in England, from Shrewsbury down to Worcester, the tanning industry was very important, and Bridgnorth was famed for its tanneries and for the quality of the leather produced there. It is probable, therefore, that John Grosvenor, one of the younger sons of the family, learned his trade there. In 1678 the town of Roxbury granted to him a lot of land "at the bridge and old mill . . . for liming leather in fee, and not to sell but for such use, and to be forfeit if it damage the water for cattle or man." (*Ib.*, p. 324.) He also held at Roxbury "the responsible office of town constable, then of great dignity and importance." (*Ib.*, p. 102.)

John Grosvenor was one of the six original purchasers from Maj. James Fitch, 1 May 1686, of the Mashamoquet grant

* Suffolk Deeds, lib. 9, fo. 140.
† The original deed is in the possession of Benjamin H. Grosvenor of Pomfret, Conn.

of 15,100 acres, which included the territory of the present towns of Pomfret, Brooklyn, and Putnam, and the parish of Abington, Conn. It is said that he was sent by the proprietors to Norwich, Conn., to pay to Major Fitch the purchase money. On 6 May 1686 the original grantees named six other associates.* These twelve proprietors were all residents of Roxbury, Mass., and on 9 Mar. 1686/7 they met to consult about the settlement of their purchase. The consent of Major Fitch to any arrangement that they might make being judged necessary, they voted that their "truely and beloved friends, Samuel Ruggles, Sen. and Jun., John White, Samuel Gore and John Grosvenor," were authorized "to treat with Major Fitch in and concerning all matters relating to said lands." On 7 Apr. these men reported that half of the land was to be laid out at once. Before the division was effected, however, Andros assumed the government of Connecticut and it seemed best to defer action. The survey and division were accomplished at last during the winter of 1693/4, and on 27 Mar. 1694, nearly eight years after the purchase, the proprietors met in Roxbury to receive their respective shares. John Grosvenor had died in 1691, but he was represented by his widow, who received the first allotment. It consisted of 502 acres, and comprised the land where the village of Pomfret now stands and the hills which surround it, including Prospect Hill, which faces the east, and the commanding eminences called Sharp's Hill and Spaulding's Hill on the west. (Cf. Larned's History of Windham County, Connecticut, vol. 1, pp. 181–185.)

Esther Grosvenor was appointed administratrix of the estate of her deceased husband, and on 17 Feb. 1691/2 filed her bond for £700. On 16 Sept. 1695 she sold 6 acres called Rock Pasture, the "Rightful Inheritance of Hugh Clarke late of said Roxbury dec^d and by the said Esther Grosvenor purchased of his son John," and 3½ acres, the "Rightful Inheritance of aforesaid John Grosvenor . . . together with Mansion house, barn, &c." On the same day she and her son William "and all other heires of the said John Grosvenner" purchased 65 acres at Muddy River, now Brookline, Mass., together with a dwelling house, the consideration being £312. On 7 Oct. 1695 they purchased 30 acres at Muddy River, "together with the house, fruit trees, wood," etc., the consideration being £150. On 15 Apr. 1701 Esther Grosvenor, William Grosvenor, Gentleman, and Susannah Grosvenor of Muddy River, and John Grosvenor of "Mashamnggabuck" in New London Co., Conn., sold "their Farme Tract" at Muddy River.† About this time, probably, the Widow Esther Grosvenor went with her family to Mashamoquin in Connecticut, where she resided for the remaining years of her life. The road to Hartford and Windham passed through the Grosvenor

* Cf. Suffolk Deeds, lib. 23, fo. 122.
† Cf. Suffolk Deeds, lib. 17, ff. 261, 262, lib. 31, fo. 198, and lib. 33, fo. 188.

land, near the first Connecticut residence of the family, which was on the western declivity of Prospect Hill, near the site afterwards occupied by Col. Thomas Grosvenor's mansion house. Mrs. Grosvenor was a woman of great courage and energy, and was held in high esteem by the early settlers of Pomfret. It is a family tradition that she was skillful in tending the sick. The so-called "Sabin" house, in which she died, is still standing, and is owned by her descendants. Her sons aided in bringing the large possessions of the family under cultivation, and identified themselves early with the growth and interests of the town.

Children, born at Roxbury, Mass.:

i.   REV. WILLIAM, A.B. (Harvard College, 1693), b. 8 Jan. 1672/3; bapt. by Rev. John Eliot 14 Oct. 1673; d. before 1733. He was minister at Brookfield, Mass., from 24 Oct. 1705 to 25 Aug. 1708, and is said to have removed from Massachusetts to Charleston, S. C.

ii. JOHN, bapt. 6 June 1675; killed by the Indians at Brookfield, Mass., 22 July 1710; m. at Concord, Mass., 27 Jan. 1708/9, SARAH HAYWARD, b. 16 June 1689, dau. of John and Anna. The estate of John Grosvenor was settled in 1724 by his brothers Leicester and Ebenezer.

iii. CAPT. LEICESTER, b. abt. 1675; d. at Pomfret, Conn., 8 Sept. 1759, in his 85th year; m. (1) at Woodstock, Conn., 16 Jan. 1711/12, MARY HUBBARD, who d. 14 May 1724, aged 37; m. (2) 12 Feb. 1728/9 REBECCA WALDO, b. at Chelmsford, Mass., 5 Feb. 1693/4, d. at Pomfret, Conn., 21 May 1753, in her 61st year. Leicester Grosvenor was a member of the first board of selectmen of Pomfret, Conn., and was elected nineteen times to that office. He was a member of the committee to select a site for the First Church at Pomfret and also of the building committee of this church. He was also ensign of the military company at Pomfret.

iv. SUSANNA, b. 9 Feb. 1680/1; m. in 1702 JOSEPH SHAW of Stonington, Conn.

v.   A CHILD, stillborn 21 Apr. 1683.

vi. SERGT. EBENEZER, b. 9 Oct. 1684; d. at Pomfret, Conn., 29 Sept. 1730; m. ANNE MARCY, b. at Roxbury, Mass., 11 Oct. 1687, d. at Pomfret, Conn., 30 June 1743, dau. of John and Sarah (Hadlock) of Woodstock, Conn. In 1710 a military company was organized at Pomfret, with Ebenezer Grosvenor as sergeant. In 1720 he was a member of the committee appointed to build the first schoolhouse at Pomfret. In 1721 the town granted to him the right to build "A pew at the east end of the meeting house." Eight children.

vii. THOMAS, b. and d. 30 June 1687.

viii. JOSEPH, b. 1 Sept. 1689; d. unm. 20 June 1738.

ix. THOMAS, d. 30 Sept. 1750; m. 22 May 1718 ELIZABETH PEPPER.

PAPERS IN CASE OF GUY VS. KING.

Communicated by HENRY F. WATERS, A.B., of Salem, Mass.

THE following documents are copied from Essex County Court Papers, Book 9, Leaf 45, &c.

Memorandum this 6th May 1653 that I Danell Kinge of Becomfeld in the County of Buckes being bound for New England have Rec. of my cosen William Guy A parcell of goods amounting to the valew of ffortey ffive pounds, ffourtene shillings nine pence starling mony which goods I have Rec: upon the account of Guy as an Adventure by him promiseing to doe my outmost indeuor for the sale of the aforesaid goods—and to make him returnes by Chrismas next if they safely arrive in the Harbor of Boston in New England they being now shipt abord in the Nue England Merchant, to which pray God blesse the Good Ship to the appointed Harbor Witnes my hand the day aboue written, Subscribed Daniell King Under is written Jn⁰ Wyatt. Dauid Sindry. Digorey Carwithen Master

vera copia   Fredᵏ Reine Not pubᵐˢ
1658

Bostown this 14 of August 1658 These presents Wittnes that I Daniell
King of Lin Sener doe aknowledge that Capt Jn° Peirce Comander of the
Ship Exchang hath bene with mee and demanded of mee a debt of aboutt
forty fiue pounds which my sone Daniell did Receive in goods of M̄ Wm̄
Guy of London: haberdasher: and my Answer is that my sone Daniell is
gone to burbados and hath carried with him goods in order to the making
the Retturne much more then I can judge will Ballance that acc°. And I
hope either by this time or very sudenly hee will Retturne a satisfacktory
acc°: This is all I haue to answer att present

Wittnes my hand　　DANIELL KING:

Wittness
Lancellot ffletcher
Ephraim Turnor

London the 8th of Aprill 1663 Wee whose names are heere underwritten beeinge at this time servants to Mr Richard Bates with Will. Guy
Daniell Kinge Junior—beeinge bound for new Ingland came to visit his
kinsman Guy & uppon discourse concerninge ye Cuntry trade Guy profferr-
ed to Adventure some goods by him, hee presently tould him what comoditis
would bee best for ye place, and turne to ye best Accompt, as he verrily
beleived, uppon which without any more A dooe, theire was a note drawne
by Kings order what goods hee would have, wch weare accordingly bought
& packt upp & delivered to ye said Kinge to his good likinge, and theire
was such seeminge honesty & Honest expressions by ye said Kinge yt hee
would make returne ye next shippinge in ould Beavor or Bever (Guy
beeinge to stand to all Hassard by sea ye goods were shipt in Cap Kirwithies
vessell) yt oure maister mr Bates had so good an opinion of his honesty yt
hee would have given him credit for above as much more And for ye
goods wee saw them & know what they cost and doe verrilie beleive theire
was not one penny got by them Havinge often heard Guy say (wee askinge
him what hee ment too sell such goods as hee bought wth redy mony they
beeinge as fresh as could possibly been had) hee Answered the profit would
bee by ye returnes the truth of wch wee doe affirme

Witness oure hands ye day & yeare above written　　JOHN WYATT
DA: SYNDRY

from Linn in New England Decembr the 28th 1660

Loueing Cusden After Respeckts prescented these earr to lett you under
stand that yours wee have receued Return you Manny thanks for your
patiente lines But beeing much troubled that wee yett cannot Answer your
ends According to your expecktations Manny ways wee have tryed By
Barbudoes By Bills of Exchange & By getting of Bever for you But as yet
canno[t] proceure anny of them But By the next shepping I hoape wee shall
find out some way or other wheerby you shall haue sattisfacktion my sonn
Ralph & my sonn Blaenny douth Intend if pleas god the liue & doe well to
com for England soe hoaping that you will bee pleased to Ad one mitt of
patience unto your Abondance which you haue had soe
　　Resting & Remaining your Euer Loueing Ante tell Death

ELIZABETH KING

PAPERS RELATING TO THE HAINES FAMILY.

[Communicated by A. M. Haines, Esq., of Galena, Ill.]

From the many valuable papers discovered by Mr. Charles Bridger, of London, Honorary Member " Society Antiquaries of New-Castle upon Tyne," and author of " Index to Printed Pedigrees of English Families," in his recent researches in England, and sent to the undersigned, he has selected the following :—The Will of John Haynes, father of Gov. John Haynes, of New-England, and abstracts[1] from the Will of Edward Cogswell, father of John Cogswell, Senior, who settled at Ipswich, 1635, and of William Thompson, vicar of Westbury, Wilts, England.

Galena, Ill.   A. M. Haines.

WILL OF JOHN HAYNES.

1606. In the name of God amen I *John Haynes*[2] of *Coddicot*[3] in the countie of *Hartf Esquier* this twentith daye of October in the yeares of the reigne of our most gratious soveraigne Lord James by the grace of God King of England ffraunce and Ireland the third, and of Scotland the nine and thirtith doe make this my last will and testament in manner and forme followinge ffirste I bequeath my soule to God that gaue it and my body to the earth from whence it came and as touching the disposition of my landes, tenementes and hereditamentes ffirst I giue and bequeathe to Charles Chilburne of *Lincolnes Inne* in the County of *Midd* esquier and ffrannces Crowley of *Graies Inne* in the said County of *Midd* esquier and Thomas Michell of *Tvinge* in the County of *Hartf* gent and George Nodes of *Shephall* in the County of *Hartf* gent. all that my *mannor* of *Olde holt*[4] wth appurtenances and all and everie the Lands tenementes and hereditaments of the same belonginge nowe or late reputed or taken as pte or number of the same sett lieinge and beinge in the severall pishes of *litle Birche, muche Birche* messiuge, *Laiermarney*[5] and *Capford* in the county of *Essex* and all those lands

---

[1] Want of space compels us to postpone these abstracts to our next issue.—Ed.

[2] John Haynes the testator died 3 Nov. 1605. His wife's name was Mary Michell. This will disproves several statements which have been published based upon tradition that nearly all of the Haineses who first came to New-England were brothers of Gov. John Haynes. See *ante*, vol. ix. 349, *et seq.* and Upham's *Salem Witchcraft*, vol. i. 109.

[3] Coddicut is near Stevenage and Welling, belonging formerly to the Abby of St. Albans.

[4] The Old Holt estate is partly in Copford Parish. Norden, in his Description of Essex, 1594, in the " Table of the Howses haning speciall names and the present occupiers of them," has " Olde holte somtyme S⸍ Tho. Tayes *now* Jo. Haynes."
Old Holt in little Birch with other lands, was sold by [Gov.] John Haynes in 1647 to Wm. Tanner, Clothier of Gt: Coggeshall. *Morant*, ii. 185.
This was undoubtedly when the Gov. was in England, on the visit which he contemplated when he made his will in Hartford. 27, 8. 1646. See Will, *ante*, vol. xvi. 167.

[5] Norden, in 1594, says, "Layre Marney hall somtyme Lord Marneys." It derives the latter part of its name from the family of Marney. "Wm. de Marney obtained license from Henry iii. [1216–1272] to enclose a park here within the precincts of the forest of Essex." It is about five miles S. W. from Colchester, and two miles from Old holte and Copford Hall:—Copford Hall, old Holt, little Birch, much Birch and Layre Marny are all in the same neighborhood.

191

tenements and hereditamentes commonly called and knowne by the name of *Palmers, Vouchers* and *Souchers* and being in the *pishes aforesaid* or some of them together with the reversion and reversions remainder and remainders of all and singular the premisses wth the rents reserved vpon any demises of them or any of them whatsoever To have and to hold all and singular the said premisses wth theire and every of their appurtenances to the saide Charles, ffranncis, Thomas and George for and during the full terme of nyne yeares from the feaste of St. Michaell th archangell last past before the date of this present will, wth liberty to take sufficient timber necessarie (for the) reparacõns of all and everie of the premisses wth out making or willinglie sufferinge any manner of waste To the intent and purpose that they the saide Charles, ffrauncis, Thomas and George, their executors and administrators shall faithfully answere and paye all the rentes yssues and profitts arisinge comminge and growinge of the said mannor and other the premisses the first yeare of the said nyne to be accounted from Michaelmas nowe laste paste to Elizabeth my eldest daughter at vpon the feast daye of the annunciacõn of the blessed Mary the Virgin and St. Michaell th archangell or wth in six weeks ensueinge everie of the said feasts at the mansion house of the mannor of *Old holt* and the Rents yssues and profitts that shalbe perceaved and taken of the said premisses the second yeare of the said terme to be paid to Mary my daughter and the rents yssues and profitts of the third yeare to be paid to Margaret my daughter and of the forthe yeare to Martha my daughter and of the fifth yeare to Deborath my daughter and of the sixt year to Sara my daughter to be paid vnto every of them at such tymes and place as is before limited for my daughter Elizabethes porcõn and that the rents yssues and profitts of the p̃misses that shalbe receved and taken then three last years of the terme aforesaid shall be equally devided betweene Philadelpha, Anne, and Priscilla my youngest daughters one whole yeares profitts to be paid to each of them three successively as they are named at theire severall ages of twenty and one yeares or dayes of their marriages w[ch] shall first happen at the mansion howse of *Old holt* aforesaid and that after the receite of the rents yssues and profitts laste aforesaid The said Charles, ffrauncis, Thomas and George their executors and administrators shall allowe and paie vnto the said Philadelpha Anne and Priscilla at theire severall ages of one and twenty yeares or dayes of marriages wch shall firste happen for the interest and increase of their said porcõns according to the rate of eight pounds in the hundred for every yeare for so many hundred poundes as they before that tyme shall have received and I give and bequeath all and singular the p̃misses from and after such estate ended to *John Haynes*[1] my eldest sonne and to the heires of his bodie lawfully begotten and for defaulte of such yssue to remayne to *Emanuell* my youngest sonne and the heires of his bodie lawfully begotten But yf John Haynes my eldest sonne shall happen to *die* before he come to the age of twenty and one yeares w[th]out yssue of his body whereby the premisses shall come and remaine to *Emanuell* brother of the said *John,* That then the said Charles, ffrancis, Thomas and George from and after the said nyne yeares shall have all and singular the

---

[1] Afterwards Gov. of Mass. and Connecticut Colonies. He was born in 1594, and died 1 March, 1653-4, in Hartford. Mather says in his "Providences," p. 260, "That he died in his sleep without being sick."
His widow, Mabel, married 17 Nov. 1654, Rev. Samuel Eaton, of New-Haven. The arms used by the Gov.'s great-grandson, Hezekiah Haynes, Esq., of Copford Hall, who died 15 Nov. 1763, were the same as those confirmed in 1578 to Nicholas Haynes of Hackney, co. Middlesex, grandfather of Gov. John—Argent 3 crescents, barry undeé azure and gules, with a Stork rising ppr. for a crest, added.

said p̄misses vntill such tyme as Emanuell aforesaid shall accomplishe the age of twentie and one yeares and the said Charles ffrancis Thomas and George shall paie and dispose of the rents yssues and profitts during that tyme amongste my said daughters and if they or any of them dye before such profitts p̄ceived having issue or issues that then the said issue or issues shall have their mothers p̄te and yf they or any of them die wth owt yssue then theire ptes to be deuided amongste the surviving sisters and theire yssues.

Item I giue and bequeath one messuage and all the freehold land therevnto belonginge or vsed or occupied wth the same com̄enly called or knowne by the name of *Haynes at Mill* situate and lyeinge in the severall p̄ishes of *muche Haddam* and *Widford* in the County of *Hartford* to *Mary* my wife dureinge her life and from and after her death to remayne to *Emanuell* my yongest sonne and his heires for ever And as towchinge all that my *mannor Lordship or farme called Walkeferes*[1] *als Wakeferes* and all and singular hereditaments therevnto belonginge or nowe or lately therew^th vsed or occupied or nowe or late reputed taken or knowne as pte p̄cell or member of the same wth theire reversions and the rents incident therevnto I giue and bequeath vnto Mary my wife for the terme of her life for her ioynture and in recompence of her dower and from and after her decease to the said Charles ffrancis Thomas and George vntill such time as Emanuell my yongest sonne should or mought atteyne to the age of twenty and one yeares to the intent that they shall dispose of all such rents yssues and profitts that should be by them or any of them thereof perceived and taken accordinge to the meaninge of this p̄sent will equally amongst all my daughters wch shalbe liveinge at the tyme of the perceivinge of such rents yssues and profitts and yf any of my daughters shall happen to be dead at the tyme of such perception and takinge havinge issue or issues of their body then the said issue or issues to haue a ratable pte as their mother should haue had yf she had been liuinge and the said premisses to be and remayne to Emanuell my sonne for one yeare and three dayes after that he should or mought have accomplished his age of twenty and one yeares and yf my said son John and his heirss shall not paie to the said Emanuell ^or the heirss males of his bodie the some of five hundred poundes within one yeares after the said *Emanuell* should or mought have accomplished his age of twentie one yeares at the *mansion howse at Wakeferes* aforesaid Then I will that my said sonne Emanuell shall haue the said premisees from and after the said yeare expired to him and the heires males of his bodie lawfullie begotten But not to have the same in possession vntill after my said wyves decease alsoe all other my lands tenements and hereditaments whatsoever not before disposed of nor bequeathed I give and bequeath to *John Haynes* my eldest sonne and to the heires males of his bodie lawfullie begotten, and in defaulte of such yssue to remayne to Emanuell my yongest sonne and his heirs for ever, and further I do make Mary my wife the sole executrix of this my last will and doe give vnto her all my goods and chattells and debts whatsoever to dispose of as shee shall thincke best In witness whereof I haue subscribed my hand in the presence of ffra: Crawley Thomas Michell Samuel Heminge John Webster Proved 7 Feby 1605–6 by Mary Haynes relict and extrix

---

[1] Jonathan Haynes (afterwards Gov.) alienated the Estate of Walkfare or Walkers with the manor and lordship, &c. and 100 acres of arable, 10 acres of meadow, 20 of pasture and 5 of wood, called the " fee farm lands," the 10 Oct. 1622 to Wm. Stone of the Temple, Esq. *Morant*, ii. 624.

PAPERS RELATING TO THE HAINES FAMILY.

[Communicated by A. M. HAINES, Esq., of Galena, Ill.]

ABSTRACT OF EDWARD COGSWELL'S WILL.

EDWARD COGSWELL of LEGH within the parish of WESTBURY co. WILTS. Clothier.   Will dated 23 June 1615; proved 12 Jan. 1615–6.

To be buried in the ch. or ch yard of Westbury.

To Margaret Marchante the wife of Thomas Marchante £20.

To Elizabeth Ernly the wife of Richard Ernle £30.

To Margery Wilkins the wife of John Wilkins £10.

To Elizabeth Marchante the daū. of Thomas Marchante 20 marks[1] at her marriage.

To the other children of my three who shall be born and living at the time of my decease £4 each.

To Elinor Smythe the wife of Stephen Smythe £40 shillings.

To Joane Freestone widow,

To Margaret Francklene widow,

To Margery Whatley the wife of John Whatley,

To Edith Stevens the wife of Thomas Stevens.

To every of these four my sisters £2.

To Henry Freestone 10 shillings.

To Edward Franklene 10 shillings.

To Robert Cogswell the son of Stephen Cogswell ten shillings.

To Margery Stevens the daū. of Thomas Stevens ten shillings.

To Edward Cogswell the son of Robert Cogswell deceased ten shillings.

To George Cogswell his brother twenty shillings.

To every of my godchildren besides these aforesaid 12 pence.

To John Cogswell[2] my son £240, beds, bedding and other household stuff, &c.

---

[1] A mark was equivalent to 13ˢ. 6ᵈ.

[2] He and his family came passengers in the ship "Angel Gabriel," which sailed from Bristol, England, 4 June, 1635, and was wrecked at Pemaquid 15 Aug. same year.   He settled at Chebacco, Ipswich, Mass., 1635, where he died 29 Nov. 1669.—See vol. xxiii. 152-3-4 *ante*.   Statements have been published that he was a merchant in London, &c., but the writer has not found any evidence of this fact.

The Cogswells had resided in Westbury and vicinity for at least 60 years before John came to New-England, and are supposed to have been cloth manufacturers.   Edward

To my son Anthony the whole estate, right and interest and term of years which I have in and to Ludborne with the appurtenances together with the Lease of the same for the term of his life to be delivered to him at the age of 23. After his death my son John Cogswell to have and enjoy the said Ludborne &c. for his life only: remainder to Jeffrey my son.

To Anthony the sum of £80 and four of my best kyne at 23.

To my son Jeffrey Cogswell all my estate right and term of years wch I have in little Horningsham[1] &c. with the Lease of the same for his life only. After his death the said little Horningsham to the party next mentioned in the said Lease to him and his assigns.

To my son Jeffrey £80 and four oxen now in the hands of Robert Northen of little Horningsham all to be delivered to him at the age of 23.

To my son John Cogswell all the right and term of years which I have to the Mylls called Ripond place situate within the parish of Froome-Selwood for his life, After his death to the party next mentioned in the Lease thereof to enjoy the remainder of the term.

I owe John Boutcher my servant £60. 10s. to be paid at any time on his demand.

To Alice my wife my dwelling house &c. so long as she keepeth her self widow and in my name After her death to my son John and his heirs forever.

To Alice my wife yearly out of Ludborne £8, after the delivering up of the same; and from Horningsham £12 yearly after the delivery of the Lease thereof to Jeffrey; so long as she keepeth herself widow and no longer.

The residue of goods and chattells unbequeathed to Alice my wife my sole executrix.

My well beloved Jeffrey Whitaker and Anthonye Selfe overseers.

Witnesses.

Robert Foster, Clerk.

Richard Painter.

Edward Cogswell.

ABSTRACT OF WILLIAM THOMPSON'S WILL.

WILL of William Thompson clerke, late of Westburie under the plaine in the co. of Wilts dec^d. First hee gave unto Elizabeth Thompson his wife

the testator, John's father, possessed mills at Frome in Somersetshire, a few miles from Westbury, which he bequeathed to John, but it does not appear that either of them ever resided at Frome.

The following record of a baptism is on the Westbury Register. "1622 Johannes Coggeswell filius Johannes Coggeswell baptizatus fuit 25 July." This is undoubtedly son of John, Sen., who was about 12 years of age when he came to New-England, vol. xxiii. 153–4, *ante*, and is the same person who wrote his father the letter from London while on a visit to England, 30 March, 1653, vol. xv. 177 *ante*, and who died on the passage home to New-England.

The following assessments are found in "Wiltshill Subsidies."

"Subsidy 7 Jas. I. (1610)

Leigh. Edward Cogswell, in goods vi. £

Dylton. Roger Cogswell, in lands xxx^s.

Subsidy. 3 Chas. I. (1628)

Lygh, John Cogswell in lands xxx^s.

Subsidy. 17 Chas. I. (1642)

Leigh, Anthony Cogswell p^d iij^s vi^d.

Robert Cogswell p^d ii iv^d.

Penly, Roger Cogswell pd x^s.

Chippenham, Ph: Cogswell, in lands xx^s."

By this it appears that Jno Cogswell was assessed in the Subsidy of 1628, but having left for New-England in 1635, his name does not appear in the subsidy of 17 Chas I. (1642).

[1] In Wiltshire on S. E. side of Frome-Selwood.

195

all his bookes made by M[r]. Greenham Rogers Perkins Dicke of the deceiptfulness of mans harte, and a booke called heaven opened;—Item he gave his sonne in law M[r] Hormsell his best cassocke and D[r] Willet on the Romaines and Samuel and his second best gowne. Item, hee gave leave to his executors to deliver to each of his five daughters one booke a piece such as his Executors and they thought fitt. Item he gave unto his sonne William Thompson Scapulas Bible this bookes of B[p] Abbotts workes. Item hee gave unto his sonne Samuel Thompson[1] Junius Bible a booke made by George Estie. Item he gave to his brother-in-law M[r] White his Best gowne, and Cloake, and such bookes of his as then weare in his possession. Item hee gave to M[r] Augustine Gauntlet his second Cassocke. Item hee gave unto John Langden one paire of new cloth hose and other of his cloathes for a suite. Item hee gave unto William Whiteacre one booke being a treatise made by the Bishoppe of Perthe. Item, hee gave to William Phippe one booke. Item, hee appointed all his debts to be paide and the remainder of his estate to be divided into fouer severall partes equallie, one fourth parte to his wife, another parte for his son William another parte for his son Samuel and the other fourthe parte for his unborn infant for their maintenance and good soe farr as their severall partes would extend by the advise direction and disposement of John White, clerke, Nicholas Phiffe[2] and *John Cogeswell*[3] to whom as his especiall friends he recomended the care for the p̃formance thereof intreatinge them to be executors of this his said last will and testament nuncupative in the presence of Elizabeth Cogeswell, M[r] George Widley and divers other credible witnesses. Date on or about the 10th of July 1623.

Byrde, quire 23.

THOMAS HALE OF NEWBURY, MASS., 1637. HIS ENGLISH ORIGIN AND CONNECTIONS.

By the Hon. Robert S. Hale, LL.D., of Elizabethtown, N. Y.

IN the Register for January, 1877 (vol. xxxi. p. 83), the writer published an article entitled " Thomas Hale, the Glover, of Newbury, Mass., 1635, and his Descendants." The article was also republished in pamphlet form. That article contained the following paragraph :

---

[1] On the Westbury Register is the following record of his baptism. " 1616. Samuell filius Willmi Thomsonn ricarie de Westburie baptizat[s] Novemb : 30."
He is the Dr. Samuel Thompson referred to in vol. xxiii. p. 154, *ante*.
[2] *Phippe?* Ed.
[3] Undoubtedly John Cogeswell, Sen., afterwards of Ipswich, Massachusetts, and the witness, Elizabeth Cogeswell, was wife of the said John, and came to New-England with him and died 2 June, 1676.

" Coffin supposes him to have been the son of William Hale, Esq., of King's Walden, Herts, England, born at that place May 15th, 1606. The birth and baptism of this Thomas appear on the family records at King's Walden, but no further entry is found there touching his life or death. No sufficient proof is found to establish conclusively the identity of Thomas of Newbury with this Thomas of King's Walden, though facts are known to make such identity probable. The question is still under investigation, and the English origin of Thomas of Newbury may become the subject of a future paper."

In pursuance of the partial promise thus made, the present article is prepared.

Coffin, in his History of Newbury (p. 304), says that Thomas[1] Hale, the emigrant ancestor, with his wife Thomasine, came to Newbury in 1635. Savage, following Coffin, gives the same date of his arrival, and that date seems to have passed unquestioned till now, though the writer in his former article stated it as matter of probability only. But the first date at which his presence in Newbury is indicated by Coffin, is August 10th, 1638, when he and John Baker were " appointed haywards" (p. 28). No entry has been found in the town or county records naming him at an earlier date than this. In determining the question of his identity, the date of his arrival is important.

Coffin speaks of his English origin and family (p. 393) thus :

" Thomas Hale resided on the south side of the river Parker. The family of Hale is of considerable antiquity and of high respectability in England. Thomas Hale of Codicote, in Hertfordshire, married Anne, daughter of Edmund Mitchell, and had three sons, Richard, William and John. Richard, the eldest son, purchased the estate of King's Walden in Hertfordshire, and died in 1620. His son William succeeded him, and died in August, 1634, aged sixty-six. He left nine children, Richard, born in 1596, William in 1597, Rowland, his heir, George, born July thirtieth, 1601, Alicia, in 1603, Winefreda, 1604, Thomas, 1606, Anne, 1609, and Dionisia, March seventeenth, 1611. The last mentioned Thomas is supposed to be the Thomas Hale who came to Newbury."

This account of his origin, though on its face conjectural, had been generally accepted, and, so far as the writer is advised, had passed unquestioned till the writer in his former article indicated his doubt of its correctness. But examinations recently completed in England by Col. Joseph L. Chester, and conducted with his well-known accuracy and thoroughness, establish beyond question that Thomas[1] of Newbury was *not* identical with Thomas the son of Richard of King's Walden, but was another Thomas Hale, son of an English yeoman, born in a neighboring parish of Hertfordshire, within a few weeks, and probably within a few days, of Thomas the son of Richard.

Of the King's Walden family it is only necessary to say that that manor was bought in 1575 by Richard Hale, citizen and grocer of London, who may be considered the "founder" of the family. Richard was the son of Thomas and Anne (Mitchell) Hale of Codicote, Herts, and seems to have gone in early life to London and there got rich in trade. His mother was Anne, daughter of Edmund Mitchell of Codicote. His paternal descent is not traced beyond his father Thomas. It is perhaps needless to add that the preposterous pedigree furnished many years ago by a pretended Herald's office in London to Dr. Moses Hale of Troy, carrying his line back through Thomas[1] of Newbury, Richard of King's Walden, and a long line of illustrious knights and gentry to " Roger de Halys " in the eleventh or twelfth century, is wholly an invention as to all material points.

The date of Richard's birth is not given, but he was first married in 1550 to Mary Lambert, the mother of his son and heir William, and died at a very advanced age in 1620. Besides his son William, he had by a second wife two sons, Richard and Robert, both of whom left issue. He left a very large estate, and was the founder of the grammar school at Hertford, still flourishing, and under the patronage of Earl Cowper, as his heir general in the female line, through his mother the late Viscountess Palmerston. Richard, son of the first Richard of King's Walden, had a son Robert, who has been by some supposed to be identical with Robert[1] the settler at Charlestown, Mass., in 1630, but this supposition is erroneous, Robert the son of Richard appearing by the records to have been living in England long after the establishment of Robert[1] of Charlestown in New England.

William, son and heir of Richard, had seven sons and four daughters (two, John and Bernard, besides those named by Coffin). Rowland the third son finally succeeded to the estate of King's Walden, two older sons having died childless. From Rowland the manor has descended in regular course to his present heir-male, now the proprietor, Charles Cholmeley Hale, Esq. The fifth son and seventh child of William was Thomas, born at King's Walden May 15th, 1606, and baptized in the parish church there 25th of same month. This Thomas doubtless died childless in the life-time of his father, not being named in the will of the latter, dated in 1632 and proved in 1634. The records of King's Walden show nothing of him after his baptism.

We return to Thomas[1] Hale of Newbury. The Mass. Hist. Soc. Collections (4th series, vol. vii. p. 19) give a copy of a letter from Francis Kirby to Gov. John Winthrop, the elder, as follows :

" *To the right worshipfull John Winthrop Esquire at his house at Boston, this dd. in New England.*

London this 10th of May, 1637.

Sir,—I wrote you lately per the Hector, wherein I sent a runlet marked with your marke, contayncinge some things your son did write to me to send him. John Wood, master's mate, did promise mee & James Downeinge that he would be carfull of it & deliver to you.

These are now to intreat you that you would be assistante to the bearer herof (Thomas Hale, my neer kinsman) in your councell & aduise to put him in the way how & where to settle himselfe in a hopefull way of subsisteinge with his family. He hath brought with him all his estate, which he hath heer or can haue dureinge the life of his mother, my sister. He had almost 200*li*. when he began to make his provision for this voyage. I suppose the greatest halfe is expended in his transportation, and in such necessaries as will be spent by him & his family in the first vse ; the lesser halfe, I suppose he hath in mony, and vendible goods to provide him a cottage to dwell in, and a milshe cow for his childrens sustenance. I suppose his way will be to hire a house or part of a house for the first year, vntill he can looke out & buy or build him a dwellinge, wherein as in other things I shall intreat you to direct him, and the courtesy that you shall doe him therin I shall acknowledge, as done to myselfe, & I shall be redy (*Deo assistante*) to endeuour to requite it in any seruice which I can performe for you heer. Thus for this present I commit you all to the protection of the Almighty, & shall ever rest

Your loving frend   FFRA: KIRBY.

I desire to be remembred to Mrs. Winthrop, to your son Mr. Jo: & his wife, & the rest of yours, also to my cosen Mary & Su: Downeinge.

My brother Downeinge will hasten to you, the next springe will be farthest, God willinge ; for he seeth that euery year bringeth forth new new difficulties ; my nephew can tell you how they haue met with many interruptions, prohibitions, & such like, which Mr. Peirce & others that went since Mr. Peirce were not troubled withall."

Indorsed by Gov. Winthrop, " Mr. Kirby."

198

The date of this letter, May, 1637, in connection with Coffin's explicit statement that Thomas[1] Hale settled at Newbury in 1635, and with the further fact that three other Thomas Hales (one probably by error for Haley) are recorded as early residents of New England, doubtless led to this letter not having been till recently regarded as having any applicability to Thomas[1] Hale of Newbury. Col. Chester's researches, however, make it quite certain that this Thomas Hale, thus introduced by his uncle Francis Kirby to Gov. Winthrop, was the veritable Thomas[1] of Newbury.

The narrative of his English origin and all that is known of his paternal descent is very brief. He was the son of Thomas Hale (whom for distinction I henceforth designate as Thomas[a] Hale) of the parish of Watton, otherwise called Watton-at-Stone in Hertfordshire, and Joan (Kirby) his wife, and was probably born at that place in May or June, 1606. No record of his birth is found, but his baptism is recorded in the parish church at Watton, on the 15th June, 1606, as "Thomas Hale, son of Thomas and Joane."

No record is found at Watton or in any of the adjacent parishes of the birth, baptism or marriage of Thomas[a] Hale. His ;wife Joan Kirby was of the parish of Little Munden, Herts, and that was probably the place of their marriage and of her birth, and not improbably of his birth as well, but the registers of Little Munden, prior to 1680, have long been hopelessly lost, and no monuments are found in the parish churches or church-yards of Watton or Little Munden of any of the name of either Hale or Kirby.

Thomas[1] Hale was the only son of Thomas[a] Hale, but he had four sisters, all born and baptized at Watton, one older and three younger than himself, whose baptisms are shown by the parish registers at Watton, as follows :

1. Dionis, baptized 15th August, 1602, and registered as "Dionis Haille." She married at Watton, 29th September, 1624, Henry Beane, and was living and had a son Henry at the date of her father's will, 11th October, 1630. Nothing more is known of them. This entry of the baptism of Dionis is the first appearance of the name of Hale in the church registers at Watton, which are preserved back to 1560. It is a noteworthy coincidence, that both William and Richard, sons of the first Richard of King's Walden, had each a daughter Dionysia, in common usance rendered "Dionis."

2. Mary, baptized 8th October, 1609, as "Marie Hale, dau. of Thomas & Joan." It is probable that she married a Whale, and had a son Joseph named in the will of her grandmother Joan Kirby, hereinafter named, as "my grandchild [doubtless meaning great-grandchild] Joseph Whale."

3. Dorothy, baptized 28th March, 1613, as "Dorothie Hale, the daughter of Thomas and Joan his wife."

4. Elizabeth, baptized 31st August, 1617, as "Elizabeth Haile the daughter of Thomas and Joan his wife."

The parish register at Watton shows the burial of Thomas[a] Hale, father of Thomas,[1] 19th Oct. 1630. The register styles him "Thomas Hale, Senior." He left a will bearing date the 11th October, 1630, and proved 9th December, 1630, in the court of the Archdeaconry of Hitchin, Herts, by Thomas Hale, the executor named in it. The original is still on file among the records of that court, is signed by the testator in a decent and legible though evidently not a business hand, is sealed with the impression of a unicorn's head, and is witnessed by ffrancis Kirby and by John Hale, the latter signing by mark. Nothing is known to connect this John Hale with the testator's blood.

In this will the testator describes himself as "Thomas Hale of ye parish of Watton-at-Stone in the County of Hartford," without addition. After the usual pious profession of faith, thanks to God, committal of his soul to its creator and his body to burial, he disposes of his personal property and his real estate consisting of eleven, and perhaps twelve, distinct parcels, probably all of small extent. Five of these parcels, designated as the house close, the backside close, the hill close, and two others, the extent and tenure of none of which are given, he devises to his wife Joane and son Thomas till Michaelmas next, conditioned that they "shall bestow necessary reparation upon my said house," and shall pay to Mrs. Cranfield the half year's rent to become due at Michaelmas on the land testator holds from her. For ten years thereafter he devises these parcels to his wife, his son Thomas to occupy the same as her tenant, paying her the yearly rent of four pounds in half-yearly payments.

Another parcel designated as the "medow and ry close conteyninge seuen acres more or lesse," he devises to his daughter Mary Hale for three years, "with all the benefit of graseinge or moweing & loppinge both in the said medow & hedges so that she do not spoile the said hedges that the said loppinge be only in the first year;" then for three years in like manner to his daughter Dorothy Hale; then for three years in like manner to his daughter Elizabeth Hale; then for one year to his daughter Dionis Beane, "or to her son Henry Beane which shall be then liveinge." He provides also that Thomas shall occupy this close as the tenant of his sisters respectively during said respective terms, paying to them respectively five pounds per year rent in half-yearly payments.

The remaining parcels of real estate, designated as two half acres of "free land (freehold) lieinge in Headen abuttinge upon the highway leadinge from Watton to Walkerne," an acre and a half in "Monsal's hearn," a "parcell of medow pasture close & orchard in Cooper's crofte abouteinge upon the river on the east & highway on the west," and one piece in Stonyfield he devises absolutely to his son Thomas, to whom he also gives all his goods and chattels "(exceptinge a bed with beddinge convenient linnen and other fittinge furniture for one chamber which I herby reserue & give to Jone my wife)." He directs payment of all his debts and the "dischargeinge of buriall and such necessary disbursements" by his son Thomas from the avails of the land and goods, and appoints him sole executor, "nothing doubtinge of his carefull performance of this my will," and requests "my brother Francis Kirby to be an overseer."

This completes our knowledge of Thomas^a Hale and of his kindred by blood, except so far as he is alluded to in the wills of his wife's kindred hereinafter named. From the brief record it is apparent that he was of the rank of yeoman of the smaller class as to property, but apparently marked by thrift, respectability, honesty, piety and prudent foresight. It is impossible to determine the value of the estate which he left, but it was evidently not large. Thomas the son undoubtedly had as heir the larger part of the estate, and the rents he was to pay his mother and sisters, nine pounds per year in all, were in that day equivalent in value to from £27 to £36 (say $135 to $180) at the present day. The widow Joan was of course entitled to dower in any of the dowable lands left by the testator, in addition to the specific devises and bequests to her, and from Kirby's letter to Gov. Winthrop it appears that Thomas[1] the emigrant would be entitled to some further property at his mother's death.

Thomas[1] was twenty-four years old at his father's death, and at that early age had his father's full confidence, a confidence which Kirby's letter shows had been fully justified up to the time of his emigration six or seven years later. At the latter date Thomas[1] had been married probably about five years, had two young children, had doubtless paid off all his father's debts, and Kirby then places the entire value of his estate at £200—equivalent to £600 to £800 at this day, besides whatever might be to fall in at his mother's death. But it is fair to note that he had probably turned his estate into cash at a disadvantage in view of emigrating. It was a humble but evidently respectable position, and doubtless a fair specimen of the average rank, social position, character and standing of the early settlers of the colony of Massachusetts Bay.

Joan the widow of Thomas[a] Hale, at some time between her husband's death and June, 1637, married a Bydes, or Bides, probably John, and was still living in October, 1640, the date of her mother's will, but was probably dead before July, 1660, the date of her brother Francis's will. After her marriage with Bydes she seems to have resided at Little Munden, to which place she was probably accompanied by her two youngest daughters, Dorothy and Elizabeth. Bydes was a man of humble social station, and nothing more is known of the widow Joan Hale after her marriage with him, except the reference to her in the wills noted below.

Of the family of Joan (Kirby) Hale our information is a little, and but a little, fuller than that of her husband Thomas[a] Hale. The name of her father is unknown. Her mother Joan Kirby, described in the records as of Little Munden, widow, made a nuncupative (oral) will, 29th October, 1640, in the presence of her three children, Francis Kirby, Joane Bides and Ruth Browne, and of John Bides, which was proved by the executor in the court of the Archdeaconry of Hitchin on the 2d December, 1640. By it she gave to the poor of Watton where she was born, 20 shillings, to the poor of Little Munden where she lived, 20 shillings, small legacies to her grandchild Ruth Cowley, to her grandchild Richard Kirby, to her grandchild Joseph Whale, to her cousin Elizabeth Isham, to her cousin Mary Newton, and to her daughter Joan Bides, and the residue to her son Francis Kirby, whom she made sole executor. The inventory attached to the will shows the entire value of her personal estate, £18, 8, 1½, of which £2, as we have seen, was given to the poor. It does not appear whether she had any real estate, as that, if any existed, would not pass by a nuncupative will.

Besides Joan Hale and Francis Kirby already mentioned, Joan Kirby the elder and her husband had children John, William and Ruth. William the youngest son died before 1660, leaving a son William and a daughter Ruth. John the second son had, by two wives, five children, the two eldest of whom (perhaps twins) were both named John, and are designated in his will as "my son John the elder," and "my younger son John." His will bears date 23d April, 1628, and was proved in the Prerogative Court at Canterbury, by both executors, 7th July, 1628. In it he describes himself as "of Little Munden, yeoman," disposes of a respectable estate, gives 20 shillings to the poor of Little Munden, provides for his wife Martha, naming her brothers Richard Ward and William Ward as trustees, and for his four sons, the two Johns, William and Richard, and his daughter Elizabeth, and appoints his brother Francis Kirby of London, and his brother-in-law Thomas Hale of Watton, executors.

"John Kirby the elder," eldest son of the above John, made his will 10th June, 1637, describing himself as "of Dane End in the parish of Little Munden, yeoman," and naming his wife Mary, his daughter Mary, and a child of which his wife was then pregnant, his brothers John and William, his aunt Ruth Cowley, and his father-in-law John Sympton, and Richard Cock of Little Munden, yeoman, which last two he named as overseers. It also named his sister Elizabeth with a bequest of £10 to her, but this entry was erased, doubtless indicating that she died before the testator. The will was proved at Hitchin, 9th October, 1637, by the widow Mary.

Elizabeth Kirby, daughter of John the brother of Joan Hale, made her will, dated 1st June, 1637, describing herself as of Dane End in the parish of Little Munden, and giving bequests to her mother, her brothers the two Johns and William, her aunt Ruth Cowley and the daughter of the latter, Ruth Cowley the younger, her aunt Joane Bydes, and *her* daughters Dorothy and Elizabeth (Hale), her uncle Francis Kirby, whom she makes executor, and his son and daughter Joshua and Sarah, these last two being residuary legatees. This will was proved at Hitchin by the executor, 2d August, 1637.

Ruth the sister of Joan (Kirby) Hale married first a Cowley, by whom she had a daughter Ruth. He died before June, 1637, and before October, 1640, she married Edward Browne. She was still living at the date of the will of her brother Francis in July, 1660, and was apparently the last survivor of the family.

It remains to speak only of Francis Kirby, the brother of Joan and the uncle of Thomas[1] Hale. A foot-note to his letters in the Winthrop papers (Mass. His. Soc. Coll. s. 4, vol. 7, p. 13) describes him as " a merchant of London, largely engaged in forwarding supplies to the colonies of Massachusetts and Connecticut, and in commercial transactions with the early settlers." All the records touching him in England, however, style him " skinner," and not merchant, the former term including dealers in leather, hides, skins, furs and peltries.

His letters to Gov. Winthrop and to his son John Winthrop, Jr., so far as published, are found in the volume of the Hist. Soc. Coll. above named, pp. 13 to 22, and in Vol. 9 of Series 3 of the same Collections, pp. 237 to 267, and range in date from 1631 to 1639. They indicate relations of great intimacy and confidence, especially between himself and the younger Winthrop; though relating primarily to business, they contain much in the way of general, local and family news, and are written in a free, pleasant and cultivated style, pretty freely garnished with Latin quotations and expressions, with a slight occasional error in inflection or orthography.

Francis Kirby's first wife and the mother of his children, was Susan, sister of Emanuel Downing (the father of Sir George), who in turn married the sister of Gov. Winthrop the elder. This connection by marriage undoubtedly led to the intimate relations between him and the Winthrops.

His business with the colonies seems to have included a general exportation of supplies of all kinds to the colonists, for which he received payment mainly in beavers' skins, for the purchase, care and shipping of which he gives frequent and minute directions.

He probably married for a second wife the widow Elizabeth Carter, mother of Joseph Carter, whom he introduced to Gov. Winthrop by a letter dated 11th April, 1639 (M. H. S. C. vol. 7, *supra*, p. 20) as " my loue-deseruinge son and faithfull servant." Carter was at Newbury the next year, 1640, when he received from Thomas[1] Hale a deed of forty acres of land in Newbury. He soon after returned to England, where he probably married, and where his daughter Eunice was baptized in St. Helen's Church, Bishopsgate, 2d July, 1643, and his daughter Mary, 8th Sept. 1644, each described in the registry as "daughter of Joseph Carter, skinner, and Eunice his wife." This notice is taken here of Joseph Carter, as being, with the exception of the wife and children of Thomas[1] Hale, and his remote alliance by marriage with the Downings and Winthrops, the only connection either by blood or marriage of Thomas[1] who is known to have ever been in America, and his stay here did not probably exceed three years. As further illustrative of the almost constant inaccuracy of Coffin, it is proper to note that he, and Savage following him, place Joseph Carter at Newbury in 1636, when he plainly did not arrive there before 1639.

Francis Kirby had three children, and only three so far as appears, viz : Joshua, Francis who died on the day of his birth, and Sarah who died before her father. He was born probably about 1590, and married about 1616, his eldest child Joshua having been born in 1617. It is significant of his character and the success which he achieved, that being the son of a rural yeoman, and probably early apprenticed to the trade of "skinner" in London, he could have achieved so early the position of a thriving and respected tradesman which he so evidently sustained from 1631 to 1639, with the degree of education and accomplishments which his letters show him to have possessed ; still more significant in this regard is the fact that his eldest son Joshua was matriculated at New Inn Hall in Oxford at the age of 17, in 1634, where he proceeded B.A. in 1637, at the age of 20 ; and M.A. in 1640, at the age of 23. Joshua took orders, and his career was a most interesting one, did our limits permit us to follow it. His persecutions, first by the puritans for his adherence to Charles I., whom he persisted in praying for publicly long after most of the puritans evidently regarded him as "past praying for," and after the restoration by the royal party for alleged undue adherence to puritan principles and practices, would seem to indicate his character as the very antipodes of the excellent and politic Vicar of Bray, as well as of the good vicar's antetype or imitator, as the case may have been, Joshua's cousin-german, Sir George Downing. His wife was Mary Balam, a sister of Balaam Balam.

Francis Kirby would seem to have met with financial reverses during the time of the commonwealth, abandoned his old business and quit his old parish of St. Helen's, where his first wife had died in 1635. Some years before his death he was appointed by the common council of London, bridge-master of Old London Bridge, and he held that post to his death. The office was a respectable and responsible one, and though indicative of fallen fortunes to Mr. Kirby, was no less indicative of the confidence and respect in which he was held by his neighbors and fellow-tradesmen. According to the old chroniclers it was an office filled by "some freeman elected by the city to look after the reparations of the bridge; he hath a liberal salary allowed him, and the place hath sometimes been a good relief for some honest citizens fallen to decay." His emoluments consisted of a salary and fees amounting to about £100 a year (equivalent to about £300 to £400 at the present day) and the use of a comfortable house at the Surrey end of the bridge in the parish of St. Olave, Southwark, known as the bridge-master's house, and readily distinguished in the old engravings of London Bridge. Here he doubtless died, and was buried in the parish church of St. Olave's, 12th October, 1661, the registry describing him simply as "Francis Kerby, bridgemaster."

His reduced fortunes were evidently somewhat improved before his death, his will indicating that he left a comfortable estate. It bears date 24th July, 1660, and was proved in the Prerogative Court of Canterbury 1st

November, 1661, by Joshua Kirby the executor. In it he describes himself as "citizen and skinner of London, now dwelling in the parish of St. Olave, Southwark, Surrey." He gives bequests to Mary, wife of his son Joshua, and to their children Godsgift, Susan, Elizabeth, Phebe, Camdena and Welcome; to his sister Ruth Browne; to the poor of Little Munden; to the poor of St. Olave's; to Elizabeth Turfett, daughter of George Turfett, the grandchild of his late wife Elizabeth, deceased; to Mary Nash, widow, late wife of John Nash; to his cousin Joseph Alport, scrivener; to his cousin William Kirby, son of his late brother William Kirby, and to his cousin Ruth Macham, sister of said William; to his cousins John Kirby and William Kirby, sons of his late brother John Kirby; to his cousin Elizabeth Goad; to Eunice, Rachel and Sarah Carter, daughters of Joseph Carter, deceased, and to his servant Mary Bradbury. He makes his son Joshua Kirby residuary legatee and devisee and sole executor, and appoints as overseer his sister Ruth Browne and his "loving neighbor, Mr. Matthew Robinson, citizen and grocer of London."

The will of Joshua Kirby, son of Francis, was made 30th May, 1674, proved at Pontefract 29th August, 1676, and registered in the registry at York. It is referred to only to note that it gives legacies of 40 shillings to each of "my brother Carter's daughters." The male line of Francis Kirby terminated with his grandson Godsgift, son of Joshua, who was educated for the Presbyterian ministry and died in 1686, unmarried, at the age of 28.

This completes the record of the English origin and connections of the emigrant Thomas[1] Hale of Newbury, so far as known or likely ever to be known. The social rank of the Hales and Kirbys, and the absence of church and church-yard monuments, and of further entries upon probate and church registers, render it improbable that more will ever be known of the generations prior to Thomas.[1] Col. Chester's labors, to which I am indebted for almost all the English records above referred to, have evidently been exhaustive and thorough.

The maiden name, parentage and birth-place of Thomasine, wife of Thomas[1] Hale, are all undiscovered, and likely to remain so, unless by accidental discovery through some records of her own family. But the identity of Thomas[1] of Newbury, who is found at that place in 1638, having a wife Thomasine and children, Thomas said to have been born in 1633, and John born 1635 or 1636, with Thomas the son of Thomas[a] and Joan (Kirby) Hale of Watton, is established beyond doubt by the following entries found in the Registry of baptisms in the parish church at Watton, viz:

"1633. Nov. 18. Thomas Hale, son of Thomas and Thomasine."
"1635. April 19. John Hale, son of Thomas and Thomasine."

In conclusion it may be added, that the name of Hale under the different forms of de la Hale, de Hale, at-Hale, Hales and Hale, has been abundant in Hertfordshire since the early part of the thirteenth century, and still is so. I find no evidence that any of the name there were above the rank of yeoman before 1560. The name also early prevailed and is still probably found in Surrey, Sussex, Norfolk, Bucks, Essex, Hants, North Hants, Kent, Salop, Somerset, Gloucester, and other counties. Of the Hales of Gloucestershire, to which family the illustrious Sir Matthew Hale, Lord Chief Justice, belonged, Atkyns, in his history of that county, says (p. 107): "The family of Hale has been of ancient standing in this county, and always esteemed for their probity and charity."

Within the first fifty years after the settlement of Massachusetts Bay, at least seven emigrants of the name of Hale, and perhaps two or three more, besides Thomas of Newbury, settled in that colony and in Connecticut, descendants of four of whom are traced to the present time. There is no evidence that any of these were of kin to Thomas of Newbury; certainly none were nearly related to him. The name was also found among the early settlers of Virginia and Maryland, and their descendants bearing the name are still found in the southern states.

HALE, DOWSETT, KIRBY, CRANFIELD. — "This completes the record of the English origin and connections of the emigrant Thomas[1] Hale of Newbury, so far as known or likely ever to be known. . . . The maiden name, parentage and birth-place of Thomasine, wife of Thomas[1] Hale, are all undiscovered, and likely to remain so, unless by accidental discovery through some records of her own family." Thus wrote the historian of the Hale family, the late Hon. Robert S. Hale of Elizabethtown, N. Y., in 1881 (*vide ante*, vol. 35, p. 375).

The following item, which adds the maiden name and date of marriage of Thomasine, was brought to my attention a year or two ago by that veteran of English research, Henry F. Waters:

"1632 Dec. 11   Thomas Hall *of Watton, apud Stone, Co. Hertford, glover* and Thomazin Dowsett, *maiden*; p. lycense" (Registers of St. Helen's, Bishopsgate, London, Harl. Soc., p. 133, Marriages).

The conclusions of the family historian are still further upset by the following items taken from the marriage records of Watton as published in volume II of Phillimore's Hertfordshire Parish Registers marriages.

"Thomas Haille & Joane Kirbie   19 Oct. 1601" (p. 87).
"John Kirbie & Joane Cranfellde 23 Dec. 1576" (p. 85).

These records add the date of marriage of Thomas[1] Hale's parents, the date of marriage of his maternal grandparents, supply the Christian name of the maternal grandfather, and the maiden name of the maternal grandmother.

Boston, Mass.   WILLIAM PRESCOTT GREENLAW.

HALE–KIRBY–DOWNING.—The Hon. Robert S. Hale communicated to the REGISTER for October, 1881, an account of the English origin of Thomas Hale * of Newbury, as established by the researches of Col. Chester. When last in England I made an important correction to the statements of Col Chester, which is interesting as concerning also the family of Downing. Col. Chester supposed Francis Kirby, brother-in-law of Thomas Hale, to have had two wives, Susan Downing and widow Elizabeth Carter. But in fact Susan Downing was the widow Carter, and the second wife Elizabeth may have been a widow Turfett. The evidence as to the first wife is the will of Richard Blades of London, 1634, who mentioned Joseph and Mary Carter, children of Susan Carter now wife of Francis Kirby, Joshua and Sarah Kirby, children of the same Francis and Susan Kirby; he also left his daughter Edith Blades to the care of Francis Kirby.

                                                  W. S. APPLETON.

*P. 196, this volume.

HAMMOND—PEACH, of Marblehead.—Richard Hammond was in Marblehead in 1670, and was undoubtedly the emigrant ancestor or one of the emigrant ancestors of the Hammonds of Marblehead. The following, gleaned from English records, probably shows his ancestry and also points to the progenitors of the Peach family of the same place :

(1) Edward Hammond and wife Catherine were living in the Parish of St. Clements, Ipswich, England, in 1571 and 1577. They had children baptized there, among whom were Mary, Susan and William.

(2) William Hammond, whose will dated 24 Jan., 1649, probated 23 May, 1650, was twice married and left a large family of children, among whom were the following :

(3) John, m. St. Clements, Ipswich, 1658, Elizabeth Crane. They had several children, among whom were sons John and William.

(3) William Hammond of Ipswich, mariner, whose will was probated, Arch. Suffolk, 13 March, 1661. Wife Dorcas, sons John and William. Daughters Hannah, Dorcas and Martha.

(3) Edward Hammond, of Ipswich, mariner, m. St. Clements, 1638, Thomasine Peach, dau. of William Peach, of Ipswich, mariner, and Thomasine Cole, his wife. Will, Arch. Suffolk, 2 Nov., 1667. Sons Jonathan, Nathaniel, Edward, Samuel, John and William; daughters Abigail and Thomasine. Sons Edward and William were mariners.

(3) Richard Hammond living in Ipswich in 1649, but no later record of him there has been found.

(3) Mary Hammond, living in 1649.

(3) Sarah, wife of John Barnes.

(3) A daughter, wife of —— Grymble, in 1649.

" The Hammonds of Ipswich were a race of hardy sea captains and themselves in great part owners of the ships they sailed in and of the cargoes they carried. They held the Manor of Newton Hall in Swilland for several generations. Edward Hammond, who died a little after the Restoration, is mentioned with approval by Matthias Candler, the genealogical Vicar of Coddenham. ' Henry Bloomfield, ' he says, ' one of the Chiefe Constables of the Hu of Thredling,' married to his second wife, ' Thomasin daughter of Thomas Coale of Ipswich, the relict of Wᵐ Peche a Mʳ of a ship neere the old Barre gates in Ipswich. She had a daughter m. to Edward Hamont, Mʳ of a ship in Ipswich, a pius man.' —*Harl. MS. 6071, p. 543.*

" A tombstone in the churchyard of St. Clement, Ipswich, has the following inscription : ' The Burying place of Captain Benjamin Hamond and Captain John Hammond, sons of Edward Hamond, in this parish.' The Shield, Party per pale, displays a quatrefoil between three demi-lions passant guardant; and the Crest above, on helmet and torse, is a wolf's head erased." (*Suffolk Manorial Families*).—F. S. HAMMOND, *Bloomfield, New Jersey.*

JOHN HAMMOND OF LAVENHAM, SUFFOLK, ENGLAND.

Contributed by F. S. HAMMOND, Esq., of Oneida, N.Y.

JOHN HAMMOND, the clothier of Lavenham, County of Suffolk, England, was born between 1500 and 1520, probably at Melford, as his father appears to have been living there before 1517. No record of his birth has been found, and there is nothing to show his age at the time of his death in 1551. It is evident, however, that his children were all young at the time, and the fact that his widow survived him for twenty-six years would indicate that he was a comparatively young man at the time of his death.

The dates of births of his children cannot be found, but William was probably the eldest son, although there is no positive evidence to prove that he was the eldest child. He is mentioned first in his father's will, and is named with his mother as executor of the will, which would indicate that he was older than his brother Thomas ; but to Thomas is left the house in Melford, while William appears to have received only £5.

The fact that William was named with his father in the deed of trust, given below, would seem to establish the fact of his being the eldest son. The following abstract of John's will was furnished by Major Henry C. Malden, a brother-in-law of Rev. Canon Thomas Scott, Rector of Lavenham, in 1897, and is dated Dec. 22, 1550:

"I John Hamond, of Lavenham, Clothier" &c.

Item, I give and bequeathe to Agnes my weif £30.

Item, I give and bequeathe to Willm Hamond my sonne £5, to be paide hym at the age of 21 yeres.

Item, I give and bequeathe to Elizabeth, Margaret, and Johane, my daughters, to every one of them £6. 8s 4d, to be paide them at the age of 21 yeres.

Item, I give and bequeathe to Thomas Hamond, my sonne my house in Melford, late John Hamonde my ffathers, holdyn by copye of Courte Rolle now of my Lady Mary's grace, to euter at the age of 21 yeres.

Item, I give and bequeathe to my said sonne Thomas £4.

I appoint my wyfe Agnes and my sonne Willm executors of this my last Will. Proved at Lambeth, June 5, 1551.

The following is a copy of the deed of trust mentioned above, dated July 25, 1548, in which one William Page of Brandeston, near Lavenham, conveys a copse and meadow to twenty-five trustees for the good of the poor of Lavenham for ever.

Indenture at Lavenham Rector.

Omnibus X^ti fidelibus ad quos hoc presens carta Indentata perve'int Will^o Page de Lavenham. Salutem in Dno sempiternam. Sciatis me prefatum Wm Page dimisisse, tradidisse, feofasse et hac presenti carta mea indentata confirmasse Will^o Rysbie, Generoso Roberto Risbie, Thome Risbie et Georgio Risbie filiis dicti Willi Rysbie, Marteno Sudeley Generoso et Marteno filio suo, Willo Grome et Willo filio suo, Rogero Grome et Thome filio suo, Thome Sexteyn, Georgio Pye et Georgio filio suo, Roberto Critost, Johni Whattoke, clothmaker, et Johni filio suo Willo Cawston, Alano Sexteyn, Johni Warde, Roberto Brinwyn, Johni Hamonde et Willo Hamonde filio suo, Roberto Lynche, Hugoni Southill, Edwo Prykke et Willo Rockeley unam peciam prati vocatam Brandeston medowe, et unam peciam bosci voc^m Brandeston Grove cum suis pertinentibus in villa de Lavenham predicta. Quae quidam pecio prati et bosci erunt ad pauperes sustentandos infra villa de Lav^m predict in perpetuum. In omnis rei testimonium huic presenti carte indentate sigillum meum opposui. Datum vicesimo quinto die July Anno regis Edwardi Sexti dei Gra Anglie ffrancie et Hiberne Regis fidei Defensoris et in terra Anglicane et Hiberne Ecclesie Capitis secundo.

(Signed) per me Willm Page
(Endorsed) Possessio et status data est in præsens Johnni Waren Nicholas Waren Thome—(illegible) Johni Vale cum multis aliis
2 Edw 6 1548

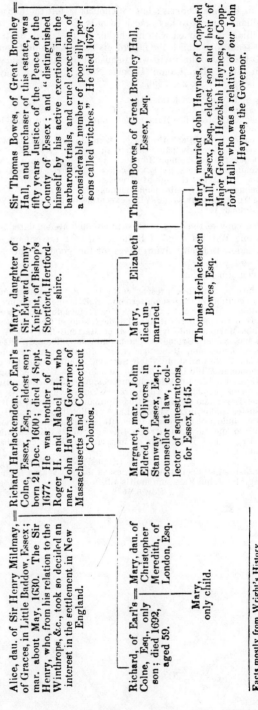

HARLACKENDEN.

Alice, dau. of Sir Henry Mildmay, of Graces, in Little Baddow, Essex; mar. about May, 1630. The Sir Henry, who, from his relation to the Winthrops, &c., took so decided an interest in the settlement in New England. = Richard Harlackenden, of Earl's Colne, Essex, Esq., eldest son; born 21 Dec. 1600; died 4 Sept. 1677. He was brother of *our* Roger H. and Mabel H., who mar. John Haynes, Governor of Massachusetts and Connecticut Colonies.

Sir Thomas Bowes, of Great Bromley Hall, and purchaser of this estate, was fifty years Justice of the Peace of the County of Essex; and "distinguished himself by his active exertions in the barbarous trials, and cruel execution, of a considerable number of poor silly persons called witches." He died 1676. = Mary, daughter of Sir Edward Denny, Knight, of Bishop's Stortford, Hertfordshire.

Margaret, mar. to John Eldred, of Olivers, in Stanway, Essex, Esq.; counsellor at law, collector of sequestrations, for Essex, 1645.

Elizabeth = Thomas Bowes, of Great Bromley Hall, Essex, Esq.

Mary, died unmarried.

Mary, married John Haynes, of Coppford Hall, Essex, Esq., eldest son and heir of Major General Hezekiah Haynes, of Coppford Hall, who was a relative of *our* John Haynes, the Governor.

Thomas Herlackenden Bowes, Esq.

Richard, of Earl's Colne, Esq., only son; died 1692, aged 59. = Mary, dau. of Christopher Meredith, of London, Esq.

Mary, only child.

Facts mostly from Wright's History of County of Essex, England. T. L. T.—*Jan.* 1836.

iiij July, **1635**. In the Defence de Loñd. Mʳ Thomas Bostocke, vrs New England p'r Cert: from the minister and Justices of peace of his Conformitie to yᵉ Govmt. of Church of Englᵈ and no Subsedy man.

Roger Harlakenden† 23 toke oathe of Allegance and Supremacie.

Eliza Harlakenden *his wife* 18   Mable Harlakenden *his sister* 21

Anne Wood	23		Wᵐ ffrench	30
Samuell Shepherd	22	*Servants to yᵉ aforesaid Roger Harlakenden.*	Eliza ffrench *his wife*	32
Joseph Cocke	27		Robert *a man servant*	
Geo: Cocke	25		Sarra Simes	30

6ᵗʰ July.   In the Defence de Loñd Mʳ Tho: Bostocke vrs. New England.

Joh: Jackson *wholesale man in Burchen Lane* 30

P'r Cert. from Sʳ Geo: Whitmore‡ and minister of yᵉ p'ish.

---

† In the *Visitation of Kent*, 1574, *Additional MSS.* (*B. M.*) *Vol.* 5532, *p.* 58 *b*, is the following pedigree :—

```
        John Harlakendon═
        of Warhorn.    │                          Richard Londinoys═
                       │                                           │
        John, of Warhorn═                                          │
            │                    │                                 │
        Thomas═Mary da: of Richard Londinoys.       Robert.        │
    │             │              │                    │
John, son and heir  William,  Elizabeth, da:═Roger, 3d═Elizabeth, da:
                    2d son.    of Hardres.  │ son.   of Blechindon.
    │             │              │            │
  Roger.       Richard.       Thomas.       Mabell.
                       Subscribed  *Roger Harlakendon.*
```

‡ The same spelt *Whittimor* in a previous page.

HARLAKENDEN FAMILY.

N. E. Hist. and Gen. Reg.   *New York, Nov. 5th,* 1860.

Mr. Editor:—After reading, in the last number of the Register, (October, 1860,) a[1] pedigree of the Harlackendens taken from the Kent Visitation of 1574, I threw into a condensed form some notes which I had previously collected relative to the same family. Seeing that these are more full in detail, besides exhibiting a material *difference* in the line of descent, I have taken the liberty to transmit a copy for your inspection, and remain   Your Obdt Servt.,

ISAAC J. GREENWOOD, JR.

The earliest mention of the name appears to be that of William Harlakenden of Wood-Church, co. Kent, who lived during the time of William the Conqueror, and died 30 April, 1081. From William was descended Thomas, living in 1408.

ARMS :—Azure, a fesse ermine between three *Eagles'* heads, erased, or, two and one.

THOMAS[1] HARLACKENDEN, living in 1408.

MOSES,[2] son of Thomas, m. Petronilla, dau. of Sir Henry Hardress, and had

1. WILLIAM,[3] of Wood-Church, co. Kent, whose son WALTER,[4] ob. s. p.
2. JOHN,[3] of Warhorn, co. Kent, m. Joan, dau. of Thomas Willis of Allington, Kent, and had

JOHN,[4] m. Joan, dau. of —— Philips of Tenterdam, and had

1. ELIZABETH.[5]
2. THOMAS,[5] of Wood-Church, father of GEORGE,[6] of Little-Yeldham, co. Essex, and others.
3. WILLIAM,[5] ob. s. p.
4. ROGER,[5] of Kenardeston, co. Kent, b. ab. 1535 ; purchased Earl's Colne, co. Essex; married four times,—1st w. Elizabeth, dau. of Thomas Hardres, Esq., by whom alone he had children ; 2d w. Elizabeth Blatchenden ; 3d w. Jane, widow of Richard Kelton and dau. of Sir Thomas Josceline ; 4th w. Anne Dewhurst, widow. He d. 21 Jan. 1602, and had
   1. MABELL,[6] m. Clement Stonard of Stapleford-Abbot, who was b. 1558, and d. 23 Sept. 1612.
   2. ROGER,[6] prob. ob. s. p.
   A-3. RICHARD,[6] of Staples-Inn. (See below.)
   B-4. THOMAS,[6] of Earl's Colne, b. 1568. (See below.)

A- RICHARD[6] HARLAKENDEN, of Staples-Inn, b. ab. 1565; m. Margaret, dau. of Edward Hubbart (Hobart) of Stanstead-Monfichet, and had four sons and seven daughters; he died, 24 Aug. 1631, and his widow being considered a lunatic the majority of the property was divided between the two surviving sons, Richard and Roger.

1. JANE,[7] the 3d dau., b. —— ; m. 17 March, 1617, Hen. Clench, Gent.
2. RICHARD,[7*] b. in 1602; married twice,—1st w. Alice, dau. of Sir Henry Mildmay, Knt., by whom he had an only son, Richard ; 2d w. Mary, dau. of Sir Edward Denny, Knt., of Bishop's Stortford, co. Herts., by whom he had three daughters. He was buried 22 Jan. 1691-2, being 89 years of age. His son—

---

* Savage, in his "Geneal. Dic.," says "he was bred at Emanuel College, Cambridge, Eng., and that he had a grant of land in Cambridge, Mass., but, as he never came out to this country, it was forfeited."

[1]The preceding article.

1. RICHARD,⁹ b. ——; m. Mary, dau. of Christopher Meredith, Gent., of London, and had an only dau. MARY,⁹* b. 22 Nov. 1653; m. 16 May, 1672, Daniel Androwes of London and Low-Leyton, co. Essex, who d. 26 Jan. 1680–1, having a posthumous son, RICHARD,¹⁰ who d. s. p. in October, 1730.
2. MARGARET,⁸ bap. 11 June, 1635; m. John Eldred, Esq., of Olivers, counsellor-at-law.
3. MARY,⁸ b. 11 Nov. 1636; ob. single.
4. ELIZABETH,⁸ b. ——; m. Thomas Bowes, Esq., of Great Bromley.
3. ANNE,⁷ bap. 21 May, 1610; m. 2 Sept. 1629, John Eden of Ballingdon, co. Essex.
4. GEORGE,⁷ b. ——; buried 6 June, 1610.
5. ROGER⁷ HARLAKENDEN, bap. 1 Oct. 1611; owned Colne Park, and other estates, in co. Essex. His first wife, Emlin, was buried at Earl's Colne, 18 Aug. 1634; he m. again, 4 June, 1635, Elizabeth, dau. of Godfrey Bosseville (Boseveile) of Gunthwayte, co. York, Esq.,—she was then 18 years of age. He embarked at London in the Defence, (Thom. Bostocke, Mʳ.,) 10 Aug. 1635, for New England, and arrived early in October, accompanied by his wife and sister Mable, and also several male and female servants; some of his male attendants, however, had evidently shipped themselves as such in order to deceive the government officials, as we find them the next year with the prefix of respect in the colony. Roger settled at Newtown, (Cambridge,) Mass., where he purchased lands of Thomas Dudley, Esq., and became a freeman 3 March, 1635–6. On the 25th of May, 1636, he was chosen an Assistant, and so continued until his death, at the same time he was appointed a magistrate for Newtown, and on 13th of December of the same year he received the post of Lieut. Col. in Col. John Haynes' Regiment, comprising the militia of Charlestown, Newtown, Watertown, Concord and Dedham. He was one of the committee appointed, 20 Nov. 1637, "to take order for a College at Newtown," but he died during the succeeding year, 17 Nov. 1638, of small pox, leaving two children. His will, written previous to the birth of his second daughter, (Sept. 1638,) appoints as executors his wife Elizabeth, his brother Richard of England, his brother-in-law John Haynes, and John Bridge of Cambridge, Mass. His lands in Essex, Eng., were left in the hands of Godfrey Boseveile, Richard Harlackenden, Henry Darby and Nath'l Bacon, Esqrs., as feoffees, giving them full power and authority to make sale of them if they should deem it fit for the better performance of his will; they were sold soon after to Sir John Jacob, Knt. Legacies were left to each of his own and natural sisters, to the children of his sister Nevile, to his cousin Sarah, to John Bridge, Anna and Mary maid servants, and to Gowldinge and Thomas Prentice. His widow, Elizabeth, subsequently m. Herbert Pelham, Esq., the first treasurer of Harvard College, (1643 to '50.) Pelham owned lands at Sudbury, Mass., as early as 1639, but returned in 1650 to England, where, according to Allen's Am. Biog., he died in 1676. The children of Roger Harlakenden were—

* Ob. 26 Oct. 1729.

1. ELIZABETH,[8] b. Dec. 1636.
2. MARGARET,[8] b. Sept. 1638.
6. MABELL,[7] the 7th dau., b. 1614, left England for the Mass. Col. with her brother Roger in 1635, being then 21 years of age. During the succeeding year, probably, she became the second wife of John Haynes, Esq., of Cambridge, Mass., (originally of Copford Hall, Essex,) who removed in 1637 to Hartford, Conn., became the first Gov. of that Colony, and died 1 March, 1654, leaving issue.—(Savage's Gen. Dic.)
7. GEORGE,[7] bap. 15 June, 1616, and d. prob. s. p.

B- THOMAS[6] HARLAKENDEN of Earl's Colne, Gent., b. in 1568; *heir* to his father, at whose death, in 1602, he was 34 years of age. Married twice,—1st w. Dorothy, dau. of John Cheney, Esq., of Draiton, co. Bucks; 2d w. Jane, dau. of Edward Hobart, of Stanstead-Montfichet, Esq. By the last wife, who was buried at Earl's Colne, 24 Nov. 1626, he had but one child, Agnes. He was buried, 27 March, 1648.
1. THOMAS,[7] b. ——; m. Elizabeth, dau. of —— Dove; he was buried at Earl's Colne, 27 Sept. 1652, leaving
   1. MEHETABEL,[8] who m. Daniel Nightingale.
   2. ALICE,[8] who m. Roger Goodall of Neyland, Gent.
2. RICHARD,[7] doctor of physic.
3. WILLIAM,[7] of Newhouse in Earl's Colne, b. ab. 1611; Justice of Peace at Cambridge, 9 Sept. 1654; m. Smythes, dau. of Edward Scroggs of co. Herts. She was buried at Earl's Colne, 28 June, 1651, and her husband on the 19th March, 1673. One son—
   THOMAS,[8] bap. 13 Dec. 1636.
4. DOROTHY,[7] b. ab. 1595, (doubtless the eldest child,) married Samuel Symonds, Esq., of Yeldham, co. Essex, of whom she was the first wife. He was afterwards Dept. Gov. of Mass.
5. ANNE,[7] b. ——.
6. MEHETABEL,[7] b. ——; m. Edward Elliston.
7. AGNES,[7] b. ——; buried at Earl's Colne, 20 Nov. 1627.

HARLACKENDEN FAMILY.

CORRECTION.—Through the kindness of Nathaniel Chauncy, Esq. of Philadelphia, I am enabled to furnish the following important correction to the pedigree (see *Reg.*, vol. xv, p. 327) of the Harlacken-* den Family.   ISAAC J. GREENWOOD, New York.

Moses[2] Harlackenden was father of
  I. William[3] of Woodchurch, co. Kent, the grandfather of Thomas[5], of the same place, who died 26th Aug. 1558, leaving a son and heir George[6], then aged 39, who m. Elizabeth, dau. of Thomas Hardres, afterwards wife of Roger Harlackenden of Earl's Colne, co. Essex.
  II John[3] of Warhorn, co. Kent, m. Joan Willis (or Willes) and had John,[4] who m. Joan Phillips and was father of Thomas[5] of Warhorn, who m. 1st Mary, dau. of Rich. Lonchnoys and granddau. of Thomas Fienes, Lord Dacre. His second wife Elizabeth was mother of Alice who m. Henry Thompson. According to the Inq. p. m. at Ashford, co. Kent, taken 11 Sep. 1564, he left sons:
   1. John,[6] aged 30; 2. William[6], aged 28; 3. Roger,[6] aged 27, the purchaser of Earl's Colne. But the will of Thomas, dated 25 Jan. 1562-3, mentions a fourth son Richard and some daughters.

*The preceding article.   212

THE ROYAL DESCENT OF MABEL HARLAKENDEN.

By a Descendant.

The alleged Royal descent of Mabel Harlakenden has never received the unqualified acceptance of careful genealogists. A pedigree is no stronger than its weakest link. That a daughter of Richard Londenoys married Thomas Harlakenden was abundantly proved, but there seemed to be no sufficient evidence of the marriage of this Richard Londenoys to a daughter of Thomas, Lord Dacre of the South. Neither Dugdale, Collins or any of the Visitations give a daughter to Lord Dacre, and it seemed significant that the shield of arms above the monument of Roger Harlakenden in the church of Earls Colne, erected in 1602, should quarter the arms of (1) Harlakenden, (2) Willis, (3) Londenoys, and (4) Oxenbridge, and should omit the much more important family of Dacre, if any descent from it could be claimed. But a pedigree of the Londenoys family, recently obtained from the British Museum (Harl. ms., 6065, fol. 76ᵇ), seems to set the matter at rest by establishing the missing link.

It appears by this pedigree that Robert Londenoys of Breade, in County Sussex, Esq., married the daughter and heir of William Oxenbridge of Winchelsea, armiger, and that Richard Londenoys of Breade, Esq., a son of this marriage, married " Catherine dau. to ye Lo. Dacres—Az 3 lions rampᵗ. or," and further, that Mary, " daugh. & sole heire to Rich. Londenoys" married Thomas Harlakenden of Warhorne in Co. Kent. Three of the children of Thomas Harlakenden are named, John " sonne & heire," William 2d son, and Elizabeth ; but as Roger, the 3d son, is not named, the pedigree was probably compiled before his birth in 1541. It is unsigned, and must be taken for what it is worth ; but corroborative evidence is found in the pedigree of the Oxenbridge family, which appears in 12 Sussex Arch., Coll. 230, where the marriage is also noted of Richard Londenoys to " Katherine daughter of Fines Lord Dacre."

The Oxenbridge family seems to have been of considerable consequence in the County of Sussex. Thomas Oxenbridge, who was of the elder branch and was first cousin once removed to William Oxenbridge of Winchelsea, whose daughter and heir married Robert Londenoys, was a sergeant at law, and had a grant of the custody of the lands of Richard Fynes, late Lord Dacre, and the wardship and marriage of his grandson and heir Thomas. This Thomas became 8th Lord Dacre, and was the father of Catherine who married Richard Londenoys. Thomas Oxenbridge was also named, with her sons Thomas and William Fynes, as one of the executors of the will of Joan Fynes, Lady Dacre, widow of Richard who died in 1486. (Testamenta Vetusta, 320.) His younger brother, Sir Goddard Oxenbridge, who was three times Sheriff of Sussex, married Ann, daughter of Sir Thomas Fines, 2d son of Richard Fynes, Lord Dacre, and Joan his wife. Sir John Fines (Fynes or Fiennes), his elder brother (sometimes but erroneously called Thomas in the early pedigrees), married Alice, daughter and co-heir of Henry, Lord Fitz Hugh. He died before 1485, in the lifetime of his father, and his son Thomas succeeded as 8th Lord Dacre, and may be confidently claimed as one of the ancestors of Mabel Harlakenden. His descent, through the Bouchier family, from King Edw. III. is, of course, unquestioned.

That no daughter is assigned to Lord Dacre in the early pedigrees has no controlling or even special significance, for younger sons as well as daughters

213

were often, if not usually, omitted, the main purpose of the compiler being to give only the direct descent.

That the arms of Dacre appear in the Londenoys pedigree would seem to preclude any suggestion of illegitimacy, and the intimate connection shown between the families of Oxenbridge and Dacres makes the Londenoys marriage a very natural and probable one, and it may be considered as fairly proven.

HARLAKENDEN.—In the REGISTER, *ante*, page 40, is an article about the royal * ancestry of Mabel Harlakenden, and references to a pedigree of the Londenoys family, in the British Museum, Harl. MS. 6065, fo. 76[b]. When in London recently I made a copy of the pedigree indexed under that number, but my conclusions are not quite the same as those of the writer of the article. The MS. is entitled "The Visitation of Essex made A°: Dni 1612, by John Raven Richmond Herald of Arms by Vertue of a Deputation from the Learned Camden Clarencieux King of Arms." That, I should think, might be considered authoritative. The writer of the article says that only three of the children of Thomas Harlakenden are named, but my copy of the pedigree shows four: John, William, Elizabeth, and *Roger*, whom the writer assumes to be left out. The pedigree calls Roger "of Earls Colne," and gives his children: Thomas, George, Roger, Richard, and Mabell. The coat of arms, also, is drawn on the pedigree: Harlakenden, quartering Willis, Londenoys and Oxenbridge. Those are the arms on Roger Harlakenden's tomb in Earl's Colne Church, and those are the arms he had a right to quarter, as descended from the heiresses of those families. Katharine Dacre was not an heiress, her brother inheriting the title, estates, &c., consequently her descendants could not quarter her arms; and the fact that the arms of Dacre do not appear on Roger Harlakenden's tomb is a proof, rather than otherwise, of his descent. At least, it does not militate in the least against it.　　　　　　　　　　　　　　　　　　　　MARY K. TALCOTT.

Hartford, Conn.

*The preceding article.

A NEW HARLAKENDEN LINE

By Sir Anthony Wagner, K.C.V.O., Garter King of Arms
and F. S. Andrus

In the summer of 1959 the late Dr. Arthur Adams drew the attention of the first named writer to a line deriving Roger Harlakenden (1611-1638) of Earl's Colne, Essex, and Cambridge, Mass., from the families of Quincy, Ferrers, Beauchamp of Powick and others, printed in Adams and Weis, *The Magna Charta Sureties, 1215* (1955), line 89, p. 73-5. He expressed doubt about certain links and asked for the position to be checked. When this had been done it was necessary to tell him that his doubts were justified. Roger Harlakenden was grandson of Roger Harlakenden (died in 1603) by Elizabeth, daughter of Thomas Hardres (died in 1556). Thomas Hardres was asserted to be son of Christopher Hardres by Dorothy, daughter of Sir John Paston of the celebrated Norfolk family. The pedigree in the 1591 Visitation of Kent, however, showed that Dorothy Paston, who was the first wife of Thomas (not Christopher) Hardres, died without issue, and that his children, including Elizabeth, who married first George and then Roger Harlakenden, were the offspring of his second marriage to Mary Oxinden.[1]

It was reported to Dr. Adams at the same time, however, that there were other lines of Roger Harlakenden's ancestry which might repay research and one of these has now turned out to give descents from royal and baronial lines. Through his mother, Margaret Huberd, Roger Harlakenden was descended from the well-known Chauncy family of Hertfordshire. Through the marriage of Sir William Chauncy to Joan, daughter of Sir Roger Bigod of Settrington (died in 1362) this brings descents from the Bigods, Earls of Norfolk, the Marshals, Earls of Pembroke, the lords of Galloway, the Kings of Scotland, Charlemagne, King Alfred and many more. The link is as follows:

215

1. JOHN[1] CHAUNCY, of Gilston, co. Hertford, aged 27 and more 5 Aug. 1479 (Inq. p.m. on his father, John Chauncy of Giltson, died 27 May 1479), died 8 June 1510, buried at Yardley, co. Hertford.

He married ALICE, daughter of Thomas Boyse, who was living 4 Nov. 1519.

Children (order of birth uncertain) among others:

    i.   JOHN,[2] of Gilston and Sawbridgeworth, co. Hertford and of Crayford, co. Kent, Lord of the Manor of Netherhall in Gilston, son and heir, died 8 June 1546 (Monumental Inscription at Sawbridgeworth). Will dated 30 Nov. 1543, proved 17 July 1546, in the Consistory Court of London. He m. (1), before 4 Nov. 1509, ELIZABETH, daughter and coheir of John Proffit of Barcombe, co. Sussex, by Alice, daughter and heir of John Horne, and widow of Richard Manfield; she d. 10 Nov. 1531 (M.I. at Sawbridgeworth). He m. (2) KATHERINE ————, who d. 30 April 1535 (M.I. at Sawbridgeworth). Issue by first wife.

    ii.   GEORGE, of Fulham, co. Middlesex. Owned land in Pevensey, co. Sussex. Will (in which he made bequests to the poor of Sawbridgeworth and Gedleston, i.e. Gilston) dated 13 Dec. 1520, proved 4 May 1521 [P.C.C. (9 Maynwaryng)]. He m. ———— mentioned, but not by name, in her husband's will.

2. iii.   WILLIAM, of Sawbridgeworth, mentioned in the will of his brother George, 1520.

2. WILLIAM[2] CHAUNCY (John[1]), of Sawbridgeworth, mentioned in the will of his brother George, 1520.

He married ———— GARLAND, who was mentioned as living in the will of her son Henry, 1557.

Children (order of birth uncertain):

    i.   JOHN,[2] mentioned in the wills of his uncle George Chauncy, 1520, and brother Henry, 1557.

    ii.   WILLIAM, mentioned in the will of his brother Henry, 1557.

    iii.   LUCY, mentioned in the will of her brother Henry, 1557.

    iv.   JOAN, mentioned in the will of her uncle George Chauncy, 1520.

    v.   MARY, mentioned in the wills of her uncle George Chauncy, 1520, and brother Henry, 1557.

3. vi.   HENRY, of Sawbridgeworth, mentioned in the will of his uncle George Chauncy, 1520.

3. HENRY[3] CHAUNCY (William,[2] John[1]), of Sawbridgeworth, mentioned in the will of his uncle George Chauncy, 1520, died in 1558.

He married JOAN, sister of Robert Tenderyng of Sawbridgeworth, in whose will, dated 20 July 1562, proved 20 March 1563 in the Archdeaconry Court of Middlesex, Essex and Hertfordshire, she was mentioned. Her will was dated 7 Nov. 1562 and proved (no date given) in the Archdeaconry Court of Middlesex, Essex and Hertfordshire (56 Raymond).

He bequeathed lease of Parsonage of Sawbridgeworth to his brother John Chauncy, in his will, dated 6 Feb. 1557, proved 5 Nov. 1558 (P.C.C. (68 Noodes)); mentioned brother-in-law William Pampyon, and also Robert Tenderyng and Richard Pille.

Children (order of birth uncertain):

i. WILLIAM,[4] mentioned in the wills of his mother, 1562, his uncle Robert Tendering, 1562, and his sister Elizabeth Huberd, 1577. M. and had issue.

ii. ALEXANDER, mentioned in the wills of his mother, 1562, his uncle Robert Tenderyng, 1562, and his sister Elizabeth Huberd, 1577. M. and had issue.

iii. MARY, m. ———— PILLE. Mentioned in the wills of her mother, 1562, and her sister Elizabeth Huberd, 1577. Had issue.

iv. A DAUGHTER, m. ———— BRIGHT, who was mentioned in the will of his mother-in-law, 1562; she was mentioned in that of her sister Elizabeth Huberd, 1577. Had issue.

4. v. ELIZABETH, mentioned in her mother's will, 1562, as "my daughter Hubbert."

4. ELIZABETH[4] (CHAUNCY) HUBERD (*Henry,[3] William,[2] John[1]*) died between 5 Dec. 1577 and 6 Nov. 1579.

She married, before 1562, RICHARD HUBERD of Birchanger, co. Essex, Churchwarden there, 1552-3, who was mentioned (but not by name) as "lately deceased" in the will of his wife, dated 5 Dec. 1577, proved 6 Nov. 1579 in the Commissary Court of London, Essex and Hertfordshire.

Children surname *Huberd* (order of birth uncertain):

5. i. EDWARD,[5] of Stansted-Montfichet, co. Essex, eldest son, mentioned in his mother's will, 1577, as having a house in Chancery Lane, London.

ii. HENRY, mentioned in the wills of his grandmother Joan Chauncy, 1562, and his mother, 1577.

iii. THOMAS, mentioned in the wills of his grandmother, 1562, and his mother, 1577.

iv. EDMONDE, mentioned in the wills of his grandmother, 1562, and his mother, 1577.

v. WILLIAM, mentioned in the wills of his grandmother, 1562, and his mother, 1577.

vi. MATHEW, youngest son, mentioned in his mother's will, 1577.

vii. ALICE, m. ———— SYMONS; mentioned in the wills of her grandmother, 1562, and her mother, 1577.

viii. ELIZABETH, m. ———— VEYSEY; mentioned in the wills of her grandmother, 1562, and her mother, 1577.

ix. JOAN, mentioned in the wills of her grandmother, 1562, and her mother, 1577.

x. JOYCE, mentioned in the wills of her grandmother, 1562, and her mother, 1577.

xi. BRIDGET, youngest daughter, under 24 and unm. 5 Dec. 1577, when she was mentioned in her mother's will.

5. EDWARD[5] HUBERD (*Elizabeth,[4] Henry,[3] William,[2] John[1]*), of Stansted-Montfichet, co. Essex, One of the Six Clerks in Chancery. Mentioned in his mother's will, 1577, as having a house in Chancery Lane, London. Mentioned in the will of his father-in-law John Southall, 1590. His will was dated 16 March 1601, proved 14 May 1602 (P.C.C. (33 Montague)), in which he mentioned the poor of Birchanger.

He married first JANE, daughter of John Southall, Citizen and Clothworker of London, who was born in Albrighton, co.

Salop, and whose will was dated 4 Oct. 1590 and proved 31 May 1592. Administration of goods unadministered 26 September following (P.C.C. (37 Harrington)). She was mentioned as deceased in her husband's will, 1601.

He married secondly ELIANOR, who was mentioned in her husband's will, 1601.

Children (order of birth uncertain):

i. SIR FRANCIS, of Stansted Hall, co. Essex, Knight, eldest son, mentioned in the will of his grandfather John Southall, 1590, and in the administration of his goods unadministered, 1592; mentioned as a minor in his father's will, 1601; m. ELIZABETH, daughter of Thomas Leventhorp, and had issue.

6. ii. MARGARET, m. Richard HARLAKENDEN of Earls Colne, co. Essex.

iii. JANE, mentioned in the will of her grandfather John Southall, 1590, and in the administration of his goods unadministered, 1592, then under 21; m., as his second wife, THOMAS HARLAKENDEN.²

iv. ELIZABETH, mentioned as under 21 in the administration of goods unadministered of her grandfather, 1592, and mentioned in her father's will 1601.

v. ANNE, mentioned as under 21 in the administration of goods unadministered of her grandfather, 1592.

vi. THOMAZINE, mentioned as under 21 in the administration of goods unadministered of her grandfather, 1592, and mentioned in her father's will, 1601.

vii. JOHN, mentioned in the will of his grandfather, 1590, and in the administration of his goods unadministered, 1592, then under 21, mentioned in his father's will, 1601.

viii. RICHARD, youngest son, mentioned in the will of his grandfather, 1590, and in the administration of his goods unadministered, 1592; mentioned in his father's will, 1601, still a minor.

6. MARGARET⁶ (HUBERD) HARLAKENDEN (*Edward,⁵ Elizabeth,⁴ Henry,³ William,² John¹*), mentioned as under 21 in the administration of goods unadministered of her grandfather John Southall, 1592. She was buried in Earls Colne, co. Essex, 4 June 1634.

She married in St. Dunstan-in-the-West, 11 Feb. 1592/3, RICHARD HARLAKENDEN of Earls Colne. He was buried there 24 Aug. 1631. His will dated 29 June 1631, proved 19 October following (P.C.C. (109 St. John)), mentioned his wife Margaret.

She had with other issue³ surname *Harlakenden*:

i. ROGER, bapt. in Earls Colne 1 Oct. 1611; d. 17 Nov. 1638; mentioned as youngest son in his father's will, 1631. He went to New England, 1635. Married twice and had issue by both marriages.

ii. MABEL, bapt. 27 Dec. 1614 [!]; mentioned in her father's will, 1631. Went to New England with her brother, 1635 [m. in 1636 JOHN HAYNES, by whom she had issue].

FOOTNOTES

1. Meredith B. Colkett called attention to another doubtful claim of royal descent for the Harlakendens through the Londenoyes-Dacres families in *The American Genealogist*, vol. 14, p. 209-214, April 1938.—Editor.

2. Thomas Harlakenden, brother of Richard, her sister's husband, married first Dorothy Cheyne, daughter of John Cheyne, of Drayton Beauchamp, co. Bucks., and had among others, Dorothy, who became the first wife of Samuel Symonds, of Great Yeldam and Toppesfield, co. Essex (later Deputy Governor of Massachusetts Bay Colony), by whom she had issue. See William S. Appleton, *Ancestry of Priscilla Baker* (1870), pedigree following p. 102.—Editor.

3. For some of Margaret Huberd's issue by Richard Harlakenden see THE *
REGISTER, vol. 15, p. 327-329, October 1861; a more nearly complete list is found in *The Topographer and Genealogist* (1846), vol. 1, p. 235.—Editor.

*Pp. 210-212, this volume.

HARRISES IN BOSTON BEFORE 1700

By Roderick Bissell Jones, Ph.D.,LL.B., Cmdr. U.S.N.R.,
of Winsted, Conn.

The Harrises of Wapping, London

(Note preliminary to material hereinafter presented)

WILLIAM HARRIS, mariner of Wapping, married DOROTHY ————,
daughter of Dorothy Lane, testatrix of 17 Jan. 1605 (THE REGISTER,
vol. 40, p. 158) and died before March 1594/5. He may have been
son of the William Harris, shipwright, listed in 1596 in the Capthall
and Wapping section of the "London Subsidies and Rent Rolls
(1596–1641)", or may have been son of Richard Harris, Sr., next
name but one to him in those rolls. Wapping on the Thames just
out the wall was, with the other hamlets of Limehouse, etc., in the
jurisdiction of St. Mary's, Whitechapel, in Stepney, Middlesex,
England. His widow married, in March 1594/5, Rowland Coitmore. See the latter's 1626 will in THE REGISTER, vol. 40, p. 158.

Children:
i.   WILLIAM,ᴬ b. before 1594/5.
ii. SAMUEL, a minor 17 Jan. 1605/6, named in grandmother Lane's will.
iii. SUSAN. . . . A Susanna Harris married, in 1609, William Ball
     (*The New York Genealogical and Biographical Record*, vol. 20,
     p. 183) in St. Mary's, Whitechapel. At least one child (surname
     Ball):
     1. *William*, named in step-grandfather Coitmore's will in 1626.
iv. DOROTHY, named with Susan in the Lane will. Named in step-
     father Coitmore's will. A Dorothy Harris married, in 1611,
     Thomas Lamberton (*ibid.*). Half sisters of the above children
     are the following daughters of Dorothy (Lane?) Harris and her
     second husband Coitmore (surname *Coitmore*):
         Elizabeth, bapt. 22 Feb. 1595/6. A granddaughter, Elizabeth
     Coitmore, was named in her grandmother Lane's will. If she was
     a second Elizabeth, b. before that 1605/6 will, she could be the
     daughter Elizabeth called a minor in father's will of 5 June 1626.
     At any rate, some daughter of his named Elizabeth married
     William Tyng, Treasurer of Massachusetts Bay Colony, and had
     by him Elizabeth 1638, Ann 1640, Bethia and Mercy 1643. Tyng
     died in Braintree, Mass., in 1653.
         Sara, called granddaughter in the Lane will. She came to
     Charlestown, Mass., about 1638. She m. Hugh Williams of
     Boston and Block Island. The History of Charlestown says she
     married a Williams. Pope says Hugh Williams' wife was Sara.
     Savage says Wm. Hilton of London married a Nowell of Charles-
     town. Sara had a stepsister who married Increase Nowell of
     Charlestown. Hugh Williams named "brother Hilton" in his
     will. Williams was unm. in 1642. They apparently had no
     children.
         A dau. to fulfill the statement in Coitmore's will "My sonnes in
     law Thomas Graves and Wm Rainsborough. . . .mariners over
     seas" (1626). This could have been a daughter of his first wife,
     Dorothy (Lane) Harris or of his second wife Catherine (Miles)
     Gray, whose daughter did marry Graves. Col. Wm. Rainsbor-
     ough, Jr., was in Charlestown for a time.

These above half-sisters of the Harris children above were also stepsisters of the following children of Coitmore's second wife, Catherine (Miles) Gray (surname *Gray*):

Parnell, m. (1) ———— Parker; m. (2) Increase Nowell of Charlestown.

Catherine, m. Thomas Graves, of Stepney, who d. in Charlestown.

WILLIAM⁴ HARRIS married in 1612 in St. Mary's, Whitechapel (Banks MS), ELIZABETH BOURNE, daughter of John and Jane (Harris) Bourne, who are mentioned (Jane as deceased) in the 11 April 1607 will of Jane's father Richard Harris, mariner, of Leigh, Essex, below London on the Thames (THE REGISTER, vol. 51, p. 109) who also names son Richard and minor children Sarah, Elizabeth, Mary, and John. William was co-executor with his mother Dorothy of the will of his grandmother Dorothy (Burton) Lane. He was said in the will of his father-in-law John Born, 4 Jan. 1618/9, to be "now gone to the East Indies" (*ibid.*, vol. 51, p. 110).

Children (named in grandfather Born's will):

   i. JOHN, b. in 1613–17.
1. ii. WILLIAM III, b. in 1614–18.

1. WILLIAM HARRIS, born in 1614/15. A William Harris, aged twenty, sailed on the *Amitie* from London 13 Oct. 1635 bound for St. Christophers and Barbados (THE REGISTER, vol. 14, p. 351). On board was a Bourne, aged twenty-one. This Harris could have been that William, born in 1614–18, son of William, Jr., and Elizabeth (Bourne) Harris and mentioned in the 1618 will of his grandfather, John Borne (*ibid.*, vol. 51, p. 110), of Wapping, London. It is here assumed that he, like so many others that were booked for the West Indies, left the ship at Boston. He was only eight years younger than his maternal great-uncle, John Harris, whom we have assumed above was the John Harris that had come to New England earlier that very year. Many of his family were to come to Boston within the next one or two years and were without doubt discussing it at this time. He, a bachelor, was free to come at once. It was Elizabeth, either his half-aunt or a stepsister of his half-aunt, that married William Tyng, treasurer of the Massachusetts Bay Colony, who died in Braintree, Mass., in 1653. His half-aunt, Sara, married Hugh Williams of Boston and Block Island. Her stepsisters, Parnell and Catherine, married respectively Increase Nowell, one of the most prominent men in the Colony, and "Admiral" Thomas Graves of Charlestown, Mass. In Charlestown by 1636 are William's step-uncle Thomas² (Rowland¹) Coitmore, whose widow married John Winthrop, Governor of the Massachusetts Bay Colony. Note below that Adam Winthrop as attorney defended William Harris (Jr.?) in a law suit.

221

It is here suggested that Mr. William Harris, merchant, of Boston, deceased in 1684, "aged about forty" and Mr. John Harris, mariner, captain, of Boston, lost at sea about 1680/2 were brothers and sons of William, born in 1614/15, son of William and Elizabeth (Bourne) Harris of St. Mary's, Whitechapel, London. The fact that there is no recorded relationship between the brothers is not surprising, because Captain John was at sea so much that his wife took a deed in his name and because both were relatively young men when they died, each leaving a single son.

    Note: When Captain John's widow set up a trust for their children in 1682 Thomas Downe witnessed it; in 1674 Downe had bought land of William Harris, the merchant, the witnesses being Jacob Eliot, whom Captain John called "my friend" and made supervisor of his will, and Theophilus Frary, the other trustee of the trust. Downe later sold to Isaac Walker. In 1679 Wm. Harris witnessed a deed to Samuel Walker. Asaph Eliot, also named by Capt. John as "my friend" to be supervisor of the Captain's will, owned land next to William Harris and bought more next to William Harris 12:245.

    Children (assumed):

2. i. WILLIAM, d. in Boston in 1684.
3. ii. JOHN, sea captain, lost at sea in 1680–2.

2. WILLIAM[2] HARRIS (*William*,[1] *William*,[A] *William*[B]) died 17 May 1684, "aged about 40 years", according to his gravestone in the Granary Burial Ground ("Pilgrims of Boston", by Bridgeman, p. 39), and administration was granted in June 1684 on the estate of William Harris, late of Boston, merchant, to the widow, Sarah (not Susan as given in Savage), who had been at least a second wife and who with Capt. Samuel Turell and William White, merchant, all of Boston, gave a £800 bond, the witnesses being Samuel Phillips and Isaac Addington, clerk (Suffolk Co. Prob. Rec., 1346, vol. 9). His estate including books, furniture, etc., was inventoried at £732–19–4 when taken 16 July 1684 by Simon Lynde and John Saffin. The widow devised land in 1702 to William Harris, calling him her "son-in-law William Harris".

    William Harris, merchant, and Sarah his wife deeded two acres of marsh in Muddy River (now Brookline, Mass.) on 13 June 1674 to John Hull. It was bounded by land of the children of Moses Payn, Daniel Turrill (by descent from his father-in-law, Elder William Colbrun), James Balston, and Thomas Gardner. Both he and his wife signed the deed 11:7, and as "Mr. William Harris", he acknowledged it. It was witnessed by Daniel Quinsey, Timothy Dwight, and Daniel Turill. The latter in 1677 sold his land to John Hull 11:9.

William and Sarah, 3 Nov. 1674, sold to Thomas Downe(s), mariner, later witness to the deed of trust for Capt. John Harris's children, land in Boston next to land of Moses Paine, Daniel Turell, and Richard Bellingham on the highway to Roxbury. The witnesses to this 1674 deed 9:76 were Jacob Eliot, father of Asaph, another witness to the trust deed and supervisor as "friend" of the will of Capt. John Harris, and Theophilus Frary one of the trustees. Downes later sold to Isaac Walker 9:183.

William witnessed, 9 July 1679, a deed 11:384 from Joshua Scottow to his son-in-law, Samuel Walker, of land, warehouses, and docks in Boston.

William and Sarah, 27 Feb. 1681/2, gave a mortgage 12:220 to Wm. Tailor on land on Mill Street and the lane to the pond, which was certified 12 Feb. 1690/1 as satisfied.

Asaph Eliot took deed 12:245 from John Barrell of land in Boston bounded by land on the highway from the Common to the Roxbury Highway and by land of Wm. Harris et al.

T. W. Harris quoted in Pilgrims, *infra*, said that all his diligence had been unable to place the William Harris, merchant, who died in 1684.

A William Harris sued in 1682 Richard Knight for money due and recovered £4.3.9.

Michael Stoakes sued a William Harris in the admiralty court in 1680. The defendant, represented by Adam Winthrop, his attorney, won (Rec. of Court of Assistants, 2:197).

A point of evidence came up in a suit by a seaman named Nathaniel Cary, 9 Oct. 1677, that he had presented a bill from his employer in Jamaica, W. I., on Mr. William Harris of Boston who had had no funds in his possession of that employer (Rec. of Ct. of Assts., 2:106).

Child:

4. i. WILLIAM,[3] born in May 1667.

3. JOHN HARRIS, mariner, died in 1680-2. John Harris, mariner, married ELIZABETH who in a deed of trust made "my brother Seth Perry" trustee 1 Nov. 1682 (Suffolk Deeds, Liber 12, p. 110). Seth had married Mehitable[2] (Jacob[1]) Eliot. She did not call Theophilus Frary, who married Hannah[2] (Jacob[1]) Eliot and who was the other trustee, brother. Elizabeth[2] (Arthur[1]) Perry was born in 1647. In the 1682 deed "Elizabeth Harris relict widow of John Harris being now upon my intermarriage" signed herself Elizabeth Harris. The list of articles covered by the deed is signed by Mrs. Elizabeth Harris. When she acknowledged the deed, 17 April 1684, before Governor Bradstreet, she is called "Elizabeth Harris now Elizabeth Barnes". In June 1682, a Nathaniel Barnes had witnessed a deed to Asaph Eliot whom John Harris named as friend in his will and made him an executor of

it. John Harris signed his will 15 Nov. 1676 (Misc. Docket 6–409 of Suffolk Co., Mass., Courts of Probate), naming wife Elizabeth and "only son John". His friends Jacob Eliot and Asaph[2] (Jacob[1]) Eliot were named supervisors in it. John Sanford (the noted scrivener) and Theophilus Frary witnessed it. The inventory of his household goods was £270, 30 Oct. 1682.

> 13 Apr. 1670 John Harris with Richard Knight witnessed a deed from Eliakim Hutchinson to Henry Kemble 8:318.
> 20 Sept. 1670 Isaac Addington deeded land to John Harris. Elisha Cook and Seth Perry witnesses. 8:37.
> 13 July 1671 he was deeded Boston land next to his own by James Bracket by a deed witnessed by Asaph Eliot, Henry Pouning, Joseph Dudley, Robert Coome, John Sanford, and Richard Codner. 7:337.
> 14 Oct. 1675 Elizabeth Harris was deeded 9:259 by John Lane, son of William and Mary (Kelloway) Lane, and by his spouse Mehitable[2] (Thomas[1] Hobart) Lane "Land . . . . neere unto . . . . Land of there father William Lane." Savage, apparently from this, erroneously called Elizabeth, daughter of William Lane. The same language is used in the 22 Dec. 1675 deed from John and Mehitable Lane to John Harris, 9:274.
> 6 May 1675 William Lane conveyed land to John Harris, Seth Perry, and Nathaniel Mann, spouse of Deborah Perry: John Lane and John Sanford witnesses. 9:193.

John Harris, mariner, was buried at sea. He is mentioned as captain and part owner of a ship in Judge Sewall's diary.

William Lane sold land next to John Harris in 1674 to Wm. Green 9:164, who sold it in 1675 to John Maryon by deed 9:162, which refers to the adjacent land of "Mr." John Harris.

Children:

i. ELIZABETH, b. 7 Sept. 1669; m. 25 Sept. 1688 JOSHUA[2] GEE, mariner and shipwright, of Boston (*The New York Genealogical and Biographical Record*, vol. 42, p. 274).
   Children (surname *Gee*):
   1. *Peter*, b. 16 Dec. 1689.
   2. *Eliza*.
   3. *Joshua*.
   4. *Mary*.
ii. JOHN, b. by 15 Nov. 1676; named in father's 1676 will, but no record of birth in Boston.
iii. SARAH, b. 2 Aug. 1677; m. —— BENET; bur. 28 April 1705. Sewall went to her funeral and added "Her uncle was Mr. Perry".
iv. JOHN, b. 27 Dec. 1680; d. 29 April 1689.

4. WILLIAM[3] HARRIS (*William,*[2] *William,*[1] *William,*[A] *William*[B]), died in Boston in September 1721 (THE REGISTER, vol. 3, p. 231), aged 54 years 4 months. He married, 11 April 1695, SARAH CRISP, daughter of Richard and Sarah (Wheelwright) Crisp, who married *inter alios*, in 1722, President William Leverett of Harvard (*ibid.*). There were eleven, including William and Sarah, that were at one time or another married to each other. In 1685 William was apprenticed to Humphrey Luscombe and William Nelson, Boston mer-

chants, the latter being William's guardian, and in 1689 he sold land "formerly assigned to Mrs. Sarah Harris (sometime Colepot)", his widowed stepmother. Thaddeus William Harris in a letter 1855 (see "Pilgrims of Boston", 1856, by Bridgman), calls him the "rich influential merchant of Boston", says he died apparently leaving no children, and was presumably the "son-in-law William Harris" to whom Sarah the widow of William Harris, died in 1684, referred in her 1702 will. He was a founder and treasurer of the Brattle Street church.

OTTERY ST. MARY ORIGIN OF THOMAS HARRIS

By Col. Edward M. Harris (USA, Ret.) of Andover, Mass.

In investigating the English origins of members of the Harris family who were present in Boston in the 17th Century, the author gave consideration to the case of Thomas Harris, called butcher, of Boston, who died leaving a will dated 3 Jan. 1697/8 and admitted to probate by the Suffolk County Court on 13 Jan. of the same year (File No. 2418).

Thomas Harris, the butcher, had been claimed as an ancestor by Edward Doubleday Harris (no relative of the author) in his "Memoir of Thaddeus William Harris, M.D." which appeared in *Proceedings* of the Massachusetts Historical Society (19:1st ser.:313), Dr. Harris having been father of the author of the memoir and sometime Librarian of Harvard. Dr. Harris was in turn the son of an equally distinguished father, the Rev. Thaddeus Mason Harris, D.D., minister for many years at Dorchester, Mass. In his memoir as well as in other publications concerning his family, Edward Doubleday Harris alleged that his presumed predecessor, Thomas Harris, had been born at Ottery St. Mary, co. Devon, England, in 1637, the son of another Thomas, born there about 1606, and that the immigrant arrived in New England about 1675. According to E. D. Harris, the identity of Thomas Harris, the butcher, had been established by "documentary evidence".

As pointed out by my friend and mentor in matters genealogical Roderick Bissell Jones in his study "Harrises in Boston Before 1700" (The Register, 106:22-4), no documentary evidence was ever produced by E. D. Harris to substantiate his allegation that Ottery St. Mary was in fact the parish from which the butcher came. [*]

Recently, in searching the files of the Suffolk County Court, this author came upon case No. 1407, an action of debt for goods sold to Jane Harris, wife of Thomas, in which George Greeneway, of Ottery St. Mary, county Devon, England, mercer, gave power of attorney to Richard Chick, also of Ottery St. Mary, under date of 13 March 1674 to receive of Thomas Harris of Ottery St. Mary, butcher, "but now of Boston, Suffolk County, New England," certain money due to Greeneway. The case further contains mention of the coming of Thomas Harris to New England in 1672, and testimony was given by Giles Dyer, aged 35. Undoubtedly this case record constituted the "documentary evidence" mentioned by Edward Doubleday Harris, but never cited.

Reference to the *Register of Baptisms, Marriages and Burials of the Parish of Ottery St. Mary, Devon, 1601-1837,* published by the Devon and Cornwall Record Society (Exeter, 1908-29) discloses the baptism of Thomas Harris on 30 July 1637, "son of Thomas and Mary". It also records the baptism on 29 Dec. 1664 of Jane Harris, daughter of Thomas and Jane Harris, as well as the baptism of a number of other children, none of whom seem to have survived to migrate to New England, except Jane. Also recorded is the baptism of George Greeneway, sone of George and Mary, on 25 March 1670;

*The preceding article.

that of Giles Dyer, son of Thomas and Jane, on 22 June 1643, and the marriage of Richard Chicke and Mary Clapp on 25 Nov. 1633.

As made evident by the late Mary Lovering Holman in her series of "Notes on Some Immigrants from Ottery St. Mary, Devon, England" (*The American Genealogist*, 16:88-95, 132-5, 205-6), emigration to New England was particularly popular in that parish, and a fertile field for those seeking the English origins of early New England families exists there. For instance, there appears in THE REGISTER (23:33) a note to the effect that Deacon John Upham of Malden, Mass., based on the evidence of then existing records, was "brother-in-law" of Joanna, wife of Robert Martin of Rehoboth, Mass., and of Richard Webb of Weymouth, Mass. In the Ottery register, however, appears recorded the marriage of one Robert Martin and Johane Upham on 16 Nov. 1618. One can therefore conclude that John Upham and Joanna Martin were brother and sister. One Richard Martyn and Elizabeth Salter were married at Ottery on 9 June 1630, quite likely he being that much younger brother of Robert who died "aged" at Rehoboth, leaving a will proved 7 May 1695 (Charles H. Pope, *The Pioneers of Massachusetts*, 1900, p. 303).

REV. JOHN HARVARD.—The late Col. Joseph L. Chester, D.C.L., LL.D., wrote me from London, April 20, 1881, in reply to a query of mine about the pedigree of Harvard :

" As to John Harvard, I have carried about with me daily for many years a little bit of pedigree in the hope of being able to perfect it. I believe that I have the will of his father, a certain Robert Harvard, who described himself as of St. Saviour's Southwark, Butcher. His will was dated 28th July, and proved 6th October, 1625, by his relict Catherine. He left three sons : 1, John ; 2, Thomas ; 3, Peter, neither of whom was then 21. So far I have been unable to trace the family further, but as it appears to be understood that John Harvard was born about 1608 or 1609, and in the neighborhood of London, and as the surname is of the rarest possible occurrence, I have always felt that this was the identical *John*. I cannot, however, yet prove it, and I dislike to put forward a mere theory. I hope to come upon further evidence some day."—ED.

JOHN HARVARD AND HIS ANCESTRY.

Communicated by HENRY F. WATERS, A.B., now residing in London, Eng.

THE Committee on English Research of the New England Historic Genealogical Society, under whose direction Mr. Waters is now pursuing his investigations in England, have on more than one occasion asserted that the method of search adopted by him—so different from that of his predecessors—would without fail enable him to bring to light what had escaped the notice of all other antiquaries. Striking proofs of the correctness of this statement have been already afforded by the remarkable discoveries Mr. Waters has hitherto made, and the following paper, in which the parentage and ancestry of John Harvard are for the first time conclusively shown, will add still another.

In 1842, the late James Savage, President of the Massachusetts Historical Society and author of the "Genealogical Dictionary of New England," went to England for the express purpose of ascertaining what could be learned of the early history of John Harvard ; but although Mr. Everett, then our minister to the court of St. James, rendered every assistance in his power, no trace of Harvard could be found, except his signature on taking his degrees at the University of Cambridge. Mr. Savage tells us that he would gladly have given five hundred dollars to get five lines about him in any capacity, public or private. Since that date others have made efforts equally unavailing.

The late Col. Joseph L. Chester, in a letter written the year before his death to the Editor of the REGISTER (REGISTER, xxxvi. 319), says that he had carried about with him daily for many years a bit of pedigree of Harvard in the hope of being able to perfect it ; that he thought he had found the will of the father of John Harvard, but could not yet prove it ; that he disliked to put forward a mere theory, but hoped to come upon further evidence some day.

At a meeting of the New England Historic Genealogical Society held in Boston June 3, 1885, a paper by Miss Frances B. James of Cambridge, Mass., was read, on "John Harvard's English Home,

228

a Caveat in Behalf of Devonshire." It contained the results of some researches made by her in the summer of 1883, in Plymtree, co. Devon, England, where there formerly lived a family of Harward or Harvard, but no claim was made by her that any relationship could be shown to exist between this family and that of John Harvard.

Mr. William Rendle, in an article in the "Genealogist" for April, 1884, on "Harvard University, U.S., and the Harvards of Southwark," gives a list of certain Harvards of the Parish of St. Saviours noted by him, but he failed to find the baptism of John Harvard, and was unable to connect him with this family of Harvards. In the South London Press for April 11, 1885, and in the Athenæum for April 18, 1885, Mr. Rendle has something further to say about the Harvards. He gives the date of baptism of a John Harvye, whom he says he believes to be the founder of Harvard College, but is unable to prove the fact, and offers no evidence to support it. These articles, however, contain nothing new. Everything of importance in them had been previously made known to us by Mr. Waters. The record of this very baptism had been already found by him, and a copy of it sent to the Committee. Mr. Rendle's knowledge of it seems to have been obtained from a person to whom Mr. Waters had mentioned it as a discovery of his own, and its appropriation by Mr. Rendle without acknowledgment and its publication in this manner was certainly a most extraordinary proceeding.

It had long been known that there was a family of Harvards in St. Saviours Parish, Southwark; that John, son of Richard, was baptized there 11 Dec., 1606; another John, son of Robert, baptized 29 Nov., 1607; another John, son of John, baptized 2 Feb., 1611; and still another John, son of John, baptized 10 April, 1614: but whether the benefactor of the College was one of these, or whether he was of Southwark at all, has not been known, until now at last the proof is presented to us by Mr. Waters. Col. Chester, as we have seen, years ago surmised that he was the son of Robert Harvard, but, like a true genealogist, waited for evidence before making a positive statement. Probably nearly every one in America who was interested in Harvard and had given the subject much thought, suspected, at least, if not believed, that he was the son of Robert Harvard of Southwark. So that Mr. Rendle offers nothing new and merely adds his belief to theirs, for which he fails to offer evidence. That Southwark was a field for persecution and therefore its people must have been ready to emigrate to New England, carries no weight, for there was persecution in other parts of England; and it would be difficult for Mr. Rendle or any other investigator to show that more people came to New England for religion's sake from the county of Surrey than from the counties of Somerset, Dorset or Wilts, in all of which Harvards were to be found. Could he say that John Harvard was not from either of these counties, or from St. Katherine's near the Tower in co. Middlesex where a family of Harvards lived, or that he was not the son of Robert Harvey, alias Harverde ot Rugby in Warwickshire?

Mr. Waters, however, is the first to show conclusively that John Harvard, from whom the College takes its name, was one of the sons of Robert Harvard of the Parish of St. Saviours, Southwark, London, and Katherine (Rogers) Harvard his wife, and that he was baptized in that Parish Nov. 29, 1607. Ample proof of this is afforded by the documentary evidence now for the first time published, to which the attention of the reader is directed. The parentage ot John Harvard is no longer a mystery. Mr. Waters gives us here, among others, the wills of his father and mother, his brother Thomas Harvard, his uncle Thomas Harvard, his aunt by marriage Margaret Harvard, his step-fathers John Elletson and Richard Yearwood, and his father-in-law John Sadler.

But although so much has been accomplished that a few months ago would have been thought impossible, much remains to be done. There are other fields of research as yet unexplored, which will richly repay all the expenditure of time and labor which a thorough investigation of them will require.

The expense of the search thus far has been met by voluntary contributions of the Alumni, particularly the Harvard Club of New York.   JOHN T. HASSAM.

MEMORANDUM That the tenth daye of July 1611 John Harvard of the pishe of Sᵗ Sauior in Southwarke wᵗʰin the County of Surrey Butcher beinge then sicke and very weake in body but of good memory, beinge moved to dispose of his temporall estate uttered theise or the like wordes in effect (in the presence of us whose names be subscribed) vizᵗ, I give unto Francis Rodgers tenn poundes —— And all the rest of my goodes and estate I giue unto my brothʳ Thomas Harvard, and I make my said brother Tho: Harvard my sole Executor, And to witnes the same we haue hereunto sett our handes Tho: Harvard his mʳke Ricᵈ Yearwood Robert Harvard his mʳke.

The above will was proved 21 July 1611 by Thomas Harvard brother and executor &c.   158, Berry
                                                    (Archdeaconry of Surrey).

Marche the 27. Anno 1622.

IN THE NAME OF GOD, AMEN. I Thomas Harvard of the precinct of Sᵗ Katherins neere the tower of London beinge sicke in bodie but of perfect memory thankes be to God doe ordaine this my last will and testament in manner and forme followinge. ffirst I doe bequeath my Soule into the handes of almightie god that gave it me, and to his sonne Jesus Christ that Redeemed me by whose death and merritts I doe trust onelie to be saved and my Sole receyved into eternall ioye. for my bodie to be committed to the Earthe from whence it came and to be buryed at the discretion of my Executrix hereundernamed And for the rest of the porcion of goodes which the lorde hath lent me duringe my life my will is my welbeloved

230

wife shall fullie and whollie enioy it whatsoeuer and to give unto my children that the lorde hath sent me whatsoever it pleaseth her into whose
handes after my decease I com̄itt all that my estate and porcion ether in
England or elsewhere beyonde the Seas and this I ordaine as my last will
and testament and disanull all former whatsoeuer making my deerly beloved wife Margarett Harvarde my sole executrix. In witnes whereof I
have hereunto put my hande. The marke of Thomas Harvard.

Subscribed and deliuered by Thomas Harvard in the presentes of us
hereunder named Edmond Swettenham   the marke of Ann Blaton.

PROBATUM FUIT TESTAMENTUM suprascriptum apud London coram vene-
rabili viro magr̃o Richardo Clarke legum doctore Surrogato venerabilis viri
domini Willimi Bird militis legum etiam doctoris Curie Prerogatiue Cantuar-
ens᷎ magr̃i Custodis siue Commissarii ltīme constituti. Vicesimo tertio die
mens᷎ Augusti Anno Dn̄i Millesimo sexcentesimo vicesimo secundo. Juramento Margarete Harvard relicte et executricis dicti defuncti in eodem testamento nominat. Cui Commissa fuit Administracio bonorum iurium et creditorum dicti defunct de bene et fideliter administrañd &c.   Ad sancta Dei
Evangelia Jurat.   78, Saville.

July the xxvi[th]: 1625

THE LAST WILL AND TESTAMENT of Margaret Harwar* of St Katherines widdowe sicke and weake in bodie but in perfecte memorie thanks be
gee geven to god in this manner and forme followeinge ; ffirst I bequeathe
my soule into the hands of Allmighty god that gave it me, and to Jesus
Christ my saviour that redeemed me hopinge and trustinge only to be saved
by his merritts death and passion and my bodie I committ to the earth
from whence it came and to be buried att the discretion of my executors
hereunder named And my worldly goodes I bequeathe in this manner and
forme followeinge ; ffirst my will and desire is that the howse I now dwell
in, commonly called by the name of the Christopher scittuate and beinge in
St Katherins neere the Tower of London be sould to the best advantage,
And to him or her that will give most money for it, And beinge sould the
money to be devided in this manner followeinge, The money to be devided
between my three daughters Margarett Harward Alse Harward, and Jone
Harward, And if any of my said daughters doe chance to dye before their
legacies come to their hands or growe due, my will is that their parte or
parts shall come to the survivors of those three; Item my will is and I bequeathe unto John Walbank my sonne the somē of Twenty Pounds of Currant English money if he be liuinge And if it please god that he be dead
then my will is that this Sonne Thomas Walbancke my Grandchilde shall
have it paid him when he comes to lawfull Age. It. my will is and bequeath unto my daughter Susan Walbanck the some of ffive Pounds to be
paid unto her when my said howse is sould It. my will and desire is that
those worldly goodes that god hath blessed me withall shall be equally devided betwixt my said three daughters Jone, Margarett Harward and Alse
Harward parte and parte alike ; every one there share ; And if any of
them happen to dye before their part come to their hands my will is it shall
come to the survivor or survivoᵣ. It. my will is and I doe give unto Thomas Wallbanck my grandchild the somē of Tenn Pounds to be paid unto
him out of my two daughters porcõns Jane and Alse. It. I give and bequeathe unto Thomas Harward the sonne of Thomas Harward my late
husband the somē of Tenn Shillins. It. my will is and I bequeathe unto

---

* This name in the original will appears invariably as Harvard.—H. F. W.

my frend Edmond Swettenham of East Smithfeild the some of ffourty
shillinges to make him one gould ringe withall to weare for my sake; And
I doe ordaine my daughter Margarett Harward my sole executrix of this
my last will and testamente; And I doe appointe and desire my two lovinge frends Robert Evebancke and Edmond Swettenham my two overseers of this my will and I doe give unto Robert Evebanck for his paines
twenty shillings;   *The marke of Margarett Harward.*
  Witnes Edmond Swettenham Rob't Ewbancke The marke of Marie
psons.

  PROBATUM fuit Testamentum suprascriptum apud London corā Magistro Thcma Langley Clico Surrogato venerabilis viri domini Henrici Marten Millitis legum doctoris Curie Prerogative Contuariensis Magistri Custodis sive Commissarii legitime constituti Nono die mensis Septembris Anno Dñi Millesimo sexcentesimo vicesimo quinto, Juramento Thome Goul-
dan Notarii Publici Procuris Margarete Harward filie et executricis in
huñoi Testō nominat Cui Commissa fuit Administraco bonorum iusium et
creditorum dci defunct de bene et fidelit Administrañd eadem Ad sancta
Dei Evangelia Jurat.   91, Clarke.

  IN THE NAME OF GOD AMEN. The eight and Twentyth daie of July
Anno Dñi one Thousand sixe hundred Twentie five, & in the ffirst yere
of the Raigne of our Soveraigne lord Charles by the grace of God Kinge
of England Scotland ffraunce and Ireland defender of the faith &c. I Robert
Harvard of yᵉ pish of Sᵗ Saviours in Southwarke in the Countie of Surrey
Butcher, being not well in body but sound in minde in memory (laud and
praise bee to allmightie god therefore) doe make and ordayne this my present last will and Testament in manner and forme following that is to saie.
ffirst and principally I bequeath and commend my soule into the hands of
allmighty God trusting through his mercie and for the meritts of his deere
Sonne my lord and Saviour Jesus Christ to haue forgivnes of all my Sinnes,
and after this life ended to bee made ptaker of life euᵗlastinge in the kingdome
of heaven And I will that my body bee decently and Christianly buried in
the pish Church of Sᵗ Saviours aforesaid, after the discretion of my executrix hereundernamed. And as touching that Temporall estate of goods and
Chattles wherewᵗʰ it hath pleased god of his goodnes to blesse, my minde
and will is as followeth vīzt, Inprimis I give and bequeath unto the
poore of the pish of Sᵗ Saviour aforesaid forty shillings and to bee payd
and distributed according to the discreōn of my said Executrix & Overseers hereunder mencōued Item I give and bequeath unto John Harvard
my Sonne Two hundred pounds To bee payd unto him when he shalbee
accomplish his age of one and Twentie yeres Item I give & bequeath
unto Thomas Harvard my Sonne the like some of two hundred pounds to
be payd likewise unto him when he shall accomplish his age of one and
Twenty yeres Item I give and bequeath unto Peter Harvard my Sonne
the like some of Two hundred pounds to bee payd likewise unto him when
he shall accomplish his age of one and Twenty yeres And if any of them
my said three sonnes depart this life before his said pte and porcōn shall
growe due to bee payd by this my will, Then I give yᵉ pte or porcon of
him deceaseinge to the residue of them Surviving equallie to bee devided
betwixt them, or wholly to the Survivor yf two of them decease And if it
shall happen all my said three Children to decease before they shall accomplish theire severall ages of twenty and one yeres as aforesaid Then and in
such case I give and bequeath unto my Cosin Thomas Harvard and his

Children ffifty pound to bee payd within three moneths next after the decease of the last Child Item I give and bequeath unto Robert Harvard my godson sone of my said cosin Thomas Harvard Ten pounds to be payd unto him when he shall accomplish his age of one and Twenty yeres All the rest and residue of my goods and Chattles whatsoever my debts (if any be) beinge first payd and my funerall expences discharged I give and bequeath unto Katherin Harvard my welbeloved wife whom I constitute ordayne and make full and sole Executrix of this my last will and Testament And it is my will that shee shall haue the use of my said Childrens porčons for theire educačon and bringing up untill the same shall growe due to them as aforesaid And I make and ordayne my good neighbour and friend Mr Richard Yearwood Citizen & Grocer of London and the said Thomas Harvard my Cosin Overseers of this my last will and Testament desireing them as much as in them shall consist and lie to see the same pformed according to my true intent and meaneing herein declared And I give unto them for theire paynes to bee taken in seeing this my will performed Twenty shillings a peece to make them rings for a remembrance Provided alwaies & I will and ordayne hereby that my saide wife shall wth sufficient Suerties wthin three moneths next after my decease or at least before shee shalbe espoused or married agayne to any other, enter and become bound in the soſħe of one Thousand pounds unto my said Two Overseers, if they shalbe both liveing or to the Survivo^r of them if either of them shallbee deceased, wth condičon to pay the pts and porčons of my said Children wch I haue before bequeathed unto them, accordinge to my true intent and meaning herein declared, and at such tyme or times as before is limyted and set downe for the payment thereof. In witnes whereof I the said Robert Harvard haue to this my p^{r}sent last will and Testament put my hand and Seale the daie and yere first aboue written, The marke of the said Robert Harverd Sealed acknowledged and delivered by the said Robert Harverd for and as his last will and Testament the daie and yere first aboue written in the presence of Ric: Sandon Scr The m^{r}ke of Richard Rayner.

Probatum fuit Testamentum suprascriptum apud London coram magistro Thoma Langley Clico Surrogato venerabilis viri Domini Henrici Marten militis legum doctoris Curie Prerogative Cantuariensis magistri Custodis sive Comissarii ltiſħe constituti Sexto die mensis Octobris Anno Dñi millesimo sexcentesimo vicesimo quinto Juramento Katherinæ Harvard Relicte dicti defuncti et executricis in huiusmodi Testamento nominãt Cui Comissa fuit administrat &c. de bene et fideliter administrando eadem, ad sancta dei Evangelia Jurat. 111, Clarke.

John Elletson citizen and cooper of London 15 June, 1626, proved the last day of June, 1626. To Mr William Quelch, clerk, sometimes minister of St Olaves in Southwarke, forty shillings, & to Mr Archer, minister of St Saviours in Southwarke, twenty shillings, within six months after my decease if they be then living. To my sister's son Stephen Hall, Bachilor of Divinity at Cambridge twenty pounds, to be paid him within six months next after my decease. To my sister Elizabeth Rigate full power and authority to dispose of the house wherein she now dwelleth for the term of two years next after her decease conditionally that a pepper corn be paid yearly therefore to my executrix. The residue of the term of years unexpired of the said house I will and bequeath unto my nephew Robert Elletson, son of my late deceased brother Robert Elletson, his executors and assigns. To my aforesaid nephew Robert all those my two messuages or

233

dwelling houses, &c. situate & being in the liberties of East Smithfield in the parish of St Buttolph's Algate, to him and to the heirs of his body lawfully to be begotten, and, for want of such issue, to his brother William Elletson & to the heirs of his body, &c., and, for lack of such issue, to George Elletson his brother and to his heirs forever, which houses I bought and purchased of Mr Norton, gentleman. And my will and mind is that my loving wife Katherine Elletsonne shall have her thirds out of the same during the term of her natural life. Item I give and bequeath unto my said loving wife Catherine Elletsou and her assigns during her natural life the yearly sum of twelve pounds of lawful money of England to be paid unto her quarterly and to be issuing and going out of all and singular my lands tenements and hereditaments whatsoever lying and being in the several parishes of Alverstoke and Rowner in the County of Southampton. To my sister in law, Mary Elletson, and her two daughters, Elizabeth Elletson and Margaret Elletson, and their assigns, during the natural life of my said loving wife Catherine Elletson, the like yearly sum of twelve pounds, &c. To my nephew George Elletson, son of my said brother Robert, all that my messuage, barns, lands & commons, &c. called or known by the name of Hemeleys, situate in the parish of Alverstoke (with remainder first to William, then to Robert, brothers of the said George), which aforesaid premises I bought and purchased of Thomas Rabenett, mariner. To nephew Robert my messuage, &c. situate in Brockhurst in the parish of Alverstocke and Rowner, &c. (with remainder to his brothers William and George, &c.) which premises I bought of Robert Nokes of Brockhurst, yeoman. To nephew William my messuage, &c. in Newton in the parish of Alverstocke, &c. (with remainder to Robert and George), which premises I bought of my brother Robert Elletson. To Thomas Elletson, son of Anthony Elletson, born at Lymehouse in the parish of Stepney, the sum of ten pounds, to be paid him at the age of one and twenty years if he shall be then living. To Robert Wilson in Southwark all such sum or sums of money which he oweth me upon one certain obligation conditionally that he give unto Mr Thomas Foster Bailiff of the Borough of Southwark, as a legacy and bequest from me the sum of three pounds, &c. within three months next after my decease, and three pounds more to the poor of the parish of St Olaves, where he is a parishioner, &c. &c. To my kinswoman Jane Merricke one quarter or fourth part of the good Bark called the Jane of Gosport, with the fourth part of the tackle, munition and apparell, which said Bark is in partnership between her husband Walter Merricke and myself. And I give and bequeath to my sister Mary Elletson and her two daughters the other quarter or fourth part of the same .Bark. To my sister Elizabeth Bygate, widow, twenty pounds yearly & every year during her natural life, to be paid her by five pounds the quarter, or within one and twenty days after the quarter day, out of the tenements which I lately purchased by lease of the wife of James Turner, holden by the masters, brethren and sisters of St Catherine's and which is situate and being in the parish of All Saints Barkin near unto Tower Hill. To my eldest brother George Elletson, dwelling in the County of Lancaster, five shillings, conditionally that he shall give to my executrix a general acquittance of all demands whatsoever from the beginning of the world until the day of the receipt of the same legacy. To my brother William Elletson, dwelling in the said County of Lancaster, ten shillings (on the same condition). To my sister Agnes Stables, the sum of twenty shillings, to be paid her upon lawful demand. To my sister Ellen Towers, dwelling in the

County of Lancaster, the sum of twenty shillings (upon lawful demand). I absolutely release and discharge Richard Edwards, dwelling at White Waltham in the County of Berks, of all sum or sums of money which he oweth me, and particularly of one specialty of thirty pounds which I freely forgive him.

Item I give unto my son in law Joseph Knapp and unto Agnes his wife, my kinswoman, all that my house, together with my buildings, yards and appurtenances thereunto belonging, and to his son John Knap after his decease, during the term of a lease which I took of Mr John James, gentleman, paying the rents, &c.; also the goods, household stuff &c in and about the said house, which is in their possession and which I left freely to them at my coming away from Mill Lane. To my said son Joseph Knapp all that my third part and bargains of boards whatsoever remaining in the County of Sussex which is in partnership between Mr Anthony Keeme, Mr Richard Waker and myself, citizens and coopers of London. To the said Joseph my best livery gown and my second cloak. Item I give and bequeath two silver cups, gilded, with my name to be ingraven upon them, to the value of twenty pounds, which shall be bought by my executrix and given to the company of coopers of the city of London within six months next after my decease. To twenty poor people which is in the Almshouse at Ratcliffe twenty shillings to be equally divided amongst them. To Mrs Suttey, my mistress, dwelling at Ratcliffe, over and above the part of the said gift of twenty shillings, the sum of ten shillings.

Item whereas Hugh Horsell of Southwarke, Innkeeper deceased, by his last will and testament did give and bequeath unto his children the sum of six hundred pounds as by his said will appeareth, of the which I have already paid the sum of one hundred pounds to Mary one of the children of the said Hugh Horsell for her legacy, as also the sum of twenty pounds which I gave with Nicholas Horsell, one of the said children, to bind him an apprentice, so that there is remaining now of the said six hundred pounds the sum of four hundred and eighty pounds to be paid unto them as in their said father's will more at large and plainly appeareth. Therefore my desire and meaning is and it is expressly my will that my executrix hereafter named shall truly pay and satisfy unto the children of the said Hugh Horsell or to the survivors of them the said sum of four hundred and eighty pounds in every point according to their father's will and to see them well educated and brought up in all things necessary in the fear of God and in learning. And I do further will that my executrix shall within one month next after my decease enter into obligation of one thousand pounds to my overseers hereafter named in every kind to see these legacies performed and the said children well brought up and educated. To the poor of the parish of Alverstocke and Gosport the sum of twenty shillings. To the poor of the parish of All Saints Barking in Tower Street, twenty shillings. To George Browne my kinsman twenty shillings to be paid upon lawful demand. I absolutely acquit and discharge Richard Graye, waterman, a bill of debt of three pounds which he oweth me. I absolutely acquit and discharge Nicholas Parsons, ostler at the Queen's Head in Southwark, of a debt of twenty and eight shillings which he oweth me. To my kinsman William Hughs and Agnes his wife one hundred pounds &c.

Item I give and bequeath unto my said loving wife Catherine Elletson the lease of all and singular the premises which I hold of the Master, brethren and sisters of St Katherines, together with all the rents and profits that shall arise by reason of the same; to have and to hold the same lease and the rents and profits thereof unto my said loving wife, Katherine Elletson, for and during the term of her natural life, she paying the rents and performing the covenants contained in the same lease on my part to be performed, the remainder of the years that shall be to come from and after the death and decease of my said wife; and the rents and profits that shall arise by reason of the same I give and bequeath unto my said kinsman Robert Elletson, son of my said brother Robert Elletson, and the issue of his body lawfully begotten. And if it shall fortune my said kinsman to die and depart this life before the expiration of the term of years in the said lease granted having no issue of his body lawfully begotten then living that then I give and bequeath the said lease and the benefit and profits thereof arising unto his brother William Elletson, his executors and assigns. The rest and residue of all and singular my goods and chattels whatsoever moveable and immoveable not before by me given and bequeathed, my debts and legacies being paid and my funeral expenses discharged I wholly and absolutely give and bequeath unto my said loving wife Catherine Elletson whom I make and ordain the sole and only executrix of this my present last will and testament, desiring her to see the same in all things performed according to my mind and meaning herein plainly declared, and I do hereby nominate and appoint my loving friends Mr Anthony Kemme, Mr George Preston and Mr Richard Waker, citizens and coopers of London, overseers thereof, desiring them according to my trust in them reposed to be aiding and assisting to my said executrix in the due " exequition " of this my present last will and testament; and I give unto each of them for their pains taking therein the sum of three pounds apiece &c. Provided always that if my said wife shall not be contented to accept of the said legacies before given unto her and to pay and perform the legacies herein by me bequeathed according to the true intent and meaning of this my present last will and testament then my will is that she shall have only so much of my estate and no more as shall justly belong unto her by the custom of the city of London and then I make and ordain my said kinsmen William Hewes & Robert Elletsonne, son of my said brother Robert Elletson, executors &c.

Wit: William Manbey Scr. Edward Thomas William Hedges.

91, Hele.

RICHARD YEARWOOD of Southwarke in the County of Surrey and citizen and grocer of London, 8 September 1632, proved 6 October 1632, and confirmed by Decree of the Court in the last session of Trinity Term 1633, After my funerals done and discharged I will that an Inventory shall be taken of all my estate in goods, chattells, wares, merchandizes plate and other things whatsoever and be indifferently valued and appraised, and that therewithall the debts which I do owe shall be first duly satisfied and paid. But because the debts which my wasteful son hath brought me unto are so great that I fear much that my personal estate will not be sufficient to satisfy the same or at the least will not be collected and got in convenient time to give that satisfaction which is fit and just much less to pay and satisfy such other legacies as by this my will I have appointed and given I do therefore will, ordain and appoint that my executors hereafter named or the survivor of them with as much convenient speed as they can after my decease for the speedier payment of my debts and discharging of my legacies shall sell and dispose all those my tenements and hereditaments situate lying & being in the parish of St Mary Magdalen of Bermondsey within the County of Surrey, near the church there, which I purchased of

Walter Oliver, being three tenements or houses &c in the several occupations of Thomas Miller Robert Fisher and John Bould their or some of their assignee or assignees. And my will is as well the leases which I bought of the same and which are in being in friends' names as also the inheritance of the said houses be sold for the uses aforesaid by mine executors or the survivor of them and by such other persons and friends who have any interest or estates in the same for my use or benefit. They shall sell &c. all that my tenement or occupation of John Blacke, in the parish of Lingfield within the County of Surrey which I bought of Edmond Rofey, and my tenement &c. in the parish of Frinsbury within the County of Kent, now or late in the tenure & occupation of —— Jones, which I bought of Henry Price. I give and bequeath unto Richard Yearwood my son all that my manor or farm with the appurtenances &c. in the parish of Burstow within the County of Surrey, now or late in the tenure &c. of Edmond Rofey &c. to have & to hold during the term of his natural life (then follow conditions of entailment on the issue of the body of the said Richard Yearwood the son). And for default of such issue to Hannah Payne my daughter during her natural life ; and after her decease to Richard Payne her second son and the heirs of his body lawfully to be begotten ; and for default of such issue to my right heirs forever. Item I give unto the poor of the parish of St Saviours in Southwark inhabiting within the liberty of the Borough of Southwark whereof I am a parishioner the sum of ten pounds &c. I give unto Mr Morton and Mr Archer ministers of the said parish forty shillings apiece. I give to William Brayne apprentice with Nicholas King grocer twenty pounds &c. to be paid unto him at the expiration of his time of apprenticeship. I give unto Margaret Dallin wife of Christopher Dallin cooper the sum of ten pounds &c. to be paid unto her in five years by forty shillings a year. To Hannah Groue daughter of Richard Groue of Middle Wiche in the County of Chester ten pounds at day of marriage or age of twenty and one years.

Item I give to Katherine my well beloved wife her dwelling in all that part of my dwelling house wherein I do now live during so long time as she shall continue a widow and dwell in the same herself if my lease thereof shall so long continue, my said wife paying therefore yearly to my executors hereafter named the sum of five pounds per annum by half yearly payments &c. And I do further give unto her all such household stuff and so much value in plate as she brought with her when I married her. And I give and bequeath unto my cousin Nicholas King grocer and Margaret his wife and the longer liver of them the lease of my now dwelling house, onely I will that my said wife do dwell and continue in such part thereof as I have before appointed during such time as aforesaid. To my loving friend and cousin Mr Stephen Street grocer ten pounds. The said Nicholas King and Stephen Street to be executors.

The residue and remainder of all my personal estate and which shall remain of my lands and tenements by me appointed to be sold as aforesaid, my debts being paid and my funeral expenses and legacies discharged, I will the same shall be distributed and divided by my executors in manner following vizt two third parts thereof unto Richard Yearwood my son if he shall be then living and that my said executors shall discern him to be reformed and become a frugal man, and the other third part thereof I will shall be divided to and amongst my daughter Payne's eight children now living vizt Edward, Richard, John, George, Anne, Timothy, Susan and Katherine, and the survivors of them ; the same to be paid to their father

237

for their uses. And I appoint my loving friends Mr Drew Stapley grocer
and my son in law Edward Payne to be overseers of this my will. And I
do give to either of them for a remembrance of my love and their pains to
be taken therein the sum of five pounds apiece.

Wit: Thomas Haruard, William Frith William Sheappard John Fincher.

13 march 1661 administration de bonis non was granted to his daughter
Hannah Payne, the executors being dead.   98, Audley.

IN THE NAME OF GOD AMEN. I Katherine Yarwood of the parrish of
St Saviours in the Burroughe of Southwarke in the Countie of Surrey
widdowe being at this tyme weake in bodie but of perfect memory praised
be God therefore doe ordayne this my last will and Testament revoakeing
all former wills and Testamentes whatsoever ffirst I bequeath my soule
into the mercifull hands of my Deare Redeemer Jesus Christ the eternall
sonne of God whoe by his holy Spirit as my trust and hope is will p^rserve
me to his heavenly kingdome; And my bodie to be interred at the discretion of my executors And for my worldly goods I thus dispose of them.
Inprimis I give to my eldest sonne John Harvard Clarke all that my messuage Tenement or Inne comonly called or knowne by the name of the
Queenes head in the Borroughe of Southwarke aforesaid with the appurtenances and all my deedes and writeings touching and concerning the same
and all my estate right title interest terme of yeares and demand whatsoever
which I have of and unto the same and of and unto everie part and parcell
thereof.   Item I give unto the said John Hervard and unto Thomas Hervard my sonne equally to be devided betweene them all my messuages Tenements and hereditaments whatsoever wth their and every of their appurtenances scituate and being in the parrish of All Saintes Barkeing nere unto
the Tower of London whereof I am possessed under two severall leases
made by the Master brethren and Sisters of the Hospitall of St Katherine's
nere the Tower of London unto John Elletson deceased ; and all my deedes
and writeings touching and concerning the same.   And all my severall and
respectiue estates right title interest terme of yeares and demaund which I
have of and unto the same, and of and unto every part and parcell thereof.
Nevertheless my will and meaneing is and soe I doe hereby appoint and declare that the said John Harvard and Thomas Harvard their executors
Administrators and Assignes shall yearly and every yeare dureing the continuance of the severall tymes in the said severall leases graunted, paye or
cause to be payed out of the rentes issues and proffits of the said last mencoed premisses at the feast of the nativity of our Lord God twentie shillings
to fower poor people that are reputed of honest conversation dwelling in the
parrishe of St Saviours aforesaid by five shillings apeece And that the
said John Hervard and Thomas Hervard their executors Administrators
and Assignes shall paye or cause to be payed the residue and remainder of
the rentes issues and proffites of the said last menconed premisses unto such of
the Children of Hugh Harsall late of the Burrough of Southwarke aforesaid
Innkeeper deceased as have not their porcons paied and was given and bequeathed unto them by the last wills & testam^{tes} of the said John Elletson and Hugh Harsall or either of them untill such tyme as the said Children shall have all their said porcons paied unto them and afterwards that
the said John Hervard and Thomas Hervarde their executors adm'strat^{ors}
and assignes shall enioye the residue of the said rentes issues and proffits of
the said last menconed premisses to their owne proper uses and behoofes
equally to be devided betweene them   Item I give to my said sonne John

Hervard two hundred and fiftie poundes in money   And I doe appoint two hundred pounds parcell thereof to be payed wth the moneys due upon one obligaĉon of the penall soᵐe of fower hundred poundes beareing date the first daye of this instant moneth of Julie made by my sonne Thomas Hervard unto my Overseer Mr Mooreton for my use condicõned for the payment of two hundred pounds at or upon the first daye of January now next ensueing   Item I give to my sonne Thomas aforesaid one hundred poundes in money   Item to the Children of my Brother Thomas Rogers I give fortie shillings a peece.   Item to the poore of this parrish of St Saviours I give fortie shillinges   Item to Mr Archer one of our Ministers I give twentie shillings.   Item to M^{ris} Moreton our other Ministers wife I give my best gould wrought Coyfe which of my two best shee please to make ·choice of   Item my Sister Rose Reason and my sister Joane Willmore to each of them I give a ring at the discretion of my executors   Item to old M^{rls} Blanchard I give my best paire of Gloves   Item to my Cosen Joseph Brocket the younger I give twentie shillings; and to my Cosen Mary Brocket I give my best scarlet Petticoate or the value thereof in money at the discretion of my executors   Item I make and ordayne my two sonnês John and Thomas Hervard aforesaid ioinct executors of this my last will and Testament. Item for the overseers of this my last will and Testament I appoint my loveing frend Mr Moreton our minister of St Saviours aforesaid for one, and to him in token of my love I give three pounds and my paire of silver hafted knyves ; And for my other Overseer I appoint my Cosen Mr Thomas Hervard Butcher of St Saviours aforesaid and to him likewise in token of my love I give three pounds   Item I give to my said executo^{rs} and Overseers eight pounds by them to be bestowed on such Christian poore as they thinke fitt   And I will that all my legacies formerly given and bequeathed except the two hundred pounds payable by the obligaĉon as aforesaid shalbe paied and deliuered by my executors w^{th}in one moneth after my decease   The residue of all and singular my goods Chattells and psonall estate after my debts payed and funeralls discharged I give and bequeath unto my said sonnes John Hervard and Thomas Hervard equally to be devided betweene them   In wittnes whereof I have unto every sheete being seaven in number put to my hand and have sealed the same this second daye of Julie in the eleaventh yeare of the reigne of our Soũaigne Lord Charles by the grace of God of England Scotland ffrance and Ireland Kinge Defender of the faith &c.   Annoɋ Dñi 1635.   The marke of
Catherine Yarwood.

Memorandum that theis wordes vizt porĉons in the seaventh lyne and John in the fourteenth lyne of the fourth sheete were interlyned and afterwards this will was read sealed and published to be the last will and Testament of the said Catherine Yarwood in the p^{r}sence of us ; Sealed and published by Katherine Yarwood aforesaid in the presence of us William Brayne Robert Greaton William Sheap.

PROBATUM fuit Testamentum suprascriptum apud London coram mrõ Johanne Hansley Cliĉo Surrogato veñabilis viri Dñi Henrici Marten militis legum etiam Dĉoris Curie Prerogative Cantuar maĝri Custodis siue Com^{rii} ltiᵐe constituti vicesimo septimo die mensis Julii Anno Dñi millesimo sexcentesimo tricesimo quinto Juramentis Johiš Hervard et Thome Hervard filiorum dcē defunctæ et executorum in huiusmodi Testamento nominatorum Quibus comissa fuit administraĉo omnĩ et singulorũ bonorũ iuriũ et creditorũ dcæ def de bene et fideliter administrando ead^{m} &c   Ad sancta dei Evangelia Jurat.   77, Sadler.

In the name of God Amen the fiefteenth daie of July Anno Domini one thousand six hundred thirtie and six And in the twelueth yeare of the raigne of our Soveraigne Lord Charles by the grace of god kinge of England Scotland ffraunce and Ireland Defender of the faith &c I Thomas Harvard of the pishe of Saint Olave in Southwarke in the County of Surry and Cittizen and Clothworker of London beinge att this presente sicke and weake in bodie but of good and pfecte mynde and memorie all laude and praise be given to Allmightie god therefore and consideringe with my selfe the frailtie and mutabilitie of this present life and the certaintie of death, And to the end that I may bee the better prepared and settled in my mynde whensoever it shall please god to call me out of this transitorie life I doe by the pmission of god make and declare this my last will and Testament in manner and forme followinge, That is to saie, ffirst and principally I comend my Soule into the hands of Allmightie god hopeinge aud assuredly beleevinge through the death and passion of Jesus Christe his only sonne and alone Saviour to obtaine Remission and forgivenes of all my Synns and to be made ptaker of everlastinge life My bodie I comitt to the earth from whence it came to be decently buried att the discrecon of my executors here under named, And as concerninge all such worldly goods Chattelles and psonall estate as it hath pleased god to endue me wth in this life I give and bequeath the same in manner and forme followinge, That is to saie Inprimis I give and bequeath unto my deere and welbeloved wife Elizabeth Harvard the some of fower hundred poundes of lawful English money to be paied unto her within six monethes next after my decease More I giue and bequeath to my said lovinge all my plate and howsehold stuffe exceptinge only my best standinge bowle of silver guilte and my great Cheste with two lockes Item I give and bequeath unto my said lovinge wife Elizabeth Harvard one Annuitie or yearely payment of thirty poundes of good and lawfull Englishe mony to be yearely due goeinge out issuinge and payable unto my said wife out of all those messuages and Tenementes with thappurtenñces And the rentes issues and proffites of them scituate lyinge and beinge att or neere Towerhill in the parishe of All Saintes Barkinge in London which I hould ioyntly togeather with my brother John Harvard by vertue of a lease to us thereof made by the M^r. brothers and sisters of the Hospitall of Saint Katherines neere the Tower of London, To have and to hould the said Annuitie or Rente charge of Thirtie poundes p Auñ unto my said loveinge wife for and duringe the tearme of her naturall life to be paied unto her att fower feastes or tearmes in the yeare, That is to saie att the feastes of Saint Michaell Tharchangell, the birth of our lord god, Thannuntiacon of the blessed virgin Marie and the Nativitie of Saint John Baptist or within one and twentie daies nexte ensuinge everie of the same feaste daies by equall and even porcons, The first paimente thereof to beginn and to be made att the feaste of the feastes aforesaid which shall first and next happen and come after my decease, or within one and twentie daies then nexte ensuinge with power to distreyue for the same Annuitie in and upon the said tenementes or anie of them, if the same añuitie shall happen to be behinde and unpaied contrary to this my will, Provided that my ffather in lawe M^r. Nicholas Kinge or his heires att any time duringe the tearme of my naturall life doe assure and conveie unto me and my heires or within six moneths after my decease to my executors hereunder named or to such pson or psons as I the said Thomas Harvard shall by anie writinge under my hand name and appointe, And theire heires and assignes, And to such use and uses as I shall thereby lymitt and declare and in such good sure

240

and sufficiente manner and forme as by learned Councell shall be advised and required All that messuage or Tenement with thappurtenñces and the rente and Reverçon thereof scituate and beinge in or neere Shippyard in the pishe of Saint Saviours in Southwarke now or late in the tenure or occupaçon of Owen Jones or his assignes Item I give and bequeath unto such childe or Children as my wife nowe goeth with or is with childe of the some of three hundred poundes of lawfull Englishe money to be paied and deliuered into the Chamber of the Cittie of London for the use of such Child and children within one yeare nexte after my decease to be imployed for the use and benefitt of such childe and children untill they shall accomplishe the age of Twentie and one yeares   Item I give and bequeath unto such childe and children as my wife goeth with or is with childe of all that my moitie or halfe parte of the lease of the said Tenem^{tes}. with thappurtenñ:es att or neere Tower hill in the said pishe of All Saintes Barkinge holden of and from the Hospitall of Saint Katherines and the moitie of my rentes and reverçons thereof, And all my estate tearmes of yeares and demaund therein charged with the said Annuity of Thirtie poundes p̃ Anñ by me herein before given unto my said wife, Prouided allwaies and my mynde and will is that if my said wife shall not be with childe att the time of my decease, or that such childe and children shall happen to miscarry or dye or departe this life before he she or theie shall accomplishe the age or ages of twentie and one yeares then in such case or cases and not otherwise I doe giue and bequeath unto the severall persons hereunder named the seu^rall legacies and somes of money hereunder menconed, That is to saie, To my said lovinge wife one hundred poundes. to my said brother John Harvard one hundred poundes. To and amongst the children of my unckle Rogers fforty poundes To my godsonn William Harvard ffiefteene poundes, To the eldest sonne of my Cossen Thomas Willmore ffower poundes to my Cossen Robert Harvard five poundes to John Brockett the sonne of Joseph Brockett ffortie shillinges, And then alsoe and in such case, I doe give and bequeath unto my said brother John Harvard my said moitie or half parte of the lease of the said Tenementes with the appu'tenñces att or neere Towerhill aforesaid and the rentes and the Reverçons thereof, And all my estate tearme of yeares and demaunde therein charged with the said Annuity of Thirtie pounds p̃ anñ by me given to my said wife, Item I doe alsoe by this my will give and bequeath unto my said brother John Harvard the sume of one hundred poundes lawfull English mony, and my standinge bowle of silver guilt and my Chest with twoe lockes before excepted, Together with my best whole suite of appell and my best cloake, And all things belonginge thereunto, Item I give and bequeath unto Mr Nichollas Morton Minister and Preacher in the pishe of Saint Saviors in Southwarke the some of fforty shillinges in recompence of a Sermon which I desire he should preach at my funerall, for the better Comforte edifyinge and instrucçon of such my freinds and neighboures and other people as there shalbe assembled, Item I giue and bequeath unto James Archer Minister twentie shillinges, Item I giue and bequeath unto Mr Osney Minister the some of twenty shillinges, Item I give and bequeath unto Mr Clarke Minister the some of twenty shillinges, Item I give and bequeath unto my said ffather in lawe M^r. Nicholas Kinge the some of three poundes to make him a ringe, Item I giue and bequeath unto my Cossen William Harvard the some of Tenne poundes, Item I give and bequeath unto my said Cossen Robert Harvard the some of six poundes, I^tem I give unto the said Joseph Brockett my seale Ringe of gould,   I will that there shalbe distributed

241

by my executors on the day of my buriall the some of ffortie shillinges, that is to saie to and amongst the poore people of Saint Saviours in Southwarke the some of twenty shillings and to And amongst the poore people of the pishe of Saint Olave in Southwarke the like some of twenty shillings Att the discreċon of my Executors where moste neede shall appeare.

Item I give and bequeath unto my Mother in lawe Margarett King ffortie shillinges and unto her twoe daughters Margaret and Hanah the like some of ffortie shillinges a peece to make them Ringes. The rest residue and Remainder of all and singuler my goodes chattelles and worldly substance whatsoever not herein before given or bequeathed, I give and bequeath in forme followinge, that is to saie, Twoe full third pts thereof unto such childe and children as my said wife nowe goeth withall or is with childe of And thother twoe third ptes thereof I fully and wholly give unto my said lovinge wife Elizabeth, and my said lovinge brother John Harvard equally betweene them to be devided pte and porċon alike. And in case my said wife shall not be with childe att the time of my decease or that such child and children shall dye before theie shall accomplishe theire age or ages of twentie and one yeares Then in such case I give and bequeath the residue and remainder of my estate my debtes funerall expences, and my legacies beinge paied and pformed unto my said lovinge wife and my said brother equally betweene them to be devided pte and porċon alike, And my will and meaniñge is that the legacies by me in and by this my last will given and bequeathed unto my said wife and such childe and children as she nowe goeth with or is with childe of is and are in full Recompence and satisfacċon of such parte of my estate shee they or anie of them shall or may claime or challenge by the custome of the Citty of London. And to the end they shall make noe clayme or challege thereby, And if they shall make such Claime or challenge by the said custome Then I will that the said legacies by me to them given shall cease and bee voide and not be paied, And I doe ordaine and make my said welbeloved brother John Harvard And the said Nichollas Morton preacher executors of this my said last will and Testament in trust for the due pformance of this my said laste will and the payment of the legacies herein included and given and especially and before all of such debtes as in right and conscience I shall owe to anie pson or psons att the time of my decease as my trust is in them, And in recompence of theire paines therein to be taken, I give and bequeath unto either of them the sume of fiue poundes lawfull englishe mony apeece, And I doe nominate and appoint my said lovinge ffather in lawe Mr Nicholas Kinge and my lovinge Cossen Thomas Harvard and my lovinge freind Mr. John Spencer Merchante to be overseers of this my will desiring them to se the same pformed accordinge to my true meaning and to be aidinge and assistinge to my said Executors with theire best advice And for theire paines therein to be taken I give and bequeath unto every one of them three poundes apeece of like mony, And I doe hereby revoke and disalowe of all former willes and bequestes by me in any wise heretofore made And this to stand and continewe for and as my last will and testament, In witnes whereof to this my said last will and testament conteyninge with this sheete, Nyne sheetes of paper, I the said Thomas Harvard have sett my hand and seale the daie and yeare first aboue written Thomas Harvard Sealed and published by the said Thomas Harvard for and as his last will and testament the daie and yeare abovesaid in the p'sence of me Richard Greene Scr: Richard Barlowe.

242

PROBATUM fuit Testamentum suprascriptum apud London coram magr̃o Willr̃o Sames legum dcõre Surrogato venerabilis viri domini Henrici Marten militis legum etiam dcõris Curie Prerogatiue Cant magr̃i Custodis sive Cõmissarii ltime constitut, Quinto die mensis Maij Anno domini millir̃o sexcentesimo tricesimo septimo Jurament Nicholai Morton Cleric executorū in humõi testament nominat; cui comissa fuit administracio omñi et singulorū bonorū iuriû et creditorū dict def de bene et fidĩe ad° ead^m ad sc^ia dei evang: iurat, Reservata p̃tate similem cõmissiõem faciefid Johanni Harvard alteri exeɔut etiam in dicto testament nominat cum venerit eam petitur.   69, Goare.

[At last, thanks to the mother that bore him, and who by her careful mention of him in her will as "my eldest son, John Harvard, clarke," has again, as it were, brought him to light, we are enabled to lift the veil that for nearly two hundred and fifty years has hidden our modest and obscure, but generous benefactor, the godfather of America's oldest University, the patron Saint of New England's scholars; to learn his parentage and birthplace, and to form some idea of his youthful surroundings. The will of his brother Thomas, to be sure (discovered by me on Washington's birth-day, 1884), furnished the first important evidence in regard to him. It will be noticed in that will, made 15 July, 1636, that he appoints his brother, John Harvard, and the Rev. Nicholas Morton, parson of St. Saviour's, joint executors; that this will was presented for probate 5 May, 1637, by Mr. Morton alone, and power granted only to him, a similar power being reserved for John Harvard, the other executor, *when he should come to seek it*. This seemed to show plainly enough the absence of John Harvard, the brother of Thomas, on that fifth of May, 1637. Well, that was the year of the first appearance of *our* John Harvard on the soil of New England, as shown by the records of Charlestown ; so that probably on that very day in May he was on his way across the Atlantic. The inference then was a reasonable one that the John Harvard named in the will of Thomas Harvard of Southwark and the wise benefactor after whom our ancient University was named were one and the same person. But it needed just the mention of him in his mother's will as "clarke," taken in connection with this fact of his absence at the proving of his brother's will, to put the matter beyond question. Here too it seems as if envious chance had sought to hide him, for in the Calendar of 1637 the name of the testator, which in the record is plaip'y enough "Harvard," was entered "Haward," a name which might be passed/ɔver by any one hunting for the name of Harvard. It was only by *gleaning* that I c/me upon it.
Again—the Register Books c/ St. Saviour's, Southwark, the parish in which our benefactor first saw the light, seem to have lent themselves to increase the mystery that has enveloped the English surroundings of John Harvard, as will appear from the following list of baptisms :*

   1601 May 31 Maryo Harverde d. of Robert, a Butcher.
   1602 July 15 Robert Harverde s. of Robert, a Butcher.
   1606 September 30 Robert Harvye s. of Robert, a Butcher.
   1607 NOVEMBER 29 JOHN HARVYE s. OF ROBT. a BUTCHER.
   1609 December 3 Thomas Harvye s. of Robt. a Butcher.
   1610 November 1 William Harverd s. of Robert, a Butcher.
   1612 September 27 Katherin Harverd d. of Robert, a Butcher.
   1613 December 12 Ann Harverd d. of Robt. a Butcher.
   1615 April 2 Peter Harvye d. of Robt. a Butcher.

Why, if his name was Harvard, should we accept the baptism of John Harvye as the baptism of our John Harvard? Here again the mother comes to our assistance. It can readily be seen that Katherine Yearwood must have been the widow of Robert Harvard and mother of the John, Thomas and Peter named in his will. It may not appear so evident that John Elletson, whose will I have given in its order of time, had married the widow Harvard before she became the wife of Richard Yearwood. The will of John Elletson makes no mention of any of the Harvard family ; yet no one can read attentively that will and the will of Mrs. Katherine Yearwood

* The first two children in the list, vizt. Mary (bapt. 1601) and Robert (bapt. 1602) were probably the children of Mr. Harvard by his first wife, Barbara Descyn, whom he married 26 June, 1600.

243

in connection with each other, without being forced to the conclusion that Katherine Yearwood must have been the widow of John Elletson and the executrix of his will, and, as such, the successor of his trust in regard to the children of Hugh Horsall, or Harsall, deceased. So convinced was I of this that almost the first object of my quest in the register of St. Saviour's, was the record of the marriage of John Elletson with the widow Harvard. And I soon found it entered thus :

1625 Januarie 19 John Ellison & Katherine Harvie.

Here we find mother and son both appearing under another and the same name, viz., Harvie or Harvye. I found too in the will of Thomas Cox, citizen and vintner of London, made 12 September and proved 21 September, 1613 (79 Capell) bequests made to sundry members of this family (John Harvard's uncles?) as follows : " I give Mrs Herverd als Harvey wife of Mr Thomas Harverd als Harvey of St Katherines Butcher six payre of best sheets," &c.—" I doe give and bequeath unto Richard Harverd als Harvey of St Saviour's parish aforesaid butcher, my now tenant, the sum of ten pounds," &c. A Robert Harvy als Harverde the elder of Rookeby (Rugby) was mentioned by Thomas Atkins of Dunchurch, Warwickshire, in his will, 41st Elizabeth. (48, Kidd.)

The burial of the father of John Harvard is thus entered :

1625 August 24 Mr Robert Harvey, a man, in the church.

The youngest son, Peter, mentioned in his father's will (of 28 July, 1625) but not in the widow's, was buried four days before the father, also in the church. where also Richard Yearwood (a vestryman) was buried 18 October, 1632, and Katherine Yearwood 9 July, 1635. John Harvard's elder brother Robert was buried the very day before his father made his will. Evidently the family were suffering from the visitation of the plague in the summer of 1625. I saw other burials entered, but did not have time to note them. All, however, I think, were buried in the church. As I passed through this venerable edifice, once the place of worship of our modest benefactor, I noticed that the great window in the South Transept was of plain glass, as if Providence had designed that some day the sons of Harvard should place there a worthy memorial of one who is so well entitled to their veneration.—HENRY F. WATERS.]

WILLIAM WARD of the parish of St Savior in Southwarke in the County of Surrey citizen and goldsmith of London 2 April 1624.

My body to be buried within the parish church of St Saviors in Southwark aforesaid. My estate shall be divided into three equal parts or portions according to the laudable custom of the city of London. One of which said third parts of my estate I do give, devise and bequeath unto my now wellbeloved wife Roase Ward. One other third part of my said estate I do give and bequeath unto my loving son Edward Ward and unto my well beloved daughter Roase Warde equally between them to be divided part and part alike (both minors). The other third part I reserve towards the payment of debts, funeral expenses and legacies &c.

To loving aunt Margaret Wood widow forty shillings per annum, in quarterly payments. To the poor of the parish of St Savior's four pounds sterling. To Mr James Archar our minister twenty shillings sterling. To the churchwardens and vestry men of the parish of St Saviors aforesaid of which society I am now a member the sum of six pounds sterling to make a dinner for them. To my good friend Mr Richard Yarwood one silver bowl of the weight of twelve ounces. Item I do give and bequeath unto my brother Mr Robert Harverd and to my friend George Garrett and my cousin William Shawarden to every of them a ring of gold to the value of twenty shillings or twenty shillings apiece in money. The remainder shall be divided into three equal parts or portions, two of which I do give and bequeath unto my said son Edward Ward to be likewise paid unto him at his age of one and twenty years, and the other third part of the said remainder I do give and bequeath unto my said daughter Roase Ward to be paid unto her on the day of her marriage or at her age of one and twenty years, which shall first happen. If both my said children shall happen to die before the legacies by this my last will bequeathed unto them and either of them shall grow due then I do will and bequeath all and every the legacies, herein by me before bequeathed unto my said children, unto my said loving wife Roase Ward and unto my cousin Elizabeth now wife of the forenamed William Shawarden equally between them to be divided &c. And I do make and ordain my said son Edward Warde and my said good friend Mr Richard Woodward executors of this my last will. And I do nominate and appoint the foresaid Robert Harvard, George Garrett and William Shawarden to be overseers of this my will.

This will containing four sheets of paper was read signed sealed and delivered in the presence of us Josua Whitfeild and me William Page Scri. Memorandum that this word Woodward was mistaken in the fifteenth line of this sheet and that according to the true intent of the said William Ward the same was meant and should have been written Yearwood who is the man mentioned to be nominated in the eighth line of the — sheet to be Richard Yearwood and mistaken by me the writer, witness William Page Scri.

Administration was granted to Roase Ward, the widow, during the minority of Edward Warde the son, 5 October 1624.   80, Byrde.

[The foregoing abstract was found in the course of my gleanings nearly a year ago, and preserved on account of its mention of Robert Harvard and Richard Yearwood. It now turns out to be very important as evidence that Robert Harvard's wife Katherine, the mother of our John Harvard, was a Rogers; for in my reading of the registers of St. Saviour's I came upon the following marriage:

1621 Oct 17 William Warde and Rose Rogers.

This I made note of at the time, not remembering this long preserved abstract of William Ward's will, but solely because I recalled that Katherine Yarwood had mentioned a sister Rose Reason, and as I fully believed the testatrix would turn out to be a Rogers, the name Rose Rogers struck me as worth noting. Rose Ward and Rose Reason were probably one and the same person.

Another most important evidence of John Harvard's identity remains to be shown. Knowing that he must have been the owner of landed property, and believing that before leaving for America (in the spring of 1637) he would be selling some of this property, I surmised that some record of such sale would appear in some of the documents preserved in the Public Record Office, although I had been informed that the Record Office had been searched for trace of John Harvard, and that it was hardly worth the while for me to make a search there. However, I laid the matter before my young friend Francis Grigson, Esq. (a son of the late Rev. William Grigson, our former corresponding member), and sought his advice. He said that my surmise was quite reasonable, and that the best field of investigation would be the Feet of Fines. No one could be kinder than he in showing me how to look for the evidence I wanted. After almost a whole day's labor, in which I found many suggestive items bearing on American names, I, at last, found an entry which led me to send for the Feet of Fines of the Hillary Term, 12th Charles I., County Surrey. The following is a copy of the first (and important) part of this document:

Hec est finalis concordia fca) in cur) Dni Regis apud Westm) in Octavis Purificac)ois Be) Marie Anno regnorum caroli Dei gra) Angli Scotie ffranc et Hibn)ie Regis fidei Defens etc a conqu) duodecimo coram Johe) ffinch Rico) Hutton Georgio Vernon et ffrancisco Crawley justic) et aliis dni Regis fidelibus tunc ibi) p'sentibus Int' Johe)m Man et Johannam uxo)m eius quer) et Johe)m Harvard et Annam uxo)m eius defore) de uno mesuagio et tribus Cotagijs cum p'tin) in Parochia Sci) Olavi in Southwarke.

The next day, after a long search, I was able to examine the Concord of Fines, relating to the same transaction, where I hoped to find the signatures of the parties to this agreement, as was the custom. This case, to my great regret, proved an exception to the rule, and I was unable therefore to get a tracing of John Harvard's autograph. However, I was enabled to fix the precise date of the transfer, vizt. 16 February, 12th Charles I. The consideration given by John and Johan Man was one hundred and twenty pounds sterling.

Here we find John Harvard appearing in February, 1636–7, as a grantor of real estate in St. Olave (where his brother Thomas was living) and with wife *Ann;* surely most important evidence that he was the John Harvard who six months afterwards was in New England with a wife Ann; and the above date of transfer and the date of probate of his brother Thomas Harvard's will undoubtedly furnish the limits of the period of time within which John Harvard left old England to take up his abode in our New England. He must have set sail some time between 16 February and 5 May, 1637. The four tenements thus conveyed were, without doubt, the same as those described in the following extract:

John Man of the parish of St. Olave in Southwarke in the County of Surrey, sea captain, 6 August 1660, proved 25 November 1661.

"I giue and bequeath all those my foure houses or Tenements with thappurtenances thereunto belonging scituate in Bermondsey streete in the parish of St Olave in Southwarke and County aforesaid which I purchased of one —— Harbert, being in the occupation and possession of one —— Greenball or his assignes at yearely Rent of eight and twenty pounds unto Mary my Loveing wife dureing her naturall life and from and after her decease to the heires of our bodyes lawfully to bee begotten forever and for want of such issue to the heires of the said Mary my wife Lawfully to bee begotten of her body forever."—H. F. W.]   180, May.

In Dei Nomine Amen. The Sixt Daye of the moneth of ffebruary Anno dñi 1637 I John Sadler of Ringmer in the County of Sussex Clerke Compos mentis et Corpore sanus thankes be to God therefore doe make & ordayue this my last will & Testament vizt ffirst I will & bequeath my poore sinfull Soule to God the father Beseechinge him of his mercy to save it for his sonne Jesus Christ his satisfaccõns sake And my Body I will to be buryed where & by whome & in what manner God hath appointed. ffor my worldly goodes I will & bequeath them in maner followinge ffirst I will and bequeath to my daughter Anne the wife of John Haruard Clarke Tweutie shillinges to be payd her after my decease when shee shall demand it. Item I will and bequeath to my sonne John Sadler Twenty Shillinges to be payd him within a moneth after my death if it be demaunded Alsoe I will and bequeath to the poore of the parish of Worsfield in the County of Salop Twenty shillinges to be distributed amongst them after my death And I will to the poore of ye pish of Ringmer abouenamed the summe of Tenn shillinges to be distributed amongst them after my departure And for the rest of my worldly goodes whatsoever legally bequeatheable I will and bequeath them to Mary my _care and loveinge wife not doubtinge of her good and godl·`diposeinge of them whome I make the sole and onely Executrix of this my will In wittnes whereof I say In wittnes whereof I haue hereunto set; my hand & seale   JOHN SADLER.

Witnesses hereunto John Shepherd John Legener.

Probatum fuit Testamentum suprascriptum apud London coram venᵇ-abili viro dño Henrico Marten milite legũ dc̃ore Curiæ Prerogative Cant Magr̃o Custode sive Comissario ltĩme Constituto vicesimo primo die mensis Octobris Anno dñi Millm̃o sexcentm̃o quadragesimo Juramento Marie Sadler Relictæ dicti defuncti et Executricis in hm̃oi Testamento noiãt Cui Comissa fuit Administrac̃o omuiũ et singlor̃um bonorum iurium et Creditorum eiusdem defuncti de bene et fideliter Administrando eadem Ad sancta dei Evangelia coram Magr̃o Esdra Coxall Clic̃o vigore Comissionis in ea parte als emanat Jurat.   Coventry, 128.

[John Sadler, M.A., whose will is given above, was instituted Vicar of Patcham in the county of Sussex, 3 November, 1608, as I have been informed by E. H. W. Dunkin, Esq., who has for years been making careful researches among the records relating to this county. In Patcham Mr. Sadler's children were baptized as follows:

Ann d. of Jn. Sadler, Mary, August 24, 1614.
John s. of Do. .... April 6, 1617.

Afterwards he was settled at Ringmer, where I find he was inducted 12 October, 1626, and was buried there 3 October, 1640.* His son John was a graduate of Emanuel College, Cambridge, M.A. 1638, Fellow of the College, Master in Chancery, Town Clarke of London and Master of Magdalen College, Cambridge, we learn from Cole's Collection (Add. MS. 5851, British Museum). From Le Neve's Fast. Eccl. Angl. we get this confirmed and with further information, under the title St. Mary Magdalene Coll. Masters. John Sadler, M.A., was admitted 1650, and deprived at the restoration.

In the same MS. Cole gives the admission of John Harvard, P. 1631, and the same year Tho. Allen P. June 22, Suff. Mr. Harvard's graduation is shown to be 1635. His pastor, Nicholas Morton, M.A. 1619, born in Leicestershire, was Dixy Fellow and afterwards chaplain of St. Mary Overies, London (i. e. St. Savior's, Southwark).

In the Sussex Archæological Society's Collection (vol. 11, p. 225) is given " A Rolle of the several Armors and furniture with theire names of the clergie within the Arch Deaconry of Lewes and Deanery of South Malling with the Deanry of Battell in the County of Sussex. Rated and appoynted the 11th day of March A° D'ni 1612 by the Right Reverend father in God Samuell (Harsnet) Lo. Bishoppe of Chichester." I extract the following item : " Petcham, Mr Jo. Sadler, vicar —— a musquet furnished."

As the widow Ann Harvard became the wife of the Rev. Thomas Allen, the following abstract may be worth noting here :

Mense Octobris 1673, Vicesimo Septimo die. Emt. Como. Thomæ Allen filio nrāli et ltimo Thomæ Allen nup Civtis Norwicen vid def hentis etc. Ad Admistrand bona Jura et cred d'ci def de bene etc jurat. Admon. Act Book 1673, fol. 128.

———

I cannot refrain from expressing the gratitude I feel towards my brother antiquaries in England for the kindly sympathy and generous assistance I have received from them ; and I desire to name especially Messrs. E. H. W. Dunkin, Francis Grigson, David Jones, Robert Garraway Rice and J. C. C. Smith, who have shown kindness without stint in this matter, as in all other matters connected with my genealogical work in England.—HENRY F. WATERS.]

247

JOHN HARVARD AND HIS ANCESTRY.

PART SECOND.

Communicated by HENRY F. WATERS, A.M., now residing in London, Eng.

IN the article in the REGISTER for July, 1885 (xxxix. 265),[*] entitled "John Harvard and his Ancestry," which formed the ninth instalment of his "Genealogicial Gleanings in England," Mr. Waters conclusively established the fact that John Harvard was one of the sons of Robert Harvard of the Parish of St. Saviours, Southwark, London, and Katherine (Rogers) Harvard, his wife, and that he was baptized in that parish, Nov. 29, 1607. In support of this statement he published, among others, the wills of Harvard's father, mother, brother, uncle, aunt, two step-fathers and father in law.

In the present paper he continues still further the investigations so successfully begun. He here gives us, with other new and important matter now for the first time published, the probate of the will of Thomas Rogers of Stratford-on-Avon, Harvard's maternal grandfather, the wills of Rose Reason, his aunt, and Thomas Rogers, Jr., his uncle, both on his mother's side, with extracts from the Parish Registers of Stratford, setting forth the baptisms, marriages and burials of the Rogers family. Harvard's grandfather, Thomas Rogers, was, at the time of his death, an alderman of Stratford, and the house which he built there in 1596 is still standing. From it John Harvard's father and mother were married in 1605. It is one of the oldest and certainly the best remaining example of ancient domestic architecture in Stratford. The illustration in this number is a heliotype copy, slightly reduced, of an excellent photograph just taken.

When it is remembered that the late Hon. James Savage, LL.D., the author of the "Genealogical Dictionary of New England," made a voyage to England for the express purpose of ascertaining what could be learned of the early history of John Harvard, and that he would gladly have given, as he himself tells us, five hundred dollars to get five lines about him in any capacity, public or private, but that all his efforts were without avail, the accumulation of material now brought to light by the perseverance of Mr. Waters is certainly most surprising. From being almost a semi-mythical figure in our early colonial history, John Harvard bids fair to become one of the best known of the first generation of settlers on these shores. The mystery which surrounded him is now dispelled. No better illustration could be given of the importance of the work Mr. Waters is doing in England, no more striking instance could be found of the extraordinary success which is attending his labors there.

*The preceding article.

The Committee earnestly hope that funds sufficient to carry on still further these valuable investigations may be speedily raised.

JOHN T. HASSAM.

MENSE APRILIS 1611.

Thomas Rogers   Vicesimo Septimo die probatum fuit testim̄ Thome
Sen.   Rogers señ nup̄ de Stratford sup̄ Avon in Com̄ Warwici
         def heñts etc. Juramento Thome Rogers filii dicti def et
         exr̄is etc. cui etc de bene etc iurat.   Probate Act Book.

[The will of which the above is the Probate Act, does not seem to have been copied into the Register, which I examined leaf by leaf, with hopes to find it. My friend J. C. C. Smith, Esq., then hunted through the bundle of original wills for that year, but in vain. That the testator was the father of Mrs. Harvard, and grandfather of our John Harvard, there can be no doubt. The extracts from the Parish Register of Stratford upon Avon, together with the wills of his daughters, &c., prove that. Among the Feet of Fines of the Easter Term, 23d Elizabeth (1581), I find a conveyance made to him by one Henry Mace, of two messuages and two gardens with their appurtenances in Stratford upon Avon. He seems to have been a prominent citizen of that borough, as will appear from the extracts I shall give from the records, and, in 1596, while he was holding the office of Bailiff, built the house still standing in High Street, now known as " Ye Ancient House," the best specimen now left in that street, or perhaps in the borough. On the front, under the broad window of the second story, appear these characters :

         T R   1596   A R

In this house, therefore, Katharine Rogers lived from 1596 until her marriage to Robert Harvard, and to it she may have come with her little son John to attend the obsequies of her father. A heliotype of this house illustrates this number.

—H. F. W.]

The Parish Registers of Stratford upon Avon commence Anno 1558. By the kind permission of the Vicar, the Rev. George Arbuthnot, M.A., I was enabled to devote the whole of one day, from the close of the morning service to the beginning of the afternoon service, to an examination of them. I took notes of the following marriages :

1562   January 31, Thomas Rogers and Margaret Pace.
1563   November 27, Henry Rogers and Elizabeth Burback.
1566   July 6, Edward Huntington and Matilda Rogers.
1570   October 15, John Rogers and Anne Salsbury.
1579   July 20, William Rogers and Elizabeth Walker.
1581   October 30, Richard Rogers and Susanna Castell.
"   November 5, Richard Rogers and Ales Calle.
1592 (?3)   December 30, Antherin Russell and Joyce Rogers.
1596   November 21, William Rogers and Jone Tante.
1600   October 28, John Nelson to Elizabeth Rogers.
1602   April 13, Lewes Rogers to Joane Rodes.
"   October 12, Francis Rogers to Elizabeth Sperpoint.
1603 (4)   January 1, William Smith to Ales Rogers.
1605   " Apriell 8, Robertus Harwod to Katherina Rogers."
1608 (9)   February 6, Henry Stanton to Phillip Rogers.
1609   July 18, Thomas Chestley to Margaret Rogers.

I looked through the record of the marriages down to 1637 inclusive, and found a few other Rogers marriages, which it hardly seems worth the while to print. Thomas, Henry, John, William and Richard Rogers had numerous children baptized and buried. Of these I pick out the children of Thomas.

249

Baptized.	*Buried.*
Margaret, September 26, 1562.	Margaret, December 1, 1562.
Elizabeth, October 28, 1563.	Johanna, February 21, 1566 (7).
Charles, March 28, 1565.	Alice, October 3, 1568.
Johanna, January 24, 1566 (7).	Anne, July 24, 1581.
Alice, September 2, 1568.	Thomas, August 13, 1584.
Joanna, October 14, 1571.	" Infant," January 15, 1591.
Joyce, February 9, 1572 (3).	Charles Rogers, " homo " March 30,
Ales, September 11, 1574.	1609 (10).
Richard, November 10, 1575.	Thomas Rogers, August 31, 1639.
William, June 8, 1578.	
Edward, February 18, 1579.	
Thomas, July 22, 1582.	
Katherin, November 25, 1584.	
Thomas, June 11, 1587.	
Rose, March 29, 1590.	
Frances, March 10, 1593.	

The burial of Margaret, the wife of Mr. Rogers, I did not find. He evidently married again; for I found the burial of " Alice wyf to Mr Thomas Rogers," August 17, 1608. His own burial is thus given :

1610 (11) February 20, Thomas Rogers, one of the Aldermen.

THOMAS ROGERS of Stratford upon Avon in the County of Warwick yeoman 27 Aug. 1639, proved at Worcester 21 May 1640. To Anne my beloved wife all that my messuage or tenement wherein I now dwell, with the appurtenances, and all other my lands and tenements whatsoever situate & being in the said town of Stratford &c. to have and to hold for life or until marriage, and, after her decease or day of marriage, to my four daughters Lydia, Alice, Ruth & Hannah & their assigns until Edward Rogers my son shall well & truly pay unto my said four daughters the sum of twenty pounds apiece, and after such payment, then to the said Edward & to the heirs of his body Lawfully to be begotten ; failing such to my right heirs forever. To the poor of Stratford twenty shillings. Towards the repair of Stratford church twenty shillings. John Whinge of Blackwell in the county of Worcester, yeoman to be the executor and my loving kinsman John Woolmer the younger and Henry Smyth of Old Stratford, yeoman, to be the overseers of this my will.

The Inventory of his goods, &c. was taken 1 October 1639 by John Wolmer the younger, gentleman, John Wynge and Henry Smith. The sum total was 86^{ll} 13^s 0^d.

The widow Anna Rogers was appointed administratrix with the will annexed and gave her bond 23 May 1640, with Francis Baggott of Witley Parva in the parish of Holt in the County of Worcester, as her surety.

WILLIAM SMYTHE of Stratford upon Avon in the County of Warwick mercer, 30 March 1626, proved at Worcester 10 May 1626. To Thomas, my eldest son my shop & the cellars lying in the Middle Row & now in the tenure of William Ayng, butcher, and also my three tenements in the Henley Street, now in the tenures of Thomas Alenn & Thomas Woodwarde and that I late did dwell in, &c. & for want of lawful issue then to Francis my son & to his lawful issue & for want of such issue to my two daughters Mary & Alice (equally). To daughter Mary twenty pounds to be paid to her within two years after my decease by my son Francis, and in consideration thereof I give to my son Francis the lease of the house wherein I now dwell, &c. To my daughter Alice Smythe all my household stuff, &c. &c. and I make Alice Smyth my said daughter executrix of this my last will & testament, and I make my brother Henry Smythe and John Wolmer overseers, &c.

The Inventory of his goods & chattels was taken 28 April 1626.

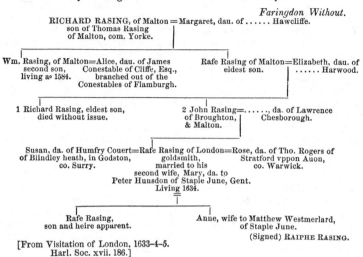

Faringdon Without.

RICHARD RASING, of Malton = Margaret, dau. of ...... Hawcliffe.
son of Thomas Rasing
of Malton, com. Yorke.

Wm. Rasing, of Malton=Alice, dau. of James
second son,   Conestable of Cliffe, Esq.,
living a⁰ 1584.   branched out of the
        Conestables of Flamburgh.

Rafe Rasing of Malton=Elizabeth, dau. of
eldest son.   ...... Harwood.

1 Richard Rasing, eldest son,
died without issue.

2 John Rasing=......, da. of Lawrence
of Broughton, Chesborough.
& Malton.

Susan, da. of Humfry Couert=Rafe Rasing of London=Rose, da. of Tho. Rogers of
of Blindley heath, in Godston,   goldsmith,   Stratford vppon Auon,
co. Surry.   married to his   co. Warwick.
    second wife, Mary, da. to
    Peter Hunsdon of Staple June, Gent.
    Living 1634.

Rafe Rasing,
son and heire apparent.

Anne, wife to Matthew Westmerlard,
of Staple June.

(Signed) RAIPHE RASING.

[From Visitation of London, 1633-4-5.
Harl. Soc. xvii. 186.]

Mense Junii 1647. Undecimo die emᵗ Comᵒ Rose Reason Relce Radulphi Reason nup poe Ste Bridgitte als Brides prope Fleetstreete Civitat London deft haben & ad adstrand bona iura et credita dict deft de bene &c. iurat.   Admon. Act. Book. Fol. 76.

[The two forms of spelling this surname are interesting for two reasons; first, as showing the loss of the guttural final *g* sound in Rasing (in connection with which it may be well to note that the crest of this family was a hand grasping a bunch of *grapes*), and, secondly, as illustrating the sound of the diphthong *ea* in *Reason*. I have seen many similar instances showing that in Shakspeare's time the word was pronounced like *raisin*. Recall Fallstaff's play on the word in Henry IV. Part I. Act ii. Sc. 4: "Give you a reason on compulsion! If reasons were as plenty as blackberries I would give no man a reason upon compulsion."—H. F. W.]

IN THE NAME OF GOD AMEN. I Rose Raysings of the Parish of Saint Bride London Widdowe being weake in bodie but of sound and perfect memorie thankes be to God doe make this my last Will and Testament in manner and forme following (videlicet) ffirst I bequeath my soule to Almighty God who gaue it me and my bodie to the Earth from whence it Came to be buried in Saint Brides Church London in Christian decentlike manner as my Executor hereafter named shall thinke fitting. Item I giue to my daughter Rose Haberly the Wife of Anthony Haberly the summe of Tenne poundes and alsoe my best Gowne and petticoate and a payre of Hollande sheetes and one douzen and to her husband twentie shillinge. Item I giue to the Children of my daughter Rose Haberley (that is to say) to Anthonie John Mary and Rose I giue fiue poundes apeece But to my Grandchild Elizabeth Haberley who is my God daughter I giue Tenne poundes. Item I giue to Katherine Wilmour my Executors Wife here after named fiue poundes. Item I giue to Joane Wilmour her Kinswoeman fiue poundes. Item I giue to John Wilmour the younger my sisters Grand-

251

Child fiue poundes. Item I giue to my Cousin Brockett's sonne Joseph Brockett in Southwarke fiue poundes and to his Mother twenty shillings to buy her a Ring. Item I giue to Marie Right That Tends me in my sicknes fiue pounds. Item I giue John Corker my Godsonne Twenty shillings and to his Mother and his brother Tenne shillings a peece. Item I giue to William Suthes the sonne of James Suthes twenty pounds to be paid att his age of one and twentie yeares. Item I giue to Master James Palmer formerly the Viccar of Saint Brides London fiue poundes. Item I giue to Master Alexander Baker of Cliffords Inne London Gentleman that Bond wherein Master Morgan and Master Powell stands bound unto my late husband Ralph Raysing which is now in suite in the upper Bench and in the Chancerie and I doe hereby giue power to the said Master Baker to sue in my Executors name for the same provided alwaies That if the said James Suches shall att anie time hereafter trouble my Executor hereafter named for any concerning mee or my late husband Ralph Raysing That then my Legacie to the said Williā Suthes his sonne shall be absolutely voyd. Item I giue to Thomas Smith the sonne of my sister Alice Smith in Warwickshire the summe of fiue pounds. And last of all I make my loueing Kinseman Master John Wilmour of Stratford upon Avon in the Countie of Warwick my full and sole Executor of this my last Will and Testament desireing him to doe all things accordingly as I haue by this my last Will required him. And the remainder of all my goods and Chattells not formerlie bequeath I doe hereby give and bequeath to my said Executor and I doe hereby renounce all former Wills and Testamentᵗˢ whatsoever and doe hereby revoake the same and publish this to be my last Will and Testament and desire that none may stand for my last Will but this and I doe alsoe giue and bequeath to Mistris Susan Annyon Widdowe the summe of Thirtie shillings to buy her a Ring. In Witnes whereof I haue to this my last Will and Testament sett my hand and seale dated This first Day of December in the yeare of our Lord One Thousand six hundred fifty and fower. Rose Raysings Signed sealed published and delivered as her last Will and testamᵗ Theise words (videlicet) and alsoe my best gowne and petticoate and a payre of Holland sheetes and one douzen of Napkins and my Bible Kinsewoeman to be paid att his age of one and twenty yeares Avon in the Countie of Warwicke being first interlined in the presence of us Susan Annyon Alex Barker.

THIS WILL was proved in London the twentith Day of June in the yeare of our Lord God One Thousand six hundred fiftie and fiue before the Judges for probate of Wills and granting Administrations lawfully authorized by the oath of John Willmour The Sole Executor named in the aboue written Will To whome Administration of all and singular the goods Chattells and debts of the said deceased was Committed he being first legally sworne truly and faithfully to administer the same. 291, Aylett.

Joh. Sadler clerk M.A. adm., on the resignation of Simon Aldriche, to the Vicarage of Ringmer, 6 October, 1626.

Archbishop Abbot's Reg. p. 2, f. 349ᵇ.

John Sadler was inducted into the possession of yᵉ vicaridge of Ringmer Octobʳ xijᵗʰ 1626.

1640 Oct. 3 buryed Mʳ John Sadler minister of Ringmer.

Ringmer Parish Register.

252

Sussex, Ringmer Vic. John Sadler 14 Nov. 1626 (to Nov. 1628), William Thomas of Lewes and William Michelborne of Westminster (his sureties). Compositions for First Fruits.

EDWARD FENNER of Auburne in the County of Sussex (13 July 1603 proved 9 October 1605) wishes his body to be buried in the parish church of Auburne and leaves all to his wife Mary whom he appoints executrix & entrusts the children to her care. 69, Hayes.

License granted 12 May 1613 to the Rector, Vicar or Curate of Stepney in the county of Middlesex to solemnize the marriage between John Sadler, clerk, and Mary Fenner, widow, late the relict of Edward Fenner, while he lived of Auborne in the County of Sussex, gen. dec'd.

Vicar General's Book.

[Albourne is a parish in Sussex near Cuckfield.—H. F. W.]

MARY SADLER of Mayfield in the County of Sussex, widow, 16 January 1645, proved 13 November 1647. " My Corpes to bee interred where ever ytt shall please God by my surviving freindes to dispose of ytt." I do nominate & appoint my daughter Elizabeth James to be my sole Executrix. And I bequeath and give unto her one hundred pounds of money which is in her husband's hands, and such bedding and chests and wearing clothes as I have (saving one chest which is full of linnen and pewter, and other small things). My will is that she shall buy & give to my grandchild Mary Russell two silver spoons of ten shillings apiece price and to Thomas Russell my grandson ten shillings of money. I will & bequeath unto my son John Sadler the money which I have in Mr William Michilborne's hands. Item I give unto my grandchild Mary James one chest of linen and pewter except two pair of the sheets and one pair of pillowcoats therein, which I give unto Anne James, and one other pair of sheets which are also in the said chest, which I give unto Elizabeth James my grandchildren. Item I give to each of my son Russell's children not before named in this my will one shilling apiece for the buying them gloves. Item I give unto my daughter Mary Sadler and to each of her children which I suppose to live in "newe" England one shilling apiece. Item I give unto my daughter Anne Allin and to her daughter Mary one shilling apiece, and this I do appoint and intend my last will and testament. 231 Fines.

ALLEN.—THOMAS, son of John Allen, dyer, of Norwich. At school under Mr Briggs eight years. Age 15. Admitted sizar litt. grat. July 6, 1624. Surety Mr Moore. Admissions Caius Coll. Cambridge.

THOMAS HERVY, citizen & " Bo'cher " of London, 16 June 1505, proved at Lambeth 3 October 1505. " I bequeth my soule to god to our blissed lady Virgyñ Mary his moder and to all the holy company of heveñ And my body to be buried in the churchyerd of Seynt Clementes in Candilwykstrete of London on the Northside of the same Churchyerd where the body of William more late Citezein and bocher of London my graundfader lyeth buried. And if it fortune that I dye or decesse owte of Londoñ thañ I will that my body be buried where as it shall please god for it to dispose. Item I bequeth to the high aulter of the said churche of Seynt Clementes for myñ offerynges forgoteñ or negligently w^{t}draweñ in dischargyng of my soule iij^s iiij^d. It I bequeth unto Margarete my wife for hir parte purparte and porcioñ of all my goodes moevable and unmoevable in redy money xl^{li} sterl and all my stuff of household and plate hole as it shalbe the day of my decesse. It I bequeth unto my sonnes Thomas Hervy and Nicholas Hervy and to the Infaunte beyng in my wiffs wombe if she now be w^t childe in redy money xl^{li} evenly to be devided and departed amonges theym and to be deliued to theym and eūry of theym whañ they or eny of theym shall cõme to their laufull ages or mariages the which money I will my moder mawde Hoppy haue the keping to the use of my said childerñ till they shall cõme to their laufull ages or mariages. And if it fortune any of my said sonnes or the Infañt in my wiffes wombe for to dye or decesse afore they or any of theym shal cõme to their laufull ages or mariages, thañ I will that the parte of hym or theym so decessyng remayne to hym or theym beyng on lyve. And if it fortune all my said childerñ to dye afore they cõme to their laufull ages or be maried thañ I will that my said moder dispose the same xl^{li} to my said childerñ before bequethed for my soule my faderes soule my childerñ soules and for all my goode frendes soules in deedes of almes and of charitie as she shall thinke best for the helth and saluacioñ of my soule. It I will that my saide moder haue the keping of my said children duryng their noonage It I will that the saide Mawde my moder take haue & receyve the proffittes and revenues cõmyng and growying of my fermes called Gubbons and Waltoñs in the Countie of Essex and of my ferme in Madebrokes long mede and Wottons croftes lying in the pisshe of Retherhith in the Countie of Surrey towardes the sustentacioñ and fynding of my said childerñ duryng their noonage and the surplusage of the same revenues and proffittes cõming & growyng of the same fermes I will it be evenly devided and depted amonges my said childerñ and Infaunt by the said Mawde my moder. It I bequeth to my suster Elyñ fflynte the wif of Johñ fflynte all my state and Tñe of years which I haue to cõme of and in my ferme called preestes m̄she sett and lying in the pisshe of Retherhed aforesaid. And I will that thendentur of the same ferme be deliued unto my said suster incontinent aft^r my decesse. Itm̄ I bequeth unto my cosyñ Thomas Hervy myñ state and termes of yeres which that I haue to cõme of and into the tenementes called the Dogge and the Shippe in Estchepe in the pisshe of Seynt Clementes aforesaid and in seynt Leonardes. And I will that thendentures of the same houses be deliued unto my said cosyñ Thomas assone aft^r my decesse as is possible. It I bequeth unto my sūnt William Anderby xx^s in money. It I bequeth unto Johñ ffelix xx^s. It I bequeth unto Richard ffelix xx^s. It I will that my moder or hir Executo^rs fynde the said Johñ ffelix to gram^r scoole and to writting scole by the space of a yere aft^r my decesse. The Residue of all my goods moevable and unmoevable aft^r my dettes paid my burying done and this my p^rsent testament in all thinges fulfilled I geve and bequeth unto the forsaid Mawde my moder she therew^t to doo ordeyne and dispose hir owne freewill for eūmore. Which Mawde my moder I make and ordeyne executrice of this my p^rsent testament. In witnesse wherof to this my p^rsent testament I haue setto my seale. Youeñ the day and yer̃ aforesaid." 36 Holgrave.

I<small>N THE NAME OF</small> G<small>OD AMEN</small> The xxixth day of the moneth of July In the yere of o^r lord god m^t v^c and viij. I Thomas Hervy bocher of the pisshe of seynt Oluff in Suthwerk in the diocise of Winchester beyng hole of mynde and memory thanked be almighty god sett make and ordeyne this my p^rsent testament and last will in man^r and fo^rme folowing ffirst I bequeth and recõmend my soule unto almighty god my creato^r and savio^r, my body to be buryed in the church of seynt Oluff aforesaid And I bequeth unto the high aulter of the same churche for my tithes & oblacioñs here before

254

necligently paid or forgoteñ ijˢ. Also I bequith to my moder church of Wynchestre iiijᵈ And I geve and bequeth to the aulter of our lady in the said pisshe church of seynt Orluff iiijᵈ. Also I bequeth to the aultʳ of seynt Anne there iiijᵈ. Also to the aulter of seynt Clement iiijᵈ. The Residue of all my goodes and catalles not bequethed nor geven after my fuñall expences dooñ and my dettes paied I will and geve unto Guynor my wif she to dispose theym after hir discrecioñ as she shall thinke moost convenyent. And of this my present testament and last will I make and ordeyne myñ executrice my said wif Thiese witnesses Sʳ William Priour Curat of seynt Oluff aforeseid William Bulleyñ grocer William Symsoñ and other.

PROBATUM fuit suprascript testm̄ corã Dño apud Lamehith xvᵒ die mens Augusti Anno Dñi Millim̄o quingētesimo octauo Jur Guynoris Relicte et executricis in huiōi testō noiãte Ac approbat & insinuat Et cōmissa fuit adm̄istraᵒ om̄ bonorum & debit dicti defuncti prefate executrici de bene & fidelit adm̄istrand Ac de pleno & fideli Inuētario citra pʳimŭ diem Septembr̄ p̄x futur exhibend necnō de plano et vero com̄pto reddend ad sca dei euñg iñ debita iuris forma iurat.   4 Bennett (P. C. C.)

WILLIAM HERFORD citizen & tallowchandler of London, 31 August 1518, proved 10 Nov. 1518.   My body to be buried in the parish church of St Olave in the old " Jure " of London in the same place where my late wife Johan resteth buried.   " And I haue bought & payed for the stone that lyeth on her.   And therefor I woll haue the same stone layed on my body & I woll have a scripture graveñ & fyxed yn the same stone makyng mension off the tyme off my deceasse requiryng the people to pray for me."   To the high altar of the same church for tythes & oblations forgotten or negligently withholden iijˢ iiijᵈ.   Towards the gilding of the tabernacle of Sᵗ John the Baptist at the south end of the high Altar of the same church xx.ˢ   Towards the maintenance of Olave's Brotherhood within the same church xijᵈ.   To the company & brotherhood of Our Lady & Sᵗ John Baptist Tallowchandlers of London my silver pot.   To John Hone my best dagger the sheath garnished with silver as it is.   To Richard Chopyn my purse garnished with silver.   " It I beqweth to Nicholas Pynchyn my best Jaket," Touching the disposition of my lands & tenements in the parish of St. Stephen in Colemanstreet I will that my wife Agnes Herford shall have them during her life and after her decease they shall remain to my children and to the heirs of their bodies lawfully begotten & for lack of such issue they shall remain to the company of Butchers of London forever, they finding forever in the same church of St. Olaves the day of my decease dirige " on nyght and masse of Requiem on the morne by note dispendyng at eūry such obyte amongyst prestes and clerkes wex Ryngyng off belles & poū people 20ˢ foreuʳ.   And if the same Company of Bouchers make defaute of and yn kypyng of the same obyte yn manʳ & forme a bouesayd then I woll that the same landes and tenñtes shall full & hole remayne to the cō-pany & felyshippe of Talow chaundelers of London foreū they doyng and dyspendyng yerely therfore an obytt yerly yn manʳ and forme as the forsayd cōpany off Bouchers ar bounde to doo yn kepyng of the forsayd Obyte as they wyll answere before God." ——— To my cousin Richard Baynbery my tawney gown furred with black, to John Kyttelwell & Robᵗ Kyttelwell either of them my single Ray gowns, to John Ryve my best dublett to William Knott my second Dublet, to William Pyper, George Chelsey & James Quick mine apprentices, so that they continue & serve out their terms well & truly to my wife their mistress, to either of them viˢ viijᵈ. when their terms of prenticehood shall be finished. To my god children that at time of my decease shall be living xii^d. The residue shall be divided amongst my wife & children accordinge to the laws & custōms of the city of London. And Executors of this will &c. I make & ordaine my said wife Agnes & the said Nicholas. To Robert Whetecroft my riding coat.

102 Bennet (Commissary Court of London).

CRISTIANA HARVYE of Shenley in the County of Hertford widow, and John Harvye, son and heir apparent of the said Cristiana, give a bond 30 June 10 Elizabeth, of one hundred pounds, to Lawrence Greene, citizen and cutler of London, that they will carry out an agreement specified in a pair of Indentures bearing date 30 June 10 Elizabeth.

Claus Roll 10 Elizabeth, Part 13.

THOMAS HARVARD of the precinct of St Katherine's near the Tower of London, butcher, conveys to Henry Rawlins of Lee in the county of Essex, mariner 29 January 1621, for the sum of one hundred and fifty pounds already received, all those three several messuages and tenements, with all shops, cellars, rollers, warehouses, backsides, entries, lights, easements, commodities and appurtenances whatsoever to the said three several messuages or tenements, or any of them, belonging, situate, &c. at the North end of Bermondsey Street, near Battle Bridge, it the parish of St Olaves, *als.* tooles in Southwark, &c. now or late in the several tenures or occupations of William Pilkington, William Hatcham and William Fells or their assigns, &c. to be delivered up the 2^d day of July next. His wife Margaret unites. (What follows seems to indicate that this conveyance is a mortgage.)

Claus Roll 20 Jac. I. Part 37.

HILL. 6 H. viij (1514) Apud Westm̃ a die Sci Martini in quindecim dies. Int^r Johēm Kyrton Nichū Tycheborñ Henr̃ Tyngylden & Johem Fowler quer. et Ricū Harvy & Cristinam uxem̃ eius deforc de uno mesuagio & uno gardino cum p̃tin in Southwerk Et preterea iidem Ricus & Cristina concesserunt pro se & hered ipius Cristine qd ipi warant pdcis Johi Nicho Henr & Johi & hered ipius Johis Kyrton pdca ten cum p̃tin contr̃ Johem Abbem monastri Sc Petri Westm̃ & successores suos &c. &c.

The consideration was twenty marks of silver.

Feet of Fines. Surrey.

Trin. 10 Elizabeth (1568). Hec est finalis concordia fc̃a in cur Dñe Regine apud Westm̃ in crastino Sc̃e Trinitatis anno regni Elizabeth dei grã Anglie ffranc & hibñie Regine fidei defensoris etc a conqu decimo, coram (&c.), Int Laurenciū Grene quer et Cristianam Harvye viduam & Johem Harvye geñosum deforc de septem messuagiis septem gardinis & una acra trẽ cum p̃tin in pochia Sc̃i Georgii in Southwarke etc. Consideration eighty pounds sterling.

Feet of Fines, Surrey.

Trinity Term 37 Elizabeth, Essex. Oliver Skinner quer. and Thomas Harvard and Johann his wife, Hugh Gullifer and Anne his wife, William Smarte, Henry West and Margaret his wife and William Spalding and Elizabeth his wife deforc,—for one acre of pasture with the appurtenances in Westham. Consideration 40^{li} sterling.

Feet of Fines.

Hillary Term 37 Elizabeth, Surrey. Thomas Harvard & Johan his wife quer. and John Leveson mil. deforc,—for three messuages with the appurtenances in the parish of St Olave alias St Toolyes in Southwark. Consideration 160^{li} st.

Feet of Fines.

Easter Term 38 Elizabeth, Essex. Christopher Poyner gen. quer. and Thomas Harvey & Johan his wife deforc, for one messuage with the appurtenances in Foxyearth & Pentrowe. Consideration 80^{ll} st.

Feet of Fines.

Easter Term 38 Elizabeth, Essex. John Jefferson and Thomas Smyth quer. and Thomas Harvard & Johan his wife & Henry West & Margaret his wife deforc, for three parts of one messuage, one barn, one garden, one orchard and twelve acres of arable land with the appurtenances, into four parts to be divided, in Westham & Stratford Langthorne. Feet of Fines.

Mich. Term 39–40 Elizth (1597) Surrey. Thomas Harvard quer. and John Anwyke and Alice his wife and William Crowcher (Crowther ?) and Agnes his wife deforc ; for two messuages, two gardens with the appurtenances in the parish of St Olave, Southwark. Consideration 80^{ll} st.

Feet of Fines.

Easter Term 40 Elizabeth, Essex, David George quer. and Thomas Herverd and Johan his wife and William Spaldinge and Elizabeth his wife deforc,—for one messuage, one barn, one garden, one orchard, twenty acres of land (arable), four acres of meadow and six acres of pasture with the appurtenances in Westham. Consideration 100^{ll} sterling. Feet of Fines.

Mich. Term 22 James I. Surrey. Robert Harverd quer. and Thomas Harverd deforc,—for three messuages, with the appurtenances in the parish of St Olaves in Southwark. Consideration 240^{ll} sterling.

Feet of Fines.

THOMAS ROWELL of the Parish of Westham in the County of Essex yeoman, 12 August 1583, proved 23 August 1583. My body to be buried in the churchyard of Westham.

" Also I doe giue vnto my sonne in Lawe Thomas Harford butcher dwellinge in London one redd cowe and he hauinge the said Cowe to giue vnto his mother in Lawe the some of xl^s." To John Bestone my wife's son all my wearing apparell. To Joane my wife all the rest of my goods & I make her Executrix.

Wit. John Hall curate, John Rowell yeoman Richard Cannon yeoman Isabell Spike widow.   306 Bullocke, Consistory Court of London."

Married, 1582, Nov. 19, Thomas Harvarde & Jane Rowell.

Register of St Saviour's Parish, Southwark.

JONE HARVARD wife of Thomas Harvard buried June 10, 1599.

Register of St Savior's Parish, Southwark.

RICHARD YEARWOOD and Katherine Ellettsone were mar^d xxviiith of May 1627.   Parish Register of Wandsworth, Surrey.

[This is the third marriage of John Harvard's mother. 1 am indebted to J. T. Squire, Esq., for his kind permission to extract the above from his MS. copy of this Register, and to my friend J. C. C. Smith, Esq., who discovered this important entry.—H. F. W.]

PETER MEDCALFE of the parish of St Olave's in Southwark in the County of Surrey clothworker 24 August 1592, proved 6 September 1592. To Mr Richard Hutton Deputy of the Borough of Southwark my best gown faced with Foynes. To my very friend Mr Thomas Lynne in Pater Noster

Rowe my best gown faced with satin. To Richard Barker my gown faced with Budge or Damask at his choice. To Peter Keseler one of my gowns faced with budge. To the poor of St Olave's in Southwark forty shillings To the poor of Redderiffe in the County of Surrey twenty shillings. To my very good friend Mr John Nokes a ring of gold with an agate cut. "Item I giue and bequeathe unto Robert Harvey a boye which I keepe the somme of ffyue poundes lawfull money of Englande to be paied unto hym at his age of one and twentie yeres. So that he be ordered and ruled by my executrix and that he do liue to accomplishe the age of one and twentie yeres aforesaied." To Symon Harvye my servant my great anvil & two of my best vices with the bellows thereunto belonging. To my other servants viz Francis, Thomas & Peter being my household servants each of them 20 shillings. Others mentioned. Wife Margaret Medcalfe to be executrix.

71 Harrington (P. C. C.)

Admon de bonis non was granted 26 (September) to Christopher Medcalf, the next of kin.

JOHN GUY of the parish of St Saviour in Southwark, in the County of Surrey, brewer (17 June 1625, proved 28 June 1625) bequeaths to Richard Harford citizen & brewer of London the sum of thirty shillings to make him a ring for a remembrance.   64, Clarke.

ROBERT GREENE of the parish of St. Savior in Southwark in the county of Surrey, yeoman (8 November 1645, proved 19 January 1645) appoints as one of the overseers of his will Mr Thomas Harvard of the said parish Butcher, calling him friend & neighbor, and gives him five pounds. In a codicil, made 11 January 1645, he bequeathes unto Robert Harvard son of Thomas Harvard (above) the sum of ten shillings. The testator had a sister Jane Marshall of Billerica, Essex.   3, Twisse.

RAPH YARDLEY citizen & merchant tailor of London 25 August 1603, proved 27 February 1603. After my debts paid and my funerals discharged I will that all and singular my goods chattels & debts shall be parted & divided into three equal parts & portions according to the laudable use and custom of the city of London. One full third part thereof I give and bequeath to Rhoda my wellbeloved wife, to her own use, in full satisfaction of such part and portion of my goods, chattells & debts as she may claim to have by the custom of the same city. One other full third part thereof I give & bequeath unto and amongst my children, Raphe, George, John, Thomas and Anne Yardley and to such other child or children as yet unborn as I shall happen to have at the time of my decease, to be equally parted, shared & divided between them, and to be satisfied and paid to my said sons at the accomplishment of their several ages of one and twenty years, and to my said daughter at the accomplishment of her age of one & twenty years or marriage, which shall first happen, &c. &c. And the other third part thereof I reserve to myself therewith to perform & pay these my legacies hereafter mentioned, that is to say, Item I give & bequeath to the poor of the parish of St Saviours in Southwark where I now dwell twenty shillings, to be divided amongst them by the discretion of the overseers of the poor there for the time being, and to such of the bachelors and sixteen men of the company of merchant tailors London as shall accompany my body to burial twenty shillings for a recreation to be made unto them, and to the Vestrymen of the same parish twenty shillings more for a recreation to be made unto them. Item I give and bequeath to my sister Palmer a ring of gold

258

to the value of six shillings eight pence, and to my cousin John Palmer her husband a like ring to the like value, and to my daughter Earby my first wife's wedding ring, and to my son Erbye her husband my best cloak, and to my cousin Richard Yearwood my black cloth gown of Turkey fashion. The rest & residue of all & singular my goods &c. I wholly give unto my said children &c. &c. Item I give & bequeath to my brother Thomas Yardley a ring of gold to the value of six shillings eight pence. And I ordain & make the said Raph Yardley my son to be the Executor &c. and the said Richard Yerwoode and my son Edward Earbye overseers.

As to my freehold lands tenements & hereditaments I will demise give & bequeath my messuages, lands &c in Southwark or elsewhere unto my said children &c.   24, Harte.

John Hall, Not. Pub., one of the witnesses.

AGNES PARKER of London, spinster, 27 November 1617, proved 9 January 1617. Brother in law Edward Smyth and sister Julian, his wife, Sister Margery, the wife of Thomas Flinte of Litterworth in the County of Leicester, glazier. To M^{ris} Elizabeth Bygate, sometime my M^{ris} the sum of twenty pounds &c. To Anne the wife of William Hughes, Elizabeth Turner, the daughter, and Elizabeth Turner, the wife, of James Turner citizen & haberdasher of London. To the poor of all Hallows Barking London where I am now inhabiting. Item I do bequeath to Mr John Ellatson & his wife for a remembrance a piece of gold of five shillings & six pence. And likewise to Mr William Bygate & his now wife a like piece of gold. And to Mr William Turner & wife another piece of gold. To Sarah the wife of Thomas Skinner ten shillings. The residue to James Turner whom I hereby make ordain & constitute my full & sole executor.
122, Vol. 23, Commissary Court of London.

ANN PALMER of London widow, 30 January 1621 proved 31 December 1624. My body to be buried in the parish church of St. Olaves in Southwark in the county of Surrey, where now I am a parishioner, as near the place where my late deceased husband was buried as conveniently may be. I give & bequeath to my son Michael Palmer all such debts duties sum & sums of moneys as are and shall be due & owing unto me at the time of my decease by Jacob Manninge Percival Manninge or either of them or by any other persons by or for them or either of them, all which debts do amount unto the sum of three score and five pounds and twelve shillings or thereabouts principal debt besides all the interest long due, the which money he caused me to lend. Item I give to John Palmer son of my son Michael Palmer three hundred pounds of lawful English money besides I have given to his master the sum of thirty pounds of like money, and unto Andrew Palmer one other son of my said son Michael Palmer twenty pounds &c. and unto Mary Palmer daughter of my said son Michael Palmer one hundred & fifty pounds of like money, and unto Thomas Palmer one other son of my said son Michael twenty pounds &c. & unto Elizabeth Palmer one other daughter of my said son Michael Palmer twenty pounds of like money. To my son William fifty pounds besides I have heretofore given him two hundred pounds and one hundred & fifty pounds before hand, which sums were intended to have been given him for a legacy ; of both which sums I do discharge him, the which may appear partly by his bond of three hundred pounds, dated 19 July 14 James &c. and partly by other writings, and I give him his plate remaining in my hands as a pledge for twenty pounds more, which twenty pounds I forgive unto him also. To John Palmer, son of my said son Michael (*sic*) two hundred pounds, besides I have given with him to his master the sum of forty pounds. To the said John Palmer, son of my said son William, the lease of my now dwelling house situate upon London Bridge, &c. &c., provided that the said William Palmer, his father, shall, from and after the end of two months next after my decease, until the said John Palmer his son shall accomplish his full age of four & twenty years, have hold & enjoy my said dwelling house, given unto his said son, paying & discharging the rent to be due for the whole to the Bridgehouse and one pepper corn yearly at the Feast of the Birth of our Lord God unto his said son if he lawfully demand the same. Reference made to the will of John Palmer, the late husband of the testatrix, and legacies to John and Mary Palmer, children of Michael, and John Palmer, son of William.

Item I give and bequeath unto my daughter Anne Faldo, late wife of Robert Faldo Esquire, deceased, two hundred and three pounds of lawful money of England and my chain of gold, and unto Thomes Faldo, her son, forty pounds, and unto Francis Faldo, her son, forty pounds, to be paid to my said daughter their mother, and by her to be paid to the said Thomas & Francis when they shall accomplish their ages of two & twenty years. To Anne Faldo, her daughter, forty pounds, and to Jane Faldo, one other of her daughters, twenty pounds, and to Elizabeth Faldo, one other of her daughters, forty pounds, at their several ages of one and twenty years or at the days of their several marriages &c.

To my daughter Elizabeth Fawcett, wife of William Fawcett, gentleman, two hundred pounds, besides four hundred pounds to them formerly given &c. and my bracelets and all my rings of gold &c.

Reference to an Obligation wherein the said John Palmer deceased (former husband of the testatrix) stood bound with the said Michael Palmer (the son) to Mr Jacob Vercelin in the sum of twelve hundred pounds, with condition thereupon endorsed to leave Mary, then wife of the said Michael Palmer & daughter of the said Jacob, if she survive the said Michael, worth in goods & chattels the sum of one thousand pounds &c.

Item I give and bequeathe unto my cousin Anne Streate and to my cousin Ellen Yarwoode twenty shillings apiece to buy them rings to wear in remembrance of me. As touching blacks to be worn at my funeral I dispose them as hereafter followeth, that is to say, I give and bequeathe unto my son Michael Palmer & William Palmer and unto my son-in-law William Fawcett and unto John Fawcett, husband of Jane Faldoe, and to my loving friends & cousins Stephen Streate and Richard Yarwoode and John Grene and Ralphe Yardley, to every of them a cloak of brown blue cloth containing three yards and half quarter in every cloak at twenty shillings every yard or thereabouts. I give and bequeathe unto my cousin Robert Poole a cloak cloth of forty shillings price, to my cousin Richard Hinde a cloak cloth, about forty shillings price and unto his wife a piece of stuff about fifty shillings price to make her a gown. Similar bequests to "my" cousin Nicholas Cowper and his wife, and cousins Anne Streate and Ellen Yarwood, and to Elizabeth Blinkensopp and Margaret Kinge and to Christopher Blinkensopp and Nicholas Kinge their husbands. Other bequests.

And I do ordain and make the aforesaid Richard Yarwoode & Stephen Streete grocers, "my cosens," full executors &c. and I appoint my loving friends John Grene Esq. and " Richard (*sic*) Yardlye Pottecary my cosen " overseers of this my will and testament, and I give and bequeath unto the said John Grene and Ralphe Yardeley for their pains therein to be taken twenty nobles apiece &c.

In a codicil dated 17 June 1624 the testatrix refers to her daughter Anne Faldoe as since married to Robert Bromfield.   111, Byrde.

Inquisition taken at St Margaret's Hill, St Savior's Southwark in the County of Surrey, 11 March 22 James I. *post mortem* Ralph Yardley, lately citizen and merchant taylor of London Deceased, who was seized, before death, in fee of one capital messuage with the appurtenances called the Horn, lately divided into two several messuages, and situate lying and being in the parish of St Savior in the Borough of Southwark, in the County of Surrey, now or late in the several tenures or occupation of George Fletcher, fisherman, and Lawrence Lunde, or their assigns; and the said Ralph Yardley, being so seized, did on the 25th day of August 1603, 1 James, by his last will in writing, give and bequeath all and singular these premisses, in English words, as follows (then follows an extract from the will). And he died, so seized, the 1st day of July 1618, and Ralph Yardley, named in the will, is son and next heir, and was aged at the time of the death of the said Ralph Yardley the father, twenty one years and more ; and the said capital messuage, into two separate messuages divided (as above) with the appurtenances, is held and, at the time of the death of the said Ralph Yardley, was held, of the Mayor, Commonalty and Citizens of the City of London in free soccage, as of their manor of Southwark, in Southwark aforesaid, by the annual rent of two shillings per annum, and is worth clear per annum, during a certain lease made by the said Ralph Yardley to a certain Richard Yerwood, citizen and grocer of London, bearing date 10 July 1603, and during the term of one hundred years, one peppercorn, and after the determination of the said lease will be worth clear and in all events and beyond reprise, three pounds per year.

Chancery Inq. p. m., Miscel., Part 4, No. 130.

[These Yardley items are interesting as showing the connection of Sir George Yardley, the governor of Virginia, to Richard Yerwood, one of John Harvard's step-fathers. I believe a little research would show that these Yardleys were of the Warwickshire family of that name. Richard Yerwood and his kinsman Stephen Street were of Cheshire, I have no doubt.—H. F. W.]

RICHARD BOWMER of the parish of St Saviours in Southwark in the county of Surrey Innholder, 7 January 1593 proved 20 March 1593. My body to be buried in the parish church of St Saviours. To the poor people of the said parish forty shillings and to the poor of the parish of St George in Southwark twenty shillings. For a sermon made at the time of my burial for me (by Mr Ratliffe if it please him) ten shillings. To the three daughters of Agnes Lackenden widow, vizt Joané, Alice and Mary, twenty shillings apiece. To Stephen Lackendon ten shillings, and to my godson, his son, five shillings. To my godson Richard Smyth of Plumpstede in the county of Kent five shillings & to my godson William Cleere of Walworthe five shillings. To my goddaughter Ellyn Beech five shillings. To Thomas Vaugham five pounds and to Henry Vaugham, brother to the said Thomas, three pounds six shillings & eight pence. To Cisly Vaugham, their sister, four pounds. To Richard Emmerson, son of William Emmerson, five shillings. To Richard Emmerson son of Humfrey Emmerson, five shillings. To Robert Rodes, youngest son now living of Roger Rodes of said parish of St Saviours, goldsmith, three pounds six shillings and eight pence, and to Elizabeth Rodes mother to the said Robert five pounds. To my kinsman

261

Peter Bowmer of Sevenocke in Kent, sadler, ten pounds. To Elizabeth Mitchell wife of Abraham Mitchell feltmaker dwelling at Horseydowne near Southwark, thirty shillings, and to my godson, her son, ten shillings. To Lambert Bowmer of the parish of St Ollifes twenty pounds, and to Robert Bowmer, his son, twenty pounds, also to the two daughters of the said Lambert now living five pounds apiece. To Henry Yonge twenty shillings, to John Yonge twenty shillings, to Gregory Francklyn twenty shillings, to Abraham Allyn twenty shillings, and to every one of their wives twenty shillings apiece to make every of them a ring of gold withall. To Richard Cuckowe ten shillings and to Peter Holmes scrivener ten shillings (for rings) and to Isaac Allen twenty shillings.

" Allso my full intente will and mynde ys : and I doe herebye giue and graunte the lease of my nowe dwellinge house called the queens heade scituate in the sayd parrishe of St. Saviors wythall my Intereste and tytle therein after my decease unto Rose my wife duringe all the yeares therein to come. Provided allwayes and my will and mynde is that the sayd Rose my wife shall haue one years respitte after my decease to pay and dischardge my legacyes herein bequeathed, and therefore I doe appoynte hereby that shee the sayd Rose shall wythin one month nexte after my decease become bounde in good and sufficyente bonde in lawe unto my ouerseers here after nominated in the some of two hundred poundes of lawfull money of Inglande that shee the sayd Rose or her assignes shall well and truly performe fulfill and keepe the tenor of this my will : and pay and discharge : all legacyes and other duetyes by me hereby given and appoynted accordinge to the tennor and true meaninge of this my last will and Testamente."

To the Society of the Vestry of St. Saviors thirteen shillings & four pence. The residue to Rose my well beloved wife whom I make & ordain my full & sole executrix. Thomas Jackson, merchant Tailor, & Miles Wilkinson, Baker, to be overseers. 23, Dixey.

ROSE BOOMER of the parish of Saint " Savyoure " in Southwark in the County of Surrey, widow, 29 March 1595, proved 9 August 1595. My body to be buried in the parish church of St Saviour's where I am a parishioner. To the preacher that shall make a sermon at my funeral ten shillings. To the poor people of the said parish forty shillings, to be distributed amongst them at the discretion of my Executor & the Collectors for the poor there for the time being. To the poor people of the parish of Bossham in the County of Sussex, where I was born, the sum of forty shillings, whereof I will that ten shillings shall be paid to Alice Reade, the widow of Richard Reede (if she be then living) And if she be then deceased then the same ten shillings to be paid to Richard Chapman. To the poor people of St John's house in the city of Winchester forty shillings. To Richard Braxton, son of Cornelius Braxton, the sum of six pounds thirteen shillings and four pence, which I will shall remain in the hands of such person as shall keep him towards his education until he shall be bound apprentice and then delivered over to use for the best profit of the same Richard and the same, with the interest, to be paid him at the expiration of his apprenticeship. And if he happen to decease before the said sum shall come unto his hands then I will to his half brother Edmond Braxton ten shillings & to his sister ten shillings, and the residue to his other two whole brethren both by father and mother, equally. To Richard Mapcrofte six pounds thirteen shillings & four pence, or if he dies to his children (in hands of his wife). To Matthew Barnard the younger, dwelling in York-

262

shire three pounds. To Matthew Barnard the elder ten shillings. To William Hildrop a piece of gold of ten shillings, for a remembrance. And a similar bequest to his brother Barnabie & his brother Richard and to John Hildrop and their sister ——, also to Johane Hoskyns, widow, and to her sister the daughter of Edward Hildroppe, and to William Braxton and —— Hardam of Chichester, son of Margery Braxton, and to Richard Wallys of Winchester, to Margaret Bathe, to John Homeade's wife of Winchester and to Richard Homeade her son, to Mrs Bird, to Mistress Denham, to Mr Thomas Thorney, of Portsmouth, to John Androwes, to Robert Boomer, to Thomas Vaughan, to his sister Cicely, to Robert Roades, & his brother Henry Clarke, and to my servant that shall attend upon me at the time of my decease, ten shillings. To Johane Allen, my daughter, fifty pounds (and certain household stuff). To Isaacke Allen, her son, & to Rosanna Allen the sum of twentie five pounds each. To my daughter Alice Francklin (certain household stuff).

"Item I will and bequeathe unto Gregorye ffrancklyn my sonne in lawe and the sayed Alice his wife (yf she the same Alice shalbe living at the tyme of my decease) all my Righte title and interest of and in so muche and suche partes and parcells of the mesuage or Inne called the Quenes hed in the parishe of Sainct Savyoure in Sowthwarke aforesayed as I lately demised by Indenture of Lease unto one Oliuer Bowker and of in and to the gatehouse of the sayed Inne nowe in the occupaçon of Bryan Pattenson: The Interest of which premisses I haue and hould by vertue of a Lease heretofore made and graunted by one John Bland unto Richard Boomer my late husband deceased and me the said Rose for diuers yeres yet to haue contynewance. Except allwayes and my meaning ys that the sayed Devise by me as aforesayed made shall not extend to certeyne garden plottes lying on the East syde of the Dytche or Common Sewer extending and passing by the Tenter yard and the garden behinde the sayed mesuage. Prouided allwayes that yf the sayed Gregory and Alice shall not permitt and suffer Abraham Allen and Jone his wife Isaacke Allen and Rosanna Allen and theire assignes peaceablye and quietly to hould and enioye the sayed excepted garden plottes according to the tenure of suche graunte and assuraunce as I haue lately made unto them That then and from thencefourthe the Devise made to the sayed Gregorye and Alice as aforesayed shall cease and be utterlie frustrate and voyde (any thinge before expressed to ye Contrary notwithstandinge)."

To my daughter Anne Younge the lease of my now dwelling house and of certain grounds at Wallworth and one hundred pounds (and certain household stuff). To my son in law John Younge and Anne his wife towards the buying of their blacks for my funeral four pounds. The same to Gregory Franckling & Alice his wife & to Abraham Allen & Johane his wife. Bequests to others. John Younge to be executor and Thomas Jackson & Myles Wilkenson supervisors.   53, Scott.

Gregory Francklin of the parish of St Savior in Southwark in the County of Surrey, citizen & sadler of London, 11 September 1624, proved 22 September 1624. My body to be buried within the church of the parish of St Savior, at the discretion of Katherine my wife & sole executrix. To the poor of the said parish forty shillings. To the Wardens of the Company of Sadlers in London four pounds to make them a supper withall.

" Itm̃ whereas I the said Gregory ffrancklin by my deede indented bearing date the Second day of ffebruary in the Thirteenth yeare of the Kings

Ma^ts Raigne aforesaid of England ffraunce and Ireland, And of Scotland the Nyne and ffortieth (ffor the Consideraçons in the said deede expressed) did graunte enfeoff and confirme unto Gilbert Kinder Cittizen and Mercer of London All that Capitall Messuage or Inne called or knowne by the name of the Queenes head Scituat and being in the p̃ish of St Savio^r in the Borrough of Southwark in the County of Surr. and one garden to the same belonging To certen severall uses in the said deede expressed As by the same more plainly may appeare, I the said Gregory ffrancklin doe hereby publish and declare that the only cause and consideraçon wch moved me to Seale unto the said deede was for that at the tyme of the making and sealing thereof I was a widdower and a sole p̃son, not having any yssue of my body then living nor then intending to marrye. Nevertheles wth a Res^ruacoñ unto myselfe in case I did marrye and had yssue, That not wth standing the saide deede, or any estate thereupon executed, the power should remaine in me to giue and dispose of the said Inne and p^rimsses at my owne will and pleasure, In such manner as I should thinck fitting. And therefore for significaçon of my will intent and meaning concerning the same, And forasmuch as it hath pleased God that I have marryed the said Katherine my nowe wiffe by whome I have yssue Gregory ffrancklin my sonne and heir who is very young and of tender yeares, unto whome I have but small meanes to conferre and settle upon him both for his educaçon and bringing upp and otherwise wch wth care I would willingly provide for after my decease, And not minding or intending that my said sonne should be disinherited or deprived of his lawfull right of and to the said Messuage or Inne doe hereby renounce and frustrate the said deede and all thestate thereupon had Togeather wth the severall uses and limitaçons therein expressed, And doe declare the same to be of noe force or vallidity at all. And doe hereby giue deuise and bequeath the said Messuage or Inne and garden wth thapp^rtenñces to the said Gregory ffrancklin my sonne and the heires of his body lawfully to be begotten, And for default of such yssue unto Gilbert Kinder and Margarett his wife and unto theire heires for ever."

Reference made to a deed indented dated the last day of August 1616 for the jointure of the said Katherine (if she should happen to survive), conveying certain tenements in the parish of St Savior in Southwark & in the parish of St Sepulchre without Newgate London and confirmation of that deed. Also to the said Katherine the moyty or one half part of the Rents Issues and Profits, when and at such time as the same shall grow due and payable of all and singular those gardens or garden plots with the Alley way or passage to the same leading and used with all the appurtenances thereunto belonging lying and being on the backside of the Messuage or Inne commonly called &c. the Queen's Head &c. now in the tenure or occupation of Isaac Allen Gen^t or his assigns. And the other moiety or half part of the Rents &c. of the same gardens and premisses I give, will and bequeath to the said Gregory Francklin, my son, at such time as he shall accomplish his full age of one & twenty years. And after the decease of the said Katherine, my wife, I give will & bequeath all the said premisses unto the said Gregory my son & the heirs of his body lawfully begotten. If my son shall happen to depart this transitory life before his said age &c. (having no issue of his body living) then the said Katherine, my wife, shall freely have, hold, possess & enjoy all & singular the same gardens & premisses &c. for & during her natural life, and from & after her decease then to the Wardens or keepers & Commonalty of the mystery or Art of Sadlers of the City of London & to their Successors forever the moiety or

264

half part of the said gardens &c., And the other moiety &c. to the Governors of the Free School of the Parish of St Saviour in Southwark, aforesaid, and to their successors forever, to this use, intent and purpose only (that is to say) for & towards the maintaining & bringing up of some one child or youth, which shall from time to time forever hereafter be born within the said parish. And I hereby will that such one always may be first taught learned and instructed sufficiently in the said free school and afterwards by them the said Governors and their successors for the time being put forth and brought up in learning, during the term of eight years, so that from time to time such one scholar may attain to the degree of M^r in Arts in one of the Universities of Oxon or Cambridge if such one scholar shall so long continue both scholar and student in either of the same, as by their discretions shall be thought most meet and convenient, whereunto I refer myself.

To the said Katherine, my wife, the lease which I hold of & from the Wardens &c. of the said mystery or Art of Sadlers &c. of all that Messuage or Tenement with the appurtenances &c. called or known by the sign of the Three Kings set, lying and being upon Snowe Hill near the Conduit there, within the parish of St Sepulchre without Newgate London, now in the Tenure or occupation of Josias Curtis, tailor &c. If she die before the expiration of the term granted by the same lease, then to the said Gregory Francklin, my son, for the time &c. unexpired. To my said son Gregory my gold seal ring (and other personal property).

Item my special will & meaning is that the said Katherine my wife shall within the space of six months next after my decease well & truly satisfy & pay or cause to be paid unto Ann Parkhurst & Katherine Parkhurst, daughters of Edward Parkhurst, late citizen & merchant tailor of London deceased & of the said Katherine my wife, the sum of one hundred pounds of lawful money of England for the redeeming of the said Gardens or garden plots, and two tenements with the appurtenances thereupon erected, which I mortgaged and stand engaged to pay the said sum by my deed as thereby appeareth.

A bequest is made to John Parvish, "my old servant," and the residue is bequeathed to wife Katherine who is made sole Executrix, and friends Richard Yerwood grocer and Robert Bucke glover are appointed supervisors, and to either of them, for their pains, a ring of gold of twenty shillings apiece is bequeathed.

Witnesses Richard Harrison, Richard Haukins, Antho: Rogers Scr., John Dodsworth, servant to Edr̃d Jackson Scr.

Probate granted to the widow 22 September 1624.

Decimo quinto die mensis Junii An° Dñi 1637° Emanavit Comissio Henrico Creswell p̄oe St Bothi extra Aldersgate London aurifabr̃ ad administrand bona iura et crēd dc̄i Gregorii ffrancklyn def iuxta tenorem et effc̄um testī prēd p Catherinam Creswell al̃s ffrancklyn al̃s Blackleech nup̃ relcam et execūt testī dc̄i Gregorii (iam etiam demort.) non plene adm̃istrat de bene etc iurat. 73, Byrde.

ANNE WHITMORE of Lambehith in the county of Surrey, widow, 9 August 1624, proved 12 October 1624. I give all my worldly goods, money, jewells, plate and household stuff whatsoever unto my grandchild Martha Smith and to the heirs of her body, lawfully begotten, provided always that if the said Martha shall happen to die and depart this life without such issue of her body lawfully begotten then my will is and I bequeath unto my grandchildren Gregory Francklin, Anne Parkhurst & Katherine

Parkhurst, the son and daughters of Katherine Francklin, wife of Gregory Francklin, to every of them the sum of ten pounds; also I give and bequeath unto Richard Smith and Thomas Bradbridge, the sons of Anne Bradbridge, my daughter, of Lambehith aforesaid, widow, the like sum of ten pounds and also to the said Anne Bradbridge the sum of forty pounds. And I nominate appoint and ordain the said Martha Smith to be sole executrix &c. And my will is that she shall within six months after my decease give unto her Aunt Katherin Francklin the sum of three pounds sterling to buy her a cup or bowl, in token of my love unto her, and I do appoint my loving friend Mr William Childe to be overseer &c. 118, Byrde.

GREGORY FRANCKLYN 19 February 1635. I do bestow all the estate that is or shall be mine upon my sister Ann, conditionally that she shall help, succor & relieve my mother in all her wants and necessities so far as she is able. And to my sister Kate I give a pair of sheets, a dozen of napkins and a towel, and to my cousin Mrs Martha Marshall a pair andirons, and to Thomas Day a piece of gold of five shillings.

Administration was granted 1 March 1635 to Anne Parkhurst natural & lawful sister of the said Gregory Francklyn of the Parish of St Buttolph without Aldersgate London deceased. 32, Pile.

HARWARD OF SOUTHWARK.—Any reference to the family of John Harvard is full of interest, so no apology is required for giving the following note:

Nichols's Collectanea Topographica et Genealogica, Vol. viii., contains an article on "The Manor of the Maze, in St. Olave's, Southwark." On page 260 are given "Extracts from the Court Rolls of the Manor of the Maze." This is dated 2 June, 1661, when John Weston was Lord of the Manor in right of his wife. A list of "Tenentes liberi" is given, ending with Thomas Harward. Then follows "Homagiu' Ss.—Joh'es Rawlinson, Bennett Hull, Jur'. Thos. Harward." Further on occurs the following entry: "Cogn'.—Ad hanc Cur' Thomas Harward cognovit se libere tenere de D'no hujus Manerii quatuor messuagia sive tenementa cum p'tin'-scituat' apud Battle Bridge in Mill Lane, infra Maneriu' p'dict' p' reddit' p' annu' 1^d. fidelitat', sect' cur', et al' servic', et fecit D'no fidelitat' ac solvit pro reddit' triginta annos ad festum Annunciac'onis beatæ Mariæ Virginis modo ult' p'terit' ij^s. vj^d.

Ad hanc Cur' p'fat' Thomas Harward sup' sacr'um suu' dat Cur' intelligi qd' antea tenebat libere de D'no hujus Manerii tria messuagia sive tenementu' cum p'tinen' scituat' apud finem plateæ vocat' Bermondsey Street infra Maneriu' p'dict' p' reddit' p' annu' iiij^d fidelitat', sect' cur', et al' servic' Quæ p'missa circa triginta annos modo ult' p'terit' p'quisivit Joh'i Harward et hereds suis qui postea p'quisivit p'missa p'dicta cum p'tinen —— Maugen de p'och Sc'i Olavie in Southwarke, et hered' suis."

The whole quotation from the Court Roll is signed

BENNETT HULL, } Jur.
THOMAS HARWARD, }

Mr. Waters in his Gleanings in the REGISTER (vol. xxxix. p. 279) gives the * will of Thomas Harvard of St. Olaves, Southwark, and in vol. xl. p. 371, are ** quotations from the Feet of Fines relative to tenements in the same parish. Possibly these refer to the places which are mentioned above; if so these notes will help to identify them. Perhaps some one more familiar with the valuable matter turned up by the careful study of Mr. Waters may be able to tell whether the John Harward mentioned in the quotations I have given above, who held the tenements in 1631, was or was not the John Harvard of everprecious memory. (Mrs.) FRANCES B. TROUP.

Offwell House, Honeton, Eng.

*P. 242, this volume.
**P. 257, this volume.

HARVARD (*ante*, xxxvi. 319 ; xxxviii. 343 ; xxxix. 185, 265).*—Rev. Francis J. Poynton, rector of Kelston, near Bath, England, whose extracts from the parish register of St. Michael's, Bath, relative to the name of Harvard, were printed in the REGISTER for April last (page 185), writes in relation to the name of Mr. Waters on " John Harvard and his Ancestry " (*ante*, pp. 265-84) :

" I have read it with interest and see that it settles the question of Harvard's parentage and birth once for all. I only wish that Col. Chester was alive to rejoice, as he would have done, to see the point cleared up. The question which I opened, in my last correspondence with Mr. Haines of Galena, still remains. Is Harvard one of the many representations of the old name Herford or Harford ? In the latter form, i. e. Harford, ' the name is legion ' in the west of England. As I said in my letter to Mr. Haines, Col. Chester may have thought the name, Harvard, scarce, because he did not think of its being a form of Harford.

" I see that Bigland's Gloucester, under Marshfield, gives an inscription to Harvard. My recent perusal of the old Marshfield parish registers down to 1715, shows that Harvard was first spelt Herford, then Harford, then Harvord or Harvard, and now Mr. Waters, from his reasearches in London, adds Harvy. Many Marshfield traders went to London, e. g. Blanchards, Crispes and Chambers. Harford too may have gone there from Bath or Marshfield."

*P. 265 is p. 228, this volume.

JOHN HARVARD AND CAMBRIDGE UNIVERSITY.—An English correspondent writes as follows :

" The two signatures of John Harvard are in the Subscription Book. Here every person, on admission to a degree, subscribed his name in token of his assent to the Royal Supremacy, the authority of Holy Scripture and the Thirty-Nine Articles of the Church of England. The declaration on these points is written, and then each person for himself acknowledges his assent to it. The order adopted is by Colleges, and Harvard's signature appears amongst those from Emmanuel on taking his B.A. degree in 1631 and his M.A. in 1635, the latter being much the better of the two. These books go back to 1613, when subscription was first required, and the originals have been preserved from that time to this day ; and, as I need not say, are of the highest interest. Subscription, properly so called, has been abolished, but persons admitted to degrees still sign the book. Amongst recent signatures of interest, that of your distinguished fellow citizen, ' Robert Charles Winthrop,' caught my eye. The Register of which Mr. Shuckburgh wrote to you (REG. xxxix. 327) as having been preserved since 1544, is the Matriculation Register, but this does not contain the signatures of the persons matriculated. Signatures go back only to the period when subscription began, which, as I have said, was in 1613.

" The only original record of the period which Emmanuel College possesses is a book with the heading ' *Recepta ab ingredientibus*,' which begins November 1, 1584, the year of the foundation of the College. This book I have examined. I transcribe the first two names in the list headed, ' From Oct. 25, 1627.' The payment on entrance seems to have been, for a fellow commoner, who is styled ' Mr.,' £5 ; for a pensioner 10 shillings, and for a sizar 2s. 6d. Thus Harvard is shown to have been a pensioner.

' from Oct. 25, 1627

Edmond Spinckes Octob. 25, Lincolneshire	0. 2. 6	
John Harverd Midlsex : Decemb. 19	0. 10. 0 '	

" The list has been conjectured to be a summary of previous more detailed entries, but I found no sufficient evidence to support this conjecture.

" It seems to me that, in this Harvard matter, confusion has arisen through lack of accuracy in designating things, and in particular that the word ' Register ' has been, and is often, used inexactly. ʼMatriculation Register of Emmanuel College ' is wrong. Matriculation is an act, the record of which is kept by the University, and not by the College of the person matriculating. Each College keeps an Admission Register, but that of Emmanuel is not existing for Harvard's date. The ' Recepta ab ingredientibus ' is the sole contemporary record of the kind which the College possesses. The Matriculation Register—which by the way I do not find has ever been consulted on this point—is not a book of signatures, whereas the Subscription Book, as its name implies, consists of nothing but signatures.

"I hope in due course we shall have a satisfactory volume touching John Harvard which will comprise all that is known of him, both on this side and on yours. It is a great mistake to isolate such a man. We want to know his surroundings, and to have grouped about him, for instance, his contemporaries at Emmanuel. I will give you an instance of what I mean by referring to two of those contemporaries. One is Sancroft, whose name is specially associated with Emmanuel, of which he became Master. Later still he was Archbishop of Canterbury, and was chief of the Seven who were sent to the Tower by James II. In spite of this hard usage he refused to swear allegiance to William III., was deprived and retired to a small patrimony at Fressingfield in Suffolk. Here he died. This on one side. On the other was Whichcote, he having taken his degree, and therefore having subscribed to the above described 'three articles,' was not only a good puritan, but was so good a republican that, thanks to the favor of the Cromwellites, he became the intended Provost of Kings, and thus had under his care that grandest monument of English ecclesiastical architecture in its latest development—royal not alone in its founder and in its benefactors, but in itself—King's College Chapel.

" This kind of matter would add, I think, much to the interest of any biography of Harvard. The influence of Emmanuel upon the University at large was great during the puritan sway. It furnished, if I remember, not fewer than twelve heads of Houses, most of whom, if not all, had, of course, to retire at the restoration."

The entry in the " Recepta," in which Harvard is recorded as of Middlesex, caused some to think that Col. Chester was wrong when he expressed the opinion that he was a son of Robert Harvard of Southwark in Surrey (REG. xxxvi. 319); but Mr. Waters's researches furnish a sufficient explanation. After Robert Harvard's death his widow married John Elletson, of London. Though John Harvard was not matriculated at Cambridge University till a year after his step-father's death, it is probable that his mother continued to reside in London till her marriage to Richard Yearwood, and that she resided there when the above entry was made.—EDITOR.

JOHN HARVARD AND CAMBRIDGE UNIVERSITY.—In the article with this heading in * the January number, after " John Harvard Midlsex: Decem. 19, 0.10.0," the following lines were accidentally omitted :

" On the same page, in a list of names is this :
' Hawered 0. 10. 0.' "
It is to this list in which the name " Hawered" occurs that the next paragraph refers:
" The list has been conjectured to be a summary of previous more detailed entries, but I find no sufficient evidence to support this conjecture."

I find that I was wrong in supposing that the entry " Midlsex " against Harvard's name in the " Recepta " indicates the residence of his mother. The following article in the New York Nation, February 18, 1886, states the matter correctly.

John Harvard: A Difficulty Solved.—To the Editor of the Nation: Sir: It appears to be clear that John Harvard was born in Surrey, at Southwark, and it is certain that when he went up to Cambridge in 1627 he was described at Emmanuel College as of Middlesex. This is the matter upon which I propose to offer some observations, with the view of removing an apparent discrepancy, for which some would account by the statement that in 1627 he was probably living in London with his mother and her husband. How far this is satisfactory will appear from what follows.

*The preceding article.

The first point of inquiry is in what manner in Harvard's time the questions addressed to a young man on entering college were put, and I think we are not without a guide which will lead us in a certain direction. When St. John's College published the first part of its Admission Register, which begins in 1629-30, it was an object of interest with me to identify, for my own information, some of the places which appear in it in a form truly grotesque. For reasons into which I need not here enter, I was led to rely mainly upon sound, and, having thus succeeded in overcoming difficulties which appeared almost insuperable, I arrived, upon independent grounds, at the same conclusion as the editor of the Register [of St. John's College], namely, that the entries were made from statements taken down from the lips of the persons admitted ; and there was no doubt uniformity of practice among the different colleges of the University.

The next point is, What was the nature of the questions? and this renders it necessary to speak of the object which they had in view. That object was not, as the man of to-day. might suppose, the mere collection of useful statistics, but was to indicate for what scholarships and other advantages, restricted to those born in a certain district, the person admitted was eligible. It is ignorance of this leading fact which has led into error those who hitherto have attempted to explain the matter. The place at which the person was residing when he went up to the University, was foreign to the scope of inquiry ; the place of birth being alone material.

The chief question, then, which was put to John Harvard at Emmanuel College was, where he was born, and the entry of Middlesex leaves no doubt that his reply was "in London." It is stated that the precise locality of his birth was the High Street of Southwark, and the statement derives corroboration from that which proceeded from his own lips. The High Street of Southwark, which extended southward from London Bridge to the spot where stood St. Margaret's Hall, formed part of the City of London, being included in the City Ward of Bridge Without, so that a person born in that street properly described himself as born in London.   z.

Cambridge, England, Feb. 12, 1886.

HARVARD.—We have received from William Rendle, F.R.C.S., of London, Eng., a communication, in which he takes substantially the ground which the editor of this periodical did in the January number, that Harvard was probably residing in London with his mother, the widow Elletson, when he was admitted to Emmanuel College, in 1627, and that the entry " Midlsex " in the *Recepta* may have been intended for his residence at the time. In our April number we quoted an English correspondent of the New York *Nation*, who asserts that this is not the correct explanation of the entry in the *Recepta*, as such entries always denote the birth place and not the residence. The same correspondent of the *Nation*, in the issue of May 20, furnishes examples to prove his position, and till instances are produced in which the residence was entered in such cases, we shall rely on his authority.

Mr. Rendle calls our attention to his own discovery of the home and birth place of John Harvard. We take pleasure in bringing this subject to the attention of our readers. Mr. Rendle, in his pamphlet on John Harvard, referred to in the REGISTER for January, 1886, page 36, describes certain " Token-books " preserved in the Vestry of St. Savior's, which contain lists of streets, courts and alleys, with the names of the inhabitants in whose families were individuals over 16 years old, to whom leaden token had been distributed implying that such persons would at their peril neglect to receive the sacrament. From these books Mr. Rendle obtains facts that convince him that the house of Robert Harvard, the father of John Harvard, was opposite the Boar's Head Tavern and Alley in Southwark. A map, showing the locality of Robert Harvard's house and other places of interest in the vicinity, is given in the pamphlet, also facsimiles of entries in the Token-books.

HARVARD.—In the printed matter relating to the ancestors of Rev. John Harvard, I have not noticed the following facts regarding their connection with the Free Grammar School in St. Saviour's, Southwark :—
Robert, the father of Rev. John Harvard, was present as a parishoner at a meeting on 20 Feb., 1615, to elect a new governor, and signed the book.

3 Jan., 1624–5, he was present and was nominated a feofee of Mr. Randall Carter's gift of an annuity to a poor scholar at Magdalen Hall, Oxford.

13 Aug., 1625, the feoffment was executed, but Mr. Harvard does not appear as one of the feoffees. The reason, of course, was his death and burial, 24 Aug., 1625.

Thomas Harvard was elected governor, 12 Dec., 1646. A new governor was chosen in the place of Thomas Harvard, deceased, on 8 Apr., 1668.

Malden, Mass.   WALTER KENDALL WATKINS.

HARWOOD-CHAFFEE-KNOLLYS. — "A list of Non-Conformists and other Dangerous Persons," dated about 1662–63 (Domestic State Papers, Miscellaneous, no. 26), contains the following passages (quoted) referring to three early Massachusetts pioneers:

"Harwood Jo. a Merc^t at Mile end Green, a factious dangerous Independ^t & ye comon Facto^r for all ye Merch^{ts} Tradeing especially to N. Engl^d who uses constantly to cou' & disguise ye shipps, Goods & persons of those of y^t Opinion in their voyages so as ye Offic^{rs} of ye Customes &c at Gravesed and oth^r places are by his interest and mony corrupted to slipp ye Oaths wch otherwise ought to be tendred to all persons going out, &c. Mr Scott."

This is undoubtedly the John Harwood who wrote to Job Lane of Malden, Mass., from Bednall [i.e., Bethnal] Green, 18 Feb. 1665/6. (See REGISTER, vol. 11, p. 108.) He was of Boston in 1645, was admitted to the church in 1647, and became freeman in 1649. He sold his estate in 1657, says Savage, to brother Thomas Scottow, and went back to England, where he was living in London in 1677. His will, dated 13 Nov. 1684 and proved in the Prerogative Court of Canterbury 22 June 1685, may be seen in abstract in the REGISTER, vol. 42, pp. 64–65. Bethnal Green and Mile End Green were formerly parts of the parish of Stepney, in the eastern part of London.

"Chaffey, a New England Preacher lives and meets in Wapping."
Matthew Chaffee, ship carpenter, is first mentioned in the New England records when he was admitted to the First Church in Boston, 7 Aug. 1636. He was freeman in 1637, a member of the Ancient and Honorable Artillery Company in 1642, and bought a farm at Newbury, Mass., in 1649. On 10 Aug. 1655 he and his wife [Sarah] were dismissed from the First Church in Boston, and no further record of him in New England has been found. In the will of Thomas Taylor of Wapping, co. Middlesex, Eng., shipwright, dated 15 Dec. 1658 and proved 10 Jan. 1658/9, there is a bequest of £5 to "Master Mathew Chafey;"* and, with one Robert Lambe, he was to dispose of £5 left to the church of Christ in Wapping. (P.C.C., Pell, 8.)

"Knowles, an Anabaptist Minister, a good Scholl^r & a trading [?] man now in Amsterdã maintained by ye Churches, & one Thibalds (his Elder) in Tow^r street correspondes wth him. to him one Riggs was recommended by Thebalds Knowles dwells in Wapping."

Hansard Knollys is said to have been born at Cawkwell, co. Lincoln, in 1598. He came to New England about 1638, was an adherent of Mrs. Anne Hutchinson, and removed to Piscataqua, where he signed the Combination in 1640. He returned to England in 1641 and was mentioned in 1658 in the will of Thomas Taylor of Wapping (*vide supra*) as "Master Hansard Knowles my son Caleb's schoolmaster."

6 Haymarket, London, S.W.   ELIZABETH FRENCH.

THE ENGLISH ANCESTORS OF EDMOND HAWES
OF YARMOUTH, MASS.

By James W. Hawes of New York City

It has been known that Edmond Hawes, described as a cutler, late of London, was among those who shipped about 5 April 1635, to sail from Southampton in the ship *James* for New England,[a] and that he arrived in Boston 3 June 1635, after a passage of about five weeks.[b] His subsequent career is known from the colonial and local records. He was in Duxbury in 1637, and was chosen constable there in 1642. In or prior to March 1645, he removed to Yarmouth, where he was active in public affairs until his death in 1693. He was one of the selectmen and town clerk and treasurer for many years, and for many years represented the town in the Colony Court. He left one son, John (who married Desire, daughter of Capt. John Gorham and granddaughter of John Howland, the Mayflower passenger), also active in public affairs in the town, from whom descended the Haweses of Yarmouth, Chatham, and other towns on Cape Cod.

Nothing, however, was known of his parentage or place of birth until the writer recently, with the pecuniary assistance of two other descendants of Edmond, Messrs. William T. Wardwell and James Anderson Hawes, of New York City, employed Mr. Gerald Fothergill of New Wandsworth, London, to make investigations.[c]

The records of the Cutlers' Company of London, recently rendered accessible, revealed that the emigrant was the son of Edmond Hawes of Solihull (a parish about seven miles southeast of Birmingham), Warwickshire, gentleman; that he bound himself, 14 February 1626–7, to Edmond Warnett,[d] a citizen and cutler of London, for the term of eight years from 2 February preceding, and that he was sworn free cutler 9 December 1634. The will of Francis Hawes (a relative, degree not known) of Belchamp

[a] Drake's Founders of New England, pp. 55–6.
[b] Winthrop's Journal (Hosmer's ed.), vol. 1, p. 152.
[c] Services were also performed by Miss P. Smith of Queen's Gardens, London. Acknowledgments are due for valuable assistance, gratuitously given, to Mr. P. E. Martineau, a local antiquary of Knowle, Warwickshire; to Rev. Robert Pemberton, author of "Solihull and its Church," of Birmingham, England; and to Mr. Frank M. Hawes, a descendant of Richard Hawes, of Somerville, Mass., who is engaged on a genealogy of the various lines of Massachusetts Haweses.
[d] Probably a relative or connection by marriage. See Waters's Gleanings, pp. 1345–7, wills of Robert and John Baker.

St. Paul, county of Essex, dated 21 November 1621, and proved in the Prerogative Court of Canterbury 2 April 1622, gives all his freehold and copyhold estates, subject to an annuity of £5 a year to the testator's sister, Anne Morris, to Edmond Hawes, youngest son of Edmond Hawes, of Solihull, gentleman.

The testator's sister and William Rastall having entered upon the lands devised and attempted to suppress the will, Edmond Hawes the younger (then 14 years of age), by Edmond Hawes the elder, his father and guardian, brought a suit in Chancery, 15 May 1622, against Anne Morris and William Rastall (an executor of the will), to establish his right, which evidently resulted in his favor. By deed, dated 12 February 1633–4, he sold his right in these estates to Sir Leventhorpe Franche, Knight, for the consideration of £250.[e] The printed parish register of Solyhull (Parish Register Society, vol. 53) shows the baptisms of Edmond and his brothers and sisters. They are all styled *Mr.* or *Mrs.*, and described as son or daughter of *Mr.* Edmond Hawes of Hillfield or Shelley, the family estates. The register also shows the marriages and deaths of certain members of the Hawes line.

The Visitation of Warwickshire made in 1619,[f] gives the pedigree of the family for eight generations down to the emigrant, Edmond (Edmond, William, Thomas, Thomas, Thomas, Thomas, Thomas).

The original of this pedigree, signed by Edmond Hawes, father of the emigrant, is in the College of Arms, London. This visitation and Burke's General Armory (p. 468) give the arms of the family as sable, a chevron argent between three leopards' faces or. For several generations they had intermarried with arms-bearing families of Warwickshire and other counties.

Hillfield Hall was rebuilt by William Hawes, grandfather of the emigrant, in 1576, and the front remains substantially in its original shape to-day. Over the front door is the following inscription, containing the initials of William Hawes and his wife Ursula:

H

W.　　V.

1576

Hic hospites, in Coelo Cives.[g]

In the parish church is an inscription laudatory of this William.

Pemberton (op. cit. p. 42) gives one more generation than the Visitation of Warwickshire, beginning with Thomas Hawes of Shirley, who purchased Hillfield about 1311.

A manuscript in the Bridges collection in the Bodleian Library at Oxford, attributed to William Belchier of Northamptonshire, reproduces inscriptions existing in the Hawes mansion in Solihull (probably about 1600 or earlier), giving the marriage of Thomas Hawes in 1465 to Ann Greswolde, with the Hawes arms impaling those of Greswolde (argent, a fess gules between two greyhounds courant sable), the marriage of Thomas Hawes in 1527 to Elizabeth Brome, with the Hawes arms impaling those of Brome (sable, on a chevron argent three sprigs of broom slipped vert), and the marriage of William Hawes in 1562 to Ursula Colles, with the Hawes arms impaling those of Colles (gules, on a chevron argent pelletée four barrulets sable between three lions' heads erased or).

e Close Rolls in Public Record Office.
f Harleian Society, vol. 12, pp. 404–5.
g Here sojourners, in Heaven citizens.

Excluding the earlier generations alluded to above, the English pedigree will be:

1. THOMAS HAWES married, 1465, ANN GRESWOLDE.[h]
Child:
   2. i. THOMAS, and probably others.

2. THOMAS HAWES (*Thomas*) married, about 1500, JOAN RAINSFORD,[i] buried 26 August, 1558.
Children:
   3. i. THOMAS.
     ii. ELIZABETH, m. ———, and had *Ann*.
     iii. CATHERINE, m. 23 Nov. 1539, WILLIAM SMALLWOOD.
     iv. ANN, m. ——— GIBBONS.
     Perhaps others.

3. THOMAS HAWES (*Thomas, Thomas*) married first, in 1527, ELIZABETH BROME, daughter of Nicholas,[j] Esq., of Baddesley Clinton, probably by his third wife, Lettice, daughter of Nicholas Catesby; and secondly, ELINOR ———, buried 12 June 1514.* He left a will filed in the Consistory of Lichfield, 27 October 1574, in which he mentions his wife Elinor, his son and heir William and the latter's son Thomas, daughter Elizabeth (wife of Thomas Jackson) and her son Thomas, daughter Hatley and her children, daughter Margaret, son-in-law Doctor Brainton, sister Elizabeth ——— and her daughter Ann, sister Catherine Wood, sister Ann Gibbons, and cousin Thomas Greswolde. His first wife was buried in the Baddesley Clinton Church, near her father, where she had an epitaph.[k]

Children, probably all by his first wife:
   4. i. WILLIAM, b. in 1531.
     ii. CONSTANCE,[l] m. THOMAS SPEHERD, yeoman; not mentioned in her father's will.
     iii. ELIZABETH, m. THOMAS JACKSON, and had *Thomas*.
     iv. A DAUGHTER, m. ——— HATLEY, and had issue.
     v. A DAUGHTER, m. DR. ——— BRAINTON.
     vi. MARGARET.

h The Greswoldes sprang from John Greswolde of Kenilworth, Warwickshire. Richard Greswolde died before 1412. Thomas Greswelde about 1438 had custody of the manor of Solihull under the Crown, and from about 1443 to about 1458 was a justice of the peace. (Dugdale, History of Warwickshire, p. 696; Visitation of Warwickshire, 1619, p. 61.)
i The Rainsford (or Raynesford) family were from Lancashire and Oxfordshire. Their original arms were argent, a cross sable. (Visitation of Oxfordshire, Harleian Society, vol. 5, p. 165; Visitation of Warwickshire, p. 48; 3 Miscellanea Genealogica et Heraldica, vol. 2, p. 158.)
j Nicholas Brome, the father of Elizabeth, was lord of the manor of Baddesley Clinton. He died in 1517, and was buried in the church there, where there was an inscription to his memory. He was Justice of the Peace for several years, and at one time Sheriff of Warwick and Leicestershire. The family was an ancient one in Warwickshire. His great-grandfather, Robert Brome, was a lawyer. His grandfather, John Brome, was member of Parliament for the Borough of Warwick in 1406. His father, John Brome, a lawyer, who bought the manor, was Under-treasurer in the Exchequer in the reign of Henry VI. (between 1422 and 1461), and held other offices. This John Brome was slain in 1468 on the porch of the White Friars' Church, London, where he was attending mass, by John Herthill, steward to the Earl of Warwick, in a quarrel over a mortgage which Brome held against Herthill. He was buried in the White Friars' Church, and there was a Latin epitaph inscribed on his tombstone. (Dugdale, op. cit. pp. 710-13.)
k Dugdale, op. cit. p. 713.
l Visitation of Warwickshire, 1619, p. 405.
*For 1514 read 1574.

4. **William Hawes** (*Thomas, Thomas, Thomas*) married, in 1562, **Ursula Colles**, daughter of William[m] of Leigh, co. Worcester, and was buried 31 Oct. 1611, aged 80 years. She was buried 26 Oct. 1615, aged 76 years. He left a will and codicil proved in the Consistory of Lichfield 14 Jan. 1611–12, in which he mentions his wife Ursula, son Edmond, a deceased son, daughters Elizabeth and Ursula, youngest daughter Constance, son-in-law William Sheldon, grandchildren William Hawes and Jane Hawes, brother-in-law Michael Colles, and the latter's son Humphrey, cousin Reginald Brome, Esq. The inventory of his estate amounted to £378 0s. 10d, and included a virginal, chessboard, clock, map, etc. His widow left a will, dated 25 March 1614 and proved in the Consistory of Lichfield 3 Nov. 1615, in which she mentions son Edmond and wife, daughters Sheldon, Hunt, Constance Hawes, grandchildren Jane, William, Ursula, and the rest of her son Edmond's children (not named), brother Mr. Michael Colles and his wife, nephew Mr. Humphrey Colles. The inventory of her estate amounted to £165 2s. 8d.

Children :

   i.   **Ursula.**

   ii. **Elizabeth**, m. 16 Oct. 1588, **William Sheldon**, of Bromsgrove, co. Worcester.

5. iii. **Edmond.**

   iv. **Thomas**, not mentioned in his father's or mother's will.

   v.   **William**, not mentioned in his father's or mother's will ; d. without issue.

   vi. **Ursula**, m. 8 Nov. 1595, **Raphael Hunt** of Stoke Green, parish of Hanbury, co. Worcester.

  vii. **Constance**, unm. in 1615.

 viii. A **son**, not mentioned in his parents' wills.

5. **Edmond Hawes** (*William, Thomas, Thomas, Thomas*) married before 1600, **Jane Porter**, daughter of Richard[n] of Bayham, co. Sussex. By deed dated 16 May 1604, with his cousin Humphrey Colles of the Middle Temple, he bought the lordship of Solihull for £1080 from Thomas, grandson of Sir George Throckmorton, Knight, and afterward sold it to Samuel Marrow, Esq.[o] He was living as late as 1653.[p]

---

[m] William Colles, the father of Ursula, married Margaret, sister and co-heir of John Hitch. He died in 1558, aged 63 years, and was buried in the Church at Leigh, where there was an inscription to his memory. His eldest son Edmond, who died in 1606, aged 76 years, had been justice of the peace, deputy lieutenant of Worcestershire, and sheriff of that county. William Colles also had a son Michael, of Hampden in Arden, Warwickshire, and Bradwell, Buckinghamshire, besides other children. The family had been seated in Worcestershire since the 14th century, and owned estates in many parts of that and other counties. (Grazebrook, Heraldry of Worcestershire, p. 124; Nash, History of Worcestershire, pp. 76, 400; Habington, Survey of Worcestershire, pp. 329–32, 399, 400, 542.)

[n] Richard Porter, of Bayham, co. Sussex, father of Jane, married Jane, daughter of Robert Whitfield, of Worth in the same county. He was fourth in descent from William Porter, of Markham, Nottinghamshire. After his death his widow married Edward Quinby, Esquire, of Titchfield, Hampshire. The Porter arms were sable, three church bells argent, a canton ermine. Crest, a portcullis argent, chained or. Visitation of Kent, 1619 (Harleian Society, vol. 42), p. 155; Berry, Kent Genealogies, p. 321; Waters, Gleanings, p. 1436 (wills of Edward and Jane Quinby).

[o] Dugdale, op. cit. p. 690.

[p] Pemberton, op. cit. p. 39.

Children:

i. JANE, bapt. 5 Oct. 1600.
ii. URSULA, bapt. 19 Jan. 1601–2; bur. Apr. 1602.
iii. LUCY, bapt. 12 Jan. 1602–3.
iv. WILLIAM, bapt. 30 Dec. 1604.
v. THOMAS, bur. 21 Apr. 1695 (an infant).
vi. URSULA, bapt. 26 Oct. 1606.
vii. MARY, bapt. 25 Oct. 1607; perhaps bur. 12 Oct. 1616.
viii. EDMOND, the emigrant, b. 1608; bapt. 15 Oct. 1612.
ix. ANN, bapt. 5 Sept. 1609.
x. JOHN, bapt. 13 Apr. 1611.
xi. ELIZABETH, bapt. 18 Aug. 1616.
xii. RUTH, bapt. June 1618.

Thomas who died in 1558, Thomas who died in 1574, William, and the latter's son Edmond, are all styled gentlemen in the records of their time.

The name seems originally to have been Hawe; at any rate it is frequently so written in the ancient records, but the emigrant and his descendants and his ancestors, at least so far back as his great-grandfather Thomas, uniformly wrote it Hawes. The name was widely distributed in England in the early part of the 17th century, and appears not only in Warwickshire and adjacent counties but also in London and neighboring counties, and elsewhere.

Besides Edmond, among the early settlers of Massachusetts were Edward Hawes, who was in Dedham in 1648; Richard Hawes of Dorchester, who came in the *Truelove* in September 1635; and Robert Hawes of Salem, Wenham, and Roxbury, in which last-named town he died in 1666. There is no evidence that these were of kin to each other, and they certainly were not nearly related to Edmond, although it seems not improbable that Richard was of the Warwickshire stock.

Respecting the emigrant Edmond Hawes, it may be observed that Winsor, in his History of Duxbury (p. 81), says the office of constable was one "of high trust and responsibility, and none were elected to it but men of good standing." In fact, in early times, constables instead of being mere peace officers, as now, had various other functions, such as acting as collectors of taxes, as coroners in summoning juries of inquest, and when a call was made for military duty impressing men for the service.

Swift in "Old Yarmouth" (p. 79), speaking of the early settlers, says: "Anthony Thacher, Edmond Hawes, and Richard Sears were certainly men of education and social standing in England"; and (p. 81): "Lawyers were not tolerated in the Colony, but conveyances, wills and other legal writings were executed by Anthony Thacher, Edmund Hawes and John Miller, according to the formulas of English practice."

A school existed at Solihull as early as 1560, when the endowment of certain chantry chapels in the parish church was devoted to the salary of a schoolmaster. Mr. Horne, a graduate of Oxford University, was master during the boyhood of Edmond Hawes, the emigrant, who was no doubt educated in this school, where Latin at that time would have been a principal element in the curriculum.[q]

q The Victoria History of the County of Warwick, vol. 2, pp. 357–60.

HAWES: ADDITIONS AND CORRECTIONS.—Mr. James W. Hawes, 27 West 44th Street, New York City, calls attention to the following changes bearing upon his article, "The English Ancestors of Edmond Hawes of Yarmouth, Mass.," in the REGISTER, vol. 65, pp. 160–4. A full copy of the will of Thomas Hawes * (Thomas, Thomas), shows that on p. 162, l. 22, "Doctor Brainton" should be stricken out and "Walter Chamber" substituted; also, among the list of children, "v. A DAUGHTER, m. DR. —— BRAINTON," should be stricken out, and the next entry should read "v. MARGARET, m. WALTER CHAMBER." On p. 163, l. 29, add "m. before 1619, GEORGE DALBY."

*Pp. 271-275, this volume.

THE ENGLISH ANCESTRY OF RICHARD HAWES OF DORCHESTER, MASS.

By Frank Mortimer Hawes, A.M., of West Hartford, Conn.

Among the sixty-seven passengers who on 19 Sept. 1635 embarked on the *Truelove*, Jo: Gibbs, master, bound from London for New England, were Richard Hawes, aged 29 years, Ann Hawes, aged 26 years, Anna Hawes, aged 2½ years, and Obediah Hawes, aged 6 months, evidently a family group consisting of father, mother, and two young children.* Richard Hawes settled in Dorchester, Mass., was admitted freeman 2 May 1638, and died probably in Jan. 1656/7, as the inventory of his estate was taken 27 Jan. 1656/7.† In addition to the two children whom he brought over in the *Truelove* he had other children who were born in New England.‡

With the meagre information derived from the shipping list, supplemented by New England records relating to Richard Hawes and his children, the contributor of this article labored for years to find the English home of this early immigrant and to learn something of his ancestry and family connections. From the fact that his son Obadiah married into the Humphrey family of Dorchester, which was known to have come from Wendover, in Buckinghamshire, the writer was impressed early with a belief that Richard Hawes probably came from that neighborhood. Accordingly, several years ago, numerous wills by testators named Hawes (with various spellings of the name), registered or filed in the Archdeaconry Court of Bucks and now preserved in the Principal Registry of Probate, at Somerset House, London, were examined, down to 1650, but without satisfactory results. Many men bearing the name of Richard Hawes lived in England in the first half of the seventeenth century; and the writer has to confess that he often pinned his faith on one Richard after another, and indeed, at one time, was very sure that a certain Richard Hawes of Ipswich, co. Suffolk, born in 1606, of the right age, therefore, to be the passenger in the *Truelove* in 1635, and apparently, from the evidence of his mother's will, living in America in 1642, must be the object of his search.§ But an examination of the Bishop's Transcripts of the registers of several Bucks parishes, in the Bodleian Library at Oxford, led to the discovery, among a number of Hawes entries in the transcripts of the registers of Great Missenden, of the baptismal records of the two children who came over with their parents in the *Truelove*, namely, Anne, daughter of Richard and An Hawes, baptized 17 Dec. 1632, and Obadiah, son of Richard and Anne Hawes, baptized 25 Mar. 1635; and recently wills in the Archdeaconry of Bucks later than 1650 have been searched and the

---

*Cf. Drake's Founders of New England, pp. 42–43 (originally published in the Register, vol. 14, in the issue for Oct. 1860), and Hotten's Original Lists, p. 131.
†Savage's Genealogical Dictionary, vol. 2, p. 380, and Register, vol. 11, p. 342.
‡Cf. Savage's Genealogical Dictionary, vol. 2, pp. 379–380.
§Time and further research may show that Richard Hawes of Ipswich was the progenitor of the Virginia line of Hawes.

will of a Richard Hawes of Great Missenden, husbandman, dated 9 Sept. 1665, has been found, which contains bequests to the testator's grandchildren Obadias Hawes and Hana Hawes in New England and to other grandchildren there, and is clearly the will of the father of Richard Hawes of Dorchester, Mass., who, it will be recalled, had died not later than 27 Jan. 1656/7.

In the present article abstracts are given of thirty-nine wills of the sixteenth and seventeenth centuries, in which information about the family connections and ancestry of Richard Hawes of Dorchester, Mass., must be sought; and these wills are followed by records of baptisms, marriages, and burials of persons named Hawes and of some of other surnames — all, with a few exceptions, earlier than the middle of the seventeenth century, found in the registers of various parishes in Buckinghamshire. On these wills and parish-register entries a pedigree has been based, which sets forth, in the usual genealogical form, the probable ancestry of the Dorchester settler.

From Probate Records*

1. The Will of John Hawys of Farnham Royal [co. Bucks] [undated]. To be buried in the Church of our Blessed Lady of Fernham Royal. To the high altar of the said Fernham 4d. To the Mother Church of Lincoln 2d. I will that there be "bakyn" at my burial half a quarter of wheat, and that half a quarter of malt be "benyd" at my said burial, and as much of each to be bestowed at the "month mynd." I will that there be bestowed at the "twelvemonth mynd" half a quarter of wheat "bakyn" in bread and half a quarter of malt "bened" also, to be bestowed among the poor folk. I will my executors do bestow yearly for the space of six years on the highways the sum of 13s. 4d. in Burnham and Fernham where is most need. To my sister's son a cow. To my sister and her son, to each a ewe and lamb. To my goddaughter which is my kinswoman a ewe and a lamb. To every godchild I have besides a ewe sheep. I will that John London be relieved of his yearly rent, 6s. 8d., and that William Smith pay but yearly for his house 5s. for six years. To each of my servants a ewe. To John Carton, Jr., a sheep. To Robert Norrys a ewe and a lamb, for to pray for me at the altar of Burnham. Executors: John Ponde and Alice, my wife. Overseer: John Eye, and he is to have 3s. 4d. for his pains. I will that John Ponde and my wife have my lease during the time of my years therein said and all my goods unbequeathed, to be divided between them in equal portions, they paying all my debts and funeral costs. Witnesses: Roger Perimar, Rychard Perimar, John Mychell, Jamys Ablem, Robert Norris, priest, Adam Wyntbathen, priest, and others. Proved 9 April 1545. (Archdeaconry of Bucks, original will.)

2. The Will of Benett Hawse of the parish of Great Wycombe, co. Bucks, dated 20 October 1545. To be buried in the churchyard of Great Wycombe. To the high altar for tithes forgotten 4d. To the Mother Church of Lyncolln 2d. To my son George Hawse my best coat, my hose, and my best doublet. To John Bussyll, my kinsman, for his loving service 8s. or one bullock to the value of the same. The rest of all my goods to

*The abstracts of wills given in this article have been abridged somewhat from abstracts made for the contributor by Miss Phemie Smith and Miss L. J. Redstone, both of London. The longer abstracts (except those of the wills numbered 38 and 39), together with abstracts of other Bucks wills by testators named Hawes (with variants), some seventy in all, have been deposited in the Library of the New England Historic Genealogical Society. For convenience in referring to them the abstracts of the wills here printed have been numbered by the contributor.

my wife, Elizabeth Hawse, she to see my debts paid, my children kept, and my body honestly buried. Witnesses: Robert Wade, priest, Wyllm. Awys, clerk and "orgayne player" in the church aforenamed. Overseer: John Greene, my neighbour. Inventory £6. 8s. 1d. Proved 3 December 1545 by the executor named in the will. (Archdeaconry of Bucks, 1546–1550, fo. 83.)

3. The Will of WYLLM. HAWIS, dated 20 October 1549. To be buried in the churchyard of Slapton [co. Bucks]. To the Mother Church of Lyncoln 2d. To every godchild 4d. To John, my eldest son, my best coat, my best shirt, best hose, and my best cape. To Richard, my son, 2 ox bullocks and 3s. 4d. To Thomas, my son Richard's son, 6s. 8d. To John, my youngest son, my best gown, my best hat, a new coffer — the lesser, and 20s. To Jane, my daughter, a red cow, my best cupboard, four pairs of sheets, four platters, a mattress, a blanket, a red coverlet, a bolster, a pan, a pot, and 20s. To Willm. Wellis, son of William Wellys, four bushels of wheat and a heifer. To John Geare a bushel of wheat and one sheep, going in Billington Fielde. To Agnes Dawbery a bushel of wheat. To Jane, my daughter, 6s. 8d. To John Cawdery my old coat, a doublet, and a pair of hose. Richard, my son, and Willm. Wellis, my son-in-law, shall after the decease of my wife have my lease of the mill, "if God do his will by her afore my feris come up." John, my youngest son, shall have part of the land that lieth in Stambrygge feldes with Wyllm Wellis, with the profits and charges together. The residue of my goods to Alis, my wife, whom I make my sole executrix. Witnesses: Robt. Amys, curate, Richard Turney, Willm. Turney, and others. Proved 14 November 1549 by the executrix named in the will. (Archdeaconry of Bucks, 1546–1550, fo. 164.)

4. The Will of THOMAS HAWIES of the parish of Prince's Rysborowe, co. Bucks, yeoman, dated 27 May 1554. To be buried in the parish churchyard aforesaid. To Richard, my son, all my horses, cart gear, and plough gear, and all things belonging thereunto. To Richard's wife all my brass and pewter, saving one little brass pot. I "give her house & all things within the same." To Thomas, the son of Henry Hawies, one quarter of wheat and another of barley and the little brass pot aforesaid. To my daughter Mary a bushel of wheat and another of barley, to be paid her at Christmas. To Henry Cocke of Pen a bushel of malt and another of wheat, to be paid him at Christmas. To all my godchildren 4s. apiece. To Robert Hawies, my son, two bushels of wheat, two bushels of barley, and my best coat. To the mendings of the "hye wayes" 20d. I make Richard, my son, and Alis, his wife, my only executors; and the rest of my goods I give to them, to bestow for my soul's health at my burial as they think good. Overseer: Henry Hawies. Witnesses: Willm. Blike, Henry Hawies, Sir John Stalworthe, priest, Alis Coker, and Agnes Loosley. Proved at Myssenden 3 October 1554 by the executors named in the will. (Archdeaconry of Bucks, 1554–1557, fo. 50.)

5. The Will of WILLM HAWES of the parish of Wingrave, co. Bucks, dated 22 August 1557. To be buried in the churchyard of Wyngrave. To Thomas Hawes, my son, a "maser," five silver spoons, my best feather bed, a cupboard, my best pot, and my best pan. To William Hawes, my son, £10 in money, to be delivered to him at the age of fifteen years, and a cow bullock, to be delivered now for his use and profit. To Alis Hawes, my daughter, £6. 13s. 4d. in money, to be delivered at the age of fifteen years. To Joan Hawes, my daughter, £6. 13s. 4d., as above, and one cow bullock now to her use and profit. To Mary Hawes, my daughter, £6. 13s. 4d., as above, and one bullock now. If either of my said children die

before they marry, such portion is to be equally divided between the survivors. My wife Agnes shall have my house and lands until my son Thomas Hawes attain the age of twenty-one; and then Thomas, my said son, shall have half the crops and half of all other things except household stuff, which I will she have wholly, except such things aforesaid. My wife shall remove no standards about the house or in the grounds, nor shall she fell trees. Sole executors: Agnes, my wife, and Thomas Hawes, my son. Overseer: My brother Thomas. If my said [son] Thomas die before he marries, my son William shall have the "maser," five silver spoons, feather bed, cupboard, pot, and pan aforesaid, and all other things bequeathed to my said son Thomas. And the £10 that is bequeathed to my said son William shall be equally divided between my children. Witnesses: Robert ——— [*illegible*], clerk, Willm. Godden, John ——— [*illegible*], ——— [*illegible*] Yllyng, John Monke, and others. Proved 1557 ——— [*illegible*]. (Archdeaconry of Bucks, 1556–57, fo. 68.)

6. The Will of JOHN HAWS of the parish of Wendover [co. Bucks], dated 20 February 1558 [1557/8]. To be buried in the parish churchyard of Wendover. To the Mother Church of Lincoln 2d. Agnes, my wife, shall have and enjoy all my freehold in Wendover during her natural life, to bring up our children. Sole executrix: Agnes, my wife, to whom I bequeath all my goods, she to dispose them as she shall think meet. Witnesses: Willm. Androw, vicar of Baldwyn, Nicholas Deping, Nicholas Welche. Proved 8 November 1558. (Archdeaconry of Bucks, 1558, fo. 113.)

7. The Will of THOMAS HAWS of Wingrave, co. Bucks, husbandman, dated 30 August 1558. To be buried in the churchyard of Wingrave. To the Mother Church of Lincoln 2d. To the high altar in Wingrave a bushel of wheat. To the church of Wingrave 3s. 4d. To John, my son, £10, when he shall attain the age of fifteen years, and a sheep now, a bedstead, a bolster, a pair of sheets, a blanket, a coverlet, my great pot, and four silver spoons, to be given him at the day of his marriage. To William Haws, my son, £10, at the age of fifteen years, and a sheep now, a mattress, a bolster, a pair of sheets, a blanket, a coverlet, and a pot, to be delivered at the day of his marriage. To Richard, my son, £10 and a sheep now, and a mattress, a bolster, a pair of sheets, a coverlet, a blanket, and a pot, to be delivered at his day of marriage. To Nicholas, my son, £10 and a sheep now, and a mattress, a bolster, a pair of sheets, a blanket, ɩ coverlet, and a pot, to be delivered on the day of his marriage. To Anne, my daughter, £6. 13s. 4d., a mattress, a bolster, a pair of sheets, one tablecloth, a towel, a blanket, a coverlet, a pot, a pan, a cauldron, three platters, three pewter dishes, two saucers, a salt, and a candlestick, at the day of her marriage, and one sheep now. If any of my children die before they marry, any such portion shall be divided among the survivors. My said children shall have, for the space of three years, half of the crop of the land late in the occupation of Benet Sharpe, and their mother shall plough and sow it, so that it bear all manner of charges and pay the rent, and she shall have one land and they the other, and, when it is sold, the money is to be divided among them. Sole executrix: my wife Joane. Overseers: Thomas Sheile and Richard Sheile, and I give them 20d. apiece for my [*sic*] pains. Witnesses: William Newark, W. Godard, Jo. Goodsped, Robt. Godsped, and others. Proved 13 January 1558 [1558/9] by the executrix named in the will. (Archdeaconry of Bucks, 1558, fo. 129.)

8. The Will of JOHN HAWSE of Cyrcot in the parish of Lincelade, co. Bucks, dated 22 January 1561 [1560/1]. To be buried in the churchyard of Lincelade. All my debts shall be paid, and, this done, the rest of

my goods shall be divided into four parts. The best part shall be at the choice of my wife Agnes. Thomas Hawes, my son, shall have the next part. My daughter Isabell shall have the third part. The fourth part shall be equally divided between Joan, my daughter, and Julya, my daughter. If either of my said children die, the other sisters and brothers shall have equal shares of such portion. Executrix: Agnes, my wife. Overseers: William Hawse, John Oveale, Hugh Partrige. Witnesses: Edward Bounker, George Boyes, Roger Lawle, John North. Proved 16 April 1561 by the executrix named in the will. (Archdeaconry of Bucks, 1561–1563, fo. 79.)

9. The Will of HENRY HAUSE of Smalde, in the parish of Sanderton, Bucks, and diocese of Lincoln, dated 17 January 1562 [1561/2]. To be buried in the churchyard of our Blessed Lady of Sanderton. To the Mother Church of Lincoln 2d. To Hugh Hause, my son, a bushel of barley. To ——— [*illegible*] Wynter a bushel of barley. To Agnes Hause, my daughter, a bushel of wheat and another of malt. To Raffe Hause, my son, a bushel of wheat. To William Hause, Sr., a bullock. To John Hause, my son, a red steer and two sheep. To my son William Hause, Jr., a red steer and three sheep. To Joan Hause, my daughter, a red cow and three sheep. To Mary Hause, my daughter, a cow and three sheep. To Helen Wynter a bushel of barley. The rest of my goods to Margery, my wife, whom I make whole executrix. Margery Hause, my wife, shall deliver to the two children of Elizabeth Stevens 20s. Overseers: John Hause and Raffe Hause, my sons, and they are to have for their pains 20d. Witnesses: Sir William Grene, parson, Thomas Ford, Thomas Wingrave. Proved 8 April 1562 by the executrix named in the will. (Archdeaconry of Bucks, 1561–1563, fo. 144a.)

10. The Will of WILLIAM HAWSE of the parish of West Wicombe, co. Bucks, husbandman, dated 26 August 1570. To be buried in the churchyard of West Wicombe. To the poor men's box 12d. All my lands in Bucks and all appurtenances belonging to the same, lying in the parish of Hutchenden, shall remain to the heirs of my body lawfully begotten; and, lacking such heirs, Richard Hawse, my brother, shall have and enjoy the same for the term of his life; and, after his decease, I will that the said tenement in Hutchenden (wherein one John Wright [?] now dwelleth) and all the lands and woods and all appurtenances thereto belonging do remain to William Hawse, the son of the said Richard Hawse, my brother, and to his heirs for ever. The other tenement, with the appurtenances belonging, now in the tenure of said Richard Hawse, my brother, lying in Hutchenden, I give and bequeath to the heirs of my body; but, lacking such, I give said tenement and appurtenances to my brother Richard Hawse for the term of his life, and, after his decease, to George Hawse, son of the aforesaid Richard Hawse, and to his heirs for ever; provided always that, whether I have heirs of my body or not, the said Richard Hawse, my brother, shall dwell in said tenement for the term of his life, paying rent for the same and for the appurtenances thereunto belonging. To Richard Hawse, my brother, a horse worth 33s., a colt coloured grey and being of the age of two years, one old long cart, with the wheels that it standeth on, the best bedstead and the mattress, a bolster, a pair of sheets, a coverlet, and a blanket. To William Hawse, George Hawse, and Henry Hawse, sons of said Richard Hawse, six sheep apiece. To William Hawse, more, a quarter of wheat and a quarter of barley. To Jane Hawse and Catherine Hawse, daughters of said Richard Hawse a quarter of barley, and to either of them a pair of sheets, two pewter platters, and a kettle holding two gallons or thereabouts. To George Hawse and Henry Hawse, to either of them, a quarter of wheat. If I have heirs of my body, then the said Richard Hawse, my brother, and William, George, and

Henry Hawse, his sons, shall not have and enjoy my lands, but they shall have 26s. 8d., to be divided equally among them. To my sister Alice Bowley a quarter of wheat. To my sister Margery Lane a great chest. To my sister Pernell Wingrave my biggest chest. To Edward Shrimpton, my sister's son, a quarter of barley. To —— [illegible], brother of the said Edward, a quarter of barley. To —— [illegible] Shrimpton, the said Edward Shrimpton's brother, a quarter of barley. To Elspeth and Agnes Shrimpton, my sister's daughters, my best bed, saving one, a pair of sheets, a blanket, a coverlet, a new cupboard standing in the house, and two pewter platters standing on the mantel. To Elspeth Shrimpton a pair of —— [illegible] worth 5s., a kettle of two gallons, and two pewter platters. To Albert Bowley a bullock. To Thomas Bowley half a quarter of wheat. To Hughe Bowley half a quarter of wheat and half a quarter of barley. To John Bowley half a quarter of wheat. To my sister Jan Clarke's [?] children, to each a sheep. To Susana, my sister Lane's daughter, a ewe and a lamb. To William Bowley, Jane Bowley, and William Spatkin three sheep. To John Lane, my sister's son, a lamb. To George Dawe a ewe and a lamb. To every of my household servants a lamb. To William West and his two sisters, to each of them a ewe and a lamb. The rest of my goods to Margery, my wife, whom I make sole executrix. Supervisors: Robert Hunt and Davy Toomer. Witnesses: Robert Hunt, Davy Toomer, William Shrimpton, William Wilkinson. Proved 10 October 1570 by the executrix named in the will. (Archdeaconry of Bucks, 1568–1572, fo. 199.)

11. The Will of JOHN HAWES of the parish of Ludgershall, co. Bucks, dated 25 May 1573. To be buried in the churchyard of Ludgershall. To my son John the crop of corn on one half yard that lieth by the house of Mr. Scudamore in Ludgershall, except one half acre of wheat which shall be paid to Alice, my daughter. To Alice, my daughter, one half acre of beans, one calf of this year's weaning, two platters, one pair of sheets, a candlestick, and a bedstead. To John, my son, two cows, a roan colt, a table board, and one platter. To Edmund, my son, my best pot, on condition it shall not be given nor sold away from the name of Hawes, and my best table. To Robert Hawes, my son, two platters and a chafing dish. To Margaret, my wife, all my goods and chattels, moveable and immoveable, not given nor bequeathed, and I make her my sole executrix. If the said Margaret shall marry, she shall pay my three daughters, Agnes, Jone, and Elyn, 20s. apiece at her marriage, to be delivered to them at the age of twenty-three years; if she do not marry, and if any die, the said portion is to be delivered to the survivors, in equal portions. Witnesses: Edward Hoyle, clerk, George Scudamore, Robert Colman. Proved 14 November 1573 by the executrix named in the will. (Archdeaconry of Bucks, 1573–1579, fo. 83.)

12. The Will of THOMAS HAWSE of Prince's Risborough, co. Bucks, dated 5 June 1574. To be buried within the churchyard of Risborough. To Umpfrey Howse, my son, £10, to be paid him by Jone Howse, my wife, my executrix, or her assigns, when he shall attain the age of twenty-four years. If my wife be called away before my son Umphrey shall attain that age, then my wife's executors shall pay the £10 into the hands of Richard Howse, my father, the Elder, of Alscote, and Richard Hawse the Younger, my brother, of Alscote, they to have the use thereof for my said son until he shall come to the said years. To Alice, my daughter, £6. 13s. 4d., to be paid her on her marriage. If said Umphrey die before he attain the age of twenty-four years, said £10 is to remain to my daughter Alice on the day of her marriage. If my said daughter Alice die before the day of her marriage, then said £6. 13s. 4d. shall remain to my wife. If both my children die before the times

appointed for the payment of their money, my said wife Jone shall retain said sums of money. Until these said times my wife Jone shall use said sums of money for the upbringing of said Umphrey and Alice; and, if she die, then said Richard Howse the Elder, my father, and Richard Howse, my brother, shall have the upbringing of my children and the use and profit of said sums. Executrix: Jone, my wife. Overseers: William Chedyngham and Nicholas Opland. Witnesses: Philippe Longford, curate, John Cooke, Thomas Roose. I owe to John Hawse, my brother, 25s. To said John, my brother, seventeen bushels of malt. I owe to said Richard, my brother, 17s. 8d. Proved 5 July 1574 by the executrix named in the will. (Archdeaconry of Bucks, 1573–1579, fo. 48.)

13. The Will of JOHN HAWES of Princes Risborough, co. Bucks, husbandman, dated 21 February 1577 [1577/8]. To be buried in the churchyard of Princes Rysborowe. To Mary, my daughter, twenty of the beeches in the wood called the Seare, to be taken within the space of three years next after my death. To Amye, my daughter, "a cowe being reed" and ten sheep, they to be appointed by my overseers and the Goodman Hawes to keep them one whole year, and she to have the profit of them wholly. To Amye, my daughter, one quarter of barley, to be paid Michaelmas twelvemonth. To Rychard Hasye and Edward Courtney, to either of them a ewe sheep. To Agnes Chaunler, my daughter, a lamb. Thomas Hewes shall have the house in which he now doth dwell for two years more, besides the first grant, and half a bushel of wheat to be paid after harvest. To John Hewes a lamb. To Cleames, my wife, the now parlour, the chamber next it, the loft over the parlour, the bed I now lie in, with all the furniture to the same, a cow, and ten sheep; and Edward, my son, is to keep said cow, a bullock, and twenty sheep, when there shall be so many bred of the same ten sheep, and to keep them as well as his own. If they cannot agree, the rest of my household stuff unbequeathed shall be equally divided between them, except the best pot, the best pan, and the malt mill. She shall have one stock of bees, the young of three hens, every year a hog, to be as well fed as his own, fourteen bushels of wheat, fourteen bushels of malt, the third part of the fruit growing upon the ground, half the "hempe plaet," and six loads of wood yearly to be brought home to her. All the rest of my goods to my son, whom I make my executor. Overseers: Thomas Clarck the Elder of the parish of Hidgendon and Hewe Dorvoell. Witnesses: Thomas Flyed, Thomas Lewees, George Clarcke, with others. Proved 14 March 1578 [? 1577/8 or 1578/9] by the executor named in the will. (Archdeaconry of Bucks, 1578, original will.)

14. The Will of WILLIAM HAWSE of Chipping Wickham, co. Bucks, dated 1 May 1582. To be buried beside my wife's grave or else where it shall please my faithful friends. All the poor and needy people that oweth me any money on the Chalk Score I do forgive them freely by these presents. I give to be bestowed among the poor of this town at my burial seven dozen of bread. To my sister Bridgett Dell 3s. 4d. To John Dell 3s. 4d. and such books as my executor shall be willing to spare — my Bible excepted, [which I give] to my executor and his wife. To Isabell Dell, my servant, 13s. 4d. To Elizabeth Wheler, my goddaughter, 20d. To my godson Christopher Oken 6d. To my godson Richard Rance 4d. The residue of my goods to William Hawse, my brother, whom I make my sole executor. Overseers: Mrs. Pinner, my landlady, and Mr. Timothy, her son. Witnesses: John Gibbons, Jeames Seman, John Dell. Proved 8 March 1582 [1582/3] by the executor named in the will. (Archdeaconry of Bucks, March 1581, original will.)

15. The Will of THOMAS HAWES of Sanderton [co. Bucks], dated 18 March 1582 [1582/3]. To be buried in the churchyard of Prince's Risborough. To my daughter Agnes one cow. To my daughters Mary and Anne all my this year's lambs, to be equally divided between them. If it shall please God to send me a male heir, the table at the Rewes, the great chest at the Rewes, a joined bedstead, and a "lattin" basin shall remain to him as standards to my house at the Rewes; but, if I have no male heir, I give the chest and the basin to my daughter Agnes. To Mary the bedstead. To Anne the table with the frame and the other chest which is here. All the rest of my goods to Jane, my wife, whom I make my sole executrix; and she shall have all the commodities and profits of rights belonging unto me of my house and free grounds at Looseley Rewes for the term of twelve years next after my decease, towards the bringing up of my children. Overseers: John Holland and George Repley. Witnesses: John Holland, George Repley, John Baldwyne, Richard Reynolds. Proved 30 July 1593 by the executrix named in the will. (Archdeaconry of Bucks, July 1593, original will.)

16. The Will of RYCHARD HAWES of Westlington in the parish of Dynton, Doe, or Doyne [co. Bucks], dated 5 June 1587. To be buried in the churchyard of Dynton. To the church of Dynton 3d. My wife shall have the use and profit of my house and all my land at Westlington during her life, if she keep herself unmarried; and at her decease or marriage I give the inheritance thereof to my son Rychard Hawes and his heirs for ever. If my wife do marry, she shall have the guardianship of my son Rychard during his minority and the use and profit of the house and land until my said son be twenty-one years of age; and, if my son die before that age, I give my house and land to Elzabeth, my wife, and her assigns for ever. To Rychard, my son, £4, to be paid when he shall attain the age of twenty-one years, one great brass pot — the biggest I have, my biggest platter, and my biggest oaken coffer. To Elzabeth, my wife, 17s. in the hands of Anthony Hawes, my brother, 20s. in the hands of Harry Towne, her brother, 40s. in the hands of William Clark of Westlington, 20s. in the hands of Francys Pollicot the Elder of Westlington, and 25s. 10d. in the hands of John Stratton of Cuddington. All the rest of my goods, moveable and immoveable, to Elizabeth, my wife, whom I make my sole executrix. Overseers: Edmund Poltur, vicar of Dinton, and John More of Westlington. Witnesses: Edmund Poulter, Francys Pollicot, John Moon, Harry Wallcot. Proved 12 June 1587 by the executrix named in the will. (Archdeaconry of Bucks, June 1587, original will.)

17. The Will of THRUSTON HAWSE of Wendover [co. Bucks], dated 20 November 1588. To be buried in the churchyard of Wendover. To Raffe Hawse, my son, my cupboard and my table, after the death of my wife. The rest of my goods to Raffe Hawse, my son, and Margery, my wife; and they are to pay all my debts and give: to Margery Hawse, my daughter, 40s., to be paid her at the Feast of Saint Michael twelve months next after my death; to John Hawse, my son, 40s., which shall be paid the next Michaelmas after my daughter is paid; to Myhyll [Michael] Hawse, my son, 40s., to be paid the next Michaelmas after that; to Thomas Haws, my son, other 40s., to be paid at the next Michaelmas after that; and to Richard Hawes, my son, 40s., to be paid to him at the Feast of Saint Myhyll next after that. To my wife the one half of my freehold during her natural life, if she do not marry; but, if she marry, my son Rafe is to have it, to him and his heirs, and he is to pay the rest of my legacies. Executors: Raffe Haws, my son, and Margery, my wife. Witnesses: Nicholas Howe, Thomas Wellche. Proved 26 September 1591 by Margery Hawse, relict of said deceased, and Ralph

Hawse, son of said testator, the executors named in the will. (Archdeaconry of Bucks, September 1591, original will.)

18. The Will of RICHARD HAWES of Allscot in the parish of Princes Risborough, co. Bucks, husbandman, dated 14 June 1590. To be buried at the discretion of my executor. To William Hawes, my son, half a quarter of wheat and half a quarter of malt, to be paid to him or his assigns within one year of my decease. To Richard Hawes and Robert Hawes, sons of said William Hawes, to each of them two bushels of wheat and two of barley, to be paid within one year after my death. To Agnes, daughter of said William Hawes, one pewter platter on her day of marriage. To William Hawes, son of the late John Hawes, a heifer, to be used to his best commodity and paid when he cometh to the age of twenty-one years. To Frances, daughter of Humfrey Caternell, one pewter platter, on the day of her marriage. To William Hawes, the late son [sic] of John Hawes, and to Richard Hawes, the late son [sic] of John Hawes, to each one lamb, to be paid with the increase thereof when the said William and Richard shall attain the age of twenty-one years. To Alice Hawes, daughter of Thomas Hawes, one bushel of wheat, to be paid within half a year of my death. To Humfrey, son of said Thomas Hawes, a bushel of malt, to be paid as above. To Amey Hawes, daughter of Richard Hawes, a calf, with the increase thereof, and one pewter platter, to be paid on her marriage day or when she attain the age of twenty-one. To the poor of Princes Risborough two bushels of malt, to be paid immediately after my burial. All the rest of my goods and chattels whatsoever I give to Richard Hawes, my son, whom I make my full executor. Overseer: My cousin Raphe Hawes, also Richard Lowsleye the Younger and William Pettipace. [Signed] Richard Hawes the Elder, his mark. Witnesses: William Pettipace of Long Wick, Richard Lowsley his mark, Robert Hooker, Ralphe Hawes his mark. Proved 17 February 1594 [? 1594/5] by the executor named in the will. (Archdeaconry of Bucks, February 1594, original will.)

19. The Will of JOHN HAWES of Sanderton, co. Bucks, dated 6 August 1593. To be buried in the churchyard of Sanderton. To my son Ralph Hawes my house at Stow, with the home close and the orchard there, to him and his heirs for ever. To my son Henry Hawes, his heirs and assigns for ever, two closes by Stow pitte, which John Winter now holdeth by lease. To my youngest son, John Hawes, his heirs and assigns for ever, a close called Long Croft. If any of my said children die without heirs, his legacy shall remain to the rest, to be equally divided between the survivors; and, if two die without issue, their legacies are to remain to the longest lived. To said Ralph a black heifer and four sheep. To said Henry and said John, to each a heifer and four sheep. To my said sons, Ralph, Henry, and John, to each £30. To Anne Hawes, my wife, my half of the lease for ten years, toward the bringing up of my said children; but, if she marry, it shall remain to my son John, and, if John die, to my son Henry, and, if Henry die, to my son Ralph. Executrix: my wife. To the poor of Sanderton 10s. To the poor of Princes Risborough 10s. Overseers: my brother Ralph Hawes and my brother Willm. Hawes the Younger, with John Winter and Julian Foorde, to help my children to their stocks; and for their pains I give to my brother Ralph 6s. 8d., to my brother William the Younger 6s. 8d., to John Winter 3s. 4d., and to Julian Foorde 3s. 4d. My four overseers shall put forth the sums of money bequeathed to my three children to their use immediately after my death, till they be twenty years of age. If my wife marry and the goods be valued at more than £30, the surplus over and above £30 shall remain to my children and be equally divided

among them. To my servant Margeret Tymberlake a bushel of barley. Witnesses: Thomas Wingrave, John Winter, Julian Foorde, Willm. Bastian, Willm. Hawes the Younger, Richard Reynolds. Proved 24 September 1593 by the executrix named in the will. (Archdeaconry of Bucks, September 1593, original will.)

20. The Will of THOMAS HAWES [undated]. I make my eldest son, Ralph Hawes, my full heir and executor of all my corn and cattle, viz., one cow, nine sheep, three lambs, six hogs. To my son John Hawes one weaning calf. To my son Harry Hawes one cow, being red and white, To my son Ralphe one bed, viz., a mattress, one coverlet — the best saving one, one blanket, one bolster, and two good pairs of sheets. I bind my son Ralphę to keep his mother in that ample manner as he is able, during her life: he shall give her apparel, meat, drink, and house room in which chamber she will. To my son Ralph timber to make him a standing bedstead. To Annys Şaunderson one ewe and a lamb worth 5s. To Elizabeth Saunderson one ewe and a lamb, two years after my decease. To my son Robert Hawes 20s., to be paid to him by my executor within one twelvemonth of my decease. To my daughter Elizabeth 20s., to be paid by my executor on the day of her marriage. To my daughters Phillipe and Isabell 20s., to be paid by my executor within three years of my decease. Witness: Nathanyell Prickett. Proved 28 April 1598 by the executor named in the will. (Archdeaconry of Bucks, 1594–1597, fo. 54a.)

21. The Will of RALPHE HAWES of the parish of Prince's Risborough, co. Bucks, husbandman, dated 1 November 1598. To be buried at the discretion of my executor. To Alice Hawes, my natural daughter, one christening sheet and seven other of my best sheets, four of my biggest platters, two coffers, and a quarter of good, sweet, and clean barley, to be delivered to her at the Feast of All Saints next after my death. To my said daughter £4, to be paid within one month after my death. To Margaret, daughter of my son Thomas Hawes, £5, to be paid to her when she attains the age of twenty-one years. To my servant now dwelling with me a bushel of wheat and a bushel of barley. To the poor of Princes Risborough 10s., to be distributed at my burial. All the rest of my goods whatsoever to Thomas Hawes, my son, whom I make executor. Witnesses: John Rene, clerk, Thomas Rose, Will. Hawes, Humfrey Hawes, John —— [illegible]. Proved 19 March 1598 [1598/9] by the executor named in the will. (Archdeaconry of Bucks, 1597–8, fo. 36.)

22. The Will of WILLIAM HAWES of Lowsley Rowe in the parish of Prince's Risborough, co. Bucks, husbandman, dated 22 November 1600. My body to be given decent burial as seemeth good to my executors. To Thomas Winter of Speene 2s. To Mary and Francis [sic], daughters of said Thomas Winter, to each 12d. To Mary, daughter of Edward Winter dwelling at Speene, 12d. To John and Bennet, sons of said Thomas Winter, to each 12d. To Hugh Hawse, my brother, dwelling at Great Missenden, 4s. To Margret, daughter of my cousin Thomas Hawse dwelling in Risborough, 5s. in money and one lamb. To my brother Thomas Hawes, dwelling at Kingshey, 4s. To John Hawes, now dwelling at Kingston-on-Thames, 13s. To Mary Gowde, my sister, who dwelleth at Brightwell in Oxfordshire, 2s. To —— [illegible] Cutler, my sister, dwelling at Renna near to He—— [illegible, ? Henley]-on-Thames, 2s. To my sister Winter 12d. To the wife of Edward Raunce, dwelling at Bledlowe, which is my goddaughter, —— [illegible]. All my other goods, moveable and immoveable, to Joane Hawse, my wife, whom I make my sole executrix. Overseer: Thomas Hawse, my cousin, to whom I give 2s. for his pains. Wit-

nesses: John Rowe, curate, John Wade, Thomas Hawse. Proved 15 December 1600 by the executrix named in the will. (Archdeaconry of Bucks, 1598–1600, fo. 1.)

23. The Will of HEW HAWSE of Great Missenden [co. Bucks], dated 17 April 1602. To be buried in the churchyard of Great Missenden. To Kynggam that married my daughter Isabell, for money I am indebted to him — which is 20s., my brown cow, and to his wife the oats I have now growing in the "pykett" lying nigh to Randdole's grounds, and to his two sons two lambs, and to his daughter one platter marked with two keys. To my daughter Elline all the rest of my goods and moveables whatsoever, indoors and out, except one sheet which I give to Susan Hore. To the same daughter Elline my pied cow and seven sheep, and to her three children three sheep. To Pettever Hogekins, husband of my daughter Elline, all my corn of what grain soever that I have now growing upon the ground, for his pains and charges he hath been at with me. Executor: the same Pettever Hodgkins. Overseer: Thomas Ives. To Thomas Hawse, son of Henry Hawes, my son, that is deceased, all my land, with the house and other commodities thereto belonging, in the parish of Little Hamden, to his use for ever, after the ending of the lease which I made with one William Black, for the rent of 13s. 4d. per annum; and the said 13s. 4d. shall be paid to Thomas Ives, my overseer, to give it for the space of thirteen years to the three children of Henry Hawse, viz., to Thomas Hawes, Henry Hawes, and Susan Hawes; and after the expiration of the thirteen years the rent of the other six years is to remain in the hands of Thomas Ives, to the use of the eldest son of Henry Hawse, which is Thomas Hawse, whereby, when he cometh to the age of twenty-one years, he may have some stock to begin the world with. The mark of Hew Hawes. Witnesses: Thomas Lorimer, the mark of Thomas Ives, the mark of Edward Edkins, the mark of Thomas Pemerton. Proved 26 October 1607 by the executor named in the will. (Archdeaconry of Bucks, 1607, 52, original will.)

24. The Will of WILLIAM HAWES of Smaleden in the parish of Sanderton, co. Bucks, dated 1 April 1603. To the amending of the church bells in Sanderton 10s., and to the poor of Sanderton a bushel of "maslyne." To John Hawes of Smaledon ten sheep, to be delivered when he shall attain the age of twenty-one years, and my black bullock, the same to be kept until she is a cow by my executor and then to be delivered for the use of said John. To said John my beech coffer; and my executor yearly at shear time ———— [illegible] sheeps' fleeces of wool. To said John £20 in money, at his age of ———— [illegible] years. To Agnes ———— [illegible], my sister-in-law, ten sheep and £10. To Edward Bristowe, my servant, a bushel of barley, one sheep, and 5s. in money. To Margaret East, my servant, one bushel of ———— [illegible]. If said John die before he attain said age, all his legacies and portions bequeathed in this my will shall remain to Ralph Hawes of Smaldoen. To said Ralphe Hawes of Smaldon in the parish of Sanderton, co. Bucks, all my meadow ground in the parish of Chinor, co. Oxford, with appurtenances, which I lately purchased of Thomas Bovingdon, with all the evidences of the same. All the rest of my goods to said Ralphe Hawes, whom I make my sole executor, to pay my debts and charges and to discharge my funeral expenses. Witnesses: John Winter, Julian Foorde, Thomas Pentres. Proved 31 March 1604 by the executor named in the will. (Archdeaconry of Bucks, 1602–1604, fo. 69.)

25. The Nuncupative Will of HENRYE HAWSE of Hutchenden, co. Bucks, tailor, dated 22 February 1603 [1603/4]. Henrye Hawse in his last sickness concerning the ordering of his lands spake these words in the presence of

———— [*illegible*] and to George Hawse, Thomas Aliborne, and Margaret Hawes, his wife, and in the hearing of his children: "I give to my wife my house & lands during her life time & afterwards to Richard my son, & I would have my wife let some part of the lands to pay my debts, & I would have my three daughters somewhat given to them." Proved 26 March 1604 by Margaret, relict of the deceased, to whom commission to administer the goods of the deceased was granted. (Archdeaconry of Bucks, 1602–1604, fo. 67.)

26. The Will of EDMUND HAWSE of the parish of Princes Risborough, co. Bucks, yeoman, dated 1 May 1606. To be buried in the churchyard of Princes Risborough. To my four sons, Thomas, Robert, Edward, and William, to every of them £10, to be paid when they shall accomplish their several ages of twenty-one years. My executor shall pay my daughter Elizabeth £20, as I promised to give with her in marriage, and shall deliver to her within a quarter of a year after my death one cow and six sheep, of the middle sort, one bedstead, one flock bed, two bolsters, two pairs of sheets, one blanket, one coverlet, one kettle, one brass pot, and two pewter platters, all such to be given with her in marriage. Also to my daughter Elizebeth a bushel of wheat. To my four sons, to each one sheep. To Agnes, my wife, one cow, six sheep of the best sort, one bedstead furnished with all kinds of bedding, two coffers, two kettles, one brass pot, one-half of all my pewter, my lesser cupboard in the hall, and a table standing in the other hall (which table shall remain to William, my son, on the death of my said wife). The residue of my goods and chattels, moveable and immoveable, quick and dead, of what kind soever, to John Hawse, my son, whom I make my sole executor. Overseers: my loving friends Robert Lacye and John Darvold, to whom I give for their pains 12d. each. Witnesses: John Hawse, Robert Lacie, John Darvold, Thomas Kinge, Edward Preston. Proved 14 July 1606 by the executor named in the will. (Archdeaconry of Bucks, 1602, 62, original will.)

27. The Will of RICHARD HAWES of Long Wicke in the parish of Prince's Risborough, co. Bucks, diocese of Lincoln, dated 5 August 1610. To be buried in the churchyard. Executor: my wife. To Thomas, my son, a powdering trough, a cupboard, a table and frame and benches, and a "bonteit." To my son Thomas 40s. To my son [Richard] £8. To my daughter Anne £10. To my son Thomas one grindstone and a spindle of yarn. My son Thomas shall have his money at twenty-one years of age, 40s., and my son Richard at twenty-one years of age, £8, and my daughter Anne at twenty-one years of age, £10. If any die before that age, their portion is to be divided equally among the rest of my children. Overseers: Frederick Boler and Henry Boler, to each of whom I give 3s. 4d. My wife shall not fell any trees either for her own use or to sell, [but] she may lop for her use of hedgings and not otherwise, nor may she "top noe trees." Witnesses: Henry Boler, Fredericke Boler, Tho: Hampton, William Abell, William Benson [?]. Proved 30 May 1611 by the executrix named in the will. (Archdeaconry of Bucks, 1611–12, fo. 19.)

28. The Will of NICHOLAS HAWES of Stewkley, co. Bucks, husbandman, dated 10 May 1614. To be buried in the church or churchyard at Stewkly. To the poor of Stewkly 20s., to be distributed at the time of my burial at the discretion of my executors and overseers. To my son and heir apparent, Richard Hawes, all my lands, closes, meadows, pastures, tenements, and hereditaments whatsoever, with the profits and appurtenances thereof, lying in the parish of Stewkly, to have and to hold to said Richard Hawes,

my son, his heirs and assigns for evermore, immediately after the death of me, Nicholas, and of Agnes, my now wife, and not before, unless my said wife marry; if she marry, I will that her term of life in the said premises do henceforth cease, and that my son Richard Hawes, his heirs and assigns, enter thereon and have and enjoy the said premises, every parcel thereof. To said Agnes, my wife, all said premises and appurtenances during her life, if she do so long live a widow and keep herself sole and unmarried. To William Hawes, my son, and to his heirs and assigns for ever, that messuage or tenement, with its appurtenances, wherein one Thomas Hawes doth now or lately dwell, situate in the parish of Wendover, co. Bucks, with the buildings, yards, and grounds to the said tenement adjoining and therewith used and occupied. I also give to said William and to his heirs for ever all that one ground lying in said parish of Wendover, commonly called Over Felde Grove, having Charlwood next unto it on the west part and one lane called Dunsmore Lane on the south, with all the profits and appurtenances at said Grove appertaining. To Nicholas Hawes, my son, and to his heirs and assigns for ever, my messuage or tenement wherein one Widow Tracher did lately dwell, with the appurtenances thereof, situate in the parish of Wendover, with the buildings, yards, and grounds to said tenement adjoining and therewith used and occupied, and also one grove of wood, with all the arable land thereto belonging, lying within the parish of Wendover, in a field commonly called Middle Feilde, with all the profits and appurtenances, lying next Sir Robert Dormers ground and the ground of the heirs of John Kipping, deceased, and the ground of the heirs of Rafe Hill, deceased, on the north part, the close of Rafe Hawes on the east part, the land now or late in the occupation of Thomas Hawes on the south part, and a grove called One Feilde Grove on the west part, to hold all the said grove of wood, with all the arable land, profits, and appurtenances thereto belonging, to the said Nicholas Hawes, my son, his heirs and assigns for ever. Provided always that the said Nicholas Hawes, my son, his heirs and assigns, shall now and ever hereafter have peaceable, quiet, and free ingress and egress and regress and free liberties and passage with men, horses, oxen, carts, and all needful things and all manner of carriages from Dunsmore Lane aforesaid unto and from said ground called Middle Feilde, in such convenient ways as are now most usually used, through the aforesaid ground by me given in this present testament to my said son Willyam Hawes. Provided always I do bequeath to Agnes, my wife, during the time she shall continue a widow, two cartloads of wood yearly out of the aforesaid ground given by me to said Nicholas Hawes and two cartloads of wood yearly out of the ground before given by me to my son William Hawes, provided said Agnes, my wife, shall not cut down nor fell any trees on the ground at Stewkley aforesaid during her widowhood, except it be needful and for the necessary repairing of the buildings in Stewkley. But if said Agnes, my wife, shall claim any dower or thirds out of my said lands, tenements, etc., in Wendover, then my gifts before herein given of my lands, tenements, etc., in Stewkly shall be utterly void, as if the same had not been given. And, to make things clear, said Agnes, my wife, within one-quarter of a year after my death, shall make two releases in the law, one to my son William, the other to my son Nicholas, of, for, and concerning her dower or thirds which by law she may have out of my said lands, tenements, etc., in Wendover, whereby her interest and right of dower may be utterly extinguished. To my son Willyam Hawes and to Nicholas, my son, to each £40. Said money is to be paid them by my son Richard out of the lands, tenements, etc. in Stewkly, £20 being paid to my son William and £20 to my son Nicholas within three years after the death of Agnes, my wife, and the further £20 to William and £20 to Nicholas within the five years next after the death of my wife Agnes. Each payment is to be made at the house where Nicholas Hawes, the testator, now resideth, situate in Stewkley. To my daughter Elizabeth Meade, now the wife of William Meade, for the first three years after my death, a cartload of wood from the land I have herein given to my son Nicholas, and, the fourth year after my death, a cartload from the land I have given to my son William Hawes. To said Elizabeth Meade 20s., to be paid within two years after my death. To her four sons, William Meade, Richard Meade, John Meade, and Nicholas Meade, 20s. each, to be paid to their parents within three years of my death. To Nicholas Hawes, son of said Richard Hawse, 20s. All the rest of my goods and chattels to said Agnes, my wife, whom I make sole executor, to pay my debts, perform my legacies, and perform my funeral in decent and comely manner. If she do marry again, then I bequeath to my three sons, Richard, William, and Nicholas, all my aforesaid goods and chattels, and I do ordain them three to be my executors. Overseers: Mr. Baldwine Sheppard of Litcote and Willyam Meade, my son-in-law, and I give them 5s. apiece for their pains. Witnesses: William Stone, Edward Elliot. Proved 19 October 1616 by Agnes Hawes, relict of the deceased and the executrix named in the will. (Archdeaconry of Bucks, 1615–1617, fo. 46.)

29. The Will of RICHARD HAWES of Alsecott in the parish of Princes Risborough, co. Bucks, husbandman, "being weak & sick in body but in perfect memory," dated 29 March 1627. To be buried in decent manner by my executor. To Cisley, my wife, my newest kettle and one little brass pot, to her use and disposing for ever, and the use of the chamber adjoining the hall, with the bedstead therein standing and all furniture belonging thereto, a long chest at the bed foot, and all other household stuff, to serve her use about my house for her life, and the milk of a cow to her own use and maintenance, while she continues in my house, and one little coffer under the stairs. To Alice, my eldest daughter, £4, to be paid within two years after my decease. To Amey, my second daughter, £6, within one year after my death. To Mary, my third daughter, £4, within three years after my death. To Faythe, my fourth daughter, 20s., within four years after my death, and one table which she already hath in possession. To Henry Hickes, my daughter Mary's eldest son, 6s. 8d. To Richard Hawes, son of Bennett Hawes, 10s. To Amey, my second daughter, one heifer of three years old, to be delivered within three years after my death. If any of my daughters die before receiving their portion, it shall remain to their children, to be equally divided among them. If my daughter Amey die without having any children before receiving her portion, her portion shall remain among her sisters and be equally divided between them. To Ann Gifford, daughter of Robert Gifford, 5s. To Mary Burthell, daughter of John Burthell, 5s. All my other goods and chattels to Benett Hawes, my son, whom I make whole executor. Overseer: Thomas Coker the Elder. [Signed] Richard Hawes, his mark. Witnesses: Thomas Coker, his mark, Robert Aptenn. 1627. [No record of probate, but merely a date: 7 June 1627.] (Archdeaconry of Bucks, 1627, 66, original will.)

30. The Will of JOHN HAWES of Litle Missenden, co. Bucks, yeoman, dated 1 December 1629. To be decently buried in the church or churchyard of Litle Missenden. To the poor of the parish 10s. To my daughter Martha Child, wife of John Child, £10, to be paid by my executor within five years of my death. To Elizabeth Child, daughter of John Child, £5, to be paid within seven years. All the rest of my goods and chattels to Elline Hawes, my wife, and John Hawes, my son, whom I make my executors. My wife shall remain in the house with my son during her life, and she shall not give away any of the goods from my son during her life, neither at her death;

but, if my son shall happen to marry and then his wife or himself shall deal crossly with her, whereby she may in any way be grieved or discontented, then I will and appoint her to take all her part of the goods and chattels afore-mentioned into her own possession and occupation, and I appoint her the loft over the hall to live in and to keep fire in, if she be not willing to live together with my son; but she shall leave all such goods to my son John at her death. Overseers: My son-in-law John Child and Nathaniell Bisco. The mark of John Hawes. Witnesses: Nathaniell Biscoe, the mark of John Child. Proved 23 April 1630 by the executor named in the will. (Arch-deaconry of Bucks, 1630, 50, original will.)

31. The Will of AGNES HAWES of Stukley *als*. Skukley [?], co. Bucks, widow [undated]. To be buried in the churchyard of Stutley [*sic*] aforesaid. To the poor of Stutley [*sic*] 13s. 4d., to be distributed by my executors and overseers. To Nicolas Hawes, son of Richard Hawes, a feather bed, one bolster, one pillow, one coverlid, a pair of blankets which belong to the bed I lie in, three sheets, the hall table and frame, the form by it, and 20s. of money, within a year after my death. To William Hawes, my son, three lands of wheat, three lands of barley, three lands of beans or pease, or £4 in money, at the choice of my executors. To William, my son, also, one cow, one heifer, a hog, one press that hath but one lid, one coffer that stands behind my chamber door, the best bedstead in the loft, and one brass pot. To Agnes Hawes, daughter of my son William, one great platter. To Eliza-beth Hawes and Katerine Hawes a platter and 20s. each, to be paid within two years of my decease. To Elizabeth Meade, my daughter, my best gown, my best red petticoat, my best russet petticoat, my best band, my best kerchiefs, my two best aprons, and my best smock. To William Meade, John Meade, Nicholas Meade, and Thomas Meade, 20s. apiece. To Richard Meade, son of Willyam Meade, £3. To Elizabeth Meade, daughter of Will-yam Meade, a coffer that stands at her grandmother's bed's head, one platter, one tablecloth, one pair of sheets, one candlestick, one saltcellar, and 20s., to be paid within two years of my death. To Katherine Hawes, wife of Willyam Hawes, a mattress that lieth on my bed. To Agnes Tomes three sheets and one blanket. To Elizabeth Burton, daughter of William Burton, one platter. To Enoch Conlye 2s. To Anne Greene, my servant, 18d. To Elizabeth Meade, my daughter, one cow, one brass kettle, one milk "kiver", and £5, to be paid within two years of my death. All the rest of my goods to Nicholas, my son, whom I make my sole executor, to dis-charge my debts and perform my funeral in decent and comely manner. Overseers: William Meade, my son-in-law, and Richard Conlye, and I give them for their pains 2s. 6d. apiece. The mark of Agnes Hawes. Witnesses: Willm. Mead, Thomas Miller. Proved 10 December 1630 [*sic*] by Nicholas Hawes, son and executor named in the will. (Archdeaconry of Bucks, 1632, original will.)

32. The will of MATTHEW HAWES of Great Missenden, in the parish [*sic*] of Bucks, dated 4 July 1632. To be buried in the churchyard of Great Missenden. To my son Thomas Hawes 20s. To my daughter Joan Howes £10, my cupboard, and my best bed, with all that belongeth thereto. All the rest of my goods to my wife, whom I make my sole executrix. The mark of Matthew Howes. Witness: Richard Howse. Proved 17 May 1633 by the executrix named in the will. (Archdeaconry of Bucks, 1633, fo. 123.)

33. The Will of RALPH HAWES of Little Kimble, co. Bucks, yeoman, dated 1 February 1634 [1634/5]. To be buried in the parish churchyard. To Thomas Hawes, my son, the chest I promised him and 5s. To my daughter Agnes Meard 12d. To my daughter Alice Freckelton 12d. John

Hawes, my son, shall, in consideration of the goods I give him, according to his best ability maintain and keep Margaret Hawes, my most loving wife, with meat, drink, and apparel during her life, and, when she is dead, shall see that she is decently interred. To each of my said children's children 12d. To my son John Hawes my cow and all the rest of my goods and chattels whatsoever, and I make him my sole executor. Overseer: Thos. Lineinge of the village and county aforesaid. Witnesses: Stephen Faber, clerk, Margaret Stalham. Proved 21 January 1636 [1636/7] by the executor named in the will. (Archdeaconry of Bucks, 1636, fo. 77.)

34. The Will of NICHOLAS HAWES of Stewkley, co. Bucks, dated 26 September 1636. To my brother William Hawes, his heirs and assigns for ever, all my land and wood in Wendover, he paying to his three daughters fourscore pounds, viz., to Agnes Hawes 40 marks, to Elizabeth Hawes 40 marks, and to Katherine Hawes 40 marks. To my brother Willyam Meade, his heirs and assigns, all my land in Stewkley for the term of twenty years, and after said twenty years I give the aforesaid ground to my cousin Nicholas Hawes and his heirs for ever. To my cousin Agnes Tomes £20. To my sister Elizabeth Meade and all her children £100, to be equally divided between them. To John Cripps 10s. To every one of my godchildren 3s. 4d. each. To my cousins Nicholas Hawes, Agnes Hawes, Elizabeth Hawes, and Katherine Hawes, £4 apiece. To the poor of Stewkley £4. All the rest of my goods and chattels to my brother Willyam Meade, whom I make my whole executor. Witnesses: Willyam Burton, John Cripps, Nicholas Hawes, Willyam Meade, Jr. Proved 15 October 1636 by the executor named in the will. (Archdeaconry of Bucks, 1636, fo. 54.)

35. The Will of JOHN HAWES of Speene in the parish of Princes Risborough, co. Bucks, yeoman, dated 19 May 1638. To be buried at the discretion of my friends. To Henry, my son, my house wherein I now dwell in Speene, with all lands belonging thereto and with all deeds, writings, and evidences to the same belonging, to him and his heirs for ever. To said Henry, my son, my table and frame standing in the hall, the cupboard, the bedstead on which I now lie, in the loft over the hall, a chest standing there also, my cauldron with two rings, and my biggest powdering "troffe." To Agnes, my wife, my house at Speene which I late purchased, with all appurtenances belonging to the same, to her and her heirs for ever. To Agnes, my daughter, 5s., the rest of her portion being already set out. To Francis [sic], my daughter, £20, to be paid at the age of twenty-one years or on her day of marriage. To my daughters Mary and Joane, to each £20, to be paid likewise. To my daughters Elizabeth, Sarah, and Abigaell, to each £25, to be paid likewise. If any of the above children die, such portion shall remain to my executrix. To John, my youngest son, a ewe and a lamb. To Edward Ayre, my godson, my daughter Agnes's son, one ewe and lamb. To the rest of my godchildren, to every one 12d. The rest of all my goods, chattels, and debts, moveable and immoveable, whatsoever, to Agnes, my wife, whom I make sole executrix. [Signed] John Hawes, his mark. Witnesses: Edward Preston, Michaell Pointer, his mark. Proved 25 June 1640 by the executrix named in the will. (Archdeaconry of Bucks, 1640, fo. 55.)

36. The Will of THOMAS HAWES of Wendover, co. Bucks, labourer, dated 30 November 1639. To be buried in the churchyard of Wendover. To my son John the house and land wherein he now dwelleth and 12d. To Elizabeth, my daughter, the house and orchard in which I now dwell, with all the housing hereunto belonging. To Alice, my daughter, the house and land thereto belonging in which Daniel Wells now dwelleth, being two

pittles of land of one and a half acre, more or less; and said Alice is to maintain a mound between the two houses, but Elizabeth, her sister, shall have at the "pitt" water so often as occasion shall serve. Alice, my daughter, shall pay her sister Prissilly, wife of Michaell Clarke, £3, within six months after my death. Elizabeth, my daughter, shall pay her sister Clarke 40s., within six months after my decease. Each of them shall pay a further £5 within a twelvemonth after my death. If the said Elizabeth and Alice refuse, then my daughter Priscilla shall have both houses, her [sic] and her heirs for ever. Elizabeth and Alice, my daughters, shall further pay my daughter Priscilla 5s. yearly for the rest of her natural life. If either die without issue, the house and all thereunto belonging shall remain to the other; and, if both die without issue, my houses shall remain to my rightful heir for ever. To my brother Richard Hawes. To John Gurman, Richard Allen, and the Widow Tomes 12d. each, to be paid by my executors within twelve months of my decease. All the rest of my goods to my executors, to pay my debts and legacies and to discharge my funeral expenses. Executors: my daughters Elizabeth and Alice. Overseers: Jonas Humfrey the Elder and John Humfrey, his son, and for their pains I give them 12d. each. The mark of Thomas Hawes. Witnesses: Jonas Humfrey, Sr., the mark of Thomas Humfrey. Proved 22 May 1640 by the executrices named in the will. (Archdeaconry of Bucks, 1640, fo. 37.)

37. The Will of Thomas Hawes, dated 22 January 1640 [1640/1]. To Thomas, my son, 5s. To his eldest daughter, Mary, 5s. To my son Edward all my working tools and wearing apparel, in consideration he shall pay to his uncle Edward 20s. To Joane, my daughter, whom I make my sole executrix, all the rest of my goods. The mark of Thomas Hawes. Witnesses: Henry Hawse, Thomas Bastian. Proved 13 March 1640 [1640/1] by Joane, lawful daughter of the deceased and sole executrix named in the will. (Archdeaconry of Bucks, 1640, fo. 174.)

38. The Will of Richard Hawes* of Misenden Magna, co. Bucks, husbandman, "being weake but of sound memory," dated 9 September 1665. "I giue . . . to the fiue Children of my Cozens Elizabeh hatch my sisters dagter of the parish of Adnum in the County of hartford six pounds a piece to be paid to them within halfe a yeare after my decease and noe soner except my executor please but if any of [t]hem should happen to die before the money is to be paid then my will is that it should remaine amoung the seruiuors of them. I giue . . . to my grand Child obadias hawes in new England twenty pounds. . . . I give . . . to my grand Child Hana hawes in new England twenty pounds. . . . I giue . . . to the rest of my grand Children in new England ten pounds to be Equaly deuided amongst them. . . . I giue . . . to the poore of great misenden fourty shillings to be paid within halfe a yeare after my decease. . . . I give towards my funerall C[h]arges forty shillings. . . . I giue to my Cozen Ane francis of Adnum in the County of harford my great brasse pan during her life and after her decease I bequeath it to my Cozens Elizabeth hatch aforesaid second sone. . . . I giue to bennet hawes of Alscut in the parish of Prince Risbourow fourty shillings to be paid within halfe a yeare after my decease. . . . I give . . . to my Cozen bennet hawes the sone of bennet hawes abouesaid the sum of forty shillings to be paid within halfe a yeare after my decease. . . . I giue to my sone in Law ten shillings   my will and meaning is that if my grand Children in new England shall within seauen yeares after my decease lawfully demand their legacies giuen aboue mencioned then my will is it should be paid with-

*This testator was the father of Richard Hawes of Dorchester, Mass., who had been dead for more than eight years when this will was made.

out further delay   all the rest of my goods and Chattells I giue . . . to my Cozen Elizabeh hatch aforesaid and of this my last will and testament I make her . . . my sole executor. . . . I giue . . . to mary Collingridg of wendor deane the daughter of william Collingridg the sum of forty shillings to be paid within halfe a yeare after my decease. . . . I giue . . . to thomas honner the sone of John honner of prestwood in the parish of misenden magna the sum of forty shillings to be paid within halfe a yeare after my decease. . . . I giue . . . Elizabeh guilford the wife of John wace [? Ware] of Chesham the sum of twenty shillings   these three legacies where given before my hand was set to this my will." Witnesses: Edward Hoare, Edward Hoare, Jr. Proved 11 January 1665 [1665/6] by Elizabeth Hatch, wife of John Hatch, niece of the testator. (Archdeaconry of Bucks, original will.)

39. The Will of BENEDICT HAWES of Alscott in the parish of Princes Risborough, co. Bucks, yeoman, "beinge sicke & weake in body but of sounde & perfect memory," dated 9 March 1666 [1666/7], 19 Charles II. To be decently buried at the discretion of my executors. To Richard Hawes, my eldest son, my cow called Blackett. To my son Benedict Hawes, his heirs and assigns for ever, all those my two acres of arable land by estimation, be they more or less, with their appurtenances, lying together in the parish of Moncks Risborough, co. Bucks, abutting upon West Meade and adjoining to the land of John Goodchild on the northeast, upon condition that said Benedict Hawes, my son, his heirs or assigns, shall, as soon as conveniently may be, discharge all my debts which I owe unto John Goodchild of Longwicke in the parish of Princes Risborough, yeoman, and unto James Stokes of the parish of Princes Risborough, husbandman, and unto James Lacey of Horsingdon, co. Bucks, husbandman, being all the sum of £31, besides interest due for the same. In case my said son Benedict, his heirs or assigns, shall fail to pay or secure my said debts unto said John Goodchild, James Stokes, and James Lacey within such convenient time as they shall think fit, then my said son Richard and his heirs shall have my said two acres of land, paying my debts aforesaid. To my said son Benedict my black cow called Nancy and my table and frame in my hall where I now dwell. To my daughter Mary Hawes my biggest kettle and my least cupboard. To my daughter Frances Hawes my biggest porridge pot and my biggest cupboard. To my grandson John Hawes my black ewe and her lamb. To my grandson Richard Hawes one ram lamb, being the lamb late of my said daughter Frances. To my grandson Henry Hawes, son of my late son Henry, 13s. 4d. of lawful English money, to be paid unto him at his age of one and twenty years. Executors: said Benedict, my son, and Mary and Frances, my daughters, and I give them all my goods and personal estate unbequeathed, my debts (except the debts aforesaid) and my legacies being paid and my funeral being discharged. Witnesses: William Blicke *alias* Pettipace, Jo. Lacey, scrivener. Proved 10 May 1667 by Benedict Hawes, Mary Hawes, and Frances Hawes. (Archdeaconry of Bucks, original will.)

THE ENGLISH ANCESTRY OF RICHARD HAWES
OF DORCHESTER, MASS.

By Frank Mortimer Hawes, A.M., of West Hartford, Conn.

From Buckinghamshire Parish Registers*

Great Missenden

Baptisms

1575 Thomas Hawes, son of William Hawes, 25 February [1575/6].
1594 Robert Hawes 22 September.
1600 Thomas Hawes, son of Samuell Hawes, 29 September.
1600 Richard Hawes, son of Willam Hawes, 14 December.
1602 Elizabeth, daug[hter] of Mathew Hawse, 24 October.

*The following entries of baptisms, marriages, and burials have been taken, unless otherwise indicated, from the Bishop's transcripts of the registers of these Buckinghamshire parishes which are in the Bodleian Library at Oxford, which have been examined for the contributor of this article by Miss E. G. Parker of Oxford.

1603 Jane Hawse, daughter of Samuell Hawse, 12 October.
1606 Richard, son of Richard Hawes, 2 November.
1608 Susan, daughter of Matthew Hawes, 3 July.
1610 Elizabeth, daughter of Richard Hawes, 3 April.
1631 Frances, daughter of Richard Hawes, 10 July.
1632 Anne, daughter of Richard and An Hawes, 17 December.
1635 Obadiah, son of Richard and Anne Hawes, 25 March.

Baptisms of Children of Other Names*

1604 Jean Cocke, daughter of Richard Cocke, 5 April.
1606 Mary, daughter of John Stevens, 19 June.
1609 Ellinor, daughter of Richard Cocke, 11 March [1609/10].
1611 Luke, son of Reginold Capen, chorister, 27 October.
1620 George, son of Richard Cocke, 16 July.
1623 Thomas, son of Thomas Hewes, 4 May.
1627 Sara, daughter of Richard Cocke, 11 June.

Marriages

1595 Samuell Hawes to Jone Chersley 10 August.
1600 Tho: Honor and Ann Hawse 11 January [1600/1].
1605 John Harding and Elizabeth Howse 10 October.
1613 George Wright and Anne Hawes 27 September.
1628 Richard Hawes and Sibbell Eldridge 29 January [1628/9].
1629 Thomas Gregory and Elizabeth Hawes 22 June.
1632 Richard Hawes and Margrett Baily 12 March [1632/3].
1634 Michaell Clarke and Priscilla Hawes 4 August.
1663 Henry Cock and Ann Haws 12 November.

Marriages of Persons of Other Names*

1608 George Barber and Elizabeth Stevens — February [1608/9].
1611 John Moudie and Elizabeth Capen 25 November.
1620 Thomas King and Elizabeth Saunders 19 June.
1624 Thomas East and Elizabeth Clarke 29 July.
1627 Thomas Stevens and Em Redding 9 October.

Burials

1600 Richard Hawes 20 January [1600/1].
1618 Elizabeth Hawes 13 September.
1619 William Hawes 31 May.
1630 Sibbell, wife of Richard Hawes, 15 June.
1632 Matthew Hawes, husbandman, 11 August.
1632 Maudlin, wife of Richard Hawes, 18 January [1632/3].
1634 Margery Hawes, widow, 13 May.
1664 Margaret, wife of Rich. Hawes, 28 January [1664/5].

LITTLE MISSENDEN

Baptisms

1604 Jane, daughter of Mathew Hawes, 14 October.
1607 Henry, son of Richard Hawse, 13 October.
1610 Susan, daughter of Mathewe Hawse, 10 July.
1628 Martha Hawse, daughter of Richard Hawse, 15 March [1628/9].
1631 Jonas, son of Richard Hawse, [*illegible*] December.
1634 Elizabeth, daughter of John and Elizabeth Hawse, 29 June.
1635 John, son of John Hawse and Elizabeth, his wife, 15 February [1635/6].
1638 William, son of Adiel Hawse and Susanna, his wife, 11 October.

*From the Withington Papers, at the Essex Institute, Salem, Mass.

1638   Joseph, son of Richard Hawse and A[*illegible*], his wife, 4 February [1638/9].

1639   Hanna, daughter of John Hawse and Elizabeth, his wife, 11 June.

Baptisms of Children of Other Names

16—   Thomas, son of John Baldwin, 11 August.

1631   Robert, son of Benjamin Winch, 6 October.

Marriages

1586   Rich. Hause and Susane Dene 10 October.*

1592   John Shrempton and Anne Hause 14 September.*

1599   John Hawes and Ellen Mortmer 22 October.*

1599   Ralfe Hawes and Sibbel, daughter of Rich Haelye, 29 October.*

1612   Richard Hawse and Mary Clarke 1 February [1612/13].

1615   Thomas Baldwine and Ann Hawes 15 May.

1618   Adiell Hause and Elisabeth Hunte 4 January [1618/19].

1628   Richard Hawse and Agnes Stevens 28 April.

1630   Beniamine Winch and Dennis Hawes 28 November.

1634   Henry Fox of Missenden and daughter of Hawes of the same ———.

1635   Adiel Hawse and Susanna Silles, without licence, 8 June.

Burials

1601   Joane Hawes, widow, 7 July.

1612   Susanna Hawse 3 June.

1626   Richard, son of Adiel Hawse, 13 October.

1627   Thomas, son of Richard Hawse, 15 July.

1629   Mary, daughter of Richard Hawse, 23 July.

1629   John Hawse 14 March [1629/30].

1632   Mary, wife of Adiel Hawse, 12 May.

1636   Elizabeth Hawes 13 July.

1639   Elenor Hawse 27 April.

1639   Richard Hawse 18 June.

Burial of a Person of Another Name

1617   Edmund Baldwine 21 March [1617/18].

PRINCE'S RISBOROUGH

Baptisms

1600   Thomas, son of Thomas Hawes, 1 June.

1600   Thomas, son of Thomas Hawes, 16 March [1600/1].

1602   Thomas, son of Richard Hawes, 18 April.

1602   Mary, daughter of Robert Howse, 16 January [1602/3].

1603   [Eli]nor, daughter of Richard Hawes, Alsk[ot], 9 May.

1604   Richard, son of Richard Hawes, 27 December.

1605   Ralphe, son of Thomas Hawes, 24 April.

1608   John, son of Thomas Hawes, 23 October.

1613   Edward, son of Thomas Hawes and Sara, his wife, 13 March [1613/14].

1615   Anne, daughter of John Hawes and Anne, his wife, 27 December.

1616   Mary, daughter of Thomas Haws and Sara, his wife, 29 September.

1617   Henry, son of John Haws and Anne, his wife, 28 September.

1619   Francis [*sic*], daughter of John Hawes, 19 December.

1624   Frances, daughter of Robert Hawes, 21 November.

1625   Richard, son of Bennet Hawes, 15 January [1625/6].

*From Phillimore's Buckinghamshire Parish Registers. Marriages, vol. 7, London, 1911.

1627 John, son of Robert Hawes, 8 April.
1627 Elizabeth, daughter of John Hawes, 8 April.
1627 Elizabeth, daughter of Bennet Hawes, 27 June.
1628 Radulph, son of Robert Hayes, — March [1628/9].
1628 Beniamin, son of Benedick Hayes, — March [1628/9].
1630 Henrie, son of Bennet Hawes, 2 May.
1632 Ann, daughter of Bennett Hawes and Ann, his wife, 21 October.
1637 Faith, daughter of Bennett Hawes, 24 January [1637/8].
1640 Frances, daughter of Bennett Hawes, 24 May.
—— —— of Bennett Hayes 25 October.*

Baptisms of Children of Other Names

1604 Em, daughter of Thomas Coker, 30 September.
1630, Alice, daughter of John Burtholl, 27 February [1630/1].
1637 Elizabeth, daughter of William Burthall, 17 September.

Marriages

1600 Hughe Bampton and Anne Hawes 4 October.
1600 Timothy Kent and Mary Hawes 5 October.
1601 Edmunde Dossett and Joan Hawes 26 October.
1605 Edmunde Haines and Elizabeth Hawes 27 January [1605/6].
1610 Robert Gifford and Alice Hawes 8 October.
1610 Robert Hawes and Joyce Graunt 2 November.
1613 John Hawes and Anne Meade 31 January [1613/14].
1615 Christopher Hicks of Chinnar, co. Oxford, and Marie Hawes of this parish "obtained a licence and were married in this church" 1 May.
1621 Robert Hawes and Clement Hazely 21 January [1621/2].
1624 John Burfold and Frances Hawes 15 April.
1640 Edward Hawes and Hannah Gold 26 November.
1642 Thomas Parslow and Frances Hawes 28 July.
—— —— and Anne Hawes "by bannes" 22 November.*

Marriage of Persons of Other Names

1615 John Haux of this parish and Susan Wingrave of the parish of Bradnam "obtained a certificate to bee married at Bradnam" 7 April.

Burials

1600 William Hawes 2 December.
1602 Agnes, daughter of Humfry Hawes, 17 December.
1605 Humfry Hawes 10 July.
1606 Edmund Hawes 10 May.
1608 The wife of Richard Hawes 19 June.
1610 Richard Hawes, husband of Anne, 21 August.
1620 Thomas Hawes his son 25 January [1620/1].
1627 John, son of Robert Hawes, 21 April.
1628 Beniamin, son of Benedick Hayes, —— [1628/9].
1630 John, son of Thomas Hawes, 24 June.
1630 Mary, daughter of Thomas Hawes, 25 June.
1640 John Hawes 22 April.
—— Thomas Hawes 5[?] April.*
1659 Henery Hawes, a child, 29 September.

Burials of Person of Other Names

1616 Mary, daughter of Richard Loosely of Alscott, 15 February [1616/17].

*Part of this entry is illegible.

1617 An unbaptized son of Robert Heys and Alse, his wife, 3 June.
1618 Jonathan Hays, an infant, 5 August.
1619 An infant, son of Robert Haies, 4 June.

WILL OF MRS. MARGARET HAWTAYNE, DAUGHTER OF LAWRENCE WASHINGTON.

Communicated by GEORGE H. HAWTAYNE, Esq., of Demarara, British Guiana.

THE following notes of the will of Margaret Hawtayne, the daughter of Lawrence Washington, mayor of Northampton and grantee of Sulgrave, an ancestor of the president, may be of interest to those to whom any information as to the Washington family is of value.

Margaret Hawtaine of Easington in the parish Banburie widdowe. Will dated 16 April 1616. To be buried at Banburie. Give to the poor of Banburie ten pounds. Bequests to Mr Wheatley minister of Banburie mr Harries* minister of Hanwell Mr Lea Mr Shorte Mr Lancaster and Mr Cleaver. Her daughter Wallopp and her eldest sonne Oliver Wallopp and her daughters Dorothy Mary and Martha. Her son Edward Hawtaine, her eldest son Henrie and Thomas his eldest son and Mary his eldest daughter.

Legacies to Robert Humphreyes of Banburie William Cooper of Banburie and to Richard Howse Thomas Burrowes and David Lawley servants of her son Henry. Her godson Thomas son of the aforesaid Richard

* "Mr Harries," minister of Hanwell, mentioned in Mrs. Hawtayne's will, was doubtless "Doctor Robert Harris pastor of Hanwell near Banbury in Oxfordshire and afterwards President of Trinity College Oxford to which he was appointed in the fatal year 1648 having before been one of the Assembly of Divines but not by any means an Enemy to King Charles the first as appears from his Sermon before the House of Commons May 25 1642." (Letter of Rev. W. Hawtayne. Rawlinson MS. Bodleian, B 76, 42 b.).

Dr. Robert Harris's son, Dr. Malachi Harris, rector of Farthinghoe, Northamptonshire, had been chaplain to Mary, Princess of Orange, mother of King William III., to whom he taught the English tongue at the Hague in Holland. At his return to England, he was made one of the chaplains of his Majesty King Charles II. His daughter Katharine married the Rev. Wm. Hawtayne, also rector of Farthinghoe, father of the Rev. Wm. Hawtayne, rector of Idelstree, now Elstree, Hertfordshire, and chaplain to the regiment of Welch Fusileers, then (1701) in Germany and Flanders, whose letter is quoted above.

Howse. Her daughter Hawtaine's servants Elizabeth Porter Mary Bull Jane Allcocke

Residue to Henrie her eldest son and sole executor.

Witnesses Henrie Hawtaine Mary Hawtaine Thomas Burrowes David Lawley

Will proved in the Peculiar of Banbury 27 September 1616 by the son Henrie sole executor.

Sum total of Inventory £399. 17. 8.

Margaret Hawtaine, or Hawtayne, was the widow of Gerard Hawtayne, described in the Herald's Visitation of 1574, as of the Ley, and also of Esington, which places are in Banbury, Oxfordshire. He was buried 19 June 1588. He was the son and heir of Edward Hawtaine and Margery, daughter of John Crocker of Hooknorton.

Gerard Hawthen (the name suffers curious changes) sold to Henry Johnson the manor of Sebford Gower (now Sibford Gore) in the parish of Swalcliffe, Co. Oxon, or the capital messuages called the "Bury Farme," where the said Gerard H. then dwelt, they having been conveyed by Robert Sapcott of Aylton, Co. Huntingdon, to one James Longworth, who sold them to Edward Hawthen, gent., father of Gerrard. Chancery proceedings were taken 14 Nov. 1590, by Johnson, to recover the deed from "one Margaret Hawthen widow of Gerard." Margaret, in her answer, avails herself of the ambiguity of the complaint pleaded by Johnson, and points out "that she knoweth not of the sale * * * and understandeth not the bill of Complaint * * for that she standeth seized in one of the Messuages by Henry Johnson's own shewinge, and he showeth not clearly which of them he alledgeth Gerrard Hawthen to have bargained and soulde to him and his Heires nor whether his Heires tooke jointlye as a purchase, or that the feoffement was in fee simple cannot be clearly knowne by the said Bill." How the matter ended I have not been able to ascertain.

In 1588 (July 23) a commission was issued to Edward Hawten, the father, and Thomas Hawten, a creditor of Gerrard Hawten of Banbury, deceased.

Margaret Hawtaine's "daughter Wallopp" was Margery, the wife of John Wallop of Bugbrooke,* Northamptonshire, whose children were five in number. Margaret Hawtayne's son Edward died without issue, and is mentioned in the will of his brother Henry (1618) as "living not in England." Henry Hawtaine, the eldest son of Margaret and Gerrard, described as of Banbury in 1606, claimed to hold of John Bishop of Lincoln, by indenture dated 12 August 1545, made to John Franchishe,† arable lands demesne in the fields of Colthorpe (Banbury), appertaining to the manor of Banbury or Esington Grange, near Banbury * * * from the expiration of a former lease made to Wm. Pearson, 7 March, 6 Hen. VIII. (1515), for the term of 50 years. Henry married Mary, fourth daughter of Sir John Doyley of Chisselhampton, Co. Oxon, and Ursula, sister of Sir A. Cope, Bart.

With the exception of a reference to Close Roll, 3 James I., where it is stated that "Laurence Washington de Soulgrave gent. owes to Thomas Adkyns de Over Winchinton Bucks yeoman fifty pounds 18 Jany 1605," I do not think I have other memoranda relating to the Washingtons. I have, however, a considerable store of notes as to my own family, in which mention is made of many persons whose names are no doubt borne by American cousins of the present day.

Lawrence Washington was admitted to Gray's Inn 1571. Gray's Inn Admission Register, p. 609. The will of Mary Beswicke of Spelmonden, Co. Kent, 8 Aug. 1653, speaks of her grandfather William Beswicke, who married Martha Washington (Waters, p. 39), and of her cozin Mr. Henry Haughton (another variation of spelling), the son of Margaret Washington and Gerrard Haytayne.

---

* By Indenture 30 Nov. 8 James I. (1610) Samuel Maunsell of the Middle Temple London in consideration of £3700 conveyed to Henry Hawtayne the manor of Bugbrooke *als* Budbrooke Northants, and a house called Palmer's house.

† John Franchishe's daughter married Richard Danvers. Their son John Danvers is described as of Colthorpe, Banbury. His son, Sir Wm. Danvers of Colthorpe, was Chief Justice of the Common Pleas, and died 1504.

PEDIGREE OF THE FAMILY OF HAYNES OF COPFORD HALL, CO. ESSEX, ENGLAND.

By A. M. HAINES, Esq., of Galena, Illinois.

[THE pedigree sent us by Mr. Haines is in tabular form. It was "compiled from the Records of the College of Arms, London, and other authentic evidences, by George Harrison, Windsor Herald." We have reduced the pedigree to our usual form for printing genealogies. Drawings of the arms of Haynes of Copford Hall and Harrison, are annexed to the pedigree. The Haynes arms are blazoned in the notes appended by Mr. Haines, of Galena. Those of Harrison are: Az. two bars erm. between six estoiles, three, two and one, ar. *Crest:* A chapeau gu. turned up erm. on either side a wing expanded ar.]

1. JOHN[1] HAYNES, of Old Hold, or Old Holt, in the parish of Copford, co. Essex; died 3 Nov. 1605; m. Mary Mitchell. Children:

  2. i.   JOHN,* of Old Holt aforesaid, and of Copford Hall, co. Essex, which he purchased of Allen Mountjoy, before 1624; m. Mary, dau. and coheir of Robert Thornton, of Hingham, co. Norfolk.

    ii.   MARY, wife of John Barley, of Clavering, co. Essex; left descendants.

2. JOHN[2] HAYNES, by wife Mary, had:

  i.   ROBERT, of Copford Hall, aforesaid, eldest son and heir; d., *s.p.* Aug. 1657.

  3. ii.   HEZEKIAH, of Copford Hall, aforesaid, a Major-General in the Civil Wars, second son, heir to his brother, Robert; entered his Pedigree at the Visitation of Essex, A° 1664; aged about 68 anno 1687; m. Anne, dau. of Sir Thomas Smithsby, of London, Hackney, and of Hampton Court, Middlesex, and widow of .... Bushel, a Turkey Merchant.

3. HEZEKIAH[3] HAYNES, by wife Anne, had children:

  4. i.   JOHN, of Copford Hall, aforesaid, eldest son and heir; aged 7 A° 1664 and 29 A° 1687; m. Mary, dau. of Major Thomas Bowes of Bromley Hall, co. Suffolk.

    ii.   HEZEKIAH, 2d son, A° 1664; died unmarried, æt circ. 24 on his return from India.

  5. iii.   THOMAS, 3d son, Citizen and Mercer of London: entered his Pedigree and Arms at the Visitation of London A° 1687, and was aged 25 years; m. Alice, dau. of John Cooke, of Great Coggeshall, co. Essex.

    iv.   JAMES, student in Christ's College, Cambridge; 4th son; aged 23 A° 1687; died unmarried.

    v.   ANNE, eldest dau., A° 1664, m. (2d wife) John Cox, of The Mount, in Coggeshall, co. Essex, and of Gray's Inn, London, barrister-at-law, sometime of Emmanuel College, Cambridge. Children:

      1. .... [5] *Cox* (dau.), m. Rev. John Harrison, M.A., Vicar of Burnham, co. Essex, who d. about 1750. Children:

        i. Rev. John[6] Harrison, M.A., Rector of Faulkbourne, co. Essex; died about 1797 [whose descendants are given for two generations in Mr. Harrison's pedigree, a copy of which will be found in the library of the New England Historic, Genealogical Society. His grandson, Fiske Goodeve[8] Harrison, to whom descended Copford Hall, was authorized, in 1840, to take the surname Fiske before that of Harrison.]

---

* Governor of the Massachusetts and Connecticut colonies.—ED.

2. *Sarah*[5] *Cox.*
3. *Hester*[5] *Cox.*
  vi. MARY, 2d dau. ; died aged about 12 years.

4. JOHN[4] HAYNES, by wife Mary, had children :
    i. JOHN, of Copford Hall, afsd. ; aged about 5 anno 1687; died *s. p.* 21
        August, 1713 ; m. Sarah, dau. of Rev. Joseph Powell, M.A., Rector
        of St. Mary, Colchester, co. Essex.
    ii. HEZEKIAH, of Copford Hall, afsd.; aged about 3 A° 1687 ; living 1713 ;
        m. Catharine Miles, widow, sister of Serjt. Wynne.

5. THOMAS[4] HAYNES, by wife Alice, had children:
    i. JOHN.   ii. JANE.

NOTES BY A. M. HAINES.

THIS pedigree gives only the descendants of John Haynes, Esq., of Copford Hall, co. Essex (who was afterwards Gov. John Haynes of Mass. and Conn.), by his *first* wife Mary Thornton. He afterwards, in New England, married Mabel Harlakenden, by whom he had several children. See REGISTER, vol. xxiv. p. 124.

The following is an extract (translated) from the Chancery Inquisition post mortem 4 James I., in the Public Record Office, London (Pt. 2. No. 90):

"Inquisition indented taken at Great Dunmow, Essex, 22 April, 4 James I. (1606), to enquire into the death of John Haynes Esq. deceased.

"The aforesaid John Haynes at the time of his death was seized in his demeine as of feeof and in all lands &c. in the several parishes of Little and Great Birch, Messing, Layer Marney, Copford and Rowen Hall, Essex. Also lands in Coddicott, and a messuage called ' Haynes at Mill' in Magna Hadham, Herts and Wedford, Essex.

"And the jurors aforesaid further upon their oath say that the aforesaid John Haynes, eldest son of the aforesaid John Haynes at the time of the taking of this Inquisition was aged 11 years, 11 months and 21 days."

This would make the birth of Gov. John Haynes, 1 May, 1594.

The Governor's only brother, Emanuel, is mentioned in the inquisition.

John Haynes the father died 3d Nov. previous to the date (taking) of the Inquisition, and was buried at Great Hadham, Hertfordshire, at which place the baptisms of his several daughters are recorded in the order in which they are named in his will, which was printed in the REGISTER, vol. xxiv. p. 422. *

The will of Gov. John Haynes can be seen in the REGISTER, xvi. p. 167, and letters of Gen. Hezekiah Haynes, the Governor's son, were printed in REGISTER, vol. xxiv. pp. 124, 324.

The armorial ensigns of the family of Haynes of Copford Hall are:

Argent, 3 crescents, paly of six undée, azure and gules. Crest:—a heron volant, body ppr. beak and legs gules. Motto :—Velis et remis.

This same coat and crest was borne by Richard Heynes of*Reading, co. Berks, a tricking of which is given in Add. MS. 4961, f. 90 (Visitation of Berkshire, 1623), the only variation being, that the beak and legs of the heron in the latter crest are *or* instead of gules and wings argent.

The above Richard Haynes's two sons, *William*[1] of London, and *Nicholas*[4] of Hackney, Middlesex, had the paternal arms and crest confirmed to them, anno 1578. The only variation from the paternal coat and crest as given in Add. MSS. 4961 f. 90, being in the heron holding up one of his feet.

*P. 191, this volume.

The grant or confirmation of these ensigns to the above-named William Haynes, is found in Harl. MSS. 1438 f. 10 B ; and that to Nicholas Haynes, his brother, in Ash. MSS. 840 f. 399, and 858 f. 204.

In the blazon of these coats of arms in Guillim's Heraldry, Morant's and Wright's Histories of Essex, Burke's Heraldic Dictionary, and in several other works in which the above authors have been copied, the *crescents* are given as "*barry* undée azure and gules," *which is an error*, as shown in the text of the original MSS. and in the trickings there given.

The crescents in *all* of the coats referred to in this article are *paly of six undée*, azure and gules, and the crest is a *heron*, and not a stork as given in some works.

The Visitation of London, A° 1687, by Henry St. George, in the College of Arms, marked K 9 f. 148, contains the pedigree and arms of Thomas Haynes, Citizen and Mercer of London, 3d son of Gen. Hezekiah Haynes of Copford Hall, and grandson of Gov. John Haynes of New England.

The arms and crest are the same as those given at the head of this pedigree, with a crescent for mark of cadency, and under the arms the following entry appears in the Visitation :

" The arms produced by Mr Haynes from a seal on the top of a silver Ink horn wch he alledged to be his fathers. In G^r Ed. Bysshe's Visitation of Essex, a° 1664 fo. 89, a Pedigree of Haynes wch pieces to this Entry, but without Arms."

The last pedigree referred to was entered by Gen. Hezekiah Haynes, in 1664, and the inkhorn was his, and the arms engraved thereon is the earliest mention the writer has found of these arms being used by the Copford Hall branch of Haynes.

MATERIAL RELATING TO THE ESSEX FAMILY OF HAYNES.

[Communicated by A. M. HAINES, Esq., of Galena, Ill.]

I.

A Full Copy of the Original Will of Hezekiah Haynes† late of Copford, Essex Dated 20 July 1693   Proved 1 Septr 1693

"In the name of God Amen   I Hezekiah Haynes late of Copford and now of Coxall in the County of Essex Esqre being in health and P'fect Memory blessed be God doe make this my last Will and Testament this twentieth day of July in the yeare of our Lorde God One thousand Six hundred Ninety three.   Imps I humbly comitt my Soule to God hopeing in his free mercy & the all sufficient Merits of Jesus Christ my only Redeem^r for the Salvation thereof   I desire my body may be privately interred & that there be not expended for my funerall above twenty Pounds.   Item as for the temporall Estate wherewith it hath pleased God to blesse me besides what is settled upon my deare Wyfe fore her Jointure & upon my children I dispose thereof as followeth:

As for my Coppehold Estate lying by Grove hill and belonging to the Mannor of Bourchers hall wherein Jeffery Hill did formerly dwell I give unto my grandchild Hezekiah Haynes, Second Son of my eldest Son John Haynes deceased & to his heires forever uppon condition nevertheless that either he, his Mother or Guardian, or the ffeoffees in trust for him doe pay or cause to be payd to my son James Haynes within Six Months after my decease One hundred Pounds of good and lawfull money of England.   But in case my son James dye before the said Six Months after my decease then my will is that he the said Hezekiah Haynes, his mother, Guardian or ffeoffees in trust shall pay or cause to be paid to my son Thomas, Citizen of London, or to his Exor's or assignes the sum of Fifty Pounds only within Six Months after my decease and deliver up to him the said Thomas Haynes his heirs or assignes the bond of Sixty Pounds wherein the said James

---

† Major General Hezekiah Haynes; born 1619; died 1693; buried at Copford Hall 1693, æ. 74.

304

Haynes stood bound to my eldest son John Haynes deceased aforesaid wch shalle in full satisfaction for the hundred Pounds aforesaid. And I desire my loveing Wyfe Ann Haynes to surrender her interest therein (the said Coppihold being taking up for her lyfe as well as my owne) to the said Hezekiah Haynes aforesaid according to this my will.

Item — I give five Pounds to the Poore of Copford to be disposed of at the discretion of my executrix both for time and manner where I desier to to be buried, — In regard I finde soe many of my relations buried there.

Item—I give to my son James One hundred and Fifty Pounds the wch with the hundred Pounds above considering his expenses & charges of his education & Monies that he hath had otherwise wch I think not fitt here to mention will make up his Portion equall'to his brothers Hezekiah & Thomas. As to the securing to Robt Simpson of Bervers five Pounds a year as long as he lives & for the payment of one hundred Pounds to the children of the said Robert I have desired Mr Buxton & Mr Jacob Cox both of Coxall to surrender the Coppihold meadow of Wiston Mill wch was in their hands in trust being aboute foure acres into the hands of John Aldam the Elder of ffoxhearth wch they have done in trust for the payment of Seventy Pounds to the Children of the said Robert Simpson and thirty Pounds more owing me by the said John Aldam of ffoxhearth wch I assigne to make up the said Hundred Pounds. Item—I give unto my deare and loving Wyfe Ann Haynes (who I do hereby appoint my Sole Executrix of this my last Will and Testament renouncing all form^r Wills whatsoever) all my Personal Estate whatsoever to enable her to discharge my debts legacies and funeral Charges in assured confidence if right remaines she will give amongst my children and grandchildren as she shall find them carry it dutifully towards her. In Witness Whereto I have sett my hand and Seale in the p^rsence of the Witnesses hereunto subscribed the day and yeare above written.

HE. HAYNES:

M^d the above written last Will and testament consisting only of one Sheet of Paper was signed sealed Published and declared by Hezekiah Haynes the Testator therein named in o^r Psence & afterward the same Will was Witnessed to in the Pre'nce of the testator by us.

JOHN LIVERMER
JOSOPH CANT
NITTIHILLS

[The original will is written on one sheet of large paper. The seal of wax is not easily describable, being indistinct. Proved by Joseph Gollifer for the executrix.   A. M. H.]

NOTE TO GEN. HEZEKIAH HAYNES'S WILL.

Hezekiah Haynes, a colonel in the British army, 1653, promoted by Cromwell to a Major-General, and appointed Military Governor of the eastern counties, 1655 (see Thurloe's State Papers for his letters). Was M. P. from Lexden Hundred Essex, A.D. 1656–7–8, and one of Cromwell's council.

At the restoration of Charles II., 1659, Gen. Haynes was reduced and imprisoned in the Tower of London, from which he was finally released the 26th April, 1662, by giving bond for £5,000 and two sureties. He was a Presbyterian Elder for the Parish of Birch (magna), and under the "Act of Declaration of Indulgence" of April 2, 1672, his house at Copford was licensed as a place of holding meetings of those of the "Presbyterian Way," and Rev. John Arger was licensed to be a Presbyterian teacher at Hezekiah Haynes's house at Copford Hall.

He was buried at Copford Hall, agreeable to a request in this will. He visited the family at Hartford, Conn., during his father's lifetime (see his letters in REGISTER, Vol. xxiv., p. 735, A.D. 1675–77].

A portrait of the general, said to be the work of Sir Godfrey Kneller, has been handed down in the Wyllys family, in Hartford, for over 200 years. He is represented in armor.

The last member of the Wyllys family possessing it was the wife of Mr. Asher Adams (she was a Wyllys) of Roxbury, Mass. About 1868 it became the property of Mr. Nicholas Brown of E. Greenwich, R. I. Upon his death it passed to his son, the late John Carter Brown, Esq., of Providence, R. I., who kindly permitted me to have it photographed in 1884. A. M. H.

II.

Will of John Haynes of Copford Hall Essex (son of Genl Hezekiah Haines) Dated 5 Septr 1691 Proved 3 Nov 1692 (Died 23 July 1692) by Mary Haynes relict.

"In the name of God Amen. I John Haines of Copford Hall in the County of Essex Esqre."

Imprimis—I give and devise unto Mary my deare and loving wife (over and above the settlement of Copford Hall and the lands thereto belonging and over and above the fferme already settled upon her) all those lands and grounds with the appurts. of about the yearly value of £8 which I lately Purchased and laide the same to the said Hill ferne and are now or late in the occupation of Edward Harman or his assigns for and during the term of the naturall life of the said Mary my Wife and from and after her decease I give and devise the said purchased lands with the appurts. unto my eldest son John Haynes and to the heires Males of his body lawfully to be begotten and for want of such issue I give the said land to my youngest son Hezekiah Haynes (died 15 Nov 1763 & was the last son of the name) and to the heires males of his body lawfully to be begotten and for want of such issue then to the heires of the body of my said sonn Hezekiah Haynes lawfully to be begotton. By settlement aforesaid have assured the said farm called Newers also Pages also the Hill farm with the appurts in Copford, Much Birch, Little Birch & Stannaway, Co: Essex, to Son John Haynes after the decease of my said wife & to his heirs & in default to Hezekiah Haynes & his heirs & in default I give same Hill farm & appurts to "my loving sister Ann Cox [through her the Harrisons obtained Copford Hall which they now possess. Her daughter married Rev. John Harrison."—A. M. H.] the now wife of John Cox Esq & to her heirs & assigns for ever.

My Mannor of ffox hearth also ffox yeard Hall "its rights & appurts. in Co. Essex with ffox hearth Mill" and the advowson and right of Patronage of the Church of ffox hearth aforesaid with the Wood called How wood containing 30 acres in ffox hearth also ffox yeard, Borely Lyston, Sudbury, Great Belchamp, Bulwer & Pantlow, together with the Mennege called Palmers with the appurts in the tenure of Widow Haman or her assigns in Copford, Great Birch, Little Birch & Layer Marney, Co: Essex, to said son John Haynes & to his heirs lawfully begotten, charged however with the payment of £500 to my said son Hezekiah Haynes at the age of 21.

And after the decease of my ffather Gen'l Hezekiah Haynes Esq and Anne his Wife my Mother or the survivor of them, when the said premises shall fall into the possession of the said John Haynes, he the said John shall pay to the said Hezekiah my son until he reaches the age of 21, the sum of £30 yearly for his Maintenance.

And also power is given to said Hezekiah to enter into possession should the £500 & £30 be in arrears and unpaid. For want of issue of the said John Haynes, I give the said Manor of ffoxhearte &c. with Palmers & appurts to son Hezekiah & his heirs & in default to "my loving brother Thomas Haynes Esq. for his life & after his death then to his first son & heirs; in default to each other son & heirs, according to age successively to the fifty son, and in default then to the said Sister Ann Cox & her heirs &c. for her own Proper use forever."

All that Messuage or tenement farm &c. called Grove Hall with the lands & appurts situate lying and being in Soles hart Ruts or near thereunto in the said County of Essex with the lease thereof &c. to my said Wife Mary for her life, and after her decease then to my son John Haynes for his life & to his heirs &c and in default to my son Hezekiah his heirs & assigns.

To said Wife all her jewels, the pictures &c as also "all the furniture in the Chamber at Copford Hall" Residue to said son John Haynes.

Overseers: "John Eldred Esq. my loving uncle" & "John Cox Esq. my loving brother in law" and to each £10. Wife to have the Guardianship of 2 sons until they are 21 and if she die before they reach that age, then "my loving Mother in Law Elizabeth Bowers" to have the charge of them. JOHN HAYNES.

Witnesses   He: Haynes
           Thomas Cox
           Charles Crane
           Thomas Bridge

NOTE TO JOHN HAYNES'S WILL.

Hezekiah Haynes, grandson of Gen. Hezekiah Haynes, and heir of his father John, died 16th Nov., 1763, *s.p.*, aged 80 years. He was the last owner of Copford Hall bearing the name of Haynes. At his death the manor passed to the Harrison family, now represented by Thos. Haynes Harrison, who inherited the estate from his uncle—Fiske Goodere Fiske Harrison—in 1872.

Monuments to his memory are to be seen in Copford church.   A. M. H.

III.

Copy of the last Will of John Haynes, of Stanway, County Essex, Clerk.

I, John Haynes Rector of ye parish of Stanway in the County of Essex, being of pfect memory do make this my last will and testament in manner and forme following Imprs I give and bequeath my soul into the hand of my faithfull Creator firmly hoping to obtaine Eternall life through the alone meritts and satisfaccon of my blessed Redeemer the Lord Jesus Christ As for my body I committ that to the ground to be decently buried in a sure hope of the Resurrection thereof and for my temporall estate wherewith it hath pleased God to blesse me I give after this manner Item I give unto my deare and loving wife Hannah Haynes all my Library of Books with all my goods and chattells whatsoever mony Bonds Bills Debts for by the with all my living stock and Instruments of Husbandry Item I nominate and appoint my said loving wife Hannah Haynes the sole Executrix of this my last will and testamn[t] requesting and humbly appointing my hon[ed] cousins John Eldred of Olivers Esq[r] and John Eldred of Earls Colne Esq[r] and Hezekiah Haynes of Copford Esq to be Assistants to my Executrix and supervisors of this my last will and testament w[h]so-

307

ever I declare this to be my last will and testament In witness whereof I have hereunto set my hand & seale this twenty fourth day of Septemb^r in the two and twentieth year of the reigne of o^r Sovereigne Lord Kinge Charles the second by ye grace & in the year of o^r Lord 1670 John Haynes I own this as my act and deed (the word Sovereigne being first interlined) in the p^rsence of me Thomas Loveddy.

Probatum fuit hoc testum apud colceste vicesimo s̃c̃do die mensis Novembr Anno Dñi 1670 Cor Robto Thompson L L Bacc Sur &c juramt° Hannae Haynes vid Ex^is in dic testo noiat Cui &c de bene &c jurat &c Solve &c.

Fish, 448.

The above will is faithfully extracted out of the records of the Commissary Court of Essex & Herts (Chelmsford Registry), 3 Aug., 1894.

NOTE.—This John Haynes was eldest son of Gov. John Haynes by his second wife Mabel Harlakenden (born at Hartford, Conn.). He graduated at Harvard, in the same class with Increase Mather. He went to England, where he became vicar of Stanaway, near Copford Hall, in Essex, where he died.　A. M. H.

IV.

Family of Emanuel Haynes, Bro. of Gov. John Haynes of New England.

From the Visitation of Herts, 1699, College of Arms, Charles Haynes.

Emanuel Haynes=Winifried, dau.
of Much Hadham, | of Sir Charles
co. Herts. Entered | Chiborne, of
Gray's Inn, 7 Feb. | Messing, co.
1619–20. Ob. 1653. | Essex.

Charles Haynes=Jane, dau. & co-heir of
of Much Hadam, æt. 28 in 1664, | Edward Serenthorpe of
Gent. Marriage license 19 Nov. | Lambeth. Spinster at
1666 (ob. 25) Clerk of Exchequer | her marriage at 28.
of pleas office. Sign document in
1689. See mss. House of Lords.

Charles, son & heir.

NOTE.—The will of John Haynes of Coddicot, Herts., father of Gov. John and Emanuel Haynes, is printed in REGISTER for 1870, Vol. 24, p. 422. I have failed to trace Gov. Haynes's line back of his father John Haynes, who died in 1605.

V

Inscription on a Monument in Coggeshall Church, Essex, England.

On the north wall of the sacrarium is a marble tablet which records quite a family history:

"Here lies (near the remains of his ancestors) the body Mr. William Boys, Gent, oldest son of the Rev. W. James Boys, late vicar of the parish. He married Hester, the youngest daughter of John Cox Esq, and Ann, his wife, who was the daughter of Major General Haynes, of Copford Hall, in this county. John Cox was of Emmanuel College, in Cambridge & of Gray's Inn London, Barrister-at-law, and (late) of Mount Hall, in this parish.

"A gentleman justly esteemed & respected as an eminent & able councellor an honest & upright man and a good Christian.

"Hester, wife of the said Mr. William Boys, departed life May 30th, 1742, aged 53 yrs., & was buried in this church, where by his own desire his remains are also interred after a long life spent in piety and good works; his great care & study in particular was to instruct the poor and ignorant in the knowledge of their Christian duty.

" Witness the many good books he dispersed for that purpose.

" Witness that charitable donation to the parish of G^t Bardfield, to perpetuate the same pious design to the end of the world. Thus lived this good man, & thus he died, July 25th 1768, aged 83 yrs.

" ' Beatus servus ille quem quam
" ' Venerit Dominus ejus invenerit ita
" ' facientem.'

" The Revd. W. John Harrison nephew & executor of the deceased, to testify his respect to his memory, caused this monument to be erected."

The Boys' family arms were a winged griffin rampant passant within a bordure.

VI.

Grave of Governor John Haynes of Hartford, Conn.

Inscription from his gravestone in the Old Parish Burying-ground (1895):

HERE LYETH THE BODY OF Y^e | HONOVRABLE JOHN HAYNES | ESQ^r FIRST GOVERNOUR OF | ye COLONY OF CONNECTICUTT | IN NEWE ENGLAND WHO DYED | MARCH ye 1 ANNO DOM 165¾. |

HERE LYETH THE BODY OF | ye REVEREND Mr JOSEPH HAYNES | MINISTER OF THE FIRST CHVRCH | IN HARTFORD WHO DECEASED | ON THE 24 OF MAY ANNO | DOM 1679 | AGED 38 YEARS.

AND OF Mrs SARAH | HAYNES RELICT OF Mr IOSEP^h | HAYNES WHO DECEASED | NOVEMBER THE 15 ANNO DOM | 1705 IN THE 67 YEAR OF | HER AGE.

VII.

Tablets in Copford Church, Essex, England.

" In a vault near this place lies the body of Hezekiah Haynes Esq. late Lord of this manor and a great benefactor to this church & Parish—a gentleman whose excellent capacity improved by a liberal education was displayed in the virtues of a good life and made him universally esteemed and his death regretted. Faithful to his God A Friend to mankind Just, generous compassionate—He passed through this mortal state with a constant cheerfulness and serenity of mind, and with a quiet conscience resigned his soul into his Maker's hands on Nov. 15th, 1763 in the 80 year of his age."

VIII.

Remarkably handsome and costly marble tablet.

" Underneath lyes the body of Mrs Catherine Haynes, the loving & much beloved wife of Hezekiah Haynes Esq., lord of this manor She dyed 1st. March 1747 aged 57. She was daughter of Owen Wynne Esq. Doctor of Laws. She was first married to Mr. Wm. Miles of Westminster by whom she had no issue, and by her late Husband had only one daughter Adriana Grace who dyed 6 weeks old. Whose person and understanding rendered her agreeable to all her acquaintance and whose well known virtues need no Remembrances and under whose happy influence Domestick affairs were conducted with the greatest prudence and economy."

The Haynes family was very ancient at Much Hadham. We find there, as early as 1523, four persons by the name of *John* Haynes, one of whom is styled "John Haynes at Mill."

"Haynes at Mill" is mentioned in the will of John Haynes at Coddicot.

The baptisms of seven of the sisters of Gov. John in the order named in this will are recorded in the parish register of Haddam, and also the burial of John Haynes of Coddicot, the testator 1605-6.

Gov. John Haynes was 11 years, 11 months and 21 days of age, 22d April, 1606 (4 James I.), Channy Inquisitions Post Mortem, Pub. Record office, London, 1877.   A. M. H.

THE MOTHER OF CHRISTOPHER HELME

By RICHARD LEBARON BOWEN, of Rehoboth, Mass.

Christopher Helme,* the early settler of Warwick, Rhode Island, and the ancestor of the well-known Rhode Island family of Helme, first appears at Exeter, New Hampshire, more than three hundred years ago, where, in 1639, together with Christopher Lawson, William Wentworth (afterwards Elder and founder of the famous New Hampshire family), and the Rev. John Wheelwright, he signed the Exeter Combination. How long Christopher Helme remained at Exeter is not known, but we do know that in 1642 the New Hampshire Plantation came under the rule of the Massachusetts Bay and that the Rev. John Wheelwright, and others, removed to Wells, Maine; also, that Christopher Helme had a lawsuit in Piscataqua, Maine, in 1642, and that in 1644 the court ordered the money sent to him, probably to Warwick, Rhode Island [Libby's *Gen. Dict. of Maine & N. H.*, p. 324]. In 1643 Christopher Helme and Christopher Lawson, apparently cousins, had both left Maine and were located at Boston where the latter, by wife Elizabeth, had a son, Thomas, born 4 May 1643 [*Savage*]. The next we know of Christopher Helme is at Warwick, Rhode Island, where he is one of the witnesses to the Indian Submission Document signed 19 Apr. 1644.

Ever since 1868, when Col. Joseph Lemuel Chester published his account of "The Wentworth Family of England" [REGISTER, vol. XXII, pp. 120–139] it has been generally known that Christopher Helme was the son of William Elmes, Gentleman, of Long Sutton, otherwise Sutton St. Mary, Lincolnshire, who married at Waltham, 1 Sept. 1619, as his third wife, Priscilla Wentworth, baptized at Waltham 14 June 1594, daughter of Christopher and Katherine (Marbury) Wentworth. Colonel Chester says "She was living in 1628, but died some time before 1648, and was buried in the parish church of Sutton St. Mary. Her husband married once or twice, but in his will, dated 21 Mar. 1648/9, directed to be buried near her, and bequeathed five pounds per annum to her son *Christopher*, if he were living . . ." [*ib.* p. 132].

Colonel Chester, and the three authorities on Maine and New Hampshire genealogy, Miss Sybil Noyes, Mr. Charles T. Libby and Mr. Walter Goodwin Davis, and other writers have accepted Christopher Helme as the son of William Elmes' third wife, Priscilla Wentworth, but Mr. Meredith B. Colket, Jr., in his *Marbury Genealogy*,† page 26, calls attention to Maddison's *Lincolnshire Pedigree*, which places Christopher Helme as the son of the first wife, and not the third, and questions his age at the signing of the Exeter Combina-

---

* Christopher Helme, the son of William Elmes, was always known in New England as "Helmes" or "Helme", which latter spelling is now generally used by his Rhode Island descendants.

The writer is indebted to his friend George Andrews Moriarty, F.S.A., for making available to him his vast store of original data on early Rhode Island settlers, without which this article would not have been so complete.

† *The English Ancestry of Anne Marbury Hutchinson and Katherine Marbury Scott* (1936), by Meredith B. Colket, Jr., with the collaboration of Edward N. Dunlop, A.B., M.S.

¹Pp. 654-673, the third volume of this series.

tion if he was the son of the third wife. This pedigree to which he refers is the source of our knowledge of William Elmes, his three wives, and his five children. Genealogists have accepted this pedigree as a source record for everything except the mother of Christopher, whom they assign as the son of the third wife instead of the first as given in the pedigree. Now if we accept nine-tenths of this pedigree as correct, we must also accept the other tenth unless we can prove it to be incorrect. Genealogists have been strangely silent on this point.

As this Harleian Society *Lincolnshire Pedigree*, edited by the Rev. Canon A. R. Maddison, M.A., F.S.A., and published in 1902, is so important, a critical study of the pedigree is necessary. The following is a *verbatim* copy:

"ELMES OF LONG SUTTON.

[MS. C. 23, Heralds' College.   Dodsworth MS. 22, f. 55.
Add. MS. 5822 (Cole).]

ARMS.—*Ermine, two bars sable, each charged with three elm-leaves or.*

John Elmes, from Northamptonshire, = Mary, dau. of William Cockson living at Long Sutton. | of Long Sutton.

William Elmes = Elizabeth, dau. of John Payne (or Baynes) of Long Sutton | of Southwell, co. Notts.

Grisill, dau. of	William Elmes of	Anne Smith,	Priscilla, dau of
Richard Spratt	Long Sutton, aet.	widow, of	—— Went-
of Barney, co.	35 in 1617; aet. 38	Reepham;	worth of Wal-
Norfolk, bur. at	in 1619; bur. at	mar. lic.	tham; bapt.
Long Sutton.	Long Sutton.	9 July 1617,	there 14 June
1st wife	Will dated 21	aet. 30	1594; mar. lic.
	March 1648-9;	2nd wife.	28 Aug. 1619,
	proved 3 April 1649.		aet. 24; bur. at
			Waltham 1 Sept.
			1619 (?). 3rd
			wife.

Thomas	William	Richard	Christopher	Mary, =——
Elmes,	Elmes,	Elmes,	Elmes, doubt-	living Gaps or
1st son,	2nd son,	aet. 21,	ful if alive	1648-9. (?) Gyps."
aet. 30,	aet. 24,	1634.	21 March	
1634.	1634.		1648-9.	

[Lincolnshire Pedigrees, vol. I, *Hart. Soc. Pub.*, vol. L (1902), p. 327.]

As to the importance of this pedigree as source evidence, every genealogist knows how untrustworthy Visitation Pedigrees often are, to say nothing of those compilations * with subsequent additions, and how frequently it is discovered that a man in producing his

---

* Canon Maddison was a careful and excellent antiquary and labored under great handicaps in editing the Lincolnshire Pedigrees for the Harleian Society. These pedigrees are the lifelong work of Mr. Arthur Staunton Larken, Richmond Herald, who died 1 April 1880. He was assisted by his brother-in-law William John, 6th Lord Monson, who in 1828 had married his sister. Both men visited many parishes in Lincolnshire and made extracts from the parish registers; in fact the nucleus of these Pedigrees is in the library of Burton Hall. Much of the data in these pedigrees is written

pedigree for the inspection of the heralds often forgot, omitted, or misnamed, his near kindred. This Elmes pedigree is no exception, and is easy to dissect. The framework is to be found in the great Lincolnshire Visitation of 1634 in the College of Arms, MS. C. 23,* to which has been added data from the Marriage License Records [Dodsworth MS. 22 f. 55] and from William Elmes' will [MS. 5822 (Cole)].

In the 1634 Visitation William Elmes entered only his three adult sons, Thomas, 1st son, age 30; William, 2nd son, age 24, and Richard, age 21, and neglected to enter his two minor children, as only too frequently happened. These two minor children, Christopher and Mary, are found mentioned in Christopher Elmes' will, dated 21 Mar. 1648/9, and have been added to his three children listed in the 1634 Visitation. If there had been only one wife the operation would have been simple, but here was a case with three wives, and the editor had no knowledge of which mother the children belonged to. When Editor Maddison put this pedigree together more than forty years ago, had he left off the line connecting these two children with the first three, as he should have done, his pedigree would have been perfectly truthful and would have saved American genealogists a great deal of trouble. But it must be remembered, however, that there are four books of 1350 pages of these pedigrees and that the editor was handling thousands of wills, pedigrees, and other documents, without much time to concentrate on any one particular pedigree, and the wonder is that there are not more mistakes. The other additions to the original 1634 Visitation Pedigree are easily seen. The entry under Christopher Elmes' name "doubtful if alive 21 March 1648-9" is the editor's interpretation of William Elmes' will leaving a bequest to his son Christopher "if he were living", meaning, of course, that he did not know where he was, consequently whether he was then living or dead. There is only one other Elmes

from memory. Lord Monson had the useful gift of being able, after reading a will over a few times, to afterwards reproduce the chief substance in writing—a most useful gift in days when the slightest attempt to make notes of a will at Doctors' Commons was at once detected and stopped by vigilant officials, and when no Department of Literary Inquiry existed.

After the death of Lord Monson, in 1863, Mr. Larken added largely to the list of pedigrees. He also, on the establishment of the Literary Inquiry Department at Somerset House, made copious abstracts of an immense number of wills. On his appointment as Portcullis Pursuivant, in 1878, he had the enlarged facilities of search in the rich stores of the College of Arms. His previous labors now bore fruit, and he was able to clothe skeleton pedigrees with flesh by means of his parish register extracts and abstracts of wills. With his ample store of abstracts of wills, post-mortem inquisitions, and extracts from parish registers, he was enabled to correct mistakes and fill up what had before been a meagre outline. These Lincolnshire Pedigrees are the result, and the originals are now the property of the College of Arms, having been bought at Mr. Larken's death.

In 1874 Mr. Larken was persuaded to publish this most valuable genealogical work, even to use his own phrase, "with all its imperfections on its head". He writes that his children are busy copying out the pedigrees for the printer. This publishing venture was a failure, and the remaining years of his life were devoted to making the pedigrees more perfect.

This Larken copy, made for publication, came into the possession of Dr. George William Marshall, Rouge Croix, who allowed the Harleian Society to publish it. As editor it remained for Maddison to rewrite the worst-written pedigrees from beginning to end if he wished to ensure freedom from errors. He also took the liberty, besides condensing and altering, of introducing some pedigrees which were not in Mr. Larken's collection. Maddison had ample opportunities of searching the Lincoln Probate Office Wills, and made abstracts of more than 3000, which abstracts he used in these pedigrees [Maddison's Preface to *Lincolnshire Pedigrees*, pp. v–xii].

* The Lincolnshire Visitations for 1666, MS. D. 23, is also in the College of Arms.

family in the four volumes of Lincolnshire Pedigrees, and in this the name Christopher does not appear.

From the above discussion of this Maddison *Lincolnshire Pedigree* it is readily seen that there is no original source authority for definitely placing Christopher Helme as the son of William Elmes' first wife; that without authority he was placed in this position by the editor of this pedigree more than forty years ago on finding the name of this additional son in the will of his father. Therefore this pedigree is of no value in proving which one of the three wives was the mother of Christopher Helme. This clears the situation, in so far as this Lincolnshire Pedigree is concerned, and advances us a step ahead for we are now no longer in the position of having to prove that Christopher Helme *was not* the son of the first wife.

Two things that do stand out in this pedigree are—first, the fact that when William Elmes made his will he left a bequest to his son Christopher "if he were living", indicating clearly that he had been out of touch with him, and had been for some time. At the time this will was made there was a Christopher Helme in New England, who had been first at Boston; Exeter, New Hampshire, 1639; Piscataqua, Maine, 1642; Boston, 1643; Warwick, R. I., 1644, where he was living in 1648/9. If he was the missing son, it is not surprising that the father in England did not know whether or not he was living.

The second significant fact is the name Christopher—especially when we know that this was the name of Priscilla (Wentworth) Elmes' father, brother, two nephews, and of her son; also, that the Christopher Helme in Warwick, Rhode Island, named his first son William, and his second son Christopher, and that there were also Christophers in the following generations.

As William Elmes married his third wife, Priscilla Wentworth, on 1 Sept. 1619, it is quite clear that Christopher, if he was the son of Priscilla, could not have been born, at earliest, before the summer of 1620 and perhaps a year or so later, in which case he would have been perhaps 19 when he signed the Exeter Combination in 1639. Mr. Colket raises this point of age.

It may be pointed out, however, that even if he was under age Christopher Helme might have subscribed to the Exeter Combination as a member of the group of first settlers. His name, together with those of ten other young unmarried men who signed the Combination, does not appear in the allotment of Exeter lands, made between 1639–1643 [REGISTER, vol. XXV, p. 60]. It may be noted that, occasionally, persons under age appear in the records in transactions which we usually associate with persons over 21. For example, Ichabod Sheffield of Portsmouth, Rhode Island, was baptized at Sudbury, co. Suffolk, on 23 Dec. 1630, but he was admitted a Freeman at Portsmouth on 10 July 1648 [REGISTER, vol. LXXVII, pp. 193–4; Records of the *Town of Portsmouth*, pp. 37–38]. John[2] Browne, son of Chad, of Providence, Rhode Island, was granted a 25-acre lot of land on 19 Feb. 1645, when he was fifteen years of age [*Prov. Town Records*, vol. II, p. 29].

From the evidence it would appear that, irrespective of age, the obvious explanation of why neither Christopher Helme's nor Christopher Lawson's name appears in the allotment of Exeter lands is that they did not remain in the town, but had moved away. They were young unmarried men, and were probably in Wells, Maine, in 1642, and we know from *Savage* that they were both living at Boston early in 1643.

The order for the divisions of lands in Exeter was passed in 1639. The record in the original book is without date, and the next succeeding record in the book is 1643, so that the list is of landholders in Exeter, New Hampshire, at some date between 1639 and 1643 [REGISTER, vol. XXV, pp. 60, 61]. In all thirty-two landholders are listed. Eleven of the signers of the compact had no land assigned them, and the reason generally given for this is that they were single men. Of this original family group Rev. John Wheelwright is listed for 80 acres, and William Wentworth for 4 acres and 20 pools —2 shares; both remained in the "Eastward" country. We also know that in 1642 Massachusetts took over the government of New Hampshire Plantation and that Rev. John Wheelwright and his followers removed to Wells, Maine.

A study of this Massachusetts Bay migration to Exeter, New Hampshire, led by the exiled Rev. John Wheelwright, the coadjutor of Anne Hutchinson, at Boston, shows some interesting family connections, and adds another link in the chain of circumstantial evidence connecting the individuals with the Marbury, Hutchinson and Wheelwright families.

Hester Hutchinson (daughter of Edward Hutchinson, and sister of William Hutchinson of Boston, Portsmouth, R. I., &c.) married Rev. Thomas Rishworth of Laceby, co. Lincoln. Their son Edward, named for Edward Hutchinson, came to New England with Wheelwright and William Hutchinson, and he, too, signed the Exeter Combination. Styled here Edward Rishworth, gent; Removed with Wheelwright to Wells, Maine, in 1640; Agent of Gorges to grant land in Wells, between the Ogunquit and Kennebunk Rivers; Selectman, Hampton, N. H., 1651, and of York, Maine (at Cape Neddick) 1656/7. Recorder of the Province of Maine under Gorges and under Massachusetts [cf. REGISTER, vol. XX, p. 360; Libby's *Gen. Dict.* * *Me. & N. H.*, p. 588].

Susanna, daughter of Edward, and sister of William Hutchinson, married at Alford, 21 Nov. 1623, Augustine Storre [REGISTER, vol. ** XX, p. 362]. Mr. Augustine Storre (son of Rev. Thomas Storre, vicar of Bilbsy, co. Lincoln, of which John Wheelwright was later vicar) was at Boston in 1638; was Assistant Ruler of Exeter in 1639, but soon vanishes, probably returning to England [cf. Libby's *Gen. Dict. Me. & N. H.*, p. 666].

Susanna, wife of Edward Hutchinson, and mother of William (husband of Anne Marbury), and of Hester Rishworth, Susanna Storre, and May Wheelwright, died at Wells, Maine, at the home of her son-in-law John Wheelwright, about 164[?] [Libby's *Gen. Dict.*

*P. 452, this volume.
**P. 454, this volume.

Me. & N. H., p. 367]. Her son Samuel also came over, was at Exeter and went to Rhode Island. Her son Edward, at Exeter, also went to Rhode Island, but soon returned to London [*ibid.*].

William Wentworth, Christopher Lawson, and Christopher Helme would appear to be grandchildren of Katherine (Marbury) Wentworth, who was sister of Rev. Francis Marbury, father of Katherine (Marbury) Scott, of Providence, Rhode Island, and of Anne (Marbury) Hutchinson, of Boston, whose husband, William, was the brother of Mary Hutchinson, the wife of Rev. John Wheelwright.

It seems quite clear that this William Wentworth, baptized at Alford, Lincolnshire, 15 March 1615/16; Christopher Lawson, born about 1616; and Christopher Helme, born perhaps about 1620, or a little later, belonged to this family group of Marbury and Hutchinson connections which settled at Exeter with Wheelwright, who besides being a family connection was perhaps their spiritual advisor in Lincolnshire, England. They appear to be all cousins, young men at the time of the signing of the Exeter Combination, and had probably come to New England with John Wheelwright and William Hutchinson, or had joined them here soon after their arrival [cf. REGISTER, vol. XX, pp. 359–67 and vol. XXII, *op. cit.*]. *

An inspection of the accompanying tabular pedigree chart shows that Katherine Marbury, who married Christopher Wentworth, had three children, each one of whom had a son named Christopher, and that two of these Christophers, and William, the brother of the other Christopher, were all in New England. This chart, besides clarifying these complicated family connections, is unique in showing that five of these families were armigerous, a record probably equaled in no other early New England family group.

SUMMARY

As the case stands today the preponderance of evidence points to Christopher Helme having been the son of Priscilla Wentworth, the third wife of William Elmes, as stated by Colonel Chester and other writers, and not of the first wife as stated by Maddison in the *Lincolnshire Pedigrees.*

His given name, Christopher, is the name of his father's third wife's father, brother, and two other relatives (also two other Christophers not shown on the chart), and Christopher of New England names his first son William, after his own father. The name Christopher Helme was not common in England, and there was only one of that name in early New England. In 1648/9 we find a William Elmes in England making his will and leaving a bequest to his son Christopher "if he were living", and at the same time we find a Christopher Helme in New England. There can be no question that the two are identical.

As for the time element, Priscilla Wentworth was married in 1619, and if her son Christopher was born shortly after, there was ample time for the Christopher Helme of Warwick, Rhode Island, to have had four small children, and to have been about 30 years of age when

*Pp. 451-459, this volume.

he died before 19 Dec. 1650. Christopher Helme's first son, William, gave a quitclaim deed at Warwick in 1661 or 1662. If he was of age at that time and his father was born in 1620, it would allow forty-one or forty-two years for his father to have married and have a son 21 years old; a short time for two generations, but not impossible. On the other hand, William was probably not of age, for he was not admitted a freeman until ten years later, 1671, a long time for a young man to wait after attaining his majority.

Moreover, the fact that Christopher Helme, if he was the son of Priscilla Wentworth, must have been under 21 when he signed the Exeter Combination in 1639 is not an insurmountable difficulty, as we have shown that persons under 21 are quite often found engaging in public acts. Mr. George Andrews Moriarty points out that this was especially true if they had attained the age of 18, which in the Middle Ages, and for some time after, was the age at which persons became enabled to do many legal acts, and that only a century before the Commission granting Protectorate powers to Somerset, during the minority of Edward VI, terminated that minority at 18 years of age [*England under the Protector Somerset*, Pollard, pp. 35–36].

We thus find a group of men closely associated in New England, *i.e.*, William Wentworth, Christopher Lawson and Christopher Helme. In England we have a brother and two sisters, *i.e.*, William Wentworth, Sr., Anne (Wentworth) Lawson, and Priscilla (Wentworth) Elmes, children of Christopher and Katherine (Marbury) Wentworth, each of whom has a son named Christopher. We further find that William, Anne and Priscilla have two married cousins, daughters of their mother's brother, the Rev. Francis Marbury, *i.e.*, Katherine (Marbury) Scott and Anne (Marbury) Hutchinson, who together with their husbands and a minister, the Rev. John Wheelwright, the brother-in-law of one of the cousins, Anne (Marbury) Hutchinson, are not only in New England, but are together with the first group in Boston (see chart) and thereafter the first group, William Wentworth, Christopher Lawson and Christopher Helme go to Exeter with the Reverend Wheelwright. All the persons in both groups were banished from Massachusetts for their religious opinions, and one of them, Katherine (Marbury) Scott, was at a later date whipped at Boston for her religious views. We further find in Exeter, closely associated with Wheelwright, Wentworth, Lawson and Helme, two other men who belonged to the group in Boston, and who went with it to Exeter; to wit, Edward Rishworth, nephew of Wheelwright's wife, born Mary Hutchinson; and Augustine Storre, whose wife, Susanna Hutchinson, was also a sister of Mrs. Wheelwright. Lastly, two Hutchinson brothers-in-law of Wheelwright went with him to Exeter, namely Samuel and Edward. There can be no doubt but what this is a family group. Perhaps it was the Marbury blood in Christopher Helme that was responsible for his being disfranchised for his contrary opinions at Warwick, Rhode Island, in 1648.

It must be noted that Canon Maddison in his Elmes pedigree states

CHART SHOWING THE FAMILY RELATIONSHIP OF NINE EXETER, N. H., SETTLERS. OF THIS FAMILY GROUP, SEVEN WENT TO RHODE ISLAND

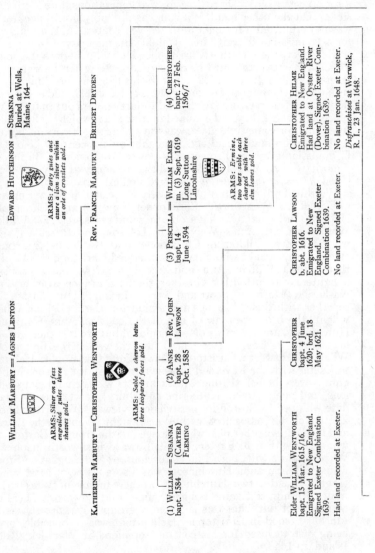

WILLIAM MARBURY = AGNES LENTON

ARMS: *Silver on a fess engrailed gules three sheaves gold.*

EDWARD HUTCHINSON = SUSANNA Buried at Wells, Maine, 164–

ARMS: *Party gules and azure a lion silver within an orle of crosslets gold.*

Rev. FRANCIS MARBURY = BRIDGET DRYDEN

KATHERINE MARBURY = CHRISTOPHER WENTWORTH

ARMS: *Sable a chevron betw. three leopards' faces gold.*

(1) WILLIAM = SUSANNA bapt. 1584 (CARTER) FLEMING

(2) ANNE = Rev. JOHN bapt. 28 LAWSON Oct. 1585

(3) PRISCILLA = WILLIAM ELMES bapt. 14 m. (3) Sept. 1619 June 1594 Long Sutton Lincolnshire

ARMS: *Ermine, two bars sable each charged with three elm leaves gold.*

(4) CHRISTOPHER bapt. 27 Feb. 1596/7

Elder WILLIAM WENTWORTH bapt. 15 Mar. 1615/16. Emigrated to New England. Signed Exeter Combination 1639.

Had land recorded at Exeter.

CHRISTOPHER bapt. 4 June 1620; brd. 18 May 1621.

CHRISTOPHER LAWSON b. abt. 1616. Emigrated to New England. Signed Exeter Combination 1639.

No land recorded at Exeter.

CHRISTOPHER HELME Emigrated to New England. Had land at Oyster River (Dover). Signed Exeter Combination 1639.

No land recorded at Exeter.

Disfranchised at Warwick, R. I., 23 Jan. 1648.

KATHERINE = RICHARD SCOTT
Whipped at Boston, 1658.
Emigrated to New England. At Providence, R. I., 1638.

ARMS: *Silver three catherine wheels sable in a border engrailed gules.*

ANNE = WILLIAM HUTCHINSON
Banished 1638.
Disarmed 1638. Signed the first compact at Portsmouth, R. I., 1638.
Capt. EDWARD, of Boston, Deputy from Kittery, Maine, 1670/1.

MARY = Rev. JOHN WHEELWRIGHT
Banished 1638. Signed Exeter Combination 1639.
Had land recorded at Exeter.

EDWARD
Possibly at Exeter 1637/8. Went to Portsmouth, R. I.; then back to London.

HESTER = Rev. THOMAS RISHWORTH
EDWARD RISHWORTH
Signed Exeter Combination 1639. Of Exeter, Wells, Hampton & York.

SUSANNA = AUGUSTINE STORRE
Assistant Ruler Exeter 1639.

SAMUEL
Grantee of Indian deed at Exeter 3 Apr. 1638. Negotiated with Thomas Gorges for land in Wells, Me., 1641. Went to Portsmouth, R. I.

All the above have been accepted by the Committee on Heraldry of the New England Historic Genealogical Society, and recorded in its Roll of Arms:

1. *Marbury*, Record No. 81. 2. *Hutchinson*, Record No. 42. 3. *Wentworth*, Record No. 44. 4. *Helme*, Record No. 348. 5. *Scott*, Record No. 297.

The above chart is an interesting example of the natural tendency among armigeri to marry in their own social class, *i.e.*, into armigerous families.

William Marbury, the father of Rev. Francis, married Agnes Lenton, probably of Aldwinkle, co. Northampton, where William's father owned property, and where a Lenton family was prominent and had arms granted, 21 Mar. 1584—*Ar. a bend erm. betw. two dolphins embowed and bendwise or.* [*Burke*, p. 601.]

Rev. Francis Marbury married Bridget, daughter of John Dryden, Esq., of Canons Ashby, co. Northampton, by his wife Elizabeth, daughter of Sir John Cope, of Canons Ashby, co. Warwick, Knt. Bridget Dryden's eldest brother, Sir Erasmus Dryden, was created a Baronet in 1619; arms—*Az. a lion rampant and in chief a sphere betw. two estoiles or.* [*Burke*, p. 302.] He was grandfather of John Dryden, the poet laureate, who was consequently Bridget Dryden's grandnephew [cf. REGISTER, vol. XX, pp. 365, 6; *Northamptonshire Families*, by Oswald Barron, F.S.A.].

Rev. Francis Marbury's daughter Katherine married Richard Scott, later of Providence, Rhode Island, who came of a long line of armigerous families [cf. *The Arms of Richard Scott*, by Richard LeBaron Bowen, REGISTER, vol. XCVI (1942)].

A granddaughter of Richard Scott's brother Frederick, Elizabeth Brand, married Sir Robert Kemp, Bart., of Ubbeston Hall, co. Suffolk [*Davy's Suffolk Collections*, British Museum MSS. Add. '19148, P.25640; cf. *The Arms of Richard Scott*, by Richard LeBaron Bowen, R. I. Hist. Soc. Coll., vol. XXXII (1939), No. 3].

Rishworth is not listed in *Burke*, but a Rushworth family had arms—*Ar. a bend betw. as eagle displ. vert. in the sinister chief, and two bedels in the dexter base.* [*Burke*, p. 870.]

A Stoor family had arms—*Ar. a pile gu. on a canton az. a cinquefoil or.* [*Burke*, p. 977.]

that Priscilla Wentworth was married by license, dated 28 Aug. 1619, aged 24 years, and that she died and was buried at Waltham, where her father resided, on 1 Sept. 1619, but *queries* this latter entry. Mr. George Andrews Moriarty suggests that this burial entry refers to the first child of William and Priscilla, rather than to Priscilla herself, and that this view is strengthened by the common custom of the period for a bride to return to her father's house to have her first child, where she could have her mother's care. Colonel Chester distinctly states that Priscilla was alive in 1628, and that she died before 1648 when her husband made his will, and he further states that in that will Christopher is identified as the son of Priscilla. If this is so, it should settle the point as to his mother. Further research is needed to determine the exact wording of the will of William Helme, and also to determine who the Priscilla Elmes was who was buried at Waltham on 1 Sept. 1619. As the case now stands the preponderance of the evidence indicates that the mother of Christopher Helme was his father's third wife, Priscilla Wentworth.

From the original records it seems easy to reconstruct the course of events that drew Christopher Helme from Boston to Warwick, Rhode Island, in 1644. He had just returned from what was apparently, so far as he was concerned, an unsatisfactory venture to the "Eastward" with the exiled Rev. John Wheelwright.

On 12 Jan. 1643 Samuel Gorton, Richard Carder, and nine others had purchased Shawomet (Warwick) from Miantonomi, the Narragansett Chieftain, and for sustaining their rights in the purchase were made prisoners by the Massachusetts Bay authorities and taken to Boston. On 3 Nov. 1643 they appeared before the General Court charged with heresy and sedition and were sentenced to jail. Richard Carder was put in irons and confined in the jail at Roxbury, not to attempt to escape "on pain of death". Finally, on — March 1644, the Massachusetts Government was glad enough to discharge the Gortonists with sentence of banishment on pain of forfeiture of life for coming back.

Richard Carder, one of the supporters of the heresies of Anne Hutchinson and Rev. John Wheelwright, was disfranchised and banished from Massachusetts Bay in 1637, went to Rhode Island, where in 1638 he was one of the eighteen purchasers of the Island of Aquidneck. On 16 Mar. 1641 Richard Carder and three others were disfranchised and their names cancelled from the roll of freemen of Aquidneck. Richard Carder was apparently acquainted with Christopher Helme; at any rate, when Carder was released from the Roxbury jail on — March 1644 and returned to Warwick, Christopher Helme went with him, for the next month, on 19 Apr. 1644, we find them both witnesses to the Narragansett Indian Deed of "Voluntary and Free Submission". From that time on the two men were closely associated in the affairs of Warwick, and after Christopher Helme's death Richard Carder bought his home lot.

Later in the year 1644, Samuel Gorton, Randall Holden, and John Greene went to England to obtain redress for their wrongs suffered from Massachusetts. They took with them the "Indian Submission", witnessed by Richard Carder, Robert Potter, and Christopher Helme, and presented it to Parliament, an account of which is found in the British Record Office, *Calendar of State Papers*, Colonial Series, vol. (1574–1660).

Christopher Helme died at Warwick, leaving a wife, Margaret, and four small children. There seems to be some uncertainty as to the exact time of his death. For more than one hundred years this date has been accepted as "before 19 Dec. 1650", as first stated by Staples in 1835 in *R. I. Hist. Coll.*, vol. II, note p. 160.

A search of the records shows the source of Staples' information. A quit-claim deed dated 13 Jan. 1661, given by "William Helmes of Warwick, eldest son and heir of Christopher Helmes and Margaret Helmes, late of Warwick, deceased", ratifies a purchase "made by Richard Carder, now of Warwick, from my Loving mother Margarett Helmes late of Warwick afore sayd deceased some eight yeares Since or ther abouts . . . which beareth date ye 19 December 1650" [Early Records, *Town of Warwick*, pp. 394, 5]. If this means his mother made the deed about eight years before, the date would be about 1653. In the early Warwick records is found a copy of the original deed, which reads: "This Deede made bearing date this 19 Day December in the year of our Lord Christ 16[torn]* . . . I Margaret Helme widow of Warwick by my Aturney Ralph Earle senr of Portsmouth on Road Iland have sould to Richard Carder . . ." [Original Records, *Town of Warwick*, p. 331].

1. CHRISTOPHER[1] HELME (*William, William, John*) born at Long Sutton, otherwise Sutton St. Mary, co. Lincoln, England, about 1620, son † of William Elmes, died in 1648/9, and his third wife, Priscilla Wentworth, baptized at Waltham 14 June 1594, died before 1648, daughter of Christopher and Katherine (Marbury) Wentworth. Christopher Helme died at Warwick, Rhode Island, probably before 19 Mar. 1650.

He married Margaret ———, who died after 19 Dec. 1650, and before 13 Jan. 1661/2. It may be suggested that her maiden name was Rouse, as she had a son Rouse who was the ancestor of the Rhode Island South County family. Rouse was an early name on the Maine coast. There was a Nicholas Rouse of Wembury, co. Devon, England, who had a house at Casco in 1630; also other families of that name at York, Portsmouth, and Falmouth (Portland).

Christopher Helme (as the name is spelled today) was the progenitor of the Helme family in America, and emigrated to New England,

---

* In 1860 the Town of Warwick Committee employed Henry Rousmaniere to transcribe the town records. In 1926, some sixty-six years later, these original town records were again transcribed for the present printed Warwick Town Records. The Margaret Helme-Richard Carder deed, appearing on page 331 of the original book, in part 2, and on page 224 of the present printed copy of the original volume, is dated "19 day December 16[ ]." That was the way it was read in 1860, and the only way it can be read today. The paper containing the last two digits of the year date is missing today just as it was in 1860. Unfortunately, when the date was transcribed in 1926 it was read as " (56) " and so appears in the present printed Warwick Town Records, which, of course, is not correct.

† Lincolnshire Pedigrees, vol. I, *Harl. Soc. Pub.*, vol. L (1902), p. 327.

probably Boston, previous to 1639. In 1639, with Rev. John Wheelwright, he was one of the founders of Exeter, New Hampshire, where he signed the Combination. He was at Piscataqua, Maine, in 1642, where he had a law suit,* and the Court, in 1644, ordered the money sent to him. He was also at Oyster River (Dover, N. H.), where he owned 500 acres of land which was purchased from him by Valentine Hill, and sold by him in November 1649, then in the possession of Darby Field [*Suffolk Deeds*, vol. I, p. 106]. He was in Boston in 1643 [*Savage*].

Not much is known about the Warwick, Rhode Island, life of Christopher Helme. Austin in his *Genealogical Dictionary of Rhode Island* gives little about this Christopher, and nothing about him previous to 1647. The following is all that the writer can find about him in the original Warwick and other Rhode Island Records:

> On 19 Apr. 1644, Christopher Helme, Robert Potter, and Richard Carder were the three English witnesses to an act and deed of voluntary and free submission to the "chief Sachems, Princes or Governors of the Narragansett" unto the Government and protection of that Honorable State of Old-England. The Indians signing were PESSICUS, his mark, chief Sachem and successor to MIANTONOMI; the mark of that ancient CONANICUS, "Protector of that late deceased Mantonomi, during the time of his non age"; the mark of MIXAN, son and heir of that abovesaid Conanicus; and the marks of AUWASHOOSSE, and TOMANICK, two of the chief councellors of Sachem Pessicus [*R. I. Hist. Soc. Coll.*, vol. II (1835), pp. 158–160].
>
> [No date] "Ordered that Mr. Potter be in Mr. Helmes rome to be layer out of the house lots . . ." [Early Records, *Town of Warwick*, p. 5].
>
> On 1 May 16[ ] "Richard Carder being an Inhabitant of the Towne of Warwicke & having his lot granted to him being about three acres more or lesse bounding Southwest upon Christopher Helme . . . Christopher Helme being received a free inhabitant of the Towne of Warwicke & having a parcell of land & confirmed for a house lott containing six acres . . . bounded Northeast on Richard Carder . . ." [Early Records, *Town of Warwick*, pp. 321, 322].
>
> "Having received our orders (this 8th August) [?1647] we have chosen [among other town officers] Chri Helmes: Sergant" [Early Records, *Town of Warwick*, p. 77].
>
> On 13 Aug. 1647 —"That Ezekiel Holman, Rufus Barton, Jo: Warner & Christopher Helmes are appointed to lay out lots & hiewayes, convenient for the Towne" [Early Records, *Town of Warwick*, p. 78].
>
> "At a towne Metteinge, 23 Jan. 1648, These are to testify that I Christopher Helme doe bind my selfe to answer all damages yᵗ may arise by the ocation of Receaving Robert Andrews † Againe into my Custody after the towne had sent him back to his master & he escaped from ye messenger . . ." [Early Records, *Town of Warwick*, p. 299].
>
> He is the fourteenth signer in a list commencing 23 Jan. 1648, and the first under date of 10 Nov. 1648, of what is apparently a list of inhabitants totaling 48 [Early Records, *Town of Warwick*, p. 73].

* Libby's *Gen. Dict. Maine & N. H.*, p. 324.

† This may be the Robert Andrew of Rowley Village (Boxford), Essex County, Mass., where he was a man of property and position. He also had land in the neighboring town of Topsfield as early as 1654, where as Goodman Andrews he took the oath of allegiance 6 May 1658. In 1661 he was in Rowley; married Grace ———, who d. 25 Dec. 1702. In his will, dated 16 May 1668, proved 2 July 1668, he directs that he be buried at Topsfield. His son Joseph was ancestor of John Albion Andrew, the celebrated Governor of Massachusetts during the Civil War (1861–1865) [*Topsfield Town Records; Essex Quarterly Court Files; Andrews Genealogy*].

"23rd January 1648 Warwick Chri: Helme: having thretened the Towne in general for going about to undermine the Towne his Act testifies the truth of his threats:

"Wee being orderly met in a towne meting doe agree and Conclude yt the said Chri: Helme is wholy deprived of all rite and Intrest in this plantation but only ye wh hee hath in present posetion apropreated, but only ye wh the Towne doth freely condesend to, by permition till hee cane mak forther provition wh wee conclud to bee by the first day of May 1649 and after that day prefixed hee is not to make use of anny comon privilige but as a transgreser liable to anser for contempt therein

"Christopher Helme you are found to [illegible] in ye some of 50 to bee levied in lands goods & chattells to answer at our Next Court of trials held in this Collony to such things as shall then and there bee charged upon you & in the meane time to stand in good behavior towards all his maety Leage people this 30th of Jan 1648

"You [   ] are to become bound to the State of England in the Asumset of tenn pound, to bringe forth the Boddy of Robert Wascote to personall apearance at the next court held at Warwicke" [Early Records, *Town of Warwick*, p. 307].

At the organization of the Colony of the Province of Providence Plantations held at Newport 20–21 May 1647, at which John Coggeshall was chosen the first president under Roger Williams' charter of 1643/4, Warwick, although not mentioned in the charter, was admitted to have the same privileges as Providence. Six commissioners represented each of the towns of Providence, Newport, Portsmouth and Warwick. There is no record of the names of the Warwick commissioners at this first meeting of the General Assembly, but there is a record of Randall Holden of Warwick being elected assistant. Christopher Helme was an important man in Warwick, for at the General Court of Election held at Providence the following year, 16 May 1648, at which William Coddington was elected president, he was the fifth member of the six Warwick Commissioners, of which John Smith,* the chairman, was elected president of the Colony the following year, succeeding William Coddington, who never qualified for the office. [Bartlett's *R. I. Colony Records*, vol. I, p. 210.]

On 23 Jan. 1648 Christopher Helme was deprived of all right and interest in the plantation (see *ante*). Apparently his wife was appointed an Inhabitant in his place, as seen by the following record:

"Ordered 8 Aug. 1648, that for Divers considerations moving the Towne there unto they have accepted of Mrs. Helme to bee an Inhabitant & to have equall priviledge with the rest of the Inhabitants notwithstanding any former order to the contrary" [Early Records, *Town of Warwick*, p. 1].

At the Court "houlden at Warwick from May 26 to the . . . (1649)":

"Ralph Erle being Presented for certayne charges in Speeches; traversseth his inditement and putteth himself uppon the tryall the verdict of the Jury is not guilty

---

* Cf. *The Providence Oath of Allegiance and its Signers, 1651/2*, by Richard LeBaron Bowen, published (1943) by the *Society of Colonial Wars of the State of Rhode Island & Providence Plantations.*

"for Christopher helmes John Greene put out & Mr. Dyer put in fore man

"Christopher Helmes upon the bill presented concerning the death of Rufus Bartin, traverseth his inditement and putteth himself upon the tryall the verdict of the Jury is we finde hime not guilty.

"Christopher helmes upon the bill presented concerning the pretended purchase of some of Warwick land traversseth his inditement and putteth himself upon the tryall the verdict of the Jury is guilty and fine given forty shillings to be payed into the publick tresurie with in xx Days of the next Session of Gene Assemblie; Judgment granted and execution thereupon for the charges of the courte.

"John Warner of Warwick called upon to answer to some charges by him made against Mr. John Smith President it was refferred to Mr. Balstone & Mr. Houldinge & Phillip Shearman to and either of them being bound in an Assumpsit of 100 li apeice to stand to the end these three made" [R. I. Court Records, vol. I, pp. 6, 7].

At this same General Court of Trials held at Warwick, 26–29 May 1649, Christopher Helme was the sixth member of a jury composed of "James Barker, Thomas Lawton, Stukly Wascot, ——— Osband, Tho: Gorton, Christo: Helmes, Ralph Erle, [Richard] Harcut, [Richard] Carder, Robert Potter, [Thomas] Thorniciaft, ——— Greene" [R. I. Court Records, vol. I, p. 7].

At a town meeting, 2 Oct. 1653, "Whereas it hath been formerly unamansly agreed upon that the necke of land joyning to the creeke next that lott granted Mr. Helmes should never bee impropriated. Now we find the Recordes defective herein, therfore we do now order that it shall never bee impropriated but left for a place for landinge for the whole Towne" [Early Records, *Town of Warwick*, p. 133].

"This Deede made bearinge date this 19 day Desember in the yeare of our lord Christ 16[—] Witnesseth that I Margaret Helme widow of Warwicke by my Aturney Ralph Earle senr of Portsmouth on Road Iland have sould to Richard Carder of Warwick that house & lot containinge six acres more or lesse lyinge & beinge in the foresayd towne of Warwick Adioyninge to the house lot of the foresayd Richard Carder Southwest to have & to houlde the sayd house & lot with all the fencinge stuffe theron & wee the foresayde Margarett & Ralph doe acquit our selves of all our right & title therein both of us our Aires or Assignes for ever I say wee the foresayd Margaret & Ralph have sould & delivered the foresayd house & lot unto Richard Carder to bee unto him & his heires for ever firme without molestation in witness wherof wee the sayd Ralph & Margaret doe set to our hands & seales
Sealed and Delivered in the
Present of
Randall Houldon   Ralph Earell
Richard Osborne   Marget Helme"
"The Words South West was Enterlined before the Sealing"
[Early Records, *Town of Warwick*, p. 331].

The town "Layd out, 9 Nov. 1660, to Richard Carder for Mr. Helmes his children six akers layinge on a little necke beyond the horse necke" [Early Records, *Town of Warwick*, p. 372].

"Itt is ordrd, 30 Apr. 1667, by ye purchasers of Shawomett neck that a hygh way of two rodde wide be Layd out A Crose ye Lotts in ye Necke so fare as ye land layed out to Christopher helmes his children on ye west side of ye swampe . . ." [Early Records, *Town of Warwick*, p. 450].

Children * born at Warwick:

i. WILLIAM,² of Warwick and Kings Town, R. I. He took the oath of fidelity at Kings Town 20 May 1671.

"This Indenture made ye 13th day of January: 1661: in the 13th yeare of ye Raine of our Souvraine lord Charles the Second of England ffrance and Ireland king &c witneseth that I William Helmes of warwicke in the Colony of Providenc Plantations in new england being Eldest Sonn and heire to Christofer Helmes and Margaret Helmes late of The Towne of warwick in the Colony afornamed nowe deceased I do by this Present Ratifie Confirme and alowe of A Certaine Purchase made by Richard Carder now of warwicke in the Towne and Collony aforenamed from my Lovinge mother Margarett Helmes late of warwicke afore sayd deceased Some Eight yeares Since or ther abouts, allso I do herby Ratifie and allow of ye deed of Sale made by my Mother Margrett Helmes aforsayd and her cartine Aturny Ralfe Earle ye elder of Poritsmouth in the Colony of Providenc Plantations aforsayd, which beareth date ye nineteenth day of Desember: 1650: father more I doe I doe acknowledge my selfe welle satisfied Contented and Payd by Richard Carder aforsayd for the six acors of land more or lese in the fore sayd deed mentioned together with the house and all apurtenances in the fore sayd deed mentioned, and I do herby thes present for me my heires Executors

"Administrators and Asignes warant the for Sayd deed of Purchase together with the Purchase it selfe to Richard Carder aforenamed his heires Executors Administrators and Asignes for ever in witnes wher of I heave her unto Set my hand and Seale the day and yeare first above written
Sealed and delivered in the:
Present of us whose names: The marke of
are underwriten the word
me over the 24th line being William Helmes
Placed there before the
Ensealing herof
Edmund Calverly
Randall Houlden
John Riss"
[Early Records, *Town of Warwick*, pp. 394, 5].

ii. CHRISTOPHER, Kings Town, R. I. He took the oath of fidelity 19 May 1671; freeman 1673.

iii. SAMUEL, freeman Kings Town, 1673.

iv. ROUSE, d. 17 May 1712; m. MARY ———, d. 9 May 1712. He was of Kings Town, R. I. At a General Court of Trials held for the Colony of Providence Plantations, begun at Warwick 14 Oct. 1662, the following bill of indictment was presented by William Harris to the grand jury against Rowse Helmes, and ten others, "for Entering forceably upon his lands and moeing his meadows."

"Whereas William harris did Indict for forceably Entrey thes severall parsones . . . and Did indict them in his owne name and yett the grand Jury found the bill and they the Indicted partyes Traversed the Indictment and put themselves to Triall by ther peares and a Jury impanelled upon them; but after the Jury weare sworne to bring in A treue verdict the persones Indicted pleaded the Elegallity of the bill of Indictment because not Exhibited in his maiestyes name not with standing which plea the Jury found them guilty and it seemeth Did not mind that plea of waight Saficient to wave such a verdict wheruppon the presoners take themselves illegally condemed and Desier that

* The data for these children, with additions are taken from Austin's *Gen. Dict. of Rhode Island* p. 322.

the Court will susspend Judgment aganst them: being his maieste
is not mentioned to be the offended party or that ther proceeds
wear Contrary to his Crowne and Dignyty but Contrary to the
Complaynnant william harris his minde: The Court are not soe
Cleare to give Judgment one the verdict. Especially Conseder-
inge that the parsones Crave the favour of the Court . . . Either
to be Cleared or Condemned " [*R. I. Court Records*, vol. II, pp.
11, 12].

He took oath of fidelity 19 May 1671; on 28 May 1671 he took
Thomas Marshall as an apprentice with the consent of the boy's
father and mother, Edward and Mary Marshall of Warwick.

On 29 July 1679 he and forty-one other inhabitants of Narragansett petitioned the King praying to put an end to those differences about the government; on 27 Oct. 1684 he took a receipt
from Thomas Marshall whose term of apprenticeship had ended;
taxed 9s. 11d. on 6 Sept. 1687; grand jury, 1687.

On 30 Jan. 1692 he sold James Carder, of Warwick, 26 acres, 12
acres, a whole right of undivided land, and a right in Commons, and
all other interests there, for £50.

He made his will 14 Mar. 1711, proved 9 Jan. 1712.   Bequests to
sons Samuel, Rouse, and William; to wife; to daughters Elizabeth
Hazzard, Mary Potter, and Mercy Watson.   Executors, wife Mary
and son Rouse. Overseers, Thomas Eldred, John Eldred, William
Knowles, and Ephraim Bull.

Inventory £284 17s. 1d., viz.: 77 sheep, 37 lambs, 4 oxen, 5 cows
and calves, 2 three years, 5 two years, 4 yearlings, horse, 5 mares,
4 colts, negro Jack £30, Nan £15, Stillyards, money, scales, gin,
4 swine, etc.

On 21 Oct. 1713 a declaration was signed by Mary Coggeshall
and Ezekiel Bull that Rouse Helme's wife died before him and that
he considering his wife's care of his son William that she would
have taken, desired her part given to his son Rouse.

Children:
1. *Samuel*,³ d. in 1728; m. Dorcas ——, d. before 1727. Will
dated 3 Sept. 1727, proved 12 Feb. 1728. Executor son
Christopher. Mentions sons Christopher, John, Samuel;
William, £70 at age; son Thomas, £70 at age; to daughters
Mary Perry, Dorcas Helme, Mercy Helme. The Town
Council to be guardian to the young children; William and
Thomas to learn to read, write, and cipher, and to be put to a
trade; Mercy to learn to read the bible.
   Children, born at South KingsTown, R. I.: (1) Mary,⁴
b. 14 June 1700.   (2) Christopher, b. 30 Mar. 1702. (3) John,
b. 11 Feb. 1704.   (4) Samuel, b. 21 Oct. 1706.   (5) Dorcas,
b. 14 June 1710.   (6) William, b. 12 Mar. 1714.   (7) Thomas,
b. 3 Jan. 1718.   (8) Mercy.
2. *Elizabeth*, d. before 1727; m. Stephen Hazard, d. 29 Sept. 1727,
son of Robert and Mary (Brownell) Hazard.
   Children (surname *Hazard*): (1) Mary, b. 20 July 1695.
(2) Hannah, b. 20 Apr. 1697.   (3) Susanna, b. 20 Apr. 1699.
(4) Stephen, b. 29 Nov. 1700.   (5) Robert, b. 12 Sept. 1702.
(6) Samuel, b. 29 June 1705.   (7) Thomas, b. 28 July 1707.
(8) Elizabeth.   (9) Sarah.
3. *Margaret*, b. in 1679; d. before 1727; m. Ichabod Potter, d. 1730,
son of Ichabod and Martha (Hazard) Potter.
   Children (surname *Potter*): (1) Ichabod.   (2) Rouse, b.
13 Feb. 1703.   (3) Thomas.   (4) William, b. 4 Mar. 1709
(5) Margaret, b. 11 Oct. 1714.
4. *Mercy*, m. Samuel Watson, d. after 1740, son of John and Dorcas (Gardiner) Watson.
   Child (surname *Watson*): (1) William.

5. *Rouse*, d. 28 Aug. 1751; m. 21 July 1709, Sarah Niles, d. after 1748, dau. of Nathaniel and Sarah (Sands) Niles. Deputy 1714, 1717, 1720, 1722; Assistant 1717, and 22 years from 1723 to 1744; clerk of the Assembly 1720; Judge of the Superior Court for over twenty years; in February 1723 he and Francis Willett were appointed by Assembly to draw a copy of all the records belonging in South Kingstown from the records of the late Kings Town; on 26 Nov. 1723 he and Francis Willett petitioned for their pay for transcribing 1230 pages, the towns of North and South Kingstown having refused to pay. Will dated 15 Apr. 1748, proved 9 Sept. 1751; Executors sons James and Rouse.

Children: (1) James,[4] b. 7 May 1710. (2) Sands, b. 21 Aug. 1711. (3) Rouse, b. 11 Feb. 1713. (4) Nathaniel, b. 17 Dec. 1714. (5) Benedict, b. 17 Feb. 1717. (6) Simeon, b. 15 Dec. 1718. (7) Benedict, b. 3 Oct. 1720. (8) Silas, b. 20 May 1724. (9) Sarah, b. 16 May 1727. (10) Jonathan, b. 14 Oct. 1729. (11) Oliver, b. 17 June 1731. (12) Samuel, b. 3 June 1734.

6. *William*.

JOSHUA HENSHAW.

ESSE QUAM VIDERI

A SKETCH OF THE LIFE OF HON. JOSHUA HENSHAW, WITH BRIEF NOTICES OF OTHER MEMBERS OF THE HENSHAW FAMILY.

[Compiled by the EDITOR.]

IT is one of the objects of the Society under whose auspices the New England Historical and Genealogical Register is published, to collect and preserve the scattered and perishable materials of History and Biography, to the end that we and our posterity may be able to obtain a correct knowledge of the history of the country. A proper sense of the obligations we owe to our forefathers for their public services should also prompt us to this course.

While much has been written concerning many of the chief actors in the American Revolution and in the scenes immediately preceding that event, little as yet has been published that illustrates to any considerable extent the part taken in that struggle by the family whose name stands at the head of this article. In order to supply this deficiency, so far as may be done at this time, the following sketch has been prepared.* An examination of the pedigree accompanying this sketch will show the high social position occupied by the ancestors of the family, both in England and on the continent of Europe. Their descendants in the United States are allied by marriage with many families of historic renown.

JOSHUA HENSHAW, the second son of Joshua and Mary (Webster) Henshaw, was born at his father's house† in Boston, August 2, 1703. Of his earlier years little is positively known, but from the fact that his father was a prominent man in Boston, and possessed ample means, it may be assumed with safety that the young man

---

* These sketches have been compiled, in part, from valuable papers prepared by the late Andrew Henshaw Ward, Esq., who at the moment of his death was engaged in compiling a Genealogical History of the Henshaw Family. For the use of these materials we are indebted to the kindness of Andrew Henshaw Ward, Esq., of W. Newton.

For the use of the engraving for the portrait (of Joshua Henshaw, 1703) accompanying this No. of the Register, we are indebted to the kindness of John A. Henshaw, Esq., of Boston.

We have found it convenient to depart from the strict chronological order in the presentation of the sketches.

† This house was built by his father, and stood on the north corner of what is now called "Hayward Place" and Washington (then Newbury) street.

was properly trained for the mercantile profession, upon which he entered at an early period of his life, and in which he acquired wealth and influence. That he was, by natural endowments as well as by education, a man of decided ability, is shown by the fact that he was so often selected by his fellow townsmen for important offices and trusts.

On the 27th day of December, 1733, he was married to Elizabeth, daughter of the Hon. Richard and Sarah (Davis) Bill, by the Rev. Benjamin Colman, then pastor of Brattle street Church, Boston. Richard Bill was at this time an influential and opulent merchant of Boston, and by this marriage Mr. Henshaw was brought into intimate social and mercantile relations with a large circle of well established families. He resided in Boston,* and, for many years after his marriage or till within a short time before the Revolution, seems to have been devoted almost exclusively to business connected with the rapidly expanding commerce of the town. We find, however, that he served frequently as a magistrate during this period: an office of great consequence then, and conferred upon a few only of the most discreet and capable men. It was not until many years after this period that the title "Esquire" came to be considered a convenient and courteous appendage to the names of even very young, and sometimes inexperienced men.

At a town meeting held March 2, 1764, of which James Otis was moderator, Joshua Henshaw was chosen first on the list of Selectmen,† and from this time forward for several years he was frequently chosen to this, the then chief elective office of the town. He was also very often appointed on special and important committees. Thus, we find him serving with Thomas Hancock, William Phillips, Joseph Sherburne and James Otis, a committee appointed May 15, of this year, to investigate the encroachments then being made upon Beacon Hill by persons in quest of gravel.‡

At an adjourned town meeting, held Sept. 18, 1765, it was unanimously "Voted, that the Hon. James Otis, Esq., the moderator, the Hon. Samuel Welles, Esq., the Hon. Harrison Gray, Esq., the Hon. Royal Tyler, Esq., Joshua Henshaw, Esq., John Rowe, Esq., and Mr. Samuel Adams, be a committee to draw up and transmit, by the first opportunity, to the Rt. Hon. Gen'l Conway, now one of his Majesty's principal Secretaries of State, and to Col. Isaac Barré, a member of Parliament, several addresses, humbly expressing the sincere thanks of this Metropolis of his Majesty's ancient and loyal Province, for their noble, generous, and truly patriotic speeches at the late session of Parliament, in favor of the Colonies, their Rights and Privileges; and that correct copies of the same be desired, that they may be deposited among our most precious archives. Also voted, that these gentlemen's pictures, as soon as they can be obtained, be placed in Faneuil Hall, as a standing monument to all posterity, of the virtue and jus-

---

* January 16, 1741–2, Richard Bill, Esq. conveys to Joshua Henshaw and wife "the house and land in Sudbury street, now in the tenure and occupation of the said Henshaw, fronting to Sudbury street on the S. S. E., there measuring forty feet; . . . on the south west on land of Thomas Cooper, late deceased, there measuring 99 feet; N. W. on Bartholomew, three needles nineteen and a half feet," &c. (Suff. Deeds, 62: 256.)

† The other members of the Board were Joseph Jackson, John Scollay, Benjamin Austin, Samuel Sewall, Nathaniel Thwing, and John Ruddock. Town Records, Vol. 4, p. 568.

‡ *Ibid.* Vol. 4, p. 594.

tice of our benefactors, and a lasting proof of our gratitude."* These communications were subsequently acknowledged† in eloquent and feeling terms by the persons addressed, and their portraits were placed in Faneuil Hall, from which unfortunately they have disappeared.‡

He was chairman of the Board of Selectmen§ who were assembled in the house of Richard Dana, Esq., opposite "Liberty Tree," Dec. 17, 1765, on that memorable occasion when Andrew Oliver, Esq., Distributor of Stamps, was compelled by an indignant community to make a public resignation of his obnoxious office. The next day the town appointed a committee, consisting of Samuel Adams, John Rowe, Thomas Cushing, John Hancock, John Ruddock, Samuel Sewall, Joshua Henshaw and Benjamin Kent,‖ with authority to employ Jeremy Gridley, James Otis and John Adams as counsel, to request Gov. Bernard to cause the courts of law to be opened again for public business.

At a town meeting held June 14, 1768, he was appointed one of a committee of twenty-one to wait upon the Governor in regard to the very serious disturbances and misunderstandings that grew out of the seizure by the Government authorities on the charge of false entry and smuggling, of "The Liberty," a sloop owned by John Hancock, and which had just then come into port with a valuable cargo.¶ On the 5th of May, 1769, he was appointed by the town on the committee, of which Richard Dana was chairman, to instruct the newly elected representatives, James Otis, Thomas Cushing, Samuel Adams and John Hancock.** The next year he was a member of the committee appointed to perform a like duty.†† This year, James Otis having been compelled by ill-health to abandon public affairs, James Bowdoin was elected in his place, as representative. At this late day, one cannot perceive what special instructions could have been needed by the men above named, but if there was any propriety or necessity for giving instructions then, surely the practice has long since most unhappily fallen into disuse.

On the 4th of October, 1769, he was appointed by the town on a committee to consider what measures were necessary to "vindicate" the town from the false and injurious representations contained in letters and memorials previously sent to the Home Government by Gov. Bernard, Gen. Gage, Com. Hood and others, which committee reported on the 18th.‡‡ On the 6th of March, 1770, the day following

---

* Town Records, Vol. 4. p. 655.
† Town Records, Vol. 5, p. 171.
‡ Drake's History of Boston, pp. 704–5.
§ They were Joshua Henshaw, Joseph Jackson, Benjamin Austin, Samuel Sewall, Nathaniel Thwing, John Ruddock, and John Hancock. Town Records, Vol. 5, p. 668.
‖ Mr. Drake adds the name of Arnold Welles. Hist. of Boston, p. 713. I here take occasion to acknowledge my constant obligations to this distinguished antiquary and historical writer. His History of Boston ought to be in every family, and the city could do no more valuable service to the people than to authorize the writer of that work to issue a new edition at the public charge, and bring the history down to the present time.
¶ Town Records, Vol. 5, pp. 98–9. Drake's Boston, under same date.
** Ibid., p. 149. Instructions reported May 8.
†† Ibid., p. 254. The instructions of this year cover nearly ten pages, folio, of the records. This paper, as well as those of the preceding years, contains a remarkable statement of the questions at issue between the Colony and the Mother Country. They are supposed to have been written by Richard Dana, chiefly. The instructions for 1764 will be found in Drake's Boston, pp. 683–4.
‡‡ Town Records, Vol. 5, p. 169. Drake's Boston, p. 771.

"the Massacre" in King street, Samuel Adams, John Hancock, William Molineaux, William Phillips, Joseph Warren, Joshua Henshaw and Samuel Pemberton were appointed a committee to wait upon the Lt. Governor* and Council, and earnestly request the removal of the troops from the town, and extorted from them an immediate compliance with the demand.†

Prior to this time, Mr. Henshaw had been a member of the House of Representatives, and in 1769 was chosen by that body a member of the Executive Council, but was rejected by Gov. Bernard on account of his well-known opposition to the measures pursued by the Government towards the Colony. At the same time ten‡ others shared the like fate, and this significant testimony to their love of country and devotion to principle gave them a still stronger hold upon the hearts of the people.

To have been thus repeatedly selected by his townsmen to participate in the discharge of duties requiring superior wisdom no less than unimpeachable integrity and undaunted resolution, in a cause, too, on whose successful issue so much depended for themselves and their children, bespeaks the degree of confidence reposed in him; while to have been associated with the most distinguished patriots of the colony upon any subject is not only evidence of the character and standing of Mr. Henshaw, but is an honor of which his descendants may well be proud.

In consequence of the enforcement of the "Boston Port Bill," and the occupation of the town by the royal troops, Mr. Henshaw, and all who like him had unreservedly staked their lives and fortunes upon the pending issue, were compelled to sacrifice property, sever business and social ties, and find places of safety outside of Boston. At this time his brother Daniel, and his own son-in-law Joseph Henshaw, were residents of Leicester in the County of Worcester, Mass. Thither he also removed, in 1774, with his wife, and boarded for a short time in the family of Rev. Mr. Conklin. From this place he removed to Dedham, near Boston, and resided there till his death, most of the time an invalid.

The following obituary notice appeared in a newspaper of the day : —" On Tuesday, August 5, 1777, died at the seat of the Hon. Samuel Dexter,§ in Dedham, from whence on the Friday following his remains were respectfully interred, the Hon. Joshua Henshaw, for years a respectable inhabitant of this town. He was a man of engaging aspect and deportment ; of solid and unaffected piety ; of untainted integrity and honor ; of sincere and steady friendship ; of great compassion for the distressed, and benevolent to all in private and domestic life. He was highly valued and beloved in public stations, and truly honorable and importantly useful as a Selectman of the town of Boston ; in his seat at the Council Board, as well as in other places of trust, he acquitted himself with prudence, fidelity and honor, ever

---

* Gov. Bernard left New England in August, 1769.

† Town Records, Vol. 5, pp. 213–16. Drake's Boston, pp. 783–4. Mr. Henshaw was one of those who advised Josiah Quincy, junior, to act as counsel for Capt. Preston and the soldiers. Memoir of the Life of Josiah Quincy, junior, p. 37.

‡ William Brattle, James Bowdoin, James Otis, Jerathmeel Bowers, Joseph Gerrish, Thomas Saunders, John Hancock, Artemas Ward, Benj. Greenleaf and Walter Spooner.

§ Ante, Vol. 8, pp. 248–9.

proving himself a warm and unshaken friend to the civil and religious rights of his country, and of those who abetted them. He was one of those uniform patriots who early opposed the encroachments of the Administration, for which he was honorably distinguished by their frowns, and he died in the pleasing hope of the success of the American cause. That stroke of sickness, under which for a number of years he was gradually failing till his death, he bore with a patience and humility, a resignation and hope which only the Gospel can inspire."

His WIFE was noted for her beauty, grace of manners, gentle disposition and benevolence. She died in Boston, September 28, 1782, aged 70 years. It is related that at her marriage there were many of the most distinguished people present, and that her bridal presents, imported from England, were rich and extensive. One or more pieces of the solid silver tea service are still in the possession of one of the family. Her portrait and that of her father, the Hon. Richard Bill, before named, are still well preserved.*

Children of Joshua and Elizabeth (Bill) Henshaw :

1. SARAH, b. Jan. 16, 1736 ; m. her cousin Joseph (of whom we give a brief sketch later in this article) at Boston, May 25, 1758 ; d. in Shrewsbury, Jan. 4, 1822, aged 86 years. They had no children.

2. RICHARD BILL, b. June 10, 1737.

3. JOSHUA, b. Feb. 16, 1746 ; grad. H. C. 1763 ; m. Catharine Hill, of Boston, March 16, 1769 ; d. in Shrewsbury, May 27, 1823, aged 78 years. Wife d. there Sept. 7, 1822, age 76 years. No children.

4. ANDREW, b. May 28, 1752 ; grad. H. C. 1768 ; m. Sarah Prince, Feb. 10, 1780. He was clerk of the House of Representatives of Mass., and afterwards clerk of the Judicial Courts, in which office he died in Dec., 1782, aged 30 years, 7 months. They had no children. He was a man of considerable attainments, polished address, and scholarly tastes. His widow m. the late John Tucker, of Boston, clerk of the Courts, and d. June 22, 1822, aged 67 years.

JOSHUA (3) entered into business with his father, in Boston, and continued thus engaged so long as the avenues of commerce remained open. He was Register of Deeds for Suffolk, from 1776 to 1786, inclusive, and during the occupation of Boston by the royal forces kept his office and resided at Dedham, to which town the public records had been seasonably removed. Upon the retiring of the troops he returned to Boston, and as was the custom of those days kept his office and the records in his own dwelling house, which was situate on the northerly corner of Orange (then a part of what is now Washington) and Harvard streets.

At the time of the great fire, April 20, 1787, this house was burned, with much valuable personal property, which he neglected, in his anxiety to save the public records. Afterwards he built a wooden house on the site of the house burned, and occupied it till he removed to Shrewsbury, in 1792. While he resided at the latter place, he was a magistrate, and of the Quorum for the County of Worcester, and transacted much official business, but declined repeatedly to be a candidate for any elective office. He was upright in his official conduct, kind in his private relations, and possessed many popular talents.

---

* History of the Bill Family, p. 143.

He distinctly remembered the events introductory to the Revolution, and delighted all within the circle of his acquaintance with interesting anecdotes of those times. Of the "Boston Tea Party" he used to say, he had seen the names of some in print for whom it had been claimed that they belonged to the " Party "; that many of these might have been lookers-on, as were a crowd of people, and yet not have participated in that transaction ; inasmuch as the enterprise was secretly contrived by a few of the most distinguished and patriotic inhabitants of Boston, and by them and their employés, all honorable men, and selected for their well known integrity and fidelity, carried into effect without molestation, in an incredibly short space of time, considering the amount of work done ; and that previous to entering upon the hazardous project they bound themselves to each other, by a solemn oath, never to reveal, directly or indirectly, the name of any of the confederates, whether as privy to, as actually engaged in, or as bound to be engaged in the enterprise. And, so well has the secret been kept, it is believed that not one of the " Party " has thus far been identified.

JOSEPH HENSHAW, the son-in-law, above referred to, was born in Boston, Dec. 20, 1727, grad. at H. C. in 1748,* and in the same year sailed for Europe, for the purpose of acquiring mercantile information. He visited various cities and commercial marts, and gained a knowledge of their staple commodities and of their wants in exchange. After an absence of two years, he returned, fitted out a vessel with an assorted cargo, and sailed for Florence as master. The voyage was successful, and on his return his father built a vessel for him, which was named after the lady whom he afterwards married. Upon the conclusion of this voyage, about 1757, he commenced trade in Boston, and became an opulent and influential merchant. In 1774, he removed to Leicester.

During the stormy period immediately preceding the Revolution, he was indefatigable with pen, speech, money and personal influence in support of the Colonial cause against the arbitrary acts of the Government. He belonged to an association of patriots composed of Samuel Adams, James Otis, Joseph Warren, John Adams, Josiah Quincy, junior, Joshua Henshaw (his father-in-law), William Molineaux and others like them, who held their meetings in private at each other's residences, where they concerted measures which eventually led to the united resistance by the greater portion of the people to the acts of the Crown. There plans were formed, letters written, manifestoes prepared, reports received, and influences set in motion for restraining the impetuous and imprudent, and for stimulating and enlisting the lukewarm friends of Liberty. The tact and skill displayed by these men, in thus prudently shaping and guiding events, has seldom received at the hands of modern writers the prominence they deserve.

He continued to reside in Leicester till near the close of the war, when he removed to Shrewsbury. There he was a neighbor of Gen. Ward, and carried on the business of a country merchant. On the 20th of October, 1774, he was chosen a delegate to the Provincial Congress, then sitting at Cambridge.† One of the instructions given

---

* Artemas (afterwards General) Ward was a classmate and intimate friend.
† Colonel Thomas Denny, his brother-in-law, the delegate from Leicester, left the Congress on account of illness, and died at home, Oct. 23, 1774.

334

him by his constituents at the town meeting presided over by his father, David Henshaw, was "to use his influence that Dorchester Point be immediately taken possession of and fortified by the Province." He was elected a delegate to the ensuing Congress, on the 9th of January, 1775. In Nov., 1774, he was chosen Colonel of Militia in place of the late Colonel Denny. He was a member of the Committee of Correspondence for his own town, and attended the Convention of Committees of Correspondence held at Worcester, Aug. 9, 1774, which continued by seven adjournments to May 31, 1775. By this Convention he was chosen one of the Standing Committee of the County, to correspond with the committees of other counties.

He repaired to the camp at Cambridge on the day following the skirmish at Concord, and on the day after his arrival was named in General Orders and assigned to duty, with the rank of Colonel. By a General Order, dated April 21, 1775, it was declared that "all officers appointed before there is a regular establishment, are appointed *pro tem.*" Subsequently he was employed in missions to the adjoining Colonies and Provinces, in collecting military stores and forwarding supplies to the army, until the British evacuated Boston, in 1776. After this, though it does not appear that he continued in the service, yet he was constantly active in behalf of the Colonies till the end of the war. During the insurrection headed by Daniel Shays,* in 1786–7, he rendered essential service to the Government of the State. He died March 19, 1794, aged 66 years. Rev. Joseph Sumner, D.D., of Shrewsbury, officiated in the funeral services.

JOSHUA HENSHAW, the father of the Joshua first mentioned above, was born in Dorchester in 1672, and married Mary Webster,† of Boston, in 1700. He settled in the latter town, and engaged in mercantile business. He was also a distiller, and largely interested in the fisheries at Canso.‡ He became a wealthy merchant. His wife is said to have been a superior woman.

At the first allotment of pews in the New South Church, Dec. 7, 1716, pew No. 27, valued at £38, was assigned to Joshua Henshaw; and pew No. 23, to Joseph Bass.§ March 10, 1716, Mr. Henshaw was one of a committee of four to state methods of procedure in the choice of the first minister‖ of said parish. Aug. 10, 1720, he was one of the Standing Committee.¶ In 1743, he built a tomb next to that of Mr. Bass, in the Granary Burying Ground, and designated it by the Henshaw Coat of Arms. He died April 27, 1747. His widow died Dec. 15, 1747.

By his will, dated April 1, 1743, he gives to his wife Mary, "all my negroes, plate, money, household goods and moveables, and other personal estate of every kind, to her sole use and behoof forever, also the sole income and improvement of all my real estate, both in possession and reversion, during the term of her natural life, and at her

---

* *Ante,* Vol. 8, 128 d—l. Vol. 18, 8–11.

† Daughter of James and Mary (Hay) Webster, and b. Dec. 9, 1672, in Boston. James Webster was a member of the Scots' Charitable Society in 1657.

‡ Hutchinson, Vol. 2, p. 240, who says Mr. Henshaw made a visit to the Governor of Louisburg in 1720.

§ Joseph Bass was a brother of Edward Bass, D.D. (the Bishop), and father-in-law of Daniel Henshaw, brother of this Joshua.

‖ Rev. Samuel Checkley, ordained April 15, 1719; d. Dec. 1, 1769.

¶ Church Records, extract from, in hand writing of Rev. Dr. Young.

decease all my said real estate shall be equally divided among my surviving children and their heirs, after each of them shall have been allowed what either of them are indebted to me, per account or otherwise. My son Samuel shall have the still house and land under the same, with a passage from the backside of his house to the still house as it is now improved by him; he allowing for said still house what men chosen to value it, shall think it worth. Further, if any of my children be dissatisfied with this my will, so as to molest and disturb my said wife in her quiet and peaceable possession and improvement of my estate as aforesaid, I do then authorize and empower my said wife to cut off said child, that shall so molest her, with the sum of five pounds in full of his proportion of my said estate." Wife, Mary, sole executrix.

JOSHUA HENSHAW,* the grandfather of the first named Joshua, was born in Lancashire, England, about the year 1643, and with his brother Daniel, born about 1646, was fraudulently abducted and sent to New England, about 1652. They came to Dorchester, Mass., where they resided during their minority.† Joshua there married, in 1670, Elizabeth Sumner.‡ Three children were born to them. In 1688, he made his will, and in the early part of the next year went to England for the purpose of recovering the large property left by his parents in the care of Peter Ambrose, their steward, who bore the imputation, not without probable grounds of suspicion, of having sent the boys Joshua and Daniel out of England for the purpose of getting possession of their property; for before they were sent away they had lived in his care and on the estate for several years, and after their departure he retained possession and died in the occupation of the estate. Wavertree Hall, extolled by Walter Scott, was a part of it.

When Joshua arrived in England he found Joshua Ambrose in possession of, and claiming the estates, as heir to his father Peter. Mr. Henshaw filed a bill in Chancery against Ambrose, but not being then prepared to prove his paternity, returned to Dorchester and procured the necessary evidence. To this bill the defendant put in his answer, and at a subsequent term of the court, in 1690, the plaintiff not appearing, the bill was dismissed with seven nobles costs. In 1692, after Mr. Henshaw's return to England, his case against Ambrose was restored to the docket, and kept there for nearly thirty years. In 1719, when it became certain that a decision was about to be rendered in favor of the plaintiff, Mr. Henshaw was invited by Ambrose to dinner, upon pretence of a desire to effect an amicable compromise, and soon after the dinner was seized with an illness, from which he died in a few hours. The suit was then dropped from the docket for want of a prosecutor.

The following is a copy of his Will:—

"In the name of God, Amen. The third Day of April Ann° Dom^{ni} One Thousand Six Hundred Eighty Eight, Annoq: R. R^s. Jacobi nunc Angliæ, etc., Secundi, Quarto.—I, Joshua Hensha of Dorchester,

---

* It does not appear when the name was changed from Hensha to Henshaw.

† The family tradition is, that the Rev. Richard Mather, who came from Lancashire, England, had the care of them, and of the money sent with them, for their support and education, and for setting them up in business.

‡ Elizabeth Sumner, eldest daughter of William and Elizabeth (Clement) Sumner; bap. June, 1652, d. in Dorchester in 1728. *Ante*, Vol. 8, 128 d.

in the County of Suffolke within his Maties Territory and Dominion of New England, Yeoman, being about to take a voyage to England, knowing the uncertainty of this Life and the hazards and dangers that do attend those that are passing by Sea, being now of a whole and disposing mind, do make and ordein this my Last will and Testament in manner following, revoking all former wills, &c.

First and principally my soul I recommend unto God in Christ Jesus my Creator and Redeemer, hoping in his grace and mercy to receive forgiveness of Sins and an Inheritance among those that are sanctified through faith in Christ. My Body I commit unto the dust, or sea, as it shall please God to dispose of me. And for that temporal Estate which it has pleased God to bestow upon me, I will that the same may be employed and bestowed as hereinafter expressed.

Imp^r. I will that all my just debts and personal Expenses (if any be) be well and truly paid and ordered to be paid by my Executrix, hereafter named, with what convenient speed may be.

Item. I give and bequeath unto Elizabeth, my well beloved wife, the use, profits and income of my whole Estate for her own comfortable Subsistence and Education of my Children, for and during the full time of her widowhood ; But upon her intermarriage only to have her thirds therein according to Law.

It. I will that my whole Estate real and personal, (debts and funeral charges being paid) shall be considered and cast into a division of eight equal parts according to the value thereof. Two parts whereof I give unto WILLIAM my Eldest son, as his double portion, and unto Each of my other Children, viz. :—Joshua, Thankful, John, Samuel, Elizabeth, and Katharin a single part or share thereof ; and if either of my s^d children happen to dye before the receiving their portion, my will is that the part or parts of such Child or Children, deceasing shall be equally divided to and among the survivours.

It. I do nominate, constitute and ordein my beloved wife Elizabeth Hensha to be sole Executrix of this my Last will and Testament. And do give her full power and authority (if need be for the payment of my just debts) by and with the advise of my overseers or some of them to dispose and make sale of any parts or parcels of my Lands, and to give a legal confirmation thereof. And I do desire and appoint my well respected ffriends and Relations—William Sumner, Senr, of Dorchester, Daniel Hensha of Milton, and John Goffe* of Boston, to be overseers of this my will, to advise and assist my wife in the due Execution thereof.

IN WITNESS whereof I have hereunto set my hand and seal, the day and year first within written.

Signed, Sealed and Published
  by Joshua Hensha to be his
  last will and Testament, in
  presence of us   JOSHUA I HENSHA, L. S.
  Jos. Jackson,
       marke
  John I T Trow,*
       marke
  Hanory A Adams.

---

* Trow and Goffe married sisters of the Testator's wife. Trow (or Tro) was then of Dorchester.

Colony of Rhode Island.

These may certify that on the day of the date heareof John Trow, Resident in Newport, aged 70 years, personally appeared before me the Subscriber, and made oath that he was Present with Joshua Hensha, and did see him sign, seal and declare the above and before written will or Testament to be his act and his last Will, and that he was then of Sound Memory and Judgement, and Joseph Jackson and Hanory Adams was present and did in the presence of the Testator subscribe their names with this Deponent as Witnesses to the s^d will. In testimony whereof I have Heareunto set my hand and affixed my seal at Newport, this 25th day of April, in the 6th year of his Maj^{tys} Reigne, George by Grace of God over Great Brittain, &c., King, Ann^o Dom. 1720.

L. S.   Sam^{ll} Cranston, Govr.''

Here follow the Letters of Administration and Certificate of Probate, signed by Samuel Sewall,* and dated, Boston, March 9th, 1723.

When Mr. Henshaw commenced his action in the Court of Chancery he obtained the aid of Robert Dale, Esq., a distinguished Genealogist, who traced the Henshaw pedigree in 1701. Copies of this paper were used in the suit. After Mr. Dale's demise, the original in Mr. Dale's handwriting and his description of the Henshaw Coat of Arms were placed in the Herald's office, London. Authenticated copies of these documents were obtained in 1844, and are hereunto annexed.

" Coat of Arms.

Henshaw,—Argent, a chevron sable between three moor-hens proper ; quartering Houghton,—Sable, three bars argent. Crest, a falcon proper,. billed *or*, beaked and membered sable, preying upon the wing of a bird, argent. Motto :—*To be, not to seem.*

Thomas Henshaw, in the reign of James I., had the Arms restored to him that had previously belonged to his ancestor, Sir Thomas Henshaw, and the crest added, and he was knighted. The ancient spelling upon the *Arms* is upon the wreath of his collar Argent and Sable, ' Falcone resting on a wing *Gould* with a crown about his neck *Gould*. Beake and Legs Sable with Belles Gould, of the first mantled Gules, Rombled Silver—the birds in the Arms are Heathcocks.' ''

---

¹ * Born in England, 1652 ; m. Hannah Hull (b. 1658), daughter of Hon. John Hull, of Boston, 1676 ; commissioned Judge of Probate 1715, and d. 1730.

Lands in Penyngton.
Worsley.
Newton in Mackenfield.
Knowsley.
Liverpool.
Ellell.
Carleton.
Sowerby.
Warton.

Houses in Lancaster.

EVAN HOUGHTON of Great Carleton, near Poulton, in the County Palatine of Lancaster, Gent. Escheat 2d May, (1610) Jac: I. He was also of Wavertre Died at Knowsley, 20 Jan. (1608) 5 Jac: I. Writ dat. 2 Dec. 6 Jac. I. 1609. = daur. of . . . Carleton of Great Carleton in Com: Palatine of Lancaster. Set qy and one ton of Carleton was not married to Hugh Singleton whose sister Margaret was wife to Lawrence, son of the eldest.

Grace, one of the sisters, died unmarried. Qy. whether Mary, heiress of Carleton was not married to Allen, whose heir Worthington married. William Carleton of Carleton.

Qy. if another sister and coheir of William Carleton

Thomas Henshaw of Derby in the County = . . . daur. to . . . Kendrick of Prescot in the County Palatine of Lancaster, or rather of Kendrick's Cross, in the same parish.
* Toxteth.

Palatine of Lancaster. Died in Toxter* Park, near Liverpool in the same County near 70 years ago.
* Toxteth.

He was 64 years old at the death of his father and upwards die capacious Inquis.

Richard Houghton of Wartre Hall and Penketh, Bakers Green House, where he died in Haighton Parish near Knowsley in the County Palatine of Lancaster. = Margaret, daur. of Henry Stanley, Esq., of Bickerstagh in the County Palatine of Lancaster. Marriage settlement dated 8 Oct. 27 surr: dated 30 Dec. ( ) 27 Eliz. (1585)

1. William Henshaw of Toxter Park, aforesaid; killed at the taking of Liverpool during the civil wars 1644. Married about 1627.*
* Probably 1637. = Katherine, daur. of Evan Houghton of Wartre Hall, in Childo Parish in the County of Lancaster. She was his only child and heir, and died 1661.

Evan Houghton of Wartre Hall in the parish = Ellen, daur. of . . . Parker of of Childo, in the County Palatine of Lancaster. Killed at the taking of Liverpool in Lancashire by Prince Rupert, during the civil war a°. 1644, where he was in prison a°. 1638. Kridgehall in the County Palatine of Lancaster, Esq; and of Derbyshire. She died after her son's wife about 10 weeks.

Dorothy, mar'd 1st to . . . Story of Windle & afterwards sed qy. to . . . .

Katherine married to . . . . . . Eliz. (1586)

2. John, who went into Ireland and died there, leaving one son deceased.

3. . . . . Drowned, unmarried.

Ellen, married to Harrison of Toxter* Park. She died 2 years ago.
* Toxteth.

Joshua Henshaw, born in Liverpool about a = Elizabeth, daur. of William Sommer year and 10 weeks before his father was killed, living a°. 1701. He was about 8 years at his mother's death, and sent to New England, a°. 1663 and came back 1688 about Apr. of Dorchester, in New England, son of William Sommer of Bucester in the County of Oxford.

Daniel Henshaw of Milton in = Mary, daur. of . . . Bull of New England, 2d son; æt. 55 New England, ann:—and about 7 years a°. 1651. Bury St. Edmund in Co. Suffolk, and widow of Nicholas Allen of Dorchester in New England.

William, æt. 30.

Joshua, æt. 28.

John, æt. 20.

Thankful, æt. 23, married to Nathaniel Leeman of Boston in New England.

Elizabeth, æt. 16.

Katherine, æt. 13.

Daniel, died unmarried and was his father's only child.

NOTE.—The original Pedigree is endorsed "Mr. Henshaw's pedigree, a°. 1701."

Extracted from the MS. Pedigrees of Robert Dale, Richmond Herald, marked "H 12," page 127, now remaining in the Herald's College, London, this 28th day of June, 1844. Signed G. W. Collen, Pursuivant at Arms, Herald's College, London.

ENGLISH ANCESTRY OF THE HIGGINSON FAMILY.

Communicated by Col. THOMAS W. HIGGINSON, A.M., of Cambridge, Mass.

I HAVE lately been informed by the Rev. E. Harlin Bates, Assistant Curate of the Claybrooke Parish, Leicester, England, of the recent discovery at Stanford Hall in that county of part of the long-missing records of Claybrooke parish. This affords for the first time the means of determining, with some approach to accuracy, the year of the birth of the Rev. Francis Higginson; a date which rested on

surmise when my life of him appeared. He was baptized, at any
rate, on Aug. 6, 1586. The parish books give also a list of his
brothers and sisters, agreeing substantially with the list preserved in
family records and given in my memoir aforesaid. The record also
supplies for the first time the date of burial of Francis Higginson's
father, the Rev. John Higginson, who was buried, it seems, on Feb.
19, 1624; this being the year suggested in my memoirs (p. 4) as
possible or probable. The name so curiously given as Dawritie and
Duwritie is unquestionably Dorothy.

Extracts from Church Registers of Parish of Claybrooke, co. Leic., England, now in possession of Lord Braye of Stanford Hall, in the same county.
All dates New Style.

Baptisms.

25 Apr. 1575 John s. of John & Elizabeth Higginson.
24 Apr. 1576 Duwritie d.   "   "
22 Sept. 1578 Presella d.   "   "
14 Dec. 1580 John s.   "   "
27 Oct. 1585 John s.   "   "
 6 Aug. 1586 ffrauncis s.   "   "
15 May 1589 William s.   "   "
18 May 1591 Catren d.   "   "
 4 Feb. 1593 Martyn & Mare "   "
24 March 1594 Nicholes s.   "   "
25 Dec. 1601 George s.   "   "
19 Mar. 1608 Nicholes s.   "   "
13 May 1610 Grace d.   "   "
 8 Dec. 1611 Elizabeth d.   "   "
23 May 1613 Judith d.   "   "
27 Nov. 1597 Nicholes s. of Edmond & Presella Higginson.

Marriages.

25 Dec. 1598 William Gilbard & Dawritie Higginson.
 5 Jan. 1607 Edwarde Androse & Elyzabeth   "
22 Apr. 1619 Thomas Coleman & Katherine   "
                  witness Nathaniell "
28 Oct. 1629 William Higginson & ffraunces Palmer.

Burials.

26 Apr. 1577 Blaunche Higginson.
18 Sept. 1577 Thomas   "
11 Apr. 1581 Nicoles   "
26 May 1585 John   "
21 Apr. 1603 George   "
30 Jan. 1612 Elizabeth   "
13 July 1613 Elizabeth   "
17 Oct. 1613 Judith   "
19 Feb. 1624 John Higginson, Vicar of Claybrooke.

N. B. In this book the following years (beginning 29 Sept.)
are missing: 1567–8, '68–9, '70–1, '73–4, '78–9, '81–2, '83–4,
'94–7.

HIGGINSON.—The parish register of St. Peter's, Nottingham, contains the following marriage record: "Franciscus Higginson duxit uxore Ana Herbert Octavo die Januarij 1615" (Phillimore, Nottingham Marriages, p. 19).

This appears to be the marriage record of Rev. Francis Higginson, minister of the First Church of Salem, and his wife Ann.

He was ordained deacon at Cawood Castle Sept. 25, 1614, by Tobey Mathew, Archbishop of York, when he was called curate of Scredingham, and was ordained priest at Bishopthorpe Dec. 8, 1614. He was collated (instituted) Apr. 20, 1615, by the Archbishop of York, the patron, to the rectory of Barton-in-fabis in the county of Nottingham, which he resigned Apr. 4, 1616 (Archiepiscopal Registry of York, Institutions Sandes, 1572 to 1619, ff. 431, 433, 437, 447; REGISTER, 52: 348). Barton-in-fabis is six miles southwest of Nottingham, near * the border of Leicestershire. From 1617, or thereabouts, to 1629, the time of his emigration, he was connected with the parish of St. Nicholas, Leicester, when he styled himself "minister" and afterwards "lecturer" (REGISTER, 52: * 848).

There was a tradition that Ann, wife of Francis Higginson, was a sister of Gov. Theophilus Eaton, but Hannah, sister of Gov. Eaton, was unmarried when named in her father's will in 1616 (New Haven Hist. Colls., 4: 186, 7: 5), and married, Dec. 5, 1622, Joseph Denman, in the parish of St. Mary Woolchurch, Haw, London, where, on Dec. 3; 1622, Theophilus Eaton married his first wife, Grace Hiller (Parish Reg. St. Mary Woolchurch). The mention of "Cozⁿ Hayler" in a letter of Col. John Higginson (3 Mass. Hist. Soc. Colls., 7: 219) and of "Tho: Hayler" (Higginson Letters, Ms.), and also the recurrence of the names Grace and Judith in the Hiller and Higginson families (REGISTER, 46: 118) ** suggests that the connection between the Higginsons and Theophilus Eaton may have been a relationship between Rev. Francis Higginson and the Hillers of the parish of St. Mary Woolchurch.   VIRGINIA HALL.

Cambridge, Mass.

*P. 253, the third volume of this series.
**P. 341, this volume.

GEORGE HINGSTON, 1631-1667

By RICHARD M. HINCHMAN, of Groton, Mass.

George Hingston, bapt. 1 Nov. 1631 at Newton Ferrers, Devon, England, died on or after 22 Aug. 1667 and certainly before 10 Oct. 1667 [? at sea or ? at Boston, Suffolk Co., Massachusetts Bay], was the son of Bartholomew Hingston and Margaret Webber.[1] He was married 25 Oct. 1660 at Newton Ferrers to Alice Greenslade.[2] He was a mariner and served aboard the ship Elinor & Christian under the command of John Shepway.[3] His brother Walter Hingston was granted administration of his estate 31 Jan. 1667/68 by Suffolk County Court at Boston.[4] An account of the estate, certified 5 Feb. 1667/68 by John Shepway, showed liabilities of £1.3s.0d. and assets of £18.12s.4d., consisting of personal effects inventoried at £4.14s.10d. and wages due from 14 Nov. 1666 to 22 Aug. 1667 in the amount of £13.17s.6d. based on 30s. per month.[5]

Although the Suffolk County probate documents spell the surname variously as Hincksman, Hinckson, Hinksman, and Hinkson, it appears probable that George Hingston was not related to Edmond Hincksman (?1614-1668) of Marshfield, Plymouth Colony, and Chelmsford, Middlesex Co., Massachusetts Bay, nor to Daniel Henchman (?1623?-1685) of Boston and Worcester, Middlesex Co., Massachusetts Bay.

REFERENCES

1. Inventory of sundry goods and money left on board the shipp Elinar & Christian belonging unto George Hinkson. Dated 10 Oct. 1667. Suffolk Co., Mass., Probate Court, file 483.

Account of the estate of George Hinkson: Certified by John Shepway, master of the ship Ellinor & Christiam. Boston, 5 Feb. 1667/68. Suffolk Co., Mass., Probate Court, file 483.

Newton Ferrers, Devon, England. Parish register, 1600-1724. Excerpts furnished by Andrew N. Stamp, son of the Rector.

2. Ibid. Was she the Alice Hingston who was married 17 Apr. 1683 at Newton Ferrers to John Cowley?

3. Account of the estate of George Hinkson.

4. Testimony that Walter Hinksman was brother to Georg Hinksman. Signed by Peetter Gee, Rich. Ford (his mark), and Walter Poore (his mark), sworn 31 Jan. 1667/68 before the County Court, Edw. Rawson, Recorder; Power of administration to the estate of the late George Hinckson, of Newtonferry in the County of Devon, marriner, deceased. Granted to Walter Hincksman by County Court held at Boston 31 Jan. 1667/68. E.R.R. ms. 1p. Ibid. This document gives the ages of Peter Gay 56, Rich. Ford 34, and Walter Poore 23.

Administration bond. Signed by Walter Hincksman with Edward Raynsford and Peetter Gee as sureties; witnessed by William Rawson and John Sanders. 3 Feb. 1667/68. Ibid.

5. Ibid.

343

THE ANCESTRY OF THE HOAR FAMILY IN AMERICA.

A Compilation from Collections made by the Honorable GEORGE FRISBIE HOAR.

By HENRY S. NOURSE, of Lancaster, Mass.[*]

THE family of Hoar, in English records generally written Hore or Hoare, from very ancient days had its representatives in several of the counties of England and in Ireland. Sometimes the name appears with the adjective *le* affixed. Between the years 1300 and 1700 thirteen members of Parliament from six different counties bore the name. English antiquaries who have made long and intelligent study of the family genealogy unite in favoring the supposition that the founder of the race was one Robert Hore who, about 1330, married the heiress of Forde of Chagford in Devonshire. In the Heraldic Visitation for the county of Devon, taken in 1620, and to be found in the Harleian MS. in the British Museum, the pedigree begins with the third Robert Hore, about 1360. This Robert married the heiress of Rowland de Risford of the parish of Chagford. The learned biographer of the famous London branch of the family, Sir Richard Colt Hoare, Bart., in his sumptuous volume "Pedigrees and Memoirs of the Families of Hore and Hoare of the Counties of Devon, Bucks, Middlesex, Surrey, Wilts and Essex, 1819," acknowledged his failure to discover a continuous pedigree from Robert of Risford, and bases his belief in this origin of the family chiefly upon the identity of the coat of arms uniformly used by all bearing the name; to wit: "Sable an eagle displayed, with two necks with a border ingrailed, argent." One antiquary has suggested a German origin to the family and calls attention to the similarity between the arms of the city of Frankfort-on-the-Main and those used in the Hoare family in England.

Captain Edward Hoare in his book, printed at London in 1883, entitled "Early History and Genealogy of the Families of Hore and Hoare," is much more positive in his assertions respecting this line of descent from Robert of Risford, but is unable to give the authority of records to vouch for his conclusions; and the many grave inaccuracies of his appendix, wherein he essays a pedigree of the American branch of the Hoar family, tend to encourage distrust in his infallibility when he discourses of matters much more recondite.

[*] To the indefatigable researches of an accomplished local antiquary, H. Y. J. TAYLOR, these pages are indebted for most of the genealogical matter relating to Gloucester and vicinity.

The defective condition or total loss of many early parish registers, and the defacement and destruction by damp or careless keeping of many early wills, make it highly improbable that the assumed connection between the Hore families of Devonshire and Gloucestershire will be discovered; and from the city of Gloucester the mother of the American branch of the family, Joanna (Hinksman) Hoare, came, in 1640, to Massachusetts. The frequent choice of the same baptismal names, and the use of the same heraldic device by both the Devon and the Gloucester branches are the only significant facts found of record. Unfortunately there is no pedigree attached to the "Visitation of the County of Gloucester," by Robert Cooke Clarencieux, King at Arms in 1583, enlarged with the Visitation of the same County in 1623, by Chitting and Philpott, deputies to William Camden Clarencieux, found in the Harleian Manuscript Nos. 1543 to 1554, although the "Arms of Hore of Gloucestershire" are given. The early presence of the family in this county, and elsewhere, is attested however by various documentary evidence, some examples of which follow:

1170. From Burke's Dictionary of Landed Gentry, p. 577, we find that William le Hore was one of the Norman Knights who invaded Ireland in 1170, and obtained grants of land in Wexford where he established a family. The pedigree in the visitation of the country begins with Thomas le Hore, who held the manor by the service of "keeping a passage over the Pillwater as often as the sessions should be held at Wexford." He had three sons: Richard, David who was high sheriff in 1334, and Walter.

1280. In the Calendar of Inquisitions, *post mortem*, *Anno* 8 Edward I. is noted: "Roger le Hore, *felo*, Ameneye, Gloucestershire." Roger le Hore held lands in Eastbrook (*see* Rudder's "Gloucester," p. 230).

1326. John le Hore is one of the witnesses to a deed, now in existence, of a tenement in Wotton, Gloucestershire, 19 Edward II.

It is noteworthy that the above dates are earlier than that of the alleged Devonshire origin.

1465. In the Calendar of the Records of the Gloucester Corporation, p. 406-7, is registered a "demise from William Hotynham, John Rudyng, clerk, and Thomas Lymark to Andrew Bye, Henry Rycard and Thomas Hoore burgesses of Gloucester, of their tenement and adjoining curtilage on the south side of Smythe strete between Sater lane and the messuage of Thomas Heyward."

1551. Alexander Hore appears as a member of the Baker's Guild.

An examination of the wills proved at Gloucester, which date from 1541 when the Court was established, gives the following:—

1544. The will of Richard Hoore of Leckhampton, husbandman, proved Oct. 10, 1545, bequeaths to wife Ellen his crops, debts, etc., leaving her to give what she pleases to the children.

1545. The will of Henry Hore of Aylburton in the parish of Lidgate, dated Oct. 23, 1545, and proved the following January, appoints his wife Christian executrix, bequeaths two pence to the Cathedral Church of Gloucester, and a cow to his daughter Agnes.

1545. The will of Robert Hoare of Leckhampton, husbandman, dated Sept. 8, and proved Oct. 10, 1545, bequeaths his soul to God, Saint Mary and all the holy company of Heaven, and mentions his wife Margery, sons Roger and Edward, daughter Jane, and Edward son of Roger.

1573. John Hore's will, proved May 27, 1573, is mostly illegible, but mentions wife Joan, sons William, Nicholas, and others "my children aforesaid." He was of Westbury on Severn.

1618. Richard Hoare of the parish of St. John the Baptist in the City of Gloucester, Gentleman, August 4, 1618, bequeaths eighteen houses with lands to his sons Richard, John and Alexander, one hundred pounds to his daughter Martha, and names wife Anne and sister Joan. This Richard was sheriff of Gloucester in 1614. By an indenture dated Sept. 4. 5. James 1. (1608) he gave in trust, for the benefit of the parish of St. Mary de Crypt, an annuity of fifty-three shillings charged upon several tenements in the city of Gloucester, to be employed in "the reparation of the Parish Church or the finding of a sufficient minnester to read divine service in the same church, and for the relief of the poor of the same parish, and other charitable uses." The trust survives, the Corporation of Gloucester annually paying fifty shillings to the parish. An ancient vault bearing the name Hoare is beneath the pavement in the south transept, near where the choir and nave join, of St. Mary de Crypt Church.

1628. The will of Richard Hoare of Norton "an old man of the adge of ffour score yeares and upward" mentions wife Maude, sons Edmond, William, Robert, Thomas, son-in-law Robert Brayne, daughter Jane, daughter Elizabeth wife of Robert Brokinnge, and her children Mary, Anne and Elizabeth, and Anne daughter of Edward. Norton is in the northern suburbs of Gloucester.

1640. The will of William Hoare "very aged" proved in 1640, is too much decayed to be legible.

1644. John Hoare of Leckhampton, husbandman, in his will mentions daughter Margaret, nephew John the son of Giles, sons Walle and Thomas and sons in law John Button and Thomas Ballaye.

1646. The will of John Hoare of Sandhurst, mentions late brother Alexander and his daughter Martha, his sister-in-law Margerie mother of Martha, and brothers-in-law Thos. Clutterbuck and Thos. Peirce.

1413. In the church of Frampton on Severn near Gloucester on a marble tablet, and in the east window of the north aisle, the Hoare arms are found quartered with the arms of Clifford and Windscombe, and the same quartering was once on a stained glass window of the parlor of Fretherne Lodge, a sumptuous mansion built by James Clifford with a design to entertain Queen Elizabeth in her "Progress to Bristol" in 1574. Fretherne is about nine miles south-west from Gloucester. Near by is the site of the residence of Walter Lord Clifford where his daughter "Fair Rosamond" was born. Fretherne Lodge, after long remaining in a state of dilapidation, was torn down in 1750. In the Visitation of 1623 it is stated that Henry Clifford of Frampton married the daughter and heiress of ―――― Hoare of Gloucestershire in the time of Henry IV. (*See* Rudder's "Gloucester.")

From the Subsidy Rolls of Gloucester in the Public Record Office, London, are these entries :―

1592. Edmund Hore of Down Hatherly, assessed for his goods.

1609. Richard Hore was assessed for goods at Norton and in the North Ward of the City of Gloucester.

1609. Charles Hoare was assessed for goods in the South Ward of the City of Gloucester and at Brockmouth.

In Alumni Oxonienses are found these entries :—

1610. John Hoare of Co. Gloucester, pleb. Magdalen Hall, matric. 16 June 1610, aged 17. B.A. 18 April, 1611, M.A. 27 Jan. 1613-4. Rector of Oddington Co. Gloucester 1616.

1628. Charles Hoare, son of Charles of Gloucester City, pleb. Magdalen Hall, matric. 12 Dec. 1628 aged 15. B.A. from Hart. Hall 16 Dec. 1630.

1624. A Thomas Hoare B.A. petitioned the East India Company, Oct. 20, 1624, for employment as a preacher. (*See* Calendar of State Papers, p. 484.)

The parish registers at St. Mary de Crypt, Gloucester, previous to 1653, are wanting, but in the Bishop's Registry are the following :—

1612. Thomas, son of Charles Hore Junior baptized June 15.

1622-3. Johan, daughter of Thomas Hoare baptized xxvj of January.

In the Church Registry are these items :—

1657. July 16, Joane Hoare, widow was buried.

1659. Oct. 21, Sara, daughter of Charles Hoare and Sara, his wife was baptized.

1664. Sept. 12, Charles, son of Charles Hoare and Sara, his wife was baptized.

1664. Nov. 8. Thomas filius Caroli Hoare et Sara ux. was baptized.

1666. Martii 14, Elizabetha filia Caroli Hoare et Sara ux. was baptized.*

1654. In Bigland's "Gloucester," p. 142, is mentioned an epitaph to "William Hoare, dyed Feb. 1654 aged 76" in the north transept of Gloucester Cathedral.

1669. The same authority, p. 168, states that in the nave of St. Mary de Crypt are epitaphs to Charles Hoare died 16 Jan. 1689, and to Elizabeth daughter of Charles Hoare died July 2.

In the St. Nicholas Registry, Gloucester City, are these entries :

1560. July 14, Margery Hore daughter of Thomas was baptized.

1569. Oct. 28, was married John Bruar unto Allys Hoare.

1590. July 31. Thomas Hoare was buryed.

1628. June Ruth, daughter of Charles Hoare was buried.

1650. —— Giles Long was married to Anne Hoare.

1662. May ye 18. John Chambers and Mary Hoare were married.

In the Registry of St. John the Baptist, Gloucester, are found :

1618. Master Richard Whoare was buried xxiiii day of August.

1619. March 22. John Hooare was buried.

1630. Mr. Thomas Clutterbuck and Mrs. Anne Hoare were married June 1.

---

* This Sara was probably that " Cousin Sarah Hoare " to whom Edmund Saunders—who from a beggar-boy rose to the position of Lord Chief Justice of the King's Bench —left five pounds by his will, 1681.

347

1634. Margery the daughter of Alexander Hoare was buried Feb. 2.

1636. Thomas Hoare and Hester Berry were married the first day of Oct.

1637. Thomas ye sonne of Alexander Hoare and Margery his wife was baptz. ye 9th. day of May.

1639. Martha ye daughter of Alexander Hoare and Margarye his wife was baptized ye 5th. day of December.

1640. Thomas Hoare of Oxinghall was married to Joane Powell of ye same, June 21.

1642. Francis, daughter of Thomas Hoare and Marye his wife was bapt. ye 7th. day of Aug.

1642. Elizabeth a twin daughter of Thomas Hoare and Marye his wife was bapt. ye 7th. day of August.

1642. Aug. 24. Elizabeth daughter of Thomas Hoare and Marye his wife was buried.

1642. Alice Drew, servant to Mr. Alexander Hoare, was buried 28th. day of June.

1655. John sone of Thomas Hoare, was buried the 11th. day of September.

1656. Edward Nesbete and Martha Hoare were married the 11th day of September.

In the Registry of St. Michael's, Gloucester, is this entry :—

1576. John the son of Thomas Hoar Bapt. 5 day of February.

At Leckhampton Registry are these entries :—

1621. Oct. 29. Walter Hoare and Margaret Faux were married.

1624. Feb. 13. Thomas Hoare and Margaret Ballinger were married.

1636. Feb. 14. Giles Hoare son of Thomas and Margaret, baptized.

1679. Aug. 6. Widow, Margaret Hoare was buried.

From Westbury Registry (Westbury is about eight miles from Gloucester) are these :—

1569. William Hoare son of John baptized, August 17.

1577. Nicholas Hoare son of John baptized, November 18.

At St. Nicholas Church, Gloucester :—

1573. Alice daughter of Edward Hoore was baptized August 23.

1594. Thomas Jones married Johanna Hore August 19.

1624. Joane daughter of Charles Hoare was baptized.

At St. Aldate's Church, Gloucester :

1641. William Hore and Mary Clark were married April 28.

1650. John Hoar was indicted in Gloucester because "custodebit coem taberna, Angl. common typling house, et ibin vendedit in domo suo cevisia et potum sine aliqua licentia."

An English gentleman of the times under consideration usually left his eldest son as well off as possible, and the younger sons were apprenticed to trades or commercial pursuits. Macaulay tells us "that the practice of setting children prematurely to work prevailed in the seventeenth century to an extent which, when compared with the extent of the manufacturing system, seems almost incredible."

In the Gloucester records of indentures the following apprenticeships are found:—

1598. Charles Hoare, son of Charles, sadler, apprenticed to his father.

1603. William Hoare, son of Richard of Norton apprenticed himself to a haberdasher.

1625. Thomas Hoare, son of Charles, Brewer, bound himself to his father.

1626. Alexander Hoare, son of Richard, bound himself to Wm. Lagg, a tanner.

1632. John Hoare, son of Charles, Brewer, bound himself to his father.

1642. Charles Hoare, son of Thomas, Brewer, apprenticed himself to his father.

In John Camben Hotten's "Lists" there appear:—

1634. Richard Hoare, among prisoners ordered transported to Virginia from London.

1685. Thomas Hoar among ninety rebels transported to Barbadoes in the Happy Return of Pool.

In the "Book-Hunter in London," by William Roberts, p. 28, it is said "a large number of books formerly in the possession of the diarist (Evelyn) have at times appeared in the auction room. Among them are two beautifully written MS. the work of Richard Hoare." Evelyn in his Diary, under date of July 12, 1649, says: "I carried over with me my servant, Ri. Hoare, an incomparable writer of severall hands, whom I afterwards preferr'd in the Prerogative Office, at the return of his Majesty." May 17, 1650, he says: "My servant Hoare, who wrote those exquisite several hands, fell of a fit of an apoplexie, caus'd, as I suppose, by tampering with mercury about an experiment in gold." The editor says in a note that specimens of Hoare's handwriting are preserved in the Prerogative Office. In the earliest edition of Sir Horace Walpole's Catalogue of Engravers, five prints illustrating Evelyn's journey from Rome to Naples are attributed to the burin of Richard Hoare, but later editors credit them to Evelyn himself.

CHARLES HOARE AND WIFE MARGERY OF GLOUCESTER, ENGLAND.

With Charles Hoare, senior, of Gloucester City, the pedigree of the American branch of the family begins, no clue to his parentage having been found. Perhaps the earliest recorded mention of him may be the item in the corporation expenditures when the Spanish Armada was menacing England, 1588: "To Charles Hoare for hyer of a horse for two dayes wch Roger Lowe had to Cisseter (Cirencester) when he went to bringe the souldiers towards portingate." A book, prepared by John Smythe of Nibley for Lord Berkeley, "containing the names and surnames of all able and efficient men in body for his Majesty's service in the wars in the

349

County of Gloucester, with their ages, Parsonable statures and armours etc.," by the Right Honorable Lieutenant Lord Berkeley, Lord Lieutenant, etc., by direction from his Majesty in the month of August, 1608, gives the following account of Charles and Richard Hoare:

"The City of Gloucester, Southward: (p. 242.)
    Charles Hoare, Sadler. 2 ca. tr.
Northward: (p. 245.)
    Richard Hore, weaver. 3 p. tr. hath a corslet furnished." Also his four servants are named and their stature given.

The figures and abbreviations appended to the names give the personal description. Thus Charles Hoare was about forty years of age, somewhat short of stature, suitable for service with a caliver, and already trained as a soldier. Richard Hore was between fifty and sixty years of age, of the tallest stature, fitted for a pikeman, and trained in military service.

Will of Charles Hoare the Elder, of Gloucester, 1632.

In the name of God Amen the nyne and twentieth day of May anno domini 1632, I Charles Hoare the elder of the City of Glouc. Sadler being weake and sicklie in body butt of Good and pfct memorie (thanks be geven to god for the same) doe make and ordeyne this my last Will and Testament in manner and forms followinge. ffirst and principalie I give and bequeath my soule unto Amightie God my creator and maker and unto Jesus Christ his only sonne and my alone Saviour and Redeemer hopinge and trustinge through his merits and bitter passion in full assurance to enjoy and inherit in the kingdom of heaven him everlastingly. And as for my body (beinge but dust and ashes) I bequeath to the earth from whence it came to be buried at the discretion of my Execut'r of my Will hoping for a joyfull resurrection both of my soule and body at the last and generall day. And as concerning my worldly goods and substance wherewith God hath bestowed upon me and blessed me wth I give and dispose in manner and form following. ffirst I give and bequeath unto my beloved Wife Margery the use and quiet possession of the house and ymplements wherein I now dwell To have and hold to her for her my said Wife and my sonne Thomas Hoare therein to dwell use and occupy during her naturall life they payinge the rent due to the City of Glouc & keeping the said howse in all needful and necessary repairs as by the lease thereof I am enjoyned. And after her decease my Will is that my sonne Charles Hoare shall have all my right and interest unto the said howse and lease thereof granted unto me from the said Citty and that he shall renew the said lease in his own name. And alsoe my Will is that the plumpe the noast and the Cisterns, glasse windows wainscot and benches with the tables board in the Hawl and the Corner Cupboard aud other Cupboards fasting to the house to remayne to him the said Charles his heirs and assigns wth the said howse at the decease of my said Wife. Provided that my sonne Charles or his assignes doe pay or cause to be paid unto my sonne Thomas Hoare or his assignes the somme of Tenne pounds of lawful English money wthin the space of fourteen dayes after he is possed of the howse and ymplements

350

And if he the said Charles or his assignes shall refuse to pay the same as aforesayd being lawfull demanded Then my Will is that my sonne Thomas shall have the said howse ymplements and lease. Item I give to my said son Thomas fyve silver spones and one silver bowle Item I give unto my son Charles my silver salt and fyve silver spones wch said plate so to my said twoe sonnes geven my Will is the same shalbe in the use and possession of my said Wife during her life and after her decease to remayne unto them Item I give to Thomas Hore Margery Hore and John Hore children of my sonne Charles Hoare ffyve pounds between them three. Item I give and bequeath unto my said sonne Thomas the lease of my Stable and Garden in Travell Lane wch I hold of the Deane and Chapter To have and to hold unto him for and duringe the residue of such term in the same lease as shalbe to come at my decease. Item I give unto Charles Hoare and to John Hoare the Children of my son Thomas Hoare the some of fyve pounds between them. Item I give unto Charles Tarne a Saddle furnished. Item I doe hereby appointe my lovinge sonne Charles Hoare to be my Executor of this my last Will and Testam't in trust and not to make any benefit of the Executorshipp to his own use and for the better providinge & maintinance of my saide wife during her naturall life my Will is & I doe appointe that my debts if any bee & funerall charges being payed and discharged by my Executor out of my estate yet unbeqeathed That all the rest of my goodes chattels Cattle household stuffe & implem'ts of household whatsoever yet unbequeathed shalbe ymploid by the appointm't of my Executors to the use benefitt & behoofs of my Wife & my sone Thomas Hoare his heirs & assignes & the benefit thereof to be yerely equally divided betweene them & soe to remayne at the disposinge of my Execut'r wth the advice of my Overseers during the life of my saide Wife and after her decease my Will is that the sayd estate off my goods & chattels shalbe by my saide Execut'r wholie conferred uppon my sonne Thomas Hoare his heirs and assignes the funerall charges of my wife being discharged first out of it within one month after her decease And that my Will may be the better pformed my Will & desire is that my said Execut'r shall wthin six weeks after my decease enter into one bond of Two hundred pounds to the Overseers of this my Will that this my Will shalbe pformed by him in all points And if he refuse to enter into such bond my Will is & I doe appoint my sayd Sonne Thomas Hoare to be Execut'r of this my Will And I doe desire my sonnes in lawe Mr. Thomas Hill & Mr. Leonard Tarne to be Overseers of this my Will & I give to each of them for their paines to see my Will pform'd a saddle a peice furnished fitt for their use And in witness whereof I have hereunto putt my hand and seele in the psence of these being witnesses.

The mke of CHARLES (H) HOARE
The mke of JAMES TILER
JOHN HOLLAND

Of the four children of Charles Hoare senior, named in this will, Thomas had two sons, Charles and John, also mentioned, but of father or sons nothing further of interest is known with certainty. The names appear in Gloucestershire annals from time to time, but the identification of personalities is not easy. Of the two daughters, wives of Thomas Hill and Leonard Tarne, the baptismal names are

351

irrevocably lost. Hill was an alderman and Tarne sheriff of the county and city of Gloucester in 1630. Thomas Hill became mayor of the city in 1640. By grant of Edward Third this city is a county by itself. A mayor and two sheriffs were annually chosen by the twelve Aldermen "and twelve other of the most legal and discreet Burgesses." (Fosbrooke's "Gloucester," p. 414.) The office of the sheriff seems to have been in social dignity on a par, at least, with that of mayor. Thomas Hill died, according to Rudder, p. 402, in October 1652, and was buried in the church of St. Mary de Crypt. His son Robert was a "goldsmith," then equivalent to banker, in Gloucester. In the will of Leonard Tarne, dated Nov. 3, 1641, with a codicil bearing date April 9, 1642, mention is made of his brothers Thomas, John and Gervase, and sister Elizabeth Cathorne, all with small families ; also of his son Thomas with daughters Elizabeth and Damaris. But by baptismal records we know that five sons were born to him :—Myles, baptized 1595 ; Charles, 1601 ; John, 1604 ; Thomas, 1609 ; George, 1613. The high standing and wealth of Leonard Tarne are attested by the great length of his last testament and by the large amount of property bequeathed. Among his possessions was the noted Raven Tavern still standing. His most noteworthy bequest was a public one : " unto the Mayor and Burgesses of the Cittie of Glouc'r. : and to their successors forever one yearly rent or sume of foure pounds of lawfull money of England to be issuinge and going out of all that pasture ground with the appurtences called or commonly known by the name of Monckleighton . . . . . the said yearly rent or sume to be paid at the ffeast of St. Thomas the apostle and upon the ffridaie next before Easter day usually called good ffridaie, by even and equall porcons . . . to be given unto fortie poore people of this cittie most needinge the same, to each of them Twelve pence a peece." Monkleighton is now a suburb covered with fine residences and known as Alexandria Road in Gloucester. Leonard Tarne was a glover with an extensive business, and there is a tradition in Gloucester that this was transferred to Worcester and finally came into the hands of the Dents.

CHARLES HOARE THE YOUNGER, AND WIFE, JOANNA HINCKSMAN.

Charles Hoare junior, the executor of his father's will, was probably the eldest son. He became a man of substance and one greatly respected in his native city, as is attested by the fact that he was one of its aldermen from 1632 to to 1638 and sheriff in 1634. His name is found in the Council minutes with "gentleman" or "generosus" affixed to it. In the lists of members of the Council for the six years before his decease his name always appears, although generally among "nomina eorum qui fecerunt defaultum," that is, were absent from the meetings. He followed the occupation of brewer, although he had served a long apprenticeship with his father, the saddler, and his will indicates that he carried on the business of wool stapling, a trade which early attained great importance in Gloucestershire, and has been pursued by members of the Hoare family there, especially at Cirencester, down to quite recent days. The original indenture of this apprenticeship, written in abbreviated Latin, is extant, of which the following is a translation:

1599. Charles Hoare son of Charles Hoare of the City of Gloucester, saddler, by act of Indenture made on the day of the Feast of St. Thomas the Apostle (Dec. 21) in the year of the reign of Queen Elizabeth the forty-first, binds himself apprentice to the said Charles & Margerie, his wife, in the trade in which the said Charles now practices, for the term of eight years following the feast aforesaid by act agreed upon verbally on each part. And the said Charles & Margerie will pay the said apprentice at the end of the time 40 shillings.

In the calendar of State Papers, vol. cccxxxiv. p. 178, 1636, is a petition of John Brown, late mayor, and Charles Hoare and Lawrence Singleton, late sheriffs of the City of Gloucester, stating that they had collected and paid over to the Treasurer of the Navy the one thousand pounds ship money imposed upon Gloucester, and asking for the repayment to them of certain expenses amounting to fifty-two pounds, which request was granted.

The date of Charles Hoare's marriage to Joanna Hinksman is not known, but it must have been shortly after the expiration of his apprenticeship. Of their children three only are named in his father's will—Thomas, Margery and John; the other three mentioned in his own will—Daniel, Leonard and Joanna—being minors in 1632. There may have been others deceased, and probably of these were Ruth, buried June 1628, and Charles graduate at Oxford 1630, aged 17. The Hincksman or Henchman family was prosperous and highly esteemed in Gloucester. A Joseph Hinxman was graduated at Oxford in 1577, and became rector of the parish of Naunton, fourteen miles north-east of the city of Gloucester. Of her immediate family we know only that she had brothers William, Walter, Edward and Thomas, and sisters Elinor Bailies and —— Founes. Thomas Hincksman, in 1634 called "late servant to Mr. Charles Hoare for the space of eight years now past," was then made a burgess, paying a fine of 10s. A Walter Hincksman about the same period was rector at Matlock in Derbyshire. The noted Captains Thomas and Daniel Henchman, who figured in the early Indian wars in New England, may have been kinsmen of Joanna, though proof of this is lacking. That there was some relationship between the early immigrants in New England bearing the names Hoare and Hinksman seems probable from the frequency with which these names are found associated. Capt. Daniel Henchman was one of the witnesses to Doctor Leonard Hoar's will, and Thomas appended his signature as witness to a power of attorney given by Daniel Hoare.

THE ANCESTRY OF THE HOAR FAMILY IN AMERICA.

A Compilation from Collections made by the Honorable GEORGE FRISBIE HOAR.

By HENRY S. NOURSE, of Lancaster, Mass.

WILL OF CHARLES HOARE (JUNIOR) OF GLOUCESTER, 1638.

Prerogative Court of Canterbury.

In the name of God Almightie Creator of all thinges and in Jesus Christ his deare and only son my most bountifull loveing Saviour and in the blessed spiritt my comforter Amen I Charles Hoare of the cittie of Gloucester being weake in body but perfect in memory blessed be my good god therefore, Doe hereby declare that my last will and testament as followeth ffirst I bequeath my soule into the handes of God that created it and my deare Saviour that soe dearlie ransom'd it with full confidence thorough his merrittes that after the end of this life it shall rest wth him everlastingly. And my bodie to the earthe from whence it came wth full assurance that at the last daie when my Saviour shall appeare in glory it shalbe by his power raised upp to the resurrection of the iust, And for the estate it hath pleased god to lend unto me of the thinges of this world I thus· dispose ffirst that with as much convenient speede as may well be all my rentes and debtes sett downe under my hand and all other if any be and can appeare to be due shalbe paid. Item I give to my brother Thomas Hoare twentie poundes, to my sister Elinor Bailies fortie shillinges, to my brother William Hincksman and Walter Hincksman and Edward Hincksman and my sister ffounes twentye shillinges a peece in gould, alsoe I give to my brother Thomas Hincksman five poundes and to my servant John Sponar at presberie five markes and to his wife five nobles and to Thomas Prichard my servant fortie shillinges and to Thomas Ade my servant tenn shillinges, Alsoe I give to Mr. Thomas Vell and to Alderman Hill and Mr. Leonard Tarne my brother lawes and my brother too new rings for my sake, and to good Mr. Workman our faithfull watchman forty shillings. Alsoe I give unto my welbeloved wife Joane Hoare ye some of three hundred and fiftie poundes and to my sonne John Hoare twoe hundred poundes and to my son Daniell Hoare one hundred and fiftie poundes and to my daughter Joane Hoare a hundred poundes and to my son Leonard Hoare one hundred poundes and my will is that my wife shall have the furniture of houshold that I have in all places at her disposing during her life and after to come indiferentlie amongst my children except the goodes at Thornebery wch was deliuered me by the sheriffe by vertue of an elegit, all wch I give unto my daughter Margerie Mathewe presentlie after my decease. Alsoe I give unto my sonn Thomas Hoare twentie poundes. Alsoe I give to the said Margery my daughter and her sonne Charles Mathewe twoe hundred poundes and my will is that soe longe as this twoe hundred poundes remanies in the stocke which I shall leave (which shalbe till my executors and overseers shall allowe thereof for her good to lett him have it,) there shalbe

354

unto her and her sonne sixteene poundes a yeare quarterly paid and my will and desire is that the stocke I shall leave unto my wife and the foure first named children with the twoe hundred poundes given my daughter shalbe used and imployed uppon the three bargaines I have taken at Encombe, Presbery and Slimsbridg and my wife and the foure children to have their maintenance out of it, and my will is that my sonne Leonard shalbe carefullie kept at Schoole and when hee is fitt for itt to be carefullie placed at Oxford, and if ye Lord shall see fitt, to make him a Minister unto his people and that all ye charge thereof shalbe discharged out of the proffitt which it shall please god to send out of the stocke and that all the rest of my estate unbequeathed all debtes and expence being discharged shalbe equallie deuided betweene my wife and my twoe sonnes Daniell and John, and Joane, and the profittes of the said stocke to accrewe unto them alsoe untill my executors and my overseers shall agree for their good to lett any of them haue their porc͂ons for their p^rferment. Only this except͟d that my sonne Leonard shall have accrue and dewe unto him out of this estate six poundes a yeare to bee paid unto him by the foresaid hundred poundes when my executors and overseers shall allowe of it to be for his preferment and if anie of my children shall die before they come to make use of their porc͂ons my will is that porc͂ons soe falling out shalbe equallie devided amongst my five children nowe with me and my sonne Thomas aforesaid and if it shall soe happen that the stocke bequeathed be not founde fitt to be imployed as I have directed but I trust ye Lord will soe blesse that happie trade of life unto them that some of them will never give over but if soe should be then my will is that my executors pay in ye porc͂ons unto them if they bee att age or els to paie it in or good securitie to my overseers and my will is that as I have agreed with Mr. Thomas Vell and p'mised there shall alwaies be really upon the groundes att Encome which I have taken of him for Eight yeares eight hundred of the best ewes to stand for his securitie untill all rentes and dewes whatsoever shalbe really paid unto him, and now deare saviour spreade thy armes of mercie over me purge away my synnes though they are many and greate and my faith weake lett thy power be seene in my weaknes and thy strength in my manifould infirmities keepe me from that evill one and Receive me to thy mercy to whom with god the father and the holie spiritt be all glorie and power and thankes giveinge both nowe and for evermore Amen this 25th day of September 1638. By me Cha: Hoare: ffurther I give unto my sonne John Hoare fortie poundes more wch shall accrewe unto him when all the other are satisfied out of the estate.

Adm͂on granted 21 Dec. 1638—to Joane Hoare the relict.*

The Mr. Thomas Vell mentioned appears to have been active in public affairs of Gloucestershire in his day, and sided with the Puritans in the early part of the Civil war; but was one of the deputation to welcome Charles II. on his restoration.

The "good Mr. Workman our faithful watchman" refers to John Workman, a native of Gloucestershire whose persecution by Archbishop Laud was, according to Laud himself, insisted upon more than any other charge at the trial of that prelate. Workman, for

* NOTE.—This will was printed in the NEW-ENGLAND HISTORICAL AND GENEALOGICAL REGISTER for October, 1891. A comparison of the printed copy with the original at Somerset House, is the authority for two important corrections now made.

certain utterances against the use of pictures and images in churches, and his condemnation of " mixed dancing," was brought before the high commission at Lambeth, suspended from the ministry, excommunicated, required to make restitution and to pay costs of suit, and thrown into prison. He then taught school to support his large family, but Laud hearing of this forbade his teaching children. He next sought a living by the practice of medicine, but died in great poverty January, 1641. The Corporation of Gloucester, in 1633, granted Mr. Workman an annuity of £20. For this act the mayor, town clerk and several of the aldermen were prosecuted in the High Commission Court. Charles Hoare was doubtless one of the offending aldermen. (Brook's "Puritans," 2, 434.)

Charles Hoare's house is still standing on Southgate street, occupied by the printing and publishing house of the Gloucester *Chronicle*.

All of the children named in the will except Thomas came to America probably within two years after the death of their father, for the first child of Margery, who married Henry Flynt of Braintree, was born in July, 1642. Their mother Joanna came with them : " the common origin of that remarkable progeny, in which statesmen, jurists, lawyers, orators, poets, story-tellers and philosophers seem to vie with each other in recognized eminence." (Charles Francis Adams in " Three Episodes of Massachusetts History".) She died at Braintree 10 mo. 21, 1661, according to Braintree Records. This date is confirmed by an entry in an almanac once belonging to Rev. Henry Flynt. "Dec. 22, 1661, ye midnight before my mother Hoar dyed and was buried ye—" She was interred in the same grave with her son Leonard, in the old Quincy burying ground. In 1892 the Honorable George F. Hoar erected a memorial to his ancestress and her daughter-in-law. It is in form a double headstone, shaped from a large, thick slab of slate. Following are the two inscriptions :

Joanna Hoare | died in Braintree | September 21st, 1651. | She was widow of | Charles Hoare, | Sheriff of | Gloucester, England, | who died 1638. | She came to | New England | with five children | about 1640. |

Bridget, | widow of President | Leonard Hoar, | died May 25, 1723 | daughter of | John Lord Lisle, | President of the | High Court of Justice, | Lord Commissioner of | the Great Seal, who | drew the indictment | and sentence of | King Charles I, and | was murdered at | Lausanne Aug. 11th 1664, | and of Lady Alicia Lisle, | who was beheaded by | the brutal judgment | of Jeffries 1685. | She was nearly akin | by marriage to | Lord William Russell. |

THOMAS HOARE, probably the oldest of the surviving children of Charles at his death, did not accompany his brothers and sisters to New England. According to the register of St. Mary de Crypt he was baptized June 15, 1612. A translation of the record of his apprenticeship to his father dated 1625, is as follows :—

Thomas Hoare son of Charles Hoare of the City of Gloucester, Brewer, binds himself apprentice to the said Charles his father by indenture dating from the day of the Feast of Purification of St. Mary the Virgin (Feb. 2,) in the year of the reign of King Charles now of England the first, for the term of twelve years etc. paying at the end of the term two suits of clothes.

The name of Thomas Hoare appears among early settlers in old Norfolk, Massachusetts, and was common in Gloucestershire; but the identity of either of the persons bearing this name with the son of Charles has not been established. One of the name was churchwarden of St. Mary de Crypt Church, Gloucester, in 1636.

MARGERY HOARE was married to John Matthews at St. Nicholas Church in Glôucester, December 25, 1633, and had a son Charles who is mentioned in his grandfather Hoare's will. She was a widow, and probably childless, when she came to New England. She married for her second husband Rev. Henry Flynt of Braintree. He is supposed to have been born at Matlock, Derbyshire, England. In politics he was of the party of Sir Henry Vane, and his theological views led him to take, for a time at least, the unpopular side in the Antinomian controversy. The inscription upon his tombstone in Quincy is as follows :—

Here Lyes interred ye Body of ye Rev'd Mr. Henry Flynt,
who came to New England in ye Year 1635, was
Ordained ye first Teacher of ye Church of *Braintry*
1639 and Died April 27th. 1668. He had ye
Character of a Gentleman Remarkable for his
Piety, Learning, Wisdom, & Fidelity in his Office.
By him on his right hand lyes the Body of *Margery*,
his beloved consort, who Died March 1686–7, her
maiden name was Hoar. She was a Gentlewoman
of Piety, Prudence, & peculiarly accomplished
for instructing young Gentlewoemen, many being
sent to her from other Towns, especially from *Boston*.
They descended from antient and good familys in England.

The ten children born to *Henry* and *Margery Flynt* as recorded in Braintree Records were :—

1. DOROTHY, b. 21. 5 mo. 1642; married *Samuel Shephard*, 1666.
2. ANNAH, b. 11. 7 mo. 1643; married *John Dassett*, 1662.
3. JOSIAH, b. 24. 6 mo. 1645; married *Esther Willet*.
4. MARGARETT, b. 20. 4 mo. 1647; died 29, 6 mo. 1648.
5. JOANNA, b. 18. 12 mo. 1648; married *Noah Newman* 1669.
6. DAVID, b. 11. 11 mo. 1651; died 21. 1 mo. 1652.
7. SETH, b. 2. 2 mo. 1653.
8. RUTH, b. 31. 11 mo. 1654.
9. 10. COTTON and JOHN, b. 16. 7 mo. 1656; died 20. 9 mo. 1656.

Mr. Flynt accumulated considerable property for a country clergyman. The eldest son, Josiah, was graduated at Harvard College in 1664, and was ordained the successor of Rev. Richard Mather at Dorchester December 27, 1671. He died at the early age of thirty-five years, September 16, 1680. His wife was Esther, daughter of Captain Thomas Willett, first mayor of New York city. Of her four children one was the noted bachelor Tutor Flynt who served Harvard College for the unexampled term of fifty-five years — 1699–1754 — and died in 1760. Her daughter Dorothy married Edmond Quincy, May 11, 1678, and thus the Quincy family derives descent from Joanna Hincksman Hoare through both of her daughters, Joanna and Margery. Mrs. Dorothy Flynt Quincy died in 1737. The house in which she lived, built by Colonel Edmond Quincy in 1685, still stands, a characteristic example of domestic colonial architecture. Among the more famous of her numerous descendants are those members of the Holmes, Wendell, Jackson, Lowell and Quincy families whose names are household words in Massachusetts, and also Gen. Terry, the hero of Fort Fisher.

JOHN HOARE must have been younger by several years than his brother Thomas, for at his father's death in 1638, his apprenticeship, a translation of the record of which is given below, had but half expired. If apprenticeships terminated when the apprentice came of age, John Hoare was but eleven years old when bound to his father.

1633. John Hoare son of Charles Hoare of the City of Gloucester, Brewer, binds himself apprentice to the aforesaid Charles his father and Johanna his wife by Indenture made on the day of the Feast of St. James the Apostle (May 11.) in the year of the reign of King Charles I. now of England etc. the eighth for the term of ten years from the feast etc. paying at the end of the term six shillings legal money of England.

John appears in Scituate, Massachusetts, as bearing arms in 1643. The historian of that town, Samuel Deane, relates that he was, while there resident, always engaged in the business of the town, and in drafting of deeds, bonds, etc., and is occasionally called a lawyer. He had lands adjoining Mosquashcut pond which he sold to the lawyer John Saffin in 1659, when he removed to Concord. His ability, vigor and originality of thought and action soon made him one of the prominent figures in Concord and vicinity, but he is found often at odds with the ecclesiastical oligarchy of the times. Whether like his sometime neighbor at Lancaster, John Prescott — to whose son he gave his oldest daughter — he sympathized with the Presbyterian criticisms of the theocratic restriction of political and religious privileges in the colony, is not known, but he strongly resembled Prescott in his persistency, enterprise and altruistic spirit. He was not only independent in speech, but rashly sharp of tongue and pen, and suffered accordingly at the hands of jealous authority. The story of his disbarment is best told by the original documents :—

In answer to the peticon or remonstrance of John Hoare, the Court finding that severall of the magistrates, and some others, are impeached for. not doing justice and other complaints of a very high nature, doe therefore order that a hearing be granted to the peticoner, and that due notice be given to the complaynant to appeare to make good his severall charges, or otherwise to give reason for the same. Notice was given accordingly to the sayd Hoare, and the sayd John Hoare appearing in Court, his peticon or remonstrance being read wth such euidences as he produced, the Court proceeded as followeth : — Whereas John Hoare, of Concord, hath presented to this Court a petition or remonstrance, wherein he complains of great wrongs and injuryes he hath susteyned as his brother's agent, by reason he could not obteyne justice in some of our Courts of judicature in seuerall actions depending betweene himself, as agent and Lieut Richard Cooke, of Boston, the Court having affoorded him large liberty and oppertunity to make good his charges, and hauing heard all his allegations together wth such witnesses as were produced to proove the same and duely weighed the case, doe judge his complaints to be groundless and unjust, and his offences to be of a very high nature, tending not only to the dishonour of God, but to the scandall and reproach of seuerall of our Courts, honer'd magestrates, and officers of Court. That due witnes may be borne against such sinfull practises, and gouerment of this jurisdiccon under his majestyes royall charter, may be upheld and mayntayned, this Court doeth order, that the sayd Hoare shall find suertyes bound in one hundred pounds for his good behauior during the Court's pleasure. and that henceforth he shall be disabled to plead any cases but his owne in this jurisdiction, and also that he pay as a fine the sume of fifty pounds for such his miscarriages, and be imprisoned till it be pajd, or security given for the same. Whereas John Hoare, contrary to express order of the Court, hath withdrawn himself from the Court before his sentence was declared, the secretary is appointed by the Court to send for him, and require the performance of the sentence of this Court to all intents and purposes therein conteyned.

(Massachusetts Records, Vol. IV. Part 11, p. 291—1665.)

In answer to the peticon of John Hoare, humbly desiring the favour of this Court to release him of his bonds of good behaviour and to make such abatement of his fine as their wisdomes shall judge meete. The Court judgeth it meete, and orders, the peticoner be released his bonds of good behaviour, and that twenty pounds of his fine be abated him.

(Massachusetts Records, Vol. IV. Part 11, p. 301--1666.)

In ans'r to the petition of Alice, the wife of John Hoare, of Concord, the Court judgeth it meete, on the petitioner's satisfying and paying in to the Treasurer to his content the sume of tenn pounds to abate the remainder of her husband's fine yet remaining and unpaid.

(Massachusetts Records, Vol. IV. Part 11, p. 387—1668.)

In 1668 John Hoare was charged before the county court of saying at the public house of Ensign William Buss "that the Blessing Master Bulkeley pronounced in dismissing the publique Assembly in the Meeting-house was nc better than vane babbling." Upon conviction of what the law of 1646 calls "the disparagement of the

Lord's holy ordinance and making God's ways contemptible and ridiculous" he was fined ten pounds. He was also called upon to answer to the Court on two occasions "for neglecting the public worship of God on the Lord's day." (County Court Files, 1668–1675.)

In November, 1675, food and fuel failed the little community of Christian Indians at Nashoba, and a committee composed of Major Daniel Gookin, Major Simon Willard and Rev. John Eliot, the selectmen consenting, caused their removal to Concord. They numbered fifty-eight men, women and children, and no man in Concord could be prevailed upon to take charge of them until John Hoare consented to do so. He gave them quarters in his own house and offices, and began the building of a workshop and palisade wherein they could labor by day and be safely kept at night. The whole land was overshadowed by the horrors of Indian warfare, and in the frontier towns the howling of a wolf or the hooting of an owl, indistinctly heard, sent pallor to the cheeks and the chill of fear to the hearts of wives and mothers; lest it might be the war-whoop of Philip's savage crew, or the death shriek of an absent son, father or husband. In the midst of the public panic came the false rumor that some of Eliot's converts were among the blood-stained murderers. Mrs. Rowlandson has informed us that she was told by her captors, and she evidently believed, that the seven persons killed at Lancaster, August 22, 1675 "were slain and mangled in a barbarous manner by one-eyed John and Marlborough's praying Indians." Yet the red men so accused, seized and taken to Boston by Captain Mosely, upon their trial proved an undoubted *alibi*. It was not strange in a time of such excitement that many of the people of Concord were greatly troubled by the presence among them of Mr. Hoare's wards. Suddenly upon a Lord's day the most brutal of the Colony captains, Samuel Mosely, appeared in the Concord meeting-house with his rough troopers, probably by invitation of the dissatisfied, and after the service declared his intention to remove the Nashoba Indians to Boston. Receiving what he considered due encouragement, he without authority and in spite of the vigorous protests of John Hoare, broke into his premises and sent "the heathen" robbed of most of their personal property, down to Deer Island under a guard of twenty soldiers. The story is told at length in Major Daniel Gookin's History of the Christian Indians. (*See* Archæologica Americana, p. 495, *et seq.*) The colonial governor and council were not well pleased by Mosely's contemptuous assumption of their powers, but did not dare to bring him to bar for his atrocious offence, nor did they recompense the brave John Hoare for his losses, which Gookin acknowledges "were considerable." Soon followed the massacre of February 10, 1676, at Lancaster, and when the governor and council sought to ransom the captive women and children they could find no efficient help until the abused Nashoba Christians came to their aid, and bore their messages to the then haughty sagamores April 3 and 28. With them on the latter date went John Hoare at the solicitation of the minister, Joseph Rowlandson. The historian, Hubbard, mentions the heroism, but forgets the hero's name who risked more than life in putting himself into the power of the merciless: "A person formerly acquainted with the Indians about Lancaster, did adventure upon the forementioned overtures, to go amongst them to try if he could not prevail with them for the redemption of the minister's wife, ... and through the favour of him who having the hearts of all in his hand, inclines them as he pleases, obtained the desired end for an inconsiderable sum, which gave encouragement to the council to send two messengers on the like errand the same week, to procure the redemption of others, not without success." These two messengers were Seth Perry sent on May 3, and Jonathan Prescott, John Hoare's son-in-law, on May 5.

Mrs. Rowlandson in her Narrative gives us a more lively picture of the trials of the embassy to the sachems at Wachuset:

On a Sabbath-day (April 30), the sun being about an hour high, in the afternoon, came Mr. John Hoar, (the Council permitting him, and his own foreward spirit inclining him) together with the two forementioned Indians, Tom and Peter, with their third Letter from the Council. When they came near, I was abroad though I saw them not; they presently called me in and bade me sit down and not stir. They then catched up their Guns and away they ran as if an Enemy had been at hand, and the Guns went off apace. I manifested some great trouble, and they asked me what was the matter? I told them I thought they had killed the Englishman (for they had in the mean time told me that an Englishman was come). They said no; They shot over his Horse, and under and before his Horse, and they pushed him this way and that way, at their pleasure, shewing what they could do. Then they let him come to their Wigwams. I begged of them to let me see the Englishman but they would not: . . . . When they had talked their fill with him, they suffered me to go to him . . . . . I now asked them whether I should go home with Mr. Hoar? they answered no, one and another of them; and it being night, we lay down with that answer. In the morning, Mr. Hoar invited the Saggamores to Dinner; but when we went to get it ready, we found they had stolen the greatest part of the Provision Mr. Hoar had brought out of the bags in the night; and we may see the wonderfull power of God in that one passage, in that when there was such a great number of the Indians together, and so greedy of a little good food, and no English there but Mr. Hoar and myself, that they did not knock us in the head and take what we had; there being not only some Provision, but also Trading-cloth a part of the twenty pounds agreed upon. . . . . . . At night I asked them again if I should go home? They all as one said No, except my Husband would come for me. When we were lain down, my Master went out of the Wigwam, and by-and-by sent in an Indian called James the Printer, who told Mr. Hoar, that my Master would let me go home tomorrow, if he would let him have one pint of Liquors . . . . . On Tuesday morning they call their General Court (as they call it) to consult and determine whether I should go home or no. And they all as one man did seemingly consent to it that I should go home except Philip who would not come among them . . . . . . About the Sun going down, Mr. Hoar and myself, and the two Indians, came to Lancaster and a solemn sight it was to me. There had I lived many comfortable years amongst my Relations and Neighbours; and now not one Christian to be seen, nor one house left standing. We went on to a Farm-house thet was yet standing, where we lay all night, and a comfortable lodging we had, though nothing but straw to lye on. The Lord preserved us in safety that night, and raised us up again in the morning, and carried us along, that before noon we came to Concord.

Before the war with the Indians was at an end John Hoare suffered an even more severe trial in the misfortune of his only son, a young man of twenty-six years. August 11, 1676, the grand jury, upon complaint of certain Christian Indians, presented and indicted Daniel Goble, Stephen Goble, Nathaniel Wilder and Daniel Hoare all of Concord, "for that they not hauing the feare of God before their eyes & being Investigated by the Divil wth other his Accomplises at or on the 7th of August last, at or neere to Hurtlebury hill, in the woods in the precincts of Concord or neere therevnto did murder & kill three Indian weomen & three Indian Children contrary to the peace of Soueraigne Lord the King, his Crowne & dignitye the law of God & of this Jurisdiction." The jury in the cases of Wilder and Hoare found a speciall verdict: "If being present & seing the fact done & concenting, it be murder then we find him gilty according to Inditement, if not not gilty." Stephen Goble was executed September 21, and Daniel Goble, September 26, several Indians suffering on the gallows the same day, as is told in the Diary of Samuel Sewall, I. pp. 21 and 22. The youths misled by them were pardoned.

11th Oct. 1676. Upon the humble peticōn of Daniel Hoare & Nathaniell Wilder, presented to this Court, acknouledging the justice of this Court, & begging pardon for their lives, the Court have granted their petition and accordingly doe remitt the sentence of death passed against them, and order, that they pay prison charges and tenn pounds apeece money, halfe towards the charge of witnesses, to be payd to the Tresurer of the Country, and the other halfe to Andrew Pittime & Swagon, ye Indians prosecuting against them: on payment whereof they are discharged. (Massachusetts Records, Vol. V. p. 117.)

In a petition to the General Court, dated June 3, 1680, John Hoare calls himself of Braintree, having taken up his residence there temporarily. He asks relief from his sentence, saying: "I am now grown old, not like long to continue in this world, and loath to leave such a remembrance upon my name or to my children." The Council voted to grant his request, but the Deputies refused consent.

The original of the following petition is in possession of the Honorable George F. Hoar:

To the Hono'rd Generall Court Now Assembled
In Boston May 24th. 1682.

The Humble Petition of John Hoare—

Humbly Sheweth that wheras in the yeare 1665 yo'r Poor Petitioner was comitted to Prison forced to find suretyes for his good behaviour and also fyned fivety pound for doing such things as I humbly conceived were but my duty and also prohibited from pleadding any bodies caus but my owne : Now yo'r poor Petitioner hath a long time layne under the smart of these sufferings and hath often moved for a release but such hath bene the unhappyness of yo'r Poor Suppliant that he hath not yet obtained such a good day the want whereof hath bene greatly prejuditiall to my Brother Mr. Daniel Hoare his Estate and so my owne and also unto my name and famyly. The perticulars in my petition then exhibited to the Honor'd Generall Court wear such as my Brother Mr Henery Flint of Brantrey & Mr Edmond Browne of Sudbury did judge would not give any ofence. And in that hope I did present it.

I Humbly now present to this Hon'rd Court that in the time of the warr I tooke the charge of about sixty Indians belonging to Nashoby by the order of Majo'r Willerd, Majo'r Gookin, Mr. Eliott, and the select men of Concord. I built them a fort that cost mee of my own estate fourty pounds and went with my teame in Hazard of my life to save and bring home there Corne and also borrowed Rey and hors for them to plant and sow which I was forced to pay for myselfe. I also made severall Journeys to Lancaster and to the Counsell and two Journies to the Indians to redeme Mrs. Rowlinson and Good wife Kettle with two horses and provisions and gave the sagamores considerably of my owne estate above whatever I received of the Countrey and by the favor of god obtained of them that they would fight noe more but in ther owne defence : Seth Perry also had severall things of mee to give the Indians that hee might escape with his life.

My sonn Daniel Hoare also was Indicted for his life yet by divine providence was spared, yet was sentanced to pay five pounds to the Indians and five pound to the Countrey tho' as I humbly Conceive he had not broken any Law.

My Humble Supplication on all accounts to this Hon'rd Court is that I might be sett att Liberty from my sentence and may enjoy the liberty of an English man, and also that the Cor't would pleas to remitt my son Daniel's sentance. And if they pleas to grant me some small parcell of Land to comfort my wife with respect unto all her sufferings by my disbursements for the Countrey as above recited.

And yo'r Petitioner shall give thanks to the Lord and you

And shall ever Pray &c

JOHN HOARE.

The magistrates consented to release John Hoare from his bonds and from the restraint laid upon him as to his pleading in the courts and also "that considering his publike service & costs in securing the Nashoby Indians at his house in Concord by order of this Court's Comittee for severall monethes in time of said warr, and for his adventuring his life to goe up to the Indians in the time of the warr the successe whereof was the Redeeming of some Captives particularly Mrs. Rowlandson" two hundred acres of land should be

363

granted his family. The deputies refused to concur and the following is the final answer of the Court:

In ans'r to the peticon of John Hoare, and on further consideration thereof the Court judge meet for his service donne for the publick etc. to grant to the wife and children of the sajd John Hoare two hundred acres of land in any comon lands from former grants, and not hindering a plantation. (Massachusetts Records, Vol. V. 359.)

John Hoare owned about three hundred acres in the western part of Concord, but exchanged the larger portion of this with Edward Wright, in 1672, for an estate in the East Quarter and for "all the right, title and interest wch Edward Wright of Concord aforesaid, husbandman, hath or should have in and to certain houses, lands and hereditaments etc. in the Lordship of Castle Browmick (?) in the County of Warwick in the Kingdom of England." (See Middlesex Deeds, IV. 409). He died April 2, 1704, and his wife Alice ——— died June 5, 1696. Samuel Sewall makes in his Diary but one noteworthy mention of Mr. Hoare. Under date of Friday, Nov. 8, 1690, he writes, "Jn'o Hoar comes into the Lobby and sais he comes from the Lord, by the Lord, to speak for the Lord: Complains that Sins as bad as Sodom's found here." We may therefore infer that neither imprisonment nor fines nor old age could put a curb upon John Hoare's freedom of speech.

The children of JOHN[1] and ALICE HOARE were three:

1. ELIZABETH,[2] married December 23, 1675, Jonathan Prescott of Lancaster, being his second wife. To them six children were born:

    i. JONATHAN,[3] b. April 5, 1677; a noted physician; m. July 9, 1701, Rebecca Bulkeley; d. Oct. 28, 1729, and had eleven children.

    ii. ELIZABETH, b. Sept. 27, 1678; m. John Fowle of Woburn.

    iii. DOROTHY, b. March 31, 1681; m. July 14, 1702, Edward Bulkeley; d. at Wethersfield, Conn., in 1748.

    iv. JOHN, b. May 13, 1683; d. Jan. 28, 1706.

    v. MARY, b. Aug. 14, 1685; m. April 16, 1702, John Miles, and had six children.

    vi. BENJAMIN, b. Sept. 16, 1687; was graduated at Harvard 1703; clergyman; d. May 27, 1777; m. (1st) Elizabeth Higginson of Salem, in 1715; (2d) Mercy Gibbs, in 1732; and (3d) Mrs. Mary (Pepperell) Colman, in 1748. By the first he had five children, of whom Benjamin m. Rebecca Minot of Salem, and had a daughter Rebecca who became, May 12, 1763, the second wife of Hon. Roger Sherman, a signer of the Declaration of Independence, and U. S. Senator from Connecticut, from 1791 to his death in 1793. Their youngest daughter, Sarah Sherman, Oct. 13, 1812, m. Hon. Samuel Hoar of Concord, and of her elder sisters, Rebecca and Elizabeth in succession became the wives of Judge Simeon Baldwin of New Haven. Rebecca was the mother of Roger S. Baldwin, Governor and Senator, who argued the famous Armistead case, and grandmother of Judge Simeon E. Baldwin. Mehitable m. for her second husband Jeremiah Evarts, Esq., the Honorable William Maxwell Evarts being her son. Martha married Jeremiah Day, President of Yale College, and was the mother of Hon. Sherman Day, author of Pennsylvania Historical Collections and State Surveyor of California.

        Jonathan Prescott d. Dec. 5, 1721, his fourth wife surviving him. His second wife, Elizabeth Hoar, d. Sept. 25, 1687.

2. MARY,[2] married Benjamin Graves, October 21, 1668.

3. DANIEL, born 1650; married July 16, 1677, Mary Stratton, daughter of Samuel and Mary (Fry), and (2d) Mary Lee, October 16, 1717. By the first wife he had eleven children:

i. JOHN,[3] b. Oct. 24, 1678, at Watertown; d. March 1, 1764, in Sudbury. By wife Ruth had ten children: 1. *Nehemiah*,[4] b. Oct. 19, 1704; d. Dec. 2, 1718. 2. *Jonathan*, b. May 30, 1706; d. Nov. 8, 1719. 3. *Oliver*, b. Oct. 14, 1707; d. May 29, 1711. 4. *John*, b. March 22, 1709; d. Aug. 28, 1711. 5. *Submit*, b. Sept. 5, 1711. 6. *Ruth*, b. Dec. 11, 1713; m. April 20, 1732, Amos Sanderson. 7. *Dorothy*, b. Feb. 22, 1714. 8. *John*, b. Jan. 2, 1715; d. Nov. 17, 1715. 9. *Josiah*, b. Jan. 2, 1717. 10. *Abigail*, b. Nov. 15, 1720.

ii. LEONARD, captain, d. April, 1771, aged 87, in Brimfield. By his wife Esther had eight children: 1. *Joseph*, b. Dec. 5, 1707. 2. *Daniel*, b. May 7, 1709. 3. *Sarah*, b. Sept. 3, 1710. 4. *Leonard*, b. Dec. 17, 1711. 5. *David*, b. Feb. 23, 1713. 6. *Charles*, b. Dec. 25, 1714. 7. *Edmond*, b. July 19, 1716. 8. *Esther*, b. April 7, 1719. Many of the descendants of this Brimfield branch of the family in 1838 took the surnames Hale and Homer.

iii. DANIEL, b. 1680; lieutenant; m. Sarah, daughter of John and Sarah (Temple) Jones, Dec. 20, 1705. She was b. at Concord, June 4, 1686. They lived a mile easterly from Concord Centre. Daniel's epitaph in the Old Concord Burying Ground is surmounted by a coat of arms— a double headed eagle—and the words " Paternal Coat Armor." The inscription is as follows:

Lieut Daniel Hoar
Obt. Feb'r ye 8th 1773 Æt 93.
By Honest Industry & Prudent
Oeconomy he acquired a hand-
Som Fortune for a man in Privet
Carrecter. He Injoyed a long Life
& uninterrupted state of health
Blessings that ever attend Exer-
Sies & Temperance.
S. N.
Heres the last end of mortal story.
He's Dead.

Lieut. Daniel Hoar had seven children: 1. *John*,[4] b. Jan. 6, 1707; m. (1st) Esther Pierce of Lexington, June 13, 1734; m. (2d) Aug. 21, 1740, Elizabeth Coolidge, daughter of Capt. Joseph, b. Jan. 5, 1720. By the first wife he had two, by the second nine children. He died in Lincoln, May 16, 1786, and his widow d. March 10, 1791. John Hoar was a resident of Lexington, Watertown and Lincoln, the changes not being wholly due to removals, but partly to alterations in town boundaries. He held various town offices, was assessor and selectman for several years, and one of the founders of the church. During the French and Indian war, July 14, 1748, at Fort Dummer, he was taken prisoner and remained a captive among the Indians for three months. He participated in the fight at Concord Bridge, April 19, 1775, being a member of the company of which his son Samuel was a lieutenant. His name leads those of the eight soldiers who made affidavit, April 23, 1775, to their experiences on the day of the fight, the first of the depositions sent to England by a fast sailing vessel from Salem.—(See *Remembrancer* I., 85.) 2. *Daniel*, m. Nov. 2, 1743, Rebecca Brooks; d. in Westminster, leaving two sons and two daughters. 3. *Lucy*, m. John Brooks. 4. *Timothy*, b. 1716; m. Abigail Brooks, Jan. 23, 1752. 5. *Jonathan*, b. 1719; graduate of Harvard 1740; major 1755, lieut.-colonel 1756, and colonel 1760, serving in the French and Indian war 1744-1763; appointed Governor of Newfoundland, etc., but died æt. 52, in 1771, on his passage from England to the colonies. 6. *Elizabeth*, m. —— Whittemore. 7. *Mary*, m. Zachariah Whittemore.

365

iv. JONATHAN, d. at the Castle, a soldier, Oct. 26, 1702.
v. JOSEPH, d. at sea, 1707.
vi. BENJAMIN, wife Esther.
vii. MARY, b. March 14, 1689; d. June 10, 1702.
viii. SAMUEL, b. April 6, 1691.
ix. ISAAC, b. May 18, 1695; m. Anna ———, and lived in Sudbury.
x. DAVID, b. Nov. 14, 1698.
xi. ELIZABETH, b. Feb. 22, 1701.

The children of John[4] Hoar, the son of Lieutenant Daniel, were :

(1) Rebecca,[5] b. in Lexington, July 1, 1735; m. May 6, 1755, Joseph Cutler.
(2) Esther, b. in Watertown, Jan. 28, 1739; m. May 8, 1760, Edmund Bowman.
(3) John, b. in Lexington, July 14, 1741; d. young.
(4) Samuel, b. in Lexington, Aug. 23, 1743; often representative, State senator 1813-1816; m. Susanna, daughter of Abijah and Thankful (Brown) Peirce; d. May 22, 1732. He had ten children: (i.) Susanna,[6] b. Feb. 22, 1774; m. Rev. Robert Gray. (ii.) Thankful, b. April 6, 1776; m. Dr. Grosvenor Tarbell. (iii.) Samuel, b. May 18, 1778; A.B. Harvard 1802, LL.D. 1838; m. Sarah, daughter of Hon. Roger Sherman, Oct. 13, 1812, and had children: Elizabeth,[7] 1814; Ebenezer Rockwood, 1816; Sarah Sherman, 1817; Samuel Johnson, 1820; Edward Sherman, 1823; George Frisbie, 1826. (iv.) Elizabeth, b. July 25, 1780; d. Jan. 14, 1811. (v.) Abijah Peirce, b. Sept. 1, 1782; m. Sarah Hartwell, and changed his name to Abijah Hoar Peirce in 1811. (vi.) Nathaniel Peirce, b. Sept. 2, 1784; A.B. Harvard 1810; d. 1820. (vii.) William, b. Sept. 16, 1786: m. Mary Bemis, and changed his name to Hanson in 1818. (viii.) John, b. April 2, 1789; m. Hannah Brooks; d. May 14, 1831. (ix.) Polly Fiske, b. July 11, 1791; m. Capt. James Farrar; d. May 12, 1813. (x.) Levina, b. Jan. 17, 1794.
(5) Elizabeth, b. in Lexington, Oct. 14, 1746.
(6) Mercy, b. in Lexington, Oct. 5, 1750.
(7) Sarah, b. in Lincoln, June 9, 1755; m. Feb. 17, 1790, Nehemiah Abbot.
(8) Leonard, b. in Lincoln, June 29, 1758; m. (1st) Nov. 10, 1785, Eunice Wheeler, who d. May 16, 1820, æt. 56; and (2d) Pamela ———, who d. 1829. He had six children: (i.) Mary Wheeler, b. May 26, 1787. (ii.) Eunice, b. Aug. 23, 1789. (iii.) Elizabeth, b. July 6, 1793. (iv.) John, b. May 5. 1796. (v.) Edmund, b. July 21, 1798. (vi.) Joseph, b. Dec. 10, 1800; changed his name to Leonard Hoar in 1831.
(9) Rebecca, b. Oct. 18, 1761; m. June 15, 1784, Joseph White of Lancaster. James Coolidge Carter, LL.D., is a grandson of Joseph and Rebecca.
(10) Mary, b. June 15, 1764; m. March 27, 1788, Thomas Wheeler.
(11) Joseph, b. July 30, 1767.

THE ANCESTRY OF THE HOAR FAMILY IN AMERICA.

A Compilation from Collections made by the Honorable GEORGE FRISBIE HOAR.
By HENRY S. NOURSE, of Lancaster, Mass.

DANIEL HOARE came to Massachusetts with the family and became a trader in Boston; at least he so speaks of himself, although
he is not found a resident or real-estate owner in the town records.
He was licensed Oct. 2, 1650, by order of the Council of State "to
export to New England three hundred birding fowling peices and
muskets upon giving security that they will not be used to the prejudice of the Commonwealth." (*See* Calendar of State Papers, 344.)
He accumulated considerable property, some of which he held in
partnership with Lieut Richard Cooke, whom he calls cousin.
This Cooke was very probably from Gloucester, as the name is
found in the records of St. Mary de Crypt. John Cooke founded
the Crypt Grammar School in 1528. The late Major General
George Cooke of Albany, N. Y., came from Gloucester. In 1650,
Daniel made his brother John and his nephew John Hull his attorneys to settle with Cooke whom, in 1663, he charges in a letter
from Hull, England, with dishonesty in his partnership accounts.
The attorneyship as before narrated, was a source of dire misfortune
to his brother John. Neither the date of birth or death of Daniel
Hoare has been discovered. Savage says he died in London. His
wife Mary writes from Hull. England, April 9, 1673, to Mrs.
Leonard Hoar asking that she would receive her son, John, into
their own family, "which would be a singular testimony of your
kindness to my husband (who I know will cheerfully pay my Bro'r;
yea more free then to a stranger), to his child, and to her that is
Your Loving Sister:" (*See* Mass. Hist. Soc. Coll. Vol. viii.
4 Series.)

LEONARD HOAR, designated in his father's will to be the scholar
of the family and a teacher in the church, although by his coming
to New England he missed the proposed matriculation at Oxford,
yet satisfied fully the spirit of the paternal wish. He was graduated at Harvard College in 1650, William Stoughton, chief justice
and lieutenant governor of Massachusetts, being the most distinguished of his eight classmates. In November, 1653, he returned
to England and it is said was there befriended by Sir Matthew Hale,
also a native of Gloucester and at that time a judge of the Common
Pleas. He was soon presented by Sir Henry Mildmay, one of the
regicides, then lord of the manor, with the benefice of Wanstead in
Essex. According to Oldmixon, Sir Henry's wife, Anne, was a
daughter of Sir Leonard Holiday, Lord Mayor of London, also

of Gloucester birth "and perhaps a Relation as well as a Name-sake" of the young clergyman. At her death, March 12, 1656, Leonard Hoar preached two sermons, "The Sting of Death" and "Death Unstung," which were printed at Boston in 1680, with a "Dedicatory Epistle to Mrs. Bridget Usher, my ever honored Aunt," by Josiah Flint. He was one of the two thousand victims of the Uniformity Act upon the restoration of Charles II., but remained in England for about ten years after his ejection, and received the degree of M.D. from Cambridge University in 1671. Among his friends in England and correspondents at a later date were the cele-brated chemist Robert Boyle and Master Samuel Hartlib to whom Milton addressed his famous "Tractate of Education." He was probably given his baptismal name in compliment to his wealthy uncle, Leonard Tarne, the Gloucester sheriff.

On July 8, 1672, Dr. Hoar with his wife landed in Boston, having been called thither with a view to settlement over the South Church, where he preached as assistant to Rev. Thomas Thacher. He brought a letter from thirteen dissenting ministers of London and vicinity commending him to the magistracy and clergy of New England as a suitable head of the college at Cambridge, the presidency of which was then vacant, and despite one or more formidable rivals he was promptly elected to that office and installed December 10, 1672, the first graduate of the institution so honored. Sewall writes that "Governor Bellingham lay dead in his House and Deputy Governor Leverett was the Chief Civil Magistrate present at the solemnity." Dr. Hoar's scholarship was of a high order, and he entered upon his difficult duties with very flattering prospects; but trouble soon began and his hopes of usefulness were speedily destroyed. Accord-ing to Cotton Mather, then an undergraduate, the students "set themselves to *Travestie* whatever he *did* and *said*, and aggravate everything in his Behavior disagreeable to them, with a design to make him Odious." He also adds that the insubordinate were countenanced in their doings by certain persons who "made a Figure in the Neighborhood," doubtless meaning some of the leading over-seers. Judge Sewall writes Oct. 16, 1674, "that the causes of the lownes of the Colledge were external as well as internal." Thomas Hutchinson says "the students were too much indulged in their prejudices against him." In Sewall's Diary, June 15, 1674, is an account of the flogging of an undergraduate before the assem-bled students in the Library, President Hoar prefacing and closing the exercises with prayer. But this was not a very unusual disci-pline in those days and Dr. Hoar is not charged with undue severity. Very probably a potent factor in the troubles was the bitter dissen-sion then waged between the Old Church and the New Church. The late Dr. J. Hammond Trumbull attributed Dr. Hoar's ill-success to the fact that soon after his coming to Boston he connected him-self with the Third Church, then newly gathered by seceders from the First Church who were synodists or advocates of the half-way covenant; thereby bringing himself into marked opposition with the governor and many among the most influential of the clergy, the magistrates and the overseers of the college.

The students having all deserted the college, "except three whose friends lived in Cambridge," Dr. Hoar was compelled to resign the presidency, which he did March 15, 1675, and as Cotton Mather writes (Magnalia, 11, 14) "the Hard and Ill usage met withal made so deep an Impression upon his Mind that his Grief threw him into a Consumption whereof he dyed November 28, 1675 in Boston." Increase Mather in his Diary records: "Nov. 28, Dr. Hoar died, having been brought into a consumption by the grief he sustained through affliction when President of the college. A solemn stroke! It will occasion (in probability) this country to be ill thought of in England, that such a man should have his heart broken among his friends in New England."

In his will, dated October 25, 1675, Dr. Hoar makes these bequests:

My just debts and funerall expenses being first paid I doe give and bequeath unto my daughter Bridget Hoar two hundred pounds in New England to bee paid her at the age of one and twenty years or at her marriage with her mother's consent . . . To my deare brother Daniell Hoar (whose zeall and perpetuall kindnesses I can never remunerate) I give those *par* acknowledgent of my stone signet and my wach. To my deare brother Jn° Hoar I give a black sute, to my deare sister Flint and sister Quinsey I give as much fine black serg as will make each of them a gown. Ont of my library I give to my Cozen Josiah Flint, Ravenelli Bibliotheca. to Cous: Noah Newman Aquinas his Sermons. and to them both the use of any Books or Manuscripts of mine in divinity, they giveing a note to returne them againe to my wife at demand. My medicall or physical writings I give to my wife's custody not to give or lend but to preserve till some of my kindred addicting themselves to those studyes shall desire and in her esteeme deserve them. Especially I respect John Hoar or any other of my Bretheren, Sisters sons or grandsons.

The inventory of his estate amounted to 1345£. 13s. 5d; the books being valued at 208£. 12s. 6d. The Noah Newman, called cousin, married Joanna a daughter of Rev. Henry Flynt, 10 mo. 30, 1669, according to Braintree Records. Doctor Hoar's printed writings are few and unimportant, consisting, besides the two sermons before mentioned, of: Index Biblicus, 1668, 1669 and 1672; Letter to Josiah Flint, 1661, printed in Mass. Hist. Soc. Collections VI., 100-108; The first of the Catalogues of Harvard College commonly called Triennial, 1674; A Letter from Cambridge, Dec. 13, 1672, to Mr. Robert Boyle, printed in Boyle's Works V. 142, Edition of 1744. The last proves the breadth of his educational views, and indicates that he had a clearer conception than was usual in his day of the value of the study of natural science. It contains what is probably the earliest recorded suggestion of modern technical education. Leonard

Hoar was the first of his family to drop the final e from the name. His tombstone in the Quincy burying ground is singularly like the one which marks the grave of his mother-in-law, Lady Alicia Lisle, in England, showing that the same taste directed its construction. The inscription upon it is as follows: —

> Epitaph wrote for the Tomb of
> Leonard Hoar Doctour of
> Phisicke who departed this life
> In Boston the 28 November
> Was interred here the 6 December
> And was aged 45 years
> Anno. Dom. 1675.

Three precious friends under this tomb-stone lie,
Patterns to aged, youth, and infancy,
A great mother, her learned son, with child,
The first and least went free. He was exiled.
In love to Christ, this country, and dear friends
He left his own, cross'd seas, and for amends
Was here extoll'd, envy'd, all in a breath,
His noble consort leaves, is drawn to death.
Stranger changes may befall us ere we die,
Blest they who will arrive eternity.
God grant some names, O thou New England's friend.
Don't sooner fade than thine, if times don't mend.

Through his wife Bridget Lisle, Leonard Hoar's life was connected with tragedies more terrible, and of broader historic interest, than that of his own failure. She was one of the two daughters of Lord John and Lady Alicia Lisle. Her father, a distinguished Puritan lawyer, gained great favor with Cromwell, and was counsel to Bradshaw, president of the High Court of Justice appointed for the trial of King Charles I., and became Lord Commissioner of the Great Seal. He for some reason did not sign the death warrant of Charles I., but was chosen by Cromwell one of the Committee of seven who prepared "a draft of a sentence with a blank for the manner of his death," and his is the first name in the list of those excepted from the Act of Indemnity, passed at the restoration of Charles II. He was assassinated, being shot in the back, on August 11, 1664, at Lausanne, Switzerland, as he was going to church, by two Irish ruffians inspired by the expectation of a generous reward from some member of the royal family in England. (*See* Memoirs of Edward Ludlow, II., p. 370, *et seq.*) Lady Alicia Lisle was one of the earliest victims of the infamous Chief Justice Jeffries, being charged with misprision of treason in aiding and concealing in her dwelling on the day after the battle of Sedgemoor, Richard Nelthorpe, a lawyer, and John Hickes, a clergyman, accused of being refugees from Monmouth's army. She declared herself innocent of guilty knowledge, and protested against the illegality of her trial because the supposed rebels to whom she had given common hospitality had not been convicted. She was then advanced in years, and so feeble that it is was said she was unable to keep awake during her tedious trial. Jeffries arrogantly refused her the aid of counsel, admitted irrelevant testimony, excelled himself in violent abuse, and so intimidated the jurors—who were disposed to dismiss the charge—that they unwillingly at last brought in a verdict of guilty. She was hurriedly condemned "to be burned alive" the very afternoon of the day of her trial, August 28, 1685, but owing to the indignant protests of the clergy of Winchester execution was postponed for five days, and the sentence was "altered from burning to beheading." This punishment was exacted in the market place of Winchester on the appointed day, the implacable King James II. refusing a pardon, although it was proved that Lady Lisle had protected many cavaliers in distress, and that her son John was serving in the royal army; and many persons of high rank interceded for her, among whom was Lord Clarendon, brother-in-law to the King. Lady Lisle was connected by marriage with the Bond, Whitmore, Churchill, and other families of distinction, and her granddaughter married Lord James Russell, fifth son of the first Duke of Bedford, thus connecting this tragedy with that of Lord William Russell, "the martyr of English Liberty." In the first year of William and Mary's reign the attainder was reversed by act of Parliament upon petition of Alicia Lisle's two daughters, Tryphena Grove and Bridget (Hoar) Usher. Among the eight great historical paintings by E. M. Ward, R.A., which adorn the corridor leading to the House of Commons, the third in the series represents Lady Lisle's arrest for relieving two fugitives from Monmouth's defeated army.

In 1892 the Hon. George F. Hoar paid a visit to the ancient home of the Lisles, and the following memoranda made at the time have been preserved: —

Saturday, Oct. 22d, Mr. Hoar, with two ladies, went from Southampton to Ringwood, about twenty miles, and drove thence to Ellingham church, about two miles and a half. The church is a small, but very beautiful structure of stone, with a small wooden belfry. The tomb of Lady Alice Lisle is a heavy flat slab of grey stone, raised about two or three feet from the ground, bearing the following inscription: —

> Here Lies Dame Alicia Lisle
> and her daughter Ann Harfeld
> who dyed the 17th of Feb. 1703-4
> Alicia Lisle Dyed the
> second of Sept 1685:

It is close to the wall of the church, on the right of the porch. In the church is seen the old Lisle pew of carved oak, and the pew of the Earl of Normanton. Opposite the pew is the pulpit, also of carved black oak, apparently ancient. The church contains a tablet to the memory of the former owner of Moyles' Court, who died in 1622.

Moyles' Court is about a mile and a half from Ellingham Church — the drive is along a beautiful lane, shaded by trees whose branches meet from the two sides, through a beautiful and fertile country, adorned by herds of fine cattle. Moyles' Court is a large two-story building, consisting of two square wings, connected by the main building. The wings project from the main building in front, but the whole forms a continuous line in the rear. As you approach it, you pass numerous heavy brick outbuildings, including several farmhouses, one of which is quite large, and apparently of great antiquity.

We were told by Mrs. Fane, wife of the present occupant of Moyles' Court, that the landed estate connected with Moyles' Court is very large, and now, or recently yielding to the Earl of Normanton, seven thousand pounds a year. The present occupant of Moyles' Court, Frederick Fane, Esq., came to reside there about 21 years ago. The house was then much dilapidated, but he has restored it in a style in keeping with the ancient architecture. The principal room is a dining hall, rising from the ground some 25 feet in height, with a gallery at one end, on a level with the second story — the walls of this room are of beautiful carved oak, the front of the gallery being ancient, and as it existed in the time of Lady Lisle. The staircase also of fine carved oak is of equal antiquity. The carved oak in the passages and some of the other rooms, has been restored by Mr. Fane from material found in the attic. There is also a curious old kitchen, with a large fire-place, with a closet in the chimney where it is said one of the persons succored by Lady Lisle was found hidden. In the cellar is a curiously carved head on a stone beam which seemed as if it might have formerly supported a mantel-piece, or shelf. It is said that this portion of the cellar was once a chapel.

Some of the chambers have been named by Mr. Fane from persons connected with the tragedy : Dame Alicia, Monmouth, Nelthrop, Hicks, Tryphena, these names being inscribed on the doors. The room is shown where Lady Lisle is said to have been seized.

Mrs. Fane told us several traditions current in the neighborhood : she says that when she first came there, there was a woman still living who told her that her grandmother had told her that she remembered seeing in her childhood Lady Alice Lisle taken past on her way to her trial at Winchester. If this be true, the two lives must have lasted at least 186 years beside a sufficient margin to enable the child to be old enough to comprehend, and remember the occurrence, and her granddaughter to be old enough to comprehend and remember the narration.

Lady Lisle was carried on horseback by a trooper to Winchester. The horse lost a shoe, and fell lame; she insisted that the trooper should stop at a smith's and have the shoe replaced, and on his refusing declared that she would make an outcry and resistance unless he did, saying she could not bear to have the horse suffer. The blacksmith at first refused. He said he would do nothing to help the carrying off Lady Lisle, but she entreated him to do it for her sake. She said she should come back that way in a few days; the trooper said, "Yes, you will come back in a few days, but without your head."

The body was returned to Moyles' Court the day of the execution; the head was brought back a few days after in a basket, and put in at the pantry window; the messenger said that the head was sent afterward for greater indignity.

There is a further tradition that when Lady Lisle heard of her husband's connection with the Court which condemned King Charles she was much distressed. It is well known that she disapproved the execution, and that she declared on her trial that she never ceased to pray for the King. The story further goes that she hastened to London, and reached her husband's

372

door, as he had just mounted his horse to join the procession for some part of the proceeding of the high court. She accosted him, but being covered with her veil he did not recognize her, and roughly thrust her away. She fell under the horse's feet, in a swoon; she was taken up and cared for by Hicks, one of the persons whom she afterwards succored, and for relieving whom she was condemned. She remained in a swoon for a long time; her husband was sent for and visited her, but, to use the phrase in which the story was told by Mrs. Fane, was very odious to her. She told Hicks that she could not repay him for his kindness in London, but if he came to the Isle of Wight, or to Moyles' Court, in both of which places she had property, she would repay him, saying, "at Moyles' Court I am Mistress." I think Mrs. Fane said Hicks lived in the Strand.

After exactly a year's widowhood Bridget Hoar married for her second husband Hezekiah Usher, Jr., November 29, 1676. Usher was a wealthy merchant of Boston, very eccentric, and, as his wife soon found, unsuited for domestic life. She lived unhappily with him until July 12, 1687, when she sailed for England with her only surviving child, Bridget Hoar, and did not return until after Usher's death which took place July 11, 1697, at Lynn. By the fall of his horse his leg was so bruised or broken as to lead to his death. Sewall writes that he " grew distracted" in his last illness, and his extravagant will indicates that his mind was not well balanced at a much earlier day. This will is printed in full in the Historical Magazine for September, 1868. It is dated August 17, 1689, at Nonaicoicus Farm, an estate of four hundred acres in what is now the town of Ayer, originally the property of Major Simon Willard. It is very lengthly and abusive in language. The following extracts concern his wife and her daughter :—

" And unto my dear wife, whom I may count very dear by her Love to what I had but not a real Love to me, which should accounting it more worth than any other outward Enjoyment; and for her covetousness & overreaching & cunning Impression that has almost ruinated me by a gentle behaviour, having only words but as sharp swords to me, whose Cunning is like those to be as an Angel of Light to others but wanting Love and Charity for me . . . . . And therefore I do cut her off from the benefit of all my Estate & do not bestow anything upon her but what the law doth allow . . . . . But as to her daughter Bridget if her mother had not been so undermining & overreaching for her I should have been willing to have done what I could for her. And do give her the Tumbler with the Arms of a Spread Eagle with two heads, (but I think one head for a body is enough,) and the Table Cloth of the best Damask, and the napkins thereto. And this Will I make to be a Warning to those women that have no Love for their Husbands, but to what they have; . . . . . "

Judge Sewall served as Madame Usher's attorney while she remained in England. In spite of the will she obtained possession of her late husband's house and grounds and there took up her residence. May 9, 1700, Sewall writes: "Madam Usher obtained Judgment for her Dower in the Mansion House against the Town House yesterday. Brick Shops and ware house are of the same title and will follow the Dwelling-house." She is invariably spoken of by her contemporaries in terms of unqualified praise, as one who ever led a charitable and blameless life. After her funeral Rev. Thomas Foxcroft, pastor of the Old Church in Boston, preached a sermon upon " The character of Anna the prophetess considered and applied ;" which was printed with a preface by Benjamin Wadsworth, president of Harvard College, in which he calls Madame Usher "a wonderful example of Christian Patience under great Pains and Bodily Afflictions." The announcement by her executors to her daughter in London of her decease and funeral, testifies to the public respect felt for her, and a schedule of the personal belongings of this gentlewoman of the seventeenth century is appended as of interest in this connection.

To the Rev'd Mr. Thomas Cotton in London.

BOSTON, June 12, 1723.

MR. THOMAS COTTON,

SIR,—These are to condole with you the loss of our worthy friend Madam Bridget Usher, who departed this life the 25th of the last Month, being Saturday at about two a Clock in the afternoon, after a fortnights Indisposition, and according to her express desire was Intere'd at Brantry May 30th, in the Grave of Dr. Leonard Hoar her first Husband, and her younger Daughter Tryphena, and the Doctrs. Mother and Sisters. The Corps was attended about half a mile in the Street leading thitherward by the Bearers, being the Honble. Wm. Dummer Esqr. Lt. Govr. and Comr. in Cheif, Saml. Sewall, Penn Townsend, Edward Bromfield, Simeon Stoddard and Edmund Quincey Esqrs. and many others, principal Gentlemen and Gentlewomen of the Town, Mr. Leonard Cotton being the principal Mourner. It pleased God to afford us a very comfortable day for the Solemnity, wherein the Executors Colo. Quincey Mr. Flynt and others Gent. with several Gentlewomen of her cheif acquaintance proceeded to Brantry on Horse back and in Coaches. The distance is very little above ten miles.

Inclosed is a true Copy of the Will though not attested as we shall send hereafter. What Estate Madm Usher has left consists chiefly in Bonds, amo. to One Thousand Two Hundred and Thirty pounds which we hope is in good hands.

We desire your speedy Direction and order as to the getting them in and disposition when got in.

We have not found one piece of money either Gold or Silver. Nor Ten Shillings in Bills of Credit, being what passes here in lieu of Money. However, we have delivered Mr. Leonard Cotton his legacy and Shall go on to pay the Funerall Expence, not waiting for the Effects of the Bonds to do it with;—With our hearty salutations of Condolence to your Self and Lady, we conclude, who are

Your Humble Servts.

SAMUEL SEWALL.

(Sewall's Letter Book II., p. 149.)   WM. WELSTEAD.

Mr. Thomas Cotton and Mrs. Bridget Cotton.

July 19th, ———.

This goes under Covert to Mr. Samuel Storke, and Se(r)ves for Covert of the enclosed Account of perticulers of what Contained in Bill of lading

Sent to him who we doubt not, but upon arrival will take care to receive and forward to you. There are Several perticulers ment[d]. in the Inventory which are already dispos[d] of here by Madam Usher's desire, according to a Schedule given by her to Mrs. Lidia Vivion, now Perkins, for that purpose. Some of the Clothes we forbear sending least they should be seized, under the Notion of East India goods. So Shall wait for your further direction about Em. Wishing what we now Send well to your hands, are with due respects.

Schedule of Articles.

An account of what was put up in Madam Usher's Chest June 29, 1725, to send to London, according to the Order of the Rev[d] Mr. Thomas Cotton, and his Lady Madam Bridget Cotton; To send by the Mary Gally, Thomas Dimond Commander.

Imprimis, One pair of Sheets, Five Table-Cloths, Thirteen Napkins; Diapar, and Damask; Nine Towells, One Pillow-bier, Seven Holland Shifts, and a Flañel one. Twelve pair of Sheets. Nine Aprons, five of them short. Nine Hoods of various sorts, one Night-Rail. Four Head-Dresses. Three pair of Pockets, one Stomacher. Eighteen Handkerchiefs; Linen, Silk, Gaws. One Red silk Purse fill'd with Knots and Girdles.

One black Paddisway Suit; One Linen Gown and Coat. One New Suit of blew Damask Lined with blew Lutestring; One Satin Night-Gown and Coat Lined with Red Lute-string; One Silk Dress Gown.

One Full Suit of Striped Satin lined with Cloth-coloured Lutestring, One Silk Night-gown, and three pairs of Stays. One pair Silk Stockings, one pair ditto Worsted, one pair of Shoes; one Scarf; two Feather screens, one black Quilted Coat, and two Silk Bonnets.

Several pieces of Earthern Ware were stowd among the Cloaths.

Two Rings delivered Capt. Dimond.

I am blest in whom my heart doth rest —

The R[t]. Honb[le] L[d]. James Russell *obt.* 22 June, 1712.

w[t]. 8 p. w[t]. 8 Grains.

Plate put into the Cotton and Linen Bag Sealed up.

One Tankard standing upon Lions; one large Plate, one Salver. One large Porringer with a Cover. One small Cann. One Candlestick and Snuffers. Two Salts. One Pepper Box. One Money-Box. One Seal &c.; One Fork, One Tabacco Stoper. One Small Tumbler. One Thimble and three Broken Pieces of Silver.

W[t]. 98 ounces, Four peny w[t]. and 7 Grains.

Books in the Box.

One Fol. English Bible, 1682. One Quarto ditto. One N.E. Psalm Book. Dr. Owen's fourth part of his Exposition on the Hebrews.

One Manuscript in Quarto. A Psalm-Book recom̃ended by Dr. Manton &c. Dyke's worthy Com̃unicant, Cole's Christian Religion: Colman on the Ten Virgins; Dr. Mather on the Beatitudes. Ryther's Plat for Mariners: Foxcroft's Godly Mans Death.

Dr. Owen on the glory of Christ. Trinity vindicated. Spiritual Songs. Funerall Sermon on Grove Hirst Esqr. Dr. Sibb's Christian Portion. Twelve sermons by Mr. Wadsworth. Dr. Patrick's Version of the Psalms. Five Sermons by Dr. Mather. Pearse his Preparation for Death. Mitchell of Glory. Mr. Tomlyn's Sermons. Doolittell of the Lord's Supper.

Mr. Pearse's last Legacy. Fox's Door of Heaven. Manuscript Octavo. Myrtle Grove. Sermons of Mr. Joseph Stephens. Grail's sum of the Holy History. Hymns and Spiritual Songs p Mr. Watts. Disce Vivere, English Letter, pages 558. Besides several small Books unbound but stitch'd only.

Boston, July 19, 1725. The foregoing is Account of what is now aboard the Mary Galley, Thomas Dimond Comander, for London; and goes consignd to Mr. Samuel Storke, to whom we inclose Bill of Lading.

SAMUEL SEWALL.

(Sewall's Letter Book II., p. 188.)   WM. WELSTEAD.

Bridget the daughter of Dr. Leonard and Bridget (Lisle) Hoar, was born in Cambridge, Mass., March 13, 1673, and married Rev. Thomas Cotton. In the litigation between Samuel Sewall, Esq., as attorney for Mrs. Bridget Usher, and Wait Winthrop, Esq., it was necessary to prove the marriage of her daughter, and the following certificate was obtained from England, and can be found in Massachusetts Archives, Vol. xiii. 22, 23.

These are to Certify that Mr. Thomas Cotton of Peniston in the County of York, Batchelor, and Mrs. Bridgett Hoar of the Parish of St Buttolph, Bishopgate in the City of London, Spinster, were Married together in the Parish Church of Alhallowes on the Wall in the City of London June 21st 1689, as appears by the Lycence for Their Marriage now remainjng in my hands, and by the Register Book of the said Parish.

Witness my hand February 17, 1692.

JOSHUA RICHARDSON, *Rect'r.*

An interesting memoir of Thomas Cotton is in Walter Wilson's "History of the Dissenting Churches," Vol. iv., p. 376-388, to which a portrait is appended. He was born at or near Wortley in 1653 and was therefore at his marriage more than double the age of his girl bride. He died in 1730, aged 77 years, and was buried in Bunhill Fields. His will mentions children : Leonard, Thomas and Alicia, and was proved August 11, 1730. His son Leonard came to America, was a teacher at Hampton Falls, N. H., and had four children. Judge Sewall mentions paying him a legacy of fifty pounds after his grandmother Usher's death. Thomas Cotton was a benefactor of Harvard College, between 1724 and 1727, to the amount in all of 500£. given for books and the increase of the president's salary. He and his wife also authorized Judge Sewall to distribute 125£. from Madam Usher's estate among poor clergymen of New England. He has descendants living in England, one of whom, Colonel Cotton of the British army has inherited two family portraits of great interest; one of Lord John Lisle, supposed to be from the brush of Sir Peter Lely, the other of his granddaughter Mrs. Bridget (Hoar) Cotton, presumed to be the work of Sir Godfrey Kneller. The name Alice Lisle is perpetuated among the daughters of the line. Judge Sewall records in his Letter Book II. 151. under date July 8, 1723, memoranda of a letter : —

To Mrs. Tryphena Grove in London p Mr. James Allen, inclosing her Ring which cost 1£. 13. 10. July 8, 1723 Sent also the Pictures of my Lady Lisle and Lady Cutler, put up in a case carefully with shreds of Paper written upon with Ink N.T.G.2 to take a Bill of Exchange. 1 Inclose two Sermons, one to Madame Grove, the other to my Lady Russell. The Rings I put in Madame Groves Sermon. Ordered him to advise with Mr. Newman.

If the portraits thus mentioned are in existence their location is unknown to the family. Madame Grove died in 1725.

JOANNA HOARE, the youngest child of Charles and Joanna of Gloucester, was baptized at St. Michaels in June, 1624. She married July 26, 1648, *Col. Edmund Quincy*, third of that name, of Braintree. He was born in England in 1627, and died at Braintree, January 7, 1698. Judge Sewall wrote in his Diary, "Seventh-day, Jan'y 8. between ten and 11.m. Parmiter comes in, and tells me that Uncle Quinsey died between 7 and 8 last night. A true New England man, and one of our best Friends is gon." His first wife died May 16, 1680, and seven months later, December 8, 1680, he married Elizabeth (Gookin) Eliot, widow of John Eliot Jr. She died November 30, 1700. By Joanna Hoar he had the following children : —

1. MARY, born 1650 (?) who married *Ephraim Savage*.
2. DANIEL, born February 7, 1651, who married *Hannah Shepard*.
3. JOHN, born April 5, 1652, and died 8 mo. 14, 1674.
4. JOANNA, born 1654; married *David Hobart*.
5. JUDITH, born 1655; married *Rev. John Reyner, Jr.*, and died March 5, 1679.
6. ELIZABETH, born 1656; married *Rev. Daniel Gookin*.
7. EDMUND, died 7 mo. 11. 1657.
8. RUTH, born 29, 8 mo. 1658; married *John Hunt*.
9. EDMUND, born 1 mo. 3, 1660; died 10 mo. 22, 1661.
10. MARTHA, born 1 mo. 26. 1665.
11. EXPERIENCE, b. 1 mo. 20, 1667; married November 24, 1693, *William Savil*.

Daniel, the only son of Edmund and Joanna Quincy who left issue, had a son John for whom the town of Quincy was named, and John's granddaughter, Abigail Smith, married John Adams, February 24, 1764, and thus became the wife of one president and the mother of another.

In James Savage's "Genealogical Dictionary," Samuel Deane's "History of Scituate" and Francis Baylies's "New Plymouth," Hezekiah Hoar, of Scituate, one of the early settlers of Taunton, and Richard Hoar, the schoolmaster of Yarmouth, are called brothers of John and Leonard. They probably came from Gloucestershire, the latter being perhaps one of those transported for participation in Monmouth's rebellion, but there is no proof of relationship to the sons of Charles.

CHARLES HOARE=MARGERY ..... OF GLOUCESTER ON THE SEVERN.

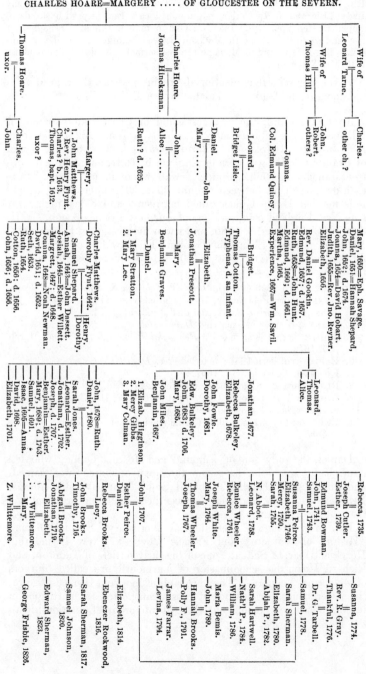

JOANNA HOAR, WIFE OF EZRA MORSE
OF DEDHAM, MASS.

By G. ANDREWS MORIARTY, A.M., LLB., F.S.A., F.A.S.G., F.S.G.

Ezra Morse of Dedham, Mass., where he lived all his life, was born there 12:5mo.:1643, son of John Morse and grandson of Samuel, the early settler of Dedham, and died there in 1697. He married, 18 Feb. 1670/1, Joanna Hoar, who died in Braintree, Mass., 21:10mo.: 1691. They had issue: Ezra, born 28 Jan. 1671/2; Joanna, born in 1673; Rev. John, born 31 March 1674 (A.B., Harvard, 1692); Nathaniel, born in 1676; David, baptized in 1681, died young; Peter, baptized in 1682, died young; Dea. David, baptized in 1683; and Dea. Seth, born in 1686.

The question to be considered is the parentage of Joanna Hoar, wife of Ezra Morse. While no positive evidence appears on this point, there is a good deal of circumstantial evidence which tends to show who she was, and I am of the opinion that the probability as to her parentage is strong. Joanna was evidently born about 1645–1650.

Two early Hoar families must be considered. First, that of Hezekiah Hoar who was of Taunton, in Plymouth Colony, in 1643. He had issue Mercy, born in January 1654; Nathaniel, born in March 1656; Sarah, born 1 April 1658; Elizabeth, born 26 May 1660; Edward, born 25 Sept. 1663; Lydia, born 24 March 1665; Hezekiah, born 10 Nov. 1668; and Mary, born 22 Sept. 1669 (Pope's Pioneers, p. 233). It is evident that Joanna could hardly have belonged in this family, as Hezekiah's chidren were born too late for her to belong in this family, and there was comparatively little connection between Dedham and Taunton, which are at a considerable distance from each other.

It may be noted that there was a Richard Hoar in Yarmouth on Cape Cod who was made a Freeman of Plymouth Colony 7 Sept. 1641, and who was among those able to bear arms in 1643. He was a proprietor, an elder, and a Court Commissioner as well as a schoolmaster, and occurs in Yarmouth in 1659 (THE REGISTER, vol. 5, p. 388). Yarmouth is a long distance from Dedham, and there is no record that he was married or had a family, so Joanna could hardly have been his daughter (cf. Pope, op. cit., p. 233).

The other family of Hoar was that of the widow Joanna Hoar, who came to New England in or about 1642 and settled in Braintree, a town adjoining Dedham. She brought with her sons John, Daniel, and Leonard, and a daughter Joanna, born about 1625, who married in Braintree, 26:5mo.:1648, Edmund Quincy, Jr. (Pope, op. cit., pp. 232–233); another daughter, Margery, married in Gloucester, England, 25 Dec. 1633, John Matthews, by whom she had a child named Charles. After the death of her husband and probably of her child, she came to Braintree and married, secondly, the Rev. Henry Flynt of that town. There is an excellent account of the English forebears of this family and of the early generations in New England in THE REGISTER, vol. 53 (1899), pp. 92, 186, 289, which is the basis of this paper. *

Charles Hoare, Jr., brewer and wool merchant, of Gloucester, England, son of a prominent citizen of Gloucester of the same name, married, about 1610–1612, Joanna Hinksman. Charles made his will 25 Sept. 1638, proved by Joanna his widow 21 Dec. 1638. They had issue Margery (above noted), Thomas, John, Daniel, Leonard, and Joanna (above noted). We must now consider this family with care. The widow Joanna came to Braintree about 1642, and brought with her her sons John, Daniel, and Leonard, and her daughters Margery and Joanna. She died in Braintree 21:10 mo.:1661 (Pope, op. cit).

*Pp. 344, 354, 367, this volume.

380

Thomas, apparently the eldest son, was baptized in Gloucester 15 June 1612, and was apprenticed to his father 2 Feb. 1625/6 in Gloucester. He is probably the Thomas Hoar who was church warden of St. Mary de Crypt, Gloucester, in 1636. He remained in England, and little is known about him. There is no evidence that he had a family or any child who came hither.

The second son, John, was born about 1619. He was the ancestor of the well-known Concord, Mass., family and will be considered later.

Daniel, the third son, came to New England with his mother. He was a trader in Boston, where he owned land. He soon returned to England, and in 1650 he was licensed to export firearms to New England. In 1650 he made his brother, John, and his nephew, John Hull (the Boston mintmaster, son of Robert Hull of Braintree, whose second wife was the widow of the first Edmund Quincy), his attorneys in New England. He never returned and Savage says he died in London. In 1673 he was living in Hull, Yorks., and on 9 April 1673 his wife, Mary, wrote to her sister-in-law, Bridget, wife of President Leonard Hoar, of Harvard in Cambridge, Mass., from Hull asking them to receive their son, John, into their family. Nothing further is known about his family or if any of them ever came to New England. There is no record of them in the New England records and it is probable that none came here.

Leonard, the fourth son, came here with his mother. He graduated at Harvard in 1650, went to England in 1653, and was inducted into the living of Wanstead, co. Essex, by Sir Henry Mildmay, the Regicide. He was ejected in 1662, studied medicine, and was M.D., Cambridge, in 1671. He then returned to New England, and was made President of Harvard 10 Dec. 1672. He died testate 28 Nov. 1675, his will being dated 25 Oct. 1675. He married in England, Bridget, daughter of John Lisle, the Regicide, and Lady Alice, daughter and co-heiress of Sir White Beconsawe, who was executed at the Bloody Assizes in 1685 by order of Jeffries, for giving refuge to some of Monmouth's men. Leonard and Bridget had only two daughters, Tryphena, who died an infant, and Bridget, born 13 March 1673, who married in England the Rev. Thomas Cotton, for many years a dissenting clergyman in London, who was buried in Bunhill Fields in 1730. They were married in London, 21 June 1689. After the death of President Hoar, his widow married Hezekiah Usher, the Boston merchant. The marriage was an unhappy one, and Mrs. Usher joined her daughter in London in 1687, but returned to New England after her husband's death in 1697. She died in Boston 25 March 1723.

We now return to John, the second son of Charles and Joanna Hoar. He was born in Gloucester about 1619, and was apprenticed to his father 11 May 1632. He came to New England with his mother and in 1643 was among those able to bear arms in Scituate in Plymouth Colony, the town adjoining Braintree. In 1659 he sold his Scituate lands, and removed to Concord, where he resided

381

until his death in 1704. However, he returned to Braintree for a short period, and as "John Hoar of Braintree, planter", he, together with his wife Alice sold land in Concord to Simon Linde and Thomas Brattle, of Boston 19 Nov. 1678 (Middlesex Deeds, East Cambridge, vol. VI, p. 408). By 5 Aug. 1680 he was back in Concord, and on that date he exchanged land there with Edward Wright and styled himself "of Concord" (*ibid.*, vol. VIII, p. 386). He married, about 1645, Alice—, and died *intestate* 2 April 1704. On 22 May 1704 administration on his estate was granted to his son Daniel Hoar of Concord. The probate papers show that Daniel had taken care of his parents since 1683 (Middlesex Probate, East Cambridge, no. 11589). Alice, wife of John Hoar, died before her husband 5 June 1696.

John and Alice had the following *known* children: Mary, born *ca.* 1648, married 21 Oct. 1668 Benjamin Graves; Daniel, gent. of Concord, born in 1650, married, first, Mary Stratton 16 July 1677, and secondly, 16 Oct. 1717, Mary Lee; he had eleven children; Elizabeth, born about 1655, married 23 Dec. 1675 Jonathan Prescott of Lancaster.

It seems quite certain that Joanna, wife of Ezra Morse, must have belonged to this family, and that she was named for the widow Joanna Hoar, who came to Braintree in 1642. Dedham adjoins Braintree and Joanna Morse died in Braintree where Joanna Hoar's two daughters lived. There is no evidence that Thomas Hoar who lived in England ever had any children or that any children of his ever came to New England. There is no evidence that Daniel had any daughter who came here, and there is no evidence that his son ever lived here. There can, therefore, be little doubt that Joanna Hoar, wife of Ezra Morse, was an unrecorded child of John Hoar,* born while he lived in Scituate about 1645–1650, as all the children of John Hoar are not surely known.

*I agree entirely with your conclusion, no other seems possible!

A. Vere Woodman, F.S.A.
Wing, Bucks., England

THE HOLDEN FAMILY OF CRANBROOK, KENT, ENGLAND.

By EDWARD S. HOLDEN, LL.D., Director of the Lick Observatory.

THE following extracts from MS. records have been collected from time to time by the kindness of many friends. They are practically complete so far as the Cranbrook Registers go, from 1560 to 1660 or thereabouts. The tombs of this family are among the very oldest in the Cranbrook church yard, and the inscriptions are nearly obliterated. I possess photographs of them. After the year 1762 the name does not appear in the Parish Registers.

EPITAPHS (Cranbrook Churchyard).

Here lieth the body of Robert Holden, of Hawkridge in this parish of Cranbroke, Gent., who departed this life the 23d. of May, Anno D. M. 1667, leavinig issve of the body of Elizabeth his wife, one sone & one davghter, viz. Robert & Mary. Aet. ....

Next this tomb is one on which the inscription cannot be deciphered and one on which the lettering can be only partially made out. It is in memory of Eliza, wife of Henry Godden, Gent., who died in May, 1705. She was the daughter of another Robert Holden.

Robert Holden, of Cranbrooke, yeoman, deceased Avgt. 27, 1653, in the year of his age 49, and left two sons, John & Robert, by his will to be brovght up in learning & piety.

383

FROM CRANBROOK REGISTERS; *Marriages.*

1562	Jan. 15;	Robert Holden & Mary Hovenden,
1585	July 5;	John Holden & Rebecca Webb,
1590	May 11;	James King & Mary Holdinge,
1604	. . . . .;	Abraham Waltier & Elizabeth Holden, widow,
1606	Oct. 7;	Richard Courthopp & Elizabeth Holden,
1614	Feb. 7;	Robert Rimmington & Clemence Holden,
1615	May 9;	Josias Colville & Elizabeth Holden,
1615	May 9;	James Holden & Elizabeth Rucke,
1623	July 29;	Richard Taylor & Mary Holden,
1626	July 23;	Richard Holden and Elizabeth Holland,
1628	Jan. 18;	John Holden & Jane Smith, widow,
1642	Oct. 11;	Richard Holden & Mary Sheafe,
1656	Nov. 24;	John Holden of Cranbrooke, husbandman, son of Nycholas Holden of Merrad[?] co. Kent, husbandman, and Marie Lane of Cranbrooke, dau. of Henry Lane of West Barmen[?] co. Kent, husbandman.

FROM CRANBROOK REGISTERS; *Burials.*

1580	June 30;	Elizabeth Holden,
1685	Oct. 6;	a crysomer of Robert Holden,
1690	April 17;	Elizabeth, wife of Mr Robert Holden,
1691	April 8;	Frances, wife of Robert Holden,
1697	June 19;	Nathaniel Holden.

FROM CRANBROOK REGISTERS; *Baptisms.*

1563	Nov. 7;	Johan Holdinge,
1569	Sep. 4;	Richard Holden,
1653-4	Feb. 15;	James Houlden, son of Richard Houlden, clothyer, & Frances Hodges his wife.
1655	Nov. 31;	Thomas Holden, son of Richard Holden of Brendon,* clothyer, & ffrances Hodges, his wife.
1656	July 12;	Richard Holden, son of James Holden of Plushinghurst, clothyer, & Sarah Sloeman, his wife.
1657	April 6;	Samuel Holden, son of Richard Holden of Brenden, clothyer, & ffrances Hodges, his wife.
1658	Aug. 30;	James Holden, son of James Holden of Plushinghurst quarter, clothyer, & of Sarah Sloeman, uxor.
1658	Sept. 12;	Samuel Holden, son of Richard Holden of Brenden, clothyer, & of ffrances Hodges, uxor.
1663	Apr. 10;	Robert son of Robert Holden,
1666	Aug. 3;	Mary, dau. of Robert Houlden & Elizabeth his wife.

FROM PARISH REGISTERS OF CRANBROOK.

Births:	1608	Jan. 15;	Anne dau. of John Holden of Hartridge,
	1609	Nov. 26;	Elizabeth dau. of Thomas Holden,
	1611	Dec. 29;	Elizabeth dau. of John Holden,
	1614	Aug. 28;	Elizabeth dau. of John Holden.

N.B. There are no other entries of Holden births in the years 1608–9–10–11–12–13–14.

Deaths: 1614   June 19, d. Elizabeth Holden, a child.

* Branden.

Christened: 1560 March 16; Cyprian Holden,
1563 Sept. 19; Marye Holden.
1565 Oct. 18; Luke Holden,
Buried: 1560 March 20; Cyprian Holden,
1568 April 5; Peter Holden.

WILLS.

Will of Mary Holden of Cranbrook widow. Mentions John Hovenden son of my brother Robert Hovenden. July 1, 1609. Proved P. C. C. 84 Dorset.

Will of Robert Holden of Cranbrook. Mentions residue of my estate to be divided between my two sons Robert Hovenden of Cranbrook, clothier, and John Courthope of same, clothier. August 20, 1653. Proved P. C. C. 370 Alchin.

Will of Robert Hovenden of Cranbrook. Mentions premises in the occupation of Richard Holden, miller [Qu. in Cranbrook?] July 11, 1656. Proved P. C. C. 329 Berkley.

Will of John Holden of Cranbrooke, clothier. Mentions my dau. Mary wife of Richard Taylor; my wife Elizabeth; my son Peter; John the son of James Holden; my cousin Richard son of John Holden: To my son Robert all my lands in Cranbrooke, Tenterden and Holden and he to be Exor. Proved Consistory Court of Canterbury Sept. 19, 1625. Vol. 48, Fo. 1.

Will of John Holden the younger of Cranbrook, clothier. To be buried beside his father and mother in the church yard there. My father Hartridge; my brother James Holden; my sisters Rimmington & Colve [Colville]; my sister Thorpe; my sister Clamponde; my sister Katherine Holden; Elizabeth Holden dau. of my brother Thomas; my brother Robert; Mary his wife; my brother Everinden; my brother James Holden; my daughters Anne & Elizabeth; to my son Richard Holden Brenden house with the woodlands and 45 acres etc.; but if he die before the age of 23 etc. Proved in the Consistory Court at Canterbury, June 13, 1623. Vol. 46, Fo. 292.

MARRIAGE LICENSES ISSUED AT CANTERBURY.

1608 Dec. 7; Thomas Holden of Cranbrook clothier & Maria Saxpes of Wartling co. Sussex J. Saxpes gent. Bondsman.

1623 Sept 11; John Holden aged 32 Bach[r] of Hawkhurst clothier & Debora Gibbons aged 34 wid. of Edward Gibbons of same, clothier.

1633 Jan 31; Thomas Holden 26 Bach[r] of Dover, husbandman & Elizabeth Hatefield 28, maiden, of same.

1635 Oct. 14; Robert Holden 28 Bach[r] of Cranbrook clothier & Mary Courthopp 24 dau. of Peter Courthopp of Cranbrook.

1667 May 17; William Peachy 30 Bach[r] of Staplehurst clothier & Mary Holden 16 maiden dau. of Elizabeth now wife of Nathl. Wilson of Kingsworth, minister.*

1639 Aug. 7; William Hovenden 27 Bachr. of Cranbrooke, clothier & Anne Holden 23 maiden dau. of Mary Holden of same.

* 1663 June 30; Nathaniel Wilson of Kingsworth co Kent clerk Bach[r] about 24 & Elizabeth Holden wid. about 40 of S[t] Mary Aldermanbury London.—From *Foster's London Marriage Licenses.*

1676   July 5;   John Holden 21 Bachr. of Lydd, husbandman, & Mary
                  Beale 20 maiden, of same.
1680   May 20;   Edmund Chillenden 24 Bachr. of Cannon St., London
                  Grocer & Elizabeth Holden 24 maiden of Westgate
                  Canterbury.

FROM THE PARISH REGISTERS OF CRANBROOK.

The following is condensed from the entries in the Parish Registers:

1577–1601; Richard Holden, Churchwarden.
1607   ; John Holden Sr., Overseer.
1610   ; John Holden of Branden, Synodsman.
1613–1614; John Holden Sr. Warden.
1622–1623; John Holden Jr. Warden.
1624   ; James Holden, Overseer.
1625   ; John Holden,   "
1626   ; Robert Holden,   "
1628   ; Robert Holden, Synodsman.
1629–30 ; James Holden, Warden.
1630   ; Robert Holden, Surveyor of Highways.
1633–34 ; John Holden, Overseer.
1635–36 ; Robert Holden, Warden.
1644   ; Robert Holden, Overseer.
1645   ; James Holden,   "
1648   ; Robert Holden, Constable.
1656–57 ; Richard Holden of Brandon, Warden.
1657   ; Robert Holden, Gent., Surveyor.
1691   ;   "   "   " , Overseer.
1700–01 ;   "   "   " , Warden.
1743–1744; Collyer Holden,* " , Warden.

The following is supposed to relate to the same family:

FROM THE PARISH REGISTERS OF ST. NICHOLAS, ACONS, NOW INCOR-PORATED WITH THE PARISH OF ST. EDMUND, KING AND MARTYR, LOMBARD ST., LONDON, E. C.

A.D. 1564 July.   John Holden married Margaret Bekensall.
1565 5 Aug.   Joane Holden daughter of John Holden (*christened*).
1568 2 May.   John Holden sonne of John Holden (*christened*).
1571 June.   Three men (names given) servants of John Holden,
                  clothworker (*buried*) time of plague.
1586 19 April. John Holden (*buried*).
1599 6 Jan.   Willim Howlding son of Willyam Howlding (*chris-
                  tened*).
1600 20 April. Sara Houlden, daughter of Willm Holden haber-
                  dasher (*buried*).
1607 12 Nov.   Jone Holden, widowe (*buried*).
1638 16 Dec   Charles Holden, the sonne of Richard Holden &
                  Amphilis (Elizabeth erased) his wife (*christened*).
1641 14 July   Elizabeth Holding, daughter of Richard Holding &
                  Elizabeth his wife (*buried*).
1644 7 July   Elizabeth, daughter of Richard Holden & Elizabeth
                  his wif (*christened*).

* This name is registered at Vestry-meetings in 1755, 1756, 1757 and 1762. After this there is no mention of Holden in the Parish records.

1645–6 10 Jan Elizabeth, daughter of Richard Holden & Elizabeth his wif (*buried*).
1647–8 31 Jan Anphilis Holden wife of Richard Holden (*buried*).
1649 26 Oct Richard Holden, the sonne of Richard Holden & Anphilis his wife (*buried*).

The above extracts are all that are recorded of the Holden families in St. Nicholas Parish between 1564 and 1649. The registers have been carefully kept and are complete, and they date from 1539 to 1812. A note at the commencement of the christening register states that in 1600 a new book was obtained into which all the previous records were copied, the entries being checked by the churchwardens.

JOHN HOLMAN OF DORCHESTER, MASS., AND HIS DESCENDANTS

By ALFRED LYMAN HOLMAN of Chicago, Ill.

THE English home of John Holman of Dorchester, Mass., the immigrant ancestor of the family which forms the subject of this article, was at Swyre, co. Dorset, a parish on the coast of the English Channel, about six miles southeast from Bridport in the same county. According to Moule's "English Counties," published in 1838, the parish contained (presumably about that time) only 43 houses and 210 inhabitants. The parish church, dedicated to the Holy Trinity, is a restoration and enlargement of the old church that has stood there for several centuries. The oldest book of the parish registers, after having been lost for many years, was discovered in the parish of Puncknowle, which adjoins Swyre on the east, and was restored to the custody of the then rector of Swyre in Feb. 1892. It includes baptisms, marriages, and burials from 1587 to 1718, and is in a most tattered condition.* This register and the will of Morgan Holman, father of John of Dorchester, Mass., are the chief sources of information about the English connections of the New England immigrant.

HENRY HOLMAN, of Swyre, co. Dorset, grandfather of John of Dorchester, Mass., is the earliest ancestor of the New England family from whom descent has been proved, and was dead in 1587. He married JOAN JOLLIFFE, who was buried in the church of Swyre 28 June 1604, daughter of William of Martinstown, Winterbourne St. Martin, co. Dorset. In one of the early parish account books at Swyre there is a reference to a bequest of £10 given by Mrs. Joane Holman of Barwick,† widow, who was buried 28 June 1604. Another item in regard to the same bequest reads: "The like somme of Tenne pounds given likewise Mris. Joane Holman widow late of Barwick in Swyre aforesaid deceased for ever to remaine to the said use and yerely imployment & yerely to yeeld 20s.," and there is also "an account showing how 24s recd for year 1614 for the use of £10 given for ever to remain in stock for use of the poor by Mris. Joane Hollman late of Barwick."

Children (order of births unknown):

   i. MORGAN, b. probably abt. 1563. See below.
  ii. ANNE, living 19 June 1614, when she was mentioned as "my sister Anne Waye" in her brother Morgan's will; m. ——— WAYE (probably HENRY WAYE). Child (probably): *Henry,* who as

---

* The marriages recorded in the parish registers of Swyre, 1588–1836, were printed in 1912 in Phillimore's Dorset Parish Registers, Marriages, vol. 6, pp. 85–96.
† A hamlet in the parish of Swyre.

"Henrie Waie Jun" was a witness to the will of Morgan Holman in 1614.

iii. WILLIAM, of East Stower, co. Dorset, and Chilcomb, co. Hants, bur. in the chancel of St. Clement's Church, Winchester, co. Hants, abt. 1624; m. SUSANNA JOLLIFFE, bapt. at Fifehead-Magdalene, co. Dorset, 4 Oct. 1583, dau. of John and Elizabeth (Newman). William Holman was named as one of the executors in his brother Morgan's will in 1614.

iv. ALICE, m. THOMAS BISHOP, s. of John and Elinor (Watkins) of Chilcombe, co. Dorset. "Mr. Thomas Byshopp" was mentioned as one of the overseers in the will of his brother-in-law, Morgan Holman, in 1614.

v. MARY (probably dau. of Henry), m. at Swyre, 29 Feb. 1595/6, RICHARD DAVIDGE, probably the Richard Davidge who was a witness to the will of Morgan Holman in 1614.

Perhaps others.

MORGAN HOLMAN (*Henry*), of Barwicke [Berwick] in the parish of Swyre, co. Dorset, Gentleman, born probably about 1563, was buried at Swyre 1 July 1614. He married at Swyre, 24 Oct. 1596, ALICE ODBERRE, who was living 19 June 1614.* As Morgan Holman of Barwick, aged twenty-five, he held in 1588 a cottage at Burton-Bradstock, co. Dorset, a parish adjoining Swyre on the west. He was churchwarden at Swyre in 1607 and overseer in 1608 and 1611. In the contributions "for the relief of our poore" in 1614 he gave 12s., the largest amount given by any one person. He held of the Earl of Bedford, by lease dated 1 Nov. 1606, for the term of ninety-nine years, "determinable vppon my life & the lives of Alice my wife and Robte my sonne," a farm at Berwick in the parish of Swyre. The house and farm buildings were situated about a mile north from the church at Swyre, and distinct traces of the old house that must have been in existence over three hundred years ago can now be seen in the present enlarged house. Extracts from Morgan Holman's will follow.

"IN THE NAME OF GOD AMEN the xixth daye of June Anno Dom 1614 . . . I MORGAN HOLMAN of Barwicke within the pishe of Swyre in the County of Dorset gent . . . Doe make and ordaine this my last will and testament . . . my body I comit to Christian buriall to be buryed in Churche of Swyre as neere my mother as conveniently it may be done to wch Church I giue the some of tenn shillings Item I giue to the poore of the same pishe to remaine as a stocke for their benifitt for ever the some of five pounds to be payed within one yeare after my decease Item I giue to my sister Anne Waye a peece of goulde of eleaven shillings to make her a ringe in token of my love to her Item Whereas I holde by lease Dated the first daye of November in the fourth yeare of the raigne of or said souaigne Lord the

---

* An Alice Holman was married at Swyre, 11 Dec. 1621, to John Napper, and an Alice Holman was buried at Swyre 23 Jan. 1628/9. One of these women — it is not possible now to determine which one — may have been the widow of Morgan Holman. Who the other one was is unknown, although it may be conjectured that, if the Alice Holman who was married to John Napper was the widow of Morgan, the Alice who was buried in 1628/9 may have been the wife of his son Morgan, for the elder Morgan Holman does not appear to have had a daughter Alice (unless perhaps there was a posthumous child of that name) and his sister Alice is known to have married, before 19 June 1614, Thomas Bishop.

Kings Matie* of the Graunt of the right honourable the Earle of
Bedforde the Farme one demesnes of Barwicke wth his apprtennes
for the tearme of fowerscore and nyntene yeares determinable vppon
my life & the lives of Alice my wife and Robte my sonne out of
wch estate my will . . . is to pvide . . . porcons and mayntennce
for my wife and children . . . I giue . . . vnto my said wife for the
terme of ten yeares nexte after my decease one annuytye or yearlye
rent of thirtye pounds by the yeare to be payed out of the said farme
and demesnes quarterlye by even porcons by myne executors herein
named if shee shall so longe liuc togcther wth the vse and possession
of soe many roomes pcell of the dwellinghouse as shall be thought
fittest for her dwelling by my said executors or the greater number of
them duringe soe longe tyme as shee shall liue sole and vnmarried
together wth th'olde garderns and halfe the fruite that shalbe
groweinge in the orchardes and after thexpiracon of the said terme
of tenn yeares . . . I giue vnto her duringe her naturall life if the
said estate shall soe longe continewe one annuyty or yearly rent of
forty pownds by the yeare to be payed out of the issues & rents of the
said farme   Item I giue and bequeath vnto John Holman my sonne
the some of one hundred poundes and to my sonne Morgan the like
some of one hundred poundes And to my sonne Thomas the like
some of one hundred pounds And I alsoe giue vnto my daughter Ann
the some of one hundred poundes wch said severall legacies . . .
shalbe raysed by myne executors . . . out of my said farme &
demesnes of Barwicke ymediately after my decease in such convenient tyme as the same may be done out of the rents and pfitts of
the same farme and to be payed vnto my said children at their seuall
ages of one and twenty yeares or dayes of marriage wch shall first
happen seuallye if my said estate in the said farme shall contynewe
vntill the same porcons may be raysed And . . . if any or either of
my said children shall dye before they or any of them shall attayne
to the full age of xxjtie yeares or daye of marriage . . . the porcon
of him or her soe dyeing shall be given & devided equallye betweene
the residue of them that shall be liveing   Item . . . vppon condicon
that Robte Holman my eldest sonne . . . shall well and trulye . . .
paye vnto my said children John Holman Morgan Holman Thomas
Holman and Ann Holman the seuall somes of fyftye pounds a peece
att their seuall ages of one and twenty yeares and shall giue bond
vnto myne executors . . . for paymt thereof accordinglye wthin
three monethes after he shalbe of the age of xxtie yeares being therevnto required by myne executors or the srvivors of them I giue . . .
the remainder of my sayd estate in the said Farme of Barewicke my
childrens porcons being raysed and my wives annuytyes payed as
aforesaid vnto my said sonne Robte Holman Provided alwaies . . .
that my said children shall be bredd vpp and mayntayned out of the
issues & profitts of my said farme vntill they shall haue attained their
seuall ages of one and twentye yeares or be placed abrode in srvice
and that my wife shall have the breeding of them duringe soe long
time as shee shall contynewe sole and vnmarried Provided alsoe
that if the said Robte my sonne shall happen to dye in the life tyme
of my said wife . . . the residue of my sonnes liveinge shall have
the residue of my said estate in the said farme then to come equally
betweene them   Item I giue . . . vnto my said sonne John the lease
of the tithes of crtayne pcells of land meadowe & pasture belonginge
to the free chappell of St Lukes wch I latelye purchased of Nicholas
Darbye Lawrence and Roger Darbye for soe longe time as shall

* 1 Nov., 4 James I, that is, 1 Nov. 1606.

incurre in the life of my said sonne John And if he shall happen to dye before thexpiracon of the said terme then I giue the remaynder therof vnto my said sonnes Morgan and Thomas equallye to be devided betweene them Provided alwaies . . . that myne executors . . . shall . . . take the yssues and proffitts of the said tythes vntill my said sonne John shall attayne vnto the age of one and twentye yeares for and towards the performance of this my last will and testament And . . . I doe hereby will . . . that myne executors . . . and the srvivors and srvivor of them shall and lawfully maye at all tymes hereafter . . . levye out of the issues and pffitts of myne estate all such some and somes of money chardges and expences whatsoeu either ordinary or extra ordinary as they or any or either of them shall . . . expende in or about the pformance of this my last will and testament or in or about any other cause matter or thing whatsoeu touching or concerninge the same Item . . . if my said children or any or either of them shall sue ymplede vex molest or trouble my said executors or either of them in any of the Kings maties Courtes at Westminster or elsewhere for or touching their or either of their dealings or intermedlinge in or about the execucon of this my will or any the matters therein conteyned . . . then he & they soe sueing impleading vexing and molesting or troubling my said executors or eyther of them shall forfeite . . . the seuall somes of twenty poundes apeece parcell of his and their legacyes hereby given . . . wch said somes of twentye pound soe to be forfeyted I giue . . . vnto my said executors towards the defence of any suite soe to be comenced Item I giue . . . vnto my brother Willm Holman my geldinge colte of three yeares age All the residue of my goods chattles and estate whatsoeu not before given or bequeathed my debtes and legacyes beinge payed and funerall expenses pformed I giue . . . vnto myne executors . . . desiringe them to sell the same or any pte thereof for and towards the paymt of my debtes and pformance of this my will and if any pte thereof shall remayne I desyre them to devide and give the same vnto & amongest my wife & children in such mann as in their discreacons they shall thincke meetest And I make . . . my loveing brother Willm Holman and my brother in lawe John Odber and my cosen Humfrey Jolyff of Dorchester Executors of this my last will and testament and I intreate my brothers in lawe Mr Robte Odber and Mr Thomas Byshopp to be Overseers of this my will And to my said brother in lawe John Odber & my cosen Humfrey Jolyff I giue to eache of them a peece of gould of twenty two shillings a peece to make them rings in remembrance of my loue to them . . . [Signed] Morgan Holman" [Seal] Witnesses: Henrie Waie Jun, Richard Davidge [Seal], Sampson Miller [Seal], Richard Jacob als Beagan. Proved 19 April 1623. (P.C.C., Swann, 33.*)

Morgan Holman's bequest of £5 for the benefit of the poor of the parish of Swyre was evidently not carried out, for in 1639 an entry in the parish account books reads: "Besides there is ffiue pounds giuen by Mr. Morgan Holman deceased wch wee [have] not received for wch we desire . . . assistance." The last allusion to this legacy occurs in 1651, and the overseers had not then received it and for the future omitted to refer to it.

* The original will is on file at Somerset House, London. It is written on two sheets, each of which is signed by Morgan Holman.

Children, baptized at Swyre:

i. JOAN, bapt. 5 Aug. 1598; bur. at Swyre 7 Oct. 1599.
ii. ROBERT, bapt. 12 Apr. 1600; m. (1) at Swyre, 29 Nov. 1622, EDITH BISHOP, dau. of Humphrey and Joan (Watkins) of Chilcombe, co. Dorset; probably m. (2) at Swyre, 4 Nov. 1644, HELLEN STROOD.
iii. JOHN, the immigrant to New England, bapt. 27 Jan. 1602/3. See below.
iv. MORGAN, bapt. 10 Aug. 1606; living 19 June 1614.
v. ANN, bapt. 27 Dec. 1608; living 19 June 1614.
vi. THOMAS, bapt. 30 June 1611; living 19 June 1614.

1. JOHN¹ HOLMAN, of Dorchester, Mass., was baptized at Swyre, co. Dorset, England, 27 Jan. 1602/3, the son of Morgan and Alice (Odberre) Holman and the grandson of Henry and Joan (Jolliffe) Holman, and died at Dorchester, Mass., between 10 June 1652, the date of his will, and 18 Mar. 1652/3, the date of the inventory of his estate. He married first, probably at Dorchester, ANNE ———, who was admitted to the church 4 Nov. 1639 and died at Dorchester 1 Dec. 1639; and secondly, probably at Dorchester, about 1640, ANNE BISHOP, baptized at Bridport, co. Dorset, England, 22 Oct. 1616, daughter of Thomas and Avis (Abbot). About two years after the death of John Holman his widow, Anne (Bishop) Holman, was married to Rev. Henry Butler, A. B. (Harvard, 1651), A.M. (Harvard, 1654), the schoolmaster of Dorchester, and soon afterwards returned with him to England. From a statement in the manuscript diary of Rev. Michael Wigglesworth it may be inferred that the marriage of Mr. Butler and Mrs. Holman took place 9 Mar. 1654/5, the entry of that date in the diary reading: "Thursd. I wēt to Boston & frō- yⁿˢ to Mr Butlers he being married." Mr. Butler, according to Calamy's "Ejected or Silenced Ministers," vol. 2, p. 611, died at Withamfrary [Witham-Friary, co. Somerset], England, 24 Apr. 1696, aged 72 years. His wife, the widow of John Holman, was already deceased on 4 Aug. 1673, when Mr. Butler, describing himself as "now or late of yeouell" [Yeovil], co. Somerset, England, conveyed to Thomas² Holman (John¹) of Milton, Mass., his interest in the estate of John Holman, and referred in the deed to "anne my late wife."*

The following entries in the "Aspinwall Notarial Records" prove that John Holman of Dorchester, Mass., was identical with John, son of Morgan Holman of Swyre, co. Dorset, England; and the second entry shows also the disposition made by John Holman of his interest in the paternal lands at Swyre.

"17 (9) 1647 [17 Nov. 1647.] John Holman of Dorch: gent, hath made &c: Mr Tho: Bishop of Bredport in the Count Dorset merchᵗ his true & lawfull Attr: to aske & receive all such Rents as are or shalbe due unto him out of Barwick fferme in the parish of Swyer in Dorsetshire by vertue of the last will &c of Morgan Holman his ffather deceased & of the receipt to give acquitt: &c: also to compound &c: & to appeare before all Lords Judges &c: to doe say sue &c: & generally to doe &c: ffurther granting his sᵈ Attr: power to alien & sell all his right & interest in & to the said Barwick fferme or any part thereof. & deed or deeds of sale to make seale & deliver in his name, and to doe all act or acts thing or things necessary & behoofefull. Ratifying

* Vide infra, 3 (p. 196). For Rev. Henry Butler see Sibley's Graduates of Harvard University, vol. 1, pp. 297-299.

hereby & confirming irrevocably whatsoever &c:" (Aspinwall Notarial Records, pp. 104–105.)

"18. (11) 1648. [18 Jan. 1648/9.] John Holman of Dorchester did grant assigne & sett over unto John Squibb of Berwicke yeoman all his right title & interest wch he the s^d John Holman now hath or of right ought to have in & unto the fferme & Demeasnes of Berwicke granted by the Earle of Bedford about the 1 (9) in the fourth yeare of King James of England &c: unto Morgan Holma for the terme of ninety nine yeares if the s^d Morgan Holman Alice his wife or Robert his son should so long live. This assignment was sealed & dd in presence of Wm Aspinwall Not publ & John Glover & Richard Collecot. 17 (11) 48." (*Ib.*, p. 190.)

John Holman, son of "Morgane Holman late of Barwick, gent.," was enrolled at Dorchester, co. Dorset, England, 25 Mar., 20 James I [1622], as an apprentice to "Wm. Jolliffe of Dorchester, wollendraper," probably one of his father's relatives.* If he served the full time of his apprenticeship, this would account for him until nearly 1630, the year in which it is believed that he emigrated to New England. Possibly he sailed in the advance ship of Winthrop's fleet, the *Mary and John*, whose passengers, landing at Mattapan in the Massachusetts Bay Colony, called their settlement Dorchester.

At a meeting of the General Court in Boston, 3 Oct. 1632, John Holman and Henry Way were authorized to receive £40 out of a fine of £45 imposed on Nicholas Frost, and to keep Nicholas Frost "in boults . . . till his ffines be paid, dureing wch time hee [Frost] is to beare his owne charges."† In Pyncheon's papers John Holman is mentioned as a collector of furs at Dorchester, Mass., in 1633. He was a landholder at Dorchester, and is mentioned often in the town records from 1 Sept. 1634 on, when Bray Clarke and John Allen were ordered to build a house "upon the Rocke by John Holman." His farm which he left by his will to his sons Thomas and Samuel and to his wife was in that part of Dorchester which was set off in 1662 as the town of Milton. He was a selectman of Dorchester in 1636, 1637, and 1642, was chosen by the General Court, 9 Mar. 1636/7, ensign for Dorchester, was a member of the "Jury of Life & Death" at a Quarter Court held at Boston and Newtown 19 Sept. 1637, and was the nineteenth signer of the original roll of the Ancient and Honorable Artillery Company in 1637. At a "Generall Court of Elections," held in Boston 2 June 1641, Lieut. Willard, John Holman, and Richard Collicott, with so many as they should receive into their society, were given a monopoly of trading with the Indians.‡

The will of John Holman, dated 10 June 1652, is as follows:

"Whereas almighty God haveing layd upon me a great affliction I thinke it my duty to dispose of that smale estate God have given me to prevent trouble for time to come: And whereas the honorable Court have established a Law the eldest sonne shall have a double portion my earnest desire is and to my greife I speak it my sonne being growne to some yeares prooveth disobedient and stubborne against me my desire is he may be deprived of that

---

* "The Inrolment of the Apprentices within the Borough of Dorchester begon 4 Apriles, 1622," in the Municipal Records of the Borough of Dorchester, Dorset.
† Massachusetts Bay Records, vol 1, pp. 100–101.
‡ Cf. Dorchester Town Records, Massachusetts Bay Records, History of the Ancient and Honorable Artillery Company, and History of the Town of Dorchester, Massachusetts.

benefitt which others may justly injoy and I give unto him my sonne John Holman the sume of fifty pounds to be paid unto him at twenty yeares of age and unto my daughter Mary Holman I give fifty pounds to be paid unto her at eighteene yeares of age or at hir day of marriage and to my foure youngest children I give fifty pounds to each of them to be paid at the age of twenty yeares to my two sonnes Thomas and Samuel Holman and to my two daughters Abigaile and Hannah Holman I give fifty pounds to each of them to be paid at theire day of marriage or at the age of eighteen yeares. As for my housing and Land at Dorchester I give to my wife dureing hir life and after hir death I give the one halfe of my land to my sonnes Thomas and Samuel Holman and the other halfe of my Land I give to my wife to despose of it as she shall see fitt: And all the rest of my estate the Legacyes being paid I give to my wife and hir I make my Executrix of this my Last Will and testament. And in case any child dye before their portion be due then to be at my wifes disposeing: my will is my foure youngest children shalbe to remaine with theire mother till they come to age mentioned on the other side and to be maintained by their mother with that wch is Left for them: now to the ful-filling of this my Last will and testament I doe appoint and order my beloved brethren Richarde Collecott and William Robeson to be overseers unto my wife and children and unto them I give power when portions shalbe due to see them paid and to be helpful to my wife in what they may.

"In testimony whereof I subscribe my hand this 10th day of the 4th moneth 1652.

John Holman."

The estate of John Holman was, for that time, a large one, the inventory, taken 18, 1 mo. 1652/3, showing a valuation of £739. 16s. The appraisers were Richard Collicott and William Robinson of Dorchester, and the inventory was "Accepted prouided ye execu-trix Appeare before the next County Court giue in securitie for the Childrens porcons." *

In his will John Holman had declared that John, his eldest son, had proved disobedient and stubborn, and instead of leaving to him the customary double portion he had bequeathed to him £50, to be paid when he should have reached the age of twenty years. The young man was born 23 Feb. 1637/8, and was therefore about fifteen years old when his father died. On 17 Apr. 1656, when he was eighteen years of age, he "came before the Magistr, & with their allowance chose *Robert Badcocke* to be his guardian." † His reason for doing this was undoubtedly for the purpose of bringing a suit to contest his father's will, and to this end he filed a petition with the General Court, in which he states that he is the "eldest sonne of his father by his former wife; mother unto your petitioner and by that parentall care and tender endevors your petitioner with the rest of the children was honestly and religiously brought up whilst his mother lived;" that he always behaved himself as a dutiful son, "the folly and vanity of child hood and youth excepted. . . . But so it came to pass your petitioners mother died and in some space of tyme his father marred another woman of good repute liveing at that tyme in dorchester by whom he had fouer children two sonnes and two daughters among whom your petitioner and his sister Mary were still continued in the family;" that he behaved himself "like a duti-

* Cf. REGISTER, vol. 8, p. 60.
† REGISTER, vol. 9, p. 142.

full sonne both to father and mother . . . excepting what by reason of folly and vanity among us children did now and then fall out as is insident unto such families where children of severall mothers are as was the condicon of godly Jacobs family and of his grandfather Abraham;" that his fathers will deprives him not only of his legal and just rights as eldest son, but defames him by characterizing him as a disobedient son; and he prays that the validity of the will may be inquired into, "whether it may not fairly appeare that my father did not resolve against me or intend it to stand in force but only to quiet my Mother & to be a terror unto me to keepe me in awe." *

The action of the General Court in regard to this petition is shown in the records of the session of 14 May 1656, as follows:

"In answer to the pet̃ of John Holman, of Dorchester, desireinge to haue his fathers will made voyd, this Court referrs it to the next County Court for Suffolk, to be heard, both p̃tyes & wittnesses, & if it appeare to the s̃d Court, vpon hearinge the case, that there is just reason to make null or alter the will of the petitionoᵣ father, then the s̃d Court to state the case, & report the grounds thereof to the next session of this Court; but if the contrary appear to the s̃d Court, vizᵗ, that the will ought to remayne in force, & the petioᵣˢ not to make any further trouble, & in that case, also, the s̃d Court to giue reasons to this Court why they app'hend the the will ought to stand in force, & also that securitie be forthwith taken by the secritary to the value of one hundred pounds, vpon the estat of Mᵣ John Holman, deceased, to be responsall for what this Court shall determine & conclude herein vpon information from the County Court."†

In connection with this suit the following declaration was made by Mrs. Anne (Bishop) (Holman) Butler, stepmother of the petitioner:

"To the Honnord Court Assembled at Boston, The Declareation of Anne Butler sume time Wife and now Executrix to Jno. Hollman late of Dorchester, etc.

"God by his providence Calling me to England to my new Husband though mor suddenly then I expected as sume of yourselves know, I thought it my Duty to leave a few lines for the Clearing of myselfe and former Husband who was Deare to me in his life time and now I hope and believe is Blessed with the Lord. Since my present husband went for England I have been informed that some persons have given in testimony against me Concerning John Hollman which is no small trouble of mind to me that there should be such Recording up family weaknesses to the dishonor of God and Grief of one another and I had rather goe many paces Backward to cover Shame than one Inch forward to discover any; and that which I am forced here to Speak I thought to have Buried had I not been forced to it for the Clearing of my selfe and former Husband: it pleased God to give me the enjoyment of my former Husband about forteen years; when I married him he had tow children the one newly taken from the Brest and the other three years and sd wch children continued with me all the time of my husbands life only a while the one was at schoole and in that time I had six children by my husband soe that our family was very great by Reason of Children and servants and my husbands calling leading him oft from whome for many weeks and months together the whole weight and Burthen of the family lay upon me to look after maters Both within and without the truth is that I am Loath to speak of it yett my very Life was a Burthen to me p' Reson of the many Troubles and distractions I met with both within and without p' Reson

* Massachusetts Archives, vol. 15, fo. 78.
† Massachusetts Bay Records, vol. 3, pp. 400–401. Cf. ib., vol. 4, part 1, p. 262.

of my husbands absence soe that it is not only Likely but Trew that I might let fall some speeches or passages that might not be according to the rule of Godly Government But it is very trew and I have caus to Bewale it that through many In Cumbrances and my own Corruption I have many ways fayled and missed it in my place. And I hope that your wisdom will consider that a woman soe offt Loste with soe many children and servants and such weight of Buseness. Tis not any Easie thing for such an one to walke according to rule in all things I desire not to Justifie my self But to bewale it wherever I have missed and it is my grief that servants and neighbors that have been in my husbands house by accident should Blarc aboroad such things as carie such a face with them as Indeed is not in them.

"And whereas I am Informed that John Hollman and others doe labor to prove that I was the caus why his father didnt give him a double portion that I must absolutely deny I never moved his father to any such thing but it was his own Voluntarie act unknown to me until such time as he read his will in my hearing I then discovered that it might be otherwise my husband was displeased with me as I supose overseers can witnes but as I said before I am unwilling to discover shame but the truth is it was John Hollmans ill carriage toward his father that was the cause his father did deprive him of a double portion it was not only the Miss carriages of his childhood for as I suppose he was seventeen years old or thereabouts when his father dyed and he being growne up to years of Descreation and his father in great affliction it was greevious to him to see his son soe to cary himselfe the wch he hath often bewaled not only to myselfe but to others allso; and Reproved and Told him the danger and Evill that wold follow and Insue such Corsess. I shall Instance in some particulars though the Lord knowes I desire nott to speake in prejudes to John Hollman but for the clearing of the truth as the Cases now stands soe farr my Declaration may have credit given to it I shall not say anything in thisse consarning his carriage towards me as his mother but only of his carage towards his father.

"His frquent Expressions the old man will never Recover it and then I shall have double portion the house and land shall be myne and his carraige hath Been very unnatnerall his father never above twise that Ivremember desired his son John to do a mean offies for him his answer was a dogs take it it stinks like poyson whereupon his father threw his slipper at him and told him with many teares that he was a curssed cham he also told him of Elis Sons and of the sins of disobedience to parents and his answer was why doe you not hang me then

"His father hath offt thretened him to have him before the Majestrate and before the Church; his father hath divers times spoaken of his death but it never brought a teare from him that I ever could perceive in soe much that his father hath offten said to him; I feare God hath reprobated thee; his father tooke it very greeviously that when he had been abroad at his Returne he would not speake to him nor aske him how he did his father told him he would make a publike example and could finde in his hart never to give him a penny he told his father to his face that he did not care Lett him do what he would and when his father lay dead in the hous he did desire to see the will that he might know what his father had given him and when he did know he wondered that his father had given him soe much.

"Much more I could have added in severall particulars but I am not willing to trouble the court in laying blemish upon John Hollman without constrainte but leave it to the testimony and Examination of others of the court see caus to call for it.

"Your worshipps to Command,

"June 28th 1656.   Ann Butler." *

* Massachusetts Archives, vol. 15, fo. 81.

John Holman was unsuccessful in his suit, as is shown by the records of the session of the General Court held in Boston, 14 Oct. 1656, as follows:

"The County Court held at Boston the 5th of August, 1656, having heard all the evidences in the case concerning Mr Holmans will in reference to John Holman, his son, according to the order of the Genll Court, May, 56, doe make this report: that notwithstanding the evidences p'duced by John Holman, which are on file, they judge the will of the s̃d Holman legally proued, & se no cause to alter the same; which returne of the County Court this Court thinkes meet to approue off in this case." *

Children by first wife, born at Dorchester:

2. i. JOHN,[2] b. 23 Feb. 1637/8.

ii. MARY, b. abt. 1639; d. after 5 Aug. 1700; m. in Boston, 29 May 1662, Gov. John Endicott officiating, SAMUEL MASON, b. in England abt. 1632, d. in Boston 20 Sept. 1691, s. of Ralph and Anne of Boston. Samuel Mason was admitted as a freeman in 1669, and his will, dated 11 Aug. 1691, was proved 23 Nov. 1691. Children, recorded in Boston: 1. *Mary*, b. 19 Apr. 1663. 2. *Anne*, b. 4 July 1665. 3. *Abigail*, bapt. 21 Oct. 1666; d. 20 Feb. 1691/2. 4. *Thomas*, b. 6 Dec. 1668. 5. *Samuel*, b. 18 Apr. 1671. 6. *John*, b. 29 Jan. 1673/4. 7. *Joseph*, b. 24 Nov. 1677. Also: 8. *Ebenezer*, mentioned in his father's will.

Children by second wife, born at Dorchester:

3. iii. THOMAS, b. 6 Aug. 1641.

iv. ABIGAIL, bapt. 20 Dec. 1642. Under her name in the baptismal records of the First Church, Dorchester, are the words: "To Taunton."

v. ANNA, bapt. 29 Sept. 1644; probably the daughter called Hannah in John Holman's will in 1652.

4. vi. SAMUEL, bapt. 6 Dec. 1646.

vii. PATIENCE, bapt. 28 Jan. 1648/9; undoubtedly d. young, as she was not mentioned in her father's will.

viii. A CHILD, dates of birth and death unknown.†

---

* Massachusetts Bay Records, vol. 3, pp. 418–419. Cf. *ib.*, vol. 4, part 1, pp. 284–285.

† In her declaration of 28 June 1656, given above, Mrs. Anne (Bishop) (Holman) Butler stated that she had six children by her [former] husband.

HOLMES.

SAML. G. DRAKE, ESQ., *Cor. Sect. N. E. Historic-Genealogical Society.*

Enclosed I send you a copy of a "Letter of Direction" concerning one of the early names of New England. John Holmes, the writer of the original, died in East Haddam, Conn., in 1734. His father Thomas, as he says, was a very aged man, being 98 years of age at his death. ANDREW F. WARNER.

"This letter of direction from John Holmes in Haddam in New England to find the place where his father was born and brought in London."

"He was son to Thomas Holmes, Councler of Grason, who lived in Saintlands parrish in Holburn, in the Keper Crown Corte in Grason lane, upper side against Grayson Walk,—his mothers maiden name was Mary Thatford—Grandfather was slain in the time of the civil wars at Oxford Sege—Our Coat of Arms are the three spurred Cocks fighting in the golden fields. My father came out of England in the time of the great plague and he thought to have gone down into Norfolk, to a place called Lyn, where he had a piece of land, One Edmund But was tenant, and had been for many years before ; but all places being guarded he could not pass, wherefore he came here unawares thinking to have returned in a few years, but it was otherwise ordered for the country proved unhealthy to him, and he was poor and low in the world—After a while he recruited and as it was ordered, married in New York to one Lucia Dudley of London daughter of Mr. Thomas Dudley who kept the laws court in Clans Street in Common garden in London ; she had two brothers—but she died about six and thirty years ago. My father died in Dec. 12th, 1724, being a very aged man.* My father so long as he lived, lived in the hopes of seeing England again, but he is dead and gone and left but only me his son being 38 years of age. This direction taken by me John Holmes on his fathers death bed."

---

* Died aged 98 years.

A LETTER OF DIRECTIONS TO HIS FATHER'S BIRTH-PLACE, BY JOHN HOLMES, OF HADDAM, CONN.—1725.

THIS Letter of Directions—from John Holmes—in Haddam—in New England—for to find—the place where his Father—was Born and—Brought vp In London : He was Son to Thomas Holmes—Councler of Grase—in* Who Liued in Saint-Tandrs†—parrich in Holborn—in the Roson Crown Cort‡—in Grasen Lain§ upper site—a Gainst Grasin walks—His Mother's Maden Name was Mary Thetford. Grandfather was Slain in the Time of the Seuel warrs—att Oxford Sege—Our : Cort : of : arms are the 3 Spord Coks fighting in a Golden feild—My father Came out of England in the Time of the Grat plage —and he thought to haue gon Down into Norfolk—to a place caled Lyn whare—we had a Small pece of Land—one Edmond Beel—was Tennant and had been for many years before but all places being garded he Culd Not pass—whear upon he Came for uirjaney‖—thenking to have Returned—in a fue years—But it was other ways ordered —for the Contry proued unhelthy to : him and he was poor and Low in the world—after a while he Recruted—and as It was ordred—Marred —in New york To one Lucrese Dodly—Dafter to—Mr.—Thomas Dodley—of London, who keep the tanes Cort¶—in—Clare Streat** in Common Gardin†† in London. She had Two—Brothers—But She Died—a bout 6—and thirty year a Go—my father Died—in Dec^m 12th—1724— Being a uery aged man—my father so long as he Liued he Liued in hopes of seeing England a Gain—But he is Dead an Gon and Left but only me his Son. being thirty—8—years—of age— — .

These Directions Taken by John Holmes on his father's Death bead.

[A copy of the foregoing Letter was inserted in the *Register*, vol. x. p. 242. This appears to have been in many particulars incorrect. D. Williams Patterson, formerly of West Winsted, Conn., but now of Newark Valley, N. Y., a well known antiquary and genealogist, has prepared an exact transcript of the original Letter of Directions, which he has had published in New York, in a tasty manner, with notes, being No. 1 of the publications of the " U. Q. Club." (See Book Notices in this number.)

Instead of making corrections and placing them in the errata, as is usual, it was thought better to reprint the Letter entire, as given by Mr. Patterson. A few explanations, taken from the notes made by the above named gentleman, are appended as foot-notes.

We learn from the genealogy annexed, in the pamphlet by Mr. Patterson, that Thomas[2] Holmes, who was the father of John,[3] the writer of the letter, died at the age of 98. John,[3] b. in New London, Conn.,

---

* Gray's Inn.
† St. Andrew's Parish.
‡ Rose and Crown Court.
§ Gray's Inn Lane.
‖ Virginia.
¶ Probably the tennis court.
** " Clare street, in London, lies nearly midway between Covent Garden Market, and Lincoln's Inn Fields."
†† Supposed to be " Covent Garden."

March 11, 1686–7, m. Feb. 11, 1706–7, Mary Willey, dau. of John and Miriam (Moore) Willey, and died in East Haddam May 29, 1734. Children : *Thomas*,[4] b. Dec. 4, 1707, m. Jan. 9, 1732, Lucy Knowlton, dau. of Lieut. Thomas and Susannah Knowlton ; *John*,[4] b. Feb. 24, 1708–9, m. Lucretia Willey, dau. of John and Elizabeth (Harvey) Willey, and had two sons and one daughter ; *Lucretia*,[4] b. July 14, 1711 ; tradition says that she m. a man named Willey, who died soon after marriage, and that then she m. Joseph Willey, son of John and Elizabeth (Harvey) Willey, and it is verified by the record, which shows that Joseph Willey m. May 22, 1727, Lucretia Willey. She had a daughter Elizabeth. He had a second wife, Rebecca, by whom he had nine children ; *Mary*,[4] b. Feb. 7, 1712–13, m. Abel Willey, son of Abel and Hannah (Bray) Willey, and had four children who are mentioned ; *Christopher*,[4] b. June 4, 1715, m. March 2, 1736, Sarah Andrews, dau. of Samuel and Eleanor (Lee) Andrews ; *Grace*,[4] b. Aug. 4, 1717, m. March 2, 1736, Robert Hungerford, son of John and Deborah (Spencer) Hungerford, and had ten children ; *Eliphalet*,[4] b. July 12, 1722, m. Jan. 25, 1742, Damaris Waterhouse. He d. Nov. 30, 1743, and his widow m. (2d) Joseph Comstock, of East Haddam, by whom she had five children ; *Sarah*,[4] b. June 14, 1726, m. Nathaniel Niles ; *Abigail*,[4] b. Aug. 1, 1729, d. Aug. 26, 1811, unmarried.

EDITOR.]

HESSET (SUFFOLK, ENGLAND) ITEMS.—Through the very polite courtesy of the Rev. Richard Morphy, M.A., Rector of Hesset, co. Suffolk, Eng., I have been given access to the Parish Register which commences 1538, and mentions several names of families which were found in the next century in New England ; and thinking they might interest, I have jotted them down. Many entries relate to the names of Hoo or How, Hoo *alias* How, Bacon, Newgate, Page, Goodrich, Chaplin, Goodwyn and Bradstreet. The latter name has interest, as one page of the Register, dated 1630, is signed *Symon Bradstreet, clerk*, who was perhaps father of Gov. Bradstreet of New England. See REGISTER, vol. ix. p. 113 ; also Savage's Dict.*

The Hoo, How, Hoo *alias* Howe entries are very numerous. This family (which resided at the Hoo and held the copyhold of Rougham Hall) and the Bacons built Hesset Church, as the evidence is still extant in black letters which commence at the East, run along the cornice of the solar, the chapel and a portion of the aisle :
" Prey for the S[owles] of Jhon hoo & Katrynne† hys wyf the queche h[at]h mad y chapel dewery deyl heyleynd y westry 8 vatytmentyd y hele.''

There is also a beautiful stone baptismal Fount at the West entrance of the church, with this inscription on the three sides of the kneeling stone :—Orate pro Adimabs ....rti. hoo et Augnetis etxis* eius q.... istum fontem feri fecerunt."

The Hoo family is very interesting, and can without doubt be connected with the Hows of Lynn and Boston. This John and Robert Hoo were no doubt brothers, the former grandfather of Walter Hoo of Hesset, whose daughter married as follows :

" Phillip Newgate† and Joan daughter of Walter Hoo, 20 Dec. 1578.

Gualtherus Hoo and Agnes Lockwood, prob. a widow and 2d wife, 7 Oct. 1561.

Abraham Church widower of Drinkstone, and Joan Lockwood, daughter (step-daughter) of Walter Hoo, 10 Sept. 1581."

In Genealogical Notes by Goodwin the will of Rev. William Goodrich of Hesset is mentioned, of which and other Goodrich wills I have copies, and have drawn a genealogical table of the family, hoping some time to have it printed in the REGISTER.

" John Goodrich‡ of Bradfield and Maria Hoo widow, 1 Dec. 1594."

The Chaplyn family of Suffolk emigrated to New England, see REGISTER and Savage.

" Thomas Hoo of Hesset and Ellen Chaplin daughter of Stephen Chaplin of Coomes, mar. at Coomes 17 November, 1657."

In will of John Goodrich of Bury St. Edmunds, co. Suffolk, Eng. (Clothier), dated April 14, 1632. His wife Margaret. My house in Burie where I now dwell, and lands in Horningsheath. To son William Goodrich the elder. To son William Goodrich the younger. To son John Goodrich. To son Jeremy Goodrich. If son John Goodrich dies before he becomes 21, then all my lands, tenements, &c. &c. to be equally divided between my son William G. the elder, William G. the younger and my son Jeremy. (Many relations mentioned.) To the poor of St. Mary Parish. To poor spiners of Drinkstone, co. Suffolk. To *Thomas* Chaplain *mercer*, and Clement Chaplain, *grocer*. To William Goodrich, son of Bro. Henry G. To cousin Robert G. of Bury St. Edmunds, *Supervisor*. To Margaret my wife, whom executrix. Wit. Richard Cooper, Robt. Brightwell, Philip Crow. Proved 16 May, 1632.

Extract Candler MSS., Ped. Chaplyn. Clement Chaplyn, a chandler of Bury St. Edmunds, went over to New England and was one of the Elders of the congregation of Mr. Hooker. Will of Clement Chaplyn of Seamer, co. Suffolk, dated 4 Dec. 1615, proved .... Feb. 1621. My son Tho. Chaplyn. My son Edward Chaplyn. Grandchild and wife mentioned.　　　　CHARLES HERVEY TOWNSHEND.
New Haven, Ct.

* According to Mather, Gov. Bradstreet's father died about 1617, some thirteen years before this date.—EDITOR.

† This vestry and chapel was no doubt built by John Hoo and Kathrin his wife, and finished before 1492, when his will was proved. Davy, Suffolk Collection, in the British Museum, gives pedigree of John Hoo, whose sister Cicily mar. John Bacon, who may have been of Hesset and the builder of the Tower of Hesset Church, whereon are his initials I. B. Queen Elizabeth's grandfather, Sir Thos. Bolyn, was grandson of Ann, only daughter of Thomas Hoo, Lord Hoo and Hasting.—C. H. T.

* This font was probably given by Robert Hoo (and Agnes his wife), whose will was proved 1510.—C. H. T.

† See the Townshend Family of Lynn in Old and New England, for Hoo and Newgate wills.—C. H. T.

‡ The Goodri*ch* Family is not the same as the Goodri*ck*, and which connected with Gov. Bellingham and Thomas Townshend of Lynn. See REGISTER.—C. H. T.

AN EARLY GOVERNOR OF NEW SOMERSETSHIRE.

By FREDERICK W. TODD, Esq., of Boston.

In the preparation of a work upon " Humphrey Hooke of Bristol, and his family and descendants in England and America during the Seventeenth Century," I have come upon some questions which have required minute study and investigation. This has resulted in the development of certain facts not hitherto generally known, or much considered by investigators, which throw some light upon an obscure period in the early history of Maine. One of these questions is in regard to the governorship of the province of New Somersetshire from say March, 1638, to June, 1640, inclusive.

Humphrey Hooke was a wealthy and influential merchant of Bristol, when that city was the largest in England next to London, and the chief commercial port in Britain. He held the office of alderman (which was a life position under the city charter), was twice mayor, and an M. P. for Bristol in the short and long parliaments. His second son, William Hooke, who came here in 1633, was his co-patentee in the Agamenticus patent, and was here representing not only his own interest therein, but the interest of his father Humphrey, his brother Thomas, and his brother-in-law Giles Elbridge. These men and a few others (notably Robert Thomson of London) were supporting the efforts of Sir Ferdinando Gorges in colonization, and furnishing a large part of the capital, of which he was then much in need. However unfortunate Sir Ferdinando may have been in his colonial enterprises — and he admits that most of them had miscarried, and that his estate had been greatly impaired thereby — there need be no doubt that he had finally associated himself with people of ample means to second his efforts, and that he had great hopes of success through his Agamenticus venture.

In regard to the financial standing of his associates, it may be stated that Alderman Hooke was lord of seven manors in Gloucestershire and Somerset, one of which had a park of over five hundred acres, and a site unsurpassed in England. None of his manorial estates had come to him by inheritance. He obtained them all by purchase, and they represented a portion of his large fortune acquired in commercial enterprises. Giles Elbridge was also a wealthy man. He had inherited the entire estate of his partner (and uncle by marriage), Robert Aldworth, one of the most enterprising and successful of Bristol merchants. Robert Thomson, brother of Sir William Thomson afterwards governor of the East India Company, was a merchant of London of ample means. He was here for a short time in 1639 on a visit of inspection, and purchased the old church edifice and ground on which it stood on State street, for £160 — site of Brazier Building, 27 State street. Mr. Savage calls him "a man of distinction in London," and says: "He was a powerful friend of Mass., and for services our Ct. made a grant to him of 500 acres." He and his brother Sir William were trustees under the will of Sir Thomas Hooke, baronet, grandson of Alderman Hooke.

But Alderman Hooke and his son-in-law Giles Elbridge were the ones upon whom Sir Ferdinando placed his chief reliance for support and assistance. The alderman was his neighbor, just across the street in Bristol, and had been more or less concerned in colonial ventures since 1610, having been at that time a member, with Lord Bacon and others, of the New Foundland Company. Edward Godfrey, in his letter to Gov. Winthrop, dated February 10, 1639, says that Alderman Hooke is "the Cheefe pattentee heere [Agamenticus], and to my Knowledge resolveth to settle it, as now he hath fayrly begun" (see Felt's *Ecclesiastical History of New England*, 1, 445–6). In view of all this it would not be surprising if we should find that Sir Ferdinando Gorges had appointed William Hooke governor of his province of New Somersetshire. Evidence to this effect from three distinct sources would seem to place this question beyond a reasonable doubt.

Every investigator admits that this particular period (1638 to 1640) in the early history of Maine is very obscure. But even the cause of this obscurity I think can be made plain. Our most important clue to "Governor Hooke" is furnished by Edward Godfrey. In the letter above referred to he states that William Hooke is now governor, and that he "is determined to leave vs, and I thinke for Nubury [it happened to be Salisbury], I presume vnknowne to you." Here again he was mistaken. He adds: "But yf our governour in the time of his government should [leave] vs distracted, and before his going home to see his parents, whose presence they [very] much desyre, it may eclipse all this light, and this place may fayll to factions. Both myne and others humble request is, you would be pleased to wright those at Nubury to forbeare their soelisatations, and that you would be pleased to wright our governour priuately, not rashly, and soe suddenly to leave vs, a people whose hartes ar soe set in reall affections one him, and to stay out his time of government."

Next we come to a deed of land from William Hooke to Henry Simson, dated March 13, 1638, and recorded in York Deeds, vi., 74, which begins: "This writing witnesseth that I, William Hooke, *now Governour*, of Accomenticus in New England." Finally we have in York Deeds, vi., 150, the following:

"I Richard Vines Steward Gen^{ll} unto S^r ffardinando Gorges K^t L^d propriet^r of the Province of Mayn doe give and Grant unto Henry Simpson his heires and assignes for ever ten Acres of marsh land upon y^e *south side* of the river Accomenticus opposite against ye ffarm of Wm *Hook Gover*: * * * In witness whereof I ye afores^d Richd Vines in ye behalf of ye s^d S^r ffardinando Gorges have hereunto set my hand this 28th day of May 1640.   Rich: Vines

Witness Will Hooke

Possession & Seizen of ye Land within mentioned was delivered to ye wthin named Henry Simpson by Thomas Gorges *Esqr* the 29 day of June 1640 — in ye p^{r}sence of Wm Hooke *Govern^r* and Richd Cornish.

A true copy of the original Transcribed & compared July: 6: 1702
                                          p Jos: Hamond Reg^r"

Here we seem to have not only the statement of Richard Vines (who had been deputy governor during the unexpired term and absence of William Gorges) calling himself *Steward General*, and calling William Hooke *Governor*, but also the *assent* to that statement of Thomas Gorges, *Esq.* (not *Deputy Governor*), who had just arrived, and not yet qualified. Mr. Vines evidently wrote the 1640 deed. The use of the double "f," as in Sir "ffardinando" in the deed, and "ffire brand" in his Winthrop letter, is peculiar to him. William Hooke appears to have lingered at Agamenticus,

403

awaiting the arrival of his successor (Thomas Gorges), although his house at Salisbury had then been completed, and his family had removed thither. He was there himself two weeks later, and writing thence to Gov. Winthrop, Gorges in the meantime having been installed.

It would seem that the chief executive officer of New Somersetshire was called "governor," and that this title should be given both to William Gorges and William Hooke. Later, however, when Sir Ferdinando was appointed governor by the royal commission, which provided that thereafter New Somersetshire should be called the "Province or Countie of Maine," the resident governor, so long as Sir Ferdinando remained in England, was to be a "deputy governor." This was the title borne by Thomas Gorges. Sir Ferdinando states that he contemplated coming here himself. Doubtless he was detained by the civil commotion in England in which, even at his advanced age, he took for a time an active part on the royalist side. After his death in 1647, the resident governors received that title in full as at first.

The obscurity that has prevailed in relation to the governorship (1638–40) is due largely to the fact that our chief sources of information have been Governor Winthrop's journal and papers, and Sir Ferdinando's account, published by his grandson, neither of which has made any mention of "Governor Hooke," or of any other governor of New Somersetshire during that period. From this statement an exception must of course be made of the Godfrey letter, which I presume was obtained by the Rev. Mr. Felt from Mr. Winthrop or Mr. Savage prior to the publication of the Winthrop papers. In regard to Governor Winthrop it may be asked: As he was in correspondence with Governor Hooke, why did he not refer to him in his official capacity, and why did he endorse the only letter we find from him during the period under discussion (the letter of January 28, 1639) "Mr. Hooke of Accomenticus," instead of "Governor Hooke," etc.? But Governor Winthrop, to be consistent, *could not* admit that Mr. Hooke was governor, for that office was a creation of Sir Ferdinando Gorges, *whose authority he disputed.* Governor Winthrop and the Massachusetts people, in 1637, after the Cleeves trouble, it will be remembered, *declined* the invitation of Sir Ferdinando to administer affairs in New Somersetshire in his behalf, "*professing to be ignorant of his right to the government of the Province*"* (Folsom, p. 52). They speak of *Mr.* Vines, and *Mr.* Hooke, and of *Mr.* Gorges (Thomas) and "his affairs," but to admit that they *were governors*, or had any valid right to that title, would be admitting that their contention in regard to Gorges was at fault. This was a vital matter with them for they claimed the territory themselves, although at that time, and before the execution of Charles I., they were necessarily somewhat guarded in their expressions upon the subject. The Massachusetts governors were the only true governors, according to their theory, and in due time they demonstrated it (?), and Mr. Godfrey had to step down and out. It is a mistake to suppose they saw a new light in 1652, and then entered upon a course of action they had not previously contemplated as wise and proper — perhaps necessary to their future peace and security. They were Puritans. New Somersetshire was an Episcopal colony, promoted by Episcopalians and royalists in sympathy with the hierarchy from which the Puritans had fled.

Gov. Winthrop makes no mention of William Gorges in his journal, and

---

* "For that it did not appear to us what authority he had to grant such a commission."—Winthrop, i., 231.

although he speaks of Thomas Gorges, who came to Boston to advise with him before going to Agamenticus, in no instance, either therein or elsewhere, does he give him his official prefix. It is always "Mr. Gorge." He says, however, that Sir Ferdinando sent him "with commission for government of his province of Somersetshire." But that (with Maine substituted for Somersetshire) was a mere statement of fact, which he did not dispute, and had no occasion or desire to conceal. It bound him in no way to assent to it as conveying any legal authority. It may be claimed that the omission of the official title, in the references to William Hooke and Thomas Gorges, was due to accident or oversight, and was not considered of much moment, notwithstanding, as I am inclined to think, the custom of the time was somewhat exacting in this respect. But whether these omissions are significant or not (and perhaps it may be doubted) the fact remains, and may be said to account in part for the "obscurity" attending the Gov. Hooke period.

Again, it may be asked: Why does Sir Ferdinand Gorges fail to mention "Gov. Hooke" if he appointed him to so important an office? But Sir Ferdinando's account is peculiar, in that it is not the detailed account we should have anticipated. Strange to say, the names of but very few people are mentioned. In the part relating to Maine, the name of Col. Norton (his old associate in the "Low-countries") is given once. A single reference, in each case, is made to William Gorges, Winthrop, Humphrey, Dudley and Vines. Other than these there are practically no names given, except those of the Plymouth Council to whom the 1635 division was made. Thomas Gorges gets no more mention than William Hooke — in short is not referred to. The offices that were instituted in 1639–40 are specified, but the names of the commissioners are not given — Hooke, therefore, gets no mention even there. Sir Ferdinando's editor calls the account in one edition "A Brief Narration," which it certainly was. Probably Sir Ferdinando would have made his account longer, and somewhat more complete, if his life had been spared. Young Ferdinando, his editor (only fifteen months old at the date of the Agamenticus grant), in his preface to the Narration, says: "This relation of my Grand-Father *was left unfinished,* * * * *myself supplied* this defect by *adding* out of the choicest authors." Further on he gives Godfrey (our principal authority for "Gov. Hooke") credit for much of the information by which he pieces out Sir Ferdinando's account.

It has been suggested that perhaps William Hooke was governor of Agamenticus — a local governor simply. But there is no precedent in English procedure for that title applied to the chief functionary of a small town or village. Young Ferdinando's account (of the situation after 1642) says: "The chief town of this Province [Maine, formerly New Somersetshire] is Gorgiana [formerly Agamenticus] which is governed by a Mayor; *the rest are only inconsiderable villages, or scattered houses.*" This statement, if correct, explains why Agamenticus, which dominated all the other towns, was selected by the lord proprietor as the seat of the provincial governor. The existence contemporaneously of both a local and provincial governor at Agamenticus is highly improbable. If this view is admitted, and we still doubt that William Hooke was the provincial governor (1638–40), and conclude that Agamenticus, unlike the other towns, had a local governor at that particular time, and so far as known at no other time, then we are forced to the conclusion either that the province was then without a governor, or that the governor's seat during that period was in one of the "inconsiderable villages." in question, both of which conclusions are equally improbable. Moreover, in the latter contingency the "inconsiderable village" in question, and the provincial governor, are equally mysterious. Their names cannot be produced in court, and they are utterly without witnesses, while "Gov. Hooke" has several of the best standing, whose testimony will not only bear the interpretation I have given it, but in my judgment is not open to any other construction, and is therefore conclusive.

WILL OF ALDERMAN HUMPHREY HOOKE OF BRISTOL, ENGLAND.

Contributed by HOWARD WILLIAMS LLOYD, Esq., of Germantown, Phila.

[THIS article was sent by the author, Mr. Lloyd, to Frederick W. Todd, Esq., 31 State St., Boston, who sent it to us with this note: "Probably you will be glad to insert in the REGISTER the enclosed draft of the will of Alderman Humphrey Hooke, of Bristol, which has been sent to me by Mr. Lloyd, Corresponding Secretary of the Pennsylvania Historical Society, with the request that I offer it to you for that purpose. I have had a similar copy in my possession for some thirty years past while working on the Hooke family—my material for which is now practically ready for publication. I have added a *note* to Mr. Lloyd's communication which in part is explanatory of certain references in the will that are likely to be of general interest.]

The will of Humphrey Hooke the elder (see note) of the City of Bristol, merchant, dated 25 June, 1658, being nearly 78 years old. To the poor of St. Stephens, Bristol, £10. To the almsmen in the Merchants Almshouse in the Marsh in Bristol £10. To the poor on the Manor of Kings Weston £10. To the poor in the East Street of Chichester where I was born, £10. To the Ministers of God's word in Bristol Mr. Towgood, Mr. Stanfast, Mr. Williamson, Mr. Bruerton, and Mr. Freeman, £3 each. To my daughter Elizabeth Creswick £1200. To my daughter Sarah Hellier £1000. To my grandson Humphrey Hooke, £300, and to his son Thomas £100.

To my grand-daughter Dorothy Aldworth £50. To my grand-son Thomas Hooke £200. To my grand-children William and Josias Hooke £40 apiece a couple of most stubborn and unruly boys and I give to their brother Jacob Hooke £100 in hope he may prove better. To my grand-children Mary and Cicely Elbridge £150 a piece and to Sarah and Giles Elbridge £100 a piece. My will is that the said Giles relinquish his interest in the City scale else this £100 shall go to the three sisters. To my grand-son William Cann £500. To my brother Edward Hooke £100. To my sister-in-law Mrs. Alice Gostlett £100. To Mary Stanlake, Ann Stanlake and Elizabeth Bickley £10 each. To Bruen Bickley the £18 which he oweth me.

To my sons Creswick, Collins, Hellier, Southwood and Jackson, and grand-sons Robert Aldworth, Humphrey and Thomas Hooke and their sister Mary Hooke £12 each for mourning. To Mr. Henry Jones, Minister of St. Stephens, Bristol £5 for funeral dues.

All my lands, houses, store houses and tenements in the City of Bristol (except 2 tenements in Broad St., and 1 in Grape Lane) which are settled by conveyance as well as that house and little Manor of Kings Weston al's Weston Lawrence in the parish of Henbury, county of Gloucester and which I bought of Mrs. Toby Edmonds to hold to myself for life and the remainder to the heirs of my son Thomas Hooke and my will is that it shall be so.

Likewise my tenements in Lawrence Weston in the tenure of Richard Wookey settled by conveyance to myself for life, to my wife for life and the remainder to the heirs of my son Thomas by Mrs. Jackson and my will is it should be so.

I give to my said wife all my manor of Kings Weston and that farm called Aytons now in the tenure of John Hollen and the farm called Hardings now in the tenure of William Hunne which I bought of Sir John Wynter, K'nt and those grounds I lately bought of Mr. Walker (Walter?) for her natural life and the remainder to my grand-son Humphrey Hooke and the heirs male of his body and in default of such heirs to the heirs male of me Humphrey Hooke forever.

To my said wife all my Manor of Frampton upon Severn county Gloucester and the farm in the said Manor in the tenure of Thomas Ager for the term of her natural life.

The remainder to my grandson Thomas Hooke son of Mrs. Jackson and to the heirs male of his body and for want of such heirs to my grandson Humphrey Hooke and to his heirs male they and every of them paying the

Lord Berkley rent and other dues. To my grandson Humphrey Hooke my Manors of Elverton al's Elberton and those of Northwick and Redwick, my three quarter parts of the Manor of Frampton Cottrell county Gloucester and also my Manor of Midsomer Norton county Somerset and to the heirs male of his body.

To my said wife my two tenements in Broad Street Bristol called the Lamb which I hold by lease of the Company of Taylors in Bristoll and all that ground in Northwick aforesaid being part of Butchers lease containing about 6 acres which I hold of Mr. Sadler for life, for her life if the leases expire not before. Also my tenement in Grape Lane in Bristol in the tenure of widow Badman and my farm in Northwick & tenement in Redwick both in the tenure of Robert Mansell and my 4 acres of land in Butchers lease for her life the remainder to my grandson Humphrey Hooke.

I appoint my wife sole executrix of this my will and give her all my goods, chattels, money, plate, jewels, rings, debts, mortgages, adventures at or beyond sea and all my personal estate whatsoever she paying my debts legacies &c.

My sons in law Henry Creswick and George Hellier and my grandsons Humphrey and Thomas Hooke to be Overseers.

I give to my grandsons William and Josias Hooke £60 a piece in addition to the £40 already given in hope of their amendment. To Cicely Tily al's Bindon £10. To my grandson William Hooke a tenement in the Manor of Kings Weston in the tenure of Catherine Stokes, widow and all the ground (except that acre which is laid to the little house) for his life after the death, forfeiture or surrender of the said Catherine Stokes. To my grandson Josias Hooke a tenement in Kings Weston in the tenure of John Stephens and that in the tenure of Jane Hill for his life after the death, forfeiture or surrender of John Stephens and Jane Hill.

Whereas there is owing to me by the Chamber of Bristol upon two of the City's scales about £550 allowing less than ordinary interesting, and defaulting [deducting] the rent I owe them, besides £100 I lent to the county of Somerset by their order as by their note appeareth, & about £30 owing me upon the Chamberlains seals all which I do give to the Mayor, Aldermen & Councill of the City provided they do pay to the Overseers of the Poor of St. Stephens every week 4/ for bread to be given to the poor of that parish & 4/ a week for coals to be given to the poor of that parish forever. And for what remaineth I give it to the Hospital of Queen Elizabeth.

I revoke my previous bequest to my grand-daughter Mary Hooke & bequeath £400 to be paid to her within two years after my decease. I give to my grandson Jacob Hooke my tenement in the Manor of Elverton now in the tenure of widow Trueman for his life after the death forfeiture, or surrender of the said widow Trueman. This will was finished 17 Sept., 1658. Witnesses, Mary Elbridge, Cicely Elbridge, Samuel Child, William Edmonds, Humphrey Hooke, Junr. Proved 20 April 1659, by Cicely Hooke the relict. Pell, 201.

[NOTE.—Alderman Humphrey Hooke of Bristol was father of William Hooke, Governor of the Province of New Somersetshire (1638-40), who died in July, 1652. From the latter are descended practically all of those bearing the name of Hooke (or Hook) in this country. I have been able to find but two exceptions among those now living. Among his descendants may be counted the Hon. William C. Whitney, and Paul D. Cravath, Esq., of New York, and the late Hon. William Appleton of Boston.

Alderman Hooke's daughter Mary was the second wife of Giles Elbridge, the Pemaquid patentee, and the Giles Elbridge mentioned in the above will was her son. Mr. Salisbury, in his Elbridge researches, was evidently not aware of these two facts. The Robert Aldworth mentioned was godson of the Pemaquid patentee of that name, and was husband of the alderman's grand-daughter Dorothy Hooke. The "stubborn and unruly boys" (then in England, but born here, and reared in the Puritan colony) were sons of William, and had been, for six years, under their grandfather's guardianship. They were probably unyielding in their adherance to Puritanism. Their grandfather was an Episcopalian, and a Royalist. Jacob (aged 18), who might "prove better," was then in this country with his mother (see General Court records).

When at the Council House in Bristol, in 1891, I was told by the Treasurer of the City that but three days previously he had drawn his cheque for that year's payment to the poor of St. Stephen's on account of Mr. Hooke's donation (as per his will) made two and a half centuries ago. It is to be hoped that the Treasurer of the City for the year 2150 will be able to make a similar statement.]

THE ORIGIN AND ANCESTRY OF REV. THOMAS HOOKER.

A paper prepared by Commander EDWARD HOOKER, U.S.N., and read before the Hooker gathering, August, 1892.

FROM whence came Rev. Thomas Hooker? Of the origin and ancestry of Rev. Thomas Hooker, we have no knowledge whatever, beyond the probability that his father's name was Thomas, and that his father had a brother named John.

It has been asserted that Mr. Hooker was born at Marfield, Leicestershire, England, but no authority is given for this assertion, and the most exhaustive searches having utterly failed to produce

409

any evidence corroborative of this assertion, the conclusion was reached many years ago that the assertion was incorrect, while the inquiries made seem to show conclusively that Rev. Thomas Hooker had nothing whatever to do with Marfield.

While the Marfield story is swept away, a mere myth of the past, no evidence has as yet been brought to light which gives any positive information as to the region from which Mr. Hooker came or the family to which he belonged, and, in the absence of all positive information regarding this matter, the only course to pursue is to collate such suggestive data as can be found, and present it in as concise form as possible, that those who wish may deduce from it their own conclusions.

From a period ante-dating the reign of King Henry VIII. and to a time long after the "Restoration," there was in the South of England a noted family of Hookers. They were possessed of wealth, rank and social position, and they intermarried with England's proud old families. They were scholars, disputants and authors whose books, written three hundred years ago, are today found as valued books of reference in the larger libraries.

From some points in these books we learn that while they were loyal to their King and undoubtedly recognized the divine authority of the kingly office, they gave careful thought to sociological matters and entertained what may be considered as at that time advanced sociologic ideas, as,—that the people were the proper source of power; that society was constituted for the greatest good to the greatest number; that all men were equal before the law.

Some time before Rev. Thomas Hooker was born there was produced a written constitution for governmental purposes, and this constitution must have been a revelation to these liberal-minded students of sociology in the south of England, for it embodied the ideas which they entertained. It elucidated the theories which they had advocated. It was a solution of the social problem to which they had, with doubtful success, devoted careful thought and laborious study, and there can be no doubt, even if no evidence existed of it, that this embodiment of their social ideas gave great satisfaction to these liberal sociologists and was carefully observed by them.

This old constitutional government continued until long after the Connecticut Colony had been founded, and their cannot be any question that Thomas Hooker and the other founders of Connecticut Colony were thoroughly acquainted with this older constitution and the success attending its working, and doubtless they had this clearly in mind when they adopted the Connecticut form of government so nearly upon the basis of this older constitution, if indeed they did not have a copy of that older constitution before them when they worked out their social problems and established their governmental forms and methods.

Here then we have a noted family of Hookers, possessing the

same characteristics for which Rev. Thomas Hooker was noted, entertaining the same sociologic ideas which he entertained and to which he gave force in the Colony of Connecticut. And around this family of Hookers we find towns, villages and parishes, bearing names which are familiar to us as names of Connecticut towns. And here too were found families having names which we find in Mr. Hooker's company, and among the founders of Connecticut.

In this family of Hookers we find that the stock names were John, Thomas, Richard, Roger, Dorothy, Joanna, Mary—the very names we find in Thomas Hooker's family.

There is little question that Rev. Thomas Hooker's father was named Thomas, and in that family of Hookers we find a Thomas Hooker, born about the middle of the sixteenth century, and who was probably between thirty and forty years of age when Rev. Thomas Hooker was born.

The Rawson family, in seeking their pedigree, find as one of their ancestors, John Hooker, a brother of the father of Rev. Thomas Hooker. And in this south of England family of Hookers we find a son John, brother of the Thomas before mentioned.

The intimate personal friendship between Thomas Hooker and John Pym can scarcely be questioned. They were of the same age, entertained the same sociologic views, and advocated the same theories and the same reforms. And many years ago the assertion was made that Anna Hooker, the wife of John Pym, was a sister of Rev. Thomas Hooker, and the assertion was also made that Rev. Thomas Hooker's wife was a sister of John Pym.

Anna Hooker, the wife of John Pym, however, was the daughter of John Hooker, and therefore could not be the sister of Rev. Thomas Hooker, whose father was named Thomas; but she may have been a daughter of that John Hooker who was a brother of Rev. Thomas Hooker's father, and thus have been an own cousin to Rev. Thomas Hooker. Of that, however, we have no positive information.

We have no evidence that assures us that the wife of Rev. Thomas Hooker was the sister of John Pym; but in view of the relations existing between the two men, and in the utter absence of all information as to who the wife of Rev. Thomas Hooker was, together with the fact that John Pym's wife was a Hooker, and the possibility that she may have been a cousin of Rev. Thomas Hooker, we may reasonably consider it at least a possibility that Rev. Thomas Hooker's wife was a sister of John Pym.

The seat of the Pym family was in the south of England, and at not a great distance from the seat of this Hooker family; and, though we have no positive evidence upon the matter, we may, from the similarity of characteristics and the community of sentiments, very properly conclude that the two families were well known and intimately associated with each other, and there is a strong probability that Anna Hooker, the wife of John Pym, was from this Hooker family in the south of England.

So far as known, no evidence exists that positively assures us that Rev. Thomas Hooker belonged to that family of Hookers, but this suggestion is presented very forcibly to us. If Rev. Thomas Hooker did not belong to that family of Hookers, then we have spread out before us one of the most wonderful chapters of coincidences the world has ever produced.

The following chart of probability is based upon the data from which this paper has been prepared :

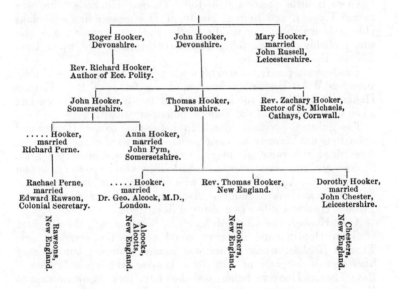

THOMAS[1] HOWELLS OF HAY AND HIS DESCENDANTS IN AMERICA

Geoffrey L. Fairs

With the continuing interest in the United States in the distinguished author William Dean Howells, demonstrated in part by the selected edition of his works being published by the Indiana University Press, it seems appropriate to give an account of his Welsh ancestry. The Howells family was intimately connected with the little market town of Hay on the banks of the river Wye on the border of Breconshire and Herefordshire. This district had already provided William Pennoyre, a Cromwellian entrepreneur and one of the early benefactors of Harvard University. It was shortly to produce John Percival Jones, a silver "king" who for many years represented the state of Nevada in the United States Senate and was one of the founders of the city of Santa Monica, California. Throughout its nine-hundred-year history, Hay has primarily been concerned with agriculture. It had no established industry of any size until the end of the eighteenth century when Thomas Howells, the great-grandfather of William Dean Howells, set up a woollen mill which eventually employed about eighty people and continued to operate until the large-scale industry in Yorkshire eliminated the smaller woollen mills in Wales and elsewhere. The Hay undertaking dealt with the whole manufacturing process, from the reception of small batches of wool from the individual farmers to the production of bales of finished flannel.

Unfortunately the factory records no longer exist, and since all of Thomas Howells's children except one emigrated to America in the early days of the nineteenth century, taking the family papers with them, local research in the history of the family has been very difficult.[1] However, considerable assistance has been rendered by a number of Thomas Howells's descendants, who have made available photocopies of relevant documents from the family archives,[2] and by two important biographies

1. Messrs R. C. Oliver of Llandrindod Wells and P. W. Coldham of Purley have provided specialist information, and Canon Ivor Davies, Vicar of Hay, has granted repeated access to the parish records. The ever courteous help of the staffs of the following libraries is also acknowledged: University of Cambridge, National Library of Wales, London Guildhall and Royal Academy of Arts, City of Bristol, The Public Record Office, and the Record Offices of Greater London, Bristol, Hereford, and Somerset. In particular, Malcolm Thomas of the Library of the Religious Society of Friends has provided invaluable information on the rules governing the Quakers of the eighteenth and nineteenth centuries, without which the family history of the Howells could not have been adequately interpreted.

2. The author is particularly indebted to Professor William White Howells of Harvard University, Dr. Pauline Skinner of Newark, Delaware, and Mr. and Mrs. David Wible of Solon, Ohio, all direct descendants of Thomas Howells, for the provision of photo-

published in the United States in the late nineteenth and early twentieth centuries.[3] These American sources, while accurate with regard to the later family history, are less reliable when referring to events in Great Britain, being dependent on hearsay. They are particularly incomplete in their identification of birthplaces, making it very difficult to check or amplify the information from parish records; this is especially the case with pitfalls resulting from Welsh place names. The problem is further complicated because of the nonconformist inclinations of the family, which meant that some children were baptized in church, some had Quaker birth certificates, and others went unrecorded.

To keep within reasonable limits, this paper deals only with Thomas Howells, his immediate antecedents, and his children. Reference to his grandchildren is restricted to the date and place of birth, where known, with the minimum of additional information necessary for clarity. Nevertheless, many of these grandchildren and great-grandchildren had lives of unusual interest and distinction.

Ancestry of Thomas¹ Howells

The ancestry of THOMAS¹ HOWELLS is obscure, partly owing to the incomplete birth records in the Hay area in the eighteenth century and partly to the vagueness of the information given in American sources. W. D. Shirk in the *History and Genealogy of the . . . Powell Families* claims that Thomas¹ was the son of a George Howells, clockmaker, born in Radnorshire.[4] W. C. Howells in *Recollections of Life in Ohio, from 1813 to 1840* says that Thomas¹ settled in Hay "near his native place in the adjoining county of Radnor."[5] Shirk refers to a longcase (grandfather) clock with "George Howells Dearfold" inscribed on the dial, and says that there is a tradition that the craft of clockmaking had persisted in the family through several generations. This clock was purchased by William Dean Howells from Thomas Howells's great-granddaughter about 1883.[6]

The registers of St. Mary Hay do record the birth in 1720 of George, son of George and Ann Howells, and there is a hamlet Deerfold on the

copies of family archives which have materially assisted his researches in Great Britain. In addition, other valuable material has been supplied by Mr. John Noyes Mead Howells of Kittery Point, Maine.

3. The biographies are William Cooper Howells, *Recollections of Life in Ohio, from 1813 to 1840* (1895; reprint ed., Delmar, N. Y., 1977) and W. D. Shirk, *The History and Genealogy of the Thomas, Joseph and Henrietta (Howells) Powell Families* (Fairfield, Iowa, 1918); details of the family's clockmaking activities in particular are given in G. H. Baillie, *Watchmakers and Clockmakers of the World*, rev. ed. (London, 1947) and I. C. Peate, *Clock and Watchmakers in Wales*, 2nd ed. rev. (Llandysul, Wales, 1975). Some supplementary information is also given in William Dean Howells, *Years of My Youth* (1916; reprint ed., Bloomington and London, 1975).

4. Page 4.

5. Page 5.

6. *The Powell Families*, 4.

Radnor-Herefordshire border (SO 377673)[7] in the parish of Lingen, but those parish registers contain no reference to either George or Thomas Howells. Nevertheless it is most certainly the place in question, since adjoining farms in the hamlet of Combe (SO 347633) were at one time owned by William Powell, steward to the Earl of Oxford, of whose will Thomas was executor.

W. C. Howells states that Thomas, with his father and a brother William, worked as clockmakers in London probably about 1750-1760, but William Dean Howells in *Years of My Youth*, says "There is no record of when my great grandfather (Thomas) and his brothers went to London and fixed there as clockmakers," suggesting that at least three brothers were involved.[8] Also in an unpublished letter of 1903 to his sister Aurelia, he says that the Deerfold clock was made by his great-great-uncle and not by his great-grandfather. In *Watchmakers and Clockmakers of the World*, G. H. Baillie claims that William became a clockmaker of distinction. Made a Freeman of the Worshipful Company of Clockmakers in 1780, he was in the same year commissioned by them to report on the accuracy of a marine chronometer designed by the famous Thomas Mudge.[9] In 1792 he received a prize from the Society of Arts for a detached clock escapement, and from 1780 to 1824 he was in a partnership with Robert Pennington. Unpublished notes by Mildred, daughter of W. D. Howells, which antedate Baillie by forty years confirm that Thomas and William were brothers.

The apprentice register of the Clockmakers Company preserved in Guildhall Library, London,[10] lists John and William Howells, both sons of John Howells of the parish of St. Catharine by the Tower, as apprentices of Thomas Sheafe in 1760 and 1765 respectively. Thomas is not mentioned—indeed the only reference to him as a watchmaker is in I. C. Peate's *Clock and Watchmakers in Wales*, which lists him in 1776 as watchmaker (probably watch repairer).[11] The registers of the Herefordshire village of Leintwardine (SO 405741), four miles north-northeast of Deerfold and three miles east of the Radnorshire border, give details of a series of births to a John and Susannah Howells between 1738 and 1749. The children surviving infancy included MARY, born 1738; THOMAS, born 1739; WILLIAM, born 1742; and JOHN IV, born 1749. The registers contain no further reference to the family after this date, suggesting that they had left the district. Baillie brackets together John Howells's father and son as clockmakers in 1765.[12] Although the evidence is circumstantial,

7. The grid references locating places in Great Britain conform to the system of the Ordnance Survey of Great Britain on the maps of the 1:25000 series (2½"/mile).

8. Page 5.

9. Page 160.

10. C. E. Atkins, *Register of Apprentices of the Worshipful Company of Clockmakers of the City of London 1631-1934* (London, 1934).

11. Page 47.

12. *Watchmakers and Clockmakers of the World*, 160.

it is probable that they were the family who migrated to London. Unfortunately the apprentice roll does not give the ages of John and William at the time of binding, which would have provided their birth dates. The only difficulty is that the Hay registers give Thomas Howells's age at death in 1824 as seventy-four, which would make his birth 1749/50 and not 1739. The gravestone gives the conflicting age of seventy-two, but Thomas may have had some reason in later life for wishing to appear younger than he actually was. Indeed it would seem more likely that he was forty years old than thirty when he successfully started up the woollen mill in Hay.

Shirk states that Thomas Howells married SUSANNAH BEASLEY (born 1744), a London Methodist; and the registers of St. Andrew Holborn record the baptism on 16 May 1773 of ANN SUSANNAH, daughter of Thomas and Susannah Howells of Fetter Lane (adjacent to Plumbtree Street). There is no record of the actual marriage, which presumably took place in a Wesleyan chapel, but the Howells family Bible gives the date as 5 September 1772. Baillie lists a number of clockmakers named Beasley, but no connection of any of them with Thomas's wife has yet been established.[13]

Thomas Howells's Career in Hay

From this point information is more precise. W. C. Howells states that Thomas and Susannah came to Hay in 1775, but gives no reason for the move. On 12 October 1775 Thomas advertised his new watchmaker's business near the Golden Lion Inn (now 21 Castle Street) in the *Hereford Journal;* and Peate lists him as a watchmaker in Hay the following year.[14] He continued only briefly in this trade, and probably before age thirty turned to woollen manufacture; by the end of the century he was firmly established in at least two sites in the town.

Thomas was an enterprising man of business as well as a mechanical engineer of more than ordinary ability—qualities that ensured his success where so many other contemporary woollen manufacturers had failed. His mill followed closely on an abortive experiment of this nature at the Trefacca settlement some eight miles west of Hay, which petered out on the death of its founder, Howell Harris, in 1773. Indeed, Thomas may well have taken on some of the weavers there or through the failure of a weavers' premium scheme introduced by the Brecknock Agricultural Society at about the same time.

Until well into the nineteenth century there were no specialist manu-

13. It would appear probable from the Church of Jesus Christ of Latter-Day Saints File Index of Baptisms in the City of London that she was the daughter of John and Susannah Beasley and baptized at St. Mary Whitechapel on 7 March 1745, or less likely the daughter of William and Elizabeth Beazley, baptized at St. James Clerkenwell on 27 November of the same year. There is, however, no reference in Baillie to the male parent in either case being a clockmaker, though Clerkenwell had many clockmakers. See also Shirk, *The Powell Families,* 4.

14. *Life in Ohio,* 1; *Clock and Watchmakers in Wales,* 47.

facturers of spinning and weaving machinery. Initially Thomas must have designed his own, relying on local blacksmiths, carpenters, and coopers to produce the required components and vats, which were then assembled under his personal supervision. His son Joseph must also have learned these skills, for W. C. Howells states that Joseph was able to produce working drawings of wool-working machinery so that the parts could be made in America. This obviated the delays in having them sent from Great Britain.[15] An unpublished diary (1863-1869) of Elinor, wife of William Dean Howells, refers specifically to grandfather Joseph redesigning and improving spinning and carding machinery in America. According to W. D. Howells, Joseph's son William Cooper Howells also inherited his father's manipulative skills.[16]

Thomas sent out his son Joseph as his commercial representative in the highly competitive South Wales market.[17] In addition, he himself made one or possibly two trips to America to sell his flannels in the rapidly developing market there. On his first visit, at the end of the eighteenth century, he was introduced to President George Washington, who tried to persuade him to settle in America and to establish a woollen industry, offering him on very favorable terms a large tract of land on the Potomac River near the new city of Washington. Thomas was undoubtedly interested, but Susannah firmly refused to leave Hay.[18] He found the prospects in America so attractive compared with the deteriorating living standards in Great Britain resulting from the French wars, that he actively encouraged his children to emigrate. He may have paid a second visit to America in 1808, accompanying Joseph and his wife and son when they left Wales.[19] At that time he was described as "Masnachydd enwog Gwalen Cymreig"—Anglice "Occupation, well-known Welsh Flannel Manufacturer"—so he must have become well known outside the immediate neighborhood of Hay. Among the Colonel Wood papers in the Brecknock Museum is a list of Freeholders of Hay dated about 1820 which includes "Thomas Howells Flannel Merchant."

After 1808 Thomas settled down in Hay, where in 1816 he became one of the original subscribers to the Hay Tramroad.[20] According to his will, in later life he lived at what had been the old George Inn in Church Street. Nothing is known of a house called "Ravenshath," mentioned as Thomas's home in one of the Howells genealogies, and this name seems a very unlikely one for the district.

15. *Life in Ohio*, 15.

16. *Years of My Youth*, 17.

17. According to W. Geraint Jenkins in *The Welsh Woollen Industry* ([Cardiff, 1969], 329), this practice was unusual, since most other manufacturers were content to process small bales of wool for local farmers.

18. Shirk, *The Powell Families*, 5.

19. B. Owen, "Ymfudo o Sir. Frycheiniog i'r Amerig 1785-1860," *Brycheiniog*, 7 (1961): 163.

20. C. R. Clinker, *The Hay Railway* (Newton Abbot, Devon, 1960), 55.

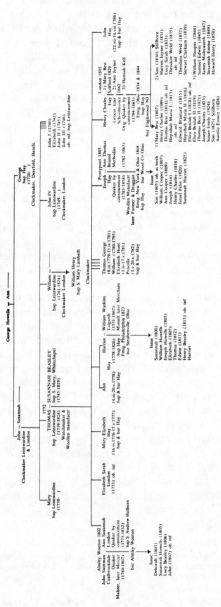

GENEALOGY OF THOMAS & SUSANNAH HOWELLS OF HAY

Also an adopted daughter or ward Henrietta Jones Howells, mar 1783, who in 1806 married Thomas Joseph Powell   (see The Family of Thomas Joseph below)

GENEALOGY OF THE POWELLS OF PRESTEIGNE, CLYRO & LLANIGON

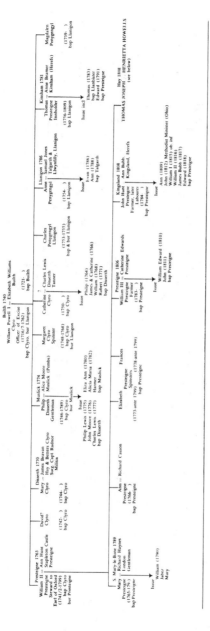

THE FAMILY OF THOMAS JOSEPH & HENRIETTA POWELL

Religious Life of Thomas and Susannah Howells

The religious life of Thomas and Susannah is complex and difficult to understand. On coming to Hay they apparently threw in their lot with the (Wesleyan) Methodists—Susannah's religion. W. Istlyn Morgan refers to a temporary demise of the Wesleyan church in Hay in 1798, and states that "Howells and his family—wife and two daughters (Susannah and Harriot) went off to the Quakers."[21] Presumably the boys Joseph (aged fifteen) and Henry (aged fourteen) were too young to qualify. All the Howells children were born in the Wesleyan period, but they were nevertheless baptized according to the rites of the Church of England, and those of them who died in infancy were buried in the churchyard. The association of the Anglicans and Wesleyans was at that time sufficiently close to make this normal. Thomas and Susannah were nevertheless extremely puritanical, as the style of their surviving correspondence indicates, and they were obviously increasingly attracted to the Society of Friends. Indeed it is stated by W. D. Howells that Thomas became a Quaker "by convincement"—i.e., by mature consideration rather than by birth—but this could not be, since the production of illegitimate offspring (see below) would inevitably bar him from full membership on moral grounds;[22] there is moreover no mention of his admittance in the local records of the Society of Friends. What is probably meant is that in general he accepted their principles. Association with the Friends became closer as the Howellses became older, and they did not witness the certificates of either of their children, Henry and Henrietta, when they were married in church. They certainly used their influence to have the births of their grandchildren recorded by the Quakers rather than having them baptized in Hay Church. Thomas was signatory in 1815 to a mortgage on a property in High Town, Hay, used as a Quaker meetinghouse.

Thomas and Susannah, like the children who predeceased them, were buried under the old yew tree in the north side of Hay churchyard. The north side was customarily reserved in Great Britain for the burial of paupers, suicides, and unbaptized infants, but this clearly did not hold in Hay, as a number of clergy and doctors, as well as the Wellingtons— Lords of the Manor—were buried on that side. Fortunately the grave is marked by a stone, since at the time of Thomas's death in 1824, his only relative living in Hay was the eldest daughter and executrix, Susannah, a practicing Quaker who would have opposed the setting up of any memorial—as would a second Quaker executor, William Enoch. It is probable, therefore, that the third executor, Henry Howells, the only son living in England at that time, erected the memorial shortly after Thomas's death. The inscription, though considerably eroded, is still decipherable:

21. W. Istlyn Morgan, "Walter Churchey (1747-1785," *Brycheiniog,* 16 (1972): 79.
22. *Years of My Youth,* 6.

Beneath this stone are
deposited the remains of
Thomas Howells of this
town, woollen manufacturer
and Susannah his wife
He died April 25th 1824
Aged 72 years
She died August 9th 1819
Aged 75 years
Also William
son of Thos. Howells
who died January 15th 1795
Aged 15 years
and one son and four daughters
who died in infancy

For this corruption must put on incorruption
And this mortal must put on immortality

I Cor. XV, 53

This inscription is incorrect in two respects: Thomas's age at death was seventy-four and two sons died in infancy.

Children of Thomas Howells

Thomas and Susannah produced a large family, most of whom died in infancy. Though the rate of mortality was very high even for the eighteenth century, the deaths could hardly be attributed to neglect, especially in a Quaker-oriented family in reasonably affluent circumstances. The situation is all the more surprising since the families of those children who did survive were both numerous and long-lived. Perhaps some factor was present conducive to premature birth, thus lessening the chances of survival, but it is idle to speculate in the absence of medical evidence.

As the births occurred regularly at almost yearly intervals, clearly there was a sufficient period between the recorded baptisms of Ann Susannah in London in May 1773 and Mary Elizabeth in Hay in June 1776 for at least one other birth. The Howells family Bible does in fact show an additional child, SARAH ELIZABETH, unrecorded in the baptismal register of St. Andrew Holborn, who only lived 10-15 January 1775.

Examination of the baptismal and burial registers of St. Mary Hay raises two problems. The first concerns the twins HARRIOT and ANN. According to the registers, Harriot was buried at Hay within a few months of birth, yet it was she who about twenty years later married William Watkins. To preserve the name, Thomas and Susannah may possibly have transferred it to the surviving twin, although a more common practice in those days was to give the name to a subsequent daughter. More likely, the curate recorded the burial incorrectly in the register, as he made other

421

wrong entries in the registers both at Hay and the neighboring parish of Llanigon.

By far the greater problem is posed by a mysterious "daughter" HEN-RIETTA, who does not appear in the Hay baptisms or in the Howells family Bible, but who according to an entry in her family Bible was born at an undisclosed place on 4 October 1783. There is no space for her in the regular series of Howells births, and indeed her stated date of birth would clash impossibly with that of JOSEPH in July of the same year. Records of over forty parishes in Brecon, Radnor, Hereford, Bristol, and London, known to have the remotest connection with the Howells, have been searched without success for evidence of her baptism; furthermore the name Henrietta does not appear in the baptismal registers of local parishes in the relevant period. A 1783 birth would seem reasonable, because two letters from the headmistress of the Quaker boarding school at Frenchay, near Bristol, where she was educated, dated 19 April and 20 December 1800, confirm that she left school between those dates. Also the fact that she witnessed the wedding of her brother Henry in London, 1805, shows that she must have been at least twenty-one years old at that time.

Why of all the Howells children was she given an expensive boarding school education—in itself a very unusual thing for a girl from a small Welsh country town—and why at her wedding in 1808 did she sign the register Henrietta *Jones* Howells when the family had, so far as is known, no connection with anyone of that name? Why also of all the surviving children did she not receive a legacy under Thomas Howells's will? This last point makes it virtually certain that she was not an illegitimate daughter, since Thomas did make specific bequests to the children of an illegitimate son. It would have been stretching Susannah's forbearance to the limit not only to accept an illegitimate daughter into the family but to give her a far better education than any of her own sons and daughters. It would seem probable, therefore, that Henrietta was an orphan or ward, with a sum of money left for her education, who was taken in by the Howells and brought up with their own children. However, no mention of her among the orphans appears in the minutes of the Frenchay Friends Women's Meetings over the relevant period.

The individual histories of Thomas and Susannah Howells's surviving children are of more than ordinary interest.

ANN SUSANNAH[2] HOWELLS in 1802 married JOHN SWETMAN (or Sweatman), son of Jerome and Elizabeth Sweatman of Coalbrookdale, Shropshire. He was a Quaker malster, later mercer. The marriage was "affirmed" at the Friends' Meeting House at Almeley Wooton in West Herefordshire, so by then Susannah must have been a full member of the Society. The marriage lasted only five years. In 1807 John died at the early age of twenty-seven and was buried in an unmarked grave at Almeley Wooton. Susannah never remarried. She died in 1854 and was buried in an unmarked grave in the Quaker burial ground at Almeley

Wooton. Quaker records in Hay show Susannah and John with four off-spring: *Deborah,* born 1803; *Susannah Howells,* born 1805; *Lucy Beasley,* born 1806; and *John,* born 1807. Of these Lucy and John died young. Deborah married William Enoch of Hay. Susannah married William Hooper of Hereford, a silk mercer, and she and her mother were among the original trustees of the Goff School in Hay, a nonconformist trust foundation which later was merged into the countrywide system of independent "British" schools. In her widowhood Susannah may have lived with her father; certainly from 1827-1830 she resided in the former George Inn at Hay, inherited under her father's will. The title deeds of the rest of the George estate show that in 1827 it was sold by a Mrs. Mary Hodson to Samuel and James Chandler and Susannah Swetman; in 1830 she sold it to her co-executor and son-in-law William Enoch, only to repurchase it from his creditors in 1843. By 1844 she had moved to St. Martin's Street in Hereford, where the local directories describe her as "gentlewoman." The records of the Society of Friends for 1831 show her and her mother-in-law as members of the Leominster and Ross meeting which included Hereford, so possibly they were living together at that time.

HARRIOT[2] HOWELLS, the only other living daughter of Thomas and Susannah Howells to survive infancy, had apparently a much more adventurous life, but unfortunately no biographer or diarist has treated this branch of the family, and few of the family records taken to America have yet come to light.

There is a tradition that Harriot eloped with WILLIAM WATKINS, and went to America. W. D. Howells mentions a letter written by Susannah Howells to "an erring" daughter who had made a runaway match and fled to America.[23] Also, the headmistress of the Quaker boarding school at Frenchay, near Bristol, while writing to Thomas Howells on 5 December 1800, specifically mentioned her former pupil Henrietta, then went on to refer obliquely to a family crisis involving another daughter, saying "I cannot but hope that she will be again restored to the joy of her disconsolate parents," which can only refer to Harriot. However, there is the birth in Hay of Susannah, William and Harriot Watkins's eldest child. She was recorded in the Digest of Births for the Worcester, Hereford, and Wales monthly meetings of the Society of Friends on 9 December 1800, only four days after the Frenchay letter was written—proof that the marriage must have taken place before that date, though when and where has not yet been discovered. This birth does throw light upon a point in a letter which Susannah Howells wrote to Henrietta just before she left Frenchay School for good in 1800: in it she gives news of the health of various members of the family saying, "Harriot and Wm. as usual."[24] Since Susannah's son William Howells had died five years previously, this

23. *Ibid.*
24. Shirk, *The Powell Families,* 9.

statement can only refer to William Watkins, and infers that they were living as man and wife with the Howellses. Nevertheless, the letter from Susannah mentioning the elopement cannot be ignored; unfortunately W. D. Howells gives no indication of its date. According to Morgan, Harriot was living at home unmarried in 1798, and the "elopement" may have taken place shortly afterwards.[25]

Little is known about Harriot's husband, William Watkins, but from his age in the 1850 Ohio census returns, hc was born in 1770-1771 "in England." In an unpublished letter written to William Cooper Howells in 1893, Paul Kester, American playright and direct descendant of William and Harriot, states that William was the son of a Watkyn Watkins of "Tuy Isa" (sic) Wales—without realizing that Ty Issa or Isaf (Anglice Lower House) was not a locality but a house or farm name and one of the commonest in Wales. It seemed possible that this Ty Issa might be some-where near Hay, since the list of the commissioners for the first bridge over the Wye at Hay in 1756 included "Thomas Watkins of Ty Issa Gentleman."[26] Examination of the registers of parishes within whose boundaries are farms named Ty Issa has revealed that William, son of Thomas Watkins of Whitelow, Talgarth, was baptized on 8 January 1771. Whitelow farm lies between Talgarth and Cwmdû (SO 164305), about a mile north of the well-known long-chambered cairn "Ty Isaf" (SO 182291). It is very probable that this is the man in question and that Kester's reference to Watkyn Watkins is to a prominent member of the family further back in the line.

The existing records are not very helpful regarding the children of Har-riot and William Watkins. The only precise information is the Quaker record of the birth of *Susannah,* December 1800, and the baptisms in Hay Church of *Elizabeth,* February 1807; *Edwin,* October 1813; and *Henry Beasley,* September 1815—the last buried (erroneously under his fore-names only) in December of the same year. The 1850 census for Coshoc-ton County, Ohio, lists only *Joseph,* aged forty-five, "born (1805/1806) England" and *Thomas,* aged thirty-nine, "born (1811/1812) England." Kester's letter gives the following *undated* births: Joseph, Susannah, Wil-liam, Elizabeth, Thomas, Edwin, and Harriet, with no mention of Henry. Thus, if the ages in the Ohio census are correct, the only birth dates re-maining to be determined are those for *William* and *Harriet.* No local con-firmation exists for Shirk's claim that Joseph was born in Hay in March 1805.[27] Assuming that this date is correct, and that William was born be-tween Joseph, 1805, and the eldest child Susannah, December 1800, there is ample room for one or two unrecorded births of other children, stillborn

25. "Walter Churchey," 79.

26. "An Act for building a Bridge across the River Wye between the Town of Hay in the County of Brecon to the opposite Shore in the County of Radnor," 29 Geo. II, Chapter 73 (Public).

27. *The Powell Families,* 54.

or dying shortly after birth. Kester states that all the Watkins children were born in Wales.

In addition to the above-mentioned baptisms, the Hay registers for 1823 record the marriage of Susannah to Charles Walker of the parish of St. Mary-le-bone, London, by license "with consent of the parents"—which suggests that the bridegroom was a minor.

Lacking precise information about the whereabouts of many of the Watkins births, no firm conclusions can be drawn about the early married life of William and Harriot. However, it appears that in the years immediately prior to their final emigration in 1823, William was employed in a fairly senior capacity in his father-in-law's factory. Like his brother-in-law Joseph, he is described in the Hay baptismal registers as "manufacturer." Undoubtedly some measure of reconciliation between Harriot and her father had taken place by 1800 at the birth of her eldest child, and that the Watkinses then lived in Hay until they finally emigrated in 1823. The absence of any birth records for some of the children may well be due to a conflict of loyalties between the Established Church and the Quakers. Possibly the first period of residence in America followed the birth of Susannah in 1800 and preceded the birth of Elizabeth in 1807.

A second estrangement between Harriot and her father is indicated by the wording of two codicils added in 1823 to Thomas Howells's will, revoking the greater part of Harriot's inheritance and even deducting the passage money advanced to her. It is not clear from the wording of these codicils whether this revocation occurred because she decided to leave for America, or whether she left because of the change in the will.

William and Harriot emigrated with their family—except for Susannah, who remained in London with her husband—first to Philadelphia and then to Ohio, where they settled in Steubenville. Little is known of their occupation except for a letter from Harriot to her son Joseph written in 1836, in which she refers to a possible extension of the family silk business.[28] William is described as "merchant" in the 1850 census returns for Ohio. He died in 1866 at the great age of ninety-six, having outlived Harriot by ten·years, and all his sons.

Of William and Harriot's children who emigrated with them, Joseph married his cousin Henrietta Powell and set up an extensive mercantile business in Evansburgh on the Ohio Canal, where he acted as banker for a wide area. His cousin Thomas, eldest son of Thomas Joseph Powell, was in partnership with him for some years. Susannah remained in London, dying as a result of a carriage accident about 1868. William became an artist and returned to London for a time. He can almost certainly be identified with a miniaturist of distinction who exhibited at the Royal Academy from 1843 to 1849, though without being elected an Academician.

JOSEPH[2] HOWELLS, the eldest surviving son of Thomas and Susannah,

28. *Ibid.,* 187, 188.

founded a family of achievement. According to W. C. Howells, he spent some of his early working life in Wales, partly helping in the mill and partly acting as his father's commercial representative and traveller in South Wales.[29] However, Howells also states that in that period he probably made two trips to America, and in 1803 attempted farming in Chester County, Pennsylvania. His name appears on a number of documents of the period as "manufacturer," and he must have acquired sufficient practical experience from his father to enable him to erect woollen mills on his own account, though without serving a formal apprenticeship. Like his elder sister Susannah, he attained full membership in the Society of Friends "by convincement."[30] In the course of travelling around South Wales he met ANN THOMAS in Pontypool.[31] She was born in Bristol, but on the death of her parents was adopted by a great-uncle and aunt named Cooper, who brought her up in the Quaker faith, though she never became a full member. As a result, when Joseph married her in Pontypool in 1805, he forfeited his own membership, though they both continued to attend Quaker meetings.[32]

There were eight children of the marriage. The two eldest, a boy who died at birth and William Cooper, were born in Hay. In his autobiography William refers to his Quaker birth certificate issued in Hay and signed by his grandmother Susannah Howells, his aunt Susannah Swetman, and the attending physician.[33] Shortly after William's birth, Joseph decided to emigrate to America, evidently hoping to profit in the infant woollen industry there. They sailed from London in April 1808.[34] At that time the British government had imposed strict regulations to prevent a brain drain of cotton and woollen specialists, particularly to the United States. To avoid detection, Joseph registered for the passage as "gentleman," but

29. Jenkins, *The Welsh Woollen Industry,* 329.

30. Howells, *Life in Ohio,* 2-5.

31. This incident is referred to by W. D. Howells in *Certain Delightful English Towns* ([New York, 1906], 119, 120) though with an inadvertent reversal of Wales and Bristol: "One day she met a young Welshman from Breconshire who had come on some affair of his father's woollen mills to the busy town. She was walking in the fields, and when they passed, and she looked back at him, she found he was looking back at her; and perhaps if it were not for this surprising coincidence, some other hand than mine might now be writing this page."

32. Howells, *Life in Ohio,* 2.

33. *Ibid.,* 3.

34. The genealogy of the Powell family as given in Burke's *Landed Gentry,* s.v. "Powell of the Chantry" in fact commences at Coel Hen of one of the three great fourth-century Strathclyde families and through him to Llywelyn Crûgeryr, following the traditional interest of all Celtic races—whether Scottish, Irish, or Welsh—in their remote ancestors. The dangers inherent in such a practice are well expressed by J. M. Lewis in *Welsh Monumental Brasses: A Guide* ([Cardiff, Wales, 1974], 13): "The pedigrees thus recorded extend beyond the limits of feasibility to include traditional figures of history such as Cunedda, Bali Meur or Urian Rheged who occur in the ninth-century 'Historia Britannorum' of Nennius." The genealogy from Rhys ap Gruffud onwards can, however, be accepted with reasonable certainty. It is of interest to note that the tradition of a descent from the ancient princes of Wales has persisted through generations of Powell immigrants in America.

426

this did not prevent him from being removed from the ship for questioning as they lay off Gravesend. He was eventually allowed to continue his journey, as there was fortunately no evidence of any apprenticeship. The remainder of the voyage was uneventful, and the ship was only out of sight of land for twenty-one days before reaching Boston.

As was customary in the Society of Friends, Joseph went armed with letters of introduction to American Quakers who had business connections in Great Britain. In anticipation of the war with Great Britain many of them were embarking on textile manufacture; Joseph contracted with a number of them to erect woollen mills, but with the inevitable delays in obtaining payment his available capital, though considerable, soon became exhausted. He had to move about seeking work, and settled temporarily in New York State, where he erected a mill at Manhattanville, then outside the city boundary. In 1812 the family again moved, to Waterford, Virginia, where another mill was installed. Then, on invitation from Joseph Steer, a Quaker, to build a mill in Jefferson County, Ohio, the family decided to take the plunge and go west. At the time of this journey there were three children: *William Cooper,* then aged six, *Anne Cooper,* aged four, and *Thomas Cooper,* one year old. After crossing the Appalachian Mountains in northern Maryland they headed west to the Monongahela River, down which they rafted to Pittsburgh; there they transshipped to travel down the Ohio River to Steubenville and so on to Short Creek. Four other children were born in Ohio: *Joseph* in 1814, who became a doctor; *Henry Charles* in 1816, a dentist; *Israel Felix* in 1820; and *Susannah Harriet* in 1825.

Joseph's engineering enterprises ceased when ratification of the peace treaty with Britain in 1815 once again allowed the import of woollens, and he turned again to farming but without conspicuous success. According to W. C. Howells, he moved successively to Mingo Bottom near Steubenville and then to Wheeling, West Virginia, the first move involving considerable pioneering work.[35] He was helped in the enterprise by his children. He finally gave up farming in 1838 and set up a book and drug store in Hamilton, Ohio, in which he was assisted by his doctor son Joseph.

Finding no Quakers in the neighborhood, Joseph joined and became a leader of "Shouting Methodists," one of the more extreme branches of Wesley's followers prominent in certain parts of Ohio in the nineteenth century. He died at Bowling Green, Wood County, Ohio, in 1858 at the age of seventy-five.

The early life of Joseph's son, William Cooper Howells, is adequately treated in his autobiography, *Recollections of Life in Ohio, from 1813 to 1840,* and his latter fifty years as a newspaper proprietor, state senator, United States consul, and friend of Presidents Ulysses S. Grant and James Garfield are covered in a prefatory note by Professor Edwin H. Cady of

35. *Life in Ohio,* 6-13.

427

Indiana University to the reissued edition of his autobiography. A full account of his distinguished career in that period has yet to be written. Although lying outside the scope of this paper, it must be pointed out that his second son was William Dean Howells.

HENRY[2] CHARLES, Thomas Howells's younger surviving son, also lacks a biographer, and such information as does exist about him is widely scattered. Fortunately a massive genealogy of his considerable family has been drawn up and is preserved in the Howells archives; this has since suggested certain fruitful lines of investigation in England. This genealogy notes that he married three times and had twenty-four children, but unfortunately there are few details of their places of birth. Moreover, nothing is known about Henry's childhood.

The first positive information is that on 22 September 1805 he married MARY BEST at St. Paul Covent Garden, London, and was described at the time as "bachelor of Hay Breconshire." His "sister" Henrietta signed the register as witness. They must have initially returned to Hay to live, because the Digests of the Quarterly Meetings of the Worcester, Hereford, and Wales Society of Friends record the birth of a daughter Mary to them there in 1807, the parents being classified as "nonmembers." The same classification held in the Bristol Digests for 1809, when a son Henry was born in Redcliffe Street in the parish of St. Mary Redcliffe, his father identified as "grocer"; but two years later on the birth of a third child Thomas, they had apparently been admitted to full membership and were living in Guinea Street in the same parish; in the meantime Henry had changed his trade to "brightsmith" (i.e., tinsmith).

Thereafter their fortunes improved radically, for in 1814 the Bristol directory refers to Henry, like the father of the Bristol poet Thomas Chatterton, as "writing master," and now living in the fashionable area of St. James Place, just north of the city center. In the following year he had taken over in the same area a "Classical and Commercial Academy" for boys five to eleven years of age, known as "Kingsdown Preparatory Boarding School," where he remained until 1827. It is perhaps significant that with this change of fortune all contact with the Quakers seems to have ceased, and there is no further record of Howells births in the Bristol Digests. Indeed, W. D. Howells, when referring to the "religiosity" of the Howells family in Hay, indicates that Henry "lived in worldly state in Bristol"—which is hardly consistent with Quaker principles.[36]

In 1827 he sold his school and purchased another, "West Bank Academy," in the northerly suburb of Cotham, which he ran until 1831. According to advertisements in the local press, both these schools had accommodation for fifty pupils. It must be assumed that in order to hold down such positions Henry would have received more education than could be provided at the Pennoyre school in Hay.

The diary of Elinor Howells supplies details of the years immediately following. Apparently on giving up West Bank Academy in 1831, he made

36. *Years of My Youth*, 13.

an experimental emigration with his family to Washington, Ohio, on the recommendation of his eldest child Mary's husband, an Episcopal clergyman living there. Henry soon moved on to Zanesville, where he became an active Abolitionist. Shirk confirms this date of emigration and quotes a pamphlet in which Henry describes his experiences as an Abolitionist, probably with some exaggeration: "Mobs composed of hundreds attacked my house by night and day with rails, tar and feathers and weapons of death to take me."[37] Later he moved to Pittsburgh, where as at Bristol he ran a boys' boarding school. He returned to Bristol in 1837, where his nineteenth child was born and where he spent the money remaining from his first wife's estate.

There were thirteen children of the first marriage, none of whom is recorded in the baptismal registers of St. James, Bristol: *Mary Best,* born 1807, *Henry Charles,* born 1809, *Thomas Best,* born 1811, *Hepsibah Maria,* born 1813, *Edward Brainard,* born 1815, *Hepsibah Maria II,* born 1816, *Eliza Beulah,* born 1818, *Eliza Beulah II,* born 1819, *Thomas Best II,* born 1821, *Joseph Charles,* born 1823, *Susannah Emily,* born 1824, stillborn son, born 1825, and *Amelia Eunice,* born 1826.

Mary Best, the elder, died in 1828 after almost continuous pregnancy, and in the following year Henry married HARRIET JOYNER of Saltford, a brass-founding village on the Avon, eight miles southeast of Bristol. The Saltford registers record Henry as widower of Westbury-on-Trym, at that time a village to the north of Bristol. His actual residence was West Park House. There were six children of this marriage: a stillborn son, born 1830, *Harriet Joyner,* born 1831, *Lucy Sarah,* born 1833, *Theodore* (?) *Weld,* born 1835, *Theodora Weld,* born 1838, and *Stewart Clarkson,* born 1839, in Bristol.

Thereafter the records are confused, since the Howells genealogy states that Henry finally emigrated in 1844, while Elinor Howells's diary gives the date as 1850. The genealogy further states that the death of Harriet, Henry's second wife, occurred in February 1842 in Allegheny, Pennsylvania, while being nursed by her friend Hannah Kell of Yorkshire; this does not fit with Henry's return to England in 1837. However, wherever the death occurred, Henry married HANNAH KELL eight months later at an unspecified place, and there were five children of this marriage: *William Hooper,* born 1844, Bristol, *Samuel Edwin,* born 1845, *James Molesworth,* born 1847, *Susanah Emma,* born 1848, and *Howard Henry,* born 1850.

When Henry finally returned to America he went to live at Eaglewood, New Jersey, where he died in 1854. His wife Hannah survived him for twenty-four years, dying in 1879.

In many ways the story of HENRIETTA[2] HOWELLS is the most remarkable of all of Thomas's children. It is unclear why she was educated at Frenchay school, so far from Hay, but it appears from surviving correspondence that the headmistress, Miss Price, had a nephew and niece in

37. *The Powell Families,* 40.

the town, and through her Quaker connections was undoubtedly known to Henrietta's "parents." Henrietta did not adjust easily to the austerities of an eighteenth-century Quaker education. On 10 April 1800 the headmistress, writing to Susannah the elder, observed "an inclination to dress" which she hoped "will not grow." Similarly, in an unpublished letter to Thomas eight months later, she predicted Henrietta going astray because of "her very lively disposition."[38]

On the completion of her schooling in 1800, she returned to Hay to help in Thomas's shop, for he operated a retail business in Castle Street as well as the factory. It was there that she probably met THOMAS JOSEPH POWELL, then a schoolboy, whose family traced a direct descent from the ancient princes of Wales through Llywelyn Crûgeryr of Crûgeryn in the parish of Llanvihangel nant Melan (SO 158592) in Radnorshire. His father, William Powell II, had been steward for the Radnorshire estates of the fourth and fifth earls of Oxford and Mortimer. He acquired considerable properties in Radnorshire, including the farms of Broadheath near Presteigne (SO 336636), Bryncôch in the parish of Llanvihangel nant Melan (SO 150608), and Maesllan in the parish of Llanbister/Llananno (SO 098736), which he bequeathed to Thomas Joseph.[39]

It is not clear how Thomas Howells came into the picture, but the connection was sufficiently close for him to be one of the executors of William Powell's will, so presumably Thomas Joseph, though still a schoolboy, would have visited Hay in connection with his inheritance. According to Shirk he fell in love with the glamorous Henrietta at first sight, and when he was of age and had become a wealthy mercer in Leominster, married her in Hay church in 1808.[40] Henrietta was clearly glad to escape from her puritan environment, and after a few months in Leominster the newlyweds set up a mercer's business in London, where they remained until 1816, except for an experimental period of farming in 1813 at Combe, Presteigne (SO 350631), probably with Thomas's elder brother William. It has not been established where they lived in London, since Shirk is too vague on this point—merely giving "High Street" and "Church Street" as their places of residence without specifying the parish.[41]

The registers of all London parishes containing both Church and High Streets at that time have been searched without success for records of the children's births. The Mormon Computer File Index of London baptisms does not record those of any of the Powell children. The baptism of one child is, however, recorded in Presteigne in 1813. Five children were born in London as well as the one in Presteigne, at the customary yearly in-

38. *Ibid.,* 9.

39. This genealogical information is derived from A. D. Powell, "Radnorshire Powells in America," Radnorshire Society, *Transactions,* 42 (1972): 52-77; A. D. Powell, "A Note on the Radnorshire Powells in America," *ibid.,* 44 (1974): 52; and G. L. Fairs, "The Powells and Howells of Radnor and West Herefordshire in the 18th and 19th Centuries," *ibid.,* 46 (1976): 51-60.

40. *The Powell Families,* 11.

41. *Ibid.,* 11.

tervals: *Thomas Howells* in 1809, *William Henry* in 1810, *Henrietta Beasley* in 1811, *John* in 1813, *Henry Charles* in 1814, and *Joseph* in 1816. Then the family emigrated to America.

The Powells' relations with Thomas Howells were not very cordial at the time of their marriage. A letter from Thomas to Henrietta dated only ten days after her wedding suggests some measure of estrangement: "I am sorry to find that you think that I am not so mindful of you as you have a right to expect, but in this you are mistaken."[42] Possibly Henrietta had expressed disappointment at his absence from her wedding; certainly neither Thomas nor Susannah signed the register. A further letter from Thomas dated shortly after their emigration complained that he had heard nothing from them either before they sailed from Liverpool or after they arrived in America.[43] Nevertheless, surviving fragments of correspondence indicate that Thomas did administer his son-in-law's Radnorshire properties after he settled in America.

The description of the pioneering days of Henrietta and Thomas Joseph as given by Shirk and Howells is absorbing. They landed at Baltimore after a very bad crossing, much worse than that of brother Joseph. The seventy-day voyage was so stormy that at one time the captain was on the point of ordering everyone into the lifeboats. They went first to Warwick, Virginia, where a daughter *Louisa* was born in 1818, and then to Richmond, where they rented a plantation. This proved unproductive, owing to extravagance, and their capital decreased alarmingly. In 1819 they decided to try their luck in the then largely undeveloped territory of Ohio.[44]

They travelled to Mingo Bottom near Steubenville in an old stagecoach purchased secondhand, and settled not far from Joseph and his family; another daughter, *Caroline* was born there in 1820. Farming continued to be unsuccessful, and they had to sell their glass and china. Following a serious fire they considered moving to Canada, but eventually decided to lease a tract of land at White Eyes Creek in the as yet unsettled area of Coshocton County, Ohio, to which they trekked with their eight children—all under twelve years of age—arriving in May 1821. Here they continued to work hard with rather more success, though Thomas had to sell his books in order to purchase a flock of sheep. Four more children were born there: *Mary Jane* in 1824, *Josephine* and *Edwin* in 1825, and *Francis Washburn* in 1828.

In 1828-1830 the Ohio Canal was constructed and provided considerable local labor, although the work was very heavy and ill paid. Thomas engaged to work on this project with the elder boys and built a log cabin on the site, where the two elder daughters officiated as cooks.

After 1830 life became easier, for Thomas was able to dispose of the Radnorshire farms of Bryncôch and Maessllan entailed under William Powell's will to Thomas Joseph's eldest son, who had become of age.

42. *Ibid.*, 6, 7.
43. PROB. 11/1688/416, July 1824. Public Record Office, London.
44. Shirk, *The Powell Families*, 12, 13.

Thomas returned to Wales for two years to effect the sales and with the proceeds purchased 1,080 acres of land at White Eyes Creek, where the family prospered.[45]

All the children except Mary Jane and Edwin, who died in infancy, married and produced large families, many of whom with their own children in turn distinguished themselves in various walks of life. Almost all became active Abolitionists, and the house at White Eyes Creek became a refuge for slaves escaping from the South and making their way to freedom in Canada. Due in part to the absence of any Episcopalian chaplaincy in the area, the children all joined the "Shouting Methodists," to the great distress of their parents, causing a division in the family which lasted for some years.

Illegitimate Children of Thomas Howells

The Howells family correspondence of the early twentieth century contains certain guarded references to verbal statements by W. D. Shirk and W. D. Howells regarding an extramarital family fathered by Thomas Howells.[46] The first evidence of the possibility of a second family comes from a discrepancy between the children recorded in the Hay baptismal registers and those listed in the Howells family Bible, together with an entry in the Elinor Howells diary previously mentioned.

The Hay registers contain the following verbatim entries:

8 March 1779. Thomas George son of Thomas and Susannah Howells baptised.
16 April 1781 Thomas Howells buried.
[the following entry being in the same hand]
27 May 1781 Elizabeth Hunt daughter of Thomas and Susannah Howells buried.

On the other hand the family Bible records Thomas Edward born 16 February 1779, and died 5 September 1812. Clearly from the Hay register it cannot be said with certainty that the Thomas Howells, buried in 1781, is the child baptized in 1779, but no other reference has been found of the death of Thomas George, nor is any reference made in contemporary family records to the existence of a son Thomas.

Elinor Howells's diary states that Thomas Howells the elder had three sons who attained adult life: Thomas, Joseph, and Charles. Son Thomas was said to have emigrated in 1807 first to New York State, and then to Missouri and New Orleans, where he served as a bookkeeper in mercan-

45. Examination of the Maesllan title deeds shows that the purchase of the land at White Eyes Creek was made by Thomas Howells Powell four months before completion of the sale of Maesllan on 23 July 1831. An earlier deed of lease of Maesllan (27 January 1830) was signed in Wales by Thomas Powell and Thomas Howells Powell of White Eyes Creek, so that Thomas Howells Powell must have originally crossed to Wales with his father at the end of 1829.

46. It should be remembered that in the late eighteenth and early nineteenth centuries in Great Britain illegitimacy was lightly regarded, and contemporary baptismal registers frequently show 20 percent of births as illegitimate (without taking into account those who were unbaptized).

tile houses, later "going on an adventure" to Jamaica where he died in 1815/16, leaving a wife and children in England.

Again the Hay registers record:

1 December 1800 Marriage by licence of Thomas Howells and Hannah Price both of Hay.
1 December 1801 Baptised Edward Thomas son of Thomas and Hannah Howells.
16 March 1802 Buried Edward Thomas Howells aged 15 weeks.
10 July 1803 Baptised Eliza daughter of Thomas and Hannah Howells.
10 December 1804 Baptised Thomas James son of Thomas and Hannah Howells.[47]

As in the case of the previous entries these latter five would be inconclusive, with so common fore- and surnames, were it not for two substantial legacies in the will of Thomas Howells the elder in favor of two grandchildren, Elizabeth and Thomas James, conspicuous as the only grandchildren to benefit directly, and the only ones specifically mentioned.

While the absence of essential data in the earlier Hay records must be regretted, it seems reasonable to assume on balance that Thomas George, like so many of the Howells children, died young, and that the other Thomas was an illegitimate son by a woman so far unidentified. A careful scrutiny of all the illegitimate births in the Hay registers over the period 1776-1800 has been made without finding anyone who might have been the mother of a second family, nor has any evidence as yet come to light about further illegitimate offspring.

The discovery of a Thomas Howells who emigrated from Hay in 1807 suggests that Thomas Howells the elder may not have made a second journey to America in 1808. The suggestion that he did rests upon a single statement by B. Owen made without any backing reference and which, because of the author's death some years ago, cannot be checked.[48] Owen was unlikely to have known of the existence of Thomas Edward, and if the reference in his paper to "well-known Welsh flannel manufacturer" was not independent but applied by him to an unspecified Thomas Howells of Hay who emigrated about the same time as Joseph, he may well have confused the illegitimate son with the father. No other evidence for a second visit has been found in Great Britain or America. W. C. Howells makes no suggestion that Thomas accompanied him and his parents when they emigrated; indeed W. D. Howells states categorically in relation to Thomas's former visit that "he certainly never returned to America."[49]

Conclusions

Considering the extremely limited opportunities in nineteenth-century Hay, the achievements of the Howells family as a whole were remarkable.

47. He was, like the daughters of Susannah Swetman, educated at the Quaker boarding school at Sidcot, presumably at his grandfather's expense.
48. Owen, "Ymfudo o Sir. Frycheiniog i'r Amerig," 151-178.
49. *Years of My Youth,* 7.

Thomas himself, coming from a family of clockmakers of distinction, turned to woollen manufacture and developed a highly successful business in an area where most other such enterprises failed. His children—apart from Henrietta and possibly Henry—must only have been educated at the local Pennoyre school, although the two elder ones would have the advantage of being taught by the scholar Edward [Celtic] Davies, who was master at that time. The children must have had additional instruction at home, cultural as well as religious. Shirk and W. C. Howells both refer to Susannah's love of poetry and contemporary literature, while Thomas must certainly have instructed his sons in mechanical engineering and commercial subjects.[50]

Thomas, however, was a strange character. On the one hand, rightly anticipating a slump in Great Britain, he actively fostered a spirit of independence in his children, encouraging them to emigrate and strike out for themselves; yet in matters of religion, he was bigoted in the extreme, even to the extent of disinheriting those children who rebelled. How much influence either of these attitudes had is difficult to assess, but the bigotry certainly had a divisive effect on the children. All with the exception of Susannah emigrated, usually after one or more trial trips and, thanks to their austere home training, all adapted themselves successfully to the rigors of a pioneering life and established a firm basis for their own families.

Ample evidence of an intense family pride is reflected in the selection of children's forenames which persisted from generation to generation. Not only were the names of Thomas's and Susannah's children used repeatedly, but they were often used in conjunction with the mothers' maiden names, demonstrating the affection in which the Welsh forebears were held by their American descendants.

One trait strongly developed in Thomas's and Susannah's children and grandchildren was a concern for minorities. Many of them were active Abolitionists, and the Powell home at White Eyes Creek contained a secret room for the temporary accommodation of slaves escaping northward to Canada. They held similar attitudes towards the North American Indians. One of Henry's daughters and her husband were missionaries to the Iroquois in Canada, where they were joined by another sister, who married an Indian chief and lived in the Six Nations reserve. Likewise, one of Harriot's sons married the daughter of a Pottawattomie chief.

This study of the Howells family in Great Britain and their early privations in America has only been possible by the provision of photocopies of early documents and correspondence which were taken to America when the children emigrated. The significance of much of this material would not be obvious to anyone unfamiliar with the district around Hay and Presteigne, but nevertheless it has provided clues to most fruitful lines of investigation which would not otherwise have occurred to the au-

50. *The Powell Families,* 4; *Life in Ohio,* 2, 3.

thor. It is highly probable that other documents still exist in family archives in America which might throw light on parts of the story which are still obscure, in particular the origins of Henrietta "Howells" and the early married life of William and Harriot Watkins. Now these papers would be scattered among sixty-six grandchildren and nearly two hundred great-grandchildren, and the difficulties of locating them are almost insurmountable. It is hoped that the publication of this paper will bring to light further relevant family correspondence.

Geoffrey L. Fairs was educated at Liverpool College and Emmanuel College, Cambridge. He is an associate of the Royal Historical Society, and a member of the Society of Genealogists.

HUNNEWELL.

By JAMES FROTHINGHAM HUNNEWELL, A.M., of Charlestown, Mass.

THE name Hunnewell, variously spelled or misspelled during some centuries past, is uncommon in England, and yet it appeared there long ago in fully two dozen places, nearly all in the southern counties.

For generations nothing about it there seems to have been known, at least publicly, in America, until the writer's research, a long one, that, besides an interest of its own, may be a help in showing persons similarly occupied how the long unknown can be found, for the writer started without a clue. By this research he has gathered enough to make a volume, but he will not now attempt to present the material. He will only mention some bearers of the name, and tell the story of his own immediate family—which has never yet been fully told, and incorrectly in the few places where it has been attempted.

A hunt for an ancestor, or somebody who might prove to be one, can be very pretty sport in old England. Of course there generally first must be research, usually a good deal of it, and then may come travel, that is more delightful, however interesting documents may have been. The writer can hardly wish any one a more charming excursion than his when he first saw his family name on an old monument in the old home-land.

A neat victoria with a liveried driver and a good horse, a sort of conveyance not apt to be found by a traveller in minor places out of England, took him six or eight miles west of Exeter. The way was over high ridges, down deep into vales, steep for that country, or anywhere else, and then higher land with a magnificent park was reached. Farther on, still by a narrow lane-like road peculiarly English, there is a wide and magnificent view—deep into and far over a great vale to the distant heights of Dartmoor, crowned by Heytor. Nestled on the swell of land, and just as English as all else, is a hamlet with little old thatched houses and an even older church, not large and yet not small.

It is Ashton in Devon, a place that through its long lifetime has been apart from the world. The church is Perpendicular, rough-cast, with a square western tower, and is, also in the old English way, surrounded by its burial ground. Internally there are five bays, a couple of aisles, a barrel vault, and most notable of all, in front of the altar, an open carved wooden screen, well designed and evidently old, having along its base thirty-two panels, in each of which, also old, is a curious painting of a saint. The storms of the Reformation do not seem to have reached this peaceful spot. Perhaps ten feet inside the porch door there is in the aisle pavement a grey stone, some five by three feet in size. On the upper part is bolted a smooth brass plate bearing, along with a little ornament, an inscription in black letters, all clean and in good order:

"In Death is Lyfe | HEAR *Lyeth* | WILLYAM HONNY | WILL G SON OF | MATHEW HONIWILL | AND IOANE HIS WYFE | DECESED THE I OF | NOVEMBER Ano | Domini | 1614."

By his will, where he is spelled Honnywell and is styled gentle-man, he directs that he shall "be buried in the parish church of Ayshton and be covered with a faire marble stone and to be engraved in brass. The sonne of the said Matthews & Joane." The result of his direction remains, as is seen, to our times. His will, a copy of which is beside the writer, shows that he was a good substantial man with relatives and friends in the region where he lived.

Many who bore his name—spelled in most of the ways that could be invented—three of these on his will and brass plate—were scattered throughout Devon in the sixteenth and seventeenth centuries, most of them quiet persons of various occupations, including, as was apt to be the case in that country, some who were husband-men or were sea-faring. Many of them were of moderate means, but, notably, several left money for the poor in their neighborhoods.

The writer has not searched, or guessed, back to Bosworth Field, let alone Hastings; nor has he tried to develope certain spelling on the Roll of Battle Abbey; this lovely Devon land seems good enough for anyone to hail from, and start from.

The name, as already remarked, appears elsewhere in England, yet its infrequency is in a degree proved by the London Directory, where for years it was not to be found. There are, however, several entries of it during the sixteenth and seventeenth centuries in the records of St. Margaret's, Westminster, and in the eighteenth it was in a great city house. Copies of all references to it in these places, known to exist, are a part of the writer's collections already mentioned. One portion may reach the eastern counties, and is as follows:

"Mary daughter of . . . . Honeywell and relict of . . . . Hawkins married as her second husband Captain Richard Hill of Yarmouth co. Norfolk an eminent Seaman in the Service of the Duke of York afterwards James the 2nd.

"She had two daughters and coheirs viz: Christian wife of Sir John Leake Kn^t Vice Admiral of Great Britian, and Elizabeth wife of Captain Stephen Martin Leake."

These entries, while interesting as showing a possible diffusion of the name, are too late (latter part of the seventeenth century.) to lead to a person who carried it to New England.

After making note it seems of all who bore the name in old England for a hundred years, an entry was found that appears to be the link between the old and the new lands.

In the Register of the Parish of St. Andrew, *Plymouth, Devon,* is the entry:

"AMBROSE Hunniwell and Jane Homes were married on the first day of November, 1659."

This entry is remarkable as the only one of an Ambrose in the full collection just mentioned, and, unlike a great many others, he appears to have left no indication of children or of will in England.

While it is quite probable that the above was not a "church wedding," St. Andrew's Plymouth is an interesting place to associate with a parting from the old world. Fronting an oblong square where the civic buildings are, it presents a large tower and grey stone walls with granite quoins and window cases. The interior, clear from end to end, has three aisles of nearly equal height, arcades with slender pillars, and vaults barrel-form panelled. Nearly all the windows have colored glass, and there are many monuments along the walls. The prevailing style is Perpendicular. It is a church worthy of an ancient and renowned port, and it is as far as well can be very English.

Two years later the name *Ambrose* is found in New England, then and there also apparently unique. There cannot be two uniques; it seems that they must be one person.

"In 1661, Ambrose[1] Hunnewell from whom the point at the Fort takes its name, resided at the lower end of Sagadahock." (Me. Hist. Soc. II, 193.) June 25, 1662, he bought land on the Sadadahock river (Indenture). About 1671, he was living on islet called Honniwells Point (Deposition). A year later he appears to have signed a petition to Massachusetts (M. H. Soc., V, 240), and July 22, 1674, to have been a grand juror at a court at Pemaquid (Do., 2d S., IV, 345), also, April 9, 1688, a selectman.

This "Hunnewell's Point" on the western shore of the mouth of the Kennebec river in Maine appears to be the land first associated with the writer's ancestors in America. It is shown on the larger maps of the State, and distinctly on the chart of the United States Coast Survey (No. 3, 1858), which also shows "Hunniwell's Beach" along the open sea in the neighborhood. No. 2, 1858, shows bearings, and No. 4, 1861, is still clearer and more minute.

The site is prominently associated with the very early history of New England. Here was the first considerable attempt at settlement, that of the Popham Colony, in August, 1607 (described in the Memorial of it, 137, etc.). It was "on the peninsular . . called by the Indians Sabino, but now bearing the English name of Hunnewell's Point." (Me. Hist. Soc., I, 29). · The colony continued there about a year (Do., V., 336). One ship with colonists sailed from Bristol (Memorial, 140), and must have brought West of England people, some of whom must have later helped to spread news about the new country. Strachey gives farther information (Mass. Hist. Soc. Coll's, IV, i., 239–40).

This Point is a dozen or more miles south of Bath, and can be reached by a pleasant steamboat excursion. It presents a great ledge of pale granite rock with grass and abundant shrubs on the sides. A long curved beach extends westward; on the other hand is the Kennebec. From the crest of the rock, site, it is said of the earliest fort, there is a great view all around south over the sea. Northward is lower, or better, land, and, on a low ledge projecting into the river, Fort Popham with two stories of granite casemates, chiefly dating from the time of the Civil War, unfinished, and a monument of an obsolete and expensive style of work. It is said to be the third fort on the spot. Altogether the scenery and view here are exceptionally imposing.

However good the country hereabouts may now be, it was in the latter part of the seventeenth century trying enough. Church says (II, 56), that by 1689, "the Kennebeck and Eastern Indians with their confederates" made war against the English in Maine, New Hampshire and Massachusetts, and forces were sent against them, including the famous captain himself. According to the Massachusetts Archives (107, 42), "The Inhabitants of Kennybeck Riuer and Sackadihock Island" petitioned the Council of Massachusetts for help, styling themselves "Your poor and humble Petitioners, being in a sad deplorable condition the Army being called home ∴ . . the most of our houses being now att this Instant in a fflame." Hence they desired "a speedy supply of men." On July 11th there was an attack near Lieut. Hunniwell's garrison. (This was Richard H., of Scarborough, of whom more elsewhere.) July 20th, a Charles Hunnewell was killed by the Indians.

AMBROSE[1] had children. They were born, and they lived, although there seem to be no extant records of their births and order.

438

The early Maine records had a hard time between dispersion or destruction during the devastating French and Indian Wars. Still, evidence quite as good exists elsewhere, and was in time found.

Naturally these children, like a great many other persons of their region, moved southward to peace and security. In Boston, 1681, appears on the tax-list an Ambrose—the first note of him there; in 1688, were a Stephen and a Richard, the latter also in 1689. Of a sister Mary there is later evidence. In 1698, at Charlestown, first appears the writer's direct ancestor Charles. Years later, the relationship of all these five is found clearly on record.

Ambrose, at Boston in 1731, deposed that about 1671 "he lived with his *Parents* upon an Islet called Honniwell's Point on the West Side of the Mouth of Kenebeck River." April 16, 1719, he, of Boston, signs "Rec^d of my *brother Stephen* Hunnewell" pay for his (Stephen's) interest in lands "on ye South Part of Sagadehoc River," including certain "made over unto my *Father Ambrose* Hunniwell."

Mary (Whitin) of Boston, "widow," conveys to her *brother Stephen* Hunniwell of Boston, Fisherman, her interest in the same, at the same date. (Stephen's pursuits are further shown in accounts of his death, that will be given hereafter by the writer.)

Richard Honnywell of Boston, conveyed same to "my well-beloved *Brother Stephen* Honnywell of Boston, Marriner." June 24, 1747, Richard Hunniwell of Boston, N. E., mason, "being aged," made his will. He gave to the ministers, Mr. Webb (Rev. John, New North Church, 1714–50), and Mr. Eliot (Rev. Andrew, Do., 1742–78), £10. each, and made bequests to *brother Charles's*[2] widow (he *d*. Dec. 14, 1737), and to brother Charles's children, especially naming Richard and Mary (living in 1747). Also £10. "to my Nephew Stephen" (a son of the above Stephen).

Thus appear Ambrose of Kennebec, and his five children (of whose number, etc., there is further evidence). Before giving an account of those who remained in Boston, and of certain ones in Maine, the writer tells the story of his ancestor Charles and of descendants from him.

Of CHARLES[2] the first record appears to be on the Charlestown Records. "1698, Novemb^r 17th Charles Hunnewell of Boston and Elizabeth Davis of Charlestown, Joyned in Marriage before the Reverend Mr Simon Bradstreet, Minister," (of Charlestown, Oct. 26, 1698, to 1741).

In Savage's Genealogical Dictionary of New England (II, 499), Charles is said to have been the son of Richard of Boston, a statement that seems to have been copied by Wyman, Ruggles, and other writers. He, however, has not the distinction of being the son of his brother, who appears to have become confused among several Richards to be mentioned elsewhere by the writer.

As already shown in this account, we find how, by looking and gathering here and there, we get the means to form a fair opinion of persons who lived long ago in quiet or secluded life, and of whom nothing like biographical notices exist. This fact we can continue to observe. General characteristics appear. Members of the present family, while good citizens through two centuries, seem to have avoided political life, and to have kept as far as could be, and as will be shown, a settled position and permanent home. Of course in such a period there have been diversities of ability and of fortune, and in these the reverse of decline has been evident.

Between 1708 and 1728, Charles bought sundry parcels of real estate in Charlestown; among them, in 1710, the house and land that for the next eighty-four years made the homestead of the writer's ancestors.

January 16, 1710, says the deed (Mid. 15, 396), he bought of Jonathan Welsh of Charlestown "Dwelling house and barne, with all the Land adjoining," given to the latter by his father's will, and situated in the second division of the town, so called (now Somerville). There were fifteen acres of land bounded south by a way leading to Menotomy. The place was about a mile northeast of Cambridge meeting-house, and three miles west by north of that in Charlestown, on what was long called "Milk Row." About fifty feet north of this road stood the house, built probably in 1691, when Thomas Welsh, father of Jonathan, had, by Selectmen's record, liberty to build. This house, as known long ago by the writer, was of wood, two stories high, and had a sloped roof. In the centre was a very large chimney, before which were a stair and the front door. On each side of these was a fair sized room with a beam across a plastered ceiling. The windows were narrow. At the back was a kitchen on which was subsequently put a second story. In front were two terraces, on the top of which the house stood, and by the road a gate flanked each side by a long hedge of lilacs fully ten feet high, and back of these by trees. The place was the most picturesque of its age, or nearly its age, that the writer remembers in the region. It was not a "colonial mansion," but it was decidedly superior to the usual old farmhouse. Long ago, also, it disappeared there, due effort to the contrary notwithstanding; poor recent buildings are now on a part of its site, and not a trace of its picturesqueness remains.

CHARLES[2] had eight children, all baptized in the First Church, Charlestown; of whom two died young, and two were unmarried. He died Dec. 14, 1737. The inventory of his estate, dated March 13, 1737–8, shows a valuation of £1304. 19. 0. Small as this would now appear, it ranks midway in a list of the estates of eighteen heads of families who were near that date best off in his native town, the largest being £4086. It shows what was then a condition in a prosperous town of Massachusetts. Millionaries had not been invented there, but as was said of the dollar that Washington is reported to have thrown across a river—money would go further then than now.

The limit of this article is reached, and the writer briefly remarks that later he proposes to give further account of early Hunnewells in Maine and in Massachusetts. The name has continued in Maine, and occasionally one who bore it thence has appeared in Massachusetts, but all who have been permanent in the latter are descended from those already mentioned. The writer's line from Ambrose[1] is Charles,[2] Charles,[3] William,[4] William,[5] and James.[6] From Richard, youngest son of Charles[3] who had a large family in Cambridge, came Walter and H. H., and the family described by H. S. Ruggles (n. p. 1892).

ORIGIN OF THE FAMILIES OF HUNT, FOWLER, BARNES, KIRKE, AND EMBREE, OF WESCHESTER, N. H., AND OF HUNT, OF CHARLESTOWN AND NORTHAMPTON, MASS.— *
No evidence has been found supporting Wyman's statement in his "Genealogy of Hunt", 1862-3, p. 160 (*American Genealogist*, 1950, p. 1), that Thomas Hunt of Westchester, N. Y., was a son of Richard Hunt of Shrewsbury, Shropshire, and that said Thomas married a woman named Cicely Pasley. This Thomas died in Westchester, N. Y., in 1695. In 1660 he had been of Stamford, Conn., to which place he had moved

*For N.H. read N.Y.

from New Haven, Conn.; this removal was by court order, dated first day, first month, 1643, because Hunt and his wife, Cicely, had "kept the councells" of one William Harding, whom the New Haven elders detested. See Hoadley's "New Haven Colony Records", 1857, p. 84, and "Records of the Colony of New Plymouth in New England", Boston, 1859, vol. 10, pp. 46, 47. Hunt's wife, Cicely, appears to have been that Cicely Clark*, who at the age of sixteen came to Boston, Mass., in 1635, in the *Planter* with that Tuttle family from Hertfordshire, who in 1639 all moved to New Haven. See the 1883 Tuttle genealogy; THE REGISTER, vol. 14, p. 305.

Hunt was representative of Westchester to the Connecticut Legislature (see Savage) before Connecticut gave up its claim to Westchester. His first son, Thomas, was born evidently in New Haven in or about the year 1640 (R. E. Dale in the *Boston Evening Transcript*, 27 May 1931, article on "Early Families of Eastchester"). The elder Hunt had come to New Haven in 1639 as an indentured servant to William Leete of Keyston, Hunts., later Governor of Connecticut. Other servants on the same trip were William Barnes and Edward Jones, who had been a servant of John Kirke of Tichmersh, Northants. See Calder's "New Haven Colony", 1934, pp. 70 *et seq.*; p. 427 of Thomas Lechford's Note Book; Steiner's "History of Guilford, Conn.", p. 24. "Westchester Court of Sessions, 1657-96", vol. II, 1924, p. 34, lists the following members of a grand jury in Westchester in 1687: "Mr. Thomas Hunt, senior, first member . . . Mr. William Barnes, 5th member . . . Mr. Thomas C. Kirke, senior, tenth member".

THE REGISTER, vol. 7, names Mrs. Susan Hunt, late wife of Robert Hunt of Charlestown, Mass., late of Sudborough, Northants, whose inventory was dated in 1642. THE REGISTER, 1876 ,gives the will of John Hunt of Sudborowe, Northants., dated in 1623, proved in 1623, naming the testator's sister, Alice, wife of Thomas Hunt of Islip, next Thrapston, Northants., and the testator's sister Helen, wife of John Fowler.

The Webster genealogy, Hartford, Conn., 1915, p. 31, states that Mary Webster, daughter of John, later Governor of Connecticut, was married in England, by 1638, to John Hunt of Sudborowe, Northants., where their son, Jonathan was born in 1637. He settled in Northampton, Mass.

The will of Thomas Hunt of Sudborowe, is in "Northampton Archdeaconry", Book V, 1st series, fo. 88. It is abstracted herewith: "5 May 1582. I Thomas Hunt of Sudborowge . . . Richard Hunt my son . . . Ellenor Hunt my daughter . . . Alice Hunt, my daughter of Islipp . . . Agnes Hunt my wife and John Hunt my son executors and if fortune that Agnes Hunt my wife and John Hunt my son could not quietly agree together . . . my goods to be divided equally . . . witnesses John Sadler, Raffe Embrie and John Blackwell" (Proved 1582).

In March 1739 Samuel Embree of Westchester left property to his daughter, Abigail Hunt (New York wills). Her husband was Samuel[4] Hunt (Samuel,[3] Joseph,[2] Thomas[1]) (Records of Grenville C. Mackenzie of Westport, Conn.).

Frost's "Underhill Genealogy" shows that Nathaniel Underhill (1690-1775) married in 1711 Mary Hunt, born in 1692, daughter of John[2] Hunt and his wife, Grace Fowler of Westchester. The daughter, Helena Underhill, may have been so named to honor Helena (Ellenor or Hellen), wife of John Fowler, *supra*.

William Barnes, the juror of 1687, *supra*, may have been the son of William Barnes, fellow indentured servant in 1639 of Thomas Hunt. Steiner's "History of Guilford, Conn.", pp. 60, 127, shows that the fellow servant, Barnes, died in 1648 or 1649. See Miss Calder's *op. cit.*, p. 223, concerning Thomas Kirke, *supra*.

There is little reason to doubt that the elder Thomas Hunt, *supra*, was a native of Thrapston, Sudborow, or Islip, Northants. The following is from the Calendar of Close Rolls, 1476: "Thomas, son and heir of Thomas Hunt of Tychemersh, Northants., to John Nicoll, grocer, of London, his heirs and assigns . . . gift etc. of all his lands in Denford, co. Northants., which came to him from his father, Thomas Hunt . . . [*ibid.*] lands in Keston, Huntingdonshire. Dated at Denford, 20 Oct. 16th year of the reign of Edward IV."

It may be noted that Denford adjoins Thrapston on the south, Keyston adjoins Thrapston on the east, and Tichmersh lies just north of both Keyston and Thrapston.

---

*According to Banks' "Planters of the Commonwealth" William Tuttle, aged 26, husbandman, of Ringstead, Northants, came to New England with his family in 1635. With them came Cicely Clark, aged 16 years. It is noted that Ringstead, Northants., adjoins Keyston, Hunts., on the west.

It seems logical to suppose that all the aforesaid Hunts, Kirkes, Fowlers, Barnes, and Embrees originated in the neighborhood of Thrapston, Northants.

Arlington, Va.   JOHN G. HUNT.

ORIGIN OF FAMILIES OF HUNT OF NORTHAMPTON AND HULL, MASS., AND BARNES OF WESTCHESTER; N.Y.:—CORRECTION AND SUPPLEMENT.—The contributor is obliged to Mr. Donald Lines Jacobus for pointing out the following facts about the note on this subject published on pages 63 through 65 of THE REGISTER for January 1959. *

The Tuttle family named therein came, not from Hertfordshire, but from Ringstead, Northants, as indicated in my footnote. See Mr. Jacobus' "Hale, House and Related Families", pp. 770-774.

The Hunts of Northampton, Mass., named in the cited note, appear to have descended from Thomas Hunt who married in Cossington, Leicester, in 1632, Margaret, daughter of John (later Governor) Webster and his wife, born Agnes Smith. The Webster genealogy cited in my note appears to have been in error regarding the origin of Jonathan Hunt (see vol. 62, *N. Y. G. B. Record,* and *The American Genealogist* for 1948, pp. 197 through 214).

William Barnes named in my note as in Westchester, N. Y., removed to that town from Southampton, N. Y. (see Southampton Town Records, vol 5, p. 225).

In addition to the above comments by Mr. Jacobus, the contributor presents the following abstract of the will of Richard Hunt of Leicester, near Cossington, who may have been related to the above Thomas Hunt who married Margaret Webster.

"27 Dec 1616—Richard Hunt . . . . my body to be buried in the ch. of Saint Nicholas, Leicester . . . . my father, Thomas Hunt, deseased . . . . Thomas Hunt, my eldest son, and his sons . . . . my son Richard and his heirs . . . . my wife, Agnes . . . . my son Edward and Joyce, my daughter, at the age of eighteen . . . . . . William Hunt and Thomas Hunt, my brethren, overseers." Proved at Leicester 20 Aug. 1621.

Wyman's Hunt genealogy cites a certificate from the Lord Mayor of London dated 1699, abstracting a deposition taken in that year showing that Richard Hunt (evidently son of the above testator) of the parish of St. Nicholas, Leicester, had a son, Thomas, born in 1602, father of John Hunt, born in 1633, formerly of Shambles Lane, St. Nicholas. Thomas, born in 1602, had a brother, John Hunt, born in 1607, father of Sarah, born in 1628, mother of Thomas Morris, a baker, now (in 1699) bound for the West Indies.

There is a possibility that this Hunt family of Leicester city was related in some way to that Thomas Hunt who married in 1632 in Cossington, above, which is very close to Leicester.

Zachary Hunt of Hull, Mass., in 1680 (THE REGISTER, 1849. p. 185)) may well have been son of Nathaniel Hunt and his wife, Mary, daughter of Sir John Bolles. Nathaniel Hunt and his wife, of Swaby, Lincs., are named in the 1665 "Visitation of Yorkshire", by Sir William Dugdale (*Surtees Society Publications,* vol. 36, page 152); their children are thus listed:

   Edward Hunt
   Nicholas Hunt
   Nathaniel Hunt

*The preceding article.

443

Zachary Hunt
Francis Hunt
John Hunt
Abraham Hunt, 6th son, born in 1641, lived in 1665 at Stainton,
Yorkshire.

"all in Ireland or forrein
countries in this year, 1665"

Arlington, Va.   JOHN G. HUNT.

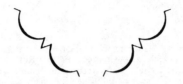

THE IDENTITY OF FRANCES, WIFE OF JOHN HUTCHINS OF NEWBURY AND HAVERHILL, MASS.—The undersigned is obliged to Mrs. Rachel Sherwin of Saugus, Mass., for pointing out that C. E. Banks, *The Planters of the Commonwealth* (pp. 198-200) indicates that in 1638 the ship *Bevis* sailed (perhaps in May) for New England, carrying two of the Dummer brothers, whose servants included "John Hutchinson, carpenter, [aged] 30, and Francis Alcock, [aged] 26". This record states that the Dummers were from Bishopstoke, Hants., and Colonel Banks states that they settled in Newbury, Mass.

John Hutchins settled there also before 1640 (*Newbury Vital Records*) and he and his wife, Frances, are named as early as 1642 in the Essex Court Records. They both again are named in the files of Essex Quarterly Court (in Salisbury, Mass.) in November 1679. For some time Hutchins was a third part owner of a mill in the area, as shown by the Essex Court Records. He was rather obviously a carpenter as proved by the same records. It is reasonable to believe that he was that "John Hutchinson" who came on the *Bevis* in 1638, especially since an "s" ending on a surname may indicate that the name at one time ended in "son". This belief is somewhat fortified by the record of a suit for debt by Mr. Richard Dummer against John Hutchins at the Ipswich Quarterly Court of September 1665. Hutchins acknowledged the debt. The Essex Court Records of 1653 show that Frances, wife of John Hutchins, was presented at the Court for wearing a silk hood, but on testimony of her being brought up above the ordinary rank she was discharged.

Savage is puzzled by the name "Francis Alcock", and says merely: "Francis Alcock, Newbury, came in the Bevis, 1638, aged 26, in employ of Ric. Dummer as Eng. Cust. ho. rec. tells, but that is sole authority for calling him of Newbury nor is any more known of him".

Does it not seem strange that the death of Francis Alcock is not cited in New England records? Or is it possible, as Mrs. Sherwin has suggested, that Francis Alcock was really Frances Alcock, a woman?

To answer these questions is our intent in this note.

First, let us note that THE REGISTER, vol. 14, p. 337, lists in the *Bevis* in 1638 the following as belonging to the Dummer party:

"John Hutchinson, carpenter, [aged] 30, servant".

"Frauncis Alcock, vizg. [aged] 26, servant".

The word "vizg." at first puzzles one, but after some study it seems that this word can only be "virg.", for in the script of the early seventeenth century the letter "r" frequently looked like a small printed "z". Hence one may conclude that "Frauncis" Alcock was a woman. In this connection let it be noted that in the 1679 court record cited above, John Hutchins' wife's name is spelled "Francis".

The disappearance of Francis Alcock from New England records after May 1638 and the appearance very shortly thereafter of Frances, wife of John Hutchins, plus the fact that they are listed next to each other in the passenger list, all suggest quite strongly that Frances Alcock married John Hutchins. Moreover, let us see what the sparse records in print concerning Southampton and vicinity state *re* the Dummers and Alcocks.

The Southampton Records Society's *Court Leet Records*, 1619, show a fine levied against an Alcock: "Refuse before the door of Mr. Alcock in St. Michael's Parish. Hence, he is fined 6 d. To be removed by Michaelmas next on pain of 12 d."

Woodward's *History of Southampton*, vol. 2, p. 115, states *re* North Stoneham (a village between Bishopstoke and Southampton): "one rector of mournful memory was Lewis Alcock who held the benefice of No. Stoneham for 55 years. In the time of Elizabeth he had been chaplain to lord Southampton ... but (because of the clamor re sequestration) he lost his living".

Venn's *Alumni Cantabrigienses* states: "Lewis Alcock, matric. pens. fr. St. John's, Lent, 1582/3. B.A., 1587/8; M.A., 1591."

Waters' *Genealogical Gleanings*, p. 200, abstracts the will, dated 1650, of Thomas Dummer of North Stoneham, Southampton, leaving a legacy for the poor of North Stoneham and Bishopstoke and naming his daughter, Margaret Clements in New England, to whom he left a legacy of 25 pounds.

Essex Court Records abstract a reference to the estate of Robert Clements of Haverhill in September 1685; his last will referred to a debt of some seven pounds "in the hands of John Hutchins for repairing the house and fencing ye home lot".

445

The son of this Robert Clements was Job Clements who was of Haverhill in 1646; he married Margaret Dummer above named in 1644 (Savage). As John Hutchins removed to Haverhill about 1661, and this town is near Newbury, it seems that he was acquainted with these Dummers and Clements. It is not at all far-fetched to suppose that his wife, Francis, was born Frances Alcock, and may have been closely related to Lewis Alcock, rector of North Stoneham, next Southampton. Alcock died 25 June 1647, aged eighty-six years (M.I.), having been rector there since 1593. His effects were administered 8 July 1647 by his next of kin, William Bennet of Wroxeter, near Shrewsbury, Shropshire; Winchester admons.

At Lichfield, Staffs., was proved in 1544 the will of Elizabeth Alcock of Wroxeter, perhaps ancestress of Lewis Alcock, above. There is at Wroxeter a small brass commemorating Thomas Alcock who died in 1627/8, whose will, dated 5 Feb. 1627/8, with codicils of 20 Feb. and 3 March following, was proved 3 April following (P.C.C., 33 Barrington). It names William Bennett, to have part of his land, Edward Alcocke, Robert Alcocke, John Alcocke, his servant, the testator's brother, Lewis Alcocke, and his sisters, Lucy (wife of ——— Clampson), and Joyce, wife of John Farmer. Bonds by Mr. Francis Garbett, clerk, and Joyce his wife, and William Bennett and Christian his wife (full abstract presented to the Society's Library).

John Hutchins of Newbury and Haverhill had children including William (married in 1661), Joseph (born in 1640), Joseph (born in 1641), Thomas (granted fishing rights in 1657) and Benjamin. The father of John Hutchins could well have been identical with, or related to, William Hutchins who in 1627 was of Stockbridge, some sixteen miles northwest of North Stoneham (Hants. Subsidy, 3 Charles I; Colonel Banks' MSS).

For information regarding the Dummers see THE REGISTER, vol. 35, p. 269,[*] also vol. 107, p. 156, for Robert Clements. [**]

Arlington, Va.   JOHN G. HUNT.

*P. 714, the first volume of this series.
**P. 957, the first volume of this series.

THE HUTCHINSON FAMILY OF ENGLAND AND NEW ENGLAND, AND ITS CONNECTION WITH THE MARBURYS AND DRYDENS.

[By Joseph Lemuel Chester, Corresponding Member of the New England Historic-Genealogical Society ; Honorary Member of the Essex and Surrey Archæological Societies, the Surtees Society, &c. &c. &c. of England.]

The writer has been able, after a long and laborious investigation, to solve the chief doubts existing in respect to the early history and connections of the family of Governor Hutchinson, several of the members of which played important parts in the affairs of New England. As has heretofore been his almost invariable experience, he has had more difficulty in clearing away the mists that have enveloped that history, growing out of doubtful traditions and careless or wilful misrepresentations, than in developing the true facts in the case when once the right clew was obtained.

Before proceeding with the history of the immediate family of the earliest emigrant ancestor of Governor Hutchinson, it will be well to state that there is not the slightest authority for connecting him with the heraldic family of Yorkshire, either with the branch settled at Wykeham Abbey in that county, or that in Nottinghamshire from which descended the famous Colonel John Hutchinson. The theory that Edward Hutchinson, of Alford in Lincolnshire, father of William the emigrant, was identical with Edward Hutchinson of Wykeham Abbey, his contemporary, is entirely baseless ; and it is quite certain that, if there was ever the most distant connection between the two families, it only existed many generations previous to their time. Edward Hutchinson of Wykeham Abbey, to whom the arms of the family were confirmed (not granted) in 1581, died early in the year 1591 ; his Will being dated on the 20th of February, and proved at York, on the 22d of April in that year ; while Edward Hutchinson of Alford survived him more than forty years. The writer has successfully traced the subsequent history of the Wykeham branch, and is able to state positively that none of its members ever had anything to do with New England, or any connection with the New England emigrants.

It is proposed in this paper to confine the investigation to four generations, ending with that embracing the children of William Hutchinson, the founder of the race in New England. Hitherto nothing has been known of his father, except that his name was Edward, and that he lived at Alford, in Lincolnshire. The writer is able to present some additional facts respecting him, and also to establish his paternity His grandfather has not been identified, and probably never can be, as he lived before the period of Parish Registers, left no Will that can be discovered, and was evidently of a very humble rank in life. We may, therefore, commence with—

I. ——— Hutchinson, probably of the city of Lincoln, who had, certainly, four sons and one daughter, viz. :

447

1. *Christopher*, who was a Clergyman. He was instituted to the church of South Leasingham on the 6th of August, 1522, and to that of Scremby (both in Lincolnshire) on the 22d of October, 1526. He died, probably, about June, 1556, as his Will was proved on the 8th of July in that year, having been made on the 18th of November, 1554, when he described himself as still " Parson of Leasingham." He bequeathed legacies to his sister and three brothers, and their children, perfectly identifying them all. His brother John was his Executor and proved the Will.

2. *Thomas*, of whom nothing is known, except that he is mentioned in his brother Christopher's Will, as having a daughter Margaret, who is also again named in her uncle William's Will as still living.

3. *William*, who, at the time of his death, was a " citizen and alderman of the city of Lincoln." On a monument to one of his daughters, in one of the Lincoln churches, he is called " Alderman and Tanner." In the ancient records of the Corporation of the city of Lincoln, he is sometimes designated as " Glover." He appears to have worked himself up from his apprenticeship to a position of some standing as early as 1540, when he was appointed to collect certain moneys in behalf of the Corporation. In September, 1541, he was elected Sheriff of the city ; in March, 1545, an Alderman ; and in September, 1552, Mayor. His Will is dated on the 4th of January and proved the 6th of March, 155$. In it he mentions his brother John (to whom he leaves his official scarlet gown, and also his interest in certain land in Whisby), his sister Remington and her husband, and his brother Thomas's daughter. His wife's Christian name was Dorothy, by whom he had three sons and three daughters, viz.: 1. Christopher, afterwards of Mablethorpe, in the county of Lincoln, yeoman, who died in 1592, having had, by his wife Anne, three sons and two daughters ; 2. Thomas, afterwards of Louth, in the county of Lincoln, yeoman, who died in 16$, having had, by his wife Anne, three sons and five daughters ; 3. William, of Horncastle, in the county of Lincoln, Merchant of the Staple, who died in 1576, leaving by his wife Elizabeth, who survived him, a daughter Margery, who subsequently married Herbert Thorndike, and was still living, with her husband, in 1611 ; 4. Margaret, who was living in 1560 ; 5. Mary, who was not fifteen years of age at her father's death ; and, 6. Margery, who married John Neale, of Horncastle, in the county of Lincoln, tanner, and died his widow in 1611. Dorothy, their mother, widow of William Hutchinson, remarried Thomas Raithbeck, of Horncastle aforesaid, yeoman, whom she also survived, finally dying herself early in the year 1592.

4. John, of whom hereafter.

5. *Alice*, married to James Remington, of Branston, near the city of Lincoln, who, in his Will, dated on the 10th of January and proved the 18th of February, 1558–9, called himself a "husbandman." She survived him, and made her own Will on the 19th of February, 1559–60, but it was not proved until the 27th of March, 1567. Her brother, John Hutchinson, was named as Supervisor of both Wills, the contents of which, as well as her husband's

description of himself, sufficiently indicate that their station in life was very humble.

II. JOHN HUTCHINSON was apparently the youngest of the four brothers above named. From the Corporation Records before mentioned it appears that he was apprenticed, on the 23d of September, 1529, to Edward Atkinson, of the city of Lincoln, glover, for seven years, which establishes his birth in about the year 1515. Like his brother William, he also, after his apprenticeship had expired, pursued such a course as to secure the confidence of his fellow citizens, and is frequently mentioned as holding minor offices of trust in connection with the business of the Corporation, and rising to the dignity of Sheriff of the city, in September, 1547. On the 11th of April, 1556, he was elected an Alderman, and, in the following September, elevated to the Mayoralty. On the 21st of October, 1558, he was elected a Justice of the Peace for an unexpired term, and on the 2d of October, 1561, that honor was again conferred upon him. In September, 1564, he was a second time elected Mayor, which office he held at the time of his death, which occurred on the 24th of May, 1565. He was buried in the church of St. Mary le Wigford, in the city of Lincoln, on the same day, and, as an illustration of the rapidity with which business was sometimes done in those times, it may be mentioned that the Corporation Records reveal the singular facts, that he died at four o'clock in the morning, and that his colleagues in office, having attended his funeral, elected his successor within sixteen hours after his decease. His Will was made on the previous 21st of April, and its bequests indicate that he had acquired considerable property. He left lands and houses to each of his sons, all of whom, as named below, he particularly mentions. To his eldest son William he bequeathed the estate at Whisby, formerly left to him by his own brother William, and also the Rectory and Parsonage of Cherry Willingham (near Lincoln), which he had doubtless acquired by purchase. His son *Edward*, and daughter Mary, he particularly commended to the kindness of his wife, who was probably their own mother. John Hutchinson had two wives. The christian name of the first was Margaret, and, from certain allusions in her husband's Will, it is probable that her surname was Browne. By her he appears to have had four sons and two daughters, viz. :—

1. *William*, named as eldest son in his father's Will, and who proved the same in 1565, which shows that he was then of full age. He married Margaret Sisson, on the 26th of August, 1565, at St. Mary Wigford's, in the city of Lincoln. She was also buried there on the 3d of June, 1580, leaving issue—John, Anne, Jane, Margaret and Susan. Her husband was buried at the same place on the 14th of January, 1583–4. His Will is dated on the 26th of February, 1582–3, when all his children were living. He mentions his brothers John, Arthur, and *Edward*, and his sisters Alice and Mary, as also his brother-in-law Edmund Knight.

2. *Thomas*, who was living, a minor, at the date of his father's Will ; but, as he is not named in that of his brother William, was probably dead before 1582–3. On the 20th of December, 1571, and the 31st of January following, he is mentioned in the Corporation Records of Lincoln, as then of Ashby, near Horncastle, and a merchant of the Staple.

449

3. *John*, a minor at his father's death, and still living at that of his brother William.

4. *Arthur*, not of age at his father's death. On the 22d of January, 1578–9, he enrolled a deed, preserved among the aforesaid Corporation Records, in which he describes himself as "of Newark [Nottinghamshire], ironmonger, one of the sons of John Hutchynson, late of the city of Lincoln, Alderman," by which he conveyed certain property to Anne Hutchynson, whom he calls his ," mother-in-law, relict of the said John Hutchynson." On the same day, being similarly described, he was admitted to the franchise in right of his birth. On the 19th of March, 1581–2, he enrolled another deed, in which he is described as "of Lincoln, Fishmonger." He was still living as late as the 10th of July, 1611, when he is mentioned in the Will of his cousin Margery Neale.

5. *Jane*, who was married before her father's death to Edmund Knight, afterwards an Alderman of Lincoln. He was buried on the 10th of September, 1584, and she appears to have died before 1583.

6. *Alice*, a minor in 1565, but married before 1583 to Thomas Dynyson. Both were still living in 1586.

The date of the death of Margaret, the first wife of said John Hutchinson, Mayor, has not been ascertained. It is possible that she may have been the mother of his other two children, but the probabilities are otherwise. The christian name of his second wife was Anne, and she had evidently been married once, if not twice before. In her Will, dated the 25th of March and proved the 18th of September, 1586, she leaves a considerable legacy to her "son William Clinte," to increase a certain sum left him by his father's Will, which amount is to remain in the hands of her "son Edward Kirkebie," until the day of said William's marriage. She also mentions her "son Thomas Pinder." The two latter, it may be presumed, were her sons-in-law, and all the evidences to be gleaned from her Will tend to show that her former husband's name was Clinte. There is nothing, however, in it to indicate her own family surname. The reasons for presuming that John Hutchinson's two youngest children were by this second wife are, first, because he especially entrusts them to her custody, while he commits the guardianship of the elder children, proved to be by his first wife, to others ; and, secondly, because in her Will, except leaving a very trifling legacy to Alice Dynison, she mentions none of the other children of John Hutchinson, but makes her "son *Edward* Hutchinson" residuary legatee, and appoints him and her "son-in-law George Freiston" (who had married Mary Hutchinson) her Executors. At all events, John Hutchinson had, by either his first or second wife, two other children, viz. :—

7. EDWARD, of whom hereafter.

8. *Mary*, who was married at St. Peter at Gowts, in the city of Lincoln, on the 13th of September, 1578, to George Freeston, of Alford, in the county of Lincoln, yeoman. They had four children, all baptized at Alford, viz. : 1. Richard, on the 19th of December, 1579 ; 2. Robert, on the 18th of March, 1581–2 ; 3. John, on the 7th of April, 1584 ; and, 4. Margery, on the 11th of September, 1586. Of these, Robert and John died in their infancy,

and were buried at Alford, and their father was also buried there on the 22d of November, 1588. His widow Mary subsequently re-married —— Cuthbert, and was still living in 1611, with her sons Richard Freeston (who had a son George) and Nathaniel Cuthbert.

III. EDWARD HUTCHINSON, the fifth and youngest son, and probably youngest child, of John Hutchinson, Mayor of Lincoln, was born about the year 1564, in the parish of St. Mary le Wigford in that city. Unfortunately, although the Marriage and Burial Registers of that parish commence as early as 1562, the Baptismal Register previous to 1621 is not now in existence, or is, at least, missing, so that the exact date of his birth cannot be ascertained. In the Corporation Records, however, during the year 1579, there appears an entry substantially as follows :—Edward Hochynson, son of John Hochynson, Alderman, deceased, enrolled apprentice to Edmund Knyght, Alderman and Mercer, of Lincoln, for eight years from the Feast of Pentecost, 19 Elizabeth [say the 27th of May, 1577]. A later record, on the 8th of February, 15$\frac{78}{79}$, says that the said Edmund Knyght came before the Mayor, and assigned over the said apprentice and his indentures to Christopher Dobson, mercer, for the remainder of their term. The object of thus antedating the commencement of the term of apprenticeship is not quite clear, but the probability is that the Mercer's Company required a service of eight years, and that, in order that the term should expire when he became of full age, his master, who was also his brother-in-law, and an alderman as well, conveniently counted the two years preceding the date of the record, during which he had perhaps lived in his family, as a portion of his actual term of service. The fact that he was so soon afterwards transferred to a new master also looks as though this view of the case was correct, and that the object of his friends was to secure his freedom at the usual age of twenty-one. This would establish the date of his birth as above given. He is mentioned in his brother William's Will in 1582–3, and proved that of his mother in 1586, when he must have been of full age. In 1592, he proved (as one of the Executors) the Will of his cousin Christopher (son of his uncle William Hutchinson), and is therein described as of Alford, and a Mercer. On the 10th of July, 1611, he is again mentioned by Margery Neale, daughter of his uncle William, who calls him her cousin, and appoints him Supervisor of her Will. After completing his apprenticeship, he must have removed almost immediately from Lincoln to Alford, and established himself there in business, where he continued until his death. His wife's name was Susan, she being thus called in the Will of Margery Neale just mentioned, who also left legacies to their daughter Hester (her goddaughter) and to their other children indiscriminately. Of her parentage nothing has yet been discovered. Edward Hutchinson left no Will, nor was his estate administered to : at least no record of either exists at the London or Lincoln Registries. This is an extraordinary and unaccountable fact, as it seems almost impossible, from his business, and the character of the matches made by his children, that he was not a man of considerable position and estate. His widow was still living in 1644, when her son John bequeathed her a small legacy. Edward Hutchinson was buried at Alford on the 14th of February, 163$\frac{1}{2}$, (not September, 1631, as is

451

stated in the account in the N. E. H. and G. Register, xix. 14). By his wife Susan he had eleven children, all baptized at Alford. As the account in the Register, just mentioned, omits some of these children, and contains other errors, it will be well to correct it from the following enumeration, the result of a more careful and thorough examination of the Alford Registers.

1. WILLIAM, eldest son and child, of whom hereafter.
2. *Theophilus*, baptized 8 September, 1588. This son is never afterwards heard of, and was not buried at Alford, but probably died in his infancy and was buried elsewhere, perhaps when his parents were on a visit.
3. *Samuel*, baptized 1 November, 1590 (not 1589). His brother John bequeathed him a small legacy in 1644.
4. *" Easter "* (Hester or Esther), baptized 22 July, 1593. Margery Neale, her father's cousin, mentioned her in her Will, in 1611. She was married at Alford on the 7th of October, 1613, to Rev. Thomas Rishworth (incorrectly Rushworth in the Parish Register and elsewhere). In his Will, dated 8 October, 1632, he describes himself as " of Laceby, in the county of Lincoln, minister of the Word of God." He had evidently been married before, as he mentions his daughter Faith Genyson, and her daughter Diana, his grandchild. He also mentions his eldest son Francis, and his son Thomas, who were probably by his first wife. His other children, viz., Susanna, Edward, Margaret and Charles, are all said to be minors, and were therefore the issue of Hester Hutchinson his second wife. These facts will throw light upon Mr. Savage's account of Edward Rishworth, evidently her eldest son. She proved her husband's Will on the 20th of November, 1632, and is no further heard of, unless, as the writer suspects, she re-married one of the name of Harneis, of Grimsby (near Laceby, and where her husband left her a house, &c.), and was the one mentioned in her brother John's Will, in 1644, as his " sister Harnis."
5. *John*, baptized 18 May, 1595 (not 1598). He was also of Alford, and described himself in his Will, dated 7 June, 1644, as a Woollen Draper. In the Alford Register, under date of 1 October, 1618, is recorded the marriage of John Hutchinson and Elizabeth Woodthorpe, who evidently had a son William baptized there 17 October, 1619. It is possible that this was John Hutchinson, son of Edward, but more probable that it was one of that name (of whom there were several) belonging to the other branch of the family. Christopher Hutchinson, certainly of the family of Edward's brother William, also had two children baptized at Alford. At all events, neither this Elizabeth nor this son William was buried there. John Hutchinson was married on the 5th of October, 1626, at Little Ponton, near Grantham, in the county of Lincoln, to Bridget, daughter of William Bury, Esq., of Grantham (by his wife Emme, daughter of John Dryden, Esq., of Canons Ashby, in the county of Northampton), and sister of Sir William Bury, Kt. She was baptized at Grantham, 1 August, 1602, and was, as will be seen hereafter, own cousin to the wife of her husband's brother, William Hutchinson. John Hutchinson was buried at Alford on the 20th of June, 1644. His wife Bridget survived him, and remained his widow, nearly 45 years. She

made her Will on the 26th of July, 1671, but it was not proved until some months after her death. She was buried at Alford on the 14th of March, 1688–9. This old Will was probably afterwards discovered, uncancelled, and, as she left no other, necessarily admitted to Probate. John and Bridget Hutchinson had ten children, all baptized at Alford, viz. : 1. William, baptized 1 February, 1627–8, and living in 1671, but apparently dead before 1696 ; 2. Edward, baptized 16 August, 1629, whose Will was dated the 19th of September, and proved the 16th of December, 1670, in which he described himself as of Alford and a " Gentleman," and he evidently died without issue and was probably buried at Alford between those dates, but there is a *hiatus* in the Parish Register including that period ; 3. Elizabeth, baptized 8 July, 1631, married at Alford 14 March, 16$\frac{48}{50}$, to William Waite of Spilsby, and living in 1671, with issue, one of whom, John, was still living in 1696 ; 4. John, baptized the 6th and buried at Alford the 10th of February, 1633–4 ; 5. John (the second), baptized 29 January, 1634–5, and buried at Alford the 2d of July, 1641 ; 6. Susanna, baptized 25 November, 1636, married about 1660 to Jeremiah Briggs, and living 1671 with issue, one of whom, Jeremiah, was still living in1696 ; 7. Anne, baptized 29 November, 1638, married in 1671 to William Wood, and still living in 1696 ; 8. Richard, baptized 24 April, 1640, and living in 1696 ; 9. Emme, baptized 4 February, 1641–2, and living unmarried in 1696 ; 10. Samuel, baptized 25 February, 1643–4 ; he became a man of considerable note at Boston, in Lincolnshire, of which borough he was an Alderman and twice Mayor : he died during his second Mayoralty, on the 2d of April, 1696, leaving issue by Catharine his wife (who died on the 16th of December following), three sons, Stephen, Edward and Samuel, and two daughters, Mary and Bridget, having had besides six other children who died young, viz., Samuel, William, John, Catharine, Samuel and Richard. These particulars are confirmed by an old broken tablet, which the writer disentombed from the sepulchral depths of the organ loft in Boston church, and a portion of the shield and crest, by which the tablet had been once surmounted, he found doing duty as an ornament in a neighboring garden. Stephen Hutchinson, the eldest surviving son of the Mayor, proved his father's Will, in 1696; and by his wife Elizabeth had several children, two of whom, Samuel and Stephen, were living at their grandfather's death. Mr. Bury Hutchinson, now an eminent barrister in London, is doubtless a direct descendant of this line.

6. *Richard*, baptized 3 January, 1597–8. There is nothing to show that he ever went to New England, although it is certain that he made investments there. He and his wife are mentioned in his brother John's Will, 7 June, 1614, as then living in London. His own Will was made on the 4th of November, 1669, in which he describes himself as " Citizen and Ironmonger of London." The writer also discovered, in the Bodleian Library at Oxford, a list of autograph signatures, of the date of 1651, supposed to be the names of subscribers to a subsidy of £90.000 per month, for six months, ordered by the Parliament to provide means for the payment of its forces. The members of the various London com-

panies appear to have subscribed liberally to this subsidy, and among the Ironmongers occur the names of Edward and Richard Hutchinson. (We subjoin a fac-simile* of the signature of the latter, by which his identity with the one of the name who appears in the early New England records may perhaps be determined.) The only reference in his Will to New England is as follows :—" To my son William Hutchinson and his heirs, my houses, lands, saw-mill, and all other my estate real and personal, debts, credits, and stock, whatsoever, in New England, which I have not, by deed or otherwise, heretofore conveyed, or settled upon my son Eliakim ; and more to William, £200, in goods sent this year for my own account." This Will was proved on the 11th of April, 1670, and he probably died shortly before that date. His widow, Mary, was then living, but has been no further traced. His sons, according to his own statement, all living at the date of his Will, were as follows : 1. Edward, named as the eldest son, who inherited his father's lands in the counties of Norfolk and Lincoln, as well as in Ireland, being apparently already in possession of the latter ; 2. Samuel ; 3. Jonathan ; 4. Ezekiel ; 5. William, above mentioned, who was not 24 years of age at the date of the Will ; 6. Eliakim, also above mentioned, who was one of the Executors of his father's Will, but did not act, being then probably in New England. The Will also mentions four daughters, three of whom were married, and two apparently then living. The first named was the wife of William Puckle, the second of Bartholomew Soames, and the third of Peter Grey. These sons-in-law were all then living. (The name of the second, according to Wotton, was Susan, and her husband was a Woollen Draper of London, the seventh son of Sir William Soame, Kt. He was afterwards of Little Thurlow, in the county of Suffolk, and by his wife Susan Hutchinson had five sons and three daughters.) The fourth and youngest daughter of Richard Hutchinson was named Anne, to whom her father bequeathed £1000 (equivalent to more than £5000 now) on condition that she married with her mother's approval. There is little doubt that the present Earl of Donoughmore descended, through the female line, from this Richard Hutchinson and his eldest son Edward, who was probably living in Ireland at his father's death.

7. *Susanna*, baptized 25 November, 1599, and buried at Alford 5 August, 1601.

8. *Susanna* (the second), baptized 9 August, 1601, and married at Alford 21 November, 1623, to Augustine *Storre*. Such is the orthography in the Alford Register, though the name seems to have subsequently undergone many variations, terminating in *Story*. She is mentioned in her brother John's Will, 1644, as his " sister *Stor*."

9. *Anne*, baptized 12 June, 1603, of whom nothing more has been

---

*

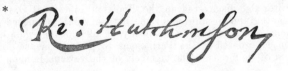

learned, unless she be the one mentioned in her brother John's Will as his "sister Levitt." Ralph Levet was a witness to the Will.

10. *Mary*, baptized 22 December, 1605. She is mentioned in her brother John's Will, 1644, as his "sister Whelwright." He further recites that he was indebted to his brother Wheelwright, by bond, for lands in Croft and Mumby (in Lincolnshire) purchased from him, and directs that the same shall be sold, and he be paid.

11. *Edward*, baptized 20 December, 1607. If he went to New England, he certainly returned before or in 1644, as he was one of the witnesses to his brother John's Will. It was doubtless he who subscribed to the subsidy in 1651, heretofore mentioned, when he was a member of the Ironmonger's Company, and probably in business in London. Both he and his wife are mentioned in his brother Richard's Will, in 1669, as still living, and probably in England, as he bequeathed to them £10, in cloth for mourning.

We now return to the direct New England line.

IV.   WILLIAM HUTCHINSON, eldest son of Edward and Susan, and subsequently the early emigrant, was baptized at Alford on the 14th of August, 1586, and evidently resided there until the time of his emigration. In the Parish Register his name occurs as Church Warden in the year 1620–1, and there is no further record of him or his family after the baptism of his youngest child in November, 1633. By his wife *Anne* (of whom hereafter) he had fourteen children, who were all baptized at Alford, and in the following order, viz. :—

1. *Edward*, 28 May, 1613.
2. *Susanna*, 4 September, 1614 : buried at Alford 8 September, 1630.
3. *Richard*, 8 December, 1615.
4. *Faith*, 14 August, 1617.
5. *Bridget*, 15 January, $16\frac{18}{19}$.
6. *Francis*, 24 December, 1620.
7. *Elizabeth*, 17 February, 1621–2 : buried at Alford 4 October, 1630.
8. *William*, 22 June, 1623 : evidently died young, but his burial is not recorded in the Alford Register.
9. *Samuel*, 17 December, 1624.
10. *Anne* (not Anna), 5 May, 1626.
11. *Mary* (not Maria), 22 February, 1627–8.
12. *Katherine*, 7 February, $16\frac{29}{30}$.
13. *William* (the second), 28 September, 1631.
14. *Susanna* (the second), 15 November, 1633.

The subsequent history of this family belongs to New England, and the writer will not trench upon the peculiar province of his brother antiquarians at home, but bring his present labors to a close by disposing finally of the doubts and difficulties that have hitherto surrounded the case of the famous *Ann Hutchinson*, wife of William, and mother of the children last named.

Governor Hutchinson's traditional reminiscences were mainly correct, her maiden name being Anne *Marbury* (not Marvury), and her father, eventually, a clergyman. Those, however, who have since interpolated "Edward," as the christian name of her father, must

455

have done so from pure conjecture, and no one has attempted to produce any authority for the assertion.

As the case possesses considerable interest and importance, the writer will perhaps be pardoned if he produces his evidences, and narrates the series of investigations by which he is now able to establish the conclusion to which he has arrived.

While examining some time ago the Parish Registers of Alford, in Lincolnshire, he took, among other extracts, the baptisms of twelve and the burials of four children, whose father's name was at first recorded simply as "Francis Marbury," but subsequently with the affix of " Gentleman." These entries extended over a period of nearly twenty years, the first date being 12 September, 1585, and the last 20 January, 1604–5. The names of these children were John, Francis, Erasmus, Anthony, "Jeremuth" (at first supposed to mean Jeremiah, a conclusion subsequently most joyfully abandoned), Daniel, Susanna, Mary, Elizabeth, Bridget, "Emme" (not Emma), and *Anne*. This last name, the time of her baptism, and the place where it occurred, being the birth-place also of William Hutchinson, naturally suggested the idea that she was the Anne Marbury who subsequently became his wife. The statement, however, of Governor Hutchinson, that her father was a clergyman, while the father of these children was distinctly and repeatedly described as a " gentleman," militated against this presumption, and the notes taken were put carefully away for future investigation. On returning to London, the Marbury pedigrees at the College of Arms were searched, but without success, and, the few Marbury Wills at the London and Lincoln Registries being equally silent, the notes were again laid aside. Afterwards, while making a protracted and thorough examination of the matriculation Registers at Oxford, the writer came suddenly upon the name of Erasmus Marbury, who was described as the son of a clergyman, and born in Lincolnshire. The date of the matriculation was the 12th of April, 1616, and the age given as nineteen years, i. e. on the last birth-day. On referring to the Alford notes, the baptism of Erasmus Marbury was found to have taken place on the 15th of February, 1596–7. Proceeding with the examination of the Registers, the matriculation of " Jerimoth " Marbury, at the same college, was found recorded on the 11th of June, 1619. He was also described as the son of a clergyman, born in Lincolnshire, and of the age of eighteen years. Again, the Alford notes were referred to, and the baptism of " Jeremuth " Marbury was found to have occurred on the 31st of March, 1601. After this, the writer could not but feel that he was on the right scent, as it seemed impossible that any other Marbury of Lincolnshire could have also had two sons with these uncommon names (and one so extraordinary as to be, in the writer's experience, unique), the dates of whose births should have so nicely agreed with those in the matriculation Register. There was, however, yet to be solved the mystery attending the different descriptions given of the father. If a clergyman, it was impossible that he could have been called for twenty years in the Alford Register a " gentleman," and it did not seem likely that a man, after gathering about him a family of fifteen children, should, so late in life, enter into holy orders. A further examination at length revealed the name of Anthony Marbury, distinctly described as the son of " Francis Marbury, Clergyman, of St. Martin's, London." He matriculated, also at the same college, on the 20th of October, 1626, at the age of eighteen, which would establish his birth in 1608. This was unsatisfactory, for the Anthony Marbury of Alford was baptized on the 21st of September, 1598, and buried there on the 9th of April, 1601, while the family disappeared from that place early in 1605, before which the baptism of no other Anthony was recorded. There were also several St. Martins in London, and it was impossible to tell which one was meant. A reference, however, to Newcourt's Repertorium soon settled this latter difficulty, for it is there recorded that Francis Marbury was presented to the Rectory of St. Martin Vintry, London, on the 28th of October, 1605, and that his successor was presented, after his death, on the 7th of June, 1611. To search the Registers of St. Martin Vintry was the next step to be taken ; but, alas ! the volumes previous to 1668 were found to be not in existence. All hope of discovering the baptism of the second Anthony, the burial of his parents, and perhaps the marriage of his sister Anne with William Hutchinson, from this source, was destroyed forever. However, another fruitless search at the Herald's College was at last followed by a triumphant success at the British Museum. In a volume of the Harleian MSS. (No. 1550, fol. 174ᵇ), being a copy of "The Visitation of Lincolnshire made in 1564 by Robert Cook, Chester Herald, continued and enlarged with the Visitation made in 1592, by Richard Mundy," is a pedigree of Marbury, in which occurs the name of Francis, to whom two wives are assigned, and by the second of which he had a daughter "*Anne* married to William Hutchinson of Lincoln." Her mother is described as " Bridget, sister of Sir Erasmus Dryden, of the county of Northampton, Kt. and Bart." The Dryden pedigree at Herald's College is also silent as to this match, but in Harleian MSS. No. 1553, fol. 13ᵇ, being Richard Mundy's copy of the Visitations of Northamptonshire of 1566 and 1619, with additions from Mr. Vincent's collections, &c., the name of Bridget Dryden occurs, and she is described as the " wife of Francis Marbury of Aufford [Alford] in the county of Lincoln."

The history of Anne Hutchinson née Marbury was, therefore, complete, and may be succinctly stated as follows, each fact being successively proved by subsequent investigations, and by evidences now in possession of the writer.

Francis Marbury was the third son of William Marbury (or Merbury, as the name is universally spelled in the old records) Esquire, of Grisby, in the parish of Burgh-upon-Bain (some 15 miles N. W. from Alford) in the county of Lincoln. (The arms of Marbury of Lincolnshire, are, Argent on a fess engrailed, gules three garbs of the first.) His mother was Agnes, daughter of John Lenton, Esq. His eldest brother Edward was knighted in 1603, and died in 1605 while High Sheriff of the county, leaving a son George, who was also knighted in 1606. His second brother, William, died without issue. He had also three sisters, Mary, Anne, and Catharine. The latter married Christopher Wentworth, who was living in 1605, and it is perhaps through this connection that the ancestry of Elder Wentworth of New England may yet be traced. (They were married, 19 August, 1583, at St. Peter at Gowts in the city of Lincoln, and he is described in the Register as a " Gentleman.") Francis Marbury first married Elizabeth Moore, by whom he had three daughters, Mary, buried at Alford 29 December, 1585; Susan, baptized at Alford 12 September, 1585, and subsequently married to ——— Twyford, of Shropshire; and Elizabeth, who was buried at Alford 4 June, 1601. This mother doubtless died soon after the birth of her youngest child, Susan, but was not buried at Alford, and Francis Marbury re-married, probably early in the year 1589, Bridget, one of the daughters (and, apparently, from the enumeration in her father's Will dated in 1584, the third) of John Dryden, Esq., of Canons Ashby, in the county of Northampton, by his wife Elizabeth, daughter of Sir John Cope, Kt. Her eldest brother, Erasmus Dryden, was created a Baronet in 1619, but the title became extinct on the death of the 7th Baronet, in 1770. John Dryden, the poet, was grandson of this Sir Erasmus, and, consequently, her grand nephew. Francis and Bridget Marbury had eleven children, all baptized at Alford, in the following order:—1. John, 15 February, 15$\frac{88}{90}$; 2. *Anne*, 20 July, 1591; 3. Bridget, 8 May, 1593, and buried at Alford 15 October, 1598; 4. Francis, 20 October, 1594; 5. Emme, 21 December, 1595; 6. Erasmus, 15 February, 1596–7, who matriculated at Brasenose College, Oxford, 12 April, 1616, aged 19; 7. Anthony, 21 September, 1598, and buried at Alford 9 April, 1601; 8. Bridget (the second), 25 November, 1599; 9. "Jeremuth" (according to the Parish Register, but "Jerimoth" as he wrote his own name in the Subscription Book at Oxford), 31 March, 1601, who matriculated at Brasenose College 11 June, 1619, aged 18; 10. Daniel, 14 September, 1602; 11. Elizabeth, 20 January, 1604–5. At least another son, Anthony (the second) was subsequently born in London, about the year 1608, who also matriculated at Brasenose College 20 October, 1626, then aged 18 years. If there was another daughter, Katharine, who subsequently married Joseph Scott, of Providence, as stated by Governor Hutchinson, she must either have been by the first wife, or else born after the removal to London.

Shortly after the baptism of Elizabeth, the last child baptized at Alford, when he was still described as a "gentleman," and after which, it will be remembered, the name never occurs again in the Alford Registers, Francis Marbury must have entered into holy orders, for, on the 28th of October, 1605, he was presented to the Rectory of St. Martin Vintry in the city of London. On the 29th of February, 1607–8, he was also presented to the Rectory of St. Pancras, Soper Lane, which he resigned after about two years, and was presented, on the 15th of January, 1609–10, to the Rectory of St. Margaret, New Fish Street, which he held, in conjunction with St. Martin Vintry, until his death, which probably occurred late in 1610 or early in 1611, as his successor at St. Margaret's was presented, "per mort. Marbury," on the 12th of February, 1610–11. It was probably at St. Martin Vintry that the marriage of William Hutchinson and his daughter Anne took place, but the loss of the early Registers of that church must ever leave this a matter of doubt.

It should be mentioned that Bridget Dryden is distinctly named in her father's Will, and also her sister Emme, who married William Bury, Esq., of Grantham, in Lincolnshire, whose daughter Bridget was subsequently married to John Hutchinson of Alford, brother of William. It is also worthy of notice that the christian names of more than half of the children of Francis and Bridget Marbury correspond with those of her brothers and sisters, after whom they were evidently named.

It will be seen, therefore, that Anne Hutchinson, by both parents, descended from gentle and heraldic families of England. The same cannot, it is to be feared, be said of her husband. While the Heralds were engaged in the Visitation of Lincolnshire, in the year 1634, Thomas Hutchinson, grandson of William Hutchinson, of Lincoln (brother of John, the ancestor of the emigrant), then living at Thedlethorpe in Lincolnshire, having made a good match with the Fairfaxes, presented his pedigree, and claimed the arms of Hutchinson of Yorkshire, but failed to establish his right to their use. The pedigree was retained among the Herald's notes, but on the original (preserved at the College of Arms) are endorsed the following ominous and significant words : "Respited for Proof." The requisite proof was evidently never furnished, nor have the arms ever since been granted or confirmed to any member of the family in this line. As this Thomas Hutchinson was himself born before the death of Edward Hutchinson of Wykeham Abbey, to whom the arms had been of right confirmed in 1581, there could have been no difficulty in establishing a connection with his branch, if any such existed, and the fact that it could not then be accomplished, and has not since been done, is fatal to the claims of the descendants of the two Mayors of Lincoln, including Governor Hutchinson himself, who clearly used the arms, not of right, but solely because they were the only arms of Hutchinson.

On the other hand, the writer may add, in conclusion, that he has successfully traced the descent of Richard Hutchinson, of Salem, another of the early New England emigrants, through the branch in Nottinghamshire, directly to the heraldic family of Yorkshire.

London, England, July, 1866.

KATHARINE MARBURY AND HER FAMILY. (Vol. xix. p. 14, and Vol. xx. p. 366.)—*
In the 19th Vol. page 14, Genealogical and Historical Register, is " a brief genealogy of the Hutchinson family," in which occurs the following : " William Hutchinson m. Ann Marbury (whose father was a minister, says Gov. H., who adds that her sister Katharine m. Joseph Scott, of Providence)."

In Vol. 20, page 366, of the Register, is an elaborate article of great research on the genealogy of the Hutchinson and Marbury families, by Joseph L. Chester, Esq., an eminent antiquarian; from which I extract the following : " If there was another daughter Katharine, who subsequently married Joseph Scott, of Providence, as stated by Gov. Hutchinson, &c."

This raises a question—Was there a Katharine Marbury, sister of Ann Hutchinson? and if so, did she marry *Joseph Scott of Providence*, or *Richard Scott of Providence?*

At first glance, these are questions of small moment—but the arbitrary use of a wrong name, in the early history of families, tends to unsettle the best established genealogies. " Truth is the historian's crown."

Bishop, in his " New England Judged by the Spirit of the Lord," tells us of Katharine Scot, of Providence, who was imprisoned in Boston in 1658, and whipped " Ten Cruel Stripes with a three-fold-corded knotted Whip," for denouncing the cruelty and intolerance of the government to Quakers, and adds, " Some of you knew her father and called him Mr. Marbury. . . . . . She was the mother

*P. 366 is p. 458, this volume.

of many children, and had been married twenty years." We have the authority of Gov. Winthrop, that a sister of Mrs. Hutchinson married a Scott, whom Callender says was Richard.

From the foregoing there would seem but little doubt of the existence of such a woman as Katharine Marbury, and that she was a sister, if Ann Hutchinson.

The first Joseph Scott known in New England (according to Savage) was son of Benjamin, of Braintree, born in 1644, six years after the marriage of Katharine Marbury. The next Joseph Scott was of Newport, admitted a Freeman in 1731, Sheriff of Newport County and Deputy in 1745. The first *Joseph Scott of Providence*, from any thing I can find to the contrary, was the great-grandson of Richard, born in 1697. It is evident Katharine Marbury could not have married a Joseph Scott.

Did she marry Richard Scott? Savage quotes Bishop as authority, that she did; and we have the same authority that Mary Scott, who married Christopher Holder, was daughter of Richard, and Katharine Scott, who received from her father, as her marriage dower, the Island of Patience in Narraganset Bay, the deed of which is recorded in the office of the Secretary of State at Providence.

Mr. Staples, in his Annals of Providence, says: "The first person in Providence who adopted the principles of the Friends, is stated by tradition to be Richard Scott; he was one of the early settlers of the town; at first he joined the Baptists, but he remained with them but a short time. His *wife Catharine* and two daughters, Patience and Mary, were also among the first members of the Friends Society."

The ancient records of the Friends in Newport has this entry: "Katharine Scott, aged about 70 years, the widow of Richard Scott, of Providence. She departed this life in Newport, the 2d of 3d month, 1687." Richard Scott died about 1679. She probably was passing her widowhood with her daughter Hannah, wife of the then Quaker Governor, Walter Clark;—and this leads me to refer to letters of Roger Williams, intimating that the wife of Richard Scott, before her death, had renounced the tenets of the Quakers, and in this connection, a letter of Richard Scott, written about 1676 (see "A New England Fire Brand Quenched"), says of Roger Williams, "I have been *his neighbor* these 38 years." Roger Williams wrote Gov. Winthrop, Oct. 2d, 1660: "*My neighbor*, Mrs. Scot, is come home from England,* and what the whip at Boston could not doe, converse with friends in England, and thear arguments, have in a great measure drawn her from the Quakers, and wholly from their meetings." Subsequently in a letter to Gov. Coddington, Williams says, "Scott was a great entertainer of Quakers against his wife's conscience (intimating that Quakers had become offensive to her), no small persecution—though one of them formerly a sufferer." Although warm friends for a time, it is known that a bitter feud existed between Roger Williams and Richard Scott during the latter part of their lives, hence great allowance should be made for what they wrote in the heat of religious controversy. I would suggest this Query to the Quaker readers of the Register: Would the Society of Friends have made the above record of the death of Katharine Scott at that early day, had she renounced their faith and doctrine?

Cleveland, Ohio, Feb. 13, 1867. MARTIN B. SCOTT.

---

* There must have been some strong motive at this early period of long and uncomfortable voyages, to have induced a woman to leave her family and cross the Atlantic back and forth; may it not have been, to procure some bequest left by her father, or the father of her husband? and may not a will be found at Doctors Commons to confirm the fact?

THE MARBURY FAMILY. Since the publication of my paper on the Hutchinson Family and its connections (Register, xx. 355), I have made some further discoveries [1] respecting the Rev. Francis Marbury, father of Anne Hutchinson. I have found his will, which was proved, not in the Prerogative Court of Canterbury, but in the Consistory Court of London. Unfortunately, it was nuncupative, and therefore gives few particulars. It was made on the 25th of January and proved on the 14th of February, 1610-11. He is described as "Preacher and Parson of St. Martins in the Vintrey, London." He bequeathed to each of his children, "beinge twelve in number," 200 marks. (This would make an aggregate of £1600, no small sum in those days.) To "Susan his eldest daughter," he gave £10 more. His wife, "Mrs. Marbury," was to "keepe all his said children at her owne charges one whole yeare after his decease, yf in the meane time she did not bestowe them in marriage or place them in service." At the end of that year such children as were of age were to have their portions, but could remain with their mother, if they chose, by paying her a proper allowance. The other children were to have their portions as they severally became of age, and in case any of them died during their minority, their portions were to go absolutely to their mother. To his maid servant he gave five marks. The residue of his personal estate he gave to his wife Bridget, whom he appointed sole executrix, and she proved the will.

This is meagre enough, it is true, but we get the important fact that there were no less than *twelve* children then living. In my paper before referred to (pp. 365-6) I enumerated *fourteen* children from the Alford Registers, of whom three were by the first wife. We also know, positively, that there was another son, Anthony (the second), who matriculated at Brasenose College, Oxford, in 1626, aged 18, and was therefore born in 1608, after the family had quitted Alford for London. We are certain, therefore, that there were no less than *fifteen* children.

I may here mention that I have found in the Registers of St. Peter's, Paul's Wharf, London, under date of 9 March, 1613-14, the burial of "Elizabeth, daughter of Mr. Marbury, Preacher, deceased," who was doubtless the second of that name, baptized at Alford, 20 Jan., 1604-5.

Now, of these *fifteen* children that we know of, I have already buried *four* at Alford, viz.: Mary, in 1585; Bridget (the first), in 1598; and Anthony (the first) and Elizabeth (the first), both in 1601. It is clear, therefore, that not only the second Anthony, but certainly one other child, must have been born in London, or there could not have been *twelve* at the date of Mr. Marbury's will.

Here comes in another valuable bit of testimony. Among the papers of the old antiquarian Randall Holme, at the British Museum, I found what appears to be the draft of a letter from him to a person in London, asking the latter to obtain some information about this very family. It is dated 2 July, 1656, and he wants the particulars in behalf of Mr. Stephen Marbury, then of Dublin, who was a son of Francis Marbury (described as a Goldsmith of London, deceased), and grandson of Mr. Marbury, "Parson of Walbrook, in London." (As Mr. Marbury was not connected with the Church of St. Stephen's, Walbrook, it may be well to mention that the stream so named ran through or near the parish of St. Martin's Vintry.)

Randall Holme gives a little sketch of the pedigree of the family, but mentions only the sons Francis (of whom we knew before) and Thomas (who, he says, was a Doctor in London), and three daughters, whose names he does not give, but who married respectively, " —— Twyford, Co. Sa." (this was of course Susan, the eldest daughter), " —— Skynner, of London," and " —— Child, a preacher." Thomas is a new name, and increases the number of children to *sixteen*.

But, what is most interesting, he says that "Parson Marbury" had "*twenty* children," and, as we must undoubtedly add Catharine Scott to the number we have already obtained, we are thus quite able to account for no less than *seventeen*. It is also an interesting fact that Randall Holme names a *Catharine* as one of the daughters of Francis Marbury, the Goldsmith.

As the will states distinctly that Susan was the *eldest* daughter, and as there is no room for the baptism of Catharine at Alford, there can be little doubt, I think, that she was among the number born in London, and must have been less than five years old at her father's death. My former remark in reference to her, quoted by Mr. M. B. Scott in the Register, vol. xxi. p. 180, was not intended to express a doubt as to her [2]

[1] P. 447, this volume.
[2] Pp. 457-458, this volume.
[2] P. 459, this volume.

461

existence, but rather to indicate her proper position in the family record. The statement in her father's will proves that the final suggestion I then made was the correct one.

I shall be happy to send verbatim copies of Mr. Marbury's will and Mr. Randall Holme's letter, &c., if any one cares to have them.

London, 20 *May*, 1867. JOSEPH LEMUEL CHESTER.

RELATIONSHIP OF THE COMBINATION SETTLERS AT EXETER, N. H., IN 1639.

[Communicated by Hon. JOHN WENTWORTH, LL.D., of Chicago, Ill.]

MR. CHESTER, in the October Number of 1866, shows that the signers of the Exeter Combination in 1639 were, many of them, of the same family; and I think, if the subject should be followed up, they would be all of the same neighborhood in England.

Wheelwright's wife was Mary, daughter of Edward and Susanna Hutchinson.

Augustine Storre (sometimes spelled Storr, Storer and Story), who was of the Combination, married Susanna, daughter of the same.

Mr. Chester finds that their sister, Anne Hutchinson, married —— Leavitt. Now Thomas Leavitt was of the Combination. Was he husband or son?

Esther, another sister, married Rev. Thomas Rishworth. Edward Rishworth was of the Combination. And Samuel Hutchinson, a brother to Mesdames Mary Wheelwright, Susanna Storre, Anne Leavitt, and Esther Rishworth, wills property in 1667 to Edward, eldest son of sister Rishworth.

These were all the Hutchinson sisters that there were.

William Hutchinson, another brother, married Anne, daughter of Rev. Francis Marbury.

And this Rev. Francis Marbury had a sister Catherine who married Christopher Wentworth; and from this Wentworth Mr. Chester hopes to trace the genealogy of William Wentworth, another of the Combination.

In the questioned deed from the Indian Sagamores in 1629, the names of Wheelwright, Wentworth, Leavitt and Storr are used. And but one other, viz., Thomas Wite (or Wright), and he was of the Combination. Of the origin of this Wite nothing is known, nor is he heard of after the Combination.

There were but thirty-five men in the Combination, and the origin of most of them is unknown, and many of them left no descendants of record.

462

GENEALOGY OF THE HUTCHINSONS OF SALEM.

[Compiled by Joseph L. Chester, Esq., and communicated by Alcander Hutchinson, Esq.]

[Arms of Hutchinson. Per pale gules and azure, semée of cross-crosslets *or*, a lion rampant argent. Crest, out of a ducal coronet *or*, a cockatrice with wings endorsed azure, beaked, combed, and wattled gules.]

The antiquity of the family of *Hutchinson* in England is very great. Its origin has been assigned to one *Uitonensis*, said to have been a Norwegian, and to have come from Normandy with William the Conqueror. This statement, however, rests upon the barest tradition, and as there are no records or evidences concerning the family for a period of more than two hundred years immediately succeeding the Conquest, it would be impossible, even if it were desirable, to claim that somewhat mythical personage as the founder of the race.

The first positive date that may be relied upon in the history of the family is the 10th Edward I. (1282), when, according to evidences extant about 1640, it was represented by *Barnard Hutchinson*, of Cowlam, in the county of York, and, as he must have been then advanced in life, it is certain that we may now (1867) trace the family back through a period embracing more than six centuries.

The authority for the first six descents rests with Sir Henry St. George, Garter King of Arms, who sometime before his death (which occurred in 1644) prepared a pedigree of the family, which, with subsequent additions, remained in the possession of the successive heirs until the present century, and was printed in the quarto edition of the Life of Col. John Hutchinson, published in 1806. So far as the present writer has been able to investigate that pedigree, he has found it strictly accurate, and it is therefore adopted without hesitation.

The descents, numerically stated, are as follow :—

I. BARNARD HUTCHINSON, of Cowlam, in the County of York, Esq., was living in the year 1282. (Cowlam is a very small parish in the East Riding of Yorkshire, the present population of which does not exceed fifty souls, and which in 1809 numbered only seventeen. As, even as early as 1282, Barnard Hutchinson was denominated Esquire (or "Armiger"), and described as of that place, there can be scarcely a doubt that he was at that time the proprietor of the entire parish, which contains an area of 2,036 acres, and that the population was composed solely of his own family and retainers.) His wife is only described as the daughter of John Boyvill, Esq. This name is that of one of the best and oldest families of Yorkshire. They had issue :

1. *John* (of whom hereafter).
2. Robert, whose wife was of the family of Newcomen, of Saltfleetby, in the county of Lincoln, one of the most ancient and respectable families of that county.
3. Mary, who married William Sutton, described in the St. George pedigree as of "Wassenbroughe." As there is no place of this name in Yorkshire, I have no doubt it means Washingborough, a small town a few miles from the city of Lincoln, and the ancient seat of the Suttons.

   It is fair to presume that by these last two matches the Hutchinsons were introduced into Lincolnshire, where they afterwards became very numerous.

II. JOHN HUTCHINSON (probably the eldest son and heir of Barnard, and also of Cowlam, although St George omitted to state either fact in his pedigree). He married Edith, daughter of William Wouldbie, of Wouldbie. I have searched the oldest Gazetteers in vain for this place. It was doubtless the name of a manor, or lordship, that has long since lost its identity. Its locality may have been in Yorkshire, but the orthography more closely resembles that of Lincolnshire. The family was doubtless a good one, as no one but a landed proprietor would have styled himself, or been called, Wouldbie of Wouldbie. Their issue were—

1. *James* (of whom hereafter).
2. Barbara, who married Lewis Ashton, of Spalding, Esq. There is no place of this name in Yorkshire, and this doubtless was Spalding in Lincolnshire, where the Ashtons remained until at least as late as the end of the 16th century, and one always described in the Parish Registers as "Esquires" or "Gentlemen."

464

3. Julia, who married Allyne Bruxbie of Shobie, Esquire. "Sho-bie" was also probably the name of a manor, whose locality it is impossible to identify at the present day.

4. Margaret, who married William Champernowne, Esq. Cham-pernowne is almost purely a Devonshire name, and it is pro-bable that through this match the Hutchinsons were intro-duced into that county.

III. JAMES HUTCHINSON, of Cowlam, only son and heir of John. He married Ursula, daughter of Mr. Gregory, of Nafferton, in the county of York, a place in the immediate vicinity of Cowlam. The absence of the christian name of her father is somewhat redeemed by the prefix " Mr." which in those days, although usually indicating a rank just below that described by the words " Esquire," or " Gentle-man," was never applied to one beneath the standing of a Yeoman. The issue of this marriage were—

1. *William* (of whom hereafter).

2. John, distinctly named as the second son, who married a daugh-ter of John Conyers, Esq.

3. Barbara, who married John Hathorne, of " Cransweke," Esq. This place was doubtless Cranswick, only a few miles from Cowlam.

4. A second daughter, whose christian name is not mentioned, who married John Ocam, Esq.

5. Eleanor, who married Thomas Brown, Esq.

IV. WILLIAM HUTCHINSON, of Cowlam, Esq., eldest son and heir of James. He married Anne, daughter of William Bennet, of Theckley, Esq. This place is probably that now called Thackley, in the West Riding of Yorkshire. Their issue were—

1. *Anthony* (of whom hereafter).

2. Oliver, who married a daughter of John Tindall, Esq.

3. Mary, who married Jervas Abtoste (probably Abtofte).

4. Alice, who married William English.

V. ANTHONY HUTCHINSON, of Cowlam, Esq., eldest son and heir of William. He had two wives. His first was Judith, daughter of Thomas Crosland, Esq., by whom he apparently had no issue. His second wife was Isabel, daughter of Robert Harvie (or Harvie Esq.), by whom he had issue as follows—

1. William.

2. *Thomas* (of whom hereafter).

3. John.

4. Richard (supposed by St. George to have gone to Ireland).

5. Leonards.

6. Edmond.

7. Francis.

8. Andrew.

Before proceeding with the line of descent of the family whose his-tory we are immediately pursuing, and which is through Thomas, the second son of Anthony last named, it will be well to trace briefly the subsequent history of the direct line, through William, last named, the eldest son and heir of Anthony, who succeeded to Cowlam. Ac-cording to St. George, he married Bridget, daughter of William Cake, of West Harlton, Esq., and had issue three daughters, viz. : 1st, Gri-zell, who married John Reeps, Esq.; 2d, Joyce, who married Thomas

465

Beed ; and 3d, Isabel, who married Thomas Cooke. He had also a son William, who succeeded to Cowlam, and married Ann, daughter of Henry Layborne, by whom he had issue two daughters, the eldest of whom married John Eplethwatt (? Applethwait), and the youngest Richard Garret ; also a son, William Hutchinson, who married a daughter of Mr. Dalton, of Kirby-over-Carr, in the county of York. This last William is described by St. George as of Wykeham Abbey, in the county of York. The St. George pedigree ends here, and leaves us to suppose that this William was the founder of the Wykeham Abbey branch of the family. This presumption I think there is good reason to doubt.

The absence of dates in the St. George pedigree deteriorates greatly from its value, but this want is relieved to a great extent by the dates which I have been able to affix to the corresponding generations in other branches of the family.

On the 4th of June, 1581, according to the record at the Herald's College, there was a confirmation of Arms to " Edward Hochinson, of Wyckham in the countie of York, Esquire, sonne and heire of Richard Hochinson." This sufficiently establishes the parentage of Edward Hutchinson, whose father was, I suspect, the Richard Hutchinson, son of Anthony last named, whom St. George supposes to have gone to Ireland. All the pedigrees of the Wykeham branch commence with this Edward Hutchinson, and if his father Richard is mentioned, his name only is given. It is fair, therefore, to presume that Edward was the first proprietor, either by purchase or otherwise, of' the Wykeham Abbey estate, and that on his accession thereto he took occasion to have the ancient arms of the family confirmed to him.

The fact that this was a *confirmation*, and not a *grant*, of arms, of itself proves that the arms had been borne by the family from time immemorial, and thus places it among the oldest Heraldic families in Yorkshire and the Kingdom. The arms thus confirmed were those since and still borne by the direct descendants of the Yorkshire line, and it is scarcely necessary to add, that those who cannot show such descent have no right whatever to bear them.

An engraving and description of the arms are prefixed to this article.

Returning to the branch in which we are immediately interested, the next in descent was—

VI. THOMAS HUTCHINSON, Esquire, who was the second son of Anthony by his second wife Isabel. He became by purchase, sometime in the reign of Henry VIII., proprietor of the principal portion of the township of Owthorpe, in the county of Nottingham, the remaining portion of which, with other lordships and manors in the same vicinity, afterwards came into the possession of his descendants. He owned also a considerable estate at Cropwell Butler, a few miles northward, and another at Colston Bassett, a few miles eastward from Owthorpe. He appears also to have had property at Tollerton, and at Ruddington, both in the vicinity of, and westward from Owthorpe. The lordship of Owthorpe alone contained 1600 acres of land.

Although in the St. George pedigree this Thomas is described as of Owthorpe, his actual residence, and that of the three succeeding generations, was at Cropwell Butler. It was Sir Thomas Hutchinson, the fourth in direct descent, who first built and occupied the mansion at Owthorpe, of which, as well as of that at Cropwell Butler, no trace remains at the present day.

Unfortunately, the Parish Registers of Cropwell Butler prior to the year 1684 were long since destroyed. These of Owthorpe are also missing prior to the year 1731. No facts in reference to the family can therefore be obtained from these sources, and the chief authorities from which the particulars in this statement are drawn, are Thoroton's History of Nottinghamshire, the Life of Col. John Hutchinson by his widow, and the wills of some members of the family.

This Thomas Hutchinson is said by St. George to have married the daughter and heir of Mr. *Drax*, of Kinoulton in the county of Nottingham. This name should undoubtedly be *Drake*, that of a good family in Kinoulton, although not proprietors of the lordship. The precise dates of their deaths cannot be ascertained, as I have been unable to discover the will of either. It is certain, however, that he was living as late as the 9th of October, 1550, on which day he proved the will of his son William. This will is dated on the 11th of the preceding June, and from the fact that the testator does not mention his mother in it, it is probable that she was then dead.

The issue of this marriage were as follows:
1. William.
2. John.
3. *Lawrence* (of whom hereafter).

The St. George pedigree mentions only the first two of these children, but I have discovered abundant evidence to establish the identity of the third. The will of the father, if in existence, or the Parish Registers of Cropwell Butler, would have doubtless at once established the fact, but the other testimony is direct and ample. The omission by St. George is not extraordinary, as his chief object was to trace the descent of the direct representatives living in his time, viz., from the eldest son. He only mentions the name of the second son, with that of his wife, while I have been able to follow that branch to its extinction. It is not strange, therefore, that he omitted the third son altogether, and it is quite probable that there was even a fourth son named Robert.

As, in my opinion, the descendants of this third son are now the only living representatives of this ancient family, it will be well, before proceeding with their history, to follow out and finally dispose of the two elder branches.

The eldest son, William Hutchinson, married a daughter of Mr. Watson, of Hareby in the county of Nottingham. He died in the year 1550, having made his will on the 11th of June in that year, which was proved at York on the 9th of October following. In this will he describes himself as of Owthorpe, where he probably resided on some portion of the family estate. He directs that he shall be buried in the Chancel of Owthorpe, which sufficiently establishes his identity, as the right to burial in that part of the church, at that time, belonged only to the proprietors of the lordship and the incumbents of the parish. The only actual relationship he mentions is that of his father, whom he calls Thomas Hutchinson, and whom he appoints his executor. Besides a few bequests to the church and to the poor of Owthorpe, Cropwell, Colston Bassett, Kinoulton, &c., he only leaves legacies to Lawrence Hutchinson, to Robert Hutchinson's wife and children, and to Edmond Drake's children, the two former being probably his brothers, and the latter a near relative of his mother. He commends his

467

wife and children to the care of his father. It is evident that he died at a comparatively early age, as his two brothers survived him, one 27 and the other 36 years. It is clear also that his widow remarried, and was living with her second husband in 1570, as will appear from the will of her son Thomas, hereafter mentioned; but I have been unable to ascertain the name of her second husband or the date of her death. Her children, by William Hutchinson, were one son and three daughters. The eldest daughter, Jane, married Thomas Ellis, Esq., of Wyham in the county of Lincoln, and a descendant of theirs was created a Baronet in 1660, but the title became extinct in the third generation, 1742. The second daughter, Isabel, married Mr. Smith, of the Monks, near the city of Lincoln. The third daughter, Elizabeth, married Mr. Bonny Eaton, of Greasby Castle, in the county of Nottingham, and was still living in the year 1599. The only son and heir was Thomas Hutchinson, who succeeded to the Owthorpe estates on the death of his grandfather. He married, first, Jane, daughter of Sir George Pierpoint, by whom he had no issue; and secondly, Eleanor, daughter of Sir George Zouch, of Codnor in the county of Derby (by his second wife Helen Lane). By her he had issue one son and one daughter. The latter, Dorothy, married John Warren (or Warring), Esq., of Eastwell in the county of Leicester, and had issue. They were both living in 1599. Thomas Hutchinson made his will on the 26th of Nov., 1570, in which he describes himself as a "Gentleman," and of Owthorpe. He also directs to be buried in the Chancel of Owthorpe. His identification is perfect, as he mentions his mother, his sister Isabel, his brother-in-law Thomas Ellis, his uncle Robert Watson (his mother's brother), his uncle John Hutchinson (and his son Thomas), &c. &c. But what is most important, he also mentions his "Uncle Lawrence Hutchinson." As all the other relationships he mentions are distinctly defined, and abundantly corroborated by other testimony, it is clear that he could have meant by his "Uncle Lawrence Hutchinson," no other than his father's brother. This will was proved at York, on the 12th of June, 1571, by his widow Eleanor, of whom I have been unable to ascertain anything further, but she evidently died before 1597, as she is not mentioned in her son's will dated in that year. This only son and heir, also named Thomas, was a minor at his father's death. He subsequently married Jane, daughter and co-heir of Henry Sacheverell, Esq., of Ratcliffe-on-Sour, in the county of Nottingham, by his wife Jane, daughter of German Ireton, Esq. (It is related by Mrs. Lucy Hutchinson, that her brother Henry Sacheverell, Esq., who succeeded to the estate of Ratcliffe-on-Sour, left it to her son Sir Thomas Hutchinson, thus cutting off his only daughter who had displeased him by her marriage. Mrs. Hutchinson adds, that Sir Thomas Hutchinson, however, generously shared the bequest with his cousin.) They had also only two children, a son and a daughter. The latter, Jane, married, 1st, Francis Grantham, 2d son of Sir Thomas Grantham, of the Black Moncks, near the city of Lincoln, and had issue, but survived him and remarried a Mr. Poulton. Her father, Thomas Hutchinson, made his will on the 14th of October, 1597, but lived till the 20th of August, 1599, when he added a codicil. His wife Jane was dead at the earlier date, as he directs to be buried near her and his ancestors in the Chancel of Owthorpe. He also describes himself as of Owthorpe, and "Esquire." He leaves his various estates in the towns hitherto mentioned to trustees (one of whom is his uncle Thomas Ellis), to the use of his children during their minority. He mentions his sister Dorothy, his aunt Jane Ellis, his aunt Eaton, and his cousins George and Thomas, sons of his great uncle John Hutchinson. In the codicil he bequeaths £200 to Mrs. Catherine Rogers, whom it had been, and still was his purpose to marry. He must have died shortly after, as his will was proved at York on the 11th of October following. He was succeeded by his only son and heir, Thomas, who was born about the year 1588. After arriving at his majority he built the mansion at Owthorpe, and was the first to take up his residence there as the head of the family, though other members of it had probably resided there before him, and it was customary for all of them to describe themselves as of that place, which was the most considerable possession of the family. He received the honor of knighthood from King Charles I. He married two wives, and had issue by each. His first wife was Margaret, daughter of Sir John Byron, Kt., of Newstead in the county of Nottingham, by his wife Margaret, daughter of Sir William Fitzwilliams, a famous Elizabethan knight. She died about September, 1619, in her 26th year, and was buried at Owthorpe, leaving two sons, John and George ; according to Mrs. Lucy Hutchinson, an elder son had died in childhood. On the 17th of December, 1631, Sir Thomas was again married, at St. Mary's Church, in the city of Nottingham, to Catharine, daughter of Sir John Stanhope, of Elvaston in the county of Derby, by his second wife Catharine, daughter of Thomas Trentham, Esq., of Rochester Priory in the county of Stafford. She was therefore half sister to Philip Stanhope, first Earl of Chesterfield. By her Sir Thomas Hutchinson had one son and two daughters, viz., Charles Stanhope and Isabella. Sir Thomas was a Royalist, and a member of the Parliament of 1643. The course of his two elder sons, which was in direct opposition to his own, so preyed upon his mind that his death was hastened thereby, and he died at London, while Parliament was in session, on the 18th of August, in that year, at the age of 55. He was buried under the Communion Table, in the Church of St. Paul's, Covent Garden. By his will, made only the day before his death, and which consists of only half a dozen lines, he disinherited his two elder sons, and gave all his possessions to his second wife and her issue. She survived him more than half a century, most of which time she passed at the city of Nottingham, living there in great splendor, and finally died in the year 1694, having reached the extraordinary age of 102 years. She was buried by the side of her husband, in the Church of St. Paul's, Covent Garden.

The eldest surviving son of Sir Thomas, who afterwards became the famous Colonel John Hutchinson, was baptized at St. Mary's Church, in the city of Nottingham, on the 18th of September, 1615. His widow and biographer gives the date of his birth, which she also says took place at Nottingham in September, 1616 ; but the Parish Register of St. Mary's distinctly contains the record of his baptism a year earlier. He was married at St. Andrew's, Holborn (London), on the 3d of July, 1638, to Lucy, second daughter of Sir Allen Apsley, Lieutenant of the Tower of London (by his third wife, Lady Lucy, youngest daughter of Sir John St. John, of Lidiard Tregoze in the county of Wilts), who was born in the Tower on the 29th of January,

1619–20. The history of Col. John Hutchinson, and the character of his wife through her biography of her husband, are so well known that I need not dwell upon them. He finally ended his illustrious career as a Government prisoner, at Sandown Castle, on the coast of Kent, on the 11th of September, 1664, and his remains were conveyed to Owthorpe, where they were buried. The period of his wife's death is unknown. Her family has long been extinct in the direct line, but merged into the noble one of Bathurst, who adopted the name of Apsley as their second title.

Col. John Hutchinson left four sons and four daughters, viz. : Thomas and Edward (twins), Lucius, John, Barbara, Lucy, Margaret and Alice (or Adeliza). There was also an earlier son John, who was born on the 6th of September, 1641, and buried at St. Mary's, Nottingham, on the 28th of August, 1647 ; and also an eldest daughter, born in 1642, who died in Nottingham Castle in her 4th year. Of the above, Edward, Lucius and the four daughters, all died without issue. Mrs. Hutchinson speaks of her daughter Orgill, and it is probable that one of the four married a person of that name. The eldest son Thomas, who (with his twin brother Edward) was born at Enfield Chase, in the county of Middlesex, on the 3d of September, 1639, married Jane, daughter of Sir Alexander Ratcliffe, who, with an only infant child, died about a year after her marriage, and her husband remained a widower till his death. The youngest son, John, also married, and had two sons, both of whom mysteriously disappeared, one of whom is said to have sailed for Russia, in command of a ship of war presented by Queen Anne to the Czar Peter, and to have been lost at sea ; while the other is traditionally said to have emigrated to the West Indies or America, where he also perished. At all events, the direct line in descent from Sir Thomas Hutchinson was long since extinct.

The second son of Sir Thomas by his first wife, viz., George Hutchinson, followed the fortunes of his elder brother John, and like him was a Colonel in the army arrayed against the Government, and also like him was disinherited. He married Barbara Apsley, a sister of Mrs. Lucy Hutchinson (his brother's wife), and had two children, one of whom was buried at St. Peter's, Nottingham, on the 22d of December, 1645. The other, named Allan, was baptized at St. Peter's, Nottingham, on the 9th of May, 1647, and died at an early age. Their mother survived her husband, and died in 1694, at the age of 75 years, and thus this branch became extinct.

Of the three children of Sir Thomas Hutchinson by his second wife Lady Catharine Stanhope, the eldest daughter was baptized at St. Mary's, Nottingham, on the 3d of May, 1634, and evidently died unmarried. Isabella, the second daughter, was baptized at St. Mary's on the 9th of September, 1635, and married there the 30th of June, 1656, to Charles Cotton, Esq., of Berisford in the county of Derby. The line was continued by Charles Hutchinson, the youngest child and only surviving son of Sir Thomas, who was baptized at St. Mary's, Nottingham, on the 15th of June, 1637. He was sometime of Willoughby on the Wolds, in the county of Nottingham, but finally of Owthorpe. He married Isabella, daughter and co-heiress of Sir Francis Boteler, of Hatfield-Woodhall, in the county of Hertford, Knight. He died on the 3d of November, 1695. She survived him many years, and died in her 92d year, on the 28th of October, 1728; both were buried at Owthorpe. They had issue seven sons and two daughters. Of these, Charles, Francis, Thomas, Boteler, Stanhope, Francis (2d), and Isabella, all died without issue, and several of them in their father's life time. Elizabeth, who survived her father, married, first, John, Lord Kennedy, eldest son of the Earl of Cassilis, and secondly, John Hamilton, Earl of Ruglen. The youngest son and eventual heir, was Julius Hutchinson, Esq., of Owthorpe and Woodhall (having inherited the latter manor through his mother). He married Betty, daughter of Col. Wm. Norton, of Wellow in Hámpshire, by his wife Elizabeth, daughter and co-heir of Sir Thomas Norton, of Coventry, Baronet. They were both buried at Owthorpe, he on the 10th of March, 1738, and she on the 2d of March, 1752. Their issue was as follows:—Boteler, who was a Colonel of Marines in 1745, and died a bachelor; Charles, who married Anne Hanson, but died without issue; Julius, who was a Fellow of New College, Oxford, and died unmarried the 6th of December, 1758, aged 41; Elizabeth and Lucius, both dead before 1718; Isabella, who married Richard Norton, Esq., of Ixworth Abbey in the county of Suffolk; Thomas, who married Anne, daughter of Sir Walter Wrottesley, Baronet, of Wrottesley in the county of Stafford, and had issue Thomas, Julius, and two daughters, who all died without issue in their father's life time; and Norton, who continued the line. He was a Captain in the East India Company's service, and died in 1781. He had two wives: the first was Elizabeth, daughter of Doctor Peter Waldo, by whom he had an only son, Julius, of whom hereafter. His second wife was Judith Scharon, whom he married in 1764, at Madras, in the East Indies. By her he had two sons and three daughters, viz.: Thomas, who was Vicar of Sabridgworth, Hertfordshire, in 1818; Norton, who was buried at Layer-Breton in the county of Essex; Cassandra, who married George Marshall, of Charing in the county of Kent; Clarissa, who married Walter Hill, of Ross in the county Herford; and Isabella, who married G. Wolfe, Esq., of Battersea in the county of Surrey. The two sons by the second wife died without issue, and the line was continued by the eldest son Julius, above-mentioned, who was sometime a Captain in the East India Company's service, but afterwards became a clergyman, and had the living of Layer-Breton, Essex, where he died and was buried. He inherited the family estates fron his uncle Thomas, and in 1792 sold the manor of Woodhall to the Marquis of Salisbury. The estate of Owthorpe had previously passed from the possession of the family. By his wife Frances he had four sons and seven daughters, viz.: Julius, who was baptized at Ware, in Hertfordshire, on the 7th of June, 1780; Henry, who was baptized at Hatfield, in the same county, on the 15th of December, 1784; Charles, who was buried at Hatfield on the 1st of August, 1786; another Charles, who was born at Sabuse near Amiens in Picardy, on the 15th of February, 1789, and baptized at Hatfield on the 24th of November, 1790; Frances; Cassandra; Mary Ann; Elizabeth; Emma, baptized at Hatfield, on the 3d of April, 1792; Henrietta Mary Clarissa, baptized at Hatfield, on the 1st of August, 1793; and Julia.

It is believed that all the sons died without issue, and thus the direct line from Thomas Hutchinson of Owthorpe (2d son of Anthony and Isabel of Cowlam), through William, his eldest son, became extinct.

It is probable that there are descendants through the female line still living, but the name on the male line has disappeared.

We now return to the second son of (VI.) Thomas Hutchinson, of Owthorpe, by his wife née Drake. This was John Hutchinson, of Bassford, near Nottingham, where he held the manor of Algarthorp, purchased and presented to him by his father. He married Mary, daughter of a Mr. Chamberlain, of whom I have been able to learn nothing further. John Hutchinson was buried at St. Mary's, Nottingham, on the 23d of June, 1586. His wife survived him many years, and dying at an advanced age, was buried at the same place on the 2d of January, 1629–30. They had issue two sons and two daughters. Thomas, the younger son, died at Alexandretta, in Syria, where he was either in business, or attached to the English Consulate. His will is dated on the 16th of July, 1607, and was proved in London on the following March. He left no issue. A daughter was buried at St. Mary's, Nottingham, as appears by her mother's will. The other daughter, Mary, married a Mr. Woolhouse, and was living in 1607, with six children. The eldest son, George Hutchinson, was married at Southwell in the county of Nottingham, on the 9th of June, 1601, to Mrs. Katherine Russell (called *Rowsell* in the Parish Register, and described as a Gentlewoman). They both died in the same year, while residing in the city of Nottingham. He died the 30th of March, and was buried at St. Mary's, in that city, on the 1st of April, 1635, and she was buried at the same place on the following 14th of November. A monumental inscription preserved by Thoroton, but not now extant, gives his age as 59 years and 3 months. They had issue one son and three daughters, all of whom were baptized at Southwell, in the county of Nottingham, viz. : John, on the 22d of April, 1602 ; Mary, on the 30th of October, 1603 ; Anne, on the 14th of July, 1605 ; and Katherine, on the 29th of June, 1608. Of Mary and Katherine I have been able to learn nothing further. Anne married a Mr. John Stanton before 1630, and both were living in 1635. John Hutchinson, the only son, was married at Basford on the 25th of September, 1620, to Susanna Jenison. He was then only about 18 years and 6 months old, and I suspect that the marriage was an unfortunate one. Mrs. Lucy Hutchinson speaks of the "unworthy branch" of the family at Basford, and must have alluded to this John, of whom she was a contemporary. They had no issue. His wife was buried at St. Peter's in the city of Nottingham, on the 29th of May, 1665. He survived her, and was buried at the same place on the 9th of May, 1677. By his will he directed the Basford estate to be sold, and the produce thereof to be given to strangers. This would indicate that his own immediate relations were all dead, or else that there were no friendly relations between them. At all events, at his death, the line through the second son of Thomas Hutchinson of Owthorpe (2d son of Anthony and Isabel of Cowlam) became extinct.

Returning now to the line of descent of the present family of Hutchinson, the next in succession was

VII. Lawrence Hutchinson, who was a younger, and probably the third son of Thomas Hutchinson, Esq., of Owthorpe, by his wife née Drake. His identity would be sufficiently established by the fact that Thomas Hutchinson, son of William, the eldest son of Thomas of Owthorpe, distinctly names him as his uncle, in precisely the same manner that he names his father's other brother, John, as well as a brother of his mother's. The connection is also confirmed by the fact that his own son, in his will, calls the then living Thomas Hutchinson of Owthorpe his cousin, exactly as he calls others cousins known otherwise to have borne that relation. Lawrence Hutchinson resided, at least at the time of his death, at Tollerton (formerly called Tolaston), a town midway between Owthorpe and the city of Nottingham, about four miles from each. His wife's name was Isabel, who was living at the time of his death, which occurred in the year 1577, as his will was dated on the 21st of July, and proved (at York) on the 9th of October in that year. They had issue :

1. Robert.
2. Thomas (of whom hereafter).
3. Agnes.
4. Richard.
5. William.

They were all living at their father's death, and are mentioned in this order in his will. It is therefore probable that

VIII. Thomas Hutchinson was their second son. He resided at the city of Newark, in the county of Nottingham. The Parish Registers of Newark now in existence do not commence until the year 1600, so that no information can be derived from that source; but, from the fact that in his will he directs to be buried in the church, and leaves what was then a considerable legacy to the poor of the parish, it may be taken for granted that he was a person in good circumstances. He died in the year 1598, his will being proved on the 11th of May in that year, and dated the preceding 1st of March. He appointed as supervisors of his will, his "cousin," Mr. Thomas Hutchinson, of Owthorpe, "Gentleman," and his cousin "Mr. Thomas Ellis, of Gray's Inn, London," thus establishing his connection with the elder branch of the family. The name of his wife I have not been able to ascertain, but she evidently died before him. Their issue were—

1. William, who died during his father's life-time. He had been married, and had children, but, from his father's will, it is doubtful if any of them were living at its date.
2. Thomas (of whom hereafter).
3. Joan.

IX. Thomas Hutchinson, only surviving son and heir of Thomas, of Newark. He inherited his father's property at Newark, but removed his residence to Arnold, near the city of Nottingham, somewhere between the years 1601 and 1605. His wife's name was Alice, and she survived her husband. He was buried at Arnold, on the 17th of August, 1618 ; having made his will on the previous 4th of March. In it he names all his children, and leaves them moderate legacies. Most of his children were doubtless born at Newark, before his removal to Arnold, and before the date when the Parish Registers of that place commence. From the manner in which they are mentioned in his will, and from other evidence, it is probable that their births occurred in the following order :

1. John, who was his father's executor, and proved his will, and was therefore of full age at that date. He was also of Arnold, and had two wives. By the first one, named Ann, who was

473

buried at Arnold on the 2d of September, 1627, he had one son and two daughters, all baptized at Arnold, viz.: Francis, on the 17th of November, 1620 ; Mary, on the 3d of November, 1622; and Isabel, on the 8th of May, 1625. On the 5th of May, 1628, he married, 2dly, Jane Melford, who lived but little more than a year, and was buried at Arnold on the 8th of July, 1629. By her he had one son, Gervase (or Jarvis), who was baptized on the 3d of July, 1629, and was buried there on the 15th of March, 1647.

2. Isabel, who was living at her father's death, and then the wife of Adam Barker.

3. Humphrey, living in 1618, and of full age.

4. Elizabeth, also living at her father's death, and of full age.

5. Robert, who was baptized at Newark on the 6th of September, 1601. He was also of Arnold. By his wife Margaret, who survived him, he had an only daughter, Joan, who was baptized at Arnold on the 23d of March, 1628, and he was buried there on the following 25th of April. The witnesses to his will, which was made only two days before his death, were his brother John, and Alice Hutchinson, doubtless the wife of his brother Richard.

6. *Richard* (of whom hereafter).

7. Thomas, who was baptized at Arnold on the 16th of June, 1605.

According to their father's will, neither of the three last named sons was of age at its date in 1618; and as we have the dates of baptism of both Robert and Thomas, between which there was a period of less than four years, it is clear that

X. RICHARD HUTCHINSON, the fourth son and sixth child of Thomas and Alice, was born about 1602 or 1603. His baptism is not recorded in the Parish Registers either at Newark or at Arnold, and probably took place elsewhere, after his parents had quitted the former place, and before they finally settled at the latter. Accident may some day reveal the exact spot, but any search for the record would be useless. He was married at Cotgrave in the county of Nottingham, on the 7th day of December, 1627, to Alice Bosworth. This name does not again occur in the Cotgrave Registers, but the family of Bosworth resided at that time at Southwell, in the same county. She was probably the daughter of Mr. Joseph Bosworth, who was in some way connected with the celebrated collegiate church of Southwell, otherwise known as the Cathedral Church of Nottinghamshire. This presumption is strengthened by the fact that her first son was named Joseph, a new christian name in the Hutchinson family, and doubtless adopted in honor of her father. In about the year 1635, Richard Hutchinson, who appears to have resided at North Muskham in the county of Nottingham, emigrated to New England with his family, and settled in the town of Salem, then in the Colony and now in the State of Massachusetts.

What confirms the presumption that Richard was born in 1602, and reduces it to a certainty, is his deposition, taken in court in June, 1660, on file in the County Court's office, of Salem, Mass., viz.: June, 1660—Cromwell versus Ruck—"The testimony of Richard Hutchinson, aged about fifty eagght." The earliest mention made of him is found in the Town Records of Salem, Mass., in 1636, about a year

474

after his arrival in the Colony, when the town of Salem made him a grant of land ; and in 1637, " It is ordered that Richard Hutchinson shall have twenty acres more than the grant already mentioned in the book of calculations, provided he will set up a plough ; " and it is asserted that at that time there were but 37 ploughs in the entire colony. In 1654, he had another parcel of land granted him, and in 1660 still another. This land, according to the deeds, was situated in the vicinity of " Hathorn's Hill," Beaver Dam brook, now called Beaver brook, which runs through Middleton into the Ipswich river.

His first wife Alice Bosworth, whom he married in England, was a member of the 1st Church of Danvers in 1636, and Richard joined in 1647, under the administration of the Rev. Francis Higginson. All of his children, seven in number, were by his first wife, four of whom were born in England. The date of Alice's death has not been ascertained. His second wife was Susannah, widow of Samuel Archer. He married her in October, 1668 ; she died the 26th of November, 1674. He married, thirdly, Sarah, widow of James Standish, of whose estate Richard was appointed administrator, April 1, 1679. Richard's will was dated January 19, 1679, and proved September 26, 1682. He was consequently 80 years of age at his decease. He mentions in his will his children Joseph, Abigail, Hannah ; his grandchildren Bethiah Hutchinson and Sarah Hadlock ; and his sons-in-law Anthony Ashby, Daniel Boardman, Nathaniel Putnam, Thomas Hale and James Hadlock ; and " lastly, I make my son *Joseph Hutchinson*, sole executor to this my last will and testament, enjoyning him, his heirs and assigns, to pay all my debts and legacies, and doe freely give unto him, his heirs or assigns, *Peter*, my servant, and all the use of my estate, both movable and imovable. This is my last will and testament made by me this 19th day of January in ye year of our Lord 1679." His children by his first wife Alice Bosworth, born in England before his emigration, were as follows :

1. Alice, baptized at North Muskham in the county of Nottingham, on the 27th of Sept., 1628, and buried there in the same year.
2. Elizabeth, baptized at Arnold (her grandfather's residence), on the 30th of August, 1629. She was a member of the First Church in Danvers, and married Nathaniel Putnam, deacon of said church, and a man of much influence in the church and town. She died in Danvers, June 24, 1688–9.
3. Mary, baptized at North Muskham, on the 28th of Dec., 1630. She was married 26th of May, 1657, to Thomas Hale of Newbury, Mass., and died October 22, 1688.
4. Rebecca, born in England about 1632. She married Mr. James Hadlock, of Salem, Mass., May, 1658.
5. *Joseph* (of whom hereafter).

It is uncertain whether the last two children were born and baptized at North Muskham, or at some other place where their parents may have temporarily resided previous to their emigration to New England. The Parish Registers of North Muskham, prior to the year 1700, are not in existence, and the dates already given were obtained from the Transcripts in the Bishop's Registry at York. These Transcripts are also very imperfect, and those for the years 1631 to 1635 are missing entirely. The probability is, however, that these two children were also born and baptized at North Muskham. Richard and Alice Hutchinson, after their arrival in New England, had three other children, viz. :

6. Abigail, baptized 25th of December, 1636, at Salem, Mass. She subsequently married Mr. Anthony Ashby, of Salem.
7. Hannah, baptized at Salem, on the 20th June, 1639. She was afterwards married, on the 12th of April, 1662, to Mr. Daniel Boardman, of Ipswich, Mass.
8. John, born May, 1643. He married, July, 1672, Sarah, daughter of John and Rebecca Putnam, by whom he had a daughter, subsequently married to Mr. Whipple. The Inventory of John's estate was taken August 2d, 1676.

The direct American line was continued by

XI. JOSEPH HUTCHINSON, only surviving son of Richard Hutchinson by his first wife Alice Bosworth. He was born in England, probably at North Muskham in the county of Nottingham, in the year 1633, according to his deposition taken in court, June, 1660, aged 27, and he emigrated with his father to New England. He settled upon a portion of his father's estate, which was conveyed to him by deed of gift during his father's lifetime, viz., March 16, 1666. It appears that he had also a grant of land from the town of Salem. He gave to his son Joseph, on the 1st of July, 1703, 54 acres of upland on the west side of Ipswich river, near Cromwell's meadow ; and on the 3d of May, 1694, he gave his son John 50 acres of land. In 1673, he was one of the Committee for building a parsonage at Danvers, and he gave the land whereon the building was erected. He was one of the signers of a petition, offered to the General Court on the 20th of February, 1689, to the effect that Salem might become a town by itself, for at that time it was merely "Salem village." He had two wives ; the name of the first has not been preserved, but by her he had five children, the first four of whom were all baptized together on the 26th of March, 1666, viz. :

1. Abigail, baptized at 1st Church Sept. 26, 1666, died young.
2. Bethiah,   "   "   "   " " "   1690.
3. *Joseph* (of whom hereafter).
4. John, baptized at 1st Church Sept. 26, 1666, married Mary Gouls, on the 7th of May, 1694, died in 1746.
5. Benjamin, baptized at 1st Church Sept. 26, 1666 ; he married, first, Jane Phillips, May 7, 1699 ; she died in 1711. He married, secondly, Abigail Foster, June 26, 1714–15. Benjamin became the adopted son of Nathaniel Ingersoll, Esq., of Danvers.

Joseph married, secondly, Lydia, widow of Mr. Joseph Small, 28 February, 1678. Her maiden name was Buxton, and she was admitted into the 1st Church at Danvers, April 27, 1690. By her he had six children, viz. :

6. Abigail, born January 14, 1679.
7. Richard, born May 10, 1681. He lived in Danvers till 1738, when he removed with his family to Maine, where a large number of his descendants are still living. In 1720, he sold his estate to James Buxton. He married Rachel Bunce, February 16, 1714.
8. Samuel, born October 9, 1682, died single.

476

9. Ambrose, born June 4, 1684. He was married to Ruth, daughter of Joseph and Lydia Leach. Letters of administration were granted to his widow Ruth and son George, September 26, 1757.
10. Lydia, born Sept. 13, 1685 ; she was married to George, son of Samuel and Mary Nourse, the 29th of April, 1709.
11. Robert, born Nov. 3, 1687. He married, first, Elizabeth, daughter of Jonathan and Lydia Putnam, on the 27th of December, 1711 ; secondly, on the 6th of June, 1717, Sarah Putnam, probably his first wife's sister.

Joseph Hutchinson, the father of these eleven children, left no will, nor has any settlement of his estate as yet been found whereby the date of his death can be ascertained.

He was succeeded by

XII. JOSEPH HUTCHINSON, his eldest son and third child by his first wife, who was baptized with his two elder sisters and younger brother John, on the 26th of September, 1666, in the 1st Church of Danvers. He was received into the church on the 4th of February, 1700. On the 19th of August, 1731, he was chosen a delegate with others to attend a Church Convention at Lynn, to dismiss Mr. Nathaniel Sparhawk, and again on the 10th of January, 1732–3, for the ordination of the Rev. John Warren. He was also one of the Financial Committee of the above named church. He resided on a portion of the estate given to him during his father's lifetime. His will was proved on the 3d of June, 1751. He had two wives. By his first wife Elizabeth, whose surname has not been preserved, but who died 21 December, 1700, aged 36, he had issue as follows :

1. *Joseph* (of whom hereafter).
2. Ruth, born February 26, 1691, living in 1766. She married, Feb. 19, 1713, Josiah, son of John and Hannah Putnam.
3. Bethiah, born December 24, 1693, who married Mr. Benjamin Putnam (son of Benjamin and Sarah), June 9, 1715, and died on the 9th of December, 1726.
4. Ebenezer, born February 20, 1695, and died unmarried.
5. Elizabeth, born February 22, 1696, "   " Feb. 18, 1702.
6. Elisha, born March 14, 1697,   "   " March 1, 1701.
7. Jasper, born January 31, 1698,   "   " February 16, 1701.
8. Elisha (2d), born December 21, 1700. He was married Jan. 12, 1727, to Ginger, daughter of Israel and Sarah Porter. He died in 1728, and left an only son Israel, who was baptized Nov. 12, 1727, at Danvers, Mass. In 1757, he joined a scouting party under Captain Israel Herrick, and explored that part of the country, now included in the State of Maine. In the following year, he was appointed Lieutenant in Capt. Andrew Fuller's company, and fought at Lake George and Ticonderoga ; in 1759, he commanded a provincial company, and was with General Wolfe when he scaled the heights of Abraham, and routed the French troops under Montcalm. When the news of the battle of Lexington reached Danvers, he hastened to the scene of action, at the head of a company of 60 Minute Men, and meeting the enemy on their retreat, he engaged them. He immediately after received a Lieutenant Colonel's commission in Colonel Mansfield's regi-

ment, and shortly afterwards was made a Colonel, which commission he held during the war of Independence. During the same year he enlisted 832 men. He was at the siege of Boston, and on the evacuation of that town by the enemy, he occupied Fort Hill. He remained there and at Dorchester Heights until October, when he was ordered to New York. He afterwards commanded Forts Lee and Washington. He crossed the Delaware with Washington in his retreat through New Jersey. On his return home, at the conclusion of the war, he was elected to the State Legislature, which office with that of Councillor he filled for 21 years. He had two wives : by his first wife, Anne Cue, of Wenham, whom he married in December, 1747, he had issue three daughters, and a son Elisha ; this son died unmarried. He married, secondly, Mehitable, widow of Archilaus Putnam, whose maiden name has not been ascertained ; by her he had a son Israel, born 6 September, 1760, who married December 15, 1785, Susannah, daughter of William and Abigail Trask, of Beverly, by whom he had three daughters and a son, the latter dying without issue. By his second wife, Eunice Putnam, whom he married July 18, 1795, he had a son Elisha, born Sept., 1799, who married, June 10, 1823, Hannah, daughter of Thomas and Sarah Morrison, of Newburyport. He resides in Haverhill, Mass. (1858), and had issue six children, viz., four daughters and two sons ; the younger son died an infant in 1836, and the elder, William Augustus, who was born 10th Nov., 1825, married Feb. 7, 1856, Mary Esther, daughter of John and Mehitable Emory, of Newburyport, by whom in the latter part of 1858 he had then no issue. Israel, William Augustus's grandfather, died 4th January, 1837, and his father, Colonel Israel, died 15th March, 1811.

Joseph Hutchinson married, secondly, on the 30th of January, 1701, Rebecca Knight, of Topsfield, by whom he had issue a daughter, viz. :

9. Elizabeth, baptized April 19, 1701, who married Benj. Buxton.

The said Joseph Hutchinson (2d) died in the month of May, 1751, and was succeeded by his eldest son and child, by his first wife, viz. :

XIII. JOSEPH HUTCHINSON (3d), who was born on the 27th January, 1689. He was of Danvers and Middleton, Mass., and paid taxes at the latter place as early as 1754. He married on the 19th of January, 1719–20, Mrs. Abigail Goodale, widow, née Elliot ; his will was proved 15th June, 1781 ; he died at a great age, having had issue as follows :

1. *Joseph* (of whom hereafter).

2. Ruth, baptized at Danvers, April 29, 1722. She married, 15th December, 1741, Stephen, son of Francis Elliot, and died the 31st August, 1826, aged 104 years.

3. Abner, baptized at Danvers, Sept. 6, 1724 ; removed to Amherst, New Hampshire, in 1758, where he died Sept. 12, 1796. He married Elizabeth, daughter of Elisha Phelps.

4. Josiah, baptized at Danvers, July 10, 1726 ; died at Middleton in March, 1782. He married, December 8, 1748, Sarah Dean.

5. Sarah, baptized at Danvers, March 31, 1728, died young.

6. Elizabeth, baptized at Danvers, Sept. 26, 1731 ; married, 7th of April, 1752, to Stephen Nichols, and died April 27, 1822.
7. John, baptized May 15, 1737, died 1830. He married on the 12th September, 1766, Lydia, daughter of Abraham and Ruth Goodell.

XIV. JOSEPH HUTCHINSON (4th), eldest son of Joseph Hutchinson and Abigail Goodale, née Elliot, was baptized in 1st Church at Danvers, in company with his sister Ruth, on the 29th of April, 1722. He resided at Middleton, Mass., where he died in the month of April, 1797. He married Hannah, daughter of David and Rebecca Richardson, for his first wife, by whom he had issue as follows :

1. Elizabeth, baptized at Middleton February 4, 1747, who was married to Ebenezer Goodale.
2. Hannah, baptized at Middleton February 5, 1749, died 1794. She married, December 26, 1765, Andrew, son of Stephen and Ruth Elliot.
3. Elisha, born at Middleton the 6th of December, 1751. He married, on the 10th of November, 1772, Sarah, daughter of Amos and Mary Buxton, of Danvers, removed to New Hampshire, and died at Amherst, 12th of October, 1800.
4. Mary, born April 10, 1754, who married Samuel, son of George and Abigail Small, 1st July, 1776.
5. *Joseph* (of whom hereafter).

XV. JOSEPH HUTCHINSON (5th), the second son and youngest child of Joseph and Hannah Hutchinson, was born in Middleton on the 3d of August, 1757, where he died December 7, 1810. He had two wives. The first was Hannah, daughter of Archelaus and Hannah Fuller, whom he married on the 2d of November, 1798, and by whom he had four children, viz. :

1. Elijah, born in Middleton February 8, 1781, where he died September 9, 1818, having married on the 3d of February, 1808, Nancy, daughter of Simon and Elizabeth Mudge, by whom he had three children, viz. : two daughters, and a son Simon who was born October 22, 1808, and died on the 27th of August, 1816.
2. *Joseph* (of whom hereafter).
3. Archelaus, born in Middleton February 28, 1784, where he died June 5, 1825, having married Eliza, daughter of Abijah and Irene Hutchinson, on the 8th of June, 1818, by whom he had a daughter, and a son Archelaus-Eustis.
4. Levi, born in Middleton May 13, 1786, where he died March 10, 1844, having married Betsey, daughter of Benjamin and Hannah Russell, May 5, 1811, by whom he had issue as follows, viz. : George Putnam, born October 12, 1812; Samuel, born 6th November, 1814 ; Benjamin Russell, born Oct. 10, 1816, and died Oct. 13, 1850 ; Simon, born August 17, 1818, and died July 12, 1845, unmarried ; Levi Russell, born December 9, 1820 ; and Alven-Elijah, born January 22, 1826.

The said Joseph Hutchinson married, secondly, Rebecca Goodale, widow, née Newhall, by whom he had issue as follows, viz. :

5. Rebecca, born September 21, 1797, who died August 27, 1821. She married March 13, 1818, Amos King, of Danvers, by whom she had one daughter Rebecca, born July 20, 1820.

6. Sarah, born April 5, 1799, who died July 4, 1816.
7. Benjamin, born May 7, 1802. He married, December 4, 1826, Martha-Abigail, daughter of Amos and Abigail King, by whom he had issue as follows : Cleaves-King, born 21st Oct., 1827 ; Susan-Elizabeth, born 2d February, 1829 ; Rebecca-Newhall, born 9th October, 1831 ; Edwin-Augustus, born January 1, 1834 ; Benjamin-Franklin, born January 19, 1836 ; William-Henry, born 7th March, 1838 ; Martha-Maria, born December 10, 1840 ; Amos-King, born December 7, 1843 ; and Frank-Dudley, born March 14, 1848.

XVI. JOSEPH HUTCHINSON (6th), son of Joseph and Hannah, was born in Middleton, Mass., the 18th of March, 1782. He had also two wives. By the first, viz., Sarah, daughter of Samuel and Elizabeth Curtis, to whom he was married on the 28th of June, 1807, he had four children, viz. :

1. *Hiram* (of whom hereafter).
2. Joseph, 7th of the name in succession, who was born in August, 1810, and died in April, 1825, without issue.
3. Elisha Putnam, born the 9th of August, 1813, who married on the 14th of May, 1836, Ruth Louisa, daughter of Joseph and Sarah Richardson. By this marriage he has the following children, viz. :

A. Joseph-Curtis, who was born July 27, 1837.
B. Walter-Derby,   "   "   " Feb. 2, 1840.
C. Ezra-Almon,   "   "   " May 22, 1842.
D. Ann-Amelia,   "   "   " June 6, 1844.
E. Julia-Louisa,   "   "   " Sept. 4, 1846.
F. Ella-Putnam,   "   "   " Aug. 31, 1848.
G. Elisha-Morton,   "   "   " Dec. 14, 1850.
H. Susan-White,   "   "   " Mar. 30, 1853.
I. Charles-Sumner,   "   "   " April 24, 1856.

4. Mary, who was born the 14th of February, 1812, was married to her cousin George Putnam Hutchinson (son of Levi), June 21, 1841, and has four children, viz. :

A. George-Henry, who was born May 23, 1842.
B. Myron-Russell,   "   "   " April 14, 1844.
C. Mary-Elizabeth,   "   "   " April 3, 1846.
D. Hiram-Lufberry,   "   "   " April 15, 1849.

Joseph Hutchinson married, secondly, Rhoda McIntire, on the 21st of June, 1820, by whom he had, viz. :

5. Sarah, who was born 15 February, 1821. She married Horatio Perry, of Danvers.

Joseph Hutchinson died at Middleton, Mass., the 10th of May, 1842, aged 60 years.

XVII. HIRAM HUTCHINSON, eldest son of Joseph, by his first wife Sarah Curtis, was born at Middleton, Mass., on the 10th of November, 1808. He was married, on the 5th of July, 1831, to Mary-Ann, only daughter of Abraham and Elizabeth Lufberry, of New Jersey. In 1853, he went to France, and became extensively engaged in manufacturing pursuits. He established two large manufactories there, and one at Mannheim, Grand Duchy of Baden, for the manufacture of India Rubber goods ; these factories were the first of any importance started in Europe, and they employed in the neighborhood of one thousand work people. He now resides (1867), in New York city. He has the following children, viz. :

1. *Alcander* (of whom hereafter).
2. Abraham-Lufberry, born at New Orleans, November 24, 1834 ; died July 10, 1835, in the Gulf of Mexico.
3. Sarah-Elizabeth, who was born at New Brunswick, New Jersey, 19th June, 1836, and married, the 8th of December, 1864, to the Right Reverend Horatio Southgate, for many years Bishop of Constantinople.
4. Mary-Frances, who was born the 1st of December, 1837, at New Brunswick, New Jersey. She married, first, on the 11th of November, 1862, Captain W. L. Gwin, of the United States Navy, who was killed on the 3d of January, 1863, while bombarding the fortifications of Haines's Bluff, near Vicksburg, in the State of Mississippi, with the Iron Clad "Benton." She was married, secondly, on the 15th August, 1864, to Henry P. Moorhouse, Esq.
5. John-Gardner, born the 5th of October, 1839 ; died the 3d of November, 1845, and was buried in Mount Pleasant Cemetery, Newark, N. J.
6. Charlotte-Carter, who was born the 29th of June, 1841, and died the following 7th of September.
7. Hiram, who was born the 25th of August, 1843.
8. Charles-Louis-Richard, who was born the 1st of October, 1859, at Paris, France.

XVIII. ALCANDER HUTCHINSON, eldest son and child of Hiram Hutchinson and Mary Ann Lufberry, was born at New Brunswick, New Jersey, in the United States of America, on the 31st of December, 1832. He accompanied his father to France in 1853. He married, at Chatillon-sur-Loing (Loiret) France, on the 19th of January, 1858, Henriette-Emma-Aimés Torrens, eldest daughter* and co-heiress of Henri-Louis, Count de Loyanté, des Bordes, près Breonin-sur-Sauldre, Chev., and niece of the Duchess de Montmorency-Luxembourg. He was for sometime Consul for the United States of America at Singapore, Straits Settlements. He now (1867) resides at Langlie, près Montarges, Loiret, and has four children :

1. Reneé-Caroline, who was born at Langlie, 14th Feb., 1859.
2. Marianne-Grizelle, "   "   "   "   2d May, 1860.
3. Barnard-Alcander-Richard de Loyanté-Hutchinson, who was born at Bellevue, près Nogent-sur-Vernisson (Loiret) on the 24th of September, 1862.
4. Hiram-Emmanuel-Henri-Dieudonné de Loyanté-Hutchinson, who was born at Langlie, on the 24th of July, 1866.

---

* Her grandfather the Count Anne-Philippe de Loyauté was one of those French officers, who came to America, and helped us to gain our Independence. He was Lieut. Colonel of Artillery and Inspector General of the Fortifications of Virginia, and member of the order of Cincinnatus, and remained in America from 1778 till the close of the war. He left his order of Cincinnatus to his son, who has transmitted it, in default of male issue, to his son-in-law Alcander Hutchinson.

RISHWORTH, HUTCHINSON, HARNEIS and WHEELWRIGHT.—The following extracts from a letter from Col. Joseph L. Chester to a friend, dated May 15, 1869, furnish some interesting facts in relation to the above families in addition to the information contained in his Hutchinson paper, *ante*, vol. xx. pp. 355–67, and vol. xxi. pp. 363–5. *

J. W. DEAN.

A recent examination of the Registers of Laceby, co. Lincoln, has put me in possession of some new facts concerning Rishworth and Hutchinson. . . .

Rev. THOMAS RISHWORTH was Rector of Laceby at least a quarter of a century, and settled there with his first wife *Bridget*. The following children by this wife were baptized there :—*Francis*, 13 Sept., 1607 ; *Faith*, 2 Dec., 1608 ; *Thomas*, 31 March, 1611 ; *John*, 30 August.

This last son, John, was buried there 13 Jan., 1613–14. Bridget, the first wife, was buried there 31 August, 1612.

He then, as I have before shown, married Hester Hutchinson at Alford, 7 Oct., 1613, and the baptisms of their children occur in the Laceby Registers, as follows :—*Susanna*, 16 Feb., 1614–5 ; *Edward*, 5 May, 1617 ; *Charles*, 19 March, 1618–9 ; *Margaret*, 28 Jan., 1620–1 ; *Charles*, 16 Nov., 1624 ; *William*, 10 March, 1626–7.

Of these children, the first Charles was buried at Laceby 28 Dec., 1619, William 15 April, 1627, and Susannah 8 Dec., 1632, three months after her father, who was buried 7 Sept., 1632.

On the 26 March, 1633, a little more than 6 months after her husband's death, his widow, Hester (Hutchinson) Rishworth, was married at Laceby to " Mr. Thomas Harnesse " [rectius *Harneis*]. . . . This Thomas Harneis, described as a gentleman, was also a widower, having buried his first wife, Rebecca, at Laceby, 23 Dec., 1630. The baptisms of eight children by his first wife are recorded and the burials of six of them—Jane and Thomas only surviving. Jane, baptized 16 April, 1622, was married at Laceby, 23 Aug., 1641, to the Rev. John Somerscales of Croxton, clerk. Thomas was baptized 4 Sept., 1628, and I have as yet no further account of him.

By his second wife Hester (Hutchinson-Rishworth), Thomas Harneis had two sons, baptized at Laceby, John, 19 Nov., 1633, and Samuel, 24 Feb., 1636–7. . . . .

Thomas Harneis, the husband, was buried at Laceby 21 March, 1636–7, about a month after the baptism of the second son Samuel. I have not yet been able to find when his widow Hester died ; but she is mentioned in her brother John Hutchinson's will, dated 7 June, 1644.

You thus get the exact data as to Edward Rishworth, mentioned by Savage, who must have emigrated young, probably with Wheelwright.

I found also, in the Laceby Register, the baptism 9 June, 1633, of " Elizabeth daughter of Mr. John Wheelwright and Mary his wife." Mr. Savage thinks this daughter was born after 1642, and at Wells. As I have before shown, *ante*, vol. xxi. p. 365, that Wheelwright had children baptized in England in 1630 and 1632, and now find another in 1633, it is absolutely certain that *if* he was in New-England in 1628, he came back to this country and remained here till his final emigration.

*Pp. 447-459, this volume.
Pp. 723-725, the third volume of this series.

THE ROYAL ANCESTRY OF ANNE MARBURY
HUTCHINSON AND KATHERINE MARBURY SCOTT

By MEREDITH B. COLKET, JR., of Cleveland, Ohio

In 1936 the contributor published a small book entitled *The English Ancestry of Anne Marbury Hutchinson and Katherine Marbury Scott.* Its primary purpose was to show the descent of two 17th century New England colonists from the English royal family, Edward I and his predecessors, together with many other great medieval families. To the contributor the basic presentation was adequately documented by contemporary evidence with one exception. Evidence that William Raleigh (ca 1420-1460) of Farnborough, Warwickshire (generation 11 in the lineage given on page 37) married a daughter of Sir Thomas Greene (1400-1462) of Greene's Norton, Northamptonshire, was based solely on pedigrees that were or could have been produced many years afterwards. Failure to find the proof had almost deterred the contributor from publishing the book, yet the evidence seemed reasonably convincing so it was put in print and may be found in several libraries. The questionable link is discussed in Appendix A, p. 53.

Not long ago the contributor was asked whether any record had subsequently turned up that might shed light on the claimed relationship. Something did turn up which was called to my attention by the late G. Andrews Moriarty about 1950. Readers of THE REGISTER may be interested in the story. Reference was made to a document quoted on page 350 of Volume III of John Nichols' *History and Antiquities of the Town and County of Leicester* to the effect that in 1432 William Raleigh shared property rights in the Greene's manor of Kegworth. The discovery was a significant one because, for the first time, a legal document connecting William Raleigh with the Greene family of Greene's Norton was cited.

The implication was clear in this printed record that William Raleigh married Elizabeth Greene by 1432 (rather than about 1440 as stated by me, *op. cit.*, p. 37). Yet if Elizabeth Greene was the daughter of the Sir Thomas Greene who was born in 1400, we have a squeeze in generations too tight to be plausible. The Raleigh-Greene relationship as presented appeared false.

Mr. Moriarty wrote suggesting that William Raleigh may well have married the sister of this Sir Thomas Greene, son of an earlier Sir Thomas Greene (ca. 1369-1417). The suggested solution would throw out the lineage to Edward I through descent from Philippa Ferrers, wife of the Sir Thomas who was born in 1400.

The contributor, however, was himself satisfied that William Raleigh was born about 1420 and presumably was unmarried in 1432. He thus urged that a search be made for the original record which Nichols cited, suggesting that the date 1432 was an error for 1452, or perhaps some other date. Mr. Moriarty subsequently corresponded with Benjamin Franklin Wilbour who was undertaking research in this matter, and some time later reported the result. Mr.

Moriarty's letter is quoted in part as follows, abbreviations being written out in full; he discusses

". . . the inquisition post mortem of Sir Thomas Greene who married Mathilda Throckmorton (i.e., the son of the Sir Thomas, died 18 Jan. 1461/2, who married Philippa Ferrers). From this inquisition it would appear that he died soon after his father on 9 Sept. 2 Ed IV (9 Sept. 1462). The inquisition was taken 3 July Ed IV (1464); the son and heir, Thomas, was then aged '3 years and more'.

"The important thing is that the inquisition recites the feoffment in question; it was presented to the jurors at the inquisition. It was stated that on 4 July 30 Henry VI (4 July 1452) John Vampage, William Wolashall, William Ralegh, John Rous, Thomas Throckmorton and John Throckmorton Esqs. were seised of the manor of Kegworth in Leicestershire and being so seised on that day aforesaid at Kegworth, they released and demised the said manor, etc., to Thomas Greene and Mathilda his wife (still surviving) to them and the heirs of their bodies, remainder to the heirs of Thomas Greene.

"Breaking this down let us examine the feoffees. John Vampage evidently belonged to the old Worcestershire family of that name who was related to the Russells of Strensham, co. Worcester. Of William Wolashall I know nothing,—perhaps he was a relative.

"John Rous married a daughter of John Throckmorton of Coughton, the Under Treasurer. Thomas Throckmorton of Coughton was his eldest son and heir and John Throckmorton was his younger brother, the ancestor of the Gloucestershire branch.

"Now Mathilda, wife of Sir Thomas Greene was a daughter of John Throckmorton of Coughton, the Under Treasurer, and hence a sister of Thomas and John Throckmorton and a sister-in-law of John Rous, the feoffees. Another sister, Elizabeth, married Sir Robert Russell of Strensham, whose great-grandmother, according to the Visitation of Worcester, was Catherine, daughter John Vampage. So you see, these feoffees, or at least 3 or 4 of them, were closely connected with Mathilda Throckmorton, wife of a Sir Thomas Greene, and this adds greatly to the probability that William Raleigh was the brother-in-law of Sir Thomas Greene and so tends to confirm the statement in the Visitation. Also you will note that Nichols erred in the date of the feoffment having read 1432 for 1452, confusing the 5 with 3; quite easy. This clears up the chronological difficulty about which I wrote you so it looks as though the statement that William Raleigh married the daughter of Sir Thomas Greene and Philippa Ferrers was O.K. . . . Incidentally, Wilbour writes me that the handwriting in the manuscript pedigree, giving the 4 last children of Thomas and Philippa is, as you said, different from that of the rest of the pedigree. So it would appear to have been added after the herald had finished."

Hitherto we had a Greene and a Raleigh pedigree, each claiming the Raleigh-Greene marriage, coupled with a chronology that made the allegation most plausible. Now we have a contemporary legal document that nicely supports the earlier conclusion.

INGALLS ANCESTRY.—In the opening pages of the History of Lynn, Mass., by Alonzo Lewis and James R. Newhall, appears the following: "'The first white men known to have been inhabitants of Lynn were *Edmund Ingalls* and his brother *Francis Ingalls.*" "A record preserved in the family of the former says, 'Mr. Edmund Ingalls came from Lincolnshire, in England, to Lynn, in 1629.'" As this Edmund Ingalls was one of my ancestors, I have been desirous of learning something more concerning HIS ancestry than is conveyed in the above. When in England this last summer, I spent a month in genealogical research, and obtained a considerable amount of information concerning a number of New England families from whom I am descended; information that has not been published in any records that I have seen, and which I conclude is not generally known. I went to Lincoln, and in searching through the old wills in the probate court attached to Lincoln Cathedral, I came upon the will of *Robert* Ingalls of Skirbeck, undoubtedly the father of the above Edmund and Francis. I consider this to have been a fortunate find, as it conclusively certifies that they came from Lincolnshire, as stated in the History of Lynn, but also gives the continued line in England, and the place from whence they came. The will is as follows:—

"In ye name of God, Amen. I, Robert Ingolls of Skirbeck, quarter of Skirbeck, in the County of Lincoln, yeoman, being sick of body but of good and perfect memorie, &c., &c. I give and bequeathe unto Elizabeth my wife during her natural life, &c. After her decease to Edmund my eldest sonne who was lawfully begotten. And for want of issue after Edmund's death to Robert, my second sonne, & for want of issue after his death to ffrancis my youngest sonne & failing issue to the natural heirs of me Robert Ingolls for ever. I give Robert Ingolls £20, and I give ffrancis Ingolls £30, both one year after my decease. I give my maid servant Anne Cleasbie £5, and to all of Henry Cleasbie's children one ewe lamb. To every one of Cousin Henry's children one ewe lamb. I give to my brother Henry a black fleeced cowe. I give to the poor of Skirbeck 10 shillings. I give one half of the balance to Elizabeth my wife during her natural life & then all to Edmund to whom I leave one half at once." Wife Elizabeth & sonne Edmund are appointed Executors. Wm. Shinfold & Robt. Harrison are appointed Supervisors of the Will and he gives them 2s. 6d. each for their pains. The will is dated 12th of July 1617, and is signed Robert Ingolls his mark. The above is only partially an exact copy, avoiding needless repetition and such matter that was of little interest.

The children of Edmund were: 1st, Robert (named after his grandfather, whose will is above); 2d, Elizabeth; 3d, Faith; 4th, John; 5th, Sarah; 6th, Henry (named after his great uncle, named in his grandfather's will); 7th, Samuel; 8th, Mary; 9th, Joseph. I am descended through Henry, the 6th child, and Mary Osgood; then through Capt. Samuel Ingalls and Mary Watts, then through John Haseltine of Chester, N. H., and Mary Ingalls; then James Haseltine of Haverhill, Mass., and Abigail Mooers (sister of Gen. Mooers of Revolutionary fame); and then John Haseltine of Philadelphia and Haverhill, and Elizabeth Stanley Shinn. Can any one give me any information concerning the ancestry of Mary Watts, who married Capt. Samuel Ingalls?

Another will which I should have included in this article is that of *Henry Ingall*, dated June 1st, 1555. In it he gives to his wife Johan. He also wills that his youngest children shall have every one £10, which was left to them (probably in the will of an earlier ancestor, which as yet I have not been able to find). If any die before coming of lawful age that share to be divided amongst the rest. Gives to the maintenance of the high altar, 12d. The balance of his effects to be divided amongst his six children. Joan, wife, executrix. Names a sonne James, and brother-in-law Thos. Wytton.

1416 Chestnut Street, Philadelphia.   CHARLES F. HASELTINE.

485

A SUGGESTION AS TO HENRY JACOB.

By the Rev. EDWARD D. NEILL, of St. Paul, Min.

HENRY JACOB, the first Congregational minister in London, Wood, in *Athenæ Oxonienses* mentions, entered Saint Mary's Hall, Oxford, A.D. 1579, at the age of sixteen, took Holy Orders, was precentor of Christ Church College, and in the last years of his life pastor of the Independent Church in London, but, that while he died at about the age of sixty years, he did not know in what place.

Neal, in *History of the Puritans*, writes that Jacob, with the consent of his church, about the year 1624, went to Virginia, where he soon died. After a search of twenty-five years the writer of this article has found no trace of him in Virginia. In March, 1623, the ship Sea Flower, on its way to Virginia, while in Bermudas harbor, was blown up by the careless communication of fire to the powder magazine, and eighteen lives were lost.

In Leroy's Bermudas there is a letter from London, to the governor of the Island, in which are these words: "The poor woman, the widow Jacob, doth still follow and importune us for the restitution of those goods of hers." The first thing on her inventory was, "a black gown lined with fur." The governor replied that he could learn nothing of the gown, but he was told that the divers found a very great chest, which in attempting to put into a boat, slipped into the sea and was lost.

May not Henry Jacob have been one of the eighteen drowned by the explosion of the Sea Flower?

THE JENKS FAMILY OF ENGLAND

By MEREDITH B. COLKET, JR., F.A.S.G., of Washington, D. C.

INTRODUCTION

Harlan Walker Jenks (1880–1942) provided in his will for the preparation of a genealogy of the Jenks family. Under the terms of the will, the "Genealogy of the Jenks Family of America" was compiled by the late William B. Browne and published in 1952. It deals with the descendants of the New England colonist, Joseph Jenks. Research was later carried on to determine, if possible, the ancestry of Joseph Jenks and that of his first wife. The present study summarizes in brief the results of this research. Much of the basic material obtained or compiled in connection with the study and photocopies of original documents cited are in the Jenks Source Books, which are to be offered to the New England Historic Genealogical Society.

We acknowledge with thanks the cooperation of Mr. Leonard Marbury and Miss Mary L. Chadwick, Vice President and Trust Officer, and Assistant Trust Officer, respectively, of the Washington Loan and Trust Company Branch of the Riggs National Bank, who were charged with handling the estate of Harlan Walker Jenks. We acknowledge the excellent research and remarkable persistence of Mrs. Dorothy Smith Coleman in following up difficult clues abroad. Her continuous support of this work has been outstanding and is deserving of the highest praise.

In addition, we acknowledge the research assistance and technical skills of a number of people. Particularly, we want to thank Dr. Arthur Adams, F.S.A, F.A.S.G., Miss Rosalie Fellows Bailey, F.A.S.G., Mr. John I. Coddington, F.A.S.G., Mr. W. E. C. Cotton, formerly chairman of the executive committee of the Society of Genealogists, Mr. Donovan Dawe, Professor E. N. Hartley, Albert E. J. Hollaender, Ph.D., F.S.A., Miss N. J. M. Kerling, Ph.D., The Viscount Mersey, P.C., C.M.G., C.B.E., F.S.A., Mr. G. A. Moriarty, F.S.A., F.A.S.G., Francis R. Sears, Esq., Dr. Jean Stephenson, F.A.S.G., Mr. Anthony R. Wagner,

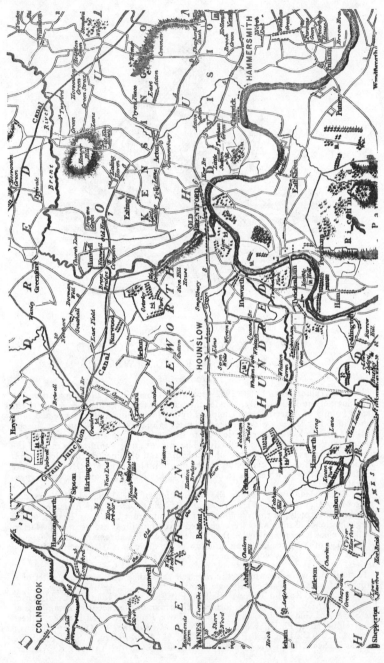

1. Early map showing the area just west of London, including Colnbrook, Hounslow, and Hammersmith, chapelries traditionally associated with Joseph Jenks.

C.V.O., Richmond Herald, College of Arms, Dr. Richard Williams, F.S.A., and Mr. A. Vere Woodman, F.S.A.

Finally, words of praise are especially due the British public officials at the Guildhall Library, Somerset House, the British Museum, the Public Record Office, and the National Library of Wales, and the staff of the Society of Genealogists, London. These persons were, without exception, courteous and generous.

The research produced far more difficult problems of identity than any the writer had before encountered. We believe that some of the problems have been successfully solved, and that sound evidence has suggested solution to the others. We hope that the results of these investigations will be of value to the descendants of Joseph Jenks and to others interested in the colonist's origin and background.

I. THE ENGLISH ORIGIN OF THE NEW ENGLAND COLONIST, JOSEPH JENKS

Joseph Jenks, the Lynn, Mass., proprietor of 1645, became associated with the iron works founded by John Winthrop, Jr., at nearby Saugus, the first successful iron works in America. Jenks invented a water mill and a distinct new type of scythe which is the forerunner of the scythe used today. He was granted a patent on his inventions by the Massachusetts Bay Colony, the first machine patent to be granted in the American colonies. He was interested in coinage, and, according to a tradition, cut the dies for the famous pine tree shilling. At an early date he negotiated with the Boston selectmen for the construction of a fire engine. In his later years he tried to build a wire factory. According to Professor E. N. Hartley of the Massachusetts Institute of Technology archaeological excavations recently carried on by the Steel Institute at Saugus reveal that Jenks was a skilled toolmaker.

Joseph Jenks founded a family of renown. Sketches of his life and of the lives of his son, Joseph, his grandson, Joseph, the colonial Rhode Island Governor, and some other family members, appear in the "Dictionary of American Biography". A descendant, Rhoda Jenks, married into the prominent Rhode Island merchant family of Brown, and had, among her descendants, Nicholas Brown, from whom Brown University derives its name, and the son of Nicholas, John Carter Brown, whose collections and gifts resulted in the John Carter Brown Library.[1] Several descendants of Joseph are named in the current edition of "Who's Who in America".

It is therefore not surprising that considerable interest has been manifested in Joseph's origin and background. Investigations were carried on in England at different periods to establish his identity, but these met with but indifferent success. As a result of the investigations, however, suggested or claimed identifications have been made in America. Joseph, whose family surname has been spelled in various ways but chiefly Jenks, Jenkes, and Jenckes, has been variously identified as:

1. A son of Arthur Jenkes of England, son of Frances Jenkes of Aston [parish of Mounslow], Shropshire.[2] This undocumented statement is improbable. The names of Arthur's children appear in both the printed 1623 "Visitation of Shropshire"[3], and in his will, which

489

was dated 18 Aug. 1638 and proved 11 Sept. 1638 in the Consistory Court of Hereford.[4] Each authority fails to list a son Joseph.

2. The Joseph whose baptism as son of Mathew Jenckes was recorded 11 March 1603/4 in the parish registers of Clunbury, Shropshire. This suggestion was presented as a clue[5], but is improbable. The printed parish registers show that "Josheph Jenckes" was buried there 6 Jan. 1605 [/6].[6]

3. The Joseph who married in the parish of All Hallows on the Wall, London, on 30 Sept. 1630, Mary Tervyn (or Turwin).[7] This identification has been presented both as a clue and as a fact[8] and was accepted by the compiler of the "Genealogy of the Jenks Family of America" (1952).

A careful examination of English records reveals considerable information about the Joseph Jenks who married Mary Tervyn.

This JOSEPH JENKS was the son of John Jenks, citizen and white baker of London though a cutler by trade.[9] If we accept the age given on his marriage license, Joseph was born about 1607. He was brought up in his father's shop in the Precinct of the Tower of London and, on 21 April 1629, became a citizen and white baker of London through paternity.[10] This affiliation with a London company gave him important business rights. Like his father, however, he did not work in the trade of that Company but became a cutler.

His marriage license, dated 29 Sept. 1630, describes him as of the Precinct of the Tower of London, cutler, aged about 23 years.[11] His bride to be, MARY TERVYN, was the daughter of James Tervyn or Turwin, citizen and currier of London. The published registers of All Hallows on the Wall, London, show that the couple were married in the church the following day. This was the church where Mary had been baptized 26 March 1611. The baptism of only one child of the couple has been found. The child, *Sarah*, was baptized in the Chapel of St. Peter ad Vincula, Tower of London, 13 Oct. 1635.[12]

Joseph's three apprentices, whom he trained in the art of cutlery, are named in the records of the Company of White Bakers: Jeremy Draper of Finchley, co. Middlesex, to serve seven years from 1633; John Noble of the same place, to serve for eight years from 1635; and John Towne of Thornton, co. York, to serve for eight years from 1637. Jeremy Draper was involved in a dispute with his master just before he obtained him freedom in 1640;[14] and later recorded his own mark with the London Company of Cutlers.[15]

Joseph used the mark of the thistle on his knife blades. His right was infringed upon by William Rush who made the mark of the pomegranate look like that of the thistle. On 16 Oct. 1638 "Joseph Jencks" described as cutler and "knyffe fforger" complained to the Cutler's Company that "diures haue and doe take the same Pound-grannett for the Thistle to the great losse and hinderance of the sayd Joseph Jencks".[16] The specific identification of Joseph as "knyffe fforger" is unusual.

On 25 Nov. 1639 Joseph Jenks was elevated to the rank of the livery of the Company of White Bakers.[17] On 9 Aug. 1641 he was taxed by the City of London as a member of the Company of White Bakers.[18] The quartridge books of the Company show that in 1641 and 1642 Jenks failed to pay his dues. In the column for the last quarter for the year 1642 is the significant marginal entry added to his name: "Dead".[19] On 7 Sept. 1642 Mary Jenks, described as the relict of "Josephus Jenks", late of the parish of St. Leonard, Shoreditch, Middlesex, was granted an administration on an estate of 48 pounds 2 shillings, in the Archdeaconry Court of London.[20] St. Leonard, Shoreditch, is a few hundred yards from All Hallows on the Wall, London.

The year 1642 was the year Civil War broke out in England. Since it is the first year that the name Joseph Jenks has been found in American records, it is conceivable that the Londoner skipped to America, leaving the presumption that he had died and the London Court was presented acceptable evidence of death. Certainly, other information harmonizes exceedingly well:

1. The name, Joseph Jenks, was rare in England in that day.
2. The colonist was traditionally stated to have been from the vicinity of London.
3. The colonist's son, Joseph, was born, according to tradition, in 1632; and this date harmonizes with the 1630 marriage date.
4. Joseph of London was a cutler, and this trade harmonizes with the trade of the Joseph, the colonist, a blacksmith who worked in edge tools.

Since, however, the alleged identification could be questioned, a thorough re-examination of records was made for clues concerning the colonist's identity. On the basis of this re-examination we are able to reject the claim that the emigrant and the husband of Mary Tervyn were identical. Following is a list of the essential American clues together with statements concerning related information from English records:

1. *American clue:* A tradition as to the place of origin of Joseph Jenks was written down in 1844 by a descendant and printed in 1855 in THE REGISTER. The descendant, The Rev. William Jenks (1778–1866) of Boston, a scholar, whose life story is told in the "Dictionary of American Biography", wrote that the colonist was: . . . traditionally stated to have come from Hammersmith or Hounslow, near London. . . .[21]

English evidence: Hammersmith and Hounslow were chapelries in the County of Middlesex, six miles apart. The former was in the parish of Fulham, the latter partly in the parish of Isleworth.

The parish registers of Isleworth, which are deposited in the Hounslow Public Library, were badly damaged by fire but the following burial entries are discernible:

[1634/5] February 29 Jone Jeankes the wife of Joseaff Jeankes was buryed.
[1638] Nov. 2 [Eliza?]beth the daughter of Joseph Jenkes.[22]

These entries were photographed through the kind permission of the incumbent.

Comment: The parish registers of Fulham are not known to be extant for the period either in original or transcript form.

2. *American clue:* According to his own testimony, in his application for a patent, Joseph was concerned in the manufacture of sharp iron instruments such as scythes and edge tools.

English evidence: The Powysland Museum, Welshpool, Wales, has an early seventeenth century sword inscribed "Joseph Jenckes" and the name "Hounslow".[23]

Comment: Hounslow is one of two places that was traditionally associated with the name of the colonist, and the name Joseph Jenks is found at an appropriate date among the parish registers of a parish that included Hounslow. The sword is described below.

3. *American clue:* A clue as to the age of Joseph Jenks appears in Massachusetts depositions of 17 Sept. 1681, and 24 June 1678 as shown in the "Records and Files of the Quarterly Courts of Essex County".[24] In the deposition first described he gave his age as about eighty-one years; in the second as seventy-six years. These depositions would place his year of birth about 1600 or 1602.

English evidence: Three miles from Hammersmith and on the west end of the City of London is the parish of St. Anne, Blackfriars. The parish registers include the following two baptismal entries:

1596[/7] Sarah daughter to John Ginkes February VI.
1599   Josephe sonne of John Ginkes August 26.[25]

Comment: That the name is Jenks is clearly shown from "London Marriage Licenses" (London, 1887), edited by Joseph Foster:

"Jenkes, John of St. Anne, Blackfriars, London, cutler, and Sarah Fulwater, of London, spinster, daughter of Henry Fulwater, of St. Anne, Blackfriars, aforesaid, cutler, gen. lic., 8 Jan. 1595/6".

The facts harmonize well in respect to age, in respect to place of birth, and in respect to trade, since trades were often carried down in families. Furthermore, the Joseph baptized in 1599 cannot easily be identified with the London cutler, Joseph Jenks, who married Mary Tervyn; for the latter's marriage license of 29 Sept. 1630, previously alluded to, gives his age as about 23, showing that he was born about 1607.

4. *American clue:* A tradition as to the place of birth of the son of the colonist, Joseph Jenks, Jr., was written down about 1813 by Esek Esten who had married a Jenks descendant. His family account was printed in issues of Dec. 12, 19, and 26, 1834, of the *Pawtucket Chronicle* and reprinted in 1926 in "A Short Sketch of the Family of Jenkses":[26]

"The Hon. Joseph Jenks, Esq. of worthy memory, was born 1632, at Colebrook (so called from the River Cole . . . a Town in Buckinghamshire. . . .)"

Philip Capron wrote in 1817 substantially the same, without, however, naming the town; and his statement was published in "The Descendants of Banfield Capron" in 1859.

English evidence: In Buckinghamshire is Colnbrook, on the River Colne, a chapelry which was chiefly in the parish of Horton. A search of the parish registers of Horton, made possible through the courtesy of the incumbent, revealed the single Jenks entry: "Joseph Jincks ye sonne of Joseph Jincks bapt. October 12, 1628".[27]

Comment: Since the date of baptism was four years earlier than the traditional year of birth of the colonist's son Joseph, Jr., a search was made to find an American source that would shed light on Joseph Jenks, Jr.'s, year of birth. This search fortunately bore fruit. The unpublished Providence Town Papers[28] in the library of Rhode Island Historical Society in Providence contain the following:

"Joseph Jenckes, Aged 81 years or thereabout, Being Engaged according to law Testifieth & Saith, that many years past (though how many this Deponant cannot Justly Remember) He did hear a report that Priscilla Harding was big with child, and that shee said it was by Tho Eustance, and that the said Eustance did Deny that it was by him that shee was with Child But not long after the sd Tho: Eustance came to this Deponant (he being then a magistrat) and Desired to be published to the sd Priscilla Harding, But the Deponant having heard the aforesd Report he Asked the sd Eustance if he did own the child to be his which the sd Priscilla was then bigg with, and he Answered that he did own it, whereupon the Deponant granted him a publication, and not Long after (the publication having stood the time apoynted by law) the sd Tho. Eustance & the sd Priscilla Harding Came to this Deponant and Desired marriage And this Deponant Doth further testifie that he did then Joyn them in marriage, & that, at the same time the sd Priscilla looked very bigg, & some weekes after he did hear that shee was Delivered of a Daughter and further saith not.

Taken upon Engagement this 27th of November 1708: before me

Joseph Jenckes Assistant"

Since Joseph Jenks, Jr., deposed giving an age that places his date of birth about 1628, it is probable that the Joseph, Jr., baptized in 1628 is the Joseph, Jr., son of the colonist.

It is interesting that Joseph, Jr's., wife, Esther, deposed in the same case giving her age as 76, or born about 1632; and it is likely that the attribution of 1632 as the year of birth of Joseph, resulted from confusing husband and wife.

A search of the Bishop's Transcripts of the Horton parish registers, which are at the Bodleian Library, Oxford, did not reveal a copy of the baptismal entry but did reveal the following marriage entry: "Joseph Jenkes and Ellen Hearne were maried the ffift day of Novembr 1627".[29]

In this instance, the incumbent failed to record a marriage in his own register, but reported it to the Bishop.

The given name of Joseph's wife, Ellen, does not correspond with the given name, Jone, which appears in the parish registers of Isleworth. This difference in name, suggests at first glance, a second marriage. This difference is discussed in the section dealing with the Hearne family.

From the information thus assembled, it is possible to reconstruct briefly the story of the early life of the colonist.

Joseph Jenks was probably born in St. Anne, Blackfriars, a parish on the edge of the Thames River at the western end of the City of London; for the baptism of Joseph, son of John Jenkes, was recorded in the registers of that parish 26 Aug. 1599. Joseph's father was a London cutler who is known to have lived in the parish as early as 1596 and as late as 1599. His mother, Sarah, born Sarah Fulwater, was the eldest daughter of a German emigrant who had come to England about 1566 and who had worked out his apprenticeship as a cutler for the London Company of Cutlers.[30]

Joseph's name is traditionally associated with Hammersmith, the chapelry in Middlesex about three miles from St. Anne, Blackfriars, but the loss of most manorial and other records has made it impossible to confirm his residence there.

The first record of Joseph as an adult that has been found is dated 5 Nov. 1627, when he married, in the parish of Horton, Buckinghamshire, about fourteen miles from Hammersmith. His eldest child, Joseph, Jr., was baptized in the parish a year later. It is probable that Joseph Jenks was not a resident of Buckinghamshire, but married his bride in the parish of her family, and, in accordance with custom, she returned to her old home for the birth of her eldest child.

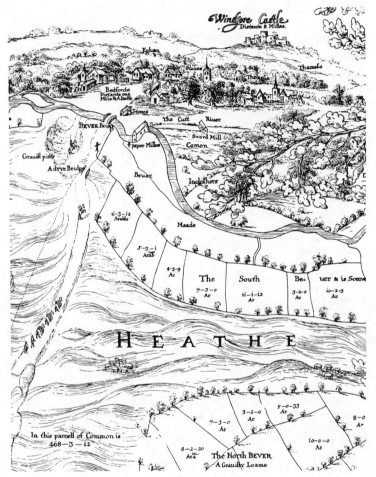

Windſore Caſtle
Diſtant 8 Miles.

John
Stones
Thames

Bedfonte
Diſtante one
Mile & A halfe

Stones
The Cutt   Riuer
Sword Mill
Comon

BEVER Bridg
paper Milles

Grauell pitts
A drye Bridge

Beuer

Incloſhers
Meade

6-3-12
Arable

5-3-1
Arab

4-3-9
Ar
The   South   Be   uer & is Souw
7-3-0   11-1-12   3-2-0   10-2-3
Ar   Ar   Ar   Ar

H E A T H E

In this parcell of Common is
468—3—12

3-2-0   5-0-33
Ar   Ar
7-3-0   8-0
Ar   Ar

10-0-0
Ar
8-2-20
Ar a   The North BEVER
A Grauelly Loame

2. *Portion of contemporary painting showing Hounslow, including
Benjamin Stone's house and sword mill, when Joseph Jenks worked there.*

Soon after his marriage Joseph Jenks was in Hounslow, Middlesex. Hounslow was between Horton and Hammersmith; all three are on the famous old London road running westward to Bath. As a cutler of German descent, Joseph was probably attracted to Hounslow by the arrival in 1629 of some skilled German cutlers who had been imported to England by Charles I to develop a sword industry worthy of the name.[31] These cutlers are believed to have come from Solingen.[32] They knew the secrets of the trade and were under oath not to divulge them upon pain of death. The German cutlers allied themselves with a powerful English figure, Benjamin Stone.

Stone was the son of a Sussex yeoman and had many years before worked out his apprenticeship with the London Company of Cutlers.[33] The account of his life in the "Dictionary of National Biography" reads in part:

> "Benjamin Stone . . . sword-maker, was an enterprising cutler of London who about 1630 established on Hounslow Heath, on the site now occupied by Bedfont powder-mills, the earliest English sword factory of which anything is known. He employed English workmen under the direction of foreigners . . . paying by the piece and finding workshops, tools, etc., as usual in the trade until recent times. His grindstones and polishing wheels were turned by a water wheel. . . . His establishment was on a scale that enabled him to produce about a thousand swords a month".

The sword factory was located in a wild desolate area that in those days was used as a rendezvous for troops. It was on an artificial stream known as the Duke of Northumberland's River, which connected the Colne River with the Isleworth River, later the Crane River, and which made possible the establishment of a number of mills, including grist mills, brass mills, and gunpowder mills.[34] The sword factory, identified as Stone's, is depicted on a 6' by 9' painting, drawn in 1635 by Moses Glover, [35] which is now in the Monastery of Sion, Isleworth, Middlesex.

Stone had great difficulty in finding a continued market for his product, and, in an effort to prevent others from copying it, applied for and received a patent on sword manufacture, one of the few patents granted by the English Government in those days. The patent, dated 9 July 1636, reads:

> "A spiall priviledge graunted to BENJAMIN STONE, swordblade maker, and his assignes, for the terme of 14 yeares next ensuing, wthin England, Ireland, and Wales, and town of Barwicke, to make and worke all manner of sword blades, fauchions, skeynes, rapyer blades, and blasts serving for rests for musketts of any fashion or kinde whatsoever, according to a way and invencon, by him devised, by the helpe of mill or mills, and the same to sell at moderate rates — paying therefore yearelie to the Crowne x¹s during the said terme; with the ordinary proviso for making this graunt voide in case it shall be found to be contrary to lawe and inconvenient to the state. Teste apud Canbury, nono die Julii, a° pd."[36]

The swords made at Hounslow during this period are considered by Dr. Richard Williams, F.S.A., the well-known British collector, among the best ever made in England.[37] Stone himself claimed that they were the best made in the Christian world. The story is told that some of Stone's swords were represented as having been manufactured at Toledo in Spain, and that one of the most experienced cutlers, Robert South, once cutler by appointment to James I, was deceived in their false representation. William Cavendish, the First Duke of Newcastle (1592–1676), referred to the surpassing excellence of Hounslow blades in two of his plays.[38]

G. E. Bate, F. R. Hist. S., gives us an interesting picture of the relationship of Stone and the cutlers who forged the swords:

> "The smith who forged the swords obtained his metal from the factory at the sword mill, took it home and in a forge by the side of his house, he forged the blade. When this was done the blades were carried to the mills situated by Baber Bridge where he was paid for the work done. At the mill the swords were ground, the stones being driven by the water wheel".[39]

Detailed information about these swords is obtainable from sword collectors and museums. There are about thirty known Hounslow swords, of which thirteen are in the collection of Dr. Richard Williams. Identified Hounslow swords are those bearing the inscription "Hounslow" on the blades. Four different kinds of swords have been found: broadswords, rapiers, horsemen's swords, and hangars. The dated swords are dated almost entirely between 1634 and 1637. From other evidence these dates appear to cover the period when sword-making at Hounslow was at its peak. Some swords bearing the inscription "London" are thought to have been Hounslow swords made before Hounslow swords became famous.

Some of the swords inscribed "Hounslow" are also inscribed with the names of the cutlers but only four different names have been found: Henry Hoppie, John Kundt, Ricardus Hopkins, and "Joseph Jenckes". Hoppie and Kundt are said to be names of cutlers of Solingen, Germany.[40]

The one sword on which Joseph Jenckes' name appears is a broadsword. It was discovered by Dr. Williams at the Powysland Museum, Welshpool, Wales, in 1938. The following account of the discovery is quoted with his permission:

> "... after a good deal of cleaning, the writer was rewarded with the discovery of a sword blade bearing the name of an hitherto unrecorded sword cutler associated with the Hounslow factory.
>
> The weapon consists of an English 17th century basket hilted broadsword. It measures 38 in. over all, the blade being 32½ in., carrying two flutes extending to the extremity. With its grip missing and its guard somewhat battered, it now weighs 1 lb. 10 ozs., the whole surface being thickly coated with black paint which collectors have come to regard as typical of a church or mortuary exhibit.
>
> Removal of this paint and much rust from a section of the blade revealed the inscription ... :

IOSEPH IENCKES

and in a similar position on the opposite side:

ME FECIT HOUNSLOW[41]

This sword, according to the Museum, had belonged to Col. William Salisbury, a supporter of Charles I, whose biography is given in the "Dictionary of National Biography". Dr. Williams had not been able to find substantiating evidence of this attribution and observed that museum attributions are often untrustworthy. There is no question in his mind, however, that the sword is an officer's sword and not a common soldier's.

At the time of the discovery of the sword, Dr. Williams expressed an interest in having it for his private collection. The Museum officials, feeling that it would be better appreciated in his collection than theirs, offered to give it to him. He stated, however, that it was too valuable a sword to be given away and offered £100 for it. The Museum, feeling that an article so valuable should not be disposed of, has retained it.

The sword may carry a secret that cannot be uncovered. Under the tang of the sword is probably the mark used by Joseph Jenks. The tang, however, is so rusted that if any attempt were made to take it apart, it would disintegrate. Rarely, according to Dr. Williams, tangs on old swords drop off leaving the cutler's mark plainly discernible.

The fact that Joseph's surname is spelled Jenckes on the sword is interesting. The first record of Joseph in New England has the spelling "Jenckes".[42] The "Dictionary of American Biography" shows that the spelling "Jenckes" was preferred by Joseph's son Joseph and his grandson, the Rhode Island Governor.

The migration of the colonist to New England may be associated with the adverse fortunes of Stone, whose name disappears from the records about 1642 when the Civil War broke out in England. But the exact date of Joseph's migration has not been ascertained. He was in Hounslow as late as 1638 when a daughter was buried. He was supposed by Col. C. E. Banks to be identical with an unnamed blacksmith who was reported on the Agamenticus (York) River, Maine, in the fall of 1641. He was evidently in Maine before 25 June 1642, when George Cleaves sailed for England and forged Joseph's name to a petition to Parliament. Joseph's name appears on New Hampshire Court records of 10 Nov. 1642 and on a deed relating to land at York River 16 March 1642/3.[43] Conceivably, he could have returned to England with John Winthrop, Jr., who was getting support for the establishment of an iron works in Saugus, near Lynn.[44] He may have induced displaced cutlers residing at or near Hammersmith to migrate. On page 82 of the 1829 edition of the "History of Lynn", by Alonzo Lewis, is the statement "The village at the Foundry was called Hammersmith by some of the workmen who came from a place of that name in England". Jenks was in Lynn by 1645.

The story of the rest of Joseph's life has been told. Nevertheless, it seems worth while to quote from his application for a patent in order to make ready comparison with the Stone patent just described:

". . . whereas the Lord hath beene pleased to giue mee knowledg in Makeing, and erecting of Engines of Mills to goe by water for the speedy dispatch of much worke with few mens labour in litle tyme my desire is to Jmproue this talent for the publike good and benifitt and Seruice of this Country; to which end my Jntention and purpose is (if God permitt)

497

to Build a Mill for making of Sithes; and alsoe a new Jnvented Saw Mill, and diuers other Engines for making of diuers sorts of edge tooles; whereby the Country may haue sush necessaryes in short tyme at farre cheaper Rates then now they can; Now yor petitioner doth humbly beseech this Honoured Court that you would please to Grant mee this priueledg; and to order that noe other person shall sett upp or vse any such new Invention or trade for the space of fowerteene yeeres without my licence; which hath been the vjuall priveledge and liberty Granted by the high Court of Parlayment in England to men that doe first sett vpon workes of this nature; least after your petitioner haue expended his estate, study, and labour, and haue brought things to perfection; Another when hee seeth it, maketh the like; and soe J loose the benifitt of that I have studied many yeeres before. . . ."[45]

The Stone patent was among the few then granted in England. The Jenks patent was the first machine patent granted in America. Both were labor-saving devices involving the finishing of sharp iron instruments by the use of water wheels.[46] Joseph apparently learned the secrets of the Solingen cutlers as developed by Stone and applied his knowledge in a practical way in the early days of manufacturing in pioneer America.

FOOTNOTES

1. For accounts of Nicholas Brown and John Carter Brown, see "Dictionary of American Biography".
2. Charles N. Jenks, "History and Trees of the Jenks Family" (1934), p. 9.
3. *Publications of the Harleian Society*, v. 29, p. 276. This is based on Harleian Manuscript 1241, fo. 164, in the British Museum.
4. See Jenks Source Books. The will is in the National Library of Wales, Aberystwyth.
5. See Banks Manuscripts, Public Library, Bangor, Maine.
6. "Shropshire Parish Registers Diocese of Hereford," v. 2, part 3, p. 190.
7. "The Registers of . . . All Hallows London Wall" (London, 1878), p. 241.
8. C. E. Banks, "History of York, Maine" (1931), v. 1, p. 142, gives this as a clue. Albert Ernest Jenks, "The British Wife of Joseph Jenks, the Patentee"; "Rhode Island History" v. 6, p. 118–27, gives this as fact.
9. Charles Welch, "History of the Cutlers' Company", London, 1922, v. 2, p. 344–5. For John's affiliation with the Company of White Bakers, see London Company of Cutlers, Minute Book, for 1626, fo. 49, in Guildhall Library, London.
10. London Company of White Bakers, Minute Book, 1617–48, #5177/4, fo. 120, *verso*, in Guildhall Library, London.
11. From the Bishop of London's Registry, 1, The Sanctuary, Westminster, London. See Jenks Source Books.
12. According to the original register in the Chapel of St. Peter ad Vincula.
13. Company of White Bakers, Court Minute Book, 1617–48, #5177/4, fo. 174, *recto*, 217 *recto*, 266 *verso* in Guildhall Library, London.
14. "16th October, 1638, Vppon the Complaynte of Joseph Jencks Cutler and knyffe fforger against William Rush also cutler and knife fforger for that he the sayd William Rush Contrary to the Rules and orders of this howse and Contrary to the graunt of this Court did and doth strike vppon his knife blades the marke of the Poundgrannett soe neare aluding to the Marke of the Thistle in so much that diuers haue and doe take the same Poundgrannett for the Thistle to the great losse and hinderance of the sayd Joseph Jencks wherefore this Court doth Commaund the sayd William not to strike the same any more but to strike the marke of the Poundgrannett in the same manner and forme as the same was first graunted and enrowled vppon the lead of stamps belonging to this howse." Charles Welch, "History of the Cutlers' Company", v. 2, p. 349; and Company of White Bakers, Register of Freemen, 1631–46, #5185, in Guildhall Library, London.

15. Charles Welch, "History of the Cutlers' Company", v. 2, p. 34.

16. *Ibid.*, v. 2, p. 349.

17. "Received of the persons hereafter named being taken into the clothing this year (vizt) . . . Joseph Jenks haveing not bine att any charge to this tyme x^s". Company of White Bakers, Audit Book, in Guildhall Library, London.

18. "Transcript of Poll Tax Commissioners, Members of City Companies 1641", p. 68, in Guildhall Library, London.

19. London Company of White Bakers, Quartridge Book 1630–59, #5179/3, in Guildhall Library, London.

20. Act Book 7, fo. 106. Photocopy made by Somerset House and filed in Jenks Source Books.

21. The Register, v. 9, p. 201.

22. See Jenks Source Books.

23. "Collections Historical and Archaeological Relating to Montgomeryshire and its Borders", v. 40, pt. 2, p. 187.

24. V. 8, p. 197; and v. 7, p. 28.

25. In the Guildhall Library, London. See photocopies in the Jenks Source Books.

26. "Wilder's Genealogical Reprints", Series M, No. 5.

27. Official copy in Jenks Source Books.

28. V. 1, no. 35.

29. Photocopy in Jenks Source Books under Hearne.

30. The records of the London Company of Cutlers are incomplete for the 16th century and do not show Fulwater's full record.

31. See Great Britain, *State Papers, Domestic* as quoted in *Apollo*, v. 29, p. 125.

32. For information about Solingen see Joseph Beeson Hinsworth, "The Story of Cutlery" (London, 1953), p. 183.

33. He was apprenticed in 1604 as son of John Stone of Sussex, according to the records of the London Company of Cutlers, Guildhall Library. An interesting account of his later life is given by Charles Welch, "History of the Cutlers' Company of London", v. 2, p. 3.

34. See Samuel Evans, "Topographical Dictionary of England" under Hounslow; and Daniel Lysons, "Environs of London" (London 1811), v. 2, p. 444.

35. See "Dictionary of National Biography".

36. . . . "Chronological Index of Patents Applied for and Patents Granted" . . . (London, 1854, v. 1, p. 21.)

37. See Jenks Source Books.

38. See "Dictionary of National Biography" under Stone.

39. "A Middlesex Medley", No. 22, New Series, in Hounslow Public Library.

40. Dr. Richard Williams, F.S.A., furnished much information on the Hounslow swords. See Clement Milward, "English Signed Swords in the London Museums", *Apollo*, v. 29, p. 125–129 (March 1939); and "Further Notes on London and Hounslow Swordsmiths", *Apollo*, v. 35, p. 93–95 (April 1942).

41. "Collections Historical and Archaeological Relating to Montgomeryshire and its Borders", v. 40, pt. 2, p. 187 (1938).

42. See State Papers, New Hampshire, v. 40, p. 7. "At a Court holden the 10° 9° Mo. 42 at Strawberry Banck . . . Joseph Jencks v^{r}sus John Phillips on accon of Case for 120' damage referd to the Court. . . ."

43. See Walter Goodwin Davis, et. al., "Genealogical Dictionary of Maine and New Hampshire". The deed mentioned recites: "Edward Godfrey of Agamenticus (York) gent. to John Alcocke of the same, planter; land on the East side of the Agamenticus (now York) River bounded S. on Joseph Gynkes, N.W. on Abraham Preble, N.E. on Common lands, S.W. on the highway. Dated 16 March 1642/3. Entered 5 Aug. 1675." (York Deeds, Bk. II, fo. 177). At Alfred, Maine.

44. See Professor Arthur Cecil Bining, "British Regulation of the Colonial Iron Industry" (London, 1933), p. 9.
45. Records of the Colony of Massachusetts Bay, v. 59, p. 26.
46. The making of weapons and the making of tools are closely allied crafts of the cutler. According to Charles Welch, "History of the Cutlers' Company", v. 1, p. 1, "The art of the cutler has consisted from the earliest ages in the making of edged weapons and tools".

Unfortunately, the facts available to us are meagre and we can only suggest a broad outline of what appears to us to be probabilities. Professor E. Neal Hartley of the Massachusetts Institute of Technology has carefully studied the American career of Joseph Jenks in connection with the restoration of the Iron Works at Saugus, and in October 1955 he made the following interesting observation on the English findings: "While your English evidence looks quite convincing, I have certain doubts going back to the fact that swords were made of steel and the tools which Jenks made at the Saugus Iron Works were done in wrought iron. It is true that the wrought iron was very good, close to steel, in fact, but both archeological and historical evidences point to an infinitesimally small use of steel at Hammersmith. I suppose the technique would have been about the same, regardless of which material was being used. It may be that it was the difficulty of obtaining steel, which had to be imported from England, that kept Jenks from becoming a sword-maker here in Massachusetts. I just don't know. In this I can merely raise a question."

THE JENKS FAMILY OF ENGLAND

By Meredith B. Colket, Jr., F.A.S.G., of Washington, D. C.

II. The Mother of Joseph Jenks

Joseph Jenks was baptized at St. Anne, Blackfriars, London, on 26 Aug. 1599, the son of John and Sarah (Fulwater) Jenks. The 1596 marriage license of Joseph's parents shows that his mother, Sarah, was a daughter of Henry Fulwater of the parish of St. Anne, Blackfriars, London.

Henry Fulwater was a Protestant who came from the Continent to England about the time of the first great wave of Huguenot migration to England. This migration was described by John Southerden Burn in "The History of the French Walloon, Dutch, and other Foreign Protestant Refugees Settled in England from the Reign of Henry VIII to the Revocation of the Edict of Nantes . . . ." He wrote that the great influx of foreigners was in the year 1567 when "upon the report of the Duke d'Alva coming into the Netherlands with 10,000 veteran soldiers the trading people withdrew from the provinces in such vast numbers that the Duchess of Parma, the Governess, wrote to Philip II that in a few days about 10,000 men had left the country with their money and goods and that more were following every day".[1]

Henry Fulwater's name was apparently first officially recorded in England in 1567 when his name appears as Harry Vallwater, a resident of the ward of Farringdon without London, who had resided in England one year.[2] His name again appears in the return of aliens resident in London in 1571 when he is shown as an apprentice to a cutler:

Farringdon Warde Without. Seincte Brydes Parrishe . . . In Bride Lane . . . Henry Fulwater, Highe Allmayne, no denizen, servant withe Ralfe Cole, cutler, hath bene in England v yeares, and in this ward so longe. Douch, 1.

3. *The mortuary sword in the Powysland Museum with part of the black paint removed showing the inscription of the maker, Joseph Jenckes. Courtesy of Dr. Richard Williams, F.S.A.*

and later:

The Ward of Farringdon Without. Seincte Brydes Parishe . . . Henrie Full-water and William Gyllam, servantes with Raphaell Cole, cutler, were borne in Lukes and [sic] Flanders, and came into this realme to worke about vj yeares past. Douche, ij. French Church.[3]

The expression "Lukes and Flanders" is puzzling. A few entries later, there is a reference to Peron Kirton, widow, born in Lukes in Flanders, who had come into the realm for religion.[4] The name "Lukes" has not been found as a place name in European gazetteers. It is possible that Lukes is meant for Liege, a city and province near Flanders; for, in Flemish, "Luik" means Liege and Het Luikse means "in the neighborhood of Liege". "Lukes" may be a shortened form of "Het Luikse".[5]

Since Henry Fulwater was described as "High Allmayne" or High German, it is likely that he was of a South German family. The surname appears in English records as Fullwater, Fulwater, Falwater, Fallwater, Volwater, and Falwattre. It is possible that it is derived from Vollwasser, voll = full and wasser = water. The name has not, however, been found in Continental records.

The nearest equivalents to Fulwater that have been found among German records are Voll(en)weider, a name Anglicized in America to Fulwider, and Fulwedea.[6] A similar surname, Clear-water, is to be found in eighteenth century New York records in neighborhoods of distinctly Continental peoples, such as Marble-town, Ulster County.[7]

It is perhaps significant that in the same small parish, St. Anne, Blackfriars, where Henry Fulwater spent most of his adult life, there was a contemporary, Richard Fewwater or Feewater.[8] Fee-water, in German, means just the opposite of Fullwater.

German authorities tell us it was common for emigrants at this time to use assumed names; and it is possible that both Fulwater and Feewater were assumed.

Henry Fulwater became a denizen by letters patent on 29 November 1571 when he was described as "Henry Fulwater, from the Dominion of the Emperor".[9] This action gave him certain limited rights of citizenship. His name appears on lists of London aliens throughout his lifetime.

The records of the London Company of Cutlers are incomplete; so we are unable to ascertain the date he completed his apprentice-ship. It is probable that it was about 1571. The apprenticeship bindings of the London Company of Cutlers show:

"Jengken phellepp son of phellep James of Lantellyan, Monmouthshire, hus-band app to henry fulwater for the term of vii yeres to beguine at the Annun-ciation of the Virgin Mary 1575.

"James long son of John Long of Grenwich [Kent] to henry ffulwater for the time of viii years to begin at the Annunciation of the Virgin Mary 1577 [Mar. 25]. Thomas marson the son of Wyllam marson of Yardley in Wor-cestershere tailor apprenticed with henry Fulwater for ye term of vii yeres to begine at ye feast of St. John baptyte 1583 in ye 25 of Queen E".[10]

Henry Fulwater had servants who were not among his apprentices. The burial records of St. Anne, Blackfriars, show the burials of Henry Fulwater's servants, Robert Hewlet and Richard Jacob in 1582 and 1595, respectively. The returns of aliens for 1576 show: "Henrie Valwater, cutler, Tyze his seruaunt"[11]; and for 1582 show "Thomas Witherspon, servaunt to Henry Fowlewater".[12]

HENRY FULWATER probably married about 1571, but the maiden name of his first wife has not been found. A London return of 1583 shows: "Henricke Fullwater, cutler, borne in Germanye, and his wife, are of the French churche. He hath a Scottish man, his servaunt, of Thenglishe churche. He hath two children, English borne. denison xj yeares".[13]

The parish registers of St. Anne, Blackfriars, record the burial of his first wife, MARGARET, 25 April 1595. His second wife, MARY, whom he married about 1596, was named in the records in 1599 and 6 June 1602.[14] He married his third wife, ANNE ———, a native of Rouen, probably in 1603. The parish register of St. Anne, Blackfriars, records the burial of Henry Fulwater 21 Sept. 1603. His widow remarried 11 Feb. 1605, according to the registers of the French Church, Threadneedle Street, London, Robert De La Tour.

Issue apparently by Margaret, baptized at St. Anne, Blackfriars, if baptismal date is given:

   i. JACOB, of St. Anne, Blackfriars, presumably one of the two children identified in the 1583 return cited above. He married, by 1612, MARTHA IRANDE (Airley?) who survived him. He was a citizen and white baker of London, but a cutler by trade and paid the fee for "translation" into the London Company of Cutlers in 1608.[15] Martha's will, dated at St. Anne, Blackfriars, 23 Aug. 1636, was proved in the Commissary Court of London 3 May 1641. Issue, bapt. at the French Church, Threadneedle Street: 1. *Bethia*, bapt. 15 Oct. 1612; 2. *Josue*, bapt. 26 Jan. 1615, evidently d. young as not named in mother's will; 3. *Marie*, bapt. 25 Nov. 1617. The evidence for the identification of Jacob as son of Henry is circumstantial.
   ii. SARAH, bapt. 19 March 1573; m. (lic.) 8 Jan. 1595/6 JOHN JENKS, cutler.
   iii. JOHN, bur. 7 Aug. 1575.
   iv. A CHILD, bur. 14 June 1576.
   v. ELIZABETH, bur. 15 Oct. 1577.
   vi. A CHILD, bur. 20 Feb. 1580.
   vii. ISAAC, bur. 8 March 1582.
   viii. EZEKIEL, bur. 12 May 1591.
   ix. JOANE, bapt. 6 Oct. 1591; bur. 16 July 1593.
   x. MARY, bur. 18 July 1593.
   xi. AQUILA, bur. 26 Nov. 1594.

Issue, evidently by Mary:
   xii. A CHILD, bur. 11 April 1597.
   xiii. A CHILD, bur. 13 Jan. 1598.

Extracts from the earliest parish registers of St. Anne, Blackfriars, London:

Baptisms

1573 Sarah Fulwater daughter to Henry fulwater March XIX.
1591 Jane daughter to Henry fulwater October VI.
1596[7]Sarah daughter to John Ginkes, February 6.
1599 Josephe sonne to John Ginkes Aug. 26.
1619 Mary Fulwater daughter to Jacob and Martha.

1575 Johne sonne to Henry fulwater Aug. 7.
1576 A Crysome of Henry fulwater June 14.
1577 Elisabeth daughter to Henry fulwater Oct. 15.
1580 A Crysome sonne to Henry Fulwater Febr. 20.
1582 Sara daughter to Richard fulwater June 4.
1582 Robert hewlet servant to Henry fulwater Noveb. 14.
1582 Isaac sonne to Henry fulwater March 8.
1591 Ezechiell sonne to Henry fulwater May 12.
1593 Jane daughter to Henry fulwater pl. July 16.
1593 Mary daughter to Henry fulwater pl. July 18.
1594 Aquila sonne to henry fulwater November 26.
1595 Margaret wyfe to Henry fulwater April 25.
1595 Richard Jacob servant to Henry fulwater May 11.
1597 A stilborne Child of Henry fulwater April 11.
1597 A Crisom child of henry falwatrs Januari 13.
1603 Henry Falwater Sept. 21.[16]

Extracts from the Registers of the French Church, Threadneedle Street, London:

Marriages 1605

De La Tour, Robert, fils de feu Louis, natif de Rouen, et Anne, vefue de feu Henry Fulwater, natifue de Rouen. Fev. 11, Mardi. (Tuesday was the 12th.)

Baptisms 1602

Gransize, Magdelaine, fille de Jan G., et de Susanne Prouue, sa femme. *Tém.* Laurent Basin, Magdelaine Chamberlain, vefue, Marye Folwattre, femme de Henry Foullwater. Juin 6.

1612

Falwater, Marie, fille de Jacob F., et de Marthe Airley, sa femme. *Tem.* George Browne, Judic Chanbrelam, femme de Gode de Laune, Agnes Temple. Oct. 15.

1615

Falwater, Josue. ——— "Josue, fils de Jacob Falwater, presente son enfant pour estre baptisé" [sic] *Tém.* Randolphe Woole, Gedeon de Laune, Sarra Broune, grandmere de l'enfant. Janv. 26.

1617

Falwater, Marie, fille de Jacob F., et de Marthe Airley, sa femme. *Tem.* Jacob Torado, Sara Dauid, Jenne Verdiere femme de Jan Baquesne, Nov. 25.[17]

Abstract of the Will of Martha Fallwater filed in the Commissary Court of London:

The Will of Martha Fallwater of the Princinct of Blackfriars in the City of London, dated 23 August, 1636. To my daughter Mary Fallwater £40. To my daughters Bethia and Mary all my plate, rings, household stuff and implements of household and all other moveable goods and the lease of my house to be equally divided between them. The rest of my estate to my daughter Bethia. My will is that the legacy to my daughter Mary shall not be paid to her until she attain the age of 21 years unless she marry in the meantime. My friends William Turges of London merchant and Francis Hulme citizen and haberdasher of London to be executors. Witnesses: George Gilbert. Francis Holmes servant to Henry Colbron scrivener, Henry Colbron. Proved 3 May 1641 by William Turges one of the executors. Power preserved to Francis Hulme the other executor.[18]

FOOTNOTES

1. P.4. It is possibly significant that many of these refugees were, like the emigrant Joseph Jenks, scythe makers. Although some went to Derbyshire, some others may have resided in the vicinity of London. Robert Eadon Leader, wrote of the Derbyshire scythe makers in "History of the Company of Cutlers in Hallamshire" (1905), v.1, p.14, "It has usually been accepted that the localisation of the scythe and sickle trades on the Derbyshire side of Sheffield, so marked a characteristic of the villages there, originated in the settlement of refugees driven out of France and the Netherlands by persecution. It was part of the policy of Elizabeth . . . to encourage this immigration . . . sickle makers were established in Eckington Parish, scythe makers in Norton Parish".

2. *The Publications of the Huguenot Society of London*, v.10, pt.1, p. 362.

3. *Ibid.*, v. 10, pt. 1, p. 421; v. 10, pt. 2, p. 3.

4. *Ibid.*, v. 10, pt. 2, p. 3.

5. Dr. Albert Gerberich kindly checked this point and corresponded with Max V. Krebs, American Consul-General, Antwerp, Belgium.

6. Dr. Karl Friedrick von Frank checked his extensive genealogical data for variants of the surname.

7. United States Bureau of the Census, ". . . Heads of Families at the First Census of the United States: Taken in the Year 1790: New York" (Washington, Govt. Print. Off., 1908).

8. This rare name appears in the unpublished parish registers of St. Anne, Blackfriars, and in the published parish register of St. Mary, Mounthaw, London. It has been found in Middlesex as early as 1554; and we have found no proof that it is of Continental origin.

9. "*Pat.*, 14 Eliz., p. 8, m. 3", *The Publications of the Huguenot Society of London*, v. 8, p. 99.

10. London Company of Cutlers, Apprenticeship Bindings, in Guildhall Library, London.

11. *The Publications of the Huguenot Society of London*, v. 10, pt. 2, p. 181.

12. *Ibid.*, v. 10, pt. 2, p. 253.

13. *Ibid.*, v. 10, pt. 2, p. 357.

14. *Ibid.*, v. 10, pt. 3, p. 51; and the register of the French Church, Threadneedle Street, as quoted.

15. London Company of Cutlers, Minute Book for 1608, p. 65, in Guildhall Library.

16. From the parish registers of St. Anne, Blackfriars, in Guildhall Library.

17. *The Publications of the Huguenot Society of London*, v. 9, pp. 5, 44, 87, 97, and 109.

18. Register, 1630–42, fo. 267.

III. THE FATHER OF JOSEPH JENKS: A PROBLEM IN IDENTITY

We have shown that there were in the vicinity of London early in the 17th century two persons named Joseph Jenks, who were cutlers by trade: Joseph, the American colonist, who was of Horton, Bucks, and Hounslow, Middlesex; and Joseph, who was of the Precinct of the Tower of London and All Hallows on the Wall, London. We have also shown that the father of each was a cutler named John Jenk(e)s.[1] One resided at St. Anne, Blackfriars, London, the other resided at the Precinct of the Tower of London. They are the earliest known members of the family who were cutlers. Following is an identification of each John and his household:

John Jenks of St. Anne, Blackfriars, London

JOHN JENKS of St. Anne, Blackfriars, London, cutler, obtained a license to marry SARAH FULWATER on 8 Jan. 1595/6. She was a resident of the parish having been baptized there 29 March 1573. Her father, Henry Fulwater, a German emigrant, was a member of the London Company of Cutlers.

Issue, baptized at St. Anne, Blackfriars:

i. SARAH, bapt. 6 Feb. 1596/7. No further record.
ii. JOSEPH, bapt. 26 Aug. 1599. The evidence for identifying him as the American colonist is summarized as follows: (1) The baptismal date harmonizes with a deposition of the colonist that places his birth in 1599 or 1600; (2) the place of baptism harmonizes with the American tradition that the colonist was associated with Hammersmith 3½ miles away; (3) the trade of the father corresponds with the trade of the colonist; (4) the German parentage of the youth harmonizes with the traditional and proved association of the American colonist with Hounslow where German cutlers worked; and (5) the name Joseph Jenks at that period was rare.

John Jenks of the Precinct of the Tower of London

John Jenks of the Precinct of the Tower of London, cutler, was born about 1576, for he was presumably 16 years of age when he became apprenticed.[2] The apprenticeship record of 1592 reads:

> Johannes Wyat presentavit Johannes Jencke esse
> apprenticum suum a festo annunciationis beate
> Marie Virginis ultimo pro 7 annis et solvit 4 d.[3]

Thus, on New Year's Day (or Lady Day, then March 25), John Jenks was apprenticed for a term of seven years to John Wyat who paid a fee of four pence for registration. The apprenticeship entry is from the records of the London Company of White Bakers. The Company recorded the apprenticeship, not because John Jenks was learning the trade of baking white bread, but rather because he was apprenticed to a man who happened to belong to the Company that had jurisdiction over the baking trade.

One would expect that John Jenks became a freeman of the Company after his seven years of apprenticeship had expired. He did not become a freeman, however, until 1604, after the expiration of twelve years. This lapse is unexplained. It is conjectured that Jenks was apprenticed to a foreign cutler who removed to the Continent; and the record of the completion of his apprenticeship was not made until his return. For the year following John's apprenticeship to John Wyatt, a John Wyatt of the Ward of Coleman Street, St. Stephens Parish, is mentioned in the London returns of aliens: "John Wyatt and his wief either dead, departed or gone out of the ward".[4] This conjecture is strengthened by the fact that knives made by Jenks in later life are regarded as having characteristic of those of foreign manufacture.

Following is a copy of the minutes of the White Baker's Company showing that John Jenks, together with a Jonas Jenks, became freemen in 1604 at the same time:

> "For appt. made freemen . . . Received of . . . John Jenks late apprtice of John Wyatt vi⁵ viii⁴ . . . Jonas Jyncks late appntice of Richard Harbert vi⁵ viii⁴".[5]

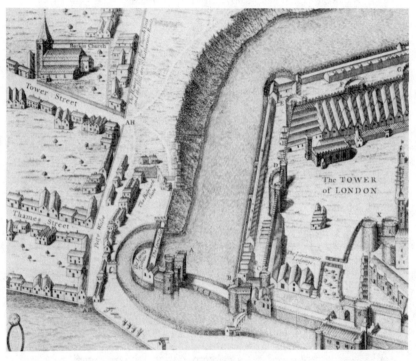

4. *Portion of the Precinct of the Tower of London, in which the Hounslow sword blades were stored, showing the Bulwark Gate where John Jenks, the knife cutler, lived. Courtesy of the Library of Congress.*

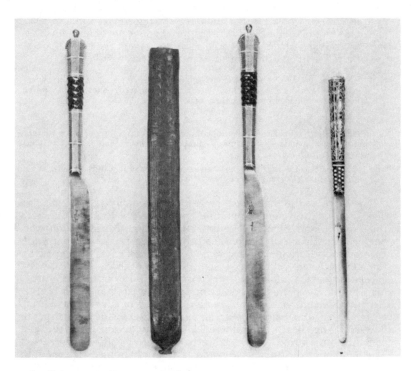

5. *Knives in the Victoria and Albert Museum showing the dagger, which identifies the work of a London cutler, and the mark of the thistle, which was used by John Jenks. Courtesy of the Victoria and Albert Museum.*

From now on John Jenks was a citizen and white baker of London, that is, a citizen of London and a member of the White Baker's Company. The Company would have little cause to record his activities, however, since he did not follow the trade of baking;[6] though he would, of course, record the bindings of his apprentices with the Company.

A London tradesman ordinarily married within a year following the date he obtained his freedom from his company.[7] Although we don't find a marriage record of this date, we know that John left a widow, Hellen, and had a son born about 1607.

John's name appears in the records of the London Company of Cutlers in 1607, shortly after James I had given the Company a charter to regulate conditions in the trade. The Company had invited cutlers who were not members to register the marks used on their knife blades. Such registration made it possible to identify the maker of any blade; and would serve to prevent the unauthorized use of a mark by another. The Company's records show:

> 15th January 1606–7. At the Court appeared theis straungers &c forreyners to whome was made acquaynted & read the charter & rules of this howse who some of them brought in their marks: . . .
>
> John Jencks the thistle
>
> 29th January 1606–7. The following additional names appear in a further list of the above date, when many makers brought in their marks and paid the registration fee:- . . .
>
> John Jencks whose marke is the thistle wch he gave in Court to Tho. Wills who claymeth the same marke formerlie XXVS. ijs. ijd.[8]

The mark of the thistle has been found on many knives that are deposited in the English museums including the British Museum, the Victoria and Albert Museum, the Guildhall Museum, and the Sheffield City Museum and in such private collections as the Howard E. Smith Collection.[9] These knives are identified as belonging to the period when John and Joseph Jenks worked. They are regarded by experts as among the most beautiful examples of craftsmanship of the period. A description of the left hand pair at the British Museum, for example, reads: "Handles of silver ornamented with filigree and enameled green and lilac translucent six petal flowers. The sheath embroidered in silver and gold with lozenges enclosing quarterfoil shaped flowers. Tassel at end. Length 9". The handles of the knives are made of a variety of materials including gold, silver, jet, ivory, inlay, and amber. They are of striking beauty and illustrate workmanship of the highest quality. An illuminating evaluation of the Jenks' knives appears in an article in "The Connoisseur", by Charles R. Beard, entitled "Wedding Knives".[10]

The mark of the thistle was used by John Jenks from at least as early as the date of its registration in 1607 to his death about 1625; and, as we have seen, was used by his son, Joseph, who protested in 1638 that another was wrongfully imitating it.

It is interesting to note that Jenks' name appears on the records of the London Company of Cutlers among strangers and foreigners. Experts regard his work as strongly influenced by foreign craftmanship. It is probable that his shop employed foreign workmen who were not formally apprenticed. The records of his own Company, the Company of White Bakers, show that he apprenticed only two workmen, William Williams on 24 Oct. 1616, and Francis Downes on 17 Feb. 1619.[11] In a list of foreign Protestants and aliens resident in England of March 1621/2, however, is the following: "The names of the Strangers Cutlers . . . English born Lambert Peterseon att Mr. Jenkes vpon Tower Dock. William Balse, is with Lambert, att Mr Jenkes".[12]

Tower Dock was in the Precinct of the Tower of London. Jenks lived in the Precinct of the Tower of London as early as 15 Sept. 1611 when he was accused of being involved in some unsavory business. The unpublished Middlesex Session Rolls show:

> 15 September, 9 James I. Josiah Ellery of Ratcliffe, shipwright, John Jinckes of St. Peters ad Vincula within the Tower of London, cutler, and Richard Peter of East Smithfield, Baker, for the said Josiah and for Bennett Haskett of Ratcliffe, carpenter, and for William Godsall of the same, yeoman, all accused by John Arnold of St. Peter's, Westminister, gentleman, with having set upon him in the highway, and taken his purse with £5 10s in it.[13]

John continued to reside at this residence. The last record of him that we have, shows that he was taxed there in 1625:

> 23 James I
> Hundred of Ossulstone
> Tower without the Bulwarke gate
> John Jenks, his goods, 4 li. Subsidy 10s. 8d.[14]

The location of the Tower without the Bulwark Gate is given in "A True and Exact Drought of the Tower Liberties Surveyed in the Year 1597" (printed in 1742.) This was the work of Gulielmus Haiward and J. Gascoyne. The few houses in the immediate vicinity of the Bulwark Gate are individually depicted. It is possible that Jenks supplied knives to the Tower.

John Jenks died sometime between 1625 and 16 August 1626, when his son, John, described as recently son of John Jenks, citizen and white baker of London, defunct, began his apprenticeship to a member of the Company of Cutlers.[15]

John's widow continued to live by the Bulwark Gate, for the subsidy lists of July 1628 reveal:

> Hundred of Ossulstone
> Tower without the Bullwarke
> Elinor Jenkes widow goodes 4 li. Subsidy 21s. 4d.[16]

Elinor (Eleanor) is a variant of Hellen (Helen), according to the "Oxford Dictionary of English Christian Names".[17] "Its relation to Helen was apparently recognized as late as 1604 when a list of Yorkshire recusants calls the same person indifferently *Helen* and *Elinor.*"

The minutes of the London Company of Cutlers tell an interesting story concerning the right of John Jenks' eldest son to the mark of the bunch of grapes. The right to this mark had once belonged to Lambert Williams, and after his death the Company permitted his widow to strike it through her servants and journeymen. She eventually sold, but without authority, the right to the mark to John Hubberd, and later, on her deathbed, willed it to her servant William Balser. The question of the title to the mark was brought before the Company. The Company refused to confirm the sale of the right to John Hubberd, "a free brother of this mystery", since he was no workman. In consideration, however, of the money paid by John Hubberd, the Company permitted him to reserve the right of the bunch of grapes to the eldest son of John Jenks "when he shall be capable so to strike the same".[18]

In 1628, following John's death, his widow, Hellen, made arrangements to convey the right to the mark to William Balls or Bales, the servant to whom it had once been willed. According to a memorandum of 6 March 1627/8, "Hellen Jenks and William Balls" agreed to its sale for VI£ sterling. According to a record of 9 Oct. 1628 "William Bales" purchased the right from "Widdo Jencks and Joseph Jencks, her son".[19]

In 1630 Benjamin Stone, the sword cutler of Hounslow, claimed the right to the bunch of grapes; but the records of the Company do not reveal the basis for his claim. Stone refused to obey an order of the Company, was adjudged in contempt, and was forbidden to strike the bunch of grapes.[20]

Known issue of John and Hellen:

    i. JOSEPH, b. *ca.* 1607; d. by 7 Sept. 1642; m. 30 Sept. 1630 MARY TERVYN. His life story has been given. Known issue: (1) *Sarah*, bapt. 13 Oct. 1635, in the chapel of St. Peter ad Vincula, Tower of London.

    ii. JOHN, b. *ca.* 1610 (evidently the John, son of John Jenkes, bapt. 6 April 1611 at nearby St. James Clerkenwell, Middlesex, according to *The Publications of the Harleian Society*, v. 9, p. 61), of the Tower of London, cutler; m. 17 July 1634[21] HANNAH GLINN. He was apprenticed to a member of the Company of Cutlers 16 Aug. 1626,[22] and became a citizen and cutler of London 12 June 1634.[23] Issue, bapt. in the chapel of St. Peter ad Vincula, Tower of London; (1) *John*, bapt. 27 Sept. 1635; and (2) *Sarah*, bapt. 16 July 1637.[24]

A comparison of the two John Jenks and their households reveals similarities too striking to be coincidental:

1. Each John was a resident of London. One John resided at St. Anne, Blackfriars, London, 1596–99. The other John resided in London as early as 1592; and from 1611 until his death he was a resident of the Precinct of the Tower of London.
2. Each was a cutler by trade.
3. Each was associated with foreign cutlers. The one married a daughter of a foreign cutler; the other had foreign cutlers in his shop.
4. Each family group was associated with a foreign cutler of the same name. John Jenks' father-in-law, Henry Fulwater, lived near a Lambert Peterson in 1571.[25] The other John Jenks' household included a Lambert Peterson in 1621/2.

5. Each family group was associated with the London Company of White Bakers. John Jenks of St. Anne, Blackfriars, had a brother-in-law, Jacob Fulwater, who was translated from that Company to the London Company of Cutlers in 1608. John Jenks of the Precinct of the Tower of London was a member of the Company of White Bakers.

6. Each had a son Joseph, a name uncommon in England at that time.

7. In each family the female name Sarah predominates. The wife and the only known daughter of John Jenks of St. Anne, Blackfriars, was named Sarah. The only known daughters of Joseph and John, children of John Jenks of the Precinct of the Tower of London, was, in each case, Sarah.

It is conceivable that the Johns were identical; for it was not infrequent in England in those days for a man to have two surviving sons of the same name. Such a theory, however, is weak. John Jenks of St. Anne, Blackfriars, was called cutler in his marriage license of 1595/6. John Jenks who came to be of the Precinct of the Tower of London was actually an apprentice at that date. Secondly, the eldest son of John Jenks of the Precinct of the Tower of London was mentioned in the minutes of the London Company of Cutlers in 1623 as not then able to wield a mark. This could not refer to the Joseph baptized in 1599, the son of John Jenks of St. Anne, Blackfriars, because Joseph was of age in 1623. For these reasons we reject the theory that the two Johns are identical.

It is also conceivable that the John Jenks of St. Anne, Blackfriars, was a widower when he married Sarah Fulwater, and that he was father of the John Jenks of the Precinct of the Tower of London by a previous marriage. The marriage license of John Jenks of St. Anne, Blackfriars, which was previously quoted, does not state whether the groom was a bachelor or a widower. If the latter was true, the two Johns could be father and son.

This inference harmonizes well with the facts, for a son often followed the trade of his father in the same city. This inference would explain the close association with foreign cutlers and, in particular, with a Lambert Peterson. It would explain the association of both family groups with the London Company of White Bakers. It would explain the recurrence of the names, Joseph and Sarah. The similarities of these two family groups can not satisfactorily be explained otherwise. We conclude, therefore, that the two Johns were probably father and son; and we shall identify them as Senior and Junior, respectively.

Who, then, was John Jenks, Sr., the father of the American colonist, Joseph Jenks? His intimate association with Continental cutlers and the fact that his name is recorded Ginkes in the parish register of St. Anne, Blackfriars, suggest the possibility that he had lived on the Continent. They also suggest the possibility that he was of European background and that his name was Anglicized to Jenks.[26]

We believe, however, that his name was Jenks or Jenkes, as given in his marriage license, and that the recording of Ginkes, which exists in the case of the baptismal records of his two children, was the result of recording an oral statement of the name made by his wife, who was of German extraction.

The identification of the forbears of John Jenks, Sr., has proved difficult. We have one important clue, however. It was shown that when John Jenks, Jr., became a freeman of the London Company of White Bakers, a Jonas Jenks also became a freeman. This appears significant for the following reasons:

1. The Jenks surname is infrequent in the London area at that day; and the appearance of two different Jenks' names on the same page of the minute book of the Company of White Bakers seems more than a coincidence.

2. John Jenks, Jr., we have inferrred, had a brother with the then unusual name of Joseph. Joseph and Jonas are Biblical names unusual for the period and when found are commonly found in the same family.

3. The Joseph Jenks, who later went to New England, had, according to tradition,[27] a son who went to Virginia. Jonas Jenks had a son Jonas who is the only known colonist of this surname who sailed for Virginia. If Jonas and Joseph are brothers, we have a confirmation of the traditional association with Virginia, except that the Virginia settler was a nephew of Joseph instead of a son.

FOOTNOTES

1. The spelling is interchangeable.

2. See Percival Boyd "Time Table of a London Merchant" in *The Genealogists' Magazine*, v. 9, p. 319.

3. Company of White Bakers, Court Minute Book, 1561–1592, fo. 281, *recto*, #5177/2, in Guildhall Library, London.

4. *The Publications of the Huguenot Society of London*, v. 10, pt. 2, p. 444.

5. Company of White Bakers, Minute Book 1592–1617, #5177/3, in Guildhall Library.

6. He is called citizen and white baker of London in the records of the Company of Cutlers in 1626 as noted below.

7. See Percival Boyd "Time Table of a London Merchant" in *The Genealogists' Magazine*, v. 9, p. 319.

8. Charles, Welch, *"History of the London Cutler's Company"*, London, 1923, v. 2, pp. 335–6.

   Letters from officials of these Museums are in the Jenks Source Books. For the Howard E. Smith Collection, see *The Connoisseur*, v. 134, pp. 164–73 (December 1954), article by J. F. Hayward, Esq., of the Victoria and Albert Museum.

10. *Ibid.*, v. 85, pp. 91–97 (Feb. 1930).

11. Company of White Bakers, Court Minute Book, 1592–1617, fo. 307, #5177/3; and 1617–1648, fo. 23, *dorso*, #5177/4 in Guildhall Library.

12. *The Publications of the Huguenot Society of London*, v. 10, pt. 3, p. 259; v. 8, p. 191, records the denizenship of Lambert Peterson from the Dominion of the Duke of Cleves, 1562.

13. Sessions Roll 506/37, 507/39/40/41; Goal Delivery Register, 1/177; and Sessions Register, 1/432, in Middlesex County Record Office.

14. Subsidy List, E 179/142/284, in Public Record Office, London.

15. "Johes Jencks filius Johes Jencks nup cy white baker defunct posiut xrofero Langton citizen and cutlerario London a dat usque octo annorum dat 16th Auguste 1626 turned over to John ffawrel of London cutler for the terme aforesaid". Minute Book of the London Company of Cutlers for 1626, fo. 49.

16. Subsidy List, E 179/142/307, in Public Record Office, London.

17. Compiled by E. G. Withycombe.

18. "6th Jan. 1622–23 (Long minute abridged). One Lambert Williams formerly had grant of the Bunch of Grapes. After his death his widow continued to strike it by her servants & journeymen 'bye the tolleracon of this howse.' The widow in her life time did take upon her to sell the mark (which was out of her power to do) to John Hubberd free brother of this Mistery. Nevertheless on her death bed she again disposed of the mark by her will to one William Balser her man contrary to the orders of this house, for 'the disposinge & allowing of all marcks to any person or persons usinge the same mysterie of Cutlers is in the said Mr & Wardeins & Assistaunts. Now for so muche as the said John Hubberd is not capable of him self beinge no worckman to stricke or have the same marck allowed vnto him And yet to give the same John Hubberd some Content for the money he paid in his owne wronge for the same marke the Court' have at his request reserved the Bunch of Grapes for the use of the eldest son of John Jencks when he shall be capable to so strike the same. Meanwhile the said mark is to 'lye dead & not to be struck by the allowaunce of this howse by any person or persons'. (Min. f. 186)". Charles Welch, "History of the Cutler's Company of London", v. 2, p. 343.

19. "6th March 1627–8. Memorandum that it is agreed betwene Hellen Jencks and William Balls concerning the marke of the bunch of Graps as followeth vizt that the sayd William doth buy the said marke of the sayd Hellen for euer payeing for the same the sum of vjl. sterling as followeth . . . and is to haue possession of the marke at the payement of first iijl. & to giue good security by bond for the other. (Min. f. 226b.) 9th October, 1628. William Bales presented the bunch of grapes wch formerly was in question for the ending of all Controversies the sayd William Bales hath purchased the same of Widdow Jencks and Joseph Jencks her sonne and had the same enrowled to him & his heires for euer in this Court. (Min. f. 229b.)" Charles Welch, "History of the Cutlers' Company of London", v. 2, p. 345.

20. "21st January, 1629–30. At this Court Beniamin Stone a free brother of this howse Came to haue the marke of the bunch of graps enrowled to him the wch alreadie is enrowled by Consent of this Court to one William Balls yet because this Court is readie to giue a just heareing Concerning the sayd marke to the sayd Beniamyn Stone their answere was that against & at the next Court those whome the same marke did alreadie Concerne should be summoned togeather & then this Court should determyne the same in the meane tyme this Court required xs. the wch he for his Contempt was formerly fyned. And at wch demaund of the sayd xs. the sayd Beniamyn Stone in Contempt refused & left the Court. (Min. f. 239b.) 11th January, 1630–1. Beniamyn Stone was forewarned to strike the bunch of Grapes. (Min. f. 247b.)" Charles Welch, "History of the Cutlers' Company of London", v. 2, p. 346.

21. "The Marriage Registers of St. Dunstan's Stepney, in the County of Middlesex," v. 1, p. 226.

22. See above.

23. Company of Cutlers, Minute Book for 1634, in the Guildhall Library. See Jenks Source Books.

24. The records are in the Chapel of St. Peter ad Vincula.

25. *The Publications of the Huguenot Society of London*, v. 10, pt. 1, p. 421. We surmise the Petersons were father and son.

26. See *Ibid.*, v. 8, p. 114, however, for a Gynkes, alias Bretein, who emigrated to England early in the 16th century.

27. THE REGISTER, v. 9, p. 201.

THE JENKS FAMILY OF ENGLAND

By MEREDITH B. COLKET, JR., F.A.S.G., of Washington, D. C.

IV. THE JENKS FAMILY OF CLUN AND CLUNBURY, SHROPSHIRE

We have shown that the New England colonist, Joseph Jenks, was baptized at St. Anne, Blackfriars, London, 26 Aug. 1599, the son of John Jenks, cutler. We have tried to show that another John Jenks, cutler, of the precinct of the Tower of London, born about 1576, was also son of John Jenks of St. Anne, Blackfriars, and half-brother of Joseph Jenks.

John Jenks of the Precinct of the Tower of London, we have noted, became a member of the London Company of White Bakers on the same day in 1604 as Jonas Jenks (*ca.* 1580–1622), and they are named on the same page in the Company's Minute book. We suspect that Jonas Jenks was related and suggest that he was a brother of John and a half brother of the young Joseph. This suggestion is greatly strengthened by the fact that Jonas Jenks had a son Jonas who came to Virginia; and there is a long standing tradition among the descendants of the New England colonist that a relative came to Virginia.[1] According to the tradition, Joseph Jenks' son, Joseph, had a *brother* who came to Virginia. If our hypothesis is correct, Joseph Jenks, Jr., had a *cousin* who came to Virginia. It should be noted that Jonas is the only early Jenks known to have come to Virginia.[2]

Two additional factors favor the suggested relationship. Both Joseph and Jonas emigrated from the London area where the Jenks surname is uncommon. Each had a Biblical name so rare for the period as to suggest they might belong to the same family group. Jonas Jenks was associated with the family at Clun, a parish in the southwestern part of Shropshire, and very near the Welsh border. For he was called cousin in the will of Richard Jenks of Clun in 1623. Richard had no sons; and of his two brothers, John and

516

JOSEPH JENCKES   ME FECIT HOVNSLO

6. *Inscription on the Jenks' Sword, Powysland Museum, Welshpool, Wales.*
Courtesy of Dr. Richard Williams, F.S.A.

William, John died without issue. William was the closest male relative of Richard and we suspect that he was the forebear of Jonas. Jonas seems more likely a grandson than a son of William for Jonas (*ca.* 1580–1622) was 45 years the junior of Richard (*ca.* 1535–1623). If the hypothesis is correct, Jonas and Joseph, the half-brothers, are sons of John Jenks, cutler, of St. Anne, Blackfriars, London, and grandsons of William Jenks of the family at Clun, Shropshire.

This suggested ancestry harmonizes with the known facts though it just barely meets the chronological test. Richard's brother, William, was born not earlier than 1536, and William's presumed son, John, must have been born about 1556 to have a son John, the London cutler, who was born about 1576.

Since we cannot prove that William had children, we should not overlook the possibility that Joseph and Jonas were of the closely related family at nearby Clunbury. Richard Jenks of Clun, in his will of 1623, named John Jenks of Clunbury. It should be particularly noted that Joseph Jenks, the colonist, who was baptized 26 Aug. 1599, was the first Jenks known to have the baptismal name Joseph. It is interesting that the second known Jenks to have the baptismal name Joseph was Joseph Jenks, baptized at Clunbury 11 March 1603/4. William, the son of the first John of Clunbury, is a possible ancestor of the London Jenks. Families of the parishes of both Clun and Clunbury sent their sons to London to learn their trades; and by the early seventeenth century the Jenkses at Clun had died out and the Jenkses at Clunbury were barely represented.

The Family of John Jenks of Clunbury

[William Jenks, Collector, was taxed on 4 pounds worth of goods at Clunbury and Brompton in 1524. Since this is the only reference to William, it is possible he is identical with the William Jenks, Collector, of Munslow. The Munslow Jenkses are of the family of the parish of Eaton-under-Heywood, which is nearby. William may be the father of John, below, and of Hugh of Clun.]

1.   JOHN JENKS, of Clunbury, is first to be found in the important subsidy of 1524, where he is described as of Kempton which is near Clun. Then and once later during the reign of Henry VIII he was taxed on 40 shillings worth of goods.

The will of John Jenks of Clunbury, which was dated 20 July 1549, was filed in the Consistory Court of Hereford, date of probate not shown. He named two sons, John, the executor, and William; his godson William, William's son; his wife Marjorie; and Henry O'Court.

Children:

2. i.   JOHN, evidently eldest son.
   ii.   WILLIAM, father by 1549. No further record. A possible forebear of the London Jenks family discussed.

2.   JOHN JENKS, of Clunbury, executor of his father's will and evidently eldest son, wrote his will on 20 Jan. 1588/9. The will was filed in the Consistory Court of Hereford, but

the date of probate has not been preserved. John named his eldest son, Richard, and his wife, Anne, in his will. The names of other sons have been ascertained from the will of his eldest son, Richard, and from a chancery proceeding discussed below.

Children:

i. RICHARD, *d. s.p.* His will, dated 9 Feb. 1588/9, filed in the Consistory Court of Hereford, named his brothers, Henry and Thomas.

ii. HENRY, named in will of brother, Richard, in 1589, and named as deceased in chancery proceeding relating to brother, John, in 1595.

iii. THOMAS, named in will of brother, Richard. No further record.

3. iv. JOHN, born *ca.* 1567, citizen and haberdasher of London.

v. MATHEW, made agreement with brother, John, about 1588. He had a life interest in a copyhold in Clunbury, according to his own deposition identified below. Described as of "Clunbury and Brompton", he was taxed 36 Elizabeth (1594–95) and 37 Elizabeth (1595–96) on property valued at 20 shillings. Known issue, bapt. at Clunbury: (1) Henrie, bapt. 19 March 1596/7; (2) Frances, bapt. 10 June 1599, presumably Francisca, who m. at Clunbury, 20 Nov. 1620, Thomas Fidian; (3) Joseph, bapt. 11 March 1603/4; bur. 6 Jan. 1605/6; and presumably (4) John, bur. 9 Feb. 1638/9; will proved C. C. Hereford, mentions several children including one son under 21, the children of Thomas Fiddian, and sister Frauncis.

3. JOHN JENKS, of Clunbury, Shropshire, citizen and haberdasher of London, was born about 1567. He was apprenticed in London to Thomas Damport (Davenport), and on 11 Jan. 1582/3 became a citizen and haberdasher of London, or freeman of the London Company of Haberdashers. One of the earliest known members of the Jenks family, William Jenks, who lived over a century earlier, was likewise a citizen and haberdasher of London.

In 1595 John brought suit against his brother, Mathew, over the handling of his property interests at Clunbury. John may have returned to Clunbury, for Richard Jenks of Clun, in his will of 1623, made a bequest to "John Jenks late of London and now of Clunbury". The Clunbury parish registers show the burial of a John Jenks 11 May 1629; and of an Anne Jenks, widow, 22 Nov. 1633.

The following entries appear to relate to his family:

29 May 8 James I (1610). Recognizances taken of John Jenckes of St. Faith's parish, London, haberdasher, et. al., for appearance of John Fryne of St. Olave's. (*Middlesex Sessions' Rolls*, II, 64.)

19 May 1616 m. lic. Jerrard Bancrofte, Gent., of St. Nicholas Cole Abbey, Bach[r] 23, and Beatrix Jenkes of St. Bennets, Paul's Wharf, dau of John Jenkes of City of London who consents. at St. Gregory's near St. Paul's.

15 Jan. 1617/18 m. lic. Robert Jenkes of St. Nicholas Cole Abbey, London, haberdasher, and Susan Stockwell of St. Mary, Somerset, London, spinster, at St. Faith's.

The Family of Hugh Jenks of Clun

1. HUGH JENKS, the only Jenks of this given name found in the sixteenth century, was presumably born about 1510–15 (eldest son

born about 1535). He was taxed at Hobendred ("Habendryd"), a small place near Clun, on four pounds in goods, 34 Henry VIII (1542/3). He paid a tax of 10d. on five pounds in goods, in 36 Henry VIII (1544/5).

Hugh's will was dated 10 July 1551. He made bequests to sons John and William, and named his wife, Anne, and son, Richard, executors. His widow described herself as Agnes Jenks of New Chappel, parish of Clun, on 12 Jan. 1569, when she made her will. She bequeathed to Richard, eldest son, John, second son, William, youngest son, and Dorothy, daughter. Both wills were proved in the Consistory Court of Hereford, but the dates of probate were not preserved.

Children:

2. i. RICHARD, b. ca. 1535.
   ii. JOHN, of Bucknell, Shropshire, d. s.p., naming his brothers and sister in his will dated 9 May 1571 (P.C.C. 31 Holney).
3. iii. WILLIAM. Presumably ancestor of some London Jenks named as cousins in will of brother Richard. See below. Administration on the estate of a William Jenks of Shrewsbury was granted in 1611 to the widow Alicia by the Prerogative Court of Canterbury.
   iv. DOROTHY, m. by 1571.

2. RICHARD JENKS, of the parish of Clun and nearby Hobendred and Kennerton, gentleman, was born *circa* 1535 (aged about 80 in 1615), died between 24 Sept. and 1 Dec. 1623, the respective dates of the signing and probating of his will.

His name appears on subsidy lists of 1570/71, 1592/93, 1593/94, 1594/95, and 1606/07. He was taxed on as much as 40 shillings in lands and 4 pounds in goods. His name appears several times in 1579 and 1580 on fragmentary manorial rolls of Clunbury preserved in the Public Record Office. These records show that he served as a juror and was involved in cases at law.

On 13 Oct. 1615, when he was "about 80", he was a plaintiff in a chancery suit, the records of which are quoted in part below. He brought suit against his son-in-law, John Middleton, and the latter's father over agreements arising out of the marriage contract of his deceased daughter, Joan.

His unusually long will of 24 Sept. 1623, named the children of his daughter. They were beneficiaries of such feudal pieces as "a cressit with a mainspike, staff, sword, dagger, headpiece thereto", and "a corselet with the furniture thereto".

Child:

i. JOAN, b. ca. 1580 (under 20 in 1597); d. ca. 1613 (d. two years before 1615); m. (contract 9 Sept. 1597) JOHN MIDDLETON of Riston. He m., secondly, Joan, widow of Oliver Redge.

Richard named a great many persons in his will, but initially made bequests to the following members of the Jenks family: "First I give the bequeath to the two sonnes of my cosen Jonas Jenks of London, deceased, called Jonas and Joshua or by what other names they are called, the some of six pownde thirteen shillings foure pence apiece. Item I doe give and bequeath to John Jenke late of London and now of Clunbury five pounde and to his three sonnes twenty shillings apiece. Item I give and bequeath to my cozen William Jenks of London Tenn pownds if he be living." It is significant that all Jenkses named had a London connection. It is possible that John, formerly of London but now of Clunbury, is the John Jenks, citizen and haberdasher of London. The identity of William is uncertain.

3. WILLIAM JENKS was living in 1571. We have suggested above that he was father of John Jenks of St. Anne, Blackfriars, and grandfather of John Jenks of the Precinct of the Tower of London, Jonas Jenks, and the American colonist, Joseph Jenks.

Jonas Jenks, who was named cousin in the will of William's brother, Richard, was of Bermondsey, Surrey, and St. Alphage, London Wall, Cripplegate, London, chandler, was born about 1580. He was in London in 1596 when he was apprenticed to a freeman of the Company of White Bakers. In 1604 both he and John Jenks, cutler, were made freemen of the Company. These two members of the Jenks family were apparently not the first Jenks to become members of the Company. Sylvia Thrupp wrote on page 102 of "A Short History of the Worshipful Company of Bakers of London": "Early in the reign of Henry VIII a baker named William Jenks was employed as an agent for the City . . ."

Jonas married at Bermondsey, Surrey, in 1612, ANN PETO. By 1617 he had moved to the parish of St. Alphage, London Wall, Cripplegate, London. He was buried there 24 April 1622, and was then described as "Mr. Jonas Jencks cunstable & a vestryman". Administration was granted on the estate of Jonas Jenks, chandler, to Ann Jenks, the relict, on 2 May 1622 in the Archdeaconry Court of London.

On 2 Dec. 1623, John Ma(u)ltby, ale-brewer, and Anne Jenks of St. Alphage, London, widow of Jonah [sic], late of the same, were granted a license to marry by the Bishop of London. Two wills of John Maltby at the parish of St. Olave, Southwark, co. Surrey, brewer, were proved in the Prerogative Court of Canterbury, the first being declared null and void. Only in the first will, which was dated 14 March 1634–35, were Jonas and Josiah named; they were described as "my second wife's sons". The second will was dated 22 June 1636, the year of his death.

Children of Jonas and Anne, the two youngest baptized

at the parish of St. Alphage, London Wall, Cripplegate,
London:

i. JONAS, b. *ca.* 1614; d. between 1 Aug. 1633, when a nuncupative
will was made, and 9 Oct. 1636, when his will was proved by Joan
Tyers, his aunt (105 Pile). The will refers to property which his
mother Anne Jenkes of London "gave to him until he became 21
or returned from VIRGINIA". He described himself as son of
Jonas Jenkes, citizen and white baker of London, and mentions
Joan Tyers of St. Mary, Maudlius, Surrey.

ii. RICHARD, bapt. 13 July 1617; bur. 17 April 1619.

iii. JOSIAH, bapt. 5 March 1619/20; presumably living 14 March 1634/5.

DOCUMENTS

(1) *Family of John Jenks of Clunbury*

The will of John Jenks of Clunbury, Shropshire, dated 20 July 1549: to
Margerye my wyffe and to John my sone all myn oxen to be indyffrently devyded
betwene them to. Item I give to John Wylcoke a blowde heyffyr of to yere olde.
Item I bequethe to John Rychards and to John Lyckas a blacke heyffyr to be
devyded indifferently betwene them to. Item I bequeth to H . . . hyrde iii s
iv d.. Item I give to John the sone of Rychard Madoc a blacke blowde yerelyng
heyffyr. Item I bequeth to [thomas] the son of John Truerper a bullock of to
yere olde. [Item I] bequeth to my godsone the sonne of Wylliam Jenks iii s iv d.
Item I bequeth to Wylliam my sone a black blowde cow, so that I wyll that
Margerye my seid wife shall have the kepyng and the profett of her duryng her
life. Item I bequeth to every oon of my god chyldern foure pence apece. Item
I geve to Margery my seid wife a blacke blowde cow, a caye mare and halff my
my [*sic*] corne and grayne beyng in mybarne and growyng in the fylds. Item I
bequeth to Sir Davyd Jones clerke to busshells of Rye. All the Resydeue of my
goods as yet unbequethed I wyll that after my funerall dyscharged my detts, pyd
and my bequeste performed that it be stowed for the welth of my soule and all
chrysten where moste nede ys by the advyse and dyscrescyon of Margerye my
seid wyfe and John my sone executors. Wytnes Sir Davyd Johannis curet of
Clonburye Harry Oconorte [?] Wyth others more. No probate act. Consistory
Court of Hereford, deposited National Library of Wales, Aberystwyth, Wales.

The will of John Jenckes of Clomberye. Dated 20 Jan. 1588–9. To be buried
in the Church of Clomberie. Ane my wife and Richard my son to be executors
to see my debts, legacies and funerals paid and discharged, any overplus when my
debts be discharged equally to be divided amongst my children. Testator owes
to Mr. Hill, vicar of Bromfelde, £6 and to Mr. Richard Vaghan, £3. Witnesses:
Henrie Court with others. No probate act. Consistory Court of Hereford.

The will of Rychard Jenckes of Clumbury. Dated 9 Feb. 1588–9. To be
buried in the church of Clumbury. To Henry Court my uncle half my sheep,
and the other half to Henry and Thomas my brethren equally to be divided
betwixt them. To Henrie Court one cow. To Mary Court, my uncle's daughter,
one heifer. All the rest of my goods to Henry and Thomas my brethren equally
to be divided betwixt them. My brother Henry to be executor. Henry Court
to be overseer. Witnesses; Henry Court, Edward Lloyd minister, with others.
No probate act. Consistory Court of Hereford.

Chancery Proceedings, Public Record Office, C 8/25/97. *Plaintiff:* John
Jenkes, citizen and haberdasher of London. *Defendant:* Mathew Jenkes, John's
elder brother, of Clunbury (Salop). *Date* 1595. *Contents:* John has property in
Clunbury and about 7 years ago he caused the land to be sown with rye and oats
which represented a value of £20. John and Mathew made an agreement according to which Mathew should receive 1/3 of the value and he promised to pay the
residue or £13.6.8. to John. At the same time John left 40 sheep, worth about
£10. on the land of Henry Jenks, another brother, together with other goods of
a value of about £10. John also lent Mathew 23s., which money never has been
paid back. John went away and left Henry as his bailiff and deputee. Mathew,
however, bought secretly the sheep and other goods which John left behind,
using the money he had borrowed from John. After Henry's death, Mathew

522

managed to get hold of more of John's property, but he refuses to pay anything to John. *The answer of Mathew Jenkes:* John has brought forward a false accusation because he wants to take away Mathew's copyhold which he holds of the Queen in the honor of Clunbury, for the term of his life. Mathew maintains that he made a different agreement with John. He only promised to sow about 6 acres of his copyhold with rye. John would receive 1/3 of the harvest, but John would satisfy Mathew for the seed. The harvest that year was very bad, but John has received 1/3 of it. Henry threshed it, for which he received 2 bushels of rye which he sold for 2s. 8d. or 3s. a bushel. In addition John bought corn from Henry. Henry had this corn as executor of Richard Jenks, his brother, who in his turn was executor of Agnes Jenkes, their mother. John sold this corn to Mathew for £4. Mathew bought 40 sheep from Henry but they were Henry's property.

The parish registers of Clunbury which begin in 1574 are published and include the following Jenks entries:

Baptisms

19 Mar. 1596–7	Henrie son of Mathew Jencks
10 June 1599	Frances dau. of Mathew Jencks
11 Mar. 1603–04	Joseph son of Mathew Jenckes

Marriage

20 Nov. 1620	Thomas Fidian & Francisca Jenkes

Burials

2 Dec. 1604	Elizabeth Jenckes
6 Jan. 1605–06	Joseph [*sic*] Jenckes
11 May 1629	John Jenkes
22 Nov. 1633	Anne Jenkes, widow
2 Feb. 1634–5	Jane Jankes, pauper
9 Feb. 1638–9	John Jenkes
5 Apr. 1644	Jone Jenckes
27 Apr. 1644	Marcy wife of John Jenckes

(2) *Family of Hugh Jenks of Clun*

The will of Hugh Jenks of Clun, Shropshire. Dated 10 July 1551. Item I bequethe to the chathedral churche of Harvord iiii^d. Item I bequethe to John my sonne ii oxen xxx^ti gotte and xx lames beyng in the custody of Meiryce ap John of the parishe of Watden. Item I bequethe to William my sonne ii oxen beyng in the custody of Gruf ap Johann of the parish of Clone. Item I bequethe to Doryte my daughter ii keyne beyng in the custody of meyn executors. Item I bequethe all the resydue of my goodes unbequethed movable and unmovable to Annes my wyfe and Richart my sonne. Item I do make and ordeyne to be meyne executors Annes my wyfe and Richart my sonne to see this my last will and testament fulfilled and to be overseeres John ap Gwelyn Ca . . . and William Stodman. In witnesse John Parson clerke my gostly fader [*sic*] Harry Ferves and John Haggley with other. No probate act. Consistory Court of Hereford.

The will of Agnes Jenks [widow] of the Newchappell in the parish of Clun. Dated 12 Jan. 1569. Item I do ordeyne and make to be my Executors Richard Jenks my eldest sonne and John Jenks my second sonne. Item I geave and bequeth unto John Jenks aforesaid my sonne my beest panne. Item I geave and bequeth unto William Jenks my yongest sonne two Ewes. Item all the resydue of my goods unbequethed I geave and bequeth unto my said Executors willinge them to be good unto Doretie my dowghter. Wittnes Nycolas Browne, John Nixon and others. No probate act. Consistory Court of Hereford.

The will of John Jenks of Bucknell, Shropshire, May 6, 1571. My body to be buried in the churche yarde of Bucknill. Item I bequeth to the poore of the parish there v^s. Item I given to my brother William Jenkes vi^li xiii^s iiii^d. Item I give to my sister Dorothie iii^li vi^s viii^d to be paied after her husband decease. Item I give to my Maister Howell Clone iii^li vi^s viii^d and one Bullocke. Item I give to Thomas Powell xx^s. I give to Richard Powell xx^s which is in the hands of Howell Clone my master. Item I give to John Powell xx^s. Item I give to Mary Powell xx^s. Item I give to Johanna Styche my god daughter vi^s. Item I give

523

to John Mason my god sonne vi^s. Item I give to Elnore his maide xvi^d. Item I gyve to Mary his maide xii^d. Item I give to William Squyre xii^d. Item I give to Guset Squire xii^d. Item I gyve to John Gor ii^s vi^d. Item I gyve to Maulde Fermor ii^s vi^d. Item I give to John Hickes two busshells of corne and two of otes. Item I give iiii shepe to Thomas Aprict of Clancadar. Item I give two shepe to Lewis Aprict of Clancadare childerne which he is the keping of Thomas Aprict. Item I give to Richard Jenckes my brother one cowe and a calf in the keping of Howell Clone my Master and more unto hym iiii kyne that I have with Thomas Aprice the one is for the first mylke and calf and two heyfers and one yerling and lx sheppes the stocke being iiii^{li} xvii^s viii^d and one rout mare and abaye fillye colte and foure fillys the one iiii yeres of aige and two fillys iii yeres of aige and one two yeres of aige and more unto hym xx shepe in the keping of Lewys a price of Clancadare the stocke xxxix^s. Item I give more to my brother Richard xl shepe which I have with Nicholas Broune, the stocke iii^{li} xiii^s iiii^d and more with hym xv shepe and vi lambes the stocke xv^s and one cowe and vi shepe with John Hickes of Sucken. Item I will and give more unto hym xx^{ti} gotes which I have with John Lewys of the parishe of Waterdeane the hire vi^s viii^d due at Barnabe next, and if the said John do pay me my xx^{ti} gotes of two yeres of aige at Seint Barnabie th appostell next commyng my will is to gyve hym vi^s viii^d and Henry Jarveyes doth owe to me iiii^{li} xiii^s iiii^d and if he do pay me at the feast of Seint Barnabe next commyng my will is to gyve unto hym xiii^s iiii^d and Nicholas Broune doth owe to me xLvi^s viii^d and W. Howelles doth owe to me xxv^s and if he do pay me at Seint Barnabe th appostell next commyng my will is to give hym v^s Jeffrey Sowuton [?] doth owe me xxiii^s iiii^d due at Seint James thappostell and he do pay me my will is to gyve him ii^s. Thomas Shery doth owe me xxiii^s at Seint Thomas thappostell next commyng and if he pay me my will is to give him ii^s. John Stiche doth owe me xxi^s and John Broune doth owe to me xx^s and I give to Richard my brother one leasne called hynde otherwise called the mydell grove for the space of iii yeres in the custody of Richard Maret and John Styche and one acre of corne in Temes felde. The rest of my goods unbequeathed moveable and unmoveable my will being fulfilled I give to my brother Richard. Item I do order and make to be my executors Richard Jenckes my brother to this my last will and testament which I trust will pay my debtes and fulfill this my last will and testament theis being witnes Richard Marete, Nicholas Broune, John Reynoulde, Christofer Mason, Vicar their with others. Proved 6 July 1571.

The will of Richard Jenkes, gentleman of Clun, Shropshire. Dated 24 Sept. 1623. First I give and bequeath to the two sonnes of my cosen Jonas Jenks of London deceased called Jonas and Joshua or by what other names they are called the some of six pownde thirteene shillings foure pence apiece. Item I doe give and bequeath to John Jenke late of London and now of Clunbury five pownde and to his three sonnes twenty shillings a piece. Item I give and bequeath to my cozen William Jenks of London Tenn pownds if he be living. Item I give and bequeath to Parnell Foxe widow late wife of James Foxe deceased twenty shillings if she be living. Item I give to Owen Bird of Bishops Easter fforty shillings which is in his owne hands and to Richard his sonne my god sonne twenty shillings. Item I give to Joyce Byrd his sister twentie shillings wherof shee hath allready sixe shillings. Item I give to Zachias Boote and to Mary Lloyd his sister twenty shillings a piece. Item I give and remitt to Elinor the daughter of Henry ap John of Clunne Twenty shillings which shee oweth me. Item I give and bequeath to the daughter of James Foxe being my goddaughter tenn shillings if shee be living. Item I give and bequeath to every of my god children hereafter named soe many of them as be lyving as followeth to Anne the daughter of William ap Owen Tenn shillings. To a daughter of William Harries of Perthrehodry Tenn shillings. To Hugh the sonne of John Cooke Tenn Shillings. To Richard the sonne of Roger Richards of Clunton Tenn shillings. To Richard the sonne of Rowland Micton ifst he be livinge tenn shillings. To Richard the sonne of George Micton Tenn shillings. To Richard the sonne of Richard Marston Tenn shillings. Item I give to Sibly granndchild of Thomas Trump of Kingsland twentie shillings. Item I give to the said Thomas Trump and Elisabeth his wife Three pounds and to his two sonnes John and William twenty shillings a piece and to his two daughters Maude and Grace twenty shillings a piece. Item I give and bequeath to Joshua Midleton the sonne of John Midleton my sonne in lawe and his heires all the lands, tenements and hereditaments whatsoever in the parish of Clunne in the County of Salop by me purchased by way of mortgage or otherwise of Thomas Harries and Elinor Harries widow his mother and all my right title and interest in and to the same and all the money layd out thereuppon yst it be redeemed. And all the lands, tenements and hereditaments in the parishe of Clunne aforesaid by me purchased by way of mortgage or otherwise of one John Griffithes and all my right title and interest in and to the same and the money layd out thereuppon yst it be redeemed And all lands, tenements and hereditaments whatsoever in Clunne in the sayd Countie of Salop by me purchased by way of mortgage or otherwise of Morris ap Owen for the some of Tenn poundes and all my right title and interest in and to the same and the money layd out there upon yst the same be redeemed. This last said land and some of Tenn pounds to be in satisfaction of parte of the three score pownds I now owe to the said Joshua by promise for his presentment in marriage and the other fifty pownds my executors are to pay yst I pay it not in my liefe tyme. Item I give and bequeath all deeds Evidents and Writeings whatsoever belonging to the aforesaid several premisses unto the sayd Joshua Midleton. Item I give and bequeath to John Midleton sonne of the aforesaid John my sonne in lawe all the lands, tenements and hereditaments whatsoever in the parish of Church Stocke in the County of Mountgomery by me purchased by way of mortgage or otherwise of one Richard ap John Thomas of Churche Stocke aforesayd and all my right title and interest in and to the same and the money laid out thereuppon yst it be redeemed And all the lands, tenements and hereditaments whatsoever in Clunne in the County of Salop by mee purchased by way of mortgage or otherwise of Rees Parsons of Clunne and all my right title and interest in and to the same and the money layd out thereupon ist the same be redeemed. And all lands, tenements and hereditaments whatsoever in the parish of Llanvayre Waterdine and in the said Countie of Salop by me purchased by way of mortgage or otherwise of Morgan Jones and Owen James and either of them and all my right title and interest in and to the same and the money layd out thereuppon yst the same be redeemed and all my lands, tenements and hereditaments in the parish of Bethowse in the sayd County of Salop by me purchased by way of mortgage or otherwise of one John ap Rees and all my right title and interest in and to the same and the money layd out thereupon yst the same be redeemed. And all lands, tenements and hereditaments whatsoever in Hobendred in the said Countye of Salop by me purchased by way of mortgage or otherwise of one John ap Lewis and all my right title and interest in and to the same and the money layd out there upon yst the same be redeemed. And all landes, tenements and hereditaments whatsoever in the parish of Llanvayre Waterdine aforesaid by me purchased by way of mortgage or otherwise of one John ap Owen and all my right title and interest in and to the same and the money layed out thereupon yst the same be redeemed. And all the lands tenements and hereditaments whatsoever with their appertenants in Hobendred aforesaid by me purchased of one John ap Rees and all my right title and interest in and to the same togeather with all Deeds evidences and writings whatsoever concerning all the sayd severall premisses. Item my meaning is and I will and bequeath the premisses to the sayd Joshua and John as aforesaid and to the respective heyres of theire bodyes lawfully begotten or to be begotten and yf either of the sayd brothers Joshua or John dye without yssue of their bodyes lawfully begotten that the survivor of them and his heires shall have the whole lands and premisses to them devised. Item I give and bequeath to Richard Midleton my graundchild a corslett with a mayne pikestaffe sword dagger headpe -te and furniture thereunto belonging, and to Joshua his brother one corslet with the furniture thereunto belonging. Item I give and bequeath all my clothes and wearing apparell to the said Joshua and John Midleton my graundchildren to be equally parted and divided betweene them. Item I give and bequeath to the said Joshua Midleton all my bedding sheets, linnens and napery and one coffer with two locks my saddle and the furniture thereunto belonging. Item I give bequeath and remitt to Francis Gilloe of Clunne twenty shillings which he oweth me by specialty and to Thomas Longwell of Bedston twenty shillings which he oweth me. Item I give to John Thomas and Margarett three of the children of John Wilcoxe late of Obley in the said Countye twenty shillings apiece. Item I give to Richard the sonne of Thomas Mitton of Clunton Tenn shillings. Item I give to the sonne of Thomas Nicholas of Kynerton being my godsonne Tenn shillings. Item Eve the daughter of David Meredith of Hobendred Tenn shillings. Item I give and remitt to Joane Fox of Kinerton twenty shillings which shee oweth mee by specialty. To Thomas Edwards of Penthrehedner twenty shillings which he oweth me by specialty. To Henry Longwell twentie shillings which he oweth me by specialty. Item I give bequeath and devise to the said Richard Midleton his executor or administrator the some of six pounds upon trust and confidence the . . . shall pay and disperse of the same the onely use of the poore of the parish of Clunne videlicet to pay and distribute it in shillings videlicet onely . . . to the said poore five shillings on Christmas day and five shillings on Easter day in bread or more as his . . . . Item I give to the poore of the parish of Bushops Caster the some of twenty shillings to be distributed by my executors with the advise and helpe of the minister and church wardens there. Item I give to the poore of the parish of Howe tenn shillings. To the poore of the parish of Bucknill thirteene shillings four pence. To the poore of the parish of B . . . five shillings eight pence. To the poore of the parish of —npton Tenn shillings. To the poore of the parish of Clunbury twenty shillings. To the poore of the parish of Kidbur— tenn shillings. Item to the poore of the parish of Church Stock twenty shillings and to the poore of the parish of Bethens Tenn shillings to be deliverd and disposed and distributed by my executors to the use of the said poore by and with the advice of the minister and church wardens in every of the said parishes. Item I give and appoynt to be bestowed for and towards my bringing home and funeralls six pounds. Item I doe give and remitt to every of my tenants and debtors by way of mortgage and every of [sic] my debtors by way of loane one quarter of a yeares loane and interest of all some and somes of money.whatsoever due to me from them at the time of my decease upon condicion that they shall and will truly performe bargayne and pay the due debt and residue of the consideracion and charges yf any be without compulsion or suite of lawe. Item I give remitt and bequeath to Robert Harries of Clunne his daughter my goddaughter forty shillings and to the said Robert forty shillings more and to his wief an [sic] other child forty shillings more which amounteth in the whole to six poundes which the sayd Robert oweth me by specialty. Item I give and bequeath to Katherine the daughter of Thomas Cooke three pownds yst she be living. Item I give and bequeath to Phillipp Byrd Shoemaker Tenn shillings. Item I give to as many men servants as shall dwell in the house with mee whhen I shall happen to decease tenn shillings a piece and to the mayd servants then being in the howse with me twenty shillings a piece. Item I give and bequeath to the said Joshua and John Midleton . . . twenty pounds a piece. Item I give and bequeath to Thomas the sonne of Roger Howells of Downe Twenty shillings and to John Lloyd of Bucknill Forty Shillings. Item I give and bequeath to Cicelly the wiefe of George Holland of Purstow gentleman five pownds and I doe appoynt the sayd George Holland overseer of this my last will and testament and for his care and paines to be taken herein as I do repose an especiall trust in him I doe give and bequeath unto him sixe pounds thirteene shillings foure pence, and lastly I doe hereby revoake and make frustrate all former and other wills and testaments by mee heertofore made. And I doe nominate constitute ordeyne and make Francis Jenkes of Kingsland gentleman, Griffin Midleton of Churchstocke gentleman, Hopkins ap Owen of Edycliffe and Roger Howells of Gilden Downe welbeloved freinds executors of this my last will and testament requiring them and reposing speciall confidence and trust in them to see this my last will and testament duly performed soe as according to my true intent and meaning nor any of my said executors shall release any of my mortgages debts or demannds or doe any important thing therein without the consent and agreement of the other and that every of my saide executors shall be . . . into severall bonds one to the other in the some of one thowsand pounds a piece for the due performance of this my will or else to revoke and not medle as executors therein. In witness whereof I have hereunto subscribed and put my seale the daye and yeare firste written witnesses to the sealing and subscribing of every lease George Holland, Ciccly Holland, Richard Holland, Timothy Holland, Signum Joshua Midleton. Witnesses to the confirming and last reading hereof Robert Midleton, Clerk, John Midleton, Timothy Holland,

Signum David Morris, Signum Johannis Bushop, Signum George Bushop, Signum Edwardi Lucas, Signum Margarette Hopton. Proved 1 Dec. 1623. Prerogative Court of Canterbury.

Abstract of Chancery Proceedings, Public Record Office, London, C8/14/53: *Plaintiff:* Richard Jenkes of Kynourton (Kinnerton near Clun), Salop. *Defendants:* Robert Middelton, John Middelton. *Date:* 13 Oct. 1615. *Contents:* On Sept. 9, 39 Elis. (1597), a marriage settlement was made between Richard Jenkes, and Edmund Middleton late of Ryston, Salop and his son and heir Robert, concerning a marriage which should take place according to "the lawes of the holy church" between John Middelton, son and heir of Robert Middelton and Jone daughter of Richard Jenkes . . . to have and to holde the . . . saide premisses after the saide marriage solemnized to the use of your sayde orator till the saide Jone shoulde accomplish the age of twenty yeares . . . Jone, Richard's daughter, died 2 years ago, leaving three sons . . . Jenkes is "now impotent and aged about 80 yeere of age" . . . *The answers of Robert and John Middelton:* Both agree that the contents of the indenture mentioned by Jenkes are correct, but in addition Jenkes promised in this indenture to pay £30 to John Middelton when he was 21 years old . . . After the death of Jone Jenkes, John married secondly "Johan Redge the relict of one Oliver Redge". She was executrix of Oliver's will.

(3) *Jonas Jenks of London and Virginia*

The will of Jonas Jenks. Jonas Jenckes son of Jonas Jenckes citizen and white baker of London deceased, dated 1 Aug. 1633. Be it known unto all men that I . . . hereby give my full power and authority unto Joane Tyres of Barnabie Street in the parish of St. Mary Maudlen's co. Surrey to keep in her custody and possession all those goods which his mother Ann Jenckes of London did give and bequeath unto him the said Jonas until he shall accomplish the age of 21 or else until his return from Virginia ratifying and confirming by these presents that whatever the said Joane Tyres shall do or cause to be done in or about the premises concerning the said goods which are due and of right appertaining unto him to warrant and defend for ever the said Joan Tyres against all persons whatsoever as if I were there personally present. Witnesses: Henry Bradford, Thomas Corington, Henry Capell. M^d that I the said Jonas Jenckes do give unto the said Joane Tyres all the said goods which appertain unto me, if it please the Lord to call me out of this life before I return unto England and the same to convert to her own use. 9 Oct. 1636 Commission to Joanne Tyeres aunt of Jonas Jenckes deceased to administer the goods etc. of deceased according to the tenor of the Deed of Gift no executor having been named. P.C.C. 105 Pile.

The Will of John Maltby, of the parish of St. Olave Southwark, co. Surrey, brewer. Dated 14 March 1634-5. To Elizabeth Maltby my daughter £100, two feather beds, one tapestry coverlet of a single story, four pair of flaxen sheets, two great chests one of them of furre and the other marked with the letters H. M. upon the cover and three window cushions. The money to be delivered at the age of 21 or within six months of the day of marriage which of them shall first happen. To Mary Sherewood my first wife's daughter and unto Jonas Jinckes and Josias Jinckes my second wife's sons and to Elizabeth Martin my cousin 12d. apiece. All the rest of my goods and chattels, money, stock of beer, leases and estate whatsoever to my wife Anne Maltby whom I make sole executrix. Witnesses: Robert Wilson, F^r Fulshares, notary public. Proved 6 Sep. 1636 by Ann Maltbie, relict and executrix. 101 Pile. P.C.C. *Note:* The above will was subsequently declared null and void by sentence, and a later will was proved in its place, as below.

The will of John Maltbie of the parish of St. Olave Southwark, co. Surrey, brewer. Dated 22 June 1636. To Elizabeth Maltby my daughter £100 the which money is now in the hands of William Wright my kinsman and for which he hath entered into bond to my said daughter to pay at a certain day. To my said daughter Elizabeth Maltbie £200 which my wife and executrix shall pay within one year next after my decease. If my said daughter die before then the said bequeasts shall be proportionately shared amongst my own brothers and sisters. To my brother Anthonie Maltbie my best Bible. To my brother Symon my best suit and cloak but one. To my sister Ellen Mason 20s. to buy her a ring. To my sister Bridget Marten 20s. to buy her a ring. To Elizabeth Marten her daughter 10s. To the poor of the parish of St. Olave Southwark where I now dwell 40s. All the rest of my goods plate leases etc. to my wife Anne Maltbie whom I make sole executrix. I make my friends John Venner and Roger Askewe overseers and give them 20s. apiece to buy them rings. Witnesses: Thomas Champion of Hurst, co. Berks., Robert Windsor scrivener, Lazerus Amis his clerk. Proved 19 Nov. 1637 by Anne Maltbie, the relict and executrix. P.C.C.

Footnotes

1. The Register, v. 9, pp. 201–2.
2. Nugent, "Cavaliers and Pioneers", lists a Jenks with a question. A careful examination of the original entry shows that the name is Jones.

THE JENKS FAMILY OF ENGLAND

By Meredith B. Colket, Jr., F.A.S.G., of Washington, D. C.

V. The Ancient Family of Jenks

Henry Harrison, in his scholarly treatise, "Surnames of the United Kingdom: A Concise Etymological Dictionary" (1918), indicates that Jenks is a shortened form of Jenkin or Jenkins; and equivalent

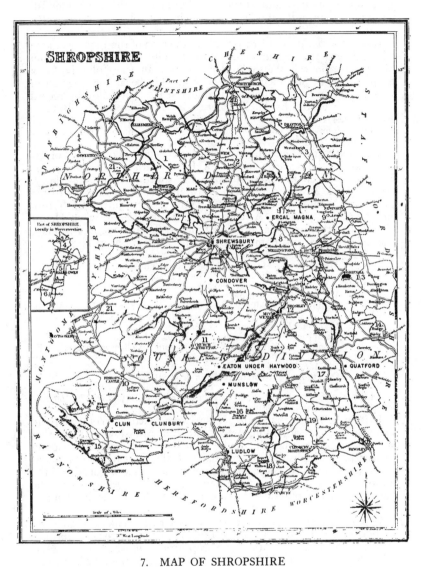

7.   MAP OF SHROPSHIRE

Showing Parishes in which 16th Century Jenks Families resided.

to Jan or John with the Low German diminuative suffix -kin or -ken added. Harrison calls attention to the prevalence of the name Jenkin(s) in Wales; and attributes this fact to the great Flemish immigration into Pembrokeshire, which took place in the twelfth century.

It is not without interest that the first person of the Jenks surname whose identity is documented by contemporary records is from Shropshire, on the Welsh border. This man was John Jenks, a draper or dealer in uncut cloth, who in 1456 became a freeman of Shrewsbury, a market town and county seat. The following record of him is reported by H. E. Forrest in the "Shrewsbury Burgess Roll" (1924):

Jenks, John (alias Sadler) of S(hrewsbury) draper, son of William of same i(ssue) Agnes, Julianna, 1456.

The next Shropshire reference to a Jenks is in Wolverton. Wolverton was in the ancient manor of Eton, parish of Eaton-under-Heywood, which is a few miles to the southwest of Shrewsbury. Here is 1521/2 Roland Jeynkys (Rowland Jenks) paid a tax to the priory at Wenlock, according to Eyton's "Antiquities of Shropshire", vol. 3, p. 318. A few years later in 1524/5, when Henry VIII levied the first great tax that touched the average Englishman, the following persons named Jenks were taxed in Shropshire:

E	179/166/130	Wenlock
	Wollerton	Margery Jenks yn goods 3 li. sub. 18s.
		Richard Jenks 40s. 3 li. sub. 12d.
		Thomas Jenks 40s. sub. 12d.
E	179/166/127	Monslow
	Aston	William Jenks, collector
		William Jenks in goods 5 li. subs. 2s. 8d.
E	179/166/127	Purslow
	Kempton	John Jenks in goods 40s. sub. 12d.
	Clombury and Brompton	William Jenks, Collector, in goods 4 li., sub. 2s.
E	179/166/131	Stottesden
	Ordynton	Richard Jenks in goods 10 li. 5s.
	North Clesbury	Robert Jenks 40s. subs. 12d.

(In the following year, 1525/6, on a list of names of collectors, E 179/166/135, was "Rowlandus Jenks de Monselowe").

It is to be noted that four persons were taxed at Wolverton and one was taxed at adjoining Aston, parish of Munslow. From other sources we know that the Jenks family of Wolverton was closely related to the Jenks family of Aston. Of the eight heads of families taxed in Shropshire, those at Wolverton and Aston constitute the majority of the taxables of the name then in Shropshire. And the Jenks name was practically non-existent in the rest of England at this early date.

It is not surprising, then, that the only early Jenks pedigree is a pedigree for the family at Wolverton and nearby Aston. It forms a part of the "1623 Visitation of Shropshire" published by the Harleian Society. The chief ingredients of the printed pedigree are two pedigrees in the British Museum, Harl. 1396, fo. 175b and Harl. 1241, fo. 41b. The published pedigree, which incorrectly attributes to the early members of the family the spelling "Jenkes" (a spelling which was not used until later), must be evaluated with caution. For its early generations cannot be documented; and experience shows that we cannot trust the earlier generations of visitation pedigrees without adequate documentation.

The pedigree begins with "Elistan Glodred lord of Ferlexland [Ferlix] between Wy and Seuerne". The Welsh scholar, Maj. Francis Jones, recognizes the claimed royal ancestor as an historical figure of the eleventh century; and recognizes the line of descent as given for seven generations to John ap Rees as one based on an ancient document of accepted validity. The Jenks pedigree, however, shows that John ap Rees was father of Jenkyn Cambray of Wollarton, who in turn, was father of John Jenkes of "Wollarton" (Wolverton). This connection has not been confirmed. It does not conform either to the Welsh or English naming system; and is plainly open to suspicion. We suspect that it was concocted by pedigree writers of later generations to please descendants.

The wife of John Jenkes of Wollarton was Alice, daughter to Stephen Bowdler. This same marriage is reported in the Bowdler pedigree as published in the "1623 Visitation of Shropshire", where Bowdler is identified as Sir Stephen Bowdler, Knt., of Hope Bowdler, a place very near Wolverton. The son of John Jenks was given in the Jenks pedigree as Thomas, his grandson as John, and his great-grandson as Rowland Jenkes of Wolverton.

Rowland Jenkes, as we have shown, is the first person in the Jenks line whose identity appears to be confirmed by original documents. The line of Rowland Jenks' descendants, as given in the pedigree, can be confirmed to a large extent from contemporary sources and, with the exception of a few minor particulars, we accept it as basically correct.

Rowland Jenks' son Richard is the first Jenks in all of England known to have left a will. It was dated in 1538, the year that Henry VIII first required that parish incumbents record baptisms, marriages, and burials. The following abstract is from an introduction to the Eaton-under-Heywood register as printed in *Shropshire Parish Register Society*, Hereford, vol. XIX, Part 3, p. i:

> We have a glympse of the Church before the Reformation in the Will of Richard Jenkes of Hatton "in the parish of Yeton in the Diocese of Hereford", dated 1538. He wills to be buried in the Church of Yeton. "I will that 12 new tapers be newe made before the Rode in the Church of Yeton". To the Church of Atton on the Hill [Acton Scott] 2 tapers. To the Church of Hope Hawther (Hope Bowdler) 2 tapers. "I will that money shall be dealed in Yeton Church and in Atton Church on Palm Sunday for my soule and all Christian soules. My eldest daughter to have my house in Hatton and all my other takings when my wife doth marry or my daughter is 15 years. My second daughter to have my landes in Auckeston [Alcaston] with part of the meadow. My wife to have my landes in Hewbrucke for life. My cosen* Thomas Jenks to have part of the meadowes end from the old hedge downwards". Executors, his brothers William and Thomas, Witnesses, John Griffyn, Thomas Jenkes, Agnes English. Proved by the Widow (the Executors renouncing) 1 June 1538 P.C.C. Richard Jenkes was a younger son of Rowland Jenkes of Wolverton.

*The "cosen" named by Richard was his nephew, Thomas Jenkes. At the time of the dissolution of the monasteries by Henry VIII, the manor of Eton came into possession of John Pakyngton of Hampton Lovett: and it was to John Pakyington that Thomas Jenkes of "Hatton" paid his rents in 1544.

Thomas had a son, George, who by 1570 advanced the fortunes of his family by marriage to Margaret Lutley, co-heiress of her brother. In 1584 George Jenkes applied to the College of Arms for a coat of arms and one was confirmed to him. George Jenkes became the first person of the surname whose right to arms was recognized by the College of Arms.

The official record of the confirmation made by Robert Cooke, Clarenceiux King of Arms, reads in part as follows:

">... being required by George Jenkes of the County of Salop Gentleman to delyver unto him the Ancient Armes belonginge to that Name and samely whereof he is descended, confirmed under the Seale of my Office, at whose request being reasonable I have made search accordingly and do fynde that he may lawfully beare these Arrmes hereafter falloinge that is to say: Argent, three bores heades coupee, and a Cheefe indented Sables, ..."

The worthy herald went on to say that he found no crest for the Jenkes family, and thereupon granted a crest to George Jenkes; and these were to be borne by the descendants of George Jenkes forever. No pedigree of George's family, according to Anthony R. Wagner, C.V.O., Richmond Herald, is filed with the College.

The descendants of George regarded this confirmation quite proudly. His eldest son, Francis, was called "armiger" in the 1592 subsidy; Francis' eldest son, Herbert, was called "armiger" when he went to Oxford. The church at Eaton-under-Heywood in which Herbert's younger brother, John, the vicar, was buried, contains an elaborate slab with the family coat of arms. (An interesting account of the Jenks inscription in the church and churchyard is given on page 43 of volume 10 of the fourth series of the *Transactions of the Shropshire Archaeological and Natural History Society*. For information about the use of the Jenkes coat of arms in Shropshire, consult "Armorial Bearings of Shropshire Families", *ibid*., vol. 6, p. 463 (1883). No evidence has been found that Joseph Jenks, the American colonist, or his immediate family claimed a coat of arms.

The examination of many early Shropshire subsidy lists, of chancery proceedings, of all Shropshire wills, 1538–1638, of practically all Shropshire parish registers, 1538–1638, has revealed but scattered Jenks references except for a few parishes. A study of the Jenks families at each of these parishes has suggested that in most cases there is a close inter-relationship of the families. Following is a list of the more important Shropshire parishes, Eaton-under-Heywood excepted, in which the Jenks family was represented, and a statement about each:

Clun: The close association of the family of Hugh Jenks of Clun with the family of Clunbury has already been shown.

Clunbury: William Jenks, collector of taxes, was taxed in 1524/5. A William Jenks, collector of taxes, was taxed in 1524/5 in Aston, parish of Munslow. We suspect that this was the same William. We have shown that the Jenks family of Aston was the same as that of nearby Eaton-under-Heywood.

Condover: William Jenks of "Doddington" died between 4 June and 24 Sept. 1562, when his will was probated (Consist. Court Lichfield). His children were Edmund, William, and Margaret. His son Edward, who married at Stapleton, had a large family.

High Ercoll: David Jenkes of "Sherlow" was involved sometime between 1533 and 1538 in a dispute over 20 acres of land (Chanc. Proc., C1/833/28). In his will, dated 28 Aug. 1574 (Consist. Court Lichfield), he mentioned his well-beloved cousin, "Adam Lutley gent. overseer". This strongly suggests a connection with the family at Eaton-under-Heywood, which intermarried with the Lutleys. David's widow, Elizabeth, was buried in 1593, aged five score years and more. William of "Obasson" in same parish, evidently a son, died an old man in 1607, leaving a large family.

Ludlow: Francis Jenks, son and heir of Richard of Quatford, was admitted to Middle Temple, London, in 1563. He married at Ludlow, in 1577, Alice Wilson, and was called gentleman and Queen's clerk of Ludlow in 1587. They had several children.

Quatford: Richard Jenkes of "The Hay" left a will of 20 May 1560 (Consist. Court of Lichfield and P.C.C. 6 Morrison) naming wife Elizabeth. According to the "1568 Visitation of London" and the "1619 Visitation of Kent", she was Elizabeth, daughter of William Blunt of Woddesley and Glose, Shropshire, by Joyce or Joanna, daughter of John Packington of Shropshire. He mentions Adam Lutley, his loving kinsman, as executor. Adam Lutley, it is noted, was a relative also of David Jenkes of High Ercoll. Richard's will also mentions land in Munslow and refers to John Pakington (to whom Thomas Jenkes of Hatton, Eaton-under-Heywood, was paying taxes). Finally, the descendants of his daughter, Margaret, who married Humphrey Wightwick, Esq., of Tettenhall, Staffordshire, quartered on their arms the same Jenkes arms as those confirmed to George Jenkes of Eaton-under-Heywood.

The above very rough summary of a detailed investigation suggests that the Jenks families throughout Shropshire came from a parent stem, and that parent stem originated in the manor of Eton.

Investigation of Jenks families throughout the rest of England for the sixteenth century reveals only scattered groups, which begin to appear about the middle of the sixteenth century. The family appears most prolific outside Shropshire in Warwickshire, particularly in the parishes of Alcester and Aston Cantlow, and in Worcestershire, particularly the parishes of Earl's Croome and Great Comberton. A few members of the family went to London, and some of these became members of the great city companies. Notable among them was William Jenks, citizen and grocer of London who, *circa* 1518–29, was surety for "Welshmen living in Wales" (Chanc. Proc., C1/586/32). A daughter, Elizabeth, married Richard Rich, knt., who in 1547 became Baron Rich of Lees (Cokayne, "Complete Peerage", 2nd ed., vol. X, p. 776). No evidence has been found that any member of the early family attained knighthood. A recent edition of Burke's "Peerage, Baronetage, and Knighthood" lists Sir Richard Atherly Jenks, 2nd Bt. 8, Connought Place, W. 2, London.

Evidence points to the fact that the Jenks family originated in the manor of Eton, Shropshire, a few miles southwest of Shrewsbury, in the fourteenth century. By the middle of the fifteenth century we find the first reference to the name in an original document. In the early part of the sixteenth century the name was scattered in more than a half dozen Shropshire parishes. During the sixteenth century, the family spread out eastward through the middle of England and some members of the family reached London. If one should draw an imaginary line between Shrewsbury and London, one would locate most sixteenth century members of the Jenks family within a few miles of this line. Such is the background of the family from which the descendants of the American colonist, Joseph Jenks, can claim descent.

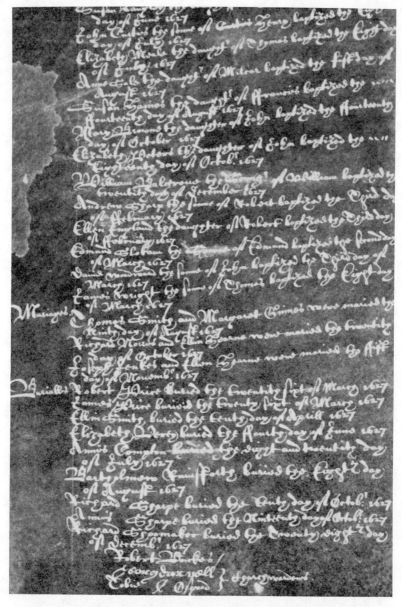

8. MARRIAGE RECORD OF JOSEPH JENKES

Portion of Bishop's Transcript of 1627.   Parish Entries for Horton, Bucks.
Courtesy of Bodleian Library, Oxford.

VI. The First Wife of Joseph Jenks

It has long been recognized that the New England colonist, Joseph Jenks (1599–1683), married twice. His first wife, whom he married in England, was the mother of Joseph Jenks, Jr. His second wife, whom he obviously married in America, was the mother of his American-born children.

The identity of the first wife has proved puzzling. From American sources it has been suggested that she was Rebecca Hudson. For Gov. Joseph Jen(c)ks of Rhode Island, the son of Joseph Jenks, Jr., is said to have written that he had a grandmother, Rebecca Hudson, of Lynn, Mass., the daughter of Thomas Hudson. American genealogical directories identify a Thomas Hudson who was at Lynn by 1638. Evidence for the claimed relationship, however, is not strong. Gov. Joseph Jen(c)ks had more than one grandmother; while tradition and documentary evidence point to the fact that Joseph Jenks' first wife died before he came to America.

The tradition, as published in THE REGISTER (vol. 9, p. 201), over a century ago, reads as follows:

> "Joseph Jenks, senior, was a widower when he came over. Our tradition states that he left Joseph, Jr., with his maternal grand-parents, whose family name I know not — after assigning a sum sufficient for his maintenance until he should be of age, when he was directed to join his father in America. But he must have arrived, it appears, before that period, perhaps when 16, and is said to have had a brother, George, or William, who 'went from England to Virginia'".

It has been shown that the colonist was traditionally associated with Hounslow, a chapelry partially in the parish of Isleworth, Middlesex, and that the parish registers include two Jenks entries, one reporting the burial of a daughter [Eliza]beth on 2 Nov. 1638, the other reporting the death of Joseph's English wife: "1634/5 February 29 Jone Jeankes the wife of Joseaff Jeankes was buryed".

It has also been shown that the colonist was traditionally from Colebrook, Buckinghamshire; that *Colnbrook* was a chapelry in Horton; and that the parish registers of Horton show only one Jenks entry, the one reporting the baptism on 12 Oct. 1628 of Joseph Jenks, Jr. The Bishop's transcripts report this also; but under a variant spelling that had hitherto escaped detection: "We doe record Joseph Gines the son of Joseph was baptized the 12th day of October 1628". The transcripts also show that on 5 Nov. 1627 Joseph Jenkes and Ellen Hearne were married.

This entry, which is on a page that is duly certified by the church wardens, appears at variance with the burial record, which records Joseph's wife as Jone (or Joan).

We are convinced that the entries for the two parishes refer to the same Joseph Jenks; but it is difficult to infer a second marriage between 1627 and 1635. Our only other recourse is to question the accuracy of the marriage entry in the Bishop's transcript for Horton.

The Bishop's transcripts, however incomplete they may be, are official documents legally authorized. They were created by a Constitution of Convocation of 25 Oct. 1597. The Constitution, which was issued by the Archbishop of Canterbury and other ecclesiastical authorities and approved by Queen Elizabeth, decreed that every year the wardens of each parish were to copy the parish register entries and send the copy to the Bishop's registry. By the canon of 1603 the copy was to be signed by the minister and wardens. Here we have a record that appears as official as the deed book in the county court house.

According to Blackstone " . . . it is a settled rule and maxim that nothing shall be averred against a record, nor shall any plea or even proof be admitted to the contrary . . ." There are two considerations, however, that face us in the present instance. First, the Bishop's transcript purports to be an authenticated copy of the parish register; yet we know that the Horton parish register does not and probably did not contain the original record. We can only assume that the Bishop's transcript was made from an intermediate paper, probably long since destroyed. Secondly, the Bishop's transcript containing the marriage entry records two weeks earlier the marriage of another Ellen Hearne. The two transcript entries read as follows:

Richard Norris and Ellin Hearne were married the
twentieth day of October 1627
Joseph Jenkes and Ellen Hearne were married the
fifth day of Nouemb^r 1627

We submit that the copyist, in transcribing the Jenks marriage, may have inadvertently copied down a part or all of the maiden's name from the previous entry instead of copying the original entry. The distinguished Bucks' scholar, A. Vere Woodman, F.S.A., after examining the transcript entries, wrote on 19 Nov. 1955 as follows: "Although the forename of Joseph's wife is probably blundered, I do not think that this is the case with the surname . . . I have met cases in which the forename was blundered but I cannot remember an instance in which the surname has been entered wrongly. The marriage entry, as it stands, is legal evidence, whether a court would allow that a mistake had been made, I cannot say!"

On the assumption that Joseph Jenks married into the Hearne family of Colnbrook, we append the following discussion of the Buckinghamshire family of the name.

The Hearne Family of Buckinghamshire

The name Hearn or Hearne, according to Henry Harrison's "Surnames of the United Kingdom: A Concise Etymological Dictionary" (1918), is a word meaning dweller in a nook or corner of land. In Middle English the spelling is "herne", in old English "hurne". The surname has many variants including Harne, Herne, Hieron, and Heron.

"The History and Antiquities of the County of Buckingham", which was written by George Lipscomb in 1847, shows several very early references to the name in Buckinghamshire. Robert le Hurne of Weston Turville was named on a tax return of 1341 (vol. 2, p. 495). Roger Heron, clerk, of the manors of Middle Claydon and Eselburgh, was named in fines of 1424 and 1427 (vol. 1, p. 177). The first Hearne will of Buckinghamshire was dated

1490. Hearne wills proved during the sixteenth century in the Archdeaconry Court of Buckinghamshire were signed by persons inhabiting the following parishes: Agmondesham (Amersham?), Chearsley, Edlesborough, Hughenden, Marsh Gibbon, Padbury, Penn, Prince's Risborough, Over Winchendon, Weston-Turville, and Wycombe.

Penn, the Buckinghamshire parish in which William Penn for a time resided, was a most important center for the Hearne family of the sixteenth century. From the branch at Penn, came the forebears of Thomas Hearne (1678–1735) of White Waltham, co. Berks, the noted antiquarian. In 1711 he was informed by his father:

> "As for our family of the Hearnes, they came from Penn in Buckinghamshire but of what antiquity there I know not at present though there be of the name there still and I believe they have been of long standing there . . . My father's name was George, the son of Wm. Hearne of Penn but what his father's name was I do not know at present [George Hearne, son of William, was baptized at Penn in 1618], but I am apt to believe that Herne, Hearon, and Hearne were all at first one family . . ."

According to J. G. Jenkins, "History of the Parish of Penn", a William Heron was named a suitor of the manor as early as 1479. The first Penn Hearne from whom descent can be traced is William Herne who is named in the 1546 subsidy.

1. **William Hearne**, of Penn, Buckinghamshire, was taxed 2d for lands in the 1546 subsidy and 2s 7d for lands in the subsidy of 1 Elizabeth 1558/9. He was buried 7 Dec. 1563. His wife's name was **Joan** ———. His will, dated 5 Dec. 1562[3?] and proved in the Archdeaconry Court of Bucks, gives his mother two sheep. She may have been Agnes Hearne, the elder, who was buried 3 April 1573. He named as overseers William Culverhouse, who was of Penn, and Jells (Giles) Skidmore, who was of Wycombe. His widow, Joan, married, secondly, 10 Nov. 1566, William West.

Children:
2.   i. **John**, m. Agnes Grove.
3.   ii. **William**, m. Sibbel ———.
      iii. **Joane**, m. 25 Jan. 1572/3 **David Shrimpton**.
      iv. **Merill**, m. 29 Jan. 1580/1 **William Grove**.
      v. **Alice**, m. 11 Oct. 1568 **Silvester Hill**.
      vi. **Sybell**, bapt. 17 July 1563; m. 22 Jan. 1591/2 **Hugh Robinson**.

2. **John Hearne** (*William*), married 6 Feb. 1574/5 **Agnes Grove**. He was a tailor as shown by the baptismal entry for his daughter, Phoebe. His wife was a member of a family most prominently identified with Penn for many generations. The couple were buried on 15 Nov. 1623 and 31 March 1628, respectively.

Children:
   i. **William**, bapt. 27 Nov. 1575; m. 4 Dec. 1609 **Susanna Ellis**. Issue: (1) *Susanna*, bapt. 24 Jan. 1612/13; (2) *Stephen*, bapt. 26 Dec. 1614; (3) *George*, bapt. 6 April 1618, ancestor of Thomas Hearne, the antiquary; (4) *Robert*, bapt. 21 May 1620; (5) *Matthias*, bapt. 24 Feb. 1624/5; (6) *Thomas*, bapt. 14 Aug. 1626.
   ii. **John**, bapt. 17 Aug. 1578, called the younger; buried 23 Jan. 1615/16. Issue: (1) *Joan*, bapt. 10 Feb. 1610/11: (2) *Edmond*, bapt. 28 Feb. 1612/13; buried 12 Feb. 1615/16: (3) *John*, named in Uncle Matthew's will.

iii. Henry, bapt. 19 March 1580/1.   Issue: (1) *Henry*, bapt. 3 March 1610/11; buried 6 Oct. 1610/11; (2) *Isaac*, bapt. 26 July 1612; (3) *Eady*, bapt. 16 Oct. 1614.

iv. Matthew, bapt. 1 Feb. 1583/4; m. Elizabeth Franklin. His will was dated 27 July 1643 and proved 2 May 1650.

v. Phoebe, bapt. 24 April 1586; m. 19 Jan. 1617/18 Henry Hill.

vi. Sarah, bapt. 13 April 1589.

vii. Mary, bapt. 25 Jan. 1592/3.

3. William Hearne (*William*) was buried 26 April 1629. He married Sibbel ———, who was buried 18 Jan. 1627/8.
  Children:
   i. Agnes, bapt. 16 April 1580.
   ii. Henry, bapt. 3 Dec. 1581 or 82.
   iii. Silvester, bapt. 8 Dec. 1583.
   iv. Mary, bapt. 17 Jan. 1584/5; buried 21 Feb. 1584/5.
   v. Merril, bapt. 1 May 1586; m. 29 May 1608 George Dosset.
   vi. Perhaps George (twin), bapt. 12 May 1588.
   vii. Perhaps Susan (twin), bapt. 12 May 1588. The register does not identify the father of these twins.
   viii. Elizabeth, bapt. 1 Oct. 1592.

The Hearnes of Colnbrook

The name Hearne is noteworthy in the annals of Colnbrook and elsewhere in the Buckinghamshire parish of Horton because of Edmund Hearne, grandson of the first Hearne to settle in the area. In his will of 1686, Edmund bequeathed to the poor of the parish each year forever £1 10s, a substantial sum for those days. The fund created under the terms of the will was administered by the parish for over two centuries and became known as Hearne's Charity. James Gyll who in 1862 published a history of the area under the title "History of the Parish of Wraysbury, Ankernycke Priory and Magna Charta Island, with the History of Horton, and the Town of Colnbrook, Bucks", tells the story of Hearne's Charity, and on page 233 wrote a very brief pedigree of Hearne of Colnbrook.

The pedigree begins with ——— Hearne who was the father of two brothers, John and George. The parish registers of Horton indicate that John had arrived by 1599 and George by 1612. If their father was indeed a resident of Colnbrook, as the pedigree suggests, we have no one to point to save an otherwise unidentified William Hearne, who with George Hearne was essoined in 1620, according to the fragmentary manorial rolls preserved at Aylesbury.

The origin of William, John, and George has been difficult to prove despite a careful search of the parish registers of many Buckinghamshire parishes. The only clue concerns Penn, the parish from which the noted antiquary, Thomas Hearne, was descended. In the Hearne family of Penn, the christian names Edmund, George, and Susan occur. In the Hearne family of Colnbrook in Horton, these same names reoccur. It is possible that the families are closely related.

Following is a pedigree of the Hearne family of Colnbrook:

1. William (?) Hearne, perhaps parent of John and George Hearne, named in the manorial records of 1620.
  Children:

538

2.   i. JOHN.
3.   ii. GEORGE.

2. JOHN HEARNE (?*William*), of the parish of Horton, was born
say about 1575. He came to Horton by 1599. In 1619 and
1621 he was, according to the few extant manorial rolls,
excused from non-appearance in court. In 1620 he was a
juryman and in 1623 a constable. He was buried on 7 Feb.
1626/7. His wife, MARGARET ———, was buried 5 June
1626. Several members of his family were victims of the
plague of 1626.

    Children:
    i. MARGARET, bapt. 21 June 1599; m. 10 March 1625 THOMAS SOUL.
    ii. MARY, bapt. 23 Aug. 1601.
    iii. JOHN, bapt. 3 Jan. 1602; presumably d. young.
    iv. JONE, bapt. 9 April 1604; presumably d. young.
    v. JONE, bapt. 19 Jan. 1605; perhaps one of the name who m. 12 Oct.
        1640 John Humperby.
    vi. SUSAN, bapt. 15 May 1608. An Ann was buried 13 Feb. 1626/7.
    vii. JOHN, bapt. 1 Nov. 1609; m. at Hillingden, Middlesex, 14 April
        1628, JOAN ALLEN. He was buried 11 Aug. 1639 as John Hieron.
        His will, dated Horton 8 April 1639, was probated 3 Oct. 1639 in
        the Archdeaconry Court of Bucks. Issue, surviving children
        named in the will were to be bound as apprentices: (1) *John*, bapt.
        22 March 1628/9; (2) *Francis;* (3) *William*, bapt. Dec. 1633,
        father of Edward and named in will of brother Edmund; (4)
        Grace, bapt. 7 Feb. 1635; apparently died young; (5) *Edmund*,
        bapt. 16 Mar. 1638; m. at Horton, in 1663, Dinah Bowry. His
        will, dated 8 July 1684 and proved 8 July 1686 (P.C.C. 96 Lloyd),
        names wife Dinah, nephew Edward, son of his brother William
        Hearne, sons-in-law (step-sons) Francis and Samuel Bowry. He
        made the bequest to which reference has been made.
    viii. ALICE, bapt. 9 March 1617.

2. GEORGE HEARNE (?*William*), apparently of Colnbrook in
Horton was evidently born about 1578. The name of his
wife is unknown.

    George Hearne came to the vicinity of Horton by 1612
when a child was baptized. He was excused in 1619, 1620,
and 1621 for non-appearance in court. In 1630 he was sworn
on a jury. He was possibly acquainted with the poet, John
Milton, who resided at Horton from 1632 to 1638. In 1639
he was named overseer in the will of John Hearne, Jr., a
fact which strengthens the statement of the pedigree that
John and George were brothers. As "George Hieron" he
was buried 22 Aug. 1643.

    Children, the identity of the first two is inferred on the
basis of the evidence given below; the younger children were
named in the Horton parish registers:

    i. ELLEN, b. *ca.* 1605; m. at Horton, 20 Oct. 1627, RICHARD NORRIS.
        Issue: (1) *Richard*, bapt. 21 Feb. 1629/30; (2) *Dorothy*, bapt. 30
        Dec. 1632; (3) *George*, bapt. 21 May 1635; buried 1 June 1641;
        (4) *Richard*, bapt. 24 Feb. 1638/9; (5) *Mary*, bapt. 12 June 1645;
        (6) *Ellen*, bapt. 27 July 1648. Ellen is obviously named after her
        mother. George is apparently named after George Hearne, one
        of the two adult Hearnes residing in the parish, and presumably
        the grandfather.
    ii. JOAN (?), b. *ca.* 1607; m. at Horton, 5 Nov. 1627, JOSEPH JENKS,

bapt. 26 Aug. 1599, the American colonist. The Bishop's transcripts show that Joseph Jenks married *Ellen* Hearne. We believe this entry to be miscopied for two reasons: (1) The previous entry in the Bishop's transcript shows that Ellen Hearne married Richard Norris; and (2) the parish registers of Isleworth, Middlesex, show that Joseph Jenks had a wife *Joan*, who was buried 29 Feb. 1634/5. If we assume that the copyist merely miscopied the maiden name of the bride, we now must ask: Who was the father of Joan Hearne? There were two adult males in the parish who were parents at the time, John and George. We know that John had a daughter Joan; but we do not have the names of the children of George baptized before 1612. John died in 1627, and George in 1643. George harmonizes very nicely with known facts and tradition. For Joseph Jenks emigrated about 1641, and his son emigrated by 1646, when he was 18, or before. According to family tradition, which is quoted again for emphasis, "Joseph Sr. left Joseph Jr. with his maternal grand-parents, whose family name I know not — after assigning a sum sufficient for his maintenance until he should come of age, when he was directed to join his father in America. But he must have arrived, it appears, before that date, perhaps when 16. . . ." As grandson of George Hearne who died in 1643, it would be quite logical for Joseph Jenks, Jr., to come to America before he came of age.

    iii. Margaret, bapt. 4 Oct. 1612.

    iv. Edward, bapt. 18 Aug. 1616.

Years later a William Hearne or Herne migrated to America. Clayton Torrence, in his "Old Somerset on the Eastern Shore", shows that Hearne was of Mattapony, Somerset Co., Md., as early as 9 Aug. 1671. He married in Somerset County, 31 Dec. 1672, Katherine Maltis or Mallis, widow. The family genealogy identifies the colonist as a London merchant.

DOCUMENTS

Transcriptions or abstracts and annotations by A. Vere Woodman, Esq., F.S.A.

(1) *Hearne entries from the Horton Register*

The register begins in 1571 and is in excellent condition to 1615 and then rather poor and obviously defective in places until 1658 when it again becomes good. The first Hearn entry occurs in 1599:

Baptisms

Margaret dau. of John Herne 21 June 1599
Mary dau. of John Herne 13 Aug. 1601
John, son of John Herne, 3 Jan. 1602 (1602/3)
Jone dau. of John Herne 9 April 1604
Jone dau. of John Herne 19 Jan. 1605 (1605/6)
Susan dau. of John Herne 15 May 1608
John son of John Herne 1 Nov. 1609
Margaret dau. of George Herne 4 Oct. 1612
Elizabeth dau. of John Herne 23 Jan. 1613 (1613/14)
Edward son of George Hearne 18 Aug. 1616
    (The above entry has been inserted in a different hand)
Alice dau. of John Hearne 9 March 1617 (1617/18)
John son of John Hearne 22 March 1628 (1628/9)
"Joseph Jinckes ye son of Joseph Jincks" 12 Oct. 1628
William Hieron son of John Hieron 8 Dec. [?]
Grace dau. of John Hieron   1635
    N.B. This entry is partially cut away.
Edmund son of John and Joane Heron 10 Mar. 1638 (1638/9)
Edward son of Edward Hieron 17 Jan. 1641 (1641/2)
    N.B. He was buried 18 Jan. the following day.
Hannah dau. of Edward Hieron 18 Sept. 1645
Edward son of Edward & Hannah Hearne "was born the 6th day of July and baptized the same day"

John Herne son of John & Catharine Herne born 12 July 1657
Katharine dau. of John & Katharine Herne born 14 Feb. 1658
(1658/9)
Edward son of John & Catharine Heron born 23 Jan. 1660/1

Marriages

Richard Holland & Margaret Heron 29 April 1639
John Humperby & Joane Hieron 12 Oct. 1640
[It is not surprising that the Jenks-Hearn marriage does not occur. Only fourteen marriages are recorded 1615-1630. (They average about four a year.) None at all occur for 1625, 1626, 1627, and 1628 and only one for 1629.]

Burials

Margaret wife of John Harne 5 June 1626 "pest"
William Harne 21 Jan. 1626 (1626/7) "pest"
Elizabeth Harne 6 Feb. 1626 (1626/7) "pest"
John Harne 7 Feb. 1626 (1626/7) "pest"
Ann Harne 13 Feb. 1626 (1626/7) "pest"
N.B. A score or more are said to have died of pest or plague 1626/7 and some in 1637; occasionally they are entered as "of Colebrook".
Grace dau. of John Hieron 7 March 1635 (1635/6)
John Hieron 11 Aug. 1639
George Heron 22 Aug. 1643
N.B. Burials from 1653-1658 are wanting.
Catharine Heron wife of George Heron 17 Dec. 1659
William son of William 18 Aug. 1670
John Hearne 17 Dec. 1670
Catharine Hearne 31 Dec. 1670

John Heron occurs as churchwarden, March 1638

(2) *Norris entries from the Horton Register*

Richard Norris married Ellen Hearne 12 Oct. 1627 (transcript)
The register records the baptism of the following children:
Richard, 21 Feb. 1629/30:
Dorothy, 30 Dec. 1632
George 21 May 1635
Richard 24 Feb. 1638/9
Mary, 12 June 1645
Ellen, 27 July 1648
George, the son of Richard Norris was buried 1 June 1641, but, although the burials were searched until 1680, no other Norrises occur.
The name George strongly suggests that his wife was the daughter of George Hearn and that her name was, as given in the transcripts, Ellen.

(3) *Extracts from the Manorial Records of Horton*

They are very incomplete, being mostly views of frankpledge.
1619 John Herne and George Hearne were essoined.
1620 George Hearne and William Herne were essoined.
      John Hearne was sworn on the jury for the King.
1621 George Hearne and John Hearne were essoined.
1622 No reference
1623 John Hearne was chosen constable for Horton for the following year (constables were also chosen for Colebroke in Horton, Chalvey, and Eaton).
1624 No reference
1626 No reference.
1630 John Hearne essoined. George Hearne sworn on the jury.
1631 John Hearne sworn on the jury.
1633 John Hearne sworn on the jury.

1636 John Hearne sworn on the jury.
1640 No reference.

(4) *Abstract of the will of John Hearne (Jr.) of Horton (Arch. Bucks)*

John Hearne of Horton, husbandman, sick in body
To John Hearne my eldest son £10
To Francis Hearne my second son £10
To William Hearne my third son £5
To Edmond Hearne my fourth son £5
The legacies to be paid at their age of 21 years and if any son die, his portion is to be equally distributed. All other goods and chattells to my wife Joane Hearne whom I make executrix. She is to give such security for the payment of the legacies as Mr. Henry Bullstrode or his son Mr. Thomas Bullstrode shall think reasonable and to bring up children until they are bound apprentices.

Overseers: George Hearne and Francis Bowry of Horton. Dated 8 April 1639.

Witnesses Thomas Wilkinson, clerk, Robert Hall, the writer. Proved 3 Oct. 1639.

THE FATHER OF JOSEPH JENKS OF LYNN:
A PROPOSED SOLUTION TO AN INTRIGUING
GENEALOGICAL PUZZLE

By Meredith B. Colket, Jr., of Cleveland, Ohio

In 1905 Dr. Edwin A. Hill wrote an article in *The New York Genealogical and Biographical Record* (vol. 36) about the Mayflower passenger of 1620, Richard More. The author identified two Richard Mores as sons of a member of the English Parliament, Samuel More of Linley and Larden. The first Richard was baptized at Shipton, Shropshire, on November 13, 1614, came to America, deposing in 1684 that he was aged about 70. The other, born circa 1627, by a second wife, inherited the family estates. The evidence presented was convincing except for the improbability that an Englishman had two sons of the same name, the elder who came to America, the younger who remained behind and inherited the family estates. This writer for one, could not bring himself to accept the thesis. But Sir Anthony R. Wagner C.V.O., D.Litt., F.A.S.G., Garter King of Arms, in an article in The Register (vol. 114, p. 163, July 1960) presented [*] conclusive evidence corroborating Dr. Hill's findings. In part it was shown that Samuel More divorced his first wife, the mother of the Mayflower passengers.

The circumstance of two children of the same given name and parents is not unique in the annals of English families who migrated to New England in the seventeenth century. A potential parallel, with the younger treated likewise as heir, is implied in the Jenks family. Joseph Jenks, a widower from England, appeared in New England in 1642. There is good evidence that he was the eldest son of John Jenks of London, cutler. There is also good evidence that another contemporary Londoner, Joseph Jenks, was son and heir of John Jenks of London, cutler. The unlikelihood of there being two John Jenks of London of the same trade and period, each with an eldest son Joseph, suggests a situation similar to that in the More family.

The two Joseph Jenks have previously been identified in the series of articles published in The Register, vol. 110, 1956, and issued also [**] in a separate reprint. It is sufficient here to summarize the information gleaned about each.

The Joseph Jenks, contemporary Londoner, born circa 1607, was son and apparently heir of John Jenks of London, cutler, and his wife Elinor. Originally a resident of the Precinct of the Tower of London, Joseph was admitted to his father's guild of white bakers in 1629, although he, too, was a cutler and once called knife forger. In 1630 he married at All Hallows on the Wall, London, Mary Tervyn. The late Colonel Charles E. Banks suspected that this Joseph was identical with the American colonist of the name and the suggested identification appeared as fact in several American publications, including William Bradford Browne's *Genealogy of the Jenks family in America*, 1952, p. 12. That this was in error is proved by

[*]P. 763, this volume.
[**]The preceding article.

the administration on Joseph's estate which was granted to his widow Mary of the nearby parish of St. Leonard, Shoreditch, Middlesex, in 1642.

Obviously the colonist who was in New England from 1642 until his death in 1683 was another Joseph Jenks. The clue to the colonist's identity came from family tradition that placed him in "Colebrook" and Hounslow. Colnbrook and Hounslow were chapelries not far from London. One was in the parish of Horton, Middlesex, the other in that of Isleworth, Middlesex. A search of parish registers revealed the following entries, the first from Horton, the latter two from Isleworth:

Joseph Jincks ye sonne of Joseph Jencks bapt Oct 12, 1628
[1634/5] Feb. 29 Jone Jeankes the wife of Joseaff Jeankes was buryed [buried 1638] Nov 2 [Eliza]beth the daughter of Joseph Jenkes

The baptism of Joseph Jr. in 1628 conforms with the deposition of Joseph Jenks Jr., of Providence, Rhode Island, son of the emigrant, stating that he was aged 81, 27 November 1708. The burial of the wife of Joseph Senior in 1635 harmonizes with the tradition that he came to this country a widower.

The sword found at the Powysland Museum with the inscription "JOSEPH IENCKES ME FECIT HOUNSLO" further substantiates the identity. Since Hounslow swords were known to be manufactured only during the 1630's, the sword was obviously made by the colonist who in America applied for a patent to make scythes.

There remains now to discuss Joseph's parentage. A search revealed the baptism at St. Anne, Blackfriars, London, of Joseph Jenks, son of John Jenks, cutler, on 26 August 1599. This record corresponds nicely with the deposition of Joseph, the colonist, on 17 September 1681, that he was about 81 years of age. It might be claimed that this was merely a coincidence and the Joseph of the baptismal record died young. But against such a supposition we marshal the following facts:

1. The Jenks surname is quite uncommon in the London area while the baptismal name Joseph is the first ever to be noted in the Jenks family of England.

2. Since Joseph the emigrant was a sword blade maker[1] in England and an inventor of scythes in New England, it is plausible to assume that he sprang from a family of cutlers.

3. Joseph's association with the foreign cutlers brought to Hounslow in 1630 by Charles I is significant in view of the fact that Sarah (Fulwater) Jenks, the mother of the Joseph baptized at St. Anne, Blackfriars, was a daughter of a foreign cutler.

We thus have two Joseph Jenks, unquestionably natives of the City of London. Each worked in a branch of cutlery, one was called knife-forger, the other sword blade maker, and each was the son of John Jenks of London, cutler. The one baptized at St. Anne, Blackfriars, in 1599, whose mother was Sarah, came to America by 1642. The other, born about 1607, whose mother was Elinor, inherited the right to the mark of the thistle and died by 1642. In THE REGISTER article previously cited a very close relationship of the two Joseph's was suspected but because of the nature of the problem, no effective interpretation was made. Now the question lies squarely before us. Could the two Josephs be half brothers and sons of the same man?

So far we have obtained but a fleeting glimpse of the John Jenks who was father of the emigrant Joseph. The records show only his marriage in London in 1596 and the baptism of two children in 1597 and 1599. Yet were he identical with the great craftsman, John Jenks of London who made such beautiful knives for the table of King James I, the mystery of this glimpse is explained. The dates allow for it; and we unearth a romantic episode in the life of a cutler's apprentice.

John Jenks, the gifted craftsman, was apprenticed to a London cutler in 1592 for a period of seven years. He well seems to be that John Jenks of London, cutler, who in 1596 married Sarah Fulwater and by so doing violated his apprenticeship agreement. The period of this matrimonial bliss lasted as late as 1599. Perhaps Sarah died and the children were adopted by another cutler, or perhaps, as in the More case, the couple separated. Under such circumstances John was free to return to his master. We have thus a plausible explanation of why it took John twelve years instead of seven to complete his apprenticeship and gain standing in his trade as a freeman. For cutler John Jenks became a citizen and white baker of London in 1604.[2]

The rest of John's story has already been told. Most London citizens married about a year after gaining their freedom. John married Elinor about 1605 and had, about 1607, a second son Joseph, who later also became a citizen, a cutler, and white baker of London. John, from 1611 until his death about 1625, lived near the Bulwark Gate in the Precinct of the Tower of London, supplying recognizable and vastly beautiful knives for the royal table, knives that are exhibited in European museums today.

The above hypothesis fits the facts like a glove and all known records of John Jenks of London, cutler, at last fall into a logical pattern.

FOOTNOTES

1. Recently, my attention has been called to a petition in which Joseph Jenks actually called himself sword blade maker. The petition, addressed to Algernon, Earl of Northumberland, was to set up a mill at Woorton Bridge (evidently over the Isleworth River, Middlesex) for making swords. It reads as follows:

To the right no^{ble} Algernon Earle of Northumberland, Lord high Admirall of England &c.

The humble peticon of Joseph Jincks, sworde-blade maker Sheweth

That yor Peticon is intended (wth yor Hono^{rs} Favour) to sett upp a new invented Engine or Blade-mill upon ye River at Woorton bridge. And having obteyne^d leave of Captaine Cripps for ye Venting of ye Water, there, hee most humbly beseecheth yor hono^r to graunt unto him a smale peece of waste ground there to sett upp a smal shudd or workhouse for his more convenience:

and hee willbe content to all for y^t the same, as yor Lordpp or any of yor Officers shall thinke meete:

Furthermore, may it please yor Hono^r to take notice that there is never an englishman in ye kingdome that cann use that profession but himselfe (except the Dutch) and hee hopes by this meanes to raise upp more english to ye same trade, and that wee shall not have hereafter so much need of Straungers, wch wilbe a further benefit^t to the comon Wealth: and therefore hee doubteth not of yor Hono^rs favour herein.

> ffor wch hee shalbe ever bound to pray
> for yor Hono^r

7°. August: 1639. his L^p gave me order to lett the peticoner have the peece of grownd to sett up his shedd or workehouse for makinge blades accordinge to his peticon to be graunted to him by lease.

The document is most revealing for it shows that Jenks of Continental ancestry on his mother's side was apparently the only Englishman who had worked among the foreign cutlers.

Although the document shows on the reverse that the petition was granted, it is evident that Jenks did not maintain a continuing operation.

The original document was among the papers in the Library of the Dukes of Northumberland (Lyon House) microfilmed for the Manuscript Division, Library of Congress, Washington, D. C. R.F. —646 R. I. le. 7 August 1639. Aln. 106/8.

I am indebted to Dr. Jean Stephenson, Fellow of the American Society of Genealogy, and Dr. Whitfield J. Bell, Librarian of the American Philosophical Society, who separately brought the item to my attention.

Another document that further helps us distinguish between the two Joseph Jenks relates to the other Joseph. It was called to my attention by Miss N. J. M. Kerling, Ph.D., of London. In the Public Record Office, London, among Passes to travel beyond seas: 24 Nov. 1629 Joseph Jencks 22 years old dwelling near the Postern gate on Tower-Hill. To Flushing on his affairs to serve as a soldier. E 157/14. This other Joseph married on the outskirts of London the following year as our records show. For siblings of identical name see *The American Genealogist*, vol. 36, p. 158; vol. 37, p. 62.

2. John Jenks became a citizen and white baker of London because the master cutler to whom he was apprenticed was a member of the White Bakers' Company. This situation was not unusual: it came about as the result of the fact that a Londoner could join his father's guild, irrespective of his own trade. Guild membership, of course, gave very desirable privileges of citizenship. Several master cutlers were at this period members of the White Bakers' Company, including Jacob Fulwater, presumed brother of Sarah who married John Jenks. Jacob found it more desirable to be a member of the London Company of Cutlers, and in 1608 paid a fee for "translation."

TWO FOUNDERS OF ROWLEY, MASS.

Contributed by TRACY ELLIOT HAZEN, PH.D., of New York City

1. JEWETT

IN this series of contributions on the pioneers of ancient Rowley, which it was vainly hoped might be completed during the Tercentenary year of 1939, it is natural to follow the account of the newly discovered lineage of Mr. Edward Carlton and of his wife, Ellen Newton,* with a re-examination of the origins of the Jewett family, from which American Carletons trace descent through the marriage of Lieut. John Carleton to a daughter of Joseph Jewett of Rowley.

The parentage of the brothers Maximilian and Joseph Jewett has been known here for seventy years, through the publication of notes by Horatio G. Somerby,† and his report has apparently been satisfactory to the Jewett Family Association ever since. Some who have the Jewett blood, though farther removed from the name, have felt that more might be learned by modern research in England, and the first approach to the original records by the contributor revealed evidence that Mr. Somerby's pioneer work had been very fragmentary and superficial. It appears as though there had been a conspiracy to suppress the fact that the family name even has been reported incorrectly, perhaps merely to please the clients who initiated the search: it is very generally written Jowett in the early records, and almost universally that spelling is retained by the army of their descendants whose names are now listed in the directory of Bradford, Yorkshire. It is contended in reply to such criticism that three hundred years ago spelling was not settled, and it makes little difference, which may be admitted. But when the Jewett Genealogy, and the recent Snow-Estes volume copying from it, put forth what purports to be a "true copy of the will" of Edward Jowet, with the surname incorrectly transcribed throughout, one begins to look for other evidences of carelessness, which are readily found. In the researches reported in this paper, the contributor has been disappointed in being still unable to carry the lineage back definitely be-

---

* See REGISTER, vol. 93 (January 1939), pp. 3–46; vol. 94 (January 1940), pp. 3–18.
† See REGISTER, vol. 22 (1868), p. 365 and *Essex Institute Historical Collections*, vol. 22 (1885), p. 1.
[1] Pp. 373-418, the first volume of this series; pp. 777-792, this volume.

yond the father of the immigrants, though a much larger body of documents has been examined than can be set forth here. If the ancient vicars or parish clerks had kept records from 1538, when the custom was initiated, or even from the beginning of the reign of Elizabeth in 1558, when the order was more generally observed, we should probably be able to go back two or three generations in this lineage. All of the Jowett wills in the York Probate Registry have been read, but they are rather few in this earlier period, and the much larger number of the first half of the seventeenth century are mostly those of collateral relatives, which do not mention the people in whom we would be interested.

Enough, however, has been found to justify a new presentation of the early family records.

FROM PROBATE RECORDS

The Will of EDWARD JOWET, 1614. In the name of god amen: the second day of ffebruary in the yeare of our lord god 1614 in the xij[th] yeare of the Reigne of our Sov'eigne Lord James by the grace of god King of England ffrance and Ireland defender of the faithe etc. and of Scotland the eight & fortieth whereas nothing is more certaine then death and nothing more uncertaine then the houre of death Therefore I Edward Jowett of Bradford wth in the dioces of Yorke Clothier, though sick, and diseased in bodie yet sound and p'fect in minde and memory I prayse god therefore do in this uncertainty of life (knowing that even in health we are subiect to death) make publish and declare this my last will & testament, in manner and forme ffollowinge, (that is to say) ffirst and principally I give up & commend my soule into the hands of allmightie god my creator & redeemer hoping & assuredly trustinge, to have full & free p'don & remission of all my sinnes, by the p'cious death, & buriall of Christ Jesus mine alone Saviour & for Justification, by his righteousnes: my bodie, I yeild to the earth to be decently buried, at the discretion of my friends. Itm My will & minde is that all my lawfull debts be paide out of my whole goods. Itm I give and bequeath two full parts of all my goods cattells chattels & creditts (in three pts to be divided) unto Willm Jowett, Maximilian Jowett, Joseph Jowett and Sara Jowett my children equally to be divided amongst them after my debts be paide & funerall expences discharged The third pte & residue of all my saide goods cattelles chattelles & creditts I give & bequeath unto Mary my wife whome I make the sole executrix of this my last will & testament And I doe intreat Willm Tayler my father in law Henry Tayler my brother in law Samuel Tayler & Trustrum Ledyard to be the supervisors of this my last will and testament Itm my will & minde is that my children shall have theire porcons paide unto them at such times as they shall sev'ally accomplish theire ages of xxi yeares or otherwise lawfully demaund the same. Lastly I doe comitt the tuicon & gov'nement of all my said children wth theire sev'all porcons duringe theire sev'all minorities, unto the said Mary my wife. witnesses hereof—

Willm Smyths * W mke Jonas A watsons * mke E ł
Lewes W watsons * mke

(York Probate Registry, original will; also recorded in vol. 33, f⁰ 587.)

Jowet [On the 12th day of July anno dni 1615 Laurence Wilson clerk, dean of Pontefract] certified concerning the probate of the will of Edward Jowet late of Bradford in the diocese of York, deceased, through the witnesses named, being sworn, and administration of the goods of the said deceased was com-

* The word *jurat* written above name of each witness.

Agreement of 1653 in handwriting of Joseph Jowett

mitted to Marie Jowet, relict of the said deceased, sole executrix named in the said will, previously sworn. There was exhibited an inventory above 40 pounds, and the said Mary and others were put under bonds. (York Registry, Act Book, Pontefract, 1615.) *

From an Unpublished Deed †

Sept. 28, 1612. Indenture between William Jewett of Thorpe in Idle, yeoman, and Elizabeth Jewett of the same place, widow, mother of the said William, of the one party, and Peter Kitson of Thorpe afsd husbandman, of the other part: Witnesseth, that the said William Jewett and Elizabeth Jewett in consideration of the sum of 104 pounds, grant, bargain, sell, aliene and confirm unto the said Peter Kitson all those two closes of land commonly known by the several names of the Hingingeroyde and Hangingroyde ynge and all those two other closes called the Browneroydes lying next to one lane there called Browneroyde lane with all the edifices and buildings builded upon the said several closes and also one full fourth part of eleven parts of all the commons moors and wastes of Idle afsd. in four hundred parts to be devided (Reserved a yearly rent of two shillings) and also doing yearly suit of service at the courts and corne mill of Idle in such manner and form as the said William Jewett and Edward Jewett deceased late father of the said William have agreed to do, and as other freeholders and tenants of the manor or lordship of Idle are charged to do. Power of entry reserved for non payment of the rent of two shillings per annum proviso for further assurance within space of seven years. (Signed) William Jewyte, Elizabeth x Jewet. Witnesses William Jowett, Roger Dornebrook, Rich. x Boothe, Wm. x Dawson, J. ridgley. Seal a lion rampant.

From the Parish Registers of Bradford, Yorkshire, 1596–1656

Marriages ‡

1600 The page of the register is signed by Willia' ⊔⊔ Jewett marke, Church warden; Caleb Kempe, vicar, April 8.

1601 Willm Jowett and Dorathie wilson, May 19.
1601 Willm Jowett and ffrances Rawson, Julie 21.
1604 Edward Jowett and Mary Tayler, October 1.
1606 Willm Jowett and Issabel Pearson, December 1.
1607 Edward Jowett and Alice Hopkinson, May 12.
1607 Willm Jowett and Ellen Patterson, June 22.
1608 William Jewett & Issabell Jewett, June 14.
1609 Edward Jewet & Aner Mawde, Februarie 6 [1609/10].
1612 Richard Jowett and ffrances Pickard, June 22.
1612 Willm Jowett and Katherine Richardson, August 16.
1613 Register signed by Callub Kempe vicar and Ric. Jowet church warden. [This apparently an autograph, though the vicar's probably is not.]

* The version of the above will printed in the Jewett Genealogy shows from internal evidence that it was transcribed from the registered copy at York. Besides minor verbal errors, it uniformly writes the surname Jowet, while the original has Jowett, except in the notations of the probate clerk, who preferred to write Jowet. The firm monogram-like initials with which the original is signed indicate a much more cultivated man than the scrawled 'marks' of the witnesses.

† An unrecorded deed, copy in possession of Mr. William E. Preston of Bradford, 1932, to whom thanks are due for the privilege of its use. A large collection of additional unpublished deeds and other documents filed in the Bradford archives at the Cartwright Memorial was examined by the contributor in 1938, through the kind cooperation of Mr. Preston.

‡ For the period 1596 to 1626 the contributor counted 49 marriage records of this family; in six cases the name was written Jewett, in three cases Jowet, in one Jewet, and in all other records Jowett. Only the names of particular interest are given above. The other early marriage and burial records are published in the *Bradford Antiquary*, vols. 1–3.

1616   William Lister & Mary Jowett (by license), Aug. 7.
1619   John Brodeley & Mary Jowett, Feb. 28 [1619/20].
1625   William Jewett & Isabel Brockden, Sept. 4.
1626   William Jowett & Ann ffield, Aug. 22.
1629   William Jowett & Grace Shawe, Nov. 10.
1632   William Jowett & Marie Denby, Nov. 30.
1634   Joseph Jewett and Mary Mallinsonn, October 1.

Baptisms

1605   Willm s. of Edward Jowet of Bradford, Sept. 15.
1607   Maximilian s. of Edward Jowett of Eckilshill, Oct. 4.
1608   Richard ye s. of Edw^{r}d Jewett of Manningham, Dec. 21.
1609   Joseph ye s. of Edward Jewett of Bradford, Dec. 31.
1610   Grace D. of Edward Jowett of Bradford, Nov. 4.
1612   Josias s. of Edward Jowett of Bradford, May 17.
1612   Ellen D. of Edward Jowett of Horton, Nov. 15.
1626   Sara d. of William Jowett of Thornton, Feb. 4 [1626/7].
1627   John s. of William Jowett of Thornton, Dec. 16.
1627   Ann d. of William Jowett of Thornton, Mar. 9 [1627/8].
1628   Joseph s. of William Jewett of Bradford, Jan. 25 [1628/9].
1630   Joseph s. of William Jowett of Bradford, Oct. 17.
1630   Lura & Susan d. of William Jowett of Thornton, Jan. 30 [1630/1].
1631   Joseph s. of William Jowett of Claiton, Feb. 5 [1631/2].
1632   Nathan s. of Willm Jewett of Bradford, Oct. 7.
1632   Marie d. of William Jowett of Thornton, Mar. 24 [1632/3].
1633   Jonas s. of William Jewitt Junr. of Thornton, Mar. 9 [1633/4].
1634   Abraham s. of William Jewitt of Bradford, Sept. 14.
1635   Sarah da. of Joseph Jewette of Bradford, Jan. 3 [1635/6].
1636   Abraham s. of William Jowett of Heaton, May 1.
1636   John s. of William Jowett of Gt. Horton, May 8.
1637   Anne d. of William Jowett of Thornton, June 18.
1637   John s. of William Jowett of Bradford, Oct. 11.
1637   Jeremie s. of Joseph Jowett of Bradford, Dec. 26.
1638   Judith d. of William Jewitt of Thornton, May 14.
1639   John s. of William Jewett of Bradford, Nov. 24.
1640   Peter s. of William Jowett of Thornton, Nov. 6.
1641   Mary d. of William Jowette of Bradford, June 20.
1642   William s. of William Jowett of Bradford, Dec. 25.
1643   W^m & Anne ch. of William Jowett of Bowling, Mar. 17 [1643/4].
1645   Judith d. of William Jowett of Bradford, Mar. 13 [1645/6].
1646   John s. of William Jowett of Bowling, Feb. 28 [1646/7].

Burials

1596   Widow of Edwd. Jowet, Jan. 28 [1596/7].
1598   Child of Edward Jowett, Apr. 14.
1602   wife of William Jowett of Eckelshill, Feb. 2 [1602/03].
1603   William Jowett of Bradford, Feb. 17 [1603/04].
1605   Wife of Edwd Jowett of Bradford, Julie 10.
1607   Child of William Jowett of Bradford, Dec. 30.
1607   Child of Edward Jowett of Bradford, Jan. 30 [1607/08].
1609   Wife of Edward Jewett of Bradford, June 11.
1613   Widow Jowett of Bradford, May 27.
1614   Edward Jowett of Barkerend, Bradford, Feb. 4 [1614/15].
1615   Widow Jowett, Bradford, July 19.
1615   Child of William Jowett of Bradford, not baptized, Aug. 30.
1616   William Tayler of Bradford, *in ecclesia*, July 12.

1616 Child of William Jowett of Bradford, n.b., Nov. 2.
1618 Edward Jowett of Bradford, Aug. 28.
1618 Mary d. Edward Jowett, late of Bradford, Sept. 10.
1618 Thomas Tayler of Bradford, *in eclesia*, Dec. 12.
1622 ffrances wife of William Jowett of Heaton, Feb. 3 [1622/3].
1626 Wife of William Lister of Bradford, May 23.
1626 William s. William Jewett of Bradford, Julie 20.
1626 Child of William Jewitt of Heaton, Dec. 1.
1627 John s. William Jowett of Thornton, Maie 7.
1627 William Jowett of Manningham, Nov. 28.
1630 Wife of William Jowett of Bradford, May 5.
1633 William Jewitt of Bradford, Mar. 4 [1633/4].
1639 Wife of William Jewett of Bradford, Feb. 26 [1639/40].
1641 William Jowett of Bradford, Apr. 12.

Among earlier records, too voluminous and detailed to print here, the contributor spent a long time in the Bradford Public Library, delving in an unindexed manuscript transcript of Court Rolls of the Duchy of Lancaster, of which Bradford Manor was a part, of the time of Henry V [1413–14], in which the only mentions for this family were several items of a William Jowet summoned to court with many others to answer for trespasses. A century later, muster rolls of the time of Henry VIII show in Bradford the names of Edward Jooet, Richard Jooet, and John Jooet [probably still pronounced Jowet, just as the name Cooper is even now pronounced Cowper in the north of England].

The unrecorded deed printed above was at first thought to give a possible clue to an earlier generation for the lineage of Edward Jowett of New England because of the conjunction of the names William and Edward Jowett. It appears, however, on closer scrutiny, to be concerned with a contemporary of our Edward Jowett, possibly a cousin. The property concerned had been long in the family, as shown by a Survey of the Manor or Lordship of Idle in 1584. Part of this property was also the subject of concern in a locally famous Chancery suit of a period too late to be of use for our pedigree.*

From all these records, however, and the numerous occurrences of the name William Jowett in the early parish registers, the contributor has arrived at the personal conviction that the father of Edward Jowett who heads the American lineage given below must have been a William Jowett, very likely that one who was buried at Bradford 17 Feb. 1603/04, and whose wife might have been the Widow Jowett of Bradford buried 27 May 1613. Since there is no actual proof at hand, this is given merely as a suggestion, which it is hoped may find support in future research. The settled pedigree must therefore still begin, as before, with Edward Jowett.

1. EDWARD JOWETT of Bradford, England, born perhaps about 1580, died at Bradford, and was buried there 4 Feb. 1614/15. He married at Bradford, 1 Oct. 1604, Mary Tayler, sister of Samuel Tayler and daughter of William Tayler (who was named supervisor

---

* See the *Bradford Antiquary*, vol. 1, pp. 198 and 268; also William Cudworth's "Round About Bradford," p. 370, and his History of Bolton and Bowling (townships of Bradford), pp. 79 and 84. 1891.

in the will of Edward Jowett, and is probably that William Tayler who was buried at Bradford, in the church, 12 July 1616).*

Edward Jowett is called in his will, dated 2 February 1614 (probably the day of his death), a clothier, which indicates that he had rather large interests in the manufacture of cloth, and perhaps held different lands and properties, since, in the record of the baptism of his second son he is called "of Eccleshill," a township which might be called suburban, though still in the extended parish of Bradford. His wife survived him, and was confirmed as executrix of his will on 12 July 1615. Left a young widow with four small children, and bereft again the next year of her father, who had been the protector of the family, what wonder that she appears, soon after this last event, to have contracted another alliance, indicated by the parish register in the record of marriage on 7 August 1616 of "William Lister and Mary Jowett (by licence)." Turning to Paver's Marriage Licenses in 1616 † one finds "William Lister and Mary Taylor, widow, of Bradford—at Bradford." In this discrepancy one may see a striking confirmation of the identity of the bride: either the groom was asked for her maiden name, or it was well known that she belonged in the family of her late father. Her further history is indicated in the record of the burial, 23 May 1626, of the "wife of William Lister of Bradford."

Children, baptized at Bradford:

2. i. WILLIAM, bapt. 15 Sept. 1605.
  ii. MAXIMILIAN, bapt. 4 Oct. 1607; d. at Rowley, Mass., where he was buried 19 Oct. 1684. He is believed to have come over with Rev. Ezekiel Rogers in 1638, and settled in Rowley in 1639, with his first wife Ann, whose family has not been identified. Their marriage is not recorded at Bradford. She was buried at Rowley, 9 Nov. 1667. He m. (2) 30 Aug. 1671 Ellen (Pell) Boynton, widow of John Boynton of Rowley, who married (3) at Ipswich, 1 June 1686, Daniel Warner, Sr., and died as his widow at Rowley 5 Aug. 1689.

  Maximilian Jewett was one of the first two deacons of the Rowley Church, ordained 3 Dec. 1639. He was a freeman 13 May 1640, and many times representative in the General Court. His long will was printed in full in the *Essex Institute Historical Collections*, vol. 22, pp. 2–4.‡

* It is surprising that no will is found for this William Tayler (who was important enough to be recorded as buried in the church) or for his son. Several Tailer and Tayler wills of this period were read, and even transcribed completely for further study, but none give any help in elucidating the history of this family.

† See *Yorkshire Archaeological Journal*, vol. 14, p. 227.

‡ His best autograph appears to be that reproduced herewith, together with his brother Joseph's, taken from their signatures to the inventory of Richard Bayley of Rowley 23 Aug. 1648, on file at Salem. See Records and Files of Quarterly Courts of Essex Co., vol. 1, p. 148.

Other signatures, described as autographs, such as the "Maxemillion Jewett", witness to the will of William Stickney in 1664, and the "Maximilion Jewett" on the inventory of the same estate in 1665, appear to have been written by other hands.

His nine children, born at Rowley, are recorded in detail in Blodgette and Jewett's *Early Settlers of Rowley*, and in the Jewett Genealogy, where the descendants bulk much more largely than those of his younger brother.

3. iii. JOSEPH, bapt. 31 Dec. 1609.
    iv. SARAH, known only by the reference in her father's will. Her baptism is not recorded.
    v. GRACE, bapt. 4 Nov. 1610.
    vi. JOSIAS, bapt. 17 May 1612. If he belongs in this family, he must have died before 4 Feb. 1614/15.

2. WILLIAM JOWETT (*Edward*), of Bradford, England, was baptized there 15 Sept. 1605. It appears most probable that he is the William Jowett who married at Bradford, 22 Aug. 1626, ANN FIELD.

Children, baptized at Bradford:

i. JOSEPH, bapt. 25 Jan. 1628.
ii. JOSEPH, bapt. 17 Oct. 1630.
iii. NATHAN, bapt. 2 Oct. 1632.
iv. ABRAHAM,* bapt. 14 Sept. 1634; probably identical with Abraham Jewett who settled at Rowley, Mass., where the inventory of his estate was taken 30 Apr. 1694; m. at Rowley, 2 Apr. 1661, ANN ALLEN, b. 8 Oct. 1643, d. at Rowley 9 Feb. 1721/22, daughter of Bozoan and Ann Allen. His eldest son was named William Jewett. (For further information see Blodgette and Jewett, and the Jewett Genealogy.)
v. JOHN, bapt. 11 Oct. 1637.
vi. JOHN,* bapt. 24 Nov. 1639. He is probably to be identified with John Jewett of Rowley, Mass., who m. (1) 2 Apr. 1661 ELIZABETH CUMMINGS (who d. at Ipswich, Mass., 9 July 1679, daughter of Isaac Cummings of Topsfield); m. (2) ELIZABETH (HOW) CHADWELL, widow of Benjamin Chadwell of Lynn and daughter of Joseph How. (Thirteen children, treated in detail in Blodgette and Jewett, and in the Jewett Genealogy.)
vii. MARY, bapt. 20 June 1641.
viii. WILLIAM, bapt. 25 Dec. 1642.
ix. JUDITH, bapt. 13 Mar. 1645.

3. JOSEPH JOWETT (later JEWETT) (*Edward*), of Rowley, Mass., baptized at Bradford, England, 31 Dec. 1609, died at Rowley, where he was buried 26 Feb. 1660/61. He married first, at Bradford, 1 Oct. 1634, MARY MALLINSON, baptized at Bradford 29 May 1606, died at Rowley and buried there 12 Apr. 1652, daughter of Richard and Sara (Waterhouse) Mallinson; and secondly, in Boston, Mass., 13 May 1653, ANN ALLEN, who was buried at Rowley 8 Feb. 1660/61, widow of Capt. Bozoan Allen.

Joseph and Mary Jowett came over, it is believed, with Rev. Ezekiel Rogers, and were among the early members of the First Church in Dorchester (admitted before "4 da.: 9 mo. 1639"), where they probably spent the first winter, removing in the spring to the new settlement at Rowley. He was a freeman 22 May 1639, and was deputy to the General Court in

---

* It must be acknowledged that no proof has been found for the assumption of the identity of the brothers Abraham Jowett and John Jowett above with the two Rowley settlers of the same names; but the suggestion by Amos E. Jewett of such an identity is so logical that it seems proper to show that the records might justify such a belief. It may be hoped that evidence in its support may be discovered in further research.

1651, 1652, 1653, 1654, and 1660; he was one of the two stewards for each of their sessions. In 1656 he is called "clothier" and later "merchant," and was active in business affairs for most of his life. As shown later, he signed his name Joseph Jowit as a witness to the will of his father-in-law 22 Sept. 1636, and even as late as 1653 he and his son Jeremiah wrote their name Jowett in an agreement preserved in the Court Files (see reduced facsimile reproduced as frontispiece of this article). Later they used the spelling Jewett which has been universal among their descendants. This sheet is reproduced because of the vivid impression it gives of the personality of the principal, who here wrote his own name four times (each time incorrectly transcribed by the editors of the *Records*).

This document (Records and Files of the Quarterly Courts of Essex County, Mass., vol. 3, p. 235, Original file, vol. 10, f° 100) is a transaction so representative of the activities of Joseph Jowett as to merit further notice here. It is an agreement, dated 18 Jan. 1653, between Joseph Jowett of Rowley and Thomas Dorman, William Emanes, Thomas Houlat, and Frances Paybody of Topsfield, for a parcel of land in Rowley in a village lately agreed on by the town of Rowley, which said Joseph Jowett sold to them for 70 pounds to be paid at Joseph Jowett's house in Rowley in corn or cattle.

Joseph Jewett's will, dated 15 Feb. 1660 and proved 26 Mar. 1661, is on file at Salem, and has been printed in exact copy, line by line, in the *Essex Institute Historical Collections*, vol. 22, p. 15. He named as executors "my Brother Maximilian Jewett, and my sonne Phillip Nellson, my sonne John Carleton and my sonne Jeremiah Jewett."

Children, the first two born at Bradford, England, the rest at Rowley, Mass.:

i. SARAH, bapt. 3 Jan. 1635/36; bur. at Rowley 17: 12 mo. 1665; m. at Rowley, 24 June 1657, CAPT. PHILIP NELSON, b. in England about 1633, d. at Rowley 19 Aug. 1691, son of Thomas Nelson. Philip Nelson m. (2) 1: 11 mo. 1666 Elizabeth Lowell, daughter of John Lowell of Newbury.

ii. JEREMIAH, bapt. as Jeremie 26 Dec. 1637; d. at Rowley 20 May 1714, aged 77 years (gravestone record); m. 1 May 1661 SARAH DICKINSON, b. at Rowley 18 Oct. 1644, d. there 30 Jan. 1723/24, daughter of Thomas and Jennet Dickinson.

iii. HANNAH, b. 15 June 1641; living at Salem as late as 27 Nov. 1706; m. (1) probably about 1658/59 LIEUT. JOHN CARLETON, b. in Yorkshire, England, about 1637, d. at Haverhill, Mass., 22 Jan. 1668, son of Edward and Ellen (Newton) Carlton of Rowley; m. (2) at Salem, Mass., 5: 8 mo. 1674, CHRISTOPHER BABBIDGE bapt. at Totnes, Devonshire, 17 Apr. 1631, living in Salem as late as 27 Nov. 1706, son of Roger and Hester (Greene) Babbidge.

iv. NEHEMIAH, b. 6 Apr. 1643; d. at Ipswich Village 1 Jan. 1719/20; m. at Lynn, 19: 8 mo. 1668, EXERCISE PIERCE, d. 13 Nov. 1731, daughter of John Pierce.

v. FAITH (twin), b. 5 May 1645; d. in infancy.

vi. PATIENCE (twin), b. 5 May 1645; m. (1) at Lynn, Mass., 29 May 1666, SHUBAEL WALKER, d. at Bradford, Mass., 22 Jan. 1688/89 and was bur. at Lynn; m. (2) RICHARD DOLE of Newbury, son of William Dole.

vii. MARY, b. 4 Apr. 1643; d. in infancy.
viii. JOSEPH, b. 1 Apr. 1656; d. at Rowley 30 Oct. 1694; m. 16 Jan. 1680/81
    RUTH WOOD, b. at Rowley 21 July 1662, d. there 29 Nov. 1734,
    daughter of Thomas and Ann Wood. Ruth (Wood) Jewett m. (2)
    26 Oct. 1696 John Lunt, b. at Newbury, Mass., 22 Oct. 1669, d. at
    Salisbury, Mass., 22 Apr. 1741, son of John Lunt.
ix. FAITH, m. at Ipswich, Mass., 20 May 1678, JOHN PINGREE, b. in
    1654, d. at Ipswich 15 Jan. 1723, son of Moses Pingry of Ipswich.

---

2. MALLINSON

This was also an old family in Bradford, Yorkshire and the surrounding region, and persists there to the present time; there were forty-three Mallinson names in the telephone directory for West and East Yorkshire in 1932. It will be seen that from the wills and parish register records immediately following a slightly more extensive pedigree may be constructed for Mary Mallinson, wife of Joseph Jowett, than has been given for her husband.

FROM PROBATE RECORDS

The Will of THOMAS MALLINSON, 1624. In the name of God Amen The last day of May in the two and twentieth yeare of the Reigne of our Soueraigne Lord James by the grace of God King of England ffrance Ireland and of Scotland the seavenn and fiftieth annoque Dni 1624 I Thomas Mallinson late of Bradford and now of Manningham in the county & dioces of Yorke yeoman knowinge the incertainty & instabilitie of this mortal life and having a care so to dispose of my personal estate as I may avoid all strife and trouble wch may hereafter growe amongst my children by reason thereof do make and ordaine this my last will and testament in manner and forme following (that is to say): principally I comend my soule into the hands of Almighty God my most mercifull father assuredly believing to haue free remission of all my sinnes through the meritts & passion of my redeemer Jesus Christ and I Comitte my body to the earth to be buried at the discretion of my Executors hereafter named hoping for a ioyful resurrection at the last day & eternal fruition of everlasting life amongst the blessed Scts in heaven: and as touchinge the disposition of my worldly goods: ffirst my will and minde it, and (after my debts and seuerall expences discharged), I do hereby give devise and bequeath unto Richard Mallinson my sonne the some of tenne pounds of lawful money of England: And I doe hereby give devise and bequeath all the residew of my goods cattells and chattells as well moveable as unmoveable unto Ellen my daughter late wife of Thomas Willson late of Bradford aforesaid deceased and unto Willm Boothe of Horton Thomas Wilkinson of Manningham aforesaid my sonnes in lawe to be equally devided amongst them the said Ellen Willm and Thomas; and I doe hereby make and ordeigne the said Ellen my daughter and the said Willm Booth and Thomas Wilkinson my sonnes in lawe joint Executors of this my last will and testam^t; In Testimony whereof I the said Thomas Mallinson have hereunto sett my hand and seale the day and yeare first above expressed These beinge witnesses Richard Wilkinson (*Jurat*) Willm Wilkinson his marke John Midgley and Willm Pearson his marke

Proved 3 Aug. 1624 on the testimony of the witnesses named and administration granted to Willm Booth and Thomas Wilkinson executors named, power being reserved for Hellen Mallinson [*sic*] daughter of the said deceased the other executrix named when she shall come. (York Probate Registry, original will; also registered in vol. 38, f° 215.)

556

The Will of RICHARD MALLINSON, 1636.   In the name of god amen the two and twentieth day of Septembʳ in the yeare of our lord god according to the course and computacon of the Church of England one thousand six hundreth thirtye and six, Seinge that nothinge is more certeyne than death and nothinge more uncertayne than the houre thereof, Therefore I Richarde Mallinson of Bradforde in the diocese of Yorke yeoman being sicke of bodye but of good and p'fecte remembrance (laude and praise be therefore given to Almightye god do ordeyne and make this my last will and testament in manner and forme followinge, ffirst and principally I give and comend my soule into thands of Allmightye god my creator and maker assuredlye trustinge and ffaithfullye beleevinge to have full and free remission of all my sinnes by the most p'cious death and blood shedding of my alone Savioʳ and Redeemer Jesus Christ the second p'son in Trinytie and by him and through his meritts to have ev'lastinge life amongst the blessed Sᵗˢ and children of god in the kingdom of heaven, And I com'itt my bodye to the earth from whence itt came and the same to be buryed in Xpian Buryall: Now my will and mynd is to dispose my goods & chattells in manner & forme followinge.   ffirst my will & mynd is and I doe give & bequeath unto Sara now my wife one payre of bed . . . wherein we used to lye one caddowe one cov'lett a payre of sheetes and the ffether bed thereupon lyeinge a boulstʳ one litle chiste a cubbarde & the pewder thereupon standinge and two other pewder dublers.   Itm my will and mynde is and I doe also give and bequeath unto the said Sara my wife for the tearme of her naturall life the plo' [parlour] wherein we use to lye & roume att the fyre in the house wᵗʰ wayes & passage & free libtye for the enioymt thereof for her owne use onely but not to assinge it to any except to Thomas Mallinson my sonne And I doe further give & Bequeathe unto the said Sara my wife for the tearme of her naturall life one Annuytie or yearly rent of ffyve pounds of lawfull English money to be yearely yssuinge & goeing forth of the residue of my messuage and all my lands & Teñts thereunto belonginge—with theyre appurtenances in Bradford nowe in my owne occupacon payable att Martynmas & pentecost yearly by even porcons and the first paymt thereof att whewther of the sayd feasts that shall first be next after my decease, yett my will is that yf I dye before martynmas next the first paymt shall not begynne untill Pentecost and my will is that yf the sayd anuytie or yearly rent shalbe arreare & unpayde aftʳ eyther of the sayde ffeastes the space of twentye dayes, that then it shalbe lawfull to & for the sayd Sara my wife into the sayde lands & Teñts to enter & distreigne and the distresse or distresses then & there found lawfully to take leade & convey away & to ympound or otherwise deteigne & kepe until the sayde yearly rent & the arrearage thereof (yf any be) shalbe fully satisfyed & payd.   And my will and mynd is that the sayde anuytie & sev'all pcells of goods hereby given to the sayd Sara shalbe in full satisfaction of her right thirds & pte as well of in & to my goods & chattells as of in and to my lands and Teñts.   Itm I give & bequeath unto Willm Goodall whoe marryed Sara my daughter the some of two shillings in full satisfaction the the childs pte of the sayd Sara and of all such rights & pte as she or he the sayd Willm Goodall her husband can or may have or clayme of in or to my goods & chattells in regard I have oferred her before.   Itm I give & bequeath unto Willm Goodall sonne of the sayd Sara my daughter the some of twelve pence & to Sara & Rosamond her two daughters two felt quishions.   Itm I give & bequeath unto Joseph Jowett whoe marryed Marye my daughter the like some of two shillings in full satisfaction of the childs pte of the sayd Marye and of all her right & pte to my goods for that I have given her or prmysed to give her a competent pte of my goods.   Itm I give and bequeath unto Sara daughter of the sayd Marye two other felt quishions.   Itm my will and mynd is that all my debts be truely payd out of my whole goods and that I be hon-

estly & decently brought forth also out of the same. Itm I give & bequeath
all the Residue and Remaynder of my goods & chattells unto Thomas Mallinson my sonne, and I doe make and ordeigne the sayd Thomas * Mallinson my
sonne sole executor of this my last will & testament and fforasmuch as I conceive that all my goods & chattells will not extend to pay & discharge my debts
and also such porcons as I have p'mysed to my daughters in marriage, Therefore my will and mynde is that the same shalbe made upp out of the rents &
p'fitts of my lands & Tents. And to that intent I give & bequeath my messuage and all my lands Tents & creditam^ts wth theyr appertenance in Bradford
unto the sayd Thomas Mallinson my sonne and to his heirs, upon condition
that he pay all my debts & my daughters porcons and such legacyes as I have
hereby given & bequeathed. In witnesse whereof I the sayd Richard Mallinson have hereunto sett my hand and seal the day & yeare first abovesayde.
Sealed & signed in the p'sence of us

Richard   +   Mallinson

his marke

(York Probate Registry, original will.)
[3 Oct. 1638 Mr. Radcliffe, clerk,] the dean certified concerning the probate of
the will of Richard Mallinson late of Bradford, in the diocese of York, deceased, through the witnesses named, being sworn, and administration on the
goods of the said deceased was committed to Thomas Mallinson son of the
said deceased, sole executor named in the said will, being previously sworn.
There was exhibited an inventory below forty pounds. (York Registry, Act
Book, Pontefract, 1638.)

The Will of EDWARD WATERHOUSE, 1598. In the name of god amen the
xiij^th day of ffebruary 1598 I Edward Watterhouse of Idle in the Countie of
Yorke yeoman do make this my last will and testament in manner and forme
following—ffirst I give and bequeathe my soule to god my maker and to Jesus
Christ my Redeemer and my bodie to be buried in the churchyard of Calu'ley
in full assurance of the resurrection to life eternall ffor my temporall goods
ffirst my mynde is that my debts being paid I give unto Sara Watterhouse my
daughter my best cupboard   Itm I give unto John Watterhouse my sonne
ij s   and to Edward Watterhouse and Isaacke Watterhouse my sonnes either
of them ij s   and to Annes Vicars iij s   Itm I give unto George Watterhouse
my sonne the one half of my farmehold wch I do now occupie in consideracon
whereof George Watterhouse shall pay unto Sara Watterhouse my daughter
iiij^li w^thin three yeares next after my death   The rest of my goods and half of
my farmehold I give unto my wife Katherin Watterhouse whome I make
executor of this my last will and testament and if my wife die and dept out of
this world before the lease be expired I give that my wife pt of the lease unto
George Watterhouse my sonne he paying yearlie therefore unto Sara Watter-

558

house my daughter vi s viij d. Theis being witnesses hereof Willm̄ ffarrowe John Wails Willm̄ Marshall and John Marshall.

And on the same day and year [25 April 1599] the said dean certified concerning the probate of this will through the witnesses named being sworn and administration of the goods of the same deceased was committed to Katherine relict of the said deceased, sole executrix named in the same will, being sworn. (York Probate Registry, vol. 27, fᵒ 569.)

The Will of WILLIAM BOOTHE the elder of little Horton, dated ffebruarie the 14th ano domine 1638. To my sonne William Boothe £12. To my sonne Robert Boothe £12. To my daughter Marie, Joseph Houlmes wife, one shilling. To my daughter Susan, Andrew Wells wife one shilling. To my sonn John Boothe one chist and my best rayment. I make my wife Marie * my executrix and I give to her all my goods and chattels.

Witnesses Isaac Balme *   William B Boothe
   Samuell Threysland   his marke
    his marke
Proved October 1639.
(York Registry, original will.)

On 21 Nov. 1644 administration on the goods of Willim Booth, late of Horton in the parish of Bradford, deceased, was granted to John Mortimer of Horton magna in the county of York, yeoman, previously sworn. An inventory above 40 pounds was exhibited. (York Registry, Act Book, Pontefract, 1644, fᵒ 39.)

FROM THE PARISH REGISTERS OF BRADFORD

Marriages

1599 Thomas Wilson and Ellen Mallynson, November 20.
1601 Richard Mallynson and Sara Waterhouse, October 29.
1606 Willm Boothe and Mary Mallynson, December 15.
1618 Thomas Wilkinson and Martha Mallinson p' licentia, february 3 [1618/19].
1630 William Goodall and Sara Mallinson, January 31.

[FROM PAVER'S MARRIAGE LICENSES

1601 Richard Mallinson and Sarah Waterhouse of Bradford, at Bradford.
1618 Thomas Wilkinson and Martha Mallinson of Bradford, at Bradford, Jan. 20 [1618/19].
1630 Thomas Mallinson and Alice Pearson of Bradford, there.]

Baptisms

1602 Thomas s. of Richard Mallinson of Eckilshill, March 6 [1602/03].

["of Eccleshall"—Bishop's transcript.]

1606 Mary d. of Richard Mallynson of Eckilshill, May 29.
1609 Sarah yᵉ D. of Rich. Mallinson of Eccleshall.
1630 Marië, d. Thomas Mallinson of Bradford, Jan. 16 [1630/1].
1633 Sara d. Thomas Mallinson of Bradford, Aug. 11.
1635 Rebeckah d. Thomas Mallinsonne of Bradford, Sept. 27.
1637 Sara d. Thomas Mallinson of Bradford, Sept. 29.

* jurat written above the name.

559

1640 Martha d. Thomas Mallinson of Bradford, Oct. 4.
1642 Thomas s. Thomas Mallinson of Bradford, May 19.
1647 Judith d. Thomas Mallinson of Bradford, May 21.

Burials

1602 The wife of Thomas Mallinson of Bradford, *in Eclia*, Jan. 29 [1602/3].
1623 Thomas Wilson of Bradford, Aug. 28.
1624 Thomas Mallinson of Manningham, *in eccles*, Aug. 6.
1638 Richard Mallinson of Bradford, May 14.
1638 William Booth, Sen. of Bradford, Feb. 18 [1638/9].
1639 Widdow Booth of Little Horton, March 30.
1641 Wife of William Booth of Little Horton, Feb. 19 [1641/2].
1643 Wife of Thomas Mallinson of Bradford, April 6.
1643 Thomas s. Thomas Mallinson of Manningham, July 15.
1643 Sara wife of Richard Mallinson of Bradford, Nov. 16.
1652 Judith d. Thomas Mallinson of Bradford, Oct. 14.
1663 Martha wife of Thomas Wilkinson of Manningham, May 11.

From the above records the following lineage is arranged:

1. THOMAS MALLINSON, of Bradford, Yorkshire, England, was a contemporary of the father of Edward Jowett, and perhaps of about the same age, born possibly about 1550–55, buried at Bradford, in the church, 6 Aug. 1624. His wife, whose name is unknown, had also been buried in the Bradford church, 20 Jan. 1602. These records, relatively unusual, indicate a family of some distinction.

The will of Thomas Mallinson, dated 31 May 1624, indicates that he had moved at the end of his life to Manningham, a township in the parish of Bradford, where dwelt his youngest daughter with her husband, Thomas Wilkinson. He bequeathed ten pounds to his son Richard, and the residue of his property to his widowed daughter Ellen and his sons-in-law, William Booth of Horton and Thomas Wilkinson of Manningham.

Children:

    i.   ELLEN, who survived her father and was named co-executrix in his will, m. at Bradford, 20 Nov. 1599, THOMAS WILSON, who was buried at Bradford 28 Aug. 1623. She may not have been the eldest child, but since her marriage is the earliest on record for all this Jowett and Mallinson group, she has been given this place here.

2. ii.   RICHARD, b. probably as early as 1580.

   iii. MARY, m. at Bradford, 15 Dec. 1606, WILLIAM BOOTH, who d. about 1639, having made his will 14 Feb. 1637, proved October 1639. In this will he named his wife Mary executrix, and left bequests to children: William, Robert, Mary, wife of Joseph Houlmes, Susan, wife of Andrew Wells, and John Booth.

   iv. MARTHA, d. at Manningham and bur. at Bradford 11 May 1663; m. there (by license), 3 Feb. 1618/19, THOMAS WILKINSON, b. about 1599–1600, son of Richard and Anne (Mortimer) Wilkinson. Thomas Wilkinson of Manningham is recorded as living 6 Apr. 1666, and then aged 66 years. (See Visitation pedigree in Surtees Society, vol. 36, p. 255.)

       Child (surname *Wilkinson*):

      1. *Thomas*, of Manningham, aged 35 years, 2 Apr. 1666; m. Anne Nutter, daughter of Ellis Nutter of the Forest of Pendle in co. Lancaster, England. Four children.

2. RICHARD MALLINSON (*Thomas*), born probably as early as 1580, was buried at Bradford 14 May 1638. He married (by license) at Bradford, 29 Oct. 1601, SARA WATERHOUSE, who was buried at Bradford 16 Nov. 1643, possibly the daughter of Edward Waterhouse of Idle, near Bradford, whose will, dated 13 Feb. 1598 and proved 25 Apr. 1599, has been printed above. He was buried in the churchyard of Calverley, whose parish registers show numerous Waterhouse records, but none early enough for the baptism of this Sara. Bradford registers also have several Waterhouse records, but there are no wills to connect them with this family. Richard Mallinson's will is of particular interest in its specific bequest to "Joseph Jowett whoe marryed Marye my daughter" and in the bequest "unto Sara daughter of the sayd Marye," which confirms the fact shown by the parish register that this small granddaughter was the only child in the family of Joseph Jowett at the date of the will, and calls attention to the inaccuracy of the American accounts which have always placed Jeremiah as the eldest child of Joseph Jewett.

Children, baptized at Bradford:

3. i. THOMAS, bapt. 6 Mar. 1602/03.
   ii. MARY, bapt. 29 May 1606; d. at Rowley, Mass., and bur. there 12 Apr. 1652; m. at Bradford, Yorkshire, England, 1 Oct. 1634, JOSEPH JOWETT, bapt. at Bradford 31 Dec. 1609, d. at Rowley and bur. there 26 Feb. 1660/61, son of Edward and Mary (Tayler) Jowett. As the will of Richard Mallinson was proved 3 Oct. 1638, Joseph Jowit could not be sworn as a witness for the probate, since he was already at sea in the *John of London* for New England.
  iii. SARA, bapt. 13 Aug. 1609; m. at Bradford, 31 Jan. 1630, WILLIAM GOODALL. They are both mentioned in the will of her father, dated 22 Sept. 1636, as well as her children, William Goodall, Sara Goodall, and Rosamond Goodall.

3. THOMAS MALLINSON (*Richard, Thomas*), baptized at Bradford, England, 6 Mar. 1602/03. He married first (by license dated 1630) ALICE PEARSON, who was buried at Bradford 6 Apr. 1643, as the wife of Thomas Mallinson of Bradford; and secondly ———.

Children by first wife, baptized at Bradford:

i. MARY, bapt. 16 Jan. 1630/31.
ii. SARA, bapt. 11 Aug. 1633.
iii. REBECKAH, bapt. 27 Sept. 1635.
iv. SARA, bapt. 29 Sept. 1637.
v. MARTHA, bapt. 4 Oct. 1640.
vi. THOMAS, bapt. 19 May 1642; bur. at Bradford 15 July 1643.

Child by second wife:

vii. JUDITH, bapt. 21 May 1647; bur. at Bradford 14 Oct. 1652.

From the records above, it will appear that the rather numerous Mallinsons of modern Yorkshire are not descended from this family, which is probably continued only in the lines of the daughters.

JOHNSON FAMILY.

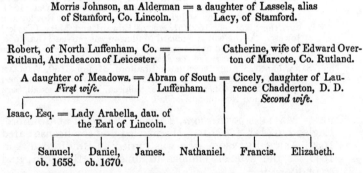

Morris Johnson, an Alderman = a daughter of Lassels, alias
of Stamford, Co. Lincoln. | Lacy, of Stamford.

Robert, of North Luffenham, Co. = ———   Catherine, wife of Edward Over-
Rutland, Archdeacon of Leicester. | ton of Marcote, Co. Rutland.

A daughter of Meadows. = Abram of South = Cicely, daughter of Lau-
First wife. | Luffenham. rence Chadderton, D. D.
                                    Second wife.

Isaac, Esq. = Lady Arabella, dau. of
the Earl of Lincoln.

Samuel,   Daniel,   James.   Nathaniel.   Francis.   Elizabeth.
ob. 1658.   ob. 1670.

The above pedigree is from Wright's History of Rutlandshire, page 38, and
also this coat of arms for Johnson, which I found in one of the Herald's Visitations
at the British Museum. The bearings are given in Wright's History :—

Arms.—Arg. a chev. sa. between three lions' heads erased gu. crowned ducally, or.

Crest.—A lion's head erased, gu. crowned ducally, or, between a plume of two
ostrich feathers, arg.

General William Augustus Johnson, a descendant, lives at "Witham on the
Hill," and his nephew, William Henry Johnson, is Rector of the Church at the
same place. I was there and at Clipsham in March, 1850.   D. DUDLEY.

P. 232, in the Pedigree of the Johnson
Family, copied from Wright's Hist. of Rutlandshire, I omitted Isaac Johnson's half
brother Ezekiel. He was born 1607, m. 1st, Anne, dau. of John Boate of North Kil-
worth, Co. Leicester, clerk, who d. 1635 ; 2dly, Thalia, dau. of Sir Edward Heron of
Cressy Hall, C. Lincoln, who d. *sine prole*. By the 1st wife, Anne, he had Margaret,
wf. of Thos. Marsh, gent. and Anne, wf. of Thos. Johnson.—*Dean Dudley.*

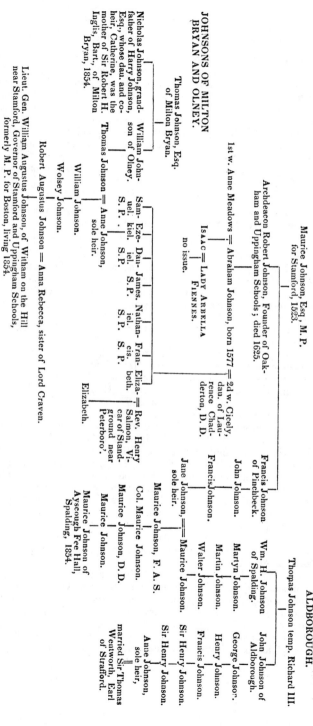

JOHNSON OF CLIPSHAM AND PINCHBECK.

Maurice Johnson, Esq, M.P. for Stamford, 1523.

Archdeacon Robert Johnson, Founder of Oakham and Uppingham Schools; died 1625.

1st w. Anne Meadows = Abraham Johnson, born 1577 = 2d w. Cicely, dau. of Laurence Chadderton, D.D.

Isaac = Lady Arbella Fiennes. no issue.

Francis Johnson of Pinchbeck.

John Johnson.

Francis Johnson.

Martyn Johnson.

Walter Johnson.

Henry Johnson.

Jane Johnson, sole heir. == Maurice Johnson.

Maurice Johnson.

Col. Maurice Johnson.

Maurice Johnson.

Maurice Johnson, F.A.S.

Maurice Johnson, D.D.

Maurice Johnson.

Maurice Johnson of Ayscough Fee Hall, Spalding, 1854.

Sir Henry Johnson.

Sir Henry Johnson.

JOHNSON OF SPALDING AND ALDBOROUGH.

Thomas Johnson temp. Richard III.

Wm. H. Johnson of Spalding.

John Johnson of Aldborough.

George Johnson.

Anne Johnson, sole heir, married Sir Thomas Wentworth, Earl of Strafford.

JOHNSONS OF MILTON BRYAN AND OLNEY.

Nicholas Johnson, grandfather of Harry Johnson, Esq, whose dau. and co-heir, Catherine, was the mother of Sir Robert H. Inglis, Bart, of Milton Bryan, 1854.

Thomas Johnson, Esq. of Milton Bryan.

William Johnson, son of Olney.

Thomas Johnson = Anne Johnson, sole heir.

Sam-uel. S.P.

Eze-kiel. S.P.

Dau-iel. iel. S.P.

James, Nathan-iel. S.P.

Fran-cis. S.P.

Eliza-beth. = Rev. Henry Salmon, Vicar of Standground near Peterboro'.

William Johnson.

Wolsey Johnson.

Elizabeth.

Robert Augustus Johnson = Anna Rebecca, sister of Lord Craven.

Lieut. Gen. William Augustus Johnson, of Witham on the Hill near Stamford, Governor of Stamford and Uppingham Schools, formerly M.P. for Boston, living 1854.

This account of the three families of Johnson, (who now quarter the arms of each other,) was furnished to Pishey Thompson by Edward Moore, Esq (cousin to the present Maurice Johnson of Ayscough Fee Hall,) who received it from his brother Maurice Peter Moore of Sleaford, who stated the pedigree upon the authority of Sir Robert H. Inglis, Bart, then M.P. for the University of Oxford.

THE JOHNSON FAMILY.

[Communicated by PISHEY THOMPSON, ESQ., of Boston in Lincolnshire, England.]

NOTE.—MR. THOMPSON, many years ago published an account of Boston, [Eng.] He is now about to publish its "*History and Antiquities*," upon which he has bestowed a great amount of labor. In the course of his researches he discovered the materials from which the following Article has been prepared. In his letter accompanying it he says, "The Johnson family is scarcely enough connected with *this* Boston, to justify the appropriation of much space therein to details respecting it. I also forward you a copy of the *authentic* pedigree of the Johnson family, and also a copy of a very curious paper in the *hand-writing of the father of Isaac*, relative to his marriage, &c. The *details* of this paper may be depended upon as being correct, but the *inferences* are, probably, too severe." Dated Boston, Lincolnshire, 2 June 1854.—EDITOR.

Extracts from a paper written by Abraham Johnson, " Gentleman and Esquire," 1638, and identified as his writing by a relative. The paper in possession of Wm Hopkinson, Esq., of Stamford, Lincolnshire.

The writer describes himself as ABRAHAM JOHNSON, Gentleman, now of Cambridge, and late of South Luffenham, in the county of Rutland, Esq. He desires searches to be made in the Herald's office, &c., for the family arms which he is entitled to bear; and apologizes for his deficiency of knowledge in that respect, through " having been deprived of the memorials thereof as touching his bearings, by his MOTHER'S ancestors, by Strangers and Adversaries, and as for those by his FATHER'S ancestors, by his *own Sons*."

The narrative recites that the writer's father was Mr. ROBERT JOHNSON, Gentleman, and his mother Mrs. MARY JOHNSON, " a Gentlewoman too. His father's education, titles, actions and good works" he sets forth, " not passing in silence his mother's worth." He himself had held the offices of High Sheriff and Justice of Peace."

ABRAHAM JOHNSON was born at *North Luffenham*, in the county of Rutland, July 6, 1577, being the only child of the ROBERT and MARY JOHNSON abovementioned. His father's father was MOORIS or MAURICE Johnson of Stamford, Gentleman. His father was Chaplain to *Sir Nicholas Bacon*, and afterwards Vicar of North Luffenham, where he resided in that capacity for nearly 50 years, never having any other church preferment. He was B. D., Prebendary of Windsor and Rochester, and Archdeacon of Leicester. " He gave 20 marks a year to the Preacher at Paul's Cross, and is there always mentioned among the benefactors and maintainers of those preachers." He founded also two Schools and two Hospitals of Christ in OAKHAM and UPPINGHAM, in the county of Rutland, *with four hundred marks Hereditaments yearly for ever*. He *died in July*, 1625.

ABRAHAM JOHNSON recites that his education was early cared for, and consisted of a thorough knowledge of the Latin, Greek and Hebrew languages, and also of the French, Spanish and Italian ones ; and of Rhetoric, Logic, Arithmetic, Geometry and Natural Philosophy ; and of Music, both vocal and instrumental. His writing seems to have been particularly cared for, having been taught by the best masters " which those times," and he " thinks any times afforded, to write Secretary, Romain,

564

Court or Chancery hand, Text hand, *Bastard* hand." He could write also, fairly, both Greek and Hebrew. All these things he had attained when he was 13 years of age.

He entered at Emanuel College, Cambridge, when he was little over 13, where he remained 4 years. He then entered as a student of the law at Lincoln's Inn, where he remained several years, when he was called to the bar. He never constantly followed the law as a profession, being more attached to "an academical life." He studied Divinity, Mathematics, Natural Philosophy, "and new, hard, profitable INVENTIONS or ENGINES, both to contrive them, and cause them to be made." He purchased a house and farm at South Luffenham, about half a mile from his native town, in 1618, for which he paid about £1,000. He was appointed Sheriff of Rutlandshire, dwelling at North Luffenham, to be near his father. In the same year he waited on his Majesty, when in these parts, and had an offer of Knighthood made him, which he did not accept, but was afterwards placed in Commission of the Peace. From this position he afterwards retired, "and used his freedom for his own studies." After an absence of 21 years he returned to Cambridge, "his honoured and dear mother;" he also occasionally resided in London.

With respect to the Arms he was entitled to bear, he says that he knows that he was descended from the *Lacy's, Earls of Lincoln*, WILLIAM LACY of Deeping St. James, in Lincolnshire, Gentleman, being his father's uncle, and always addressing him as *nephew*. He was also allied to the *Smiths of Standground*, near Peterborough. His father always called the representative of that family, (*Robert Smith*,) uncle and patron, having been appointed his guardian by his father, Maurice Johnson. His family was also connected or allied with the *Bevills* of Sawtry, in Huntingdonshire, and the Clarkes of Elmington, in Northamptonshire. His father had three wives; the first was Susanna *Davers*, whose brother, *Jeremy Davers*, was a fellow of Clare Hall, Cambridge. This first wife did not live more than a year with his father, and died without issue. The second wife was mother to the writer, and was *Maria Hird*, sister to *Richard Hird*, who was Steward to *Sir Francis Walsingham*, Secretary of State to *Queen Elizabeth*. He knows that, by his mother, he is descended from or allied to the *Byngs* of Kent, and with the *Gamages* of London, and the *Woodwards* of Hoddesdon, of whom *Sir John Woodward* was called the *Royal Merchant*. ABRAHAM JOHNSON gives a long account of a quarrel between the different branches of his *mother's* family, during which the personal estate, "consisting of movables, books, writings and papers, coats, seal rings, jewels and medals," were abstracted by a dishonest executor.

ABRAHAM JOHNSON married 1st, *Anna Meadows*, dau. of Robert Meadows of Stamford. The Meadows were allied to or descended from the *Wimbleby* and *Loveday* families. This lady was the mother of ISAAC JOHNSON,* who emigrated to America; "he was, in courtesy, written Esquire, after he had married the Lady ARBELLA" (not Arăbella) "FINES, one of the sisters of the now Earl of Lincoln, who both went into New England to inhabit, and in a few months after their arrival, both died there, never leaving any issue." "That over high match," continues Abraham Johnson, "was not blessed by him, nor assented to, but forbid-

---

* There was no other child by this marriage, excepting a daughter, Mary, who died a child.

den by him, who foresaw and foretold the inconvenience which fell out accordingly, proving uncomfortable to themselves and injurious to him and his second now wife, and their six sons and a daughter ; because his father" (Isaac's Grandfather) "being of some 82 years, and in infirmities, and not continuing so dèeply wise as he had been in his former consistent age, and green old age ; and always contrary to the principles he had given him (Abraham) in charge, that he would not marry above his own degree, w^h he fortified with many reasons—was misled by meddling, tatling women with an opinion of raising his house, nobody knows how high. Whereas he (Abraham) had so convinced his said father, that he seemed satisfied, that there was an inherent greatness or nobleness of blood in the lady w^h was not impartible or derivable to his son, or any child he might have by her. But eagerly pursuing till they had got a clandestine marriage, never daring to own or tell the father *who* married them ; they had got the GRANDFATHER to state all his lands upon the said Isaac and his heirs, (except a *quillet* not worth taking up, which he had cast upon the right heir) with an utter prostration of him the father, that he did not 40 years before his death, estate any land upon him in fee simple or fee taile, no not so much as for his life, or for years. And if he did for years, he w^d and did ask him to part with it again, w^h he, in his obe- dience to him, did. And at his death (the grandfathers) they got him— using a lewd fellow that was his Clerk—(one *Richard Butcher,*) who being worthless, when he came to that service, yet without that wealth w^h he got while he was in it, bought the Towne Clerkship of Stamford, from w^h he was afterwards put, for his ill deserts ; and who is an enemy to good ministers and religion and goodness—to make the said *Isaac* also his Executor, and not so much as any valuable legacy given to ABRAHAM JOHNSON the father. So the said son in his covetousness and ambition, unnaturally got from him and kept from him, his father's whole estate in lands, annuities, houses, cattle, corn, plate, &c., esteemed at some £20,000. And besides by this manner, the said grandchild carrying away all the Grandfather's books and papers, and *coats* and *seal-rings*, whereof he had been a great gatherer and hoarder. Living sometime at his manor of Clipsham in Rutlandshire, (worth about 500^{lbs} p' year.) Sometimes at Boston, 30 miles off in Lincolnshire, sometime, at Sem- pringham one of the Earl of Lincoln's houses. Sometime at Tuttershall, another of his houses, and sometimes at London, using strangers in his business, and making many strangers his * * * *, who scarcely knew any of his family but himself, and who scarcely any of his family knew but himself. The said *Abraham Johnson* is thus deprived of such knowl- edge of his pedigree, and of such marriages and other things as might better satisfy and instruct him, and enable him to direct the intended en- quiry for the better. Whereas, now that very chief coat the Johnsons bear—viz. Argent, a Chevron Sable between three Lion heads coupé Gules, crowned Or between two ostrich feathers Argent, is taken from him and all his, and is either lost, or in some stranger hand they know not who nor where. The grandfather's picture was, and, he really thinks is still, left at Boston, in a strange Gentleman's house, that never knew *Robert Johnson,* nor had any cause to care for him. And diverse of his chief books and papers ISAAC took with him into New England, in which expedition he spent from £5,000 to £6,000. And was so sett upon it, that had he again come over, as he intended the spring after, he had sold every foot of land his grandfather left him ; and whether any writing be there or no that conduceth to these things, he knows not. But chiefly by being deprived of these books and papers he is very deficient as above too plainly appears. But he verily thinks ISAAC had some good memorials of all these things, for his Grandfather was a great and painful putter down of any comment almost that concerned him, though some but of mean nature. Therefore it is not to be thought but that he had set down the marriages and alliances of former times. The rather seeing he was careful to obtain the exemplification or attestation of our before described bearing of the three Lions' heads &c.

"The mother of the said Isaac being taken from him ere she was 20 years old, who was so obedient to him, and loved him so well that in his conscience and full persuasion he believes had she lived, she w^d either have dissuaded the Grandfather and the son of her own bowels from such unnaturelness against him his father, or else mourned for it. When he was some 27 or 28 years of age he married *Elizabeth Chaderton* the sole child and heir apparent of *Laurence Chaderton* Gent^n and of Cicely his wife—He had by this second wife—*Samuel, Ezekiel, Daniel, James, Nathaniel* and *Francis,* and one daughter *Elizabeth* married to Henry Salmon a Gent^n of Cheshire, a Scholar and Divine, and Vicar of Standground near Peterbro'. Their eldest child was a daughter named Elizabeth.

THE JOHNSON FAMILY OF LUTTERWORTH, ENGLAND.—In the history of Lutterworth,[*] rendered famous in the life of Wickliffe, occurs the name of Archdeacon Johnson, Rector of North Luffenham in 1591, and who was an eminent divine and founder of the schools of Oakham and Uppingham. It is an interesting fact, in the history of this ancient family, that Isaac Johnson and his wife Arabella Johnson, of Clipsham, co. Rutland, England, were among the founders of Boston, New England. He, with his wife and sixteen others, sailed from Yarmouth in 1630, and settled in Boston, America. Isaac Johnson left the whole of his property to support the christian church gathered in America. Bishop Ryder was succeeded by the Rev. R. H. Johnson as Rector of Lutterworth and Vicar of Claybrooke. The Rev. R. H. Johnson, M.A., was of a distinguished family, and the son of the Rev. Robert Johnson, Rector of Wistanston and Hamstall Ridware, who married the sister of the 6th Earl of Craven, and was a member of the great " Lunar " Society. His son married in 1808 to Miss Boughton, the second daughter of Sir C. R. Boughton, of Rouse Leach, co. Worcester. He died in the month of October, 1870, and was buried at Claybrooke. Possibly the above notes may prove interesting to the descendants of Isaac Johnson, now residing in America. This family I have not given in my account of John Eliot and his friends at Nazing and Waltham Abbey, published in 1882.   W. WINTERS.

Church Yard, Waltham Abbey, England.

[*] By F. W. Bottrill, 1882.

News Letters from Joseph Meade to Sir Martin Stuteville Jan. 1626–
April 1631 (British Museum Harley Manuscript 390 (D'Ewes Collections)).
fo. 525, letter from Joseph Meade† to Sir Martin Stuteville‡, dated Christ College, Cambridge, 5 December 1630.

[extract]
"This weeks [London] letter relates the arrivall of many more [letters] from
New-England reporting (as my author heard) the lady Arabella's death & that
divers have exasperated the natives against them & disagree among themselves
as well about Civill government as in Church business, to the hazard of all their
endeavours: I hear also that Mr. Wilson (a minister about Sudbury) had formerly
(a month or more since it was related) written to his wife that those who were
for New-England must not look for venison & but bring selfe-denying spirit, &
be content to dine with a messe of pease-pottage, & sup with a dish of water
grewell. That one of their company being sick could not by any meanes procure
so much as a messe of milk without charge of other victualls. That divers of
better fashion, especially women, were dead."

*[marginal note by Meade]
"The Earle of Lyncolnes sister, wife to Mr Isaak Johnson. Shee dyed of a
burning feaver & distempered in ye head, was sick a fortnight & as was thought
caught it by taking cold going in a dewy morning to ye cowes. Alas good Lady.
This I saw since out of a letter from hir husband written to his father, & this
sume thereof sent to Mris Chadderton. The same letter says that Mr. Higginson
ye minister who wrot the book, is also dead & another gentlewoman."
fo. 551, the same to the same, dated Christ College, 20 May 1631.

[a postscript]
"I forgot to tell you this 2 or 3 weeks that Mr Isaak Johnson is also dead in
New England som . 6 . weeks after his Lady. And so the lands will come to
Mr. Samuel, Dr. Chadderton's grand child, who was once at Dalham."

London, England.   Franklin M. Wright.

---

†Joseph Mead[e] (1586–1638) of Berden, Essex, Bachelor of Divinity, Christ's College, Cambridge, 1618. King Edward VI fellow at Christ's College, 1614–1638, and Mildmay Greek Lecturer, 1618–1638. A noted scholar in his day, and author of numerous works on mystical divinity
and prophecy. (J. Peile *Christ's College Register*, vol. I (Cambridge, 1910), pp. 245–247; see also
D.N.B., *sub. nom.*)

‡Sir Martin Stuteville (Stotevill) of Dalham in Risbridge Hundred, co. Suffolk, of which manor
his family had been possessed since 1417. Sir Martin was born at Dalham about 1569, son and
heir of Thomas Stotevill, Esq., and Anne Whitney, his wife, and died 13 June 1631. Stuteville
was an intimate friend of Joseph Mead and the latter spent much time at Dalham. Mead's news-
letters to Sir Martin fill two folio volumes at the British Museum (Harl., 389, 390) and cover the
years 1620–1631. Each week Mead had a news-letter from London which he forwarded to Sir
Martin with his own comments added.
Stuteville was on intimate terms with Sir Simonds D'Ewes and his family, and is mentioned
in the latter's "Autobiography", *passim*.
References for Stuteville — W. A. Copinger "Manors of Suffolk", vol. 5 (Manchester, 1909),
pp. 217–218; Metcalfe's Visitations of Suffolk (Exeter, 1882), pp. 68–69; 103.

FRAGMENTS CONCERNING THE JONES FAMILY.

[Collected by J. GARDNER WHITE.]

ZACHERYE JOHNES, Gent. buried July 7, 1597, had issue, 1. *Catharine*, baptized at St. Dunstan's in the West, London, December 28, 1594. 2. *Raphe*, baptized June 6, 1596, buried at St. Dunstan's in the West, London, July 30, 1597.

HENRY JOHNES, Gent. had issue, 1. *Thomas*, baptized at St. Dunstan's in the West, London, November 23, 1596. 2. *Elizabeth*, baptized April 18, 1598.

WILLIAM JONES, Vicar of Bolder, Co. Southampton, had a son, 1. *Henry*, a clockmaker, who died Nov. 20, 1697, aet. 63. He and others of his family were buried at St. Dunstan's in the West, London. Arms: az. on a bend Gu. three spread eagles Ar. in chief a mullet Or.

THOMAS JONES purchased "The King's Head" in Chancery Lane, London, January 10, 1647.

ALEXANDER JONES purchased "a house" in Blowbladder Street, London, and certeine lands in Camberwell, Surry Co., Sept. 27, 1647.

HUMPHRIE JONES and HENRY JONES purchased the manor and lordship of Istervin, Flint, and Denb. Co., May 23, 1648.

JOHN JONES, Esq. and Geo. Twistleton purchased several manors in York Co., March 23, 1649, and the said Jones also purchased the manor of Gogaith, Hertf. Co., July 18, 1650, and the manor of Llandevy Brevye, Bishopric of St. Da., Nov. 1, 1650.

JOHN JONES of London, buried at St. Mary the Virgin, Marlborough, March 29, 1743, had *thirty-one* children born and baptized, one of whom, 1. *Elizabeth*, married Wm. Greenhill, of Greenhill, Middlesex. Their seventh son, and *thirty-ninth* child, petitioned Government in 1698.

RODERICK JONES was buried at Farndon, Co. Chester, 1639.

THOMAS JONES, of Crew, was baptized at Farndon, Co. Chester, 1703.

WILLIAM JONES, Gent. of Crew, was buried at Wrexham, 1703.

Rev. GRENT JONES succeeded Rev. Mr. Wake, 1715. His wife *Elizabeth*, was buried at Ogbourn St. Andrew, Wilts, January 25, 1720.

WILLIAM JONES, buried January 8, 1748-9, in the parish of St. Mary the Virgin, Marlborough, had issue, 1. *Ann*, baptized April 24, 1722, buried in the Church, Oct. 20, 1741. 2. *Elizabeth*, baptized February 24, 1725.

Sir THOMAS JONES, Knight, had a daughter who married Rev. Mr. Meyrick, Dec. 14, 1739.

THOMAS JONES of Oswestry married *Mary* ——, who died April 13, 1752, aet. 45, at Ellesmere, Co. Salop. *Elizabeth Jones* died at Ellesmere, Co. Salop, February 11, 1771, aet. 35.

Rev. LEWIS JONES, Vicar of Rhuabon, Co. Denbrigh, and Rector of Llanymowddy, Co. Merioneth, married *Susan* ——, who died a widow, 1795, aet. 73.

THE ANCESTRY OF JOHN JONES, 18th CENTURY BOSTON MERCHANT

By A. E. DE COUËT, of Shepton Mallet, England

Among the papers bequeathed to the Society of Genealogists (of London) by the late Rev. T. C. Dale is a typescript book containing, with a few other items, "The Life of Cadwallader Jones, Collector General of Customs to King Charles I, and his descendants". That Mr. Dale intended to complete this work is shown by a number of manuscript notes obviously added from time to time, but, if the general outline was clear, there remained, at Mr. Dale's death, a rather serious gap in the chain of evidence.

John Jones, great-grandson of Cadwallader, was very difficult to trace. That he had four children was proved by his father's will, but whom, where, and when he married, when and where he died, was a mystery.

The will of a first cousin mentions him as "believed to be in New England". Mr. Dale concluded that perhaps he had died there.

Since then, further research, mainly in Bristol, gave added strength to this belief, and it was thanks to Mr. Walter Goodwin Davis, who first identified Cadwallader's great-grandson with John Jones of Dorchester, a Boston Merchant, and to Professor Arthur Adams, who found both John Jones' will and that of his wife Hannah, that the pedigree could be satisfactorily completed.

The following account is largely drawn from the Rev. T. C. Dale's book, sometimes in his own words.

1. CADWALLADER JONES was, at his name implies, of Welsh extraction, and, it seems, the first of his line to adopt a surname. There is in existence a pedigree according to which he belonged to the family of Rhirid Flaidd.

570

However this may be, he came to England during the first half of the seventeenth century, and married, after 18 July 1643 and before 1646, ANNE BLUET, the second but eldest surviving daughter and co-heiress of John Bluet (1603-1634), of Holcombe Rogus, Devon, Esquire.

On the 8 Dec. 1642 he was granted by patent the reversion of the office of Collector of Customs, etc., in the Port of Sandwich*, and King Charles I, in a letter written from Oxford on the 23 March 1643/4†, calls him "the Collector General of our Customs".

In 1645 he was in Exeter, then besieged by Sir Thomas Fairfax, from whom he received a certificate that he was entitled to the benefits of the Articles of Capitulation, when the City surrendered in April 1646.

Cadwallader Jones was an object of suspicion to the Commonwealth Government. He had declined to take the National Covenant and the Negative Oaths, producing a medical certificate that he was ill and unfit to move. On the 9 March 1649/50 the Council of State issued a warrant to apprehend him and bring him before the Council*, but with what result does not appear.

In February 1647/8 he had applied to the Parliamentary Committee for Compounding the Estates of Delinquents for permission to compound. For this purpose he had to make an exact return of all his possessions, which has thus come down to us. Although mostly in Somerset, they included his part in some manors in Devon and Dorset.

In February 1650 he paid the £483.15.0 imposed (one-tenth of the estimated value of his estate) and the estate was discharged.†

He seems to have ruined himself in raising the money to pay his fine, for he was outlawed in Exeter in November 1653, in London in the same year and again in London in 1655, upon pleas of debt.

In April 1660 when King Charles II was in Breda about to return to England, Cadwallader Jones sent him a petition stating that "his late Majesty did by letters patent under the Great Seal confer upon your petitioner the Customer's place of Sandwich and of all the ports, etc., there unto belonging in the County of Kent for his life". He petitioned for a confirmation of that grant.* He evidently received this confirmation for a warrant to swear him in was issued from the Treasury that 6 Sept. 1660.

On 12 Oct. 1663, he received a grant from the Crown of the Manor and lands of Wondy, or Undy, in Monmouthshire, for 31 years at a rent of £19.19.2½.†

*Patent Rolls, Charles I, 18th year, Pt. 3.
†State Papers: Domestic: Charles I.
*State Papers: Domestic: 1650, p. 529.
†State Papers; Interregnum- G 205/765 and G 4/189.
*State Papers: Domestic: Interregnum 220/120.
†Patent Rolls.

Soon after this he became involved in serious difficulties with the Treasury, as surety for a late Receiver of Hearth Money for the County of Devon, William Harris, who had defaulted.

Faced with a liability to the Crown of £2,500 which he could not discharge, Cadwallader Jones was at length suspended from his post of Customer of Sandwich, by a Treasury Warrant of the 1 Feb. 1668/9, and finally, by Warrant of the 16 July 1669 committed to the King's Bench prison.

His wife petitioned the King for his release, at first unsuccessfully, but, on 1 April 1672, there is an order that Mrs. Jones may have her husband discharged on paying £300, the profit of his office to be received for the King till the money be paid.

On 10 July 1672, a warrant is issued for his release and on the 30th of the same month an order is given to restore him to office.* He did not, however, long enjoy this change of fortune, as before the year had ended he was buried in Ashbrittle. There also his wife was buried in 1683.†

They left five children. William, their eldest son, having died young:

i.   CADWALLADER.
ii.   JOHN, who seems to have lived in Pugham in the parish of Burlescombe, Devon, and of whose line nothing is known after 1691.
iii.   STEWART, d. unm. (will dated 31 Oct. 1688 proved 26 Jan. 1688/9).
iv.   DOROTHY, m. in 1665, as his second wife, GEORGE HELLIER, of Whitchurch, Binegar, Somerset.
v.   ANNE, m. in Ashbrittle, 2 Oct. 1681, HUMPHREY HELLIER of Binegar, son of the above George Hellier, by his first wife, Sarah, daughter of Humphrey Hooke, of Bristol.

2. The second, but eldest surviving son, CADWALLADER, was born about 1654. He succeeded to his mother's share of the Bluet estates, but they were heavily encumbered by a settlement made by his parents on 18 April 1659 by which £4,000 was to be raised to be divided equally between their younger children.* This caused protracted litigation between Cadwallader Jones and his brother-in-law, George Hellier, which seems only to have ceased with the death of the contestants.

On the 30 April 1677 the following license to marry was issued by the Bishop of Bath and Wells: "Cadwallader Jones, of Ashbrittle, Esquire, aged 23, and Elizabeth Hippisley, widow; to be married at Blagdon, Burrington, or Cameley". They were married at Blagdon Church, 10 May 1677.

The bride was the only child of John Creswick, a prosperous merchant of Bristol, by his first wife, Elizabeth, daughter of Hugh Browne, Alderman of Bristol. She had previously married Richard Hippisley of Stone Easton, co. Somerset, who died in 1672.

*See Calendar of Treasury Books, under dates given above.
†Will dated 17 May 1683; proved (P. C. C., Drax 114) 9 Oct. same year.
*Chancery Proc., 9/107/41.

Cadwallader Jones made his will 17 Sept. 1687. It was proved (P.C.C. Fane 88) 2 May 1692. His wife survived until 1698, in which year (8 November) administration of her effects was granted to her father, John Creswick, as guardian of her eldest son, John Jones, a minor, she having died intestate.

On the chancel arch of Cameley Church hangs a monument to Cadwallader Jones, with the chevron and the three wolves' heads of Jones impaling the lion rampant of Creswick.

The inscription runs: Hic jacent cineres CADWALLADER JONES Armigeri Laetam Anaetaein Exspectantes, Atavis Nobilibus tum parentis tum Maternis oriundi, filii Natu maxmi Cadwallader Jones de Grenham in Agro Somersetensi, obiit 13 Aprilis 1692.

Cadwallader and Elizabeth (Creswick) Jones left four sons and two daughters:

i.   JOHN, b. in or about 1679; m. ELIZABETH, daughter of Edward Clarke, of Chipleigh, Somerset, and had one (surviving) son, *Edward*, at whose death in 1753, this branch of the family became extinct in the male line.
ii. BLUET, bapt. at Cameley, 12. Nov. 1683; m. at St. Thomas' Church, Bristol, 30 Aug. 1708, SUZANNA, elder daughter of John Smith of Bristol by his wife Suzanna, daughter of Philip Brome of Isle Abbotts, Somerset. His branch ended in the male line with the death of his grandson, another Bluet Jones, 21 March 1836.
iii. WILLIAM.
iv. CADWALLADER, bapt. at Cameley 2 March 1688. Matriculated at Gloucester Hall (now Worcester College), Oxford, in May 1708. B. A., 1710. Took Orders and became Vicar of Ubley, Somerset, in 1716. He was buried there 20th June 1721,
v.   ELIZABETH.
vi. ANN.

3. The third son, WILLIAM, was baptized at Cameley 27 Oct. 1685. He was apprenticed by indenture of 13 Nov. 1702 to Thomas Grove, of Bristol, linen draper, and Mary, his wife.* He married by license, at the Church of St. Thomas, Bristol, the 23 April 1707, MARTHA, born 26 July, baptized 2 Aug. 1685, buried at St. Augustine's, Bristol, 31 Oct. 1714, daughter of John Smith, and sister of Suzanna, wife of his own brother, Bluet Jones.

William Jones was buried, also at St. Augustine's 23 March 1748. He left only a rough note of his will, giving £1,000 to his grandson and namesake and to his three granddaughters, Hannah, Martha, and Suzanna, £500 each at twenty-one. Residue to his son, John Jones, in view of a bond given on marriage to his (John's) mother, and he to be executor. He desires his brother Smith (Councillor Smith) and Captain Jefferies to manage his affairs till his son "comes over himself." This will, dated 15 Sept. 1747, was proved (PCC Lisle 286) the 23 Sept. 1749, by the testator's son, John Jones.

4. JOHN JONES, baptized at St. Nicholas, Bristol, 23 Jan. 1708, only surviving child (his two sisters, Mary, baptized 8 Aug. 1712,

*Bristol Apprentice Books.

573

and Martha, baptized 21 Oct. 1714, having both been buried 24 Oct. 1714) went to New England, and having settled in Boston, married there, 2 Sept. 1734, HANNAH, born 24 Sept. 1715, daughter of Abraham Francis by his wife Hannah Fayerwether. His will, dated 22 March 1770 (codicil 21 Jan. 1772), was proved 6 Oct. 1772. In it he mentions his wife, Hannah, his son William, his daughter Suzanna Welles* and his grandsons John Jones Spooner, William Spooner, Joseph Waldo, and John Jones Waldo.

The will of his wife, Hannah, dated 3 Dec. 1781, proved 23 July 1782, mentions her son William Jones, in the City of Bristol, in the Kingdom of Great Britain, her daughter Suzanna Welles, wife of Arnold Welles, her grandsons, John Jones Spooner, William Spooner, Joseph Waldo, and John Jones Waldo, Hannah Jones, daughter of her son William, her great-granddaughter, Hannah Spooner, and Hannah Francis Oliver, daughter of Daniel Oliver.

5. The only son, WILLIAM JONES, married at Blandford, Dorset, 5 Jan. 1762, JANE, daughter of Edward Madgwick of Blandford, by his wife, Jane, daughter of Henry Kittier, of Ringwood, Hampshire. He died 1 Dec. 1805, leaving seven children:

i. WILLIAM, b. *circa* 1769; said to have d. unm. Matriculated Brasenose College, Oxford, B.A., 1793. In Holy Orders.

ii. JOHN MADGWICK, b. *circa* 1770; d. *s.p.* 17 May 1832; m. SARAH LLOYD. Matriculated Brasenose College, Oxford, B.A., 1792, M.A., 1795. In Holy Orders, and for more than twenty years curate of St. Bride's, Fleet Street, London.

iii. JANE, buried in the church of All Saints, Bristol, in 1801; m. at Weston-in-Godano, Somerset, 17 March 1783, PEREGRINE STOCKDALE, of Bristol.

iv. HANNAH, m. THOMAS BIDWELL, of Coaxdon Common, under Axminster, Devon.

v. SUZANNA, m. RICHARD SAVAGE, of Moorfields, London.

vi. MARTHA, m. at St. James' Church, Bristol, 5 Jan. 1802, JOHN PENKIVIL, of Plymouth Dock, Devon.

vii. FRANCES, b. *circa* 1773; m. at St. James' Church, Bristol, 14 Aug. 1798, WILLIAM JAMES, of Chard, Somerset.

APPENDIX.

Notes on the Bluets of Greenham and Holcombe Rogus.

The Bluets were long established in the west of England. The Manor of Greenham came to them by the marriage of Sir Walter Bluet to Christian, heiress of the Greenham (or Grindham) family. The great-grandson of this marriage, John Bluet, married Maud, daughter and co-heir of John Chiselden (died in 1420), who brought him the Manor of Holcombe Rogus, Devon.

On 30 Aug. 1553, Lady Mountjoy, fourth wife, and widow, of William Blount, 4th Baron Mountjoy, added to her will (dated 4 April 1552; proved 17 Nov. 1553) a codicil by which she gave to her daughter Dorothy (who married another John Bluet, fifth in descent from Maud Chiselden's husband) all her jewels, her gown of velvet and her gown of satin, and to her son John Blwett [*sic*] her "best colt in Cary or Almysford Park."

---

*Suzanna Jones m. 23 Dec. 1760 Arnold Welles. Her sister, Martha, m. 11 March 1762 Joseph Waldo.

Lady Mountjoy was daughter of Thomas (Grey), First Marquess of Dorset, and great-aunt of the unfortunate Lady Jane Grey, whose nine days reign ended on the scaffold.

Richard Bluet, son of John Bluet and Dorothy Blount, married Mary, 5th daughter of Sir John Chichester, of Raleigh, by his wife, Gertrude, daughter of Sir William Courtenay, of Powderham; which Sir John, through his mother, Elizabeth, daughter of John Bourchier, Earl of Bath, was sixth in descent from Thomas, Duke of Gloucester, youngest son of Edward III.

Their son, Arthur Bluet, married Joan, daughter of John Lancaster, of Bagborough, Somerset, by his wife, Dorothy, daughter of Thomas Carew, of Crowcombe, and had a son, John Bluet, who by Elizabeth, his wife, daughter of Sir John Portman, of Orchard, Baronet, left four daughters, his co-heirs:

1. Anne, bapt. at Holcombe Rogus 8 Sept. 1625; m. Cadwallader Jones,
2. Mary, m. (1), Sir James Stonehouse, Baronet; m. (2), Sir John Lenthall, son of Sir William Lenthall, the famous Speaker of the House of Commons.
3. Dorothy, m. Henry Wallop, from whom descend the Earls of Portsmouth.
4. Suzanna, m. John Basset, of Umberleigh.

John Bluet died in 1634, intestate. His daughters, being minors, became wards of the Crown during their minorities. His wife survived him by less than three years. Her will, dated 18 March 1635/6, was proved the 20 May 1637 (P.C.C. Goare 63).

She desires to be buried in the church of Holcombe Rogus "without great solemnity, near my late loving deceased husband" and asks her executors that there may be "a decent Monument set up in remembrance of us both". To her daughter Anne she leaves her best bed and bedspread with all its furniture, her best petticoat with embroidered sleeves and stomacher to it, her coloured waistcoat wrought with silk and gold, her best pane, her holland child-bed sheet and pillow-ties to it, and one dozen of silver plates. Her daughter, Mary, receives similar gifts.

She appoints as her executors, her brother, Sir William Portman, and her sister, Grace Portman, and earnestly desires them "to have special care and regard to the religious and moral education and breeding of all my children and that they may live and be brought up together with them in the fear of God".

John and Elizabeth Bluet were buried in the Bluet Chapel of Holcombe Rogus Church, under a monument thought to be one of the finest in the West Country.

REV. ROBERT JORDAN.

[By W. H. WHITMORE.]

We have mentioned, in a preceding article, one of the noble deeds of Rev. Robert Jordan. This gentleman and Rev. Richard Gibson were the pioneers of Episcopacy in Maine. Mr. Gibson left the country about the year 1642, but Jordan remained at the post of duty, and never relinquished his stand as a churchman, or his professional character. It is one of the strange omissions in Rev. Dr. Sprague's Annals of the American Pulpit,— an appropriate memoir of so distinguished and faithful a churchman. He was the soul of the opposition to Massachusetts, and a chief supporter to the Royal Commissioners and the anti-Puritan polity. It is much to be desired that the Hon. Wm. Willis of Portland, out of his abundant knowledge, would furnish a fitting tribute to the memory of this indefatigable missionary and leader of the forlorn hope of Episcopacy in Maine. He was from the west of England, perhaps from Melcomb, where a merchant of the same name, Robert Jordan, dwelt. He was born, perhaps, about the year 1611, and came to Maine, (Richmond's Island,) as early as 1640.* This island, near the entrance to Portland harbor, was an important commercial plantation, under the government of Mr. John Winter, whose only child, Sarah, became the wife of Mr. Jordan. By this marriage Mr. Jordan became one of the great land-proprietors and wealthy men of that region, a source of influence which he failed not to exert in favor of his church and politics.† The Rev. Richard Mather, on his voyage from England in 1635, touched at Richmond's Island and noted the fact in his journal.‡ Mr. Thomas Willett of New Plimouth, and afterwards mayor of New York, had, just before the time of Mather's visit, escaped to Richmond's Island, having been driven by the French from Penobscott, and took passage in the ship with Mather for Massachusetts. Of Jordan's family I have learnt the following particulars:—By wife Sarah he had John, who m. Elizabeth, dau. of Elias Stileman ; Robert; *Dominicus*, who m. Hannah, dau. of Ralph Tristram of Saco, and was killed by Indians in 1703 ; Jedidiah, Samuel, and Jeremiah. Dominicus had issue, with others, *Elizabeth*, who m. Capt. Humphrey Scammon and had Dominicus, who, by wife Rebecca, dau. of Capt. Daniel Smith, had *Elizabeth*, wife of Col. Thomas Cutts, father of Hon. Richard Cutts of Washington, and father-in-law of Dr. Thomas Gilbert Thornton, many years marshal of Maine.

By the kindness of George D. Phippen, Esq., of Salem, we are enabled to present a document which throws considerable light upon the Jordan pedigree.

He has in his possession a tabular pedigree of his family and connexions in England, prepared at a very early date, by Joseph Phippen or Fitzpen, eldest son of David Phippen the emigrant, and who probably accompanied his father to this country in 1635. He was living at Falmouth in the neighborhood of Jordan as early as 1650, and to him Jordan made one of his earliest conveyances of land.

This document was copied in 1768, upward of a century after its first preparation, and re-copied in 1808, the latter copy being the earliest now in existence. It has upon it the arms of Peirce, Holton, Jordaine, Fitzpen, and Fitzpen impaling Pie, and Burges impaling Pie ; these arms are

---

* Willis's Portland, I., 154; Folsom's Saco and Biddeford, 79.
† Maine Hist. Coll. v. 228.   ‡ Mather's Journal, ed. 1850, pp. 27–30.

arranged around an emblazoned caption, the text of which had become illegible before the copy of 1808 was taken, as also much of the contents of the numerous bordered enclosures which follow the arms, and which formerly contained the several pedigrees and connexions; enough of which, however, still remains to more than prove this assertion, and which is remarkably corroborated and defects therein supplied by the Herald's Visitation of Cornwall in 1620, now preserved among the Harleian manuscripts in the British Museum. These enclosures, where the margins are not obliterated, are occasionally connected in pairs by two intervening hearts, implying marriage as fully as could be done by written language. From two of said enclosures we learn that "Robt. Jordaine Gent. left issue Robert," and that he married "Cokers —— of —— —— in Blandford," for his first wife; "a second wife brought him issue, Henry."

Two other tablets state, that "Robt. Jordaine, merchant in Melcomb, left issue, Cokers, Jane and Edward," and that "Robt. Fitspen" married "Cicely Jordaine." The Herald's Visitation of 1620 explains that this Robt. Fitspen was of Weymouth, in Dorsetshire, and the father of David Phippen above mentioned; and that his wife Cicely was the "daughter of Thomas Jordon," also of Dorsetshire. The parish records of Melcomb Regis, the adjoining town to Weymouth, record their marriage "18 Sept. 1580," and also state that "Robt. Jordan was burried there, Oct. 12, 1589." It therefore appears somewhat more than probable that Joseph Phippen, who was somewhat conspicuous in the early days of Falmouth, now Portland, was induced to leave Massachusetts proper, and settle there, from advantages held out by the Rev. Robt. Jordan, undoubtedly his relative.

We would also say that the record of the Phippen Family, prepared by Mr. Phippen, is the most beautifully executed MS. we have ever seen. We trust he will soon have it printed, with engravings of the above, and other arms and illustrations with which it is emblazoned; for his copy must remain unique, as only a labor of love could prompt the taste and care so visible on every page of his volume. The colors of some of the charges of the arms mentioned are apparently wrong, and that of the shields omitted, which errors may have arisen from the fancy of the copyist. We give them as they are, noting variations :—

1. PEIRCE.—Two bends *sable*. This ordinary was used in several forms by the family of Pearse. See BURKE.

2. HOLTON.—On a bend *or*, three eagles displayed. BURKE gives the field *azure*, and the eagles *gules*.

3. JORDAINE.—A lion rampant, between nine cross crosslets. BURKE says, *azure*, and between three crosses *or*.

4. FITZPEN.—Two bends *azure*, in chief three escallops. In another section of the same document these arms are given as described by Burke, viz.: argent, two bends *sable*, escallops of the second.

5. PYE.—Three escallops in fesse. BURKE gives several coats, the fields and charges of different colors, but puts them *on* a fesse. This may be owing to the obliteration of the lines of the fesse.

6. BURGESS.—A fesse chequy *argent* and *gules*, in chief three cross crosslets. BURKE has not this coat precisely, but has various modifications.

PEDIGREE OF JOSELYNE.

[Communicated by S. G. Drake.]

To the Editors of the Register.

You will notice that the names, especially that of *Joselyne*, in this Pedigree, are spelt in various ways. I need not apprise you that I "follow copy." The original is in tabular form, as are most of the Visitations, but I have reduced it to narrative, as more convenient to print.

I presume this to be the Pedigree of our Henry Jocelyn, or Josselyn, of New England; but that I leave for the Josselyns to determine.

James Joselyne[1] m. Jane, da. and heir to Wm. Chastelyn, who had who had Henry,[2] m. to a da. and heir of Sr. John Hyde, Kt. Their son, Ralph,[3] m. Maude, da. and heir of Sir John Hyde, Kt. Their son,

John,[4] m. Katherine, da. and heir of Sr. Tho. Battell. Their son, Thomas,[5] m. . . . . . Maud who m. 2d Nicholas Vohres. Thomas,[5] had by . . . . . Maud, Thomas,[5] who m. Alice, da. to Willm Leston. Their son, Ralphe,[7] m. Maude, da. to John Sutton als. Dudley and had Jeffery[8], m. to Margaret, da. to Robt. Rockell. By this marriage was Thomas Josslyne,[9] who m. Maude, da. of Adam Brancktell. Their son Jeffere Joselyne,[10] m. Katherine, da. of Thomas le Braye, and had Sir Thomas Joslyne,[11] Thomas Joselyne,[11] and Sir Ralph Joselyne[11] Lord Maior of London, 4, E. 4, Kt. of ye Bathe and Seile. Thomas Joselyne[11] m. Alice da. to Lewis Ouke, and had Ralphe Joselyne,[12] who m. . . . . . da. of . . . . . Bardolfe, and had Ralphe Joselyn,[13] and John Josselyne[13] who obi. 17 H. 8. Ralphe[13] m. Katherine, da. and heir to Richd. Martyn. John[13] m. Phillip da. to William Bradary, Esq. Ralphe[13] had by Katherine, Gabrell Joselyn,[14] Jefferey Josselyn,[14] and John.[14] Jeffery[14] had Thomas[15] m. to Elizabeth, da. to Nicholas Hadesley, Esq. who had Thomas,[16] m. to Mary, da. to Thomas Parker of Essex, who had Thomas,[17] of Horley in Essex, now living, 1614. He is m. to Jane da. to Edward Saunders of Charlewood, Com Surry, Esq.

John Josselyne,[13] who m. Phillip, had by her, Anne,[14] Sir Thomas,[14] of Hyroodin in Com Essex, who m. Dorothy, da. to Sr. Gefferey Gattes, and Jane[14] m. to Nicholas Wentworth. Sir Thomas[14] had by Dorothy, Lenard,[15] Thomas,[15] John,[15] Richard,[15] Mary,[15] Jane,[15] Lenard,[15] Thomas,[15] Edwaid,[15] and Henry,[15] 4th son. Richard[15] m. 1st. Alice, da. to John Shaltan, and 2d to Ann da. of . . . . Lucas of Borye, and had by this 2d wife, John Joselyne[16] m. to . . . . da. to Willm Wysman of Mayland, who had John[17] Edward,[17] Thomas[17] and Robert ;[17] Winnefrid,[16] m. to Richd. Doddesworth, Richard,[16] 7 yeres ould one Barthelmew da: 1579, 1st son, m. to Johne da. to Robt. Atkinson, by whom he had Sr. Robert[17] of Hadhall, com. Hartford, living 1634, with wife Bridgett, da. to Sr. Willm Smyth, and has William,[18] eldest son, Roberd,[18] Frances,[18] Bridget,[18] and Dorothy,[18]. The other child. of Richard[15] by Ann, are Jone,[16] m. Francis Rerd,* Mary,[16] m. to Thos. Renett, and Rebek."

Edward Josslyne,[15] son of Sir Thomas Josselyne,[14] m. . . . . . da. to . . . . . Lambe, Com. Middlesex, & had Henry,[16] Thomas,[16] Jane,[16] Dorothy,[16] Ann,[16] Elizabeth,[16] Margaret,[16] m. to Peter Gates, 1st da., and Wynefred,[16] m. to . . . . . Syday of Gates ; Henry,[15] brother of Edward,[15] m. Ann da. and co-heir to Humphery Foxoll, and had Sir Thomas Josselyne,[16] who m. . . . . . da. to John Franke, widdow, and had a da.[17] m. to a son of Sr. Nicholas Lusher of Surey, and Ann,[17] m. to . . . . . Allen of Hortford.

Jane,[15] da. of Sir Thomas Josselyne,[14] m. 1st, Richard Kelton, and 2d, Roger Harlackenden, of Cawarth Henton, Com. Kent.

NOTE.—The Visitation from which the above is copied was originally made in 1614. Additions were made to it in 1634. On the cover is written this :—" T Vizitation of Hartfordshire taken by Sr. Henry St. George Richmond Herraulde Aano 1634 being deputy to Sr. John Borough Garter and Sr. Richard St. George Clerenceaulx Kinges of Armes."

London, Eng., October 20, 1859.

---

* Whether *Rerd* or *Berd* I am not quite certain.—*Transcriber.*

HENRY JOSSELYN, THE FIRST AND ONLY ROYAL CHIEF MAGISTRATE OF MAINE.

By William M. Sargent, A.M., of Portland, Me.

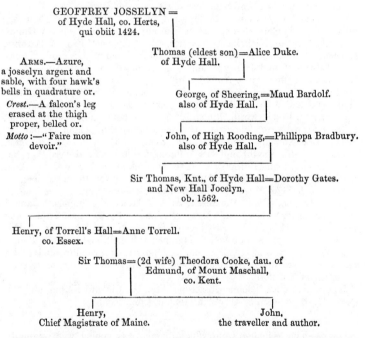

GEOFFREY JOSSELYN =
of Hyde Hall, co. Herts,
qui obiit 1424.

Arms.—Azure,
a josselyn argent and
sable, with four hawk's
bells in quadrature or.

Thomas (eldest son)=Alice Duke.
of Hyde Hall.

Crest.—A falcon's leg
erased at the thigh
proper, belled or.

George, of Sheering,=Maud Bardolf.
also of Hyde Hall.

Motto :—"Faire mon
devoir."

John, of High Rooding,=Phillippa Bradbury.
also of Hyde Hall.

Sir Thomas, Knt., of Hyde Hall=Dorothy Gates.
and New Hall Jocelyn,
ob. 1562.

Henry, of Torrell's Hall=Anne Torrell.
co. Essex.

Sir Thomas=(2d wife) Theodora Cooke, dau. of
Edmund, of Mount Maschall,
co. Kent.

Henry,
Chief Magistrate of Maine.

John,
the traveller and author.

Henry Josselyn, whose pedigree is traced above, arrived in New England in the ship "Pide-Cow," at Piscataqua, in 1634,[*] as chief agent for Capt. John Mason, the Patentee. He continued to act in that capacity until the death of Mason in 1635; undertaking the discovery of Erocoise [i. e. Champlain] Lake in the Laco-

---

[*] See Mason's letter of 5 May, 1634, to Gibbons, endorsed, "received July 10th," two days after the arrival of the ship.

nia Patent. He intended to settle himself at Newichewannock [Berwick, Maine], but because of his patron's death and the subsequent confusion of his affairs, he removed to Black Point (Scarborough) in 1635.*

There was probably some agreement between him and Sir Ferdinando Gorges, the Patentee of that region, relating to private grants of land; and such lands as he became possessed of this way added to Capt. Thomas Cammock's Patent,—part of which was devised to him, and the remainder of which he became seized of by marrying the widow Margaret Cammock in 1643,—made him the owner of a considerable portion of that township, and he thus became the most extensive proprietor who has ever lived in Scarborough.

He resided with Captain Cammock until the latter's death, and afterwards in the same house, near the "Ferry Rocks," which is supposed to have stood over the old cellar near "Garrison Cove" on the neck, and which was at the time of the Indian troubles in 1675 converted into a garrison, to which many of the inhabitants resorted with their families. The situation of this garrison rendered it one of the strongest in the Province—and it might easily have been defended against any number of Indians.

In 1635 Josselyn was a Commissioner under William Gorges; and again under the Patent of 1639 under Thomas Gorges. In 1645 chosen vice-Deputy Governor under Richard Vines as Deputy Governor; at Vines's departure from the country, he became acting Deputy-Governor, and held the last General Court under the authority of Gorges, at Wells, July, 1646.

He was heartily attached to Gorges and his cause, but he preferred to obey Rigby rather than to disturb the promised peace of the Province by unavailing contention. He was appointed among the Judges of Lygonia, with Cleeves and Jordan. Strongly opposed to the authority of Massachusetts, he held out for five years; was arrested and obliged to give bond to appear before the General Court, which he did, as did Jordan, in 1657; submitted to Massachusetts July 3, 1658, and, with Henry Watts, was appointed a Commissioner for the Town; was Associate and Town Commissioner in 1661; but in 1662 Josselyn and Shapleigh refused to take the oath of office. as Associates for the Province, and in the contest which followed was backed up by his fellow-townsmen; but being again elected Commissioner by his townsmen in 1664, was then accepted by the Massachusetts authorities.

Soon after young Gorges's application to the King, he appointed Josselyn one of twelve Magistrates under his authority. In 1664 he was appointed a Royal Justice by the four Commissioners sent over by the King, and there being eleven of them, the Commission-

---

* Mason did not die till late in 1635. His will was made Nov. 26, 1635, and proved Dec. 22.—EDITOR.

ers directed that in case the Justices were equally divided Josselyn should have the casting vote; thus constituting him the Chief Justice of the Province. He was its first, and only Chief Magistrate ever appointed by Royal authority. With the establishment of the royal government in the Province, the jurisdiction of Gorges ceased and was never resumed. This royal government, with Josselyn at its head, continued till 1668.

Long and bitterly partisan accounts of the particulars of the usurpation of authority by the Commissioners of Massachusetts and their deposition of the subject of this sketch in that year have been written. Suffice it here to say that this terminated his public services in this region.

Living the retired life of a gentleman planter till August, 1676, he was, with numbers of his neighbors, then surprised and besieged by the Indians in his garrison-house. Accepting the invitation of Mogg Hegone, their chief, to a parley, he found on his return that all the garrison, except his own family, had rowed away in boats. Surrendering, he was treated with a kindness and consideration by the savages that evinced their appreciation of his undeviating justice and many kindly acts shown them in the past, and was allowed to depart to the eastward.

Exhausted at his age by the protracted civil contests; disgusted with their results; viewing the destruction by savage hands of the accumulated industries of a lifetime, and considering the impracticability of immediate resettlement, he cast in his lot with the more favored maritime settlement at Pemaquid, appearing there immediately upon the establishment of the Duke of York's government in 1677—in which it is inferable he was an active participant, as he appears continuously acting as a Justice, considering, doubtless, his old commission valid anywhere in his Majesty's domain. He was reinvested, or newly commissioned, however, by the Governor of New York in 1680; and subsequently received other distinguishing marks of consideration and confidence.

He was as distinguished for uprightness and probity amidst his new surroundings as of yore; *Cœlum non animum mutant qui trans mare currunt;* and while perhaps not as conspicuous a figure thereafter as in the previous annals, his honorable reputation made new friends, and he seems never to have alienated old ones—while a letter of Governor Andros to Ensign Sharp in command at Pemaquid, September, 1680, shows that official appreciation but confirmed the estimation of his neighbors, and extended the fostering aid of judicious patronage to a tried and proven public servant, alleviating his necessities as a merited mark of royal recognition of the gentleman and scholar, the Magistrate and Governor, than whom we have never had one more worthy and seldom one so pure. He writes:

582

As to Mr. Jocylne whom I would have you use with all fitting respect Considering what he hath been and his age. And if he Desire and shall build a house for himself to lett him choose any lott and pay him ten pounds towards it or if he shall Desire to hyre soe to live by himself then to Engage and pay the rent either of which shall be allowed you in yor account as aloe sufficient provision for himself and wife as he shall desire out of the stores.

In the scarcity of records that have survived the chances and changes of those troubled times, the nearest approximation to the time of his death is that it was shortly before May 10th, 1683, for Captain Brockholls, writing that day to Lawrence Dennis, speaks of him as deceased.

" No storied urn nor animated bust," no epitaph even, marks his unknown resting place, but in the hearts and memories of his successors is he ever justly famed.

NOTE.—I have to express my very great obligation to Lt. Col. John Henry Josselyn, of Ipswich, England—a practising lawyer and Town Councillor there—for the construction of the above used pedigree, from his own printed pedigree of this family, by which it appears that the subject of the above sketch and Col. Josselyn are " second and eighth " cousins ; also for many valuable citations from his MS. collections; from these I quote his opinion : " I have a note that Henry Josselyn, of the County of Kent, was admitted to Corpus Christi College, Cambridge, 1623. This might very well have been your Henry before he went to America, and his being described as of the County of Kent is consistent with his being the son of Sir Thomas, whose second wife (Henry's mother) came from that County." " For genealogy of the elder branch of our family, refer to title ' Earl of Roden ' in ' Burke's Peerage ' of 1883 and subsequent years. The genealogy given in editions prior to 1883 is incorrect. Sir Bernard corrected the 1883 edition after a correspondence I had with him about it." " The proper arms of the family are those borne by the Earl of Roden and by ourselves, viz." [description as at the head of this article]. " It would seem to be probable that Thomas Josselyn, fourth son of Ralph of Roxwell, co. Essex, whose will (dated 4 Aug. 1626, and proved 4 May, 1632) is identical with the Thomas Josselyn who embarked for America in ship ' Increase,' 17th April, 1635. I base this theory on the coincidence that the family names Dorothy, Mary, Nathaniel and Elizabeth, are repeated in the issue of the last named Thomas. As regards the name ' Abraham,' given by said Thomas to his eldest son, it may have been the name of his (Thomas's) father-in-law, for what more likely than that a woman bearing the Scriptural name ' Rebecca ' should have had an ' Abraham ' for her father? Roxwell is adjoining parish to Willingale Doe in which is Torrel's Hall. But I cannot trace the origin of this branch of the Josselyn family, nor its connection, if any, with the Torrel's Hall branch. Search of registers might do it." *Vide passim* REGISTER, xiv. 15 ;*' Tuckerman's Introduction to John Josselyn's ' New England Rarities.' "

This last citation erroneously states that " Sir Thomas Josselyn .... did not come to this country "—a mistake previously made by Mr. Southgate in his " History of Scarborough " ; while Sir Ferdinando Gorges, by

*The preceding article.

implication, states the contrary in this extract: "Whereas Sir Thomas Josselyn Knt was named chief in the said Commission and Ordinances [dated Mch. 10: 1640] Now for that I am informed he is returned into England he is left out of the Commission and my Cousin Thomas Gorges put in his place and the same power given unto him as to the said Sir Thomas Josselyn." (From the files of the Maine Historical Society—MS. copy of State Papers, 40: e.)—W. M. S.

ROGER KENYON AT BLOCK ISLAND.—In his Lancashire Pedigrees, London, 1873, the late Joseph Foster, Esq., in giving an account of the noble family of Lord Kenyon of Gredington, states that Roger Kenyon, son of Roger Kenyon of Peel, Esq., was educated at Cambridge and died *s. p.* The elder Roger Kenyon was governor of the Isle of Man and M. P. for Clitheroe, and his son Roger was born, according to Dugdale's Visitation, 29 Feb. 1659/60. He was the eldest son, the ancestor of Lord Kenyon being the fourth son of the elder Roger, Thomas, who was born in 1668. That the younger Roger did not die *s. p.*, but married on Block Island and had a son Roger, is conclusively proved by the Block Island records, together with certain letters in the Kenyon Manuscripts, printed in the Fourteenth Report of the Historical Manuscripts Commission.

The Block Island records give the marriage, 11 Oct. 1683, of Roger Kenyon and Mary Ray and the birth of their son Roger, 23 Jan. 1684/5. This Mary Ray was born on Block Island 19 May 1667, and was the daughter of the venerable Simon Ray, one of the founders of the Block Island settlement, by his wife, Mary Thomas of Marshfield. Their granddaughter Catherine Ray, the wife of Gov. William Greene of Rhode Island, in writing of her grandfather's family in a letter dated at Warwick, R. I., 5 Mar. 1793, states that her grandfather's eldest daughter Mary "married an Englishman, who carried her to England, and she was the first American lady introduced to the king and kissed his hand." On 20 Oct. 1707 Sarah Dickens entered upon the Block Island records an oath that at the request of Mr. Roger Kenyon she wished to state that she saw his father, Roger Kenyon, married to his mother, Mary Ray, and that the said Roger Kenyon was the reputed son of Roger Kenyon Esquire of ―――― in Lancashire. In the original record the name of the residence of this Roger Kenyon is almost illegible, but it appears to be Mareshere or possibly Manchester.

In the Kenyon Manuscripts there is a letter, dated at Liverpool, 19 July 1683, from Edward Tarlton to Roger Kenyon at Peel, reading: "My son Edward, beinge arrived from Barbados, gives me account that your sonne took occasion to leave Barbados and is safely arrived at New York, in America, where he teacheth gentleman's children, and is engaged there to continue for two or three yeares, by covenant with a gentleman there." Other letters in the collection show that this son's name was Roger, and that he subsequently returned to England and became a fellow of Cambridge University. In a letter, dated at Stockport 5 Apr. 1694 and addressed to his mother, Alice Kenyon, he writes that owing to his opposition to the then Government he had left the University and was at a farmer's house, learning the art of husbandry. He concludes with these words: "where I am very well employed in learning the art of husbandry' and courting my landlord's daughter against the days prohibiting matrimony be over." It is clear, therefore, that at this date Mary (Ray) Kenyon was dead, and that Roger purposed to marry again. Other letters prove that he had been sold for some misdemeanor and transported to Barbados, whence he drifted to New York and thence to Block Island.

It would appear that the son Roger, born in 1684/5, sent to Block Island for proof of his father's marriage, and this explains the deposition of 20 Oct. 1707. This son died probably *s. p.* Shortly after the date of Roger Kenyon's marriage a John Kenyon was at Westerly, R. I., only a few miles from Block Island, and was taxed there in 1687, and from this John the numerous Kenyons of that section are descended.

Newport, R. I.   G. ANDREWS MORIARTY, JR.

EXTRACT FROM ENGLISH PARISH REGISTERS RELATING TO KING AND HAINES FAMILIES.

Communicated by Rufus King, Esq., of Yonkers, New York.

Baltonsborough Parish, Somerset.

Children of Richard Kinge.
William, bap. June, 1540.
Richard, " July, 1545.
Mary, " February, 1551.
Christian, " " "
Rafe, " ———, 1556.

1620, William King, Senior, buried.
1620, Richard Hayne, churchwarden.
1621, Stephen Kinge, "

The Curate of Baltonsborough states that there are many later entries of the name King.

East Coker Parish, Somerset.

1595, Edward Kinge married.
1596, Bartholomew, son of Edward Kinge, bap.
1598, John, " " " "

Gillingham Parish, Dorset.

1594, Sept. 2, William Kinge, son of Christopher Kinge, bap.

Combe-Hay Parish, Somerset.
Baptisms.
1587, Nov. 14, John Heynes.
1588, Mar. 16, George Heynes.
1589, " 28, —— Hayne (christian name illegible).
1591, May 20, Marie Heynes.
1592, Dec. 10, Alice Heynes.
1593, Feb. 17, Dorothy Haines.

Shapwick Parish, Somerset.
1592, Jan., Anna, filia Jois Tayler, als Kinge, bap.
1593, ——, William Kinge and Margereta Showell, mar.
1594, ——, Margereta, dau. Will'mi Kinge, bap.
1594, ——, " uxor " " bur.
1595, ——, " dau. " " "
1596, ——, Petra, son Petri Kinge, bap.
1597, ——, Will'mus Hatch and Bridgitta Kinge, mar.

Dundry Parish, Somerset.
1633, Dec. 2, Mary, dau. William King, of Littleton, bur.
1640, Ap^r. 2, William King, bur.
1641, Ap^r. 14, William King, bur.

Glastonbury, S^t. Benedict Parish, Somerset.
1622, Oct. 28, William Parsonns and Rose King, mar.
1623, June 1, Rose, wife of William King, bur.

Glastonbury, St John's Parish, Somerset.
1623, Mar. 8, Richard Kinge, bur.
1629, Aug. 20, Richard Kinge, bap.
1629, Mar. —, Elizabeth Joan Kinge, bur.

Worminghall Parish, Oxfordshire.
Baptisms.
1562, Jan. 4, Richard Kynge.
1564, Feb. 12, Elizabetha Kynge.
1566, Apr. 10, Phylipp Kynge.
1567, June 20, Alivia Kynge.
1568, Oct. 23, Phillippe Kynge.
1570, June 11, Thomas Kynge.
1572, Apr. 20, Dorithea Kynge.
1575, Oct. 3, Edmund Kynge.
1591, Jan. 17, Henricus filius John Kynge.

Marriages.
1616, Nov. 7, Stephanus Radford et Agnetes Kinge.
1623, Jan. 29, Thomas Kinge and Maria Cook.
1631, Nov. 10, Laurentius Kinge et Sarah Rippinghall, vidua.
1647, Nov. 8, Johannis Philips, et Sara Kinge.

Burials.
1577, July 14, Edwardus Kynge.
1592, Jan. 14, Phillipus Kynge.
1606, Mar. 22, Elizabetha Kynge.
1632, Jan. 5, Elizabetha, filia Laurentii King.

KING.—The following extracts from the Parish Register of Southold, Suffolk County, England, relating to the King Family, have been communicated to the REGISTER by Rufus King, Esq., of Yonkers, N. Y.:—

1602, Dec. 12, William King and Judith Cocke, married.
1603, Sep. 21, Judith, dau. of W. and J. King, baptised.
1604, Feb. 3, Henry, son of W. and J. King, baptised.
1607, Oct. 23, Eliza, dau. of W. and J. King, baptised.
1609, Sep. 28, William King, buried.
1614, Jan. 16, Edmund Awstens and Susan King, married.
1620, Jan. 10, Robert Howse and Margaret King, married.
1622, Nov. 14, Mary, daughter of William and Ann King, baptised.
1633, Oct. 12, John, son of Jeffery and Sarah King, baptised.
1635, Nov. 5, Joseph, son of Jeffery King, baptised.
1638, Oct. 18, Child of Jeffery King, buried.
1639, Aug. 7, Henry King, buried.

ENGLISH RECORDS OF THE KING FAMILY OF SUFFIELD, CONN.

By CAMERON H. KING, ESQ., of San Francisco, Cal.

IN the REGISTER, vol. 46, page 370, appeared a brief genealogy of "The King Family of Suffield, Connecticut," by the late Edmund Janes Cleveland, Esq., of Hartford, Conn. At that time, though it was stated by Mr. Cleveland that William King, the father of James King of Suffield, lived in Uxborough [which should have been Ugborough], Devonshire, England, nothing was definitely known concerning either the place or date of the birth of that James, the founder of the family in America.

Within the past year I caused a search of the parish registers of Ugborough to be made, and have discovered therein the entries of the marriage of the father and mother of James King, and the baptism of James and his elder brother William.

The following is translated from a certified copy of these entries, which are in Latin, sent me by the vicar, Rev. William Edward Windle, M.A., Ugborough Vicarage, Ivybridge, Devon.

Marriages.

1548—John Hayman and Mary Kynge were married 27 day of August
1621—William King and Christia Lapp were married 27 of September
1642—William Kinge and Agnes Elwill* were married 16 of October

Baptisms.

1584—Robert, son of William Kinge and Margaret his wife was baptized 27 March

* The father and mother of James King of Suffield.

1643—William,* son of William Kinge and Agnes [his] wife was baptized the last day of December

1647—James,† son of William Kinge and Agnes his wife was baptized 7 day of November

The foregoing were all the entries which I requested the vicar of the parish to certify, but the following, translated from the Latin entries, also appear on the parish register.

Baptisms.

1549—William, son of Thomas Kynge

1577—Alicia and Joanna, daughters of William and Margaret Kinge

1581—Thomas, son of William and Margaret Kinge

Burials.

1579—Joanna, daughter of Thomas Kinge.

1662—Agnes, wife of William King.

The parish registers show no connecting links between William and wife Margaret Kinge and the William Kinge who married Christia Lapp in 1621, nor between the latter William and the William Kinge who married Agnes Elwill in 1642, and whose children were *William*, baptized Dec. 31, 1643, and *James*, baptized Nov. 7, 1647, afterwards of Suffield, Conn. It would seem probable, however, that all these were successive generations of the same family. An examination of the adjoining parish registers might perhaps make this clearer.

There exists an old parchment, dated in the year 1389, made by a Roger Kynge, showing that he then lived at Dodbroke [about seven miles from Ugborough], Devonshire, which relates to the sale by him in that year of a property near the "Redepitte," near the font of St. Thomas the Martyr in the burg of Dodbrooke, and bearing his seal in red wax. The seal is about an inch in diameter, and the design thereon appears to be a tree and on either side two distinct branches rising from the ground independently. There are several witnesses to the document, the first being the "prepositus" of the burg of Dodbrooke. The wording on the parchment is in monkish Latin, and very legible. This ancient parchment is now in the possession of Harvey James[6] King, Esq. (Roger,[5] Lieut. Eliphalet,[4] Capt. Joseph,[3] James[2] of Suffield, Conn., William[1] of Ugborough), who obtained it quite recently from R. Palmer Sanderson, Esq., of Lily Grove, Lancashire, England. The Christian name Roger occurs very early, and frequently afterwards, among the descendants of the Suffield family. The Ugborough parish registers of baptisms and marriages are from 1538, and that of burials from 1542.

In Mr. Cleveland's article, the first wife of James King of Suffield was erroneously given as Elizabeth Emerson. It should have been Elizabeth Fuller (see REGISTER, vol. 53, pages 335–6). She was the daughter of John and Elizabeth (Emerson) Fuller, and grand-daughter of Thomas Emerson the immigrant.

The contributor is compiling a genealogy of the King family of Suffield.

* William King of Suffield.
† James King of Suffield.

HANSARD KNOLLYS, AND HIS LETTER OF PUBLIC ASSURANCE.—1639.

[HANSARD KNOLLYS was born in Chalkwell, Lincolnshire, about the year 1598. When he left the university at Cambridge, where he graduated, he was chosen master of the "free school" at Gainsborough,* in his native county. In June, 1629, he was ordained by the Bishop of Peterborough, first deacon, and then presbyter, soon after which the Bishop of Lincoln presented him to the living of Humberstone, in Leicestershire, which he held only two or three years, when, having conscientious scruples in regard to a conformity to the Church of England, he resigned his living into the bishop's hands. About the year 1636 he left that church and joined himself to the Nonconformists. Being followed by persecution wherever he went, in his native country, he sought shelter in New England, and arrived in Boston in 1638. He sympathized with Rev. John Wheelwright in his religious doctrines—was accused in Boston of having Antinomian views, and subsequently went to Dover, N. H., where he preached four years. Being recalled to England by his aged father, he arrived safely in London, Dec. 24, 1641. He taught a few scholars in his own house upon Great Tower hill, till he was chosen master of the free school in St. Mary Axe. There, in the course of one year he had no less than one hundred and fifty-six scholars. He quit the business of a teacher ; entered the parliament army and preached to the soldiers, but soon left the army and returned to London. He preached in Suffolk, where he met with renewed persecutions—was imprisoned in Newgate eighteen weeks—removed into different parts of England and Wales, went to Holland, from thence to Germany, and back again to Rotterdam, from whence he returned to London ; was again engaged in preaching and teaching school, and died after a short illness, Sept. 19, 1691, in the 93d year of his age.

His wife died April 13, 1671, and afterwards his only son. The remains of Mr. Knollys were interred in Bunhill Fields. Rev. Thomas Harrison published a sermon upon his death, and the Rev. Benjamin Keach an elegy on the same occasion. Mr. Knollys published several works, the titles of which, twelve in number, are specified in Brook's *Lives of the Puritans*, and Wilson's *History and Antiquities of Dissenting Churches*. Some account of the Life of Knollys, written with his own hand, to the year 1672, as also, his *Last Legacy to the Church*, was published after his decease.

Gov. Winthrop calls Knollys " a weak minister," " an unclean person," &c. It is not in our power, of course, to disprove these allegations. We have no doubt, however, that Winthrop was strongly prejudiced against this " preacher of antinomanism so called," and it may be magnified his failings. The presiding public functionaries did not like

---

* This school was founded by Queen Elizabeth, who permitted any of her liege subjects to endow it with lands or other property, not exceeding in value £30 per annum. See Carlisle's *Endowed Grammar Schools in England and Wales*, Vol. i. 797.

to be thwarted in their plans, or disturbed, in the least, in their schemes of policy. Opposition to their measures would naturally at once be frowned upon. True, Knollys, by letter at least, maligned the government, but " he afterwards made an ingenuous and satisfactory confession." Let it also be remembered, that he arrived at Boston, " a persecuted fugitive, in a state of utter destitution. He had sacrificed every thing for conscience sake. His child had died on the passage. His wife's money was all expended." " Few living men now would blame him for writing sharply to his friends of the oppressive system under which he suffered on his first coming here." Besides, some of the charges brought against him were undoubtedly untrue. His enemies would not be expected to speak of his virtues, and we know that small faults or suspicions of failings even, passing through malicious channels, are often swollen into the deepest of sins. We are aware that our opinion in regard to the merits or demerits of this noted man will have but little weight. One who esteemed him says :—" He bore his sufferings with the greatest courage and cheerfulness ; and behaved with meekness towards his enemies. In the whole of. his life he exhibited a bright pattern of Christian piety. He did not confine his affections to Christians of his own party, but loved the image of God wherever he saw it. And so circumspect was he in the whole of his behaviour as to command the reverence of those who were enemies to his principles."

See Brook's *Lives of the Puritans*, iii. 491 ; Wilson's *History and Antiquities of Dissenting Churches* (which contains also a portrait of Knollys), ii. 571 ; Crosby's *English Baptists*, i. 334 ; Harrison's *Sermon on the Death of Knollys* ; Eliot's *Dictionary* ; Drake's *History of Boston*, pp. 220, 242, 254, 256, 378 ; Sprague's *Annals of the American Pulpit*, Vol. vi. Baptist.

The following " letter of Public Assurance," as it is termed, was copied from the first volume of Suffolk Registry of Deeds. It is without signature. EDITOR.]

Massa. 11 : 29 : 1639. Wheras, Mr. Hansard Knolles, of Dover, vpon Pascay., hauinge, by letters into England greatly Scandelized ye Church and Civill State of this Jurisdiction, and beinge vpon better consideration brought to see the greatnesse of his offence and there vpon hath oft and earnestly craued Libertye that he might come to giue Publq. satisfaction : *

---

* " At his first coming hither," says Winthrop (see Savage's edition of Winthrop's Journal, i. 326), he " wrote a letter to his friends in London, wherein he bitterly inveighed against us, both against our magistrates and churches, and against all the people in general (as by the copy of his letter sent over to our governour may appear). The governour gave him notice thereof, and, being brought to a better judgment by further consideration and more experience, he saw the wrong he had done us, and was deeply humbled for it, and wrote to the governour to that effect, and desired a safe conduct, that he might come into the bay to give satisfaction, etc. for he could have no rest in his spirit until, etc." [Winthrop had just stated, that Mr. Knollys was denied a residence in the Massachusetts on account of his being found inclining toward the views of the " familistical opinionists," in whose company he came over from England ; that he went to Pascataquack, where he began to preach, but Mr. Burdett, their governor and preacher, " inhibited him ; " so he removed to Acomenticus, and there gathered a church of which he became a pastor ; " and Capt. Underhill being their governour, they called their town Dover."] Gov. Winthrop proceeds, " which being sent him," (that is, " a safe conduct " " to come into the bay," &c.) " under the governour his hand (with consent of the council), he came, and, upon a lecture day at Boston (most of the magistrates and elders in the bay being there assembled), he made a very free and full confession of his offence, with much aggravation against

591

I haue thought fit, by the advise and consent of the rest of the Councell, to graunt him these letters of Publq. Assurance: by wch he shalbe in peace and saftye wthin this Jurisdiction, duringe the time of his cominge, stayinge, and returninge, free from any arest ore other molestation, by, ore from, any Auth^{ty}. heere, he demeaninge himselfe well, accordinge to the order of such Publq. Ass^{ce}. p^rvided, that he shall not staye wthin this Jurisdiction aboue tenn dayes, after notice giuen him by the Governo^r, Depty Govr., this Assurance to be in force till the ende of the thirde month next, and noe longer.

   To all Publiq. Officers
and others within this
Jurisdiction whom this
may concerne.

himself, so as the assembly were well satisfied. He wrote also a letter to the same effect to his said friends in England, which he left with the governour to be sent to them."

On the first page of the first book of Suffolk Deeds, is a letter, chiefly in characters, entitled, "Copie of A letter sent to England from Mr. Hansed Knollys, To Mr. Robert Simson, and bearing date: ye 19: of 12 month Anno 1639." This may be a copy of one of the letters referred to by Gov. Winthrop.

JACOB KUHN AND HIS DESCENDANTS: ADDITIONS

By George Kuhn Clarke, LL.B., A.M., of Needham, Mass.

To the Register, vol. 51, pages 441–447 (October 1897), the present writer contributed an article entitled "Jacob Kuhn and His Descendants," in which the information then available about the Kuhn family, for several generations substantial citizens of Boston, was presented in genealogical form, beginning with Jacob[1] (or John Jacob) Kuhn, said to have been a native of Gochsheim, then in Württemberg but now (since the time of Napoleon I) in Baden, who came to America, with his family, about the middle of the eighteenth century. A reprint of that article, together with nearly three closely printed pages of "Additions and Corrections," was issued in March 1898. When the article was prepared in 1897, the writer had only one document brought to this country by the immigrant, viz., a testimonial written at Karlsruhe in Baden and signed on Shrove Tuesday, 1736, by Georg Jacob Finck, Johann Daniel Nothardt, and Johann Bernhardt Lamprecht, in whose employ Johann Jacob Kuhn, son of Johann Michael Kuhn, master butcher of Gochsheim, had been from Shrove Tuesday, 1735, to Shrove Tuesday, 1736. They wish him well and recommend him as well behaved and reliable. [Seal.]

On 12 Feb. 1921 the writer of this article came into possession of a collection of old family papers, including eight documents brought to America by the immigrant and a letter addressed to him after he arrived here. Translations of these papers have been made, and from these translations the following abstracts of the more important documents have been prepared:

1. Certificate of the baptism of Johann Jacob Kuhn [the immigrant] in Gochssheim [then in Württemberg but since the time of Napoleon in Baden]: "Anno 1715 the 10th Nov. was here begotten and born and baptized in Christ. Johann Jacob the still living parents are Johann Michael Kuhn, a citizen and butcher here and his wife Anna Barbara. Baptismal Godparents were Johann Jacob Kienl[?] Brother and mistress Maria Catharina, daughter of Herr Loventz Deschurus[?] at that time village mayor of Unteröwisheim. Which in fidem with my own signature. Gochssheim, the 15th April 1740 M Georg Friedrich Brotbrett city minister here."

[It is unfortunate that the surname of the godfather is not clear, as there is a distinct word in German for brother-in-law, and he may have been brother of the whole blood of the child's mother. Gochsheim or Gochssheim is eighteen miles northeast from Karlsruhe.]

2. Indenture of apprenticeship for Johann Jacob Kuhn. This testifies to his good standing, his father a master butcher, the son to be one. Dated at Gochssheim in Creichgau, 8 December 1734, and signed by Johann Heinrich Woelffing and two others, also guild officers. [Seals.]

3. Dismissal and certificate of good character and ability of Johann Jacob Kuhn, signed at Heidelberg [then in the Palatinate but since 1802 in Baden], 24 August 1738, by Johannes Hauck, Johann Georg Hiller,

and Philipp Spengel, citizens and master butchers of Heidelberg, in whose employ Kuhn had been from Shrove Tuesday, 1736, until St. Bartholomew's Day, 1738. [Seals.]*

4. Dismissal and recommendation of Johann Jacob Kuhn, who served under her as butcher's man from Shrove Tuesday, 1739, to Shrove Tuesday, 1740, given by Julianna Becker, widow of the mayor and innkeeper "To the Golden Ox," and dated at Königsbach, 13 March 1740. [Seal.]

5. Authentication. Hanss Michäel Kuhn citizen and butcher's [sic] son [of] Johann Jacob Kuhn, who settled in Königsbach under the benignantly gracious Esquire Sanckt Andra, the above-mentioned Kuhn can after his father's death raise paternally and maternally (so God should not send war or fire over this place so that one can [continue to] reside) sixty to seventy gulden ready cash. To this testifies 19 July[?] 1740 Mayor in office here Chrisoph [sic] Farrenschon.

[Apparently this paper gives us the name of the *grandfather* of the emigrant to America. The names "Hanss" and "Johann" are often used as identical by the Germans.]

6. Certificate of church membership for Maria Margaretha Kohler, given 3 May 1752 and signed by F.[?] D.[?] Beuthen[?], pastor of the Evangelical Reformed Church.

[In this certificate the pastor names three villages or parishes which cannot be found in German gazetteers or on maps. Perhaps it was issued to the mother or other near relative of Anna Maria Barbara Kohler, wife of Johann Georg² Kuhn (see REGISTER, vol. 51, p. 442, No. 2, John George² Kuhn), and was brought to this country by her family.]

7. Attestatum for Johann Jacob Kuhn and his wife Anna Margretha, born Wettach. It begins "I, Alexander Magnus, Baron of St. André, Master of Königsbach and Kochendorff, Imperial and Royal Hungarian Lieutenant, also Knight of the Princely August Deeded [sic] Order of Baden, add herewith for general knowledge that I am sponsor of this Johann Jacob Kuhn, master of the trade of butcher, until now my subject and citizen here in Königsbach, [who is] of the Evangelical Lutheran religion, [is] at present forty years of age, [and has] humbly submitted to me, that he has resolved with God for the improvement of his maintenance, to move with his wife and four children to the American [land], the so-called new land, and in this land to settle." He further testifies that Johann Jacob Kuhn is a native of the small town of Gochssheim in Württemberg, that his wife Anna Margretha is forty-four years old, the legitimate daughter of the late Jacob Wettach, citizen and baker, that she has a special parochial certificate of baptism, that she is "of Christian and respectable parents," [and that they (Johann Jacob Kuhn and his wife Anna Margretha)] "entered here the wedded state in which they are now living, and have with them a fine son, Johann Georg going on 15 years, Johann Jacob, 12 years old, a little daughter, Anna Maria, 5 years old, [and] a little son, Johann Michael, 3 years old." This curious document, covering two long pages and half of another, is complimentary to Johann Jacob Kuhn and family, and wishes them good fortune. One of the paragraphs states that they "have conducted themselves so respectably and well that nothing bad or ill, but on the contrary only everything good, can be said about them," and that "moreover the aforesaid Kuhn and his lawful wife, Anna Margretha, and the children are not related or attached in bondage to any one, but are free and exempt." Then follow kindly wishes,

*This is a large and impressive illuminated parchment.

594

and the Baron recommends them to all persons whom they may meet "on their journey." "To testify to the truth of the statements in this document, I have signed with my own hand and have affixed my inherited noble seal in public. This [has been] given and [has] taken place at Königsbach, situated near Durlach in the Canton Creichgau, the 16th of May 1755. [Signed] V St. André." [Seal.]

[This document entirely changes the order of the births of the children of Jacob[1] (or John Jacob) Kuhn, as printed in the REGISTER (vol. 51, p. 442), and fixes the date of the emigration as 1755, *not* 1754. It was not the *eldest* son who was drowned with his father, 28 Nov. 1763, but the *youngest*, a boy of eleven years. The traditional surname of Jacob[1] Kuhn's wife, "Weddock," is replaced by "Wettach." It is possible that he never lived at Königsberg in East Prussia, and that his eldest son was not born there, but at Königsbach in Baden.]

8. Long invocation or prayer for the journey [to America] and [for success] in the new land, beginning with the words, "In the name of God the Father, and the Son and the Holy Ghost," and closing with "Amen." It is dated in 1755, and is signed by Joh. Michael Kuhn [father of the emigrant], who apparently wrote the whole document, and by Johann Friderich [*sic*] Kuhn [probably a near relative].

9. Letter from Johann Georg[2] Kuhn, then in his sixteenth year, to his parents, brothers, and sister in Boston, dated at Nantucket 16 May 1756 and directed to Johan Jacob Kuhn in Boston.

Besides the new light thrown on the family history and ancestry of Johann Jacob[1] Kuhn, the immigrant ancestor of the Kuhn family of Boston, by the documents of which abstracts have been given above, the following additions and corrections should be made in the article on this family published in the REGISTER in October 1897 and in the reprint made in 1898:

Johann Georg[2] (or John George) Kuhn (No. 2 of this Kuhn family), now known to have been the eldest son of the immigrant, was at the age of twenty-one a mariner employed on small coasting vessels. His schooner left Nantucket on 28 Dec. 1761, and it took her sixty hours to reach Boston. On 9 Nov. 1762 he sailed from Boston to Kennebeck "in order to go to live there with Captain Patison." It took him from 7 June to 13 June 1763 to sail from Kennebeck to Boston "with Captain Wilson." From 30 Jan. to 5 July 1764 he was in the service of Nehemiah Davis (at a place not named), and then moved to Boston, where he lived about six months in Mr. Pitman's house, then, in January 1765, moved to Mr. "Kumber's" house, and on 8 Oct. moved once more to Edward Baker's house in Gibbons Court. Sailing from Boston 2 June 1766 on a sloop, Capt. Thomas Homer, master, for Cape Fear "in North Carolina," he had a passage of twenty-five days, and was two days at Brunswick, N. C., then two weeks in Wilmington, then back to Brunswick for four days, and thence to Boston, where he arrived 2 Aug. 1766, "and got my discharge." Evidently Brunswick County then had a port. The interior Brunswick is now the only town of that name in North Carolina. He refers to "the Reverend Mr. Smith Germane minister," who preached "the first time" on 9 Sept. 1770. "His quarter began September the 16th, & I paid my quarter [?] October the 14th." Other items in his journal relate to the Rev. Mr. Smith, who attended his first burial service on 22 Oct. 1770, that of George Stephens, who was drowned 20 Oct. He also records some marriages and deaths outside his family. He lived in Boston during the entire period of the American Revolution. One George Kuhn was of the German Colony at Broad Bay before 1760 (History of Waldoboro, Maine, page 51), but the present writer has not identified him. John George Kuhn, in the record of his marriage on 24 June 1762, written in German, calls his wife "Maria Barbara," a name which is puzzling, as her grandchildren, who were closely associated with her, have told the writer that her name was Anna, and one of them was named for her. Perhaps she had several Christian names, given in compliment to one or more godmothers, as was, and is, a German custom. One record of her death calls her Anna B., a combination which may account for the name *Barbara*.

Jacob[2] Kuhn, second son of the immigrant, died 17 Sept. 1808, aged 63 years (Records of St. Paul's Church (Protestant Episcopal), Newburyport, Mass.). He married first, 10 Nov. 1768 (intention also recorded), Mehetabel Stockman, who died in October 1781 (Records of the First Religious Society in Newburyport); secondly Anne Moody (called "Mrs." in the intention), who died in February 1799, aged 44 years (gravestone on Old Burying Hill); and thirdly Abigail Pike (called "Mrs." in the intention), who died 12 Oct. 1806, aged 54 (Records of the First Religious Society in Newburyport). In 1778 he was paid ten shillings for two days and a half spent in collecting blankets for the Army (Mrs. E. Vale Smith's History of Newburyport, 1854).

Jacob[3] Kuhn, son of Jacob[2] and Anne Kuhn, died 24 Apr. 1795, aged 8 years, 4 months (gravestone on Old Burying Hill).

The husband of Emily[4] Kuhn (No. 4, v, of this Kuhn family) was Isaac W. Goodrich, who, together with two children by his first wife and two children by his second wife, was buried in a tomb in the Granary Burying Ground, Boston. The site of this tomb is now covered by the kitchen of the Union Club, and the bodies have been removed to Mount Hope Cemetery.

Catharine[4] Kuhn (No. 4, viii), who married B. F. Foster, died in London.

John Michael[4] Kuhn (No. 5, iii) died or was buried 27 Nov. 1816, aged 4 years. Ogden Codman, in his "Gravestone Inscriptions and Records of Tomb Burials in the Central Burying Ground, Boston Common," 1917, calls him George Michael; but his brother and sisters were probably correct as to his name. His brother, Albert[4] Kuhn (No. 5, iv), died or was buried 15 Nov. 1822, aged 8 years. Both are buried in Tomb No. 114, in the Central Burying Ground, Boston Common.

The wife of John[4] Kuhn (No. 7) was Mary Newell Phipps, daughter of Jesse and Elizabeth (King) Phipps and sister of Capt. William K. Phipps.

Emeline Chester, wife of George Cole[4] Kuhn (No. 8), was born in Boston 20 Mar. 1818, and died in Salem, Mass., 13 Dec. 1850, daughter of Charles Christopher and Eunice (Wilson) Chester (see Chester Genealogy). Her son, George Albert[5] Kuhn (No. 8, iii), was born 12 Dec. 1845.

ANCESTRY OF JOHN LAKE,
HUSBAND OF MARGARET (READE) LAKE

By Walter Goodwin Davis, B.A., LL.B., of Portland, Me.

From several references in the Winthrop family correspondence it has long been known that John was the given name of the husband of Mrs. Margaret (Reade) Lake, the stepdaughter of Rev. Hugh Peter and the sister-in-law of Gov. John Winthrop, Jr., and Deputy Gov. Samuel Symonds, who emigrated to New England previous to 1635, lived with her sister, Mrs. Winthrop, in New London, Conn., and died at Ipswich, Mass., in 1672. Through her two daughters, Hannah (Lake) Gallop and Martha (Lake) Harris, Mrs. Lake has many descendants in America.

In 1891 Charles H. Browning, in his "Americans of Royal Descent," identified John Lake with John, son of Richard and Anne (Morrelly) Lake and half brother of Sir Edward Lake, Bart., members of a family of Lincolnshire gentry; and through them Browning traced John Lake's descent from numerous royal personages. A comparison, however, of known facts regarding the Lincolnshire Lakes and John Lake, husband of Margaret (Reade) Lake, definitely proves Mr. Browning's identification to be erroneous; but, in spite of at least one clear demonstration of these facts in the Genealogical Department of the *Boston Evening Transcript* (J. D. F. in answer to A. H. M. A., *3037.3, 19 Feb. 1913), this "royal descent" is still appearing in genealogies dealing with descendants of the Gallop and Harris families.

Very briefly, the destructive argument is as follows: Sir Edward Lake died in 1674, aged 77, and was born, therefore, about the year 1597. He had two younger half brothers whom he mentioned in his will, Thomas and John, the former being the Capt. Thomas Lake who was a selectman of Boston, Mass.; and it was this Captain Lake's son who was the baronet's heir. Capt. Thomas Lake was killed by Indians in 1676, and his gravestone in the Copp's Hill Burying Ground, Boston, states his age at death as 61. He was born, therefore, about the year 1615, and it may be inferred that his brother John was born about two years later, in 1617. Now that John Lake and Margaret Reade were married and had two children in 1623, when John Lake of the Lincolnshire family was at most only six or seven years old, is proved by the will of Mrs. Lake's father, Edmund Reade of Wickford, co. Essex, made in that year, wherein they are mentioned.*

Luckily, however, the Winthrop correspondence produces a clue by pursuing which the husband of Mrs. Margaret Lake is definitely identified. On 18 Jan. 1661/2 Mrs. Lake wrote to Gov. John Winthrop, Jr., who was then in England, asking him to ascertain whether her "sister Breadcale" of Lee, Essex, was still living. From this starting point it was not difficult to establish the fact that John Lake was a member of a family seated for several generations at Great Fanton Hall, North Benfleet, co. Essex. Although they held several Essex manors, the Lakes appear to have been of the rank of yeomen, or, at best, minor gentry, and there is no evidence at the College of Arms or in the Visitations of Essex that they were entitled to coat armor. Great Fanton Hall, a large farmhouse of no architectural pretension, was still standing in 1925, although sadly threatened, on the London side, by the on-coming tide of suburban bungalows.

The following abstracts of records from English sources throw light on the history of this Lake family; and the information derived from them is summed up in a brief pedigree in the usual genealogical form.

From Probate Records

1. The Will of Thomas Sandell of Basselden [Basildon], co. Essex, yeoman, dated 10 October 1593. To be buried in Basselden churchyard. To my son John Sandell one-third of all my lands holden by knight's service. To my wife Elizabeth my tenement called Sayers for life, and then to my son Thomas and the heirs of his body, with reversion to my son John. My mother's third being set off and my son John's third, with the dowry of my wife in all my lands holden by knight's service, the remainder shall be to my executor for ten years, and then to my son John. To my wife her dwelling in this my capital house till Michaelmas after my decease, twelve kine, forty ewes, one ram, all the goods she had when I married her and has made since, my ambling young mare, my horse, "Buttun," three loads of timber for the repair of Sayers, etc., and she is to have the bringing up of all the four children we have had between us. To my son John all my stuff in the parlor and all the glass. To my daughter Joan, Anne, and Elizabeth £20 each at marriage or at the age of eighteen, with the right of survivorship if any die before. To my daughters Mary, Thomasin, and my youngest daughter, Anne, £20 each, to be delivered to my wife towards their education, and, if any die, my son Thomas is to have her portion. If my mother die before my son John is twenty-one, my executors are to take the land she had till he is of age. If John die before he is twenty-one, then all my lands shall descend to my son Thomas, he paying to my daughters living £40 apiece, to my sister Stauterford's [*sic*] children £10, to my sister's son, Roger Dowe, £10, to my sister

*Cf. Ancestry of Priscilla Baker, by the late William Sumner Appleton, 1870, p. 119.

598

Lacke's son, John Lacke, £10, and to his sisters, Elizabeth and Sybell Lacke, £10. The Widow Ivyt is to have her dwelling in "Jacke at woods" for life for £4 a year. To my servant Alice Radlynne a tenth profit of my tenement called Bacons for five years. To my boy Chatterton my red bullock with the white face. To my cousin Ann Pake a bullock, in consideration of 20s. due to her of my father's gift. To Abraham Richbell 3s. 4d. To Widow Chatterton 3s. 4d. To Widow Marrage 3s. 4d. To my daughter-in-law Elizabeth Ladde a bullock. Residue to Thomas Taylor of Stornedowne and my brother Richard Sandell, my executors, for the education of my children. Overseers: my brother William Hurte and Mr. John Paschall. Witnesses: Arthur Denham, Alexander Paschall, Jo: Paschall. Proved 11 April 1594 by the executors. (Consistory Court of London, Sperin, 85.)

2. The Will of JOHN LAKE of North Bemflete [North Benfleet], co. Essex, dated 10 December 1596. To be buried in North Bemflette church or chancel. For making of forms and other things necessary and convenient in and about the chancel of the said church, 20s. To the parson of the said church, for a Communion Book or Psalter, 10s. To trimming and mending the porch buttresses of the said church and chancel, 20s. To each of the eight people who carry my body to the church 12d. To the poor of Bemflette and of the parishes of Runwell, Wickford, and Rawrethe, co. Essex, to each parish 20s. To the poor of Rayleigh, co. Essex, 40s. To Widow Castle, my mother-in-law, who now dwelleth with me, the bed whereon she usually lieth, furnished with all things belonging thereunto, as it now standeth, and 20s. To my wife Mary Lake all my goods, household stuff, and implements in my house called Fanton Haule, in Bemflette, except the leases of my manors or farms of Fanton Haule aforesaid and Bonefields *alias* Boneviles, in Bemflette, my ready money, and all other my writings, bonds, evidences, scripts, and muniments, which are to go to my executor. To my wife all goods and household stuff in my kitchen, bolting house, "woll" house, granary, or north end of my house of Fanton Haule aforesaid, and in my house in Kemps Crofts, also all my butter, cheese, bacon, and other provisions, all my calves, milk of my kine, and all my ewe sheep on my farm of Fanton Haule, and also free use of my mansion house, Fanton Haule, and my new house in Kemps Croft, etc., for a month after my decease, whereupon [various articles specified] are to be carried by my executor to Bonefelds *alias* Bonviles for my said wife. My said wife is to pay my executor £6 yearly for the premises [Bonefelds] and to enter into a bond, and, if she refuses, the legacy to her is to be void and my executor is to pay her 100 marks. To my brother Richard Lake, who dwells with me, pasture of one horse for life, my best black nag, and also his meat, lodging, washing, and entertainment for himself in my house for life. To Nicholas Stelewoman £21 left him by John James, late of Hockley, co. Essex, on the day appointed in the said will. To Dorothy Luther, daughter of Henry Luther, deceased, £20, and my wife is to educate her. To Elizabeth, Frances, and Joan Luther, the other daughters of the said Henry, £20 each, at the age of eighteen or marriage. To every godchild 2s. To Thomasine Drywood, dwelling with John Brooman of South Bemflette, £10, £4 thereof being what I owe her. To my cousins John and George Porter £10 each. To every one of my brothers' and sisters' children, except the said John and George Porter, the children of my brother Robert Lake, Richard Lake, the son of my brother Richard Lake, Joan Ducket, the wife of Robert Ducket, who owes me £20, the which I forgive him, and John Brooman of South Bemflette, to everyone of the other I give £5. To Simon Prisceley, my servant, a bullock and

sheep which were Robert Lone's, deceased, and £10. To every man and
maid servant, except those before and after named, 6s. 8d. To Richard
Lake, son of my brother Richard Lake, lands in Wickford and South
Hannyngfield which I late bought of Robert Vane of Sinocke, co. Kent.
To John Brooman of South Bemflette, my kinsman, my house and lands
in South Bemflette which I bought of Thomas Wyat, late of Thundersleye,
co. Essex. To Elizabeth Lone, daughter of Margaret Lone of Rayleigh,
widow, the houses, lands, etc., which I purchased of John Camber of Til-
burie; but Foulk Evans, tailor, is to have his free use and occupation of
all those rooms which he now has for life, without paying any rent for the
same, and Elizabeth Lone is to make a lease for twenty-one years to
Henry Julian which I have promised him. To Anne Castle, who dwells
with me, £10 at twenty years. To Anthony Lone, who dwells with me, £10
at twenty years, and my executor is to educate him in the meantime. My
tenement at Layndon called Nokes, which I late bought of Thomas Anger,
and the residue to John Lake of North Bemflette aforesaid, the son of my
brother Richard Lake, whom I make sole executor. Overseers: Mr. Edmund Reade of North Bemflette, Mr. Richard Mason, parson of Rawrethe,
and Mr. Thomas Jobie, parson of Thundersley, and they are to have 20s
each. Witnesses: William Harryes, Isaac Gilbert, Thomas Meredithe.
Proved by the executor 7 April 1597. (Commissary Court of London
for Essex and Herts.)

3. The Will of RICHARD LAKE of North Bemflette [North Benfleet],
co. Essex, dated 17 September 1599. To be buried in the church or
churchyard of North Bemflette. To the poor of the parish 5s. To every
godchild 12d. To every servant dwelling with my executor 12d. To my
brother William's wife 5s. To my sister Greene and my sister Cracknell
12d. each. To the children of George Reignolde which he had by my
daughter £10, to be paid to the said George for their use. To my son
Richard Lake £20. To my daughter Phennynge and her children £10
equally between them. To my daughter Lachyngdon and her children
£10 equally between them. To my son-in-law Thomas Lachyngdon all
the debts he owes me. To my daughter Joan Ducket and her children the
£21 which her husband Robert Ducket owes me, and to her two children
two of my best platters. To my son Richard Lake, to my daughters Margaret Phennynge and Sybille Lachyngdon, and to my executor my chest
of linen and certain pewter. To every one of my brothers' and sisters'
children 5s. Residue to my eldest son, John Lake, and he is to be executor. Witnesses: Edmund Portwaye and Thomas Meredithe. Proved by
the executor 11 October 1599. (Commissary Court of London for Essex
and Herts.)

4. The Will of JOHN LAKE of North Bemflet [North Benfleet], co.
Essex, yeoman, dated 29 November 1612. To be buried in such place as
my wife and friends shall think good. To the poor of North Bemflet 10s.
To the poor of Nevendon 10s. To Elizabeth, my wife, my manor of Little
Bastable Hall, now in the tenure of one Jeremy Rogers, during her natural
life, a third part, however, being reserved unto John Lake, my eldest son,
with all the quitrents and profits of the courts, and he is to pay a third part
yearly of the £28 which is due to be paid out of the said manor to my
sister Blage for her thirds, and my wife is to pay the rest. To my wife
Elizabeth all the household stuff in the said house of Bastable Hall, all the
bedding and furniture belonging to the bed in the parlor at Fanton Hall,
with one great chest and a trunk standing in the chamber over the parlor
and all that is in them, my gelding, three kine, ten sheep, and all the brass

and pewter. My wife shall have her dwelling with my son John during the term of Jeremy Rogers's lease of Bastable Hall, if she marrieth not, without paying anything either for her diet or dwelling, if she like thereof. Otherwise she is to have the house where Abraham Turke dwelleth to herself during the said term. To Richard Lake, my son, the lease of Bonfields, when he shall accomplish the full age of twenty-one, the bed, bedding, and furniture, as it stands in the chamber over the parlor, and one chest. To Thomas Lake, my son, my messuage and tenement called Jacat-Hoods [*sic*], in Basseldon, Fobing, and Vange, in the tenure of Edward Ivitt, and my wife is to have the use of the said land and the bringing up of my said son Thomas during his minority. To Elizabeth Paschall, my daughter, two kine, and to each of her sons, Andrew and Thomas Paschall, a sheep. To Sibell Bentten, my daughter, £100 and one cow or £3 in money, at her choice. To Tamsen Lake, my daughter, £100 at the age of eighteen or at marriage. To Anna Lake, my daughter, £100 at the age of eighteen or at marriage, and my executor shall bring up my said daughter Anna until she accomplish the age of sixteen, and my wife is to see her set to school at the charge of my executor. To Tebetha Lake, my brother Richard's daughter, 40s. at twenty-one. To all of my servants in my house 2s. each. Residue to John Lake, my son, whom I make sole executor. Overseers: Andrew Paschall and Andrew Bentten. Witnesses: Thomas Man, Abraham Turke, Robert Castell. Proved 30 January 1612/13. (Commissary Court of London for Essex and Herts.)

5. The Will of ANDREW PASCHALL of Nevendon, co. Essex, gentleman, dated 9 November 1613. To my wife Elizabeth my lands in Nevendon and Basseldon, and she is to bring up my son Andrew, allowing him for his maintenance and good education £20 a year, and, when he is twenty-one, the lands are to be divided between my said son and wife. If my wife does not marry again, she is to enjoy my mansion house; but, if she marries, my son is to have the same and all my lands, allowing my wife half the revenues and rents for life. To my sister Anne Reynoldes £30, if she makes no claim to any legacy left to her by her father. To my cousin Marie, daughter of my said sister, £10 at the age of twenty-one or at marriage. To the poor of Nevendon 10s. Residue to my wife Elizabeth, and she is to be sole executrix. Overseers: my kinsman Thomas Bretton of Laynedon, co. Essex, gentleman, and Thomas Man of South Bemfleet, yeoman. Witnesses: John Woode, John Browne, T. Gibbonson[?]. Proved 25 February 1613/14. (Commissary Court of London for Essex and Herts.)

6. The Will of ELIZABETH LAKE of Nevendon, co. Essex, dated 1 May 1616. To the poor of Basseldon 5s. To the poor of Nevendon 5s. To the poor of Northbenflet 5s. To my daughter Elizabeth Paschall 44s. To my daughter Sibell Benton 44s. To my daughter Tamson Lake £10. To my daughter Anne Lake £10, to be paid into the hands of John Lake, my son, upon this condition, that he shall pay for the education and bringing up of my daughter Anne from her age of sixteen years to her age of eighteen years. To my daughter Elizabeth Paschall my best gown. To my sister Slaterford 31s. To my servants Richard Woodly, Dorothy Sworder, and John Wood 2s. each. Residue to my son Thomas Lake, who is to be sole executor. Overseers: my sons John Lake and Richard Lake, to whom [I give] 22s. apiece. To each of my daughter Benten's children a sheep. To Andrew Paschall, my daughter's son, a sheep. To Anne Lake, my daughter, a trunk. To William Purland a lamb. Witnesses: Jeremy Rogers, Thomas Man, Thomas Playle. Proved 3 June 1616. (Commissary Court of London for Essex and Herts.)

7. The Will of ELIZABETH BRIDCAKE, widow, of Leigh, co. Essex, dated 10 July 1651. To my son Andrew Paschall 20s. To Cleere Paschall, his wife, 20s. To each of my said son's children now living, to wit, Andrew Paschall, Thomas Paschall, Cleere Paschall, and Elizabeth Paschall, and to John Bundocke and Elizabeth Bundocke, children of my daughter Cleere Bundocke, 40s. each. To Mr. Argor and his wife 20s. each. To my daughter Cleere Bundock my house I now dwell in for her life, then to her daughter Elizabeth, and, if Elizabeth die without issue, to her brother John Bundock. To Cleere Bundock all my goods, and what remains of them on her death to Elizabeth Bundock. Executors: my daughter Cleere Bundock and my cousin Mr. Thomas Harrison. Witnesses: Thomas Salmon, Anne Goodland, Thomas Fenner. "Since the sealing and subscribing by the executrix [sic, ? testatrix] her will is that her brother John Lake shall receave of her executors the summe of twenty shillings within three months after her decease." Proved 28 August 1651.

8. The Will of THOMAS LAKE of Nevendon, co. Essex, clerk, dated 18 February 1651/2. To my brother John Lake, for his life, my tenement and lands called Mangers *alias* Bacons, in Basseldon, which I late bought to me from one Thomas Dennys and Jeremy Croxton; and after the decease of my said brother the said tenement and lands are to go to my second son, John Lake, and to the heirs of his body, and, in default of such issue, to my youngest son, Peter Lake, and his heirs, and, in default of such issue, to my nephew Richard Lake, son of my late brother Richard Lake, deceased. To my son Peter Lake all my tenement and lands called Great Bradmore and Little Bradmore, in the parish of Stock, co. Essex, which I lately bought of my kinsman Richard Sandell, tailor. To my son Thomas £10 and my bedstead standing in the parlor of my dwelling house [and various other articles of furniture]. To my son John £60 [and various articles of furniture]. To Elizabeth Sandell, daughter of my cousin Richard Sandell, all my childbed linen. To my cousin Richard Sandell's other four children, namely, Thomas, Richard, Susan, and Eleanor, 20s. each. To my cousin Richard Sandell a silver-gilt cup, with a cover. To William Bushe of Nevendon 10s. To Richard Sandell a mortgage I have in lands in the parish of Downeham, belonging to one William Knightsbridge, for the use of my son Peter. Residue to my son Peter, and Richard Sandell is to be his guardian and my executor. Overseers: my brothers-in-law Robert Sumpter of Leaden Roodinge and Francis Sumpter of White Roodinge. Witnesses: Raphe Frithe, John Frithe.

Administration *cum testamento annexo* was granted to the overseers 8 April 1652, the executor having died before he took upon himself the execution of the said will. (P. C. C., Bowyer, 77.)

FROM PARISH REGISTERS

NORTH BENFLEET, CO. ESSEX, 1572–1635

Baptisms

1590   Johes Lake filius Johis Lake Juniors et Elizabethe ux 26 September.
1591   Elizabetha lake filia Johis et Elizabethe Lake   12 December.
1592   Sibilla Lake filia Johis et Elizabethe   11 February [1592/3].
1594   Richardus Lake filius Johis Lake Junioris et Elizabethe 18 November.
1596   Thomasina Lake filia Johis Lake et Elizabethe   14 October.
1597   Margareta Lake filia Johis Lake et Elizabethe   12 March [1597/8].
1600   Thomas Lake filius Johis Lake et Elizabethe   21 October.
1604   Anna Lake filia Johis Lake et Elizabethe   10 February [1604/5].

1618   Sarah Lake daughter of Richard Lake & Sarah his wife 13 September.

1620   Elizabeth Lake daughter of Richard Lake & Parnell his wife 10 August.

1621   Ann daughter of John Lake & Margaret his wife 3 July.

1622   Ann daughter of Richard Lake & Parnell his wife 1 July.

1623   Elizabeth daughter of John Lake & Marget his wife 5 June.

1624   Martha daughter of John Lake & Margaret his wife 20 July.

1629   Samuell sonne of John Lake & Margaret his wife 29 March.

1630   Elizabeth daughter of John Lake & Marget his wife 17 February [1630/1].

Marriages

1578   Willmus Dixon et Helena Crosson servientes Johis Lake 8 November.

1589   Johes Lake et Maria Castle de North Benfleet 28 April.

1591   Thomas Lachyngdon et Sibilla Lake 11 October.

1592   Robertus Ducket de Thundersley et Johanna Lake 10 April.

1597   Johannes Greene de Rawreth et Marie Lake 26 May.

Burials

1588   Elizabetha Lake ux Johis Lake 10 March [1588/9].

1590   Filius Johis Lake senioris aqua non renatus 9 March [1590/1].

1592   Robertus Lone gener Johis Lake 4 December.

1596   Johannes Lake senior 12 March [1596/7].

1599   Richardus Lake senior 24 September.

1608   Robertus Lake filius Johis Lake de Basselden 13 August.

1612   ―――― Lake 10 December.

1616   Elizabeth Lake Widdow 4 May.

1618   Sarah daur. of Richard Lake 5 October.

1622   Parnell the wife of Richard Lake 14 October.

1622   Sara the wife of Richard Lake seniore 17 December.

1623   Elizabeth daur. of John Lake 31 August.

1625   Rebecca Lake 4 October.

1629   Samuel Lake 19 March [1629/30].

Rayleigh, co. Essex

Baptisms

1579   Johne son of Johne Lake a joyner 12 April.

1580   Joane the daur. of Johne Lake 30 April.

Marriage

1576   Johne Lake and Sisbell Hedendon 22 September.

Runwell, co. Essex

Baptism

1574   Susan Lake daughter of Robert 22 August.

Marriage

1558   John Lake and Elizabeth Lone 3 February [1558/9].

Burials

1563   A servant of John Lake.

1574   Susan Lake daughter of Robert 8 October.

1598   Margaret Lake, infant, 24 July.

603

SOUTH BENFLEET, CO. ESSEX

Baptisms

1635 Elizabeth Lake daughter of John and ———— his wife 22 September.

1636. Emund [*sic*] Lake the base son of John Lake and Elsabeth Browne 26 March.

Burial

1636 Edmund the base son of John Lake and Elizabeth Browne 5 September.

WICKFORD, CO. ESSEX

Baptisms

1597 John Lake son of Richard Lake 19 February [1597/8].

1602 Mary Lake daughter of Richard Lake 6 March [1602/3].

1606 John Lake son of Richard Lake 24 August.

1607 Edward Lake son of Richard Lake 20 December.

1617 John Lake son of John Lake 6 July.

1618 Thomas Lake son of John Lake and Margaret 18 January [1618/19].

1620 Richard the son of John Lake of Northe Bemfleet and Margaret 21 May.

Burials

1599 Goodwyfe Lake 22 September.

1605 John Lake 17 July.

1606 John Lake 16 September.

1608 Edward Lake the sonne of Ric' Lake 13 February [1608/9].

1620 Richard Lake the sonne of John Lake & Margaret 22 May.

On the foregoing records the following short genealogy is based.

1. ———— LAKE, who lived in the first half of the sixteenth century, was the father of *at least* four sons and two daughters.

Children:

    i.   JOHN, of North Benfleet, co. Essex, the testator of 10 Dec. 1596 (Will No. 2), d. *s.p.*; bur. at North Benfleet 12 Mar. 1596/7; m. (1) at Runwell, co. Essex, 3 Feb. 1558/9, ELIZABETH LONE, probably a widow,* who was bur. at North Benfleet 10 Mar. 1588/9; m. (2) at North Benfleet, 28 Apr. 1589, MARY CASTLE, who m. (2) at North Benfleet, 26 May 1597, John Greene of Rawreth, co. Essex, and was living 17 Sept. 1599, when she was mentioned as "sister Greene" in the will of her brother-in-law, Richard Lake (Will No. 3).

            After his first marriage John Lake appears to have lived at Runwell, where one of his servants was buried in 1563. Between that date and 1578 he moved to North Benfleet, where he held the manors of Great Fanton and Boneviles and other property. Great Fanton Hall, a large farmhouse, was still standing in 1925. He also owned land in the neighboring parishes of Rayleigh, South Benfleet, Wickford, Laindon, and South Hanningfield.

            In his will, after the usual formal directions and charitable bequests, he makes John Lake, the son of his brother Richard, his chief heir and executor. Other legatees were his mother-in-law, Widow Castle, his brother Richard Lake, his nephews John Porter, George Porter, and John Brooman, the children of

—————
*Robert Lone, "son-in-law" (*gener*) of John Lake, was buried at North Benfleet 4 Dec. 1592.

his brother Robert Lake, Elizabeth Lone and Anthony Lone (doubtless related to his first wife), and various servants and persons of unspecified relationship.

2. ii. RICHARD.

iii. ROBERT, probably of Runwell, co. Essex, in 1574.
Children:
1. *Susan*, bapt. at Runwell 22 Aug. 1574; bur. there 8 Oct. 1574.
Other children, living 10 Dec. 1596, when they were legatees in the will of their uncle, John Lake (Will No. 2).

iv. WILLIAM, living 17 Sept. 1599, when his wife was a legatee in the will of his brother Richard (Will No. 3).

v. A DAUGHTER, m. —— PORTER.
Children (surname *Porter*):
1. *John,* } both legatees in the will of their uncle, John
2. *George,* } Lake, dated 10 Dec. 1596 (Will No. 2).

vi. A DAUGHTER, m. —— BROOMAN.
Child (surname *Brooman*):
1. *John,* of South Benfleet, co. Essex, 10 Dec. 1596, when he was a legatee in the will of his uncle, John Lake (Will No. 2).

vii. A DAUGHTER (perhaps). Richard Lake, in his will dated 17 Sept. 1599 (Will No. 3), leaves 12d. to his "sister Cracknell," who may have been a sister who had m. —— Cracknell or a sister-in-law.

2. RICHARD LAKE, of North Benfleet, co. Essex, the testator of 17 Sept. 1599 (Will No. 3), was buried at North Benfleet 24 Sept. 1599. He was apparently a widower, living with his brother John at Great Fanton Hall in 1596; and, as the very full parish registers of North Benfleet contain no baptismal records of his children, it is obvious that his married life was passed in another parish, possibly Rawreth, co. Essex.*

In his will he mentioned his brother William's wife, his "sister Greene" (the widow of his brother, John Lake), his "sister Cracknell," his sons John and Richard, his daughters Margaret Phennynge, Sybil Lachyngdon, and Joan Ducket, his son-in-law Robert Ducket, the children of his deceased daughter and George Reignolde, and the two children of his daughter Joan Ducket.
Children:

3. i. JOHN.

ii. RICHARD, a legatee in the will of his uncle, John Lake, dated 10 Dec. 1596 (Will No. 2), and in that of his father, dated 17 Sept. 1599 (Will No. 3); living 17 Dec. 1622; m. SARA ——, who was bur. at North Benfleet 17 Dec. 1622.
Children:†
1. *Tabitha,* under twenty-one on 29 Nov. 1612, when she was named as a legatee in the will of her uncle, John Lake (Will No. 4).
2. *Sarah,* bapt. at North Benfleet 13 Sept. 1618; bur. there 5 Oct. 1618.

*The registers of Rawreth have not been examined, as the financial demands of the present incumbent are prohibitive.

†The baptisms of four children of a Richard Lake, who was possibly identical with Richard Lake (2, ii), son of Richard, are recorded in the parish registers of Wickford, co. Essex. These four children were: 1. John, bapt. 19 Feb. 1597/8. 2. Mary, bapt. 6 Mar. 1602/3. 3. John, bapt. 24 Aug. 1606. 4. Edward, bapt. 20 Dec. 1607; bur. at Wickford 13 Feb. 1608/9.

iii. A DAUGHTER, d. on or before 17 Sept. 1599, when her husband and children are mentioned, as living, in her father's will (Will No. 3) ; m. GEORGE REIGNOLDE.

iv. MARGARET, a legatee, with her children, in her father's will, dated 17 Sept. 1599 (Will No. 3) ; m. before 17 Sept. 1599 —— PHENNYNGE.

v. SYBIL, a legatee, with her children, in her father's will, dated 17 Sept. 1599 (Will No. 3) ; m. at North Benfleet, 11 Oct. 1591, THOMAS LACHYNGDON, who was living 17 Sept. 1599.

vi. JOAN, a legatee, with her two children, in her father's will, dated 17 Sept. 1599 (Will No. 3) ; m. at North Benfleet, 10 Apr. 1592, ROBERT DUCKET of Thundersley, co. Essex, who was living 17 Sept. 1599.

3. JOHN LAKE (*Richard*), of Great Fanton Hall, North Benfleet, co. Essex, yeoman, the testator of 29 Nov. 1612 (Will No. 4), born probably about 1565, was buried at North Benfleet 10 Dec. 1612. He married ELIZABETH SANDELL, the testatrix of 1 May 1616 (Will No. 6), who was buried at North Benfleet 4 May 1616, whose family held the manor of Little Bastable, in the neighboring parish of Basildon, co. Essex, about 1589.

In addition to his inherited manors of Great Fanton and Boneviles in North Benfleet John Lake acquired from his wife's nephew, John Sandell, then living at Kempton, co. Herts, "all that manor of Litle Barstable Hall *alias* Bassildon Hall . . . in Bassildon, co. Essex, with all the lands thereto belonging . . . and all other its appurtenances in Bassildon, Vaynge and Fobbinge, co. Essex, . . . also three crofts containing forty acres called Sawyers in Bassildon . . . and two other parcels of land called Hockleyes and Undermundes in Vayinge" for the sum of £1,121 (Indenture of 1 Mar., 2 James I [1 Mar. 1604/5], Close Roll, 2 James I, C 54/1800). By his will Little Bastable went to his wife and his son John, with certain reservations to satisfy the dower of his "sister Blage" (the widow of his brother-in-law, Thomas Sandell, the testator of 10 Oct. 1593 [Will No. 1]), Boneviles was bequeathed to his son Richard, Jac-at-Hoods [*sic*], one of the Sandell properties in Basildon, Fobing, and Vange, to his son Thomas, while Great Fanton, the family homestead, went to John. Substantial legacies were made to his daughters Tamsen and Anna Lake and smaller ones to his daughters Elizabeth Paschall and Sybil Benton and his niece Tabitha Lake.

Elizabeth (Sandell) Lake, who at the time of her death was residing at Nevendon, co. Essex, the home of her daughter Elizabeth Paschall, made her son Thomas the executor of her will, and bequeathed to her sons John and Richard, her daughters Elizabeth Paschall, Sybil Benton, and Tamsen and Anne Lake, her grandson Andrew Paschall, her two Benton grandchildren, and her three servants.

Children, baptized at North Benfleet :

4. i. JOHN. bapt. 26 Sept. 1590.

ii. ELIZABETH, the testatrix of 10 July 1651 (Will No. 7), bapt. 12 Dec. 1591 ; d., a widow, between 10 July 1651 and 28 Aug. 1651, when her will was proved ; m. (1) ANDREW PASCHALL of Nevendon, co. Essex, gentleman, the testator of 9 Nov. 1613 (Will No. 5), who d. between that date and 25 Feb. 1613/14, when his will was proved; m. (2) JOHN BREADCAKE of Leigh, co. Essex, mariner, who d. in 1636, when he was in command of the ship *Thomas,* on a voyage to or from Gibraltar (Chancery Proceedings, Charles I, 15/45, Vassall *v.* Breadcake, 13 June 1637).

Andrew Paschall bequeathed to his wife Elizabeth, his son Andrew, his sister Anne Reynolds and her daughter Marie, his kinsman Thomas Bretton of Layndon [Laindon], co. Essex, and various servants.

Elizabeth (Lake) (Paschall) Breadcake left her estate to her children, Andrew Paschall and Clare Bundock, and her grandchildren. In a codicil to her will she mentioned her brother John Lake.

Child by first husband (surname *Paschall*) :

1. *Andrew,* m. Clare ———. Both were living 10 July 1651, when his mother made her will, and they had four children then living, viz., Andrew, Thomas, Clare, and Elizabeth Paschall.

Child by second husband (surname *Breadcake*) :

2. *Clare,* m. ——— Bundock. She was living, with two children, John and Elizabeth Bundock, 10 July 1651, when her mother made her will.

iii. SYBIL, bapt. 11 Feb. 1592/3; living 1 May 1616, when she and her two children are legatees in her mother's will; m. before 29 Nov. 1612, the date of her father's will, ANDREW BENTON.

iv. RICHARD, bapt. 18 Nov. 1594; d. before 18 Feb. 1651/2, when his brother Thomas, in his will (Will No. 8), left a reversionary interest in the Basildon property to his (Thomas's) nephew Richard Lake, son of his (Thomas's) late brother, Richard Lake; m. before 1620 PARNELL ———, who was bur. at North Benfleet 14 Oct. 1622. He was probably the "out-dweller," Richard Lake, who was recorded in 1636 in the Essex Ship-Money Returns as owning property at Laindon Hills.

Children :

1. *Richard,* living 18 Feb. 1651/2, when he was mentioned in the will of his uncle, Rev. Thomas Lake (Will No. 8).

2. *Elizabeth,* bapt. at North Benfleet 10 Aug. 1620.

3. *Anne,* bapt. at North Benfleet 1 July 1622.

v. THOMASINE (TAMSEN), bapt. 14 Oct. 1596; living unm. 1 May 1616, when her mother made her will.

vi. MARGARET, bapt. 12 Mar. 1597/8; probably d. young, as she was not mentioned in her father's will, dated 29 Nov. 1612. Perhaps she was the Margaret Lake, infant, who was bur. at Runwell, co. Essex, 24 July 1598.

vii. REV. THOMAS, A.B. (University of Cambridge, 1621/2), A.M. (*ib.,* 1625), the testator of 18 Feb. 1651/2 (Will No. 8), bapt. 21 Oct. 1600; d. between 18 Feb. 1651/2 and 8 Apr. 1652, when administration on his estate, *cum testamento annexo,* was granted to the overseers named in his will; m. ——— SUMPTER, who d. before her husband made his will.

He was admitted a pensioner at Peterhouse College, Cambridge, 7 July 1618, and matriculated the same year. He was ordained deacon at Peterborough 21 Dec. 1623 and priest on the following day. He was probably the Thomas Lake who was living at Laindon, co. Essex, in 1636, where were also members of the Sumpter family, as recorded in the Essex Shop-Money Returns. In 1638 he was presented to the living (vicarship) of Leyton, co. Essex, by Lady Lake, widow of Sir Thomas Lake of Stanmore, co. Middlesex,* and in 1645 he was sequestered to the

*Lady Lake (Mary Ryder) was a daughter and coheiress of Sir William Ryder, Knight, who was Lord Mayor of London in 1600; and from him she inherited the manor and advowson of Leyton. Her husband, Sir Thomas Lake, Knight, M.A., who was born about 1567

rectory of Wickford, co. Essex, the incumbent, Rev. Charles Grey, being a prisoner of the Parliamentary forces. Lake was summonsed for examination as to his fitness by the Assembly of Divines, but relinquished the rectory, which was thereupon sequestered to the use of Rev. John Banning. (Cf. Venn's The Book of Matriculations and Degrees . . . in the University of Cambridge from 1544 to 1659, Venn's Alumni Cantabrigienses, and Proceedings of the Committee on Plundered Ministers, 1644/5 [British Museum, Additional MSS., 15669, folios 150b, 160b, 172b].)

In his will he styled himself of Nevendon, co. Essex, clerk, bequeathed to his brother John Lake, his sons Thomas, John, and Peter Lake, his nephew Richard Lake (son of his late brother, Richard Lake), his cousin Richard Sandell, and Richard Sandell's five children, viz., Elizabeth, Thomas, Richard, Susan, and Eleanor, and appointed Richard Sandell his executor and his brothers-in-law, Robert Sumpter and Francis Sumpter, overseers.

Children:
1. *Thomas*, living 18 Feb. 1651/2, when their father made
2. *John*, his will.
3. *Peter,* a minor 18 Feb. 1651/2, when his father made his will.

viii. ANNE, bapt. 10 Feb. 1604/5; a legatee in the will of her father, dated 29 Nov. 1612 (Will No. 4), and in that of her mother, dated 1 May 1616 (Will No. 6).

4. JOHN LAKE (*John, Richard*), of Great Fanton Hall, North Benfleet, co. Essex, baptized at North Benfleet 26 Sept. 1590, was living in 1657, but died before 18 Jan. 1661/2 (*vide infra*). He married, about 1616, MARGARET READE, born 11 July 1598 and baptized at North Benfleet 16 July 1598, died at Ipswich, Mass., between 30 Aug. 1672, when her will was dated, and 24 Sept. 1672, when it was proved, daughter of Edmund and Elizabeth (Cooke) Reade of Wickford and North Benfleet, co. Essex.*

John Lake was a legatee in the will of his uncle, Thomas Sandell, dated 10 Oct. 1593 (Will No. 1), was named as residuary legatee and executor in the will of his father, dated 29 Nov. 1612 (Will No. 4), was mentioned and named as overseer in the will of his mother, dated 1 May 1616 (Will No. 6), was a legatee in the will of his sister, Elizabeth Breadcake, dated 10 July 1651 (Will No. 7), and was a beneficiary in the will of his brother, Rev. Thomas Lake, dated 18 Feb. 1651/2 (Will No. 8). By an indenture dated 4 June 1622 he sold Little Bastable Hall and its appurtenant properties in Basildon, Fobbing, and Vange, co. Essex, to Richard Chester of Leigh, co. Essex (Close Roll, 20 James I). It would seem that he disposed also of the North Benfleet manors before 1636, as his name does not appear in the North Benfleet list of landowners in the Essex Ship-Money Returns in that year. He was prob-

and died in 1630, was a son of Almeric Lake of Southampton, co. Hants, and a brother of Right Rev. Arthur Lake, M.A., D.D., Bishop of Bath and Wells, 1616–1626. Sir Thomas Lake was made Clerk of the Signet by Queen Elizabeth about 1600, was knighted by James I in 1603, and was a Member of Parliament in 1604, 1614, 1625, and 1626, Privy Councillor in 1614, and Secretary of State in 1616. There was probably no relationship between him and the Lake family of North Benfleet. The statement in Alumni Cantabrigienses that the patron of Leyton, in 1638, was a Lake of the Wilston family, in Tring, co. Herts, is incorrect.

Vide supra, p. 113, for Reade entries from the parish registers of North Benfleet.

ably the Mr. Lake who was recorded as of Basildon in this same return.

Sometime between between 1631 and 1635 John Lake's wife, Mrs. Margaret (Reade) Lake, left him and emigrated with her sisters and their families to New England, taking with her her two daughters, Ann and Martha Lake. For many years she lived in the family of her brother-in-law, Gov. John Winthrop, Jr., at New London, Conn., and is mentioned repeatedly in the Winthrop family correspondence. The last decade of her life was spent at Ipswich, Mass., the home of her daughter, Martha (Lake) Harris, and of her brother-in-law, Deputy Gov. Samuel Symonds. In 1654 Rev. Hugh Peter, Mrs. Lake's stepfather, wrote from London to John Winthrop, Jr.: "John Lake is alive and lusty;" and in 1657 he stated to the same correspondent: "John Lake live[s] still." * In 18 Jan. 1661/2 Mrs. Lake wrote from Wenham, Mass., to her brother-in-law, Governor Winthrop, who was in London: "Might I not bee to troublesome to you I would have desired yors. to have done mee yt courtesy as to have inquired concerning my husbands death, & how hee ended his dayes, as also to have inquired of my cousen Thomas Cooke, whether hee knew whether their was any thing left mee or no. . . . I would desire you inquire whether my sister Breadcale [sic] who dwells in Lee [Leigh], in Essex, bee liveing. You may heare of her, if liveing, at Irongate where boats weekly come from Lee."† No will of John Lake has been found. His widow in her will, dated 30 Aug. 1672, left her property to her daughters Hannah Gallop and Martha Harris, and to her grandchildren.‡

Children:

i. JOHN, bapt. at Wickford 6 July 1617; mentioned in the will of his grandfather, Edmund Reade of Wickford, dated 20 Nov. 1623;§ probably that son of John and Margaret (Reade) Lake who was mentioned as dead by Mrs. Lucy Downing, when she wrote, on 30 Jan. 1657/8, from Edinburgh to Fitz John Winthrop: "Your uncle, Collonell Reade, was, a month or two since, with us, . . . and [said] that God had takne [sic] a sonn of his sister Lackes that was with him, and was very hopefull for further preferment."||

ii. THOMAS, bapt. at Wickford 18 Jan. 1618/19, of whom nothing further has been discovered.

iii. RICHARD, bapt. at Wickford 21 May 1620; bur. there 22 May 1620.

iv. ANN (called HANNAH in New England records), bapt. at North Benfleet 3 July 1621; migrated with her mother to New England; m. about 1642 CAPT. JOHN GALLOP, who had served in the Pequot War in 1637 and was killed in the Narragansett Swamp Fight in King Philip's War, 19 Dec. 1675, son of John and Christabel Gallop of Boston, Mass. They lived successively in Boston, New London, Conn., and Stonington, Conn. Ten children.

*See *Collections of the Massachusetts Historical Society*, Fourth Series, vol. 6, p. 115, and vol. 7, p. 204 (The Winthrop Papers).
†*Ib.*, Fifth Series, vol. 1, p. 99 (The Winthrop Papers).
‡Probate Records of Essex County (Mass.), vol. 2, p. 289.
§Cf. Ancestry of Priscilla Baker, by the late William Sumner Appleton, 1870, p. 119.
||*Collections of the Massachusetts Historical Society*, Fifth Series, vol. 1, p. 44 (The Winthrop Papers). Col. Thomas Reade was the Parliamentary governor of Stirling Castle.

<ol type="i" start="5">
<li>ELIZABETH, bapt. at North Benfleet 5 June 1623; bur. there 31 Aug. 1623.</li>
<li>MARTHA, bapt. at North Benfleet 20 July 1624; migrated with her mother to New England; living in 1687, when her husband made his will; m. at Ipswich, 15 Nov. 1647, THOMAS HARRIS of Ipswich, son of Thomas Williams *alias* Harris of Winnisimet and Elizabeth, his wife. Eight children.</li>
<li>SAMUEL, bapt. at North Benfleet 29 Mar. 1629; bur. there 19 Mar. 1629/30.</li>
<li>ELIZABETH, bapt. at North Benfleet 17 Feb. 1630/1; probably d. in infancy.</li>
</ol>

LEVERETT. — In Savage's Genealogical Dictionary of New England, vol. 3, p. 84, a list is given of thirteen children of Elder Thomas[1] Leverett of Boston, Mass., with the dates of their baptisms in Boston, co. Lincoln, Eng. This list of baptisms is said to have been sent to Gov. John[2] Leverett by a friend as an attested copy of the entries in the registers of the English Boston. Of these thirteen children Savage believed that all but the third, fourth, and sixth died young, for it is known that only John, Jane, and Anne are found in New England records. The attention of the Editor has been called to the printed parish registers of Boston, Eng., 1557–1638, recently published by the Lincoln Record Society; and from them it is possible to correct a few errors in the dates as given by Savage and to supply the burial records of eight of the thirteen children, the two sons Thomas and James being still unaccounted for. The printed registers show also that the wife of Elder Thomas Leverett was Anne Fitche, and not Anne Fisher, as the name is given in the Leverett Memorial (Boston, 1856), p. 24, and in the pedigree facing p. 289 of vol. 12 of the REGISTER. The facts disclosed by the Leverett entries in the parish registers of Boston, Eng., prior to 1639, are as follows:

Christenings

1612 John son of Thomas Leveritt gent' 16 August.
1613 Jane daughter of Tho. Leuerett 9 August.
1614 Jane daughter of Thomas Leveritt 6 January [1614/15].
1616 John son of Thomas Leverit gent' 7 July.
1618 Thomas son of Thomas Leverit gent' 30 July.
1619 Anne daughter of Thomas Leveret gent' 9 January [1619/20].
1621 James son of Thomas Leveret 28 June.
1622 Sara daughter of Thomas Leveret 26 September.
1623 Marie daughter of Thomas Leveret 5 February [1623/4].
1627 Jabes son of Thomas Leveret 6 September.
1628 Israell son of Thomas Leverett 25 September.
1630 Elisha son of Thomas Leveret gent' 3 July.
1632 Nathaniell son of Thomas Leveritt gent 12 April.

Marriages

1596 [Mr.]† John Anderson and [M'ris]† Jane Leveritt 7 October.
1610 Thomas Leveritt and Anne Fitche 29 October.

Burials

1612 John son of Thomas Leveryt 9 January [1612/13].
1613 Jane daughter of Thomas Leverett 10 August.
1623 Marie daughter of Thomas Leveret 27 February [1623/4].
1624 Sara daughter of Thomas Leveret 14 February [1624/5].
1629 Issraell son of Thomas Leveret 3 July.
1630 Jabes son of Thomas Leveret [gent']* 15 February [1630/1].
1630 Elisha son of Thomas Leveret gent' 12 March [1630/1].
1632 Nathaniell son of Thomas Leveritt aldermant† 22 November.

† The word in brackets is an addition from the Bishop's transcripts of the parish registers.

THOMAS LEVET OF EXETER AND HAMPTON

By Victor Channing Sanborn, Esq., of Kenilworth, Ill.

A surprising fact about the early settlers of New England is that so few records were kept of their English homes and ancestry. Where no identifying record has survived three centuries of time, a connection can often be traced through neighbors and friends in the first twenty years of sojourn here. But sometimes an early immigrant cannot thus be linked with a group. Then, unless the family name be uncommon, the search for English ancestry is blind indeed.

The name of Levet is not uncommon, and there is some doubt whether a connection exists between Thomas Levet of Exeter and Hampton and any group of early New England settlers. Thomas Levet was born in 1616, as appears from his death record and from a deposition of his, made in 1676 in the case of Drake v. Colcord (Mass. Ct. Assts., File No. 1566). He was thus born in the same year as William Wentworth, Christopher Lawson, and Edward Rishworth. He is first found among the signers of John Wheelwright's Exeter Combination of 1639, where his name appears between those of James Wall and Edmund Littlefield. For we must regretfully abandon belief in the Wheelwright Deed of 1629, where the name of "Thomas Levitt" appears as a grantee, with Wheelwright, Augustin Storre his brother-in-law, Thomas Wight, and William Wentworth. This fraudulent deed was brought forward in 1707 to support the anti-Masonian claims, but its only genealogical use is to connect the grantees, between whom a relationship was doubtless at that early date known to exist.

In tracing the English ancestry of our Thomas Levet, three clues present themselves: (1) The tradition connecting him with Wheelwright, the Hutchinsons, and Wentworth. (Wentworth Genealogy, vol. 1, p. 76.) (2) What is known of other early Levets in New England. (3) The affidavit of Abraham and Nathaniel Drake in 1691, that Colchester, co. Essex, was the English home of Levet's wife and, perhaps, of Levet himself. (Register, vol. 21, p. 316.)

The Wheelwright-Hutchinson tradition points to Lincolnshire, since that county furnished the entire Wheelwright connection. Lincolnshire is singularly lacking in Levets, though a few references to the name are found. The will of John Hutchinson in 1644 mentions his "sister Levitt," and Ralph Levet was a witness (Register, vol. 20, pp. 362–363). * This led Col. Chester and Hon. John Wentworth to believe that our Thomas was a son of this Ralph Levet. But Canon Maddison found in the Bilsby transcript the marriage of "Ralfe Levit and Anne Hutchinson" on 25 Jan. 1631/2. Doubtless this Ralph Levet was rector of Grainsby, Lincolnshire, in 1635, and belonged to the Melton line, as we shall see. He was the father of Francis Levet, rector of Little Carlton, mentioned in the next paragraph. But he could hardly have been the father of our Thomas Levet, who was born in 1616.

In Suffolk Deeds, book 10, fo. 215, is a deed from John Wheelwright, 22 Oct. 1677, conveying to Richard Crispe all his messuage in Mawthorp, parish of Willoughby, Lincs, and lands in Burnethorpe and Hog-

*Pp. 454-455, this volume.

strope, which were in the tenure of John Banister, and were purchased of Francis Levet, gent., of North Willingham, Lincs. This seemed a distinct clue, but the registers of North Willingham contain no Levet entries. Francis Levet, undoubtedly the son of Ralph of Grainsby, was rector of Little Carlton, Lincs, from 1662 to 1711. This was a Hutchinson and Thorndike parish. (REGISTER, vol. 51, pp. 120 *et seq.*) The transcripts of Great and Little Carlton have been searched, and from 1662 to 1710 those for Little Carlton are signed "Fran: Levet, rector." They show that "Francis Levett, Clerke, and Elizabeth Marris" were married 10 Dec. 1662. Their children were:

i. ELIZABETH, bapt. at Great Carlton 15 Dec. 1663.
ii. ANNE, bapt. at Little Carlton 11 Aug. 1667.
iii. RALPH, bapt. at Little Carlton 18 Feb. 1669; bur. 10 May 1674.
iv. MARY, bapt. at Little Carlton 9 Mar. 1670/1; m. at Great Carlton 22 Feb. 1693/4 RICHARD OGLE.
v. THOMAS, bapt. at Little Carlton 1 May 1673; bur. 5 May 1673.
vi. RICHARD, bapt. at Little Carlton 14 Feb. 1673/4; bur. 16 Feb. 1673/4

On 18 Feb. 1673/4 Elizabeth, wife of Francis Levet, was buried; and 3 July 1711 "Mr. Francis Levett, Rect^r," was buried. The will of Francis Levet is filed at Lincoln (vol. for 1711, fo. 60), and in it he leaves bequests to his three sons-in-law, Michael Johnson, William Eldinor, and John Harrison, and to his Johnson and Eldinor grandchildren. The will is sealed with the arms of the Melton Levetts.

A few scattered notes exist of other Lincolnshire Levets. The will of Robert Levitt of Lincoln in 1565 gives nothing of value, unless the bequest to Isabella Symkinson connects this Levitt with the Doncaster Simpkinsons. James Levit was ordained deacon by Thomas Cooper, Bishop of Lincoln, in 1583. At Foston and Allington in southern Lincolnshire was a family of Lovetts, which can be traced for a generation or two, but this gives no apparent clue.

William Wentworth of Exeter came from Lincolnshire, but was descended from the Yorkshire line. Near their ancestral home lived a Yorkshire family of Levetts, belonging to the lesser landed gentry, seated at Normanton for some generations, and acquiring in the fifteenth century a fair estate, though not the manor, at High Melton. These Normanton and Melton Levetts intermarried with the Wentworths. Their pedigree* appeared in the Visitation of Yorkshire of 1612, and is printed in Hunter's Deanery of Doncaster. It has been amplified by a descendant, Mr. Milner-Gibson-Cullum, in 3 *Miscellanea Genealogica et Heraldica*, vol. 1,† and is in part as follows:

* It would seem possible to construct a pedigree of the Normanton and Melton Levetts extending two centuries farther back than the pedigree printed herein. Thus we find in 1249 a Hamond de Lyvet. In 1272-1307 lived a Nicholas de Lyvet, who held from John de Vesci the manor of Hooton, later Hooton-Levet, as well as fees in Wickersley and Pickburn; he is mentioned in Kirkby's Quest. In 1327 we find a William Levet of Hooton-Levet, who married Constantia, daughter of Roger de Wickersley and granddaughter of Richard fitz Turgis, who with John de Busli founded the Cistercian Abbey of Roche. In 1377 John Levet, son and heir of William Levet, sold to Richard Barry of London all his ancestral rights in Roche Abbey. In 1392 lived William Levet of Tylse, who was a feoffee of Thomas de Barley. In 1420 William Levet and Elizabeth his wife lived in Hooton-Levet. These Levets sold Hooton-Levet to the Cliffords, and perhaps removed to Normanton, where we find a William Levet who was admitted in 1447 to be a tenant of the prior of St. John of Jerusalem. He it is who heads the pedigree of the Normanton and Melton Levetts.

† Many records also of this family, including (in a somewhat different form) some, but not all, of the abstracts given below on pp. 69-70, have been communicated to the same volume by Mr. Milner-Gibson-Cullum.

LEVETT OF NORMANTON AND MELTON, YORKSHIRE

ARMS.—Sable, a fess battled on both sides between three leopards' heads erased argent.

WILLIAM LEVETT of Normanton, 1477 = ——

WILLIAM LEVETT = Elizabeth, dau. and ROBERT ELIZABETH, m.
of Normanton, 1480, and | coheir of Robert Thomas Gargrave,
of Melton, *jure uxoris*, 1488 | Syward of Melton father of Sir
Thomas

WILLIAM LEVETT = Anne, dau. of
of Normanton and Melton | John Barnby

WILLIAM LEVETT = Elizabeth, dau. and coheir
of Normanton and Melton, b. abt. 1500; | of William Wentworth
d. 1576; bur. at Sprotborough of Sprotborough

NICHOLAS LEVETT = Anne, dau. of
of Normanton and Melton, b. abt. 1520; | Ralph Westby
d. 1598; bur. at Rotherham of Ravenfield

RALPH LEVETT = Elizabeth, dau. of ANNE, JANE
of Normanton and Melton, | George West of m. Francis
b. abt. 1545; d. 1581; | Barnborough and Hallom
bur. at Melton Aughton

THOMAS LEVETT = Elizabeth, dau. WILLIAM, bapt. 1574;
of Melton, | of Robert m. Elizabeth (Vickars
bapt. 1572; d. | Mirfin of or Wray) Sheppard;
1623; bur. at | Thurcroft d. *s. p.* 1638;
Melton lived at Bentley

ROBERT, bapt. 1576; = Frances, dau. of CATHERINE, bapt. 1578;
d. 1655; bur. at | John Nalson m. Wm. Strelley
Normanton of Snydale
GERTRUDE, b. 1580;
a quo the Levetts d. 1585
and Hansons of
Normanton ELIZABETH, m.
John Morley

THOMAS LEVETT = Margaret,* RALPH, = Anne, dau. of
of Tixover, Rutland, | dau. of John bapt. 1600, | Edward Hutchinson
bapt. 1594 | Lindley of Rector of | of Alford
Leathley Grainsby

FRANCIS LEVET, =
Rector of Little Carlton |

JOHN, = Mary, dau. and PETER, JANE, b. 1607; m.
LL.D. | coheir of b. abt. 1611; Andrew Goodhand
Emmanuel d. 1672; of Lincolnshire;
Mote of Vicar of d. 1627
Melton Cantley

THOMAS LEVET of
Exeter and Hampton

* This match is given by Brooke and Hunter; but I think that the husband of Margaret Lindley was really Thomas Levett of Sussex, who died at East Betchworth, Surrey, in 1616, leaving a will (P. C. C., Cope, 118) and a widow Margaret, sole executrix.

The last Levetts living at Melton were the children of the Thomas Levett who died in 1623. An abstract of his will follows, together with the answer of his son John to a Chancery bill, showing what became of the Melton lands.

The Will of THOMAS LEVETT of High Melton, gent., 7 October 1622. I give to my wife Elizabeth £40, over and above her portion of my goods. To Thomas Levett my son and heir apparent all glass and seeling in or about my house at Melton. To Ralph Levitt my second son £20, to be paid within one month after he shall commence Maister of Arts in one of the Universities of Cambridge or Oxford. And whereas I have a spetiall desire to have my two younger sons, John Levett and Peter Levett, to be educated and brought up at their books, whereby they be furnished with knowledge and learning to become profitable members in God's Church or the commonwealth of this land; I do hereby pray and desire my said wife, my eldest son Thomas, and my second son Ralfe to be aiding and assisting to the said John and Peter therein. And therefore, rather to allure them to their books and to assist them in their studie, I do bequeath to the said John Levett £20, to be paid to him w^thin one month after he shall take the degree of Maister of Arts in Cambridge or Oxford. [Same bequest to Peter Levett.] To my daughter Jaine Levett £40, over and besides her portion. The bequests to my three younger sons to be raised out of lands in Cadeby purchased of Richard Waterhouse. If this devise be insufficient in law, then I do require my eldest son to consider how chargeable his own education hath been to me and how much to the hindrance of his younger brethren's preferment, and therefore I do pray him to give way to this devise. My wife to be executrix. My brethren Robert Mirfin of Thurcroft and William Levett of Bentley to be supravisors. To my good friend Henry Saxton,* clerke, 10s., in thankful remembrance of God's blessing by him as a secondary cause in the indoctrinating of my children. Proved 1 May 1623. (York Wills, vol. 37, fo. 234.)

WHITAKER v. FITZWILLIAMS, LEVETT et al., bill dated 26 October 1653: Thomas Whitaker, exr. will of John Whitaker, late of Melton-on-the-Hill, complains that John Levett, Dr. of Lawes, being seized of a capital messuage there, did on May 10, 1638, lease the same to the said John Whitaker for 21 years at £61 pr. ann. The said John Whitakers did continue tenant and much improved sd. farme and continued to pay his rent until he understood that the said Dr. Levett had conveyed the reversion thereof to Richard Berry, Dr. in Phisicke, since decd., after wch time he did with the consent of Dr. Levett pay the rent to Dr. Berry. Sd. John Whitakers made his will and appointed your orator and John Whitacers his son exrs. and demised to your orator sd. farme and your orator pd. rent to Dr. Berry. Dr. Berry, dying about June, 1651, demised sd. farme to John Fountaine, Esq^e † and since then your orator has pd. rent to sd. Fountaine, saving that sometimes by consent of Dr. Levett, Dr. Berry, and Fountaine your orator and his father pd. to Thomas Fitzwilliams of Doncaster £16 pr. ann., the interest on £200, lent on some small pt. of the farme by sd. Fitzwilliams. And after the death of his sd. father, your orator being an illiterate person brought up only to husbandry, the sd. Fitzwilliams, being an attorney and often Under Sheriff for the County of York, repaired to your orator and required him to seale some writings, which he said were only to secure the payment of sd. interest; but now he pretendeth they are bonds wh. he threatens to put in suit. The sd. Fitzwilliams did combine with the said Dr. Levett (who married Mary, one of the daughters and coheires of Emmanuel Mote decd.) and with Anne and Dorothy Mote, two other daughters of sd. Emmanuel Mote, so that Feb. 13, 1651, a bill was drawn by which the said Anne and Dorothy Mote claimed that the sd. Emmanuel Mote was seized in fee of the manor of Melton and of this farme; and upon the marriage of the sd. Mary to Dr. Levett, and his agreement to pay £500 to sd. Anne and Dorothy, the premises were settled on the sd. Dr. Levett; but the sd. Anne and Dorothy lately discovered that on July 30, 1635, their father conveyed the premises to sd. Fitzwilliams for £200. Prays writ of subpœna commanding defts. to appear and set forth the truth, etc.

* Henry Saxton was vicar of Conisbrough from 1615 to 1665 and is buried in Conisbrough church.
† John Fountayne of Melton married Elizabeth, daughter of Major John Monkton and a grand-niece of Dr. Richard Berry.

Answer of John Levet, Dr. of Lawes, one of the defendants, 9 February 1653/4: Defendant did at the time mentioned in the Bill believe that he was seized of the capital messuage and lands expressed in the Bill as in fee; for he did not know that Mr. Emmanuel Mote had mtgd. any part of them to the defendant Mr. Thomas Fitzwilliams; and deft. believeth that John Whittakers, compts.' father, was privy to the mortgage. The deft. leased said lands, etc., to the said John Whittakers, who continued as such tenant until such time as Doctor Berrie got his interest in it. The deft. upon trust and agreement with the said Dr. Berrie (then a great professor of his love to the Levets for Mr. Thomas Levet's sake, to whom he did acknowledge himself beholden for the greater part of his fortunes) did make a conveyance of his manors and lands in Melton (a part being the said messuage and lands) with other lands in Cadeby, Wildethorpe, and Bentley, unto the said Dr. Berrie for the securing of what money he had lent the deft. or his brother Thomas Levet, which loans were about £3300. And for the purchase of the said lands (in Melton only) deft. had £10,000 proffered him by Arthur Ingram the elder, as also by Sir John Melton, and indeed had sold them to the latter, but afterwards because he could not get his moneys in the sd. Sir John desisted from perfecting the purchase. After, the said Dr. Berry (contrary to the trust reposed in him) enrolled the conveyance and endeavored to eject deft., etc., and John Fountayne has ejected the Deft. (Chancery Proceedings, 1649–1714, Bundle 17, Bridges.)

Thomas Levett, the eldest son and heir of Melton, matriculated at Lincoln College, Oxford, in 1610, and proceeded B.A. 1612/13. In 1621 he was entered as a barrister at Lincoln's Inn, and he was still of Lincoln's Inn in 1626. According to Foster's Alumni Oxonienses he was B.C.L. of Orleans University, 1626.

The Calendars of State Papers (Domestic), James I, vol. 11, p. 438, contain an interesting letter from Matthew Dodsworth to Dr. More, dated 3 Jan. 1624/5. Matthew Dodsworth was chancellor to the Puritan Archbishop Toby Mathew of York, and was father of Roger Dodsworth the antiquary. Perhaps Dr. More was Robert More, Puritan vicar of Guisley, whose daughter married Capt. Christopher Levett. The letter states that Dodsworth is willing to accede to Dr. More's wish "that Thomas Levett, student of Civil Law, may share his patent as Judge of the Admiralty in the Northern Counties, being an able and honest man. It is said that the offices of Chancellor and Commissary of the Archbishop of York are now for the Tyme disposed of, but they say they are settled in trust for Mr. Levett, as they lately were for Sir Tobie Mathew" [the Archbishop's son]. Before 1633 Thomas Levett had moved to Tixover, co. Rutland, a small hamlet in the smallest county of England. Here, on 21 May 1633, he sued Richard Bullingham of Ketton (Chancery Proceedings, Series 2, Bundle 408, No. 95). Bullingham was the grandson of Bishop Bullingham, and had sold the tithes of Ketton to Levett for twenty-one years, but had previously charged the premises with certain payments, unknown to Levett. In 1639–40 Thomas Levett was high sheriff of Rutlandshire. The State Papers (Domestic), Charles I, vol. 15, p. 465, contain the following abstract of a letter from him to the Council, dated 17 Feb. 1639/40:

" Upon December 20 I received instructions for levying the ship money: and, on January 20, the Lords' second letter, requesting me to pay by February 20 such moneys as I should by that time have collected. I have lain sick here in London since Martinmas (November 11): Nevertheless I have by my agents been framing my assessment, and, I hope, by diligence, to bring in the whole money for my small county by April 1st."

Thomas Levett of Tixover is said in all the printed pedigrees to have married a daughter of John Lindley of Leathley. It is certain that in 1613 Margaret, the only daughter of this John Lindley, was married to

"Thomas Levit, Esq.," who is named as son-in-law and supervisor in John Lindley's will, dated 31 May 1613 and proved 30 June 1614. (York Wills, vol. 33, fo. 144.) If this were Thomas of Tixover, it was an early marriage, for he was but nineteen at the date of the will, and had taken his B.A. at Oxford only very recently, on 8 Feb. 1612/13. But this marriage of 1613 would permit the birth of our Thomas Levet in 1616. In connection with Rutlandshire it is significant that this will of John Lindley mentions his "cousin Sir Guy Palmes," who represented Rutlandshire seven times in Parliament from 1614 to 1640. Arthur Lindley, the oldest son of John Lindley, married a daughter of Sir John Garrard, Lord Mayor of London. Two of her sisters married Lincolnshire men, one Sir John Reade of Wrangle, and the other Francis Hamby of Tathwell. It is curious to note that the granddaughter of this Arthur Lindley married the son and heir of Robert Hitch, Dean of York, and thus a grandson of Capt. Christopher Levett, the explorer.

Hunter's Deanery of Doncaster states that Roger Dodsworth, the antiquary, "was intimate with Levett of Tixover, who gave him a Chartulary of the Cluniacs of Pontefract." This was the Chartulary of St. John of Pontefract, published by the Yorkshire Archæological Society. On this volume, in Dodsworth's own hand, is the record that it came to him "ex dono Tomae Levett de High Melton, in anno 1626-7." Probably Thomas Levett died at Tixover before 1655, for in Dugdale's Monasticon, of which the first edition was printed in 1655, is an abstract of a deed concerning Roche Abbey with this caption, "ex autographo penes Thomam Levet nuper de Tikesover in com. Rutland." The parish registers of Tixover were included with those of Ketton up to 1740. These have been searched, but no reference to Thomas Levett has been found. The registers have suffered much from damp, and the ink is so faint that many pages could not be deciphered.

John Levett, third son of Thomas Levett of Melton, was born about 1605. He was admitted pensioner at Christ's College, Cambridge, in 1623. Peile's Register states that he had studied at Conisbrough and Haughton. He proceeded LL.D. in 1633 (*per lit. reg.*), and became a somewhat celebrated lawyer at York, but he seems always to have been financially embarrassed. In 1636 he married Mary, daughter and coheir of Emmanuel Mote, who owned the manor of Melton. Through this marriage John Levett acquired a considerable estate, including the manors of Melton and Bentley, charged with payments to the sisters of his wife. A collection of abstracts of deeds in *Topographer and Genealogist*, vol. 3, pp. 519–526, shows that by 1637 John Levett had sold Bentley manor to Sir Arthur Ingram, who in turn sold it to Bryan Cooke of Doncaster. The manor of Melton was offered to Sir John Melton in 1640, but as he failed to complete the purchase it went to Dr. Richard Berry, together with the Levett lands in Bentley and Cadeby, in satisfaction of large sums of money which Dr. Berry had lent to John and Thomas Levett. Hunter's Deanery of Doncaster quotes many letters from Dr. Berry. In one of them, dated 7 Dec. 1649, he says that a general release has been sealed between him and Levett; and in one dated 4 Mar. 1650 he says that Dr. Levett had promised to remove his wife and children out of Melton Hall and to yield possession, with all the demesne lands. Dr. Berry was the son of William Berrie of Walesby, co. Lincoln, and was B.A. of Lincoln College, Oxford, in 1606, M.A. 1609, and B.Med. 1614. He also obtained a diploma from Padua in 1620, and seems to have been a man of means, though John Levett says " he was beholden to Mr. Thomas Levett for the greater part of his fortune." Dr. Berry married in 1637 Prudence, only daughter and heir of the unhappy Thomas Gargrave, and lived at Hodroyd, near Felkirk, where he acquired a large estate. His nephew, Major John Monkton, was the ancestor of the present Viscount Galway, and of General Robert Monckton, who was wounded with Wolfe at Quebec.

On 9 July 1640 James Morley sued John and Thomas Levett for £2700, for his interest "in certain cole mines lying in Harraton and Riccleston, co. Durham." Morley claimed that he had in 1639 sold his interest for £300 a year for 21 years to Thomas Lewis of York and Thomas Levett of Tixover, and that they had "acknowledged a statute staple of £5000 in consideration thereof;" that in June 1639 Thomas and John Levett had agreed to purchase this £300 a year for £2700, but that Sir John Melton, John Levett, and Thomas Levett combined to deprive Morley of his money. (Chancery Proceedings, Charles I, Bundle M. 46, No. 18.) This matter of the Harraton collieries came before Cromwell's Committee for Compounding in 1651-2, and on pp. 2127-9 of the Calendar appears the petition of Thomas Wray et al. and the answer of John Levett and Josiah Primate. On 21 Jan. 1652/3 "John Levett, D.C.L., of York" begs an allowance for attending on the Committee.

Both John and Thomas Levett were probably Royalists, and they appear on the Calendars of the Committee for Advancing Money (pages 769 and 1142). In each case, heard in 1649-50, both brothers were cited to appear, but neither appeared, and the resulting fine was ordered to be levied by distress on John Levett's estate.

Ralph Levett, second son of Thomas Levett of Melton, was baptized at Melton 3 Jan. 1600. Following his father's wish, he matriculated at Christ's College, Cambridge, as a pensioner, in July 1617. This was the college of John Milton, and John Wilson of the First Church in Boston took his degree there, as did Ezekiel Rogers, the founder of Rowley, Mass., and Thomas Jenner of Roxbury, Weymouth, and Saco. Ralph Levett took his B.A. in 1620/1, and proceeded M.A. in 1624, in which latter year he was ordained a deacon at York. Perhaps he had a curacy in Yorkshire, but he was soon associated with Lincolnshire. It may be that he knew Wheelwright at Cambridge, for they were there at the same time, though Wheelwright took his M.A. at Sidney Sussex College in 1618, one year after Ralph Levett was matriculated at Christ's College.

On 25 Jan. 1631/2, as shown above, "Mr. Ralfe Levit and Anne Hutchinson" were married at Bilsby.* She was a daughter of Edward Hutchinson of Alford and therefore a sister of the second wife of John Wheelwright. Perhaps Wheelwright himself performed the ceremony. In 1633-34 "Radulphus Levet, rector," signs the transcripts of Grainsby, Lincolnshire. On 3 Apr. 1635, when the former rector, Thomas Humphrey, was buried, "Ralph Levitt, M.A.," was presented to the rectory of Grainsby by Frances, widow of Sir William Wray†. (Lincoln Presentation

* Canon Foster has found in the Bilsby transcripts some new data about John Wheelwright. On 22 May 1628 his daughter Susanna was baptized; she it was who married Edward Rishworth. On 18 May 1629, the day after the date of the Wheelwright deed, John Wheelwright's first wife, Mary Storre, was buried. Canon Foster has also found in the transcripts of Hogsthorpe, 6 July 1620, the marriage of Robert Towle and Elizabeth Lawson, and in those of Willoughby, 24 June 1624, the marriage of Georgius Dearebarne and Helena Robinson.

† These Wrays of Glentworth were a notable Puritan family of Lincolnshire, originating in Yorkshire and connected with the Wentworths and with the Melton Levetts. The father of Sir William was Queen Elizabeth's Lord Chief Justice, Sir Christopher Wray, who married a daughter of Nicholas Girlington. The Girlingtons were lords of the manor of Mumby, and of them John Wheelwright held land in Mumby. Frances Wray, a granddaughter of Sir William, married in 1640 the famous Sir Harry Vane, a lifelong friend of Wheelwright.

Deeds, 1635, p. 25.) The Grainsby transcripts for 1636–37 are missing. That of 1638 is signed "Radulphus Levet" and that of 1639 "Raph Levet." The transcripts for 1640–48 are missing. In 1649 the signature is "R. Levet, rector." The years 1650–63 are missing, and the year 1664 is signed by William Jackson. The transcripts show that on 6 July 1638 Thomas Levet was buried, and on 11 Dec. 1638 "Thomas Levet, son of Raph Levet and Ann his wife," was baptized. No record has been found of this Ralph Levet after 1649. He was the father of Francis Levet of Little Carlton, for whose marriage and children see p. 67 above.

Wheelwright was dismissed from his Bilsby vicarage in January 1632, and in 1636, with a party of relatives and friends, sailed for New England. What more natural than that Ralph Levett should entrust to his brother-in-law Wheelwright a near relative, perhaps his only nephew? John Levett's answer to the bill in Chancery shows that he and his brother Thomas had borrowed £3000 from Dr. Berry on the Melton estates. Evidently the family inheritance was beginning to go under the hammer before 1640, in which year Sir John Melton and Sir Arthur Ingram died.

If then we assume that Ralph Levett of Grainsby did entrust a near relative to his brother-in-law Wheelwright for the New England venture, what was the exact degree of relationship? Let us analyze the family of Ralph. His only brothers and sister were:

A. Thomas Levett, the oldest son and heir, baptized at Melton 8 July 1594. (*Vide supra.*) My theory is that our Thomas Levet was his son, born in 1616.

B. John, born about 1605 (*vide supra*); living in 1665; too young to have been the father of our Thomas Levet.

C. Peter, born 1610–11. In Peile's Register we find that as the son of Thomas Levett of Melton he was admitted pensioner at Christ's College, Cambridge, 27 Jan. 1628/9. He had attended the Rotherham School under Mr. Thomas Bonner. He proceeded B.A. 1632/3, M.A. 1636, and became vicar of Cantley, near Doncaster, where he died in 1672. Perhaps in 1666 he was vicar of Boynton, co. York. He was too young to have been the father of our Thomas Levet.

D. Jane, born 1607; married in 1627 Andrew Goodhand of Kirmond in Lincolnshire, near Grainsby. His great-uncle Nicholas married Judith Harneis, the sister of Thomas, who married Esther Hutchinson. Jane Goodhand died in 1632, and is buried at Melton.

In the next preceding generation of Melton Levetts we find that Thomas Levett, the father of Ralph, had only the following brothers and sisters:

A. William Levett of Bentley, Yorkshire, born 1574; married Elizabeth Vickars or Wray (widow probably of Thomas Sheppard), who died 1635, leaving a will which mentions daughter Dorothy Sheppard, grandchild Thomas Sheppard, and nephew William Vickars. William Levett himself died 1638. His will is not extant, but his inquisition post mortem gives as his next heir his nephew Thomas Levett of Tixover, and says that William Levett made his will 14 May 1638; in it he left his lands to "my cozen Thomas Levet son of my brother Robert Levet." Apparently he had no children and did not wish his lands to go to his spendthrift nephew of Tixover.

618

B. Robert Levett of Normanton, born 1576; married in 1605 Frances, daughter of John Nalson of Snydale, a hamlet of Normanton. His children are thus recorded on the Normanton register:

  i. KATHERINE, daughter of Robert Levett of Snydale, bapt. 30 June 1607; d. 12 May 1610.
 ii. THOMAS, son of Leavett of Snydale, bapt. 3 Sept. 1609.
iii. ELIZABETH, daughter of Robert Levett of Snydall, bapt. 21 July 1611.
 iv. JOHN, son of Robert Levett of Snydall, bapt. 21 Sept. 1613.
  v. ELIZABETH, daughter of Robert Levett of Normanton, bapt. 9 Oct. 1617; bur. 3 Apr. 1625.
 vi. THOMAS, son of Robert Levett of Normanton, bapt. 1 May 1619. He is said in Mr. Gibson-Cullum's Levett pedigree to have married Joanna, daughter of John Jaques of Epworth, co. Lincoln, and to have been the progenitor of the Normanton Levetts and Hansons.
vii. MARIE, daughter of Robert Levett of Normanton, bapt. 3 July 1621.
viii. ROBERT, son of Robert Levett of Normanton, bapt. 7 Nov. 1622; bur. 19 Mar. 1625.
 ix. RALPH, son of Robert Levett of Normanton, bapt. 28 Aug. 1625; bur. 14 Oct. 1625.
  x. AGNES, daughter of Robert Levett of Normanton, bapt. 15 April 1627; bur. 29 July 1627.
 xi. JANE, daughter of Robert Levett of Normanton, bur. 20 May 1627.

Robert Levett himself was buried at Normanton 26 Jan. 1655/6 No will is extant. According to the records shown above he had two sons named Thomas, of whom one was born in 1609, and the other in 1619. If, as was sometimes the case, he had two surviving sons named Thomas, it is possible that one of them was our Thomas Levet; but his brother William, in his will referred to above, leaves his land to Thomas, "son of my brother Robert Levett of Normanton"; therefore in 1638 Robert had apparently but *one* son Thomas.

C. Catherine Levett, born 1578; married William Strelley of Strelley.

D. Elizabeth Levett, born ————; married John Morley.

Apparently in this generation there are no possibilities for our Thomas Levet, unless we assume that Robert had two surviving sons named Thomas, and that one of them was our ancestor—a rather violent assumption. The children of this generation would be cousins of Ralph Levett of Grainsby.

Going back one generation, we find that Ralph Levett of Melton, the grandfather of Ralph of Grainsby, had no brothers and but two sisters, Anne and Jane. There are no possibilities here, and the relationship is moved one degree farther off.

William Levett of Normanton and Melton, the great-great-grandfather of Ralph of Grainsby, married Elizabeth, daughter and coheir of William Wentworth of Sprotborough. No will is extant. His administration is on file at York. The son and heir, Nicholas Levett, born in 1524, survived his own son Ralph and died in 1598. We find no record of brothers or sisters.

Thus in five generations of the Melton Levetts there is apparently but one possibility for our Thomas Levet, namely: he may have been a son of Thomas of Tixover and a nephew of Ralph of Grainsby, the brother-in-law of John Wheelwright. The dates for such a theory harmonize so well, and the probability of a Wheelwright and Wentworth connection is so strong, that until proof to the contrary is shown I feel convinced that this is our line. Could the wills of any of the four sons of Thomas Levett of

Melton be found, this theory might be confirmed or upset. But in spite of a careful search at both principal and diocesan registries, no probate proceedings for any of the four sons have been discovered. Probably Thomas and Ralph Levett died during the confused Commonwealth period, from 1650 to 1660. But John Levett was living in 1665, and Peter Levett, we know, died in 1672.

In the exhaustive search for Levetts in Lincolnshire and Yorkshire I desire to thank my friend Canon C. W. Foster, editor of the Lincoln Record Society. Canon Foster's suggestions have been most helpful, and have resulted in tracing the Melton Levetts into Lincolnshire. With his aid a thorough search has now been made of Lincoln Subsidy Rolls, Wills and Administrations, Institutions and Presentation Deeds, etc.

Among other early Levetts in New England the explorer, Capt. Christopher Levett, whose life has been so ably written by Hon. James Phinney Baxter for the Gorges Society, comes first. He bore the same arms as the Melton Levetts, and the Visitation of Dorset in 1623 gives his pedigree (2 *Miscellanea Genealogica et Heraldica*, vol. 2, p. 354). There may have been a connection between the families, but Christopher was descended not from the Melton Levetts, but from another line, the Levetts of Bolton Percy.

The pedigree in the Visitation of Dorset began with "—— Levett of Harbord, co. York," who had three sons, Richard, William, and Percival. This undoubtedly means Harewood, in the West Riding of Yorkshire. William Levett of Harewood died in 1569. A Chancery proceeding was begun by his oldest son Matthew in 1570 (Levett *v.* Levett, Series 2, Bundle 116, No. 40). It recites that by his second wife William Levett of Harewood left four sons, Richard, William, Percival, and Charles. These are undoubtedly the sons of "—— Levett of Harbord," and Percival was the godson and cousin of Francis Levet of Bolton Percy, mentioned in his will of 1614/15. William of Harewood was probably* the son William mentioned in the will of his father Richard of Bolton Percy in 1567. This establishes the following pedigree:

1. JOHN LEVETT of Bolton Percy, whose will was proved 1526 (York Wills, vol. 9, fo. 364), married AGNES ——.
    Children:
    i.   WILLIAM; his will of 1546 mentions sons *Guy, Francis, John.*
    ii. JOHN, a clerk; under 23 in 1526; admon. in 1575.
    iii. ROBERT.
  2. iv. RICHARD, executor of his father's will.
    v.   ISABEL, m. —— KENDALL.
    vi. ALISON, m. —— PICKERING.

2. RICHARD LEVIT, of Appleton in Bolton Percy, whose will was proved 1567 (York Wills, vol. 17, fo. 759), married first ELLEN ——; and secondly CONSTANCE ——.
    Children by first wife:
    i.   HENRY, of Appleton; will proved 1597.
  3. ii. WILLIAM.
    iii. KATHERINE.

*There was also a branch of the Levetts at Holme and Lund in the East Riding, in which Matthew and William were family names. It may be that William of Harewood came from this line, but their wills do not indicate this, and the mention of a godson Percival Levet in the will of Francis Levet seems to connect the line of Christopher with the Bolton Percy family.

iv. ISABEL.
v. ROBERT.
vi. JAMES.
vii. ELLEN.

Children by second wife:

viii. THOMAS.
ix. MARGARET.

3. WILLIAM LEVETT, of Harewood, married first ANNE ———; and secondly JOAN YNGLANDE. Admon. 6 July 1569 (Dean and Chapter Vacancy Act Book, 1568–70, fo. 165).

Children by first wife:

i. MATTHEW.
ii. ELIZABETH, m. WILLIAM NAWTE.
iii. ANNE, m. JOHN WARDMAN.
iv. KATHERINE, m. OTHO WARDMAN.

Children by second wife:

v. RICHARD, Mayor of Doncaster. His will of 1618 mentions only one son, *William*, Alderman of Doncaster, whose will of 1643 mentions two sons, Robert and John, and four daughters.
vi. WILLIAM, twin brother to Richard, of whom there is no further record.
4. vii. PERCIVAL, b. 1560.
viii. CHARLES, probably of Scrayingham, m. GRACE AMPLEFORTH.
ix. JOAN, m. THOMAS USHER.

4. PERCIVAL LEVETT, born 1560, was freeman of York 1581, innkeeper, and sheriff of the City of York 1597. He was buried at St. Martin's, Micklegate, 13 Feb. 1625. He married ELIZABETH ROTHERFORTH, daughter and heiress of Alexander.

Children:

i. MARY, bapt. 1581; m. JOHN SMITH of Cottingham.
ii. RUDDERFORTH, bapt. 1582; d. 1584.
iii. GRACE, bapt. 1584; m. WILLIAM TODD of York.
5. iv. CHRISTOPHER, b. 5 Apr. 1586.
v. PERCIVAL, merchant of York; had nine children, but no child named Thomas.
vi. ANNE, m. (1) 1623 CHRISTOPHER TOPHAM of York, perhaps uncle of the Toppans of Newbury; m. (2) 1627 JOSEPH MICKLETHWAITE of Swyne, great-grandfather of Viscount Micklethwaite.

5. CAPT. CHRISTOPHER LEVETT, born 5 Apr. 1586. He is the well-known explorer who sailed to New England in 1623, and again in 1630, in the *Porcupine*, and died at sea in 1631. He married first MERCY MORE, daughter of Robert, rector of Guisley, York; and secondly FRANCES LOTTISHAM, daughter of Oliver, of co. Somerset.

'Children by first wife:

i. SARAH, b. 1610; m. ROBERT HITCH, rector of Normanton and dean of York.
ii. REBECCA, b. 1612; d. young.
iii. MARY, b. 1613; d. unm. 1644. Her will, proved 1644/5, mentions all her kindred (York Wills).
iv. JEREMIAH, b. 1614; rector of Leyton in Essex; m. EDITH ———; d. 1650.

Children by second wife:

v. TIMOTHY, b. 1617; of West Lydford in co. Somerset. Will dated 1650, proved 1669, mentions wife FLORENCE, children *Mary* and *Joan*.
vi. ELIZABETH, b. 1619; d. unm.

621

Thus the line of Christopher Levett contained no near relative named Thomas. It may be that our Thomas Levet was a distant connection, but this is unlikely.

New information concerning Christopher Levett's last voyage to New England is contained in a Chancery proceeding begun in 1631 by his widow against Thomas Wright and Robert Gough of Bristol, owners of the ship *Porcupine*. The proceedings give in detail the sailing agreement and mention the grant of 6000 acres to Levett.

Concerning John Leavitt of Hingham, Mass., Mr. Sheldon Leavitt, Jr., writes that the earliest known record appears in Dorchester, Mass., where in 1634 land was granted to him by the town. In 1636 he was made a freeman of Hingham, where first a house-lot and in the course of time much other land was granted to him. His first wife (possibly, according to Pope, the Mary Lovitt of the Dorchester Church) died at Hingham 4 July 1646, and he married for his second wife, 16 Dec. 1646, Sarah, daughter of Edward Gilman, then of Hingham, Mass., and later of Exeter, N. H. For many years he was a deacon of the church at Hingham and a selectman of the town, which he represented for several sessions in the General Court. He died in 1691, leaving a will, filed in Boston, in which he calls himself "a tayler," and spells his name as above. Some of his children moved to Exeter, and became the ancestors of a distinguished family of Leavitts there, among whom was Dudley Leavitt, the compiler of an excellent Farmer's Almanac. I can find no reason for believing that any connection existed between these Leavitts and our Thomas Levet. Perhaps John Leavitt came from the Essex Levitts, for whom see the next paragraph.

The affidavit of Nathaniel and Abraham Drake (*vide supra*) has led some to believe that our Thomas Levet, like his wife Isabel Bland, came from co. Essex. In Essex there were several families of Levitts, one of which, the Levitts of Messing, had some connection with New England through the Whites. (REGISTER, vol. 55, pp. 22 *et seq*.)* It may be that John Leavitt of Dorchester and Hingham came from one of these Essex lines, but a careful search of Essex wills reveals no Thomas Levet who could be our Exeter settler.

Thus a systematic investigation of these three sets of clues gives no positive proof of the ancestry of our Thomas Levet of Exeter and Hampton. The most probable line is that of Lincolnshire and Yorkshire, connected with both Wheelwright and Wentworth.

But if Levet were a protégé of John Wheelwright, he did not follow the Antinomian to Wells in 1642. The removal of their pastor scattered the Exeter settlers in that year, and in 1643 we find Thomas Levet at Hampton, next neighbor to Exeter, where his name is signed to a petition against Lieut. William Howard.

The list of grants and possessions in the old Hampton town records, made about 1644, in the beautiful handwriting of William Howard, the town clerk, shows that before that date Thomas Levet had married Isabel (Bland), widow of Francis Asten of Dedham and Hampton. The record follows:

II. 58. House lots and other ground granted &c. unto the several inhabitants of Hampton, compiled Anno 1644.
THOMAS LEVITT OF HAMPTON.
1. 5 a. of upland for a house lot granted unto Fras. Asten the former husband of Thomas Levitt's wife, lying betw. upland of Saml. Getchell, some-
*Pp. 730 *et seq*, the third volume of this series.

622

times Will. Hunton's, before that John Philbrook's to the West, and the upland of Thomas Sleeper's sometimes Chr. Lasone's.

2. 5 a. of upland granted to Thomas Levitt.
3. 10 a. upland in the North plan of upland.
4. 6 a. meadow granted to the above named Fras. Asten, former husband of Tho. Levitts wife, lying between the meadow & marsh of Timothy Dalton N.E., and Will: Howard S.W.
5. 3 a. meadow bought of Anthony Taylor, betw. A. T. & Taylor's River.
6. 6 a. salt Marsh granted unto him, betw. Widow Husse N., & Will. Maston S.
7. 5 a. salt marsh bot. of Anthony Taylor.
   Additions to Anno 1658.
8. 5 a. bought, granted to Edw. Palmer.
9. Granted to Tho. Levitt 2½ a. swamp betw. swamp of Sam. Getchell & Timothy Dalton.
10. 5 a. salt marsh gr. to John Sanders.
11. 4 a. upland bot. of John Samborne.
12. 11 a. salt marsh beyond Falls River.

The Norfolk County record of the birth of James Levet in 1652 calls him "son of Thomas and *Elisabeth* Levitt," but this is a clerical error, repeated in Pope's Pioneers of Maine and New Hampshire. We may safely assume that the only wife of our Thomas Levet was Isabel Bland, daughter of John Bland of Watertown and Martha's Vineyard. John Bland was a stepson of Jeremiah Norcross, and his mysterious *alias* of "John Smith" has been explained by Dr. Charles E. Banks, in his History of Martha's Vineyard, vol. 2, pp. 41–46. It is possible that John Bland and the Hampton Drakes were of Yorkshire origin.

The old pronunciation of the family name was Lovitt. In spelling it our Thomas Levet seems to have used interchangeably "Levet," "Levitt," and "Levit." These are the forms in which the name of Ralph Levett of Grainsby appears: "Levet" when he signed his name, "Levitt" when others wrote it. In the case of our Thomas Levet the uncertainty of Colonial orthography is increased by the fact that apparently he could not write, and always signed by a mark, so that his name was spelled and written by some one else. It is "Levitt" in the Exeter Combination, written by his relative Wheelwright, and also in the record of a deed in 1659, in the "Wheelwright Deed," the Hampton record of 1644, and the Drake deposition. In signatures of 1654 and 1657 and in the Martha's Vineyard power of attorney it is "Levit." In the testimony in Drake *v.* Colcord, 1676, and a jury verdict of 1680 it is "Levet," and so distinctly in the wills of both Thomas and Isabel. In the Hampton petition of 1643 it was probably also "Levet"; a copy of this petition is in the Massachusetts Archives, and in it the scrivener has spelled the name "Livet."

In 1647, when Wheelwright was called to the Hampton church, Thomas Levet was already there. He lived in Hampton until his death in 1696, a quiet, useful citizen, seldom prominent in town matters. He was perhaps a tanner, though the only deed from him in the old records describes him as a "planter." He appears in 1654 with Robert Smith as an appraiser of the estate of George Haborne or Rabone, who was one of the Wheelwright group and probably a Lincolnshire man. In 1657 Thomas Levet and Godfrey Dearborn witnessed the will of Susan, widow of George Haborne and then the wife of Thomas Leader of Boston. Dearborn, who followed Levet from Exeter to Hampton, was a Lincolnshire man. (REGISTER, vol. 60, p. 308.) Levet's stepdaughter Isabel married Philip [1] Towle,* who came to Hampton when Wheelwright was there.

---

* Towle was probably a Lincolnshire man, perhaps from Habrough. Many Towle wills are filed at Lincoln, but they throw no light on his ancestry. Several Towles are still living in Lincolnshire.

[1] P. 640, the first volume of this series.

Thomas Levet served as selectman of Hampton in 1657 and 1667, and was constable in 1664. He served on several juries, and took the oath of allegiance to Massachusetts in 1678. He was "freed from Training" in 1681, probably on account of age or disability. In 1683, with eighteen others, he signed a petition that their poll-tax be abated, because of old age, "many about seventy, some above eighty, others near ninety, being past labour and work." In 1685 he signed Weare's petition against Cranfield. The Dukes County records show a power of attorney dated 16 Apr. 1691 from Thomas and Isabel Levet to their son John, authorizing him to deal with Isabel's share of the Bland estates in Martha's Vineyard. Apparently some dispute between John Levet and another coheir, Elias, son of Philip Watson, was settled by a division in 1699. John Levet's name in subsequent conveyances of the Vineyard land is spelled "Levit," "Lovet," and "Leavit." Thomas Levet died 28 Nov. 1696, "aged about* eighty," the town record says, and his will and inventory are on file at Concord, N. H. (Probate Records, vol. 2, p. 26, and vol. 3, p. 125.) An abstract of his will, dated 9 July 1692, is as follows:

To loving wife the thirds of all lands and meddows, etc., with housing convenient during her life. To wife two cows, two swine, three sheep, my brass and puter, the thirds of all my corn. To son Hezron Levet 100 acres at the new plantation, £20 formerly given him, and 5s. after my decease. To Hezron's son Thomas Levet £10, to be paid him at the age of one and twenty. Residue of lands and housing to sons Aretas and John Levet equally, John to divide and Aretas to choose. To son Aretas all in his house and half the wedges, half the cross cut saw, and half the tools about husbandry, with his house that he now lives in. To son [John] Levet the other half the tools mentioned with all carpenter tools and his house and ground. To son James Levet £10. To three daughters, Isabella Towle, Jemima Knowles, and Kezia Tucker, 5s. apiece. Executors: wife and son John Levet. Witnesses: Abraham Drake, Senr., Abraham Drake, Junr., Robert Drake.

Inventory, £210.1.0, includes all buildings, housing, barn, and house-lot containing 10 acres. 15 acres upland. 25 acres mead and marsh. 5 acres upland and swamp. 4 shares commonage. 60 acres in the North Division. 100 acres in New Plantation. Appraised by Abr. Drake, Senr., and John Smith.

Isabel Levet, widow, died 9 Feb. 1698/9, aged about 87, and her will and inventory are filed at Concord. (Probate Records, vol. 3, p. 165.) An abstract of her will is as follows:

To daughter Isball Toule one cow, one box of linen, and my wearing clothes. To daughter Jemima Knowls one cow and one sheep. To grandchild Sarah Knowls one sheep. To daughter Keziah Tucker 12s. All my puter and brass to be equally divided among my three daughters. Residue to son John Levet, sole executor. Witnesses: John Smith, Senr., and John Smith, Junr.

Inventory taken by Thomas Roby and John Tucke, £76.11.9, including "an estate at Mathes Vineyard."

The "three daughters," Isabel Towle, Jemima Knowles, and Kezia Tucker, were the three children of Isabel Bland by her first husband, Francis Asten.

The children and grandchildren of Thomas Levet may be arranged in a pedigree as follows:

1. THOMAS[1] LEVET had
    2. i.   HEZRON,[2] b. 1644.
    3. ii.   ARETAS, b. abt. 1646.
    4. iii. JOHN, b. abt. 1648.
    5. iv.   JAMES, b. 10 Nov. 1652.

* The old record is torn here, so that it cannot be definitely stated whether it says "above" or "about."

2. HEZRON[2] LEVET (*Thomas[1]*), born in 1644, according to a deposition, resided at Hampton, and died there 30 Nov. 1712. He was a tanner and shoemaker. He married, 25 Sept. 1667, MARTHA TAYLOR, daughter of Anthony of Hampton.

On 15 Feb. 1702/3 Hezron Levet and his son Thomas, who like his father was a tanner, made an agreement by which the son was to take over all his father's house, tanyards, and lands, and to maintain his father and mother in comfort "beside what my father shall get by his practis and my mother by stilling." The son also agreed to make certain payments to his four sisters. Both father and son signed their names "Levvit" to this instrument. (N. H. Deeds, vol. 13, p. 237.)

Children:
i. LYDIA,[3] b. 5 Aug. 1668; m. MEPHIBOSHETH SAMBORN.
ii. JOHN, b. 26 Nov. 1670; m. SARAH HOBBS, daughter of John.
iii. JAMES, b. and d. 1673.
iv. MOSES, b. 30 Jan. 1673/4; m. MARY CARR.
v. THOMAS, b. 8 May 1677; m. ELIZABETH ATKINSON of Newbury, daughter of John and granddaughter of Theodore Atkinson.
vi. MARY, b. 20 Oct. 1679; m. CAPT. BENJAMIN THOMAS, son of James of Dover.
vii. ABIGAIL.
viii. SARAH.

3. ARETAS[2] LEVET (*Thomas[1]*), born about 1646, resided at Hampton, and died there 14 Jan. 1739. He married, 1 Aug. 1678, RUTH SLEEPER, daughter of Thomas, an early settler of Hampton. He was a farmer, and served in King William's war. No will or inventory of Aretas Levet has been found. On 25 Dec. 1710 he conveyed to his sons James and Thomas certain lands at Hampton. The estate of Thomas Levet, the father, was finally divided in 1725 by Sergt. John Levet and James, the son of Aretas. (N. H. Deeds, vol. 74, p. 154.)

Children:
i. LUTHER[3] (a daughter), b. 1679; d. 1684.
ii. ELIZABETH, b. 1680; d. 1684.
iii. MEHITABEL, b. 8 June 1682; m. ROBERT ROWE of Hampton.
iv. JAMES, b. 1683; m. (1) 20 Feb. 1717 ANN BRACKETT, daughter of Capt. Anthony; m. (2) HANNAH ———.
v. THOMAS, b. 15 Jan. 1685/6; m. 24 Nov. 1714 ELIZABETH LOCKE, daughter of Nathaniel of Hampton.
vi. ELIZABETH, b. 2 Aug. 1690; m. JAMES SAMBORN, son of Nathaniel.
vii. RUTH, b. 19 May 1693; m. STEPHEN SAMBORN, son of Stephen.

4. SERGEANT JOHN[2] LEVET (*Thomas[1]*), born about 1648, died 1726/7. He married DELIVERANCE ROBIE, granddaughter of Henry Robie of Hampton, of the family of Robie of Castle Donington, Leicestershire. He served in several campaigns against the Indians. His will, dated 23 Dec. 1726, is filed at Concord, N. H. (N. H. Wills, vol. 7, p. 638), and leaves to wife Deliverance the improvement of his estate; to daughter Deliverance, at age of 18 or at marriage, one-half the estate; if she has a male heir her share is to go to him; if not, it is to go to John Levet, son of "cousin" Thomas and grandson of Aretas. The estate, inventoried at £1029, included a halberd and some books.

Child:
i. DELIVERANCE,[3] b. 6 May 1719; m. JEREMIAH CLOUGH of Salisbury.

625

5. JAMES[2] LEVET (*Thomas[1]*), born 10 Nov. 1652, died at Portsmouth, N. H., 4 Apr. 1718, and is buried in the Point of Graves Cemetery there. He married about 1692 SARAH PARTRIDGE, widow of Nehemiah of Salisbury and Portsmouth, a brother of Governor William Partridge. Her maiden name does not appear, but she was a kinswoman of Anthony Ellins, an early settler of Portsmouth, who in 1668 conveyed land at Portsmouth to Nehemiah Partridge and his wife Sarah, "my kinswoman."

Little has been known of James Levet, perhaps because he left no children, but he was the richest of his family. In 1668, at the age of sixteen, he removed to Portsmouth, then the most aristocratic settlement in the new province. There he was the clerk of Henry Dering, a Portsmouth merchant, and before that a tavern-keeper at Hampton. Dering soon removed to Boston, but James Levet remained at Portsmouth. His name was generally spelled "Lovet," that being the usual pronunciation of the name. He was selectman of Portsmouth in 1696/7 and again in 1708, deputy sheriff in 1694, coroner in 1697, and constable in 1706. In 1705 he was overseer of the will of Roger Rose. His will, dated 1 Apr. 1718 (N. H. Wills, vol. 10, p. 5), leaves all his property to his wife Sarah, and is witnessed by Thomas Beck, Jr., Elizabeth Furber, and Ann Barn. The widow Sarah Levet made her will 10 Nov. 1733 (N. H. Wills, vol. 14, p. 421), leaving bequests to grandsons Nehemiah Partridge and William Partridge, to granddaughters Sarah McBride and Abigail Chapman, to great-granddaughters Sarah Partridge and Abigail Partridge, to Sarah Braughton, daughter of Abigail Chapman, to great-granddaughter Sarah Beck, to granddaughter Mary Beck, to Mary, wife of Nehemiah Partridge, and to Mary, wife of William Partridge. The residue she left to Samuel Beck, who had married Mary Partridge. Her inventory is a long one and includes a silver tankard.

ANCESTRY OF THOMAS LEWIS AND HIS WIFE
ELIZABETH MARSHALL OF SACO, MAINE

By WALTER GOODWIN DAVIS of Portland, Maine

LEWIS, OF SHREWSBURY, SHROPSHIRE

LEWIS ARMS

Thomas Lewis, the patentee of Saco in the Province of Maine, was a native of Shrewsbury, co. Salop, where his father was a wealthy merchant and his grandfather a prosperous yeoman named Lewis ap Jevan, whose sons, abandoning the Welsh system of nomenclature, adopted their father's Christian name for their English surname.

In 1623 two heralds from the College of Arms, Robert Tresswell, Somerset, and Augustine Vincent, Rouge Croix, deputies of William Camden, Clarenceux, made a visitation of Shropshire, accompanied by John Withie, a painter of arms. No Lewis pedigree appears in the original visitation at the College, nor is one included in the copy in the Harleian mss. in the British Museum* made contemporaneously by Withie. However, in a manuscript collection of Shropshire pedigrees, seemingly based on the visitation of 1623 but with many additions, now in the library of Shrewsbury School, there is a pedigree of the Shrewsbury family of Lewis.

The date of the Shrewsbury School manuscript is difficult to determine. One pedigree is thought to be in the handwriting of John Philpot who obtained the office of Somerset Herald in 1624. The manuscript is said to have come from the library of John Warburton, a later Somerset, and to have been bought by Richard Hill Waring, Esq., who in turn sold it to Jonathan Scott, Esq., of Shrewsbury. Mr. Scott gave it to the School in 1766. In preparing its printed volume, "Visitation of Shropshire, 1623," the Har-

*Harleian ms. 1936.

Home of the Marshall Family of Shrewsbury

leian Society made use of the School manuscript as well as of the Withie manuscript.

The Lewis pedigree deals quite fully with Lewis ap Jevan, his children and grandchildren, and lists one great-grandchild who was baptized in 1607, which roughly dates it. In all important particulars this portion of the pedigree can be verified by public records.

In the early part of the nineteenth century two Shrewsbury antiquaries, Joseph and George Morris, made the history and genealogy of Shropshire their life work, and Joseph Morris compiled a tremendous collection of pedigrees which are now in the possession of Leonard Peele, Esq.* Morris prepared a pedigree of Lewis of Shrewsbury which amplifies and extends that in the Shrewsbury School manuscript.

Back from Lewis ap Jevan in both pedigrees stretches one of those extraordinary lines of descent, covering twelve generations and more than four centuries, which are familiar to students of Welsh and border genealogy. How much faith can be placed in these long Welsh ancestries is a matter of honest disagreement.† Obviously few if any of them can be proved by documentary evidence, and some antiquaries reject them altogether. On the other hand it is a well recognized fact that the Welsh as a people were keenly interested in their descent — the great number of these long lists of ancestors is evidence of that fact — and it is distinctly possible that pedigrees were committed to memory from generation to generation. All of us who in childhood learned by rote the rough verses beginning "William the Norman and William his son" have done much the same thing. In any event and for what it may be worth, the descent of Lewis ap Jevan, as given in the Shrewsbury School manuscript and by Mr. Morris, is here set forth: (*See opposite page.*)

Rhys Sais, who appears at the head of the pedigree by Morris, was an actual person who was living at the time of Norman conquest. Of him Mr. Eyton, the highly respected mediaeval scholar and historian of early Shropshire, says: "I have already spoken of Rys Sais, a Welsh noble, who was living at the time of the Norman Conquest. He was called Sais, or Saxon, either because he understood the Saxon language, or had served in England, or (still more probably) because of his English predilections. He is said to have divided his possessions among his sons in 1070. His sons are again authentically mentioned in 1079, when they slew Urgeney ap Sitsylht, a Welsh noble. Tudor, the eldest son of Rys Sais, is believed to be the person mentioned in the above quotation from Domesday."‡

*Mr. Peele kindly allowed the contributor to examine them in 1933.

†See The Value of Welsh Pedigrees, by H. J. T. Wood in *The Ancestor*, 4:47; 6:62; also, a dissenting opinion, The Origin of the Carews, by J. Horace Round, *The Ancestor*, 5:47.

‡In Domesday the following is in the description of the parish of Whittington: "Tudor quidam Walensis tenet de Comite(Rogerio) unum Finem terrae Walensis et inde reddit iv libras et v solidos."

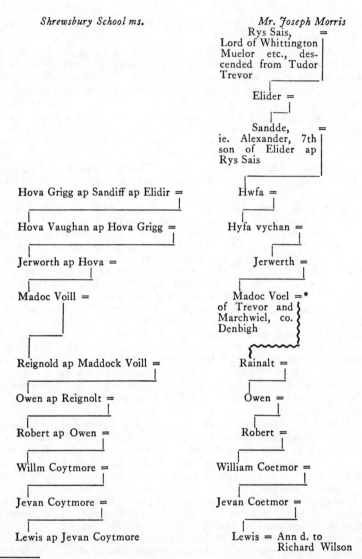

Shrewsbury School ms.	Mr. Joseph Morris
	Rys Sais, =
	Lord of Whittington
	Muelor etc., des-
	cended from Tudor
	Trevor
	Elider =
	Sandde, =
	ie. Alexander, 7th
	son of Elider ap
	Rys Sais
Hova Grigg ap Sandiff ap Elidir =	Hwfa =
Hova Vaughan ap Hova Grigg =	Hyfa vychan =
Jerworth ap Hova =	Jerwerth =
Madoc Voill =	Madoc Voel =*
	of Trevor and
	Marchwiel, co.
	Denbigh
Reignold ap Maddock Voill =	Rainalt =
Owen ap Reignolt =	Owen =
Robert ap Owen =	Robert =
Willm Coytmore =	William Coetmor =
Jevan Coytmore =	Jevan Coetmor =
Lewis ap Jevan Coytmore	Lewis = Ann d. to
	Richard Wilson

The estate or commhot which he had consented to hold under Earl Roger was probably part of Maelor Saesneg, called Saesneg or Saxon, to distinguish it from Maelor Gymraeg, or Welsh Maelor. It had perhaps been held by Rys Sais himself, under a Saxon suzerain, and had taken its name either from that circumstance or from his tenure thereof. Bleddyn, the elder son of Tudor, is further stated to have inherited Maelor Saesneg, and from him many Welsh families derive their descent. We have seen that Wronou, a younger son of Tudor, is alleged to have been the father of Roger and Jonas de Powis. . . . There can be no doubt that the King's resumption of Whittington Castle in 1165 was in order that he might confer it on Roger de Powis. The Welsh genealogists assert Roger de Powis to have been a son of Wronou, son of Tudor, son of Rys Sais, and make Tudor to have been Domesday lord of Maelor Saesneg, now in Flintshire. This story is so entirely consistent with chronological tests and with certain circumstances which probably were unknown to the Welsh genealogists that I cannot hesitate to accept it as the truth. ("History of Shropshire," Eyton, XI: 30, 31, 48, 49.)

*The waving line indicates illegitimacy.

Tudor Trevor and Elidir ap Rhys Sais lived centuries before the common use of coat armor, but later generations obligingly endowed them with arms. To Tudor Trevor was assigned — Per bend sinister, *ermine* and *erminois*, over all a lion rampant *or* — and to Elidir ap Rhys Sais — *Ermine*, a lion rampant *azure*. Both of these coats, or slight variations of them, were borne or quartered by many Welsh and border families, the Eytons of Eyton, the Edwardes of Kilhendre and of the College at Shrewsbury, and the Hoziers of Woodcote and Shrewsbury all claiming male descent from Elidir ap Rhys Sais and using the second of the two. To the Lewises of Shrewsbury both of our manuscript sources give — *Ermine*, a lion rampant within a border, *azure*.

Also in the library of Shrewsbury School is a roll of arms in which "Robert Owen, gentleman, an herald at arms", as he was called in the register of St. Chad's when he was buried in 1632, collected the coats of the several bailiffs, stating that he was "authorized by the court marshall of England a deputy herald of this and several adjacent counties", which is not to be taken seriously. Two of Lewis ap Jevan's sons, Thomas and Andrew Lewis, had served as bailiff, and Mr. Owen gave their coat as *Gules*, a chevron *ermine* between three Saxons' heads couped at the neck, proper. When Michael Lewis, a son of Thomas Lewis, made his will in 1644 he used an armorial seal, the first and fourth quarters of the shield bearing a chevron between three heads.*

Shrewsbury in the sixteenth century was an aristocratic town, many of its merchants being sons of the Shropshire and Staffordshire squirearchy and gentry. The wealthy merchants whose immediate forebears were of the yeomanry, like the Lewises, often married into the established families. They doubtless became very conscious of the outward marks of caste, and adopted arms, either based on some more or less remote genealogical claim, or as fancy dictated, without the by-your-leave of the College of Arms, and after several generations of use on tombs and seals the arms became "respectable" and possibly recognized in some later visitation of the heralds.

1. LEWIS AP JEVAN of Almer Park, near Shrewsbury, co. Salop, and included in the parish of St. Mary of that town, was probably born between the years 1500 and 1510. He seems to have been a wealthy yeoman, possibly with interests in Shrewsbury where his children lived and took an active part in civic affairs. He married ANNE WILSON whose father is given as Richard Wilson in the pedigree of the Lewis family prepared by Mr. Morris. He died in 1558 and his widow survived until 1573.

The will of Lewys ap Jevyn, dated May 25 and proved August 23, 1558, directs that he be buried in St. Mary's

---

*This coat was also used on their eighteenth century tomb in St. Chad's church at Shrewsbury by a family named Griffiths, and is credited in Burke's "General Armory" to Griffiths of Penrhyn, co. Carnarvon.

church or churchyard. To my wife Anne, my taking in Almer Park for life and three pastures called the Hydes for her widowhood, then to Richard my son. To my wife, also, six oxen, a plough and a wain and all that belongeth to husbandry, twelve kine, six young beasts and forty sheep, also all my household stuff, all corn in barn and field and six spoons for life, she to leave Richard half my household stuff and the spoons, and, if Richard die before her, to any other child she pleases best. To my sons Richard, John and Andrew 100 marks each, but if all die before they receive their parts, then to Thomas and Elyn. To Elyn my daughter, £20 and to her sister Johan Proud £5, and to Lewys her son £5. To my wife Anne, my silver salt for life, then to my son Andrew, also my two mares. To Lewys Proud, my godson, a croft I have in mortgage from one Griffith ap John of Ditton for £3 and he pays 20s. a year for three years. To Dorothy Harneg, a two year old heifer and a one year old. To my man Harry, 10s. My takings in Newton to my son Richard, except three leaseholds to my wife during widowhood. To each of my sons, forty sheep. To Elizabeth Houffe, twenty sheep and two heifers, or 40s. To Dorathe Wilson, 40s. and a year old heifer. To Thomas Wolf, a yoke of bullocks of four years. If any of my sons be not ordered by my executors and overseers, they can take from his part as he shall deserve. To John Ellys, 5s. To Margery Betton, the twenty sheep her father hath and six. more. To my god-daughter Margery Kemanson, six sheep. To Jevyn, my man, six sheep. To Meredith that was my servant, six sheep. The rest of my goods to be distributed among my children. Executors: George Prowde, Richard Capper and my son Thomas. Overseer: Richard Samforte. To each of them, 20s. Witnesses: Mr. Thomas Beton, John Clarke of Berwylke, Sir John Butterrey, my ghostly father.*

The will of Anne Lewes of Almer Park in St. Mary's, Salop, widow, made Feb. 27, 1564(5) and proved August 27, 1573, directs that she be buried in St. Mary's church. To my son Andrew Lewes, £20 which Mr. Richard Sanford of the Yle doth owe me. To my son John, £10 in Thomas Manning draper's hands and twenty sheep. To my son Thomas Lewes all my interest in the wood I bought at Woolascott, also £6 to make it worth £20, and my gray colt. To my son Richard Lewes my sown crop of corn, four oxen, a wain and all other instruments of husbandry. To my daughter Ellen Proude, a silver goblet for life, then to Jone Proude's daughter if she like, if not, to George Proude, her son, also my white bag of leather and all in it. To my son Thomas, one coverlid and a pair of sheets. To my son Andrew, one coverlid and a pair of sheets. One half of my household stuff to be equally

---

*Prerogative Court of Canterbury, 37 Noodes.

divided between my sons Thomas, John and Andrew. To
my daughter Ellen Prowde, twenty ewes and twenty lambs.
To my servants Thomas Woolfe and Roger Cruxson, all my
cattle with Jeffrey ap Richard and 10s. equally. To my
servants Thomas ap William and Thomas, a yearling heifer
each. To Lewis Prowde and Marie Prowde, a cow each.
To my sister Ellen Wilson, two kine. To my maids Anne
and Marye, a two year old heifer each. To my god-daughter
Anne Willaskott, a ewe and a lamb. To my god-son George
Proude, twenty sheep. All my goods, plate, etc. unbequeathed to my three [sic] sons and my daughter Ellin Proude
equally. To my son Thomas, six silver spoons I bought
myself. To Richard and Thomas Woolfe, ten sheep. To
Ellin Proude my daughter and Jone Proude her daughter,
all my kerchiefs etc., so she give Ellin Wilson two. To my
brother William Wilson, one ox. Executors: Richard Keepar,
George Prowde and my son Thomas. To Richard Keepar,
a filly with a star in the forehead. To Andrew, a colt, and
to Ellin Prowde my mare and saddle. To Jane Armedg,
daughter to Richard Armedg, £4 at age of fourteen. I forgive
Richard Armedg* and Dorothy Harnidge his wife the money
they owe. The twenty sheep given to my god-son George
Prowde to be divided among all Ellen Prowde's children.
To my sister Ellen Wylson £4 to her marriage, so that she
marry not Reynolde Gittins. To my god-son Richard Hig-
gens, a ewe and a lamb. To George Yrishe, a ewe and a
lamb, and to Thomas Yrish('s) wife, a table cloth. To Jane
Ellis, a yearling calf. Witnesses: George Proude the writer
hereof and others.†

Children:

1. i.   ELLEN,[2] b. about 1535; m. before 1558 GEORGE PROWDE, son of
        Richard Prowde, mercer, of Shrewsbury. He came of a family
        which had been seated at Sutton, co. Salop, as tenants of the
        priory of Wenlock at least since 1483, and which bore as arms
        "Or, a chevron barry of six gules and sable." He was admitted to
        the Drapers' Company April 6, 1553, and was elected bailiff in
        1569. In 1568 he erected a fine half-timbered house in Shrews-
        bury, which is still standing in a quadrangle reached by a passage
        on the right side of Shearmen's Hall on Milk Street.‡ George
        Prowde, gent., was buried at St. Julian's Jan. 1, 1591/2, and Mrs.
        Ellnar Prowde, widow, on April 29, 1616.
             The will of George Proude of Shrewsbury, draper, was made
        Dec. 24, 1591, and proved March 14, 1591/2. The house I dwell
        in and the house where Thomas Cowper dwelleth to Thomas
        Lewis, my brother, to be sold for the preferment of my two daugh-
        ters Catherine and Alice. To my wife Ellen, all my tithe corn and
        hay of Betten and Alkmere for life, then to my son Lewis and his

*Richard and Dorothy Harnage and their daughter Jane are presumably the Richard Harnage
of Shenton and his wife Dorothy (Kinaston of Shotton) who had a daughter Jane as shown in the
Harnage pedigree in the Visitation of Shropshire, 1623, Harleian Society, xxviii, 216.
†Prerogative Court of Canterbury, 26 Peter.
‡"Old Houses of Shrewsbury", H. E. Forrest, 1920.

heirs. The house I have in Fish Street to my wife for life, then to my son Richard, and, if my son Lewis do not suffer him quietly to enjoy it, then the tithes given to Lewis are to go to Richard. Also to my wife, all my plate and household stuff. To my daughters Katherine and Alice, the benefits of my lease of Monckey for the first six years, for the seventh year they are to go to my son Thomas, for the eighth year to my son Richard, for the ninth year to my son Roger. Every one of my children is to have the benefit of the said lease for one year: 1st Lewis, 2d Marie, 3d William, 4th Elizabeth, 5th Roger, 6th Catherine, 7th Alice, 8th Richard. Executors: my wife Ellin and my son Lewis Proude. Witnesses: William Proude, Thomas Proude, William Midlecote.*

The will of Ellen Prowde, widow, of the parish of St. Julian's in Shrewsbury, was made Oct. 23, 1610, and proved in 1616 in Litchfield. She directs that she be buried in the churchyard of St. Julian's, as near to her husband as may be. To my son Lewis Prowde my best carpet and eight cushions. I owe my son Thomas Prowde £6: 13: 4 and he is to have six of my best silver spoons, also my window cushion, in satisfaction of the same. To my son-in-law Richard Steeventon a silver cup and to his daughter Mary a pair of purled flaxen sheets. To William Medlycot's son Thomas, my great pot. To my son William Prowde, £6: 13: 4 and to his son Lewis Prowde one great pot and to his daughter Ellen Prowde one other great pot. To my daughter Katheren Phillips, the bedstead, table and hangings in the painted chamber, and to her daughter Mary a feather-bed and two bolsters. To my daughter Katheren Phillips, my damask table-cloth and six damask napkins, and to her son Edward Phillips my cup-board in the hall and to Andrew, her other son, a cruse covered with silver. To Ales my daughter, my best pair of flaxen sheets and best scarlet gown to make her a petticoat, and to Daniel Gittins, her son, my best cruse covered with silver. To my son Richard Prowde, the bedstead and bed whereon I lie, and to George Prowde, his son, my andirons in my hall. Whereas there is due unto William Hollewell his children, by my late husband, George Prowde, his will £3: 2: 0, my will is that Mary, Anne and Elizabeth be paid 9 s. each and all the rest of his children be paid their part. To Joseph, Andrew, Stephen, Judith and Martha Medlicott, children of my son-in-law Medlicott, £10 equally divided, which £10 I have in keeping of my son-in-law Edward Phillips. The rest of my goods to my daughter Katherine Phillips. Executors: Andrew Lewis and my son-in-law Edward Phillips. Witnesses: Roger Phillips, Richard Evans. Inventory of £35: 13: 4 entered Feb. 1616(7) by William Medlicott, William Phillips and Ronale Thomas.†

Children, born in Shrewsbury:

1. *Lewis Prowde*, b. before 1565. He was a scholar of Shrewsbury School in 1571, and matriculated at Cambridge, a pensioner from St. John's College, at Easter, 1576. On Jan. 23, 1577/8, he was admitted to Lincoln's Inn and was called to the bar in 1586. He was made a Bencher of the Inn in 1602, served as Autumn Reader in 1606 and was its treasurer in 1614, in which year he was elected Member of Parliament for Shrewsbury. He had been justice of assize for three shires in Wales, and with Sir James Whitelocke steward of the manors and lands of Westminster Abbey. He married Ursula Trappes, daughter of Francis Trappes, late of St. Michael Bassishaw, London, on Dec. 24, 1590. He

---

*Prerogative Court of Canterbury, 20 Harrington.
†Litchfield Registry of Probate.

was buried in Westminster Abbey Jan. 16, 1616/7, at the entrance of St. Benedict's Chapel. Letters of administration, in which he was called "late of St. Giles in the Fields," were issued to Thomas Prowde Feb. 7, 1616/7.

2. *Mary Prowde*, b. before 1565; probably m. William Holliwell and had children mentioned in her mother's will in 1610.

3. *Joan Prowde*, b. before 1565; d. before 1591; possibly m. Richard Steeventon and had a daughter Mary mentioned in her mother's will in 1610.

4. *William Prowde*, entered Shrewsbury School in 1571; m. May 20, 1589, Anne Sotherne, daughter of Gilbert Sotherne; tanner and burgess of Shrewsbury in 1590; buried at St. Chad's Nov. 13, 1628.

5. *Thomas Prowde*, bapt. at St. Alkmund's June 17, 1562; a scholar at Shrewsbury School in 1571; living in 1615. He matriculated at Cambridge University in Lent, 1579/80, a pensioner from Trinity College, was elected a Fellow in 1585 and was granted many degrees — B.A. 1583/4, M.A. 1587, B.D. 1594 and D.D. 1615. He was vicar of Trumpington, co. Cambridge, in 1595 and resigned the same year, rector of Little Gidding, co. Huntington, 1597–1598, rector of Cheadle, co. Stafford, 1600–1601, vicar of Enfield, co. Middlesex, 1601–1616 and rector of St. Andrew Wardrobe, London, 1608–1615, being buried there Feb. 20, 1615/6. He was married twice, his second wife being Agnes (Howe?).

   The will of Thomas Prowde, D.D., made February 10, 1615, was proved February 22, 1615. He directed that he be buried in the church of St. Andrew's in the Wardrobe in which parish he was living. To his son Robert, £50 and books and apparel which are to be sold by the testator's brother Lewes Prowde, his cousin Rowland (Helme?) and his cousin Robert Jeffreyes who are to have a care for the setting out of Robert's portion for his maintenance and education. To his three children by his now wife, £10 apiece when eighteen. To his mother Allen Prowde, £5 for a gown. To his brother William Prowde, £5 for a gown. To his cousin Lewes Prowde, son of his brother William Prowde, £5. To his cousin Martha Medlicott, £5. To his father-in-law Master Howe, £5. Residue to wife Agnes Prowde, executrix. Witnesses: William Nayler, John Cooke, Gyles Harrys.*

6. *Elizabeth Prowde*, bapt. at St. Alkmund's Oct. 13, 1563; m. William Medlycott Dec. 11, 1587, at St. Julian's; her husband and six children named in her mother's will in 1610.

7. *George Prowde*, bapt. at St. Alkmund's Jan. 1, 1564/5, and buried there April 13, 1565.

8. *Richard Prowde*, bapt. at St. Alkmund's April 20, 1566; d. young.

9. *Roger Prowde*, bapt. at St. Julian's Dec. 19, 1567; not mentioned in his mother's will in 1610.

10. *Catherine Prowde*, bapt. at St. Julian's July 31, 1569; m. Edward Phillips, son of Hugo and Elizabeth (Owen) Phillips, Feb. 7, 1596, at St. Julian's. Edward Phillips, gent., was buried Nov. 12, 1618, and Mrs. Katherine Phillips Aug. 3, 1650, at St. Julian's. Their son Edward married Anne Milton, daughter of John Milton, scrivenor, of London, and sister of the poet.†

---

*Prerogative Court of Canterbury, 41 Cope.

†Visitation of Shropshire, 1623, Harleian Society, 29: 397.

11. *Andrew Prowde,* bapt. at St. Julian's Jan. 10, 1570/1, and buried Aug. 20, 1574.

12. *Alice Prowde,* bapt. at St. Julian's Sept. 28, 1572; m. Richard Gyttens Dec. 29, 1599, at St. Julian's.

13. *Richard Prowde,* bapt. at St. Julian's Feb. 7, 1573/4; m. Eleanor Waring;* mentioned with his son George in his mother's will in 1610. He was admitted to the Drapers Company in 1600 and was buried at St. Chad's Oct. 24, 1622.

2. ii. RICHARD.
3. iii. THOMAS.
4. iv. ANDREW.
   v. JOHN. As "Johannes ap Leus" he was entered in Shrewsbury School in 1563 and as "Johannes Lewis" in 1565. He was a shearman or finisher of cloth, and was a burgess of Shrewsbury in 1582. He married ELEANOR EYNES, daughter of John Eynes. "John Leweis, Sharman, in the barker street", was buried at St. Chad's Jan. 12, 1621.

   Children:†
   1. *Thomas.*
   2. *Bartholomew.*
   3. *Lucy.*
   4. *Mary.*

2. RICHARD[2] LEWIS (*Lewis[1] ap Jevan*) was born presumably at Almer Park, near Shrewsbury, about 1540. He married MARJORIE IRELAND, daughter of Thomas Ireland, Esq., of Adbrighton, co. Salop, and sister of Robert Ireland of Shrewsbury, the builder of the great half-timbered townhouse known as Ireland's Mansion and still one of the most interesting structures in the town. His second wife, whom he married May 8, 1586, at St. Mary's, was MARY LLOYD, widow of David Lloyd and daughter of John Evans of Dreff. He was buried July 14, 1587, at St. Mary's.

Ric'us Lewys was in 1563 a brother of the Guild of the Sacred Trinity in Shrewsbury, which had been founded by Edward IV. As Richard Lewis, son of Lewis ap Jevan, he was made free of the Drapers' Company in 1566‡, and was a burgess of Shrewsbury. He was lessee of the tithes of Almer Park in 1578. In the General Muster of 1587 Richard Lewis, gent., appears among the Drapers, having in armor "a Calliver, one bowe and a sheffe of arrowes".§

The will of Richard Lewes of the parish of St. Julian, Salop, draper, made July 7 and proved November 28, 1587, directs that he be buried within the church of St. Mary. To his son Nathaniel he left 100 marks in money to be paid to his brother Richard Evans and his wife Mary Lewis, they to have the use thereof and keep the boy until he was eighteen. In case of Nathaniel's death the 100 marks was to be repaid

---

*Morris's pedigree of Prowde.
†Their names and that of their mother are from the pedigree of the family by Morris.
‡Shrewsbury Drapers' Apprentices, Shropshire Archaeological Society, 50:1.
§Shropshire Archaeological Society, 2nd Series, 3:114.

to the use of all of his daughters, they to be governed by the executors. To Nathaniel, a lease of three pastures and a pool, held of John Hetton of Great Berwick. To his daughter Elizabeth Lewis, £40 and a house now in building in St. Mary's over against the almshouses. To his daughters Susanna, Sara, Alice, Margaret, Mary and Deborah Lewis, £40 each. To all of his daughters, the lease of a farm at Aston Abbots, co. Salop, to be sold for their benefit. "I am bound with my brother Thomas Lewis to Richard Evans for payment of £100 to my wife Mary Lewes. I give my brother £100 to discharge this bond." To his wife, all the wearing apparel, rings and jewels she had before marriage, and one black cow. To his maid Ann Heyward, one black cow in the custody of the widow of Hugh Peers of the Castle Foregate, also a ewe and a lamb. To his servant Richard Goodale, his servant Josia Griffith and to William Leicester, son of John Leicester, a ewe and a lamb to each. To his servant Katherine, one brown heifer. To his maids Cicely and Joan, a ewe and a lamb each. To his man John, a ewe and a lamb. To his brother Richard Evans and his brother Andrew Lewis, a colt each. If his wife Mary is with child, it is to have £30. Residue to all his children equally. "I am bound to pay £110 to my wife's two daughters. If she take in discharge the goods of her late husband David Lloyd then I give her £13: 6: 8." Executors: brethren Robert Ireland Esq. and Mr. Thos. Lewes gent. to whom 40s. each to make a ring. Witnesses: Richard Owen, Thos. Chareton, Andrew Lewes, Wm. Roberts scrip.*

Children by first wife:

i. ELIZABETH.[3]
ii. SUZANNA, possibly m. at St. Julian's July 1, 1600, RONDULPH KYN- NASTON, gent.
iii. SARA, m. Hugh Jones and was mentioned in the will of her uncle Thomas Lewis in 1604.
iv. ALICE.
v. MARGARET, living, unmarried, in 1604.
vi. MARY, living, unmarried, in 1604.
vii. DEBORAH, living, unmarried, in 1604.
viii. JOSEPH, son of Richard Lewys in St. Chad's, buried in St. Julian's Jan. 4, 1586/7.

By second wife:

ix. NATHANIEL, bapt. Feb. 19, 1586/7, at St. Julian's; apprenticed in the Drapers' Company in 1603.

3. THOMAS[2] LEWIS (*Lewis[1] ap Jevan*) was born about 1545, presumably at Almer Park, near Shrewsbury. He married about 1580 SUSANNA IRELAND, daughter of Thomas Ireland, Esq., of Adbrighton, co. Salop, and a sister of the wife of his brother Richard Lewis. In the register of St. Julian's under the date March 25, 1605, is the entry "Thomas Lewys gent. dyed one of ye Baylyffs of our towne". Mrs. Susanna Lewis was buried at St. Julian's on February 5, 1628/9.

---

*Prerogative Court of Canterbury, 72 Spender.

Lewis was admitted to the Drapers' Company in 1573. In the General Muster of June 10, 22 Elizabeth (1580) Thomas Lewis, gent., appears under the heading "Free of noe occupation within the Town". He owned a jacke, a sallett and a bill. Again in the General Muster of 1589 his name is listed under the same heading, owning a corslet and a collyver. His servant William Manninge is also listed.* Shrewsbury was governed by two bailiffs elected annually by the burgesses, and Thomas Lewis served as bailiff in 1581, 1589, 1600 and 1604.

When the Visitation of Shropshire of 1585 was taken by Richard Lee, Portcullis, Thomas Lewis was "disclaimed"; that is, his "gentility" was stated to be a pretense. The local church and civic authorities continued to give the Lewises the distinction of "Mr." and "gentleman", however, and no member of the family was disclaimed when the Visitation of 1623 was taken.

The will of Thomas Lewis of the Parish of Saint Julyans within the town of Shrewsbury, gent., was made February 15, 1604/5, and proved May 1, 1605. To my wife Susan, all my lands for life, three tenements under the Wilde in Shrewsbury, three tenements in Coleham, a suburb of the said town, and a tenement in the Abbey Ferriot; also all my household stuff, plate excepted, to bestow at her decease upon her children; also three silver tonns, three small silver wine cups and my second silver salt; also £400. To my son Thomas, all my lands before named at his mother's death, with reversion to my sons Daniel, Samuel and Michael and then to my right heirs. To my son Thomas, pastures near the Bott of Camery held of Mr. John Baker, a pasture called Brinthredinoke held of Mr. Roger ap Hugh, a pasture adjoining called Caneworth, £100 and my best gelding or mare. To my son Daniel, £40 in the hands of his master, Mr. Robert Stephens, draper, and £160 to be paid him £40 a year. To sons Samuel and Michael £200 each, to be paid them £40 a year. To my brother John Lewis, 40 s. To my man Thos. Davyes, 5 marks. To my maids Lowry Hughes, 40 s., and Alice Parre, 20 s. To my boy servant John, 10 s. To the poor of Shrewsbury £5 (£1 to each parish). To my wife Susan, six best silver spoons. To my sister Prowde, 40 s. My brother Andrew Lewis owes me £100 and I remit half if he pay the other half punctually £40 a year [sic]. I owe my cousin Nathaniel Lewis 100 marks which his father left him and it is to be made up to £100. To my cousin Margaret Lewis, whom I owe very near £120, 40 s. to buy her apparel. To my cousins Mary Lewis and Debora Lewis, to whom I owe like sums, 40 s. to them also. To my cousin Sara Jones daughter, if

*Shropshire Archaeological Society, 2nd Series, 2: 259.

she live to the age of ten, £5. Residue to all my children at the discretion of their mother. Executors: wife Susan and son Daniel. Overseers: brother George Ireland and brother Andrew Lewis. Witnesses: William Banes, Samuell Lewis.* Children, baptized in Shrewsbury:

i. THOMAS,[3] bapt. at St. Julian's Feb. 18, 1581/2; m. SARAH DUTTON, daughter of Rowland Dutton of Hatton, co. Chester, who was possibly buried at St. Julian's June 5, 1649. He was probably that Thomas Lewis who was a scholar at Shrewsbury School in 1591 and 1592. He was a churchwarden of St. Julian's in 1612, and was admitted to the Mercers' Company Oct. 8, 1613.
Children (possibly others):
1. *Edward*,[4] bapt. at St. Julian's June 21, 1607. He was executor of the will of his uncle Michael Lewis in 1644, being called a clerk in that document.
2. *Mary*, "daughter of Mr. Thomas Lewis", buried at St. Julian's Aug. 3, 1649.

ii. DANIEL, bapt. at St. Julian's May 31, 1584; m. at St. Alkmund's June 2, 1612, SARAH STEPHENS; buried at St. Julian's June 3, 1635. Possibly his widow was the Mrs. Sara Lewis who was buried at St. Julian's June 5, 1649. Daniolt Lewes, son of Thomas Lewes of Salop, yeoman, was apprenticed to Robert Stephens in 45 Elizabeth (1602–1603). He was admitted to the Drapers' Company in 1609, was a burgess of Shrewsbury and was elected bailiff of the town in 1629. He was a churchwarden of St. Julian's in 1626.
Children (possibly others):
1. *Thomas*,[4] bapt. at St. Alkmund's June 6, 1613.
2. *Robert*, bapt. at St. Alkmund's Oct. 16, 1614. A Robert Lewis m. at St. Julian's March 22, 1635, Blanche Corbet, who was buried at St. Julian's Nov. 19, 1675. The pedigree by Morris assigns this Robert to Thomas and Sarah (Dutton) Lewis, but there is no other evidence that Thomas had a son Robert. Robert, aged 17, son of Daniel Lewis, draper, was apprenticed to a member of the Drapers' Company in 1631. He was named in the will of his uncle Samuel Lewis in 1637.
3. *Joshua*, bapt. at St. Chad's March 21, 1618/9.

iii. MARY, bapt. at St. Julian's May 29, 1586; m. WILLIAM KING, gentleman, Feb. 10, 1604.

iv. SAMUEL, bapt. at St. Julian's Aug. 5, 1587; m. (1) MARY GARDNER, daughter of John Gardner of Shrewsbury; m. (2) ISABEL (MILWARD?); buried at St. Julian's May 9, 1637. He was in Shrewsbury School in 1600 and 1602, and was admitted to the Mercers' Company in 1613. He was a churchwarden of St. Julian's in 1618.
The will of Samuel Lewis of the town of Shrewsbury, gentleman, directs that he be buried in the church of St. Julian's. He left all his goods and chattels, both in his dwelling house and those in the custody of his mother-in-law Alice Milward of Merrinall in Shrewsbury and due to his wife Isabel under the will of her father, to be employed to pay his debts. To Robert Lewis, son of his brother Daniel, £5. To the three children of his brother Michael, £5 each. To his brother-in-law William King and his cousin Edward Lewis, £5. Executors: brother-in-law William King and nephew Edward Lewis, clerk. Witnesses: James Peddey, Daniel Porter, John Bennett. It was dated April 17, and proved June 10, 1637.† His children must have been otherwise provided for.

---

*Prerogative Court of Canterbury, 30 Hayes.
†Prerogative Court of Canterbury, 94 Goare.

Children:
1. *Nehemiah*,[4] bapt. at St. Julian's April 25, 1620, and buried there May 12, 1648. As son of Samuel Lewis of Shrewsbury, gentleman, he matriculated at Oxford, from Brasenose College, July 24, 1635, aged 15, and received his B.A. from St. Alban's Hall June 18, 1639.
2. *Thomas*, bapt. at St. Mary's March 6, 1622. He was apprenticed in the Drapers' Company in 1640, as son of Samuel Lewis, late of Shrewsbury, mercer.
3. *Mary*, bapt. at St. Julian's April 13, 1632.

v. MICHAEL, bapt. at St. Julian's Aug. 24, 1589; m. ALICE EDWARDS, daughter of Thomas Edwards of Greet and of the College, Shrewsbury, Esq., and sister of Sir Thomas Edwards, Bart.; buried at St. Julian's July 22, 1644. He was a scholar at Shrewsbury School in 1600, and was admitted to the Mercers' Company June 20, 1625. In 1638 he was an assistant or councillor of the town government under the charter granted by Charles I.

The will of Michael Lewis of Shrewsbury, gentleman, was made July 12, 1644, and proved Jan. 10, 1644/5. He directed that he be buried in the church or chancel of St. Julian's. To his wife Alice, £40 to be paid within four days of his death, three silver bowls, two silver salts, eight silver spoons valued at £12, the best bedstead and feather-bed and £5 to buy her a mourning gown. To his two children, Daniel Lewis and Anne Lewis, £50 each to be raised out of his brass, pewter, etc. Residue of all personal estate to his executor Mr. Lewis Davies. Witnesses: Launcelot Forster, Richard Hayward. Mr. Davies renounced probate and Alice Lewis, the widow, was granted administration. The will was sealed with an armorial seal, a quartered coat: 1 & 4, a chevron between three heads; 2 & 3, in chief (or on a chief) three roundels, in base an animal or bird.

Children:

1. *Thomas*, bapt. at St. Julian's Oct. 19, 1623; d. before 1644.
2. *Daniel*, bapt. at St. Julian's Dec. 6, 1627; buried in St. Julian's Feb. 26, 1655/6.
3. *Edward*, bapt. at St. Julian's Jan. 22, 1628/9; buried at St. Julian's Jan. 25, 1630/1.
4. *Anne*, living in 1644 and was probably the Mrs. Anne Lewis, spinster, buried at St. Julian's April 30, 1686.

vi. RICHARD, bapt. at St. Mary's July 6, 1592; buried at St. Julian's Sept. 25, 1597.

4. ANDREW[2] LEWIS (*Lewis*[1] *ap Jevan*) was presumably born at Almer Park near Shrewsbury about 1550. His mother entered him in the third class of Shrewsbury School in 1562, and, if he remained there to complete his course, he may have known two boys who came to the school in 1564 and gained lasting fame at the gallant court of Queen Elizabeth — Sir Philip Sidney and Sir Fulk Greville. As "Andrew Lewys, son of Lewys ap Jevan and apprentice of George Prowde", his brother-in-law, he was admitted to the Drapers' Company of Shrewsbury in 1573* was a burgess of the town by 1582 and a bailiff in 1607. Andrew Lewis, draper, was listed in the General Muster of June 10, 22 Elizabeth (1580), as the possessor of a sword and dagger, and in the Muster of 1587 he, "gentleman", had "a bowe, a sheff of arrows and a

---

*Shropshire Archaeological Society, 4th Series, 11:143.

skull".* He married about 1580 MARY HERRING, daughter of Mr. William Herring of Shrewsbury, vintner and draper. "Mr. Andrew Lewis one of the Alldermen of Salop" was buried at St. Mary's Sept. 31, 1617. "Mris Mary, wife of Mr. Andrew Lewis" was buried at the same church Jan. 20, 1628/9.

The will or administration papers of Andrew Lewis were probably entered in the court of the Peculiar of St. Mary's, of which no records survive for this period.

Children:

    i.   JANE,[3] bapt. at St. Julian's July 9, 1581; probably d. in infancy.
    ii.   ROBERT, admitted to the Drapers' Company in 1605; d. of the plague and buried at St. Mary's Oct. 21, 1607.
5. iii. THOMAS.
    iv. MARY.†
    v.   ELEANOR.
    vi. SAMUEL, bapt. at St. Mary's Aug. 22, 1591; d. of the plague and buried at St. Mary's July 28, 1604.
   vii. ELIZABETH, bapt. at St. Mary's May 27, 1593; probably d. before 1623.

5. THOMAS[3] LEWIS (*Andrew,*[2] *Lewis*[1] *ap Jevan*) was born in Shrewsbury in the 1590 decade. As he was a benefactor of Shrewsbury School in later life he was undoubtedly a pupil there, but he cannot be the Thomas Lewis, "gen. f. & h." (gentleman's son and heir) who was entered in 1599, as his elder brother Robert was alive in that year. However, boys named Thomas Lewis were in the school in 1600, 1603 and 1605 and some of these entries must refer to him. As Thomas Lewis, son of Andrew Lewis, draper, he was apprenticed to a member of the Drapers Company in 1607‡, but his principal business, after his apprenticeship ended, was that of vintner, or wine merchant. His grandfather Herring, who was a vintner, left no sons, but two of his grandsons, Thomas Lewis and Thomas Woley, who was also a vintner, probably inherited his business. In 1618/9 he was the owner or lessee of the Sextry, a tavern and inn in the Sextry Shut, managed by his partner George Cleeve who "lived there in good sorte and fashion".§ The Sextry, now known as the Golden Cross, is still one of the taverns of Shrewsbury. As a burgess of the town he was called Thomas Lewis, vintner, in 1619, and Thomas Lewis, draper, in 1620. It was in 1625 that he, vintner, was listed among the benefactors of Shrewsbury School.

Thomas Lewis and ELIZABETH MARSHALL were married at St. Chad's on August 29, 1618. By this marriage he must have added to the not inconsiderable means which had come

---

*Ibid., 2nd Series, 2:259; 3:114.

†She and her sister Eleanor were named in the Herring pedigree in the Visitation of Shropshire of 1623.

‡Shropshire Archaeological Society, 50: 1.

§*Cleeve* vs. *Price,* Court of Requests, Bundle 35, part III, 1618/9. The papers in this suit, in The Public Record Office, London, read by Col. Charles E. Banks, gave the initial clue to the location of Thomas Lewis and George Cleeve in Shrewsbury.

to him as his father's only son when Andrew Lewis died in 1617.

When and how Lewis became interested in emigration to New England is, of course, unknown. Capt. Richard Bonython, the son of a Cornish squire and later Lewis's associate, may well have known Sir Ferdinando Gorges during his many years of command at Plymouth, and Gorges was an outstanding advocate of colonial expansion in America. Bonython's mother was born Eleanor Millington and spent her last years with Millington kinsmen in Shrewsbury where she was buried at St. Chad's on January 10, 1628/9. Bonython, visiting his mother, may have excited interest in Sir Ferdinando's transatlantic plans, and it does not require much imagination to see Capt. Bonython, Thomas Lewis, Arthur Mackworth, George Cleeve and possibly Michael Mitton, all of whom became great resident landowners in Maine, seated around a table in the Sextry, deep in discussion of their coming adventure.

On February 12, 1629, the Council for the Affairs of New England in America, otherwise known as The Plymouth Company, granted by patent to Thomas Lewis, gentleman, and Capt. Richard Bonython a tract of land on the north side of the Saco river in what was known as the Province of Maine, extending four miles from the mouth of the river and eight miles inland. Of Lewis the patent states that he "hath already been at the charge to transport himself and others to take a view of New England . . . for the bettering of his experience in advancing of a Plantation," and so it is fair to presume that he had some previous knowledge of his future estate.*

June 28, 1631, found Mr. Lewis arrived from England and entering into the possession of his property, livery of seisin being given by Mr. Edward Hilton of New Hampshire, one of the several commissioners nominated in the patent by the Council. Mr. Lewis then proceeded, in his turn, as attorney for the Council, to give Mr. Hilton possession under his patent to Piscataqua, in New Hampshire, which document he probably brought from England with his own. The exact location of Mr. Lewis's residence is uncertain, but it is probable that he lived on Rendezvous Point near the old graveyard in the house which was later the property of his son-in-law, Lieut. Gibbins. Richard Vines, who had received a similar patent for land on the south side of the Saco river, had settled upon his grant in 1630, building his house at Winter Harbor, now known as Biddeford Pool, and surrounding himself with a goodly number of planters. The patents on both banks of the river were known by its name, Saco. The Plymouth Company did not send out a governor to ad-

---

*The original patent is among the manuscripts in the library of the Maine Historical Society.

minister the affairs of the colony. The planters seem to have taken matters into their own hands, however, and to have entered into an agreement or "combination", the terms of which have not survived, which constituted the basis of self-government, the document embodying it being in the custody of Mr. Lewis.

In 1635, the Council, after granting a patent to Sir Ferdinando Gorges which included within its limits all of their former jurisdiction, gave up their charter to the throne. The new over-lord, calling his province New Somersetshire, appointed Capt. William Gorges its governor, and granted commissions as counsellors to the most prominent patentees and gentlemen then residing within its borders, among them Mr. Lewis. The new government, sitting also as a court of law, convened "in the house of Capt. Richard Bonython in Saco, this 25th day of March, 1636, present, Capt. Richard Bonython, Capt. William Gorges, Capt. Cammock, Mr. Henry Jocelyn, Mr. Thomas Purchase, Edward Godfrey, and Thomas Lewis, Gents." The session seems to have been a stormy one for Mr. Lewis. He and Capt. Bonython had had a dispute with Mrs. Joan Vines, the wife of the Winter Harbor patentee, who was apparently abroad at the time, in regard to the title to one of the islands in the river. The court dealt with the case as follows: "To the request of Mrs. Joan Vines, and an order of Sir Ferdinando Gorges as per the same at large appeareth, and other circumstances us inducing, concerning the difference between Capt. Richard Bonython and Mr. Thomas Lewis against Mrs. Joan Vines, concerning the planting of corn on the island where she planted formerly, and an order left by her husband how to plant: It is ordered for the preservation of the public peace and the general good of the country, that Mrs. Joan Vines shall peaceably plant what she hath formerly planted and what more she can plant. Also Capt. Richard Bonython and Mr. Thomas Lewis to plant what they can except where Mrs. Vines planteth and for trial of the title to said island, to rest till further trial may be made thereof, and this we register, ratify and confirm, although Mr. Thomas Lewis did opprobriously, in open court, lacerate and tear an order made to that purpose." On the third day of court Mr. Lewis brought suit for slander against Mr. Thomas Williams, and Williams was bound to answer at the next term, under a penalty of £100. The adverse decision on the Vines case seems to have incensed Mr. Lewis against the new government. He retained possession of the old combination, quite possib'y opposing it to the authority of Capt. Gorges, for under the date February 9, 1636/7, we find the court ordering "that Mr. Thomas Lewis shall appear the next court day at the now dwelling house of Thomas Williams, there to answer his contempt, and to show cause why he will not deliver up the Combination belonging to us."

Mr. Lewis also appeared before the same session of the court, of which he still remained an official, first as defendant in an action by John Richmond for trespass, and second, in what appears to have been an issue of veracity with Clement Greenway. Greenway's affidavit states that on "the 5th July 1635 Mr. Thomas Lewis did hyre the said Greenway his servant called Peter Hogg till the midst of March following, and the said Lewis was to pay this deponent seaven£ for his servants hyre, and this deponent saith that he did not promise that the said Hogg could caulk boats very well." This case went against Mr. Lewis, and he had to pay damages of £4.*

Mr. Lewis died between 1637 and 1640, probably before 1639, as his name does not appear on the list of Counsellors appointed by Sir Ferdinando Gorges after the confirmation of his patent by a royal charter in that year. The court of 1640 ordered that "Francis Robinson executor of the last will and testament of Thomas Lewis, late of this plantation, deceased, upon the delivery of the goods and chattels now in his custody belonging to the said testator, unto his creditors, shall be allowed of such reasonable charges as have been by him expended upon two of the children of said testator since his death." The will is not filed or recorded among the Maine probate records, and a search in the Prerogative Court of Canterbury, where a colonial will might possibly be filed, has been productive of no result. Mr. Robinson, the executor, was a man of some importance, being a magistrate of the province in 1645.

Mr. Lewis's widow, Elizabeth Lewis, survived him only a short time. From the letter of Rev. Richard Gibson to Gov. Winthrop, from which quotations are made later, it would seem probable that she and her daughters did not join the patentee in Maine until 1637. Her name appears in a partition agreement, dividing a portion of the patent, dated October 8, 1640, entered into by Capt. Bonython individually and with Francis Robinson, as "Executors In Trust for Ye last will & Testament of Elizabeth Lewis", and "Elizabeth and Judeth the daughters of the above named Elizabeth Lewis." From this document we are able to determine that Mr. Lewis left his Maine estate to his wife, who in her turn left it by will in trust to Capt. Bonython and Robinson for her two daughters. Her will is also missing.

Children, baptized at St. Chad's:†

*Province and Court Records of Maine, Maine Historical Society, 1928, I:5.
†Correcting The Ancestry of Charity Haley, Walter G. Davis, 1916, pp. 54–5.

i. MARY,[4] bapt. June 28, 1619; m. in Saco in 1638 REV. RICHARD
   GIBSON. Richard Gibson, A.B., Magdalen College, Oxford, was a
   Church of England clergyman who had been sent out in 1636 by
   Mr. Robert Trelawny of Plymouth to guard the spiritual welfare
   of his plantation at Richmond's Island, several miles to the east-
   ward of Saco. He found it impossible to agree, however, with Mr.
   Winter, the manager of the Trelawny patent, although he seems
   to have gained the confidence and friendship of the fishermen and
   planters, and he was soon devoting a part of his labors to the
   Saco settlement. In 1637 he is stated in the court records of New
   Somerset to hold an order settling "the controversies about the
   Island", which probably refers to the dispute between Mrs. Vines
   and Lewis and Bonython. His marriage with Mary Lewis does
   not seem to have been the result of a very romantic attachment.
   Writing from Richmond's Island on Jan. 14, 1638(9) to Governor
   Winthrop of Massachusetts Bay, he says "By the providence of
   God and the counsell of friends, I have lately marryed Mary,
   daughter of Mr. Tho. Lewis of Saco, which marriage was thought
   a fitt meanes for the closing of differences and settling an order
   both for religion & govermt in these Plantations. Howbeit, so it
   is for the present, that some troublous spirits, out of miss-affection,
   others, as is supposed for hire, have cast an aspersion upon her,
   & generally avouch that shee so behaved her selfe in the shipp
   which brought her from England hither some 2 yeares agoe, that
   the block was reaved at the mayne yard to have duckt her, and
   that she was kept close in the ships cabin 48 houres, for shelter
   and rescue, which tends to her utter infemy, the greif of her
   freinds and my great infamy and hinderance. . . . My humble
   suite to your Wopp is . . . that you would please to call before
   you George Burdett of Boston, shoemaker, Anne his wife, and
   others whom they can name, which came over in the ship with
   her, and examine them of these things whereof she is accused.
   . . . I married the mayd upon long demurres, by advize of friends,
   and if these imputations be justly charged upon her, I shall
   reverence God's afflicting hand, and possesse my selfe in patience
   under God's chastiseing. If false, both shee and many shall have
   cause to blesse God for you, and for that govermt which shineth
   from you to us. . . . Richard Gibsonn, minr of the Gospell at
   Richmond Island & Saco."

   One of the troublous spirits was undoubtedly John Bonython,
   the only son of the Captain, who gave the colony constant trouble
   and was finally outlawed in 1645 by the Provincial Court in which
   his father sat as a magistrate. In the court held in June 1640,
   Richard and Mary Gibson sued John Bonython for slander, charg-
   ing that, in addition to making scandalous charges against Mrs.
   Gibson, he had on April 28th, 1640, in the house of Thomas Lewis,
   deceased, called Mr. Gibson "a base priest, a base knave, a base
   fellow." The plaintiffs obtained a verdict, the damages being
   assessed at £6: 6s: 8d. At the same session John Bonython sued
   Mr. Gibson for debt, declaring that he owed him £5 on a bill
   due May 1, which Mr. Gibson, through his attorney, Francis
   Robinson, the executor of his father-in-law's estate, partly acknowledged, and asked that the matter be referred to arbitration.
   Mr. George Cleaves and Mr. Arthur Mackworth were appointed
   arbitrators and Mr. Gibson's corn, growing in Saco, was pledged
   as security for the payment of their award. By 1640 or 1641
   Mr. Gibson left Richmond's Island and Saco and became first
   minister of the settlement at Piscataqua. Here, however, he
   came into conflict with Puritan Massachusetts. As Governor
   Winthrop says, "He being wholly addicted to the hierachy and
   discipline of England . . . did marry and baptize at the Isle of

Shoals which was found within our jurisdiction." Gibson further increased the dislike of the Governor by writing his colleague, Rev. Mr. Larkham of Dover, denying the title of Massachusetts, and when later in the year he arrived in Boston,'being apparently about to sail for England or some other colony,' he was thrown into jail, where he remained until he acknowledged the charges and threw himself on the mercy of the court, "whereupon, in regard he was a stranger and was to depart the country in a few days, he was discharged without any fine or other punishment."

ii. SUSANNA, bapt. Nov. 2, 1620; no further record.

iii. MARGARET, bapt. April 22, 1622; no further record.

iv. ELIZABETH, bapt. April 7, 1623; m., presumably in Saco, ROBERT HEYWOOD, planter, of the parish of St. Thomas, Barbadoes. He may also have been a native of Shrewsbury, where Heywood was not an uncommon name. Elizabeth Heywood inherited from her father and mother a joint title with her sister Judith in the patent at Saco. Her brother-in-law James Gibbins managed her Maine property for several years under a power of attorney* but eventually the entire Lewis half of the patent vested in Mrs. Gibbins, presumably through the purchase of Mrs. Heywood's interest. Robert Heywood died before 1680.

Elizabeth Heywood of the Town of St. Michael in the Island of Barbadoes, widow and relict of Robert Heywood of the parish of St. Thomas, planter, deceased, made her will Jan. 10, 1680, and it was proved Oct. 23, 1682. To her son-in-law Thomas Hase and Elizabeth his wife, she left a piece of land and a house on Palmetto street in St. Michael's. To her son-in-law William Charles and Martha his wife, a piece of land and a house on Palmetto street in St. Michael's. To her son John Heywood, a piece of land with new houses thereon. To her sons Robert and Thomas Heywood, equally, her dwelling-house wherein she was living, with land and out-buildings. To her son Nathaniel Heywood, a house and land on Palmetto street in St. Michael's. To her son Richard Heywood, a negro boy named Daniel. To her daughter Martha Charles, and, after Martha's death, to the testator's granddaughters Elizabeth Hayes, Frances Charles and Katherine Heywood, a negro girl named Tabby. To her daughter Hester Orpen, a feather bed and bolster, to be delivered to her after the death of her husband John Orpen, and not before. To her grandson Richard Heywood, son of her eldest son Richard Heywood, mariner, a piece of plate "to be sent home". To her daughter Hester Orpen, £3 in case she should be in want and under certain conditions. Executors: son-in-law Thomas Hase, a son John Heywood.

Children:

1. *Elizabeth Heywood,* m. before 1680 Thomas Hayes of Barbadoes.

2. *Martha Heywood,* m. before 1680 William Charles of Barbadoes.

3. *Richard Heywood,* mariner, married and the father of a son, Richard, in 1680.

4. *John Heywood,* m. Aug. 12, 1677, Mr. John Heywood and Mrs. Mary Whitehead; children bapt. 1681–1688 in Barbadoes. A John Heywood was Chief Marshal of His Majesty's Court of Common Pleas for the parishes of St. James and St. Thomas in 1699, and Chief Justice of the Court of Common Pleas in 1704.

5. *Hester Heywood,* m. (1) before 1680, apparently against her mother's wishes, John Orpen. In 1680 John Orpen and wife had 3 hired servants and apprentices, 2 bought servants and 5 negroes. Mr. John Orpen was buried Nov. 6, 1696. As

---

*York Deeds, 11: 5.

Mrs. Hester Orpen, she m. (2) Nov. 21, 1701, Mr. Richard Turner.

In his will, dated Nov. 19, 1687, Thomas Lewis Esq., of the parish of Christ Church, Barbadoes, left to Hester, wife of John Orpin, an annuity of £15 sterling during her natural life. That the testator was a Lewis of the Shrewsbury stock, and a cousin in some degree of Elizabeth (Lewis) Heywood is an inescapable conclusion.*

6. *Robert Heywood*, m. Mary ———— and had daughter Susanna bapt. Jan. 21, 1681; buried Oct. 23, 1694 in Barbadoes.

7. *Thomas Heywood*, m. Nov. 23, 1680 Mary Harding; children bapt. 1687–1699. She must be the Mary Heywood of St. Philip's parish, widow, who made her will Feb. 4, 1729, proved Aug. 19, 1730, naming sons Harding, Richard, John and Nathaniel Heywood, daughters Elizabeth and Mary Heywood, grandson Thomas Heywood and the children of her son Richard Heywood. She directs that her dwelling be the home of all the children during minority, but, as it is impossible that any of her own children were minors in 1729, she must have included the grandchildren. Of the sons, Richard Heywood of St. Michael's parish, wheelwright, made his will May 21, 1730, proved March 8, 1735/6, naming his wife Prudence (Prudence Hart, married Oct. 10, 1714), and children Thomas (an acre of land at St. Philip's, given me by the last will of my mother Mary Heywood), John, Robert, Richard, Charles, Elizabeth and Margaret Heywood, and his brothers John Heywood and Richardson Hart. Nathaniel Heywood of Christ Church, planter, made his will Oct. 22, 1735, proved April 22, 1736, naming his brothers Harding, Richard and John Heywood, his sisters Elizabeth ("one black heifer now at Rendevous

---

*Thomas Lewis, Lieut. Col. of Col. Christopher Lyne's regiment, and a member of the Royal Council of Barbadoes at the time of his death, made his will Nov. 19, 1687, and it was proved in Barbadoes on June 12, 1690. To his wife Joan Lewis he left an annual income of £400, to be raised out of two plantations with the land, negroes and buildings thereunto belonging, in the parishes of Christ Church and St. Philip's. Also to his wife, the sole use of three rooms in the house wherein he was living, *i.e.*, the chamber over the porch, the great room or chamber and the room with the balcony adjoining, with free passage to and from the same. Also to his wife, two negro men, Matthias and Lawrence, a boy Tony, and six women, Sarah, Joane, Nicho, Jonney, old Winney and young Winney, all being house negroes. "And where as I have an Estate in the Kingdom of England consisting either in Land Tenement hereditaments goods and chattels readie money or moneys put out to Interest either in my own name or in trust for me," I do hereby give this estate to my beloved wife Joan Lewis. To Hester, wife of John Orpin, an annuity of fifteen pounds sterling during her natural life. To Elizabeth Dillon, now living with him, maintenance until she is 21 or married, at which time £15. If his wife is enceinte, the entire estate in Barbadoes to the child. Sole executrix: wife Joan Lewis. Witnesses: (Major) John Dempster, (Capt.) John Adams, (Lieut. Col.) Tobias Frere, (Mr.) Christopher Lytcott, James Mowatt. In depositions made by the witnesses it appeared that Lewis had "brothers" John Dorne and Tobias Frere and a "cousin" Thomas Sutton. Either Mrs. Lewis was in England at the time of her husband's death or she went there immediately afterward, for she applied for and got administration on her husband's estate from the Prerogative Court of Canterbury on Nov. 18, 1689, until such time as she could produce his will, the letters being addressed to "Joan Lewis widow relict of Thomas Lewis, Esquire, one of the councillors in the Island of Barbadoes." As stated above, the will was not proved in Barbadoes until June 12, 1690, whereupon it must have been sent to Mrs. Lewis who proved it in London in October 1690. The will is not on file or recorded in the Prerogative Court of Canterbury, and possibly it is buried among the papers of a suit in Chancery involving the estate in England.

Lieut. Col. Thomas Lewis had married Joan Frere at Christ Church on Jan. 13, 1687, the year in which he made his will. She was a daughter of John and Ann Frere and had been baptized in Barbadoes on Oct. 1, 1663. Lieut. Col. Tobias Frere was her brother and her sister Anne Frere had married at Christ Church on Aug. 22, 1678, John Dorne, which accounts for the "brothers" Frere and Dorne mentioned in the affidavits. The "cousin" Thomas Sutton was probably a son of John Sutton and Margaret Lewis who were married March 18, 1669. Whether Thomas and Margaret Lewis were native Barbadians or whether they had come from England is not known. A Thomas and Mary Lewis had a son Thomas baptized at Christ Church on Aug. 11, 1645, who may possibly have been the future councillor. This earlier Thomas Lewis, gentleman and merchant, was a great landowner as the Barbadoes deeds, 1640–1654, testify. Some of his deeds were witnessed by a man of the very Salopian name of Eyton. Lewis could very well be that Thomas,

647

plantation", doubtless named by his grandmother for her father's home on the Saco river in Maine) and Mary, his nephew Robert Heywood, his niece Margaret Heywood, and John, Richard, Nathaniel, Elizabeth, James and Prudence, children of his brother Richard Heywood.

8.   *Nathaniel Heywood*, Mr. Nathaniel Heywood m. Mrs. Alice Homeyard Nov. 11, 1683; Mr. Nathaniel Heywood buried Sept. 6, 1704; children bapt. 1686–1691/2.   He was a merchant in 1683 when he and his brother Richard, mariner, sold their share in their father's plantation and his slaves and negro children to their brother-in-law Thomas Hayes.*

v.   ANDREW, bapt. Feb. 22, 1624/5 and buried Nov. 15, 1625, at St. Mary's.

vi.   JUDITH, bapt. Oct. 23, 1626; m. in Saco about 1646 JAMES GIBBINS. From her many Maine families can trace descent..†

vii.   ANDREW, bapt. March 25, 1628; d. young.

---

son of Daniel Lewis of Shrewsbury who was bapt. at St. Alkmund's in 1613.   He would have been a second cousin of Elizabeth (Lewis) Heywood.
   Lewis was an extremely common name in Barbadoes in the seventeenth century.   From 1644 to 1700 there are 68 Lewis burials, 45 Lewis marriages and, to 1690, 37 Lewis baptisms in the island records.   Like Lieut. Col. Lewis, other Barbadian Lewises were extremely wealthy.   In 1679 Edmund Lewis of Christ Church had 214 acres of land, 8 white servants and 72 slaves; Capt. John Lues of St. Joseph had 152 acres, 1 servant and 70 slaves; Morgan Lewis of St. Peter, who later returned to Bristol, England, and died there, had 40 acres, 5 servants and 100 slaves.

*Barbadoes Deeds, 13: 455.

†See "Genealogical Dictionary of Maine and New Hampshire", Noyes, Libby, Davis,1928–1939, p. 259.

ANCESTRY OF THOMAS LEWIS AND HIS WIFE
ELIZABETH MARSHALL OF SACO, MAINE

By Walter Goodwin Davis, of Portland, Maine

Herring, of Shrewsbury, Shropshire

HERRING ARMS

The Herring family of Shrewsbury, co. Salop, of which Thomas Lewis' mother was a member, had its origin in Coventry, co. Warwick, from which city William Herring came to Shrewsbury about 1550. There is no Herring pedigree in the official Visitations of Shropshire of 1584 and 1623 at the College of Arms, but one appears in the copies of each of these visitations which are in the Harleian manuscripts in the British Museum and which are used as the basis for "The Visitation of Shropshire, 1623", published by the Harleian Society.

The first of these is Harleian ms. 1396, in which the Herring pedigree is on folio 164b. This manuscript was written by John Withie, a painter who accompanied the two deputy heralds, Robert Tresswell (Somerset) and Augustine Vincent (Rouge Croix) when they were in Shropshire viewing the arms and pedigrees of the Shropshire gentry, and the information contained therein is at least contemporary. The second pedigree is in Harleian ms. 1241, on folio 143. This is a copy by Thomas Hanford of Wigmore, made in 1661, of the visitation of Shropshire made in 1584 by Richard Lee (Richmond), marshal to Clarenceux, copied and *augmented* by Jacob Chaloner of London in 1620. Obviously the Herring pedigree is an *augmentation*, which does not diminish its relative credibility. A third Herring pedigree is included in the vast collection of genealogies of Shropshire families made by Joseph Morris of Shrewsbury in the early nineteenth century and now in the possession of Leonard Peele, Esq. These three pedigrees, which vary

St. Chads Church. 1778.

slightly in unimportant details, form the skeleton of the following account of the Herrings, which by good fortune can be clothed with much corroborative evidence from the public records.

The Herring arms, doubtless assumed without formality, are given in both of these Harleian manuscripts, and also in the extra-ordinary heraldic manuscript in the library of Shrewsbury School in which Robert Owen, gentleman, collected "the arms of the bailiffs of Shrewsbury" before his death in 1632. Few of these coats would pass the tests of the College of Arms, but they demonstrate a step in the process by which wealthy merchant families gradually rose to the status of gentry, through the consent of their fellows, the acquisition of country property and the assumption of arms, their pretensions being, perhaps, regularized at the next visitation of the heralds. The Herring coat, as given by Owen and by Withie, is *Azure,* semée of cross crosslets, six herrings hauriant, *or.*

1. WILLIAM HERRING, of Allesley, co. Warwick,* was presumably born about 1460. He married, according to the pedigrees, Alice Pickering. Allesley is a parish about two miles west of Coventry.

    Children:

    2. i. RICHARD.[2]

    ii. DOROTHY, m. Roger Cotton of Whitechurch, co. Salop, draper. In the Cotton pedigree in the visitation of Shropshire, Harleian ms. 1396, Roger Cotton is stated to have been the third son of Thomas Cotton of Whitchurch Coton and Alkington whose brother William Cotton was an alderman of Coventry. William Cotton, corvisor, witnessed the will of Richard Herring, Dorothy Herring's brother, in 1544, and Thomas Cotton, corvisor, received a legacy therein.†

    ? iii. THOMAS. Thomas Heryng, draper, of Coventry, who made his will on January 7, 1536/7, naming Mr. Richard Herynge a supervisor, was undoubtedly a member of this family and may have been a son of William Herring although he does not call Richard brother. He commends his soul to Almighty God, our Lady St. Mary and all the holy company of Heaven, and directs that his body be buried in Trinity church. To the high altar, 12d. To the altar of John, 4d. To our Lady's altar, 4d. To the altar of Corpus Christi, 4s. To the reparation of the church of Holy Trinity and for his burial there, 8d. To either of the mother churches, 2s. To either of the friars, 3s. 4d. To the craft of the drapers, 4d. To the craft of the butchers, 4d. I will to have a priest to sing for my soul and all Christian souls at Jesus altar at Trinity church for the space of a whole year and he is to sing once in the week a dirge and mass of requiem and also a mass of the five wounds, and he is to have for his wages £5: 6: 8. To Agnes Johnson, his servant, a black gown, lined, and 13s. 4d. To Thomas Banbroke, a mattress, a pair of sheets and a coverlet. To every servant in his house, 4d. To Margaret Herynge, his wife, a messuage which lyeth in the city of Coventry with all the appurtenances in Spone Street for her life, and on her departing to put it to what use it

---

*"Owsley minor" in Harleian ms. 1396 and in the Joseph Morris pedigree, and "Owsley major" in Harleian ms. 1241.

†Dorothy Herring appears in Mr. Morris's pedigree only.

shall please her so that their souls be prayed for, the souls of their parents and all Christian souls. Residue to wife Margaret, executrix. To Mr. Richard Herynge and Richard Kyenynge, supervisors, 3s. 4d. each. Witnesses: William Weit, Curat, John Brown, Robert Andros, with others. Proved March 8, 1536/7.*

2. RICHARD[2] HERRING (*William[1]*) was presumably born in Coventry about 1490. He married Margaret Carrington, according to all three of our pedigrees.

Richard Herring, mercer, was sheriff of Coventry in 1517, bailiff a year later, mayor of the city in 1527, master of Trinity Guild in 1529 and a member of the city corporation in 1542.†

The will of Richard Hearing of Coventry, mercer, was made April 19 and proved October 13, 1544. He directs that he be buried in Trinity church in Coventry in the south aisle under St. Anne's chapel. He makes bequests to various altars, to the mother church and to several craft guilds. To his daughter Dorothy, £13: 6: 8, part in plate and household stuff and part in money, at the discretion of his executrix. To every of his other children, £10 each at twenty-one. To his daughter Elizabeth, one plain piece of silver and three silver spoons on her day of marriage. To his wife Margeret, all lands and tenements called free charter land in the lordship of Allesley until his son and heir Julynes be twenty-one years of age, then Julynes is to enjoy the same, with remainder for lack of heirs to the testator's son William. To his wife, his copy lands in Allesley for life, and then his son William shall have a tenement in the east end of Allesley in the tenancy of John Bradesall, his son John shall have a parcel of land called "the hudds" and his daughter Dorothy shall have a parcel of land called Ardens. Julynes, his son and heir, shall have all the residue of the copy lands after the death of the testator's wife. To his son William Hearing, a messuage in the town of Nuneaton, co. Warwick, called "the sign of the bear." To Sir John Carrington, priest, a black gown. To his godson Richard Smyth, a silver spoon with a gilt image. To every woman servant, a kerchief of cloth. To William Ligh, his bay gelding. To Thomas Coton, corvisor, three yards of black cloth. To Trinity Church, two streamers. To Allesley church, two streamers. To the church wardens of Allesley, 4s. out of a piece of land in Allesley called "hormesche". To Master Cuthbert Joyner, 5s. To William Holbach of Fillongley, three yards of black cloth at 13s. 4d. To John Mylnor, bailiff of Allesley, three yards of black cloth at 13s. 4d. To the said William Holbach 5s. yearly "that he shalbe a frynd & counsayler to my wyfe and chyldren." To John Hill of Counden, 3s. 4d. yearly for ten years. Twelve poor men shall bear twelve

*Lichfield Probate Registry.
†"Trinity Guild of Coventry", Dugdale Society, 1944, p. 93.

tapers containing a pound of wax at his funeral and every of them shall have 4d. Residue to wife Margaret, executrix. Supervisors: Mr. Cuthbert Joyner, mercer, William Holbach of Fillongley, John Milner of Allesley. Witnesses: Richd Warner, barber, William Cotton, corvisor, William Lighe, surgeon, with divers others.*

Children:

    i.   Dorothy.³
    ii.   Elizabeth.
    iii. Julynes.†
3. iv. William.
    v.   John.

3. William³ Herring (*Richard,² William¹*), a minor in 1545 and married by 1556, was born about 1530, presumably in Coventry. He left his native city and settled in Shrewsbury, co. Salop, where he became a vintner or wine merchant. There he married by 1556 Elizabeth Mackworth, daughter of Arthur Mackworth, lord of the manor of Meole Brace, a few miles from the city.‡

The Mackworth family of Shropshire, a branch of the Mackworths of Mackworth, co. Derby, and unquestionably of "gentle blood", is surprisingly not included in the visitations of Shropshire of 1584 and 1623. Coming to Shropshire in the fifteenth century the Mackworths acquired the manor of Meole Brace, near Shrewsbury, and engaged in the trade and civic activities of that town, apprenticing their sons to drapers and vintners. The Arthur Mackworth whose

---

Ibid.

†Either Julines or John Herring was the father, or more probably the grandfather, of the eminent Puritan divine, Rev. Julines Herring, who was born at Flambere Mayre, co. Montgomery, in 1582. His family returned to Coventry in 1585. He was educated by Mr. Perkin, the minister at Morechurch, co. Salop, and at the grammar school at Coventry, and entered Sidney Sussex College, Cambridge, when he was fifteen. After obtaining his M.A. he returned to Coventry where he studied divinity under Humphrey Fenn, vicar of Holy Trinity, took orders from an Irish bishop and became a popular preacher in Coventry. Obtaining the living of Calke, co. Derby, he remained there eight years, attracting so many hearers that the church would not hold them, but was compelled to resign the living because of his scruples as to ceremonies. In 1618 he went to Shrewsbury, hired the Drapers's hall for meetings and was appointed lecturer at St. Alkmund's. He was watched by spies but escaped persecution by the ecclesiastical courts, although Archbishop Laud is reported to have said that he "would pickle that Herring of Shrewsbury". While at Shrewsbury he is said to have refused several offers of a pastorate in New England. Complaints were finally lodged against him and the Bishop of Litchfield, although sympathetic, was obliged to suspend him. After instructing from house to house a Miss Gellibrand, daughter accepted an invitation to become co-pastor of the English church at Amsterdam in 1636. He had much difficulty in escaping from England and did not arrive in Amsterdam until September, 1637, where he was warmly welcomed by the magistrates of the city who paid the expenses of his journey. He died in Amsterdam March 28, 1644, "a hard student, a solid and judicious divine and in life a pattern of good works." He had married, when at Calke, a Miss Gellibrand, daughter of the English pastor at Flushing, Holland, by whom he had thirteen children. (Dictionary of National Biography.)

Some member of this Herring family, possibly one of Rev. Julines Herring's sons, emigrated to Jamaica where a Col. Julines Herring was a wealthy planter in the eighteenth century and is an ancestor of the Earl of Halifax, the former British Ambassador to the United States.

‡This marriage is given in both of the Herring pedigrees in Harleian mss. 1241 and 1396 which were drawn up when at least one son-in-law (Thomas Wolley) and many grandchildren of William Herring were living in Shrewsbury, and, although it does not appear in the Mackworth pedigrees in which few daughters are entered, it is most probable.

daughter Elizabeth married William Herring would seem to be the Arthur Mackworth whose wife was Mary Barker, according to Mr. Joseph Morris's account of the family. A later Arthur Mackworth was a neighbor, associate, and presumably a cousin, of Herring's grandson, Thomas Lewis, in Maine in 1630.

In 1563 William Herringe of Shrewsbury, vintner, son of Richard Herringe of Coventry, was admitted a burgess of the town and his children's names and ages were recorded. They were Margaret, aged six, Mary, aged five, Elizabeth, aged two, and Eleanor, six months old.* On April 19, 13 Elizabeth (1572), William Hearinge, son of Richard Hearinge, late of Coventry, was admitted to the Drapers Company, the principal trade guild of Shrewsbury, on payment of a fine or fee of £10.† He was the elected one of the two bailiffs of the town in 1580. In a general muster roll, taken June 10, 22 Elizabeth (1581), Herring was listed as the possessor of armor consisting of a bill, a sallett, a pair of splints and a jacke. In another muster roll of 1587, in which the names of the citizens were given under the heading of their trade companies, William Hearinge, gent., appears among the drapers, possessing in armor a corslet and a pike furnished.‡ This was the year in which the Armada threatened, after the "singeing of the King of Spain's beard" at Cadiz.

Herrings' first wife died before 1578/9 when at St. Julian's church in Shrewsbury "William Herrynge and Beatrydge Higgons" were married on February 24. She was the daughter of George Higgins, who was bailiff of Shrewsbury in 1584.§ "Beatryche, wyffe of Wm Herringe, gent.", was buried at St. Julian's on August 15, 1586. His third marriage took place at the same church on October 7, 1587, the bride being "Ellnor Jones, wydd." She was the daughter of John Hancocks and widow of Thomas Jones.‖

William died late in 1593. Administration of the goods and chattels of William Hearing, late of Shrewsbury, deceased, was granted to George Taylor on December 5, 1593, and an inventory of £40: 11: 7 was taken two days later by Edward Lloyd, Richard Teggyne, Myles Puller and Thomas Lloyd.¶ Presumably he had disposed of his property by marriage settlements and gifts to his daughters before his death.

"Ellnor Herringe, wyddowe," was buried at St. Julian's on December 25, 1600.

---

*Shrewsbury Burgess Roll, edited by H. E. Forrest, Shrewsbury. 1924.
†Shropshire Archaeological Society, 4th Series, 11: 142.
‡*Ibid.* 2nd Series, 2: 259; 3: 114.
§The Herring pedigree by Joseph Morris.
‖*Ibid.*
¶Lichfield Probate Registry.

654

Children, by first wife:

i. Margaret,[4] b. about 1557; m. Robert Churley of Boulde.*
ii. Mary, b. about 1558; m. Andrew Lewis of Shrewsbury (*see Lewis*).
iii. Elizabeth, b. about 1561; m. Thomas Wolley of Shrewsbury, son of Ralph Wolley of Minshull Vernon, co. Chester. Wolley was a vintner, possibly succeeding to his father-in-law's business, and was a bailiff of Shrewsbury in 1611. She was buried at St. Julian's on Nov. 26, 1620, and he on Nov. 15, 1628.
iv. Eleanor, b. about 1563; m. Francis Yonge.†
v. Jane, m. Ralph Dannett.‡
vi. Ralph.||
vii. Magdalen, m. Richard Fawkener.¶
viii. Sara, d. *s.p.*

MARSHALL, of SHREWSBURY, SHROPSHIRE

MARSHALL ARMS

Marshall is not an uncommon name in England and there were Marshall families in Shrewsbury and the surrounding Shropshire parishes from a very early period. In 21 Henry III, on the morrow of St. Edmund, a fine was recorded between Henry Bozsard, plaintiff, and Ralph Marshall, tenant of three bovates of land and appurtenances in the parish of Bureton.§ In 1444 Richard Marshall was elected one of a council or board of assistants to the bailiffs of Shrewsbury. The sixteenth century finds several Marshalls in local religious offices. Richard Marshall *alias* Baker resigned as Abbot of Shrewsbury in 1529, while, when the collegiate body of St. Chad's church in Shrewsbury was dissolved by the act of 1 Edward VI (1547), two of the ousted prebendaries were Richard Marshall and William Marshall. John Marshall was curate of St. Chad's from 1553 to 1558. In 1529/30 the heirs of Thomas Marshall were tenants of the Drapers Company "of serten grounde one sainct Johns hyll," then in occupancy of Thomas Donne.*

A pedigree of the Marshall family with which we are concerned appears in the great genealogical collections of Joseph Morris, the indefatigable Shrewsbury antiquary of the early nineteenth century, and is as follows.

At first glance the first generation of the pedigree looked extremely traditional, but it has been possible to prove it completely by public records.

---

*So given in the Joseph Morris pedigree, but "Churley de Vulle" in Harleian ms. 1396, and "Churle of Onley" in Harleian ms. 1241.
†"Elianora ux. Fransisci Yonge" in Harleian ms. 1396.
‡"Jana nupta Rad'o Danat 5 fil." in Harleian ms. 1396.
||He appears only in Joseph Morris's pedigree, and, if he existed, presumably died in infancy.
¶"Magdalena ux. Ricardi Fawkener" in Harleian ms. 1396.
§Shropshire Archaeological Society, 4th Series, 4:166.
*History of Shrewsbury, Owen and Blakeway, I: 215; II: 203; Shropshire Archaeological Society, 4th Series; 8: 55; 9: 266.

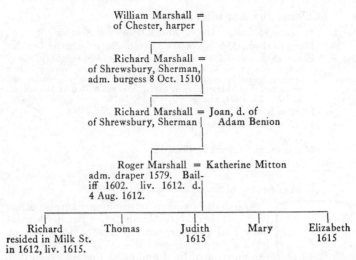

William Marshall = of Chester, harper

Richard Marshall = of Shrewsbury, Sherman, adm. burgess 8 Oct. 1510

Richard Marshall = Joan, d. of of Shrewsbury, Sherman | Adam Benion

Roger Marshall = Katherine Mitton
adm. draper 1579. Bail-
iff 1602. liv. 1612. d.
4 Aug. 1612.

| Richard resided in Milk St. in 1612, liv. 1615. | Thomas | Judith 1615 | Mary | Elizabeth 1615 |

1. WILLIAM MARSHALL of Chester, harper, was possibly a musician attached to the cathedral choir. He was presumably born between 1450 and 1460 and may have been a native of Shrewsbury, co. Salop, where there had been Marshalls living from very early times, with strong church connections.

   Child:
   2. i. RICHARD.²

2. RICHARD² MARSHALL (*William¹*) was presumably born in Chester about the year 1485. He was admitted a burgess of the town of Shrewsbury, co. Salop, on October 8, 1510, the record on the Shrewsbury Guild Merchant Roll reading as follows: "Ricardus Marshall de Villa Salop' Sherman filius Willelmi Marshall de Comitate Cestrie harper admissus est liber Burgensis Ville Salop' et Juratus prout moris ibidem similiter qui per sacramentum suum dicit quod habet exitum Johannem filium quasi etatis trium quartiorum unius Anni qui quidem Johannes ab hoc libertate penitus est exceptus et dismissus."*

   Children:
   i. JOHN,³ b. about 1509/10.
   3. ii. RICHARD.

3. RICHARD³ MARSHALL (*Richard,² William¹*) was presumably born in Shrewsbury between 1510 and 1530. He married, according to the pedigree, Joan Benyon, daughter of Adam Benyon of Shrewsbury.

*Richard Marshall of Shrewsbury, shearman, son of William Marshall of county Chester, harper, is admitted a free burgess of Shrewsbury and sworn there according to custom: he says on oath that he has issue a son John, of about the age of three-quarters of a year, which John is wholly excepted from this freedom. (Shropshire Archaeological Society, 3d Series, 5:107.) Nothing more is known of him.

They may have been the Richard Marshall and wife Joan, with son Roger, of the following records. On April 20, 20 Elizabeth (1578), Richard Norton of Forieta Monachorum (the Abbey Foregate), corvisor, and his wife Anna, daughter of Thomas Lloyd, sometime of Salop, draper, deeded to Richard Bedowe, butcher, various properties on the High Pavement (now Castle street) in Shrewsbury, including a messuage and garden near the cemetery of St. Chad's church now in the tenure of Richard Marshall. On October 28, 22 Elizabeth (1580) Norton and his wife gave a power of attorney to Richard Baynes, Merchant of the Staple, to prosecute Richard Bedowe, Joan Beche *alias* Marshall, widow, Roger Beche *alias* Marshall and others for unlawfully detaining the above property.*

Obviously Richard Marshall had died between April 20, 1578, and October 28, 1580, leaving a wife Joan and a son Roger. There may have been any one of several reasons for the use of the *alias*.

The Benyon family of Shrewsbury was probably founded by Robert Benyon who was admitted a burgess in 1451, described as son of Deys ap Eignon of Rowton in the parish of Allerbury. He was a bailiff of Shrewsbury in 1475 and represented the town in Parliament in 1478 and 1484. Thomas Bennyon, a young lawyer, who made his will in 1585, left a doublet to Roger Marshall who was a witness.† Roger also witnessed the will of Thomas Benyon of Shrewsbury, draper, made in 1587, which left to "my cousin Roger Marshall 40s."‡

Child:

4. i. ROGER.⁴

4. ROGER⁴ MARSHALL (*Richard*,³ *Richard*,² *William*¹) was born about 1561. His parents entered him in Shrewsbury School in 1571, and in 17 Elizabeth (1575) he was apprenticed as Roger Marshall, son of Richard Marshall of Salop, to Michael Chambers, draper.§ In the General Muster Roll of June 10, 22 Elizabeth (1580), he was listed as Roger Marshall, servant of Michael Chambers, gent.‖ Although he was a burgess of Shrewsbury by 1587 he was not admitted to the Drapers Company until March 2, 40 Elizabeth (1597).¶

There is a distinct probability that Marshall spent the interval between his freedom from apprenticeship (about 1582) and his admission to the Drapers Company in 1597 in the study and practice of the law in London. In 1595

---

*Shropshire Archaeological Society, 2nd Series, 12: 199, 200.
†Prerogative Court of Canterbury, 20 Windsor.
‡*Ibid.*, 49 Spencer.
§Shropshire Archaeological Society, 4th Series, 11: 149.
‖*Ibid.*, 2nd Series, 2: 259.
¶*Ibid.*, 4th Series, 11: 147; 49: 222.

the Lords of Queen Elizabeth's Privy Council arbitrarily imposed on several cities a tax for the furnishing of the Royal Navy. In the case of Shrewsbury it amounted to £66: 13: 4 and the highly irregular proceeding met with local opposition "even in that obsequious reign". Roger Marshall, in London, represented Shrewsbury before the Privy Council and in a letter to the bailiffs of the town, dated March 8, 1595, he stated that "we have byn manie tymes before their hono^rs" and answered their demands. He tells them that Worcester had already submitted to the tax and that the Council will require the like of Shrewsbury "wherefore I beseech you, with all convenient speede, to sende me up word what I shall doe herein, and I doe verely thinke the sooner I heare from you, the better shall I proceed in o^r sute, and with the lesse charge." He was successfull to the extent of having the assessment reduced to £40.*

About 1590 Roger Marshall married Katherine Mytton, daughter of Edward and Ann (Skrymsher) Mytton of Weston-under-Lizard, co. Stafford. Katherine (Mytton) Marshall came of a family which flourished in Shrewsbury in the fourteenth century, when her ancestor Thomas de Mutton was bailiff in 1352 and 1360 and represented the town in Parliament in 1366. Thomas's grandson, Sir Richard de Mytton, knight, by his marriage with Margaret de Pesale, daughter of Sir Adam de Pesale, acquired the manor of Weston-under-Lizard, co. Stafford, which became the seat of many generations of Myttons and is still the home of their direct heir, the Earl of Bradford. Katherine Mytton's great-great-grandmother, Constance Beaumont, who married John Mytton of Weston, dowered her descendants with one of those fantastic mediaeval ancestries, which, when the necessary link is proven, almost bore the researcher with a spate of grandeur. All of the "points" desired by specialists in mediaeval ancestry are there — descents from King Henry III (not so desirable as Edward III, to be sure), a Knight of the Garter (John, Lord Beaumont), several sureties of Magna Carta and, of course, from Charlemagne by numerous lines. The great houses of Berkeley, Beauchamp, de Vere, FitzAlan, Warrenne, Despencer, Ferrers, Marshall, de Clare, Neville, Mortimer and Zouche are all represented and many others only less distinguished. Sir Walter Blount, who appears in Shakespeare's "Henry IV", is there, and through his Spanish wife, Sacha de Ayala, there is even a descent, we are told, from the Islamic Kings of Mecca!†

Some time before his death Marshall became a Merchant of the Staple of England. He was bailiff of Shrewsbury in 1602.

*"History of Shrewsbury," Owen and Blakeway, II: 556-5.

†Collections for a History of Staffordshire, William Salt Society, New Series, Vol. II; The American Genealogist, XIX: 10.

The house in which Roger and Katherine Marshall lived has been identified by Mr. H. E. Forrest, the authority on the ancient buildings of Shrewsbury, and the old half-timbered building, still retaining the original wood frame, though the small bricks now filling the spaces are quite modern, stands on Milk street and is now used as auctioneers' offices.

Roger Marshall died in Shrewsbury on August 4, 1612, and was buried in St. Chad's church, which was destroyed in 1788. Sir William Dugdale, however, noted the monuments and arms remaining in the church in 1660, and copied the inscriptions.*

"Neere the pulpit in the middle isle is this inscription engraved on a plate of brass fixed in a gravestone:

Here lyeth the body
of Roger Marshall
gent. late merchant
of the Staple of England Bailiff and Alderman of this town of Salop. who
took to wife Katherine one of the daughters of Edward Mitton of Weston under
Kirwed Esq. and had yssue two sonnes Richard
and Thomas and three daughters Judith Mary and Elizabeth and deceased the 4th day of August
1612

Two shields: on that to the left of the spectator, a bend engrailed; on that to the right, the former coat impaling 1 and 4, a spread eagle (*Mitton*), 2 and 3 a cross fleuree and a canton charged with a wolf's head, (*Pesale*)."†

The first coat, for Marshall, is the same entered in the roll of the bailiffs of Shrewsbury kept by "Robert Owen, gentleman, an herald at arms" as he was described at his burial in St. Chad's on November 8, 1632, and now in the library of Shrewsbury School. Owen, "bearing singular affection to the place of his nativitie" collected the "escouchions" of the several bailiffs, stating that he was "authorized by the court marshall of England a deputy herald of this and several other adjacent counties", which must not be taken too seriously. He describes the coat of Roger Marshall as *Gules*, a bend engrailed *or*. Marshall quite possibly assumed this coat after his marriage into the armorial family of Mytton.

Roger Marshall, "Burges and Alderman of the town of Shrewsbury in the Countie of Salop", made his will on

*Lady Dugdale, Sir William's wife, was a great-niece of Katherine (Mitton) Marshall.
†"History of Shrewsbury," Owen and Blakeway, II: 235.

August 3, 1612, the day before his death. To his executors he left all that messuage in the tenancy of Roger Brown, weaver, in the said town, to be sold. To his wife during her widowhood, for the maintenance of his children, the messuage in which he then dwelt and all his other lands, with remainders to his son and his heirs male, then to his son's issue female, then to his eldest daughter Judith and then to his daughter Elizabeth. If Judith succeeded to the property she was to pay Elizabeth £100. To his wife, a debt of six score pounds from John Blackmore, late citizen and goldsmith of London. Roger Brown was to retain his tenancy for his life. His gowns and wearing apparel were to be sold. Residue to his children equally, provided that his wife should have the use of all his household goods during her lifetime. At her death or remarriage his son was to pay to his two daughters the value of two parts of the goods, or to the survivor one-half. Executors: his wife and his friend John Garbett. Witnesses: John Browne, draper, Edward Mytton, Richard Nettles, William Byrche, Katheren Largdoxe, George Baugh. Proved October 17, 1612, by Catherine Marhsll, relict, and John Garbet.*

Children:

i.   JUDITH,⁵ m. at St. Chad's June 8,⁵1618, George Perch, who was bapt. at St. Mary's July 12, 1584, son of John Perch of Shrewsbury and his wife Eleanor (Sherrer). Both his father and grandfather were Merchants of the Staple of Calais.†

Children, baptized at St. Mary's:

1. *Eleanor Perch*, bapt. March 25, 1619.
2. *John Perch*, bapt. at St. Chad's Nov. 19, 1620; buried at St. Mary's April 10, 1624.
3. *Thomas Perch*, bapt. Jan. 10, 1621(2).
4. *Katherine Perch*, bapt. Aug. 20, 1623.
5. *John Perch*, bapt. May 22, buried May 23, 1625.

ii.   MARY, d. before 1612.

iii.   ELIZABETH, m. at St. Chad's Aug. 29, 1618, Thomas Lewis, and with him emigrated to New England, settling in Saco in the Province of Maine (*see Lewis*).

iv.   RICHARD, b. about 1597. He was entered at Shrewsbury School in 1603, and was a burgess of Shrewsbury in 1618. His marriage record has not been found, but at St. Chad's on March 9, 1620/1, "2 children of Mr. Richard Marshalls was christened".

v.   THOMAS, d. before 1612.

*Prerogative Court of Canterbury, 82 Fenner.
†Visitation of Shropshire, 1623, Harleian Society, 29: 395.

THE DESCENT OF MARGARET LOCKE, THIRD WIFE OF DEPUTY GOVERNOR FRANCIS WILLOUGHBY.

By Col. JOSEPH L. CHESTER, LL.D., of London, England.

[IN the REGISTER for January, 1876, was printed an account of *
the Willoughby family, by Isaac J. Greenwood, Esq., of New
York, who gives, among other notes from the will of Margaret, the
third wife of Deputy Governor Willoughby, the following, viz. :
that she left "to her sister *Elizabeth Lock* £100, due her out of
rents in England." This sentence, meeting the eye of Col. Chester
of London, threw a flood of light upon what had long been a genealogical mystery to him. In working out the family history of
Mr. P. A. Taylor, M.P. for Leicester, his intimate friend, and a
warm friend to the United States, descended from Daniel Taylor,
a wealthy merchant of London, a great Cromwellian, and one of
the Commissioners of Customs during the Commonwealth, Col.
Chester found that Daniel Taylor married a second wife named
Margaret ; and after many years he discovered that she was a daughter of William Lock, of Wimbledon, Surrey, Gent., and found reason to suppose, from some of the family papers, that she had re-married a Willoughby. The sentence above quoted from Margaret
Willoughby's will gave the needed clew, and opened a place for her
in the Lock pedigree, which Col. Chester had already drawn up,
including "all the Locks who ever lived in England." The following abstract of these researches of our learned fellow-countryman was
kindly sent by him to Mrs. Salisbury, wife of Prof. Edward E.
Salisbury, of New Haven ; and is by her contributed to the REG-
ISTER, with some few notes added by her husband. Mrs. Salisbury
is a lineal descendant, both on the side of her father Judge Mc-
Curdy, and that of her mother Sarah Ann Lord, of Lyme, Conn.,
from Gov. Willoughby by his third wife Margaret, through their
daughter Susannah, wife of Nathaniel Lynde, of Saybrook, Conn.,
a brother of the first Chief Justice Benjamin Lynde, of Massachusetts.

The paper here published, while interesting to a wide family-cir-
cle, cannot fail also to attract the notice of students of our colo-
*P. 809, the third volume of this series.

nial history, to whom the name of Gov. Willoughby must have become familiar. Col. Chester's authorship will give it additional value for comparison with the "Historical Account of the Locke Family in England," reprinted from the "Gentleman's Magazine" for 1792, Vol. 62, which is appended to the "Book of the Lockes" by John Goodwin Locke, a member of the New England Historic, Genealogical Society, published at Boston in 1853. Prof. Salisbury's notes give some additional details respecting certain persons of the name in England, drawn from this last named work, and point out a difference or two between the two statements. But Col. Chester's paper will be found distinguished by a completeness and thoroughness, genealogically considered, beyond comparison with the older account.]

I. *William Locke* (Lock, Lok, or Loke, as the name was indifferently spelt in early times) had two sons, viz., John Locke, citizen and mercer of London, who died in 1519, leaving no issue, and

II. *Thomas Locke*, also citizen and mercer of London, who died in 1507. By his wife Joanna Wilcocks, of Rotheram, co. York, who died in 1512, and was buried with her husband in Mercer's Chapel, he had an only son, viz.,

III. *Sir William Locke*, Knight, Alderman of London, who was born about 1486, as he was admitted to the freedom of London, at the end of his apprenticeship, in 1507. He succeeded to his father's business and estate, and became an eminent tradesman and citizen. He received the royal appointment of Mercer to King Henry VIII., with whom he was an especial favorite,* having a key to the King's Private Chamber, and occasionally entertaining him at dinner at his house in London. There are records in existence showing materials furnished by him to the royal household, including Queen Anna Boleyn and the Princess, afterwards Queen, Elizabeth, as also Will Somers, the King's Jester. After being several years an alderman, he was elected Sheriff of London in 1548, and was knighted on the 3d of October in that year, but died before it was his turn to become Lord Mayor.

Sir William Locke married four wives :
- 1st. Alice, daughter of a citizen and fishmonger of London named Spencer, who has not yet been identified. She died in 1522, and was buried in Mercers' Chapel.
- 2d. Catherine, daughter of William Cooke, of Salisbury. She died in childbed of her eleventh child (Sir William's twentieth) 14 Oct., 1537, and was buried at Merton, in Surrey.
- 3d. Eleanor, widow of Walter Marsh. They were married at St. Lawrence, Old Jewry, London, 13 May, 1540, her first husband having been buried there the preceding 20th of January. She died in 1546, having had no issue.
- 4th. Elizabeth, widow of Robert Meredith, citizen and mercer of Lon-

---

* In the 25th year of Henry VIII., William Locke "undertook to go over to Dunkirk and pull down the pope's bull which had been there posted up by way of a curse to the King and kingdom. For this exploit the King granted him a freehold of £100. per annum, dubbed him knight, and made him one of the gentlemen of his privy chamber." The crest—" A hand ppr. holding up a cushion or "—given by Burke to the Lockes, with the shield described by Col. Chester at the end of this paper, probably symbolizes this exploit as an upholding of the Protestant pulpit.

don, and formerly wife of —— Hutton. Their marriage-license was granted 28 January, 1547–8, her husband Meredith having been buried at St. Lawrence, Jewry, 9 Jan., 1546–7. She survived Sir William Locke, having no issue by him, and was buried in Mercers' Chapel, London, 5 Dec., 1551. The curious feature of this marriage was that she was the second wife and widow of Sir William Locke's own son-in-law, Robert Meredith having first married a daughter of Sir William by his first wife, as will be seen hereafter.

Sir William Locke died at the age of about 64, on the 24th, and was buried in Mercers' Chapel 27 August, 1550. (In the "Diary of Henry Machyn," published by the Camden Society, will be found an account of his burial, at page 1, and at page 12 an imperfect one of that of his last wife.)

By his second wife, Catherine Cook, Sir William Locke had eleven children, viz., Dorothy, Catherine, John, Alice, Thomazin, Francis and a second John, of none of whom is there anything of particular interest to record. The first two married tradesmen in London, and the others died without issue.

Elizabeth, one of the daughters, married, first, Richard Hill, citizen and mercer of London, and second, after his death in 1568, the Right Rev. Nicholas Bullingham, Bishop of Worcester. By her first husband she had thirteen children, one of whom, Mary, married Sir Thomas Moundeford, and was mother of Bridget, who married Sir John Bramston, Lord Chief Justice of the King's Bench.

Rose, another of the daughters, married, first, Anthony Hickman, of London, Esq., and second, Simon Throckmorton, of Brampton, co. Huntington, Esq. By her first husband she was ancestress of the Earls of Plymouth, their grandson Dixie Hickman having married Elizabeth, eldest daughter of Henry, fifth Lord Windsor, and had a son Thomas, who succeeded his uncle (by limitation of the patent) as seventh Lord Windsor, and was created Earl of Plymouth, 6 Dec., 1682. The title became extinct only on the death of the eighth Earl, 8 Dec., 1843.*

Of the sons,† Michael Locke became a merchant of eminence in London, and was twice married: first, to Joane, daughter of William Wilkinson, Sheriff of London, and second, to Margery, widow of Dr. Cæsar Adelmare, by whom she was the mother of the celebrated Sir Julius Cæsar. Michael

---

* This daughter of Sir William Locke, in certain "memoires" originally inserted in a family Bible, and long carefully preserved in the female line of her descendants, "says that in the tyme of her first husband, Anthony Hickman, after the death of Edward the Sixth, Queen Mary changinge the relligion, her husband and her elder brother Thomas Lock, beinge merchants and partners, they lived to geather and sheltred manie of the godlie preachers in theire house ; but the Queen inioyninge all to come to mass, and persecutinge the refusers, they were forced to let them goe, giuing them monie ; she mentions Hooper, Fox, Knox, and one Reinger. for which her husband and brother beinge questioned before the commissioners (she calls them high commissioners) were committed close prisoners to the Fleete, and then shee tells how they gott out ; . . . . after which she says her husband went to Antwerpe, tooke a house there at 40 pounds rent, sent for her, but she being with child could not goe, but went into Oxfordshire to a gentleman's house . . . wher she was deliuered ; names not the child . . . but says she went to Cranmer, Latimer and Ridlie, prisoners then in Oxford, to know whether she might christen her child in the Popish manner. They answered her that baptisme was the least corrupted in that church, and therefore she might . . . but she says she put sugar instead of salt into the handkercher which was to be deliuered vnto the priest, after which she went to Antwerpe to her husband, left 2 houses of her husband's, well furnished, one in London, another at Rumford, taking noething but one feather bed" . . . etc.

† This is in conformity with the statement of the "Gentleman's Magazine," and not with that of the author of the "Book of the Lockes," who conjectured that this Michael was a *brother* rather than a *son* of Sir William. From Michael was descended, in the fourth generation, the philosopher John Locke, born Aug. 29, 1632.

Locke had by his first wife five sons and three daughters, the eldest of whom, Zachary Locke, Esq., died in 1603, being then Member of Parliament for the Borough of Southwark.

The interesting fact in the history of Michael Locke is that he was the original patron of the celebrated Sir Martin Frobisher in his earliest expeditions.* He was living as late as 1611.

The other son, Henry Locke, was also a citizen and merchant of London. He married Anne Vaughan, and had issue a daughter Anne, who married Robert Moyle, of Cornwall, whose descendants intermarried with the St. Aubyns and Prideauxs, among the best families in that county ; and two sons, viz., Michael, to whom the historian Hakluyt left a legacy in his will ; and Henry Locke (or Lok), a poet of some note in his day, an edition of whose scarce productions was issued in 1871 by the Rev. Dr. Grosart (nearly the whole of the biographical introduction to which I had the pleasure of furnishing, and which upset all the conjectures and theories of previous writers).

We now return to the children of Sir William Locke by his first wife, Alice Spencer, who were nine in number, eight sons and one daughter, viz. :

William, Peter, Richard, and William, the first, second, fourth and fifth sons, all died in infancy or childhood, before their mother. Philip, the seventh son, died in 1524, unmarried. Edmund, the sixth son, lived until 1545, but died unmarried. One of the old heralds added to the entry in one of the visitation-pedigrees : " He died for love of Sir Brian Tuke's daughter."

Matthew Locke, the eighth son and youngest child, but second surviving, was a citizen and mercer of London, and married Elizabeth Baker, by whom he had an only daughter Elizabeth, who married Richard Candler, Esq., and had an only daughter Anne, who married Sir Ferdinando Heyborne, Kt., one of the Gentlemen of the Privy Chamber to Queen Elizabeth. Matthew Locke died in 1552.

Joane (or Jane, for she is called both), the only daughter, married Robert Meredith, citizen and mercer of London, who, after her death, remarried Elizabeth Hutton, widow, who in turn, after his death, remarried Sir William Locke, father of his first wife. From this Robert Meredith and Jane Locke descends the present Earl of Romney, through their daughter Mary, who married Richard Springham, whose daughter Magdalen married Thomas Marsham, whose son was Sir John Marsham, Baronet, whose grandson was created Lord Romney in 1716, whose grandson was created Earl of Romney in 1801.

We return now to the third son, but eldest and only surviving child, of Sir William Locke, by Alice Spencer, his first wife, viz. :

IV. *Thomas Locke*, who was born on the 8th of February, 1514–15, and became, like his fathers, a citizen and mercer of London. He married,

* In the Cottonian Library is a MS. written by this Michael Locke, in which he says that at the age of thirteen " he was sent over the seas to Flanders and France, to learn their languages, and to know the world, since which time he has continued these 32 years to travel in body and mind, following his vocation in the trade of merchandize, passing through many countries, had the charge of and captain of a great ship of more than 1000 tons, three years in divers voyages; and that he has more than 200 sheets of MSS. of his travels."

Hakluyt's Voyages contain a " History of Sir Martyn Frobishere's Voyage for the Discovery of a Passage towards Cathay, in 1574, written by Michael Locke, Locke himself being a great adventurer therein ;" and Hakluyt speaks thus of the map: " The mappe is master Michael Locke's, a man for his knowledge in divers languages, and especially in cosmographie, able to do his country good, and worthy in my judgment, for the manifolde good partes in him, of good reputation and better fortune."

19 Jan., 1544–5, at St. Peter's, Cheapside, London, Mary, daughter of Simon Long, of the Isle of Wight, who, after his death, remarried Dr. Owen, and subsequently Sir William Allen, Kt., Alderman of London. In 1552–3 he obtained from King Edward VI. a grant of the Rectory of Merton, co. Surrey, which remained in the family for about one hundred years, when it was sold.* His line had their residence during this period at Merton Abbey, some members of it, however, continuing in business in London. He died at his London house, which was in Walbrook, and was buried in Mercers' Chapel, 30 Oct., 1556. His issue were five sons and two daughters, viz., William, Rowland, Matthew, John, Thomas, Mary and Anne, some of whom died before their father, and of the others no subsequent trace has been found, except the third son, viz. :

V. *Matthew Locke,* who, as eldest (and probably only) surviving son, succeeded to the estate at Merton. He was born about 1558. He married Margaret, third daughter of his stepfather, Sir William Allen (his mother's third husband) by his first wife Joan, daughter of John Daborne, of Guildford, co. Surrey. He died in June, 1599, as " Matthew Locke, Esquire, of Merton," and was buried with his fathers in Mercers' Chapel, London. His widow remarried Sir Thomas Muschampe, Kt., of London, and of Mitcham, co. Surrey, whom she also survived. She died 25 Aug., 1624, and was buried with her first husband in Mercers' Chapel.

Their issue were as follows :

1. Thomas Locke, who succeeded to the estate at Merton, which he sold in 1646. He died about February, 1656–7, leaving a widow Jane and several children.
2. Robert Locke, who continued the business in London, where he died. He was buried at St. Alphage, 9 Sept., 1625, and appended to the entry of his burial in the Parish Register are the descriptive words " a good parishioner." By his wife Elizabeth, who was living his widow as late as 1647, he had four sons and three daughters, viz., Matthew, William, Robert, Thomas, Mary, Elizabeth and Margaret, of whom Thomas and Margaret died before their father, and William died before 1647. At this last date Matthew and Robert were still living, the former being then a citizen and scrivener of London, as also Mary, married to Hugh Justice, and Elizabeth, married to Edward Mason.
3. Francis Locke, who was living in 1599, but of whom I find no later trace.
4. *William Locke,* of whom hereafter.
5. Mary, who was still living in 1623, wife of Edward Thrille.
6. Elizabeth, who was living in 1599, but died unmarried before 1623.
7. Anne, who died unmarried between 13 April and 23 May, 1623, and directed in her will to be buried in Mercers' Chapel.

The fourth son of Matthew Locke and Margaret Allen, viz. :

VI. *William Locke,* was sometime of Merton, and afterwards of Wimbledon, co. Surrey, his condition, as near as I can make out, being that of a country-gentleman in comfortable circumstances. He married Susanna, one of the daughters and coheirs of Roger Cole, of St. Saviour's, Southwick, co. Surrey, Gentleman, one of the Proctors of the Court of Arches. In 1623, the date of the Heralds' Visitation, they had only a daughter Mary living, from which it is evident that the marriage had taken place not very long before. This daughter Mary probably died young, as she was not named in her father's will, which was made 10 June, 1661, and of which the following is a full abstract :

* Merton estates seem to have been held by members of the Locke family at an earlier period, perhaps even as early as 1291, certainly in 1499. The author of " Book of the Lockes " says he thinks " it is evident that they belonged to the Lockes before 1552, as the second wife of Sir William Locke was buried there, Oct. 14, 1537, and Sir William himself in 1550."

I, William Lock, of Wimbledon, co. Surrey, Gentleman—As to the houses in St. Saviour's, Southwark, given and bequeathed by my father in law Mr. Roger Cole to Susanna my wife and her children, whereas there is an agreement between my children that said houses shall remain to such of them as I and their mother shall appoint, on condition of my settling on the rest of them portions of a greater value than the divisions of said houses would amount to, which portions I have made good to my three eldest daughters, Hannah, Susannah and Margaret, whom I have bestowed in marriage, and whereas I shall lease an estate in land for Thomas my son, and provide otherwise for Elizabeth my daughter, I now appoint that five brick tenements, and another known formerly as the Gaden House, all on the ground given by Mr. Roger Cole as aforesaid, shall remain to my daughter Sarah Lock and her heirs forever, and the two other houses in said parish, next the Thames, in tenure of Mr. Robert Bowes, I give to my daughter Jane Lock and her heirs forever—To my wife Susanna 4 brick tenements, called Beane Acre, in Lambeth, co. Surrey, she giving £200 thereout to my daughter Elizabeth—To the poor of Wimbledon, £3—All residue to my wife, whom I appoint my executrix.

The will was proved in the Prerogative Court of Canterbury, 7 June, 1664, by Susanna Lock, relict and executrix. She was still living 25 Oct., 1670, when she proved the will of her daughter Jane, after which I have failed to find any further trace of her. All that I have been able to ascertain concerning their children is as follows:

1. Thomas Locke, only son, who was still living 19 March, 1669–70, with two children, Henry and Susanna.
2. Mary, who, as we have seen, evidently died young.
3. Hannah, who married, before her father's will, Thomas Bragne. Both were living 1669–70.
4. Susanna, who married at Wimbledon, Surrey, 8 Oct., 1657, the Rev. James Stephenson, then the Puritan Vicar of Martock, in Somersetshire, who was ejected in 1662 (see an account of him in Palmer's " Nonconformists' Memorial," ii. 371), to whom she was second wife. She was buried at Martock, 25 April, 1662, leaving two daughters, Susanna and Mary, who were both living in 1669–70.
5. *Margaret*, of whom hereafter.
6. Elizabeth, who was still unmarried at the date of her sister Margaret's will, 21 Aug., 1680.
7. Sarah, who was living unmarried in 1661, but evidently died before 19 March, 1669–70, as she was not named in the will of her sister Jane.
8. Jane, who died unmarried. She made her will 19 March, 1669–70, as of Wimbledon, Surrey, " one of the daughters of William Locke, Gentleman, deceased." The following is a full abstract of it:

> To my dear and honourable mother Mrs. Susanna Locke, £20—To my brother Mr. Thomas Locke £10.—To my sister Mrs. Hannah Bragne £20—to *my sister Mrs. Margaret Willoughby* £10.—To my sister Mrs. Elizabeth Locke £20—To *Francis and Susanna the two children of my sister Willoughby* each 50 shillings—To Susanna and Henry Locke, the children of my brother, and to Susanna and Mary, the children of my sister Stephenson, each 20 shillings—To the poor £5, at the discretion of my brother Mr. Thomas Bragne—To the poor of Wimbledon 40 shillings—All residue to my mother Mrs. Susanna Locke, and I make her my executrix.

The will was proved in the Prerogative Court of Canterbury, 25 Oct., 1670, by the executrix.

I have searched every possible source for the wills of the mother Susanna, and Thomas the son, in vain, and, as they were not named by Margaret Willoughby in her will, the presumption is that they died before her.

We now return to the fourth daughter and fifth child of William Locke and Susanna Cole, viz.:

VII. *Margaret Locke*. She was first married at Clapham, co. Surrey, 8 August, 1654, to Daniel Taylor, a wealthy citizen and haberdasher of London, descended from an ancient family in Huntingtonshire, ancestor of

Peter Alfred Taylor, Esq., for many years and still M.P. for Leicester. She was Mr. Taylor's second wife, he having buried his first on the preceding 3d of February. He settled upon her a considerable jointure, and died within a year after the marriage, being buried in London on the 20th of April, 1655. She had no issue by him. She remarried, probably in London (exactly when or where it is impossible to ascertain, owing to the deficiencies and irregularities in parish-registers at this precise period), certainly as early as 1659, Francis Willoughby, Esq., who had been some years in New England, but had returned to England, and was one of the two members for the borough of Portsmouth in the last Parliament of the Commonwealth, which assembled on the 27th of January, 1658–9, and was dissolved on the 22d of April following. In the parish-register of St. Olave, Hart Street, London, is an entry that their son Francis was born 29 Feb., 1659–60. They shortly after emigrated to New England, and the rest of their history must there be sought.

The maternal descent of Margaret Locke-Taylor-Willoughby was as follows:

I. *William Cole*, of Hittisleigh, co. Devon, living 1243, whose heir,
II. *Roger Cole*, was of Chumleigh, in the same county, and was living as late as 1301, in which year he is supposed to have been slain in an expedition against the Scots, as also his son and heir
III. *Roger Cole*, whose son and heir
IV. *John Cole* was summoned to represent the county of Devon in Parliament in 1323-4, and was living in 1341. His son and heir
V. *Sir John Cole*, of Brixham, was in the military service, and was knighted on the field, in France, 25 July, 1380. He married Anne, daughter and heiress of Sir Nicholas Bodrigan, Kt., of Gorrans, in Cornwall, by whom he had issue
VI. *Sir William Cole*, Kt., who married Margaret, daughter of Sir Henry Beaupell, Kt., and was father of
VII. *Sir John Cole*, Kt., who attended the Duke of Gloucester at the battle of Agincourt, 25 Oct., 1415, and is supposed to have then received his knighthood. By his wife Agnes, daughter of Sir —— Fitzwarine, Kt., he had four sons, of whom the third,
VIII. *William Cole*, had two sons, the younger of whom,
IX. *William Cole*, was father of
X. *John Cole*, of Sudbury, co. Suffolk. (Thus far the descent is from the elaborate pedigree drawn up in 1630 by William Segar, Garter King of Arms. What follows is in the outline from the Heralds' Visitations, but elaborated from my own researches.) He married Elizabeth, daughter of John Martyn, by whom he had five sons. Our line is through the second son, viz.
XI. *William Cole*, of Sudbury, who married Catalina, daughter of Ferdinando de Gallegos, a Spaniard of noble extraction, by whom he had two sons, the eldest of whom died without issue, when the second became heir, viz.
XII. *Roger Cole*, of St. Saviour's, Southwark, co. Surrey, who signed the Visitation-pedigree of 1623, naming his wife as Anne, daughter of Edward Maisters, of Rotherhithe, co. Surrey; his sons Roger, Roger (the second) and John, as all dead without issue; and his three daughters, viz., Elizabeth, married to William Plaud, of London; Catalina, then unm.; and
XIII. *Susanna*, then *wife of William Lock, of Merton, co. Surrey.*

It will be seen, therefore, that, Susanna Cole being a coheiress, her husband William Locke was entitled to impale her arms, which are—Argent, a bull passant gules, armed Or, within a bordure sable bezantée.

The arms of Locke are—Per fesse azure and or, in chief 3 falcons volant of the second.

It follows, also, that the descendants of Francis Willoughby and Margaret Locke, who are entitled to bear arms, have the right to quarter these two coats.

London, 27 Feb., 1880.

667

Joseph Long, Robert Longe

JOSEPH LONG, son of Joseph Longe, gent., of Broad Magna, Dorset (Dorchester), England, who early settled in Dorchester, New England (Mass.). Record of his arrival has not been found, but he may well have been one of the original settlers who arrived in June 1630 on the "Mary and John", with Winthrop's fleet, coming from Dorchester, England, where his father was a member of the Dorchester Company. His wife was Mary, daughter of William Lane, who was in Dorchester, Mass., as early as 1636. She married, secondly, Joseph Farnsworth, and thirdly, Joseph Wilcox, Jr. Her will, dated 3 April 1671, is on file at Hartford, Conn.

Joseph had brothers Giles, Jasper, and William, and sisters Elisabeth and Anne, all dead in 1655, except William Longe, gent., a younger half-brother, then living in Dorchester, England. Joseph returned to England for the settlement of his father's estate, and was last heard of from London prior to 22 May 1651, on which date the court in Massachusetts Bay Colony, believing him dead, gave his wife liberty to remarry.

The father, Joseph Longe, of Broad Magna, Dorset, appears to be identical with Joseph Longe of Frome Bassett, Dorset, 1606, son of Gyles Longe, innholder of London, Holborn St. Sepulchres Next Newgate, whose will in 1607 names a sister Elizabeth, a brother John, London innholder, kin Gyles and John Longe, London innholder, and children Robert, White Swan Inn, Anne, Richard, White Swan Inn, JOSEPH, Jacob (or James), and Gyles. Robert Longe, 1590-1663, innholder of Charlestown, Mass., Dunstable, and St. Albans, near London, is thought to belong to this family. (See No. III, *infra.*)

Joseph and Mary (Lane) Long were parents of Joseph (d. 26 Aug. 1676, Dorchester, Mass.; m. 3 Dec. 1661, by the Governor to Mary —————), and Thomas (Estate administered 4 Feb. 1711/12, Hartford, Conn.; m. (1) 1666, Sarah Wilcox, b. 1648; m. (2) Sarah Elmer). Many Connecticut and Vermont Longs trace back to Thomas, but no descendants from Joseph have been traced beyond his children.

Authorities:
New England Families in England, Emmerton & Waters
THE REGISTER, 9:140,100:220; 100:328; Mass. Archives, 9:16
Records of the Colony of Mass. Bay, p. 232
Long Family of Dorchester and Conn., by Mary (Wood) Bates, 1931 (MSS at NEHG Soc. Library.)

III

ROBERT LONGE, innkeeper, died at Charlestown Mass., 9 Jan. 1663/4, aged 73. He appears to belong to the London family of innholders, referred to in No. II *supra*, and left London 7 July 1635 on the "Defense", bringing with him a certificate signed by the minister and justice of the peace at Dunstable, Bedfordshire, listing the names and ages of his second wife, his ten children, and his servants. His first wife was Sarah, 1595-1631, daughter of John and Margaret (Willmote) Taylor, whom he married 5 Oct. 1614. His second wife was Elizabeth, aged 84 in 1687. (Surname and date of marriage not found.) His children were Michael (m. Joanna —————), Sarah (m. Abraham Hill), Robert (m. Elizabeth Hawkins), Elizabeth (m. James Parker), Anne (m. James Converse), Mary (m. Simon Kempthorn), Rebecca (m. Elias Rowe), John (m. Mary Norton; Mary Nowell), Zachary (m. Sarah Tidd; Mary Burr; Sarah Foster), Joshua (no marriage recorded), Hannah (m. Henry Cockery; Luke Perkins), Ruth (m. William Whalen), and Deborah (no marriage found); all born between 1615 and 1642. In 1636 he started the "Three Cranes Inn" or "Grand Ordinary" at Charlestown, which remained in his family for nearly a century. The building had been built in 1629 at the foot of town hill. It was occupied by the First Church of Charlestown and later was called the "Great House" and used as the Town Hall. It was burned down 17 June 1777, when Charlestown was set afire by British troops evacuating the city. The Long family on Nantucket, and probably other parts of the coast, trace back to him.

On the registers of the Cathedral at St. Albans, near London, are recorded the births of six of his children between 1615 and 1629, as is his first marriage. They also record births to John Longe, a sidesman, of Marie 1594, and John 1596, and the marriage in 1619 of John Longe (Jr.) to Dorothy Robbins (d. 1641) and 2nd to Elizabeth Simmons; there were born to him John 1624, Thomas 1627, Robert 1630, Gyles 1635 (d. in infancy), and Ann 1643. The register also recites births to a Richard Longe of Elizabeth 1608, Francis 1609, Richard 1612, and Jane 1614. The registers begin with 1594, and it is very probable that Robert, born 1590 (of Charlestown), and Richard, married before 1608, were also sons of John, the sidesman, and born before the registers were commenced in 1594, and thus brothers of the recorded Marie 1594 and John (Jr.) 1596. Names, vocation, and dates strongly suggest that these Longs belong to the London family of innholders treated in No. II, *supra*. It is possible that John Longe, St. Albans sidesman 1594 (probable father of Robert Longe, Charlestown innholder, b. 1690), was identical with John Longe, London innholder, 1607, the brother named in will of Gyles Longe (probable grandfather of Joseph Long, to Dorchester about 1630).

Authorities:
  Genealogies and Estates of Charlestown, Wyman
  Registers of St. Albans Cathedral, England

LONGE FAMILY DESCENDANTS: ADDENDA.—In the July, 1946, *Register* (C: 220), Prof. G. Andrews Moriarty tells of a lawsuit in Dorchester, England, Derby vs. William Longe et al. in 1655. It names his father as Joseph, who had by a former wife, Elizabeth, Giles, Jasper, Joseph and Anne. That William received lands in Broad Magna, Dorset, and Joseph "who died in New England" is thought to have had issue as he had two hundred pounds from his father's estate.

In the Records of the Colony of Mass. Bay, p. 232, and Mass. Archives (9: 16) we find that on 22 May 1651 the Court granted Mary Longe of Dorchester (Mass.) liberty to remarry upon consideration of her petition and supporting affidavits reciting that her husband Joseph Long went to England to see his brother William about a legacy from their father's estate; that he was last heard from a London when he wrote that he was proceeding the next day; that his brother William stated he had not seen or heard of him; that other efforts to locate him in Er land were unavailing and he was thought to be dead. Mary was a daughter of William Lane to Dorchester, Mass., by 1636, and married (2) Joseph Farnsworth, and (3) John Wilcox, Jr. Her will dated 3 April 1671 is on file at Hartford, Conn.

The will of Joseph Farnsworth (9 *NEHG Reg* 140) filed 1 Jan. 1659/60 names his wife Mary and "her two children which she had by her other husband, namely Joseph Long and Thomas Long". Joseph died 1676, Dorchester, and Thomas died 1712, Windsor, Conn., both leaving issue.

Another generation is probably given in "New England Families in England" by Emmerton & Waters, which gives the will of Gyles Longe, innholder of London, Holborn St. Sepulchres Next Newgate, 1607, which names sister Elizabeth, brother John, children Robert, Anne, Richard, *Joseph* (of Frome Basset, *Dorset*, 1606), and Jacob (or James). Other wills are included in this work of the London family of innholders to which Robert Long, 1590–1663, innkeeper, of Charlestown, Mass., Dunstable and St. Albans, near London, is thought to belong.

Washington, D. C.   HALLOCK PORTER LONG,

LOVERING FAMILY.

[Communicated by THOMAS B. WYMAN, Jr., Esq., of Charlestown.]

In Bond's Watertown record is made of Thomas Loverin of Watertown, son of William of Aldham, co. Suffolk, and John L. of Watertown, who came from Dedham, co. Essex. The following abstracts of documents on the Middlesex Inferior Court files for 1704 give more light relative to the Lovering family. The first is a power of attorney given by David Loverin, Citizen and Draper of London, the only surviving son of William L. late of Aldham, near Hadleigh in the county of Suffolk, England, to John and Samuel Marion of Watertown in New England, to take possession of property falling to him as heir of Thomas Loverin deceased, by virtue of his will dated 13 Aug. 1692. This power of attorney is dated 10 Mch. 1703, and has, against David Loverin's name, a round seal, bearing these arms :—On a bend, three martlets ; on a canton in the sinister chief, a rose.

2d   A Certificate of John Sponer, rector, and Joshua Horrex and Caleb Wade, churchwardens, of Aldham, "that the persons whous names are hereunder written were the sons and daughters of William Loverin, formerly of the Parish of Aldham in the co. of Suffolk, and Susanna his wife, and were baptized as appears by the register kept for the parish, William Loverin bapt. 6 Sept. 16 [torn off] John, 20 Feb., 1622; George 20 Jan'y 1624 : *Thomas*, 30 Nov., 1626; Jonathan, 10 Sept. 1629 ; Susanna 19 Jany, 1631 : *David* 20 May, 1633; Elizabeth 21 Aug., 1636 ; Edward, 8 Jany, 1637.

Burials in the church yard of the aforesaid parish:
Edward Loverin, buried 24 June, 1639 ; John, 16 Mch., 1663 ; William 1 Dec., 1666, Susanna Close. 10 Jany, 1681.

3rd. Deposition of Henry Nelson apothecary, aged 88 years, and Richard Buddle, gentleman, aged 46 years, both of Aldham, and John Beare of St Sepulcbre's parish, London, upholsterer. Nelson knew William Loverin and his family. Mr L. frequented Arthur Gale's house in Hadleigh when he served as an apprentice to Mr Gale, an apothecary. Knew that Thomas Loverin was put as apprentice to a clothier at Dedham, six miles from Aldham, and set up his trade at Dedham. In the year 1667 he went to New England, afterwards returned to Dedham and in about six months went again to New England. Richard Buddle m. Susanna, daughter of Susanna Close, the daughter of W^m. Loverin. The testimony is that David is the only surviving heir of William Lovering. Sworn before Samuel Dashwood, Mayor of London; witnesses, Francis Harding and John Butler. John Butler confirmed his testimony at Boston before Judge Addington, 22 Oct. 1703.

ABSTRACTS OF ANCIENT ENGLISH WILLS, IN THE NAME OF LUNT.

[Copied by HORATIO G. SOMERBY, Esq., of London, and communicated by Hon. GEORGE LUNT, of Boston.]

FROM the Registry of Probate at Ipswich, County of Suffolk :

1. Walter Lunte, of Holbrooke, in Suffolk, made his will April 9th, 1460. Proved May 6th, 1468. Mentions his wife Agnes, and sons John and William.

2. John Lunte, of Holbrooke. Will dated Jan. 20th, 1469–70. Proved Feb. 17, 1469–70. Son Roger. Appoints his wife Christian, Robert Lunt and William Alby, Executors.

3. Alice Lunt, of Holbrook, widow, late wife of John Lunt. Will dated Feb. 28th, 1521–2. Proved March 21, 1521–2. Appoints her son, John Pylborough, Executor, and makes him principal legatee.

4. Joan Lunte, of Orford, County of Suffolk, widow. Will dated Aug. 18th, 1540.

From the Registry of Wills at Chelmsford, in the County of Essex :

5. Robert Lunt, of Tarling, in Essex. Will dated Feb. 18th, 1566. To his son, Henry, not sixteen, his apparel and that which was his own mother's. Daughter Margery, not sixteen. Brothers Thomas and John. Appoints his wife, not named, Executrix, and his brother Thomas Supervisor.

From the Registry of Wills at Chester. Wills of persons of Lancashire were proved at this office :

6. Gilbert Lunt, of Letherland, in the parish of Sefton. Will dated July 15th, 1568. Daughter Isabel Harris. Daughter Margery and Richard Walley, Executors.

7. Humphrey Lunt, of Maghull, Co. Lancaster, Yeoman. Will dated 29th Elizabeth (1587). Proved Oct. 7th, 1592. Desires to be buried within the Chapel at Melling (Westmoreland), near the place where his wife is buried. Legacies to a great many individuals other than Lunt. To his servant, John Lunt, £4. To his servant, Ellen Lunt, £4. To Bryan and Ellen Lunt, children of Anthony Lunt, the former £5, the latter £3, when twenty-one. To the children of Paul Lunt, viz., Thomas and Andrew, each £3. To Jane Lunt, £4. To the poor of Liverpool, 40s. To Humphrey Lunt, his nephew, all his lands, houses, &c., in West Derby, &c.; mentions his houses in Liverpool. If Humphrey dies without heirs, then the aforesaid property to Bryan, son of Anthony Lunt. Legacies to old Nicholas Lunt and Richard Lunt. Appoints his nephew, Humphrey, Executor.

8. William Lunt, of Ince Blundell, in the parish of Sefton, County of Lancaster, Husbandman. Names sons John and Robert, and their children. Appoints his sons Executors. Will dated May 16th, 1604. Proved Aug. 18th, 1604.

9. Alice Lunt, of Rainsforth, County of Lancaster, widow. Will dated July 16th, 1616. Proved April 9th, 1648. Desires to be buried in the Church at Prescot. Legacies to several persons.

10. Anthony Lunt. Will dated July 22d, 1617. Proved July 28th, 1617. Desires to be buried in the Church of St. Oswold, in Chester, where his last wife was buried. Names brothers Humphrey and Richard ; nephews Anthony, John and Richard Lunt ; sister Elizabeth Banks. Appoints his brothers Humphrey and Nicholas Executors.

11. Edward Lunt, of Aughton, County of Lancaster. Now wife Jennet. Eldest brother William. Brother Henry. Youngest brother Thomas. Sister Catherine and her daughter Jane. Will dated Dec. 11th, 1629. Proved Aug. 17th, 1632.

12. Hugh Lunt, of Babington. Will proved Nov. 4th, 1648. Wife Hannah and son Henry, Executors.

[Note.—All persons of the name of Lunt, in this country, so far as known, are descended from Henry Lunt, who was one of the original settlers of Newbury, Essex County, Mass., in the year 1635. His will, recorded at Ipswich, is dated in 1662, and provides well, as Savage (Gen. Dict.) says, for his widow and seven children. The widow afterwards married Joseph Hills, Speaker of the House of Representatives.

The name of Lunt is of Scandinavian origin. In Denmark it is well known, and is spelled Lundt. It seems likely that it is derived from some of the early Danish invaders, or incursionists into England. Most of the Christian names of the legatees mentioned in the will of Humphrey Lunt (No. 7), and some of them not very common, as, for instance, Paul, Andrew, Richard and Nicholas, have been borne by descendants of Henry Lunt, of Newbury. The sum of 40s. "to the poor of Liverpool" marks a not uncommon bequest of the period. In the year 1639, Burton, author of the "Anatomy of Melancholy," left 40s., by will, to "the poor of Higham." In 1587, the date of Humphrey Lunt's will, Liverpool had about three thousand inhabitants.]

DESCENT OF GEN. DOUGLAS MACARTHUR FROM EMPEROR CHARLEMAGNE

Marcellus D. R. von Redlich, LL.B., LL.D., Ph.D., of Chicago, Ill., the eminent authority on mediaeval history, has prepared the following descent, with the citation of sources, of the line of descent of Gen. Douglas MacArthur from Charlemagne, King of the Franks and Emperor of the West.

1. CHARLEMAGNE, King of the Franks and Emperor of the West, b. 2 Apr. 747; d. 28 Jan. 814; m. in 771 the Swabian Princess Hildegard, d. 30 Apr. 783,

2. PEPIN, King of Italy, b. in April 773; d. 8 July 810; father of

3. BERNARD, King of Italy from September 813 to his abdication in December 817; b. about 797; d. 17 Apr. 818; m. Cunigunde, d. about 835,

4. PEPIN, Count of Senlis, b. in 817/18; d. after 840; father of

5. HERBERT I, Count of Vermandois, b. about 840; was murdered about 902; m. Berthe de Morvois,

6. HERBERT II, Count of Vermandois and Troyes, b. about 880–890; d. about 943; m. Liegard, daughter of Robert I, King of France,

7. ALBERT I, the Pious, Count of Vermandois, b. about 920; d. in 987/88; m. Princess Gerberga, granddaughter of Henry I, the Fowler, King of Germany,

8. HERBERT III, Count of Vermandois, b. about 955; d. about 1000; m. as her second husband Irmgard (Ermengarde), daughter of Reinald, Count of Bar,

9. OTHO, Count of Vermandois, b. about 1000; d. 25 May 1045; m. Pavie,

10. HERBERT IV, Count of Vermandois and of Valois, b. about 1032; d. about 1080; m. Adela de Vexin, daughter of Raoul III, the Great, Count of Valois, Vexin, etc.,

11. ADELAIDE (ADELHEID), Countess of Vermandois and of Valois, m. Hugh, the Great, Duke of France and Burgundy, Marquis of Orleans, Count of Amiens, Chaumont, Paris, Valois, Vermandois, etc., son of Henry I, King of France, by Anne, daughter of Yaroslav I, Grand Prince of Kiev,

12. ISABEL DE VERMANDOIS, Countess of Leicester, d. 13 Feb. 1131; m. as her second husband William de Warenne, second Earl of Surrey, d. about 1135–1138,

13. GUNDRED DE WARENNE, m. first, Roger de Newburgh, second Earl of Warwick, Crusader; d. 12 June 1153, son of Henry, first Earl of Warwick,

14. WALERAN DE NEWBURGH, fourth Earl of Warwick, d. about 1204–1205; m. secondly Alice, daughter of John de Harcourt and widow of John de Limesi,

15. ALICE DE NEWBURGH, m. William, Baron Mauduit, of Hanslope, co. Buckingham, d. in April 1257,

16. ISABEL DE MAUDUIT, sister and heiress of William de Mauduit, Earl of Warwick, m. William, fifth Baron Beauchamp, of Elmley Castle,

17. WALTER DE BEAUCHAMP, of Beauchamp's Court in Alcester, co. Warwick, and of Powick, co. Worcester, Steward of the Household of Edward I, King of England, d. in 1303; m. Alice de Tony,

18. GILES DE BEAUCHAMP, of Beauchamp's Court in Alcester, d. in October 1361;
    m. about 1329 Catherine, daughter and heiress of Sir John de Bures,
19. JOHN DE BEAUCHAMP, d. between 1378 and 1401; m. Elizabeth, d. in 1411,
    probably daughter of Sir John St. John,
20. SIR WILLIAM DE BEAUCHAMP, of Powick, co. Worcester and of Alcester, co.
    Warwick, Constable of the Castle of Gloucester, Sheriff of Worcestershire
    and later of Gloucestershire, d. before 1431; m. before March 1414/15
    Catherine, daughter and co-heiress of Gerard de Ufflete,
21. SIR JOHN DE BEAUCHAMP, K.G., created Baron Beauchamp of Powick 2 May
    1447; Justice of South Wales; Lord Treasurer of England, 1450–1452; d.
    9–19 Apr. 1475; m. about 1434 Margaret, sister of Richard Ferrars,
22. SIR RICHARD DE BEAUCHAMP, second Baron Beauchamp of Powick, d. *s.p.m.s.*
    19 Jan. 1502/3; m. 27 Jan. 1446/47 Elizabeth, daughter of Sir Humphrey
    Stafford, Knt., of Grafton, co. Worcester, a descendant of Emperor Charle-
    magne,
23. ANNE DE BEAUCHAMP, d. in 1535; m. Sir Richard Lygon of Arle Court, co.
    Gloucester,
24. SIR RICHARD LYGON, m. Margaret, daughter of William Greville of Arle Court,
    co. Gloucester,
25. HENRY LYGON, d. about 1577; m. Elizabeth, daughter of Sir John Berkeley
    of Upton St. Leonard, co. Gloucester,
26. ELIZABETH (or ISABEL) LYGON, m. Edward Basset of Uley, co. Gloucester,
27. JANE BASSET, d. about 1631; m. Dr. John Deighton of St. Nicholas, co.
    Gloucester, d. about 1640,
28. FRANCES DEIGHTON, bapt. at St. Nicholas, co. Gloucester, England, 1 Mar.
    1611; d. in Taunton, Mass., about February 1705/6; m. at Witcombe
    Magna, co. Gloucester, England, 11 Feb. 1632, Richard Williams, bapt. at
    Wotten-Under-Edge, England, 28 Jan. 1607, d. in Taunton, Mass., about
    August 1693, one of the original purchasers of Taunton in 1640, Deputy to
    the General Court in 1646 and later,
29. BENJAMIN WILLIAMS, d. by 1705/6; m. 18 Mar. 1689/90 Rebecca Macy,
    daughter of Capt. George Macy (one of the original purchasers of Taunton,
    Mass., in 1640) and his wife, Susanna, daughter of the Rev. Nicholas Street,
30. CAPT. BENJAMIN WILLIAMS, served almost constantly throughout the French
    and Indian War in Colonel Gridley's and Colonel Thomas' regiments as
    Company Captain, b. in Taunton 31 July 1695; d. 5 Apr. 1775; m. in Boston,
    25 Jan. 1727, as her second husband, Abigail (Parsons) Johnson,
31. DEBORAH WILLIAMS, b. in 1737; d. 2 May 1774; m. 13 or 27 Dec. 1764 Gregory
    Belcher, served in the French and Indian War, 2 Nov. 1759 to 15 Mar. 1760,
    in Capt. Stephen Whipple's Company, b. 26 Jan. 1738/39, son of Rev.
    Joseph Belcher and his wife Deborah Hunt (daughter of Rev. Samuel Hunt)
    and grandson of Dea. Gregory Belcher,
32. BENJAMIN BELCHER, b. in Easton, Bristol Co., Mass., 17 Sept. 1765; d. 17
    Dec. 1833; m. in Taunton, Mass., 1 Jan. 1792, Sarah (or Sally) Barney, b.
    in Taunton 26 June 1771, d. in Chicopee, Mass., 14 Oct. 1867, daughter of
    John Barney of Taunton,
33. BENJAMIN BARNEY BELCHER, b. in Taunton, Mass., in 1793/94; d. in Chicopee,
    Mass., 5 Sept. 1859; m. (1) about 1817 Olive ———, d. 13 Sept. 1845,
34. AURELIA BELCHER, d. in 1864; m. about 1844, as his second wife, Arthur Mac-
    Arthur, b. in Glasgow, Scotland, 26 Jan. 1815, d. in Atlantic City, N. J., 24
    Aug. 1896, City Attorney, Milwaukee, Wis., in 1851, Lieutenant Governor
    of Wisconsin in 1855, Judge of the second Judicial District of Wisconsin,
    and Associate Justice of the Supreme Court of the District of Columbia,
    1870–1888,
35. LIEUT. GEN. ARTHUR MACARTHUR, b. in Chicopee Falls, Mass., 2 June 1845;
    d. in Milwaukee, Wis., 5 Sept. 1912; m. in Norfolk, Va., 19 May 1875, Mary
    Pinkney Hardy, daughter of Thomas A. Hardy of Norfolk, Va.,
36. GEN. DOUGLAS MACARTHUR, b. in Little Rock, Ark., 26 Jan. 1880.

AUTHORITIES:

Generations 1 to 12—Prof. Dr. Erich Brandenburg's "Die Nachkommen Karl des Grossen", 1935; Marcellus D. R. von Redlich's "Pedigrees of Some of the Emperor Charlemagne's Descendants", vol. 1, pp. 120–121.

Generations 12 to 16—G. E. Cokayne's "The Complete Peerage", vol. 8, pp. 53–56. Also see Marcellus D. R. von Redlich's "Pedigrees of Some of the Emperor Charlemagne's Descendants", vol. 1, pp. 120–121.

Generations 17 to 19—George E. Cokayne's "The Complete Peerage", New Edition, vol. 2, p. 46, note (f).

Generations 20 to 22—George E. Cokayne's "The Complete Peerage", New Edition, vol. 2, pp. 46–47.

Generation 23—Ibid., note (e). Also see vol. 2, p. 41.

Generations 23 to 28—Marcellus D. R. von Redlich's "Pedigrees of Some of the Emperor Charlemagne's Descendants", vol. 1, p. 158; Visitation of Gloucestershire (1623), pp. 204–206, as to Generation 26; Waters' "Gleaning in English Wills" as to Generations 27–28. Also see "The Ancestor", October, 1904.

Generations 28 to 36—Conklin Mann's article "Some Ancestral Lines of General Douglas MacArthur" in *The New York Genealogical and Biographical Record*, July 1942, pp. 170–172 and Charts between pp. 172–173.

DESCENT OF GEN. DOUGLAS MACARTHUR CORRECTION.—I am grateful to Mr. Edgar R. Stickney for the following correction relative to my article entitled "Descent of Gen. Douglas MacArthur from Emperor Charlemagne" in the October 1943 issue of the REGISTER: *

"Item 14—Alice, second wife of Waleran de Newburgh, fourth Earl of Warwick, was not a daughter of John de Harcourt but of Robert de Harcourt."

This doesn't in any way invalidate the descent as set forth in my article, the line being through Waleran de Newburgh and not through his wife's line.

Chicago, Ill.   MARCELLUS D. R. VON REDLICH.

*The preceding article.

DIPLOMA OF THE CREST OF LANCELOT MANFELD—1563.

[COMMUNICATED BY REV. WILLIAM TYLER, OF NORTHAMPTON.]

The following is a copy of a diploma of the Crest, granted in 1563, by William Flower, Esq., Norroy King of Arms, to Lancelot Manfeld, Esq., to be attached to the ancient Arms of his family:

TO ALL AND SINGULER as well nobles and gentils as others to whome these presentes shall come, be seene, heard, read, or understoode Will͞ flower Esquire otherwise called Norroy principall herald and kinge of Armes of the East West and North partes of the realme of England from the ryver of Trent northward, sendeth greetinge in our Lord God everlastinge. WHEREAS Lancelot Manfeld of Skirpenbeck in the countie of Yorke Esquire is well borne and descended of worthie progenitors bearinge signes and tokens of their race and gentrie called Armes which lykewise unto him ar due by just descent and prerogative of birth from his auncestors: He yet not knowenge of any Creast or Cognoysance properly belonginge unto his auncient Armes (as unto very meny auncient coates of Armes) he now hath required me the said Norroy kinge of Armes to assigne unto his said auncient Armes a Creast or Cognoysance meete and lawfull to be boren without prejudice or offence to any other person. IN CONSIDERATION WHEROF for a further declaration of the worthinesse of the said Lancelot Manfeld and at his instant request I the said Norroy kinge of Armes by vertue of myne office and by power and authoritie to me comitted by letters patentes under the greate seale of England haue assigned given and graunted unto the said Lancelot Manfeld to his auncient Armes beinge Gueules a bend cotized argent betweene six Crosse-crosseletts fiche gold: For his Creast or Cognoysance upon the healme on a Torce or wreathe argent and gueules, A man's arme the sleeve asure turned up at the hand ermyne the hand proper colour houldinge a Clubbe gold: with Mantelles thereunto appendant gueules doubled or lyned argent. WHICH ARMES AND CREAST or Cognoysance and every part and parcell thereof I the said Norroy kinge of Armes do by these presentes ratifie confirme give and graunt unto the said Lancelot Manfeld his ofspringe and posteritie for ever: he and they the same to have hold use beare enjoy and shew foorth at all tymes and for ever heerafter in shild cotearmoure penon standard seale signet glasswyndowes buyldinges or any plate jewelles or houshold stuffe with their distinctions and differences due and accustomed accordinge to the laudable custome and usage of this realme of England touchinge the bearinge of Armes at his and their libertie and pleasure without the impediment lett or interruption of any person or persons. IN WITTNESSE wherof I the said Norroy kinge of Armes have heerunto subscribed my name with myne owne hand and sette to the seale of myne office the twentieth day of Septembre In the yere of our Lord God one thousand fyve hundred sixtie three: and in the fifte yere of the reigne of our most gracious Sowvereigne lady Elizabeth by the grace of God Queene of England France and Ireland Defendo^r of the faith, &c.

Pr moy WYLLAM FLOWER, Esquyer

(L. S.)   alis Norroy Roy d' armes.

The diploma is on vellum, handsomely written in German text, with the Arms and Crest beautifully emblazoned in the margin; and with the exception of the loss of the seal, is in a fine state of preservation. In the margin at the top, the arms of France and England quarterly are emblazoned, in honor, as is supposed, of the reigning monarch, by whom they were borne; on one side of which, is the red rose of the house of Lancaster, and on the other, is the fleur de lis of France.

The family of PHELPS, resident at Windsor, Conn., from the early settlement of that town, to which their ancestor WILLIAM PHELPS, *Esquire*, removed from Dorchester, Mass., have had the diploma in their possession through successive generations, and the same is now in the hands of Mr. John Grant, a Tutor in Yale College, whose mother is of that family. The Windsor family of Phelps claims descent from the Lancelot Manfeld, Esq. to whom the Crest was granted, through the marriage of an ancestor of theirs to his daughter or grand-daughter. Mr. Grant obtained the diploma from Mr. Hiram Phelps, of Windsor.

PARENTAGE OF OLIVER MANWARING. — Oliver Manwaring, of Salem, Mass., and of New London, Conn., called in the Essex Deeds "seaman" and "mariner," died 3 Nov. 1723, aged 89. (Hempstead's Diary.) It is the purpose of this note to show that he was probably identical with an Oliver Maynwaring who was baptized at Dawlish, co. Devon, England, 16 Mar. 1633 [1633/4]. (I was indebted to Miss Susan T. Martin for my first clue.)

The early Norman immigrants into England from Mesnil Guerin in the Cotentin held manors near the border between Cheshire and Shropshire. They were inland people, not seafarers. The Maynwarings were a "county family" from the start.

It is probable that our later Manwaring immigrant into New England came from some obscure cadet branch that had rooted itself near the coast or at least on tidewater. Such a branch can be found at Exeter, co. Devon, appearing in the Visitation of Devonshire of 1620; and an offshoot of this branch persisted for more than a hundred years at Dawlish, a fishing hamlet halfway between the harbor at the mouth of the River Exe and the mouth of the Teign.

No other known branch of this family, in London or elsewhere, made such a continuous use of the given name "Oliver" from the sixteenth century on. There was formerly, in the chancel of the parish church at Dawlish, a heraldic ledger-stone which showed the line of Oliver, [Esse], Oliver, and Oliver Maynwaring, 1672-1740. when the last heir male. at least in the local senior line, died. (See Incledon's Church Notes, North Devon Athenæum, Barnstaple.) A more extended pedigree may be found in the *Devon & Cornwall Notes & Queries*, which gives yet another earlier Oliver in the line of descent.

Dawlish was a peculiar of the dean and chapter of Exeter Cathedral, and the probate records are scanty. No probate instrument has been found at any registry for Oliver Maynwaring, who died 14 Mar. 1672, but there is an administration for Esse Maynwaring, who died 13 May 1674. The will of Oliver Maynwaring, who died 11 Feb. 1740, son of Esse and grandson of Oliver Maynwaring aforesaid, makes no reference to blood kin elsewhere.

Oliver Maynwaring, the cadet son of Oliver Maynwaring, gentleman (who died 14 Mar. 1672), and his wife Prudence Esse (daughter of Henry Esse, gentleman, and his wife Lovely Moyle, of Clyst Formizon, *alias* Sowton, co. Devon), was baptized at Dawlish 16 Mar. 1633 [1633/4]. (Transcripts of the Parish Registers of Dawlish, in the Diocesan Registry, Exeter.) His parents were married in 1618. Below are given in parallel columns the chief considerations which make it probable that this Oliver Maynwaring, son of Oliver and Prudence (Esse) Maynwaring, was identical with Oliver Manwaring of New London, Conn., who died in 1723.

Of Old England	*Of New England*
Oliver Maynwaring, baptized at Dawlish, a fishing village in Devon, 16 Mar. 1633 [1633/4].	Oliver Manwaring, seaman, mariner, died 3 Nov. 1723, aged 89.
His mother's name was Prudence. His grandmother's name was Lovedy. His father's name was Oliver.	His third daughter was named Prudence. His fourth daughter was named Love. He had a son named Oliver.
The family were poor and proud gentlefolk. They farmed the tithes. They were buried in the chancel.	In his lifetime he established his two sons with estates elaborately tied up.
This Oliver was uncle to a nephew Oliver, son of Esse Maynwaring. This nephew Oliver was baptized at Dawlish 28 July 1663, and lost heavily when the French vessels raided East Teignmouth in 1690. He lived until 1740.	In his will he mentioned "that Bond from my nephew Oliver Manwaring in England."

Boston, Mass.

HOWARD MENDENHALL BUCK.

677

THE ANCESTRY OF MARY MAPLETT, WIFE OF SAMUEL GORTON OF NEW ENGLAND

Communicated by GEORGE WALTER CHAMBERLAIN, M.S., of Malden, Mass.

THE wills of Mary Mayplett of London, widow, and Dr. John Maplett of Bath, co. Somerset, were discovered in England by the late Henry FitzGilbert Waters, Esq., and abstracts of them were published in the REGISTER in 1890 and 1892. They proved that the wife of Samuel Gorton, whose controversies with the authorities of the Plymouth Colony and the Massachusetts Bay Colony have been often described, was not Elizabeth (———), as Austin and others had stated, but Mary (Maplett). These wills seemed also, as a contributor to the REGISTER (vol. 51, pp. 199–200) pointed out, to justify the * assertion of Gorton that his wife "had bin as tenderly brought up as was any man's wife then in that towne [Plymouth in New England]." The same contributor suggested that Mary (Maplett) Gorton might have been the granddaughter of Rev. John Maplet of Northall, co. Middlesex, through his son John. The wills of this Rev. John Maplet and his son John have recently been found, and they, with certain entries in the registers of the parish of St. Lawrence Jewry, London, show that this suggested ancestry of Mary (Maplett) Gorton is the correct ancestry. Abstracts of these wills and of the two discovered by Mr. Waters, with other English records, are given below, and are followed by a brief pedigree showing the descent of Mary (Maplett) Gorton and her brothers and sisters from Rev. John Maplet of Northall.

The Will of JOHN MAPLET, Clarke, Vicar of the parish church of Northall, in the County of Middlesex, 30 August 1592. To be buried in the chancel of the parish church of Northall. To John Maplett my son £50, when he shall attain the age of twenty-one years. To Margaret Maplett my daughter 40 marks at the age of twenty years or on her day of marriage. To Ellenn Maplett my daughter, to Mary Maplett my daughter, and to Thomas Maplett my son, to each 40 marks to be paid likewise. If any die, such portion to be divided equally among the survivors. To John Maplett my son one feather bed, two down pillows, my silver pott, and one silver spoon. To the residue of my children above-named one silver spoon. To Milchizedek Leaper my wife's son £10, to be paid at once. To Margaret Powell my maid 20s. To Elizabeth Meridon my maid 6s. 8d. To Matthew Randall my man 13s. 4d. To the parish church of Northall "my Bible of the greatest Vollome." To the poor in Northall 20s. To repairing the Queen's Highway in Northall 20s. Residuary legatee and executrix: Ellen Maplet my wife. Supervisors: George King and Henry Wheeler of Northall. Witnesses: George King, Henry Wheeler, Nabuchodonizer Knightes, and Margaret Wheeler. (P.C.C., Scott, 70.) Proved in the Consistory Court of London, 11 September 1592, by William Mannsfielde, notary public, proctor for Ellen, relict and executrix of the said John Maplett, deceased, to whom administration on the goods of the said deceased was granted. (Consistory Court of London, Vicar-General's Books, 1592.)

Administration on the goods of said deceased, according to the aforesaid will, was granted in the Prerogative Court of Canterbury, 7 November 1595, to Mathew Randall, dwelling in the County of Middlesex, yeoman, because

*Pp. 77-78, this volume.

the said Ellen had died before all the goods had been administered by her. (P.C.C., Scott, 70.)

In the Consistory Court of London, 11 November 1595, commission was granted to Matthew Randall, late husband of Ellen Randall alias Maplett, deceased, formerly relict and executrix of John Maplett, Clerk, late Vicar of Northall in the County of Middlesex, deceased, to administer the goods of the said John Maplett not administered by the said Ellen his executrix. (Consistory Court of London, Vicar-General's Books, 1595–1597, fo. 32b.)

The nuncupative Will of Mr JOHN MAPLETT of the parish of St. Lawrence in the old Jury [London], 11 January 1629 [1629/30]. Memorandum that on the 11th day of January, 1629, about seven o'clock in the morning, Mr John Maplett of the parish of St. Lawrence in the old Jury sent for Mr William King of the same parish to come and speak with him, he being sick in body but sound in mind & memory, and he told Mr King that he prepared himself for another world, but that his desire was to make known that he appointed his wife Mary Maplett his sole executrix, & did give her his whole estate to dispose of to his children as she thought fitting, and did also bequeath to his daughter Mary Gorton forty shillings: Mr King urged him to give a better legacy to his said daughter but he answered again that he had given her a great portion in marriage, & that he knew not how his estate would fall out. Therefore he concluded this to be his last will & testament. [Witnesses:] John Maplett, William Kinges, Elizabeth ffreeman, William ffreeman, John Maplett, Susanna Kinge. Proved 15 January 1629/30 by Marie Maplett, relict and sole executrix nominated in said will, William Kinge and Susanna King bearing witness that this was the last will and testament made by said deceased. (P.C.C., Scroope, 6.)

Administration on the goods of MATTHEW RANDALL, late of the parish of Elinge, co. Middlesex, deceased, intestate, was granted 23 November 1630 to William Randall, lawful son of said deceased. (Commissary Court of London, Administration Act Book, 1629–30, fo. 115b.)

The Will of MARY MAYPLETT of London, widow, 7 December 1646. Unto my daughter Mary Gorton, wife of Samuel Gorton living in New England, all the money which her said husband Samuel Gorton doth owe me, and a breed of cattle which he hath of mine, and £10 to buy her mourning. To my daughter Elizabeth Ham and to her husband William Ham £10, between them, to buy them mourning. To my sister Elizabeth Freeman, widow, £6 to buy her mourning. To my grandchild Samuel Chapleine, son of my said daughter Elizabeth Ham by her former husband, £20, which I have lent to the Parliament. To Mrs. Joane Joyner 20s. To Mrs. Elizabeth Warrington 10s. To Mrs. Elizabeth Swann, widow, 10s. The residue to my son John Mayplett, whom I make executor. Proved 10 April 1647. (P.C.C., Fines, 69.) [For a somewhat longer abstract of this will see REGISTER, vol. 44, p. 384, and Waters's Genealogical Gleanings in England, vol. 1, p. 461.]

The Will of JOHN MAPLETT of the city of Bath, Somerset, Doctor of Physick, 13 April 1670. Unto my dear sister Mrs. Mary Gorton of New England 20s., and to each of her children 10s. apiece. Unto my dear sister Mrs. Elizabeth Ham of London, widow, 20s. To my dear daughter Anne Maplett £400 at marriage, if she marry with her mother's good liking and consent, otherwise only £5. To her younger sister my daughter Elizabeth £300 (on same condition). To my aforesaid daughter Anne Maplett all land and houses in Bristol brought to me by her mother at our marriage, being formerly part of the estate of her brother Mr. Walter Williams (after her mother's decease). To my wife my house in Bath with the tenement and gardens thereto belonging all lately bought of Mr. Thomas Fisher, to be her own forever. She to be executrix. Signed 31 July 1670. Proved 7 February 1670 [1670/1]. (P.C.C., Duke, 24.) [For a somewhat longer abstract of this will see REGISTER, vol. 46, p. 153, and Waters's Genealogical Gleanings in England, vol. 1, p. 565.]

FROM THE PARISH REGISTERS OF NORTHOLT (FORMERLY NORTHALL), CO. MIDDLESEX

Marriages*

1584 Thos. Rowsse and Jone Randoll 17 July.
1584 Thos. Freeman and Alys Larchyn 29 November.
1589 Geo. Kynge and Jone Rowsse 28 February [1589/90].
1590 Nabucodoneser Knyghte and Alice Archer 24 September.
1592 Mathewe Randoll and Hellen Maplett [*day and month missing*].

FROM THE REGISTERS OF THE PARISH OF ST. LAWRENCE JEWRY, LONDON, 1538–1638

Christenings

1606 John son of John Maplet haberdasher 15 February [1606/7].
1607 Elizabeth daughter of John Maplet hab: 7 February [1607/8].
1608 Mary daughter of John Maplet haberd. 12 March [1608/9].
1610 John son of John Maplett haberdasher 24 February [1610/11].
1613 Thomas son of John Maplet haberdasher 23 January [1613/14].
1615 Elizabeth daughter of John Maplet haberdasher 28 May.
1616 Sara daughter of John Maplet haberdasher 23 February [1616/17].

Marriage

1603 John Maplet and Hellen King 25 April.

Burials

1603 Ellen wife of John Maplett haberdasher 24 November.
1605 A stillborne child of John Maplett haberdasher 17 May.
1608 John son of John Maplet haberdasher 26 April.
1629 Mr Maplett 18 June [*sic*, ? 18 January 1629/30].

From the foregoing records and other authorities referred to below the following pedigree has been compiled:

1. JOHN MAPLET, clerk, the testator of 1592, was matriculated as a sizar of Queen's College, Cambridge, in Dec. 1560, was admitted to the degree of Bachelor of Arts in 1563/4, was a fellow of Catharine Hall in Aug. 1564, received the degree of Master of Arts in 1567, and was instituted to the rectory of Great Leighs, co. Essex, 26 Nov. 1568. This benefice he exchanged for the vicarage of Northall (now Northolt), co. Middlesex, on 30 Apr. 1576, and he was buried in the chancel of Northall church on 7 Sept. 1592. He was the author of treatises on natural history and astrology. He married ELLEN ———, who was probably widow of ——— LEAPER, her son, Milchizedek Leaper, being named as a legatee in Rev. John Maplet's will. Ellen, widow of Rev. John Maplet, married at Northall, between 11 Sept. 1592 and 24 Mar. 1592/3, Matthew Randall, later of Ealing, co. Middlesex, yeoman, probably the person called "my man" in Rev. John Maplet's will. She died before 7 Nov. 1595, and Matthew Randall died intestate before 23 Nov. 1630, when administration on his goods was granted to his son William.†

* The marriages at Northolt, 1575–1812, have been printed in Phillimore's Middlesex Parish Registers, Marriages, vol. 2.
† See brief notice of Rev. John Maplet, with reference to authorities and with some account of his writings, in Dictionary of National Biography, reissue, vol. 12, p. 997, and compare REGISTER, vol. 51, p. 200.

(P. 77, this volume.)

Children:

2. i. JOHN, probably the elder son, under 21 on 30 Aug. 1592.
   ii. MARGARET, under 20 on 30 Aug. 1592.
   iii. ELLEN, b. in 1575/6 (Dict. of Nat. Biog., *loc. cit.*); under 20 on 30 Aug. 1592.
   iv. THOMAS, b. in 1577 (*ib.*); under 20 on 30 Aug. 1592.
   v. MARY, b. in 1581 (*ib.*); under 20 on 30 Aug. 1592.

2. JOHN MAPLET (*John*), of London, haberdasher, the testator of 1629/30, under 21 on 30 Aug. 1592, was buried in the parish of St. Lawrence Jewry, London, 18 Jan. 1629/30. He married first, in that parish, 25 Apr. 1603, ELLEN (or HELEN) KING, who was buried there 24 Nov. 1603; and secondly MARY ———, the testator of 1646, who died between 7 Dec. 1646 and 10 Apr. 1647.

Children by second wife, recorded in the parish of St. Lawrence Jewry, London:

   i. A CHILD (stillborn), bur. 17 May 1605.
   ii. JOHN, bapt. 15 Feb. 1606/7; bur. 26 Apr. 1608.
   iii. ELIZABETH, bapt. 7 Feb. 1607/8; probably d. young.
   iv. MARY, bapt. 12 Mar. 1608/9; m. before 11 Jan. 1629/30 SAMUEL GORTON, afterwards well-known in the history of New England; a legatee in the will of her brother, Dr. John Maplett, which was signed 31 July 1670.
   v. JOHN, the testator of 1670, bapt. 24 Feb. 1610/11; d. at Bath, co. Somerset, 4 Aug. 1670; m. probably ——— WILLIAMS, who d. in Feb. 1670/1, aged 35. From Dictionary of National Biography, reissue, vol. 12, p. 998, it appears that he "was educated at Westminster, whence in 1630 he was elected to Christ Church, Oxford. He graduated B.A. on 8 July 1634, M.A. on 17 April 1638, and M.D. 24 July 1647." He was a teacher and writer of some note, was for two different periods principal of Gloucester Hall (now Worcester College), and at one time practised medicine at Bath in the summer and at Bristol in the winter. In Bath Abbey a tablet was erected to his memory, and another to his wife and children, John, aged 3 years, and Mary, aged 3 months. Children (order of birth not known): 1. *John*, d. aged 3 years. 2. *Mary*, d. aged 3 months. 3. *Anne*, living unm. 31 July 1670. 4. *Elizabeth*, living unm. 31 July 1670.*
   vi. THOMAS, bapt. 23 Jan. 1613/14.
   vii. ELIZABETH, bapt. 28 May 1615; living in London, a widow, in 1670; m. (1) ——— CHAPLEINE; m. (2) before 7 Dec. 1646 WILLIAM HAM, who was living 7 Dec. 1646 but d. before 13 Apr. 1670. Child by first husband: 1. *Samuel*, living 7 Dec. 1646.
   viii. SARA, bapt. 23 Feb. 1616/17.

MAPLETT: ADDITIONS. — Since the publication of the article entitled "The Ancestry of Mary Maplett, Wife of Samuel Gorton of New England," in the present * volume of the REGISTER, pp. 115–118 (April, 1916), an examination of the parish registers of Northolt (formerly Northall), co. Middlesex, England, for the years 1560–1605, has brought to light the following Maplett entries, in addition to the marriage record of Matthew Randall and Ellen Maplett already printed:

Christenings

1575 Ellen Maplett dawghter of John Maplett 2 February [1575/6].
1577 Thomš Maplett son of John Maplett 25 June.
1581 Mary Maplett dawᵗᵉʳ of John Maplett 28 November.

Burial

1592 John Maplett p'son of Northall 7 September.

In the records at Haberdashers' Hall in London the following entry has been found:

"John Maplett, free by George Brough, 4ᵗʰ April 1600."

This shows that John Maplett, the father-in-law of Samuel Gorton, was admitted to the freedom of the Company of Haberdashers, after he had served his time as an apprentice to George Brough. A careful search has been made for the entry of the apprenticeship, but it has not been found.

29 Hillside Avenue, Malden, Mass.   GEORGE WALTER CHAMBERLAIN.

NOTES ON PERSONS CONNECTED WITH AMERICA, FROM WILLS OF MARSHALLS IN THE PREROGATIVE COURT OF CANTERBURY, ENG.

By GEORGE W. MARSHALL, LL.D., F.S.A., of London, Eng., editor of "The Genealogist,"
and Corresponding Member of the N. E. Historic, Genealogical Society.

WHEN perusing a few months since Mr. Hassam's very valuable "Abstracts of early deeds on record at Boston," in vol. xxxii. p. 181 of the REGISTER, I read with much interest the deed of settlement made by Sybill Marshall, of Lenham, co. Kent, and John Marshall her son, of a certain messuage, &c. to the use of the said John, and Mary, daughter of Ralph Patritch, his wife, and his heirs. On referring to my notes on the surname of Marshall, I found that I had one of the will of this John Marshall, and as the deed has been deemed of sufficient value to find a permanent place of record in the REGISTER, I assume that no better can be found for a copy of the will, which is registered in the Prerogative Court of Canterbury, *Berkeley*, 401, and is as follows:

"This is the last Will and Testament of me John Marshall of Lenham in the County of Kent, Mercer, made the Eight daie of October one Thousand Six Hundred ffiftie Six. I make Marie my wife sole Executrix of this my last will. And my will is that she shall not sell or dispose of anie of my goods without the consent of my good friend Mʳ Michael Beaver. Also my will is that the said Mʳ Beaver shall sell anie of my lands & Tenemtˢ where he shall please for the payment of my debts and the raysing porcõns for my Children and for the maintenance of them and my wife as he shall Think ffit or see cause. Witn's my hand and Seale the daie and yere abouesaid.   JOHN MARSHALL."

Proved by Marie Marshall the relict 20 Novʳ 1756.

ᵏThe preceding article.

I am unable to connect John Marshall with any family of the name in Kent; it does not appear to have been common in that county. His mother Sybill may have been the person mentioned in the will of Marie Marshall, of Maidstone, co. Kent, spinster, dated April 10, 1671, and proved by "Master" Joseph Studley, the sole executor, 26 September following, in the Prerogative Court of Canterbury. (Duke, 114.) This testatrix bequeaths to " my aunt formerly named Jane Cox, now the wife of . . . . Williams of St. Martins, wheeler, £100." "To my cousin Thomas Milway eldest son of my cousin Ambrose Milway of Maidstone, £200." Mentions "Ambrose Milway the younger, son of the said Ambrose Milway"; "Anne wife of John Bigg of Farleigh"; "Sibilla Beacon, daughter of Theodore Beacon"; "Master Joseph Whiston"; "My aunt Mayers of London"; "MY LATE MOTHER Mʳⁱˢ SYBILLA MARSHALL, HER WILL." Directs her lands at Fator-Bridge, Merstham, and Chiddingstone to be sold. The will of Sybilla Marshall was not proved in the Prerogative Court of Canterbury; it will probably be found in some local registry.

The difficulty of tracing the descents of persons whose misfortune it has been to possess a surname so common as Marshall, is, I hope, a sufficient apology for adding to this note the following abstracts of wills proved in the Prerogative Court of Canterbury relating to Marshalls having some connection with America. I can vouch that they are all which can be found in these, as I have examined the wills of every one of the name from its first occurrence in 1415 to the year 1760. If they add a missing link to any of the valuable genealogies which fill the pages of the REGISTER, my time will not have been wasted.

CHARLES MARSHALL, the well known Quaker, author of several works. Died 15 August, 1698. Buried in Bunhill Fields. An account of him will be found in Josiah Smith's "Catalogue of Friends Books," vol. ii. p. 142, &c. Will (Pett, 45), in which he is described as late of Middlesex, and now of the City of London, Practitioner in Physick, dated 6 August, 1698. Wife Hannah Marshall, one of the daughters of Edward Prince, late of the City of Bristoll, Ironmonger, devisee of lands at Tetherton in the parish of Bromhill, co. Wilts. To son Beulah Marshall lands in Pensilvania in America. To son Charles Marshall coppermines in Cumberland. Daughter Mary Scott. Sons Richard Scott, and James Honour. John Marshall, son of my late brother Richard Marshall deceased. Mentions his grandchildren, but not by name. Proved by relict, 25 March, 1699.

MARY MARSHALL. Will (registered Fox, 121) of Mary Marshall of London, widow, "infirm of body and that increased by my grief for the death of my late dear and loving husband Mʳ Joseph Marshall," dated 16 January, 1715. To be buried in the parish church of St. Mary Aldermary as near husband as may be. My cousin Dannetta Dellingham, daughter of my late uncle Dannet Foorth deceased. My cousin Sarah Tukes, daughter of my late uncle Thomas Foorth deceased. My cousin Mary Terry, widow of Stephen Terry deceased. My cousin John Meade. My cousins

Matthew, Samuel, Robert, Francis, Rebecca, and Mary Meade, sons and daughters of my late uncle Richard Meade deceased. My cousin Rebecca Shrimpton, wife of Epaphras Shrimpton of Boston in New England. My cousin Matthew Rolleston of Friday Street, London. My cousin Debora Rolleston his sister. My cousin Samuel Rolleston brother of the said Mathew Rolleston, £500 if he shall be bred a dissenting minister, but if not then only £100, to be paid him at his age of 21 years. My cousin Dannetta Dellingham's two daughters. The two daughters of my cousin Elizabeth Wildbore, daughter of my late uncle John Foorth. My cousin Elizabeth Baker, wife of James Baker. My aforesaid cousin Mary Terry's son and daughter. Richard Baker Citizen and Skinner of London and Anne his wife. The three children of Widow Smith, who was the neice of Martha Lathum deceased. Joseph Higgison son of my neice Elianor Higgison. My brother Benjamin Marshall. My neice Anne Marshall. My cousin Sarah Foorth, daughter of my late uncle Dannett Foorth. My cousin Joseph Reynolds, writing master. To Sir Nathaniel Meade, ten guineas— The same to Doctor Richard Meade. Mr Tongue and Mr Newman, ministers of Salters Hall, £10 each. Elizabeth Johnson, widow. My cousin Mary Meade, wife of Robert Meade, son of my uncle Mathew Meade. To Mrs Anne Ashley, my gold watch. Mrs Anne Clarke, daughter of Mr Clarke the dissenting minister. Mrs Rebecca Bedford. Eighty rings of 20^s apiece amongst such of my relations and acquaintance as my executor shall think fit. Cousin William Meade of Aylesbury, co. Bucks, gent., exor. He proved the will 15 June, 1716.

How Rebecca Shrimpton was cousin to the testatrix, I am unable to explain, neither can I connect her with any family of Marshall whose pedigree is known. Her "late dear and loving husband" was buried at St. Mary Aldermary, London, 25 March, 1715. His will (Fagg, 54) in which he is described as Citizen and Skinner of London, is dated 23 Feby 1714–15. He mentions his brother Benjamin Marshall of Moorfields, Clockmaker, and his wife Mary, and their daughters Anne Marshall and Eleanor "who is lately married." Gives £100 to ten poor dissenting ministers. Mentions Mr Richard Baker of Lawrence Pountneys Lane, London, Skinner; Mr John William Lutkin of London, Merchant; and Mr William Doldren, of London, Skinner. Appoints his cousin William Mead of Aylesbury, co. Bucks, gent., executor, and his (testrs) wife Mary executrix. Both proved the will 28 March, 1715.

Benjamin Marshall, above mentioned, is described in his will dated Octr 1731 (Bedford, 143), as Citizen and Clockmaker of London. Mentions his daughter Elinor and her present husband Jonathan Higginson. Ann Hayward. Appoints his wife Elizabeth Marshall executrix and residuary legatee. By a codicil dated 3 Jan^y, 1731, the legacies given to his daughter and son in law are " revoked because they have lately given me much fatigue and trouble." The will was proved by the relict 11 May, 1732.

ROBERT MARSHALL of the parish of St. Olave Southwark, co. Surrey, Gent., in his will dated 12 April, 1718 (Tenison, 147), and proved 4 July 1718, by John Domine the executor therein named, mentions " Goods, moneys, etc., out of the estate of John Wright lying and being in Maryland." It does not appear that he was in any way related to John Wright, and it is therefore unnecessary to notice him further.

Persons Connected with America, &c. (vol. xxxiii. p. 217).—Allow me to add [1] the following administration, accidentally omitted in my previous notes. Administration of the goods of Henry Marshall of Boston in New England deceased, unmarried, was granted by Prerogative Court of Canterbury to Richard Marshall his cousin and next of kin, 9 January, 1733. This administration was cancelled, and administration granted to Sarah Percival, widow, his aunt and next of kin, 22 Nov. 1733.

Errata to above mentioned Notes :—p. 217, last line, for " 1756 " read " 1656 " ; [2] p. 218, third line from foot, for " Tukes " read " Jukes " ; p. 219, the will of Benjamin Marshall is dated 15 Oct. 1731.　　　　Geore W. Marshall.

London, England.

[1] The preceding article.
[2] Pp. 217, 218, 219 are pp. 682, 683, 684, this volume.

MASCARENE FAMILY PAPERS.

S. G. Drake, Esq.

Dear Sir,—The accompanying letters will explain themselves with a very little assistance on my part. The first, written by a son of Paul Mascarene, (for so many years acting Governor of Nova Scotia, and as such interested in many of the most brilliant deeds of the New England troops, elicited from his nearest relative the touching record of the hardships endured by one of the Huguenots. These documents, in their present translation, were obtained from the surviving branch of the Governor's descendants. I hope to be able to furnish in your next number a sketch of Paul Mascarene, drawn from original documents, and a record of his descendants.

I remain with much respect, your friend,   W. H. Whitmore.
Boston, April 27th, 1855.

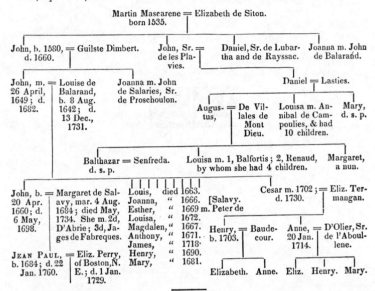

[Copy of my letter to Mr. Mascarene, (the person who told me of him could not tell me his Christian name.) Memo. This was wrote to him in French.—J. M.]   *London, 30th Sept.,* 1763.

Sir,—The person who has now the pleasure of writing to you, is a native of North America, though descended, as he imagines, from a branch of your family. Some affairs of my father's, who died near four years past, calling me to England, I was very desirous of finding whether there were any of his relations living in Languedoc, whence he came, I think from Castras. For this purpose I was recommended by a gentleman to one Mr. Bose, who I was told came thence, and knew a family of my name, and I accordingly applied to him a few days past, who told me there was one, and gave me a proper direction for a letter.

I remember to have seen a memorandum which my father left behind him, and which is in my possession at home, containing some account of his Family, Birth, Education, &c.; but my departure for England being somewhat sudden and unexpected, I had not time to look for it. All that I know is, that he was born in Languedoc in the year 1684, about which time there being a persecution of the Protestants, my grandfather fled with him to Holland, but I think, if I remember right, left my grandmother behind him, she having embraced the Catholic faith. My father having lived sometime in Holland, and after my grandfather's death having had his Education under care of Mr. Rapin, he came over to England, obtained a commission, and from here went to America with some Troops in the year 1711, and was employed in Nova Scotia, where he was by degrees advanced to the Commission of a Colonel, and was also for some years Lt. Governor and Commander-in-Chief of the Province of Nova Scotia till the year 1750, when, finding himself pretty far advanced in years and infirm, he obtained his Majesty's leave to dispose of his commission and retire to his family, which resided in Boston, New England. However, as he still retained his rank in the Army, he was advanced to the Commission of a Major General some years before he died. He married in Boston and has left behind him three children, namely, two daughters and myself. His name was Jean Paul Mascarene, but was known generally by the name of Paul. I am the only male survivor of the family bearing the name, except a son which I have, and who is named Paul after my Father. This, Sir, is all the information I can furnish you with, and if from the circumstances given you of my father's birth, and my grandfather's removal with him to Holland, you can trace the family, I shall esteem it a favor if you will be kind enough to give me any intelligence respecting it, and whether there are any of my grandfather's successors living, or any collateral branch, as I shall be very desirous of forming a correspondence with them as well as with you. I expect to return to New England in the Spring : in the meantime a letter in answer to this will be esteemed as a great obligation conferred on, Sir, your most humble and

Most obedient servant, JOHN MASCARENE.

Please direct for me at the New England Coffee House, Threadneedle street, London.

Castras, Nov. 14, 1763.

Sir and Dear Nephew,—It is not possible for me to express to you the pleasure I felt in receiving your letter of the 30th Sept., which came to hand the 16th Octo. I was fearful that not only your father might be dead, but also lest he should not have left any successor behind him. The last news I had of him was in 1720 ; his letter was dated from Placentia in Newfoundland, where he at that time commanded. The public newspapers in 1748 informed me that one Mascarene was advanced to the rank of Major General of the English troops, but I was uncertain whether it was your father or any of his children. At length, my Dear Nephew, we have found each other ; and your letter acquainted me that you are not only desirous of knowing your pedigree, but also of having a correspondence with your nearest relation, which I accept of as being the nearest, and the only one who can inform you of what you are desirous of knowing, having very carefully preserved all the letters and writings of your grandfather, whom I shall give you some account of in the sequel of this : it would have been more easy for me to have done this, had God been pleased to have preserved to me my sight, which I have lost since 1744. A dungeon, where I was confined seven months on account of my religion, did not a little contribute to this loss, and I am now almost wholly deprived of the benefit of reading; however, the cause of this deprivation of my sight is what helps to soften the calamity, and makes me support it with patience and resignation. The history of that excellent man, John Mascarene, your grandfather, (whom you could have but a very imperfect knowledge of from the minutes which your father left, as he himself could not have acquired any particular information, having left France when he was but eleven years old,) I shall endeavor to make known to you, and that you may be the better able to understand it, I send you a genealogy,* which I carried no further back than the father of your great-grandfather: this history is too deeply engraved in my heart for me to forget it. There is not an aged person in the place (I mean those who think as we do) who is ignorant of it; and at the same time scarce a young person who is not desirous of knowing it, which puts me often upon reciting it; all those to whom I relate it admire his constancy and resolution;—in a word, your grandfather is looked upon as a model of virtue, and one who has carried Christian heroism to the highest pitch, and who, in short, quitted everything to follow his God.

The following is an abbreviation of his history :—

John Mascarene was born the 20th of April, 1660. He pursued his studies closely, and especially made himself acquainted with that religion which was of great assistance to him in all his misfortunes: he was Counsellor to the Parliament, that is to say, to the Chamber of the Diet, which subsisted a long while at Castras. He was married to Margaret de Salavy the 4th of April, 1684, from which marriage proceeded John Paul, your father. I must give you some particulars of his birth, in order to which you will observe that the revocation of the Edict of Nantes was in October, 1684, and before this revocation was published orders were issued for soldiers to be quartered at discretion, at the houses of such as would not abjure the Protestant religion; your grandfather was threatened with a preference above others, which indeed they could not help doing. The situation of his wife, who was then near lying-in, determined him to go to a farm-house which he had, about four leagues from ——, and near to the highest mountain we have, and which is called the Nose, whither he had fortunately time to make his escape with his wife, and his estate left to the discretion of a company of Dragoons, who finding themselves disappointed in not being able to exercise the barbarity against your grandfather and grandmother, sold all the moveables, cattle, hay, straw, and in short everything they could find, and made strict search to find your grandfather; which he being informed of, resolved to flee as soon as his wife was brought to bed, which happened at the end of the year 1684, (I do not exactly know the time), when she was delivered of a son, afterwards named John Paul, your father, who was born on the aforesaid mountain, in the cottage of a peasant, with whom he remained some time, and was concealed till he was weaned. The fire of persecution being a little cooled, his grandmother took him and brought him up with her, and was continually in fear lest he should be taken from her. I shall here leave your father, who lived in this manner till he was eleven years old, to return to your grandfather, who, in his flight, took the road to Bordeaux. It was at the beginning of February, 1686, that he left his retreat, and arrived without any accident at Agen, the 20th of February, the same year, a little town situated on the Garonne, about thirty leagues from Castras. Here he took

---

* This genealogy is at the beginning of this article. The French names are liable to be misspelt in copying.

688

passage in a packet boat, on the said river, for Bordeaux, whither he intended to go in order to procure some assistance and continue his journey. Scarce was he got into the boat when an officer of the regiment of Turin, who commanded a detachment, inquired of this excellent man whether he were not one of those who professed the Protestant religion. "Pardon me!" answered he. "I order you, in the king's name," said the officer, "to follow me with that lady, who, I suppose, is your wife." "That is true," said your grandfather; on which they both followed the officer, who conducted them to the prison at Agen. They searched my uncle and found some pocket books in which he had a quarter of a sheet of paper, on which was figured a quadrant, and, among other things, three addresses for different persons, one at Geneva, another at the Hague, and a third in London. These three addresses were the principal grounds of accusation against him. Divine Providence, which guided him in all his actions, caused him, by way of precaution, to make the officer and his deputies who arrested him, take particular notice of the papers which they had found upon him. This precaution was of great service to him, and though the President was present to hear his examination, he would not answer to any of the interrogatories which were put to him, but insisted upon being sent before his natural Judge; but when the pocket book was produced there was found in it a song in the Gascon tongue, in ridicule of some conversions which at that time had taken place. He was under the necessity of declaring that he did not understand that tongue, that he had neither written nor read nor heard anything of the said song, but that it had been put there by the officer or sergeant who were called upon by him to witness to the papers which they had found upon him, and which, as was before said, he had made them take particular notice of, and he still persisted in his demand of being sent before his natural judges. The President, not being willing to act in this affair, sent him before the Judge at Castras, who was appointed to try criminal cases, where, after many interrogatories made to him at different hearings, the Judge questioned him respecting the aforementioned song. He protested, as I said before, and demanded that the officer, sergeant and others who apprehended him, should be brought face to face, to which demand the judge paid no regard, but pronounced sentence upon him the 19th of August, 1686—condemning this noble champion to the Galleys for life, and fining him the sum of 3000 livres for the King's use, besides the confiscation of all his estate. This sentence did not terrify him. He very calmly appealed to the Parliament and uttered these words: "God quitted everything for my sake, and expired upon the cross;—it is right that I should make him that little sacrifice to which I am condemned; I am persuaded he will never forsake me so long as I am faithful to him."

Are you not impatient to know what became of Margaret de Salavy, your grandmother, whilst your grandfather was in this critical situation? I will tell you. I have said nothing of her since her being arrested with her husband at Agen, where she separated herself from that worthy man and demanded from the President at Agen her enlargement. The offer made was to abjure her religion, which was accepted, and she was set at liberty and returned to Castras, where she led a life which I shall pass over in silence, lest I should exceed the bounds of that moderation which is necessary should be preserved for the sex. Her son, who arrived at Geneva, 14th Dec., 1696, empowered her, in quality of his only successor, to take possession of all his effects, and her abjuration made this matter very easy. Louiza de Balarand, who was an only daughter and very rich, and had some considerable mortgages upon the estate of your grandmother, threatened your grandmother to go to law with her in order to recover upon the said mortgages; the justice of her demand terrified your grandmother, or rather her adherents, and by the intermediation of their mutual friends, an instrument was signed the 28th of Oct., 1698, by which your grandmother gave up all she was possessed of, saving her dowry and the interest upon it, and a right of succession to two brothers of your good father, which amounted to twenty thousand livres, and the enjoyment of a country house and house at Angly, which together yielded more than 300 livres a year rent. I should have observed to you that she took possession of all the moveables and effects which had been concealed, and those which were saved from the plunder of the Dragoons. But let us finish this disagreeable account to return to my dear uncle; however I must make you acquainted with the two husbands who succeeded my dear uncle. After the foregoing transactions, she retired to Angly, of which I have before told you, and in 1699 she married Mons. D'Albie, with whom she lived about three years, and had no children. The third marriage was with Mr. Jacques de Fabriques, grandson of Mons. Toussand, minister; the said Mr. de Fabriques had joined the said Mons. Toussand in Holland, (where he had retired). As the climate, I suppose, did not suit him, the said Mr. Fabriques returned to France and married your grandmother in 1704, by which marriage she had two children. She died at Castras in 1734, having without doubt taken possession of all she could; so far, indeed, that Louisa de Balarand could not come at sufficient to discharge her mortgages, as I shall have occasion to tell you presently. In the meantime let us finish this disagreeable history and return to my dear and respected uncle whom I left in prison at Castras. After having appealed from the sentence of the judges, he was in consequence thereof carried to the Parliament of Toulouse, where he was obliged to undergo several particular interrogatories. He defended his cause with the assistance of Mr. Davie, an advocate, and I have the instructions which he gave to the said Mr. Davie, with his case stated. Amongst other questions which were put to him, the affair of the song, found among his papers, was not forgotten. The letters for Geneva, the Hague and London, were, said they, a proof that he intended to leave the kingdom. He denied it, and cited the 12th article of the Edict of Revocation, which permitted all those who would not abjure the Protestant religion, to retire into any part of the kingdom they pleased; that in consequence of this indulgence he was retiring to Bordeaux for some time, in hopes that the king would be pleased to pronounce some more favorable sentence on those who maintained the Protestant faith. The several hearings he had before, were nothing in comparison to a public one on the 7th May, 1687, where he appeared on the stool in the presence of all the chamber appointed for the trial of criminal causes, composed ordinarily of the judges. The humble posture in which he was placed,—the chains on his legs,—the presence of fourteen judges,—did not in the least terrify him. He maintained an admirable firmness and composure of mind, heard all his judges, and answered each of them without the least discomposure, and when at last he was obliged to enter into a controversy, he defended himself extraordinarily well, till he obtained from the court (a thing unknown before) leave to interrogate one of the judges who proposed a question to him. He confounded the judges, upon which the court, having their eyes on the President, asked

690

him if he had taken care to instruct himself well. To which he answered, "Yes!" "Do you persist in your faith?" "Yes," answered he; "I am ready to follow my God wherever he shall please to call me; he has quitted everything for me; it is just that I should quit everything for him."

They sent him back to the palace prison, and the day after removed him to that of the Hotel de Ville. 'Tis thus they deal with those criminals who are destined for execution; 'twas there my dear uncle that the end of all his troubles was near; but when three days were elapsed, and no notice given him of his destiny, he resumed courage, and afterwards understood that an arrest had intervened, which was put to a Notary to be finished upon the appeal and the letters which had been sent to quash proceedings against him. He passed about a year in the prison of the Hotel de Ville, in soliciting a definitive sentence, without being able to obtain it. His utmost care, money, and friends, were employed, but in vain. I have his hearing on the stool, written by his own hand, which I always read with fresh pleasure, and may possibly send it to you hereafter, with an elegy on his wife, and a prayer in verse beginning with these words: "O King of kings, thou power supreme!" He composed this prayer in the prison of the Hotel de Ville, after his hearing before the Parliament of Toulouse; his troubles, his confinement, and his trust in God were the subjects of it.

At last, in the beginning of April in the year 1688, after having retained this worthy prisoner for two years and two months,—would you believe it?—they conducted him to the place whither he was going when he was arrested. The * * * of April, 1688, early in the morning, the Lieutenant of the patrol, an officer of the Bourgeois, which was quartered at Toulouse, came into my uncle's chamber, whom he found in bed. "Come, sir," said the officer, "you must rise immediately." To which my uncle answered, "Give me time to say my prayers, and then I am ready to go whithersoever God shall call me." He did not doubt but that his last moment was near. In half an hour the officer returned, and asked him if he was ready. "Yes," answered my uncle. The officer took a handkerchief out of his pocket, with which he blinded him and put him in a litter, into which he also got himself, and carried my uncle to the frontier of France, and forbade him, in the King's name, to return thither again. He thanked the officer for the care he had taken of him, and told him it was scarce worth while to have detained him two years and at last carry him whither he desired to go; that he comforted himself under all his sufferings, as he looked upon them as nothing in comparison to the glory that was to be revealed, and which he had a firm faith that he should enjoy. He arrived at Geneva, April 10th, 1688, having nothing at all with him but what he carried on his back. My grandmother sent him all the assistance that was in her power. I have spared no cost to obtain a copy of the proceedings against him, but it is not to be found in the Records of the Parliament. I have always been of opinion that it was lodged in the hands of Mr. De Levin, the Recorder, and this family is extinct. I should have been very glad to have found it, to conclude the account of this dear uncle. He lived ten years in a strange country, and died at last at Utrecht, the 6th of April, 1698, and though his son arrived at Geneva, the 14th of December, that is to say, sixteen months before his death, he had not the satisfaction of seeing him. M. de Rapin took care to instruct him in the language, and he arrived at Utrecht two days after the death of his father. Thus finished the career of this worthy and virtuous confessor at the age of 38 years.

Let us now proceed to John Paul, your father, who was brought up, as I have before informed you, by Louisa de Balarand, my grandmother, and by Cæsar Mascarene, my father, as Margaret de Salavy took very little care of him. Jean Paul having arrived to the age of eleven and in a capacity of travelling on horseback, my father, to gratify my uncle, who, in all his letters, solicited my mother to send his son; my father, I say, hazarded the journey at the latter end of Nov., 1696. He made the young lad dress himself in a green livery, with a design of making him pass for his lacquey; he had been exercised for that purpose, and had succeeded well under his instruction. Another person who was trusty, and who had served him before, (named la Graudem), was the groom. Everything being prepared, they took the route of Lyons, and instead of going to St. Esprit, they went to a village near it called Sciffel, a little below the fort de Puluse, where they were to pass the Rhone without being seen, as it was not possible to pass the bridge of St. Esprit without a passport, which my uncle had not. It was necessary, therefore, to make interest with a barge man, in order to pass the Rhone. He addressed himself to one who was carrying hay from Sciffel to the other side of the river, who engaged to carry Paul and his portmanteau; but as for my father and the groom, they being obliged to remain at Sciffel, were forced to submit to it. Paul, with as much resolution as a man of twenty-four, quitted his green livery to take on him the habit of a sailor; they hid his portmanteau in a bundle of hay, and after taking their leave of each other, Paul took the oar; by which means he safely passed the Rhone and took the road to Geneva, where he arrived, I can't tell how, the 14th Dec., 1696. He was received by Mr. Rapin, who took care of his education, as I have before informed you. I forgot to tell you that my father went alone from Castras to Angly, where he had two country seats, and Paul some days after joined him. The day that Paul set out from Castras was the same that my father left Angly. Paul had a recommendation to Mr de Caill at Angly; who was a very good friend of my father and your grandfather. Paul remained concealed some days with Mr. de Caill, and as no news was heard of him, there was a story at Castras that he had been stolen away. My grandmother made strict search after him; my father went into the country, and instead of searching for Paul, he took the route of Lyons with Paul, whom he was at no loss to find. They learnt at last that he was at Geneva, but there was none of his friends who knew how to get there. I have this information from my father. This evasion caused a good deal of trouble to my grandmother; they put all her effects under an arrest; that is to say, the King took possession of them, and she had no sooner redeemed them, than they were arrested again, and in short she was obliged to ransom them three times in less than six years.

In 1702, my grandmother, from eleven children which she had, finding herself with only Cæsar, her youngest son, had an inclination to have him married, which she effected in the same year; and by the marriage contract gave him all her estate. This alteration of property did not excuse my father from the arrest which had been made: he took all the pains he could, and was at a considerable expense to get quit of it, and he succeeded at length so far as to obtain a dismission with liberty to dispose of his estate, with the consent of Louise de Balarand, his mother, on account of the mortgages she had on the estate of her deceased husband. This was done, and he obtained a decree in the year 1719, when he was left in quiet till the year 1730, when he died. Three years after, they pretended to have lost his discharge and the decree, and put his estate again under arrest, and I was obliged to produce the decree which I had of the Register, which made me easy. It was happy for me that my father gave up a sum of money to obtain this decree, without which I should have been in danger of losing all my estate.

You see here, my dear nephew, the sorrowful history of your and my family. It is a subject for a large volume. As your letter required of me the detail which I have given you, I did not think it proper to speak of it to any one ; and as it will make a considerable packet, I was afraid lest it should excite the curiosity of some one ; and have taken the precaution to send it to Pezeras where there is at this time a fair. For the future I shall write you by the way of Bordeaux, where I have some mercantile friends, and there are often English vessels which arrive there, especially the beginning of March and October, when there is a considerable fair; by this way I can send you some of your grandfather's writings. But to conclude, I am obliged to Mr. Bose for the pleasure he has given me. I beg you would give my very humble services to him ;— his house is opposite to my wife's, (daughter to Mr. Baudicour.) You may tell him that his sister is well. You would give me pleasure in sending me your profession, and I beg you would inform me by first opportunity. I shall be pleased to know also if your sisters are settled— and the names of their husbands with their professions. There are many refugees in London from Castras. General Ligoneer is uncle to one of my friends ; a sister of another friend, daughter to Mr. Dubisson, married an ambassador, whose name I do not recollect ; M. de Lugage, who, I believe, is in trade, and others whom I cannot at present remember. I shall close this in desiring you to excuse the incorrectness of this letter ; I indicted it myself but cannot read it. My sister, who is a widow and lives with me, is a proof, by right inheritance, of the misfortunes which have attended our family to this very day. My sister, I say, committed this to writing. I am, my dear nephew, with the most sincere esteem, your most humble and most obedient servant, MASCARENE.

I forgot to tell you that your grandmother, after her last marriage, maintained the same principles in which she was brought up. I ought likewise to acquaint you that our family is one of the most ancient in this country, and passes for such. It has been always in the Law or the Army ; but more in the first than the latter. Tell me, I pray you, what town you reside in, as well as how I may direct to you, without which I shall make use of the directions you have already given me. Mine is, to Mascarene, advocate in particular at Castras in upper Languedoc. My wife, sisters, and daughters, made me promise to say many things to you from them, and to assure you of their friendship. Our respects, I pray, to madam, your spouse, and sisters. We embrace the dear family.

Memorandum for entering my coat of arms at the Heraldry Office.

Paul Mascarene, born at Castras in Languedoc, in the kingdom of France, was naturalized in England in the session of 1706 ; was made Lieutenant in the same year (1706) and gradually rose in the Army to the Post of Lieutenant Colonel, and continued in the Service to the year 1750, having been for the last seven years Lieutenant Colonel to Lieutenant General Philipps' Regiment of Foot, Lieutenant Governor of Annapolis Royall, and in the absence of the Governor, Commander-in-chief over the Province of Nova Scotia in North America; when, being aged and infirm, he obtained his Majesty's leave to resign, and his Majesty was graciously pleased to give him a Commission of Colonel of Foot, to hold his rank as such in the Army.

Beareth Argent, a Lion, rampant, gules, with a Chief Azur charged with three mullets Or and a mullet of the same for Crest,
By the name of   MASCARENE.

MASCARENE FAMILY PAPERS.

S. G. DRAKE, ESQ.,

DEAR SIR.—I hand you with this some more papers relating to Governor Mascarene, being a continuation of those published in the Register for July, 1855.*

You will observe that, though the name of Mascarene is extinct, yet the descendants, through the female lines, bear the names of some of the most distinguished Boston families.   I remain yours, truly,   W. H. WHITMORE.

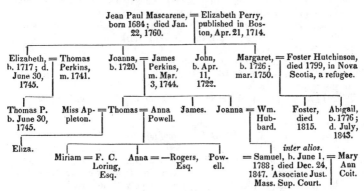

JEAN PAUL MASCARENE was born at Castras in Languedoc, France, but being obliged to leave his family and country when very young, he fled first to Geneva, and thence to England. There he was naturalized in 1706, and in the same year made lieutenant. The earliest mention of him in Boston is in 1714, at which time he is described as of Great Britain. He probably resided in the town of Boston until the date when the present extracts from his letters show him as an emigrant to Nova Scotia. The imperfect examination which I have been able to make, has not revealed the cause of his determination to go to that province, but perhaps the death of his wife, and a proper anxiety to increase his income, may have had weight with him. Indeed, he writes to his daughter very soon after his arrival, " I have often represented to you that while I live you may expect to live in no want, but that at my death you will find a great alteration in your circumstances, and therefore I wanted, whilst it was in my power, to lay up something for my children, to make this alteration seem the less grievous to you." As to his duties and actions in his new home, the following extracts will afford an indication.

These extracts are gleanings from a letter-book, still preserved by his descendants, and kindly loaned me by them. They are, of course, unconnected, and are, in fact, of interest chiefly, as the honest sentiments of a prominent actor in a series of intrigues, the results of which were of great importance to New England. The MS. from which they are copied is numbered 3 in the series, and thus commences abruptly, and contains reference to matters previously mentioned. There is a letter from Mascarene to Gov. Shirley, dated April 6, 1748, at Annapolis, printed in the General Description of Nova Scotia. In Parsons's " Life of Sir William Pepperrell," there are two or three letters mentioned, but none of importance.

June 7, 1740, writing to his daughter Eliz., he says:—1 am not sure that this title of commander-in-chief over this Province will be of any ad-
*The preceding article.

695

vantage to my income, butt rather an increase of charge, and as another person may chance to be soon named att home to succeed me, this airy title may soon vanish and leave me, perhaps, worse in my circumstances than I was.

June, 1740, writing to Dr. Douglass:—I have kept my station pretty well, notwithstanding some blocks thrown in my way, for to you only be it said, I have to do with something like a Proteus or a weathercock, which, though it shows fair wind to-day, may not do so the next.

Sept. 29, 1740, to the same:—We have had a report here by Thom. Donnell, who says he heard it from Mr Wm Clark, that Lt Col Cosby is Lt Govr of the Province, but little credit is given here to it nor will it be on such a slender authority, that he will be allowed to act here as such. This however has elevated him, and made him act too rashly in the matter of the foresaid bills.

Dec., 1740, to his daughter Eliz.:—I seldom, of late, visit at Lt Col Cosby but keep up a very friendly intercourse with Capt Handfield and Lieut Amhurst and others of our officers.

December 1 to 23, 1740, to Dr. Douglass:—You perceived in my last that a coldness between Lt Col Cosby and I would naturally ensue from his proceeding towards me. It has continued some time, and is to like to do so, so far indeed as to interrupt any familiar conversation betwixt him and me, butt not as yet, and I hope will not break upon the peace and quiett the place has enjoyed since my arrival. The affairs of our Government go on in an easy manner hitherto, and without interruption.

March 18, 1741, to the same:—I have had no conversation at all for these six months past with our Lt Col who endeavors to swell his power by military honors and other ways, thereby to depress mine. We shall soon see what news will come from home, and till then I shall hold in as much as possible.

Our French subjects here keep under obedience and in peace, and our civil government has been hitherto carried on with tolerable decency. I impatiently expect some lights from home for regulating my future proceedings. Lt Col Cope having —— directed to C—— by the title of Lt Gov of the Province makes him believe himself to be such, as has gained the belief of others so far as to dread it.

April 20, 1741, to Dr. Douglass:—You'll see by the enclosed copy of Lt Col Cosby's letter and my answer, what steps he would take if it was in his power to get me away from hence, and how he was mistaken in thinking I was not taken notice of at home in the station I have sustained. His expectations, which he has kept here very warm all winter, are very much cooled since he has had my answer to his letter; butt as he, leaving nothing undone, and makes use of any means that may promote his views, I am always oblig'd to be upon my guard. He has not dared to refuse from being putt up att the fort gate a proclamation issued a few days ago, prohibiting the exportation of provisions to any other port than what belongs, and is within his Majesty's Dominions, bearing my title of President of the Council and Commander in Chief for the time being of this Province.

You'll see three of our council by this opportunity. I would have them received with civility, if they visit my family, butt without any great fuss, being under no great obligations to them, especially to Phillips, who, as farr as he could, has sett himself in opposition to me.

June 15, 1741, to the same :—Our affairs here go att the old rate. Lt Col Cosby now and then breaks out, but my moderation and coolness of temper, I have, much against his will and desire, kept every thing quiet and in peace.

Aug. 4, 1741, to the same :—Our mighty expectations are vanished ; the Governor in his letter to me doth not so much as mention the new instruction he wrote me in his last he would apply for towards new set-tling the government. He writes to me, indeed, in a very civil manner, as att the head of the council, butt is cautious in giving me hopes of ex-pecting anything for my trouble. The agent is pretty much on the same strain, but more open in his telling me of the little hope there is for the Lt Col and I to obtain the post of Lt Gov of this Province, there being some persons of interest putting in for it, and that as the Governor intends for these parts, the management of the affairs of this Province will continue lodg'd in me till his Ex. arrival.

This is the substance on my side. On the other if I may judge by ap-pearances and circumstances no very great satisfaction has been given. For hopes which are very uncertain conditions hard are imposed, embar-rassments by delays of paying Bills, &c. As for my part I have a fair acct from the Agent, my bills all paid to December last, to which time the acct reaches, and £62 stg balance, so that I am not crampt that way. The Lt Col endeavours to keep up his Interest here by giving out that he is certainly to be att the head of the Province, which I don't doubt his Father-in-law will endeavour to support amongst you. Great endeavours have been used to gain the members of the Council from me, even by the greatest courtshipp paid to irreconcileable Enemies. This sometimes has obtained so farr as to cool the Zeal with which some us'd to act their part before ; but the Engine he thought would effectually procure his Ends was his ordering me to Canso. You have seen how I withstood his attack last spring ; he has since renew'd it, to which I writt an answer in stronger terms than I did before, which to the surprise of every Body he refus'd to receive from the hands of the officer I sent it by. Had I comply'd, an effectual end would have been putt to the Civil Establish-ment of this Government and the whole power lodg'd in the military.

In the midst of all these struggles and many underhand practices used to weaken the authority on which I act, I have kept my temper and whilst fire and tow was on one side I took care to oppose coolness and steadiness on the other. This indeed begins to be tiresome especially as I do not find the support I might reasonably have expected from home and there-fore if at the return of our members they will not joyn in a representation of our case att home, I shall be obliged to represent by myself that the King's Authority over His Majesty's Subjects in this Province cannot be supported with due weight in the circumstances we are now in. In which representation I must make use of another channel than that of Messrs Wilks and Kilby who I am afraid are too much influenced by our Agent Gould, or too remiss on my ac. The New Governour may afford me a conveyance of my letters to the Duke of New Castle by enclosing them and making one word of mention only of them. I have writ a letter of compliment and congratulation to him. If you could have some discourse with him on this head and acquaint me with the result it would be a help to my farther proceeding.

Nov. 23, 1741, to the same :—As for what relates to Great Brittain the letter you sent me inclosed has given me hopes that my affaires there are

697

in a good way and that my acting here is not reckoned so insignificant as a certain Person of ours would fain make it appear. I shall endeavour to build on that foundation and also make use of the Channell you have open'd for me with Governour Shirley.

My antagonist here has received a very sharp letter from our Agent wherein as I have heard his turbulent temper is in plain words laid to his charge, and said to be the means which has debarr'd him from obtaining any rule in civil authority.

We have here as well as in other Places what is call'd corruption.

I go on however hitherto in the Duty of my office of President and Commander in chief over the Province and by all means in my power endeavor to avoid or remove the blocks laid in my way, in which I have hitherto happily succeeded.

April 12, 1742, to the same:—A little vessel from Salem, trading up this bay without caution, was surprised by some roving Indians and plundered. I am now taking his examination with the assistance of the Council. Whether this beginning of troubles amongst us will have any consequence, I don't know, nor how our French subjects will behave in case of a warr with France. I have done my part to keep them in due decorum and have not been wanting in making representations att home suitable to our condition.

28th:—Since my writing the foregoing I have received letters from Manis which acquaint me that the Inhabitants as soon as they heard of the Robbery before mentioned, fitted out a Vessel, manned her with 20 hands and went in pursuit of the Indians, and recover'd a good part of the goods; on which the master returned there again and had a faithful ac of his goods so recovered, had them delivered into his hands and is since returned hither. This is farr from being pleasant to my opposer who I am apt to believe rather wishes all in confusion than any credit shall accrue to my administration of the affaires of this Province, by the influence it has in bringing the People to a sense of their Duty. It is certain they never acted with such a vigour in any the like occasion which has happened even in times of the most profound peace.

Nov. 23. To Dr. Douglass:—We were like to run into a great confusion on acct of our Provisions and are not out of it yet. The Lt Govr of the Garrison having undertaken to provide Beef instead of Pork and fresh bread instead of Bisq^t &c the Oxen droven for twenty miles from Mavis in bad roads soon fell away, and prove when killed wretched meat, which occasions murmuring amongst the men of ill consequence and if continued may turn to mutiny; they have had no peace for these twelve months, six months whereof by giving them Credit for Rhumm on the settlers has been patched up, butt six months remain expected to be paid in specie.

[Note. Lt Col Cosby d. Dec. 27, 1742, leaving a widow and six children. Gov. Mascarene then applied for both posts of Lt Col. and Lt Gov. feeling that the late controversy being thus ended, it would be most advantageous to have the military and civil power under one control.]

July 26, 1743, to Dr. Douglass:—It will be sufficient to tell you that our Commissary here has been obliged to apply to Mr Borland for Fifty Quintals of Bisq^t which accordingly he has received and to buy what he could here from the officers who had any thing due and would part with it att the rate of a groat sterling for every man's allowance, which is more than I believe Mr Borland receives. All this to prepare himself for a survey I long ago intimated to him I would order on the Provisions.

This survey is over and he is still deficient. As I am not of a revengefull nature and what I do is more to prevent such embezzlements for the future, I shall be satisfied when all is put to rights again. By a letter I have received from Capt Heron who commands att Canso exery thing there is well and if he tells true he has behaved better than was generally expected. He acquaints me with the arrival of Capt Robert Young of the Kingsale who brings not other Public news than what we have had before butt tells in regard to us that on representations made to the King in Council it had been ordered that the Regiments in America Gibraltour and Port Mohan should be relieved for the future every three years to begin from 1843. If this is true a new scene of action will be open for me which makes me the more impatient to hear from England Especially in answer to my last application which must be att this time in agitation att home and to which I may expect answers by the return of our fall vessels in September.

Extracts of Letters from Gov. Belcher to Major Mascarene, 1740, 1741.

Sir,—Sometime the last Month I received your Favour of the 27th March, by which I was glad to find you safely arrived at Annapolis Royal and that you had been well received at the head of His Majesty Province of Nova Scotia. * * * I see you had issued a Proclamation for the Settlement of the Civil Government until your further Orders. * * * *

Boston, May 2, 1740.
Maj Mascarene.
To the care of the young lady
his Daughter Miss Betty.

Honoble Sir,
Your most obedient, &c.
Jonathan Belcher.

The following letter shows the standing of his son-in-law :—

Boston, *May* 19, 1741.

I have had the pleasure of knowing you personally for 2 and Thirty years past. I can say without flattery, such things [animosities among the officers of the Government] cannot be imputed to Major Mascarene's Conduct. * * * I Congratulate you, Sir, upon the Marriage of your pretty and worthy daughter to as good a husband as this part of the world could oblige her with.

Maj^r Mascarene. Jonathan Belcher.

At his death his estate was valued at £5688. 15. 10. 1. and his wife's at her death at £1440. His house stood on School Street.

His son John Mascarene (whose signature is here given) was b. April 11, 1722. He m. Margaret Holyoke, whose pedigree is here inserted.

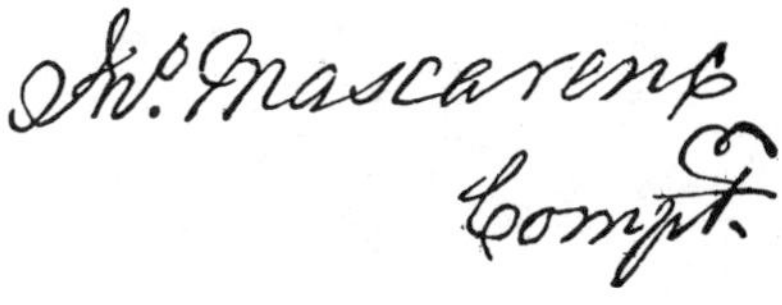

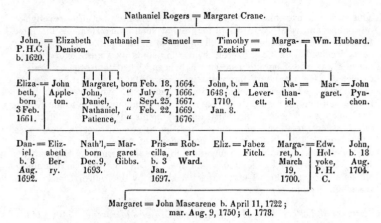

Nathaniel Rogers = Margaret Crane.

John, = Elizabeth	Nathaniel =	Samuel =	Timothy = Ezekiel =	Marga- = Wm. Hubbard.
P.H.C. Denison.				ret.
b. 1620.				

Eliza- = John Apple- beth, ton.
born
3 Feb.
1661.

Margaret, born Feb. 18, 1664.
John, " July 7, 1666.
Daniel, " Sept. 25, 1667.
Nathaniel, " Feb. 22, 1669.
Patience, " 1676.

John, b. = Ann
1648; d. Lever-
1710, ett.
Jan. 8.

Na- = than- iel.

Mar- = John garet. Pyn- chon.

Dan- = Eliz- iel, abeth
b. 8 Ber-
Aug. ry.
1692.

Nath'l, = Mar- born garet
Dec. 9, Gibbs.
1693.

Pris- = Rob- cilla, ert
b. 3 Ward.
Jan.
1697.

Eliz. = Jabez Fitch.

Marga- = Edw. ret, b. Hol-
March yoke,
19, P. H.
1700. C.

John,
b. 18
Aug.
1704.

Margaret = John Mascarene b. April 11, 1722;
mar. Aug. 9, 1750; d. 1778.

He was Comptroller of the Customs in 1760. His son, the last of the name, lived and died in Dorchester.

LETTER OF JEAN MASCARENE, 1687.

Communicated by SAMUEL EPES TURNER, A.M., of Baltimore, Md.

Letter to M. Devie, his Attorney, written from the prison of the Hotel de Ville, December 1, 1687.

[IN the REGISTER, vol. ix., pages 239–47, and vol. x., pages*
143–8, will be found some papers of the Mascarene family, with a
tabular pedigree. The following letter of instructions and poem,
in French, from the same collection, have been translated and furnished us by Mr. Turner. This letter is mentioned in one from
Paul Mascarene to a relative dated "London, 30th Sept. 1763,"
which is printed in the article first referred to above. Those who
wish to know the later history of Jean Mascarene will find it in the
letter of Paul. He was kept in prison till April, 1688, when he
was carried to the frontiers of France and released, but forbidden
to return to that country. He arrived in Geneva, April 10, 1688,
from which place he removed to Utrecht, where he died April 6,
1698, aged 38.—EDITOR.]

Sir,
    I have cast my eyes upon you to pray you to defend my rights and
put them in evidence, because I know of no attorney more enlightened by
study and by experience, more honorable, or less likely to be influenced by
an ill-governed and ill-advised religious zeal.
    I make profession of the Reformed Religion, and I am in prison accused
of having violated the edict of the King, which forbids his subjects to depart the kingdom.
    2. I was arrested at Agen the 20th or 21st of February in the year
1686 (my wife with me) by the Lt. Chevalier de Gramond, lieutenant of
dragoons, and conducted by him and several other officers, accompanied by
soldiers, to the Logis de St. Jacques; thence, after separation from my
wife, I was led to the prison of the Presidial of Agen, with others that had
been arrested. An hour later I was visited by a sergeant and a soldier of
the Touraine regiment, who took my tablets from me after I had opened
them in the presence of the goaler. There was nothing in the tablets but
a bit of card board on which a diagram was drawn. These tablets were
taken to the officers in command of the troops then in Agen.
    3. Two or three days afterward I was examined by an official in a gown,
who was addressed as "Lieutenant of the Presidial of Agen." I appealed
from him to my natural judge, but although I had determined not to answer any of his questions, I could not restrain myself when he showed me
my tablets and I saw written in them a sonnet in the Gascon dialect in
derision, as he said, of the conversions that were made. I presume that the
officers of the Touraine regiment, through whose hands my tablets passed,
had written it there. I contented myself with protesting that I had neither
composed, written, read nor heard mention of the said sonnet, and that it
had been foisted into my tablets after I had handed them over to the ser-
*The preceding two articles.

701

geant and soldier, as I called both them and the gaoler to witness. My protest was recorded upon the sonnet itself.

4. After a second hearing, some twelve or fifteen days later, during which I kept urging my appeal, I was sent to Castres, together with M. Dupuy, now a prisoner in the Conciergerie under the same charge with me. He was arrested the same day that I was, and it was then that I made his acquaintance.

After we had been some days in the prison of Latoucandiere at Castres, M. Barbara, the criminal judge, proceeded to my hearing.

5. He asked me if it were not true that I had left my house in Castres at the beginning of the summer of 1685, to go into the country. I replied that I had passed the summer with my wife at my farm near Angles, attending to my haying and harvesting, and enlarging my house, which had previously contained but one room, so as to pass comfortably one or two months there every summer.

6. He asked me if after returning to Castres towards the end of the summer I had not again gone to my farm. I answered in the affirmative.

7. He asked me why I had left my country house with my wife about the 10th or 12th of October, 1685. I answered that my wife was then pregnant, expecting to be confined in seven or eight days, and was much alarmed at the rumors current that Castres and Angles were to be given up to the soldiery, as the neighboring towns had already been, and afraid that our house would be occupied by them.

As it was impossible for me to reassure her, and I saw that her life and our child's life were in danger, I sought an asylum for her among some peasants in the mountains near Nove, where we passed part of the winter. Here she was delivered of a male child, which was named Jean Paul Mascarene (he is now at Castres).

8. He asked me why I had gone to Toulouse. I replied that the news that twenty of the Conismark (*query*, Königsmark) regiment had sold my cottage and all the hay and straw on my farms, together with my furniture, and had been detailed in the night to arrest us, so increased my wife's fears that we were obliged to depart. This was the more necessary because we could no longer remain in that locality by reason of an ordinance of the Intendant which forbade harboring those of the Religion under the penalty of 500 livres fine.

I said, moreover, that Article XII. of the edict of the King revoking the Edict of Nantes, gave us liberty to go into all the cities of the kingdom without molestation on occount of our religion.

9. He asked me why I had not stayed at Toulouse, and why I had embarked on the Garonne in the mail-boat. I answered that thinking it impossible to remain in Toulouse with safety because I was well known there, I determined to go to cities where I was not known, where I could wait until it should please the King to ordain some abiding measures with reference to his subjects of the Religion called Reformed, for although it was forbidden by his Majesty to disturb them, nevertheless some persons abused their power and seized the opportunity to persecute such as they had grudges against. That my wife could not then travel conveniently on horseback, because she was not fully recovered from an illness consequent upon her lying in, and hence I concluded to embark on the Garonne in the boat that runs regularly to Agen. Arrived at Agen I feared for my safety there, because I was known to Lt. de Romeus, a native of Castres, who commanded the troops quartered in the city by virtue of senior Captaincy,

and because I saw several other officers who knew my wife and myself, and heard that people of the Religion had been arrested there.

Thus I was compelled to embark at once on the boat for Bordeaux. We were no sooner aboard, than the Lt. Chevalier de Gramond accosted me and asked if I did not profess the Religion called Reformed. On my replying that I did, he commanded my wife and myself in the King's name to follow him, and we obeyed.

10. M. Barbara, the criminal judge, then asked me explicitly if it were not true that I had intended to depart the kingdom. I replied that I loved my country too well to leave it, unless forced to do so.

11. He next asked me if I had not planned with M. Dupuy of Caraman, M. de Moulens and wife, the Lt. Candier and wife, resident at Bruniquet, three leagues from Montauban, and the Lt. Malabion (now at Castres), to depart the kingdom. To this question I replied in the negative, and added that I did not know M. Dupuy or the Lt. Candier or his wife at all, and that I only knew M. de Moulens and wife by sight—that the three former lived at the distance of nine or ten leagues from my place of residence, the latter at the distance of twelve or fifteen leagues.

I acknowledged that on my arrival in Toulouse I had met the Lt. de Malabion, who told me that he was bound to the fair at Bordeaux with the horse that he was then riding (the horse belonged to the judge, M. Barbara). I was surprised afterwards to find the Lt. de Malabion on the boat, and asked him what he had done with his horse.

12. The judge next asked me what was my object in going to Bordeaux. I replied that I went because I could not safely remain at Agen, and was in hopes to pass a few days there unnoticed and in quiet, at least during the fair, which was to begin in seven or eight days. (I intended to stop in La Reale or elsewhere in case I found the safety and rest that I was seeking.)

Four of my tenants from different farms testified that I set out from my farm at Carrelle where I had passed the summer, but that they did not know whither I went. One of them said that I set out in the night with my wife. My testimony in that regard you will find in section 7.

Two of the town council of Angles testified that a sergeant and twenty soldiers of the Conismark (query, Königsmark) regiment, in command of a commissioned officer, went to my farm at Carrelle, and that one of them on his return to Angles said that they had not found me. See again my testimony in section 7.

A certain Darraquy tutor in a gentleman's family testified that when I was asked by the gentleman with whom he lived whether I would not change my religion, I replied that I was convinced of the truth of my religion and hoped to be faithful to it all my life. I not only admitted this fact to M. Barbara when he confronted me with this witness, but I told him that if he would take the trouble to ask me the same question, I should ever make the same reply.

By judgment rendered in the month of April, 1686, M. Dupuy and myself were sentenced to the galleys for life, our property was confiscated and a fine of a thousand pounds imposed to be paid into the royal treasury.

Later we had to appear before the Parliament of the Presidency of Toulouse, and some days thereafter we were separated. M. Dupuy remained at the Conciergerie, while I was transferred to the prison of the Hôtel de Ville, from which I write to you.

A year after, viz. May 7th of the present year, 1687, we had a hearing at La Lelette, where the Councillors of the Chamber of Parliament asked me some questions concerning the matters specified above, but occupied most of the time of the hearing in discussing affairs that have nothing to do with our present business.

Although my religion passes for a crime, and I know well that but for my religion I should not be in my present condition, I make bold to justify this so-called crime, and choose rather to be the criminal that I am than to recover all that I have lost.

All discussion apart, I am persuaded of the truth of my religion, my conscience refuses what is offered me, and I have an uncontrollable aversion to hypocrisy.

It is my opinion that all that can bring us to embrace any religion is the knowledge that we have of God and of what he has done for us, the love and gratitude that we feel towards him, our recognition and our love of truth, our fear of infinite and eternal misery, and our hope of perfect and eternal happiness.

In all my hearings I omitted mention of an affair in which my wife was concerned, that gave us good reason to fear seizure and maltreatment. You will perhaps consider its bearing upon my case important, and hence it will not be improper for me to digress here.

I married Marguerite de Salavy three years ago. Four years ago a certain young man named Calvet gave her a blow in the public street. On account of this insult a warrant was issued for his arrest, and he was arrested and carried to the prison of La Tourcaudiere, where the relatives and friends of the said Mlle. de Salavy, now my wife, were obliged to stand guard over him, because the gaoler would not be responsible for his safe keeping by reason of the insecurity of the prison and his fear of the said Calvet. He was tried before the proper officials at Castres, and sentenced to six years in the galleys. This sentence was about to be carried into execution, when by the decree of the Parliament, issued upon his appeal, it was commuted and he was sentenced to beg Mlle. Salavy's pardon in her house at Castres, in the presence of such persons as she should choose, and was banished the city and faubourgs for one year.

The father of the said Calvet was consul of Castres in 1685, when the soldiers came there, and as it was a time when those who had authority abused it to satisfy their private animosities, he boasted that the first fifty dragoons that entered Castres should be detailed to plunder our property and persecute us at our small farm at Carrelles, where we then were, and where our only shelter was one room. Picture to yourself the feelings of a woman expecting to be confined in two or three days, on hearing such news as this.

The same Calvet was afterwards the cause of our quitting the place where my wife was brought to bed. He happened to meet on his road a man from the farms of Poussines, and inquired of him particularly my whereabouts, saying that he was one of my intimate friends and wished to know where I was in order to offer me his services and pass a few days with me. We learned that he had gone to Castres to inform his father the Consul that all he had to do was to send the soldiers, and that they could not fail to secure our persons this time as they had failed before. He had already had the satisfaction of seeing our property seized and made away with.

From the data that I have given you, and from the other points that shall be furnished if we have time, please make up a brief, putting all other business aside as long as necessary for attention to this, because the Procureur General spoke to my Procureur, M. Manou, to-day, of bringing the case up soon, and our trial may take place on Saturday next. Nevertheless, we must take time enough to have the brief printed and to distribute it.

If there is need of our having a personal interview, I beg you will come to see me here, assuring you that whatever time you employ in my behalf shall not be time lost to you. If there are any expenses to be met other than for the trial of the case, I pray you advise the bearer of this letter, for I am resolved to use all the influence of my friends and connections, all that I can claim of them and all that is left to me, to make good my defence, leaving the issue to the will of God. If I must suffer, I shall suffer more patiently knowing that I have not to blame myself for neglect in any respect. To my thinking it is as much a man's duty to sacrifice his possessions to save his life, as it is to sacrifice both life and possessions to save his soul.

I am, Sir,

Your very humble and very obedient servant,

Mascarene.

I do not remember, Sir, that there was anything said in the course of my trial about the Lt. Calvet referred to in the summary that I sent you of my case, because it never entered my head that M. Barbara could impose any penalty upon me, and I was accordingly at no great pains to justify my actions. If, however, you think that matter of some importance, I can prove what I advance as follows.

It is on record that Lt. Calvet was consul in 1686. The reasons that he and his son had for ill feeling towards my wife and myself are evident from the sentence recorded in the ordinances of Castres, which condemned the latter to the galleys at the suit of Marguerite de Salavy, now my wife, and from the arrest of judgment upon his appeal recorded at the Chamber of Parliament, which changed the penalty and condemned him to ask her pardon, and to banishment for one year. The threats which he publicly made can likewise be proved. To the best of my recollection, when I sat in the prisoner's dock in the Chamber of Parliament on May 7th of the present year, 1687, one of the judges asked a question that bore so directly upon this matter that I made mention of it; but of this I cannot be sure.

The Sr. Barbara condemned me on the presumption that my desire to go to the neighborhood of Bordeaux and my embarking on the Garonne were due to an intention to depart the kingdom. But my journey was made for another reason, and was due to the persecution of a private enemy.

What right had he to condemn me out of his imagination? Even if his theory had ground, it would be at most but putting it that I had the intention of departing the kingdom, and I have always heard say that intentions are not punished in France.

I was arrested at Agen forty or fifty leagues from the frontier, and you might say in the heart of the kingdom. Admitting that I had such intention, I should have had plenty of time to change my mind, and might reasonably have done so, knowing as I did that even since the edict of the King revoking the Edict of Nantes, those who professed the Religion called Reformed could remain in all the cities of the kingdom without being molested on account of their religion. There was nothing then to fear but the resentment of individuals and the malice of those who abused their power.

It is clear that M. Barbara took part against me from the fact that when my three neighbors were brought to confront me (I think they were the first witnesses produced), it was discovered that he had couched their depositions in his own words according to his own fancy, instead of using the words of the witnesses. When he read the deposition of the first witness, it was worded somewhat as follows: " Such an one, shoemaker, deposes that Sr. Mascarene set out from his house in Castres to go to his country house in order not to change his religion according to the will of the King." The witness was much astonished and exclaimed that that was not what he had testified—that he had said that I set out from Castres to go into the country with my family, but what the business was that called me away he did not know, not having the gift of divination so as to be aware of what passed in my mind. Sr. Barbara threatened in my presence to put him in irons and to hang him, but the witness persisted, and declared that though he should hang for it he would only testify to what he knew, whereupon Sr. Barbara corrected the record of his testimony.

As he had treated the depositions of the other two witnesses in the same way (they were then waiting in another room in the prison), under pretence that my presence at the correction of the testimony of the first witness had annoyed him, he sent me into another room before calling them in. The record of their testimony afterward had nothing to say as to the design with which I left Castres.

The truth of what I affirm will appear from the erasures that will be found in the original trial papers.

My name is Jean Mascarene. I am a native of Castres. At the time of my first hearing I was about twenty-six years old. I was twenty-seven years old the 26th day of April last.

[*The Metre is that of the Original.*]

CANTICLE COMPOSED IN THE PRISON OF THE HOTEL DE VILLE IN 1687.

> Oh King of Kings, oh Sovereign Power divine,
> In thee alone I trust. Thine ear incline,
> Show forth in me thy all resistless might
> Before thy foes, and shame them with the sight.
>> And to my heart be given
>> Sustaining strength from heaven
>> From thee, its very source,
>> That neither trip nor fall
>> Arrest my walk in all
>> Yet left me of my course.
>
> My mid career of life they roughly stay
> And shut me from the blessed light of day,
> And fouler means ere long they may employ
> To shake my courage and my faith destroy.
>> Within these gloomy walls,
>> Where everything appals,
>> As through the dark I peer
>> No hope can I descry.
>> Each moment to my eye
>> Presents new forms of fear.
>
> Weakness and error are within me met
> To turn me from the path that I have set.
> Deign with thy spirit so to point the way
> That nought can tempt my feeble steps astray.
>> In thought of coming bliss
>> May I lose sight of this,

706

The world, which I resign ;
Though bound and girt with ill,
The marty's crown be still
Held up to me—be mine.

Well Satan knows that such a sacrifice
From out his hands must snatch the wished-for prize.
He bids me hence transgress my country's laws,
And thinks to filch the justice from my cause.
Oh, Lord, his plans confound
And bring them all to ground.
The blindest then shall see
How thy pure, holy word
Doth suffer wrong in me.

Thee have I followed, thee would follow still,
To live without thee have nor strength nor will.
Behold thy creature's cheerful offering,
Peace, liberty and life, my all I bring.
I know that but thy nod
Thy power bounds, Oh God,
And that thy providence,
Though all mankind oppose,
Can shield me from my foes,
Secure me from offence.

But though thy hand rend not this massy wall,
Nor ope these doors, nor draw these bolts, but fall
On me, and but strike off these galling chains
To give in death release from all my pains,
Yet let me not repine,
Assist my strength with thine,
Grant steadfast faith and bold,
My trembling hope to stay,
And on the awful day
My constancy uphold.

THE ENGLISH HOME OF CAPT. HUGH MASON
OF WATERTOWN, MASS.

Communicated by CHARLES FRANCIS MASON, A.B., of Plymouth, Mass.

HUGH MASON, tanner, aged 28, with his wife Hester, aged 22, came to New England in the spring of 1634 from Ipswich, co. Suffolk, in the *Francis*, and settled in Watertown, Mass. He was admitted freeman 4 Mar. 1634/5, held various town offices, including that of selectman, which he held for twenty-nine years in all, was a deputy to the General Court ten years, and was captain from 1652 until his death on 10 Oct. 1678. His widow died 21 May 1692. They were the ancestors of a large and well-known New England family.

The late J. Henry Lea communicated to the REGISTER, vol. 54, page 189, abstracts of records found in one of the Act Books of the Prerogative Court of Canterbury, which showed that on 16 May 1702 a commission was issued to Benjamin Franklin,* attorney for John and Joseph Mason, sons of Hugh Mason, late of Watertowne in New England, deceased, to administer during the absence and for the use of said sons, and that on the same date a commission was issued to the said Franklin, attorney for John and Joseph Mason, sons of Hester Mason, widow, late of Water Towne in New England, deceased, to administer during the absence and for the use of said sons.

The clue given by these records published in the REGISTER has been followed by the contributor of the present article, and has led recently to the discovery in the Public Record Office, London, among the records of proceedings in Chancery, of documents that connect the Watertown settler and his wife with the borough of Maldon, co. Essex. Abstracts of these documents, giving, in present-day spelling (except for proper names), whatever statements are of genealogical interest, follow.

FROM CHANCERY PROCEEDINGS†

19 June 1702. To the Right Honorable Sir Nathan Wright, Knight, Lord Keeper of the Great Seal of England.

Humbly complaining shew unto your Lordships your orators, JOHN and JOSEPH MASON, sons of Hugh Mason, late of Water Towne in New England, in parts beyond the seas, yeoman, and of Hester his wife, both deceased, which Hester was one of the daughters and devisees of Thomas Wells the Elder, deceased, and one of the sisters and coheirs of Thomas Wells, son and heir of the aforesaid Thomas Wells, late of Maulden in the county of Essex, yeoman, likewise deceased, and Benjamine Franckling of London,

---

*This Benjamin Franklin, who appears also in the records of the Chancery case given below as "Benjamine Franckling of London, dyer," was an uncle of Benjamin Franklin, the American statesman and philosopher, who in his autobiography calls him a "silk dyer of London." He was born at Ecton, co. Northampton, 23 Mar. 1650/1, a son of Thomas and Jane (White) Franklin, emigrated to Boston, Mass., in 1715, whither his younger brother Josiah, father of the American patriot, had preceded him in 1684, and died in Boston 17 Mar. 1727/8. He left two quarto volumes of his own poems. — J. GARDNER BARTLETT.

†Preserved in the Public Record Office, London. These documents are in Chancery Proceedings before 1714, Mitford's Division, Bundle 469/3.

dyer, administrator not only of all the goods, chattels, rights, and credits which were of and did belong to the said Hugh Mason at the time of his death but also of all the goods, chattels, rights, and credits which were of and did belong to her, the said Hester, who survived the said Hugh Mason, at the time of her death, that the said Thomas Wells, the father, in his lifetime, that is to say, on or about the seventeenth day of December, which was in the year of Our Lord 1624, being seised in fee or of some other estate of inheritance of and in all that piece or parcel of meadow or pasture land called or known by the name of Little Portland, containing by estimation four acres and a half, more or less, with the appurtenances, lying and being in Mauldon aforesaid, and which was then in the tenure or occupation of Michaell Coop[er] or his assigns, and also of and in all that messuage or tenement in which he then dwelt, lying and being in Fulbridge Street in Maulden aforesaid, and the houses, buildings, stable yards, gardens, and orchards thereunto belonging or therewith then used as part, parcel, or member thereof, with the appurtenances, made his last will and testament in writing, duly executed, and bearing date on or about the said seventeenth day of December, in the said year of Our Lord 1624, and thereby he devised in these or the like words, that is to say, I devise and give unto my son Thomas Wells and to the heirs of his body lawfully to be begotten all that my close or parcel of meadow or pasture called Little Portland, containing by estimation four acres and a half, more or less, with the appurtenances, lying and being in Mauldon aforesaid, and which is now in the tenure and occupation of Michaell Cooper or his assigns; and, for default of such issue of his body, then I will the one half of the said parcel of meadow or pasture, with the appurtenances, to remain unto Hellene, my daughter, now wife of Moses Catmer, shoemaker, and to her heirs, and the other moiety of the same to remain unto Hester Wells, my youngest daughter, and to her heirs for ever. Item, I do devise and give the messuage in which I dwell and the houses, buildings, stable yards, gardens, and orchards thereunto belonging or therewith used as part or parcel thereof, with the appurtenances, in manner following, that is to say, the one half of the said messuage, gardens, orchards, and premises thereunto belonging, with the appurtenances, unto the said Hellene, my daughter, and to the heirs of her body lawfully begotten, and the other moiety of the said messuage and premises, with the appurtenances, unto the said Hester Wells and to the heirs of her body lawfully to be begotten; and if both my said daughters happen to die without issue lawfully begotten, then I will the said messuage and premises, with the appurtenances, shall remain to the said Thomas, my son, and to his heirs and assigns for ever. And your orators further shew that the said Tho: Wells, the father, also in his said will devised the care and education of his said younger children, Hester and Thomas, unto his brother-in-law, Simon Raye, until they and either of them should be of competent age and years and of ability of body to be put forth and placed in service, as by the said will, had your orators the same to produce to this Honorable Court, more fully might and would appear. Soon after the making of which said will, that is to say, about the end of the month of December, in the year of Our Lord 1624 aforesaid, he, the said Tho: Wells, the father, departed this life, being then unmarried, and leaving issue, the said Hellene, Hester, and Tho: Wells, his only children, and after whose death, about the third day of February following, the said Simon Raye proved the said will, whereof he was therein made executor, in due form of law, and took on him the burthen and execution thereof, and afterwards, that is to say, about the month of December, in the year of Our Lord 1631, he, the said Tho: Wells, the son, departed this life, being then under the age of twenty-one years and unmarried and leaving no issue of his body and without making any disposition of his estate, the said Hellene and Hester surviving him, whereby the est te devised and that pertained to him as aforesaid, by the said will or by descent, came to them, the said Hellene and Hester, as devisees by the said will or as sisters and coheirs of him, the said Tho: Wells, the son. And the said Hellene and Hester or those who were intrusted to do the same on their behalf entered into and became seised of his said premises. And afterwards, that is to say about the month of January, in the year of Our Lord 1632, she, the said Hester, intermarried with Hugh Mason, then of Maldon aforesaid, tanner, and since of Water Towne in New England, in parts beyond the seas. And your orators further shew that the said Hugh Mason and Hester, sometime after their marriage, that is to say, about the year of Our Lord 1633 or the year of Our Lord 1634, went out of this Kingdom of England into New England in America, in parts beyond the seas, aforesaid, and afterwards, that is to say, the 29 day of September, in the year of Our Lord 1654, being then in England, the said Hugh Mason, by his deed then dated, demised and granted unto one Giles Cole of Maldon aforesaid all that his moiety of the said piece or parcel of land called Little Portland for the term of the natural life of him, the said Hugh Mason (in case she, the said Hester, should so long live), at the yearly rent of three pounds per annum, which rent the said Giles Cole in his deed then made and duly executed did for himself and his assigns covenant and agree with the said Hugh Mason well and faithfully to pay to the said Hugh Mason accordingly. . . . Afterwards, that is to say, in the year of Our Lord 1655, she, the said Hellene, wife of the said Moses Catmer and one of the daughters of the said Thomas Wells, the father, departed this life without making any disposition of her share of the said premises or any part thereof and without issue of her body, the said Hester surviving her, whereby her share of the said premises did descend unto her, the said Hester, according to the said will or as next heir at law to her, the said Hellene, after whose death the said Hugh and Hester Mason entered and became seised of all the said premises in right of her, the said Hester, in fee, etc.

The answer of BENJAMIN SMITH, one of the defendants to the bill of complaint of John Mason and Joseph Mason, etc. The said defendant saith that John Cole of Swilland in the county of Suffolk, yeoman, being seised and in peaceable possession of a moiety of a certain close of land called Portlands, containing by estimation four acres, more or less, in the parish of St. Peter's in Maldon, of an estate of inheritance in fee simple, being, as this defendant believes, part of the lands and tenements in the complainants' said bill of complaint mentioned, . . . in the tenure or occupation of John Paine, gard[e]ner, or his assigns, abutting on a parcel of land called Beau Meade towards the north, etc.

No record of the birth or marriage of Hugh Mason is to be found in the registers of the Maldon parishes, but the following entry in the register of the parish of St. Mary, in Maldon, may refer to a kinsman of the Watertown settler:

1631 Joseph Mason and Mary Houatt married 1 November.

For his success in this search the contributor of this article is greatly indebted to the advice of J. Gardner Bartlett of Cambridge, Mass., the well-known specialist in English research and a member of the Committee on Publications of the New England Historic Genealogical Society, Vincent Burrough Redstone, F.S.A., of Woodbridge, co. Suffolk, England, a member of the Committee on English Research of this Society, and the latter's daughter, Miss Lilian J. Redstone of London.

MATHER (*ante*, xxxii. 339).—In the REGISTER for July, 1878, I inquired what evidence there is besides the statement of the late Samuel G. Drake, Esq., that the father of Thomas Mather of Lowton, ancestor of the Mathers of New England, was named John. I find among some manuscripts of Mrs Hannah Mather Crocker, (wife of Josiah Crocker and youngest daughter of Rev. Samuel Mather), author of "Observations on the Rights of Woman," formerly belonging to the late J. Wingate Thornton, Esq., and recently presented by his heirs to the New England Historic, Genealogical Society, the following statement in Mrs. Crocker's handwriting :

" Mr. Richard Mather was born in Lancaster, in a small village called Lowton, in the year 1596. The family can be traced to John. Thomas was his son, and Richard was son of Thomas. The chair in the antiquarian room belonged to Thomas. Richard sat in it when a child. He was married 1624. His children that were born in Europe sat in the chair before he came to this country—Samuel, Timothy, Nathaniel, Joseph. The last named sat in it when he brought the chair to America. Eleazar and Increase were born in America. They both sat in the same chair. The chair descended to Increase, and all his children sat in the same. It came in line to Cotton Mather; his children all sat in the same. It descended to his son Samuel, and his children sat in the same chair. His youngest daughter was the only child that had any children, and she has had ten children sit in the chair, and several grandchildren. As the regular line of Mathers has run out, she wished the chair to be deposited in the antiquarian room with the venerable shades, that those who come after her may look to the rock from whence they were hewn, and find an ancient seat to rest any chip of the old block in, as she flatters herself there may in some future day a sprig spring from the root of Jesse ; and the tribe of Levi may return to their rest, after she is at rest in another world."

This was probably the rough draft or a copy of a letter to the Rev. Abiel Holmes, D.D., as I find the following letter of Dr. Holmes addressed to Mrs. Crocker filed with it :

" Cambridge, 5 Sept. 1822.

" I thank you, my respected Friend, for your ' authentick account of the Mather's small Chair ' in the Antiquarian room. It was very acceptable to me, and I mean to make a good use of it. Such relics impressively associate former times and events with our own ; and the tradition or history of them ought to be exact. Nothing offends a chronologist like an *anachronism*. Somebody told me at the room, it was Richard Mather's chair, and, as I understood him, *the chair* in which he sat on his passage to New England. I was sure there was an error *somewhere*—you have made all clear.

" I thank you, Madam, for the suggestion respecting several manuscripts. You do me honour in the confidence reposed in me.—Neither my own health nor my wife's is at present very good, and we are thinking of a journey ; but when I can pay my respects to you, it will give sincere pleasure to,

" Madam, your respectful and obliged Friend,   A. HOLMES."

In my query above referred to, I stated that it was my impression that Mr. Drake told me that he derived his information from the late Horatio G. Somerby. I remember distinctly that Mr. Drake told me, when he showed me a proof of his article in the REGISTER, that some one, whom he named, gave him the information. I am now inclined to believe that he said it was Mr. Thornton, who probably derived his information from Mrs. Crocker's memorandum above printed.   J. W. DEAN.

ABSTRACTS OF THE WILLS OF THE MATHER FAMILY, PROVED IN THE CONSISTORY COURT AT CHESTER FROM 1573 TO 1650.

By J. PAUL RYLANDS, Esq., F.S.A., of Birkenhead, England.

SAMUEL CLARK, in his account of "The Life and Death of Mr Richard Mather who dyed Anno Christi 1669," says :—"Richard Mather was born in a Village called Lowton, situate in the Parish of Winwick in the County of Lancaster, Anno Christi 1596. His parents Thomas and Margaret Mather were of ancient families in

Lowton aforesaid ; but by reason of some unhappy Mortgages, they were reduced into a low condition in regard to their outward estate."

Much has been written about Richard Mather and his descendants ; but very little is known of his forefathers, who were probably resident in Lancashire for several centuries, as the name occurs in early documents as Madur, Madowr, &c. The family does not appear to have been of sufficient importance socially to attract the attention of the Heralds at their visitations, although Cotton Mather states that the armorial bearings of his family were *Ermine, on a fesse wavy Azure three lions rampant Or;* Crest :—*On the trunk of a tree lying fesseways Vert, a lion sejant Or;* bearings which are also attributed to Madder of the County of Stafford in Burke's "General Armory."

It was with a view of adding something to the family history of the Mathers that, a number of years ago, I made a series of genealogical abstracts from the wills at Chester, in conjunction with the late Mr. Charles Bridger ; and the abstracts then made have been recently supplemented by others made by Mr. William Fergusson Irvine of Birkenhead, thus forming a complete series from the year 1573 to the year 1650. Unfortunately these wills do not, so far as I am aware, increase our knowledge of Richard Mather's ancestry, but they may help to bring some new facts to light from other sources ; and in the hope that this will be the case I offer them to the New-England Historic Genealogical Society. For the same reason I will allude to the marriage of Ralph Rylands, then of Westhoughton, but afterwards of Culcheth in the parish of Winwick, yeoman (who died in November, 1633), and Mary Mather of the parish of Winwick, which was solemnized at Deane Church, 25 May, 1613 (Transcripts at Chester). This Mary, in her will, proved at York 20 November, 1645, desires "to bee buried at my parishe Church of Winwicke in my ancestors buriall [place] and neare unto Raphe Rylandes my late husband"; and I have very little doubt that she was a relative, probably a near one, of Richard Mather, the "Pilgrim Father," because her place of burial suggests that she was one of the Lowton Mathers, and also because her husband, being a man well-to-do in the world, would be likely to choose his wife from the better educated branch of the Mather family. Their third son Ralph, who was born in 1622, was living with Henry Mather at Culcheth in 1641, and, on 19 May, 1644, he married Alice Mather at the chapel of Newchurch in Winwick parish ; Alice was, perhaps, Henry's daughter, and a relative of her husband.

It is also worth noting that Margaret Byrom, of Lowton, widow of Henry Byrom, in her will, dated 18 April, 1648, mentions her son Henry, her sister Jane Green, her sister Anne, wife of Roger Bate, and her brother Richard Mather.

An entry in Warrington Parish Registers of the baptism, on 9 December, 1610, of "Christian, daughter of George Mather, Gent.," shows that the wills at Chester do not give all the contemporary information that could be desired. Probably, when the Record Society of Lancashire and Cheshire carries out its intention of printing the early Marriage Licences, which begin in the year 1608, we shall know more of the history of the Mathers of Lowton and their alliances, and so obtain a clue which will lead us to other fields for investigation.

Elianor Mather, of Ince, near Wigan, Widow, 1573.

xiii. daie of August 1573. I ELIANOR MATHER widowe, being sicke & weake in bodie, but praised bee god of good & perfecte Remembrance, do make this my laste will & testament in mannere & forme following—firstlie & cheeflie I bequeath my soule into the hands of Almightie God, etc—my bodie to be buried in my Parishe Churche as nighe to my late husband as may conveniently be done. And as for my worldie goodes which God etc. Firstly. I bequeath unto my sonne Chrōfer Mather my best fether bedde & bolstar, one pillowe & one matteresse belonginge to said bedde, one cou'let [coverlet] etc etc. & one panne of pewter. Item. I give unto Adam Bancke all the corne nowe growing in the higher heye & my plows & harrowe, one of my hoggs, & halfe a bushell of malte & a wyndle of meale. Item: I give unto my god daughter Elianᵣ Bancke one acre of ote [oats] growinge in the Emmefeld. Unto my daughter Elizabeth Penningtn̄ one other acre and to Xpofer Bancke & Thomas Bancke, one other acre with corne. Item: I give unto my saide sonne Chrofer Mather three of my eldest kyne, & the rest of my kye & cattel I give unto the saide Elianᵣ Bancke. Item. To Jenitt Laythwatt one payre of shets one cou'let & one Blanckett. All the rest of my householde stuffs & implements I give unto the said Elen Bancke. Small bequests to William Cartwrighte & John Burscoughe. My bedgowne & best hatte to my dau. Elizabeth Penyngtn. Item: To Richard Reyner & John Michell vi yardes of flaxen clothe, and to the children of Chrofer Mather vi yardes of the same clothe. Item: I give unto Sᵣ Raufe Stotte, clerke xiiiˢ. iiiiᵈ. and to Sᵣ Thomas Baron iiiˢ. iiiiᵈ. I ordaine & make my said sonne Chrofer Mather & Adam Bancke the Executor of this my laste Will & Testament. Overseers. James Bradshaw & Roger Hyndeley unto whom I give iiiˢ iiiiᵈ. apeece.

Witnesses: James Bradshawe
Roger Hyndley
Robert Gerrarde withe others.

Hec sunt debit q. mihi debent

Imprimis:	Richarde Haughton	xˢ.	
Item	William Haddocke	vˢ.	
"	John Higham		xixᵈ.
"	John Burscoughe	viˢ.	viiiᵈ.
"	William Man		viiiᵈ.
"	John Laythwatt for rente.	vˢ.	
"	Olyu' [Oliver] Man̄	iiˢ.	viiᵈ.
"	John Molyneux	ivˢ.	

A true inventorie of all goodes etc of Elianor Mather of Ince. Praised by John Hyndley, William Ince, Rauffe Perpoyne & Jas. Morrys, taken 23 August 1573.

713

Item.   corne in the felde   [?   ]
Item.   iii acres of ote in emmefelde   iiii^{li}.
Item.   one acre of barlie pease & ote   xxvi^s. ix^d.
        etc etc. Summa Totalis   xli^{li}. x^s. ii^d.
Item.   I owe unto William Molyneux   iii^s. iiii^d.
[on dorso is written].   Expences at the buriall & the p'bat of the tista-
ment.

Item.—paide for a mortuary   ———
Item.—paid unto the prests clarks &   }
        for other charges at the burialle } xlix^s. viii^d.
Item: paide for provinge of the will.   ———.
Proved 6 Sept. 1573, by Adam Banks.

Richard Mather, of Orford, near Warrington, 1576.

In the name of God Amen.—the twentieth daie of April in ye yeare of
our Lorde God etc etc one thousand five hundred & seventy-sixe—I RICHARD
MATHER, of Orforthe in the parish of Warringtū in the Countie of Lancastre
husbandman doe make this etc.—leaves his bodie to be buried " in the
Parish Church or churcheyarde " [of Warrington] " at the descrecion of my
executors & friends."   After payment of debts & funeral expenses his property to be divided " equallie betweene Ellyn my lovinge wyfe, Henry my
son & Jane Mather my daughter " " and the saide children & goodes to be
at the rule & gou'mente of the saide Ellyn my weyfe untyll they come to
bee of lawfull yeres of descrecion " " if either of my children die in their
minoritie," share to be " equallie divided between my wyfe & the othere
childe."   Henry & Jane my said children to be Executors.   " William
Ashton gentleman, & Thomas Mather my brother" appointed " oūseers
for ye true execution of this my laste will & Testament."
          Witnesses :   Wm Ashton.   Lawrence Clerk.
                          Thos Mather.   Seth Lawton.
                          Hamlet owen.   John Ashton.
                          John Erlam.   with others.
          Hec sunt debit que ego pred^{ts} Richardus Mather debeo.
Imprimis : I owe to Thomas Penkethman of Warrington } iiii mke [marks]
               iiiij barrelles of heringe   }
             Hec sunt debetaque mihi debentur.
Imprimis : Hughe Leche of Avonley [Alvanley] in the
             Countie of Chester husbandm̄ for lynnen
             clothe of me had & boughte the summe of   xiii^s. viii^d.
Item :   John Page of Warington oethe me for sackecloth   xx^s.
Item :   Richarde Lyon & James finche   xxiii^s.
             suertie to me for him.
Item :   John Bolton of Robae [Roby] oethe
             me for clothe to this daie   liv^s.
Item :   George Paynter of Newton   ii^s. vi^d.
Item :   John Sadler of Warrington   xxvii^s.
Item :   Robt Spencer of Warrington   iv^s. vi^d.
Item :   Oliu' Southworth   xxvi^s. viii^d.
Item :   M^{res} Sibell Burche, widowe   iii^s.
Item :   Randle Yate oethe me   iv^s. viii^d.
Item :   Ellis ap John   xvii^s.
Item :   Mr Bailiffe of Werington   iii^s. ix^d.

| Item: | John Owen oethe me | v^s. |

Item: John Owen oethe me   v^s.
Item: Edmund Griffye als Ivie [?]   xx^s.
Item: Hughe Stirrop of Newton oethe me &
    Mr Bailiffe suertie for the half thereof   xviii^s. ix^d.
Item: James Hanes [?] of Budworth P^rishe   vii^s.
Item: The Executors or Adminst of Wm Hulme
    late of Burtonwood   iv^s.
Item: Edmund Wright͞m unpayde in
    parte for clothes [cloths]   xv^s.

Inventorie praissed 29 April [1576] by Robert Holbroke, Thomas Smyth, John Clarke, & Seathe Lawton.

Summa totalis   clxvi^{li}. xvii^s. vi^d.

Roger Mather, of Leigh, Lancashire, 1582.

ROGER MATHER of the Parish of Leigh, 3 March 1582. To be buried at Leigh.* Wife Katherine. "To little Roger Mather one great brasse potte." My 5 children. Exors, Wm Boydell, & James Mather my son. Witnesses: James Corlesse, Edward Corlesse John Holcroft Junr.

The debts mention :—

My son Henry Mather,	John Batesbie,
Edward Flitcroft,	Wm. Risleye,
James Halle,	Jas Corlesse,
My daur Ann Mather,	Wm Boydell,
Jhoane Boydell,	Nicholas Mosse,
Oumffraye Birchshooe [Birchall],	Wm. Bayrume, [Byrom]
Geoffrey Strange,	John Holcroft.

Inventory by John Mosse, Roger Flitcrofte, James Corlesse, Wm. Moyle, £10..9..7. Proved 24 April, 1582.

Symond Mather, of West Leigh, Lancashire, 1588.

SYMOND MATHER of Westleigh,† yeoman, 18 April 30 Eliz. [1588] Was old. To be buried in the middle of the parish Church of Leigh in the accustomed burial place of my predecessors. My son Jeffrey Mather. My 2 maidservants Isabel, & Margaret Mather. My 2 children Jeffrey & Robert Mather. My sons in law John Partington of Tyldesley, James Haughton, William Liptrotte, & Jas. Mo͠ne [Mann]. Richd Arrowsmith of Leigh mentioned. In the entail are Edward, Henry, John, Nicholas, & Richard, sons of my son in law James Haughton, of Arburie. There is also in the entail Anne wife of James Scarisbricke of Downholland. Exors, Sons in law James Haughton of Arburie & William Liptrott of West Leigh. Supervisors, the worshipful Mr James Scarisbricke of Down Holland gent, & John Partington & James Mo͠ne of Tyldesley my sons in law Witnesses: Richard Arrowsmyth, John Mather, Jarvice Lowe.

Debts name :—Richard Geste, Nicholas Mather, Symond Mather, Margaret Mather, John Pinnington, John Partington son in Law.

Inventory by Hugh Hinley, George Hurste, Robert Arrowsmyth, & Symond Bradshaugh, 26 April 1588, £120 : 32 : 8. [sic]. Proved 30 April 1588.

---

* He was buried at Leigh church, 5th March, 1581-2. (Stanning's Parish Registers of Leigh, 1558-1625).

† Symon Mather was church-warden of Leigh in 1552, and he was buried there 24 April, 1588.

RICHARD MATHER, of Lowest Hulton, in the parish of Deane within the Co. of Lancaster, 8 Augt 1593. My bodie to the earth whereof yt was made & the same to bee buried at my p'ishe Church of Deane. Debts paid remainder to be divided into three parts. One part I to have myself, the seconde parte to Annes my wyff, the third part to Mrgreat Partington my daughter. Reversion of my part equally Emongs Raphe, Ellyn & Ales p'tington my daughter Margreat her children at the sight of my Executors. After my Lease wch I have from Mr William Wartton of Wartton Hall be expired my good will thereof to my daughter Margreat her children to wyte [wit] Raphe Partington and for want of hym to Ellen Partington for want of her to Alise Partington naturall* systers to the s^d Raphe. Executors:— Annes Mather my wyff & Thomas Eccarselaie [Eckersley] my brother in law. Debts which I the Testator do owe.

Item to the right worshipfull Mr Raphe Ashtonn of great lever	xxvj^s.	viij^d.
Item to James Crompton of Lostock	xj^s.	
Item to Richard morres of great boulton for flax	xxx^s.	
Item to Charles p'tington my son in law	xxvj^s.	
Item to the said Charles [Partington]	xj^s.	iiij^d.
Item to Thomas Eccarselay	ij^s.	xj^d.
Item to James Mather my brother	x^s.	

Debts owing unto mee the Testator.

Item William Macand dwelling upon Bakersgreen being the Rev^rsion of money for the prise of a mare wch I the Testator sould hym the som of xiij^s. Witnesses Richd Lie [Leigh], gent Thomas Bordmann, Willm. Warttonn & Thomas Warttonn.

Inventory p'sed 14 Aug by Tho Hurst, James Edge Willm Warttnn and Raphe Sweetlove.

Proved 22 Aug. 1593, by Thomas Eccarsley power reserved to Agnes the relict.

Gilbert Mather, of Adlington, Lancashire, 1593.

GILBARTE MATHER of Adlington, [in the parish of Standish] co. Lanc. drover, 19 May, 1592. My body to the earth to be layed in Christian buriall at Blackrood. To Jane Greene als Mather bastard daughter of mee the sayed Gilbert vj^l. xiij^s. iiij^d. To Cicelie Greene als Mather, one other bastard daughter of mee the sayed Gilberte vj^l. xiij^s. iiij^d. with benefit of survivorship. If both dye s^d xiij^l. vj^s. viij^d. amonges three of my Children or survivors of them viz Anne Mather, Katherin Mather, and one Margaret Stones als Mather, one other bastard Daur of mee the sayed Gilbert. To repairiage of the Church or Chappell of Blackrood. To my verie good Mr James Anderton of Lostocke Esquier my gould ringe. After Debts paid the rest amonges my children viz Raphe Mather Anne Mather Katherin Mather & the sayed Margarett Stones als Mather my bastard daur. I make John Mather by brother, and Raynold Mather my exōrs & my verie good M^r [master] overseer. To Raphe Mather my sonne all my landes &c when 21. Profits during his minority to be taken by my Exōrs, & Thos Anderton, gent, & Hugh Greenhalgh for use of my said children Raphe, Anne, Katherin, and Margarett Stones als Mather. No Witnesses.

---

* Natural here means actual, and does not signify illegitimacy.

Inventory £ 143:16:4 praised by George Allenson, Peter Mather, Robte Worthington, & John Breres.
Proved 25 Oct 1593 by John Mather, Reginald Mather having renounced.

James Mather, of Radcliffe, 1596.

3ᵈ daie of October, 1595.—I, JAMES MATHER of the parishe of Radcliffe in the Countie of Lancaster:

My body to Parish Church or Churchyard of Radcliffe.—mentions "one house & certaine lands, which I & my wyffe & my eldest sonne Raphe Mather enjoy," "the property which I houlde of the most worshippful my Mʳ and landeslorde Richard Ashton of Mydleton, Esquire."—to be employed "for the goode education & bringing upp of my younger children untill my sayde sonne accomplishe the age of 21 years."—mentions further —"my brother Hughe Mather his widdowe"—"John Fletcher"—"Mʳ Fox my Lord derbie his steward"—"Ellyn Mather my wyffe"—"my five children"—leaves to "my younge sonne Thomas Mather xlˢ"—"my eldest daughter Elizabeth Mather xlˢ"—"my seconde daughter Marye iiiˡⁱ"—"my youngest daughter Ann Mather iiiiˡⁱ"—"My saide wyffe & my two sonnes" executors—"my brother Hughe Mather & my cosin Randle Mather overseers."

Debts owinge unto Mʳ James Mather amountinge to 38ˡⁱ. 7ˢ. 6ᵈ.

[*inter alia*] Item: Hughe Mather, 48ˢ. 7ᵈ.
Item: Edwarde Tyldsley my brother-in-law, 18ˢ.
Item: Thomas Tyldesley my brother-in-law, 10ˢ.
Item: Ux Wme Mather my mother-in-law, 2ˢ.

Witnesses. Roberte Kenyonn, Randle Mather, Samuel Mather, Hughe Dyggle, ffrancke Wrooe, scripsit.

Inventorie 14 November, 1595, by Hugh Mather, Edward Tyldsley, Ellys Walker & france[is] Wrooe.

Summa totalis cixˡⁱ. xviiˢ. viᵈ.

Proved 6th February 1595[-6].

Ralph Mather, of Radcliffe, 1597.

The 2 October, 1597. I, RAUFFE MATHER of the Parishe of Radcliffe in the Countie of Lancaster, tanner—beinge sicke & weake in bodie etc. etc.— "bodie to be decentlie buried in the Parish Church yard of Radcliffe,"— property to be divided into "two equalle partes, whereof I doe reserve the one parte to my owne specialle use,"—"and as for the other part I doe hereby will & devise the same unto my several children, equallie amongst them namely, Gabriel Mather, Habraham Mather, Samuell Mather, Reynould [Reginald] Mather, & Sara Mather:" "of my owne parte I doe give to my daughter Sara iiiˡⁱ"—"to Renould Mather iiiˡⁱ"—"to Habraham Mather & Samuel Mather either of them xlˢ apeece."—"I alsoe give unto Samuel Mather which I am grandfather to xiiˢ."

"Rest & remainder amongst aforesaid five children"—"Habraham Mather, Executor."

Witnesses. "Hugh Mather th' elder"
"Thomas Mather"

Dettes owinge unto said Rauffe Mather.

Imprimis: William Bowcher. 4ˡⁱ. 9ˢ. 8ᵈ.

Richarde Manchester is surtye of 40ˢ of the sᵈ monye which Wᵐ Bowcher doth owe.

717

Inventorie made 7th October, 1597, by Hugh Mather, George Kerkeman, William Macant & Wm Kenion.

Summa totalis, clxxx^{li}. ii^s. vii^d.

Peter Mather, of Anderton, 1598.

In the name of God Amen—on the xiv. daie of September, Año dñi 1598.—I PETER MATHER—of Anderton in the Countie of Lancaster, yōman, sicke in bodie etc. etc.—1st I commit my soule into the hands of Almighty God etc. etc.—bodie to the earthe whence it came & as touchinge the desposing of such worldlie goodes etc.—divides property into 3 parts—" whereof I leave one parte unto Margarett my wyffe—another thirde parte unto Margaret Woodwarde my daughter & the other thirde part I reserve unto myselfe to dispose off at my pleasure."—" And of my saide parte I doe give & bequeath unto Robte Rigbie my servante liii^s. iiii^d.—" Item: Unto Ellyn my servante xx^s."—Item: "unto Hugh [torn] ightgall [Nightgall] tenne shillinge."—" Item: I give unto Reynould my brother all my apparrelle & clothes for my bodie."—Item: I give unto everie childe which I am godfathere unto ii^s. for a Remembrance."—" Item: I give unto Margaret my grandchild x^{li}. to be employed to her best use."—Remainder after payment of debts funeral expenses etc. equally between—"Margaret my wiffe & Margaret Woodwarde my daughter."—" I appointe & ordaine my well-beloved wyffe Margaret & my deare friende Henerie Hodsinson my true & lawfulle Executor."

> Witnesses. George Houlme.
> Reynould Mather.

Dettes which I doe owe.

Imprimis: To Margaret Nightgall my cosin, iii^{li}.

Dettes owinge unto me without specialtie.

Imprimis: William Anderton Esquire, my
maister oweth me in lente

monie,	24^{li}. 6^s. 8^d.
Item: Peter Makinson in lente monie,	9^s.
Item: William Platt in lente monie,	5^s. 6^d.
Summa totalis,	xxv^{li}. iii^s. ii^d.

Inventorie of Peter Mather late of Anderton yeoman, praissed by Arthur Houlme, Regynald Mather, James Rivington & Robte Rothewelle 20th daie Sept. in 44 yeare of our gracious soveraigne ladie Queene Elizabeth, by the grace of God, Queen of England, Scotland, France & Ireland, etc. An. dñi. 1598.

[inter alia] Item: Y^e halfe of five scour [score] & six sheepes in the custodie of Robert Pilkington gent, x^{li}.

Sum tot—clxxxxiiii^{li}. xiiii^s. 1^d.

The summe oweinge sett under the will is, xxv^{li}. iii^s. ii^d.

Sum tot. cc.xix. xvii^s. iii^d.

Annes Mather, of Hulton, widow, 1600.

ANNES MATHER, of Lowest Hulton, " wyddow wth in the p'ish of Deane, 1599 [1600] 20th Januarie. Bodie to the earth to be buried at my p'ish church of Deane. Debts paid, the residue to Thomas, John, & Margaret Farneworth &c. Apparell to the children of Charles p'tington. Reversion of all my part of goods &c. to Charles P'tington & Margaret his wife towards the bringing up of theyre children. And I appoint Charles p'tington my son in law sole Exor.

718

Debts wch I do owe

To Margaret Mather wyddoe,   xx^s.
" Ellyn P'tington,   xx^s.

Witnesses: Jas. Pendleburie, Clerk.
      Ric: ffarneworth.
      Thomas Eccarselaie.

Inventory of those goods wch in Right Annes Mather of Lowest Hulton wydow latelie decessed of Right had interest in . . . . trulie saide pplie to her in her Lyff tyme did app'taine taken forth . . . . of Richard Mather her husband who decessed Anno Dom̃i 1593 . . . . vid one third ptt of the saide Inventorie of good presed devided & sum̃ed xxjth daie of Januarie & by us is prised Richard Farneworth Lambart p'tington Roger Eccarselaie & Thomas Eccarselaie.

Md. The shapon App[ar]ell for the bodie of the decedent prised unto xxx^s.

It the pt of the goods due forth of her husband his last will & Inventorie the some of xij^{li}. xiij^d. iiij^d.

Proved 22 January 1599[-1600].

John Mather, of Lowton, 1601.

John Mather of Lowton 22 Apr. 1601. To be buried at Winwick. Son-in-law Richard Greisse & Agnes his wife. Son Richard and his children.
Brother Nicholas.
Dau. Ann shall have 40^s which her aunt Jane gave her.
Brother James & his son John.
Anne. Coarlles [Corless].
Exors: Richard my son, Ric. Greisse my son-in-law & Richd Corlles my son-in-law.
Supervisor, Wm Byrom.
Witnesses: James Crofte.
      Wm Mather.
      Nicholas Lythgoe.
Among debts are ment^d Symonde Mather, my sister Margaret.
Inventory, 24 April 1601, by Symonde Mather Henry Stirroppe, Ric^d Gleover Jervesse Winterbothome. £45 18. 0.
Proved 6 May 1601.

William Mather, of Westhoughton, 1602.

William Mather of Westhoughton, yeoman. 8 June 44, Eliz. 1602. To be buried at Deane. Goods divided into 2 parts—first pt to self, 2^d part to Agnes my wife. After debts etc. paid rem. of my pt. to be divided in 4 pts:

1st. to Jas Anderton my brother-in-law.
2. to Ellis my brother.
3. to Elizabeth my sister.
4. to Margaret Mather my brother's daur.

To Arthur Woodward 40^s.
To Henry Woodward, David Woodward, James Woodward, Thurston Woodward & Margaret Woodward 40^s.
To Richard Lich & his children £5.
To Agnes my wife one close of ground which I have taken of Jas Browne of Westhoughton Esq. for her life & after her deče to Margaret Mather & her father during life of s^d Margaret.

719

To Agnes my wife one close of ground for 8 years that I have taken of Oliver Rigby—if she die before expiration of s^d term then to David Woodward.

To s^d David Woodward the same close for 15 years after s^d lease of 8 yrs has expired.

Exors: James Enderton [Anderton?], Ellis Mather my brother & Agnes my wife.

Witnesses, Charies Leigh, Ric^d Woodward, Henerie Rothwell.

Among debts are named—Jas Morres of Lostocke, Wm Plate, Wm Talior of Hinley [Hindley], Christopher Harte, John Grcgorie & wife, Ric^d Gregorie, Hugh Rigby, Ric^d Woodward.

Inventorie. 15 June 1602 by Jas Ma[r]kland, John Scotte, Henerie Hampson, Jas Woodward, Chas Leigh, Ric Lithe. Mention of lands taken of Wm Banester, Ric^d Greene, John Gregorie & Oliver Rigby.—Ric^d Woodward.—Hugh Rigby. £102. 2. 0.

Proved 19 Ju— 1602.

William Mather, of Warrington, 1603.

WILLIAM MATHER of [Conies' Corner] Warrington, Yeoman, 18 Decr 1602. To be buried within the parish church of Warrington. To William Brocke, son of Richd Brocke of Bunbury all the goods in the closet in my house in Warrington. Whereas I owe to the said Wm Brocke 18s. I give him in consideration "one Whyte Bullocke about the age of two years." To my wife Johanne Mather all my tack of ground &c. which I hold under any persons whatsoever with all my goods chattels, &c. &c.

Exors: Johanne my wife & Richard Brocke of Bunbury my brother in law.

Witnesses: Wm. Waringe, Nycholas Bate, John Fletcher. In the debts &c. are named, Gilb^t Hylls, John Blundell, Lawce Hallywell, Robt Woods, Mercer, Edward Woodward of Eccles, Hy: Holbrocke Senr, Peter Ellam, Thos. Allen.

Inventory 29 Dec. 1602 by Thos Mather, Thos. Richardson, John Barns & Randull Pynyngton.

Proved 3 January 1602[-3].

Richard Mather, of Hulton, 1693.

RICHARD MATHER of Middle Hulton, 18 Oct. 1600. To be buried at Deane. Wife Elizabeth. Sons (both Exors) Henry and James.

Witnesses: Simon son of Roger Edge, John Godbear.

Debts name: John Mather and John Marshe.

Inventory 27 Sept. 1602 by Richard Edge, Symond Mather, Robert Spakeman, Ralph Higson. £46. 10. 0.

Proved 3 Feby. 1602[-3].

Gabriel Mather, of Kearsley, 1605.

In the name of God Amen. I, GABRIELL MATHER of Kersley in the Countie of Lancaster, blacksmyth, sicke in bodie etc.—leaves "bodie to be buried in ye Parish Church of Deane." Property into three equal parts.— "One third parte to Margaret Mather my wyffe" & "another thirde parte to my two sonnes Henry & John Mather."—One other thirde part I reserve unto myselfe."

"Item—I give & bequeath unto my mother Anne [Emme?] Mather one paire of gooses."—"To Richard Mather sonne of Thomas Mather my brother, iii^s. iiii^d."—"Margerie Mather my sister."—"I give and bequeath

720

unto the younge sonne of my brother Samuell, my godson, iii^s. iiii^d."—
"John Howell [Hawell?] my Father in lawe."—"Robert Granger cooke of Leaver."—" George Woode."

Executors: Margaret his wife & "Henerie Scolcroft of ffarnworth."—

16th Oct. 1604.

Gabriel Mather   his
mark.

Witnesses: Arthur Seddon. James Hoope. Edward Seddon. George Seddon. Thomas Greene.

Dettes owing unto testator.

[*inter alia*]   John Crompton of tasker.
Alexander Crompton.

Inventorie by Thomas Dodson & Ric^d B'thwell, taken 26 October 1604. Proved 6 June 1605 by Margaret Mather widow, the relict.

ABSTRACTS OF THE WILLS OF THE MATHER FAMILY, PROVED IN THE CONSISTORY COURT AT CHESTER FROM 1573 TO 1650.

By J. PAUL RYLANDS, Esq., F.S.A., of Birkenhead, England.

Hamlet Mather, of Radcliffe, 1609.

9 July, 1606 [or possibly 1608]. "In the name of God, Amen. I, HAMLET MATHER of the Parish of Radcliffe being sicke & weake in bodie but praissed be God of howle & sounde mynde & always consideringe the uncertaine houre of death do make this my laste Will & Testamente in manner & forme following. Firstly and before all other thinges I doe leave my soule into the handes of Almighty God my maker, and my bodie to be buried in the Parish Church of Radcliffe and as for the goodes and cattels, which God hath seen fit to lende unto me, I do dispose of them as here followeth." Divides goods in two equal parts, one he reserves to himself and the other part he leaves between his 3 "sonnes, Richard, Henry and James Mather"; to "Henerie" he leaves his "land at Radcliff Bridge." Small bequests to "my servante mayde Anne Mather," my servante man Wᵐ Harrington" and "my daughter-in-law Katherine Mather wife of Henry Mather my son." Mentions "Richard Mather whiche I am unkell unto."

Executors, his 3 sons Richard, Henry & James.

Overseers, "Bartholomew Fletcher & Randall Mather."

Dettes which I doe owe.

[inter alia] Imprimis: Tᵒ Sʳ Richard Asheton knighte   xxˡⁱ.

Witnesses. Hugh Allence clarke. John Whorrockes [Horrocks.] Hugh Seddon Senʳ Samuell Mather with others.

Dettes oweinge unto me Hamlet Mather.

from James Mather, Henerie Mather, Richard Mather [probably his 3 sons], Hugh Sharpplews, Grace Dygby [or Dygly] my sister, Hamlet Sandyfourth, Francis Sharpplews, Hugh Mather.

Inventorie praised by Barthom Ffletcher, Henry Walker, James Diggel of the parish of Prestwich & Hugh Seddon of the parish of Yᵉ Deane.—6 May 1609. Summa totalis 397ˡⁱ. 4ˢ. 8ᵈ.

Proved 15 May 1609.

Symond Mather, of Lowton, 1609.

In the name of God Amen the xxiijᵗʰ day of November in the yeare of oʳ Lord God 1609, and in the yeare of the raigne of James Kinge of England the seaventh & of Scotland the xliijᵗʰ I SYMOND MATHER of Lowton

722

in the p'rishe of Winwick yeoman whole of mynd and sicke of body (thanked bee God) doe make my last will & Testament in mann' & forme followinge,—ffirst I bequeath my soule to almightie God my redeemer & maker & my body to bee buried in the p'rishe Churche of Winwicke or Church yard in my buriall place.—ffirst I dispose of my wourldly goods wch I am possessed of in this mann' following.—ffirst I give to the free schoole of Winwick xx^li wch said some of money to be put unto the hands of the right worshiple Sr Peter Legh, Knight & to his heires to see that the vse of it bee payde to the free schoole of Winwicke for ever & if hee will not, then to returne unto my executor againe Itm I give ten pounds unto Burtonwood Chappell to bee put unto the hands of Edmund Taylier & the ou'seers of the said Chappell & shall bynd themselves & theire heires executors, admirators & assignes for ever to pay the vse of the same some of ten pounds unto Burtonwood Chappell to the mentinence of Gods service there for ever Itm I give unto the poor, halt, blynde, & lame twelve shurts or Smocks during the naturall lyefe of Alice my wiefe yearly—Itm I give to my servant Elizabeth Twisse xx^s. Itm I give to my servant John Twisse xx^s. Itm Ellis Cleaton [Clayton] xx^s. Itm I give to my servant Richard Mather xx^s. It I give to Thomas Robothome Curat of Winwicke vj^s. viij^d. The rest of my goods vnbequeathed my debts payd my funerall expences discharged, I give unto Alice my wiefe whome I ordeyne constitute & make my trustie & wellbeloved wyfe my executrix to see my will fulfilled & satisfied in all points. Ou'seers Thoms Corlies, John Banke. Witnesse hereof, John Grysse, Thoms Corlies, John Twisse & Thomas Robothome.

Debts owinge unto mee Symond Mather.

		li	s	d
Imprimis.	Thoms Hurst,		xxx^s.	
It	John Hasleden of Goulborne,		viij^s.	viij^d.
It	Thoms Turner,		xliiij^s.	
It	Hughe Stirroppe,	vj^li	vj^s.	viij^d.
It	Richard Gloouer [Glover],		xl^s.	
It	Richard Corlies of Pinington,		xl^s.	
It	Willm Boydel of Pinington,		xxxiij^s.	iiij^d.
It	Henry Sedowne [Seddon],		xxxvij^s.	
It	Edward Wood,		viij^s.	
It	John ffraunce,		xlv^s.	
It	John Crouchley,		ix^s.	
It	Ric. Doumbell,	iij^li.	iij^s.	iij^d.
It	John his sonne,		xl^s.	
It	Richard ffitchet,		iiij^s.	vj^d.
It	Ric. Shawe,		xviij^s.	
It	Thoms Taylier,		xij^s.	
It	the wiefe of Ather Asheton,		xxx^s.	
It	the wiefe of Ric. Liptrot,		xl^s.	
It	Ric ffraunce,		vj^s.	
It	Thoms Boulton of Kenion,		xlvj^s.	viij^d.
It	Edward Parpointe,		x^s.	
It	Raphe Birche,		ix^s.	iiij^d.
It	Thoms Twisse,		xl^s.	
It	John Gryss,	iij^li.	xx^s. [sic]	
It	Robt Grysse,	viij^li.	iiij^s.	
It	Ric. Grysse,	vij^li.		

It	Tho Kerfoote,		xx^s.	
It	John Ainsworth & his wife,	iij^{li}.	vj^s.	
It	John Ridyord,		xiiij^s.	
It	the wiefe of Charles Baxter,		xx^s.	
It	Tho Eden,		xvij^s.	v^d.
It	Tho Ridyord of the pale,		v^s.	iij^d.
It	John Maddocke,		l^s.	
It	Wm Parr,	iiij^{li}.		
It	Wm. Luther a͞ls Baines,		xiij^s.	iiij^d.
It	John Widdowes,	iij^{li}.		
It	Symond Kay,		xxxiij^s.	iiij^d.
It	Nicholas Goulden,		xx^s.	
It	the wiefe of Peter Hynd,		xxvij^s.	
It	Richard Mather of Pyle dytch,	iij^{li}.		
It	Gernice Winterbothome,		xx^s.	
It	Widdowe Wilsone of Newton,		xij^s.	
It	Raphe Wood	xl^s. upon a powne.		
It	Mr. Henry Byrom, ⎱	iij^{li}.	xvij^s.	
	& Mrs. Byrom his wife ⎰			
It	Richard Wood,		ix^s.	

Proved 14 Decr 1609 by Alice Mather sole extrix. Endorsed. Be yt knowne unto all men that I Symond Mather of Lowton yeoman have knowne the way betwixt Wi͡llm. Byrom & Tho͞ms Corlies now in suite three score years & odd & neu^r knewe nor hard at anie tyme Tho͞ms. Corleis or his predecessors to be lett stopped molested or hindered for going that waye but now of late & to testifie that this is true I have sett my hand to the same in the prsence of Thoms Robothome Curit of Winwicke, John Grysse John Twisse wth divers others.

Inventory prased by Hewe Sterroppe, Thomas Turner, Thomas Corlies, & Richard Baxter, 7 Dec. 1609, ccxx^{li}. xxix^s. x^d. besydes the readie money —vj^{li}. xiij^s. iiij^d.

Abraham Mather, of Radcliffe, 1613.

" In the name of God Amen, on the one & twentieth daie of September in the yeare of our Lord God one thousand six hundred & thirteen. I ABRAHAM MATHER of Radcliffe, Countie of Lancaster tanner, beinge visited by the hande of Almightie God sicke and weake in bodie, but of sound & p'fect minde for which praise be to God, make & ordayne this my last will & Testament in manner & form followinge—

Firstly & chiefly I bequeathe my soule to God the Father to Jesus Christe my Redeemer through whose merrittes I trust to see a glorious resurrection & to the Holie Gost the Santifier. & my bodie to be buried in decente Christian burialle in the parish church of Radcliffe.

And As for the disposinge of those temporalle & worldie goods which I doe possess it is my will that they be divided in to two equalle p'tes— one parte of which I doe will & bequeath to my wyffe Jane & the other I reserve to myself to be disdosed off in manner & forme followinge.

To my Brother Reginald Mather	13^{li} 6^s 8^d
To Samuel Alens & his sistar Rosamund Alens to either of them	40^s
To my godson Abraham Macone [Makant]	10^s
To all my god children	3^s 4 apeece.

To Samuel Mather his two sonnes Samuell &
    Christopher Mather   6ˢ 8 apeece.
To the poore of yᵉ Parish of Radcliffe   40ˢ

The house & grounde the which I rente from The Ryght worshipful Richard Assheton of Midleton I do give & assigne to my lovinge wyffe Jane."

In case of his wife's death the house & grounde to come "To Abraham Mather my nefue, which now dwelleth with me if he be come to the age of 20 yeares" in which case—"Abraham Mather my nefue to pay to the sayd Reginald Mather his unkell the summe of 6ˡⁱ. 13ˢ. 4ᵈ.

To Samuell Mather my brother those two closurs or closes of grounds which layeth by Ralph Undisworth's house which my Father boughte of Roger Tyldesle for ever—and the house wherein I now dwell & all the reste of my grounde to my nefue Abraham Mather." If Abraham die all to his brother Reginald.

Executrix   His wife Jane Mather.

Witnesseth   Reginald Mather.   Abraham Mather.   John Herdman. William Herdman.   George Kyrkman.

Inventorie praised by foure honeste sufficiente men.   George Kerkman Wᵐ Macon Geffre Lomax & John Herdman on the 24 Sept. 1613.
                Summa Totalis £87. 18. 0.

Humphrey Mather, of Wigan, 1613.

HUMFREY MATHER of Wigan.   Tanner 3 May, 1611.   To be buried at Wigan.   Land leased from Gerrard Massie D.D Rector of Wigan, Wife Ellen—Eldest son Roger.   Sons—Roger, William, James, Nicholas, 3 Daurs, Grace, Jane, Elizabeth, Son in Law John Scotte (Stott?] Brother of ½ blood Thomas Banks   Servant Henry Asmall.   Cousins Wm. Gardner, Wm. Mather, Peter Marsh.   Exix. wife.   Overseers, Dr Marshe & 3 cousins above named.   Witnesses: Gerrard Massye.   Wm Gardner. Peter Marsh.

Many names in Inventory which is dated 9 Dec. 1612.

Proved 9 Decʳ. 1613.

William Mather,* of Turton, 1614.

"On the 23 daie of March 1613 WILLIAM MATHER of Turton in the Countie Palatine of Lancaster husbandman,† being sicke in bodie, uttered his laste Will & Testamente in the followinge wordes or wordes like unto them—in the presence of the witnesses whose names are below written." He divides his property into 3 parts—1ˢᵗ part to Margaret his wife, 2ᵈ part between his sons "Nicholas, John, Richard, William & James equallie"— 3ᵈ part, after payment of his debts, funeral expenses, etc., to be divided "equallie between my three youngest sonnes—that is to saye, Richard William & James Mather."

Executors.   Margaret his wife & John Mather his son.

Witness at the utteringe of the words   Alexander Horrocks.

Inventory valued March 31ˢᵗ 1614 [probably meant for 1613 O. S. as the will is endorsed as proved 1613] by Christopher Horrocks, James Walnighte [?] Lawrence Browlawe Junior & James Roskowe [Roscoe].
                Summa totalis £165. 08. 04.

Proved 28 April 1614 by all the executors.

---

* This will is wrongly endorsed Nicholas Mather.

† Husbandman at this period generally meant what we now call a tenant-farmer.

Ralph Mather, of Atherton, 1614.

RALPH MATHER of Atherton in the parish of Leigh, 28 Feby. 1613[-14]. To be buried at Leigh,* Goods to be divided into 3 parts. First part to Elizabeth my wife. Second part equally among my children. My sons, Roger Mather, & Raufe Mather, my Daughters, Ellen Mather, & Margaret Mather. Third part to myself, for legacies, Debts &c. Residue to son & daus. Ralph, Ellen, & Marg^t. Mather equally. Exors Elizabeth my wife and Rauf my son. Overseers—Henry Greene & Symon Smith.—Item, to my brother John Mather, 6^s 8^d to my Brother Richard Mather 6^s 8^d to my sister Elizabeth Mather, 3^s 4^d.

Names mentioned among Debts—Henry Denton, John Reeve, James Meaneley, John Rogerson, Wm. Hulton Esq, Raufe Mather my son, Raufe Sothworth, Wm Hurste, John Hulton, John Houghton, Wm Echcersley, John Smith, cobler, The late wife of Robert Rigby.

Inventory by John Bradshawe, Rd Sothworth, John Astley, Chas. Greene, Rt. Morris, Rd. Battorsbie, 26 may 1614.

Proved 14 June 1614.

Ellen Mather, of Wigan, 1614.

ELLEN MATHER of Wigan, widow, 30 April 1614, late wife of Humphrey Mather late of Wigan, Tanner, To be buried at Wigan. My son Christopher Anderton. My brother Lawrence Maudisley. My sister Jennit Morrice. My cousin Ellen Langshawe. Elizabeth wife of Matt Markland, Elizabeth wife of Peter Marsh. My six sons, Christopher, Lawrence, Roger, William, James, & Nicholas. Overseers to have tuition of son Lawrence, & also of s^d Roger, W^m. James & Nicholas Mather, my younger sons. Roger to be a tanner.

Exor. Christopher Anderton.

Overseers. D^n Gerrarde Masseye D.D. Rector of Wigan & Peter Marsh of Wigan, Gent.

Witnesses: Peter Marsh. Matt. Markland. Thos Briggs.

Proved 7 Sept 1614.

Gowther Mather, of Winwick, 1616.

GOWTHER MATHER of Winwicke husbandman 2 June, 13 James 1615. To be buried in my buriall within the parish church of Winwick. Goods to be divided into 3 parts, one for myself, the other for my wife & the third for my son Thomas Mather, in regard the rest of my children viz. Margaret & Jane my two daurs. already have had good portions. To daur. Jane Burton 5s. To daur Margaret Bretherton 5s. To Margaret Holcroft my granddaur, 1 black cow stirke of a year old. To Thomas Mather my grandson, 1 lamb &c. To Margerie Mather my mother in Lawe 5s. Residue to wife Anne Mather.

Exors. Son Thom^s. Mather & Gregorie Frend, Gent. Witnesses Nicholas Scaresbricke, Adam Coller, & Thomas Golden. Persons named under debts &c. Matthew Bretherton. Exors of Rich. Milner, Cather. Mason. Wm Towers. The officers at Winwicke, Thomas Golden, Mr Gregorie Frend, which he disbursed for me abt. my suit with John Kerfoote 35s. Tho. Golden, Hy. Towers, Hy. Sothworth, Roger Par, Humfrey Parr.

Inventory 10 June 1615 by adam Coller, Henry Towers, Matt. Bretherton, & Tho. Burton £100. 3. 9.

Proved 18 Oct. 1616, by Thomas Mather.

The renunciation of Gregory Friende is enclosed in the will.

* He was buried at Leigh church in May, 1614.

726

Ellis Mather, of Toxteth, 1617.

In the name of God Amen. I, ELLIS MATHER of Toxteth within the Countie of Lancaster within the Realme of England husbandman, beinge in p'fecte health & memorie praysed bee God for y[e] same, yet calling to mynd the uncertaintie of mans life & that there sh[d] bee no contention or variance about those goodes which it hath pleased God to bestowe on mee here, I do therefore ordaine & make this my last will & testament in manner & forme following. First I commit my soule into the handes of Allmightie God, hoping by the sufferings of Jesus Christ to be saved & to enjoy a joyfull resurrection with the reste of Gods children & so to be blessed for evermore.

Item I will that my bodie be committed to the Earthe in honeste comelie burriall. Item, my goodes & chattels landes & tenements debts wheresoever due & howsoever, my will ys that they be disposed of In manner & forme following, viz my messuages & tentes with all howses barnes & buildings etc in Toxteth with all other my landes & tenements goodes & chattels to bee put to the ordering & disposing of my trustie & well beloved friendes William Banester of Liupoole [Liverpool] Alderman, William ffoxe of Toxteth, Randle Mather my unkle & Myles Mather my brother to the uses hereafter mentioned & noe otherwise. viz the moitie of my house & grounds in Toxeth to be ockupyed & used to the behoofe of Myles Mather my eldest son. The said Myles paying to my younger children the full wholl summe of twentye pounds of Lawfull Englishe money to be devyded by equal p'portion among them at such tyme as he shall come to the full age of twentye & one yeares.

Item: the other moitie to the use & behoofe of Elizabeth my wyffe for & towards the education & bringing up of my children in the feare of God.

Item. My will ys that my Lands & buildings in the Speake fielde bee used & ockupyed to the moste commoditie & profit of Richard, Thomas, William & Edwarde my naturall* children during all my tearme of yeares & Interest in the same & what further tearme may be had in the same to be to the p'fermente of my sonne Richard.

Item: My will is that my goodes & chattels be devyded into 3 parts, the first part whereof I give & bequeath unto Elizabeth my wyffe; the seconde to my children; the thirde I reserve to myself out of which besydes my bringinge out & discharging of my debts, the residue I give & bequeath unto my abovenamed younger children.

And to the end this my laste will & testamente according to my desyre may be p'formed I doe appointe & ordaine the abovenamed W[m] Banester & W[m] ffoxe my true & lawfull executors hoping they will bee faithful & trustie herein. Item. my will & Desyre is that my brother in law Thomas Hodgsonn would be pleased to be overseer of this my will & Testament to see the same in all pointes p'formed.—my hand & seal the xv daie Sept. A D. 1616.

Debts oweinge unto mee.

John Tarleton on reckoninge between hym & me	50[li].	
W[m] Griphith for a mare & a colte	4[li].	
Alexander Warde of Boulton		12[s]
Richard Partington for a mare to paye at Mich. 1617	3[li].	
Ned Reshton		20[s]
Bartin Mather my unkle due at purificato 1617	7[li].	

* Natural here does not mean illegitimate.

727

John Windle oweth 10^{li} to Bartholemew Thomson }
  which I am suretie for. }

My brother Hodgson about   4^{li}.

Dettes oweinge by mee.

To Mr Darbie of Liu'poole   13^{li}.

  Witnesses Edward Rushton Ellis Mather

          Thomas Woodes [this is only a copy]

1617. A true and perfect Inventorie of goodes & chattels of Ellis Mather of Toxteth, as they were prysed & valewcd by John Walker, Wm Horrockes, Wm Gill & Myles Mather the xix daie of Dec. 1616.

Summa totalis 134^{li}. 2. 11.

Proved January xxx. 1616[-17] by Executors.

John Mather, of Astley, 1617.

"John Mather of [Astley in] the p' rishe of Leigh. 25 May, 1617. To be buryed in my parishe church of Leighe* in my owne buryall [place] there as neare vnto my wyffe as may bee." After debts paid "one halfe of my goodes amongst all my fyve children and also that my three youngest children have every one of them 20^s over and besides their parts." Residue of other part to said children. Lamberte Partington of Tyldesley and Thomas Withington of Astley Exors.

Debts which I owe

Roger Younge	vi^l.		
Lamberte Smethurste		vi^s.	
John Gest	iij^l.	x^s.	
ux. Thome Rysley	iij^{li}.	vi^s.	viij^d.
Lamtle Partington		xl^s.	
Jane Worsley		liij^s.	iij^d. ob
Gyles Dunsteere to be paid at Martinmas	iij^l.	iij^s.	viij^d.
Mr. Henrie Trapes, [Trapps]		xxiiij^s.	ix^d.
Lamberte Tyldesley		xx^s.	
Christopher Astley		xxiiij^s.	
William Hope	iij^{li}.	ij^s.	viij^d.

Debts oweinge to me

James Astley	iiij^{li}.	xiij^s.	iiij^d.
George Holcrofte		xxx^s.	
John Walkden		xv^s.	

  Witnesses:

Lamberte Tyldesley

Robert Cluarthe [Cleworth]

Tho. Morse.

Inventory £64-2-8 prysed & valued by Christopher Astley, Hughe Mather, John Walkeden & Symond Mather, 29 May, 1617.

Proved by Executors, 4 July, 1617 (called of Astley in the parish of Leigh).

Thurstan Mather, of Hindley, 1619.

Thurstan Mather of Hindley. 22 February, 1618-19. To be buried at Wigan, Son Philip. Lease from Xpofer Stanynoght & others. My wife Margery. My 3 children Hamphrey, Jane and Elizabeth, Grandchild Gilbert. Exors, wife Margery, son Philip. Overseers, my master Mr. Abraham Langton, & friend Wm. Latchford.

* He was buried at Leigh Church, 29 May, 1617.

Witnesses: Ja. Massye, Adam Aspull, Wm. Latchford, Randle Latchford, Abraham Langton.

Inventory 8 April, 1619, by Peter Langton, Wm. Langton, Richard Greene of Hindley, yeoman, Richd Ashton of Abraham yeoman, £135 : 1 : 0.

Proved 24 Nov. 1619.

Richard Mather, of Bedford, Lancashire, 1621.

RICHARD MATHER, of Bedford, Leigh, 17 January 1620[-1.] To be buried at Leigh.* All lands tents &c in Bedford to Allyce my wife during her life, if she remain unmarried—if she marry or live unchaste &c then &c to the heirs of my own body, Failing to Hugh Mather, son of Hugh Mather of Tildesley & his heirs male, failing to James, another son of the said Hugh, failing to Thomas another son of the said Hugh, failing to John eldest son of the said Hugh, failing to the right heirs of the said Hugh. I give to Ellen Cawdall my sister, wife of Thos Cawdall the sum of 20^s. Rest of goods to Alice my wife & I make her exor.

Debts owing to me Richard Mather.

First. Ellis Greene oweth me for bord wages of himself for one quarter of a yeare after three pounds the yere the some of   xv^s.

Item. Hugh Mather my father-in law   vi^{li}.

Inventory 20 March 1620, £59 10. 10. by Christ Astley, John Ouldham, Thomas Nailer, Wm Crompton.

Proved 22 March 1620[-21.]

Joane Mather, of Warrington, Widow, 1621.

" In the name of God Amen, on the laste daie of September in the yeare of our God 1621. I JOANE MATHER, of Warrington in the Countie of Lancaster wydowe, sicke in bodie but of good & p'fecte minde God I thank therefore doe make & ordayne this my laste will & testament in manner & form followinge.

Before all other thinges I leave my soule into the hands of Allmighty God the Father.—to Jesus Christe the son my redeemer & the Holie Ghost the spirit my sanctifier & my bodie to the earth from whence it came.

Item. I give & leave to Sister Hyde, £10

"   "   "   " my brother W^mBrock, £10.

"   "   "   "   "   " Ric^d Brock of Bunbury, £10.

"   "   "   " his daughter Mary Brock, one of my beste gownes & £5 in money.

I give & bequeathe to Joane Bowden als. Johnson one fether bed one coveringe one blankett & one greate potte also one Petticoate & one und^rcoate which I usually weare."

A small bequest to "my god daughter Jane Gryce." "The reste & remainder of my goodes moveable and immoveable quick & dead I will & bequeath to Wm Brocke my nephewe & his children."

Executors: "My brother Richard Brocke & nephewe Wm Brocke."

Witnesseth. John Wright, Lawrence Shepherd, John Bulling, Wm Brock, Anne Hyde, Joane Bowden.

Invent. by Lawrence Massie, John Dunbabyn, Ric^d Toppinge & Richard Boardman. 1st Oct 1621.

Summa totalis 219^{li}.

* He was buried at Leigh Church, 18 March, 1620-21.

729

John Mather, of Newton in Makerfield, 1624.

JOHN MATHER of Newton in Makerfield [in the parish of Winwick] yeoman 22 March 20 James [1623]. To be buried at Winwick. Thomas son and heir apparent under age. Margaret my now wife. John Mather of Lowton my natural father to have property in Newton and Golborne during the minority of Thomas. Immen Mather my daughter named.
Witnesses Thomas Liptrot, Henry Byrom.
Inventory "praysed by foure honeste men" Hy. Byrom, Richard Baxter, John Johnsonne, & Thos. Storrope [Stirrop], 1 April 1624, £55. 10. 8. An addition to the inventory made 28 Mar. 1625–6; in it are mentioned John Mather father of the deceased, Richard Mather his youngest brother, Jane Hasleden his sister in law, Wm Mather his brother. Thos Mather, Roger Greene his brother in Law & his children, John Ridyard, blacksmith, Margaret Mather and his Fellow Churchwardens [of Winwick].
Proved May 1624.

Raphe Mather, of Warrington, 1625.

RAPHE MATHER of (Conies Corner] Warrington yeoman.
Inventory 13 Oct 1624. £231. 17. 6.
His father-in-laws house. House at Conies corner. Richard Baxter. Goulden Cooke. John Cooke. Peter Spakeman. M^r [or W^m] Bispham. Ellen Spakeman, his sister-in-law. John Higginson. Thomas Miller. Peter Spakeman's field. Raphe Mather of Radcliffe Bridge. John Cook of Winwick. Thomas Highfield. James Boyde. Wm Mather & wife. Thomas Mather his father. Margery wife of s^d Thomas. John Dytchfield. M^r [or W^m] Brooke.
Appraised by Thomas Bisphome. Nathan Ashworth. Geffrey Wilkinson. Henry Mather.
Proved 19 Sept. 1625.

Richard Mather, of Lowton, 1626.

RICHARD MATHER of Lowton, yeoman, 21st Sept. 1626. One third of lands etc to Catherine, my nowe wife for life. The other two thirds to my son John Mather during the life of s^d Catherine, & after her decease my son John to have all lands etc to him & his heirs for ever. Son Nicholas Mather.
Exors John Mather, son.
Overseers Hamlet Warburton my son-in-law & Hy Winterbothome of Kenyon Senr.
Witnesses: Nicholas Mather. John Mather. John Winterbothome.
Inventory by Hy Byrom, John Mather, Geo Darwell, Hy Winterbothome, 29 Sept. 1626. £52. 8. 8.
Proved 12 Oct. 1626.

ABSTRACTS OF THE WILLS OF THE MATHER FAMILY, PROVED IN THE CONSISTORY COURT AT CHESTER FROM 1573 TO 1650.

By J. PAUL RYLANDS, Esq., F.S.A., of Birkenhead, England.

Gabriel Mather, of Radcliffe, 1627.

" In the name of God Amen. I, GABRYELL MATHER of Radcliffe C⁰ of Lancaster Yeoman beinge sicke & weake in bodie but sounde & howle in mynde thanks be to God therefore, & knowing the mortalitie of this bodie & that it is appointed unto all men once to dye, do make & ordayne this my laste will & testament in manner & forme following : firstly & chieflie I leave my soule in the hands of God the Father etc "—

" And as concerninge the goodes & chattels, which it hath pleased God to blesse me withall, my will & minde is that accordinge to the custome of the province wherein I nowe dwell, the same be devyded into 3 equall partes, namely, one third parte commonlie called the deathes p'te I reserve unto myself. Another parte accordinge to the custome I leave unto my wife Elizabethe & the other Third p'te & Remaynder I give & bequeathe unto my six children (that is to saie) unto Raphell, Zacherie, James, Abraham Gabriell & Dorothie equallie to be devyded amongst them."

" To all my grand children iˢ apeece—to all my god children the same.—

" It is my mind & will that my two youngest children Gabriell & Dorothie to wit have xxˢ apeece towards their education "—

" Item. I leave to my sonne Gabriell xlˢ more."

" Item I leave to my sonne Zacherie iiiˡⁱ."

" Item I leave to my mayde Jane Battersbie xxˢ."

" I doe give to my sonne James two bays of howsinge wherein he nowe dwelleth, he mayntaininge the same tenantable duringe the remainder of my lease."

" I ordayne & constitute my loveinge wife Elizabeth & my son Abraham Mather my sole Executors."

Witnesseth—Roger Hardman, James Mather.

Inventory taken " 17 daie of October 1627 by Richard Partington, Thomas Mather Edward Allen & James Mather."

[inter alia] " Memᵈ There is a p'cell of lands which we contende to be a chattel taken by the deceased of the Worshipfull Mʳ Raphe Asshton of Middleton, contain, 21 acres for 21 yeares for 45 pounds ffyne [fine*] which did beginne the 25 March, laste paste.—

Summa totalis 96ˡⁱ iˢ 0ᵈ.

Henry Mather, of Hulton, 1629.

HENRY MATHER of Middle Hulton, co. Lancaster, husbandman, 20 Sept 1627. To be buried at Deane, in my father's burial [place] Debts paid

---

* Fine, here a payment in one sum, instead of an annual rent.

&c. Goods &c to be divided into 3 parts. First part to myself. Second part to Anne Mather now my wife. The third part to all my children, equally divided. Out of my own part, after payment of funeral exps &c. residue to Ralph Mather & James Mather, two of my youngest sons. Exors. Anne Mather, my wife, and Richard Mather my eldest son " and I humblye desyre the right worshipfull my verye goode Ladye, the Ladye Dame Dorothie Lighe [Legh] to be sup'vysore of this my last will.

Witnesses   [Signed]
Thomas Marshe,   HENRYE MATHER.
Adam Grundye,

Inventory taken, 28 May 1629 by Richard Edge, John Russell[?] Thomas Edge, Adam Grundye.

Debts owing by testator,

Ralph Mather his sonne	£1 .. 8 .. 0.	
Elizabeth Earsleye	£1 .. 2 .. 0.	
Funeral Charges at the house & the Church }	£2 .. 18 .. 0.	

Proved 9 April, 1629 by the exors.

James Mather, of Pennington, 1631.

JAMES MATHER of Brockhurst in Pinington [in the parish of Leigh, Lancaster] husbandman 1st Nov. 1630 To be buried at Leigh. And whereas I am seized of a tenement &c. in Brockhurst in Pennington for a certain term of years as by Indenture of lease—now I give the sd lease to Henry Mather my eldest son according to promise at his marriage to Margaret his wife, he the sd Henry paying to his younger brethen, viz. Richard Mather, Thomas Mather, and John Mather &c. And as for goods, &c. to be divided into 2 equal parts. One I reserve for myself the other part I give to my 4 sons, Henry, Richard, Thomas, & John—&c &c.

Makes Henry & John, exors.   [a copy]
Witnesses. Tho Corloes, John Domvill, George Alston.

Inventory 24 June 1631 by Tho Corlaes, Geffrey Mather, Robert Wotmoughe James Greene. £55 .. 14 .. 10.

Proved 25 July 1631.

John Mather, of Lowton, 1633.

JOHN MATHER of Lowton yeoman. 29 Oct. 8 Charles 1632. To be buried at Winwick. Whereas Richard Holland, late of Denton, co. Lanc, Esq deceased by lease dated 16 June 4 James [1606] did for a consideration therein contained lease a tenemt. &c in Lowton wherein I the sd John Mather did then & now dwell for fourscore years if I the sd John Mather party to these p'sents Thos. Mather & John Mather sons of me the said John Mather or any of them so long live at a rent of 17s per annum. Now this my will witnesseth that I the sd John Mather, for the preferment of my wife & children do assign to Margaret now my wife &c. Thos Mather my son. Whereas John Mather late of Newton in Makerfield yeoman deceased by his will dated 22 March 21 James [1624] did give to me John Mather &c lands in Newton & Golborne, co. Lanc, to me after the decease of the sd John Mather of Newton until such time as Thomas Mather son & heir apparent of the sd John M. of Newton is 21. Now for the maintenance &c of the sd Thos. Mather my grandchild & Immen Mather his sister &c. I devise to Roger Harte of Westhoughton co. Lanc, yeoman, the s^d property in Newton & Golborne, to have & to hold until my said Grandchild Thomas Mather shall be 21. To Anne wife of Robert Batte, of Croft my natural* daughter £3. The residue to my son William Mather & Imen & Margaret my daughters equally.

Exors : son Richd Mather & John Hindly of Aspoule [Aspull].

Among Debts &c are mentioned,

Margaret Hale, Anne Hynde, Elizabeth Forster, Roger Fraunce, Henry Hiltom, William Baxter, Jas. Shawe, Humfrey Houghton, and testator's children William, Richard and Margaret.

Inventory by Hy. Byrom, Rd Baxter Tho: Corles, & John Lyptrotte, 16 April, 1633. £154 ·· 4 ·· 6.

Named in the inventory are,

Peter Peterson, Humphrey Houghton, Anne Hynde, Marg^t Hale, Anne Holland, James Shawe, Elizth Forster, Richard Pare [Parr].

Proved 24 April, 1633.

William Mather, of Warrington, 1633.

WILLIAM MATHER of Warrington Yeoman, 26 Aug. 1633. To be buried in our usual burying place in the churchyard of Warrington. Wife Margaret. Money owing by Thomas Middlehurst of Warrington. Land late in the occupation of John Holcrofte of Warrington, Son Wm Mather. Land late in occup^n of Edward Wilson of Warrington, Son Thomas Mather† Daur Jane. Lands late in occup^n of Richard Abraham, Richard Clarke, Mr. Thos Bispham, Nathan Ashworth schoolmaster & Thomas Littlemore, all of Warrington. Exors. "Nathan Ashworth Schoolem^r of the Free Grammer School of Warring[ton]."

Witnesses : Raphe Holland, Edward Wilson.

WILLIAM MATHER.

Proved 15 Sep. 1633.

Immen Mather, of Lowton, Spinster, 1633.

IMMEN MATHER of Lowton, of the parish of Winwick, spinster 5 Oct. 1633.

My Mother. My Sister Alice Harte. My sister Jane Greene. My sister Margaret Mather. My nephew Thomas Mather & his sister Immen Mather. My godchild Robert Harte. My godchild Anne Liptrote. My brother Wm. Mather. My brother Richard Mather executor.

Witnessess :—John Byrom.   the mark Manuell
              Richard Mather.   of Immen Mather.
              John Winterbottom.

Inventory 20 Oct. 1633, by Hy. Byrom, & Rd. Baxter.

The Debts name :—

John Liptrote, Robt. Tickle, Rafe Hasleden, Roger Culcheth, John Morris, Thomas Corleis. £65 ·· 1 ·· 5.

Proved 5 Nov. 1633 by the exōr.

---

* Natural here does not mean illegitimate.

† "Thomas Mather, the attorney," was buried at Warrington, 2 July, 1659.—(Beamont's "Warrington Church Notes," page 81.) Another Thomas was an Ironmonger at Warrington about the same time.—("Wills at Chester, 1660-1680," Record Society's publications, vol. 15, p. 182.)

William Mather, of Warrington, 1634.

A true & lawfull Inventorie of all the goodes & cattels chattels & debtes moveable & immoveable of WM MATHER late of Warrington in the Countie of Lancaster Yeoman dec^d, taken & prised the xiiii day of September An Dom 1633, by these honest & credible p'sons, to wit, Richard Bordman, John Pennington, John Lether & Thomas Fletcher.

In the house.

[*inter alia*] One Joyned chaire, one Twiggen chaire, two throwne chaires, 8 stooles & two little children's chaires.　　　　　　　　　　　　xi^s.

The following rooms are mentioned Butterie, Kitchen nearer chamber at the stairehead, further chamber—Parlor.—Stable.

"In the house at Conies Corner, on Warrington heath side." "In the shoppe." "In chamber over shoppe."

Item: A Tacke of Grounde in Arpley being Two Acres from Thos Mather of the streete.　　　　　　　　　　　　　　　　　　　　x^li.

Item: One house called Sharth House　　　　　　　　　　　xl^li.

Item: Two closes of late ymproved heath ground called by the names of the nearer & the further intack containing by estimation 4 ac. & a half for a terme of yeres.　　　　　　　　　　　　　　　　　　　xxxv^li.

Item: Two closes of late ymproved heath ground, late in occupation of Roger Hughes & Ric Crosbie 3 acres.　　　　　　　　　　　xvi^li.

Item: A parcel of ye late Thos Bulling & Elizabeth Yale, & called The Homes 2 acs. for a terme of yeres　　　　　　　　　　　　xvi^li.

Item: One mortgage of a ten^t from Thos Penkethman Jn^r to s^d Wm Mather for use of children of Thos Thelwall of Holme consideration being £50.

Item: Due by Ellice Macon sen^r & E. M. Junr　　　　　4^li. 6^s.

Item: Due by Thos Littlemore on the annun^cton of our Blessed Ladie Marie, The Virgin, next　　　　　　　　　　　　　　30^ll.

Item: Due by John Launder & the Exors of John Eden.　21^li. 7^s.

Item: In apparrell for the dec^d his back.　　　　　　　　vi^ll.

Smma totalis cclxxii. vii. x.

pr^d x April 1634.

Elizabeth Mather, of Lyme, 1634.

Administration of the goodes & chattles of "ELIZABETH MATHER of Lyme, Countie of Chester wydowe" granted July, 1634, to her daughter Alice Mather, being of the age of 20 years.

Overseers, "John Bretherton, John Leigh of Lyme & Humphrey Barlow de eadem in Countie of Chester yeoman, consanguines."

[On dorso—John Leigh & Humphrey Barlow]

A true & p'fect Inventorie of the goodes &c. that were Elizabeth Mather's late of Lyme Countie of Chester widowe. Praissed by Richard Steele Thomas Chantler & George Mann of Lyme aforesaid 6th July 10th yeare of Charles by the grace of God King of England, Scotland, France & Ireland def of the faith etc.

[*inter alia*] Item: All her app'ell [apparel]　　　　　xxxx^s.

Item: One tacke of ground　　　　　　　　　iii^li. x^s.

Item: Hemp & Too [tow]　　　　　　　　　　xl^s.

Item: All sorts of Lynnens　　　　　　　　　xxxx^s.

Summa totalis £50. 10^s.

Richard Mather, of Whitefield, 1635.

In the name of God Amen 2 Oct. 1626 I RICHARD MATHER of Whitefield in yᵉ parish of Prestwich [cum Oldham] Countie of Lancaster fustian webstar—My " bodie to Parish church yard of Prestwich."—" And as for suche goodes as I had leafte me by my parentes, it is my will & mind & I do give & bequeath them unto my unkell Mylles Mather." To " my measter Richard Rostern 20ˢ." " Item: My brother Thomas to have that one barne & parcel of ground which was left me by my Father. My executors to enjoy the same to the daye of the Purification of the Blessed Virgin Mary next after the date hereof. Till my brother Thomas shall come to 21 years."
" To Margaret Rosterne 5ˢ."
" To my two brethern Wᵐ Mather & Edward Mather."
Executors John Horrocke of the out wood & Mylles Mather my brother.
Witnesses. John Horrock [?] of Toxteth.
          Edward Rostern.
Proved 30 Sept. 1635, by Miles Mather.

John Mather, of Atherton, 1635.

A true & p'fecte Inventorie of all the goods & chattels that were JOHN MATHER'S, late of Atherton [in the parish of Leigh, Lancashire] deceased, not yet administered by vertue of an Assignment made to the said John Mather & one Bradshawe by Ralph Thropp [Thorp] late of Atherton aforesᵈ in trust to certaine uses & Lymittacions as thereby it my appeare, which said Assigmᵗ being for 70 yeares determinable uppon . . . . hath been valued by us whose names are here under written to the summe of Foure pounds
Witness our hands
          Henry Aked
          Gyles Green
          Ricᵈ Thorpe
[endorsed 1635.]

Richard Mather, of Pennington, 1636.

RICHARD MATHER of Brockhurst in Pennington [in the parish of Leigh] co. Lancʳ husbandman, 29 Sep 1636. To be buried at Leigh. Wife Anne enceinte. Children Roger & Anne. Brother John Mather. Brother in Law John Farnworth. Wm Wood.
Exors: bro: in law Jno Farnworth & Brother Hy Mather.
Witnesses:
William Wood ✕ his m'k, Oliver Leigh ✕ his m'k, John Sorocold, Henry Mather.

Debts mention:—

Wm. Urmeston Junʳ, Thoˢ Houlden of Eccles, Nicholas Valentyne, Thoˢ Boydell, John Hasleden, George Mouncke's [Monks] Evan Haydock, Henry Mather, Gawther Kenion, Geoffrey Mather Senʳ, Thoˢ Hardman of Barton, Alex Radcliffe, John Sorocold, Ellen Haslegreeve alias hole. Tho. Batterbie "litle Ann."
Inventory 1 Oct. 1636, by Robert Watmough, John Mather, Richard Wood, Thomas Farnworth. £99 ·· 9 ·· 2.
Proved 18 Nov. 1636, by Hy. Mather.

Samuel Mather, of Radcliffe, 1638.

In the Name of God Amen, the two & twentieth daie of March in the yeare of our Lord God 1635. I SAMUEL MATHER of the Parish of Radcliffe, cloakworker, infirme & weake in bodie but sounde & clere in mynde & memorie, do make this my laste will & testament in manner & forme followeth.

Firstly & before all other things I bequeath my soule in to the hands of Allmighty God, etc. & my bodie to be buried in the Parish Church or Churchyard of Radcliffe.

After payment of funeral Expenses—property to be divided into "three parts, except my howsing & backside which I hould by lease from the Right Worshippfull Raphe Assheton, situate & being in the Parish of Radcliffe, which I give & dispose unto my sonnes Christopher & Abraham."

Mentions, "The bay next Richard Fletchers house"—"Anne my wife."

"to Elizabeth Mather my grand daughter one gowne which was Dorothie's my late wifes.

"To Rachael & Dorothie Mather my grand daughters 5ˢ.

"To Richard, Samuel, John, Abraham & Christopher Mather my grandsons 3ˢ 4ᵈ apeece."

"To James Yate, Elizabeth Yate & Richard Yate my wife's children 3ˢ 4ᵈ apeece.

"To Sarah my brother Renald's daughter 3ˢ 4ᵈ.

Executors Christopher & Abraham Mather.

"My kinsman Abraham Mather overseer."

Witnesses.   Hamlet Sandiforth.
             Thomas Harobinn.
             Richᵈ Davenport.

Inventory 1638 by Abraham Mather, Richard Walker, Richard Manchester, Richard Hardman.   Summa totalis, £110.6.4.

Proved 6 June 1638, by Christopher Mather, Exor.

William Mather, of Lowton, 1638.

WM MATHER of Lowton husbandman.   18 Aug 1638.   To be buried at Winwick.   To sister Margaret Mather £100.   To brother Thomas Mather &c. brother Richard Mather & Jane wife of Brother Richard Mather.   To Thomas Mather which I am uncle to.   To Immen Mather which I am uncle to.   To sister Jane Greene.   Sister Alice Harte.   Sister Anne Batte. Exor Sister Margaret Mather.

Witnesses :—John Byrom, Henry Byrom.

Inventory taken 3 Sep. 1638 by Hy Byrom, Thomas Corles, Henry Corles.

Proved 5 Sep 1638.

John Mather, of Tyldesley, 1638.

In the name of God Amen, on the 7ᵗʰ daie of March 1638 I JOHN MATHER of Tildesley, Parish of Leighe [Lancashire] husbandman—leaves "bodie to be buried in the Parishe Church of Leighe.

"Item.   Whereas my eldest sonne John had 10ˡⁱ lefte him by the laste will & testament of Richard Woodborne deceᵈ his late unkell, & whereas I had the monie, I will that it be repaid him."

Goods into 3 parts. 1ˢᵗ reserves to himself, 2ᵈ part to Margerie his wife & 3ᵈ part equally amongst his children.

His 1ˢᵗ part he wishes after payment of funeral expenses etc. to go to his 4 youngest children namely, William, Hugh, Anne & Margaret.

Executor. " My sonne John & my lovinge wife."

Witnesseth. Thomas Hulton, Ricᵈ Ashley, William Vallentyne.

Inventory by Thomas Hulton, Wᵐ Vallentyne Ricᵈ Partington, Lambert Gall [or Sale], James Mather, 1 April 1638.

Summa totalis 58ˡⁱ 9ˢ 6ᵈ.

Proved 8 October[?] 1639 by Margery Mather, widow, the relict.

John Mather, of Lowton, 1638.

John Mather of Lowton, 25 Nov. 1637. My sons Richard, Nicholas & John (the last under age). My wife Elizabeth. Brothers in law George Darrowe and Hamlet Warbottonn.

Exors. wife Elizabeth & son Nicholas.

Debts mention :—

Nicholas Mather my brother, Roger Croft, Richard Wood, Ralph Chaddocke, Elizabeth Sharlocke, Widow, Thomas Battersbie.

Inventory, 5 Dec. 1637, by James Greene, George Darrow, Thos. Torner, & Richard Holcroft of Lowton, yeoman. £63 ·· 13 ·· 11½.

Witnesses :

mark of Richard Holcroft
H. T. Henry Taylor his mark
Richard Leigh.
Roger Mason.

Proved 1638.

Hamlet Mather, of Manchester, 1639.

In the name of God Amen the eighte daie of January in the yeare of our Lord God 1639 I Hamlet Mather of Manchester in the Countie of Lancaster, servant to Gyles Siddall being sicke in bodie & Infirme, but of sound mynde etc. Property in three parts. I reserve the 1ˢᵗ parte for my self & I take unto my selfe therefrom Tenne Pounds for my discharge in the bringeing of me forthe.* It is my will that the seconde parte be devided to my kinsfolk—first I give and bequeath to my brother Henerye Mather £4—to his sonne Richard Mather 20ˢ—to my brother Richard Mather £4—to my Aunt Mary Horraxe [Horrocks] £4—and the gould receved of the Kinges majᵗⁱᵉ.† Item. I give to her sonne John Horraxe & his wife 13ˢ. 4ᵈ. Item. I give to her grandchild John Horraxe £3. Item: I give to her one daughter Margaret Butterworth the coffer that is at John Rowbotham's house. Item: I give to her daughters Dorothie Wolworke & Elizabeth Towneleye either of them 6ˢ 8ᵈ. I will that the 3ᵈ part be divided between my friends. I will & bequeath to my master Gyles Siddall £10. Item: To Abraham Bouker [Bowker] now servant to James Johnson, my cloake & my beste shuite. [suit] Item: To James Slater that presse of myne which is in his house & 3 of my beste bands that hee

---

* That is for his funeral.

† The " gould " here referred to was a small gold coin given by the King when the recipient was " touched " for the " King's evil," or scrofula. From the Inventory to this Will it appears that the gold coin was a half sovereign given by Charles I. to Hamlet Mather.

can chuse. Item: To Mary Bouker now servante to Gyles Siddall 20ˢ. Item: what is left over the 20ˢ to him that shall preach at my Buriall, to go to my master Gyles Siddall. I desire that Gyles Siddall my master be my Executor.

Witnesses. Ricᵈ Meare Edwᵈ [?——] Thos Briddocke [Brideoake].

A true & perfecte Inventorie and Indent of the Goods & chattels of Hamblet Mather late of Manchester in the Countie of Lanc deceased; Appraized by George Crannige Richard Halliwell vintner, Nathaniel Lownds & James Slater the xiii daye of April in yᵉ year of our Lord God 1640. Among many other items is:—

Item: One peece of gould given unto him by the Kings' Maj' for the Kings ewell. [evil]   xᵈ

Summa totalis   49ˡⁱ.   14ˢ.   6ᵈ.

Exhibit' xx Aprilis 1640.

Proved 14 Feb. 1639 [—40.]

The Rev. Richard Mather, of Castle Northwich, 1640.

In the name of God Amen. I RICHARD MATHER of Castle Northwich within the Chapelry of Witton in the Countie of Chester clerke.—being sicke in bodie but of perfect memorie praisse & laud be to God therefor do make & ordayne etc. I commit my bodie to the earth to be interred within the chancell of the Cappell of Witton aforesᵈ Imprimis To my deare lovinge wife Elizabeth Mather, all that my messuage & tenement situated in Warrington Countie of Lancaster, with th' appert's for the terme of her natural life, if she continue in my name & keepe herselfe sole & unmarried & live in a chaste comely & discreet manner. Mentions "all my children duringe their minority." "To my sonne Samuel Mather when he attains yeares of discretion"—"my sonne Benjamin"—"my daughters Martha, Mary & Hester Mather."—Executrix, his wife. "My worthy friends Mʳ Burrowes viker of Runckhorne [Runcorn] Mʳ Richᵈ Pigot of Witton aforesᵈ Thomas Robinson of Northwich, Peter Venables of Lostocke—my brother-in-law Richᵈ Wroe & my Lovinge kinsman Nicholas Mather of Warrington overseers."

9ᵗʰ Sept. 1640.

Witnesses. Ricᵈ Pigott.
Thos Robinson.

[A note is enclosed—as follows:]

A note of all such bookes as I Richard Mather clerke doe give unto the overseers of my will & other speciall friends as followeth:

To Mʳ Burrowes. Docʳ Dauenant [Davenant] upon the Collects.

To Mʳ Pigot, Rogers Catichisme & the treatis[e] of the sacraments, both bound up together.

To Thos. Robinson. Elton upon the viiiᵗʰ of Romans.

To Peter Venables such a booke as Mʳ Pigot shall think fitt & so also for my brother Wroe—cosen Nicholas Mather—Wᵐ Venables his sonne—& other friends whom I have mentioned to him.

To Mʳ Robert Venables the younger Renalls three . . . . . . [?] in one volume.

[Signed] RICHARD MATHER.

Inventory—27 Sept. 1640 by Richard Pigot Thomas Robinson Peter Venables Wᵐ Venables Nicholas Mather [all signatures].

Summa totalis £51. 14ˢ. 9ᵈ.

Thomas Mather, of Eccleston, 1641.

In the name of God Amen, I, THOMAS MATHER of Eccleston neare Croston in the Countie of Lancaster Bricklayer*—etc. Property into 3 parts—reserves one part—2^d part to his wife [Margery.] 3^d part to his 3 sons Adam John & William 1^s to every godchild.

Item I give to every one who shall owe me any money with consideration att the tyme of my death, a third pte of the use or consideration.

Rest & remainder equallie between his two sonnes. John & William.

And whereas I have a messuage & tenement situate in Asley in the parish of Leigh within the Countie of Lancaster I do leave the same to Adam my son & whereas I have a messuage & tenement for the term of 4 score & 19 years I do leave the same to Margery my wife & Adam my sonne, equallie between them. Mentions " An Indenture made by Alice Gradell of Ulnes walton widow & Christopher her son, both deceased."

I herewith grant & assign the new house lately erected att the east end of my new dwelling house unto my son William.—& the lofte of my house unto my s^d sonnes John & William.

Also that messuage which I hold on lease from Richard Ld Viscount Molyneux dec^d & by the demise of Wm Diconson of Heskyn gent called by the general names of Loe close & The Longe Butts.—I bequeath unto Margery my wife.

Margery my wife to mayntaine W^m my son in clothes meate & drinke so long as he is apprentice to Richard Wareing.

Witnesses   Robt. Hodson.
         Ric^d Wareing.

Dettes oweing unto me the s^d Testator

From Robert Spencer	40^s
" John Simpson	20^s
" Rob^{te} Kokker	10^s

Inventory by Robt Hodson of Ulnes Walton yeom̄ James Mather of Tildesley yeom̄ Ric Waringe & James Blackborne of Eccleston yeom̄ 7 March 1640[-1].

Sum tot. £212. 8. 6.

Proved 10 March 1641[-2.]

Ellen Mather, of Atherton, 1647.

Feby 1646-7. Administration of goods of ELLEN MATHER of Atherton, granted to Ralph Mather.

Bondsman, Wm Bennet.

William Mather, of Warrington, 1647.

21 Oct 1647. Administration of goods of Wm MADDERS of Warrington, granted to Edward Evered.

Endorsed. Administration of the goods of Wm Mather late of Warrington, 1647.

Geoffrey Mather, of West Leigh, Co. Lanc., 1648.

23 Oct 1648 : Administration of goods of JEFFRAY MATHER, late of West Ley, Yeoman, granted to John Williamson of West Ley [Leigh] husbandman.

---

* The " Bricklayer " of 1641 was the equivalent of the modern " builder " and " contractor."

Joan Mather mentioned & described as his widow & relict.

Inventory, by William Grundy, Heath Radcliffe, Roger Ranikares & John Greene.

Summa totalis, 35^{li}. 00^s. 04^d.

William Mather, of Warrington, 1649.

30 Jan 1648[-9]. Administration of goods of Wm MATHER, late of Warrington, granted to Margaret Mather, widow, mother of deceased.

John Mather of Warrington yeoman bondsman. [Signed]

John Mather.

William Mather, Junior, of Warrington, 1649.

Administration of Goods of Wm MATHER junior, late of Warrington granted to Margaret Mather, mother of deceased.

Bondsman, Edward Evered jun^r of Warrington 4th April 1649.

Robert Mather, of West Leigh, co. Lanc. yeoman, 1618.

[From the original will in the possession of Mr. J. P. Earwaker, M.A., F.S.A.]

In the Name of god Amen vpon the xxixth day of May In the yeares of the Raigne of our Sou^raigne Lord James By the grace of god kinge of England ffraunce and Jreland the ffyfteenth and of Scotland the ffyfty, the Defender of the ffaith &c 1617, I Robert Mather of westleighe in the County of Lancaster yeoman feellinge my selffe sick and disseased in bodie yet of a good and p'fecte memorie Lawde and praise bee to the almightie for the same Doe constitute ordaine and make this my p'sente Testamente and last will in manner and forme ffollowinge viz. ffirst and aboue all thinge J commend my soule into the mercifull Custodie of my Lord and Saviour Jesus Christe by whose ffree mercy and grace I do assuredly truste to bee saued and my body to bee buried in Christian buriall* And as concerneinge all such goods as god hath geven mee the vse and Custodie of, J will the same to bee bestowed in such manner and forme as heareafter in theis p'sente is menconed and Expressed That is to saie ffirst I giue and bequeath vnto Wiłłm, John, Marie, Anne and Jenett p'tington [Partiugton] Children of John p'tington of Tildisley eu^rie oue ij^s vj^d a peece And vnto Christopher, Elizabethe, Ellin and Wiłłm Manne Children of James Manne of Tildisley afforesaid eu^rie one ij^s vj^d.   And vnto Jenet, Katherin, Margrett, Elizabeth and Anne Liptrott dawghters of Wiłłm Liptrott of westleighe aforesaid eu^rie one ij^s vj^d And vnto Richard Hawghton Nicholas and Anne Hawghton Children of James Hawghton late of Arburie deceased eu^rie one ij^s vj^d   And vnto Symon Mather Geffrey Mather Robert John James and Ellin Mather Children of Geoffrey Mather my Brother eu^rie one v^{li} equally to bee devyded amongst them and the survyv^r and Survyvo^{rs} of them, and to bee paid vnto them at such tymes as they shall and doe come to and accomplishe the ffull age of Twenty and one yeares and in the meane tyme to bee vsed for the most gaine profitt and aduantage of the said Children of my said brother Geoffrey Mather by my executors hereafter named, Itm I giue vnto Symon Mather aĺs Morton my base sonne the some of xiij^{li} vj^s viij^d And yf my said sonne happen to dye before he shall or doe attaine to the age of xiiij yeares then and in such Case J doe geue and bequeath the same some of

* He was buried at Leigh Church, 4th June, 1617.

xiij^{li} vj^s viij^d vnto the said sixe Children of my said brother Geffrey Mather
and to bee vsed and delyu^{r}ed [delivered] vnto them in such manner and forme
as ys mente Concerneinge there [their] other former Legacyes, Jtm. J geue
& bequeath vnto Elline Mather ats Morton my base Dawghter the sume of
vj^{li} xiij^s viij^d And if she happen to dye before she doe or shall come to the
age of xiiij yeares Then and [in] such Case J doe geue and bequeathe the
same some of vj^{li} xiij^s viij^d vnto the said sixe Children of my said brother
Geffrey Mather And to bee vsed and delyu^{r}ed [delivered] vnto them in
such manner & forme as is mente concerninge there [their] other former
Legacies, Jtm. J geve vnto Anne Mather nowe wyfe of the said Geoffrey
Mather my Sister in lawe v^{li}. Jtm. J giue vnto Robert Whittell ats Brown-
lowe Wi$t$$t$m Manne & Rob'te Whittell whom J am godfather vnto eu^{r}ie
[every] one xij^d and vnto my said brother Geoffrey Mather J giue my
truncke and vnto the said Anne my Cheeste [chest] Jtm. J gyve and bequeath all the Residue of my goods Cattells Chattells & Debts ouer and
besydes the dischargeinge of my ffunerall expences and legacies hearein
Conteynned & men$\bar{c}$oned vnto the said Geoffreye Mather my Brother. Jtm.
J constitute ordeyne and make the said Geoffrey Mather my brother and
James Sorrowcoulde my True and Lawfull Executo^{rs} to execute p'forme &
ffulfill the same in all things as my Trust is in them aboue others.

Sealled signed & pupplished   [Signed with marks
in the p'sence and sight of   probably intended for
Geoffrey Mather, Junior ⎫ [all good   the letters R. M.
Robert Mather, Jū. &   ⎬ signatures]   and sealed with an
John Whittells.   ⎭   illegible seal.]

An indorsement in Latin to the effect that the Will was proved before
David Yale, Doctor of Laws, Chancellor of the Supreme Court and Spiritual
vicar of Thomas [Moreton] Bishop of Chester, 4th July 1618, by the
executors in the Will named; a full and true inventory to be exhibited.

NOTE BY THE EDITOR OF THE REGISTER.

Mrs. Hannah Mather Crocker, author of "Observations on the Real Rights
of Woman" and other works, was a daughter of Rev. Samuel and Mrs. Hannah
(Hutchinson) Mather, and a granddaughter of Rev. Cotton Mather, author of
the "Magnalia." She was born at Boston, June 27, 1752; married April 15,
1789, Joseph Crocker, H. C. 1774, born Feb. 24, 1749, died Nov. 13, 1797. She
died at Roxbury, July 10, 1829. Her descent from John[1] Mather of Lancashire
is through Thomas,[2] Rev. Richard[3] Mather of Dorchester, Rev. Increase,[4] Rev.
Cotton,[5] and Rev. Samuel[6] Mather, her father. She left in manuscript a volume
of "Reminiscences and Traditions of Boston," now in the possession of the
New-England Historic Genealogical Society. From this volume we quote the
following :

"Mr. Richard Mather was born in Lancaster in a small village called Lowton
in the year 1596. The family can be traced to John. Thomas was his son, and
Richard was son of Thomas.

"The chair in the Antiquarian room [i.e. the rooms of the American Antiquarian Society, Worcester, Mass.] belonged to Thomas. Richard sat in it when
a child. He was married in 1624; his children that were born in Europe sat in
the chair before he came to this country—Samuel, Timothy, Nathaniel, Joseph.
The last named sat in it when he brought the chair to America. Eleazer and
Increase were born in America. They both sat in the same chair. The chair
descended to Increase, and all his children sat in the same. It came in line
to Cotton Mather. His children all sat in the same. It descended to his son
Samuel, and his children sat in the same chair. His youngest daughter [Han-
nah, the writer of these notes] was the only child that had any children, and
she has had ten children sit in the chair, and several grandchildren."

"As the regular line of Mather has run out, she wished the chair to be deposited in the antiquarian rooms with the venerable shades, that those who come after her may look to the rock from whence they were hewn, and find an ancient seat to rest any chip of the old block. As she flatters herself, there may at some future day a sprig spring from the root Jesse, and the tribe of Levi return to their rest, when she is at rest in another world."

Rev. Increase Mather, in his "Life and Death of Mr. Richard Mather" (Cambridge, 1670), says: "There is in the Parish of Winwick, the County of Lancaster, a small country town or village called Lowton, in which village Richard Mather was born, Anno 1596. His parents, Thomas and Margaret Mather, were of ancient families in Lowton aforesaid, but by reason of some unhappy mortgages they were reduced to a low condition as to the World." He does not give the name of the father of Thomas.

His son, Rev. Cotton Mather, in his "Parentator: Remarkables of Increase Mather" (Boston, 1724), does not give even the name of the father of Richard. There was a Jeremiah Mather in Boston in 1681, between whom and Rev. Richard Mather no connection has been traced. See REGISTER, vol. 36, page 402.

SOME DEEDS OF THE MATHER FAMILY OF WEST LEIGH, LANCASHIRE, 1609 to 1632.

By J. PAUL RYLANDS, Esq., F.S.A., of Birkenhead, England.

BY the kindness of Mr. J. P. Earwaker, M.A., F.S.A., I have had an opportunity of examining a bundle of fifteen old documents relating to the Mathers of West Leigh, which belong to Mr. W. Ecroyd, of Lomeshaye, Nelson, Lancashire; and I have made the following abstracts of them. The seals appended to the deeds are of very little interest, being (with the exception of that to the bond of 3 February, 1617, which displays the arms of the Lancashire family of Byrom of Byrom Hall, differenced by a crescent) merely fanciful figures of birds and quadrupeds.

The signatures of Geoffrey Mather, Symond Mather, and Geoffrey Mather junior, are in the style of handwriting used by fairly educated persons in the seventeenth century; those of Sorocolds, Alexander Radcliffe and William Crompton suggest a higher standard of education. The tracings of the Mather signatures, which I send,* may be of service hereafter for purposes of identification when more is known of the early history of the family.

Symond Mather, of West Leigh, yeoman, whose will is printed in the REGISTER under date 1588, was the father of Geoffrey Mather the elder and Robert Mather of Newstead, co. Notts., who are named in the deeds. Robert returned to West Leigh and died in 1617; his will is also printed in the REGISTER.

Geoffrey Mather, the elder, married at Leigh Church, 12 December, 1591, Anne Parr, and their children, Symond (who was buried at Leigh 28 September, 1617), Geoffrey, Ellen, Robert, John and James, are all named in the deeds, they were baptized at Leigh Church, and the records of these baptisms will be found in "The Registers of the Parish of Leigh, Lancashire, 1558–1625, edited by J. H. Stanning, M.A., Vicar, 1882," together with the marriages of Margaret Partington, Jane Liptrott, and Ann Monne or Man, the sisters of Geoffrey Mather the elder. The marriage of another sister to James Haughton of Arbury in Winwick parish is not recorded in the Leigh registers.

The property owned by Geoffrey Mather passed at last to the Sorocold family. One of the Sorocolds is mentioned in Roger Lowe's Diary :—" March 1672-3. 7 friday night died Capt. [John] Sorrowcold an old cannibell that hath orethrowne many families but he hath now arrived at his one [own] place, abundance of gold and silver is found under his handes." ("Local Gleanings relating to

---

* They are preserved by the New-England Historic Genealogical Society.—EDITOR.

Lancashire and Cheshire," Vol. I., pp. 191, 215, Vol. II., p. 31, where some notices of the Sorocolds will be found.) There is an interesting remnant of the feudal system in the lease of 7 July, 1632.

I have added some genealogical memoranda of Gilbert Mather of the Soak in Hampshire, who was born in Lancashire in 1522, which were communicated to "Notes and Queries"; and an abstract of a Writ dated 1417, from the Risley Charters, which mentions Mathew and Richard Mather of Culcheth in Winwick parish, the name being written "le Madour."

I have not met with any armorial seal of the Mathers bearing the arms attributed to them; but in 1706 Abraham Mather and Richard Mather witnessed a deed to which the parties were Richard Clough of Kenyon, in the parish of Winwick, Chapman, of the one part, and Thomas, Viscount Fauconberg of the other part, and Clough used an oval seal bearing the letters A. M. above a heater shaped shield displaying *a chevron between three pairs of compasses*, which was evidently Abraham Mather's seal. The arms of the Carpenters' Company of London, granted 6 Edw. VI., A.D. 1552, were *Argent, a chevron engrailed between three pairs of compasses Sable*, and it is probable that this coat is intended to be represented on Abraham Mather's seal.

Abstracts of Deeds relating to Geoffrey Mather of West Leigh, co. Lancaster, yeoman.

20 December 41 Eliz. 1598. *Counterpart of a Lease* (not executed) by Geffraye Mather and Richard Arrowsmyth, of Westleigh, co Lanc., yeomen, to Roberte Grenehalghe, of Lawton [Lowton] co. Lanc. yeoman, of 12 acres of land in West Leigh, called "the furthest eyes, the old medowe, the little dam, and the ferdell crofte," 6 closes; and liberty during the term for Robert Grenehalgh to drive cattle through "the meane eyse nowe in the holdinge of Gefferay Strange and Thomas Corlus leading towards Lawton Common," as also through other ground of the said Geoffrey Mather "leading towards Westleigh mylne or leigh." Term 10 years from 25 Decr 1598. Consideration £55 fine and 10s. 6d. per annum. There is a recital of an Indenture dated 2 Sept. 20 Eliz. whereby James Scaresbrecke of Down Holland, co. Lanc. gent., and Anne his wife, demised the premises to Symond Mather deceased [who died 1588] father of the said Geoffrey for 60 years if the said Anne Scaresbrecke should so long live. There is also a recital of an Indenture dated 10 March 26 Eliz. whereby Symond Mather assigned the premises to the said Richard Arrowsmyth, apparently as a trustee for Symond.

28 April 1609. *Bond* from Geffrey Mather of West Leigh, yeoman, and Robert Mather of Newsteede, co. Nottingham, yeoman, to James Sorowcolde of Newton in Makerfield, co Lanc., in £80, conditioned for the performance of covenants in an Indenture of even date. Witnesses to Geffrey Mather's signature: Jhon Assheton, Thomas Thelwall, Richard Grundy, and Roger Jameson. Witnesses to Robert Mather's signature: Rich: Vrmstonn, John Thomasson, Ja: Sorocoulde Junr, 1 die Martii 1610.

2 April 1615. *Demise* from James Massye of Hindley, co. Lanc., gent. to Geoffrey Mather of Weastley, yeoman, for 400 years, at a peppercorn rent, of lands called Geoffrey Mather's house in West Leigh, being 9 closes called "the furmoste eyes, hough, newe meadowe, twoe marled earthes, Hampsone meadowe, the entrye, the greate dame meadow, and the fardyle crofte," 21 acres 3 roods, theretofore demised to James Sorocoulde for 400 years (2 other closes called Jeppe greasse and crofte by Greenes, 2½ acres, theretofore sold to Richard Arrowsmith and his heirs excepted). Witnesses: Christofer Stanynoghte, Christofer Strange.

12 April, 1615. *Deed Poll* by which Geoffrey Mather of West Leigh assigns to Thomas Parr of P[en]kett, co. Lanc. yeoman and Gerrard Johnson of . . . . . . co. Lanc. innkeeper, for the maintenance of Anne wife of the said Geoffrey and his children Ellen Mather, Robert Mather, John Mather, and James Mather, certain lands which James Massye of Hindley had leased to the said Geoffrey, called Geoffrey Mather's house in West Leigh with fields called "the furmost eyes, hough, new meadow, the entrye, the great dam meadow, and the fardyle croft, 21 acres 3 roods, theretofore let to James Sorocould, two parcels called Jeppe grease and Croft by Greenes (2½ acres) theretofore sold to Richard Arrowsmyth and his heirs excepted. Witnesses: Henry Byrom, Richard Arrowsmith's mark, Roger Ranicar's mark, Henry Raynolds.

30 May 1615. *Deed Poll*, in latin, by which James Massie of Hindley, co. Lanc., Esq. for good causes and in performance of the confidence reposed in him by Geoffrey Mather of Westleigh, yeoman, grants to Simon Mather, son and heir apparent of the said Geoffrey, and his heirs, a messuage in West Leigh in the occupation of Geoffrey and all those closes &c theretofore assured to James Sorocoulde of Pynnington, gent, and Richard Arrowesmith of West Leigh, husbandman. Ralph Southworth and Henry Byrom of Westleigh, gents. are appointed the attorneys to deliver seizin to Simon Mather. Witnesses: John Pattin(?), William Blackburne, Henry Asheton, Ja: Sorocoulde, Ja: Sorocoulde Junr, Robert Whittell. This is a copy attested by Ja: Sorocoulde and Ja: Sorocoulde Junr.

10 January 1615[-16.]. *Demise, by way of mortgage*, by Geoffrey Mather of West Leigh, yeoman, and Symon Mather of West Leigh, yeoman, son and heir of the said Geoffrey, to James Sorocould of Brockhurst in Pynnington [in the parish of Leigh] co: Lanc. yeoman, of the old meadow, the damm, the little damm meadow, the lower barn heys, the two widdows field and the foure acre, in all 18 acres of land in West Leigh, for 400 years; consideration £357. Witnesses: Rich. Vrmstonn, Rich. Man, Robt. Watmoughe, Henry Moese, Thomas Boydell, Ja: Sorocoulde Junr, George Sorocoulde, John Sorocoulde, Gouth^r Kirfote.

10 January 1615–16. *Demise, by way of mortgage*, by Geoffrey Mather of West Leigh yeoman, and Symon Mather of West Leigh yeoman his son and heir apparent to James Sorocoulde of Brockhurst in Pynnington, co. Lanc. yeoman, of 2 closes in West Leigh called "the Healey Eyes and the lytle cowe hey" 6 acres, for 3 years, to secure £30, to be repaid at the rate of £10 a year. A provision consolidates with this a demise by way of mortgage of even date. Witnesses: Rich: Urmstonn, Robert Watmoughe, Henry Moese, Thomas Boydell, Ja: Sorocoulde Junr, Rich Man.

3 February 1617[-18]. *Bond* from Geoffrey Mather of West Leigh, yeoman, son of Geoffrey Mather, of West Leigh, yeoman, to James Sorocoulde, of Brockhurst in Pennington, yeoman, in £70, for the performance by Geoffrey Mather the father of covenants in an Indenture dated 10 Jan.

1615[–16]. Witnesses: Robert Watmoughe, Gowther Kirfoote, Thomas Corles, Ja: Sorocoulde, Junr.

1 May 1618. *Demise, by way of mortgage,* by Geoffrey Mather the elder, of Weasley, yeoman, and Geoffrey Mather the younger, his son and heir apparent, to James Sorocoulde, of Brockhurst in Pynington, yeoman, of Higher Barne Hey in West Leigh, 3 acres, for 400 years; consideration £50 : 5 : 6. Witnesses: Richard Vrmstonn, Nycholas Lythgo, George Sorocoulde.

1 May 1618. *Bond* from Geoffrey Mather the elder and Geoffrey Mather the younger, to James Sorocoulde, in £80, for the performance of covenants in an Indenture of even date. Witnesses: Rich: Vrmstonn, Nycholas Lythgo, George Sorocoulde.

20 March 1620[21]. *Defeazance* of lands in West Leigh, between James Sorocolde, of Brockhurst in Pynnington, gent., Rauffe Sorocolde, of Newton in Makerfield, co. Lanc., gent., and Robert Watmough, of Lawton [Lowton] co. Lanc., yeoman, of the one part, and Geoffrey Mather, of Westleigh, gent., and Geoffrey Mather his son and heir apparent of the other part. Reciting an Indenture of bargain and sale of even date to Ralph Sorocoulde and Robert Watmough and their heirs [as trustees] by the appointment of James Sorocoulde, of "the oulde medowe, the dam, the litle dam medowe, the twoe barne heyes, the twoe widowes fields, the foure acre, a parcel of land lying upon the north side of the great cowe hey, and one parcel in the west end of the Henley Eyes (one little parcel of land and one usual way leading from the dwelling of the said Geoffrey to Strange Common excepted). And reciting that the lands were formerly granted to James Sorocold his executors &c by lease for a great number of years, it was agreed that if the said Geoffrey Mather or his heirs should pay to James Sorocoulde either £24 : 1 : 6 for each acre, or a certain specified sum for each field (amounting in the whole to £466 : 3 : 2) that as such payments were made such parts of the premises should be reconveyed by James Sorocoulde, Rauffe Sorocoulde and Robert Watmough to Geoffrey Mather &c. Witnesses: Alexander Radclyffe, Rich: Vrmstonn, Richard Grundy, Wm Crompton.

20 March 1620[–21]. *The Counterpart,* witnessed by Henry Byrom, Alexander Radclyffe, Wm. Crompton.

15 June 1621. *Deed of feoffment,* between Geoffrey Mather, of Westleigh, gent., and Geoffrey Mather his son and heir apparent of the one part, and Richard Urmeston, of Pynington, gent., and William Crompton, of Bedford [in the parish of Leigh] co. Lanc. yeoman, of the other part, of lands in West Leigh, to the use of Geoffrey Mather the elder for life, and after his death as to one half to the use of Anne his wife for her life, and as to the other half and the reversion of the former half to the use of Geoffrey Mather the son, his heirs and assigns. Power of Geoffrey the father to grant by deed or will an annuity of 40 shillings, charged on the lands, for any future wife or wives of his (one Alice Swan of Pynnington only excepted) for her or their life or lives. Witnesses: Roger Ranicker's mark, Richard Grundy, Christopher Strang, Richard Man's mark. Memorandum endorsed that on 16 June 1621 possession was given to Richard Urmeston and William Crompton in the presence of the same witnesses.

4 March 1624–5. *Deed of feoffment,* between Geoffrey Mather, of West Leigh, yeoman, Geoffrey Mather, of West Leigh, yeoman, his son and heir apparent, and Ann Mather, wife of Geoffrey the father, of the one part, and George Sorocold, of Brockhurst, yeoman, of the other part, of lands in

West Leigh; consideration £112. Alexander Radclyffe and William Crompton appointed attorneys to deliver seizin. Witnesses to the signatures of Geoffrey Mather the father and Geoffrey Mather the son: Alex: Radcliffe, Thomas Corles son of James, Robert Tickle, William Tickle, Ja: Sorocolde. Witnesses to the signature (mark) of Anne Mather: Henry Byrom, Alex: Radcliffe, Roberte Watmoughe, Ja: Sorocolde, Wm: Crompton, Jo: Sorocolde, Thomas fforbor. Memorandum endorsed that on 30 April 1625 seizin of the lands was given by Alexander Radcliffe and William Crompton to George Sorocold in the presence of Henry Byrom, Ja: Sorocolde, Robert Watmoughe, Geffrey Mather [the elder] Thomas fforbor, Jo: Sorocolde. Memorandum endorsed that on 7 July 1632, seizin of a close of land, parcel of the within mentioned lands was delivered by Alexander Radcliffe and William Crompton to George Sorocold in the presence of: Richard Grundy, Robert Watmoughe, Geffrey Mather [the elder] Christopher Strange Junior's mark, Jeffrey Mather [the younger].

7 July 1632. *Counterpart of a Lease*, by George Sorocolde, of Ashton in Makerfield, co. Lanc. yeoman, to Geoffrey Mather, of West Leigh, yeoman, for the lives of Geoffrey Mather the elder, Geoffrey Mather the younger, and James Mather another son of Geoffrey the elder, of a messuage in West Leigh, and the little cow hey, the higher barn hey, land situate at the east end of the Henley eyes, land at south east corner of the great cow hey, 2 closes called Pingotts, the rood land situate in a meadow called Hart's meadow; in all 15 acres 1 rood large measure; rent 22s. 10½d. per annum. There is a covenant by Geoffrey Mather during the term that he his executors or assigns will "beare carry and showe one muskett peece wth the furniture thereunto belonging when & as often as the s^d George Sorocoulde his heirs or assigns shall be comanded to showe a muskett with the furniture thereof as aforesaid for such landes as the said Geffrey Mather the father & Geffrey Mather the sonne have sould unto James Sorocould the late father of the said George and unto him the said George, hee the said George Sorocold his heirs & assignes upon his and their costs & chardges fynding & provyding from tyme to tyme the said muskett peece & furniture aforesaid during the said terme." Witnesses: Henry Byrom, Richard Grundy, Alex: Radcliffe, Roberte Watmoughe, Wm. Crompton, Jeffrey Mather Junr.

Extracts from the Parish Registers of Leigh, in the County of Lancaster.

The Rev. J. H. Stanning, M.A., Vicar of Leigh, has kindly sent for publication the following extracts relating to the Mather family, in continuation of the Mather entries in his " Registers of the Parish of Leigh, Lancashire, from February 1558 to March 1625," printed in 1882.

Marriages.

1627 May 15. John Mather & Ellen Cowdall.
1627–8 February 11. John Mather & Katherine Partington.
1632 November 10. Jeffrey Mather & Ellen Arrosmyth.
1637 August 1. James Mather & Elizabeth Strange.
1638–9 January 27. Symond Mather & Margaret Flightwood.
1639 July 3. John Mather & Margaret Smith.
1639–40 February 8. Richard Grundie & Ellin Mather.

Burials.

1625 April 7. John Mather de Atherton.
1626 May 13. John Mather de Bedford.

1626-7 Jany 12. ux[or] William Liptrott de Westleigh.
1630 April 10 [20?]. John Mather de Astley.
" October 10. Jeffrey Mather al[ia]s Collier.
1631 June 24. James Mather de Pinington.
1638 October 16 [?] James Mann of Tilesley.
1639 March 29. Jefferie Mather of Westley.
1644 July 25. James Mather of Tildsley.
1665 April 22. Gentkin Mather de Abram.
1666 May 12. Abram Mather de Radclife parish.
" May 20. A da[ughter] of Henry Mather de Pinington.
1666-7 March 20. Margery Mather, widdow de Tildsley.
1668 July 11. Simon Mather de Lowton.
Sep. 20. John Mather of Westleigh.
1671-2 March 10. Richard son of Richard Mather of Shakerley.

Gilbert Mather of Soak, Hampshire.

The following genealogical memoranda were communicated to *Notes & Queries* (8th S. IV. October 14, 1893) by Mr W. D. Macray. They occur in the calendar prefixed to a Roman Breviary, printed at Lyons in 1556, now in the Bodleian Library, and have been inserted by one Gilbert Mather. The writer's own name, Gilbert Mather, occurs in several parts of the volume, which, in 1566, was possessed by one Ambrose Barnabye.

Jan. 13. 1544. I was maryed at Eastone
Jan. 20. 1561. Gilbertus Mather filius meus natus fuit.
Feb. 9. 1551. Nata fuit Alicia filia mea apud Chilbolton.
Feb. 26. 1542. I cam[e] fyrst to Winchester.
March 19. 1547. Natus fuit Thomas Mather filius meus
March 26. 1548. Sepultus fuit predictus Thomas.
April 5. 1539. I cam[e] fyrst to Chippen[ham]
April 15. 1554. Natus fuit Henricus filius meus.
April 17. [or 19] 1546. Natus fuit Thomas Mather senior filius meus.
June 3. 1553. I toke possessyone of my howse in the Soke [Hampshire].
June 15. 1522. I was borne at Weryngtone in Lancashere
July 6. 1568. Natus fuit Gilbertus Mather filius meus
July 10. 1539. I was bounde prentise in Norwiche.
Sept. 20. 1553. I cam[e] into my howse in the Soke fyrst to dwell after I had bowght the same.
Sept. 27. 1549. I cam[e] to Chilboltone [Hampshire] to dwell.
Oct. 3. 1545. I was sworne tenante at Chilboltone.
Nov. 12. 1549. Nata fuit Elizabeth filia mea apud Chilboltone.
Dec. 15. 1546. I cam[e] into the Soke to dwell there, being tenante to Richard Harrold.

From the Risley (co. Lancaster) Charters.

16 August, 5 Henry V. (A.D. 1417) WRIT to the Sheriff of Lancashire commanding him to attach James son of Ric. de Radcliff of Radcliff to answer Nicholas de Risley of Risley, wherefore he with Ric. de Radclyf of Radclyf, Armiger, Oliver de Entwissel of Bury, Gentilman, John de Rothwell of Radclyf, yoman, John Atkinson of Pilkington, yoman, Thomas Acson of Pilkington, yoman, Wm. le Walker of Radclyf, yoman, *Mathew le Madour of Culcheth*, husbandman, *Ric. le Madour of Culcheth*, husbandman, and Roger de Hertleghes of Culcheth, by force and arms broke the close of the said Nicholas at Risley and him took and imprisoned at Radclyf and took away four cows and other enormities then did.

THE PARENTS OF REV. RICHARD MATHER.

WILLIAM FERGUSON IRVINE, Esq., honorary treasurer of the Parish Register Society, 4 Eaton Road, Birkenhead, England, writes to the Editor of the REGISTER under the date of March 19, 1900, as follows:

DEAR SIR:

Adverting to the Notes on the Mather Family, printed in the REGISTER in 1893, from the pen of Mr. J. Paul Rylands, I now send an extract from the Parish Register of Warrington, which looks very much as if it might refer to the marriage of the parents of the Rev. Richard Mather. You will remember, doubtless, that Samuel Clark, in his Life of Mather, says that "his parents Thomas & Margaret Mather were of ancient families in London." Richard himself was born in 1596.

The entry is as follows:

1591. September.
Thomas Mather & Margrett Abrā the same [*i.e.* married 30th day].

The entry is made in a little larger hand writing than that preceding and succeeding it, and so looks as if they were people of more consequence than the usual run of folk.

There was a family of Abrams or Abrahams in Warrington at the time who were strong Puritans; at all events their children in the first half of the 17th century were, so that this also tends to confirm the supposition.

Yours truly,
WM. FERGUSON IRVINE.

THE MAVERICK FAMILY.

By Isaac John Greenwood, A.M., of New York city.

Some twenty years since, looking over the late Col. Joseph L. Chester's MS. catalogue of Oxford graduates, my attention was drawn by him to the name of "John Maverick, 1595, Exeter College, from Devon, Minister."

Foster's Catalogue, much fuller in details, reads as follows:

"Maverick, John of Devon, cler. fil., Exeter Coll., matric. 24 Oct. 1595, aged 18; B.A. 8 July 1577; M.A. 7 July 1603; then in orders, rector of Beaworthy (s.w. of Hatherly), Devon, 1615. (See Foster's Index Eccl.)."

This was undoubtedly "the godly Mr. Maverick," whom Roger Clap, born on the Devonshire coast, at Salcomb (between Sidmouth and Branscomb), speaks of as living "forty miles off," and who, after establishing a congregation at Dorchester, N. E., died Feb. 3, 1636-7, being, according to Winthrop, "near sixty years of age."

Though we hear nothing of his wife, she is alluded to in 1665, by Col. Cartwright, in his "Memorial* concerning the Massachusets," who observes:

"If any of the commissioners think it more convenient for them to stay in those parts, that they may haue leue to do so. For Mr. Maverick hath his mother, wife, children & brothers living there, and nether estate, nor employment here."

And Samuel Maverick, writing from Rhode Island Oct. 9, 1668, to Secretary Sir William Morice, says that his mother "presents her humble service." (See Sainsbury's Calendar of Colonial Papers, vol. 3, p. 415, No 1288). This Secretary Morice, who died in

---

* Clarendon Papers, N. Y. Hist. Soc. Coll., 1869, p. 108.

Dec. 1676 aged 74, was son of Jevan Morice, fellow of All Saints College, Oxford, of an ancient Welsh family, doctor of laws and chancellor of Exeter, Devon, in 1594, and ancestor of the extinct Baronets Morice of Werrington, Devon, on the borders of Cornwall, a few miles s.w. of Beaworthy.

The widow Maverick, in 1668, must have been well advanced in years, since by his own deposition,* taken in December, 1665, her son Samuel was then "aged 63 yeares or therabouts."

Samuel, the eldest son of the Rev. John Maverick, born about 1602, had settled in New England as early as 1624,† near the confluence of Charles and Mystic Rivers, where with the help of his neighhor, David Tomson,‡ he had built a small fort. He was an episcopalian and loyalist, and frequently embroiled with the colonial government; finally, after one of his several voyages to the old country, he was, in April 1664, appointed one of the four Royal Commissioners to visit the colonies and inquire into grievances. For his services he received from the Duke of York, through a grant from Gov. Lovelace, a certain house and lot in New York City, on the Broadway. This gift he acknowledges in a letter of Oct. 15, 1669, to Col. Rich. Nicolls, his associate in the Commission, and we hear not of him again till in a deed of Mar. 15, 1676 (recorded Albany, L.1, p. 133), his trustees, John Laurence and Matthias Nicolls, of New York, confirm to William Vander Scheuren this same property on Broadway, which the latter had bought from the Deacons of the City, by whom it had been purchased at a public sale made for the benefit of Maverick's daughter, Mary, wife of Rev. Francis Hooke of Kittery. Neither the time nor place of Maverick's death, nor the depository of his will have been, as yet, ascertained. No records of so early a date are preserved by the Dutch Church, who evidently held the lot for a short period, but, after a careful examination of conveyances in the City Register's office, the writer has satisfactorily located the position of the Maverick Lot. May 30, 1667, Gov. Nicolls granted a lot on Broadway to Adam Onckelbach, which is described in later deeds as bounded south by house and lot of William Vander Scheuren, and which finally in Oct. 1784, when known as No. 52 Broadway, was sold to John Jay, Esq., the future governor, who here erected a fine stone mansion. At this time the lot adjoining to the south was in the tenure and occupation of John Slidell, save some 64 feet on the easterly or New Street end, which had been sold in 1683 by Vander Scheuren to William Post (L. 13, p. 8; L. 35, p. 170). Slidell's sons in 1819 sold the greater portion of the lot, facing on Broadway, with a frontage of $21\frac{1}{3}$ ft., and a depth 110 ft., to

* Suffolk Deeds, iv., 328.
† Letter of May 30, 1669, to Rev. Sampson Bond, at the Bermudas; a native of Northill, Cornwall.—Mass. Hist. Soc. Coll., 4th s., vol. viii, p. 318.
‡ Thomson's widow, Amias (Coles) is supposed to have married Maverick.—Reg., v. 47, p. 76.

Robert Lenox; while the remaining few inches, with a lot adjoining to the south, known as No. 48, was sold by them on the same date to David Gelston. From the foregoing facts we gather that the original Maverick Lot was 26¼ feet wide, located on the easterly side of Broadway, running through to New Street, and beginning 125 feet south from the Church Street (afterwards Garden Street, and now Exchange Place); and that it corresponded with the present No. 50 Broadway.

Though extinct in the New England States, the Maverick family has existed for the past one hundred and fifty years in New York City, where Andrew Maverick, a young painter, 24 years of age, was admitted a freeman July 17, 1753; his name occurring on the Poll List of Feb., 1761. He was baptized at the New Brick Church, Boston, Feb. 9, 1728-9 : one of the numerous family of John[4] Maverick (Paul[3], Elias[2], Rev. John[1],) an importer of hard woods on Middle Street (now Hanover St.), at the sign of the "Cabinet and Chest of Drawers," John's grandson Samuel (son of Samuel deceased), an apprentice of Mr. Isaac Greenwood, ivory turner &c., was mortally wounded, March 5, 1770, in the Boston Massacre. Andrew, who came to New York, married about 1754 Sarah, dau. of Peter and Bethia Ruston or Rushton, and Mr. Rushton, in a will of 1765, proved Aug. 14, 1767 (L.25, p. 534), leaves his entire estate, after the death of his wife Bethia, to his grandson Peter Rushton[6] Maverick.* The latter, born in the city April 11, 1755, a silver-smith, etcher and engraver, was in Aug. 1775 an Ensign in Capt. M. Minthorn's Co., of Col. John Jay's 2d Reg't of N. Y. Militia, and on July 23, 1788, represented the Engravers in the N. Y. Federal Procession; he died in Dec. 1811, and was succeeded by his three talented sons, Samuel,[7] Andrew[7] and Peter.[7]

The name Maverick, one of unusual occurrence, is akin doubtless to Morris, Morrice, or Maurice; we get nearer to it in the original Welsh Mawr-rwyce, "a valiant hero."

Nath. Maureick,† chief clerk of the Town Clerk, London, died 24 November, 1630, and John Mavericke was a settler located in Charleston, S. C., in 1672.

One other entry to the name is given by Foster:

"Maverick, Radford,‡ of Devon, pleb., Exeter Coll. matric. 17 Nov. 1581 aged 20; rector of Trusham (n. of Chudleigh), 1586, and vicar of Islington, Devon(?) 1597. (See Foster's Index Eccl.)."

* Dr. John Greenwood of N. Y. writing in Nov., 1803 to P. R. Maverick, alludes to a lot on Middle St., Boston, belonging to estate of his late father, Isaac G., and which adjoined land of Maverick's grandfather.
† Smith's Obituary, Camden Soc. Pub.
‡ Radford was a Devonshire family name.

REV. JOHN MAVERICK (*Register*, xlviii., 207). [*] The following interesting memorandum has been forwarded through the courtesy of the Rev. Arthur Burch, connected with the Diocesan Registry, Exeter. John Maverick, clerk, M.A., was instituted to Beaworthy, Aug. 30, 1615, at Silverton, co. Devon., by William Cotton, Bishop of Exeter, on the death of John Norrice, and on the presentation of Sir Jonn Arscott. The next Rector, John Crought, B.A., was instituted March 24, 1629, the living being then vacant through the free resignation of John Mavericke, the last possessor thereof.   I. J. G.

MAVERICK.—Let me correct an error in my note in the October (1895) number of the REGISTER, upon Rev. John Maverick. Instead of living at Okehampton, as I carelessly stated, Maverick was rector of Beaworthy, a parish about eight miles to the northwest of Okehampton. The present rector of Beaworthy, the Rev. F. A. Willis, LL.D., writes me, Sept. 25, 1895: "After searching the registers of this parish I have failed to find the name of Maverick in any of them, but this is hardly to be wondered at, as the date of his incumbency is so long ago as 1615."

"Edmandus Arscotte" should read "Edmundus."

Through the continued kindness of the historian of Plymouth (R. N. Worth) I am enabled to announce the discovery of the place and time of the marriage of the Rev. John Maverick, and the name of his wife. The Ilsington register contains the entry of John Maverick's marriage to Mary Gye, October 28, 1600. "Guy," says Mr. Worth, "is not a name current in the locality, and her presence in Ilsington is only reasonably explained by her marriage."

New Castle, N. H.   FRANK W. HACKETT.

A MAVERICK ITEM.—From vol. 4, page 31, of the Smith manuscripts in possession of the Society of Genealogists of London:

Will of William Gallop of St. Jame's Parish, Barbados, gentleman.

About to take a voyage to England. To Kinsman Thomas Gallop. To his nieces Henrietta, Deborah Ruth and Elizabeth Gallop. To nephew Samuel Gallop. Sister in law Ruth Gallop widow. Kinsmen Robert Osborne Esq. Mr. Isaac Thorpe and Mr. William Thorpe. To children of brother Samuel Gallop. To sister in law Mary Gallop who is to live in his mansion house or elsewhere in Barbados. To kinsman Robert Gallop. Sister Mrs. Howard deceased and her daughter Ann Howard. To niece Katherine Maverick and brother in law Nathaniel Maverick. To brother and sister Maverick a gold mourning ring. Sisters Ruth and Mary Gallop.

22 Sept. 1715   proved 6 April 1716.   P. C. C. 33 Jenison

Samuel Maverick witnessed the codicil of the will of William Dott in on St. Andrew Barbados 9 Oct. 1701.
P. C. C. 25 Dagg.

This indicates that Mary, wife of Nathaniel[4] Maverick (Captain Samuel,[3] Nathaniel,[2] Samuel[1]) of Babadoes was a sister of William Gallop. Perhaps these Gallops were related to Capt. John Gallop of New England.

Ogunquit, Maine   G. ANDREWS MORIARTY.

*P. 750, this volume.

JOHN MAVERICK AND SOME OF HIS DESCENDANTS: ADDITIONS.—A footnote in THE REGISTER, vol. 96, p. 363, October 1942, gives an abstract of the will of Henry Harding of Barbodos, dated in New York 10 Sept. 1742, which names his wife Elizabeth and only daughter Isabella. It would seem that the latter may have been a granddaughter of Nathaniel Kingsland of Barbados, whose will, dated 14 March 1685, names his daughter, Isabella, wife of Henry Harding, gent. This will is abstracted in *The American Genealogist*, vol. 36, p. 106-107, April 1960.

Arlington, Va.   JOHN G. HUNT.

DOROTHY MAY AND HER RELATIONS.

Communicated by Capt. CHARLES HERVEY TOWNSHEND, of "Raynham," New Haven, Conn.

RICHARD CLOPTON, of the knightly family of Clopton of Melford and Groton, County Suffolk, England (the latter manor and patronage of the church for some years previous to the settlement of New England was in Governor Winthrop's family), had, with other issue, a son and heir William Clopton (of whom hereafter) of Groton, and daughter Frances Clopton, married to Martyn Bowes, second son of Sir Martyn Bowes, knight, goldsmith, Lord Mayor of London, son and heir of Thomas Bowes, "an inhabitant of Ye City of York." This Martyn Bowes, son of the Lord Mayor, 1645, had a daughter Cordelia, who married John May of Shouldham Abbey, County Norfolk, who was son of John Mey or May, Bishop of Carslile.*

In the Harleian Manuscripts, B. M., Visitations of Essex, 1634, 1083, fol. 4, I find this note: "This John Mey or May was Doctor of Divinity and Master of Catherine's Hall, Cambridge, and was consecrated Bishop of Carslile by John Elmer, Bishop of London, deputed thereunto by the Archbishop of York, September ——, Anno 1577. He died in the month of April, A.D. 1598." In this visitation his son, John May, is called of Kings Lynn, County Norfolk, Esq., who had a daughter, Elizabeth, wife of John Sedgwick of Wisbach in the Isle of Ely, County Camb. and of Lynn Regis, County Norfolk, who had male issue, viz.: Edward, John and William Sedgwick, all living in 1619, and some of whom may have settled in New England and connect with the noted General Sedgwick of colonial times. This John May or Mey of Shouldham Abbey and Kings Lynn, Norfolk, in the visitation of Norfolk, 1555–1613, Harleian Manuscript, 1552, fol. 94, is recorded as having by wife Cordelia Bowes the following issue, viz.: *Margaret May*, married to Richard Faucet, *Francis May, o. b., Farnneru (Jacomye?) May, Francis May, Henry May*, 1st son, *John May*, 2d son, *Stephen May*, 3d son, and *Dorothy May* who was probably first wife of William Bradford (the Pilgrim Governor of Plymouth Colony) who was drowned Dec. 7th, 1620, from the "Mayflower" in Provincetown, Cape Cod Harbor, while her husband was absent on an exploring expedition, and whose banns, according to the Lyden Holland Records, 15th Nov., 1613, to William Bretfoot (Bradford) fustian worker from Oosterfeldt in England, affianced to Dorothy May from Witcsbuts (Wisbach Co. Cambᵈ near Lynn, Co. Norfolk); these banns are again recorded November 23d and 30th, and we find from his marriage registered in the Pulboeken at Amsterdam, he was a fustian worker. The full entry is as follows: "1613 Nov. 9th, William Bradford of Austerfield, fustian worker, 23 years, living at Lyden, where the banns of marriage were laid, it was declared that he had no elders (*i. e.* parents) and Dorothy May, 16 years, of Wisbech. The attesting witness is Henry May.† We may mention that four years earlier Dorothy May's sister *Jacomye May*, also of Wisbach in Cambridge, was married to Jean de l'Ecluse, a book printer from Rouen, who was an elder of the Ancient Church of Amster-

* See Biographical Sketch of Bishop May. Willis's Survey of Cathedrals, Vol. I., pp. 298-9.

† The Dutch spelling is very difficult to decipher, but a glance at the original is sufficient to satisfy one of the meaning thereof.

dam, having come over from the French Church of know evils existing among them."*

Among the English residents of Holland during the early part of the 17th century was a certain John May and wife; of the latter, Ephraim Paget, minister of St. Edmond's, Lombard Street, London, in his "Heresiography,† or a Description of the Hereticks and Sectarie, mentions 'Mistress May, who used to in her house sing (psalms) being more fit for a common brawl,'" as he termed the singing of psalms. Again he says: "By reason of such uncouth and strange translations and the meeter used in them the Congregation was made a laughing stock unto strangers."

In a letter to Governor Bradford from Roger White, a brother-in-law of the Rev. John Robinson, written from Holland in December, 1625, mention is made of John May, your (Governor Bradford's) "father in law."

In Mary E. Perkin's "Old Houses," Norwich, Connecticut, I find a Bradford Pedigree giving John Bradford, son of Governor Bradford and Dorothy May. This son John by wife Dorothy May married Martha Bourne, daughter of Deacon Thomas Bourne and Martha . . . ? of Marshfield, Mass. She died in 1678 without issue, and Martha, his wife, married before 1679, Lieutenant Thomas Tracy — no issue.

Returning to the before-mentioned William Clopton, of Groton, County Suffolk, to show his family relationship with others interested in New England settlement, he had issue: Anne Clopton, bapt. 29 of January, 1580, and married John Mateson‡ of Boxted, Suffolk, and Walter Clopton, a grocer of London, bapt. June, 1585, who married Margaret Mateson, a sister of aforesaid John Mateson, and she secondly Robert Crane. This Walter Clopton came to New England with his relation, Governor Winthrop, in 1630 and returned home soon after. His elder brother, William Clopton, was baptized 9th of April, 1584, and married at Whatfield, Suffolk, 3d August, 1615, Alice, daughter of Edmund D'Oyley, of Shottisham, Norfolk, esquire, and Pond Hall, Hadleigh, County Suffolk, whose cousin, Elizabeth D'Oyley of the Chislehampton, married Edward Goddard, Esquire, of Englisham, County Wilts, whose family, about 1630, emigrated with Governor Winthrop to New England. This Edmund D'Oyley and Thomas Goodwin, of Stoneham, County Suffolk, were trustees for Henry Townshend,§ of Breakon Ash, whose second wife, Anne Calthrone, was sister to Mary, wife of Edward D'Oyley, brother of Edmund

---

* See Pilgrim Fathers of New England, by John Brown, p. 126. Also H. C. Murphy's History, 1859, p. 261.

† The first edition was printed in London, 1645, and the sixth edition, from which the above is abstracted, was printed in 1661 by William Lee and sold at his shop the Turk's Head in Fleet Street.—C. H. T.

‡ This name, in deeds and inquisitions, is spelt *Maydston, Maistone.*

§ Henry Townshend's first wife was Margaret Forth, daughter of Robert Forth, LL.D., by whom he had two sons, Robert and Thomas.

D'Oyley, uncle of Alice D'Oyley, wife of William Clopton, a brother of Thomasine* Clopton, second wife of Governor Winthrop. Another daughter of William Clopton was Bridget, bapt. 29 January, 1581, and married 27 June, 1598, John Sampson of Sampson Hall, Kersey, County Suffolk, whose son, Robert Sampson, came with Governor Winthrop to Boston, and were relations of Henry Sampson and Humility Cooper, cousins of John Tilly, the Mayflower pilgrim, and as the surnames, Tilly, Cooper, Carver and Sampson are all found in the same neighborhood in County Suffolk, the tradition seems sustained that these families were all connected with the Forth family, from which Governor Winthrop married his first wife.

ORIGIN OF THE MERRIAMS AND OTHER FAMILIES OF CONCORD, MASS.

[Communicated by WILLIAM S. APPLETON, A.M., of Boston, Mass.]

I COMMUNICATED to the REGISTER for April, 1868, a short account of the Merriam family, at the end of which I remarked that we could not say, with certainty, whence in England came the three brothers of this name. In July, 1868, I made researches, which convince me that I found their home and father in Kent, and which also induce me to believe that there was a large settlement of Kentish families in the town of Concord, Mass.

First, as to the latter point, Shattuck says:—William Buss had a brother in Tunbridge, Kent; Thomas and James Hosmer came from Hockhurst (i. e. Hawkhurst), Kent; Simon Willard came from Horsemonden. Savage says:—William Hartwell, Concord, came, says tradition, from Kent. Now not only are these good Kentish names, but Barrett, Brooks, Fletcher, Fowle, Hayward, Wheeler, Wood, all names of early inhabitants of Concord, are instantly met with in the county of Kent.

The Merriam family I believe to be descended from William Mirriam of Hadlowe, Kent, whose will I found at Rochester. It was written 8 September, and proved 27 November, 1635. He was a clothier, and owned lands in Hadlowe, Goodherst, Yalding, and Tewdly (Tudeley), all small villages near Tunbridge. He mentions his daughters Susan, Margaret, Joane and

---

* Mary Clopton, sister of Thomasine, the second wife of Governor Winthrop, married Thomas Dogget or Daggett, of Boxted, County Suffolk, who settled in New England, and was connection of the Dagget family of Martha's Vineyard.

Sara, as well as grandchildren of the name of Howe, children of a deceased daughter; his wife Sara; his sons Joseph, George and Robert; granddaughter Mary, daughter of George; grandson William, son of Joseph; and appoints his son Robert sole executor.

I examined the church-registers of Hadlowe, Yalding and Tunbridge, but obtained little information from them; of Tudeley no early register is known to be in existence. At Hadlowe "William Miriam was buried September 23, 1635." At Tunbridge, George Miriam and Susan Raven were married October 16, 1627; they had Mary, b. and d. 1628; Mary, b. 1630; Elizabeth, b. 1635; Joseph, b. 1637.

These facts and names agree very closely with what I previously printed about the Merriams in this country. The three sons of William are all found at Concord: George with a wife Susan, and both Joseph and George with children born in England, but not exactly corresponding with those now named. Joane, their sister, undoubtedly married a Day, and was mother of Isaac, mentioned in the former article. The name of Day was common in the Kentish villages I visited. I would certainly advise all genealogists, who are on the hunt for the ancestry of settlers in Concord, to begin their English investigations with the county of Kent.

PEDIGREE OF MINER.

The following curious pedigree of Lieut. Thomas Miner, or Minor, of Connecticut, was sent us last year by Frederick P. Tracy, Esq., of San Francisco, Cal., who copied it, some years previous, from the original manuscript, then in the hands of J. Hammond Trumbull, Esq. The latter gentleman, having been requested to correct the proof by the original, has kindly consented to do so; and his corrections have much increased the reliability of the printed copy. Mr. Trumbull writes, that "Lieut. Thomas and his immediate descendants (all of them good penmen) uniformly wrote the name Minor." "The original manuscript," he adds, "was deposited, some years ago, in the library of the Connecticut Historical Society, in accordance with the wish of Deacon Asa Miner of Stonington, a descendant of the sixth generation from Lieutenant Thomas,[1] through Deacon Manasseh,[2] (b. 1647)—Deacon Thomas,[3] (b. 1683)—Thomas,[4] (b. 1707)—Deacon Thomas,[5] (b. 1749), married Lucretia Safford, 10 Oct. 1771."

The several arms impaled with Miner have been described by Mr. Trumbull. His descriptions of them will be found appended.

An Herauldical Essay

Upon the Surname of Miner.

It is more praise worthie in noble and excellent things to know something, though little, than in mean and ignoble things to have a perfite knowledge. Amongst all those rare ornaments of the mind of man, Herauldrie hath had a most eminent place; and hath been held in high esteem, not only at one time and in one climate, but during all times and through those parts of the world where any ray of humanitie and civilitie hath shined: for without it, all would be drowned in the Chaos of dissorder. Neither is she so partial that money shall make the man. For he ought not to be accounted a perfite Herauld except that he can discerne the difference betwixt a Coat armoriall obtained by valour or purchased by money. *Scutum Gentilitium Palud [amentum et Cristatum]* honorable not mercenary as appears by this coat of the MINERS.

The reason (as GARCILLASSO sayeth, Page 432) is this;—Edward the third going to make warre against the French, tooke a progresse through Somersett; and coming to *Mendippi Colles Minerarij*,—Mendippe hills in Somersett, where lived one HENRY MINER, his name being taken both *a denominatione loci et ab officio*, who with all carefullness and Loyalltie having convened his domesticall and meniall servants, armed with battle axes, proffered himself and them to his masters service; making up a compleat hundred. Wherefore he had his coat armorial GULES (signifying *Minius*, red, another demonstration of the original surname:) A FESSE (id est, *cingulum militare*, because obtained by valour) BETWIXT THREE PLATES ARGENT, another demonstration of the arms: for there could be no plates without MINES. It is folly to suppose such a surname as MINOR to have any coat of armes, It being contrary, yea contradictory, in termes—that *Minors* can obtain paternal coats or atchievements unlesse it be presupposed that *Major* was his father.

BARTAS, a French Herauld, says MINER is a word contracted in Dutch—**min=heir,** that is *my Master,* or *Lord,* and gives his reason for the plates to be dollars, or pieces of eight, abundance of which will make any Hollander (albeit born upon a Dunghill) to be titled **min=heir;** but ye crest, reason aforesaid and chronologie proves the first. And albeit Heraulds differ in the descriving (says FORDON, page 342) of this surname

759

of Miner, and time with the various dialects of severall counties, have almost made it to be another name; yet if ignorance would strive to eradicate *Ancestrie*, it cannot do it in this coat, the name and colours making so much proofe, with the place (sayes Baker) 1. the place where the original came from,—Mendippi Colles Minerarij. 2^ly The field Minius. 3^ly The charge Minerall, [4^ly] The circumstances and actions upon record relative to the crest, being a battle axe, armed at both ends Minerall.

Herauldrie is a thing not of yesterday, or which may be otherways found out, being already condescended upon by all nations, and, as it were, established, *Jure Gentium*, among the Greeks, Romans, Germans, French, Spainiards, English, Scots, Danes, and Hungarians, &c. Fordon, the great Antiquarian, sayeth, that the King's Secretary returned the for's'd Henry Miner, a compliment for his loyaltie, in these words, "Oceanus (Quamvis magni Fluvij multique Torrentes sint ei Stipendarij) non dedignatur recipere *minores* Rivulos &c.," *id est,*

The ocean (though great rivers with many currents pay him tribute) disdains not also to receive the Lesser if loyall brooks which by one only Urne pour themselves into its bosom.

This Henry died in the year 1359, leaving behind him Henry, Edward, Thomas, and George, Miners, of whom little is to be said, save only that Henry married one Henreta Hicks, [A] daughter to Edward Hicks of Glocester, of whom, as appears by the paling of their armes, are the Hicks of Beverston Castle in Glocester descended; and had issue William and Henry. William married one Hobbs [B] of Wiltshire, and had issue Thomas and George. Henry, the 2^d son, served Richard the second, *anno* 1384. Thomas, 1399, married one —— Gressleys, [C] daughter of Cotton, in the countie of Stafford, and had issue Lodovick, George, and Mary. Lodovick married Anna Dyer, daughter of Thomas Dyer [D] of Staughton in the *Com.* Huntington, and had issue—Thomas, borne 1436, and after that twins, being 22 years after the birth of the said Thomas; and the twins George & Arthure, who both served the house of Austria, the younger married (as Philipe Comines relates) one Henretta de la Villa Odorosa. Thomas married Bridget, second daughter to Sir George Hervie [E] *de* St. Martins in *Com.* Middlesex, and died 1480, leaving his son William, and daughter Anna Miner, in tutorage to their mother Bridget, whom she resigned to her father, and turned to a monstericall life in Datford, where she remained during her life. William married Isabella Harcope [F] *de* Frolibay, and lived to revenge the death of the 2 young princes murdered in the tower of London, upon their inhuman uncle Richard the 3^d. It was said of this William Miner that he was "*Flos Militiæ*," the flower of chevallrie. He left behind him 10 sons, William, George, Thomas, Robert, Nathaniel, and John; the rest are not recorded. The 2 last went over to Ireland, 1541, when King Henry the 8 was proclaimed I king of Ireland. Nathaniel maried one Fitzmaurice neigh Catherlough, in the province of Leinster in Ireland. John married to Joselina O'bryan, daughter to Teig O'bryan of Innis in the county of Clare; whose posteritie remains there, in the name of Miner, bearing the same coat. George married and lived in Shropshire. Thomas in Hereford. William, the eldest son, had issue—Clement and Elizabeth Miners, and was buried at Chew-Magna, the 23 day of February

Anno Domini, 1585 ; and lies interred in the Priests Chancell, about four foot from the wall, with this inscription 𝔥𝔢𝔦𝔯——𝔢𝔱𝔥——𝔪 𝔪𝔶𝔫𝔢𝔯 ——𝔬𝔣——𝔭𝔰𝔥——𝔬𝔟𝔦𝔦𝔱 𝔯𝔯𝔦𝔦𝔦 𝔣𝔢𝔟𝔯𝔲' 𝔪𝔡𝔩𝔯𝔯𝔯𝔟 : this and no more legible upon the stone, with the coat expressed in the margin, at this sign *, but by the records and registers of the said church, it is evident

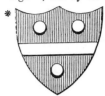

that his name was WILLIAM MYNER, they both agreeing in the same date and place, and must needs have been the head of the same family, as by the paternal coat clearly appears. CLEMENT his son succeeded his father in heritage, and married ——— and had issue CLEMENT, THOMAS, ELIZABETH, and MARY MINERS ; and departed this life the 31 of March, 1640, and lyes interred in Chew-Magna in the countie of Somersett.

CLEMENT the eldest brother married SARAH POPE [G] daughter of JOHN POPE of NORTON-SMALL-REWARD, in the countie of Somersett, and had issue WILLIAM and ISRAEL. This Clement was buried at Burslingtown in the Countie of Somersett. THOMAS his brother is now alive at STONING-TOWN, in CARNETICUTE COLLONEY, in NEW ENGLAND, *Anno Domini* 1683, and has issue, JOHN, THOMAS, CLEMENT, MANASSAH, EPHRAIM and JUDAH MINERS, and two daughters MARIE and ELIZABETH. WILLIAM MINER, eldest son of CLEMENT MINER, married SARAH, daughter of JOHN BATTING [H] of Cliffon in Gloucestershire, and lives *Anno* 1683, in Christmas Street in the city of Bristoll, and has issue WILLIAM and SARAH MINERS. ISERAELL, the second son, married ELIZABETH, daughter of THOMAS JONES [I] of Burslingtown in the countie of Somersett, and has issue CLEMENT, THOMAS, SARAH, JEAN, and ELIZABETH MINERS, *Anno* 1683. And now having done with the description Genealogicall I hope that

τον τις ἒ τηλόθι ναίων

Even every ingenious stranger makes mention

Τιμᾶ ανηρ αγαθος

and if I have used any old or ancient words, yea words now differently syllabicated, I may excuse myself with QUINTILIANUS, ' *verba a vetustate repetita, non solum magnos assertores habent, sed etiam afferunt orationi majestatem aliquam, non sine delectatione,*' and for the Ingenious Reader I am ; not caring that every peasant should venture his sick-brain'd opinion upon this essay, knowing well that *ars nominem habet inimicum præter ignorantem,* but if he will take this counsell †

——— *ἰι δέ γαρ πα - - άν*
Νηίς. φυς Μυσεων ῥιψο ἁ μη νοέις

and keeping himself silent, he may parse for a witt ; while on the contrary his too much garrulity shows his nakedness, as much as *Prester John*‡ who describes himself from the loijns of SOLOMON, or FRITHULF from Seth : but I shall be very much beholden to the learned reader, who if he can give more satisfaction in this essay would for the honor of antiquitie (who now lyes *in profundo Democratis Puteo*) mend the errata Chronologicall, and see if he can describe the surname from a longer time ; it being

---

† [In the margin.] If thou hast no taste in learning medle no more with what thou understandest not. [The Greek, of which this is a translation, is nearly illegible in the manuscript.]

‡ DAMIAN. A GOES "De moribus Æthiopum."

supposed that HENRY MINERS name, before the Kings Progresse in Somersett, was BULLMAN, but how certain however I know not, but leave it to some other whose experience and learning exceeds mine ; desiring nothing more than that herauldrie should be restored to its pristine splendor and truth, and not to be abused by every common Painter and Plaisterer, who before they will lose a fee will feinzie a coat of armes to the loss of the estates, goods, and sometimes their very name

"Quid non mortalia pectora cogis auri sacra fames."

But—

"Emblemata ad voluntatem Domini Regis sunt portanda et non alias," and Herauldrie stands in need of the doze φαϱμαxωδης, and now I will conclude, with RALPH BROOKE, Esquire, and York Herauld,

> " To make these names alive again appeare
> Which in oblivion well neigh buried were,
> That so our children may avoid the jarres
> Which might arise about their ancestors,
> And that the living might those titles see
> With which their names and houses honored be;
> Yet I have hope of more acceptance from
> Those future times that after me shall come,
> For when beneath the stroke of death I fall
> And those that live these lives examine shall,
> Detraction dying, you that doe remain
> Will credit me and thank me for my pain
>
> Virg. ———si quid novis rectius
> Candidus imparti ; si non, his utere mecum."

[A marginal note on the original is as follows :—]

" This Coat of the Miners of Chew I attest to be entered at Bath in Somersett by Clarenceux the 4 of K. James the first, which visitation is in custody of me, 1606.   Alex: Cunninghame."

[NOTES.—The Miner arms are impaled with those of the following families at the sides of the pedigree against the places where we have inserted the respective letters :—

A. " With *Hicks*,"—gu. a fesse wavy, between three fleurs-de-lis or.

B. " With *Hobbs*,"—ar. two bars sable, in each of the three compartments, three birds gu. [Burke gives Hobbes, of Sarum, co. Wilts, " sa. on a chev. or, betw. three *swans* ar. as many lions heads erased." Perhaps the artist designed to represent swans, in this sketch,—but swans gules would be *raræ aves*,—and the birds do not look swan-like, though they might pass for *ducks*.]

C. " With *Gressley*,"—barry of six, gules and ermine. [Gresley, of Coulton, co. Stafford, " *Vaire* gu. and erm. *Burke*.]

D. " With the *Dyers*,"—Per fesse indented, gu. and or. [I have little doubt that this *ought* to have been, Or, a chief indented, gu. ; but the drawing is as I have given it.]

E. " With the *Hervies*,"—gu. on a fesse ar. three trefoils slipped.

F. " With the *Harcops*,"—sa. a chevron betw. three lions(?) rampant ar.

G. " With the *Popes*,"—per pale or and az., on a chev. between three griffins(?) heads erased, as many fleurs-de-lis, all countercharged.

H. " With the *Battings*,"—ermine, a fesse sable.

I. " With *Jones*,"—ermine, a chevron sable.]

762

THE ORIGIN OF THE MAYFLOWER CHILDREN: JASPER, RICHARD AND ELLEN MORE

By Anthony R. Wagner, C.V.O., D.Litt., F.A.S.G., Richmond Herald,
College of Arms, London, England

The problem of the children Jasper, Richard and Ellen More and their nameless brother, who sailed on the *Mayflower* in 1620, has long intrigued New England genealogists. By good fortune, the answer to this puzzle became known to me in January 1959 and some account of the discovery was given in the London *Times* of 30 June 1959. It was thought, however, that a somewhat fuller account of the evidence would be of interest and it is by the courtesy of Mr. Jasper More of Linley Hall, Shropshire, the owner and discoverer of the crucial document, and by that of *The Times* that I am able to communicate this.

The principal facts hitherto known are given in an article by Dr. Edwin A. Hill, "The English Ancestry of Richard More of the Mayflower", which appeared in 1905 in the *New York Genealogical and Biographical Record*, vol. 36, pp. 213-219, 291-301. William Bradford in the account which he put on paper in 1650 of "the names of those which came over first in the year 1620 . . . and their families" (Bradford's "History of Plimoth Plantation", ed. 1901, pp. 531, 534-5) tells us that Mr. John Carver brought with him on the voyage "a child that was put to him, called Jasper More"; of Mr. William Brewster that "a boy was put to him called Richard More"; and another of his brothers; of Mr. Edward Winslow that "a little girl was put to him, called Ellen, the sister of Richard More"; that "Mr. Carver and his wife dyed the first year; he in the spring, she in the sommer; also his man Roger and the little boy Jasper dyed before either of them, of the commone infection"; and finally that "Richard More his brother dyed the first winter; but he is maried, and hath 4 or 5 children, all living".

Richard More (or Moore, as he spelt it) settled in Salem in 1639 and died in 1698-9 leaving issue.[1] On 27 Sept. 1684 he made a deposition (THE REGISTER, vol. 50, p. 208), giving his age as "seaventy yeares or thereabouts" and stating "that being in London att the House of Mr Thomas Weston Ironmonger in the year 1620. He was from thence transported to New Plymouth in New England." This fixes his birth in or about 1614.

In 1899 the parish register of Shipton, Shropshire, was printed by the Shropshire Parish Register Society. A copy of this came to the hands of Dr. Edwin A. Hill, who noticed in it three baptismal entries which fitted the Mayflower children. They were those of *Ellinora Moore filia Samuelis Moore de Larden* on 24 May 1612, of *Jasperus Moore filius Samuelis Moore de Larden Generosi* on 8 Aug. 1613 and of *Richardus Moore filius Samuelis Moore de Larden et uxoris ejus* on 13 Nov. 1614. There was also that of *Maria Moore filia Samuelis More et Caterinae uxoris ejus de Larden* on 16 April 1616.

Now the Mores of Linley and Larden are among the oldest families of the gentry of Shropshire. Samuel More, the father of the children baptized at Shipton, appears in the "Dictionary of National Biography" as a commander on the side of the Parliament in the Civil War. He was born in 1594, the son of Richard More of Linley. In 1610, aged only 16, he married his third cousin Catherine, daughter and heir (since her brother's death in a duel in 1607) of Jasper More of Larden. Since the bride was 23 it looks as if the marriage was arranged to keep Larden in the More family. By 1627, however, Samuel More had married a second wife by whom he had seven children. The eldest of these, another Richard More ultimately succeeded his father at Linley and Larden.

There were thus alternative mysteries. If the children baptized at Shipton were the Mayflower children, why were they shipped overseas and deprived of their inheritance? If they were not the Mayflower children, what became of them? On the whole it seemed that they must be the same, but it was hard to suggest a plausible explanation. Dr. Hill indeed thought that it would be natural for a man of Puritan sympathies, who had lost his wife and been left with young children, "to seek a safe asylum for his helpless, motherless children, in the new commonwealth about to be founded beyond the seas by men of his own religious and political faith". Others, however, found this hard to swallow.

The present Mr. Jasper More of Linley is seventh in descent from Samuel More by his second marriage. He and I were schoolfellows, so that, when I became interested in this problem, my first step was to ask his opinion. This was that, though the identity of the Mayflower children with those baptized at Shipton seemed probable, it was hard to find a plausible explanation of the facts and that all was therefore still surmise. It was, accordingly, with the greatest

---

[1] For his descendants see Walter Goodwin Davis, "The Ancestry of Phoebe Tilton, 1775-1847", Portland, Maine, 1947, pp. 97-9.

interest that I heard from him in January 1959 that having been kept indoors by snow he had been searching among his archives at Linley and found a document which seemed to solve the problem. Shortly afterwards he came to London and left the document at the College of Arms for my inspection. In the evening he came to my house and I read it to him. I was by now fully satisfied that the problem had been solved. The document, written on six sides of paper measuring 7½ by 11½ inches, reads as follows:

To the right Honorable Sir James (L)ee knight and Baronett Lord chief Justice of England.

A true declaracon of the disposinge of the fower children of Catherine More sett downe by Samuell More her late husband together wth the reasons movinge him there unto accasioned by a peticōn of hers to tht Lord cheif Justice of England

In July ao dñi 1620 by the appointm^t and direccōn of the said Samuell More the fower children of the Petitioner Katharine More were brought up to London by a servant of the father of Samuell and delivered to Philemon Powell who was intreated to deliver them to John Carver and Robert Cushman undertakers for the associats of John Peers for the plantacōn in Virginia The same moneth and yeare the said Carver and Cushman receaved the Children and did covenant and agree to transport them into Virginia & to see that they should be sufficiently kept and maintained wth meate drinke apparrell lodginge and other necessaries and that at the end of seaven Yeers the should have 50 acres of land a peece in the Countrey of Virginia for performance whereof they entered into Articles and they together wth one Mr. Weston an honest and sufficient Merchant gave bond to Mr Paul Harries cosin germane of the said Samuell in the some of 120^11 as by the Articles of agreement and bond more at large appeareth the said Paul Harris beinge intreated as a friend in trust to take the bond and Articles in his name the said Samuell being at that time wth his Lord at Bath, The saide Samuell also trusted his said cosin wth the money to pay them wch was onely paied vizt 80^11 and also 20^11 more in adventure wth wch 20^11 and the proffit that should arise therefrom the portion of such of the children as should best please was purposed to be enlarged

The reasons movinge to this manner of disposinge of the said children are as follow

1. Imprimis the comōn fame of the adulterous lief of the said Katherine More wth on Jacob Blakeway a fellow of meane parentage & condicōn wch continued longe before the said Samuell suspected it, and after it was knowne to the said Samuell the apparent likenes & resemblance of most of the said children in their visages & lineaments of their bodies to the said Blakeway./

2. Itm after such time as the said Samuell had forborne the company of the said Katherine and had forewarned the said Blakeway of her company upon certeine knowledge of her lewdnes they notwithstandinge continued priuately to meet together & the said Catherine iustified her actes wth Blakeway as beinge her husband before god alledginge a precontrack wth him before her marriage wth the said Samuell affirminge her accompanyinge wth the said Blakeway lawfull but her marriage wth the said Samuell unlawfull wch contract though she could not sufficiently prove by witnesses yet it was all one before god as she sayed./

3. Itm the foresaid consideracōns movinge the said Samuell to resolve to seperate himself from the said Catherine who through the continuance in sinne became impudent. In April 1616 The said Samuell (hauinge by fine and other assurance in law cutt of his estate tayle in his lands and setled it) came to London to the right honorable the Lord Zouch wth whom he hath euer since continued hauinge taken care for the maintenance of the said children & their educacōn in the Countrey wth certaine tenants of the said Samuell's father and in the towne where he dwelleth unto wch children

765

the said Catherine often repayred and there used diuers exclamacōns & slaunders & did teare their cloathes from their backes by reason of w^{ch} & other her continued lewd demeanor the said Samuell's parents were continually vexed & greiued they forbearinge to take the sd children into their house to avoide her slaunders (yf it should have pleased god to visit any of them wth death) of beinge murtherers of them: and wth all to shunne the continuall sight of their great grief of such a spurious broode./

4. Itm̄ the said Blakeway & Catherine growinge more & more impudent & purposinge to obteine a diuorce and to marry (as it seemeth) procured themselves to be cited before the chauncellor of the diocosse wth whom they practized by some friend to obteine a sentence of diuorce & for license to entermarry & wth all by that meanes to free the said Blakeway from any informacōn in the high Comission court for the said offence/

And before the Chauncellor they brande the children further by a confession wch was enacted by these words 14th Junii *1616*, tam prefatus Jacobs Blakeway quam antedicta Katherina More comperuerunt quibus articulo sive crimine incontinentiae vitae sive adulterii iudicialiter objecto fatebantur se insimul plures et iteratis viribus incontinentur vixisse ac adulteriū una comississe./

5. Itm̄ the said Blakeway (beinge articled against in the high Comission court for the adultery aforesaid) exhibited letters testimoniall conteininge the said confession of adultery & a cōmutacon of pennance therefore into the some of 20^{11} but it beinge further proved that he had (contrary to the monicōn of the Chauncellor & his oath) accompanied wth the said Catherine since the time of his comutacōn (vizt) since 14° Junii 1616 in secret and obscure places (the said Blakeway to free himself from punishment in the said high comission Court and before the Councell of the Marches of Wales where also he was informed against) procured the kings Maties pardon for adultery wth Catherine the wief of Samuell More under the great seale./

6. Item the said Blakeway hauinge obteined a pdon caryed himself more and more insolently affrontinge the said Samuell's friends & hauinge soe longe continued the company of the sd Catherine in the howses & about the grounds of the sd Samuell to the intollerable provocacōn of his friends by the advise of his councell learned in the lawes he tooke an accōn of tresspasse against the sd Blakeway for breakinge & entringe his house & grounds at Larden & treadinge his grasse to the valew of 10^{11} & doinge other enormities to the sd Samuell to his damadge of 1000^{11} to wch accōn he pleaded not guilty & upon the evidence at the assisses before Mr Justice Warburton in the Lent 1618 the adultery of the said Blakeway wth Catherine beinge proved the Jury brought 400^{11} damages after wch verdict the said Blakeway pleaded errors in arrest of Judgm^{t} yet notw^{th}standinge after many argumn^{ts} of the errors iudgment was awarded in the king's bench but the sd. Blakeway to prevent execucōn fledd./

7. Itm̄ the said Catherine hauinge refused to accept of her children & reasonable maintenance wth them & hauinge twenty markes a yeere maintenance from the said Samuell by the consent of her friends soe longe as she should absteine from the company of Blakeway yet neuerthelesse she not onely frequented his company but assisted him in his suites by her self & friends wch moved the said Samuell hauinge forborne any suite against her seeinge her impenitent & incorrigible to sue in the Court of audience to be diuorced from her wch suite longe depended & many comissions upon new & friuolous allegacōns were executed to putt the said Samuell to the most charge he bearinge the charge both of pl. & deft. And at leingth upon manifest proofe in trinity tearme 1619 sentence of diuorce was given./

8. Item the said Catherine after the said sentence appealed in to the Court of deligates from the sentence for determininge of wch appeale there were assigned the Lords Bishops of Rochester & Elie Sr William Bird Sr James Hussey Sr John Amy & Dco^{r} Gooche wch comissioners upon all the proofes at fower severall daies informacōn fower of them beinge present whereof the said Bishop of Ely was one did affirme the former sentence to be iust in trinity tearme 1620 all wch charge & vexacōn the said Catherine (w^{th}out

care of her reputacon or of her children) hath malitiously caused and although at all times the said Samuell and his frinds haue binne willinge to end suites & to agree upon a seperacōn wthout the publique & chargeable course of law, and to make it appeare to the world that neither he nor his friends desired to gaine any thinge by the match wth her but to depart wth all the proffitt to her & her children and to make any indifferent friends iudges thereof yet she hath still refused & endeuoured his subuersion & intollerable vexacōn alledginge & exclayminge wth Crocadills teares that she brought a great estate of land and that the said Samuell causlessly casteth her of and disinheriteth her children whereas in trueth by the said Match the estate of the said Samuell & his father is ruined the whole estate of land that came by the said Catherine's mariage beinge worth not above 100¹¹ p annū all wch Jasper More the said Katherines father enioyed duringe his lief & reserved an . . . markes p annū thereout of payeable after his deceasse to Elizabeth his wief duringe her lief who yet enioyeth the same soe that there cometh clerely by the said match but 33¹¹- 6^s - 8^d p annū for which Richard More father of the said Samuell gave to Jasper 600¹¹ besides the losse of the preferrment of the said Samuell beinge his sonne & heire and as it hath fallen out great & troublesome suites & vexacons have ensued & continued these six yeares there beinge eleven yeares compleat since the said match. The premises considered that these children are be [*sic*] branded in their favour wth apparent likeness to the sayd Blakeway and also not only by fame but by testimony of witnesses that proue the very acte of adultery in the mother wth a base fellow, both their confessions & that iudicially before their ordinary the sentences & actes of soe many Courts, verdicts at comōn law, & a pardon from the Kinge procured all caused and forced by the cariages of Blakeway and Katherine or willingely donne by them as plentifull testimony wittnesseth The said Samuell upon good and deliberate advise hath thought fitt to settle his estate upon a more hopefull issue & to provide for the educacōn & maintenance of these children in a place remote from those partes where these great blotts & blemishes may fall upon them and therefore tooke the opportunity of sendinge them when such yonge ones as they went over wth honest & religous people, but such is the restlesse spirit of that wicked woman who cannot be contented to continue her lewde lief but still by complaints bringeth the [passages?] of her lewd life to be published in all places & [countrys?] wch yf there were any modesty lefte she would desire to hide and wch the said Samuell to his great grief is forced by way of his [owne?] defence to discover./

[The document is endorsed:—
".................. Katherine
Mores petition to the
Lo Chief Justice ....
the disposing of her children to
Virginia."]

Though the appearance and internal evidence of the document and its entire consistency with the facts already known left me in no doubt of its authenticity, it was clear that this might in fact be tested by referring to the public records for confirmation of facts therein stated. Mention is made in it of the following legal proceedings:

(1) In or before April 1616 Samuel More cuts an entail and resettles his lands by fine. A record should be found in the Feet of Fines in the Public Record Office.
(2) Matrimonial proceedings on the initiative of Jacob Blakeway and Catherine More before the Chancellor of the Diocese of Hereford in June 1616. The record of this should be in the Bishop's Registry at Hereford.
(3) Proceedings against Blakeway in the Court of High Commission subse-

quent to June 1616. Records of this Court are in the Public Record Office.

(4) Proceedings against Blakeway before the Council of the Marches. The Records of the Council appear to have perished.

(5) Samuel More's action against Jacob Blakeway for trespass and damage at Larden before Mr Justice Warburton at the Lent Assizes 1618. The record should be in the Assize Rolls in the Public Record Office.

(6) Unsuccessful plea by Blakeway for arrest of judgment in the Court of King's Bench. This should be found in the King's Bench Records in the Public Record Office.

(7) Suit by Samuel More in the Court of Audience for divorce from Catherine ending in sentence of divorce in Trinity term 1619. The Records of the Court of Audience appear to have perished.

(8) Unsuccessful appeal by Catherine against this sentence in the Court of Delegates.

This last was looked for first. The Records of the Court of Delegates are in the Public Record Office. The following references to the case were noted in the Act Books.

Del. 4/8. 1619-21
fo. 77ʳ   3 Dec. 1619
fo. 95ᵛ   28 Jan. 1619-20.
fo. 101ᵛ   17 Feb. 1619-20.
fo. 110ʳ   5 May 1620
fo. 116ᵛ   10 May 1620
fo. 123ᵛ   19 May 1620
fo. 128ʳ   29 May 1620
fo. 132ᵛ   14 June 1620
fo. 138ʳ   19 June 1620
fo. 146ʳ   30 June 1620
fo. 152ʳ   5 July 1620
fo. 153ʳ   8 July 1620 Porrection of Sentence.

These were not examined but the Definitive Sentence was turned up in the Sentence Book Del. 5/6. 1618/22, m.85. It is dated 8 July 1620, and at great length, and with much verbiage declares Catherine's representations insufficient and her appeal dismissed. It bears the names and signatures of the delegates mentioned in the eighth paragraph of Samuel's draft petition. Of the facts of the case it says nothing, but the correspondence appears sufficient to confirm the general truth of Samuel More's account.

Nothing has yet been learned of the fate of Catherine More and Jacob Blakeway, though Blakeways long continued at Shipton. It will, however, be evident that there is ample room for further research. One of the most striking features of this story is the way in which it brings home to one the immense potential value to genealogists of a class of record seldom used because it is unindexed, uncalendared and hard of access—the records of the ecclesiastical courts.

THE ROYAL DESCENT OF A MAYFLOWER PASSENGER

By Sir Anthony Wagner, K.C.V.O.

Garter King of Arms, College of Arms, London, England

Ten years ago I was able to present in The Register (vol. 114, [*] p. 163-168, July 1960) evidence which settled the long vexed question of the parentage of the "Mayflower children", Jasper, Richard and Ellen More. This was a declaration made in or about 1620 to the Lord Chief Justice of England by Samuel More (1594-1662) of Linley, Shropshire, a commander on the Parliament side in the Civil War, 'of the disposing of the four children of Catherine More by Samuel More her late husband together with the reasons moving him thereunto'. The document had been found among his family muniments in January 1959 by my friend and former schoolfellow, the present Mr. Jasper More of Linley, Member of Parliament for Ludlow.

It tells a sad but fascinating story. Samuel More had been married in 1610 when only sixteen to his third cousin Catherine More, the heiress of Larden, then aged 23, presumably in order to keep that property in the family. Between 1612 and 1616 four children were born and baptised as Samuel's before he became aware of "the common fame of the adulterous life of the said Katherine More with one Jacob Blakeway, a fellow of mean parentage and condition" and noticed "the apparent likeness and resemblance of most of the said children in their visages and lineaments of their bodies to the said Blakeway".

The declaration then tells of Catherine's efforts to obtain a divorce from the ecclesiastical court in order to marry Blakeway, of her rejection of her children, and of how Samuel first boarded them with a tenant of his father's and then covenanted with "honest and religious people" "to transport them into Virginia and to see that they should be sufficiently kept and maintained with meat drink apparel lodging and other necessaries and that at the end of seven years they should have 50 acres of land apiece in the Country of Virginia".

So they sailed in the Mayflower as wards of John Carver, William Brewster, and Edward Winslow. Only the boy Richard More (1614-1699) survived childhood; he, as is well known, in time settled in Salem and left descendants. It always seemed to me that he, of all the Pilgrims, could be shown to be of royal descent and I planned, if ever I had occasion or leisure, to investigate this point. When asked by the Editor of The Register in September 1969 if I could provide an article connected with the Pilgrims I resolved to make a search. Two lines have so far emerged; one legitimate and fairly well documented from David I, King of Scotland, from the Saxon Kings, from a sister of William the Conqueror and from Charlemagne; the other, at the present much less well documented, from John de Botetourt, now believed to have been a natural son of Edward I, King of England (cf. *ibid.*, vol. 119, p. 99, April 1965). Others will perhaps be able to improve on this beginning.

[*]The preceding article.

First Line

1. MALCOLM III, King of Scotland 1058-1093, mar. 1068 [St.] Margaret, dau. of Edward the Aetheling, son of Edmund Ironside, King of England, a descendant of King Alfred (AR, p. 19).
2. DAVID I, King of Scotland 1124-1153, mar. 1113 Maud, dau. of Waltheof, Earl of Huntingdon, by Maud (d. 1130-1), niece of William the Conqueror (CP, vol. 6, p. 638-642).
3. HENRY, Earl of Huntingdon (d. 1152), mar. Ada (d. 1178), dau. of William de Warenne, Earl of Surrey, by Isabel, dau. of Hugh, Count of Vermandois, a descendant of Charlemagne (ibid., p. 642; AR. p. 65).
4. DAVID, Earl of Huntingdon (d. 1219), mar. 1190 Maud, dau. of Hugh, Earl of Chester (CP, vol. 6, p. 646-7).
5. ADA mar. Sir Henry de Hastings of Ashill, Norfolk (d. 1250) (ibid., p. 345).
6. SIR HENRY DE HASTINGS of Ashill (d. 1268/9) mar. Joan, dau. of Sir William de Cantelou (ibid., p. 345-6).
7. SIR JOHN DE HASTINGS of Abergavenny, Lord Hastings (b. 1262, d. 1312/3), a competitor for the crown of Scotland, 1292, mar. Isabel (d. 1352/3), dau. of William de Valence, Earl of Pembroke (ibid., p. 346-8).
8. ELIZABETH mar. Sir Roger de Grey of Ruthin, co. Denbigh, Lord Grey (d. 1352/3) (ibid., p. 152-3).
9. JULIANE (d. 1361) mar. 1329/30 John Talbot of Richard's Castle co. Hereford (d. 1355) (ibid., vol. 12, pt. 1, p. 630).
10. JOHN TALBOT of Richard's Castle (d. 1374/5) mar. Katherine (d. 1381) (ibid., p. 631).
11. ELIZABETH (d. 1407) mar. Sir Warin l'Arcedeckne, Lord Arcedeckne (d. 1400) (ibid., vol. 1, p. 187; vol. 12, pt. 1, p. 631).
12. ELEANOR (d. 1447) mar. 1385 Sir Walter Lucy of Newington, Kent (d. 1444) (ibid., vol. 8, p. 261-2).
13. ELEANOR mar. Thomas Hopton of Hopton, co. Salop (see no. 9 in the Second Line) (ibid., p. 263).
14. ELIZABETH (b. 1426/7, d. 1498) mar. 1st, Sir Roger Corbet of Moreton Corbet, co. Salop (d. 1467). She mar. 2ndly, John Tiptoft, Earl of Worcester, who d. 1470, and 3rdly, Sir William Stanley, K. G., who d. 1494/5 (ibid., vol. 12, pt. 2, p. 845).
15. JANE mar. Thomas Cresset of Upton Cresset, co. Salop. Will dated 20 Aug. 1520 (Shropshire Archaeological & Natural History Society Transactions, 4th Ser., vol. 6, p. 216).
16. RICHARD CRESSET of Upton Cresset mar. Jane, dau. of Walter Wrottesley (d. 1473) of Wrottesley, co. Stafford (College of Arms, MS. Vincent 134, fo. 257: William Salt Society, New Ser., vol. 6, pt. 2, p. 400).
17. MARGARET mar. Thomas More of Larden, co. Salop (College of Arms MS. C. 20, fo. 137, Visitation of Shropshire 1623).
18. JASPER MORE of Larden, will dated 27 May 1611, proved 25 May 1614 (P.C.C. 42 Lawe), mar. Elizabeth, dau. of Nicholas Smalley.
19. KATHERINE MORE mar. Samuel More of Linley, mother by Jacob Blakeway of an illegitimate son called:
20. RICHARD MORE, of Salem, passenger in the Mayflower.

Second Line

1. EDWARD I, King of England 1272-1307, had an illegitimate son:
2. JOHN BOTETOURT, Lord Botetourt (d. 1324), mar. about 1285 Maud, dau. of Thomas FitzOtes of Mendlesham, Suffolk (Hailes Abbey Chronicle, British Museum MS. Cotton, Cleopatra D. III, fo. 51; Handbook of British Chronology, Royal Hist. Soc., 2nd ed. (1961), p. 35; CP, vol. 2, p. 233-4).
3. MAUD (d. 1391), said to have been dau. of 2, mar. 1327 Reynold, Lord Grey of Wilton (b. 1311, d. 1370) (CP, vol. 6, p. 176-7).
4. HENRY, Lord Grey of Wilton (b. ca. 1340, d. 1396), mar. 1379 Elizabeth (d. 1402), said to be dau. of Gilbert, Lord Talbot, of Eccleswall, co. Hereford (ibid., p. 177-8).
5. RICHARD, Lord Grey of Wilton (b. ca. 1393, d. 1461), mar. 1st (it is said) Blanche, dau. of Sir Philip de la Vache. Had no. 6, below, been his son by

770

the second wife, Margaret, dau. of William, Lord Ferrers of Groby (as asserted in MCS, p. 85), there would be a legitimate descent here from Edward I. Since, however, that marriage took place in 1427, this is chronologically impossible (CP, vol. 6, p. 178-9).

6. ALICE (stated in College of Arms MSS, Vincent 51, fo. 40 and 134, fo. 134, and by Owen & Blakeway, *History of Shrewsbury*, vol. 2, p. 139 to have been dau. of no. 5 above, but in Harleian Society edition of the *Visitation of Shropshire*, p. 254, to have been dau. of Sir Richard Pembridge, K. G.) mar. Sir William Burley of Bromcroft, co. Salop (d. 1470), Speaker of the House of Commons 1436-43 (DNB, vol. 7, p. 376: Shropshire Archaeological & Natural History Society *Transactions*, 4th Ser., vol. 6, p. 232).

7. ELIZABETH mar. 1st, Sir John Hopton (*ibid.*, p. 233).

8. SIR WALTER HOPTON mar. Joan, dau. & coheir of Sir Walter Mortimer (College of Arms, MS. Vincent 134, fo. 134).

9. THOMAS HOPTON mar. Eleanor, dau. of Sir Walter Lucy (see no. 13 of the First Line above).

Abbreviations

CP   = *Complete Peerage*, new edition (14 vols.), 1910-1959.
AR   = F. L. Weis, *Ancestral Roots of Sixty Colonists* (1951).
MCS = A. Adams & F. L. Weis, *The Magna Carta Sureties*, 1215 (1955).

MORSE-CHICKERING CORRECTION.—In volume 83, page 290 of THE REGISTER, when giving the family of Samuel Morse of Dedham, I stated that his son, John of Dedham, married Annas' sister of Francis Chickering of Dedham. This marriage was taken from the Morse Genealogy by Mr. J. Howard Morse and Miss Emily W. Leavitt, and I did not verify the same, as it had no bearing upon the parentage of Samuel Morse and his English ancestry, with which my article was concerned. Recently Mr. Jacobus wrote to me and queried this marriage, whereupon I made a study of the question, which convinces me that it is most doubtful if Annas, wife of John Morse, was a Chickering. Miss Leavitt based her statement upon the fact that John Morse in his will (printed in THE REGISTER, vol. 8, p. 278) called Francis Chickering "my brother".

The account of the English ancestry of the Chickerings (THE REGISTER, vol. 69, pp. 226–229) and the will of Henry Chickering of Ringesfield, co. Suffolk, father of Francis Chickering, dated 11 July 1626, proved 7 July 1627 (cf. THE REGISTER, vol. 63, p. 282), fails to disclose a sister of Francis Chickering named Annas. Francis did have a sister, name unknown, who was married to one Nicholas Wolnough, when their father Henry made his will. It is, of course, possible that her name was Annas and that she married secondly John Morse but this seems a rather remote possibility and the chances are greatly in favor of some other combination to make John Morse call Francis Chickering "my brother". Their wives may have been sisters or again they may have been merely "brothers" in the church. At any rate the evidence was not sufficient to justify Miss Leavitt in stating without qualification that Annas, wife of John Morse, was sister of Francis Chickering.

Ogunquit, Maine.   G. ANDREWS MORIARTY, F.S.A.

The Identity of John Newcomen, Slain in 1630 at Plymouth, New England.—
The compiler is greatly obligated to F. G. Emmison, F.S.A., County Archivist, Essex
Record Office, for numerous suggestions concerning the text which follows.

It should be understood that Newcomen is, and was in the seventeenth century, a
rare surname; there is little doubt that most members of that family were related to
Martyn le Newcomen of Saltfleetby, Lincolnshire, who died in 1536; see the several
"Visitations of Lincolnshire", and "Lincolnshire Pedigrees" (Harleian Society), vol.
51, pp. 713, 714.

After studying all references to the name Newcomen given in Marshall's "Index to
British Pedigrees", and in the continuation thereof, Whitmore's "Genealogical Guide"
(1953), one is able to eliminate every John Newcomen in New England in the year
1630 except one; he was that John Newcomen, fourth son of Stephen Newcomen,
named below. It must not be pretended, of course, that a study of works cited in
Marshall and Whitmore exhausts the field of possible identification, for it is well
known that the great majority of the members of most families never were listed in
any of the heralds' pedigrees. There are reasons, however, presented later in this
paper, which strongly suggest that the identification below is correct.

Stephen Newcomen, who took his B.A. degree at Cambridge in 1586, was born at
Barwick-in-Elmet, Yorkshire, son of John Newcomen of Saltfleetby, Lincolnshire, by
his wife, Alice Gascoigne. Stephen was vicar of St. Peter, Colchester, Essex, from 1600
until his death in 1629 (Venn's Alumni Cantab.). His will was proved 31 May 1631
(Vicar General's Book, London County Council, Record Office, County Hall, London,
fo. 108a), by his widow, but the original is not extant, nor does a transcript survive.
His first wife, whose name is not known, was dead before 1625, for in that year was
born to his second wife, Stephen's fifth son, Stephen the younger. By his first wife, the
elder Stephen had had four sons, who included:

i. Thomas Newcomen, born in 1608; the unpopular Royalist rector of Holy
Trinity, Colchester 1628, and can on of Lincoln, 1660. He was hated by the
Parliamentarians (Dict. Nat. Biog.).

ii. Matthew Newcomen, D.D., born in 1610, was also educated at Cambridge.
A famous nonconformist, he evidently became "infected" by those same
elements at Cambridge that had influenced William Brewster of Plymouth,
New England. After 26 years in Dedham, near Colchester in Essex, he was
ejected as minister there in 1662 and removed to Leyden, where he died in
1669 (ibid).

iv. John Newcomen (fourth son); neither the date of his birth nor anything
further is known of him.

Most of the foregoing account is culled from Miss C. Fell Smith's article on "The
Essex Newcomens" (Essex Review, published at Chelmsford, vol. ii, 1893, pp. 35-40).

Savage tells us that John Newcomen as a youth was waylaid and killed in Plymouth,
New England, by John Billington, who therefore was executed in October 1630. Also
see Smith's "Bradford of Plymouth", and Willison's "Saints and Strangers". Savage
also names Elias Newcomen constable at the Isle of Shoals, in New England, in 1650.

Now an Elias Newcomen attended Magdalene College, Cambridge, where he received his M.A. degree in 1572; in 1600 he was incumbent at Stoke Fleming, Devon;
he died in 1614. He was second cousin of Dr. Matthew Newcomen named above (Dict.
Nat. Biog.). This Elias, who was a schoolmaster, had translated, around 1575, an
account from the Dutch, describing the stirring events in the Netherlands; from this, it
would seem that he might well have had great sympathy with the Dutch Protestants

772

in their struggle for independence. It is quite possible that Elias Newcomen, who in 1650 was a constable in New England, was related to the schoolmaster of the same name who died in 1614, for both names, "Elias" and "Newcomen" were rare; the combination is highly significant.

To return to John Newcomen, Stephen's fourth son: we know that his mother had died before 1625; John himself seems to have been born around 1614 if we may judge from the baptismal dates of his older brothers. Thus, in 1630, he would have been an orphan. It may well be that his stepmother had no great love for him; the unpopularity of his brother. Thomas, rector of Trinity, Colchester, might well have swung him into sympathy with the Puritans, who were numerous in Colchester, and it is quite probable that he would have aligned his own ideas to the Puritan tenets of his brother, Matthew. This nonconformity would have encouraged removal to Plymouth, New England, where a community existed that was greatly admired by most English nonconformists.

Further, the youthful John, slain in 1630 in New England, seems to have been there without his parents. There is a definite reason for thinking that the Brewsters sponsored him there. Young John was, as shown above, grandson of Alice Gascoigne. She was aunt of Mary Wentworth; this Mary was named in the will of her father, Thomas Wentworth, bailiff of Scrooby, Nottinghamshire, dated 27 March 1574, and proved 5 Feb. 1576/7, by his widow, Grace, born Gascoigne, who married soon after Wentworth's death, Thomas Troughton, gent. (Gascoigne and Wentworth pedigrees, in Foster's "Pedigrees of County Families of Yorkshire"; "Ducatus Lancastriae, Calendar of Pleadings", vol. 3, part 4, p. 46; Yorks. Fines, Hilary term, 1575/6).

Grace Gascoigne, widow of Wentworth, is thus named in the will of her brother, Richard Gascoigne of "Barnbow", Yorkshire, esq., dated 1 April 1590, proved 28 April 1593, which leaves "the daughters of my sisters Elizabeth Thompson and Grace Troughton . . . that my executors shall pay with that sume to every one of my sisters Troughtons thre daughters the sum of xiii li., vi s., viii d. apiece" ("Barwick in Elmet Wills," published, pp. 27-31).

Many years ago, Mr Walter Burgess, in his "John Robinson, the Pastor of the Pilgrims" (1920, p. 80), supposed that the above Mary Wentworth (daughter of Grace Gascoigne Wentworth Troughton) married William Brewster of Plymouth, New England, whose father succeeded her father as bailiff at Scrooby manorhouse. This dentification is not only plausible, but is made more than probable, by the fact that Jonathan Brewster (first son of William of New England) named one of his daughters Grace; likewise one of his granddaughters was named Grace (Jones' Brewster genealogy).

If Burgess' identification was correct, and Mary Wentworth was the wife of William Brewster, the elder at Plymouth, New England, it is then true that Brewster's wife was second cousin of John Newcomen, orphaned son of Stephen Newcomen of Colchester, Essex. It is reasonable, in the light of the foregoing, to believe that this young John would have been sponsored in New England by his cousins, the Brewsters, and that he was the victim of Billington's fury.

Further, the delay from 1629 to 31 May 1631 in proving the will of Rev. Stephen Newcomen, may well have been because John (probably a legatee) had been murdered in New England in the interim, and proof had to be adduced thereof.

Arlington, Va.   JOHN G. HUNT.

MEMORANDA CONCERNING THE NEWGATE FAMILY.

Communicated by CHARLES HERVEY TOWNSEND, Esq., of New Haven, Conn.

JOHN NEWGATE was a merchant and prominent citizen of Boston. He was admitted freeman of Massachusetts, March 4, 1634–5. At the time the Book of Possessions was compiled, he had in Boston, "One house and garden containeing about three quarters of an Acre, bounded with Henry Fane northwards; the new field westwards and southwards; Anne Hunne, vid. George Hunne, eastwards."* Savage, in his Genealogical Dictionary, says that he was "b. 1580, in Southwark, near London bridge." An abstract of his will, dated Nov. 25, 1664, and proved Sept. 11, 1665, is printed in the REGISTER (*ante*, xiii. 333–5). The name is sometimes spelled *Newdigate*.

The following abstract of the will of John Newgate of Bury St. Edmunds, co. Suffolk, Eng., dated 12 Oct., 1642, on record in England, proves that our John Newgate had a brother bearing the same christian name, who resided in Bury St. Edmunds. I have often found two and three brothers named John in the same family.

Being of sound mind & perfect remembrance &c. &c. To be buried at discresion of Executrix. To Sarah loving wife the use of house, Lands & other property in Bury St. Edmund for life. Then to brother Joseph Newgate for life—After decease of said Joseph, "Then the same to be and remain unto my brother John Newgate now living resident in the parts beyond the seas called New England & to his heirs forever."

All the rest of his movable property to wife Sarah & her heirs forever.

Appoints wife Sarah Executrix.   Signed   JOHN NEWGATE.

Wits. William Halstead
      Thomas Bull
      Robert Walker

Proved in the Archidiaconal Court of Sudbury, co. Suffolk, on the 5 Oct. 1649, by the oath of the Executrix, wife of Thomas Frost.

In the will of Robert Newgate the elder, of Great Horningsheath, next Newton, co. Suffolk, probably grandfather of John Newgate of Boston, dated May 23, 1608, I find mention of sales of lands to Mr. Revell. Now this Mr. Revell may have been the John Revell, a merchant of London, who loaned to the Plymouth Colony money through Isaac Allerton, their agent, in 1626, and who was chosen Assistant to the Massachusetts Bay Colony, Oct. 20, 1629, and was one of the five undertakers appointed with Gov. Winthrop to reside in New England where he went in the "Jewell," one of· Winthrop's fleet, landing there in June, 1630; but returned home next month with Mr. Vassall and Mr. Bright in the "Lion" of Bristol. Perhaps it was through this Mr. Revell that John Newgate happened to emigrate.

We find among the names of Gentlemen mentioned in Blomefield's History of Norfolk, and Fuller's Worthies of England, as early as the year 1400, the name of Newgate. The family held considerable estates at Holkham, Wells, and adjoining parishes in the county of Norfolk.

* Second Rep. Record Commissioners of Boston (1877), p. 170.

In 1433 a certain William Newgate, gentleman, is mentioned. Again in 1501, another William Newgate is recorded as being seized of a messuage, 200 acres of land, 40 acres pasture, and the appurtenances, in Apton and Apelton in the same county. These estates were enlarged by others which came by marriage with the Bedingfield, Congham, Watson and other families; also by grants from the crown. Charles I. granted Robert Newgate salt marshes in Holkham, with power to enclose the same, for £150 paid to the king, to be held of his manor of East Greenwich by fealty only in free and common soccage. In this grant, boundaries by the sea are mentioned.

In 1659 a certain Edmund Newgate, of Holkham, sold his estates for £3400 to John Coke, Esq., of Holkham, ancestor of Earl Leicester. This Edmund Newgate, in 1664, records his pedigree at the College of Arms (without a coat), as Newgate alias Newdegate of Wighton, co. Norfolk, where he still held estates. In 1667–8, Nathaniel Newgate, of London, merchant (son of John Newgate, of Boston, in New England, who was formerly of Horningsheath, near Bury St. Edmunds, co. Suffolk), in his will dated Sept. 8, 1668, calls himself Newgate *alias* Newdegate. It is probable that these two gentlemen were near relatives, and may have had some evidence of their relationship to the Surry family of Newdegate, and decided to add the *alias*.

The following is an extract from the will of John Pynner, gentleman, of Bury St. Edmunds, co. Suffolk, dated April 26, 1639 :

Items In consideration that *John Newgate of Bury St. Edmunds, maultster* divers & sondry times hath come to and resorted to Comfort & confer with me in the time of my sorrow, &c. &c. I doe give & bequeth unto him the said John Newgate the sum of four pounds lawfull money of England, to be paid unto him within one year next after my decease.

The will of Philip Newgate, of Great Horningsheath, Ickworth, co. Suffolk, proved Aug. 10, 1636, is witnessed by John Newgate, *probably the maulster* of Bury St. Edmunds.

I have copy of all the Norfolk, Suffolk and London Newgate wills ; also extracts from the Parish Registers.

The will of Alice Newgate, of Claye next Sea, co. Norfolk, widow, dated Nov. 20, 1623, probate (dated May 4, 1624) by Michael Pead, with letters of attorney for Joseph or *Joshua Newgate*, executor, now in parts beyond the seas, in Anchusen or Enkhesen in the kingdom of Holland. This may have been the *Joshua Newgate* who died in Boston, Nov. 20, 1658.

A Christopher Newgate is mentioned as a subscriber to the Virginia Adventure, 1619 ; amount of subscription, £25. This may have been the Christopher Newgate, merchant of London, owner of ship "Barbara," 1632–3. State Papers, year 1633, page 354.

775

CHURCH OF ST. AUGUSTINE. HEDON. YORKSHIRE

THE ANCESTRY OF ELLEN NEWTON, WIFE OF EDWARD CARLTON OF ROWLEY, MASS.

Contributed by Tracy Elliot Hazen, Ph.D., of New York City,
for the Tercentenary Celebration of Rowley

The first of these contributions* presented a detailed account of three generations of the forbears of Edward Carlton, and somewhat problematical indications of two earlier generations, to carry the line back to the 14th year of King Henry VIII (1522). The present article will record four generations of the ancestry of Mr. Carlton's wife, Ellen Newton, tracing her line clearly back to the death of her great-great-grandfather in the seventh year of Henry VIII (1515). It will be seen that a main thread of the evidence is the continuity of land tenure, most important in old English lineages, where it can be traced.

The origin of this Newton family cannot be determined with certainty, but there can be little doubt that the surname had its beginning, as in the case of the Carleton family, in one of two small hamlets in the parish of Aldbrough, bordering on the North Sea, northeast of Hull (see sketch map in REGISTER, vol. 93, p. 10). East Newton and West Newton are "recorded in Domesday as in the manor of Aldbrough, and are no doubt so named from their relative position to it as New towns." (Poulson, History of Holderness, vol. 2, pp. 27, 31–32.) In the ninth year of Edward I Thomas de Newton held here 2 carucates, where 48 make a knight's fee. 15 Edward I Thomas de Newton, of Aldburgh Newton, held 4 bovates in demesne, and 12 bovates of land in service. Temp. Henry III Thomas de Neuton held, of the King *in capite*, 4 oxgangs of land *in Dominio* in Neuton, with three tofts, by knight service. 19 Henry III Thomas de Newton gave to Meaux Abbey 2 closes in East Newton. In the same year the heirs of Thomas de Newton held in this place in demesne, half a carucate and in service, one carucate and a half, as of the fee of Albemarle.

The documents on which this pedigree is based are set forth in the following pages. For the first three generations the setting was

---

* See REGISTER, vol. 93 (January 1939), pp. 3–46.

(Pp. 373-418, the first volume of this series.)

[1] P. 381, the first volume of this series.

entirely rural; in the next two generations the families centered about the fine old Church of Saint Augustine (known as the "King of Holderness") * in Hedon, in the southeast part of Yorkshire, where, at the early age of thirty-six, the father of Ellen Newton, two years after her birth, attained the dignity of the office of mayor, and was thereafter alderman.

From Inquisitions Post Mortem †

Inquisition post mortem John Newton, York, 1529. Inquisition taken at Great Dryffeld in the aforesaid County on the xiij[th] day of September in the xxi[st] year of the reign of King Henry VIII before Peter Vavasour knight Ralph pulleyn Walter Grymston and laurence fforster commissioners of the lord King after the death of John Newton gentleman by the oath of William Newton [and eleven other jurors named] who say on their oath that the aforesaid John Newton named in the aforesaid commission was seized in . . . ‡ iiij acres of land meadow and pasture with their appurtenances in Riell and Preston in the aforesaid County which are worth by the year in all issues beyond reprises iiij li vi s And of one messuage and two closes of meadow and pasture with the appurtenances . . . which are worth by the year in all issues beyond reprises xxvj s viij d and also of one messuage and ij closes of pasture in Heddon and Paull with appurtenances which are worth by the year in all issues beyond reprises xxvj s . . . bovate of land x acres of meadow xx acres of pasture and iij s iiij d of free rent with their appurtenances in Ryell aforesaid which are worth by the year in all issues beyond reprises lviij s viij d And of two bovates of land and pasture with the appurtenances in Preston aforesaid which are worth by the year in all issues beyond reprises xxxiiij s vij [d] . . . And further the aforesaid Jurors say that the aforesaid messuage one bovate of land x acres of meadow xx of pasture and iij s iiij d of free rent with their appurtenances in Ryhill are held of Thomas, Earl of Rutlond as of his manor of Rosse by knight's service And that the aforesaid iiij bovates of land meadow and pasture with appurtenances in Ryhill and Preston and one messuage with one close in Paull are held of the lord King by reason of the forfeiture of Edward late Duke of Bukingham as of his manor of Bristwyk by knight's service And the aforesaid messuage and two closes with appurtenances in Skeklyng are held of the lord King in bondage by copy of Court [Roll] by reason of the forfeiture of the aforesaid late Duke of Bukingham as of his aforesaid manor And that the aforesaid ij bovates of land meadow and pasture with appurtenances in Preston are held of the Abbot of Thorneton by fealty And also that the aforesaid close with appurtenances in Heddon aforesaid is held of the mayor of the town of Heddon in free Burgage And further they say that the aforesaid John Newton named in the said commission neither had nor held nor did any other persons have in tenure for his use any other lands or tenements in the county aforesaid on the day on which he died And that the aforesaid John Newton died on the ninth day of June in the seventh year of the reign of the lord now King [1515] And that John Newton is his son and heir and was at the time of this inquisition of the age of

---

* The photograph of this church which appears in the frontispiece was made in August 1938, especially for the purpose of this paper, with the kind permission of the Vicar, by Messrs. Turner and Drinkwater of Hull; it had to be taken just before twilight in order to secure the best lighting on this north front.

† Preserved in the Public Record Office, London.

‡ . . . indicate words omitted because of illegibility or torn condition of the original document. This inquisition was so exceptionally difficult because of its faintness and worn condition that I was obliged to avail myself of the expert assistance of Miss Lucy Drucker, whose reading at critical places was entirely convincing, once it had been pointed out.—T. E. H.

xiij years x months and six days and more. (Chancery Inquisitions Post Mortem, Series II, 49/26.)

Inquisition post mortem John Newton, 1587. Inquisition taken at York Castle in the county of York on the xxx[th] day of November in the xxix[th] year of the reign of the lady Elizabeth by the grace of god Queen of England France and Ireland defender of the faith etc. before William Hildyard esquire eschaetor of the lady Elizabeth in the county aforesaid by virtue of a writ of *diem clausit extremum* for inquiring after the death of John Newton late of Ryall in the county aforesaid deceased by the oath of [15 jurors named] who say on their oath that the aforesaid John Newton on the day of his death was seized in his demesne as of fee of and in one messuage five and a half bovates of arrable land meadow and pasture with the appurtenances in Ryall and Camerton in the said county of York as of and in three and a half bovates of arrable land meadow and pasture with the appurtenances in Preston in the said county of York. And existing so seized he died therein seized. And further the jurors say on their oath that the messuage and other aforesaid premises with their appurtenances in Riall and Camerton aforesaid are held and at the time of the death of the aforesaid John Newton were held of Henry Constable knight as of his manor of Burstwick by knight's service and that they are worth by the year in all issues beyond reprises xxx s. And that the three bovates of land in preston aforesaid are held and at the time of the death of the aforesaid John Newton were held of the said Henry Constable knight as of his manor of Burstwick by knight's service . . . and they are worth by the year in all issues beyond reprises xxxvi s viij d and that the aforesaid John Newton died about the xxviij[th] day of April in the xxix[th] year of the reign of the said Queen And that John Newton is the son and next heir of the said John Newton and was at the time of the death of his father of the age of about two years and three months And that the aforesaid John Newton deceased on the day of his death held no other lands or hereditaments of the Queen nor of any other person in the county aforesaid. (Chancery Inquisitions Post Mortem, Series II, vol. 215, no. 271.)

Inquisition post mortem Ellen (Newton) Bracks, 1635. Inquisition taken at York Castle in the County of York on the twenty-ninth day of August in the thirteenth year of our lord Charles by the grace of god King of England Scotland France and Ireland and defender of the faith etc. before Darcye Washington Esquire eschaetor for inquiring after the death of Elianor Bracks late of Headdon in the county aforesaid widow deceased by the oath of [15 jurors named] who say on their oath that the aforesaid Elianor Bracks named in the said writ on the day on which she died was seized in her demesne as of fee of and in the Manor of Ryhill and Camerton with all the rights members and appurtenances belonging to the said Manor in the said county of York And also of and in five bovates of arrable land meadow and pasture with their appurtenances and certain lands commonly called fforby landes containing by estimation a half of one bovate of land with the appurtenances in Ryhill aforesaid and also of and in three bovates of arrable land meadow and pasture with their appurtenances in Preston in the said County and that the aforesaid Elianor Bracks named in the aforesaid writ existing thus seized of the premises as above set forth, on the fifteenth day of September which was in the year of our Lord one thousand six hundred thirty five died of such her estate therein so seized. And further the said Jurors on their aforesaid oath say that the aforesaid manor of Ryhill cum Camerton with the appurtenances are held and at the time of the death of the aforesaid Elianor Bracks were held of the said lord King in chief as of his honor of Albemarle by knight's service (vizt) by a sixteenth part of one knight's fee and were worth by the year in all issues beyond reprises thirteen shillings and four pence and that the other

779

premises with the appurtenances in Ryhill aforesaid are held and at the time of the death of the aforesaid Elianor Bracks were held of the said lord King in chief as of his honor of Albemarle by knight's service and are worth by the year in all issues beyond reprises six shillings and eight pence And that the said three bovates of land in Preston with the appurtenances are held and at the time of the death of the aforesaid Elianor Bracks were held of the said lord King as of his Abbatt of Thorneton in the County of Lincoln by knight's service and are worth by the year in all issues beyond reprises ten shillings And that ffrancis Newton is her relative and next heir (namely) son and heir of Thomas Newton who was brother of John Newton who was the father of the aforesaid Elianor Bracks named in the aforesaid writ and he was at the time of the death of the aforesaid Elianor Bracks named in the aforesaid writ of the age of fifty years and more . . . [Signed] Darcye Washington Esr. (Chancery Inquisitions Post Mortem, Series II, vol. 558, f° 82.)

FROM PROBATE RECORDS

The WILL of PETER FLINTON.   21 Nov. 1574, I Peter flinton of Garton in Holdernes, sicke in bodie.   To be buried w^thin the churche earthe of Garton. To my cosyn Edwarde fflinton of Hull his wyfe and his children x li. . . . To Mr. Peter Tresholde my landlorde two olde angeles trusting that his worshipp will se my executors or assigns may enioye one lease that I did take of his worshupp . . . To everie one of my godbarnes . . . Itm̄ I do gyve to Thomas Newton my sone in lawe vi li xiij s iiij d in consideration that he shalbe good to John Troughite . . . To everie one of my brother Johans children not married xl s. . . . Itm I gyve to Elizabeth Newton my doughter all my leases duringe all my yeres wth all my rights and interest that I have in any of them excepte of one lease to me morgaged of one tenamente of Willm Thomsons wyfe wch lease I do gyve to John Troughite . . . to the said John Troughite fyftie poundes.   I will that Thomas Newton my sone in lawe shalbe bounde in obligacon to my brother John flinton wth sufficiente suertie to give to my doughter Elizabeth Newton at hir pleasur to her childe or children or any other frende & yt beyinge so gyven by hir Then the said Thomas Newton to pay the same to suche p'sons as the same shalbe given.   The reste of all my goods to Elizabeth Newton my doughter whom I mayke executrix.   Witnesses John flinton, M'tine Rawson, Richarde Moore, Peter Hardie, Roberte Dickson Store, Thomas Samson, and Willm Crossetwalys.   Proved 22 July 1575; administration to Elizabeth, the daughter, sole executrix named.   (York Registry, vol. 19, f° 811.)

The WILL of JOHN FLINTON.   17 December 1584, I John fflinton of Garton in Holdernes.   [To numerous servants (?) and poor.]   I give to Elizabeth Newton my nece a sorelld amblinge meare wch I bought of Thomas Squier and to eyther of her two Boyes ane ewe and a lambe trusting that she will helpe my executors to that wch she her husband and his executores owethe me.   To my sonne M'maduke fflinton fortie pound and my owne graye geldinge.   To my doughter Elline Standover . . . Thomas Standover my sonne in lawe. Residue to M'maduke Grimston of Grimston Esquier, John Catterall of Holme gentleman and Thomas Mosley of York merchant, whom I make executors.   (York Registry, vol. 23, f° 275.)

The WILL of THOMAS NEWTON.   15 Sept. 1583, I Thomas Newton of Garton in Holdernes in the Countie of Yorke Gentleman sicke in bodie.   To be buried w^thin the churche yeard of Garton aforesaid.   To the poure people w^thin the p'ishe of Garton twentie shillinges, to be equallie dyvided amongst them wher most need is.   To Elizabeth Newton my wyfe her feoffement and the third of all my goods. The reste of all my goodes wth my leases not geven nor bequiethed my detts being paid my legacies and fun'alles discharged and allowed, I give them unto ffraunces Newton, John Newton and the child yet beinge in the mother's wombe my children whom I make my full and whole executors joyntlie altogether of this my last will and testament. Itm I ordeyne and make John Newton my brother the gardion of my said sone ffraunces Newton. Itm I make and ordeyne Jerome Newton my brother gardion of my sone John Newton and also I make M'maduke Grimston of Grimstone Garthe gardion to the child yet beinge in my wife's bodie if yt shall please god that the said child do lyve and my wyfe well delivered of the same. Thes beinge witnesse John Newton, John Gwyre & John fflinton with others.

Proved 6 May 1584 and administration granted to Jerome Newton and John Newton the tutors or curators for the use and benefit of ffraucis Newton and John children of the said deceased, named as executors in said will, right being reserved to the offspring existing in the womb of Elizabeth Newton, mother of the said offspring. (York Probate Registry, vol. 22, f° 666.)

The WILL of MRS. MARGARET NEWTON of Flinton, 1587. In the name of God amen the xxviij^th day of August In the yeare of our Lord god a thousand fyve hundrethe foure score and seaven, I Margaret Newton of fflinton in Holdrenes in the countie of Yorke gentle woman sicke in bodye but of good and p'fect remembrance thanks be to god doe make this my last will and testament in manner and forme followinge. ffirst I bequethe my soule to almightie god my saviour by whose deathe I trust to have Remission of all my synes and my bodye to be buried at the discresion of my executors. Itm I give and bequiethe to Margaret Grymstone my servante my best gowne and my best petticott, Also I give to Isabell Grymstone my brother wyfe my russett gowne and my next best petticott. Also I give to Margaret Grymstone a whyt whye in the pasture thre yeares old. Also I gyve to Margaret Grymstone my servant the bedstead that I lye in a mattris a coverlett that lyethe on the Bed a paire of harden sheets a Boulster. Also I give to Ranse Rawsone fowre kye the best that he will choyse. Also I give to my brother Christofer Grymstone an acre of wheat and an acre of pease. Also I give to my brother Christofer Grymstone daughters ffrances Grymstone Isabell Grymstone and Elline Grymstone everye one of them thre shillinges fowre pence. Also I give to Mr. Marmaduke Grymston my Landslord my stoced horsse trustinge his worshippe wilbe good to my sonnes as to lett them the farme againe that I Dwell in. Also I give to the poore ffolkes in Humbleton sixe shillinges eyghte pence. And I give to the poore in ffytlin sixe shillinges eyghte pence. And in Esternewicke and Deane Thorpe sixe shillinges eyghte pence. Itm I give to everye poore house in flinton eyghte pence. Also I give to Elline Becke my syster my Blewe worssett kirtle. Also I give to John Newton sonne of John Newton my sonne twentie shillinges to be paid by my executor when John Newton comes to be of one and twentie yeares of aige. Also I give to Robert Newton and Elline Newton and Lanncelott Newton everye one of them thre shillinges fowre pence. Also I give to George Gryscrofte, Thomas Deighton, Henrye Litster, Willm Squier, John Mycaell, John Comynge, my s'vantes everye one of them twelve pence. Also I give to John Newton, ffrancis Newton sonnes of Thomas Newton to be paid when they come to be of thaige of one and twentie yeares eyther of them thre shillinges foure pence. Also I give to Christopher Englishe two shillinges sixe pence. Also I owe Heirome Newton twelve poundes for Rent of wadsorthe house. The Rest of my goodes unbequiethed I give to ffrancis Newton and Hierome Newton my sonnes whome I make my whole executors of this my last will and testament. Thes witnesses Robert Wright, Christofer Grimston, Thomas Wood.

And 13 December 1588 the dean of Holdreness certified concerning the probate of this will through the said witnesses above named, being sworn, and administration was granted to the executors named in the said will. (York Registry, vol. 23, f° 936.)

The WILL of JOHN NEWTON, 1587. In the name of god amen The xxiij[th] day of marche in the yeare of our lord god a thousand fyve hunderthe eyghtie seaven I John Newton of fflinton in the P'ishe of Humbleton in Holderness in the countie of yorke gentlemā sicke in bodie but of good and p'fect remembrance thanked be god do make and ordeyne this my last will and testament in manor and forme followinge. ffirst I bequieth my soule to almyghtie god my maker and redeamer trustinge most faithfullie that by and throughe the merritts death and passion of my Lord and Saviour Jesus Christ to have remission and forgiveness of all my synes, and as touchinge the buriall of this my bodie I leave yt to the order and discretion of my executors hearin this my p'sent Testament to be named. Itm I give to my brother ffrancis Newton my sonne Launclott Newton, and he to learne hym his occupatōn and I will that he have a yocke of oxen fyve kye and the howshold stufe that he haith of myne, and my brother ffrancis to have yt unto Lawnclott come to the age of xxi[tie] yeares. Itm I give to Ranse Rawsone one cowe that John Todd haithe in his coustedie. Itm I give to Marie Newton my wyfe the third of my Lands wch the Lawe doth alowe and I will that she have an other third pte of my Landes to my sonne John Newton come to xxi[tie] yeares of aige to paye all my dettes withall and the other third pte to be due to the cheefe hed of the fee. Itm I give to Isabell Grymston a cowe, and she to have other two kye one geve by Thomas Newton and the other by Elizabeth Shipwright wch I have in kepeinge. Itm I give to M'garet Grymstone one haroked whye in the houste. Itm I give to Elline Grymstone a brandied whye in the garth. Itm I give to Xpofer Grymstone one acre of wheat at ferre Burton holes and the peas at the hyther burton holes. Itm I give to Willm̄ Cooke foure shillinges that he owes me. Itm I give to Margaret Grundall tenne shillinges. Itm I give to Martyne Browne foure shillinges. Itm I give to Alice Sanderson thre shillinges foure pence. Itm I give to Isabell Medley thre shillinges foure pence. Itm I give to John Walker a cowe for and considerynge his wages to Martynemas next the price thirtie shillinges. Itm I give to Robte Dumbler his Ladies day Rent wch is viij s. Itm I make and ordeyne my brother Hyerome Newton guardian of my sonne Robte Newton. Itm I make and ordeyne Marie Newton my wife guardian of my daughter Elline Newton. Itm I praye and desyer Mr. Marmaduke Grymston even as my trust is in hym that he will buy my sone John Newton of Sr Henrie Counstable by cause I would have him brought upe in that house as my father was. Itm I give to John Armytaige thre shillinges foure pence. Itm I give to everie poure house in fflinton eyght pence. And to everie poure house in Humbleton foure pence. Itm I give to Robte Newton my sonne foure pounde sexe shillinges eyghte pence in the yeare after my mother her decesse wch she is possessed upon for and duringe hir lyfe naturall. Itm I give to my sonne Launnclett a house in the tenor and occupacōn of Willm̄ Wadfurth and one other house in the tenor and occupacōn of Ranse Hanstey wth all their appurtenances thereto belonginge nexte and immediatlie after the decease of the said Launclett then the same to be and remaine to my sonne and heire forever. Itm I give to Maister Marmaduke Grymstone my good will of ffrances my brother sonne and his porcōn untill he come to aige. Itm I give to John Newton my sonne a gray year aige fillie. Itm I give unto my brother Hierome Newton halfe of a farme in Garton praysed to thirteene pounds sexe shillinges eyghte pence the whole farme. And he to paye for the halfe of yt as yt is praysed to me in the porcōn of ffrances Newton my brothers sonne.   Itm I give to Sʳ Xpofer Inglishe two shillinges sexe pence.   Itm I make and ordeyne Mr. Marmaduke Grymstone and Hierome Newton my brother the sup'visores of this my last will and testament.   The rest of all my goods not geven nor bequiethed my legacies and funalles discharged and alowed I give them unto Robte Newton my sonne and Elline Newton my daughter whome I ordeyne and make my joynt and whole executors of this my last will and testament.   Itm I give to everie one of thes witnesses of this my p'sent will and testament tenne shillinges.   Thes beinge witnesses Hierome Newton, Robt Weight and Willm Sledde.

And on the fifth day of the month of October in the year of our Lord one thousand five hundred eighty seven the dean of Holderness certified concerning the probate of this will by the witnesses above named being sworn.   And administration of the goods of the same was committed unto Marie Skipsey alias Newton for the use and accommodation of Robert and Ellene children and executors named in the will of the said deceased during their minority. (York Registry, vol. 23, fᵒ 544.)

16 June 1591 Christopher Grymston was admitted to the tutorship or curatorship of Robert and Ellen Newton children of John Newton of fflynton deceased, and of their goods, rights, and portions during their minority, having been sworn in form of law, and the aforesaid Christopher Grymston and others were placed under bond.

On the same day, administration of the goods, rights, and credits which belonged to William Skipsey late of Ryall in Holdernes, deceased, was committed to Mary, relict of the deceased, sworn in form of law, and the said relict and others were put under bond.   (York Registry, Act Book, Holderness, 1591.)

[15 April 1600] the said dean certified that he had committed the tuition or curation of Lancelot ffarmer alias Newton, twenty years of age, supposed son of John Newton late (while he lived) of fflinton in the diocese of York, deceased, and the administration of his goods, rights and portion, to Cuthbert Leeche, previously sworn, and the aforesaid Cuthbert and others were put under bond.   (York Registry, Act Book, Holderness, 1600.)

The WILL of ELLEN (NEWTON) BRACKS, 1638.   In the name of God Amen September the ffift [1635] I Hellen Brackes of Headon in Holmderse widdow being sicke in body but of good & perfect remembrance.   To be buried in the church of Sct. Augustine in Headon aforesaid besides that place where my husband lyeth buryed.   Whereas I heretofore about the nynth day of October anno dni 1633 did make an estate in trust to Mʳ Christopher Hollme of Paullhollme Esq. and unto Mʳ ffrancis Edgar of Wynestead clerke of all my freehold land within the towne ffeilds and territoryes in Preston Rihill & Cammerton unto the use and behoofe of my neeces Hellen, Mary, Elizabeth & ffrances Newton the daughters of my brother Launcelot Newton dec: with promise that all the said lands and estate of them should remaine in my own power to revoke and disanull duringe the tyme of my natural life att my will and pleasure as by the severall deeds and the Lands conteyned may appeare now my will and minde is that the said severall deeds and the lands conteyned in them shalbe ratifyed and confirmed and I doe ratify and confirme the same according to their several uses unto my said neeces and to their heires for ev'.   Item I give unto my neece Hellen Newton x li.   Unto the children of my coosen Elizabeth Burstall viz. to William Robert and Hellen Burstall x li to be equally divided amongst them & my will is that it shalbe put forward for their benefitt till they accomplish lawful age.   Unto Mʳ Edgar, to his wife &

to his children ffower old angells of gold. Unto Mʳ Christopher Hollme a
twenty shilling peece of gould. Unto Mʳ William Burstall & to his wife
each of them x s. To James Atkinson my nephew v li in three years. To
Jane Atkinson twenty shillings. To Thomas Little x s. To my two servants
to each ij s vi d. To Isabell the daughter of Mʳ John Burstall a gold ring.
To my neece Elizabeth Newton a gould ring. To my neece ffrances Newton
a gold ring which her grandmother gave unto mee. To my coosens ffrancis
and John Newton to each of them xx s. To the poor of Headon xxx s, of
Preston xxx s, of Burstwicke xxx s, of Ryhill xx s. To my sister Gilby x s.
To my neece Mary Newton x s to make her a ring. To Thomas Cole and
his wife to ech of them 5 s. To Henry Cuppledicke & his wife five shillings
each. Item all the rest of my goods unto Elizabeth Newton and ffrances
Newton my two neeces whome I do make the joynt executrices of this my
last will and testament.

Witnesses: ffrancis Edgar clerk, Thomas Little.

her mke
[Signed]   Hellen **E** Brackes

[1 October 1635] the said Mʳ Edgar certified concerning the probate of this
will through the witnesses named, being sworn, and administration of the
goods of the said deceased was committed to Elizabeth Newton and ffrances
Newton, relicts, coexecutrices named in the same will, being previously
sworn.   (York Registry, original will; also registered in vol. 42, fᵒ 674.)

From Feet of Fines *

Final agreement made in the King's Court at Westminster, in the quinzaine
of Easter, 5 James I [1607] before the King's justices there, between Lancelot
Farmarye alias Newton, plaintiff, and Robert Braxe and Helen his wife,
deforciants, of the annual rent of ten pounds issuing out of the manor of
Ryhill, and from 24 acres of land, 10 acres of meadow, and 30 acres of pasture
in Riall and Camerton, whereof a plea of covenant was summoned in the
same court, that is, that Robert and Helen granted the said rent to Lancelot
and rendered the same to him in this court to have and to hold to him and the
lawful heirs of his body, and Robert and Helen and the heirs of Helen warrant
him and his said issue in the same against themselves and the heirs of Helen
forever. For which grant etc., Lancelot has given Robert and Helen
200 pounds sterling.   (Feet of Fines, Yorks, Easter, 5 James I.)

Final agreement made in the King's Court at Westminster, in the quinzaine
of Easter, 8 James I [1610] before the King's justices there, between Lancelot
Newton, plaintiff, and John Burrell and Jane his wife, deforciants, of a
messuage, a garden, an orchard, and a rood of land in Headon, whereof a
plea of covenant was summoned between them, that is, that the said John
and Jane acknowledged the same to be the right of Lancelot, as of their gift,
and that they had remised and quitclaimed for themselves and the heirs of
Jane to the said Lancelot and his heirs forever. And further for themselves
and the heirs of Jane have granted to warrant Lancelot and his heirs therein
against themselves and the heirs of Jane forever. For which acknowledge-
ment etc., Lancelot has given them forty pounds sterling. (Feet of Fines,
Yorks, Easter, 8 James I.)

A Fine of Edward Carleton and Ellen (Newton) his wife, of property in
Ryhill and Camerton, Easter, 14 Charles I [1638], was printed in the Register,
vol. 93 (January 1939), p. 13. (P. 385, the first volume of this series.)

* Preserved in the Public Record Of

FROM LAY SUBSIDIES FOR CO. YORK, EAST RIDING (1520–1630)*

16 Henry VIII [1524] (202/167) Assessment
Holym
    On John Newton for his lands xij d.
    On Stephen Newton for his goods xij d.
[Margin worn away]†
    [On J]ohn Newton for his goods xij d.

33 Henry VIII [1541/2] (203/192)
Patterryngton
    John Newton in goods [valued at] xx li. [subsidy] x s.

Hollome
    Stephen Newton in goods [valued at] xx li. [subsidy] x s.

Halseham
    Edmund Newton in goods [valued at] xx li. [subsidy] x s.

[Flinton does not occur]

7 Edward VI [1553] (261/1)
Lyssyt
    Thomas Newton in goods [valued at] vj li. [subsidy] iiij s.

5 Elizabeth [1562/3] (203/273)
Patrington
    John Newton in goods [valued at] xx li. [subsidy] xxxiij s. iiij d.

Flynton with Etherwyke
    Maystres Newton in lands [valued at] xxx s. [subsidy] iiij s.

14 Elizabeth [1571/2] (204/296)
Awbroughe cum Bewick
    Henry Newton is worth in goods iij li. [subsidy] iij s.

Flinton and Etherwick
    Margaret Newton widow is worth in lands xxx s. [subsidy] ij s.

40 Elizabeth [1597/8] (204/340)
[Pat]rington
    John Neweton in lands [valued at] iiij li. [subsidy] xvj s.

Flinton and Ethernewicke
    Jerrome Neweton in lands [valued at] xxx s. [subsidy] vj s.

Lissett
    Thomas Neweton in goods [valued at] iij li. [subsidy] viij s.

FROM THE PARISH REGISTERS OF HUMBLETON, YORKSHIRE

Baptisms

1578 Elizabeth fillia Bryan Brax May 22.
1584 John fillius John Newton Feb. 14.
1586 Robert fillius John Newton Sept. 28.

Burials

1587 John Newton Aprill 2.
1587 Margrit Newton Decemb. 14.
1587 John fillius John Newton Jan. 13.
1599 Jayne uxor Herom Newton Januarie 5.
1602 Isabell Braxe ux Briani Oct. 15.
1608 Jerome Newtone ffebruarie 22.

* Preserved in the Public Record Office, London. The early subsidies are so very difficult that the contributor had them all done by Miss Lilian J. Redstone. It is disappointing to find so few Newton items. Subsidies of 4 and 5 Edward VI and 22 James I furnish lists for Ryhill, Paul, Preston, Skeckling, Garton and Humbleton, and the last also Flinton, but no Newton names occur.
† The place name worn away in the subsidy of 1524 Miss Redstone suggests might be Patrington. Without having seen the original document, the contributor ventures the guess that it might be Ryhill, which occurs in the subsidy of 1541/2, but without any Newton.

785

1611 Bryan Braxe Januarie 11.
1622 Elling the wyfe of Robart braxe the iijth of december.
1625 Robertus Brax nove' 21.
1653 Thomas Newton of Lelley-dike bur. Sept. 6.

Marriages

1587 Willm Skypsey & Marye Newton July 18.
1604 Robert Braxxe and Elline Newton June 10.

FROM THE REGISTER OF GARTON, YORKSHIRE

1585 Marmaduke Todde & Elisabeathe Newton maried the 3 day of July.
1589 Jone Newton buryed ye xviij Julye.
1689 Jane Newton was buried 7 ber 15.

FROM THE REGISTERS OF HEDON, YORKSHIRE

1560–1670

Baptisms

1580 Henry Newton sone of ffrancis Newton was baptized April 20.
1582 Gabriell Newton sone of ffrancis Newton was baptized Maie 4.
1582[/3] Michaell Newton sone of ffrancis Newton was baptized ffebruary 24.
1611 Thomas the sonne of Lancelot New[ton] * was baptized the 18th day June.
1614 Ellen the daughter of Lancelot Newton was baptized on St Matthias day Anno Dni one thousand six hundred and fower teene I say A° Dni 1614.
1617 Marg'ry daughter of Launcelot Newton alderman was bap: May 2.
1619 Elsabeth ye daughter of Launcelott Newton Alderm. bapt. Januar. 2.
1619 Ellen ye daughter of John Newton was bapt. Januar. 30.
1621 John ye sonne of Richard Newton was baptized Apr. 7.
1621 Thomas ye sonne of John Newton was bapt. Oct. 24.
1621 ffrances daughter to Lancelote Newton was bapt. Jenuarie day 2.
1623 William sonne to John Newton baptized Aprill day 12.
1627[/8] Jane the daugh of Richard Newton was baptized March 22.

Burials

1619 Ellen ye daughter of Richard Newton was buryed Sept. 30.
1619 Ellen ye daughter of John Newton was buryed Febr: 23.
1622 Mr Lanclotte Newton Alderman was buryed Aug. 30.
1632 Marie Newton gent was buryed March 12.
1635 Ellen Bracks gent. was buryed September 16.
1657 John Newton was buryed ffeb: 19.
1667 Mary the wife of Rich. Newton was buried Novemb. 22.
1669 Margarett ye wife of Thomas Newton buried March ye 6th.

Marriages †

1617 Richard Newton & Maude Prawokr (?) were marryed Sept. 4.

From the foregoing documents and records the subjoined pedigree is derived.

---

* It appeared certain to me that a syllable "ton" had been clipped off from "New" at the right margin of the page in the rebinding of the register. No "New" family items were found in this register elsewhere.
† No Newton marriages 1560–1616.

1. JOHN NEWTON, gentleman, died 9 June 1515, probably as a comparatively young man. His chief seat appears to have been at Ryhill, near Hedon, in the southeast part of Yorkshire, where he was seized of a messuage, one bovate of land, ten acres of meadow and twenty acres of pasture, held of Thomas, Earl of Rutland, as of his manor of Roos. As set forth in his inquisition post mortem, taken in 1529, about fourteen years after his death, he was also seized of a messuage and close in Paull and a messuage and two closes in Skeckling, held of the King as of his manor of Burstwick, and of lands in Hedon and Preston. There is no definite indication of the identity of his wife, who evidently survived him; but from the circumstance, disclosed later in the will of his grandson, that his young son was brought up in the house of the lord of the manor of Grimston Garth in Garton, the suggestion may be ventured that John Newton may have married a daughter of the main line of the Grimston family, and that she returned to her paternal roof after the death of her husband. This conjecture is possibly strengthened by the fact that no record is found of the guardianship of the young heir, or of his livery of seisin on attainment of his majority. Walter Grimston, named as one of the King's Commissioners in the inquisition, was the head of the family at this time, and might have been the father or brother of John Newton's wife. The William Newton who was one of the jurors may have been a near relative, possibly identical with a William Newton, gentleman, who sold to William Maunsel of York one bovate of land in Humbleton 23 Henry VIII, or he may have been a member of the Newton family of Patrington. No other children are of record, save the "son and heir" named in the inquisition, born about five months after the death of his father.

Child:

2. i. JOHN, b. on or about 7 Nov. 1515.

2. JOHN NEWTON (*John*), born on or about 7 Nov. 1515, died rather early, like his father, probably before the date of the lay subsidy of 1562/3, when his wife (who was MARGARET GRIMSTON) was taxed for lands at Flinton as "Maystres Newton," and certainly before the subsidy of 1571/2, when she was called "Margaret Newton, widow." She evidently lived chiefly at Flinton, a hamlet in the parish of Humbleton, where she was buried 14 Dec. 1587. In her will, dated 28 Aug. 1587, and proved 13 Dec. 1588, she gave bequests to her brother Christopher Grimston and his daughters, to her sister Ellen Becke, and to other Grimstons. She also bequeathed to John, Robert, Ellen, and Lancelot Newton (children of her eldest son), and to John and Francis Newton, children of her (deceased) son Thomas Newton; her sons Francis Newton and Jerome Newton were named executors. This will furnished the clue to the parentage of the testatrix: she was clearly the daughter of John Grimston of Aldbrough, gentleman,* who died in July 1534 (desiring to be buried in the

* A brief abstract of John Grimston's will, with notes on his ancestry, appeared in *Publications of the Surtees Society*, vol. 45, page 251. For this reference, and confirmation of the connection, I am

church of St. Michael at Garton), by his wife Elizabeth Eure, described in old pedigrees as the "daughter and heiress of Mr. Every of the Bishoprick;" her exact connection with the notable Eure family is not shown in the pedigrees of that family.

In the list of vicars of the parish of Preston is found a *Dominus* John Newton, instituted 5 June 1546 by the Subdean of York, and on 25 June 1546 also instituted as vicar of St. Augustine's Church at Hedon (sometimes regarded as a chapel of Preston). It seems possible that the Grimston family would have had sufficient influence to secure the appointment of their kinsman John Newton to such a benefice. It is surprising that no will or inquisition post mortem can be found for this John Newton.

Children, as shown by their own and their mother's wills:

3. i. JOHN.
4. ii. THOMAS.
5. iii. FRANCIS, b. about 1551.
    iv. JEROME, who was buried at Humbleton 22 Feb. 1608. JANE, his wife, had been buried at Humbleton 5 Jan. 1599. Their marriage does not appear to be recorded. With his brother Francis he was named residuary legatee and executor in his mother's will, 28 Aug. 1587; he was given half of a farm in Garton by the will of his brother John, dated 28 March 1587. He was taxed for lands at Flinton in the subsidy of 1597/8. No record of children found.

3. JOHN NEWTON (*John, John*), of Flinton, was buried at Humbleton 2 April 1587 (according to the parish register). The dates in regard to his death and will appear to be not altogether reliable. The inquisition post mortem calls him "late of Ryall," indicating that he retained the family estates there inherited from his grandfather, although he lived at Flinton, near his mother. The fact that the Ryhill estates were held of Sir Henry Constable, Knight, explains the desire expressed in his will by John Newton that "Mr. Marmaduke Grimston will buy [the guardianship of] my son John Newton of Sir Henry Counstable" because he preferred to have him brought up in the Grimston house, as his father had been. In this will, dated 23 March 1587, proved 5 October 1587 [according to the records] he provided for the four children named below, and to Marie Newton his wife gave "the third part of my lands which the law doth allow and another third part of my lands until my son John Newton come to the age of 21

---

indebted to the late Rev. Charles Moor, D.D., of London, the accomplished genealogist of the Grimston family, who has given me much additional information. John Grimston was a younger son of Thomas Grimston and Elizabeth Newark, and grandson of Walter Grimson of Grimston Garth by Elizabeth, daughter and coheiress of Sir John Portington, Knt. From Walter the line is carried back to 1150 (about eleven generations) in a paper by Dr. Moor, published in *The Genealogist*, n.s. vol. 29, 1913; he has furnished corrections to the pedigree in recent editions of Burke's *Landed Gentry*. The most interesting of these "corrections" is in the marriage of Thomas Grymeston who died in 1462 (father of Walter just mentioned) to Alice, daughter and heiress of Walter Flynton, probably a grandson of another Walter de Flynton aged 30 in 1342, who was the son and heir of Sir Herbert de Flynton by Cecelia, daughter and co-heiress of Sir Walter de la Lynde of Hartley Manor, Dorset.

years to pay all my debts withal." Although he named his son Robert Newton and his daughter Ellen Newton joint executors, the Court appointed Marie Skipsey alias Newton administrator for the use and accommodation of the children Robert and Ellen Newton during their minority. The Humbleton register discloses that the widow Marie Newton rather promptly, on 18 July 1587, had taken a second husband, William Skipsey, with whom she probably removed to Ryhill, perhaps the better to care for her lands there; she was appointed administrator of the estate of William Skipsey, late of Ryhill, deceased, 16 June 1591, and on the same day the guardianship of her children Robert and Ellen Newton was committed to Christopher Grimston (presumably their great-uncle).

The name of John Newton of Flinton is in a list of gentlemen at Glover's Visitation of Yorkshire in 1585, but he failed to have his pedigree recorded: without doubt he could have settled for us the name of his grandmother.

Children:

6. i. LANCELOT, b. about 1580.
   ii. ELLEN, d. 15 Sept. 1635 (Inq.p.m.) and was buried at Hedon 16 Sept. 1635; m. (by license) at Humbleton, 10 June 1604, ROBERT BRAX or BRACKS, who died before his wife, and was buried in the Church of St. Augustine, Hedon, though the register has not preserved the date. He was perhaps the son of Bryan and Isabel Braxe of Humbleton, born too early for record in the parish register. As Robert Brackes his name appears on the list of mayors of Hedon in 1614 and 1625. In her inquisition post mortem it is shown that Ellen Bracks held the Manor of Ryhill and Camerton, not previously mentioned as a Newton possession, and other lands in Ryhill and Preston apparently inherited through her father from her great-grandfather. She had possibly herself purchased the manor; the history of this manor is involved in much obscurity.* However, the inquisition and will of Ellen Bracks together form the keystone of this Newton pedigree. She had in 1633 made estate in trust for the benefit of the four daughters of her deceased brother Lancelot Newton, which was confirmed in the will. The "sister Gilby" and nephew James Atkinson named in the will probably represent relationships through her mother's second marriage to William Skipsey. The fact that the original will displays a capital **E** used as her mark in lieu of signature is sufficient confirmation that her name was Ellen, rather than the Helen used by the scribes.
   iii. JOHN, bapt. at Humbleton 14 Feb. 1584, bur. there 13 Jan. 1587; named in the will of his grandmother, and in the will and inquisition post mortem of his father.
   iv. ROBERT, bapt. at Humbleton 28 Sept. 1586; probably d. unm. By his father's will given to the guardianship of his uncle Jerome Newton, on 16 June 1591, together with his sister Ellen, he was placed by

---

* For example, in Yorkshire Fines (Yorks. Arch. Soc. vol. 8, pages 13, 164) the purchase of the manors of Ryall and Camerton by Henry Constable Kt. in 1594, is listed, and in 1601 purchase of a fourth part of the same manors by the same plaintiff. Earlier fines of 1559 and 1566 record the sale of the manor of Ryall, but no clear indication of continuous ownership, and no mention of purchase or sale by a Newton. (Yorks. Arch. Soc. vol. 2, pages 234, 319.) It was suggested that this matter might have been worked out for the Victoria County History, but when the Commission which has that project in hand very courteously put before me all their memoranda, nothing was found beyond the records set forth above.—T. E. H.

the Court under guardianship of Christopher Grimston. Nothing is known of him later.

4. THOMAS NEWTON (*John, John*) of Garton, died shortly before 6 May 1584, when his will was proved. He married, before 21 Nov. 1574, ELIZABETH FLINTON, daughter of Peter Flinton of Garton, in whose will of that date she was named executrix; she and her two boys were also beneficiaries in the will of her uncle, John Flinton of Garton, 17 Dec. 1584. Elizabeth Newton married secondly, at Garton, 3 July 1585, Marmaduke Todd. In the account of the Flinton family in Poulson's Holderness, the coat of arms attributed to Thomas Newton is the same as that described in Foster's Visitation of Yorkshire 1584/5 by Glover, for William Newton of Holderness: "Sable, three pairs of shin-bones in saltier, 2 and 1, the sinister surmounted of the dexter, argent."*

NEWTON

Children, probably born in Garton, but before the beginning of the parish register:

   i.   FRANCIS, mentioned in the inquisition post mortem of Ellen (Newton) Bracks in 1635 as then "of the age of fifty years and upward," but certainly born before 1585. He was declared next heir of Ellen

* In an old manuscript volume in the library of York Minster, under a heading "A collection of divers Gentlemen's coats of arms of Yorkshire blazoned by Edmō Yarburgh Esqᵗ" is found under Holderness: William Newton: Sable a Parrot proper with a Ring about his neck Legs gules inter 6 mens Thybones saltire ways argent. Our illustration is adapted from a tricked drawing in another part of the same manuscript volume, where it is clear that shin-bones, rather than thigh-bones, are represented.

The parrot was doubtless added to difference one branch, perhaps that of Patrington, in which William was a frequent name. Numerous wills for several generations of Newtons of Patrington are preserved in the York Probate Registry, but unfortunately they fail to furnish evidence as to the earlier history of the Newton family. It may be inferred from the citation of the arms of Thomas Newton that our family of Ryhill and Flinton was lineally descended from the eldest branch, to which the arms were granted, a matter on which we have been able to get no light from the College of Arms. It may be of interest to compare the simpler coat of Sir Isaac Newton illustrated in A. R. Wagner's Historic Heraldry of Britain, published in connection with the New York World's Fair.

Bracks, and the relationship there set forth was most useful in constructing this pedigree. No trace of his marriage and family has been discovered.

ii. JOHN, mentioned, together with his brother Francis, in the will of their cousin Ellen Bracks in 1635. He is probably the John Newton buried at Hedon 19 Feb. 1657, who had children recorded there: 1. *Ellen,* bapt. 30 Jan. 1619; buried 23 Feb. 1619. 2. *Thomas,* bapt. 24 Oct. 1621. 3. *William,* bapt. 12 Apr. 1623.

iii. JONE, buried at Garton 18 July 1589, is perhaps the posthumous child indicated in Thomas Newton's will and probate.

5. FRANCIS NEWTON (*John, John*) of Hedon, was born about 1551. This date is derived from Depositions taken at Headon, Co. York, 15 September 26 Elizabeth [1584] before commissioners for the Court of Chancery,* in which Francis Newton of Headon, yeoman, aged 33 years, was a witness for Henry Constable, esquire, in two suits brought against the latter, apparently by his tenants. Francis Newton answered interrogatories showing his familiarity with the towns of Wythornsey, Thorne, Esyngton, Kylnesey, and Skefflinge, as part of the Manor of Burstwick, saying that for the last thirteen years he had been Clerk of the Courts for those towns. Francis Newton appeared as a witness to the marriage of Michael Constable and Margeria Logley at Brandesburton, 23 May 1581. (Parish Register.) He is recorded in Park's History of Hedon as being mayor in 1584; Mr. Francis Newton, mayor, attended Glover's Visitation in 1585. John Newton (3) in his will of 1587, committed the guardianship of his son Lancelot to his brother Francis Newton; the fact that the guardianship of Lancelot was granted by the Court on 15 April 1600 to Cuthbert Leeche, may indicate that Francis Newton had died about this time. It is strange that no settlement of his estate is found, and nothing as to his children, beyond their baptism in the Church of St. Augustine, Hedon.

Children:

i. HENRY, bapt. 20 April 1580.
ii. GABRIEL, bapt. 4 May 1582.
iii. MICHAEL, bapt. 24 Feb. 1582/3.

6. LANCELOT NEWTON (*John, John, John*) of Hedon, born about 1580, was buried at Hedon 30 Aug. 1622. He married at Barmston, 3 Jan. 1610, MARY LEE, who appears to have survived her husband, and is probably the "Marie Newton, gentlewoman," who was buried at Hedon 12 March 1632. As noted above, Lancelot was given by his father's will into the charge of his uncle Francis until the age of 21, to learn his occupation, and in that way probably he went to Hedon to live. He was given two houses in the same will. By 1607 he was able to purchase by fine, from his sister Ellen and her husband Robert Bracks, a considerable income arising out of

* Chancery Depositions (County) C.21/F.21/20; C.21/C.48/5. Preserved in the Public Record Office, London.

her property in the ancestral town of Ryhill and Camerton. Three years after his marriage, in 1613, he is recorded as being a bayliff in Hedon, and in 1616 he was mayor. (Poulson's Holderness, vol. 2, p. 148; Park, G. R. History of Hedon, p. 81.) At his death he is recorded in the parish register as "Mr. Lanclotte Newton, Alderman." These glimpses of his career indicate that he must have been a man of force and character.

Children, baptized in the Church of St. Augustine, Hedon:

i.   THOMAS, bapt. 18 June 1611; probably died in infancy.

ii.   ELLEN, bapt. 24 Feb. 1614; m. at St. Martin, Micklegate, York, 3 Nov. 1636, EDWARD CARLTON, born in Hornsea, bapt. at Beeford 20 Oct. 1610, son of Walter and Jane (Gibbon) Carlton. As set forth previously in the Carlton article, Edward Carlton and Ellen his wife by a fine dated 9 April 1638 (see REGISTER, vol. 93, page 13) sold considerable land, which had been her property, in Ryhill and Cammerton. Shortly after this date they emigrated with the company of Rev. Ezekiel Rogers, to become pioneer settlers in Rowley in 1639. The often repeated tale that the Rogers company came over on the ship *John of London*, which also brought Stephen Daye with the first printing press to reach English North America, finds confirmation in Johnson's Wonder-Working Providence (page 128. 1654 [Ed. Poole, 1867]). The tercentenary of this press is commemorated in a postage stamp issued just one month after the celebration at Rowley (24–27 August 1939).*

iii.   MARGERY, bapt. 2 May 1617; perhaps the same as Mary, named in the will of her aunt Ellen Bracks. No burial of a Margery is found in the parish register, twice searched for such items.

iv.   ELIZABETH, bapt. 2 Jan. 1619; living in 1635.

v.   FRANCES, bapt. 2 Jan. 1621, only about eight months before her father's death.

These last two, Elizabeth and Frances Newton, were named residuary legatees and joint executrices in the will of their aunt Ellen Bracks, 5 Sept. 1635, while their sister Ellen, namesake of the aunt, was merely remembered with a bequest of ten pounds. Ellen had perhaps already gone to York, possibly with a relative on the Lee side, this family having thus far eluded search.

A year ago, at the beginning of the Carleton article, it was indicated in a footnote that the new pedigree established for the pioneer Edward Carlton provided for him a much richer historical background, in his inheritance through Neville of Thornton Bridge, and more especially through Gascoigne and Neville of Oversley, going back to John of Gaunt and other royal lines.

In this epilogue it may be noted that it seemed unnecessary in the present article to attack the purely supposititious wife ascribed to Edward Carlton in Captain Percival Carleton's "Memorials" in 1869, and since unquestioned here. American descendants will be quite willing to abandon the baseless legend of "Ellen, daughter of Sir Thomas Denton" in favor of this clear Newton ancestry. Ellen Newton, daughter of a forceful man who had made his own way to success in his community, may be believed to have made her own important contribution in the settlement of Rowley. Furthermore her inheritance through the ancient Grimston line discloses vistas for future exploration. In particular the ancestry of Sir John Portington, with several divergent pedigrees in the field, is most intriguing for those who pursue "endless genealogies."

* An ancient press, claimed to be the original press of Stephen Daye, is preserved in the library of the Vermont Historical Society, and although this claim has been called in question by Samuel Eliot Morison in a note in his Founding of Harvard College, the endorsement of the Post Office Department and the display of the press at the Graphic Arts Exposition in New York will satisfy Vermonters as to its authenticity.

NOYES INSCRIPTION AND MEMORANDA.

By JAMES ATKINS NOYES, A.B., Ph.B., of Cambridge, Mass.

A PHOTOGRAPH of the light-brown stone tablet which covers the remains of Rev. James Noyes in the ancient Palmer burying ground upon a sloping hill on the east side of Wequetequoc Cove, midway between Stonington, Connecticut, and Westerly, Rhode Island, is reproduced in fac-simile on the opposite page. (The next page.)

Rev. James Noyes was a son of Rev. James Noyes of Newbury, Mass., and grandson of Rev. William Noyes, rector of Cholderton, Co. Wilts., England. He was born in Newbury, Mass., 11 March, 1639–40; was graduated at Harvard College, 1659; ordained 10 Sept. 1674, as the first minister of Stonington, Conn.; married 11 Sept. 1674, Dorothy, daughter of Thomas and Anna (Lord) Stanton. Rev. James Noyes was one of the founders of Yale College.

The photograph was taken in 1889 under the direction of Judge Richard A. Wheeler of Stonington, Conn. The tablet was recut before the photograph was taken.* George W. Marshall, LL.D., Rouge Croix, Heralds' College, London, says that the only Noy–Noye–Noyes arms recorded are those of William Noy of Buryan, Co. Cornwall, England, who died 1593, and whose grandson was William Noy, Attorney General to Charles I. These arms were granted by Robert Cooke, Clarencieux, and the blazon is as follows :†

Coat—Azure 3 crosses botony in bend Argent.
Crest—On a chapeau Azure turned up Ermine a dove Argent in the beak an olive branch Vert.

The epitaph was written by Rev. Eliphalet Adams, Harvard College 1694, who died 1753; pastor in 1720 of the First Congregational Church, New London, Conn. The original draft was in 1889 in the Sunday School Library Room of the First Congregational Church, Stonington, Conn.‡

Rev. William Noyes, rector of Cholderton, Co. Wilts., Eng. (a town 11 miles from Salisbury), matriculated at University College,

---

* These arms appear to be wrongfully assumed by this branch of the family. Also the bend here is reversed, probably a mistake of the stone cutter.

† This blazoning differs from that in Vivian's Visitation of Cornwall and Burke's General Armory; but is that on record in the Heralds' College, London.

‡ *References.*—Heraldic Journal, Boston, 1866. Vol. II., p. 84. New-England Historical and Genealogical REGISTER, Vol. XIII., pp. 26–189. Caulkins's History of New London, Conn., p 285. Wheeler's Hist. First Church, Stonington, Conn., p. 294. Ed. E. Salisbury's Family Hist. and Gen., Vol. I., Pt. l, pp. xvii., 262, 265, 316, 309; Vol. III., supplement, Pedigree Charts, *Lord*, V., VI. Sibley's Harvard Graduates, Vol. II., p. 45.

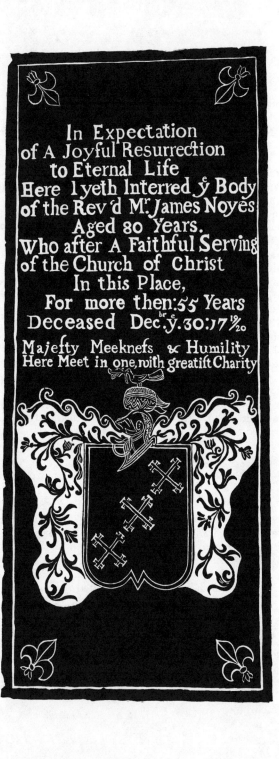

In Expectation
of A Joyful Resurrection
to Eternal Life
Here lyeth Interred ẙ Body
of the Rev'd Mr. James Noyes
Aged 80 Years.
Who after A Faithful Serving
of the Church of Christ
In this Place,
For more then:55 Years
Deceased Dec:ẙ.30:17¹⁹/₂₀

Majefty Meeknefs & Humility
Here Meet in one, with greatift Charity

Oxford, 15 Nov. 1588, æ. 20 years, and was graduated B.A. 31 May, 1592. He married Anne Parker. He died intestate before 30 April, 1622, when an Inventory was made and widow app. adm. 28 May, 1622. (Court of Archdeacon of Sarum). She bur. at Cholderton, 7 March, 1657, æ. 82 yrs. (per Parish Register). Her will is at Somerset House, London (Wootton, 130), and mentions sons James and Nicholas in New England. Will made 18 March, 1655, proved 21 April, 1658, at London.

Their sons, Rev. James and Deacon Nicholas Noyes, in March, 1633, embarked for New England in the *Mary and John* of London, with their cousin Rev. Thomas Parker, and were among the settlers of Newbury, Mass., May, 1635.

Rev. James Noyes, born in England about 1608; matriculated at Brasenose College, Oxford, 22 Aug. 1627, but was not graduated; died at Newbury, Mass., 22 Oct. 1656, æ. 48; married 1633, Sara, eldest daughter of Mr. Joseph Brown of Southampton, Co. Hants, Eng. She died 13 Sept. 1691, at Newbury, Mass. His will made 17 Oct. 1656, proved 26 Nov. 1656, mentions wife Sara and children, brother Deacon Nicholas Noyes and cousin Rev. Thomas Parker. Inventory of estate amounting to £657 11s. 4d. Her will made 11 Nov. 1681, proved 29 Sept. 1691. Inventory of estate amounted to £1108.*

The branch of the Noyes family of East Mascalls, Co. Sussex, England, represented by Thomas Herbert Noyes, B.A. Ch. Ch. Oxford, claim the following arms :†

Coat—Azure 3 crosses crosslet in bend Argent.
Crest—On a chapeau Gules turned up Ermine a dove Argent in the beak an olive branch Vert.

Dr. Marshall is of the opinion that these arms have been wrongfully assumed.

In the Visitation of Berks at Heralds' College, *no arms are entered* with the partial pedigree of this family.

A cut of the arms of Noyes of East Mascalls from the Archæological Collections of Co. Sussex, 1857, vol. ix., page 340, is given in the margin.

* *References.*—Registrum Universitatis, Oxon, II., p. 166; III., 171. P. 565 Hist. Newbury, Co. Berks., England, by W. Money. Founders of New England, by S. G. Drake, p. 68. Old New Eng. Traits, by G. Lunt, App. II. and III. Mather's Magnalia, Ed. 1853-5, Vol. I., p. 484. Coffin's Newbury, 15, 23, 312, 356. Reminiscences of a Nonagenarian, by S. A. Emery, p. 114. Savage's Gen. Dict., Vol. III., p. 296, Noyes. REG., xlii., 64, Will of Widow Anne Noyes; xlii., 403, Burial of Mrs. Anne Noyes. Parish Notes, by Rev. E. P. Barrow, rector of Cholderton in 1889, page 8. N. Y. Gen. and Biog. Rec., xx., p. 66, 139.—Foster's Alumni Oxonienses.

† *References.*—Burke's General Armory, Burke's Landed Gentry of Great Britain and Ireland, Walford's County Families, Fairbairn's Crests of the families of Great Britain and Ireland, Lower's Patronymica Britannica, Archæological Collections of Co. Sussex, England, Notes and Queries, London.—2d series, Vol. ii., 169-478; 2d series, Vol. vii ; 35; 4th series, Vol. i., 390-566; 4th series, Vol. ii., 13-587. The Genealogist, Vol. vi., 1882, p. 67.

MAJOR GENL SIR DAVID OCHTERLONY BART. G.C.B.

THE SCOTCH ANCESTRY OF MAJ.-GEN. SIR DAVID OCHTERLONEY, BART., A NATIVE OF BOSTON, IN NEW ENGLAND.

By Walter Kendall Watkins, of Malden, Mass.

The Scotch furnished a large number of people who early colonized New England. It was on the 10th of September, 1650, that the Council of State in England considered as to the disposal of the Scotch prisoners who had been taken at the battle of Dunbar, just one week previous ; and within the following week a scheme had been propounded for the transportation of some of them beyond the seas, while others, on the proposition of Cromwell, the Lord General, were to be sent to Ireland. These last numbered some two thousand, but it was not thought best to send to Ireland the Highlanders, " by reason of their affinity to the Irish." Down and Antrim were counties filled with Scots who had made a first lodgement there in the time of Henry VIII., while in Ulster were also many Scots, as all British landholders, by the articles of the Ulster plantation, were bound to bring households out of England and Scotland to people their lands. From these Scotch settlements in Ireland the New World, during the eighteenth century, received a large Scotch-Irish emigration.

23 Oct., 1650, the Council of State requested the admiralty committee to examine whether or not the Scotch prisoners were being sent to places where they would be dangerous to the English Commonwealth. The proportion for New England was to be shipped forthwith, " as their ship is ready and the place is without danger."

11 Nov., 1650, Sir Arthur Hesilrigge, who was in the North, was ordered to deliver 150 Scotch prisoners to Augustine Walker, master of the "Unity," to be transported to New England.

797

On 6 Feb., 1649–50, she was ready to sail from Boston, as on that date a bill of health was attested for the "Unity," Augustine Walker, master. Her captain was of Charlestown, where he was admitted to the church in 1640, and where, by his wife Hannah, he had the following children: Hannah, born 1640; Samuel, born 1642; Augustine, born 1646; James born 1647. He died before 8 Aug., 1654, when an inventory of his estate was taken, and adminstration granted to George Bunker and Edward Burt, whose sale of certain lands was confirmed by the General Court in 1656. At this time complaints were heard in regard to the treatment of Scotch prisoners on board vessels lying in the Thames, and the justices about Blackwall were ordered to receive some sick Scotch prisoners into their pest houses, to be cured at the expense of some persons who had fetched them from the North for transportation to the foreign plantations.

24 March, 1651, the Council wrote Hesilrigge, regarding the Scotch prisoners remaining at Durham under his care, that 300 be delivered to Col. Rokeby, and 200 to Lieut. Col. Killigrew, who had been given license to transport them beyond the seas, and they undertaking that no use be made of the prisoners to the prejudice of the Commonwealth. Assistance was to be given in shipping them away.

The lot under Rokeby were destined for France. The prisoners were confined in Durham Castle and shipped from Newcastle. In London they were confined in the Tiltyard at Greenwich, and the East India House and yard at Blackwall. Among the troops detailed to guard the prisoners in London, was a troop of horse under Major Stephen Winthrop, the fourth son of Gov. John Winthrop of Massachusetts.

In 1651, the Scotch taken at Worcester and other places were added, and a commission was formed, 16 Sept., 1651, to have power to dispose to the plantations all the prisoners under the grade of a field officer. 22 Sept., 1551, those prisoners at Liverpool, Chester and Stafford were ordered sent to Bristol to be sent abroad.

At York Castle many prisoners were confined. 2 Dec., 1651, an infectious disease broke out among those in London, who had been ordered to the plantation and inquiry was made as to why they had been left behind, and it was ordered there be paid for their subsistence 4d. a day for privates, and 5s. per week for officers.

Of a shipment from London, 11 Nov., 1651, in the "John and Sarah," John Green, master, bound for Boston in New England, of a lot of nearly 300 Scotchmen consigned to Thomas Kemble of Charlestown, we have not only the record but nearly a complete list of the names of those who were thus forced to assist in the colonization of a new country. The consignee was a merchant of Charlestown, where he first appears as receiving his human freight, and from the proceeds of which he doubtless purchased his house and warehouse in Charlestown, and his interest in saw mills at Dover and on the Piscataqua. The consignors were Robert Rich of London, John Beex and William Green. In this ship was a quantity of provisions, ironwork and household stuff, free of duty by ordinance of Parliament, shipped by Robert Rich, who had, a year previously, shipped on the "Speedwell" a cargo mostly of linens and cloths valued at over £2000.

On the 6 Jan., 1657, a score or more Scotsmen gathered together in Boston "to make a box" in which each was to place sixpence quarterly, and twelve pence was to be paid by new members on joining, the same to be for the relief of themselves when necessary, or of any of the Scotch nation they saw cause to help. One of good report, fearing God and hating covetousness, was chosen as boxmaster. This was the founding of the Scots Charitable Society, which still exists in Boston.

On its rolls we find entered, year by year, the names of its members, and in many cases from whence in Scotland they came. Many of the names became prominent in the affairs of the town and province : Duncan Campbell, book binder; Francis Borland and John Borland; George Jaffray of Piscataqua; George Bethune; John Hamilton, postmaster-general ; William Douglas, M.D.; Thomas Inches; Robert Auchmutie; John Smibert; John Scollay ; Thomas Handyside Peck; William Hyslop; George Traill, and scores of others, who became more or less prosperous in their adopted country. A large number enrolled were but transients among the population of the largest and most prosperous port of the Northern Atlantic coast, which always had a floating population of mariners and soldiers. Thus, under date of 1739, appears " Peter McKenzie, Cromarty, son to ye Earl of Cromarty." We fail to find him, however, among the progeny of any of the Earls of Cromarty of that period given in Douglas's Peerage of Scotland, and are forced to consider him either an imposter or an example of a Scotch bar sinister. Under date of 1752 we find the name of " David Ochterlony, Montrose." Though there were members of the Ochterloney family living at Montrose at this time, his residence there was only for a short period, and it probably was the port from which he sailed to New England. He was the second son of Alexander Ochterloney, Laird of Pitforthy, and Elizabeth, daughter of David Tyrie of Dunnydeer.

The records showing the antiquity of prominent Scotch families, in their completeness and the amount of data furnished, compare favorably with those of England. The modes of procedure of the courts, and the forms of the Presbyterian Church, in Scotland, being different from those of the Courts and of the Established Church in England, the Public Records also vary. The Parish registers contain not only the vital records, but, in many instances, the minutes of church meetings, with entries similar to those found in our church records in New England, which seem therefore to have been modelled more after the Scotch Presbyterian form. The Probate matters are to be found in twenty-two Commissariat Courts covering the territory of Scotland, the earliest about 1550. These are supplemented by the Records of Retours and Service of Heirs, which go back to 1545, and are similar to the Inquisitions Post Mortem of England. The Saisine records are those of land rights, and date from 1600.

For earlier matter, there are the Great Seal records, Privy Seal, Chancery, Exchequer, Court of Sessions, and Burgh records, Sheriff Courts, Regality Courts, Barony, and Bailie Courts, Diligence records, Register of Arms, &c.; while the earliest must be extracted from the records of the abbeys, and from family archives. From these sources the following facts relating to the Ochterloney family have been gathered.

The English prefixes " Auchter " and " Ochter " are corruptions from the Gaelic " Uachar," meaning upper or top. Ochterloney belongs to Forfarshire, meaning " the elegant top or summit." Between 1226 and 1239, Walter, son of Turpin, exchanged the lands of Othirlony, which had belonged in heritage to his ancestors, for those of Kenny in the parish of Kingoldrum, Forfar, possessed by the Abbey of Aberbrothock. They had been bestowed on the Abbey by a charter of William the Lyon, and confirmed by Alexander III., and again by King Robert Bruce.

In Kingoldrum, at the present time, the locality is still known as the farm of Meikle Kenny; while Kyrkton, also mentioned in the charter of con-

799

firmation to John de Othyrlony, of 3 Sept., 1351, is still identified in the farm of Kirkton, in the same parish.

The family were of some prominence at an early day. Walter Ochterloney is recorded as having sworn fealty to Edward I., in 1296, following the example of Baliol who swore fealty to Edward, at Norham Castle, in 1292.

In 1342, Johanne Ochterloney was Sheriff of Forfar.

In 1351, there appears in the Register of the Abbey of Aberbrothock a confirmation to John Ochterloney, by the Abbot, of the lands at Kenny.

In 1391, William Ochterloney made a gift of the relief of Melgund.

The Register of the Abbey recites in 1409 that William and Alexander were the sons of William Ochterloney.

In the Register of the Great Seal of Scotland, under date 4 Nov., 1444, in a confirmation charter of lands in Kelly, we find William de Ouchterloney of Kelly, while under date 18 Dec., 1467, we find the King confirms the charter of William de Ouchterloney of the same, who conceded to William de Ouchterloney, son and heir of Alexander de Ouchterloney, the lands of Balnahardis, with those of "Rattoune Raw" in the Barony of Ochterloney.

It was just previous to the confirmation of 1444 that probably Kelly came into the Ochterloney family by marriage with a Stewart, hence the quartering of the Stewart arms, as shown in the ancient arms of Ochterloney. John Ochterloney of Guynd, *circa*, 1682, furnished to Sir Robert Sibbald, Geographer for the King, an account of Forfarshire, in which he included some remarks about the Ochterloney family and their intermarriages. The Stewart marriage is the first he alludes to, but if it is the one given above, he errs in calling the family that of Stewart of Rosyth, Fife, as it was Stewart of Kellie.

Another statement, that his grandfather saw a letter from Sir William Wallace directed to his trusty friend the Laird of Ouchterloney, requiring him to repair with his friends and servants to his aid, has been greatly doubted (Spottiswood Miscellany, p. 350). In 1445, the annual rent from Panmure to William Ochterloney of Kelly was £8, 6s., 8d.

After this date Kelly is called "Kelly alias Ochterloney," or "Ochterloney alias Kelly."

In a confirmation of the lands of Kennymykle, 12 Apr., 1466, by Walter, Abbot of the monastery at Aberbrothock, to Alexander de Ochterloney, son and heir of William de Ochterloney, Master of Kelly, which confirmation also mentions a previous charter from Malcolm the Abbot to the same, there is also mention of Mariote de Drummond, wife of Alexander Ochterloney.

She was probably the daughter of Sir Malcolm Drummond, ancestor of the Earls of Perth, by his wife Mariota, daughter of Sir David Murray, Lord of Tullibardin. Sir Malcolm Drummond died in 1470. A record of the Drummonds, some of whom intermarried with the Royal family of Scotland, is given, back to about the year 1100, in Douglas's Peerage of Scotland.

Still later, 6 May, 1493, by the Register of the Abbey, David the Abbot shows the possession of the lands of Kennemekle by the Master of Kelly, and states that James de Ochterloney is son and heir of Alexander de Ochterloney.

13 May, 1517, the King conceded to William Ochterloney of Kelly the lands of Lochle and Inchgromnell, in Glennesk, Forfar. 8 Sept., 1525, the King, for good service, conceded to William Ochterloney of that ilk,

and Margaret Gardyne his wife, lands of Petcourent in Kerrimuir, Forfar, which were those of Archibald, Earl of Angus.

28 Oct., 1525, the Abbot conceded to Alexander Ochterloney, son and heir apparent to William Ochterloney of Kelly, and to Elizabeth Leyrmount the wife of Alexander, the lands of Kennemekyle in Kyncoldrun, Forfar.

10 June, 1530, the King confirmed to Alexander Ochterloney of the same ilk, and Elizabeth Leirmonth his wife, the lands of Kelly alias Ouchterloney.

7 Dec., 1547, Queen Mary conceded to James Ochterloney, son and heir apparent of Alexander Ochterloney of the same, lands in the barony of Ochterloney alias Kelly.

In a Retour of Inquest, 30 Oct., 1560, taken at the front gate of the monastery of Arbroath, the name of William Ochterloney of Setoun appears, with others.

23 Nov., 1591, the King confirmed, for good service, to William Ochterloney of the same, the lands and barony of Auchterloney alias Kelly.

4 July, 1603, the King conceded to William Ochterloney, apparent of the same, and Katherine Scrymgeour his wife, the lands of Ochterloney with lands in Rescobie.

20 Jan., 1603, the King ratifies two charters: (1) John, Lord Hamilton, commendator of Aberbrothock, to William Ochterloney and Barbara Rait his wife, of the lands of Seyton in Aberbrothock, dated 31 Apr., 1586; (2) John, Marquis of Hamilton, to James Ochterloney, son of the said William Ochterloney, and Isabell Peirsoin wife of said James Ochterloney, dated 26 Dec., 1601.

In the Commissariat of Edinburgh, under date 6 March, 1598, we have "the Testament Dative and Inventory of the Estate, of Barbara Rait, relict of umquhile W^m. Auchterloney, of Wester Seytoun, wthin the prochin of St. Vigien, Forfar, who quha decessit in the month of October the yeir of God jaji clxxxxvii yeirs" * * * * " Follows the dettis awin to the deid. Item ther wes awin to the said umqle barbara rait relict of umqle Wm Auchterloney of West^r Seytoun be Wm Auchterloney of Kellie resten of one yeiris añuelrent the sowme of xl^{li}. Itè be Wm Rait of Halgrene pfme to his obligachm II^c lxvi^{li} xiii^s iiii^d " * * * " Mr John Rait Sevito^r to my lord of Edzall is becû caú un " (become cautioner). Gilbert Auchterloney, her lawful sòn, was her executor.

James Ochterloney of Wester Seytoun was witness for Wm Rait of Hailgrene and Robert Rait his second son, under date 13 July, 1599, for the lands of Conansythe, Inverkeillour.

In the Inquisitionum Retornatarum, under date 22 Oct., 1631, we find William Ochterloney of Wester Seatoun is heir of his father, James Ochterloney of Wester Seatoun.

5 March, 1639, John Ochterloney is heir of William Ochterloney of Wester Seaton.

From the family papers of the Wester Seaton branch, we are informed that the wife of John Ochterloney was Margaret Pearson, and their son, James Ochterloney, married 1 Feb., 1671, Elizabeth, daughter and heir of James Gairden, Esq., of Midstrath in the parish of Birs.

James Ochterloney had a grant, 3 Aug., 1698, of Wester Seaton, and, on the same day, of Tillifroskie, in the parish of Birs.

Wester Seaton, which had then been in the family for over a century, is in the parish of St. Vigeans in Arbroath, and it is still identified in a farm.

The present house is a modern one, but the site of the old mansion of the Ochterloney family can be identified.

James Ochterloney died before 21 Feb., 1727, and is buried at the church of Birs. By his wife Elizabeth he had:

 i. ALEXANDER, b. 14 Feb., 1673.
 ii. JOHN, b. 8 April, 1674.
 iii. JAMES, b. 4 July, 1679; m. James Irvine.
 iv. HELEN, b. 1680.
 v. JAMES, b. 15 Sept., 1681.
 vi. PETER, b. 22 Nov., 1683.
 vii. MARGARET, b. 1684; m. 1715, J. Melville.
 viii. MATTY, b. 1685.
 ix. ISABEL, b. 1687.
 x. DAVID, b. 22 Jan., 1690; d. Feb., 1739.
 xi. ELIZABETH. b. 1692.
 xii. ANNA, b. 1693.
 xiii. ALEXANDER, b. 16 Sept., 1695; of whom later.

David Ochterloney of Tillifroskie, born 21 Jan., 1690, died 1739, and is buried at Birs. He married Mary, daughter of Peter Forbes of Balfour in the parish of Fettercairn, and she died in Feb., 1739, and was carried to the grave with her husband.

On 14 Jan., 1744, Peter Ochterloney of Tillifroskie was served as Heir General to his father, David Ochterloney of Tillifroskie. 26 Sept., 1755, he was served as Heir Special, in Tillifroskie, Boghead, Rammahagan and Birs, to his father David, who died in 1739.

The eight children of David and Mary (Forbes) Ochterloney were:

 i. PETER, who m. Margaret, dau. of Thomas Buchan, Laird of Auchmacoy, and had five children.
 ii. DAVID, a captain in General Monkton's regiment of foot, who was unm., and d. of wounds received at the Siege of Quebec, Aug., 1754.
 iii. JAMES, a twin of David, d, in Feb., 1739.
 iv. ALEXANDER, a planter in the Island of Dominica, where he d. 25 May, 1779. He m. Mary Ann, dau. of John Gordon of Dominica, and had two daughters.
 v. ELIZABETH, who m. Francis Douglas of Aberdeen and Abbots Inch, son of Robert Douglas of Blackmiln, Logie Coldstone. He was an author, of whom a sketch is given in "Eminent Scotsmen," by Irvine.

Sir Robert Douglas of Glenbervie, the author of the earliest published Scotch Peerage and Baronage, and a kinsman and contemporary of Robert of Blackmiln, states the latter's descent from John, son of Sir Archibald Douglas of Glenbervie, a grandson of Archibald, 5th Earl of Angus, commonly known as "Bell the Cat." Francis and Elizabeth (Ochterloney) Douglas had one son, Robert, a merchant at St. Domingo, and five daughters, one of whom, Bethia, married Hugh, son of John Cochrane, Baillie of Paisley. Hugh and Bethia (Douglas) Cochrane were the grandparents of the late Alexander Cochrane, formerly in business with the late Gov. Thomas Talbot, at Billerica, Mass., and founder, in 1859, of the Cochrane Chemical Works at South Malden, now Everett, Mass.

 vi. MARY, who m. Alexander Dyce of Aberdeen, and had five sons and three daughters.
 vii. ANN, who m. Andrew Tate.
 vii. BETHIA, who m. Charles Tate, an advocate in Aberdeen.

Alexander Ochterloney, born 16 Sept., 1695, son of James and Elizabeth (Gairden) Ochterloney, married 1 Nov., 1721, Elizabeth, daughter of David Tyrie of Dunnydeer; she died 23 July, 1749. He was Laird of Pitforthy, Brechin, Forfarshire. In this parish are still to be found the farms of East

Pitforthie and the Mains of Pitforthie.   His five sons and two daughters were :

   i.   GILBERT, of Newtown Mill and Pitforthy, who m. 25 Sept., 1745, Maria, dau. of William Smith, Professor of Philosophy at Aberdeen. He d. without issue, 6 Feb., 1786.

   ii.   DAVID, b. 30 Oct., 1765; of whom presently.

   iii.   JAMES, who d. on the Isle of Man, 8 March, 1760, leaving a daughter, *Elizabeth*, wife of Alexander Fairweather of Brechin, and afterwards of Philadelphia.

   iv.   ALEXANDER. Lieut. of the " Juno," killed by an accident at Quiberon Bay in 1760; unm.

   v.   CHARLES, who d. in Bengal, in 1755.

   vi.   ELIZABETH, who d. unm., in 1782.

   vii.   JANE, who m. 17 Sept., 1748, John Lyon, Esq., of Forgandenny and Castle Lyon, North Britain. She d. in April, 1775, leaving issue.

David, second son of Alexander and Elizabeth (Tyrie) Ochterloney, was a captain in the merchant service, residing for a while at Montrose. Probably Boston was one of the many ports visited by him in his voyages. Five years after his first appearance in Boston, 4 June, 1757, his intention of marriage was published to Katherine, daughter of Andrew Tyler of Boston, by his wife Miriam, a sister of Sir William Pepperell. On 27 June, 1762, he purchased a brick house with about 1500 sq. feet of land, on Back Street, which at that time was that part of Salem Street from Hanover Street to Prince Street.*   Meanwhile three sons and a daughter were born : David, Gilbert (d. 1780), Alexander (d. 1803), and Catherine (d. 1792).

The eldest of these was David, born 12 Feb., 1758, who was to revive the glory of the name in a new locality.

Burke's " Extinct Baronetcies " states that Gilbert Ochterloney, the second son, died in 1763. The following extract from the Gentleman's Magazine tells a different story.   Under Deaths, 16 Jan. 1780, " Gilbert Ochterling, (Ochterloney), esq. ; a very amiable youth, aged about 16. He died at the house of his father Isaac Heard, esq. in the college of arms.   [The eighth line in our last, p. 51, col. 2, is a mistake.] "   This last refers to a death item of the preceding month, " at the Heralds College, Isaac Heard, esq."

Capt. David Ochterloney, the father, continued his career as a mariner, but a few years after locating permanently in Boston he died, in 1765, at St. Vincent.   His will, made at the time of his marriage, was probated 7 March, 1766, and left everything to his wife " Katrin ; " but his debts made his estate insolvent, and it was not till 1791 that a sum was realized to close up the estate, by a dividend of six and a half pence on the pound, to his creditors.

His widow went to England, where she married second, Sir Isaac Heard of London, Norroy· and Garter King of Arms, and Gentleman of the Red Rod to the Order of the Bath.

Sir Isaac Heard, born 10 Dec., 1740, at Ottery St. Mary, Devonshire, did not die till 29 Apr., 1822.   During his official career as Garter King at arms he proclaimed the titles, &c., at the funerals of six generations of

---

* The late Rev. Edward G. Porter, in his " Rambles in Old Boston, N. E.," pp. 346–9, states that the old house still standing on the corner of North and Centre Streets was owned by David Ochterloney, and he gives it the name of the Ochterloney-Adan house. The house was only mortgaged to Ochterloney by his mother-in-law, Mrs. Miriam Tyler, in 1762, about the time he bought his Salem Street house.   Tradition states that Sir David Ochterloney was born in a house on Queen (Court) Street.

the House of Brunswick. He proclaimed George IV. as King, at Carlton House, 31 Jan. 1820.

The son David, born 1758, was a scholar at the Latin School in Boston when his father died, in 1765. At the age of eighteen he went to India as a cadet, and in 1778 received an appointment as Ensign. In 1781 he was Quartermaster to the 71st Regiment of Foot. He attained the rank of Major in 1800, Lieutenant-Colonel in 1803, and Colonel in 1812. His commission as Major-General bears the date of 1 June, 1814. In 1817 he received the thanks of both Houses of Parliament, and after nearly fifty years of uninterrupted military duty, through impaired health he was forced to resign, with the intention of returning to England, but while at Meerut, for a change of air, died 15 July, 1825. He was Deputy-Adjutant-General at the Battle of Delhi, after which he was sent as Envoy to the Court of Shah Alum. For his conduct in the Nepaulese war he was created a Knight Commander of the Bath, and 7 March, 1816, was made a baronet. These distinctions were the occasion of researches in the family history, by Sir Isaac Heard, his stepfather, which resulted in an account of the family back to about the year 1650. This account was kindly placed at the disposal of the writer, by the present baronet, and was confirmed, and added to his own researches.

The arms granted were: Azure, a lion rampant argent, holding in his paws a trident erect or, and charged on the shoulder with a key, the wards upward, of the field; a chief embattled or, thereon two banners in saltire, the one of the Mahratta states vert, inscribed Delhi, the other of the states of Nepaul; the staves broken and encircled by a wreath of laurel proper.

In the patent, granted 1816, the title did not descend, and was re-created, 8 Dec., 1823, and the limitation was extended to Charles Metcalf Ochterloney, of Delhi, son of Roderick-Peregrine and Sarah (Nelley) Ochterloney. Sir Charles married 31 Dec., 1844, Sarah, daughter of William P. Tribe, of Liverpool, and was succeeded by his son, the present baronet, Sir David Ferguson Ochterloney, to whom the writer is indebted for courtesies and hospitality on many occasions.

The arms of the Ochterloney family used in past centuries are those described in the account of John Ochterloney, *circa* 1682:—Azure, a lion rampant argent, within a border gules entoure of eight buckles or. Above the shield a helmet mantled gules and double argent, and on the torse for a crest an eagle displayed azure with an escallop in her beak argent. The motto "Deus mihi adjutor." These arms were registered by John Ochterloney of Guynd, and two of his kinsfolk, in 1672–1678. Then the Stewart quartering previously used, namely, or a fesse chequy argent and azure, was dropped.

In 1779 there was certified to, in the College of Arms, London: "Azure a lion rampant argent charged on the side with a key in pale of the field and holding in the dexter paw a trident or. Crest, a swan rousant argent ducally crowned or, collared and chained of the last, charged on the breast with a rose gules." This was probably the work of Sir Isaac Heard.

The crest last given has been modified in recent years, inasmuch as the breast is charged with a buckle gules instead of a rose, and the wings and body debruised by a bendlet sinister wavy azure. The motto is "Spe labor levis."

Other branches of the family have flourished in Scotland, but the limits of this sketch prevent a detailed account of them.

We have carried out the line of the Wester Seyton branch, from that at Kelly in the middle of the 16th century; and less than a century later, in

1614, William Ochterloney sold Kelly, and the family became seated at Guynd in the parish of Carmilie, six miles west of Arbroath. This was held by the Ochterloney name till the death of John Ochterloney, in 1843, when it went to his nephew, James Peirson.

In 1826, John Ochterloney contested with the government the right of sepulchre, for members of the family, under the high altar of the Abbey of Arbroath, the government having acquired the ruins for preservation. It was decided against him. On the death of Mr. Peirson, by his request Guynd went to Col. T. H. Ochterloney, of the Montrose branch of the family, John Ochterloney of Montrose having married Ann Ochterloney of Guynd, in the previous century.

In 1654, John Ochterloney of Hospitalfield was heir of his father, John of Guynd, in the towns and lands of Hospitalfield, more widely known as the "Monkbairn" of Sir Walter Scott's "The Antiquary," the scenes of which are laid in the vicinity of Arbroath.

A short account of the localities in which the Ochterloney family resided might be of some value, in view of the fact that it is usually impossible to find in gazetteers the localities mentioned in ancient deeds and charters of Scotch families, the names being those of estates, and the parish is often never mentioned.

John Ochterloney, in his account of Forfar, states that Balmadie in the parish of Rescobie, belonging to the Lairds of Ochterloney, was the manor house of the family, and their burials were at the Kirk of Rescobie, until they purchased Kelly. We have seen, however, by the earliest charters, etc., that before they acquired Kelly, they had the lands of Kennymykle in the parish of Kingoldrum. A reference to his account of Kingoldrum fails to find any mention of the family having had lands in that parish, though he has made frequent reference to their connection with other parishes. Resobie is three miles from Forfar, but the parish is six miles long, and the Mains of Ochterloney, so called, is at the extreme south-east end, six miles from Forfar towards Arbroath. To the north-west of Forfar is Kingoldrum, and the farms of Meikle Kenny and Kirkton are about ten miles north-west of Forfar.

From Kingoldrum we pass to Kelly, which is in the parish of Abirlot. Kelly Castle, a fine example of an old Scotch manor, is three miles from Arbroath. It is owned by the Earl of Dalhousie, who inherited it from the Earls of Panmure, and is now leased to a Dundee tradesman. Wester Seyton is in the parish of St. Vigeans, and now included in Arbroath. It is a farm which is north of that place, on a high cliff, and has been farmed by the Francis family for about a century. The modern house does not stand on the site of the old mansion.

From Wester Seyton to Tillifroskie is a distance of some forty miles northward, to the Forest of Birse and the Valley of the Dee. It is reached by the railway running between Aberdeen and Ballater. Tillifroskie belongs to the Farquharsons, Lairds of Finzean, and is a farm that still retains the name.

The next move of the family was south some eighteen miles to Brechin, ten miles north-east of Forfar and seven miles west of Montrose. There the Laird of Pitforthy held sway at the present farm of the Mains of Pitforthie, which is near the celebrated Glencadam Whisky Distillery. It is but a short journey to Montrose; but the succeeding generation was to be born three thousand miles to the westward, and then the scene changed to India. Thus we have the wanderings of a Scotch family for six centuries.

EXTRACTS FROM THE BISHOP'S TRANSCRIPT OF THE REGISTERS OF THE PARISHES OF BEDFORD COUNTY, ENGLAND.

MADE BY FREDERIC A. BLAYDES, ESQ., SHENSTONE LODGE, BEDFORD.

Communicated by RUFUS KING, Esq., of Yonkers, N. Y.

AMPTHILL—Redborn Stoke.

Baptism.

1602, Sep^t 29, Jhephrie, son of Thomas Wodell

CRANFIELD, Redborn Stoke.

Baptisms.

1602, Feb 24, W^m. son of Willm Wodell of Warleyend
1602, Oct. 10, John, son of Wm. Wodell de Elm
1602, Ap^r 25, Dorothy, dau. of Richard Wodell of the Arke
1602, Ap^r 17, Elizabeth, dau. of Richard Wodell
1603. Apr. 3, Elizth Odle, dau. of Isaace Odell
1603, Apr. 10, Henry Odle ye son of Thomas Odle
1603, " 25, Annye Odle, ye dau. of Robte Odle
1603, Aug. 28, Elizabeth Odle, ye dau. of Abraham Odell
1603, Dec. 11, Johan Odle, ye dau. of Wyllm. Odle
1603, Feb. 28, Henry Odle ye son of Richard Odle
1605, Apr. 2, Sara, dau. of Isaac Woddell
1605, June 2, Richard, son of Will'm Woddell de Wharleyend
1605, June 23, Elizabeth, dau. of Richard Woddle
1605, Oct. 19, Thomas Woddell son of Richard
1605, Nov. 23, Abraham, son of Abraham Woddell
1605, Feb. 20, Thomas, son of Willm Woddle
1607, Jan. 3, Tho. son of Abraham Odle
1607, Mar. 13, Mary, dau. of William Odle
1608, ... Judith, dau. of Isaac Odle
1608, ... 25, Elizabeth, dau. of Wm. Odle
1608. . . . . . 28, Clement, dau. of Wm Odle
1609, Dec. 17, Richard, son of Thomas Wodell
1609, Jan. 28, Alce, dau. of Inocent Wodell
1610, Mar. 25, Agnes, dau. of Abr. Odell
1610, Mar. 10, Robert, son of Wm. Odell
1611, Aug. 4, Isaac, son of Isaac Woodell
1611, Oct. 12, Elizt^h. dau. of Richd Woodell
1611, Oct. 21, Mary, dau. of Abraham Woodell
1611, Dec. 6, Rich^d son of William Woodell

1612, July 12, Agnes, dau. of Thom. Odell
1612, Jan. 17, John, son of Innocent Wodell
1612, Jan. 24, Isaac, son of Abraham Wodell
1612, Feb. 14, Susan, dau. of Wm. Wodell
1612, Feb. 28, Sara, dau. of Ric. Wodell
1613, Aug. 22, Margaret, dau. of Isaac Wodell
1614, Jan. 8, Frances, dau. of Richard Wodell
1615, Apr. 2, Marie, dau. of Tho⁸. Odell
1617, Apr. 6, Thomas, som of Tho⁸. Odell
1617, Jan. 6, William, son of Wm Wooddell
1620, Aug. 27, Sarah, dau. of Thos. Odell
1620, Oct. 15, Sarah, dau. of Thos. Odell
1621, Feb. 10, William, son of Inocent Odell
1622, Jan. 7, John, son of Thomas Odell
1623, Feb. 15, Thos., son of Thom Odell
1624, Mch. 20, Thomas, son of Thos. Wodell

Marriages.

1610, Nov. 29, Richard Wodell and Alce Mason.
1620, May 18, Geo. Barret and Joane Odell
1620, Nov. 30, John Carter and Grace Odell
1621, Nov. 26, William Armes and Agnes Odell
1621, Jan. 24, John Steen and Joane Odell

Burials.

1603, Ap. 28, Henry Odle son of Thomas
1605, Aug. 7, Sara, dau. of Isaack Woddell
1609, Sep. 6, Thomas, son of John Wodell
1610, May 5, Annis, dau. of Wm. Odell
1611, Nov. 3, Mary, dau. of Abraham
1612, Mar. 30, John Wodell
1613, Mar. 10, Susanna, dau. of Wm. Wodell
1615, June 22, William Odle of Worley
1615, Aug. 13, Agnes Odle, widow
1615, Oct. 24, Elizabeth Odle
1616, Jan. 18, Richard Wodell
1617, Apr. 10, Joane Woddel, wife of Richard
1617, Apr. 25, Richard Woddel, de esche
1618, Sep. 5, Alce, wife of John Odill
1618, Sep. 23, Thomas Odle
1619, Apr. 2, John Odell
1621, Nov. 8, William Odell
1624, Nov. 18, William Wodell
1625, Sep. 21, John Woddell
1625, Jan. 25, Thos. son of Thos. Woddell

MARSTON-MORETAINE—Redborn Stoke

Baptisms.

1602, Sep. 19, Mary, dau. of Wᵐ Odell
1602, June 6, Eliztʰ. dau. of Tho⁸. Odell
1603, May 25, Thomas, son of Roberte Odell
1603, June 13, John, son of John Odell

807

1604, July 22, Robt., son of Robt Odell
1606, March 1, John, son of William Odell
1607, July 20, Gilbert, son of Robert Odell
1610, Apr. 17, Johan, dau. of Robert Odell
1611, Jan. 2, Marg^t., dau. of John Odell
1611, Sep. 29, Richard, son of Willm. Odell
1614, Sep. 4, Ricus, fil. Robti Odell
1615, Ap^r. 11, Richard, son of John Odell
1616, Jan. 1, Richard, son of Stephen Odell
1618, Dec. 20, Sarah, dau. of John Odell
1619, May 2, Thos. son of Stephen Odell
1621, July 22, John, son of John Odle
1622, Dec. 25, Ann, dau. of John Odle
1624, June 20, William, son of Stephen Odell
1624, Sep. 26, William, son of John Odell, Senr.
1624, Jan. 1, Tho., son of John Odell

Marriages.

1604, Nov. 30, Richarde Odell and Judeth Persevall
1607, Nov. 23, John Odell and Katherine Neale
1611, Feb. 20, Stephen Odell and Joane Basterfield
1618, Ap^r. 19, John Odell and Elizt^h Cooper
1619, Oct. 11, John Asseldon and Agnis Odell
1620, Oct. 23, John Odell and Suzan Stanbridge
1622, Oct. 22, John Odell m. Em. Dobes.
1624, Apr. 9, John Taylor and Elizth Odell

Burials.

1603, May 25, Thomas, son of Robert Odell
1607, Aug. 7, Agnes, wife of John Odell
1611, July 13, Marie, dau. of William Odell
1615, Sep. 11, John Odell
1616, Feb. 22, Katheryn wife of John Odell
1617, Feb. 23, Joane Odell, widdow
1618, May 24, Margaret, wife of Robert Odell
1618, Dec. 23, Sarah, dau. of John Odell
1620, Mch. 7, William Odell
1620, " 16, Richard son of John Odell
1621, Sep. 23, Mary Odle
1621, Dec. 25, Agnes, wife of Thos. Odle
1622, May 12, Elizabeth, wife of John Odell, Senr
1625, June 26, Johannes fil Johis Odell
1625, Feb. 12, Stephanus Odell

KEMPSTON.

Baptism.

1604, Feb. 24, Robert, son of John Odill

Marriage.

1620, Nov. 2, Thomas Odell and Em. Radwell

Burial.

1605, Oct. 20, John Odell his wife was bur

SALFORD.

Baptisms.

1605, Nov. 10, Marie dau. of John Odill
1607, Mar. 29, John, son of John Odell
1610, June 3, Richard son of John Odell
1611, Jan. 26, Edward, son of John Odell
1613, May 9, Elizabeth dau. of John Odell
1616, July 21, Johan, dau. of John Odell
1619, Oct. 3, Joane, dau. of John Odell

Marriages.

1603, Dec. 5, John Odill and Johane Bingley
1611, Dec. 2, Jeremie Pearce and Mary Odell of Cranfield

Burials.

1611, Mar. 31, Richard Odell
1618, Apr. 30, Johan, dau. of John Odell
1621, July 1, Agnes Odle, widow

SUNDON

Baptism.

1606, Mar. 1, George, son of George Odell.

RIDGEMONT

Baptism.

1608, Nov. 4, Ellena, filia Thomas Odell

Burials.

1609, Feb. 23, Thomas, filius Thomas Odell
1616, Jan. 11, Elizth. Odell
1617, Jan. 30, Thomas Odell

FLITWICK

Baptisms

1617, Feb. 27, George, son of Thomas Odell
1619, Jan 23, Alice, dau. of Thomas Odell

Marriage

1614, Nov. 10, Thomas Wodell and Eliz[th] Collope

Burial

1619, Feb. 3, Alice Odell

STEVINGTON

Baptisms

1614, Nov. 6, Richard, son of John Odell
1616, May 26, Maria, filia Johis Odell
1619, Nov. 25, John, son of John Odell
1621, May —, Thos., son of Tho.
1623, Oct. 25, Hellenor, dau. of John Odell
1625, Dec. 7, Grace, dau. of Tho. Odell

Baptisms

1617, May 25, Maria, dau. of John Odell

Marriage

1619, Sep. 13, Johes Odell and Rebecca Whisson

Burial

1618, June 24, Anna, ux Johis Odell

HARLINGTON

Baptisms

1622, Oct. 6, William, son of William and Frances Woodell
1624, Mar 20, Thomas, son of William and Frances Odell

Marriage

1617, Feb. 5, Wm Woodell and Francis Brinkloe

Burial

1625, Mar 26, Thos., inf. son of W^m and Frances Odell

HULCOT, *Baptism*

1617, Aug. 17, John, son of Rich. Odell

Marriage

1621, Nov. 1, Thomas West, of Soulbury, Com. Bucks and Susan Odell

Burials

1620, July 2, Anne dau. Richard Odell
1624, June 7, Jane, wife of Richard Odle

WOBURN

Marriages

1624, Oct. 18, Richard Odell and Katherine Cranfield
1619, Jan 28, Peter Lord and Dorathy Odell

MILBROOKE

Baptisms

1620, Jan. 14, Robert, son of Thomas Odell
1622, Apr. 7, Elizabeth dau. of Thomas Odell
1625, Jan. 1 Marie dau of Tho. Odell

HUSBORN CRAWLEY.

Marriage.

1620, July 10, John Odell and Elizabeth Turney

Baptism

1621, Oct 21, Elizabeth, dau. of John Odell

Burial

1621, Oct. 26, Elizabeth, dau. of John Odell

WOOTTON

Baptisms

1623, Aug. 11, John and Elizabeth children of Thomas Barker and
  Elizabeth Odell his wife

1625, Sep. 11, Alice dau. of John Odell and Agnes Hill

1625, Jan 8, John Son of John Odell and Ann Hill

Burial

1623, Aug. 11, Elizabeth Odell, wife of Thomas Barker

TODDINGTON

Marriages

1624, Oct. 7. George Odell and Jane Smith

1624, Nov. 25 Henry Odell and Elizabeth Godfrey

Burials

1624, July 2, Isabell wife of Henry Odell

1624, Dec 26, Henry Odle

1624, Jan. 30 Elizabeth wife of Henry Odell

LIDLINGTON

Marriage

1624, Jan. 17 John Odle and Marie Hill

CADDINGTON

Baptism and Burial

1625, Sep. 25, Richard, son of Richard Odle and bur. Oct. 3

SOUTHILL

Burial

1625, July 27, Joane wife of Edward Odell

OGIER FAMILY.—I was most interested to see in the Editor's Notes (THE REGIS-
TER, vol. 120, p. 142, April 1966) the reference to President Johnson's descent from
the Huguenot family of Ogier; as my wife is descended from them also. The
Editor has since kindly sent me copies of the pages relevant to this descent from

Mrs. Johnson's *A Family Album*; and, as he observes no definite statement is there given of the parentage of Amy Ogier, the great-great-grandmother of the President.

The chart gives her as daughter of William Osier (rightly Ogier). But the text (pages 111-12) only says that Amy Ogier was born 28 Feb. 1799 in North Carolina; adding that she was a descendant of Louis and Catherine (Creuze) Ogier, who came to Carolina with their nine children in 1774; and that all Ogier descendants in America are descended from Louis, Thomas or John Ogier, three of the sons of this couple. Dates make it certain that Amy must be a daughter, not a grand-daughter, of one of these three; and therefore she was not a daughter of William Ogier.

There is a good, if rather confused, account of the Ogier family by H. H. Sturmer, *Some Poitevin Protestants in London: notes about the families of Ogier from Sigournais and Creuzé of Châtellerault and Niort* (1896). From this it appears that Louis Ogier and Catherine Creuzé had no less than sixteen children, but not one was called William. Of their sons only Louis and Thomas seem to have left descendants in America; and as Thomas did not marry until 1804, five years after Amy was born, it is very probable that Amy was a daughter of his elder brother Louis.

This Louis Ogier was born in London in 1753, and became a factor in Charleston, S.C., where he died 13 Nov. 1820. He married 2 Oct. 1783 Susan [or Susannah] Martin, second daughter of the Rev. William [John] Martin [deceased], who died 14 Nov. 1827 at Charleston, aged 63 (*South Carolina Historical and Genealogical Magazine*, vol. 18, p. 89, April 1917. Amongst their children were two daughters, Jane Ogier, baptized 9 April 1798 at Charleston, and Elizabeth Martin Ogier, baptized 21 Feb. 1802 in Charleston. So they could well have had a daughter in between: Amy Ogier, whom we know was born 28 Feb. 1799. This should be possible for someone having access to Carolina records to prove. Data relating to the Charleston Ogiers is to be found in the reference cited above, vol. 17, 1917, vol. 20, 1919, 28-29, 1927-1928 and vols. 31-33, 1930-1932.

It is surely significant that Amy Ogier called her second son Martin (Butler), I suggest after her mother's family. Further Louis Ogier had a great-aunt Aymée Ogier (Auger), born 6 Dec. 1692 at Chassay l'Eglise, France, after whom his presumed daughter Amy was probably called. If the above suggestion prove acceptable the Ogier ancestry of Amy Ogier was as follows:

Louis Ogier. Born 1753 in London. Died 13 Nov. 1820 at Charleston, S.C. M.I. Circular Church.

Louis Ogier, silk merchant. Born 16 July 1726 at Moncoutant, Lower Poitou. Married 18 July 1751 at St. John's, Hackney, London. Naturalized 20 Dec. 1753. Died 8 Oct. 1780 at Ashley River, Charleston, S.C.

Catherine Creuzé. Born 12 Dec. 1732 in London. Died 17 July 1808 at Clapton in Hackney, and buried in the family vault at St. John's, Hackney. M.I.

Pierre Ogier, silk weaver. Born 1680 at Sigournois, Lower Poitou. Married 1710. Emigrated in 1730, five years after he had been denounced by a royal agent, the Abbé Gould, as a most dangerous man, who contemplated escaping from France and had already sent two of his children to England. Died December 1740 in London.

Catherine Rabaud. Born 1688 at Moncoutant. Died 1744 in London.

Pierre François Creuzé, jeweller. Born 30 July 1690 at St. Symphorien in Saintonge. "Escaped from France only with his life, in the reign of Queen Anne." Married 25 Nov. 1722 at the Artillery Chapel, Spitalfields, London. Died 24 Jan. 1758 at Clapton, and buried in the family vault at St. John's, Hackney, which he had built in 1743. M.I. Will (P.C.C. 33 Hutton) dated 5 Jan., proved 3 Feb. 1758.

Elizabeth Giboreau. Born 11 Jan. and baptized 23 Jan. 1704 at the Artillery Chapel. Died 30 Aug. 1766, and buried with her husband. M.I. Will (P.C.C. 331 Tyndall) dated 27 Sept. 1765, proved 10 Sept. 1766. All her household goods, linen and china, together with a pearl necklace and diamond stay buckles, were left to her daughter Catherine Ogier.

Pierre Ogier (Auger), merchant of Chassay l'Eglise and farmer at Benêtre in Sigournois. Born 1645 or 1655. Married 1678. Died 1697.

Jeanne Bernardin, of Moncoutant. Born 1658. Emigrated in 1700. Died 1738.

François Creuzé, of St. Symphorien. Son of François Creuzé, a merchant and protestant convert (died 31 Jan. 1687), and Marthe Violette. Born about 1650. Married 1682, and abjured protestantism in the same year.

Marie Laidain.

Jean Giboreau, from the province of Beauce. Flour-dealer, of Red Lion Street, Stepney, in 1704.

Susanne le Bailly.

Further information on the Creuzé family is to be found in *The Herald and Genealogist*, vol. 1, p. 259, 369 (1863); H. & P. Beauchet-Filleau, *Dictionnaire des Familles du Poitou*, vol. 2, p. 743 (1895); *The Genealogist*, N.S. vol. 27, p. 114-115 (1911).

Nothing certain seems to be known as to the origin of Pierre Ogier. His granddaughter Louise Ogier married a Courtauld, and from this marriage descends the well-known Courtauld family. The early Courtaulds of St. Pierre d'Oléron in Saintonge were connected with an Ogier family of that place. Pierre Ogier, saulnier, witnessed a Courtauld marriage contract 11 June 1602. He was presumably identical with the Pierre Ogier, l'aîné, son of Marc Ogier, who appears in another Courtauld marriage contract the following day (S. L. Courtauld, *The Huguenot family of Courtauld*, vol. 1 (1957)). Possibly the Ogiers of Sigournois were descended from this family.

Family tradition, surely worthless, would derive the family from Ogier the Dane. This hero "revolted against Charlemagne, fled to Lombardy and resisted the imperial forces for seven years. He was at last taken prisoner and imprisoned at Rheims. He was released in order to fight against the Saracen giant Brehus, or Braihier after which he had a conqueror's career in the East. He was then carried off by Morgan la Fay, who made him immortal, and he either still lives at Avalon, or sleeps in a mountain, like Barbarossa, ready to be awakened in time of need" (M. Letts, *Sir John Mandeville* (1949), p. 108).

The name Ogier was not uncommon in France in the early middle ages. Its occurrence, with many examples, is discussed by P. Boissonade, *Du nouveau sur la Chanson de Roland* (1923), p. 350-5.

Bryn Cadwrfa, Montgomery, Wales.   CHARLES EVANS.

A CONTRIBUTION TO THE HISTORY OF THE FAMILY OF OSGOOD.

[Communicated by OSGOOD FIELD.]

FEW of the early New England families have increased more in the land of their adoption than the Osgoods, while the name is almost extinct in the mother country and will be sought for in vain in the counties of Hants and Wilts, where the family originally flourished.

Scattered notices of the American branch have appeared in various publications, but I have never met with anything approaching to a complete account of the family, or an attempt to trace their ancestry in England.

It is partly with the hope that some competent genealogist, who has more ready access than the writer to New England records, will publish a full and detailed account of the descendants of John and Christopher Osgood, that the following contribution to the history of the family is made.

At a very early period in English history we meet with the names Osgot, Osgotus and Osgod. They are probably of Danish or Scandinavian origin. I have found them in two or three instances before the Conquest, and in the Domesday survey persons bearing them appear as holders of land in a dozen different counties, including Hampshire and Wiltshire. In the latter county Osgot was a "tenant in capite," that is, a holder of land direct from the crown, showing that he was a person of some consequence.

Apparently the family remained in Wiltshire, for in 1295 Robertus Osegod was returned a burgess for Chippenham.

On the book-plate of my grandfather, the Hon. Samuel Osgood, the arms of the family are thus given : or, three garbs ; crest, a demilion rampant supporting a garb. The coloring of the garbs is not shown by the engraving. These arms, worked in tapestry, are said to have been taken over from England by John Osgood.

Berry's " Encyclopedia Heraldica " gives the arms of Osgood thus : " Three garbs within a tressure flay and counter flay gules ; crest, a demilion rampant ppr., supporting a garb gules." Probably the former are the original arms and the latter since borne by a younger branch of the family, with the tressure, &c. for " a difference."

For a century preceding the departure of John and Christopher Osgood for New England, the parishes of Upper and Nether Wallop in Hampshire appear to have been the chief seats of the family, and from these places they doubtless found their way to other parts in the neighborhood, either in the same county or the adjoining one of Wilts.

Unfortunately the parish * registers in those places anciently the

---

* In the register of Upper Wallop the burials date from 1538, with a chasm from 1625 to 1664. Marriages from 1541, Baptisms from 1684. These are from parts of registers collected together about one hundred years ago, by the then clergyman, who mentions in a note that it was all that remained of the ancient register of the parish of Upper Wallop. The parish register of Nether Wallop does not begin till 1628, and contains no names of Osgood.

residences of the Osgoods, are very defective, most of the early ones being lost or destroyed; thus depriving me of the only positive means of connecting some of the earlier branches of the family. Several of the wills, also, of persons dying in Hampshire which were proved and deposited in the Registry at Winchester, are missing, as shown by the calendar, which has been preserved, dating from 1530. Enough, however, exists to show pretty conclusively the descent of John Osgood, the New England emigrant, from Peter Osgood, whose will was proved in 1534. From this date to 1660, there were thirteen wills of persons of the name of Osgood, proved at this court, seven of which only, viz., those in italics, can now be found. Peter of Wallop, 1534. Peter of Nether Wallop (perhaps the same individual as last), 1534. Richard of Wallop, 1543. Robert of Ibsley, 1567. William of Nether Wallop, 1582. *Peter* of Over Wallop, 1585. *Henry* of Over Wallop, 1591. *Margaret* of Nether Wallop, 1595. Richard of Upper Wallop, 1607. *William* of Fordingbridge, 1614. *Richard* of Shipton, 1626. *Robert* of Wherwell, 1630. *Peter* of Romsey, 1639.

We gain some further facts from the Subsidy rolls, by which it appears that in the 14th year of the reign of King Henry the Eighth (1522), Richard Osgood, of Over Wallop, was assessed to the King's subsidies for goods to the value of £15, and in the same year Peter Osgood, of Nether Wallop, was assessed for goods valued at £10. In the 13th of Elizabeth (1570), Henry Osgood, of Upper Wallop, and William Osgood, of Nether Wallop, were assessed. In the 39th Elizabeth, Robert Osgood, of Wherwell, is among those of that place who were assessed, and again in the 18th of James I. (1620). In the same year occur the names of Peter. Osgood of Romsey, and Henry Osgood of Upper Wallop. William Osgood, of Shipton, was assessed 4th Charles I. (1628).

Probably Peter Osgood, of Nether Wallop, who was assessed in 1522, and whose will was proved in 1534, was the father or grandfather of Peter Osgood, whose will, dated Jan. 10, 1585-6, was proved Feb. 21st of the same year. The latter, after making bequests to his parish church and the mother church at Winchester, gives small legacies to his sons Robert and Richard, and to his daughters Margaret and Elizabeth. He also bequeaths to his son Peter 20 pounds, articles of household furniture, and a house called Great house when 21 years of age; and to his son John, half his "tolles," his timber and his hops. He names his wife Elizabeth and makes his son Richard executor and residuary legatee. The burial of Peter Osgood is recorded in the parish register of Upper Wallop, Jan. 26, 1585-6, in letters thrice the size of any other entry, from which I infer that he was the principal parishioner. In 1598, July 30, the burial of Elizabeth Osgood occurs, in the same register. She was doubtless the widow of Peter Osgood.

Robert Osgood, son of Peter, and named in his will, was that Robert of Wherwell (a parish adjoining the Wallops), whose will is dated Aug. 25, 1630, and was proved Nov. 17th of the same year. He describes himself as of Cottingworth, in the parish of Wherwell, and after a bequest to the parish church, leaves £60 to his youngest daughter Dorcas, to be paid on the day of her marriage, £20 to his daughter Mary, and small legacies to his wife Joan, and his son

Robert. There is a gift of £10 to Edward Abot, and of £20 to Elizabeth, wife of John Bartlett. He appoints executors his son Stephen and daughter Mary. In a list of debtors attached to the will, is the name of John Osgood, and £4.9.0. was the amount of his indebtedness. The legacies to Edward Abot and Bartlett's wife, are so considerable for that period, that I infer they had married daughters of the testator. I would observe, in passing, that the Abbots were among the early families who settled at Andover, Massachusetts.

Cottingworth is a large farm in Wherwell, of about 360 acres. It formerly belonged to the Osgoods, and a sketch of their ancient residence, which is still standing, is in my possession.

John Osgood, named as a debtor to Robert's estate, was doubtless his eldest son, and the same that emigrated to New England and settled at Andover.[*] He had probably received his portion of the estate, before the date of the will, as also his brother Stephen, and they are therefore not named among the legatees.

The earliest parish register of Wherwell dates from 1634. In 1636 the following entry occurs : " Elizabeth Osgood, the daughter of John Osgood, was baptized the 14th of November and of Sarah his wife." The name of Osgood does not occur again in the register during the next 50 years. We shall see hereafter that John Osgood, of Andover, Mass., left at his death a daughter Elizabeth, whose age would correspond to that of the above child, and also, in all probability, a widow Sarah.

In her Majesty's State paper office is the following document, written by Dr. Stanley, who was at that time head master of the famous school at Winchester.

" NOBLE SIR,

I am earnestly solicited by John Osgood, to write unto you again about His intended journey to New England, that he may have the liberty to goe. I told Him I had written the last weeke, but that would not satisfy Him because He could not be sure that Letter was Delivered, or that the way would be open to Him. I desire you, therefore, that you would be pleased, if you have not done it already, to take order that He may passe, as He intended ; because I would by noe means hinder him in his iourney though it may be He would be his best friend that should doe it. I take my leave and rest.

Your Servant to dispose of,

March 23d, 1637.[†]   EDWARD STANLEY.

Your sonne is very well.

Yᵉ bearer of this letter will, as I am told, pay any monys, that shall be due in this business."

Superscribed.	*Endorsed.*
" To my Honourable friend, Mr.	" R. 3d Aprilis 1638.
Nicholas[‡] one of yᵉ clerks of	Mr. Dr. Stanley school-
Yᵉ counseyl in King's Street	master at Winton.[§]
near yᵉ axe yard in Westminster."	for a passe for
	Jo : Osgood."

---

[*] For the early generations of John Osgood's descendants, see vol. xiii. pp. 117–21.—ED.
[†] i. e., 1637–8.
[‡] Sir Edward Nicholas, principal Secretary of State to Charles I.
[§] The old name of Winchester.

Shortly after the above letter was received by Nicholas, the ship Confidence sailed from Southampton for New England, and the following names occur in the list of her passengers, dated 14th April, 1638. Sarah Osgood, of Herrell (Wherwell) *spinster*,* and four children, together with William Osgood and William Jones, both children under 11 years of age, and Margery Packe, servant.

This Sarah was undoubtedly the wife of John Osgood ; but why she is called *spinster* in the list of passengers is not easily explained. Possibly it is a clerical error, or her husband may have been refused permission to leave England, being a subsidy man, and consequently obliged to resort to some deceit to enable him and his family to secure their passages. Such practices were not uncommon at that period.

We next find John Osgood's name among the persons who were admitted freemen in Massachusetts on the 23d of May, 1639. Soon after he settled at Andover, which place was so named by its first inhabitants from and of the principal towns in Hampshire, in the vicinity of which lie the 2 Wallops and Wherwell, the last named parish being less than 4 miles distant from it. John Osgood died at Andover Oct. 24, 1651, in the 57th year of his age, and Sarah Osgood, whose death is entered in the town records April 8, 1667, was doubtless his widow. New England authors mention the following children of John Osgood : John, born 1632, Mary, Elizabeth, Stephen, 1638, Christopher, 1643, and Hannah, 1644.

Among the early settlers of Ipswich, is found Christopher Osgood,† concerning whom the following facts may prove interesting. In the parish church of St. Thomas in Salisbury, Wilts, occurs the following :

" 1599, October X. pofer Osgood married to Eliz : Brockwell the 30.''

In the registry of wills, at Salisbury, is that of Elizabeth Osgood, widow, dated June 18, 1612, and proved the same year. She desires to be buried in the church yard of St. Thomas, and names her son,‡ Matthew Mayland, Margaret, wife of Edward Noble, Priscilla Hicks, son-in-law Thomas Roberts, and friends John Hicks and John Upton.

I am indebted to Mr. Harrison, of the College of Arms, for the following copy of a pedigree in a private collection there. He says, in transmitting it, that he believes Christopher was the name of the father of Christopher, William and Mary, and as the name is an uncommon one, I would suggest that Christopher of Salisbury was father of Christopher of Marlborough, and grandfather of Christopher of Ipswich.

It would appear, from the pedigree, that this branch of the family is extinct in England in the male line.

---

* For some observations on the meaning of this word, see vol. xiii. pp. 117 and 284.—ED.

† For the early generations of the descendants of Christopher Osgood, see vol. xiii. pp. 200-2.—ED.

‡ i. e., Son-in-law.

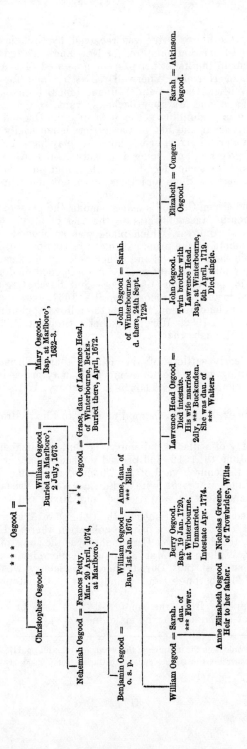

* * * Osgood =

Christopher Osgood.

William Osgood =
Buried at Marlboro',
2 July, 1673.

Mary Osgood.
Bap. at Marlboro',
1652–3.

Nehemiah Osgood = Frances Petty,
Mar. 20 April, 1674,
at Marlboro,?

* * * Osgood = Grace, dau. of Lawrence Head,
of Winterbourne, Berks.
Buried there, April, 1672.

John Osgood = Sarah.
of Winterbourne.
d. there, 24th Sept.
1729.

Benjamin Osgood =
o. s. p.

William Osgood = Anne, dau. of
Bap. 1st Jan. 1676. *** Ellis.

William Osgood = Sarah,
dau. of
*** Flower.

Berry Osgood.
Bap. 19 Jan. 1720,
at Winterbourne.
Unmarried.
Intestate Apr. 1774.

Lawrence Head Osgood =
Died intestate.
His wife married
2dly, *** Buckenden.
She was dau. of
*** Walters.

John Osgood.
Twin brother with
Lawrence Head.
Bap. at Winterbourne,
5th April, 1719.
Died single.

Elizabeth = Conger.
Osgood.

Sarah = Atkinson.
Osgood.

Anne Elizabeth Osgood = Nicholas Greene.
Heir to her father.   of Trowbridge, Wilts.

On referring to the parish register of St. Mary's in Marlborough, Wilts, which begins in 1602, I find the following entries :

Baptized, 1632–3, March 17, Mary, daughter of Christopher Osgood.
Married, 1632, April 21, Christopher Osgood and Mary Everatt.
" 1633, July 28, Christopher Osgood and Margery Fowller.
Buried, 1633, April 21, Mary Osgood.

In the register of St. Peter's in Marlborough, which dates from 1611, are the following entries :

Buried, July 2, 1673, William Osgood.
Married, April 20, 1674, Nehemiah Osgood and Frances Petty.
Baptized, Jan. 1, 1676, William, son of Nehemiah Osgood.

It would appear from the register of St. Mary's that Christopher Osgood lost his first wife soon after the birth of his daughter Mary, and again married a few months after.

On the 24th March, 1633,* his name occurs in the list of passengers for New England by the Mary and John, of London, who then took the oath of allegiance and supremacy, and on the 6th May, 1635, he was admitted freeman by the Massachusetts General Court.

Christopher Osgood settled at Ipswich, shortly after his arrival in New England, and died there in 1650, leaving, it is said, a widow Margery, and children, Mary, Elizabeth, Abigail, and Christopher born in 1643. After his death his widow Margery married her fellow townsman Thomas Coleman, who also came from Marlborough, Wilts. Her father Joseph Fowler followed his daughter to New England, and settled at Ipswich.

The following extracts from the papers of my grandfather, Samuel Osgood, may be of use to any one who should undertake a fuller account of the family.

Peter Osgood, of Andover, and Sarah his wife, daughter of Benjamin Johnson, had the following children :

Isaac,	born	27 January,	1743–4.
Peter,	"	24 June,	1745.
Samuel,	"	3 February,	1747–8.
Sarah,	"	11 do.	1749–50.
Joseph,	"	3 December,	1751.
Susannah,	"	23 August,	1754.
Isaac,	"	15 July,	1756.
Joseph,	"	30 May,	1758.
Lydia,	"	22 March,	1760.
Timothy,	"	17 do.	1763.

The above Samuel Osgood married, first, 4 Jan., 1775, Martha Brandon, who was born Dec. 25, 1753, and died without issue 13 Sept., 1778. His second wife, whom he married May 24, 1786, was Maria, relict of Walter Franklin, of Franklin Square, New York, and daughter of Daniel Bowne, of Rocky Hill, Flushing, N. Y., where she was born March 4, 1754. Samuel Osgood had the following children by his last wife :

---

* i. e., 1633–4.

819

Martha Brandon, born 6 Feb., 1787, m. Hon. Mr. Genet, French
                          Minister to Washington.
Juliana,   " 14 Aug., 1788, m. Samuel Osgood, her cousin.
Walter Franklin,   " 24 Mch., 1791.   [of New York.
Susan Kittredge,   " 12 April, 1795, m. May 17, 1821, Moses Field,
Caroline Matilda,   " 27 Feb., 1799, died young.
London, July 28, 1865.

THE OSGOOD FAMILY.—*To the Editor of the New England Historical and Genea-*
logical Register. Sir—In an article of mine in your No. for January, 1866, I stated, *
on the authority of New England writers, that the first John Osgood, of Andover,
Mass., left a son named Christopher. Both Farmer, and Abbot in his History of
Andover, mention this as a fact. I should be glad to know if there is any good
authority for this statement. It is well known that there was a Christopher Osgood
in Andover, at an early date ; but inasmuch as the above John Osgood does not
mention any son of that name in his will, while Christopher Osgood, the first of the
family who had settled at Ipswich, does, I am led to suppose that the two Christophers were father and son.

Apparently both of the emigrants from England, name in their wills all their
respective children living at the time. That of John Osgood, dated 12th April,
1650, in the 54th year of his age, speaks of his sons John and Stephen, and daughters Mary, Elizabeth, Hannah, Sarah and Rebeccah, and his wife Sarah. Christopher's will is dated April 19, 1650, and names his son *Christopher*, daughters Mary,
Abigail, Elizabeth and Deborah, and wife Margery.

I spoke of the name of Osgood being derived from the Danish or Scandinavian.
I think, however, that there are equally strong grounds for supposing it to be of
Saxon origin.

I avail myself of this opportunity to correct two slight errors in the article
referred to. In speaking of the arms, as given in Berry's " Encyclopedia Heraldica," the paragraph should read—" three garbs within a double tressure flory and
counterflory gules," instead of " within a tressure flay and counterflay gules." At
page 25, line 17, for " and of the principal towns," read " one of the principal
towns."

I have received several communications from descendants of William Osgood, of
Salisbury, Mass., who, it is said, built a barn at Newbury in 1640, for Mr. John
Spencer, requesting information as to his English ancestry, and I regret that my
ingestigations have not enabled me to trace his parentage, &c. to my satisfaction.
He could not have been the William Osgood, described as a " child under 11 years
of age," who accompanied Sarah Osgood to New England in the ship Confidence, in
April, 1638, unless his age was accidentally or purposely misstated.

He may possibly have been one of the persons of that name referred to in the following wills:—Ann Osgood of West Woodhay, Co. Berks, widow of Richard
Osgood of same place, in her will dated May 16th, 17th James 1st (1620), appoints William Osgood one of the overseers of it. Richard Osgood, of Shipton, in
his will dated May 23, 1625, appoints his son William executor.

West Woodhay is about 6 miles W. S. W. of Newbury, and about 10 miles N.
of Andover. Shipton, Hants, is about 8 miles west of Andover, and 10 or 12 miles
N. E. of Salisbury.   OSGOOD FIELD.
76 Mark Lane, London, September 13, 1867.

*The preceding article.

820

The name Otis. — Hereditary surnames, were not assumed in England till after the Norman Conquest (1066) and then only gradually and by families of rank ; so that it is difficult to trace the pedigree of any family beyond the 13th century. Another difficulty arises from the loose orthography which obtained up to the time of Elizabeth and even later. At the commencement of the 15th century there was much confusion in family names, and surnames were not permanently settled before the era of the Reformation.

In Hollingshed's copy of the Roll of " Battel Abbey," is " Fitz-Otes." As Latin was the language employed by the clerks of early times, proper names were almost uniformly Latinized from the 11th to 16th century. Camden gives a list of Latinized surnames in his " Remains," p. 130. In Wright's " Court Hand Restored " is a more copious list, in which is " Filius Odonis — Fitz — Otes." The method adopted by the old Normans to distinguish families was prefixing to their names the word Fitz, a corruption of *Fils* and that derived from the Latin *Filius,* as the Scotch employed Mac — the Welsh Ap — meaning respectively, *the son of.* Verstegan supposes that those names with Fitz superadded, to have been Netherlanders.

Our investigations among English records are too limited to enable us to trace any lengthened pedigree of the Otis Family previously to the arrival in this country of the emigrant ancestor. And it would be useless to speculate upon the origin of the name Otis, or, without any evidence of the fact from historical records, to jump to the conclusion that we must needs be descended from some stalwort Norman who " hacked his way to eminence and fortune through the serried ranks " of the Saxons at Hastings, because a name similar to that we bear happens to be on the Battle Roll. Even *identity* of surnames is not always proof of the consanguinity of the parties bearing it, for in some instances two families have derived their surnames from one *place.* Names of the monosyllabic kind were borrowed generally by the Anglo-Saxon race from local places — other names from Natural objects, as coney, otter, &c., many from avocations, etc.

We have already expressed the opinion that the families of Oates and Otes were in no way connected with the family of Ottis or Otis. The former are and always have been of one syllable, while the latter are distinctly two. Besides, affinity of Arms in Heraldry distinguishes families with nearly if not quite the certainty of surnames. It will be seen on examination that the arms of these two families are widely different in their character and bearings.

Extracts from the Parish Register of St. John the Baptist, Glastonbury, Co. of Somerset, England. The register commences in 1603. *Baptisms:*

821

Alicia Oattis, dau. of John, 23 June, 1604.
William Ottis, son of James, 5 Dec., 1610.
Joan Ottis, dau. of John, 1 Dec., 1612.
Maria Ottis, dau. of James 2, Jan. 1615.
Hannah Ottis, dau. of John, 16 Aug., 1618.
Flora Wottis [Ottis ?] dau. of James, 3
    April, 1612.

Elleanor Ottis, dau. of James, 15 April, 1609.
Joan Ottis, dau. of John, 15 Dec., 1610.
Elizabeth Ottis, dau. of John, 12 Nov., 1614.
Richard Ottis, son of John, 27 Feb., 1616.
James Ottis, son of James, 31st May, 1617.
John Ottis son of John, 14 Jan., 1621.
Joan Ottis, dau. of James, 23 July, 1621.

Marriages: — William Oattis and Agnes Awstin, 7 Jan., 1606.
James Oattis and Flora Awstin, 1 Aug., 1608.
Burials: — Maria Oattis, wife of William, 1 Dec., 1605.
Joan Ottis, dau. of John, 22 Dec., 1611.
Joan Ottis, dau. of John, 21 Dec., 1612.
Agneta Ottis, widow, 6 June, 1614.
Elizabeth Ottis dau. of John, 31st March, 1615.
James Ottis, son of James, 14 March, 1618.

Extracts from the Parish register of Othery, near Bridgewater, Somersetshire :

Elizabeth Otis, dau. of Anthony, Baptised 19 Oct., 1561.
Thomas Otis, son of   "   "   21 Aug., 1567.
Sibella Otis dau. of   "   "   16 Oct., 1569.
John Otis, son of   "   "   29 April, 1627.
Joan Otis, dau. of   "   "   3 May, 1629 ; buried 6 Sept., 1630.
Anthony Otis, son of   "   buried 18th Jan., 1653.

From this it is seen that the derivation of John Otis of Hingham, Mass., is not from Barnstable, in Devonshire, or from Hingham, in Norfolk, but from Glastonbury, in the Co., Somerset. Glastonbury is about five miles S.S.W. from Wells, the seat of the Bishop, so a much more probable place for breeding early non-conformists. Besides, Glastonbury was one of the very highest spots for sanctification in the days of prevalence of the Romish superstition. It will be seen that John *had* a son Richard, but we have heretofore given our reasons for believing he was not the Richard of Dover, N. H. If Richard Otis of Dover, be not a son of John of Hingham, Mass., born (as above) in England, 27 Feb., 1616-17, it may be some gratification to presume that the same John, (the first) was probably son of Richard of Glastonbury, (whose Will is dated 1611) and that Stephen (Will dated at G., 1637,) was his brother, each giving a son the name of the grandfather.

Lechford, a Lawyer getting into difficulty, or out of occupation among the colonists, went home and "wrote a book against them," * wherein he says, "they refuse to baptise old Ottis grand children, an ancient member of their own church." And Tudor, in his life of Otis, says, "as twelve years after a minute of the baptism of Mary Otis [dau. of second John] is made in the Journal of Rev. Peter Hobart, the difficulty, whatever it was, had been removed." "Old Ottis" — John[1] — had grand children by one, if not two daughters before Lechford wrote. Mary[3] (Gill,) mentioned in the grandfather's Will, and old enough to marry John Beal, 14 Nov., 1660, was not baptized before Jan., 1644, and her sister Sarah[3], who m. John Longley, 3 Jan., 1666, was baptized at the same time. (The other child, Thomas Gill[3], m. Susanna Wilson, in Dec., 1673.) The refusal of Lechford therefore, may be applied to both these children. We know, that unless one of the parents was of the church, the offspring would not be admitted, in those times, to baptism. Many instances are known, where, three, four, and even six children were baptized at once, after the father or mother had just united with the church.

Notice. — It is proposed to publish in pamphlet form, a corrected and enlarged edition of the Genealogy heretofore printed, being the descendants of John Otis. This is presumed to be sufficient notice to all descendants who may see this, to send a full account of their families to the compiler of this, or to the Editor, Mr. Samuel G. Drake, Boston.

Who was James Otis, 2d Lieutenant in Capt. John Jones company of Col. James Reed's regiment, 2d regiment under Gen. Washington at Cambridge, 1776 ?
Who was Joseph Otis, private, wounded at Morrisianna, Feb., 1781, residence, Branford, Ct. Enlisted 1 January, 1777 for the war and received half pension ?

* Plaine Dealing, Newes from N. E., written in 1641.

PEDIGREE OF REV. JOHN OXENBRIDGE, OF BOSTON.

A correspondent has sent us a tabular pedigree showing the descent of Katherine Harby, supposed to be the mother of Rev. John Oxenbridge, of Boston, from King Edward I, of England, through two of his sons and one of his daughters, namely: King Edward II, Edmund, Earl of Kent, and the Princess Joan of Acres.

"I do not seek," writes our correspondent, "to claim a distinguished lineage for *all* our Puritan ancestors, for their hold on our veneration and respect is too well founded to need the aid of such; and when we build up an imposing pedigree and load their names with fictitious honors they neither sought nor cared for, we are apt to forget the simple virtues that best adorn their memories. Too much has been attempted in this way; opinions the most absurd have been advanced serving only to make their authors contemptible in the estimation of those not personally interested—and yet, when accident or patient research has revealed some well authenticated fact not previously known, it is proper that it should be recorded for the benefit and instruction of others.

Rev. John Oxenbridge, pastor of the Old South Church, was we are told, the son of Daniel Oxenbridge, M. D., of Daventry, Northamptonshire, England. In Baker's Hist. of N., vol. 2d, page 19 (a copy of which is in the Boston Public Library), we find that this Daniel O. married Catharine, dr. of Thomas Harby, *and had issue*, but the names of their children are not there given ; but as John O. was born in 1608-9 and his father died in 1642, I think it extremely probable that Catharine Harby was his mother, especially as we are not told that Daniel O. had other wives.

On referring to Burke's Royal Families, vol. 2d, pedigrees 116 and 124, the lineage of this lady may be satisfactorily traced ; from these we learn that she was descended in two direct lines from King Edward III; through his sons, John of Gaunt, Duke of Lancaster, and Edmund, Duke of York; she was the fifth also from Lady Alice Neville, dr. of Richard, Earl of Salisbury, and sister of the renowned 'king maker,' and inherited the blood of the Montacutes, Beauchamps, Holands and Throckmortons.

I think I may with confidence assert that the old Puritan divine, whose remains rest in the King's Chapel Burial Ground, was descended from many of the noblest families of England. N. F. C."

WILL OF DANIEL OXENBRIDGE.

THE following most important will supplements the interesting group of Oxenbridge wills given by Mr. Waters in the REGISTER for January, 1890. As this will may be considered a document in the history of old England (the Long Parliament having passed a vote of thanks and, I believe, decreed a monument for the initial bequest), and as the testator is so closely connected with New England, it is worth printing in full. I append a brief note concerning the connections of the testator and his brother, Rev. John Oxenbridge.   LOTHROP WITHINGTON.

30 LITTLE RUSSELL ST., W. C., LONDON.

COMMISSARY COURT OF LONDON, REG. NO. 29, Fo. 239.

I DANIEL OXENBRIDGE of London now resident and merchant in Liverne being at this present in a weake Estate of Body but of a good memorie and sound minde doe make this my last and only Will and Testam^t to be performed if it shall please God at this or any other time to call mee out of this life ffirst I humbly assigne my soule to God its maker . . . . &c & next my Body I comitt to the Earth in such decent manner to be buried as shalbe by my friendes thought fitt. I then constitute and appointe after the time of my decease my Executors John Throckmorton, Charles Longland & John Collyer desyring their care and paines to see effected what here of them is required First I give to the Right Honble the Lords and Com̃ons now assembled in parlm^t in or neere London & to their use for the prosecution of their designes One Thousand pounds Sterlinge to be paid halfe in six monthes and the other halfe in twelve monthes after the daye of my decease. More to severall godly people impoverished by the said distractions in England I give One hundred and fiftie pounds to be disposed of according to the discretion of my brother Mr. John Oxenbridge and Mr. Thomas Doubty our Minister here residing ffor or towards the buying of a burying place for the English nation in Liverne I give fiftie pounds to my brother-in-law Mr. William Langhorne Twenty pounds to my sister his wife fiftie pounds to his son Daniell fiftie pounds to each other sonne or daughter they may have at the time of my death thirtie pounds to my Broth^r-in-law Mr. Caleb Cockcroft fortie pounds to my sister his wife fortie pounds to each of their children livinge at my decease Twentie pounds to my Broth^r-in-law Mr. Hunt and my sister his wife Eightie pounds To my Broth^r Mr. John Oxenbridge minister two hundred pounds readie money if hee requests it and to his wife and sonnes one hundred pounds besides what may be due to him

824

in my bookes. To my brother Clement Oxenbridge all my part proceed
of the Tynfarme wch is valued at six hundred and ninetie pounds sterlings
or there abouts be it more or lesse. To my mother eight hundred pounds
besides all lands Houses Testements (*sic*) as in or neere London or in the
Countie of Northumberland are left me by my father her deceased husband in the same manner as it is left unto mee thereout of it discharging
such debts and Legacies as were thereon enjoyned mee as by my Fathers
will maie appeare   To my sister M^ris Catherine Henly one hundred pound
To her daughter Katherine ffowler one hundred and fiftie pound   To
my Coozen M^ris Henry Barnard (*sic*) and his wife thirtie pounds and to
my Coozen Mr Nicholas Searle and his wife a lyke some that is thirtie
pounds to each of their wifes in all one Hundred and twentie pounds to
you foure   To Mr. Job Throckmorton foure hundred pounds   To his
wife a chaine of pearles in my deske containing as I conceave 490 pearles
or what they are   To my three freinds Mr. Phillipp Williams Mr. Charles
Longland and Mr. Tho: Doubty one hundred pounds apeece that is three
hundred pounds to them three   To William Reymes a hundred Dollers   To
Mr. Robert and Nicholas Abny fiftie dollers apeece for a poore remembrance of mee   To Mr Samuell Bonnels fiftie pounds sterling   To
Thomas Dethicke one hundred Dollers   To John Collyer three thousand
dollers   To Leonard Digge fiftie Dollers   To Robert Barbor and Edward
Rett one hundred dollers apeece   To George Dethicke my servant a hundred dollers   To Richard Browne one hundred Dollers   To John Con
fourtie dollers   To Joanna woman servant thyrtie dollers   To the Gover-
no^r & Mad^na ffran^a five dollers apeece   To Angelina 10 dollers   To John
Batt^a the boy five dollers   To Sig^r Gualtero Vandercoort and his wife
fourtie pounds between them to buy a ring in my remembrance   The advance of my estate to be given to my forenamed Execuato^rs for their paines
in this business   Be it noted that the pounds sterling are to be reduced
into dollers at fiftie pence the doller and by a doller is meant a peece of
eight effective of Spayne   Lord receave my Soule

5th ffebry 1643   Witnesses present at the readinge of this Will to Mr
Daniell Oxenbridge in his House on the 6th ffeb^ry 1643 and wee heard him
say hee confirmed it as his will   beinge demanded if he confirmed this as
his will he answered I doe I doe   ffrancis Read Thomas Barnsly Ralph
Duke Thomas Crathorne Robert Barbor Tho: Banks John Bommer

Wee Thomas Doubty Charles Longland Phillipp Williams and John
Collyer being present with Mr Daniell Oxenbridge on the ffirst day of
ffeb^ry about twenty foure houres or a little after did at his request heare
him declare Verbatim the words written parte on this and parte on the other
syde of this paper in words and desired John Collyer to write them downe
to make out of them a will in as good forme as in short time hee could
Wee testifie further that what is in the will hereto annexed under the
hand of John Collyer and consented by the said Oxenbridge this morning
the 6th of ffeb^ry and attested by the seaven Witnesses therto subscribinge is
the true Import of what this paper contains according to the intent of the
Testator and it was in our company by him confirmed and in Witness of
the truth of what wee write hereunder each hath to y^t I read that
Joines these two sheetes of paper   Sett his seale the 6th of ffeb^ry 1643 as
before Thomas Doubty Charles Longland Phillip Williams John Collyer.

Probatum fuit &c. . decimo sexto die Mensis Martij anno dm̃ Juxta &c
1643 [1643–4].   Willmo clarke leg &c &c Arthuri Ducke leg com &c
Juramento Johi Throckmorton prin Execut &c Nec non de veros Com^p

825

fuerens Carolo Longland et Johi Collyer execut etĩa in humoi Testamᵒ
noĩat cum venerunt eam in debita juris forma petitis.

[The testator was a junior son of Dr. Daniel Oxenbridge of London. His
two brothers John and Clement were of much mark. Clement may be almost
said to have been the founder of the English post office service. As to John,
he was a pioneer in Guiana, Jamaica, Bermuda, &c., a leading spirit in the Commonwealth in England, an intimate of Milton and Cromwell, fellow of the Eton
college, and finally minister of Boston in New England. The brother-in-law
Caleb Cockcroft died the same year (1644), and the widow married the famous
solicitor general, Oliver Saint John. Another sister mentioned, Mrs. Henley,
afterwards was wife of the noted General Philip Skippon. Her daughter
mentioned in the will, Katherine Fowler, was the poetess, the "matchless
Orinda." I have traced back many hundreds of the direct ancestors of this
illustrious family, and have quite a collection of wills bearing on the immediate
family connections of Rev. John Oxenbridge, including the will of the paternal
grandmother of his wife Frances Woodward. This will shows that her father
Ezekiel Woodward orginated not in Worcestershire, as stated by Antony à
Wood, but in Hereford, a shire as yet little explored by genealogists. I trust
to publish some of these additional Oxenbridge notes later on.—L. W.]

THE ENGLISH ANCESTRY OF ROBERT PAGE
OF HAMPTON, N. H.

By George Walter Chamberlain, M.S., of Malden, Mass.

In 1860 Samuel Gardner Drake, one of the founders of the New
England Historic Genealogical Society, published his The Founders
of New England, and on pages 44 to 48 of that volume he reproduced "a Register of persons" who desired "to passe into forraigne
partes . . . by vertu of a commission granted to Mʳ Thomas
Mayhew, gentleman."

One of the entries which was published reads as follows :

"Aprill the 11th 1637. The examinaction of Robertt Page of Ormsby
in Norff. husbandman, aeged 33 yeares and Lucea his wife, aged 30
yeares, with 3 children, Frances, Margrett, and Susanna, and 2 Saruants,
William Moulton and Anne Wadd ; the one aged 20 yeares the other
15 yeares, and are all desirous to passe for New England to inhabitt and
Remaine."

826

In the REGISTER for 1872 (vol 26, p. 75) Dr. William Prescott of Concord, N. H., communicated the results of his investigations concerning the parentage of Robert Page in his introduction to his descendants. From the fact that what Dr. Prescott published corresponds with the English Notes of the late Horatio G. Somerby, it is inferred that they were the result of the latter's English gleanings. As the parish registers of Ormsby St. Margaret do not begin until 1675 and the register of Acle till 1664, the establishment of the Page pedigree was regarded as difficult. Recent researches enable me to carry it back to a period as early as 1550 with certainty. The pedigree is based upon the following English wills:

Will of ROBERT PAGE of Acle made May 8, 1450. I Robert Page desire my body to be buried in the churchyard of St. Edmund King and Martyr at Acle. To the high altar 12 pence. To the emendation of the sd church 8s. To the light of the Blessed Virgin Mary in sd church 6d. To the Brotherhood of St. Edmund King and Martyr 2s. The residue of my goods I give to my executors. I appoint Nicholas Hardy and Margaret my wife my executors. Proved at Norwich May 16, 1450, by Nicholas Hardy with power reserved to Margaret wife of the deceased. (Consistory Court of Norwich, 1448–1455, Alleyn 41.)

Will of JAMES PAGE of Acle made December 2, 1534. To be buried in the churchyard of St. Edmund King and Martyr in Acle. To the Church of St. Mary burgh within Flegge [Fleggborough] 6s. 8d. To the reparation of the Church at Ridlington a quarter of malt. The residue of my goods and chattells whatsoever, I bequeath to my executors and I ordain Henry Page of Acle and James Hall, mariner, of Burgh in Flegge executors. Witnesses: William Corbet, Thomas Calne, with others. Proved at Acle, January 16, 1535, by the executors. (Archdeaconry Court of Norwich, 1529–1536, fo. 152.)

Will of ROBERT PAGE of Acle in Norfolk, husbandman, made April 20, 1587. My body shall be buried in the church-yard at Acle. I bequeath to Edmund Page my son my houses, tenements and lands in Acle with all pertaining thereto, to him and his heirs forever. To Robert Page my son £10, to be paid 20s. yearly for ten years. To Cicely Page my daughter £5, 20s. to be paid each year until £5 is paid. To Margaret Page my daughter £5 to be paid in like manner. I will that Martha my wife shall have for life the house where John Taylor now dwelleth, and 10s. yearly, to be paid 5s. half yearly or as she may need. Also the "hole" furniture, one table now in the house where Gosling dwelleth, etc. All the rest of my goods, cattells, implements and stuff of household I bequeath to the disposition of my executor, and I appoint Edmund Page my son my sole executor. Witnesses: Peter Downhill, Ralph Cootes, John Plum, William Smith, William Johnson, and John Downing. Proved in Acle, May 15, 1587, by the executor. (Archdeaconry Court of Norwich, Barnes, 1587.)

Will of ROBERT PAGE of Ormesby, Co. of Norfolk, husbandman, made July 1, 1617. My body shall be buried in the churchyard of the parish of Ormesby St. Margaret's. To the sd church of St. Margaret's 12d. To Margaret Page my wife my house and land with all appurtenances thereto belonging, situate and being in Acle in the Co. of Norfolk for the term of her life.

After her decease the sd house and land and all appurtenances thereto belonging to Robert Page my son, he paying all such legacies in such manner as is hereafter mentioned. To Thomas Page my son £5, to be paid by the said Robert Page two years after the decease of Margaret my wife. To Rebecca my daughter £5, to be paid by the sd Robert Page four years after the decease of Margaret my wife. To Henry Page my son £5, to be paid by the sd Robert Page six years after the decease of Margaret my wife. If it happen the said Robert Page my son does not pay the aforesaid legacies in manner and form aforesaid, my will and mind is that he or she who shall be unpaid their legacy shall reenter and possess the aforesaid house and land with all belonging until the "fearme" of the aforesaid house and land in Acle shall satisfy and pay their aforesaid legacy of £5. To Francis my son £7, Margaret my wife to pay it in manner following, viz. 40s. when the sd Francis attain the age of 21 years, and £5 when he shall attain the age of 24 years. My will is that my wife Margaret shall enter into two several bonds unto the sd Francis for the payment of the said seven pounds within five days after my death. The rest of my goods and chattels, movables and immovables, unbequeathed, I give to Margaret my wife whom I make sole executrix, to pay my debts and funeral charges and prove my will within one month of my death. If she shall refuse, then I ordain Francis my son to be my sole executor and Margaret my wife to be void. Any of my children departing this life before their legacy is due, their legacy shall be divided among the survivors. If Robert my son depart this life before Margaret my wife, then I will my son Thomas have the house and land in Acle and pay the aforesaid legacies that Robert should have paid. Witnesses: Ralph Smith, William Larwood, and Edward Boughton. Proved July 23, 1617, by the executrix. (Archdeaconry Court of Norwich, 1617.)

Will of FRANCIS PAGE of Ormesby St. Margarett in Norfolk, husbandman, February 4, 1666. To Rebekah Rix my sister my piece of ground lying in Ormesby on the north of the tenement where I now dwell, with all the rights and appurtenances thereto belonging, which I purchased of Clement Harcocke, deceased, estimated to be about five roods, to her and her heirs forever. To my said sister all my goods whatsoever, and I appoint her sole executrix. The mark of Francis Page. Witnesses: William Worde, and William Bryspoole. Proved at Norwich, April 5, 1667, by the executrix. (Archdeaconry Court of Norwich, 1666-7.)

From the foregoing wills the line of descent appears to be as follows:

1. ROBERT[1] PAGE of Acle, co. Norfolk, husbandman, born before 1550, died between 20 Apr. and 15 May 1587. He married MARTHA ———, who was living 20 Apr. 1587, at the date of her husband's will, as were the following children:

    i.   EDMUND[2], inherited the homestead in Acle, and was appointed executor 15 May 1587.
2. ii.   ROBERT.
    iii.   CICELY.
    iv.   MARGARET.

2. ROBERT[2] PAGE (*Robert[1]*) of Acle and of Ormsby St. Margaret, co. Norfolk, husbandman, was born as early as 1577. He died at Orms. by between 1 and 23 July 1617, and was probably buried in the churchyard of Ormsby St. Margaret.

"Roberte Page & Margrett Goodwynge" [Goodwin] were married in the parish of Hemblington, 16 July 1598 (Norfolk Parish Register Marriages, vol. 1 p. 22). As Hemblington is only four miles from Acle, and as this Page was the only person of the name there married, he is probably the Robert Page of Acle. Margaret Goodwin was perhaps the daughter or sister of Francis Goodwin of Hemblington in 1585.

Children:

3. i. ROBERT[3] PAGE, b. abt. 1604.
   ii. THOMAS, probably not the Thomas Page, a " gentleman," who was at Saco in the Province of Maine from 1637 to 1641.
  iii. REBECCA, bapt. at Ormsby St. Michael, 16 May 1608; m. ——— RIX, and was living 5 Apr. 1667, probably in the vicinity of Ormsby.
  iv. HENRY, living 1 July, 1617.
   v. FRANCIS, under age 1 July 1617; husbandman; d. in Ormsby St. Margaret betw. 4 Feb. 1666 and 5 Apr. 1667, probably leaving no descendants.

3. ROBERT[3] PAGE (*Robert[2], Robert[1]*), born about 1604, who was to inherit the Page homestead in Acle after his mother's death, emigrated to New England in 1637. He married, about 1628, LUCY ———, who died at Hampton 12 Nov. 1665, aged 58 years; and he died there 26 Sept. 1679, aged 75 years. The family lived at Salem, Mass., from 1637 to 1639, after which year they lived at Hampton.

Children:

   i. MARGARET[4], b. abt. 1630; lived at Hampton; d. 13 July 1699.
   ii. FRANCIS, b. abt. 1633; d. at Hampton, 15 Nov. 1706.
  iii. SUSANNA, b. abt. 1635.
  iv. REBECCA, bapt. at Salem 1 Sept. 1639; d. 27 May 1673.
   v. THOMAS, bapt. at Salem 1 Sept. 1639; d. 8 Sept. 1686.
  vi. HANNAH, b. abt. 1642; d. 6 Aug. 1704.
 vii. MARY, b. abt. 1644; d. 8 Mar. 1700.

On 24 June 1673, Robert Page of Hampton conveyed land by a deed in which he called Edward Colcord of Hampton his brother and Colcord's wife Ann his sister. The author of the Colcord Genealogy published in 1910, p. 7, states that Edward Colcord married Ann Page. The foregoing pedigree shows that there was no Ann Page for him to marry. According to the Genealogy, Ann Colcord was the mother of ten children born between 1641 and 23 July 1667. From this fact she must have been born between 1621 and 1626. As the father of Robert Page of Hampton died before 23 July 1617, she could not have been his posthumous daughter. She may have been a half sister to Robert Page, or a sister or half sister to his wife Lucy, or Lucy may have been a sister or half sister to Edward Colcord. It is clear that Colcord's wife Ann was not Ann Page. She may have been Ann Wadd, aged 15 years in 1637.

The fact that Robert Page of Ormsby, 1617, was the son of Robert Page of Acle, 1587, appears to be clear from the fact that the Ormsby man owned a home in Acle in 1617. The inquisitiones post mortem, if preserved, would probably give more light on this point.

The foregoing and other data seem to indicate that the Acle family is not recently descended from the Saxthorpe family of this surname.

CORRECTION FOR THE PAINE PEDIGREE, VOL. IV., P. 331-2.

[Communicated by Miss Caroline Whiting, of Dedham, Ms.

Thomas Payne born 1612, died Aug. 3, 1686 ; it was his *grandson* who died Sept. 6, 1686.

Thomas Payne b. 1644, d. between Jan. 24, and Feb. 25, 1725-6, and *not* " 3—2—1697." His will was dated Jan. 24, and proved Feb. 25, 1725-6. He m. 1. Rebecca Peck, April 25, 1671. She died 28—9—1682. He soon, probably, m. a second wife, named *Margaret*—as appears thus :—" Thomas, son of Thomas Payne, d. Sept. 6, 1686." " *Margaret* Payne died Sept. 16, 1686." (Probably an infant) " Thomas, son of Thomas and *Margaret* Payne, born Sept. 5, 1687." " Thomas Payne d. April 3, 1697." (Probably, the preceding.) " Thomas Payne (Sen.) and Mary Lamson m. Aug. 20, 1689." " Mary, dau. of Thomas and Mary Paine, born Oct. 16, 1693." She married Josiah Smith, and was the only surviving child of her father. " Mary, wife of Thomas Pain died April 5, 1718." " Mary Payne died Oct. 25, 1694 :—Probably **Mary** Day, wife of John Payne. Josiah and Mary (Paine) *Smith*, of Dedham, had, 1. Mary, b. Nov. 6, 1716, m. a Mr. Graves. 2. Rebekah, b. Nov. 14, 1722, m. Thomas Payn, of Needham, Nov. 22, 1744. 3. Thomas, b. Feb. 15, 1725, m. Rebekah Wilson, of Dedham, Jan. 8, 1756. *Their* son, Josiah Smith, m. Sarah, dau. of Sam'l Lewis, and inherited the Paine homestead, which is now in possession of *his* only son Thomas Smith. Thomas and Rebecca (Smith) Payn, of Needham, had child. : *Samuel, Rebecca, Anna* and *Phebe*, who signed a receipt Nov. 26, 1785. This Thos. Payne of Needham, was probably a grandson of John and Mary P. of Dedham.

THE FAMILY AND ANCESTORS OF THOMAS PALMER
OF BOSTON, N. E.

[Communicated by CLIFFORD STANLEY SIMS, Member of the Society of the Cincinnati of New Jersey, of the Historical Society of Pennsylvania, and Cor. Member of the N. E. Hist.-Gen. Society.]

In looking over Burke's *Landed Gentry,* I stumbled upon the enclosed account of the Palmer family, one of which, Thomas Palmer by name, emigrated to Boston, N. E.

"The Family of Palmer, whose patriarch, William le Palmer, was a Crusader under Richard Cœur de Lion, was from a remote period established in the county of Sussex; but a branch of it was settled at Marston as early as the year 1559."

JOHN PALMER of Marston, co. Stafford, living in 1566, a scion of Palmer of Yorkshire, had three sons: 1, Robert of Hill, co. Beds. father of Sir William Palmer, knt. of Wardon street; 2, William of London, and afterwards of Wanslip; 3, John of Marston, who had two sons—Robert, a Hamburgh merchant, and Thomas of Marston. John Palmer's second son,

WILLIAM PALMER, Esq., of Wanslip, co. Leicester, d. about the year 1636, leaving by Barbara Archdale, his wife, 3 sons: 1, Archdale his heir; 2, Sir William of Hill, co. Beds. carver to King Charles I; 3, John of Temple Hall, co. Leicester, the eldest son.

ARCHDALE PALMER, Esq., of Wanslip, served as high sheriff of Leicestershire, in 1641. He m. Martha, dau. of Thomas Smith of London, merchant, and by her, who d. in 1679, had issue: 1, William his heir; 2, Archdale in holy orders; 3, Thomas of Engorsby; 4, Samuel of London; 5, Joshua, M. D.; 6, Barbara m. first to Samuel Sleigh, Esq., and second, to John Morswood, Esq. of Alfreton; 7, Martha, wife of Richard Lloyd, a citizen of London. Mr. Palmer d. in August, 1673, aged 63, and was succeded by his son

WILLIAM PALMER, Esq. of Wanslip, who m. twice. By his first wife Elizabeth, dau. of Wm. Danvers, Esq., of Swithland, he had 4 sons: 1, Archdale, his heir; 2, Henry, d. s. p.; 3, William, M. D. m. Mary Hough and their dau. Mary m. Coote Molesworth; 4, Thomas of Boston in New England, who m. Abigail Hutchinson and had 2 sons, Eliakim and Thomas, and a dau. Sarah m. to Mr. Lewis. Wm. Palmer d. 18th April, 1692, aged 56, and was succeeded in the Wanslip estate by his son Archdale. The English branch of the family is now seated at Nazing Park, co. Essex.

PALMER.—It is known that William Palmer, who was of Watertown, Mass., in 1636-37, of Newbury, Mass., in 1637, and of Hampton, N. H., in 1638, conveyed, 10 Mar. 1645/6, all his property in Hampton and Newbury to John Sherman of Watertown and his wife Martha, who was Palmer's daughter, in place of an estate in Great Ormesby, Eng., which was Martha's by inheritance. (Cf. Pope, Pioneers of Massachusetts, page 342.) At my request Mr. J. Gardner Bartlett, the well-known authority on the English ancestry of early American settlers, has examined the records in the Archdeaconry Court of Norwich, co. Norfolk, Eng., and has found, under date of 28 July 1636, that one William Palmer of Ormesby St. Margaret's was presented for not attending church and was cited to appear on 28 Sept. following. On his failure to appear he was excommunicated. He is not found later in the records there, and there seems to be no doubt that he is identical with the William Palmer who was at Watertown a few months later and who in his deed of 1645/6 mentions the estate at Great Ormesby which was the inheritance of his daughter.

Boston, Mass. WILLIAM LINCOLN PALMER.

PALMER.—In Phillimore's "Norfolk Parish Registers, Marriages," vol. 3, p. 88, is the following marriage entry, from the parish registers of Ranworth:

"William Paulmer, p. Omesbye, & Mary Stamforth 30 Jan. 1608" [? 1608/9]

This entry, which was found by me several years ago in the library of the New England Historic Genealogical Society, the book in which it is printed having been published in 1907, will probably be of great interest to the descendants of William Palmer and of his son-in-law, Capt. John Sherman, both of whom were at Watertown, Mass., about 1636.

Immediately below the entry of the marriage of William Paulmer and Mary Stamforth is recorded the marriage of John Goodwins and Mary Paulmer, 19 July 1610, and the Ranworth registers contain also several records of Stamforth marriages.

Malden, Mass. GEORGE WALTER CHAMBERLAIN.

PARKERS OF AMERICA.

Communicated by WILLIAM S. APPLETON, A.M., of Boston.

IN his researches concerning the family of Parker, the late H. G. Somerby made abstracts of a remarkable group of wills, for which we are now indebted to the kindness of the Hon. F. E. Parker.

Dorothy Parker, of Mildenhall, Wilts, in her will written 10 Oct. 1649, bequeaths £200 to her "son Mr Thomas Parker at New England," and mentions her daughters Sarah, wife of Thomas Bayley, and Elizabeth, wife of Timothy Avery, and four children of Sarah Bayley, viz., John and Benjamin Woodbridge, Sarah Kerridge and Lucy Sparhawke. This was the mother of Rev. Thomas Parker, of Newbury, but who was Lucy Sparhawk?

Robert Parker, in his will, written 13 Nov. 1671, proved in 1673, mentions property in Bosham, Midhurst and Southampton, sons George and John, daughters Abigail Martin, Margaret, Ann and Constance, and says, "Item if any of my daughters are willing and will renounce their legacy in England and goe to Virginia in America, I doe hereby will that that daughter shall have for her portion whatsoever due to me my heires or assignes with my Plantation, housing, orchards and stocks running all purchased with my Penny with all right of my Patent to her and heires forever with Patent and other things concerning my Estate is in the hands of Mr John Wise at Ocnancok in Northampton county in Accomake the Plantation in Anduen River."

William Parker, in his will written 3 Jan. 1673, proved in 1673, leaves to his daughter Elizabeth "one negro woman, 12 female cattle and 2 breeding mares in Maryland;" to his son William, "a stock of sheep in Maryland;" to his wife Grace 1 negro woman, 1 English servant and 8 female cattle, besides his part of ships Richard and Martha, &c., and mentions his daughters Thomasine Kent, Mary Parker, Sarah Edmonson and Dorothy Whittle, also "tobacco in Maryland."

Joan Parker, of St. Savior, Southwark, Surrey, in her will written 24 August, 1674, proved in 1675, mentions many relatives named Parker, and gives to her "brother Henry Curtis of Sundbury in New England, to his wife, and 3 sons Ephraim, John and Joseph," each 20 shillings, also to her said brother her little silver tankard and six silver spoons.

Alexander Parker, of George Yard, Lombard Street, London, in his will written 6 March, 1689, proved in 1689, desires that all his estates, lands and tenements in the kingdom of England and in the province of Pennsylvania be sold and the proceeds divided amongst his five children, Mary, Ellen, Elizabeth, Alexander and John.

WOODBRIDGE AND PARKER.—Since the Woodbridge Genealogy in this number (*ante*, p. 292) was printed, an article entitled "Parkers in America" has been handed us by Mr. Appleton, and will be found on page 337. *

It will be seen by the abstract of the will of Dorothy, widow of the Rev. Robert Parker, that her daughter, who married the Rev. John[1] Woodbridge, was named Sarah, and that after the death of Mr. Woodbridge she married Thomas Bayley. Besides her sons, the Rev. John[2] and the Rev. Benjamin[2] Woodbridge, she had, it seems, two daughters, Sarah Kerridge and Lucy Sparhawk. In reply to the query of Mr. Appleton, Who was Lucy Sparhawk? I would suggest that she may have been the wife of the Rev. Edward Sparhawk, of Black Notley in Essex, who had a wife Lucy. (See Davids's *Annals of Evangelical Nonconformity in Essex*, p. 432.) He was ejected under the Bartholomew act. Sarah Kerridge, also, may have been the wife of an ejected minister, as there was a Rev. Mr. Kerridge ejected from Wooton Fitz-Pain in Dorset, who had a son Rev. John Kerridge, M.A., ejected as a schoolmaster at Lyme Regis in Dorset, afterwards a dissenting minister at Culleton in Devon. See Palmer's *Nonconformist's Memorial*, ed. 1778, vol. i. pp. 460 and 487. It is possible that the Rev. Thomas Baylie, B.D., ejected from Mildenhall in Wiltshire, who died in 1663, aged 81 (*Ibid.*, vol. ii. p. 508), may have been their step-father.

Mrs. Parker's other daughter, Mrs. Elizabeth Avery, we are informed by the late Hon. James Savage, LL.D. (Mass. Hist. Coll., 3d Ser. viii. 288), printed a book containing what her brother Thomas considered religious errors. A letter to her by him, touching her opinions, was written at Newbury in N. E., Nov., 1648, and printed in England the next year, with a preface by their nephew, the Rev. Benjamin Woodbridge.—ED.

WOODBRIDGE.—Many years ago, my kinswoman, Mrs. M. C. Caswall, then wife of Rev. Henry Caswall, D.D., of Figheldean Vicarage, near Amesbury, Wiltshire, England (now his widow, residing at Franklin, Pa.), procured for me the following extracts from the parish register of Stanton :

" John Kerridge & Sarah Woodbridge marryed ye 27th of Decemb. 1632."

" 1637. John Woodbridge Rector of this parish buryed the 9th of December, 1637."

One of these records confirms the supposition (*ante*, p. 342) concerning the —— Kerridge who married Sarah Woodbridge, and the other gives the date of the death of Rev. John Woodbridge (*ante*, p. 292) more nearly than it is generally known.

*The preceding article.   L. R. PAIGE.

THE FAMILY OF GEORGE PARKHURST
OF
WATERTOWN AND BOSTON, MASS.

By Edson Salisbury Jones, Esq., of Port Chester, N. Y.

The main facts that have long been known concerning George[1] Parkhurst of Watertown and Boston, Mass., are that he first appears of public record, in America, at Watertown, under date of 10 May 1642, when it was ordered that a highway should be laid out by his house. He is not mentioned in the four grants of land between 25 July 1636 and 9 Apr. 1638, inclusive, and the date of his acquisition of the house lot is not disclosed by extant records; but Dr. Bond believed that the plot was Parkhurst's homestall of 16 acres. On the same date he was granted a farm of 56 acres. These lands appear to be all that he acquired by purchase or grant — his other holdings coming by a later marriage. Seven deeds, of record in the registries of Suffolk and Middlesex, show the disposition he made of some of the property.

The time of his arrival in America is unknown, and no evidence has been seen that a wife accompanied him; but unquestionably certain of his children came hither. Savage thought that George,[2] Phebe[2] (who married Thomas[1] Arnold), and perhaps other issue emigrated with their father; and Bond named the same two children, and conjectured that Joseph of Chelmsford was also his son.

One of the early proprietors of Watertown was John Simson, who was buried there 10 June 1643, leaving two sons, John and Jonathan, three daughters (born at Watertown 1634–1642/3), and a widow, Susanna, whom George[1] Parkhurst soon married. By this union he acquired all the real estate of the deceased, except a small parcel alienated by the widow and 6 acres of upland, which she transferred to William Page on 9 Nov. 1643, acknowledging the deed on 28 Nov. of the same year. As Parkhurst sold 2 acres of the Simson land on 16 Nov. 1644, the marriage took place between these dates. Probably he soon removed from Watertown, as he was of Boston on 4 Oct. 1645, when he conveyed 6 acres; and he seems to have remained there (though possibly he returned to Watertown for a time) as late as 13 June 1655, when he sold 12 acres (in two parcels) of what had been Simson's land for £21. The last conveyances were made by permission of the General Court, granted 23 May 1655 in response to his petition, and two thirds of the sum realized were to be retained by Mr. Richard Brown for the benefit of Susanna's two Simson sons until they should come of age. After the date of the last-mentioned deeds the public records of Massachusetts disclose no reference to George[1] Parkhurst, as far as the present writer is aware.

As regards this petition, "A true copy of the original lying in the General Court Files in the year 1655" is to be seen in File no. 3175 of the Superior Court, Boston, in connection with a suit brought in 1695 concerning some land that had been John[1] Simson's; and in the same file is an affidavit by George[2] Parkhurst, made 30 July 1695, in which he calls himself "aged 78 years or thereabout," and refers to "my honored father George Parkhurst Deced, which married Jno Simsons Widdow." The petition of George[1] asserts that he was then [1655] "near 67 yeares old;" that he, his wife, and most of her children were in destitute condition; that she had had ten children during her twenty years' residence in America — seven sons and three daughters [five sons by Parkhurst, therefore]; that she had gone to London, England, with six of her children, but found her mother, brothers, and sisters unable to do what she had expected; that four of her children had remained in America, two of whom seem to have been bound out [Jonathan Simson was in the service of Richard Brown in 1659, according to the latter's will, and probably the other child was Benjamin[2] Parkhurst]; and that the petitioner desired to sell the land [apparently all that remained] in order that he might go to the aid of his wife. It is very probable that he returned to England, and that, too, as soon as possible after 13 June 1655.

Of the issue born abroad, we have been certain of George[2] and Phebe,[2] by reason of Thomas[1] Arnold's deed of 30 Mar. 1655 (also signed and acknowledged by his wife, Phebe Arnold) to "George Parkhurst my brother in law of Watertown" for 30 acres there "that I bought of our Father George Parkhurst and his wife Susanna," this instrument having been signed "In the presence of George Parkhurst our Father."

In 1873 the late William H. Whitmore, Esq., contributed to the REGISTER (vol. 27, pp. 364–369) an article entitled "The Dalton and Batcheller Pedigree," in which he expressed conclusions as to the names of seven of George[1] Parkhurst's children, resulting from a study of copies of records, letters, and documents. The chief of these was an indenture of 22 Mar. 1663/4 between Ruth Dalton of Hampton, Mass., widow of Rev. Timothy Dalton, and Nathaniel Batcheller, her "constituted heir," whereby all her lands were conveyed to Batcheller upon his agreement to pay her £10 per year during her life and stipulated sums to others after her death. Among the latter were six persons, who, the writer thought, were very probably the issue of George[1] Parkhurst, as follows: Deborah Smith, wife of John; Elizabeth Merry, wife of Joseph; Phebe Arnall, wife of Thomas; Joseph Parkers; George Parkers; and Mrs. Mary Carter, wife of Mr. Thomas of Woburn.* The name of the seventh child was derived from a letter of "Georg Parkis" of Watertown, dated "the 25 of June '69," to his "Loueing Cous[e] Bashelder," asking the latter to pay "my brother Beniamen, fife pounds of that twenty

* Old Norfolk Co. Deeds, vol. 1, fo. 169 (reverse). The surname "Parkers" for Joseph and George is in accordance with the record. Batcheller's first wife (married 1656) was Deborah Smith, daughter of John and Deborah.

which will bee due to me from my ant Dolton." This was endorsed: "My unkell Gorg. Parkes his letter: sent by benjeimen Parkes." Whitmore gave also an abstract of a receipt from "Josieph Parkis of Chemford in New Inland" for £20, "reseved of Nathaniell Bachiler, exsecutor to the last will and testiment of my Ant Dalton deisesed;" also an abstract of a power of attorney from Thomas Arnoll of Providence, for himself and wife Phebe, to collect a legacy of £20 bequeathed by the will of Mrs. Ruth Dalton to Phebe Arnold; and, lastly, a copy of a receipt by John Wyman to Batcheller for the equivalent of £14, "by ordier of my father in law Thomas Carter," given to "my mother in law, Merri Carter by Mrs. Ruth Dalton of Hampton deiseised," which was endorsed: "Cosen John Whayman's aquitens about my unkell Carter's Legassy."

As will soon appear, there should be no doubt that Deborah, Elizabeth, Phebe, Joseph, George, and Mary, mentioned in the foregoing indenture, were among the issue of George[1] Parkhurst, and were born in England. Mrs. Ruth Dalton seems to have been a sister of their mother — not of George,[1] else probably she would have named his later children.

There is certainty that one son, by Susanna, was "Daniel of George Parkhurst member of Ch. of Watertowne aged about 11 days," who was baptized in Boston 10, 4 mo., 1649, because George[2] and Sarah Parkhurst had a daughter, Sarah, born 14 Sept. 1649, according to the Watertown records. The Boston church records also give "Joshua of ———— Parkis of Watertowne," baptized 7, 1 mo., 1652, and "Callib of Mr. Parkis of Watertowne," baptized 26, 12 mo., 1653. Whether Joshua and Caleb were sons of George[1] or George[2] it is difficult to decide upon this evidence, though not improbably the former was the father. If so, he would seem to have been living at Watertown at the times, or the word "Church" was omitted from the records. He and Susanna were of Boston on 3 Oct. 1651, when she declared that she had previously sold land. This statement was acknowledged by both on 30 Oct. 1652 before Increase Nowell, but their residence at the latter date does not appear.

Benjamin would seem certainly to have been Susanna's son. The present writer recalls no mention of him in New England records; but a Benjamin, whose surname is variably spelled Parkis and Parkest, appears as a grantee of lands in Woodbridge, N. J., in 1670. In 1681 Benjamin Parkis received a commission as captain-lieutenant for Elizabethtown, N. J., which adjoined Woodbridge; on 16 Feb. 1683/4 an inventory of the personal estate of Benjamin Parkis of Elizabethtown, gentleman, was taken; and on 10 Mar. 1683/4 administration on his estate was granted to his widow, Martha. In 1686, 1690, and 1696 a Benjamin Parkis appears as owner of Elizabethtown land; in 1701 Benj: Parkhurst signed a petition as one of the residents of New Jersey; and on 9 Dec. 1721 Benjamin Parkhurst of Elizabethtown, weaver, made his will, which was proved 8 Dec. 1722 and named wife Mercy and children Martha, Mary, Hanna, Benjamin, John, and Samuel.*

* These New Jersey items may be found in the printed New Jersey Archives, vols. 2, 21, 23.

In the parish registers at Ipswich, co. Suffolk, Eng., the following baptisms of nine children of George[1] Parkhurst have been found, the first in the parish of St. Stephen, the second in that of St. Mary-at-the-Quay, the third to the seventh, inclusive, and the ninth in that of St. Margaret, and the eighth in that of St. Mary-le-Tower:

1612 Phebey Parkhurst the daughter of George Parkhurst of the Key Parish and of Phebey his wiffe 29 November.
1614 Mary ye Do: of Georg Parkhurst was baptized at St. Lawrens 28 August.
1616 Sammewell sone of Gorge P'rust [Parkhurst *in later hand in margin*] 2 February [1616/17].
1619 Deborah Dawter of George P'rust [Parkhurst *in later hand in margin*] 1 August.
1621 Geordge son of Geordge Parkhurst 5 June.
1623 John Sonne of George Parkehurst 19 October.
1625 Abigail Daughter of George Parkehurst 1 January [1625/6].
1628 Elizabeth Parkisse daughter of Geo. Parkisse, borne in St. Margette, 18 May.
1629 Joseph Sonne of George Parkehurst 21 December.

It will be observed that six of these nine Christian names agree with the six mentioned in the indenture between Ruth Dalton and Nathaniel Batcheller, and that the name of the mother of the first was Phebe. Very probably all of them were her children. In Ipswich and vicinity search has been made for the marriage of George Parkhurst and Phebe ———, but without success. When the first two children were baptized, the father was living in the parish of St. Mary-at-the-Quay, where possibly, or probably, the marriage took place. Unfortunately, no marriages earlier than 1653 were to be found in 1902 in extant registers of this parish. Seemingly the family removed to the parish of St. Margaret after the birth of the second child, and there remained until the baptism of the ninth. No burial record of Phebe, wife of George, or of Samuel, John, or Abigail, as issue of George, was found, but there are some gaps in the registers. The family may have removed from Ipswich to a place as yet unknown; and in such place or in its vicinity Phebe[2] may have married Thomas[1] Arnold* and Mary[2] may have married Thomas[1] Carter. Rev. Thomas Carter was a native of co. Suffolk and a graduate of a school at Bury St. Edmunds. Rev. Timothy Dalton, husband of Ruth, was rector of Woolverstone, about five miles southeast from Ipswich, in the first third of the seventeenth century, and there several of his children were baptized. Many of the early inhabitants of Watertown, Mass., embarked at Ipswich when they emigrated.

Below is given an abstract of what is believed to be the will of the father of George[1] Parkhurst:

The Will of JOHN PARKHURST of the parishe of Saynte Marye Keye, in the town of Ipswich, co. Suffolk, Clothier, 29 Mar. 1610. To wife Sara all household stuff, as bedding, brass, pewter, linen, and woollen, and the annual rent of

---

* The writer of this article thinks it not improbable that Thomas[1] Arnold was a co. Suffolk man, and questions the assumption that he embarked for Virginia in 1635. He was probably not a half-brother of William[1] Arnold, and the alleged ancestry of these two men, printed in the REGISTER in 1879 (vol. 33, pp. 432 *et seq.*), is erroneous, as will be shown in an article to be published in a future number of the REGISTER.

£8, to be paid half-yearly for life. To son George Parkhurst all shopstuff, all my implements of trade as a shearman, all my books of what title and print, and all the rest of my goods and stock, movables and immovables. To son John Parkhurst 100 marks at the age of twenty-one. To daughter Thamar Parkhurst the annual rent of £5, to be paid her half-yearly for life. To daughter Hellen Parkhurst £50 at the age of twenty-one or marriage. To daughter Sara Parkhurst £40 at the age of twenty-one or marriage. My executor to put forth to best profit the portions of said John and Hellen, for their further education and bringing up. Son George, sole executor. "Cousin" Nicholas Babbe of Nedeham Markett, supervisor, and he is to receive 20s. for his pains. My executor is to give to the supervisor a bond of £300, for the faithful performance of my will. Witnesses: Nicholas Babbe, scriptore, Jn° Parkhurst, Samuell Pecke, Edward Catherall. Proved 7 June 1611. (P.C.C., Wood, 50.)

Of the children named by John Parkhurst in his will, the baptism of only one has been found in the Ipswich parish registers, namely, Hellen, daughter of John Parkhurst, 1598/9, 7 [? January]y, in the parish of St. Mary-at-the-Quay; and this is the earliest baptism of a Parkhurst recorded in that register, which begins in 1559. It would seem that the testator may have previously resided elsewhere than at Ipswich. In Wodderspoon's "Memorials of the Ancient Town of Ipswich," it is stated that in 1576 there were four companies there, among them that of the Drapers, which included clothiers. If the records of this Company be extant, they may shed light on the parentage of the testator, John Parkhurst.

The earliest Parkhurst disclosed by any of the Ipswich parish registers is Christopher, whose daughter Anne was baptized in 1569, in the parish of St. Nicholas. Probably he was the Christopher who was appointed in 1561 by the Bishop of Norwich, John Parkhurst (inducted in 1560), as keeper of the Bishop's Palace in Ipswich, where dwelt the bishops when they were in that part of their diocese.

The registers of Oxford University show Richard and William Parkhurst as taking the degree of M.A. in 1505/6; John as B.A. in 1506; Symon, Oliver, and John (of Langton) as enrolled there in 1510; Robert as B.A. in 1519/20; and John (subsequently Bishop), son of George, as B.A. in 1528. The last-named died in 1574/5, aet. 63; and therefore he was born about 1511 — and in Guildford, as stated in his will, dated 1 Feb. 1573/4 and proved 4 March 1576/7 (P.C.C., Daughtry, 10), in which he named brothers Christopher (and his son Christopher) and Nicholas (and his son John) and "other of my brothers' children, whom I would fain have brought up in learning;" sisters Helen, Agnes, Alice, and Elizabeth; brother Beckingham; and cousin Margaret Crampton and her husband, Richard Crampton.*

The earliest seat of any Parkhurst family, so far as known, was in Guildford, co. Surrey, where parish registers show many of the name from 1541 onward. George Parkhurst was mayor of Guildford in 1522, 1529, and 1536; George, Jr., died there in 1540, leaving a will, which mentioned a wife and an unnamed child. In the vicinity

* Helen Parkhurst married Thomas Beckingham, and their daughter, Margaret, became the wife of Richard Crampton. The will (1580) of this Richard Crampton mentioned, among others, his brothers-in-law Richard and Nicholas Babbe.

were others, as John of West Clandon, whose will (1523/4) named a wife, four daughters, and sons John and Thomas; Henry of Shere, in 1525 (others are found there later); and John of Leatherhead, in 1525. The will (1558/9) of one John mentioned brothers Raff and Robert. Some Parkhursts were of Godalming. Others, as early as 1553, were of co. Kent,* and Rev. Robert Parkhurst was of co. Sussex in the same year. Richard and Thomas were of London in 1569 and 1584 respectively, when administrations on their estates were granted — that on the estate of the former to his brother, Anthony Parkhurst. Many Parkhursts were armigerous, as is shown by the Heralds' Visitations.

It seems probable that John Parkhurst, the Ipswich clothier and testator, was descended from co. Surrey stock, and very likely from the Parkhurst family of Guildford, where the clothing trade flourished; but proof is needed to substantiate this conjecture.

A theory has been advanced that the earliest co. Surrey Parkhursts migrated thither from the Isle of Wight. The present writer has seen nothing to indicate this. The theory was based upon the presence on that island of Parkhurst Forest, which was said to have been so named in Domesday Book; but it is called therein "parco Regis." In certain pipe rolls in the time of Henry II it appears as "foreste de Witingelega." In 1545 it was called Caresbroke Forest. It was also known as Avington Forest.

The surname *Parkhurst* was very probably derived from the residences of men in, at, or near a park hurst (park woods, or wooded park), of which there were many in early times; and the variations in spelling of the surname may have included *Parkes* (pronounced in two syllables) and others.

---

* In the Visitation of Kent, 1619, a Parkhurst family is headed by John of Lenham, whose will is dated in 1577. He had sons Anthony (aet. 67 in 1599), Richard, Robert, and James.

The Origin of the Family of Parris[h], of the Barbadoes and of Massachusetts, in the seventeenth century.—Waters' "Genealogical Gleanings in England" (1901), pp. 143, 144, gives the will of John Parris of the Barbadoes, Esq., dated 1660, naming his brother Thomas' sons Thomas, Samuel, and Martyn, all three nephews being under the age of twenty-one years. He also named Sarah, daughter of his brother Richard Parris, deceased, "Thomas Martaine, son of my cousin Thomas Martaine of this island", and "John Parris, eldest son of my brother Thomas"; he shows that the brother Thomas was in 1660 in London, and also names his sister Rebecca.

Mr. G. Andrews Moriarty, pp. 354, 355, vol. 49, *The Essex Institute Historical Collections* (1913), adds the will of the above testator's brother, Thomas Parris, Esq., dated in 1673 at Barbadoes Island, and proved in London. The latter testator names his eldest son John Parris, then in England, and his four other children, Thomas, Ann, Elizabeth, and A———.

Both Waters and Moriarty show that the legatee John Parris, named in the foregoing wills, was a minister at Ugborough, near Plymouth, and that his son Thomas Parris (son of John, the minister) was identified with the Parris family of Pembroke, Danvers, and Salem, Mass., in the seventeenth century, one of whose descendants was Martin Parris.

It is apparent that the foregoing Parris family were related to the Thomas Martin of Freiston, near Boston, Lincolnshire, mentioned below:

The will of Marie Parrish of Boston, Lincolnshire, dated 1629, ... Consistory Court of Lincoln, 1632, No. 477:

"I, Marie Parrish of Boston, widow. . . . my body to be buried in the parish church of Boston . . . to John Parrish of Freeston, my sonne, sixe acres of arrable lande . . . . in Butterwick and Freeston. . . To Susan Parrish, my daughter . . . my daughter Leake . . . Anne Leake, Rebecca Leake & Saray Leake, my grandchildren. . . . Andrew Leake and Elizabeth Leake, my grandchildren . . . Marie Meeres, Marie Storre, Alice Blythe and Marie Blyth, my kinswomen . . . James Storre of Boston, my kinsman. . . . Nathaniel Leake and Marie Murford, my grandchildren . . . my freinds Thomas Martyn of Freeston and Nicholas Brandon of Boston, supervisors . . . Witnesses: Thomas Martyn, Nicholas Brandon, William Murford, John Kinsle, Tho: Scott". Will dated 5 Nov. 1629, proved at Lincoln 15 Feb. 1632/3 (Lincolnshire Archives Committee) (unpublished).

Lincolnshire Records Society Publications, vol. 3, Boston Parish Registers, include the following: "Buried, December 25, 1632, Marie Parrish, gentlewoman". The Bishop's Transcripts, published by the same Society, include the entry below:

"Married January 25, 1625/6, John Parrishe of ffrieston, aged 22 years, and Anne Martin, aged 22 years, daughter of Thomas Martin of (Freiston), yeoman".

The testatrix, Marie Parrish, *supra*, well could have been that Marie Mountford named in the 1592 "Visitation of Lincolnshire", subject Mountford, who married, first Richard Banks; and, secondly, John Parish. She is named as a widow 2 Sept. 1620 in the will of her brother, Thomas Mountford. Their parents were Henry Mountford of Kirton in Lindsey and Gainsborough, Lincolnshire, and Dorothy, buried in 1574, daughter of———Curteys of Nottinghamshire. The Mountfords, an armigerous family, are said in this visitation to descend from the family of that name of Kylnhurst, Warwickshire (evidently Yorkshire; see Foster's edition, "Glover's Yorkshire Visitation", p. 248; *Harleian Society Publications*, vol. 12, pp. 54 through 56.) Her husband I think to have been that John Parish of Toft Grange, in the parish of Kirkby on Bain, Lincolnshire, gentleman, whose administration was dated 1616. Kirkby on Bain lies ten miles northwest of Boston, while Freiston is about four miles east of Boston.

From the evidence that Governor Bellingham of Massachusetts (a native of Boston, Lincolnshire) performed the marriage ceremony in New England of Joanna Quarles, (apparently niece of Mabel Quarles Whittingham, of Boston, Lincolnshire) (see THE * REGISTER, vol. 111, p. 72), and the fact that he also officiated at the marriage of John Parrish and Hannah Jewell in Braintree, Mass., in 1664, and from the above wills, it would seem possible that the above testator, Thomas Parris, of the Barbadoes, esquire, had also a nephew or cousin named John, the resident in 1664 of Braintree, Mass.

While John Parrish of Braintree, *supra*, did not leave a son Thomas, or a son Martin, he did leave a son Samuel (eldest son), and grandchildren Abigail, Dorothy, and Rebecca, all names identified with the family of Parrish of Freiston, Lincolnshire, above.

Based on the foregoing, the following pedigree is advanced:

I. THOMAS MOUNTFORD of Kirton in Lindsey, Lincolnshire, m. ISABEL CHIPLEY of Northamptonshire. He descended, it is said, from a younger son of the Mountfords of Kylnhurst, Yorkshire. They had:

II. HENRY MOUNTFORD of Gainsborough, Lincolnshire, who married DOROTHY, daughter of———Curteys of Nottinghamshire. They had:

III. MARY MOUNTFORD, who married, secondly, JOHN PARISH.
He seems to have been that John Parish of Kirby on Bain, Lincolnshire, gentleman, administration of whose goods was granted in 1616. She is styled "widow" in the will of her brother, Thomas Mountford, in 1620. She is believed to have been that "Marie Parrish, gentlewoman", who was buried at Boston, Lincolnshire, 25 Dec. 1632, and who left the following children:

    i. JOHN (see IV, below).
    ii. SUSAN, evidently she of that name who married 1 Jan. 1633, at Boston, Lincolnshire, GEORGE MACHAN.
    iii. A DAUGHTER, who married one———LEAKE, and had children Anne, Rebecca, Sarah, Nathaniel Leake, and perhaps another child, Marie, possibly wife of William Murford.

IV. JOHN PARRISH was born in 1603 or 1604. He married at Freiston, 25 Jan. 1625/6, ANNE (also then aged 22 years), daughter of Thomas Martyn, yeoman, of Freiston, No will or administration can be located for John or his wife. Their children evidently included the following:

    i. THOMAS (see V, below).
    ii. JOHN PARRIS, esquire, of the Barbadoes, a planter, whose will, dated 1660, is cited above.
    iii. RICHARD PARRIS, deceased by 1660, whose daughter Sarah was living in 1660.
    iv. REBECCA, living in 1660.

V. THOMAS PARRIS, in 1660 of London, was in 1673 living in the Barbadoes, where he made his will. His children were:

    i. JOHN (see VI, below).
    ii. THOMAS, aged under 21 years in 1660.
    iii. SAMUEL, aged under 21 years in 1660.
    iv. MARTYN, aged under 21 years in 1660.

VI. JOHN PARRIS, a dissenting minister at Ugborough, near Plymouth, England, living in England in 1673, was father of

VII. THOMAS PARRIS, of Pembroke, Mass., father of

VIII. The Rev. Mr. SAMUEL PARRIS of Salem and Danvers, Mass. See the works by Waters and Moriarty, cited above.

Arlington, Va.   JOHN G. HUNT.

P. 891, the third volume of this series.

The Origin of the Family of Parris[h], of the Barbadoes and of Massachusetts, in the Seventeenth Century: Correction.—The contributor of the note on this subject in The Register, vol. 112, p. 158, is grateful to Mr. Walter G. * Davis of Portland, Maine, for pointing out the fact that the Parrish pedigree presented therein is in error. Specifically, the will of Thomas Parris, dated in 1673, refers to his eldest son John, and John's four children, Thomas, Ann, Elizabeth, and A———. Moreover, the Rev. Samuel Parris of Salem Village was born in 1653, and was the legatee under age named in the will, dated in 1660, of his uncle John. Consequently, this Samuel, generation eight of the pedigree given in the cited note, patently could not have been descended, as indicated, from John Parish of Freiston.

A further important fact is that Mr. Thomas Parris was Assistant Justice in Barbadoes in 1631 (The Register, vol. 39), as pointed out by Mr. Davis. It is probable that this Thomas Parris was the testator of 1673 whose will is cited.

By way of amends for the serious mistake made by the contributor, he will make a special search of Chancery suits in which persons named Parris (or variants) occur; briefly, it may be stated that John Parys and Elizabeth, his wife, daughter and heir of Richard Wylkys occur, about 1543, re lands in Devon, in Early Chancery Proceedings, vol. 51, p. 189, Great Britain, Record Office, Lists and Indexes.

Lastly, the contributor is especially grateful to Mr. Davis because by eliminating the Barbadoes family of Parris[h] from known kinship with Marie Parish of Boston, Lincolnshire, he has allowed the contributor now to suggest the great possibility that Marie Parrish (whose will, dated in Boston in 1632, names John, her son, of Freiston, Lincolnshire, nearby) was indeed the grandmother of John Parrish who married in Braintree, Mass., in 1664, Hannah Jewell. As shown in the cited note in The Register Governor Bellingham (native of Boston, Lincolnshire) officiated at this marriage, and there is great possibility that he was acquainted with the parents (in England) of either John Parrish of Braintree, Mass., or his wife, Hannah Jewell; for as shown, Bellingham had officiated in New England at another marriage in which the bride, Joanna Quarles, evidently was a niece of a resident of Boston, Lincolnshire, where Bellingham had been recorder before moving to the New World.

It is known from "The New England Ancestry of Dana Converse Backus" (1949), p. 96, that Thomas Jewell, father of Hannah who married John Parrish above, was from Kingston, Surrey.

Arlington, Va.   John G. Hunt.

*The preceding article.

The Origin of the Family of Parris[h], of Barbados and of Massachusetts * in the Seventeenth Century: Addition.—On page 240 of the July 1959 issue of *The preceding article.

843

THE REGISTER the family of Parris who lived in Barbados is shown not to be related to the Parish family who lived in and near Boston, Lincs., as far as is known.

The will of John Parris of Barbados, Esq., dated in 1660, named "Thomas Martaine, son of my cousin Thomas Martaine of this island".

The will of Thomas Martine* of Barbados, dated 1 April 1661 and probated 15 Dec. 1662, shows that the testator:

1. Was in 1661 bound for England in the ship *Barbados Merchant* of Plymouth, Capt. Caleb Came, Commander.

2. Names his sons Thomas, John, Richard, William and Joseph Martin, and daughter Abigail Martin, each aged less than fifteen years.

3. Names his wife, Abigail Martine.

4. Names his sisters, Ione Mortifield of Newton and Agnis Nicholls of Dartmouth, both of the county of Devon.

5. Appoints as overseers "my trusty and wellbeloved friends, Mr. John Parris, Mr. Henry Baker and Mr Richard Bickford".

6. As executors appoints his wife and Mr. Francis Godfrey.

This will was witnessed by John Wilson and John Roope (the original now at Barbados Registration Office).

The pedigree of Roope of East Allington (five miles west of Dartmouth, Devon) is cited in Sims' *"Index of the Heralds' Visitation in the British Museum"* (1849).

The above facts, plus the fact that John Parris, nephew of John Parris above, was a dissenting minister in Ugborough (six miles northwest of East Allington) point directly to a Devon origin for both the Parris and Martin families of Barbados.

The following entries from the Devon Subsidy Roll (a copy of which is included in the Banks mss in the Rare Book Room, Library of Congress) may assist interested persons in determining exactly where, within Devon, these Parris and Martin people may have originated.

From Devon Subsidy Roll of 1624

In Broadclist, near Exeter
    Wilmott Martin, widow
    Edward Martinfield and Edward Martinfill
    John Martin
[*Note*: Devon wills, not now extant, included that of John Martin of Broadclist, dated 1619; perhaps husband of Wilmott Martin, above.]
In Newton Abbot
    Thomas Martyn
    John Martin jr.
    Wilmote Martyn, widow
In Abbots Carswell, next Newton Abbot
    John Martin, sen.
At Berry Pomeroy, near Paignton (five miles south of Newton Abbot)
    Margaret Parris†
At Plimton St. Mary
    John, Mary, Walter and Thomas Bickford, and Katharine Parris†
At Plimton Morris
    John Marteine

An armigerous Martin family, several of whom lived in Exeter, are discussed in "A View of Devonshire in MDCXXX", by Westcote, page 596. This work, however, does not name Wilmote Martin above, who may well have been ancestress of the Martins of Barbados.

The Inquisitions Post Morten of Thomas Martin, 1628, and of John Martin, 1626, both of Devon, are extant, and would perhaps yield valuable data to persons wishing to develop the Martin pedigree.

---

*The full text of this will has been presented to the Society.

†The above two women are the only persons surnamed Parris listed in the Devon Subsidy Roll of 1624.

In Hotten's "Original Lists", it is noted that Thomas Martin, aged 17 years, was to travel to St. Christophers, Barbados, in 1635 (p. 70), and that Thomas Parish, clothier, aged 22 years, was to be transported to New England in the *Increase* in 1635 (p. 65). Chances are that these two men settled in Barbados and were somehow related.

There is some possibility that the aforesaid family of Martin of Barbados was related to the Martins named in THE REGISTER, vol. 86, pp. 251, 252, for the names Thomas and Richard are found in each family. Moreover, each was acquainted with the Bickford family. Rattery, Devon, where the testator, Henry Martyn, clerk, resided, is not far from Ugborough; Totnes, where his son, Richard, a merchant, resided, is not far from Dartmouth and Newton Abbot, identified with relatives of the family of Martin of Barbados.

Arlington, Va.   JOHN G. HUNT.

PAYNE FAMILY RECORD, &C.

THE following curious record of the Payne or Pain family, who came early to Salem, and finally settled at Dedham, Ms., has been put into the editor's hands, by a lady of the latter place, with liberty to publish it. Although we apply the very common term *curious* to this record, it is truly a *very uncommon curiosity*, according to our antiquarian notions of things in that line. The writing, from which this copy is made, was begun in the reign of Queen Elizabeth, and was added to, from time to time, as the family of which it is a record, increased or diminished; and when the family came to New England, they undoubtedly brought it with them, as the entries upon it show a different hand as well as a different date, the last of which is, as will be seen, 1636.

(COPY.)

𝔄°. 𝔡𝔫𝔢. 1580 𝔄°. 𝔎𝔢ⁿᵉ. 𝔊𝔩𝔦ʒ. 22. 𝔭. 𝔪𝔢. 𝔗. 𝔉.

A trew and perfight note of the birth day and hower of the Childrine of Thomas Payne and Katheren his wyffe : And allso the day of ther mariage.   ⱷ : ⱷ : ⱷ

Quos deus coninuxit nemo seperat.

Memorandum quod ego Thoma duxi vxorem meam' katheren harssant filiam Thome harssant de Cransford : Apud Cooklie in die solis Que fuit vicesimo die Mensis Julÿ añño Regni domine Elizabethe Regine nunc Anglie : vicesimo : et in anno Domine 1578.

Nativitas Henri payne sonne to the aforesaide Thomas Payne and Katherin his wyffe was borne into this worlde vppon friday : Betwene the howers of. 7 : and. 8. of the clocke in the after noone, which was the last day of Juli in the xxi yeare of the Raigne of our Soveraign Queene Elizabeth : and in the yeare of Christes Incarnation 1579 : the which said Henri Payne died and yelded his soule vnto allmightie god vppon saterday betweene the howers of. ii. and xii : in the nighte. which was the 26 : day of September 1579.

Nativitas John Payne sonne to the aforesayd Thomas and Katherin was Borne into this worlde vppon thursday Betwene the howers of one and two of the clocke in the afternone which was the xxvii day of October and in the yeare of raigne of our soveraign ladie Queene Elizabethe the xxij ; and in the yeare of our lordgod. 1580 :

Nativitas Marie Payne the daughter to the aforesaid Thomas and Katherin was borne into this worlde vppon monday beynge the 25 day of March betwyn the howers of 2 & 3. of the clocke in the morninge and in the yeare of our lord god 1583. anno Regni Regine Elizabethe nunc anglie 25. The which said marie payne died and yelded her soule vnto almighty god in the saied yere.

Nativitas Robarte Payne sonne to the aforesaid Thomas and Katherin was borne into this worlde vppon sonnday beinge the 7 day of June, in Anno done 1584 betwyne the howers of three and foure of the clocke in the morning. Anno Rene Elizabeth xxvj.

Thomas Payne sonne to the aforsaid Thomas and Katherin was borne into this worlde vppon sonday beinge the xi day of December, 1586. betwyne the howers of v and vj of the clock in the afternoone. Anno Rene Elizabet xxix.

(In another and later hand.)

Katherin Payne the wife of Thomas Payne deceased the xviii of May : 1620.

Thomas Payne first aboue sayd departed this life the xiiiith day of Apriell : 1631. in the fourscore and eleuenth year of his life.

Thomas Paine & Elizabeth were maryed on xxij nouembeer Anno 1610.

Mary Payne the Daughter of the said Thomas was borne on the xij of october Anno 1611.

Thomas Payne his sonne was borne on the xviii day of January 1612.

Elizabeth payne was borne the xx daie of January Anno 1614.

Peter Payne was borne the xiiij day of March Anno 1616.

Dorothy payne was borne the vj of December Anno 1618.

John payne was borne the 26 of August 1620.

Sara payne was borne the vij of march, 1621.

Nathaniel payne was borne the xxi July 1626.

Nathathaniell Payne departed this life the sixt of Aprill 1636 of the age of nine yeares : going for ten.

The last entry on the paper, as above given, there is no doubt, was made at the time of the death which it records.

From this record, and several old papers from the same source, the following brief tabular pedigree has been mainly compiled.

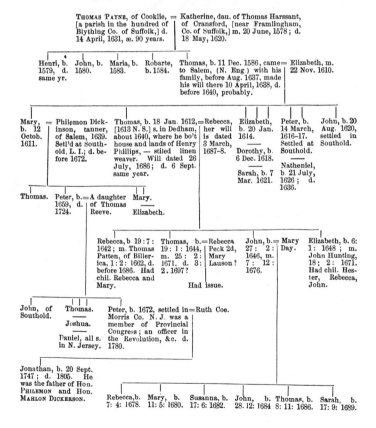

FACTS RELATIVE TO THE PEASE FAMILY.

Sam'l G. Drake, Esq.   *Albany, December* 19, 1853.
The enclosed matter relating to my family seems too valuable to lose. By giving it a place in the Register you will oblige us all. Most truly   FRED. S. PEASE.

We are under obligations to H. G. Somerby, Esq., for the collection of the following interesting particulars of our family in England.

From the records of Nayland, Co. Suffolk, are :—

Baptisms—1577, Elizabeth, daughter of John Pease,   Sept. 29.
       1579, Henry, son of   "   "   March 8.
       1582, John, son of   "   "   Dec. 2.
       1585, Thomas, son of   "   "   Dec. 17.
       1584, Amey, daughter of John Peese,   Dec. 20.
       1589, Robert, son of   "   "   Oct. 28.
       1592, William, son of   "   "   June 11.

Marriages—1576, John Peece, to Jone or Joan Smith,   Nov. 4.
       1637, John Pease, single, to Eliz'h Weede, singlew'n, Aug. 14.

Burials—1587, An infant of John Pease, unbaptized,   Aug. 19.
       1597, Amy Pease,   Oct. 24.
       1594, John Pease, householder,   Dec. 18.
       1597, John, son of John Pease,   June 8.

From the parish register of All Saints, Sudbury, Co. Suffolk :—
Baptized—1567, April 22, Margaret, daughter of Thomas Pease.
       1572, Nov. 16, Anne,   "   " Thomas Pesse.
       1576, April 22, Richard, son of Thomas Pease.

Buried—1583, April 2, Thomas Pease.

From the parish register of St. Savior's, Southworth, Co. Surrey :—
Married—1606, July 19, Richard Pease to Mary Clements.

From the parish register of St. Olave, Southwark :—
Baptized—1615, Aug. 27, William, son of Richard Pease, butcher.

From the parish register of St. Martin-in-the-Fields, London :—
Married—1629-30, Feb. 4, William Pease to Joan Bromlecome.

From the parish register of Cottenham, Co. Cambridge :—
Married—1615, Oct. 16, John Peasse to Elizabeth Essex.

From the parish register of Epping, Co. Essex :—
Baptized—1604, June 10, Robert, son of Robert Pease.
      1606-7, Jan. 18, Susan, daughter of Robert Pease.
      1608-9, March 5, John, son of   "   "

From the parish register of St. Margaret :—
Baptized—1625, Dec. 21, at Lynn, Joan, daughter of John Pease.

EXTRACTS FROM WILLS.

Arthur Pease, of Bullethorpe, in the parish of Swillington, Co. York, badger. Will dated Sept. 17, 1612. Wife Jennet. Children : Francis, William, Thomas, John, George and Elizabeth. Appoints daughter Elizabeth, executrix. Proved at York.

Thomas Peace, of Oaldecot, Co. Nottingham, Yeoman. Will dated Sept. 2, 1615. Mentions his brothers William of Nether Woodhouse ; Henry ; Hugh, and his sons John and Thomas ; and John. Proved at York.

Thomas Pease of Little Preston, in the parish of Rippax, Co. York, husbandman. Will dated June 28, 1624. Desires to be buried in the church of Swillingham. Wife Anne ; daughter Anne ; brother Robert. Mentions Thomas, son of Arthur Pease. Proved at York.

George Pease of Kingston-upon-Hull, merchant. Will dated Oct. 15, 1630. Eldest son William. To son Robert, £150 ; daughter Elizabeth Thompson ; daughter Anne Leach ; daughters Susannah and Jane Pease ; sister Alice Leake ; brother George, and his son George. Proved at York, March 2, 1631.

Richard Pease, of Potters Pury, Co. Northampton. Will dated June 6, 1601. Wife Mary ; sons Thomas and William. Proved at Northampton, July 16, 1601.

Robert Pease of Kettingdon, laborer. Will dated Dec. 11, 1593. Wife Jane. Children : Jude, William, John, Dennys, Mary, Alice and Anne, all under 21 years of age. Proved January 17, 1598, at Chelmsford, Essex.

Thomas Pease, of Stanford, yeoman. Brother John and his son William, and three daughters, Margaret, Elizabeth, and Joan. Wife Mary. Brother-in-law John Casse of Hatfield. Will proved at Chelmsford, 17 Sept. 1646.

Robert Pease, of Wittlesey, Co. Cambridge. Will dated Oct. 16, 1585. Wife Anne. Daughter Elizabeth Tomlyn. Proved at Cambridge, 3 Dec. 1586.

John Pese of Little Porland, Co. Norfolk. Will dated Dec. 29, 1539. Daughters Jone, Katherine and Anne. Proved in the Archdeacon's Court of Norfolk, July 16, 1540.

The compiler of the Memoir of the Pease Family has become convinced that there is no ground for the assumption that the name was derived from or formed part of the name Peabody. See page 27, Vol. III.

PEASE ANCESTRY.

In volume iii. page 30, N. E. Hist. and Gen. Reg., there is mention of John Pease, aged 27, and Robert Pease, aged 27, who came from Ipswich, England, to Boston, on board the ship Francis, in April, 1634, and removed to Salem, where they were known to have been in 1637.

It was assumed that John was ancestor of the families embraced in the account which was published in that volume, and his name was accordingly placed at the head. But further research and more reflection have served to transfer this honor to Robert.

Mr. Somerby, to whom much is due for his researches in England, writes under date of June 6, 1854, that while making some genealogical investigations in Essex, he met with the will of Robert Pease, of Great Baddow, and considering it worth the trouble, he visited that place and made extracts from the parish register.

Robert Pease of Great Baddow, Co. Essex, Locksmith. Will dated May 10, 1623. Mentions his wife Margaret, sons Robert and John, daughter Elizabeth, son-in-law Abraham Page, and brother-in-law Francis King. Will proved June 12, 1623.

From a long list of baptisms, marriages and burials, dating from 1540 to 1623, the following have been selected :—

John, son of Robert Pease, baptized May 24, 1593.

John, infant son of Robert Pease, buried January 10, 1599.

John, son of Robert Pease, baptized Nov. 20, 1608.

There is no record of the baptism of Robert, the other son mentioned in the will, and Mr. Somerby thinks he must have been baptized in some other parish.

It would be imprudent to assert positively that the John and Robert whose names are in the will, are the same who came in the Francis; but it seems not improbable that Great Baddow is the locality, and the family of Robert Pease that to which the ancestry of the family may be traced.

Great Baddow is in what is called the Hundred of Chelmsford, about thirty miles north-east from London, on the thoroughfare to Ipswich, the most convenient place of embarkation from that neighborhood, and old Norfolk and Essex here were settled chiefly by people from counties of the same name in England.

FREDERICK S. PEASE.

Albany, 21 *January*, 1856.

850

THE PECK GENEALOGY.—In a notice of this work in the REGISTER for January last (pp. 96-7) I am asked for more particulars in relation to the tabular pedigree it contains, and the identification and connection of my branch of the name with it.

I said in my history all that I thought it necessary to say in relation to the pedigree or the connection of my branch of the name with it. In relation to the identification of this branch of the name and its connection with the pedigree, the will of Robert Peck, of Beccles, the father of Joseph, the emigrant ancestor to this country, which I give, contains evidence, taken in connection with the pedigree, that no one should doubt. In relation to the pedigree, I stated that it could be found in the British Museum, and gave as authority for its correctness the certificate of officers at the Herald's College, which there accompanies the coat of arms and pedigree as follows :

20th Nov. 1620.

Visum agnitum et in munimenta Collegii Heraldorum relatum die et Anno supra scriptis. Testamur hoc

> Henry St. George, Richmond.
> Henry Chitting, Chester.
> John Philpot, Rouge Dragon.

They testify that they had seen or examined it and knew it to be correct. I considered this sufficient authority for its correctness and the best I could give, and supposed it would be satisfactory to others. No one who had examined the pedigree and certificate, with whom I had conversed or corresponded upon the subject, ever doubted its authenticity or correctness.

In relation to Mr. Somerby and Col. Chester, to whom allusion is made in the notice above referred to, I will say that with Col. Chester my correspondence is of recent date and designed mainly for information in relation to the present generations of the Pecks in England and the ancestors of the Connecticut Pecks.

With Mr. Somerby, whose sanction to the pedigree, it is stated in the notice referred to, would be sufficient, I have been in correspondence for about 20 years, my correspondence with him and other persons in England upon these subjects having commenced in 1850 or '51, and continued with intervals to the present time. During his residence in England he has furnished me with much information upon these subjects, such as heralds' visitations, pedigrees of the different branches of the name, coats of arms, crests, copies of wills, extracts from parish registers, probate records, &c., which, instead of giving in this history, I have preserved for another work. Mr. Somerby has examined this pedigree and the subject thoroughly, and has never expressed a doubt as to its authenticity and correctness, or of the connection of Joseph Peck, the emigrant ancestor of the Massachusetts Pecks, with it. To show his opinion of the pedigree, and that he did sanction it, I give a few extracts from his letters. In 1853, on sending me a copy of this pedigree, he writes, " I assure you that few families in England, and none in America, have one so complete and extensive." In answer to my questions in relation to the identification of this branch of the name with the pedigree, he writes, " The will of Robert Peck, of Beccles, the father of your ancestor Joseph, proves, positively, that the pedigree I sent you is correct. In his will he speaks of his son Robert at Cambridge. [See the genealogy, page 23.] Now we know there was but one Robert Peck at Cambridge, and he was afterwards the minister at Hingham, who, with his brother Joseph, emigrated to America." Again he writes in answer to my questions, " Everything in the pedigree perfectly agrees in regard to dates, Christian names, &c. I feel as well convinced that the document is correct as if I were living at the time and personally acquainted with the individuals mentioned therein." Other extracts from his letters, as full and as much to the point, might be given, but I presume these will be sufficient to show that Mr. Somerby sanctioned the pedigree, and he is not the only expert who has examined and copied it, with the coat of arms and the herald's certificate for me. It is in the library of the British Museum, and can be found in the "Additional Manuscripts, No. 5524, fol. 152," and was evidently prepared at much expense for Nicholas Peck, the elder brother of Robert and Joseph, who possessed, after his mother's decease, the most of his father's and uncle's estates. Those who have examined this pedigree agree in its being very extensive and complete. It impales the arms of over thirty families, into which the Pecks married. These arms, of which I have fac-similes, I could not find room for in my history, but design the drawings for a work which I hope to publish in relation to my branch of the name in England, and the ancestors of the Connecticut Pecks, whose descendants my history contains. I have also in preparation a genealogical history of the Ballous of this country, upon which I have been engaged for many years, and shall be thankful for records of families and information in relation to persons of the name.

Woonsocket. R. I.   IRA B. PECK.

THE IDENTITY OF ROBERT AND ANN PECK, WARDS OF ELDER WILLIAM BREWSTER IN LEYDEN IN 1610.—Elder William Brewster, born about 1566, was the son of William and *Prudence* Brewster. In 1610 he and his wife, Mary, had living with them as wards, Robert and Ann Peck, brother and sister, from Launde (see Willison's "Saints and Strangers").

Marriage registers at Sutton cum Lound, Notts., which lies about three miles southeast of Scrooby (the home of Elder Brewster), include: "At Lounde: 15 June 1589-Robert Pecke and June Jenyver".

This Robert Pecke may be he who lived in Everton, Notts., about two miles north of Lound, whose will, dated and proved in 1598, is preserved at York. It states:

"I, Robert Pecke of Everton, husbandman . . . my body to be buried in the churchyard of Everton . . . I give the poor of Everton 3/4. I give William Pecke my son 7/6/8. I give George Pecke, my son, the same. I give Thomas Pecke my son the same. I give *Prudence* Pecke my daughter the same. I give *Ann Pecke* my daughter the same. I give Thomas Hodgson 10/-bequeathed to my mother. I give Thomas Sympson half a rood of Rye. I give Hercules Moore 12d. I give *Robert Pecke* my eldest son a couple of black stears. I give Prudence my wife and Robert my son all residue and make them executors. I make Richard Perkin guardian of my son Robert during his minority. Witness Anthony Phan, clerke, Richard Harrison, and William Fletcher".

It seems quite possible from the foregoing that the above testator, Robert Pecke, married (perhaps secondly) Prudence, who may well have been sister of Elder William Brewster; their two children, Robert and Ann, appear to have been Elder Brewster's nephew and niece, and wards in 1610.

Arlington, Va.   JOHN G. HUNT.

HERBERT PELHAM, HIS ANCESTORS AND DESCENDANTS.

By Joseph Lemuel Chester, LL.D.

HAVING recently had access to a contemporaneous document which throws considerable light upon the history of the Pelham family, I have supplemented the information therein contained by the results of further independent researches, and now propose to place the whole in convenient shape for preservation. So little, comparatively, has been known of Herbert Pelham, and his history after quitting New England, and the brief accounts of him contain so many inaccuracies, some of them serious, that I cannot doubt that any addition to our stock of knowledge about him and his descendants will be acceptable. It is not very much, indeed, that I have to offer, and perhaps the chief value of the present narrative will consist in its settlement of hitherto doubtful dates and the correction of long existing errors.

The document to which I have referred is a richly emblazoned parchment roll, some yards in length, now in the possession of an aged maiden lady of Castle Cary, in Somersetshire. It was originally compiled by her ancestor, Samuel Bennet, Esq., of Shepton Mallet in that county, and is thus headed : " Register of severall of the ancestors of Samuel Bennet and his wife Katherine, with their several alliances by marriage, for four generations, Anno Dom: 1693." At this date he was about forty years old, and had probably been accumulating facts respecting his ancestry for many years, which, in 1693, he arranged and thus placed on record. He evidently continued to make additions to the roll until his death in 1735, after which the same was done by his successive descendants into whose hands it passed as an heir-loom. It is, however, only with the original portion of it that we shall have to deal. His wife was a Shute, and the greater portion of the roll relates directly to the families of Bennet and Shute, but it also includes accounts of a number of families with which they were allied by marriage, and among them that of Pelham. It may be as well to say at once that Herbert Pelham, senior, sometime of New England, was the great-uncle of Samuel Bennet's wife, she being Catharine, daughter of Thomas Shute, Gent., and Catherine his wife, who was a daughter of Rev. James Ashton by Catherine sister of Herbert Pelham.

Samuel Bennet was imbued with the true spirit of the genealogist, and must have had access to family records, and searched parish registers, for it is rarely that the early portion of the roll does not give the precise dates of birth, baptism, marriage, death, and burial of the persons named in it. During twenty years' experience I have never before seen so perfect a pedigree of the 17th century. It is, however, entirely in narrative form, and it is only when reduced to the tabular form, which I have done, that its wonderful completeness can be fully comprehended. I may add that I have had the opportunity, in many instances, of testing the statements by a direct reference to parish registers, and so far have not detected a single error.

The present possessor will not allow the roll, or any entire portion of it, to be printed; and it would possess no particular interest except to the families immediately concerned, while to Americans its importance is confined to the Pelhams. I have, however, been allowed to copy it entire, and, under that express stipulation, to make such use of its details as I see fit. From the statements in this roll, and such other facts as I have been able to glean from other sources, I now propose to present what I believe to be the true history of Herbert Pelham.

As a specimen of the style of the Bennet roll, I will quote *verbatim* the commencement of the account of the Pelham family. It reads thus :

"By my Wife's Mother's Father. There were three brothers of the Pelhams, one called Black Pelham, the other White Pelham, the other only by the name of Pelham. Sir William Pelham of Brockleby in Lincoln was the Black Pelham, and mother Shute's mother for the White Pelham; so are also the Pelhams of Compton in Dorset. My g. g. grandfather Herbert Pelham his father's name was Anthony, and this Anthony Pelham's son and grandson married with Elizabeth and Penelope West, daughters of Lord Delaware."

This is all that the roll says respecting Anthony Pelham, with whom I shall commence my narrative, and with whose descendants, rather than his ancestors, we are especially concerned.

I. ANTHONY PELHAM was the fourth and youngest son of Thomas Pelham, of Laughton, co. Suffolk (son and finally heir of Sir John Pelham, Kt.), and brother of William Pelham, ancestor of the Earls of Chichester and Yarborough, through the ordinary histories of which peerages his antecedents can be readily traced. The accounts which describe him as of *Buxted*, in Sussex, are entirely wrong. It does not appear that any Pelham ever lived at Buxted, and certainly this Anthony did not. It would be well to draw black lines in Berry's Sussex, p. 316, over his entire bit of pedigree, for almost every one of its statements is erroneous. He did not live at Buxted, did not die in 1577, and had no son Robert. His residence was in the parish of Warbleton, and the name of his seat was, as he himself spelt it in his will, "*Buxstepe.*" In his day a mansion of some pretensions, it still exists as a farm-house, and is now known as Bucksteep. It was really the inheritance of his wife, and only became the property of the Pelhams by his bequeathing to her son, by a former husband, other property in exchange. His wife Margaret, whose maiden name was Hall, was, when he married her, the widow of one Pierce, by whom she had, with other issue, this son, Thomas Pierce, with whom the exchange was effected.

She was buried at Warbleton on the 9th of December, 1560. Anthony Pelham made his will on the 5th of April, 1563, describing himself as "of Buxstepe, in the parish of Warbulton, Esquire." The following is a full abstract of it:

To the poor of Warbleton and Dallington, £30.—My overseers, viz., my son in law William Morley, my cousin John Lunsford, and Barnard Randall, to have the use of all my personalty during the minority of Herbert my son, for the purchase of lands for him when 21 years of age—My manors, lands, and tenements in the counties of Kent, Sussex, Surrey, Dorset, Lincoln, Northumberland, and York, or elsewhere, to my said overseers until my said son Herbert be of age—To Thomas Pierce, my late wife's eldest son, certain lands, &c. in Westfield and Ore, co. Sussex, in lieu of my house and lands where I now dwell, called Buxstepe, which were the inheritance of Margaret my wife, and would by common law have descended to said Thomas Pierce—If my said son Herbert die without issue, then Buxstepe to go to said Thomas Pierce, and all my other lands to my nephew John Pelham and the heirs male of his body, with remainder to heirs male of the body of his father Sir Nicholas Pelham, Kt., remainder to my right heirs—My said son Herbert to be my sole executor.

This will was proved, 26 February, 1566-7, in the Prerogative Court of Canterbury, by Herbert Pelham, son of the testator, the executor named.

Anthony Pelham had by his wife Margaret only two children, at least who survived. His daughter Anne became the second wife of William Morley, of Glynde, in Sussex, whose line terminated in heiresses in the second generation. His only son, viz. :

II. HERBERT PELHAM, had barely attained his majority when he proved his father's will, and hence was born in 1546. He was twice married, and by both wives had thirteen children, although the usual accounts allow him but four, and assign three of those to the wrong wife. His first wife was Catherine, daughter of John Thatcher, Esq., of Priesthawes (not *Preshull*), in the parish of Westham, co. Sussex, by Margaret, daughter of Sir Goddard Oxenbridge, Kt. By her he had one daughter and two sons, viz. :

1. *Margaret*, who married Sir Thomas Palmer, of Wingham, co. Kent, Kt., and was mother, among other children, of Herbert Palmer, the celebrated Master of Queen's College, Cambridge.
2. *John Pelham*, who, on the 28th of January, 1608-9, had a license from the Bishop of London to marry Catherine, daughter of John Yardley, Esq., of Henley, co. Warwick, spinster, aged eighteen. He was described as of the Middle Temple, Gentleman, a bachelor, aged twenty-four, son of Herbert Pelham, Esq., of Warbleton, Sussex. He was, therefore, born in 1584, and it may be assumed that his father's first marriage took place about 1580. I have failed to ascertain the subsequent history of this John Pelham, but he certainly died before his father, leaving at least no male issue, as will subsequently appear.
3. HERBERT PELHAM, of whom hereafter.

The exact date of death of Herbert Pelham's first wife Catherine does not appear. He married, secondly, at Wherwell, in Hampshire, Elizabeth West, eldest daughter of Thomas, second Lord De la Warr, by Anne, daughter of Sir Francis Knollys, K. G., Treasurer of the Household to Queen Elizabeth. According to the Bennet roll,* she was born 11 September, 1573, and baptized at Wherwell, her sponsors being Queen Eliza-

* As an instance of the accuracy, minuteness and importance of this roll, I may mention that it gives the precise days of birth of no less than thirteen children of Lord De la Warr, many of whom do not appear in the peerages, with the names of their sponsors. It is probably the only record of them, as the parish register of Wherwell, of that period, has long since disappeared.

beth herself, the Countess of Lincoln, and the Earl of Leicester. She was married at Wherwell, to Herbert Pelham, 12 February, 1593–4, being then only twenty years and five months old, while her husband was about forty-eight. By her Herbert Pelham had the following issue:

4. A daughter, born at Offington, 25 September, 1594.
5. A daughter, born at Michelham, 25 March, 1595.
6. A daughter, born 26 March, 1596.

> These three daughters, according to the Bennet roll, all died in their infancy ; and, as no Christian names are assigned them, probably at their birth, and hence unnamed and unbaptized.

7. *Thomas Pelham* (eldest son by the second wife, and not, as hitherto stated, by the first wife), who was born at Chichester, 23 Jan. 1597–8. He married at Salisbury, 4 September, 1621, Blanche Eyre, who died in 1667. They lived at Compton-Valence, co. Dorset, and had a numerous family, whose history and alliances are set forth in the Bennet roll, but which are omitted here as possessing no special interest for American readers.

8. *Anthony Pelham*, who was born at Michelham, 5 March, 1599–1600. He became a clergyman. His will, dated at Fordington, co. Dorset, 29 April, 1659, was proved 27 July following. He named his children, but his wife was evidently dead. He was probably minister at Fordington during the commonwealth period, and hence his name does not appear in the official list of incumbents.

9. *Anne* (fourth daughter and sixth child by the second wife, and not, as usually stated, by the first wife), who was born at Hellingly, in Sussex, 22 March, 1601–2. She was married at Fordington, co. Dorset, 2 May, 1621, to the Rev. Edward Clarke, Vicar of St. Mary Magdalen, Taunton, co. Somerset, to whom she was second wife. They had three daughters, who all subsequently married clergymen in Devonshire, and a son John who was buried at Taunton, 23 June, 1630. On the 19th of December following she died, and two weeks later he also, both being buried in his church.

10. *Elizabeth* (also by the second wife, though hitherto otherwise stated), who was born at Hellingly, 27 April, 1604. She was married at Salisbury, 4 September, 1621, to John Humphry, Gentleman, usually described as of Chaldon, co. Dorset, but who, according to the Bennet roll, was then living near London.

11. A son, born at Dokinfield, 10 April, 1606, whose christian name is not given, and who probably died in infancy.

12. *Katherine*, who was born at Dokinfield, 22 August, 1607, and buried at Warbleton, 17 March, 1608–9.

13. *Jonathan Pelham*, who was born at Cralle, in Warbleton, 6 Feb. 1609–10, and baptized at Warbleton on the 11th of the same month. He died unmarried, and a creditor administered his estate, the letters being dated 2 May, 1634, when he was described as late of Fordington, co. Dorset.

The time of Herbert Pelham's death has never before been correctly stated (Berry says 30 July, 1625), but I have discovered the Inquisition *post mortem*, which fixes the date as 12 April, 1620, and also the confirmatory evidence of the record of administration of his estate, the letters being granted to his son Herbert on the 27th of May in that year, when he was described as late of Fordington, co. Dorset. After occupying several different residences in Sussex, all, however, in or near Warbleton, he appears to have passed the last few years of his life at Fordington, where some of his children continued for some years afterwards. His widow Elizabeth evidently took up her residence with her own eldest son Thomas, at Compton Valence, Dorset, where she died, 15 January, 1632–3, and was buried. Her monumental inscription describes her as in her 59th year, which perfectly agrees with the date of her baptism as given in the Bennet roll.

We now return to his third child, and second but eldest surviving son, by by his first wife, Catherine Thatcher, viz. :

III. HERBERT PELHAM. By his father's Inquisition *post mortem*, dated 9 April, 1621, he was found to be his son and heir, which proves, as has before been said, that his elder brother John died *vita patris*, leaving no male issue. He married, about 1599, Penelope West, fourth daughter of Thomas, second Lord De la Warr, and consequently his stepmother's younger sister. She was born, according to the Bennet roll, 9 September, 1582. When or where she died I have so far been unable to ascertain, but the same authority states that they "had 16 children, most of them born in Sussex or Lincolnshire."* The roll specifically mentions twelve of them, and adds: "The rest of the 16 children, some of them dead-born, some died unbaptized." I have otherwise identified two not named in the roll, making 14 in all, and the remaining two were probably still-born, a class of children which the compiler always carefully included throughout the entire roll. These children were as follows:

1. HERBERT PELHAM, of whom hereafter.
2. *William Pelham*, second son. He makes a nuncupative will on or about 8 August, 1667, leaving all his possessions to his brother Herbert, who took out letters of administration under it, 7 January following, when the testator was described as a bachelor. He was probably not far from sixty years of age at his death. There can, I think, be little doubt that he was the William Pelham named by Savage as being in New England from 1630 to 1647, and in England in 1652.
3. *John Pelham*, third son, of whom the roll says nothing more, but who was clearly the John Pelham, aged 20, who, with his sister Penelope, emigrated to New England in 1635. He would have been born in 1615. Savage does not dispose of him, and I find no later trace of him in this country.
4. *Anthony Pelham*, fourth son. I find that I have his baptism at Boston, co. Lincoln, 24 May, 1621 ; but I fail to trace him later.
5. *Edward*, fifth son. No more in the roll.
6. A son, who lived and died in London, unmarried.
7. A son, who also lived and died in London, unmarried.

The roll affords no further information about the last two, and it is clear that the seven sons are not placed in strict chronological order. Probably the last two should come somewhere between the others. I give the daughters as they are enumerated in the roll:

1. *Margaret*, eldest daughter. She was living unmarried at the date of the will of her brother-in-law Ashton, 3 May, 1647, and appears to have been buried at Bures, in Suffolk, in 1661.
2. *Catherine*, second daughter, who was born at Dokenfield, in Sussex, 22 Aug. 1606, and married at Compton, in Dorset, in 1631, to the Rev. James Ashton, of Kilmersdon, co. Somerset. He died before Michaelmas, 1647, aged 52. She died the 19th, and was buried 21 April, 1659, both in Kilmersdon church. They had two sons and three daughters, who all died young except the second daughter, Catherine, who married 25 Aug. 1658, at Kilmersdon, Thomas Shute, Gent., and their second daughter, Catherine, born the 30th, and baptized 31 March, 1661, was married there, 15 May, 1683, to Samuel Bennet, the compiler of the roll referred to.
3. "*Helenor*, third daughter, lived till she was 19 or 20 years old : she had a black Pudding arm." I quote the roll *verbatim*.
4. *Penelope*, fourth daughter. The roll, in another place, says : "My great aunt Penelope Pelham is married to Mr. Belingham, Gent. : they live in Boston, in New England." She was, of course, the wife of the well-known Governor Richard Bellingham, whom she survived nearly thirty

* The accounts hitherto have assigned them positively only one son, possibly two more, and two daughters; but certainly there were no less than ten children living at their father's death.

years, dying at Boston, 28 May, 1702. She was born about 1619, her age being given as sixteen at her emigration in 1635.

5. "*Elizabeth*, youngest daughter, 70 age, lives with her sister Penelope, at Boston, New England." Again I quote the roll *verbatim*, and for a special purpose. The date of the roll is simply 1693, and this entry may have been made anywhere between 25 March, 1693, and 24 March, 1693–4. If her age were given with precise accuracy, she would have been born in 1623, or before 24 March, 1623–4. In the parish register, of Boston, co. Lincoln, under the date of 8 July, 1624, occurs the baptism of "Elizabeth, daughter of Herbert Pelham, Esq.," and there can be no reasonable doubt that this is the entry of her baptism. Neither can there be any doubt that it was she, and not her brother Herbert's second wife, who, according to Savage, died 1 April, 1706, in her 84th year, and was buried at Marshfield, Mass. That it was not the latter will be abundantly proved hereafter. She was really, therefore, not quite 82 at her death.

The two other daughters not named in the roll were :

6. *Anne*, who was buried at Boston, co. Lincoln, 10 March, 1622–3, and

7. *Martha*, who was baptized at Boston, 6 March, 1622–3, and buried there, 19 April, 1624. Both are in each instance described as daughters of Herbert Pelham, Esq.

Like his father, this Herbert Pelham died intestate, as did his wife, who probably survived him, so that we are without the information that might have been afforded by their wills, and hence the value of the details contained in the Bennet roll. He appears to have been somewhat of a wanderer, and almost as having no settled home, which is the more strange when we consider his very large family. When he administered his father's estate in 1621, he was described as of Hastings in Sussex, but most of his children had been born at other places in that county. He had inherited from his father the manor of Swineshead, in Lincolnshire, but he evidently never lived there, as the register of the parish does not contain a single entry of his family. The last year of his life, and rather more, was spent at Boston in Lincolnshire, and he was buried in the Rev. John Cotton's church, not in 1625 as is usually stated, but, according to the parish register, on the 20th of July, 1624. His Inquisition *post mortem*, dated 20 June, 1625, says that he died "the last day of July last past," a discrepancy of at least eleven days. He was never knighted, as has been hitherto stated. In every record of him that has been discovered, down to that of his burial in the Boston register and the Inquisition *post mortem*, nearly a year later, he is invariably described as "Herbert Pelham, Esquire."

We now return to his eldest son, viz. :

IV. HERBERT PELHAM, of whom the Bennet roll only says : "My great-uncle Herbert, eldest son of my great-grandfather and great-grandmother, Herbert and Penelope Pelham, married Mrs. Waldgrave, of Essex, a great heiress, buried her, married again, and had by both his wives four sons and six daughters." His first wife's name has hitherto been erroneously stated as Elizabeth. Their marriage license, granted by the Bishop of London, describes her as *Jemima* Waldegrave, spinster, aged about twenty, daughter of Thomas Waldegrave, of Bures *ad montem* in Essex, Esquire. Herbert Pelham is described as of Boston, co. Lincoln, Esquire, a bachelor, aged about twenty-six. He was born, therefore, in 1600, and this date is confirmed by his father's Inquisition *post mortem*, when he was found to be son and next heir, and aged twenty-four at his father's death. Jemima Waldegrave was not, as has been hitherto stated, daughter and coheir of Thomas Waldegrave by Elizabeth, daughter of Robert Gurdon of Assing-

858

ton, who were her grandparents, she being the second daughter and coheir of their son Thomas, who inherited Ferriers Court, in Bures, co. Suffolk, and whose wife was Margaret, daughter and heir of John Holmstead, of Halstead, co. Essex, Esquire. By her Herbert Pelham had issue as follows:

1. WALDEGRAVE PELHAM, eldest son, of whom hereafter.
2. *Nathaniel Pelham*, second son, baptized at Bures, 5 Feb. 1631-2. He is said to have graduated at Harvard College, and to have died in New England, in 1657. His father, in his will, dated 1 January, 1672-3, directs that a year's rent of certain premises shall be paid to Josias Winslow, in satisfaction of a debt which " he says my son Nathaniel Pelham *owes* him," but the rest of the will gives no intimation that he was still alive, and the word was probably a clerical error for *owed*.
3. *Jemima*, eldest daughter. The Bennet roll says that she " married Samuel Kem, called Maior, Alesbury, six miles from Oxford." This is one of the very few instances in which I have found the roll not strictly accurate, but I am able to set it right from my own Collections. Her husband was the Rev. Samuel Kem, B.D., Rector of Albury, near Oxford, and the record of the publication of their intended marriage occurs in the register of St. Martin in the Fields, London, under the date of 19 January, 1653-4. In his own parish register of Albury, Mr. Kem made the following entry, under the date of 10 February in the same year : " Mr. Samuel Kem, pastor of this parish, and Mrs. Jemima Pelham, eldest daughter to Harbert Pelham, Esq., of Ferriers Court, co. Essex, in the parish of Buers, co. Suffolk, were published three times in Albury Church, and they were married, and proclaimed husband and wife, by Mr. Jacob Roswell, J. P., in Trinity parish in London, the following 10th of February." She did not long survive, for three and a half years later, Mr. Kem, with his own hand, wrote the following entry in the Albury register : " Jemima Kem, eldest daughter of Herbert Pelham, Esq., of Essex, and second wife of Mr. Samuel Kem, B.D., and Rector of Albury, died the 20th day of August, 1657, and was buried at her father's church, in the chancel, of Buers in Suffolk." Mr. Kem married a third wife in 1659, and buried her in 1661, after which I have no knowledge of him. He appears to have had no issue by Jemima Pelham.
4. *Penelope*, second daughter. The Bennet roll says : " My cousin Penelope Pelham, second daughter, married *William* Winslow, of Boston, New England, and lives there." This should of course read *Josiah* Winslow. The inaccuracy is, so far, the only serious one I have discovered in the entire roll, and is readily rectified. She was baptized at Bures in 1633, married in New England in 1657, died there 7 December, 1703, and was buried at Marshfield, Mass. Her age could have been only 70, instead of 73, as hitherto stated.
5. *Catherine*. The Bennet roll says : " My cousin Katherine Pelham, youngest daughter by the first wife, lived and was married." She was living at the date of her father's will, 1 January, 1672-3, as Katherine Clarke, but her husband is not otherwise named.

It seems probable that all these children went with their father to New England in 1638, and that when he finally returned to England he left behind him only Nathaniel and Penelope. I have not been able to ascertain when their mother died, or where she was buried, but it was doubtless before the emigration, as Herbert Pelham's second marriage must have taken place, in New England, the following year. His second wife was Elizabeth, daughter of Godfrey Bosvile, of Gunthwaite, Yorkshire, and widow of Roger Harlakenden, who had died in New England in November, 1638, leaving two young daughters, Elizabeth and Margaret. The Bennet roll does not name her, but after mentioning Catherine, youngest daughter by Herbert Pelham's first wife, says : " Next, his children by a second wife," and enumerates them as follows:

859

6. "*Edward Pelham*, my cousin, son of my great-uncle Herbert, and brother to Waldgrave Pelham by the father's side, is married and lives at Boston, New England." As he either remained in New England, or returned there after arriving at maturity, his history must there be sought.[*] He will be found mentioned in his father's will. I cannot but note, however, that if he graduated at Harvard College in 1673, and died in September, 1730, as is stated, he must have been upwards of thirty years of age at his graduation, and nearly ninety at his death.

7. "*Herbert Pelham*, my cousin, was second son of my great uncle Herbert, by his second wife." He appears to have been born in New England, 3 October, 1645, and buried 2 January following.

8. *Mary*, who is said to have been born in New England, 12 Nov. 1640. The Bennet roll says : "My cousin Mary Pelham, the eldest daughter of my great uncle Herbert by his second wife, died in Essex, unmarried."

9. *Frances*, who is said to have been in New England 9 Nov. 1643. The Bennet roll says : "My cousin Frances Pelham, second daughter of my great uncle Herbert by his second wife, lived and was married in Essex." She was doubtless the wife of Jeremiah Stonnard (or Stannard) whom her father named in his will as his son.

10. *Anne*, of whom the Bennet roll says : "My cousin Anne, third daughter by the second wife, died unmarried, in Essex." She was living at the date of her father's will, 1 January, 1672-3.

Besides these ten children, there was clearly another son, viz. :

11. *Henry Pelham*, who is distinctly so called in his father's will. He appears to have been buried at Bures in the latter part of the year 1699, and his widow Elizabeth took out letters of administration to his estate, 10 June, 1700. Her will, dated 30 Dec. 1713, was proved 3 February following. They seem to have had an only son William, who was baptized at Bures in 1677, and whose will, dated 3 February, 1714-15, was proved 16 May following, by his widow Elizabeth. He left two young children, Henry and Elizabeth, the latter being baptized at Bures in 1713.

I can find no evidence that Herbert Pelham had still another son, William, as has been sometimes stated, but it is not impossible. At all events, he was not named in his father's will.

Knowing that Herbert Pelham did not make the slightest allusion to his second wife Elizabeth in his will, I always doubted that it was she who, according to Savage and others, was buried at Marshfield, Mass., in 1706 ; and, after a careful search, I discovered that on the 25th of August, 1659, letters to administer the estate of Elizabeth Pelham, late of Ferriers, in Bures, co. Essex, were granted, by the Prerogative Court of Canterbury, to her husband Herbert Pelham. There can of course be no doubt as to her identity, and thus a double mystery is cleared up, as I have shown when and where she really died, and that it was her husband's sister who was buried at Marshfield in 1706. Of her daughter by her former husband, Margaret Harlakenden, I have found no trace, but her other daughter, Elizabeth Harlakenden, will be mentioned hereafter.

Herbert Pelham does not appear, as suggested by Savage, to have been a lawyer, but simply a country gentleman. Certainly he was not educated at Oxford. The Herbert Pelham who matriculated at that university in 1619, and accepted by Mr. Savage as the emigrant, is distinctly declared in the register to have been the son of a Knight, which his father never was. They were distant kinsmen, the Oxford student being the son of Sir William Pelham, of Brocklesby, co. Lincoln.

Herbert Pelham survived his last wife fifteen years, dying at the age of 73, and was buried at Bures, 1 July, 1674. He made his will on the first of January, 1672-3, but for some reason it was not proved until 30 March,

* See REGISTER, xxvi. 401.—EDITOR.

1676. As the last record of one whose name is closely connected with the early history of New England, a full abstract of it may prove acceptable. The incorrect orthography of it must be attributed to the scrivener who wrote it. Omitting only the mere verbiage, it reads thus :

I, Herbert Pelham, of Ferrers, in Bowers Hamlet, in the County of Essex, Esquire, etc.—To my son Waldegrave Pelham all those lands, tenements, &c. with the rents and arrearages, which belong to me by virtue of a settlement of James Thacker [rightly *Thatcher*], late of Perist-Hawes [i. e. *Priesthawes*] in Sussex, Esq., or by virtue of any settlement of William Thacker or John Thacker, sons of said James Thacker, or by any other ways or means whatsoever, which were settled by him or them upon Katherine Pelham my grandmother, sister of said James Thacker, and descend upon me as heir of said Katherine Pelham—Whereas I have settled my manor of Swinstead *alias* Swinestead [rightly *Swineshead*] in Lincolnshire, on my said son Waldegrave and his heirs male, I now confirm the same—Whereas, by my Indenture dated 12 December 1667, I have settled, after my decease, a certain farm in Swinstead North-End, my will now is that the yearly rent of said farm be paid as follows : to my sister Penelope, wife of Richard Bellingham, Esq., £30. per annum for her life ; to Elizabeth Pelham my sister £10. per annum for life ; and the remaining £10. per annum to my daughter Penelope Winslow for life—If my son Edward Pelham survive my sister Bellingham, he to have, after her decease, £10. per annum thereof, and, after the death of both of my said sisters and my said daughter, he to receive the whole of said rents for life, and, at his death, the whole of said lands to come to my said son Waldegrave and his heirs male, with remainder to the heirs male to Edward Pelham, remainder to Henry Pelham and his heirs male, remainder to my right heirs—Whereas I have settled by my deed upon my said son Edward, for his life, my lands at Smeeth Hall, being 480 acres, part of the Eight Hundred Fenn, and a house and land in Chapel Hill, in Lincolnshire, my will is that he shall not receive any rents thereof until my debts are paid, and then the first year's rent shall be paid to my daughter Anne Pelham ; the second year's rent to my sons Henry Pelham and Jeremiah Stonnard (viz. £20. to my son Stonnard and the residue to my son Henry) ; the third year's rent to my son Josias Winslow, in satisfaction of a debt which he says my son Nathaniel Pelham owes [*sic*] him ; the fourth year's rent to my daughter Penelope Winslow, if living, or to her children if she be dead ; the next three year's rent to be paid " into the hands of my son Winslow for the use of my son Edward Pelham, to be paid unto him in New England, if he reside there, upon the conditions hereafter expressed, that is to say, if he said Edward Pelham so behave and demean himself that he can procure either the hands of the Governor and four of the Magistrates or Assistants of the Colony of the Mattachusetts Bay, or of New Plymouth Government, that he is now grown serious, sober, and solid, and follows his study, and avoids all idle and profuse company, and that they verily conceive there is a real change in him for the better, and not only to attain his ends thereby, then, upon such certificate," &c., said three years' rent shall be paid to him by my son Winslow, and afterwards said Edward shall receive said rents for life ; " but, if in all these years he will not be reclaimed," &c., then the first year's rent after said three years shall be paid to my said son Waldegrave, the second to my daughter Winslow, the third to my daughter Clarke, the fourth to my daughter Anne, the fifth to my son Henry, and then to begin again with my son Waldegrave, &c.—All my lands in Oweneboy, in the barony of Kirricurry, co. Cork, Ireland, to my said son Henry and his heirs male, with remainder to Edward Pelham, remainder to my said son Waldegrave, remainder to my right heirs—My daughters Katherine Clarke and Anne Pelham, each to have £25. per annum for life out of my lands in Wigtoft in Lincolnshire, and my son Henry Pelham the residue of the rents thereof for life, and, at the death of either, his or her part to be paid to the use of Waldegrave Pelham and Herbert Pelham, my grandchildren, for their lives—" To my son Edward Pelham all my lands, tenements and hereditaments in New England, in the Mattachusetts Bay in America, scituate, lying and being in Cambridge, Watertown, Sudbury, or elsewhere within the said Colony, which are laid out unto me, as also all other which are due to me from any of the said towns, or from the country, which are not laid out unto me, together with all

861

such rents and arrearages of rents as shall be due unto me at the time of my death for any lands letten within the said Colony "—All my plate in New England to my said son Edward, with one great silver tankard which was given him by his grandfather Godfrey Bosevile, Esquire—All other brass, bedding, linen, with all my books, and other utensils and moveables, which I have in the Mattachusetts Bay in New England, to be divided between my son Edward Pelham and my daughter Penelope Winslow—To my daughter, the wife of Mr. Guthlach Tolliot, the cabinet that was her mother's, and to her daughter Elizabeth a silver cup—I appoint my son Waldegrave Pelham my sole executor.

The only portion of this will not already referred to, and necessary to explain, is that relating to the mysterious daughter, wife of Guthlach Tolliot, who, in the only account of the Pelham family in which I have seen him mentioned, completely loses his identity by being strangely metamorphosed, no doubt from accidental causes, into *Cuthlac Elliot.** She was not Herbert Pelham's own daughter, but his second wife's eldest daughter by her former husband, being no other than the Elizabeth Harlakenden who was born, according to Savage, at Cambridge, Mass., in December, 1636. I find among my Collections the record of their marriage, at St. Augustine's, London, 2 February, 1659–60, he being described as of St. Mary le Bow, London, and she as "Elizabeth Harlackinden, of Bures St. Mary in Essex."

It now only remains to follow out briefly the history of Herbert Pelham's eldest son by his first wife, Jemima Waldegrave, viz.:

V. WALDEGRAVE PELHAM, who was baptized at Bures, 26 September, 1627. The Bennet roll says: "My cousin Waldgrave, eldest son of my great uncle Pelham, by his first wife Mrs. Waldgrave, lives at a house called Ferriers, near Buers Town in Essex." He was admitted to the Inner Temple in November, 1647, and married Abigail, daughter of Thomas Glascock, of Hedingham Sible, Essex. She was buried at Bures in 1698, and he late in 1699. Letters to administer his estate were granted, 28 February following, to his brother Edward Pelham, who, it thus appears, was then in England. Their children were as follows:

1. *Waldegrave Pelham*, who was baptized at Bures 6 June, 1667, and evidently died in infancy.
2. HERBERT, of whom hereafter.
3. *Waldegrave Pelham*, second of the name, who was baptized at Bures in 1670. He died unmarried, and a creditor administered to his estate, 19 May, 1703.
4. *Penelope*, who was living unmarried, 28 February, 1699–1700, when she renounced administration to her father's estate.
5. *Margaret*, who was also living unmarried at her father's death, but who renounced administration to her brother Waldegrave's estate, 19 May, 1703, then as Margaret Jenison.
6. *Jemima*, who died unmarried, and was buried at Bures in 1721.
7. *Abigail*, ⎫
8. *Elizabeth*, ⎬ who apparently all died young.
9. *Mary*, ⎭

The second but eldest surviving son, viz.:

VI. HERBERT PELHAM, died in 1746, and, according to his monument at Bures, in his 77th year. His widow, Sarah, was buried there in 1748.

* The author of the account of the Pelham family in the *Heraldic Journal* for April, 1867 (iii. 84–9), to which we suppose Col. Chester refers, quotes this name as from the will of Herbert Pelham, and probably obtained it from the copy communicated to the REGISTER for April, 1864 (xviii. 172–5), where the name appears, "Cuthlach Elliott."—EDITOR. *

*Pp. 964–967, this volume.

They appear to have died intestate, as I can discover no will or record of administration of either in any of the courts of London or Essex. Their issue were as follows :

1. *Waldegrave Pelham*, who was baptized at Bures in 1703. He died, apparently unmarried, and was buried at Southwell, in Nottinghamshire, 20 May, 1763.
2. *Sarah*, who was baptized at Bures in 1705, and buried there in 1714.
3. *Herbert Pelham*, who was baptized at Bures in 1707, and buried there in 1729.
4. *William Byatt Pelham*, who was baptized at Bures in 1709, but of whom I can discover nothing further.
5. *Nathaniel Pelham*, who was baptized at Bures in 1713, and buried there in 1736.
6. *Elizabeth*, who was baptized at Bures in 1716.

It may, I think, be assumed with tolerable safety, that unless there are descendants of Edward Pelham of New England, the male line of Herbert Pelham became extinct in the last generation recorded, and probably on the death, in 1763, of the last Waldegrave Pelham.

124 Southwark Park Road,
London, S. E., England.

PELHAM.—Since Col. Chester's article in this number of the REGISTER, on "Herbert Pelham and his Descendants," has been printed, and the printed sheet sent him, the editor has received from him a letter from which the following is an extract :

"The conclusion in my last paragraph, page 295, seems to be shaken by the statement in the REGISTER, vol. xxvi. p. 401, but I have no knowledge of that Herbert Pelham, who made the claim in 1761, and called himself the only son of Waldegrave. If he substantiated his claim, then the Waldegrave Pelham buried at Southwell, Notts, in 1763, must have been another person altogether. I did not attempt to pursue the family later, and only used the facts I had before me. Perhaps the discrepancy may lead to discussion, and the real facts come out."

Col. Chester suggests that the difference of eleven days in the records of the death of the second Herbert Pelham (*ante*, p. 290, lines 36 and 37) may be owing to one date being given in old style and the other in new, though the difference of the styles then was only ten days. This reduces the discrepancy to one day. The letter furnishes the following corrections of typographical errors :

Page 289, *line* 16, should read, "He made," not ma*k*es "a nuncupative will," &c. [2]
Page 293, *line* 21, should read "heirs male *of* Edward Pelham," not *to*. *Line* [5] 35, should read "if *the* said Edward Pelham," not "if *he*."

HERBERT PELHAM (*ante*, xviii. 172 ; xxxiii. 290).—Besides what I have written about Herbert Pelham on pp. 163, 317, 318, 319, 419 and 517 of my book [Annals of Nonconformity in Essex, *ante*, xx. 192], I find notes of his being named in Scobell, ii. 66 and 406. He was also one of the magistrates who signed the committal of James Parnell to Colchester jail for disturbing the congregation at Coggeshall in this county. Parnell himself gives the warrant in his "Fruits of a Fast," &c. pp. 250–2. I also find that Pelham frequently signed entries of marriage on the parish registers of the neighborhood.   THOMAS W. DAVIDS.

4 St. George's Square, Upton, London, E., England.

[1] P. 858, this volume.
[2] P. 857, this volume.
[5] P. 861, this volume.

THE PENROSE FAMILY OF WHELDRAKE AND BALLYKEAN AND THEIR DESCENDANTS IN BOTH HEMISPHERES

By GEORGE E. McCRACKEN, Ph.D., F.A.A.R., F.A.S.G., of
Drake University, Des Moines, Iowa

The genealogical account now to be presented is remarkable in that from one Elizabethan yeoman, who died in 1572, it has been possible to trace, not only descendants who belong to the landed gentry of Ireland but also others among the early Quaker immigrants to Pennsylvania. Wheldrake mentioned in the title is a parish some miles southeast of York; Ballykean is the name of an estate near Redcross in the Rathdrum district of County Wicklow, Ireland, once owned by members of this family who were ancestral to both the Irish and the American groups mentioned.

This family shows no possible connection with another Penrose family of Pennsylvania which stems from the shipwright, Bartholomew Penrose (1674-1711), a native of Bristol, son of another Bartholomew Penrose who was in turn son of a Capt. Thomas Penrose, originally of Fowey, Cornwall, later an officer in the navies of both Oliver Cromwell and Charles II.* The name is, however, undoubtedly Cornish in origin but no explanation of how people with a Cornish name came to be living in the sixteenth century in York-

---

*On the Bartholomew Penrose family see William Penrose Hallowell, *Records of a Branch of the Hallowell Family including the Longstreth, Penrose, and Norwood Branches* (Philadelphia, 1893), pp. 145 ff.; Josiah Granville Leach, *History of the Penrose Family of Philadelphia* (Philadelphia, 1903), the fundamental treatment of this family; Col. George H. Penrose (U.S.A.), *A Genealogical Chart, being Supplement to the Penrose Family (published in Philadelphia in 1903) and containing certain information of the older generations therein not contained* (New York, no date, but *ca.* 1930) , an important addition to Leach's genealogy; Frank Willing Leach, article in the Philadelphia *North American*, Sunday, 30 June 1907; George Norbury MacKenzie, *Colonial Families in the United States of America* (Baltimore, 1917), 6:374-379, a pedigree of the late U. S. Senator Boies Penrose (1860-1921), whose nephew, Boies Penrose II, of Devon, Pa., has been very helpful; C. P. Keith (*Pennsylvania Magazine of History and Biography*, 25:285f.).

shire has been found. The Penroses of Wheldrake were not, however, the only people of the name in Yorkshire—the name is found in a number of other Yorkshire localities between 1569 and 1700, though no connection with the Wheldrake group is proved.

The present head of the British descendants of this family is Joscelyn Denis Penrose, Esq., of Woodhill, Milton-under-Wychwood, Oxfordshire, whose cooperation in this study has been great. He most generously sent across the sea an elaborate tabular pedigree of his own compilation, though he possessed no duplicate. He also made available a transcript of a precious document of the eighteenth century: a letter from one Richard Savage, then living at Wheldrake, to one of the Irish Penroses, whose descendants passed it to Mr. Denis Penrose's father. The text as it now stands contains, besides a list of Penrose christenings taken by Richard Savage from the Wheldrake register, some interpolated material which could not have been available to Savage when he wrote. In the transcript below both the christenings and the interpolation are omitted—they will be utilized later at the proper points.

Friend. This is a true copy of the Register belonging to the parish of Wheldrake, from the year 1603 to the year 1666. [Here follow 41 christenings, including three sets of twins, and the interpolation.] Friend please to observe that John son of John born in the year 1605, was father to one [our?] mother mentioned in the last 3 Lives. I am Richard Savage now living in Wheldrake, Son of Catherine, daughter of John Penrose. William Hotham now living in Storpeate two miles from Wheldrake is son of Elizabeth daughter of John Penrose. Grace is now living Gainsborough 30 miles from York and hath one daughter called Anne Clarke. As for the place you call Wolverton we know nothing of, but there is a place called Alverton [now Elvington] on the other side of the River Derwent whither I sent to examine the register, but there is no such name as Penrose in it. As to their estate there hath been more than there is at present, for John son of John, having been an extravagant man, would have spent all if he could, but his wife's friends prevented him by getting it made fast to his children, which in some of them is since improved.

Wheldrake, 5 miles from York
  July 9th 1742
      I am your friend
        Richard Savage

This Richard Savage could hardly have been identical with the well-known poet of the same name. Wheldrake on modern maps appears to be eight miles, not five, from York, but Savage's house may have been nearer the city than the center of the parish.

Acknowledgment must be made also of assistance from Mr. Denis Penrose's son-in-law, Hugo Read, of Heathy Lea, Baslow, Bakewell, Derbyshire; James Ronald Penrose, of Watford, Hertfordshire; Prof. John Insley Coddington, Miss Ida C. Townsend, Mr. Walter Lee Sheppard, Jr., and Prof. William A. Russ.*

---

*Partial accounts of the family will be found in the following bibliography to which reference will be made as occasion demands: Ellwood Roberts, *Old Richland Families* (Norristown, 1898), pp. 205-209; Albert Cook Myers, *Immigration of the Irish Quakers into Pennsylvania 1682-1750* (Swarthmore, 1902), and his *Quaker Arrivals at Philadelphia 1682-1750* (Philadelphia, 1902); W. H. H. Davis and

1. THOMAS[1] PENROSE or PENROS, as the name is spelled in the Bulmer Act Book, when administration was granted on his estate to his widow ALICE ———, 19 Nov. 1572, was apparently a yeoman, and was of Wheldrake.

Probable child:

2. i. NICHOLAS, d. in Wheldrake in 1591.

2. NICHOLAS[2] PENROSE (*Thomas[1]*) died in Wheldrake, intestate, administration being granted 20 April 1591 (Deanery of Bulmer) to his son John who died himself in 1607 without having finished administration, after which, on 20 Dec. 1614, administration was again granted on Nicholas's estate to Richard Penrose and John Penrose, natural and lawfull sons of said deceased (Bulmer Act Book). Nothing is known of his wife.

Children (all known):

3. i. JOHN, bur. in Wheldrake in 1607.
  ii. ?WILLIAM, of Wheldrake, lic. to m. in 1598 MARGARET LONSDALE, widow, of Wheldrake (*Yorkshire Archaeological Society*, 10:47) and she m. (2), in 1616, when of All Saints Pavement Parish, York, James Crocker of Huntington (*ibid.*, 14:232).

3. JOHN[3] PENROSE (*Nicholas,[2] Thomas[1]*), buried in Wheldrake in 1607, was granted administration on his father's estate in 1591 but left it unadministered at his own death. His undated will (York Probate, 30:428) was probated 31 Oct. 1607 by son Richard Penrose: to everyone of my children 20s, being eight in number, to be paid by son Richard Penrose; to John Penrose, son of son Philip Penrose, 20s; to Hester and Anne, daughters of Richard Williamson, bedstead and clothes whereon I ly; to Anne Williamson, my hatt; rest of goods, leases, chattels, to said son Richard Penrose, executor; witnesses: George Howsman, clerk, John Penrose, Thomas Penrose.

Children:

4. i. RICHARD, d. ca. 1627-8.
5. ii. THOMAS, d. ca. 1649.
  iii. HENRY, had a son Mark, bapt. in Wheldrake 28 April 1605.
6. iv. JOHN, d. ca. 1634-5.
7. v. WILLIAM, d. in 1617.

Warren S. Ely, *History of Bucks County, Pennsylvania* (New York-Chicago, 1905), 3:293-296, 699 f.; Mary Paul Hallowell Hough, assisted by Anna Hallowell Penrose, *The Hallowell-Paul Family History*, etc.(Philadelphia,1924); Clarence Vernon Roberts, *Early Friends Families of Upper Bucks* (Philadelphia, 1925), chapter xxvii, pp. 396-415, a work which entirely supersedes that of Ellwood Roberts; George E. McCracken (*The American Genealogist*, 29:242-245, 35:234-236). The various editions of Burke's *Landed Gentry* contain accounts of Irish and English Penroses, all of whom belong to this family. In the following pages reference to "Roberts" always refers to Mr. C. V. Roberts' admirable volume, cited above.

vi.   EDWARD, m. in Wheldrake, 21 June 1607, MARGARET LEEDES, and
       had a son *William*, bapt. there 2 March 1610.
8. vii.   PHILIP.
viii.   ANNE, m. RICHARD WILLIAMSON.

Children: 1. *Hester*, mentioned in grandfather's will. 2. *Anne*,
mentioned in grandfather's will. 3. ? *William*, not mentioned in
grandfather's will but on some of the charts of James Ronald
Penrose.

4. RICHARD⁴ PENROSE (*John*,³ *Nicholas*,² *Thomas*¹), named eldest
    son in his father's will, probated it in 1607, and after 20
    Dec. 1614 was, with his brother John, administrator of his
    grandfather Nicholas's will. His own will is dated 3 Jan.
    1627/8, probated 19 Feb. 1628/9 (York Probate 40:355) by
    wife ALICE ————, and directs burial in Wheldrake church-
    yard, not church, a clear indication that the family was not
    of the gentry; to daughter Mary Penrose one black cowe
    and £5 out of farm, to be paid by son Robert when he
    enters on farmhold; to son John Penrose first three yeare of
    the Paddocke or 20s to be paid by his mother and 20s more
    out of farmhold by son Robert Penrose; to sons Richard
    and John Penrose the chamber over the howse to lye in
    during the time they are unmarried; to wife Alice farmhold
    during widowhood, also residue, and she is named execu-
    trix; witnesses: William Walker, Thomas Roome, Robert
    Penrose.

    Children:

i.   ROBERT, eldest son, perhaps m. in Wheldrake, 13 Sept. 1636, AIMS-
      TISS WEFFE; probably the Robert of Sutton on Derwent whose
      widow Ann [Aimstiss?] took admin. 20 April 1661.
ii.   MARY, bapt. in Wheldrake 25 May 1603; in father's will 1627; m. in
      Wheldrake, 25 Nov. 1635, WILLFREY HARRISON.
iii. MATTHEW, bapt. in Wheldrake 6 June 1604.
iv.   JOHN, bapt. in Wheldrake 9 April 1606; unm. in 1627.
9. v.   RICHARD, no baptism found.

5. THOMAS⁴ PENROSE (*John*,³ *Nicholas*,² *Thomas*¹) witnessed his
    father's will in 1607. His wife DOROTHY is named in the un-
    dated will probated 30 Aug. 1649 by Anne Penrose, one of
    the executors. Burial is directed in Wheldrake churchyard;
    to eldest son Robert Penrose land which I took of Mʳ
    Stabler Haxby; to son Mathew Penrose land which I have
    in the Banckes (except what I have hereafter given to my
    wife): to son William Penrose, farmehold (excepting what
    I have given to my wife and daughter Anne Penrose): to
    son William Penrose foure oxen, two swine and calves, a
    new wayne and a new plow with all gear, son William to
    maintain wife Dorothy with meat & drink and I give her one
    third of all goods and lands; to sons Mathew and William
    two payre of wayne blades between them and my own
    waine; to wife Dorothie Penrose during her life two cowe-

867

gates in the Banckes and two of my best kine and a third part of the fruit; to daughter Anne my farm till my son William enters, two of my oldest oxen, five young beasts and one cowe; to grandchild Janie Raymes, daughter of George Raymes, one little whie; to grandchildren Richard and William Coates 6/8 to buy them books; rest of goods unbequeathed to Dorothy Penrose and daughter Anne Penrose, executrices; witnesses: George Blanshard, George Walker, Mathew Penrose.

Children; all but Hester's baptism found in Weldrake:

10. i.   ROBERT, bapt. 24 Oct. 1604.
    ii.   THOMAS, (twin?) bapt. 3 Feb. 1606; bur. in 1607.
    iii.   RICHARD (twin?), bapt. 3 Feb. 1606; bur. in 1609.
11. iv.   MATTHEW, bapt. 7 Oct. 1608.
12. v.   WILLIAM, bapt. 21 Oct. 1610.
    vi.   MARY, bapt. 6 Feb 1613; m. there, 19 Jan. 1635, John Coats, and had sons Richard and William.
    vii.   ANNE, bapt. 17 Feb. 1616; probated father's will 1649; evidently a woman skilled in farm management.
    viii.   HESTER, no baptism found; m. in Wheldrake, 19 Oct. 1630, GEORGE RHAMES or RAYMES, and had daughter *Jane*.
    ix.   THOMAS, bapt. 6 June 1620; bur. in 1625.

6. JOHN[4] PENROSE (*John*,[3] *Nicholas*,[2] *Thomas*[1]), witness of his father's will in 1627, was a labourer of Newton-on-Derwent, buried in Wilberfoss, both places near Wheldrake. His will, dated 28 Dec. 1634, was probated by his wife MARY, 12 May 1635 (York Probate 42:507), power being reserved of making the like grant to the other executors. He directs burial in the churchyard of Wilberfoss; to sons William and Thomas all that part of Westwood which belongeth to me after decease of my wife; to son William Penrose the interest of this my dwelling in Newton after decease of my wife; residue of goods and chattels unbequeathed after payment of funeral expenses and debts to wife Mary Penrose and sons William and Thomas Penrose, named executors; witnesses: William Williamson, Robert Hart and John Robinson.

Children:

    i.   WILLIAM, named in father's will, 1634.
13. ii.   JOHN, bapt. in Wheldrake 2 May 1605.
    iii.   THOMAS, named in father's will, 1634; perhaps m. in Wheldrake, 26 Sept. 1624, ALICE CHAMBERS; probably father of *Elizabeth*, bapt. in Wheldrake 22 Aug. 1631.

7. WILLIAM[4] PENROSE (*John*,[3] *Nicholas*,[2] *Thomas*[1]), of Thorganby, a place a little south of Wheldrake, died intestate, administration granted to wife ALICE, 20 June 1617. Also, tuition of the goods and portions of Thomas Penrose, Edward Penrose and Mary Penrose, natural and lawfull children of said deceased, was granted to said Alice Pen-

rose, widow, relict of the deceased (Bulmer Act Book). The marriage to Alice took place at Wheldrake, 26 Nov. 1609, the surname being read by the rector as "F——ton."

Children:

14. i.   THOMAS, bapt. in Wheldrake 23 Aug. 1610.
    ii.   EDWARD, named in father's probate and in brother's will, when he had daughters *Alice* and *Jane*.
    iii.   MARY, named in father's probate and called Mary Savadge in her brother's will, then having two children.
    iv.   ALICE, named in brother's will as Alice Martin, having children *Robert* and *Anne*.

8. PHILIP[4] PENROSE (*John*,[3] *Nicholas*,[2] *Thomas*[1]) had married by 1607 and then had a son John who was named in his grandfather's will. It is possible but not certain that he was the Mr. Philip Penrose of the City of York whose history is now set down with a strong caution that it may not belong here. Mr. Philip, in any case, married, first, at Holy Trinity Church, Goodramgate, York, 18 Nov. 1587, ELIZABETH WILSON, her death not found; and secondly, JOAN ——, buried in the high quire of St. Michael le Belfrey, York, 29 Sept. 1623. Mr. Philip was himself buried at Holy Trinity, 4 March 1633/4, leaving a will calling himself Philip Penrose the Elder of the City of York, gent., dated 28 Jan. 1633/4, probated 4 April 1634, directing burial in the Church of Holy Trinity, Goodramgate; to son John Penrose my Office House in the Minster Garth of St. Peter, he to buy a ring for his wife to wear for my sake; to daughter Mary Connyears £6; sons Philip and John shall beare charges of my funeral; residue to son Philip Penrose and daughter Judith Penrose, and Philip is to be executor; witnesses: John Lawrence, William North, Vincent Bovell, Roger Caely, Richard Hatter. This Philip was not a clergyman, or he would not have been called "gent.," but he probably occupied some lay position of trust under the Archbishop of York. The son John, shown below, certainly belonged to the Philip Penrose under discussion; if that Philip was not identical with Mr. Philip, then both, at least, had sons John.

Children:

15. i.   JOHN, no baptism found.
    ii.   PHILIP, bapt. Holy Trinity, Goodramgate, 29 May 1601; bur. there as Mr. Philip 26 Feb. 1649/50, probably father of the Mary, bur. in the high quire of St. Michael le Belfrey, 6 July 1623.
    iii.   JUDITH, bapt. Holy Trinity, Goodramgate, 3 July 1603; m. there, as 2nd wife, 8 Sept. 1634, BYGOT BLADES, who had m. (1), St. Michael le Belfrey, 24 Nov. 1616, Elizabeth Dent, bur. Holy Trinity 3 Aug. 1632, mother of all the known children. Mr. Bygot Blades was bur. Holy Trinity 20 June 1643.
    iv.   MARY, bapt. Holy Trinity 6 March 1605/6; called Mary Connyers in her father's will.

869

9. RICHARD[5] PENROSE (*Richard,*[4] *John,*[3] *Nicholas,*[2] *Thomas*[1]),
unmarried in 1627, was probably the testator of Wheldrake,
3 Sept. 1660, will probated 9 May 1665 (Prerogative Court
of York, 37:61, not examined).

Children, baptized in Weldrake:

i. MARTHA, bapt. 25 Oct. 1636.
ii. ALICE, bapt. 29 Oct. 1637.
iii. JOHN (twin?), bapt. 4 May 1640.
iv. MARY (twin?), bapt. 4 May 1640.
v. ESTHER, bapt. 23 April 1641; probably m. there, 23 Nov. 1665,
ROBERT SMITH.
vi. JOHN (twin?), bapt. 7 Aug. 1644.
vii. ELENOR (twin?), bapt. 7 Aug. 1644.
viii. MARY, bapt. 18 June 1647.

10. ROBERT[5] PENROSE (*Thomas,*[4] *John,*[3] *Nicholas,*[2] *Thomas*[1]),
eldest son, was baptized in Wheldrake 24 Oct. 1604, and is
therefore identifiable as the ancestor of all the later Penroses in this study, because Wicklow Friends records say he
was born in October 1604. He married JANE ———, died in
Ballykean, co. Wicklow, Ire., 2 Aug. 1680, buried in Ballymoran Friends Burying Ground. No probate has been
found for him in Yorkshire or Ireland, and there is no positive evidence that he ever came to Ireland or was a Friend,
but there is a persistent tradition in the family of his son
Richard to the effect that Robert Penrose came to Ireland
in the time of Cromwell, and this tradition has been
generally attached to Robert Penrose No. 18. The tradition
would, however, be better applied to Robert Penrose No.
10, as the inheritance of Ballykean would then seem more
logical.

Children, baptized in Weldrake:

16. i. WILLIAM, bapt. 2 Oct. 1627.
17. ii. RICHARD, bapt. March 1630.
18. iii. ROBERT, bapt. September 1632.
iv. ELIZABETH, bapt. 2 April 1637; not found in Ireland.
v. JANE, bapt. 25 April 1640; not found in Ireland.
vi. ALICE, bapt. 8 Jan. 1642; d. in Ballykean 3 March 1690.
vii. JOHN, bapt. 24 Aug. 1645; not found in Ireland.

11. MATTHEW[5] PENROSE (*Thomas,*[4] *John,*[3] *Nicholas,*[2] *Thomas*[1])
was living in 1649. Nothing is known of his wife.

Children, baptized in Weldrake:

i. MATTHEW, bapt. 22 April 1644.
ii. MARY, bapt. 26 Oct. 1645.

12. WILLIAM[5] PENROSE (*Thomas,*[4] *John,*[3] *Nicholas,*[2] *Thomas*[1]),
baptized in Wheldrake 21 Oct. 1610, was probably the
William of Sutton-on-Derwent whose will, dated 24 June
1668, probated 19 May 1679, directs burial at Sutton-on-
Derwent and names wife HESTER as executrix; 12/- each to

son Robert Craven and daughter Elizabeth Craven; 5/- each to grandchildren William Craven and Thomas Craven, and to cousin Jane Lister.

Children, baptized in Weldrake:

i. THOMAS, bapt. 6 Oct. 1647; not in father's will.
ii. ELIZABETH, bapt. 6 Feb. 1651/2; m., quite young, ROBERT CRAVEN and had sons *William* and *Thomas.*
iii. JANE, bapt. 12 March 1653.
iv. DOROTHY, bapt. 22 Oct. 1656.

13. JOHN[5] PENROSE (*John,*[4] *John,*[3] *Nicholas,*[2] *Thomas*[1]), baptized in Wheldrake 2 May 1605. He married there, 19 Jan. 1629/30, KATHERINE LOURNEDALE. His descendant, Richard Savage, says that he was extravagant but was prevented from dissipating his substance by his wife's friends, and that, by 1742, when Savage made the statement, the situation of some of the family had been improved. This John was probably the Mr. John of York, buried at Holy Trinity, Goodramgate, York, 19 Oct. 1654, with a wife, Mrs. Katherine, buried there 26 March 1638.

Children:

19. i. JOHN, m. in Wheldrake, 26 July 1655, ELIZABETH FAWCETT.
ii. ANNE, bapt. in Wheldrake 27 Oct. 1632.
iii. ELIZABETH, bapt. in Wheldrake 7 June 1635.

14. THOMAS[5] PENROSE (*William,*[4] *John,*[3] *Nicholas,*[2] *Thomas*[1]) was baptized in Wheldrake 23 Aug. 1610, and was named in his father's probate. He was probably the cordwainer of the Parish of St. Crux, York, who made his will 8 Dec. 1662, no date of probate, directing burial in that parish. Second son John Penrose is to get £40 at age 21, this to be put into the hands of Robert Martin of Sutton on Forest, Yorkshire; 22/- at age 21 to the two daughters, Alice the eldest and Jane the youngest, of his brother Edward; 5/- to sister Mary Savadge and 2/6 to each of her two children; to sister Alice Martin's two children, Robert and Anne, 12d; executors: wife JANE and eldest son Thomas, also residuary legatees. Thomas is under age and a messuage in Collygate in Christ's Parish is mentioned; witnesses: William Penrose, William Lasonbye, Robert Huthwett.

Children:

i. THOMAS, under age in 1662.
ii. JOHN, under age in 1662.

15. JOHN[5] PENROSE (*Philip,*[4] *John,*[3] *Nicholas,*[2] *Thomas*[1]) is mentioned in his grandfather's will in 1607 but no baptism has been found. If we have rightly identified his father as Mr. Philip Penrose of York, then this John married, first, by license dated 4 Aug. 1618, at St. Cuthbert's, FAITH TATTER-

SALL, of that parish (*Yorkshire Archaelogical & Topographical Journal*, 14:473) ; and secondly, THOMASINE WHINCOP, baptized 20 Sept. 1598, daughter of the Rev. Thomas Whincop and widow of John Vaux who died in 1643 (*ibid.*, 12:431 n.) .

Children: all by first wife:

i. JOHN, bapt. 17 March 1619/20, Holy Trinity, Goodramgate, York.
ii. KATHERINE, bapt. 26 Feb. 1621/2, same church.
iii. ELIZABETH, bapt. 1 Dec. 1624, same church.
iv. ABIGAIL, bapt. 1 Nov. 1626; bur. 3 Dec. 1628, same church.
v. NATHANIEL, bapt. 24 Oct. 1629; bur. 25 Oct. 1629, same church.

16. WILLIAM[6] PENROSE (*Robert,[5] Thomas,[4] John,[3] Nicholas,[2] Thomas[1]*), eldest son, was baptized in Wheldrake 2 Oct. 1627, but no record has been found of him in Ireland. He may have been the William Penrose buried at St. Michael le Belfrey, York, 2 Jan. 1677/8, who was probably the William who married at All Saints Pavement, York, 30 Jan. 1653/4, ALICE RAW. She likewise was probably the Alice Penrose who married at St. Michael's, 21 May 1678, William Fesher.

Probable children:

i. ELIZABETH, bapt. All Saints Pavement 27 Feb. 1654/5; bur. St. Michael's 2 March 1657/8.
ii. ?ELIZABETH, baptism not found; of St. Michael's when m. there, 2 April 1684, to WILLIAM PRESTON of Duninton.
iii. ?MARGARET, bur. St. Michael's 21 March 1700/1; perhaps the Margaret who had a son *William*, bapt. St. Michael's 16 May 1693.

17. RICHARD[6] PENROSE (*Robert,[5] Thomas,[4] John,[3] Nicholas,[2] Thomas[1]*), second son, baptized in Wheldrake in March 1630, was murdered in his house, probably in Ballykean and certainly in co. Wicklow, Ireland, 27 April 1686. "His house had been broken into by thieves, who robbed it and mortally wounded him, and one William Walsh, being at the said robbery, was taken and hanged at Wicklow Assizes." According to Wicklow Friends records, he was born in Alverton *alias* Elverton, now called Elvington, a parish near Wheldrake. The interpolation in Richard Savage's letter states that he crossed over to Ireland in September 1665 but there are conflicting accounts which make his brother Robert (No. 18) cross over in 1658. He married in Ireland, 25 April 1667, ANNE STORYE, who died in Ballykean 8 May 1682, perhaps as the result of childbirth two months earlier, daughter of John Storye of Churchtown, co. Dublin.

Book W-5 of Wicklow Friends records states under "Sufferings" that in 1673 "Richard spoke to a priest, reading the words, 'I know that my Redeemer liveth,' and asked how he knew. The priest indited him at the next Assizes, and he is not yet released." Again, in 1678, "Richard 3 months in prison for refusing to take the oath." Both Anne and Richard were buried in the "burying place of the people of God at Ballymoran in the County of Wicklow." At his death, his children, now orphans, were 18, 14, 13, 9 and 4 years of age.

Either he or his brother Robert was owner of the property called Ballycaine, Ballycane, or Ballykean Penrose, just north of the village of Redcross in the Rathdrum District of co. Wicklow. The spelling Ballykean, here adopted, is that found on the 1909 Survey and there are three Ballykean Townlands: Ballykean (Penrose), Ballykean (Annesley), and Ballykean (Stringer). The Ballykean Penrose property consisted of 360 acres and adjoined the Annesley and Stringer properties. No evidence of a documentary nature shows how the property came into the Penrose family. Hearsay claims that Robert Penrose (No. 18) came to Ireland as one of the Cromwellian soldiers 'planted' on Irish soil. It would appear that both Richard and Robert lived in Ballykean, and if descent of the property after their deaths is any indication, as it ought to be, it was the descendants of Richard who clearly remained in Ballykean for some time after his death, whereas there is evidence, sometimes of a conflicting nature, that Robert Penrose (No. 22), son of Robert (No. 18), the supposed Cromwellian soldier, moved about in Ireland considerably before he came to America in 1717. It does not seem to be known just when the property passed out of the Penrose family. In the latter part of the eighteenth century a descendant of William (No. 21) visited Ballykean from Waterford and wrote a poem about it, so perhaps the family was living there then, but in 1837 the *Topographical Dictionary of Ireland* shows the house as then occupied by a Mrs. Foot. The farm was a few years ago occupied by a Swiss gentleman named Ernest Miville, married to an Irish wife, who operated it as a stud farm. There is an older house, supposedly of the seventeenth century, now used as a stable, and a larger house which looks like eighteenth century construction to me, or, as it appears to Mr. Hugo Read, who has seen it, as I have not, early nineteenth. Mr. Read says that immediately opposite the main entrance gate, on the other side of the road, is a small building about 30 by 18 feet, in a small garden of about a third acre. From its style he estimates the date of construction as about 1720-1730. It appears to have been a single building, later converted into a two-room cottage, and now used as a store. Mr. Read thinks this might have been a meeting house erected on land given by Daniel Penrose (No. 23). Mr. Read has been much interested in the legal history of the various Penrose properties in Ireland and has been extremely helpful in this regard. See my articles in *The American Genealogist*, 29:242-5, 35:293-4. The Wicklow Friends records are now in the Strong Room of the Eustace Street Meeting in Dublin where they were examined for me by Mrs. Olive C. Goodbody of Warriston, Glenageary, co. Dublin. This Richard Penrose was ancestor to all the British Penroses hereafter mentioned.

Children:

20.   i.   JOHN, b. in Ballykean 13 April 1668.
    ii.   JANE, b. in Ballykean 25 Feb. 1672; witnessed brother's marriage.
    iii.   RICHARD, b. July 1673/4 [according to Savage interpolation: 5 March 1673]; d. in Ballykean 4 Sept. 1699; bur. in Balymoran.
21.   iv.   WILLIAM, b. in Ballykean 18 Aug. 1676.
    v.   MARY, b. in Ballykean 3 March 1681/2.

18. ROBERT[6] PENROSE (*Robert,*[5] *Thomas,*[4] *John,*[3] *Nicholas,*[2] *Thomas*[1]), third son, born in Alverton *alias* Elverton, now called Elvington, Yorkshire, in September 1632, died in Ballykean, co. Wicklow, Ire., 10 Nov. 1677. He is supposed to have crossed over to Ireland in 1659, perhaps 'planted' as a Cromwellian soldier, in which case he was not yet a Friend, and it is clear that he became a Friend in co. Wicklow (see below). He must certainly have lived and died in Ballykean but whether it was he or his brother Richard (No. 17) who owned the property is not known. On 25 March 1669, i.e. after the arrival of his brother in Ireland, he married ANNA RUSSELL, died in Ballykean, probably as the result of childbirth, 5 April 1676, daughter of John Russell of Kilmackart in Carlow, of whom nothing else is known.

The Kilmackart Friends records are silent on these Russells who may not have been Friends. By 1673 Robert and Anna Penrose had, however, become Friends, for in Wicklow records there is this "Testimony: Robert Penrose and Anne his wife lived at Ballycaine, and received Truth early in the breaking forth of it in the County, and some Meetings at first held at their house and was very servicable in their day and died in Unity with Friends and left a good savor behind them." Both were buried at Ballymoran. On 26 May 1673 Robert was committed to prison for refusing to take an oath, there ten weeks. He and his wife are ancestors of all the Penroses of Pennsylvania hereafter described. See my articles in *The American Genealogist*, 29:242-5, 35:293-4.

Children, born in Ballykean:

    i.   ANNE, b. 16 Nov. 1670; d. 19 Aug. 1702; m. 12 Feb. 1687/8 NICHOLAS CHETAR *alias* CHAYTOR, uncle to Mary Chaytor, wife of her brother Robert (No. 22).
22.   ii.   ROBERT, b. 16 June 1673.
    iii.   MARY, b. 5 April 1676, d. 24 June 1686.

19. JOHN[6] PENROSE (*John,[5] John,[4] John,[3] Nicholas,[2] Thomas[1]*) was probably the man of that name who married in Wheldrake, 26 July 1655, ELIZABETH FAWCETT.

> Children, baptized in Weldrake:

i.   ELIZABETH, bapt. 22 Oct. 1656.

ii.   CATHERINE, bapt. 20 July 1657; m. ——— SAVAGE and had son *Richard,* who was living in Wheldrake in 1742 when he corresponded with the Irish Penroses.

iii. ELIZABETH, bapt. 12 Aug. 1663; m. ——— HOTHAM, and in 1742 their son *William* was living in Storpeate near Wheldrake.

iv.   GRACE, bapt. 20 Sept. 1666; had in 1742 a daughter *Ann Clarke* then living in Gainsborough in Lincolnshire, thirty miles from York. Whether Ann's maiden or married name was Clarke is not clear.

20. JOHN[7] PENROSE (*Richard,[6] Robert,[5] Thomas,[4] John,[3] Nicholas,[2] Thomas[1]*), born in Ballykean, co. Wicklow, 13 April 1668, died in Cools in that county, 23 Dec. 1731. He married at the house of John Wickham in Kilmurray, co. Wicklow, 21 Feb. 1687/8, MARY HALL, born 8 June 1664, died 13 Jan. 1728, daughter of Daniel and Dorothy Hall of Ballyterge, co. Wicklow. Intentions were declared at the Men's Meeting, Balykean, 23 Dec. 1687, 3 Feb. 1687/8; at the General Meeting, Casteldermot, 31 Feb. 1687/8 [day obviously wrong], and the General Meeting for the Province of Leinster, 11 Feb. 1687/8. The marriage certificate was signed by Jean Penrose and the marks of Dorothy, George, Daniel and John Hall. Mr. Read thinks the number of intentions unusual and supposes that this means that the marriage was opposed by John's aunt Alice, then the only senior member of the family still living, but three intentions are usual, and perhaps the couple happened to attend the fourth meeting and embraced the opportunity to increase the legality of the marriage. At the date of marriage John was not quite twenty, his wife nearly four years older, and he was an orphan.

John, his daughter Dorothy, and his first cousin Robert (No. 22), were among the witnesses to the wedding of William Evans and Hannah Eves, somewhere in co. Wicklow 22 March 1709 (Albert Cook Myers, *Immigration of Irish Quakers* [Swarthmore, 1902], p. 357).

> Children:

i.   ANNE, b. 31 Sept. 1688; d. 3 March 1689.

ii.   DOROTHY, b. 5 Jan. 1690; d. 27 March 1717.

iii. MARY, b. 31 Aug. 1693; d. 13 Jan. 1728; m. 17 Aug. 1715 WILLIAM SPARROW.

iv.   JOHN, b. 14 Feb. 1695; d. in Lamstown, co. Wexford, 30 June 1727; m. 20 Oct. 1720 CATHERINE DAVIS. James Ronald Penrose says he had a son *John* who m. ——— Neale; that their son John was teacher at Mountmellick School about 1820, and J. Denis Penrose mentions the son and grandson but calls the son Richard.

v.   RICHARD, b. 10 Oct. 1700; d. 11 Dec. 1717 at his master's house in Dublin, bur. Stephens Green. He was doubtless an apprentice when he died.

23. vi.   DANIEL, b. 6 June 1709.

21. WILLIAM[7] PENROSE (*Richard*,[6] *Robert*,[5] *Thomas*,[4] *John*,[3] *Nicholas*,[2] *Thomas*[1]), born in Ballykean 18 Aug. 1676, died 22 Feb. 1746. He married 20 June 1701 MARGARET GODFREY, daughter of John and Anne (————) Godfrey of Waterford.

Following the death of his father when he was ten, William must have been apprenticed to a tanner, for we find him styled in 1704 a 'skin[n]er.' The occupation of his first cousin Robert (No. 22) is unknown, but that Robert's like-named son (No. 29) was likewise a tanner. We do not know how wealthy the Godfrey family was but by 1704, when our William was aged 28, he was able to take a twelve-year lease of John's Gate House in Waterford with the adjoining tanyard and garden. This house was situated just behind the gaol at John's Gate and immediately within the old city walls. The lease calls him skinner, as stated, and shows that he was already in possession of the house when the lease was signed. The owner was Rebecca Dennis, widow of Samuel Dennis of Waterford, merchant, and the rent was £10/10s per annum. Eight years later a new lease was signed for 99 years at a rent of £8 a year, because a part of the garden had been excluded, and this time William is called a merchant. He was evidently appointed executor to the estate of Rebecca Dennis's son Samuel and was left the house for his life-time with reversion to William's own son Samuel (No. 25) of the remainder of the lease term. It then became part of what is known as the "Joint Estate" (see below). In 1703, one year before the first lease, Rebecca Dennis had leased for 999 years at £1/6s. per annum a plot of land just to the north of the garden of John's Gate House for building a Quaker meeting house, lessees Samuel Cooke of Stonwell, co. Tipperary, merchant; Stephen Collett of the same, skinner; David Hutchisson of the City of Waterford, joynor. Then in 1709 a lease 'for lives renewable for ever' was granted by the same Rebecca, at £1/10s. per annum, of a vacant lot to the west of the meeting house site and running up to the city wall, with frontage on Bowling Green Lane (now Manor Street), lessees William Penrose and Francis Annesley of the City of Waterford, merchants, Robert Wickham of the same city, maltster. It was because this lease included part of William's garden that his rent was reduced and a longer term given. William himself wrote on his copy of the new lease the following:

Memorandum that the piece of ground that is within mentioned part of the meeting house and eleven feet leading from the corner of the tanyard in a direct line to the town wall granted to me during my life and my children after me provided we come to the meeting and be esteemed to be honest men as a minute made in the meeting book will appear which was made by the men's meeting in Waterford about the year 1712 or 1713 which I was willing to let and hereafter have that ground fearing I might leave this house and yard and that some that might not be of our Society might take it which might not be convenient. Witness my hand this 4th 8mo. 1714.

William Penrose

In order to understand what happened to the properties of the Penrose family, it will now be well to have details of the Dennis family, whose last male survivor died in 1775, and whose whole properties in Cork and Waterford came eventually to the Penroses in one form or another. The chart printed on page 251 was prepared by Mr. Hugo Read on the basis of his own intimate knowledge of the history of these properties. Various daughters who did not inherit are omitted.

The two Dennis properties were, first, that of John Dennis which came to Cooper Penrose (No. 36) through his marriage, together with a very profitable timber merchanting business, including Woodhill, co. Cork, an estate purchased by Dennis from the widow of Sir John Dickson Haman, Bart. The other property was the 'Joint Estate' in Waterford, belonging to Samuel Dennis, which was left to the daughter Temperance but with reversion, if she died unmarried, as an undivided estate, between (a) John Dennis, (b) James Dennis, and (c) Samuel Penrose (No. 25), who was himself not a Dennis descendant but father to the two Penroses who married the Randall girls. These ladies, also, were not Dennis descendants but their great-grandmother, Bridget Harrison, had been wife to the first James Dennis. The first property came to Cooper Penrose directly, and the second was purchased from Matthew O'Hea after the death of his wife Susanna Dennis, granddaughter of the second James Dennis, while the third was left in equal shares to William Penrose (No. 39) and his brother Samuel (No. 38). Samuel sold out his share when he left Waterford on the occasion of the marriage of his son Samuel to Mary Hawkes (or about that time), and so it was again merged in his brother William's estate and descended to Robert William Penrose (No. 78) from whose trustees Joscelyn Denis Penrose (No. 103) purchased what remained of it in the year 1960. Thus, all the remaining property of the Dennises is now vested in Joscelyn Denis Penrose and he still has the rents from the sites of John's Gate House and the Old Meeting House in Waterford (about £10 per annum!).

The Dennis property in Cork has fared better. Though Woodhill was sold about 1936, and the property is now used commercially, some land around it is still held, as is also the majority of the old Dennis property in the Kyrl's Quay area of Cork. But Cooper Penrose added to this substantially during his time by investing on the north bank of the River Lee in Cork, immediately to the north of Penrose Quay, and these rents are substantially owned today. On the other hand, the Waterford line which stemmed from Samuel (No. 25), William (No. 39), Jacob (No. 60), and Robert William (No. 78) invested in leasehold property very largely from Waterford Corporation, and these have now for the most part run out, like the original investment of William (No. 21) in the New Quay area.

Children:

	i.	REBECCA, b. probably 6 March 1701/2; d. 3 April 1728; m. ISAAC JACOB of Waterford.
	ii.	RICHARD, b. 14 Feb. 1703.
24.	iii.	JOHN, b. 23 May 1706.
25.	iv.	SAMUEL, b. 1 Aug. 1708.
26.	v.	FRANCIS, b. 8 Oct. 1710.
	vi.	MARY, b. 26 Feb. 1712; d. 19 Sept. 1717.
	vii.	WILLIAM, b. 26 March 1715.
	viii.	JOSEPH, b. 14 March 1716; d. 20 Aug. 1717.
	ix.	JOSEPH, b. 26 June 1718; d. in 1730.
	x.	BENJAMIN, b. 5 Aug. 1720; d. in 1724.
27.	xi.	GEORGE, b. 5 Nov. 1722.
	xii.	ELIZABETH, b. 22 April 1724; m. JOSEPH BOYLE of Cork.

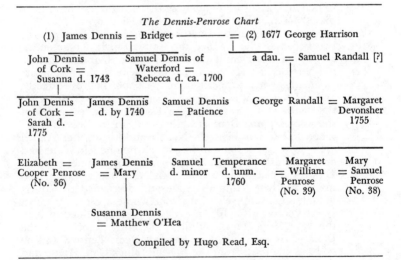

The Dennis-Penrose Chart

Compiled by Hugo Read, Esq.

22. ROBERT[7] PENROSE (*Robert,*[6] *Robert,*[5] *Thomas,*[4] *John,*[3] *Nicholas,*[2] *Thomas*[1]), second child and only son, born in Ballykean, co. Wicklow, Ireland, died in Pennsylvania at

an unknown date subsequent to 21 May 1735, when he and wife Mary signed the marriage certificate of their son Joseph (No. 30) in Maiden Creek, Berks County. It is possible that he was the Robert Penrose who signed the certificate of marriage of his son Richard, also at Maiden Creek, on 10 June 1747, though this signer may have been the son of the same name, who was then living in Bucks County but could have gone to Maiden Creek for the wedding of his brother. The late Albert Cook Myers, *Immigration of the Irish Quakers into Pennsylvania 1682-1750* (Swarthmore, 1902), pp. 289 f., is wrong in surmising that Robert was born about 1670 in Back Lane, Dublin. He was doubtless relying on a statement of Ellwood Roberts, *Old Richland Families* (Norristown, 1898), p. 205, where Ballykean appears in the corrupted spelling of "Blackane." While yet in Ireland, Robert Penrose married 29 May 1695 MARY CHAYTOR, born in 1677, daughter of Christopher Chaytor by his wife Margaret Jolley. Her name has appeared as "Mary Clayton" in all accounts which appeared before my article in *The American Genealogist*, 29:242-245 where, for the first time, the true reading, as found in Wicklow Friends records, was published. On the Chaytor family see *The American Genealogist*, 37:232 f.

The late Miss Anna Jordan of Quakertown, Pa., possessed a list of births of the children of Robert and Mary (Chaytor) Penrose in which the birthplace of the first, sixth and tenth children was given as Clanmaning, so from 1697 to 1715, Robert and Mary would appear to have been living there. There is also evidence that the son Joseph was born at Munnef or Munduff. Mr. Myers (*op. cit.*, 357) cites a marriage certificate of William Evans and Hannah Eves who were married in co. Wicklow, 22 March 1709, and among the witnesses was a Robert Penrose who must have been this one. He also cites (p. 289) a certificate of Dublin Two Weeks Meeting dated 21 May 1717 for Robert, Mary, and two daughters Margaret and Ann, and one son Christopher, and this was duly deposited in Philadelphia Meeting on 25 Oct. 1717, but the original cannot now be found. No record of this certificate was found in Dublin by Mrs. Goodbody but she did find a record of a certificate from the Men's Meeting, dated the same day, applicable only to the eldest son Christopher, who had been apprenticed to a Friend and was now released to go to America.

Upon their arrival in America, the family resided for a time in Philadelphia but then removed to Marple Township, then Chester, now Delaware County, the dates being given variously: 29 2nd mo. 1720 and 27 9th mo. 1724 (*Publications of the Genealogical Society of Pennsylvania*, 7:250) or 25 10th mo. 1724 and 27 3rd mo. 1726 (Hinshaw's *Encyclopaedia of American Quaker Genealogy*, 2:620 f.) . I take it that the first certificate pertains to Robert (No. 22) and the second to his son of the same name (No. 29). At Goshen Monthly Meeting, Chester County, there was received on 3 6th mo. 1726 a certificate of Darby Monthly Meeting which reads as follows: "Whereas Robert Penrose having requested a certificate for himself and his wife into the verge of your Meeting . . . he came from Ballykennon [sic] in Ireland (on recommendation of members there) which was accepted by Philadelphia Monthly Meeting and from thence recommended to us . . . they having had their residence with us for some time." On 30 5th mo. 1734 Robert Penrose and family were received at Gwynedd Monthly Meeting from Goshen Monthly Meeting. On 3 10th mo. 1734 Robert was appointed in Gwynedd as an overseer of Oley Preparative Meeting. These references in Gwynedd do not mean that they were actually living in Gwynedd, for that meeting then included considerable territory in Berks County, probably the area later in Maiden Creek Meeting. Morton L. Montgomery, *History of Berks County* (Philadelphia, 1886), p. 1022, says that Joseph Whyley and Robert Penrose were among the first settlers of Maiden Creek in 1732. There is, however, no record of probate or death of either Robert or Mary in Berks County. Miss Jordan's list gives the dates of their deaths, respectively, as 25 May 1774 and 2 March 1795, but these dates must be those of the son Robert (No. 29) and his wife, also named Mary. A woman who married in 1695 could hardly have survived her wedding a whole century. C. V. Roberts correctly states that there were thirteen children but is able to name only five. Ten names are found in Wicklow records, but the final three, born in this country, can be supplied from Miss Jordan's list—where the original is since her death I do not know—my knowledge of the list is from a copy supplied by a descendant of Steadman Penrose.

Children:

28.	i.	CHRISTOPHER, b. in Clanmaning, Ire., 24 March 1696/7.
29.	ii.	ROBERT, b. in Ireland 11 March 1697/8.
	iii.	MARGARET, b. in Ireland 24 Sept. 1699; to America with parents in 1717; m. (1) (intentions, Philadelphia Monthly Meeting, 29 April 1720, wedding 27 May 1721), JOHN SMITH of Darby.
	iv.	ANNE, b. in Ireland 20 Dec. 1701.
	v.	JOHN, b. in Ireland 29 Aug. 1703; d. 30 March 1714.
	vi.	MARY, b. in Clanmaning, Ire., 9 Sept. 1705; d. 29 March 1708. James Ronald Penrose's chart says she was b. in Culross Fife.
	vii.	PHEBE, b. in Ireland 9 Sept. 1707; d. 19 Jan. 1714/15.
30.	viii.	JOSEPH, b. in Munnef or Munduff, Ire., 21 Aug. 1709.
31.	ix.	WILLIAM, b. in Ireland 6 Oct. 1711.
	x.	JOHN, b. in Clanmaning, Ire., 20 Jan. 1715/16; not found in America.
	xi.	MARY, b. in Philadelphia 6 Oct. 1717; d. 10 July 1759, according to Miss Jordan's list. She certainly m. JOHN WILEY of Maiden

Creek, who d. August 1755, leaving two children, and I think she had previously m. in Oley (Exeter Women's Meeting), 24 April 1740, Isaac Wright, unless this was her mother.

Children (surname *Wiley*): 1. *Penrose*—his name appears frequently in wills, marriage certificates, etc., as witness. 2. *Martha*.

xii.   PHEBE, b. in Darby 25 June 1720; d. in September 1736, according to Miss Jordan's list. Her birth antedates the certificates of removal to Darby.

32. xiii.   RICHARD, b. in Darby 26 May 1722.

23. DANIEL[8] PENROSE (*John*,[7] *Richard*,[6] *Robert*,[5] *Thomas*,[4] *John*,[3] *Nicholas*,[2] *Thomas*[1]), youngest child and the only one whose descendants have been traced far, was born in Stephens Green 6 June 1709, according to James Ronald Penrose's charts; died in Ballykean 25 Nov. 1740, buried in Ballymoran. He married 17 Oct. 1725 GRACE DAVIS. He had a coat of arms, gave land for the Ballykean Meeting House, doubtless not the first building so used, but the first specifically built as a meeting.

Children:

33. i.   RICHARD, b. in Moortown, co. Wexford, Ire., 17 July 1726.
34. ii.   JOHN, b. 14 July 1728.
35. iii.   WILLIAM, b. in Ballykean 14 July 1730.
      iv.   DANIEL, b. in Ballykean 8 Sept. 1731; d. there 15 Aug. 1738, bur. in Ballymoran.
      v.   FRANCIS, b. 14 Oct. 1734; d. 31 May 1805; m. 21 Nov. 1759 SUSAN PIM; moved from Ballykean to Edenderry and back again, and had son *John Pim Penrose*, b. in Ballykean 22 April 1763. He may have been the Francis of whom Hugo Read has found a single lease in Cork ca. 1780.
      vii.   MARY, b. 5 Aug. 1736; d. 14 Aug. 1738, bur. Ballymoran.
      viii.   SAMUEL, b. 15 June 1738; d. 19 Dec. 1738, bur. Ballymoran.
      ix.   DOROTHY, b. 7 April 1740; m. 28 July 1760 JOSEPH EVES.

24. JOHN[8] PENROSE (*William*,[7] *Richard*,[6] *Robert*,[5] *Thomas*,[4] *John*,[3] *Nicholas*,[2] *Thomas*[1]), born 23 May 1706, died 17 Sept. 1739 aet. 33. He married in Carlow, 12 Sept. 1732 or 1733, ANNE COOPER, born 7 Nov. 1713, daughter of Edward Cooper of Cooper's Hill (formerly Iragh) by his wife Ann Inglefield, daughter of John Inglefield of Dublin. After John's early death, his widow probably returned to her mother in Carlow, but we next hear of her leasing a house in George Lane, Dublin, in 1746. The son William, having completed an apprenticeship with a firm of merchants, began to trade in his own name at this address. As a marriage settlement, William (No. 21) had settled on John (No. 24) some of his property investments in a leasehold site held from the Corporation at New Quay, behind George Street, together with a half interest in his merchant business.

Children:

36. i.   COOPER, b. 12 April 1736, 4:45 P.M.; d. in 1815.
37. ii.   WILLIAM, b. 29 Nov. 1737, 9:00 A.M., d. 1802, unm.

iii. MARGARET, b. 3 Nov. 1738, 1:25 A.M., d. Ballitore, co. Kildare, 31 Dec. 1744.
iv. JOHANNA ANNA *alias* JOHN ANNE, b. posthumously 28 Oct. 1739; m. RICHARD PIKE; no issue.

THE PENROSE FAMILY OF WHELDRAKE AND
BALLYKEAN AND THEIR DESCENDANTS IN
BOTH HEMISPHERES

By GEORGE E. McCRACKEN, Ph.D., F.A.A.R., F.A.S.G.,
of Drake University, Des Moines, Iowa

25. SAMUEL[8] PENROSE (*William,[7] Richard,[6] Robert,[5] Thomas,[4] John,[3] Nicholas,[2] Thomas[1]*), born 1 Aug. 1708, died 11 April 1765. He married 2 Jan. 1749 ANNA BEALE, born 7 Nov. 1713, daughter of Thomas and Mary (Pike) Beale of Cork. He was of John's Gate, Waterford. See Burke's *Landed Gentry of Ireland* (1912), 753 f.

Children, first six born in Waterford:

i.		MARGARET MARIA,[9] b. 15 Nov. 1750.
ii.		WILLIAM, b. 20 Dec. 1751; d. young.
iii.		ANNE, b. 17 Dec. 1752; d. 1754.
38.	iv.	SAMUEL, b. 10 Aug. 1754.
	v.	ELIZABETH, b. 12 April 1756.
	vi.	ANNE, b. 17 June 1757; m. 1773 ——— Watson.
39.	vii.	WILLIAM, b. 29 May 1758.
	viii.	MARY, b. 24 Oct. 1764.

26. FRANCIS[8] PENROSE (*William,[7] Richard,[6] Robert,[5] Thomas,[4] John,[3] Nicholas,[2] Thomas[1]*), born 8 Oct. 1710, died 13 Nov. 1775. He married 20 July 1757 ELIZABETH BEALE, born 11 July 1716, died 11 Dec. 1771, daughter of Thomas and Mary (Pike) Beale of Cork, and sister of his brother Samuel's wife.

Children:

i.		MARY,[9] b. 28 March 1739; d. in August 1779; m. THOMAS BARCROFT who was associated with her brother William in the Waterford glass works. They had a son *Ambrose Barcroft*.
ii.		THOMAS, b. 9 May 1740.
iii.		MARGARET, d. 1 Oct. 1774; m. 21 Sept. 1773 WILLIAM STRANGMAN, associated with her brother William in the glass works.
iv.		JOHN, d. 13 Jan. 1794.
	v.	ELIZABETH, b. 26 Oct. 1743; m. SAMUEL CHERRY.
40.	vi.	WILLIAM, b. 22 Dec. 1745.
	vii.	FRANCIS, d. 22 June 1749.

27. GEORGE[8] PENROSE (*William,[7] Richard,[6] Robert,[5] Thomas,[4] John,[3] Nicholas,[2] Thomas[1]*), born 5 Nov. 1722, died 8 May 1796. He married 12 Jan. 1749 ELIZABETH DUCKETT. With his nephew William (No. 40) he founded the Waterford glass works.

Children:

i.		JANE,[9] b. 28 Dec. 1750; d. 8 June 1752.
ii.		JOHN, b. 15 Dec. 1751; d. 28 June 1752.
iii.		SARAH, b. 20 April 1753; d. 22 Nov. 1755.
iv.		WILLIAM, b. 18 Aug. 1754; d. 2 Dec. 1755.
v.		MARGARET, b. 10 May 1756; m. (1), SAMUEL PIM; m. (2), SIMON MAX.

vi.   ELIZABETH, b. 15 Oct. 1757; d. in 1832; m. in 1775 HENRY RIDGEWAY.
vii.   JANE, b. 28 July 1761; d. 18 June 1762.
viii. CHARLOTTE, b. 17 Nov. 1762; d. 14 Nov. 1765.
ix.   REBECCA, b. 4 Jan. 1764; d. 17 May 1819, m. (1), JOSHUA FORBES; m. (2), in 1791 Abraham Neale, b. in co. Kildare 5 Feb. 1756, d. 20 July 1813 (see *Miscellanea Genealogica et Heraldica* 4th ser., vol. 1, p. 5, 1906).
41. x.   GEORGE, b. 17 Aug. 1765.

28. CHRISTOPHER[8] PENROSE (*Robert,*[7] *Robert,*[6] *Robert,*[5] *Thomas,*[4] *John,*[3] *Nicholas,*[2] *Thomas*[1]), eldest son, was born at Clanmaning, Ireland, 24 March 1696/7, and was early apprenticed to a Friend, David Tomlinson (*Publications of the Genealogical Society of Pennsylvania*, 3:234 Jan. 1906). In 1717, however, when near the end of the term, he was released to go to America with his parents, and given a certificate by Dublin Men's Meeting dated 21 May 1717. He married ca. 1719, at Middletown Monthly Meeting (now Delaware County), ANNE HUNTER, daughter of Peter and Jane (———) Hunter (certificate to marry requested of Philadelphia Monthly Meeting, 26 Dec. 1718, granted 30 Jan. 1718/19). No full list of his children can be given but Gilbert Cope, *The Smedley Genealogy*, 1901, p. 227 f., reports two daughters—there may have been more children.

Children, all found:

i.   ANN,[9] m. at First Presbyterian Church, Philadelphia, 24 April 1745, JOSEPH BLACK.
Among possibly others they had child (surname *Black*): 1. *Margaret*, b. 3 April 1748; bur. 26 July 1816 (Middletown Meeting); m. by lic. dated 26 Oct. 1768 David Regester. Children (surname *Regester*): (a) Robert, b. 20 Oct. 1769; d. 18 April 1852; m. Sarah Williams. (b) Joseph, b. 6 Jan. 1771; d. 26 June 1835; m. Sarah Russell. (c) John, b. 3 Oct. 1775; d. 10 April 1850; m. Priscilla Hoopes. (d) David, b. in 1778; d. 1 Jan. 1864; m. Jane Leonard.
ii.   JANE, m. when almost 21, 10 Nov. 1742, WILLIAM BURN, aged ca. 22.
Children (surname *Burn*): 1. *Mary*, b. 20 Nov. 1743; d. in infancy. 2. *Joseph*, b. 8 Nov. 1744; m. 2 Dec. 1766 Jane Lownes, daughter of George Lownes. 3. *Mary*, b. 27 Feb. 1746/7; d. young. 4 *William*, b. 30 Feb. 1749/50; d. in infancy. 5. *Rachel*, b. 15 May 1751; d. 15 March 1830; m. James Dunwoody. 6. *Isaac*, b. 4 July 1753; d. 4 July 1831; m. (1), Margaret Green; m. (2), Elizabeth Vernon. 7. *William*, b. 29 June 1756; d. 8 Feb. 1787; m. Rachel Worrall.

29. ROBERT[8] PENROSE (*Robert,*[7] *Robert,*[6] *Robert,*[5] *Thomas,*[4] *John,*[3] *Nicholas,*[2] *Thomas*[1]), second child and second son, a tanner, born in Ireland, probably at Clanmaning, 11 March 1697/8, died in Richland Township, Bucks County, Pennsylvania, 25 May 1774, founder of the Richland Penroses. He did not come to America in 1717 with his parents and some of the other children, but brought a Dublin certificate calling him Robert Penrose Jr., dated 10 May 1721, which he deposited at Philadelphia, 25 May 1724. He was probably the second of the two Robert Penroses who took certificates from Philadelphia to Darby as stated above in his father's sketch. As a wife is men-

tioned in these certificates, he must have had a wife unknown
to his descendants. What became of her and whether she had
children is unknown, but at Springfield Meeting in present
Delaware County, he married, 13 Sept. 1733, when he was aged
33, a young woman fourteen years his junior, MARY HEACOCK,
born 26 May 1712, died 2 March 1795, daughter of Jonathan
Heacock by his wife Ann Till, whose ancestors on both sides
are well described by Clarence Vernon Roberts, *Early Friends
Families of Upper Bucks*, 1925, p. 396-415, which work also contains an excellent, though not complete, account of the descendants of this couple. Both Robert and Mary signed at Maiden
Creek on 21 May 1735 the marriage certificate of his brother
Joseph. He was in 1743, and again in 1747, before Richland
Meeting for irregular conduct (excessive drinking), but was re-
instated on 21 Sept. 1749.

Children:

42. i.   JONATHAN,[9] b. 1 March 1735/6.
43. ii. JOSEPH, b. 10 Aug. 1737.
44. iii. JOHN, b. 19 Jan. 1739/40.
45. iv. WILLIAM, b. 15 April 1742.
    v.   ROBERT, b. 6 May 1744; d. intestate in 1792, a carpenter, shown in 1790
         Census (1/1/0). His estate was divided between the seven brothers
         and one sister (Mary Fell).
46. vi. SAMUEL, b. 21 Aug. 1748.
    vii. BENJAMIN, b. 30 Dec. 1749/50; living in 1792.
    viii. MARY, b. 5 May 1753; m. 8 Dec. 1774 EDWARD FELL of Springfield Town-
         ship, Chester County. They removed by certificate dated 16 Feb. 1775
         to that county, and she was living in 1792.
47. ix. JESSE, b. 2 May 1755.

30. JOSEPH[8] PENROSE (*Robert,[7] Robert,[6] Robert,[5] Thomas,[4] John,[3]
Nicholas,[2] Thomas[1]*), born in Ireland, according to James
Ronald Penrose's chart at Munnef, according to the Memorial
cited hereafter, at Munduff, 21 Aug. 1709, died at Maiden
Creek, Berks County, Pa., 2 March 1791, in his 82nd year. In the
Collections of the Genealogical Society of Pennsylvania is a
copy of a record taken from a Bible formerly owned by an unidentified Miss or Mrs. Penrose (died in Williamsport, Pa., ca.
1933), and purchased by George H. Neff of Sunbury, Pa., for a
small sum. This confirms the spelling Munduff and the dates
as given. He married at Maiden Creek, at a public meeting in
the meeting house, 21 May 1735, SARAH WILY or WILEY, daughter of Joseph Wiley. The marriage certificate is signed by both
Joseph and Sarah Penrose (the couple), and then in customary
form from right to left by the following witnesses: Robert Penrose [groom's father], Jos. Wily [bride's father], Mary Penrose
[groom's mother], Abigail Wily [bride's mother?], Robert Penrose Jr. [groom's brother], William Penrose [another brother],
Richard Penrose [another brother], Mary Penrose [wife of Robert Jr.], Phebe Penrose [groom's sister], Ann Wily [groom's
sister-in-law, not yet married?], John Wily [groom's brother-in-

law and bride's brother?], and by Thos Ellis, Sismore Wright, Jacob Holco[m]be, Frances Parvin, Thomas Parvin, the last five not clearly related. Joseph Penrose left a will dated 22 Aug. 1784, probated 6 May 1791 (Berks Wills, 3:171), mentioning son Isaac Penrose; beloved wife Sarah Penrose (£6 yearly); daughter-in-law Elizabeth Penrose, widow of son Joseph deceased, and his children; land on the south side of the great road from Reading to Easton [athwart which lies Maiden Creek Township]; daughter Abigail and husband George Rush, property for six years from 24 Jan. 1784; daughter Sarah Reed and heirs, £5 [sic]; daughter Phebe £50 [sic], daughter Mary £50 [sic], both obviously unmarried; beloved wife executrix, and son Isaac Penrose executor; signed, not by mark; witnesses: John Hutten, Owen Hughes, Penrose Wiley. See Morton L. Montgomery, *History of Berks County*, 1886, 1022. Exeter Monthly Meeting Minutes (D19, p. 364) contain a Memorial for Joseph Penrose dated 24 Sept. 1794 which was to be forwarded to the Quarterly Meeting, as follows:

He was born at Munduff in Ireland the 21st day of the 6th Month, 1709 and when young came to Pennsylvania with his parents, Robert & Mary Penrose. And after some years, having settled at Maiden Creek, a branch of this Monthly Meeting, where through the early Extendings of Divine Love and a concern to improve the talent committed to his Trust, he became qualified for weighty services in the Church; filling up the stations of Overseer & Elder with circumspection and Christian gravity. He was often successful in his Endeavors to compose Differences (among Friends) being of an affectionate and winning Disposition, cheerful & loving in Deportment, plain and pertinent in Expression. . . . Few have been more generally beloved than he was by all ranks of People within the Circles of his Acquaintance, so that we believe he in good degree experienced the saying of David 'When a man's ways please the Lord he maketh even his Enemies to be at peace with him.' He was afflicted with a paralytic Disorder some years before his decease which nearly disabled him . . . which circumstance (though trying) he bore with patience and resignation, and seemed to be waiting for his Dissolution . . . which was on the Second day of the Third Month, 1791, in the eightysecond year of his age. He was attended by many Friends and Neighbors to our Burying Ground at Maiden Creek.

Children:

48. i. ISAAC,⁹ b. ca. 1750.
49. ii. JOSEPH.
    iii. ABIGAIL, d. 31 Aug. 1782; m. shortly before 30 May 1781 GEORGE RUSH, son of William Rush deceased. Despite the date of her death, the will of her father seems to imply she was still living in 1784.
    iv. SARAH, m. shortly before 25 Nov. 1760 THOMAS REED, probably dead by 1784.
    v. PHEBE, unm. in 1784.
    vi. MARY, unm. in 1784.

31. WILLIAM⁸ PENROSE (*Robert,*⁷ *Robert,*⁶ *Robert,*⁵ *Thomas,*⁴ *John,*³ *Nicholas,*² *Thomas*¹), born in Ireland 6 Oct. 1711, died in Huntington Township, Adams County, Pa., ca. 1785. He married in 1738, under the care of the Exeter Monthly Meeting, ANN WILEY, died 26 Feb. 1804, probably a daughter of Joseph

and Abigail Wiley of Maiden Creek. He was granted a certificate for himself, his wife, and his children Hannah, Thomas and John, on 27 May 1762, and on 28 Oct. 1762 a similar certificate was granted for his children Jane, William and Susannah, in both instances to go from Exeter Meeting to Warrington Monthly Meeting in York County. No certificates were found for daughters Mary and Phebe, however, but the wife was doubtless the Ann Penrose who took another certificate to Warrington dated 27 Dec. 1764, returned on certificate in 1765, and was granted still another to Warrington on 30 Nov. 1774. Myers (*op. cit.*, 169) shows William as one of the patentees for Warrington Meeting House, 22 Jan. 1767; elsewhere (289 f.) he tentatively identifies him as son of Robert and Mary, and says that he later removed to Huntington Township, Adams County, where he and his wife both died.

Children:

i. MARY,[9] m. in Warrington, 21 Oct. 1762, THOMAS EDMUNDSON, son of Caleb and Mary.
ii. JANE, m. in Warrington, 3 May 1764, JEDIAH HUSSEY, son of John.
iii. PHEBE, m. in Warrington, 13 May 1766, THOMAS LEECH, son of Samuel, late of Newberry.
50. iv. THOMAS.
v. WILLIAM, no further information except that his wife REBECCA was received on certificate from Warrington at Philadelphia 12 Feb. 1785, and marked "since died."
vi. JOHN, perhaps the John in York County, 1790 Census (1/1/-).
vii. SUSANNA, m. in Warrington, 17 May 1781, DAVID CADWALLADER.

Children:

32. RICHARD[8] PENROSE (*Robert*,[7] *Robert*,[6] *Robert*,[5] *Thomas*,[4] *John*,[3] *Nicholas*,[2] *Thomas*[1]), born at Darby, Chester County, Pa., 26 May 1722, died a yeoman in Catawissa Township, then Northumberland, now Columbia County, 14 April 1799. He left a will dated 16 Aug. 1797, probated 26 Nov. 1799 (Northumberland Wills, I-218). He married, doubtless at Maiden Creek, 29 Oct. 1745, reported 31 Oct. 1745, MARGARET WRIGHT the younger, born 11 Feb. 1720/1, died 20 May 1802 aged 81/5/9, daughter of Sizemore and Margaret Wright. Both are buried at Roaring Creek near Catawissa. In 1790 he appears in Northumberland County (2/0/2) immediately above an Isaac Penrose doubtless his own son. A sketch of Richard appears in the Alfred R. Justice Collection at the Genealogical Society of Pennsylvania.

Children:

i. MARY,[9] b. 8 Aug. 1746; d. 25 July 1748.
ii. PHEBE (twin), b. 21 Jan. 1747/8; d. 19 Feb. 1747/8.
iii. ROBERT (twin), b. 21 Jan. 1747/8; d. 5 Aug. 1748.
iv. WILLIAM, b. 9 July 1749; d. 26 May 1750.
v. MARGARET, b. 8 Feb. 1750/1; d. 1 March 1751/2.
vi. MARY, b. 22 Nov. 1752; d. 24 March 1789; m. 14 Aug. 1778 SAMUEL HUGHES.

vii.   ROBERT (twin), b. 11 March 1755; d. 1824; m. 14 April 1775 REBECCA
       THOMAS, daughter of Thomas and Martha Thomas of Robeson Meet-
       ing, where the wedding took place. He was shown in Northumberland
       County in 1790 on the same page as his father (1/1/3).

viii. RICHARD (twin), b. 11 March 1755; d. 17 May 1784; m. at Robeson
       Meeting, 13 March 1778, SARAH EVANS, daughter of Robert and Mary,
       both deceased, and she m. (2), shortly before 25 April 1787, John
       Williams, and as such a former daughter-in-law is mentioned in his
       father's will.

ix.   ISAAC, b. 27 July 1757; m. out, and dismissed by Exeter Monthly Meet-
       ing 29 Dec. 1791.

x.   HANNAH, b. 26 Jan. 1759. According to evidence in her father's will, the
       statement of Mr. Justice that she m. —— GEORGE and went to
       Virginia seems to be disproved.

xi.   JOHN, b. 15 Sept. 1760; d. 25 Feb. 1769.

51. xii.   THOMAS, b. 20 Sept. 1767.

33. RICHARD[9] PENROSE (*Daniel,*[8] *John,*[7] *Richard,*[6] *Robert,*[5] *Thomas,*[4]
John,[3] *Nicholas,*[2] *Thomas*[1]), born at Moortown, co. Wexford,
Ireland, 17 July 1726, died at Brittis, co. Wicklow, 14 Dec. 1756,
buried at Ballymoran. He married 15 June 1749 MARY MARTIN.

Children:

52. i.   DANIEL.[10]
     ii.   THOMAS, m. ca. 1793 —— ——, and had *Isabella* and *Maria* (m.
           —— Sharp).
     iii. RICHARD, removed to Waterford, and had, *inter alios,* son *John* who
           had also a son John.
     iv.   GRACE, m. 11 Aug. 1777 ARCHIBALD NEVINS.
     v.   SARAH, m. ca. 1796 —— ——.

34. JOHN[9] PENROSE (*Daniel,*[8] *John,*[7] *Richard,*[6] *Robert,*[5] *Thomas,*[4]
John,[3] *Nicholas,*[2] *Thomas*[1]), born at Moortown, co. Wexford,
Ireland, 14 July 1728, died 20 Jan. 1759. He married in Febru-
ary 1750 MARY NEALE.

Children:

53. i.   SAMUEL NEALE,[10] b. 1755.
54. ii.   WILLIAM.

35. WILLIAM[9] PENROSE (*Daniel,*[8] *John,*[7] *Richard,*[6] *Robert,*[5] *Thomas,*[4]
John,[3] *Nicholas,*[2] *Thomas*[1]), born at Ballykean 14 July 1730,
died in Dublin 15 April 1783, buried at Ballymoran. He married HANNAH THACKER.

Children:

i.   HANNAH,[10] b. 13 Sept. 1754; d. 24 July 1807; m. in 1774 WILLIAM CHAP-
       MAN.
ii.   GRACE, b. 24 Aug. 1756; d. 6 Nov. 1802; m. 21 April 1778 AERY JESSOP.
iii.   ELIZABETH, b. 29 June 1758; d. 10 March 1785; m. 7 Jan. 1783 JAMES
       MORRISON.
iv.   FRANCIS, b. 28 April 1764; d. 24 Dec. 1783.

36. COOPER[9] PENROSE (*John,*[8] *William,*[7] *Richard,*[6] *Robert,*[5] *Thomas,*[4]
John,[3] *Nicholas,*[2] *Thomas*[1]), born at 4:45 P.M. 12 April 1736,
died 25 Feb. 1815. He married in 1763 ELIZABETH DENNIS, born
11 Nov. 1742, died 20 Jan. 1807, only child of John and Sarah
Dennis of Cork. On the Dennis family see No. 21. Cooper Pen-

rose was the last of the Quakers in this line and used a Cornish coat of arms. He was first apprenticed to his uncle Samuel (No. 25) in Waterford but was later taken into partnership with his father-in-law John Dennis of Cork. To the old Dennis property in the Kyrl's Quay area of Cork, he added substantially by investing on the north bank of the River Lee in Cork, immediately to the north of Penrose Quay, and in 1780 he began the rebuilding of Woodhill. He made a trip to France to buy art and succeeded in getting the famous French painter, Jacques Louis David, to paint his portrait, said to be one of the few occasions when David painted any but royalty and nobility on commission. The portrait descended to Joscelyn Denis Penrose who, after the sale of Woodhill, sold it to a dealer. It is now the property of the Putnam Foundation Inc., and is on exhibition in the Metropolitan Museum of Art in New York.

Children:

	i.	JOHN DENNIS,[10] b. 14 Nov. 1763; d. 2 March 1767.
	ii.	COOPER, b. 18 Feb. 1765; d. 8 Oct. 1765.
55.	iii.	JAMES, b. 8 Oct. 1766.
	iv.	SARAH, b. 19 Oct. 1767; d. 16 Jan. 1770.
	v.	WILLIAM EDWARD, b. 23 Sept. 1768; d. unm. 3 May 1841.
	vi.	ANNE, b. 4 Feb. 1771; d. unm. in Lincoln 11 April 1827.
	vii.	ELIZABETH, b. 18 July 1774; d. unm. in 1862.

37. WILLIAM[9] PENROSE (*John,[8] William,[7] Richard,[6] Robert,[5] Thomas,[4] John,[3] Nicholas,[2] Thomas[1]*), born at 9:00 A.M., 29 Nov. 1737, died unmarried in 1802. In 1758 he became a merchant in George Lane, Dublin, in a property which had been leased by his widowed mother twelve years previously. He appears to have been still in Dublin in 1762, because there is a deed of partnership for a Sugar House entered into in that year, William's share being £600. There is also a partnership deed of 1773 between Cooper and William Penrose and James Fisher, to take over the timber merchanting business in Cork which Cooper had previously run in partnership with his father-in-law John Dennis who had just died. This William is described as "Late of the City of Dublin Merchant but now of the City of Cork," and there is a strong presumption that this must have been Cooper Penrose's brother, so that it is probable that it was not he who was mayor of Waterford in 1770, as stated in the notes of James Edward Penrose (No. 89).

38. SAMUEL[9] PENROSE (*Samuel,[8] William,[7] Richard,[6] Robert,[5] Thomas,[4] John,[3] Nicholas,[2] Thomas[1]*) was born 10 June 1754. He married 25 July 1775 MARY RANDALL, died 6 Dec. 1793, daughter of George and Margaret (Devonsher) Randall, as shown above in Sketch No. 21.

Children:

| 56. | i. | SAMUEL,[10] b. 14 June 1776. |
| 57. | ii. | GEORGE RANDALL, b. 10 Sept. 1777. |

iii.   MARGARET, b. 15 Dec. 1778; d. unm.
iv.   ABRAHAM DEVONSHER, b. 6 Dec. 1779; m. BRIDGET WELSTED, daughter of John Welsted of Ballywalter, co. Cork, by his wife Bridget Hawkes (sister of Mary Hawkes, wife of No. 56). He had a son who d. *s. p.*

v.   ELIZABETH, b. 8 Dec. 1780; m. WILLIAM HAWKES.

58. vi.   WILLIAM, b. 3 Jan. 1782.

vii.   ANNE, b. 11 Nov. 1783.

viii.   JOHN, b. 29 May 1784.

ix.   MARY, b. 22 Aug. 1785; d. in November 1787.

x.   SARAH, b. 14 Dec. 1786; m. Samuel Hawkes.

xi.   JAMES, b. 18 Jan. 1788; d. 11 Nov. 1788.

xii.   FRANCIS RANDALL, b. 27 March 1789; d. 5 April 1790.

xiii.   MARIA TERESA, b. 21 April 1792.

39. WILLIAM[9] PENROSE (*Samuel,*[8] *William,*[7] *Richard,*[6] *Robert,*[5] *Thomas,*[4] *John,*[3] *Nicholas,*[2] *Thomas*[1]), born 29 May 1758, died after 1794. He married first, in 1779, MARGARET RANDALL of Cork, daughter of George and Margaret (Devonsher) Randall, as shown above in Sketch No. 21; and secondly, 14 Jan. 1790, ANN GOFF, daughter of Jacob Goff of Horetown, co. Wexford.

Children by first wife:

i.   ELIZABETH,[10] b. 24 April 1780; d. unm.

ii.   ANNE, b. 1 Sept. 1781; d. unm.

59. iii.   SAMUEL, b. 6 Sept. 1782.

iv.   MARIA, b. 22 Nov. 1783; m. ——— Jacob.

v.   GEORGE, b. 5 Sept. 1785; d.*s.p.*

vi.   JOHN, b. 16 March 1787; d.*s.p.*

vii.   MARGARET, b. 26 May 1788; d. unm.

Children by second wife:

viii.   WILLIAM HENRY, b. 1 Dec. 1791; d. in infancy.

60. ix.   JACOB, b. 4 March 1792.

x.   HENRY, b. 22 Feb. 1794; d.*s.p.*

40. WILLIAM[9] PENROSE (*Francis,*[8] *William,*[7] *Richard,*[6] *Robert,*[5] *Thomas,*[4] *John,*[3] *Nicholas,*[2] *Thomas*[1]), born 22 Dec. 1745, died 12 Jan. 1799. He married 15 Feb. 1778 RACHEL NEVINS, born 1 Jan. 1755, died 12 Sept. 1794, daughter of Thomas and Rachel (Pim) Nevins. With his uncle George (No. 27) he founded the Waterford glass works.

Children:

i.   ELIZABETH,[10] b. 21 March 1779; d. 10 June 1846; m. 12 Dec. 1805, according to James Ronald Penrose, ANTHONY ROBINSON (a different man from the one who m. No. vi below?).

ii.   FRANCIS, b. 25 Aug. 1780; d. 20 Nov. 1861; sold the glass works in 1799.

iii.   WILLIAM, b. 10 Aug. 1784.

iv.   JOHN PIM, b. 20 Dec. 1789; d. 29 Dec. 1821. Note by J. Denis Penrose (1950): "He is the man who passed on to Robert Penrose of Riverview, Waterford [No. 78] the information relating to the Yorkshire Penroses which his grandfather Francis must have got from Savage in 1742. My father got a copy of this information from Robert in 1894 at Riverview Ferry Bank, Waterford."

v.   THOMAS, b. 6 Jan. 1787; d. 10 Jan. 1787.

vi.   SUSANNE, b. 3 Sept. 1791; d. 19 Sept. 1814; m. 19 Sept. 1814 ANTHONY ROBINSON of Moate. [Note: this makes her die on her wedding day and one of the dates is probably wrong.]

41. GEORGE[9] PENROSE (George,[8] William,[7] Richard,[6] Robert,[5] Thomas,[4] John,[3] Nicholas,[2] Thomas[1]), born 17 Aug. 1765, died 29 March 1846. He married DEBORAH PIKE. Upon getting the Phillipstown estate left to him by John Duckett, he took the name of Duckett.

Children:

i. GEORGE PIKE,[10] b. 20 April 1794.
ii. JOSEPH PIKE, b. 23 Dec. 1795.
iii. MARY PIKE, b. 2 Feb. 1797; m. DR. HARTFORD of Carter Coar or Crae.

42. JONATHAN[9] PENROSE (Robert,[8] Robert,[7] Robert,[6] Robert,[5] Thomas,[4] John,[3] Nicholas,[2] Thomas[1]), born in Richland Manor, Bucks County, Pa., 1 March 1735/6, died in Richland Township, 1797, testate, leaving a will dated 7 April 1795, probated 7 Nov. 1797 (Bucks County Wills, 6:48). He leaves wearing apparel to his three sons; the beloved wife is unnamed but she gets furniture, a room to occupy, etc. The plantation in Rockhill where testator now lives, formerly property of brother Robert, is mentioned. Son Isaiah is to pay for this £340 in installments of £66, £66, £76/13/4, £76/13/4, which is £53/13/4 less than the total. Son-in-law John Walton gets 5/- [his wife in 1786 was named Hannah and she was still living in 1792 but how much longer is unknown], granddaughter Alice Richards [whose parents are unidentified], £10; daughter Mary, £33/6/8 [one-third of £100]; son David gets £66 out of a larger sum now due from him; son Robert £66 [£66/13/4 is one-third of £200]; daughter Martha, £60; daughter Sarah, £60; executors, brother William Penrose and son Isaiah; witnesses: Everard Foulke and George Shaw. Jonathan married at Richland Meeting, 10 May 1759, MARTHA JAMES, whose parentage still remains unknown, despite vigorous efforts to determine it. Jonathan was a farmer and weaver, residing on the John Morgan farm, which means, probably, that Morgan was owner of the farm about 1920. In the 1790 Census of Bucks Jonathan is shown with four males above sixteen, three females, in his household.

Children:

i. ISAIAH,[10] b. ca. 1760; d. s.p. ca. 1815; perhaps m. ANN ———. He left a peculiar will (Bucks County Wills, 9:223 and file): Isaiah Penrose i giv unto my brother robert Penrose my wearing close—what he ose me and my watch and desk a[s] well. I give unto Ann Penrose too hund Pounds and my tea kettle and my arm chair and my puter plats and my bible and bed tick close and resude of my estate to be equol between my three sisters Phebe Mary Martha I desire that Robert would pay my debts out of what I left him and this to be my will what I have wrote is my desire that mit stand isaiah Penrose. Abel Roberts [husband of sister Martha] was sued on 6 Dec. 1817 for what he owed the estate and the will was admitted to probate in the Court of Common Pleas as part of this suit. The jury found for the plaintiff with 6 cents damages and 6 cents costs. The will is merely a few scraps of paper containing also some accounts. The actual papers do not throw any light on who Ann Penrose was.

ii. DAVID, b. ca. 1763; living in 1799; m. MARY HARTZELL, of Rockhill Township; six children. For continuation of this line, see Roberts, *op. cit.*, p. 400.

iii. ROBERT, b. ca. 1765; d. unm. 16 Feb. 1829; will dated 28 July 1827, probated 25 Feb. 1829, devises to nephews Joseph and Samuel Penrose, and Joseph Smith, and to niece Anna Smith.

iv. MARY, perhaps unm. in 1795.

v. PHEBE, perhaps unm. in 1795.

vi. MARTHA, b. 25 Feb. 1772; d. 18 April 1855, bur. Richland Meeting; m. ca. 1796 ABEL[8] ROBERTS, b. Milford Township 27 Sept. 1770, d. 17 April 1837, bur. Richland Meeting, son of John[2] Roberts (Edward[1]) by his wife Margaret Enochs. Eleven children; for continuation of this line see Roberts, *op. cit.*, p. 432-467.

vii. SARAH, probably unm. in 1795.

viii. A DAUGHTER, m. ———— RICHARDS, parents of *Alice Richards*, granddaughter mentioned in Jonathan Penrose's will; she became second wife of that George Shaw who witnessed said will (for her children see Roberts, *op. cit.*, p. 521).

ix. ?HANNAH, m. in 1786 JOHN WALTON and was punished for marrying out. John Walton is called son-in-law in Jonathan Penrose's will. His wife in both 1786 and 1792 was named Hannah, but they removed to Northampton County and have not been traced further.

43. JOSEPH[9] PENROSE (*Robert,[8] Robert,[7] Robert,[6] Robert,[5] Thomas,[4] John,[3] Nicholas,[2] Thomas[1]*), born in Richland Township 10 Aug. 1737, died there 22 Aug. 1824. In 1768 he married ELEANOR ————, evidently not originally a Friend, since she applied for membership at Richland Meeting 15 June 1773, and was accepted 16 Sept. 1773. She died 12 Aug. 1822, aged ca. 90, in which case she must have been five years senior to her husband who was probably the Joseph in the 1790 Census of Bucks (1-1-3) next after William Penrose.

Children:

i. ISRAEL,[10] b. 31 Dec. 1768; living in 1827; m. 21 Oct. 1790 SUSANNA FOULKE, b. 5 Nov. 1766, daughter of Thomas and Jane (Roberts) Foulke. Seven children; for continuation of this line, see Roberts, *op. cit.*, p. 400 f.

ii. JANE, b. 7 Jan. 1771; d. 4 Dec. 1822; m. 4 Aug. 1806 SAMUEL PUGH, farmer, of Richland, d. in June 1819. Son and daughter.

iii. BENJAMIN, b. 3 Jan. 1773; d. in September 1777.

iv. JOSEPH, b. 27 Jan. 1777; d. 19 Nov. 1835; m. 20 May 1802 MARGARET JAMISON, b. 11 June 1779, d. 23 Oct. 1811, daughter of John and Jane (Crosly) Jamison. Four children; for continuation of this line, see Roberts, *op. cit.*, p. 401.

44. JOHN[9] PENROSE (*Robert,[8] Robert,[7] Robert,[6] Robert,[5] Thomas,[4] John,[3] Nicholas,[2] Thomas[1]*), born in Richland Township 19 Jan. 1739/40, died there 12 Feb. 1813. He married 8 Nov. 1764 ANN ROBERTS, born 16 April 1745, died 28 April 1841, daughter of John and Martha (Roberts) Roberts. In 1790 there was one householder between him (3-3-6) and his brother Joseph.

Children:

i. MARTHA,[10] b. 13 Oct. 1765; d. 20 March 1849; m. 30 April 1795 AMOS

RICHARDSON, farmer, of Rockhill, d. 10 Feb. 1850. All six children d. unm.

ii. ENOCH, b. 1 Aug. 1767; d. 22 Aug. 1842; m. (1), 26 Nov. 1801 MARTHA EDWARDS, b. 6 July 1776, d. 8 May 1804, daughter of William and Meribah (Gaskill) Edwards; m. (2), at Exeter Monthly Meeting in July 1812, ESTHER TOMLINSON, d. 28 Feb. 1842. One child by first wife, four by second; for continuation of this line see Roberts, *op. cit.,* p. 402.

61. iii. NATHAN, b. 1 April 1769.

iv. RACHEL, b. 7 Feb. 1771; d. 9 March 1797; m., as first wife, 26 Jan. 1795, GEORGE SHAW, b. in 1768, removed to Ohio; he m. (2), Alice Richards who was a granddaughter of Jonathan Penrose (No. 42). Rachel d.*s.p.*

v. JANE, b. 3 Nov. 1773; d. unm. 21 May 1848.

vi. THOMAS, b. 2 May 1775; d. 3 Dec. 1854; m. 11 March 1796 RACHEL HILLMAN, d. 5 April 1855. Six children; for continuation of this line, see Roberts, *op. cit.,* p. 403.

vii. JOHN, b. 7 Feb. 1777.

viii. ANN, b. 22 June 1779; d. 2 July 1872; m. 4 April 1799 GEORGE HICKS, b. 12 June 1770, d. 20 Aug. 1847, son of William and Hannah (Shaw) Hicks. Eleven children; for continuation of this line, see Roberts, *op. cit.,* pp. 272 f.

ix. EVAN, b. 2 April 1782; d. 11 Feb. 1861; m. 23 April 1807 REBECCA BALL, b. 2 March 1789, d. 5 Jan. 1852, daughter of Aaron and Margaret (Hicks) Ball. Four children; for continuation of this line, see Roberts, *op. cit.,* p. 403.

x. MARY, b. 9 May 1785; d. unm. 16 Dec. 1849.

45. WILLIAM[9] PENROSE (*Robert,*[8] *Robert,*[7] *Robert,*[6] *Robert,*[5] *Thomas,*[4] *John,*[3] *Nicholas,*[2] *Thomas*[1]), born in Richland Township 15 April 1742, died 26 Jan. 1808. He married 8 Nov. 1770 MARY ROBERTS, born 30 Nov. 1748, died 30 Nov. 1843, daughter of John and Martha (Roberts) Roberts. If one disregards the eleven intercalary days, she died on her 95th birthday. In 1790 William (2/0/4) lived next to his brother Joseph.

Children:

i. ABIGAIL,[10] b. 11 Sept. 1771; d. 14 Aug. 1854; m. Oct. 1799 EVAN ROBERTS, b. 20 April 1775, d. 26 March 1849, son of David and Phebe (Lancaster) Roberts. Four children; for continuation of this line, see Roberts, *op. cit.,* p. 434.

ii. MARGARET, b. 5 May 1775; d. unm. 31 Oct. 1826.

iii. SARAH, b. 21 Nov. 1778; d. 26 Aug. 1860; m. 4 April 1811 Caleb Edwards, b. 23 Oct. 1782, d. 7 Oct. 1862, son of William and Meribah (Gaskill) Edwards. Four children; for continuation of this line, see Roberts, *op. cit.,* 115.

46. SAMUEL[9] PENROSE (*Robert,*[8] *Robert,*[7] *Robert,*[6] *Robert,*[5] *Thomas,*[4] *John,*[3] *Nicholas,*[2] *Thomas*[1]), blacksmith, born in Richland Township 21 Aug. 1748, died 2 Feb. 1833. He married 9 Oct. 1777 SARAH ROBERTS, born June 1758, daughter of Abel and Gainor (Morris) Roberts. In 1790 he had two males above sixteen, three below, and four females in his household.

Children:

i. ABEL,[10] b. 7 Aug. 1778, d. 7 Dec. 1824; m. (1), 1 April 1802 KEZIAH SPEAKMAN, d. 11 Nov. 1803, daughter of Joseph and Catherine (Dennis) Speakman; m. (2), 2 May 1805 ABIGAIL FOULKE, b. 18 May 1779, d. 23 June 1851, daughter of Everard and Ann (DeHaven) Foulke, and she m. (2), 11 Sept. 1828 Jesse G. Heacock. No issue by any of these marriages.

ii. GAINOR, b. 14 March 1780; d. 22 Feb. 1865; m. RICHARD JARRETT, d. in 1827, son of Jonathan and Hannah (Mather) Jarrett of Horsham. Seven children; for continuation of this line, see Roberts, *op. cit.*, p. 404.

iii. WILLIAM, b. 14 March 1782; d. 20 Nov. 1823; m. in 1810 HANNAH JARRETT, b. 1 Oct. 1783, d. 24 March 1850, daughter of William and Ann (Lukens) Jarrett. Seven children; for continuation of this line, see Roberts, *op. cit.*, p. 404.

62. iv. EVERARD, b. 7 Oct. 1784.

v. MARY, b. 11 May 1787; d. 19 Sept. 1795.

vi. BENJAMIN, b. 16 Sept. 1791; m. RACHEL FRATT.

vii. SUSANNA, b. 21 Aug. 1793; d. 8 Aug. 1799.

viii. SAMUEL, b. 10 Aug. 1796; d. 16 June 1797.

ix. MARGARET, b. 20 Sept. 1798.

x. MORRIS, b. 16 June 1801.

47. JESSE[9] PENROSE (*Robert,*[8] *Robert,*[7] *Robert,*[6] *Robert,*[5] *Thomas,*[4] *John,*[3] *Nicholas,*[2] *Thomas*[1]), born in Richland Township 2 May 1755, died in Ohio 7 March 1836, buried near St. Clairsville. Mr. Roberts knew that he took a certificate to Exeter Monthly Meeting, Berks County, dated 21 Sept. 1775, and that he was still living in 1792, but nothing more. He married at Maiden Creek, Berks County, 17 May 1780, SARAH STARR, died 25 Nov. 1840 aet. 80, also buried near St. Clairsville, Ohio, daughter of Meredith Starr of Maiden Creek Township. Jesse, wife Sarah, and children Mary, Abraham, Benjamin, and Joseph, took a certificate dated 30 May 1787 to Crooked Run Meeting in Virginia; the parents and Abraham, Benjamin, Joseph, Phebe, William and Sarah, took another dated 28 Feb. 1803 to Redstone in Pennsylvania, received there 3 June 1803. Jesse and Sarah were again transferred to Plainfield Monthly Meeting in Ohio by certificate dated 30 Dec. 1814, received there 27 May 1815.

Children:

63. i. ROBERT.[10]

ii. ABRAHAM, disowned for disunity, Redstone, 2 March 1804.

iii. BENJAMIN, disowned for disunity, Redstone, 2 March 1804.

iv. JOSEPH, with wife MARY, granted certificate 28 Dec. 1810 by Redstone to Miami (Ohio), received 27 March 1811; disowned at Springborough Monthly Meeting for joining the Hicksites, he on 28 April and she on 24 March 1829.

v. PHEBE, m. —— CONNER, disowned therefor, Redstone, 28 Sept. 1810.

vi. WILLIAM.

vii. SARAH, m. —— WORKMAN, disowned therefor, Redstone, 3 March 1815.

48. ISAAC[9] PENROSE (*Joseph,*[8] *Robert,*[7] *Robert,*[6] *Robert,*[5] *Thomas,*[4] *John,*[3] *Nicholas,*[2] *Thomas*[1]), born ca. 1750, died at Maiden Creek, Berks County, 16 March 1837 aet. 86/4/3. He married first, ELIZABETH ——, died 16 Nov. 1784; and secondly, 11 May 1791 ELEANOR PARVIN, died in 1842 aet. 80.

Children by first wife:

i. MARY,[10] b. 8 July 1775.
ii. SARAH, b. 3 June 1776.
iii. ANN, b. 16 Aug. 1777.
iv. MARGARET, b. 26 Nov. 1778.
v. SAMUEL, b. 17 Aug. 1781.
vi. JOSEPH, b. 19 March 1783; d. 3 May 1786.

Children by second wife:

vii. JOSEPH, b. 13 March 1792; d. 17 July 1874.
viii. THOMAS, b. 7 Oct. 1793.
ix. PHEBE, b. 26 June 1795; d. 26 Jan. 1869; m. JOHN WRIGHT.
x. SARAH (twin), b. 20 Dec. 1796; m. at Exeter, 3 Nov. 1830, JEREMIAH LEE, son of Isaac.
xi. MARY (twin), b. 20 Dec. 1796.
xii. ISAAC, b. 12 Feb. 1799; d. 18 July 1803.
xiii. EPHRAIM, b. 14 July 1801; d. 8 Feb. 1876.
xiv. ELLEN, b. 9 Nov. 1803; d. 16 Sept. 1874.

49. JOSEPH[9] PENROSE (*Joseph,[8] Robert,[7] Robert,[6] Robert,[5] Thomas,[4] John,[3] Nicholas,[2] Thomas[1]*) died, *vitâ patris,* 15 June 1784 aet. 36. He married at Maiden Creek Meeting, 16 Nov. 1774, ELIZABETH TOMLINSON, who died 11 Jan. 1824, daughter of William and Anne Tomlinson.

Children:

i. MARY,[10] b. 8 July 1775.
ii. SARAH, b. 3 June 1776.
iii. ANN, b. 26 Nov. 1777; d. 15 May 1807.
iv. MARGARET, b. 26 Nov. 1778.
v. SAMUEL, b. 17 Aug. 1781.

50. THOMAS[9] PENROSE (*William,[8] Robert,[7] Robert,[6] Robert,[5] Thomas,[4] John,[3] Nicholas,[2] Thomas[1]*) married at Warrington Meeting, York County, Pa., 11 May 1775, ABIGAIL CADWALLA-DER, daughter of David Cadwallader, later of Loudon County, Virginia. He was in Huntington Township, York County, in 1790 (1/4/3), one from John Penrose on the same page.

Children:

i. AMOS,[10] b. 13 March 1776.
ii. HANNAH, b. 29 April 1779.
iii. ANN, b. 22 June 1781.
iv. WILLIAM, b. 9 May 1784.

51. THOMAS[9] PENROSE (*Richard,[8] Robert,[7] Robert,[6] Robert,[5] Thomas,[4] John,[3] Nicholas,[2] Thomas[1]*), born 20 Sept. 1767, died in Ohio (Deerfield Meeting), 29 Jan. 1853 aet. 86. He married SARAH HIBBS, died in Deerfield Meeting 28 May 1848 aet. 72. They first resided in Catawissa but when that meeting was part of Muncy Monthly Meeting took a certificate dated 23 Dec. 1812, covering the parents and first seven children, received at Short Creek, Ohio, 23 March 1813. By certificate dated 22 May 1827 the parents and two youngest children removed to Deerfield Meeting, and by somewhat later certificates so did Thomas, James and John.

Children:

i.   HANNAH,[10] b. 27 May 1797; m. in Short Creek, 2 May 1816, BENJAMIN STANTON.
       Children (surname *Stanton*): 1. *Charles Osborn,* b. 19 July 1817. 2. *Mahlon,* b. 22 June 1819. 3. *Ruth,* b. 10 Feb. 1821. 4. *Thomas,* b. 25 Feb. 1823.

     ii.   MAHLON, b. 7 June 1799; disowned for marrying out, 23 May 1821.

64.   iii.   RICHARD, b. 18 May 1801.

65.   iv.   JAMES, b. 2 July 1803.

66.   v.   THOMAS, b. 12 April 1805.

67.   vi.   JOHN HUGHES, b. 24 April 1807.

     vii.   JACOB HIBBS, b. 21 Oct. 1809, called Jason by Mr. Justice.

     viii.   SARAH ANN, b. 3 March 1813; m. (1), in Deerfield, 21 Feb. 1821 [*sic:* date probably copied wrongly] EMLEN GRIFFITH; m. (2), 20 Aug. 1845 ELISHA HOLLINGSWORTH. No issue by either marriage.

68.   ix.   JOSEPH, b. 26 April 1817.

52. DANIEL[10] PENROSE (*Richard,[9] Daniel[8] John[7] Richard,[6] Robert,[5] Thomas,[4] John,[3] Nicholas,[2] Thomas[1]*), of Brittis, co. Wicklow, died 27 March 1820. He married 14 Nov. 1800 ANNE DOYLE of Gayfields, Dublin.

Children:

69.   i.   GEORGE, [11] b. 29 Sept. 1801.

     ii.   MATILDA, b. 21 June 1809; d. 26 Oct. 1888; m. 9 April 1833 FRANCIS FRY.

53. SAMUEL NEALE[10] PENROSE (*John,[9] Daniel,[8] John,[7] Richard,[6] Robert,[5] Thomas,[4] John,[3] Nicholas,[2] Thomas[1]*), born in 1755, died in February 1816. He married 29 Jan. 1782 ELIZABETH SHANNON.

Children:

70.   i.   SAMUEL NEALE,[11] b. 5 Nov. 1782.

     ii.   JOSEPH JACOB, b. 5 May 1784; d. 7 Nov. 1858.

     iii.   SARAH, b. 8 June 1786; d. in January 1792.

     iv.   ANNE, b. 11 June 1788; d. 1 July 1803.

     v.   MARY, b. 18 June 1790; m. 20 Aug. 1813 JOSHUA PEET.

     vi.   ELIZABETH, b. 23 Aug. 1792; d. in 1864; m. 12 June 1816 THOMAS GOODBODY.

71.   vii.   GEORGE ROOKE, b. 10 Aug. 1794.

     viii.   THOMAS, b. 19 Jan. 1796; d. 28 Jan. 1797.

72.   ix.   FRANCIS, b. 3 Nov. 1800.

THE PENROSE FAMILY OF WHELDRAKE AND BALLYKEAN AND THEIR DESCENDANTS IN BOTH HEMISPHERES

By George E. McCracken, Ph.D., F.A.A.R., F.A.S.G.,
of Drake University, Des Moines, Iowa

54. William[10] Penrose (*John,[9] Daniel,[8] John,[7] Richard,[6] Robert,[5] Thomas,[4] John,[3] Nicholas,[2] Thomas[1]*) died in October 1791. He married at Cork, 3 June 1777, Mary Osborne.

Children:

i. Mary,[11] b. 14 May 1778; d. 20 Sept. 1783.
ii. Sarah, b. 30 May 1779; d. 24 April 1787.
iii. Samuel, b. 9 July 1780; d. 26 Oct. 1780.
iv. John, b. 31 Dec. 1781.
v. William, b. 15 March 1783.
vi. Mary, b. 12 Oct. 1785; d. 10 Nov. 1786.
vii. Samuel Neale, b. 22 Aug. 1787; d. 13 April 1789.
viii. George, b. 3 Oct. 1788; d. Sept. 1790.
ix. Mary Anne, b. 11 Oct. 1790; d. 30 March 1793.
x. Margaret, d. 21 May 1792.
xi. William Henry, d. 21 May 1795.

55. James[10] Penrose (*Cooper,[9] John,[8] William,[7] Richard,[6] Robert,[5] Thomas,[4] John,[3] Nicholas,[2] Thomas[1]*), born 8 Oct. 1766, died

19 April 1845, and was of Woodhill. He married 12 July 1794
LOUISA PETTITOT FITZGERALD, died 28 Oct. 1854, daughter of
Robert Uniacke-FitzGerald of Lisquinlan and Corkbeg, sister
and eventually the heiress of her only brother, Lieut. Col.
Robert Uniacke-FitzGerald who died without issue in 1832. See
Burke's *Landed Gentry*, 1939, p. 1788, where this couple is
credited with only seven daughters.

Children:

    i.   LOUISA,[11] b. 16 July 1795; d. 16 Sept. 1855.

    ii.   COOPER, b. 23 Sept. 1796; d. unm. 29 Jan. 1862, succeeded to Woodhill in 1845.

    iii.   ELIZABETH, b. 14 July 1798; d. 12 July 1800.

73. iv.   ROBERT UNIACKE-FITZGERALD, b. 1 July 1800.

    v.   FRANCES ANNE, b. 21 June 1802; d. 4 Aug. 1867; m. 24 June 1835 the REV. GEORGE GUMBLETON, Vicar of Affane (Cappoquin), d. in 1860.
        Children (surname *Gumbleton*): 1. *William E.*, b. in Woodhill 2 March 1840; d. unm. 3 April 1911. 2. *George, D. L.*, b. 4 June 1843; d. *s.p.* in Littlestones-on-Sea 25 May 1894; m. ―― Skinner.

74. vi.   JOHN DENNIS, b. 31 Aug. 1804.

    vii.   ANNE (twin), b. 17 March 1807; d. 26 Feb. 1885; m. 27 March 1855 T. B. L. STEWART, d. *s.p.* 1 Jan. 1874.

    viii.   GERALDINE (twin), b. 17 March 1807; d. 5 Jan. 1881; m. in 1842 the REV. JAMES GORDON of Florida, co. Down, b. in 1794, d. *s.p.* 12 Nov. 1867.

    ix.   GERTRUDE, b. 5 Feb. 1809; d. 19 March 1894; m. 4 Aug. 1835 SIR JAMES TAYLOR INGHAM, b. in 1805, d. in 1890, second son of Joshua Ingham of Blake Hall, Yorkshire. See Burke's Landed Gentry, 1939, p. 1208 f.
        Children (surname *Ingham*): 1. *Louisa Pettitot FitzGerald*, b. 19 Jan. 1837; d. 2 Dec. 1839. 2. *James Penrose*, b. 2 June 1838; d. 28 Nov. 1879. 3. *Geraldine Marion*, b. 29 July 1840; d. unm. 13 Feb. 1912. 4. *Matilda Jane* (twin), b. 7 Feb. 1842; d. 17 April 1843. 5. *Gertrude* (twin), b. 7 Feb. 1842; d. unm. 24 June 1906. 6. *Alice Martha*, b. 5 April 1844; d. unm. 25 June 1923. 7. *Robert Wood*, b. 8 May 1846; d. 10 Jan. 1928; m. his first cousin, Mary Elizabeth Penrose.

    x.   HENRIETTA, b. 15 Feb. 1811; d. unm. 16 May 1880.

    xi.   SARAH ELIZABETH, b. 5 March 1813; d. 12 Jan. 1895; m. 3 Dec. 1840 CAPT. ROBERT ST. LEGER ATKINS, b. in 1802, d. 26 Aug. 1858, of Waterpark.
        Children (surname *Atkins*): 1. *Robert St. Leger*, b. 12 Nov. 1842; d. unm. 10 March 1888. 2. *Louisa Pettitot St. Leger*, b. 6 Jan. 1845; m. 18 June 1868 George Moore. 2 sons and 5 daughters. 3. *Mary St. Leger*, b. 7 May 1847; d. 9 March 1935; m. 12 Sept. 1874 John Borlase Warren. 3 daughters. 4. *Delta St. Leger*, b. 19 Feb. 1849; d. unm. 5 May 1877.

    xii.   JAMES WILLIAM EDWARD, b. 26 Nov. 1816; d. unm. 24 April 1842.

75. xiii.   WILLIAM, b. 3 Nov. 1818.

56. SAMUEL[10] PENROSE (*Samuel*,[9] *Samuel*,[8] *William*,[7] *Richard*,[6] *Robert*,[5] *Thomas*,[4] *John*,[3] *Nicholas*,[2] *Thomas*[1]), born 14 June 1776, died 3 March 1869. He married in June 1799 MARY HAWKES, daughter of John Hawkes of Sirmount, co. Cork.

Children:

76. i.   SAMUEL,[11] b. in 1804.

    ii.   JOHN, b. in 1805; m. HESTER GOLLOCK, daughter of Thomas Gollock of Elmglyn.

    iii.   BRIDGET, d. 9 Dec. 1859; m. MASSY HUTCHINSON WARREN.

    v.   MARY, d. unm.

57. GEORGE RANDALL[10] PENROSE (*Samuel,*[9] *Samuel,*[8] *William,*[7] *Richard,*[6] *Robert,*[5] *Thomas,*[4] *John,*[3] *Nicholas,*[2] *Thomas*[1]), born 10 Sept. 1777, died 19 Jan. 1864. He married MARGARET PIM, died 16 April 1856, daughter of Samuel and Margaret Pim.

Children:

i. SAMUEL GEORGE,[11] b. 28 Sept. 1819; d. young.
ii. JOHN PIM, b. 28 Oct. 1822, d. *s.p.* in 1889; m. at Limerick, in 1853, ANNE ROBINSON.
iii. DEVONSHER GEORGE, b. 22 May 1824; d. unm. in 1870.
iv. MARGARET MARIA, b. 16 Aug. 1825; d. unm.
v. ANNA ELIZA, b. 10 Sept. 1828; d. young.

58. WILLIAM[10] PENROSE (*Samuel,*[9] *Samuel,*[8] *William,*[7] *Richard,*[6] *Robert,*[5] *Thomas,*[4] *John,*[3] *Nicholas,*[2] *Thomas*[1]) was born 3 Jan. 1782. The name of his wife is unknown. See Burke's *Landed Gentry of Ireland,* 1958.

Child:

i. SIR GEORGE DEVONSHER (Kt. Bach.); m. (1), MARY MOLLOY, d. in 1884, daughter of Keiran Molloy; m. (2), MARY GERTRUDE DUNNE, d. in 1912, daughter of Jeremiah Dunne of Dublin.

59. SAMUEL[10] PENROSE (*William,*[9] *Samuel,*[8] *William,*[7] *Richard,*[6] *Robert,*[5] *Thomas,*[4] *John,*[3] *Nicholas,*[2] *Thomas*[1]), born 6 Sept. 1782, died in 1811. He married ELIZABETH SPARROW of Oaklands, died in 1842, daughter of Richard Sparrow. She married, secondly, Sir Richard Keane, Bart. See Burke's *Landed Gentry of Ireland,* 1912, p. 556.

Child:

77. i. WILLIAM HENRY,[11] b. 8 July 1810.

60. CAPT. JACOB[10] PENROSE (*William,*[9] *Samuel,*[8] *William,*[7] *Richard,*[6] *Robert,*[5] *Thomas,*[4] *John,*[3] *Nicholas,*[2] *Thomas*[1]), born 4 March 1792, died 15 Oct. 1869. He married in 1826 SARAH ANNE COOKE, daughter of Robert Cooke. Captain Penrose was of Adelphi, Waterford, and was an officer in the 33rd Regiment. See Burke's *Landed Gentry of Ireland,* 1912, p. 556.

Children:

78. i. ROBERT WILLIAM,[11] b. in 1827.
ii. HENRY, b. in 1830; d. unm. in 1860.
iii. JACOB, b. in 1831; d. in 1868; m. MARION ELIZABETH COOKE.
     Children: 1. *Donald William Henry,*[12] living in 1921. 2. *Marion Annette Georgina,* d. unm. 25 Jan. 1884.
iv. ANNE, d. unm. 31 Oct. 1881.
v. MARIA, d. unm. 4 Jan. 1894.

61. NATHAN[10] PENROSE (*John,*[9] *Robert,*[8] *Robert,*[7] *Robert,*[6] *Robert,*[5] *Thomas,*[4] *John,*[3] *Nicholas,*[2] *Thomas*[1]), born in Richland Township 1 April 1769, removed in 1820 to Yonge, Upper Canada, where he died before 1835. In 1794 he married HANNAH HICKS, daughter of William and Hannah (Shaw) Hicks.

Children:

i. MARTHA,[11] b. 6 June 1795; m. JOHN SMITH.
ii. LAVINIA, b. 5 Oct. 1798; m. 20 April 1815 WILLIAM HEACOCK, b. 19 Jan. 1790, d. 7 Nov. 1877, son of Jesse and Tacy (Thompson) Heacock. Two children; for continuation of this line see Roberts, *op. cit.*, p. 254.
79. iii. NATHAN, b. 24 Nov. 1800.
iv. TACY, b. 18 March 1808.
80. v. WASHINGTON HICKS, b. 17 Sept. 1809.
vi. WILLIAM, b. 18 Oct. 1812.

62. DR. EVERARD[10] PENROSE (*Samuel,*[9] *Robert,*[8] *Robert,*[7] *Robert,*[6] *Robert,*[5] *Thomas,*[4] *John,*[3] *Nicholas,*[2] *Thomas*[1]), a physician, born in Richland Township 7 Oct. 1784, died in Hilltown Township 30 Aug. 1823. He married a woman named BRIDGET but she was apparently not the mother of his children.

Children:

81. i. STEADMAN,[11] b. 2 Feb. 1808.
ii. WILLIAM, minor in 1823.
iii. SARAH, minor in 1823. She and her brother William appear as Dr. Penrose's children in Roberts, *op. cit.*, p. 404, but what evidence Mr. Roberts had for their existence has not been found. The only probate records for Dr. Penrose discovered in the Bucks County courthouse in 1961 were guardianship papers of Steadman Penrose which prove that he was son of the physician.

63. ROBERT[10] PENROSE (*Jesse,*[9] *Robert,*[8] *Robert,*[7] *Robert,*[6] *Robert,*[5] *Thomas,*[4] *John,*[3] *Nicholas,*[2] *Thomas*[1]) was not included in the certificates granted from Crooked Run to Redstone, as he was doubtless already married. It should be pointed out that placing him in this posiiton is not quite certain. With wife RACHEL he took a certificate from Young Street Monthly Meeting, Upper Canada, including children Jesse, Mark, Isaac, Edwin and Sarah, dated 13 April 1815, to Short Creek, thence to Plainfield by another dated 22 Sept. 1822. Since this was the meeting which Jesse[9] Penrose also joined, it is probable that we are right in identifying Robert as Jesse's son. Rachel and Sarah were disowned for joining Hicksites at Stillwater, 24 Oct. 1829, but Rachel and Jesse were granted a certificate at Concord to go to Clear Creek, Ill., 21 Oct. 1846, Sarah and Rachel having come to Concord from Plainfield 3 Oct. 1828, received 24 Dec. 1828. Another Short Creek certificate dated 26 Nov. 1818 gives Robert's name as Albert but he has the same wife and children.

Children:

i. JESSE,[11] certificate from Plainfield to Concord dated 23 Oct. 1828, received 19 Nov. 1828; disowned for joining Hicksites 26 Dec. 1829; went with mother to Illinois in 1846.
ii. MARK, condemned for marrying out, 14 Jan. 1847, but went to Clear Creek 18 Feb. 1847.
iii. ISAAC, disowned for joining Hicksites, Stillwater, 24 Oct. 1829.
iv. EDWIN, m. under Plainfield auspices at St. Clairsville, 5 March 1828, MARY SPENCER, daughter of Nathan and Ann Spencer of Belmont County, Ohio; disowned for joining Hicksites, 1829; their children

900

appear in three certificates, one to Alum Creek, Delaware County, Ohio, 1841.

Children: 1. *Lavinia.*[12] 2. *Eliza.* 3 *Ann.* 4. *Robert* or *Rachel* (once as Robert, twice as Rachel). 5. *Nathan Linville.* 6. *Jesse,* b. after 1846.

    v.   SARAH, received from Plainfield at Concord 24 Dec. 1828; disowned as Hicksite in 1829; m. —— WARD, condemned for so doing, Concord 22 Nov. 1837.

64. RICHARD[10] PENROSE *(Thomas,[9] Richard,[8] Robert,[7] Robert,[6] Robert,[5] Thomas,[4] John,[3] Nicholas,[2] Thomas[1])* born, probably at Catawissa, Pa., 18 May 1801, died 27 April 1883, buried at Pennsville, Ohio, then elder of Deerfield Meeting. He was restored to membership at Deerfield, by consent of Short Creek, 18 June 1833. His wife was ANN ELIZABETH SWICKARD, also an elder at Deerfield when she died 24 March 1884 aet. 75.

Children:

    i.   JOSEPH,[11] d. 2 May 1892 aet. 63; became Friend 13 March 1834.
    ii.   JASON, became Friend 13 March 1834; m. in Deerfield, 24 May 1854, MARTHA HARMER.
        Children: 1. *Charles,*[12] b. 5 April 1855. 2. *Rachel Ann,* b. 23 Nov. 1857. 3. *William H.,* b. 2 Feb. 1861. 4. *Hannah S.,* b. 23 April 1867.
    iii.   MARGARET, b. 25 July 1836; d. 5 May 1840 aet. 3.
    iv.   BARCLAY, b. 8 April or May 1841; d. 20 April 1920, bur. Pennsville; m. in Stillwater MARY GILBERT, b. 1 Jan. 1843, d. 11 Jan. 1929, daughter of Joel and Elizabeth (Smith) Gilbert.
        Children: 1. *Oliver J.,*[12] b. 14 June 1862. 2. *Elizabeth.* 3. *Mahlon.*
    v.   HANNAH, b. 10 Oct. 1843.
    vi.   MARY, b. 9 July 1848.

65. JAMES[10] PENROSE *(Thomas,[9] Richard,[8] Robert,[7] Robert,[6] Robert,[5] Thomas,[4] John,[3] Nicholas,[2] Thomas[1])*, born, probably at Catawissa, 2 July 1803. He married ca. 1833 REBECCA FARMER, born 3 Jan. 1805, died 8 Aug. 1855, buried Salinesville, Ohio, daughter of John and Mary Farmer of New Garden Meeting, Ohio.

Children:

82.   i.   WILLIAM,[11] b. 7 Nov. 1834.
    ii.   MARY, b. 30 June 1836; m., perhaps, —— NAYLOR, disowned Deerfield 16 Sept. 1858.
    iii.   SARAH, b. 8 July 1838.
    iv.   MERIBAH, b. 3 June 1840.
    v.   THOMAS, b. 7 May 1842; condemned for marrying out 17 Nov. 1859.
    vi.   RHODA, b. 27 Feb. 1844.

66. THOMAS[10] PENROSE *(Thomas,[9] Richard,[8] Robert,[7] Robert,[6] Robert,[5] Thomas,[4] John,[3] Nicholas,[2] Thomas[1])* was born 12 April 1805. He married at Deerfield Meeting, Ohio, 24 Nov. 1830, MARIA CLENDENON. Thomas and his wife died in West Branch, Iowa, both aet. 75.

Children:

    i.   CLARKSON T.,[11] b. 22 Sept. 1831.
    ii.   OSBORN, b. 4 Nov. 1833; m. in Deerfield, 22 Aug. 1855, but in Pennsville, SUSAN A. WOOD, daughter of Joshua and Esther Wood of Washington County, Ohio.

901

iii.   ISAAC C., b. 1 April 1836; m. in Pennsville, 19 Aug. 1857, MARY JANE NAYLOR, daughter of Abraham and Rachel Naylor.

iv.   WILLIAM W.

v.   JAMES.

vi.   EMLEN G., b. in Chesterfield, Morgan Co., Ohio, 22 Aug. 1844; living in 1910 in Tama, Tama Co., Iowa, where he was a hardware merchant; m. JENNIE E. STODDARD, daughter of Joel Stoddard, and had a son *Frank B.*, b. in July 1871; living in 1910 in Tama. See R. J. Caldwell, *A History of Tama County, Iowa* (Chicago-New York), 1910, 2:557. An obituary in *Annals of Iowa* (18 [1931-33] 79) adds that he had been councilman and mayor of Tama, served two terms as state senator (beginning 1893) and d. in Tama 20 Nov. 1930.

vii.   HANNAH.

JOHN HUGHES[10] PENROSE (*Thomas,*[9] *Richard,*[8] *Robert,*[7] *Robert,*[6] *Robert,*[5] *Thomas,*[4] *John,*[3] *Nicholas,*[2] *Thomas*[1]), born, probably at Catawissa, 24 April 1807, died at Deerfield, Ohio, 2 May 1852 aet. 49. He married first, at Cross Creek, 28 April 1830, ANNA CREW, died 12 Dec. 1840, buried Pennsville, daughter of Jacob and Elizabeth Crew of Jefferson County, Ohio, recorded Plymouth-Smithfield Monthly Meeting; and secondly, at Short Creek, 24 April 1844, HANNAH M. LIGHTFOOT, daughter of Samuel and Rachel Lightfoot of Jefferson County. She may have been the Hannah who married at Deerfield, 22 Dec. 1852, Edward Maule, unless this was her step-daughter.

Children by first wife:

i.   SARAH ELIZABETH,[11] b. 16 April 1832; disowned for marrying out, Deerfield, 14 Feb. 1856.

ii.   HANNAH, b. 21 Aug. 1834; perhaps m. Deerfield, 22 Dec. 1852, EDWARD MAULE, unless this was her step-mother.

iii.   JACOB, b. 25 July 1836.

iv.   JOHN D., b. 27 Sept. 1840.

Children by second wife:

v.   MARY, b. 9 Oct. 1846.

vi.   CHARLES, b. 2 Dec. 1848.

vii.   JANE, b. 6 Nov. 1851.

68. JOSEPH[10] PENROSE (*Thomas,*[9] *Richard,*[8] *Robert,*[7] *Robert,*[6] *Robert,*[5] *Thomas,*[4] *John,*[3] *Nicholas,*[2] *Thomas*[1]), born 26 April 1817, died 25 Nov. 1894 aet. 76. He married first, at Pennsville, Ohio (recorded Deerfield), 22 Aug. 1838, MARY GILBERT, daughter of Abel and Rebecca Gilbert; and secondly, at Pennsville (recorded Deerfield), 20 May 1846, MILDRED WORTHINGTON, daughter of William and Elizabeth Worthington of Muskingum County, Ohio.

Children by first wife:

i.   ELVIRA,[11] b. 9 Oct. 1839; m. 30 Dec. 1858 ASHER MOTT.

ii.   ALBERT, b. 24 Feb. 1841.

Children by second wife:

iii.   SARAH, b. 22 Feb. 1850; d. 25 April 1858.

iv.   LINDLEY, b. 18 May 1852; disowned for marrying out, 18 Oct. 1880.

v.   ELIZABETH, b. 24 Oct. 1854; m. 24 Oct. 1877 NATHAN BURGESS.

vi.   John Addison, b. 30 Sept. 1857.
vii. Eliza Jane, b. 24 Feb. 1865; m. ———— Cook, disowned for marrying out 19 Sept. 1887.

69. George[11] Penrose (*Daniel,[10] Richard,[9] Daniel,[8] John,[7] Richard,[6] Robert,[5] Thomas,[4] John,[3] Nicholas,[2] Thomas[1]*) was born 29 Sept. 1801. He married Abigail Barker of Ontario, Canada.

Children:

    i.   Thomas,[12] b. in 1827; d. in 1844.
83. ii.   James Doyle, b. in Canada 30 Aug. 1829.
    iii. Sarah Eliza, b. 4 Oct. 1834; d. in 1849.
    iv. George Cooper, b. 14 Sept. 1837.

70. Samuel Neale[11] Penrose (*Samuel Neale,[10] John,[9] Daniel,[8] Daniel,[7] Richard,[6] Robert,[5] Thomas,[4] John,[3] Nicholas,[2] Thomas[1]*) was born 5 Nov. 1782. He married in 1804 Charlotte Harmon.

Children:

    i.   Charlotte,[12] d. 2 Jan. 1814.
    ii.   Frances Elizabeth, b. in 1817; d. 20 Oct. 1858.
    iii. George. Had son and daughter unknown.
84. iv. Edward, b. in 1810.
    v.   Henry Joseph, b. in 1816; went to sea ca. 1846.

71. George Rooke[11] Penrose (*Samuel Neale,[10] John,[9] Daniel,[8] Daniel,[7] Richard,[6] Robert,[5] Thomas,[4] John,[3] Nicholas,[2] Thomas[1]*), born 10 Aug. 1794, died 23 June 1865. He married 3 March 1824 Anne Thacker.

Children:

    i.   Anne Shannon,[12] b. 10 July 1825; d. 19 Aug. 1890; m. 2 June 1863 Joseph Beale.
    ii.   Barker Thacker, b. 25 Oct. 1826; d. 19 March 1903; m. in 1855 Fanny Crawford.
85. iii. Frederick George, b. 2 Aug. 1828.
    iv. Alexander, b. 17 Aug. 1830; m. Dora Trumbell.
    v.   Jane, b. 29 May 1832; d. unm. in Monkstown 29 Aug. 1907.
    vi. Henry, b. 14 June 1836; d. in 1863; m. Elizabeth Gilbert.
    vii. Samuel, b. 14 April 1838; went to Australia, married a widow, and had five children.

72. Francis[11] Penrose (*Samuel Neale,[10] John,[9] Daniel,[8] Daniel,[7] Richard,[6] Robert,[5] Thomas,[4] John,[3] Nicholas,[2] Thomas[1]*), born 3 Nov. 1800, died in 1863. He married in 1831 Anna Slater.

Children:

    i.   Robert Samuel,[12] d. unm.
    ii.   Elizabeth, d. unm. 8 Nov. 1902.
    iii. Francis, d. in 1842.
    iv. Adelaide, d. unm.
    v.   Edward Henry, came to America.
    vi. Dinah or Diana, d. young.
    vii. Frederick, d. young.
    viii. Anna, m. the Rev. Canon French of Stokestown.

73. ROBERT UNIACKE FITZGERALD[11] PENROSE (*James,*[10] *Cooper,*[9] *John,*[8] *William,*[7] *Richard,*[6] *Robert,*[5] *Thomas,*[4] *John,*[3] *Nicholas,*[2] *Thomas*[1]), born 1 July 1800, died at Lismore 12 June 1857. He married 14 Feb. 1830 FRANCIS MATILDA AUSTEN, daughter of the Rev. Robert Austen by his wife, the Hon. Matilda Sophia Cokayne, daughter of the Hon. William Cokayne, youngest son of Charles, 5th Viscount Cullen. Upon inheriting the FitzGerald property in 1834, he took as his name ROBERT UNIACKE PENROSE-FITZGERALD, of Corkbeg and Lisquinlan. See Burke's *Landed Gentry*, 1939, p. 1788.

Children:

	i.	MATILDA SOPHIA GEORGINA,[12] b. 9 April 1838; d. 3 Jan. 1903.
86.	ii.	ROBERT UNIACKE, b. 10 July 1839.
87.	iii.	CHARLES COOPER, b. 30 April 1841.
88.	iv.	JAMES HENRY BRABAZON, b. 1 July 1843.
	v.	GERALDINE FRANCES LOUISA, also called MAE, b. 17 Jan. 1846; d. aet. over 80 years.

74. THE REV. JOHN DENNIS[11] PENROSE (*James,*[10] *Cooper,*[9] *John,*[8] *William,*[7] *Richard,*[6] *Robert,*[5] *Thomas,*[4] *John,*[3] *Nicholas,*[2] *Thomas*[1]), of Woodhill, sometime rector of Magourney, born 31 Aug. 1804, died 4 Feb. 1894. He married 3 May 1849 HARRIET HARDY, born 3 Oct. 1828, died 14 Aug. 1922, daughter of the Rev. John Hardy. He inherited the property after the death of his elder brother Cooper, since the second brother Robert had taken over the FitzGerald property (see No. 73). See Burke's *Landed Gentry*, 1939, p. 1788.

Children:

89.	i.	JAMES EDWARD,[12] b. 15 Feb. 1850.
	ii.	MARY ELIZABETH, b. 24 Jan. 1851; d. in March 1938; m. her first cousin, JUDGE ROBERT WOOD INGHAM, J. P. and D. L., of Sugwas Court, Herefordshire, b. in 1846, d. 10 Jan. 1928, son of Sir James Taylor Ingham by his wife Gertrude Penrose (daughter of No. 55). See *Burke's Landed Gentry*, 1939, p. 1258 f.

Children (surname *Ingham*) : 1. *Louisa Geraldine*, b. 5 Nov. 1877; m. 20 Sept. 1905 Philip Bartholomew Barneby, of Trewyn, Abergavenny, second son of William Barneby of Saltmarsh, Castle Bromyard. Three sons, one daughter. 2. *James Geoffrey Penrose*, b. 26 Nov. 1878; d. in 1959; m. 14 Jan. 1913 Zelda Raney Dalrymple, daughter of Walter Francis Dalrymple. Children: (a) Clarence, b. 15 Oct. 1913; d. 21 Jan. 1914. (b) Ellinor Mary, b. in 1916. (c) Nevill Robert Penrose, b. 29 Jan. 1919. 3. *Gertrude Katherine*, b. 26 March 1879; d. 6 Jan. 1897. 4. *Robert John FitzGerald*, b. 16 Nov. 1880; d. 1 July 1917, of wounds in action; m. Ella Prendergast Triscott, daughter of Brig. Charles Prideaux Triscott, R.A. Children: (a) John Oliver, b. 1 Dec. 1912. (b) Priscilla Beatrice, b. 12 Dec. 1913. 5. *Oliver Edward Uniacke*, b. 13 April 1883; d. 12 Sept. 1911. 6. *Wilfred Rawdon*, clergyman, b. 17 Sept. 1887; m. 19 April 1928 Margaret Nancy Waring, daughter of Herbert Fuller Waring of Farningham, Kent. From 1938 he was rector of Batsford with Moreton-in-Marsh, Gloucestershire. Children: (a) Susanna Mary, b. 27 April 1932. (b) Robert Benjamin Fuller, b. 4 May 1936. 7. *Lancelot Gordon*, b. in May 1889; d. after 1933; m. 16 Feb. 1916 Mary Helen Cooper, daughter of Col. Francis Edward Cooper of Markree Castle, co. Sligo.

Children: (a) Robert Cooper, b. 3 Dec. 1916. (b) Patricia Mary Alice, b. 5 April 1919. (c) Susan Ella, b. 8 July 1927.

iii.   LOUISA JOSEPHINE PETTITOT, b. 26 May 1852; d. in 1938; m. 1 May 1886, her first cousin, JAMES HENRY BRABAZON PENROSE-FITZGERALD (No. 88).

90.   iv.   JOHN TREVENAN, b. 12 Nov. 1853.

91.   v.   COOPER, b. 8 March 1855.

92.   vi.   EDWARD RAWDON, b. 8 Sept. 1856.

     vii.   FRANCES ANNE HENRIETTA, b. 31 May 1859; d. 28 Jan. 1950; m. (1), 9 Aug. 1883, the REV. JOHN MYTTON THORNEYCROFT, d. 22 Dec. 1886; m. (2), 28 Jan. 1909, COL. MAURICE MORGAN MORRIS, R.A., d. 26 May 1934.

     viii.   ROBERT FITZGERALD, b. 7 March 1864; d.s.p 6 Aug. 1914; m. 7 Feb. 1903 Hilda Lovett Robertson. He was a captain in Roberts' Horse, Boer War.

75. WILLIAM[11] PENROSE (*James,[10] Cooper,[9] John,[8] William,[7] Richard,[6] Robert,[5] Thomas,[4] John,[3] Nicholas,[2] Thomas[1]*), born 3 Nov. 1818, died 12 July 1898. He married 9 Aug. 1849, when of Glenmore, HELENA TOWNSEND, daughter of E. Townsend, M.D.

Children:

i.   LOUISA PETTITOT,[12] b. 24 Oct. 1851; m. 15 Aug. 1885 CHARLES FREEMAN. She became a Fellow of the Royal Astronomical Society.

ii.   ELIZABETH, b. 26 June 1853; d. 25 March 1927; m. 31 May 1884 the REV. ARTHUR SLOMAN, Rector of Sandy, Beds., and Canon of St. Albans, b. 18 Oct. 1851, d. 20 Dec. 1919.
     Children (surname *Sloman*) : 1. *Harold Newenham Penrose*, b. 22 April 1885; m. 19 Dec. 1912 Mary Trinder. One son. 2. *Arthur Eric*, b. 21 April 1890; m. 2 Nov. 1915 Carmen Guze. One daughter.

iii.   MAYE, b. 1 May 1862; d. unm. 1 Nov. 1917.

76. SAMUEL[11] PENROSE (*Samuel,[10] Samuel,[9] Samuel,[8] William,[7] Richard,[6] Robert,[5] Thomas,[4] John,[3] Nicholas,[2] Thomas[1]*), of Shandangan, co. Cork, was born in 1804. He married in 1827 his first cousin, SARAH WELSTEAD of Ballywalter, co. Cork.

Child:

93.   i.   SAMUEL,[12] b. in 1829.

77. WILLIAM HENRY[11] PENROSE (*Samuel,[10] William,[9] Samuel,[8] William,[7] Richard,[6] Robert,[5] Thomas,[4] John,[3] Nicholas,[2] Thomas[1]*), of Low Park, Dedham, Essex, and of Lehane, co. Cork, J, P., born 8 July 1810, died in 1896. He married, first, 16 July 1840, the HON. GEORGIANA ISABELLA KEANE, died 12 April 1854, youngest daughter of John, 1st Lord Keane; secondly, in 1856, LOUISE HYDE, d. without issue in 1857, daughter of John Hyde of Castle Hyde, co. Cork; thirdly, in 1858, ANN AGNES LILLINGSTONE, d. 13 May 1860, daughter of Charles Lillingstone of The Chantry, Ipswich; and fourthly, in 1863, ELIZABETH WATHERSTON, living in 1912, youngest daughter of Capt. Robert Tait Watherston, R.N., of Pirn, Midlothian.

Child by first wife:

i.   HENRY FRANCIS KEANE.[12]

Child by third wife:

ii.   ELIZABETH HARRIET ANNE AGNES.

Children by fourth wife:

iii.   ELIZABETH W. TAIT.
iv.   WILLIAM WATHERSTON, b. 29 Oct. 1863.
v.   ROBERT TAIT, b. 29 March 1865.
vi.   EDWARD SAMUEL, b. 13 March 1868.
vii.   ARTHUR CRUDEN, b. 4 Nov. 1870; d. in Dec. 1884.
viii.   JOHN ERNEST, b. 18 Nov. 1872.

78. ROBERT WILLIAM[11] PENROSE (*Jacob,*[10] *William,*[9] *Samuel,*[8] *William,*[7] *Richard,*[6] *Robert,*[5] *Thomas,*[4] *John,*[3] *Nicholas,*[2] *Thomas*[1]), of Riverview, Ferry Bank, and Seaville, Tramore, co. Waterford, born in 1827, died 22 Aug. 1911. He married in 1872 FRANCES ALICE SANDFORD, daughter of the Rev. William Sandford by his wife Susan Alice Lyster, eldest daughter of John Lyster of Ballymeelin.

Children:

94. i.   WILLIAM ROBERT,[12] b. in 1873.
ii.   HENRY HERBERT, b. in 1874.
iii.   ARTHUR JOHN, b. in 1875; d. in 1892.
iv.   EDWARD ALICK, b. in 1877; d. in Sept. 1957. He was agent for the family property in Waterford for some fifty years and left a daughter and a widow, the latter in 1960 the only person of the name Penrose living in Waterford.
v.   JOHN SAMUEL SANDFORD, lieutenant R.N., b. in 1879; d. in 1914; m. in 1910 IRENE HESTER SMITH, eldest daughter of Henry Joshua Smith of Pinehurst, Cape Colony, by his wife Dorothea Sueur, daughter of John le Sueur of Rosedale, Cape Town, South Africa.
vi.   MABEL FRANCES, d. 30 Sept. 1911; m. in 1904 the REV. EDWARD NEVILL, Rector of Fenagh.
      Child (surname *Nevill*) : 1. *Rhoda Frances.*
vii.   SUSAN ALICE.
viii.   FRANCES AMELIA.
ix.   SAR ELIZABETH, m. DAVID HAWKINS.
x.   EMILY KATHLEEN, m. the REV. W. SHAW.

79. NATHAN[11] PENROSE (*Nathan,*[10] *John,*[9] *Robert,*[8] *Robert,*[7] *Robert,*[6] *Robert,*[5] *Thomas,*[4] *John,*[3] *Nicholas,*[2] *Thomas*[1]) was born 24 Nov. 1800 but nothing more was known of him to Mr. Roberts. In later records he is generally called Nathan R. Penrose, but what the middle initial stood for is unknown. He died sometime in 1887 while a resident of Beaver Meadows, Carbon County, Pa., leaving a brief will which bequeaths all his property to unnamed children; there is a certificate of the executors which asserts that he left absolutely no personal property. A series of deeds in Luzerne and Carbon Counties permits us to name his children and give a brief account of his life. He evidently married CASEY or CACY or CAS ANN [was it Tacy?] BARNES, daughter of Joseph and Ann Barnes of Northampton County, who settled property on their daughter which was afterwards sold by her heirs. He first purchased property in Salem Township, Luzerne County, which adjoins the Borough of Berwick, Columbia

County, upstream, in 1827, but in 1847 he bought property in Banks Township, Carbon County, where the Borough of Beaver Meadows now stands. In 1859 some of his property was sold for debt by the Carbon County sheriff. After his death the heirs allowed the County Treasurer to sell property for taxes but one of them bought it in and then released it soon afterwards.

Children:

i. HANNAH,[12] m., as second wife, JOSEPH J.[6] FOULKE (Samuel,[5] Everard,[4] Thomas,[3] Hugh,[2] Edward[1]) , b. 16 Nov. 1818; d.s.p. 13 Dec. 1894.
ii. MARY L., unm. in 1877.
iii. GEORGE WASHINGTON, m. EUPHEMIA B. ——; living in Weatherly, Pa., in 1892.
iv. LYDIA, m. (1) , JOHN BEACROFT; m. (2) , by 1890, —— HOYTE; was of Beaver Meadows in 1890.
v. JOHN B[ARNES?], in 1890 of Washington, D. C., unm.
vi. MARIA, m. J. W. HEART, HEARTH, or HEATH; in 1888 was of Wichita, Kans.
vii. SUSAN ANN, m. WILSON S. BETTERLY, of Stockton and Hazleton, Pa.
viii. EVALINA, m. HENRY TREVASKIS.
ix. EMMA, m. WILLIAM PHILLIPS.
x. JANE, perhaps not the youngest, m. JAMES H. ALLEN of Beaver Meadows. Carbon County Orphans Court file 94 contains petition and guardian's bond, 14 Nov. 1849, for Jane P. Penrose, minor under 14, N. R. Penrose her next friend [had her mother just died?]. She bought property as Jane P. Penrose of Beaver Meadows in 1870, and in 1874 as Jane P. Allen sold another property to her father.

80. WASHINGTON HICKS[11] PENROSE (*Nathan,[10] John,[9] Robert,[8] Robert,[7] Robert,[6] Robert,[5] Thomas,[4] John,[3] Nicholas,[2] Thomas[1]*) , born 17 Sept. 1809, died 22 Jan. 1878 aet. 68, buried in Greenwood Cemetery, Frankford, Philadelphia. He married SARAH DALBEY, born 17 Feb. 1822, died 15 Jan. 1900, buried with her husband, daughter of Abner and Sarah (Shaw) Dalbey.

Children:

i. NATHAN,[12] b.11 Sept. 1847. It is barely possible that he was the Nathan of Philadelphia, with wife who had been Alice Horton, shown in a Luzerne County deed dated 7 March 1881 (Luzerne Deeds, 222:566).
ii. MARY JANE, b. 5 April 1849.
iii. DANIEL DALBEY, b. 14 April 1851; d. 11 July 1851.
iv. ELLA, b. 7 June 1858.

THE PENROSE FAMILY OF WHELDRAKE AND BALLYKEAN AND THEIR DESCENDANTS IN BOTH HEMISPHERES

By George E. McCracken, Ph.D., F.A.A.R., F.A.S.G.
of Drake University, Des Moines, Iowa

81. Steadman[11] Penrose (*Everard,*[10] *Samuel,*[9] *Robert,*[8] *Robert,*[7] *Robert,*[6] *Robert,*[5] *Thomas,*[4] *John,*[3] *Nicholas,*[2] *Thomas*[1]), born in Hilltown Township, Bucks County, Pa., 2 Feb. 1808, died near Sacramento, Calif., 27 Oct. 1850. No success has been had in explaining his unusual first name; there were Steadmans in Philadelphia in 1768. Probate records of Bucks County show, a year after the death of Dr. Everard Penrose, that on 12 Dec. 1824, David Johnson was appointed guardian of "Stidman" Penrose, minor son above fourteen of Everard Penrose deceased; there is also on file a release of said guardian by Stidman Penrose of Richland, blacksmith, now aged 21, dated 6 Feb. 1829. Thus, there can be no doubt that Steadman was a son of Everard. It is hardly possible, however, that Steadman was the son of the only known wife of Everard, namely, the Bridget, wife of Dr. Penrose, as shown in a deed dated 24 Nov. 1814, recorded 21 Sept. 1815 (Deeds, 44:150). When Steadman was presumably two years old, his father joined with others in a deed dated 28 May 1810 (Deeds, 39:304), but no wife appears with Everard in that deed, though a wife is mentioned for another Penrose grantor. It would seem clear that the doctor married Bridget, whoever she was, between 1810 and 1815, when he already had a son by another mother. Descendants of Steadman Penrose have no tradition concerning Bridget, but they do have a unanimous belief that Steadman's mother was Ann Dalbey, born, doubtless in Bucks County, though probably not in Richland, 24 May 1778, died in Benton County, Iowa, 2 Sept. 1846 aet. ca. 68, buried in the Strawn Family Cemetery in Linn County which adjoins Benton. She had married, in the only marriage claimed for her, probably in Bucks County but where is unknown, 8 Oct. 1818, when Steadman was about ten, the weaver William[4] Ball, born Monday, 7 Feb. 1785, about 5:00 A.M., died in Benton County 6 Aug. 1857, likewise buried in the Strawn Cemetery, son of Nathan[3] Ball (John,[2] John[1]) by his wife Mary Satterthwaite. According to C. V. Roberts (*op. cit.,* 54) William Ball lived from 1819 to 1844 on a lot on the Hellertown Road purchased of Abner Dalby, but then removed to Quakertown where, as Mr. Roberts supposed, both William and Ann died on dates approximately the same as those given above. It is clear that no one had told Mr. Roberts that the Balls had removed to Iowa. Ann died before any Iowa census was taken but William Ball is shown as aged 66 in the 1850 Federal Census

and as aged 71 in the 1856 State Census, residing in the household of Steadman's widow. In Mr. Roberts' sketch of Steadman (p. 408 f.), it is stated that Steadman removed with his
mother and stepfather, first to Ohio, then to Iowa, but the
older generation is not identified nor connected with the
Balls. The dates given above are taken from a Bible now the
property of a descendant (Ruth Coffman), once owned by
Steadman's daughter Ann (No. i, below). This Bible also
shows that the parents of Ann Ball were Nathan and Abigail
Dalbey, and that Abigail Walton, wife of Nathan Dalbey,
died 29 May 1820 aet. ca. 64. She was Abigail Hicks, born 21
April 1756, second daughter of William[2] Hicks (George[1]) by
his first wife Margaret Evans, and she married, secondly,
Enoch Walton, who survived her and died without issue 20
Sept. 1828 (Roberts, *op. cit.*, p. 272, 578). Search at Doyles-
town in 1961 for probate and deeds of Nathan Walton was
unsuccessful; Enoch Walton's probate does not mention his
step-daughter. The Bible cited also records the deaths of
John Shaw, Jr., and his wife Elizabeth, the latter William
Ball's sister, and is very full for the Virden family into which
the younger Ann Penrose married, but it does not mention
Steadman Penrose or his wife, and the only reference to any
Penrose in it is the fact that the maiden name of Mrs. Ann
Virden (No. i, below) is given as Penrose. That Mrs. Ball
was Steadman Penrose's mother is also confirmed by a small
notebook once owned by Mrs. Steadman Penrose, with the
entries in the hand of her son Lewis (No. 95).

Steadman Penrose married in Pennsylvania, 31 Oct. 1830,
MARY STRAWN, born in Haycock Township 3 May 1808, died
in Whitewater, Colo., either 3 Oct. or 6 Nov. 1882, a few days
after she had arrived there on a visit to her daughters. She
was the daughter of Enoch[3] Strawn (Jacob,[2] Lancelot[1]) by
his first wife Rebecca Raudenbush; she married, secondly,
27 Oct. 1859, Benedict J. Kenyon, born in Rhode Island, in
July 1806, died in Iowa in 1895, son of Corey[4] Kenyon (Benedict,[3] John,[2] John[1]) by his wife Waitey (Moon) Barber, and
he had married, first, 30 Oct. 1826, Abigail Champlin. Benedict and Mary were separated before her death. Steadman
Penrose appears in a fragmentary census of Benton County
in 1848; but when gold was discovered in California, he
caught the fever and went in search of it, only to die soon
afterwards. His widow appears in another fragmentary
census of Benton County in 1852 and in the Federal Censuses
of 1850, 1860, and 1870, and in the State Census of 1856 (the
1880 Federal Census was not examined). See *The American
Genealogist*, 35:232, 235 ff., Oct. 1959; also *History of Benton
County*, Iowa, 1878, p. 564.

Children:

i.   ANN,[12] b. in Bucks County, Pa., 27 Feb. 1832; d. in Whitewater, Colo.,

18 July 1894; m. probably in Shellsburg, Iowa, 15 May 1857, DANIEL VIRDEN, d. in Colorado 15 March 1910 aet. 84, son of William Virden, b. in Delaware 26 Jan. 1787, d. in Waterloo, Iowa, 27 March 1855, and Martha Williamson, b. in New Jersey 29 Jan. 1793, d. in Waterloo 11 Feb. 1886 aet. 93.

Children (surname *Virden*) : 1. *Genetta*, b. in Logan, Dakota Co., North Dakota Territory, 3 April 1858; d. 14 May 1858 aet. 6 weeks, buried in Nebraska. 2. *Stella Antoinette*, b. in Logan 20 Nov. 1859; d. 25 Jan. 1861 aet. 1/2/5. 3. *Mary Etta*, b. in Shellsburg 16 April 1861; d. 17 June 1957 aet. 96; m. (1) ——— Shutt; m. (2) ———Brumley. 4. *Rose Ella*, b. in Canon City, Colo., then Fremont County, Colorado Territory, 14 Dec. 1862, the first white child born there; d. 25 Nov. 1948 aet. 85; m. William H. Coffman, b. 25 Sept. 1853, d. 7 May 1952. Children (surname *Coffman*) : (a) Fred, b. 30 Oct. 1888. (b) Ernest, b. 4 May 1890. (c) Glen, b. 7 June 1891. (d) Ruth, b. 30 Dec. 1902; living unm. in 1961. 5. *Louis Edwin*, b. in Shellsburg 22 Aug. 1865; drowned in Gunnison River, Colo., 18 Sept. 1885 aet. 20/0/27. 6. *William Steadman*, b. in Jefferson County, Colorado Territory, four miles west of Denver, 27 Aug. 1867; d. *s.p.* in Arizona. 7. *Arthur*, b. in Araphoe County, Colorado Territory, 2 Sept. 1868; d. 25 Oct. 1868 aet. 0/7/4, buried east of Denver. 8. *Elgin Penrose*, b. in Araphoe County 22 Nov. 1870, eight miles northwest of Denver; went to Alaska in the gold rush and was never heard from again. 9. *Elbert Daniel*, b. in Bear Creek, Jefferson Co., Colorado Territory, 22 Dec. 1872, eight miles southwest of Denver; m., but d. *s.p.*, injured in a rodeo accident in California. 10. *Louanna Martha*, b. in Jefferson County 18 May 1874; living in California in 1961; m. ——— Selzell.

95. ii. JOSEPH, b. in Bucks County 2 April 1837.
    iii. WILLIAM, b. in Iowa 26 May 1842; killed in the Battle of Shiloh, member of Co. D, 8th Iowa Volunteer Infantry, 6 April 1862.

96. iv. LEWIS, b. in Iowa 22 Nov. 1844.
    v. MYRA or MIRAETTA, b. in Iowa 8 April 1847; d. in Buena Vista, Colo., 23 June 1936; m. in Denver City, Colo., 25 Aug. 1867, ROBERT SHROPSHIRE, d. in Grand Junction, Colo., 18 Nov. 1927.

Child (surname *Shropshire*) : 1. *Clyde Evans*, b. in Shellsburg 21 Aug. 1871; living in 1961; m. in Whitewater, Colo., 25 Aug. 1892, Ada Anderson. Children, b. in Whitewater: (a) Winnie E., b. 7 March 1893; m. in Whitewater, 12 March 1913, Vida C. Laramore. (b) Robert Ray, b. 29 Sept. 1892; d. in Havre, Mont., in August 1939; m. there, in 1931, Gertrude ———. (c) Bessie M., b. 6 March 1897; d. in Seattle, Wash., 22 Dec. 1951; m. in Grand Junction, in April 1917, Roy Moore. (d) Elmer C., b. 4 April 1899; d. in Chico, Calif., in May 1943; m. in Grand Junction, in 1929, Faye Anderson. (e) Gladys L., b. 16 March 1902; m. in Fruita, Colo., 1 June 1920, Lee Willey.

82. WILLIAM[11] PENROSE (*James*,[10] *Thomas*,[9] *Richard*,[8] *Robert*,[7] *Robert*,[6] *Robert*,[5] *Thomas*,[4] *John*,[3] *Nicholas*,[2] *Thomas*[1]), dealer in farm machinery, born in Morgan County, Ohio, 7 Nov. 1834, died at his home in Burlington, Iowa, funeral, 3 Feb. 1908 at the First Presbyterian Church, Burlington. He married 9 June 1858 OLIVIA THOMPSON, born Columbiana County, Ohio, 11 March 1839, died before her husband. He removed to Burlington in 1868 and appears, at various addresses, in the Burlington directories for 1870, 1871, 1885-7, and in the 1870 Federal Census of Third Ward, Burlington, but he was not found, as he should have been, in the Iowa Census of 1885 and 1895. His obituary appeared in the

910

Burlington Hawkeye, Sunday, 2 Feb. 1908; see also *History of Des Moines County, Iowa*, 1879, p. 656.

Children:

i. JAMES R.,[12] b. in Ohio in 1859; living in Burlington in 1908; was in 1884-5 a bookkeeper for his father; in the 1915 Iowa Census he is aet. 53, residing in Burlington, with his wife called M. J. PENROSE, aet. 49, b. in Ohio, her father b. in Virginia; and they had an 18-year-old daughter *Elizabeth E.*, also b. in Ohio.

ii. REBECCA LELIA, b. in Ohio in 1862; aet. 8 in 1870, aet. 52 in 1915; an artist in 1884-5, in 1915 House Secretary for the Y. W. C. A.; apparently d. unm.

iii. JOHN T., b. in Ohio in 1865; in 1885-6 bookkeeper for his father; in 1908 living in Springfield, Ill.

iv. WILLIAM C., b. in Iowa after 1870; living in 1908 in Mediapolis, Iowa.

v. MARY L., b. in Iowa after 1870; living in 1879, not living in 1908.

83. JAMES DOYLE[12] PENROSE (*George*,[11] *Daniel*,[10] *Richard*,[9] *Daniel*,[8] *John*,[7] *Richard*,[6] *Robert*,[5] *Thomas*,[4] *John*,[3] *Nicholas*,[2] *Thomas*[1]), born in Canada 30 Aug. 1829, died 24 Sept. 1897. He married 17 Nov. 1854 ANNIE BOWLES. He lived in Mitchelstown, co. Dublin, Ireland. See Burke's *Landed Gentry*, 1939, p. 1788.

Children:

i. SARAH ELIZA,[13] b. 20 July 1855; d. in Waterford 26 Jan. 1931; m. 20 April 1914 LEONARD GEORGE SOUTHWELL.

ii. GEORGE, b. 7 April 1857; d. unm. 21 Feb. 1930, lived at Waterford, bur. Jordans.

iii. ROBERT WILLIAM, b. 21 Jan. 1859; d. unm. 30 Sept. 1916.

97. iv. JAMES DOYLE, b. 9 May 1862.

v. ELIZABETH JOSEPHINE DOYLE, b. 14 Dec. 1864; d. young.

98. vi. ARTHUR EDWARD DOYLE, b. 6 April 1869.

99. vii. HENRY WALTER, b. 12 Oct. 1870.

viii. ALFRED ERNEST, b. in Downham Market, co. Norfolk, 8 March 1874; m. 2 Feb. 1905 MABEL WIGGINTON, b. 12 March 1879.

84. EDWARD[12] PENROSE (*Samuel Neale*,[11] *Samuel Neale*,[10] *John*,[9] *Daniel*,[8] *Daniel*,[7] *Richard*,[6] *Robert*,[5] *Thomas*,[4] *John*,[3] *Nicholas*,[2] *Thomas*[1]) was born in 1810. He married 20 Jan. 1838 SARAH EDGAR.

Children:

i. SAMUEL,[13] b. in 1839; d. 19 Sept. 1843.

ii. JOHN, b. 2 April 1840; m. MARY GRATTAN.

100. iii. HENRY JOSEPH, b. 13 Aug. 1842.

iv. BARTHOLOMEW, d. young.

85. FREDERICK GEORGE[12] PENROSE (*George Rooke*,[11] *Samuel Neale*,[10] *John*,[9] *Daniel*,[8] *Daniel*,[7] *Richard*,[6] *Robert*,[5] *Thomas*,[4] *John*,[3] *Nicholas*,[2] *Thomas*[1]), born 2 Aug. 1828, died in Monkstown, Dublin, 23 June 1911. He married 4 April 1856 JANE ISABEL MALONE.

Children:

i. MARGARET MANLIFFE,[13] b. 11 June 1860; d. 15 Oct. 1871.

ii. HERBERT FREDERICK, b. 9 May 1862; d. 5 Feb. 1925; m. 15 April 1902 MARY JANE SCHROEDER.

911

iii. GEORGE ROOKE, b. 28 Oct. 1865; m. 6 Feb. 1902 HENRIETTA CHARLOTTE CLARK.
iv. LUCY BARRINGTON, b. 5 April 1871.
v. FRANCIS SINCLAIR, b. 11 Nov. 1876; m. 3 Nov. 1915 AGNES FINLAYSON McKECHNIE, and had *Pearl Ines* (b. in 1916) and two other daughters.

86. SIR ROBERT UNIACKE[12] PENROSE-FITZGERALD, Bart. (*Robert,*[11] *James,*[10] *Cooper,*[9] *John,*[8] *William,*[7] *Richard,*[6] *Robert,*[5] *Thomas,*[4] *John,*[3] *Nicholas,*[2] *Thomas*[1]), born on 10 July 1839, died 10 July 1919. He married 13 Sept. 1867 JANE CODRINGTON, daughter of General Sir William Codrington, G.C.B., Commander-in-Chief of British Forces in the Crimea, 1855-6. He was created a baronet on 4 Aug. 1896 but, as he died without issue, the baronetcy became extinct at his death, and his estate in Corkbeg, co. Cork, was left to his nephew, Robert Francis Uniacke Penrose-FitzGerald (No. 101).

87. ADMIRAL CHARLES COOPER[12] PENROSE-FITZGERALD (*Robert,*[11] *James,*[10] *Cooper,*[9] *John,*[8] *William,*[7] *Richard,*[6] *Robert,*[5] *Thomas,*[4] *John,*[3] *Nicholas,*[2] *Thomas*[1]), born 30 April 1841, died 11 Aug. 1921. He married, 29 Nov. 1882, ELIZABETH or HENRIETTA HEWSON, daughter of the Rev. Francis Hewson.

Children:

101. i. ROBERT FRANCIS UNIACKE,[13] b. 8 Sept. 1886.
102. ii. JOHN UNIACKE, b. 27 July 1888.
iii. MARY ELIZABETH, b. 8 Sept. 1883; d. 2 Feb. 1937.
iv. LAURA FRANCES, b. in March 1885.

88. JAMES HENRY BRABAZON[12] PENROSE-FITZGERALD (*Robert,*[11] *James,*[10] *Cooper,*[9] *John,*[8] *William,*[7] *Richard,*[6] *Robert,*[5] *Thomas,*[4] *John,*[3] *Nicholas,*[2] *Thomas*[1]), born 1 July 1843, died 14 Aug. 1922. He married 1 May 1886, his first cousin, LOUISA JOSEPHINE PETTITOT PENROSE, born 26 May 1852, died in 1938, second daughter of the Rev. John Dennis Penrose of Woodhill (No. 74).

Children:

i. CHARLES BRYAN,[13] b. 3 Dec. 1887; m. EVELYN HUNTER JONES.
ii. EDWARD UNIACKE, b. 18 Dec. 1888; m. 11 Jan. 1934 ISABEL WILFORD, daughter of Sir Thomas Mason Wilford of Wellington, New Zealand. He had a daughter *Sarah,* b. 30 Jan. 1935.
iii. NESTA FANNY HARRIET, b. 7 Jan. 1890.
iv. HERBERT JAMES COOPER, b. 15 Aug. 1891; d. 12 Oct. 1916, killed in action.
v. MAURICE JOHN, b. 8 April 1894; d. 26 July 1916, killed in action.

89. JAMES EDWARD[12] PENROSE (*John Dennis,*[11] *James,*[10] *Cooper,*[9] *John,*[8] *William,*[7] *Richard,*[6] *Robert,*[5] *Thomas,*[4] *John,*[3] *Nicholas,*[2] *Thomas*[1]), born 15 Feb. 1850, died 22 Sept. 1936. He married 13 Dec. 1880 ETHEL CHARLOTTE COGHILL, born 13 May 1857, died 1 June 1938, eldest daughter of Sir Joscelyn Coghill, 4th Baronet, by his wife Katherine Frances, second daughter of John, 3rd Lord Plunkett. For many years he managed the Irish estates of the Dukes of Devonshire. He

912

was assiduous in the collection of genealogical information concerning the family and has thus made possible the story of the Irish Penroses in this study. See Burke's *Landed Gentry*, 1939, p. 1788.

Children:

i. KATHERINE ST. AUBYN,[13] b. 6 Nov. 1881; unm.
103. ii. JOSCELYN DENIS, b. 19 Oct. 1882.
104. iii. NEVILL COGHILL, b. 27 Feb. 1884.
iv. ETHEL MARY JUDITH YORK, b. 27 Jan. 1885; m. 18 Feb. 1928, as second wife, Lieut. Gen. SIR GEORGE RICHARDSON, d. *s.p.* 9 April 1931.
105. v. EVELYN COOPER, b. 15 Dec. 1886.
vi. HONOR ASHLEY PETITOT, b. 19 Sept. 1887; m. 19 Sept. 1914 RUPERT BARKLEY-SMITH, youngest son of Harry and Harriet (Stanlet) Smith of Wimbledon.
Children (surname *Barkley-Smith*) : 1. *Hugh Penrose*, b. 2 Dec. 1915. 2. *Anthony Rupert*, b. 19 Dec. 1917. 3. *Brian*, b. 5 Nov. 1920; killed in action, World War II.

90. THE REV. JOHN TREVENAN[12] PENROSE (*John*,[11] *James*,[10] *Cooper*,[9] *John*,[8] *William*,[7] *Richard*,[6] *Robert*,[5] *Thomas*,[4] *John*,[3] *Nicholas*,[2] *Thomas*[1]), sometime rector of Gawsworth, Barnard Castle and Petworth, born 12 Nov. 1853, died 2 Oct. 1926. He married 2 April 1885 ANNIE CHARLOTTE MCNEILL, eldest daughter of Edmund McNeill of Craigdunn.

Children:

i. MARY ESME VIOLET,[13] b. 1 March 1886; d. 6 Jan. 1901.
ii. EDWARD JOHN MCNEILL, b. 2 Oct. 1888; d. 25 April 1915, killed in action at Ypres.

91. BRIG. COOPER[12] PENROSE (*John Dennis*,[11] *James*,[10] *Cooper*,[9] *John*,[8] *William*,[7] *Richard*,[6] *Robert*,[5] *Thomas*,[4] *John*,[3] *Nicholas*,[2] *Thomas*[1]) of the Royal Engineers, C.B., C.M.G., born 8 March 1855, died 12 April 1927. He married 16 May 1885 SYLVIA ALICE GREENE, born 23 Oct. 1868, second daughter of Thomas Greene (son of Richard Greene, Baron of the Exchequer in Ireland) by his wife Sylvia Maria Coghill, daughter of Admiral Sir Josiah Coghill, Bart., by his wife Anna Maria, daughter of Chief Justice Bushe.

Children:

i. PHYLLIS MARY,[13] b. 24 Feb. 1886; m. 9 June 1915 ARTHUR KENRICK DICKENSON HALL, son of the Rev. F. Hall, Rector of Manby, Lincolnshire.
Children (surname *Hall*) : 1. *Geoffrey Penrose Dickenson*, b. 19 July 1916. 2. *Roger Kenrick Mantagie*, b. 12 Aug. 1917.
ii. SYLVIA JANET, b. 8 Nov. 1887; m. 6 May 1911 HERBERT DE LISLE POLLARD-LOWSLEY, b. 20 April 1877, d. 30 Oct. 1936, younger son of Lieutenant Colonel Barzillai Lowsley.
Children: 1. *John Inglis Penrose*, b. 30 March 1912; m. in 1936 Sylvia Marion Lind. 2. *Sylvia Patricia*, b. 18 Jan. 1915; m. 8 Oct. 1935 James G. Broomhead Walker (div.) . 3. *Anne Pamela*, b. 19 Oct. 1919; m. 7 July 1942 Thomas Donald Kellock, M.A.
iii. CONSTANCE MONICA, b. 15 Feb. 1889; m. 4 May 1916 JORDAYNE CAVE-BIGLEY.
Child (surname *Cave-Bigley*) : 1. *Peter Jordayne*, b. 19 June 1919.

913

92. LIEUT. COL. EDWARD RAWDON[12] PENROSE (*John Dennis,*[11] *James,*[10] *Cooper,*[9] *John,*[8] *William,*[7] *Richard,*[6] *Robert,*[5] *Thomas,*[4] *John,*[3] *Nicholas,*[2] *Thomas*[1]), born 8 Sept. 1856, died 31 Jan. 1926. He married 29 Oct. 1891 KATHERINE HARRIET THACKWELL, eldest daughter of Maj. Gen. William de Wilton Roche Thackwell and granddaughter of Lieut. Gen. Sir Joseph Thackwell, fourth son of John Thackwell of Wilton Place by his wife Judith Duffy. By royal decree of 20 Oct. 1904, Colonel Penrose took the arms and name of Thackwell, and the surname has henceforth been Penrose-Thackwell.

Children:

i. MARY GERALDINE HARRIET,[13] b. 22 Sept. 1892; m. 19 March 1915 JOHN HELLIER DE ROUGETEL.
ii. ELENOR MAUD CHARLOTTE, b. 14 Dec. 1897; m. 29 April 1922 LOUIS DE SOISSONS.
iii. WILLIAM JOHN RAWDON, b. 17 Jan. 1900.
iv. MARJORY HELEN FLORENCE, b. 15 Oct. 1902.
v. GEOFFREY JOSEPH ELLIOTT, b. 28 March 1904.

93. THE REV. SAMUEL[12] PENROSE-WELSTEAD (*Samuel,*[11] *Samuel,*[10] *Samuel,*[9] *Samuel,*[8] *William,*[7] *Richard,*[6] *Robert,*[5] *Thomas,*[4] *John,*[3] *Nicholas,*[2] *Thomas*[1]), of Shandangan and Ballywalter, born in 1829, died in 1918, and took the name of Welstead upon the death of his uncle, John Welstead, of Ballywalter, when he succeeded to the property in October 1896. He married in 1857 MARY ELIZABETH O'CALLAGHAN, died in 1904, daughter of Henry Davis O'Callaghan, J. P., of Nadrid, co. Cork.

Children:

106. i. SAMUEL QUAYLE,[13] b. in 1861.
ii. HARRY HUGH, b. in 1862; d. 13 Aug. 1955; m. in 1889 MARY ELIZABETH LEWIS, d. 23 Aug. 1942, daughter of Henry Lewis of Kinsale, co. Cork.
iii. FRANK PHILIP, b. in 1864; m. 14 May 1891 HENRIETTA MARY TIBBS, daughter of the Rev. Philip Tibbs, D.D., of Kilmacdaugh, and had daughter *Iris* who d. unm.

94. WILLIAM ROBERT[12] PENROSE (*Robert William,*[11] *Jacob,*[10] *William,*[9] *Samuel,*[8] *William,*[7] *Richard,*[6] *Robert,*[5] *Thomas,*[4] *John,*[3] *Nicholas,*[2] *Thomas*[1]) was born in 1873. He married in 1889 ISABEL MONTSERRAT NEVILL, daughter of Edward Nevill of Bawnmore, New Ross, co. Wexford, by his wife Eleanor Colles, daughter of Alexander Colles of Milmount.

Children:

i. ROBERT WILLIAM EDWARD,[13] b. in 1909.
ii. FRANCES ISABEL SUSAN ELEANOR.
iii. BEATRIX WILLIE.

95. JOSEPH[12] PENROSE (*Steadman,*[11] *Everard,*[10] *Samuel,*[9] *Robert,*[8] *Robert,*[7] *Robert,*[6] *Robert,*[5] *Thomas,*[4] *John,*[3] *Nicholas,*[2] *Thomas*[1]), born in Quakertown, Pa., 2 April 1837. died in

Shellsburg, Iowa, 2 May 1902. He married there, 11 Feb. 1859, PHOEBE REBECCA JONES, born in Coshocton, Ohio, 31 Oct. 1840, died in Long Beach, Calif., 17 Oct. 1935, daughter of James and Barbara (Walters) Jones.

Children, born in Shellsburg:

i. JAMES STEADMAN,[13] b. 17 Nov. 1859; d. 9 Nov. 1860, bur. in Strawn Cemetery, Linn County, Iowa.

ii. WILLIAM OSCAR, b. 26 Jan. 1861; d. there 2 Aug. 1937; m. OLIVE THOMPSON, not related to the husbands of Nos. v-vi.

iii. ADELLA DELILAH, b. 7 Sept. 1862; d. in Grand Junction, Colo., 1 Sept. 1952; m. HENRY WELLINGTON SCHNEYER or SNYER, b. in Glendale, Mass., 9 July 1861, d. in Grand Junction 26 June 1943, fifth child of John Frederick Schneyer (1822-1870) by his wife Catherine Margaret Oppel (1818—ca. 1888).

iv. LAURA, b. 25 Dec. 1864; d. in Long Beach, Calif., 20 March 1951; m. OTTO THOMPSON.

v. MARY BARBARA, b. 18 Oct. 1867; d. in Long Beach, Calif., 26 June 1944; m. —— THOMPSON, brother to Otto.

107. vi. LEWIS EDWIN, b. 26 July 1870.

vii. JOHN ALBERT, b. 6 Oct. 1874; d. in Los Angeles, Calif. 28 March 1938.

viii. ANNIE MYRTLE, b. 24 May 1879.

96. LEWIS[12] PENROSE (*Steadman*,[11] *Everard*,[10] *Samuel*,[9] *Robert*,[8] *Robert*,[7] *Robert*,[6] *Robert*,[5] *Thomas*,[4] *John*,[3] *Nicholas*,[2] *Thomas*[1]), born in Benton County, Iowa, 22 Nov. 1844, died in Shellsburg, Iowa, 10 June 1923, buried in the Strawn Cemetery in Fayette Township, Linn County. He married in Muscatine, Iowa, 4 July 1871 SARAH ELIZABETH CLECKNER, born in Pike County, Ohio, 13 May 1844, died in Fayette Township, Linn Co., Iowa, 9 Feb. 1930, daughter of Samuel Cleckner, born 31 Jan. 1815, died in 1887 aet. 72, by his wife Nancy Shropshire, born 31 Aug. 1806, died in 1895, supposedly aet. 85.

Children:

108. i. HARRY JEFFERSON,[13] b. 17 June 1872.

ii. MARY ELIZABETH, b. 9 April 1874; d. in Tacoma, Wash., in July 1947; m. in August 1912 SYLVAN CHANDLEY. For many years she supported herself and daughter as a kindergarten teacher, in Philadelphia, among other places, and while there, visited relatives at Quakertown, one of whom made the classic remark: "Others call thee Bessie but we will call thee Elizabeth."

iii. ANNIE FLOY, b. 4 March 1878; living in Seattle, Wash., in 1962; m. the REV. NELSON C. WEHRHAN, a Congregationalist minister. One daughter Lois.

97. JAMES DOYLE[13] PENROSE (*James Doyle*,[12] *George*,[11] *Daniel*,[10] *Richard*,[9] *Daniel*,[8] *John*,[7] *Richard*,[6] *Robert*,[5] *Thomas*,[4] *John*,[3] *Nicholas*,[2] *Thomas*[1]), born 9 May 1862, died in Oxhey Grange, Watford, Hertfordshire, 2 Jan. 1932. He married, 19 April 1893 the HON. ELIZABETH JOSEPHINE PECKOVER, daughter of Alexander, 1st Baron Peckover, born 16 Aug. 1830, raised to the peerage, 20 July 1907, died 21 Oct. 1919, after which the title became extinct. Lord Peckover had married, 8 April 1858, Eliza Sharples, died 7 Aug. 1862, only child of Joseph Sharples of Hitchin, Hertfordshire, banker, by his

wife Elizabeth Ransom. Besides Mrs. Penrose, Lord Peckover had daughters Alexandrina and Anna Jane.

Children:

109. i. ALEXANDER PECKOVER DOYLE,[14] b. 12 Aug. 1896.
110. ii. LIONEL SHARPLES, b. 11 June 1897.
111. iii. ROLAND ALGERNON, b. 14 Oct. 1900.
112. iv. BERNARD EDMUND, b. 20 Sept. 1903.

98. ARTHUR EDWARD DOYLE[13] PENROSE (*James Doyle,*[12] *George,*[11] *Daniel,*[10] *Richard,*[9] *Daniel,*[8] *John,*[7] *Richard,*[6] *Robert,*[5] *Thomas,*[4] *John,*[3] *Nicholas,*[2] *Thomas*[1]), born at Windmill Hall, Herstmonceux, 6 April 1869, died at Herstmonceux 6 Feb. 1947. He married 17 March 1914 MAUD BEATRICE KITSON.

Children:

i. KENNETH KITSON,[14] b. 17 Dec. 1914; m. MARIAN MARSHALL.
ii. EDWARD VICTOR, b. 13 Dec. 1915; m. 20 Aug. 1941 FREDA IRENE MARY HAYWARD.
iii. JOAN, b. 27 May 1917.
iv. IRENE, b. 30 May 1918.
v. ERIC ROBERT, b. 24 Nov. 1919.
vi. JEAN, b. 27 Oct. 1921.
vii. GWENDOLEN, b. 23 March 1923.
viii. CLARENCE RUPERT, b. 22 Oct. 1924; d. young.

99. HENRY WALTER[13] PENROSE (*James Doyle,*[12] *George,*[11] *Daniel,*[10] *Richard,*[9] *Daniel,*[8] *John,*[7] *Richard,*[6] *Robert,*[5] *Thomas,*[4] *John,*[3] *Nicholas,*[2] *Thomas*[1]), born at Mitchelstown, Castleknock, 12 Oct. 1870, died in 1920. He married 26 Oct. 1902, ANNIE BARTON.

Children:

i. HENRY BARTON,[14] b. 18 Sept. 1905; m. 24 Sept. 1932 SYBIL WOODHEAD, b. 17 Sept. 1903.
    Children: 1. *John Barton,*[15] b. 13 Aug. 1934. 2. *Janet Elizabeth,* b. 13 Jan. 1938. 3. *Patrick Edwin,* b. 13 Jan. 1938.
ii. JAMES RONALD, b. at Hillside, Herstmonceux, 30 April 1910; now of Watford, Hertfordshire; m. 16 June 1934 BERTHA RACKHAM. He has long studied the history of the Penrose family in England, Ireland, and America, and has generously provided copies of beautiful tabular pedigrees which have been used in this study.
    Children: 1. *Raymond James,*[15] b. in Watford 22 Oct. 1935. 2. *Ann Margaret,* b. in Croxley Green 31 Jan. 1939. 3. *Mary Josephine,* b. in Watford 27 Aug. 1944. 4. *Robert William,* b. in Watford 5 Aug. 1948.
iii. GEORGE RICHARD, b. 6 March 1912; m. in September 1933 RENE WILSON.

100. HENRY JOSEPH[13] PENROSE (*Edward,*[12] *Samuel Neale,*[11] *Samuel Neale,*[10] *John,*[9] *Daniel,*[8] *Daniel,*[7] *Richard,*[6] *Robert,*[5] *Thomas,*[4] *John,*[3] *Nicholas,*[2] *Thomas*[1]) was born 13 Aug. 1842. His wife's name is unknown.

Children:

i. EDWARD A.,[14] b. 26 Aug. 1874; m. 6 April 1910 GERTRUDE LUNHAM.
ii. EVALINE M., b. in 1876.

iii. FLORENCE JANE, b. in 1877; m. in November 1903 ROBERT [?].
iv. SARAH JOSEPHINE, b. in 1880.
v. WILLIAM HENRY, b. in 1882.
vi. JOHN WARE EDGAR, b. in 1883; m. BEATRICE QUICKLY.
vii. JAMES GOOD, b. in 1887.
viii. ANNIE ELIZABETH (twin), b. in 1891.
ix. FRANCES HENRIETTA INGHAM (twin), b. in 1891; m. JAMES RANDS.

101. ROBERT FRANCIS UNIACKE[13] PENROSE-FITZGERALD (*Charles Cooper,[12] Robert Uniacke,[11] James,[10] Cooper,[9] John,[8] William,[7] Richard,[6] Robert,[5] Thomas,[4] John,[3] Nicholas,[2] Thomas[1]*) was born 8 Sept. 1886. He married 29 Feb. 1916 MABEL FRANCES WARNE TOWER, daughter of Francis Tower of Dunedin, New Zealand.

Child:

i. ELIZABETH CONSTANCE,[14] b. 20 Aug. 1918; m. 22 March 1947 LIEUT. COM. VERNON NORTH GRAVES, R.N.
  Children (surname *Graves*): 1. *Janice Penrose*, b. 29 Dec. 1947. 2. *Sarah Frances*, b. 30 Oct. 1950.

102. REAR ADM. JOHN UNIACKE[13] PENROSE-FITZGERALD (*Charles Cooper,[12] Robert Uniacke,[11] James,[10] Cooper,[9] John,[8] William,[7] Richard,[6] Robert,[5] Thomas,[4] John,[3] Nicholas,[2] Thomas[1]*), born 27 July 1888, died on active service 13 Dec. 1940. He married first, 30 July 1919, CECIL MARY GOLDIE-SCOTT, died 13 Aug. 1920; and secondly, 11 July 1925, EUGENIE BEATRICE GWENDOLINE ALLPORT HOWARD, daughter of James Howard.

Child by first wife:

i. CECIL PHILIPPA UNIACKE,[14] b. 13 Aug. 1920, B.A., M.R.C.V.S.

Children by second wife:

ii. MICHAEL JOHN ROBERT UNIACKE, b. 21 May 1927; m. 29 July 1954 NUALA MARY CASSIDY, daughter of Patrick Joseph Cassidy of Dublin.
  Child: 1. *Timothy Michael*,[15] b. 1 Nov. 1956.
iii. GERALDINE PATRICIA, b. 2 April 1929; m. 22 Oct. 1955 PHILIP ROBIN CHAWORTH-MUSTERS, son of Douglas Chaworth-Musters of Bedford.
iv. ROMAYNE, b. 9 Aug. 1932.

103. CAPT. JOSCELYN DENIS[13] PENROSE, J.P. (*James Edward,[12] John Dennis,[11] James,[10] Cooper,[9] John,[8] William,[7] Richard,[6] Robert,[5] Thomas,[4] John,[3] Nicholas,[2] Thomas[1]*), now of Wood Hill, Milton-under-Wychwood, Oxfordshire, was born 10 Oct. 1882. He married 24 Sept. 1913 EDITH FLORENCE PRESTON, youngest daughter of Maj. Arthur John Preston of Swainston, co. Meath, by his wife Gertrude Mary Knight, daughter of Richard Knight. Captain Penrose served in the Boer War and in World War I. He has made generous contributions to this study.

Children:

i. RUTH ESME,[14] b. 16 March 1915; m. 5 Oct. 1939 HUGO ERNEST GILDART

917

READ, b. 31 Aug. 1908, only son of Ernest Read, C.B.E., of London. Mr. Hugo Read, like his father-in-law, has made liberal contributions to this study.

Child (surname *Read*) : 1. *Susan Brigid*, b. 1 Sept. 1943.

ii. JOHN DENIS FITZGERALD, b. 23 Dec. 1919; m. 15 April 1950 ANNE ROSEMARY NICHOLSON.

Children: 1. *Rosemary Ruth*,[15] b. 7 May 1951. 2. *Nicholas James Dennis*, b. 21 Sept. 1953.

104. NEVIL COGHILL[13] PENROSE (*James Edward*,[12] *John Dennis*,[11] *James*,[10] *Cooper*,[9] *John*,[8] *William*,[7] *Richard*,[6] *Robert*,[5] *Thomas*,[4] *John*,[3] *Nicholas*,[2] *Thomas*[1]) was born 27 Feb. 1884. He married 29 April 1909 NELLIE OSLER, daughter of Alfred Clarkson Osler of Edgbaston.

Children:

i. JOAN CATHERINE,[14] b. 11 Sept. 1911; d. 27 May 1940; m. in August 1936 JOHN ROTHERAM.

Child (surname *Rotheram*) : 1. *Jill*, b. 20 Sept. 1937.

ii. BARBARA COGHILL, b. 10 Sept. 1913; m. 1 June 1946 JOHN DOUGLAS PYE SMITH STIRLING, b. 7 Aug. 1918.

Children (surname *Stirling*) : 1. *Elizabeth Anne*, b. 22 March 1947. 2. *Jacqueline Susan*, b. 13 March 1949. 3. *Wendy Margaret*, b. 13 Sept. 1950.

iii. JOSCELIN HUGH, b. 15 Aug. 1915; m. 7 July 1941 KATHARINE ELLEN FORSYTH, daughter of Alexander and Ellen Forsyth of Kenilworth, South Africa.

Children: 1. *David Hugh*,[15] b. 4 Dec. 1942. 2. *Judith Joan*, b. 11 July 1945. 3. *Alison Mary*, b. 2 July 1948. 4. *Janet Katherine*, b. in March 1954.

iv. SUSAN, b. 18 March 1918; m. 27 April 1950 JAMES VAN SETON HENDERSON of Wargrave.

v. DESMOND JAMES, b. 24 May 1920; d. 24 Nov. 1944, killed in action, a lieutenant in the Dragoon Guards.

105. EVELYN COOPER[13] PENROSE (*James Edward*,[12] *John Dennis*,[11] *James*,[10] *Cooper*,[9] *John*,[8] *William*,[7] *Richard*,[6] *Robert*,[5] *Thomas*,[4] *John*,[3] *Nicholas*[2] *Thomas*[1]), born 15 Dec. 1886, died 19 July 1938. He married 29 Aug. 1928 LAURA POWER, daughter of Robert Power of Lismore, co. Waterford.

Child:

i. DERRICK ROCH,[14] b. 8 June 1929; resides now at Edensor, Bakewell, Derbyshire; m. 11 Aug. 1955 ZOE LOUISE BECHER, eldest daughter of Brigadier Ralph Frederick Richard Becher, C.B.E., of Castlehaven, co. Cork.

Children: 1. *James Godfrey*,[15] b. 7 Aug. 1957. 2. *Rory Desmond Fane*, b. 25 April 1959.

106. SAMUEL QUAYLE[13] PENROSE-WELSTEAD (*Samuel*,[12] *Samuel*,[11] *Samuel*,[10] *Samuel*,[9] *Samuel*,[8] *William*,[7] *Richard*,[6] *Robert*,[5] *Thomas*,[4] *John*,[3] *Nicholas*,[2] *Thomas*[1]), of Ballywalter, born in 1861, died 22 Nov. 1925. He married in 1888 ELEANOR GRACE FLEMING, died 12 March 1956 aet. 88, daughter of the Rev. Canon Thomas H. Fleming of Ballinakill, co. Galway.

Children:

i. SAMUEL RICHARD,[14] b. 14 June 1889; captain, Royal Irish Regiment, D.F.C., killed in action in August 1918.

918

ii. REGINALD HUGH, b. 23 April 1891; colonel in the Indian Army; m. 13 May 1918 GERTRUDE EUGENIE PERFECT, daughter of George Perfect of Bara Banki, U.P., India.
Children: 1. *Rosemary Geraldine*,[15] b. 13 April 1919. 2. *Eleanor Mary*, b. 18 March 1924.

107. LEWIS EDWIN[13] PENROSE (*Joseph*,[12] *Steadman*,[11] *Everard*,[10] *Samuel*,[9] *Robert*,[8] *Robert*,[7] *Robert*,[6] *Robert*,[5] *Thomas*,[4] *John*,[3] *Nicholas*,[2] *Thomas*[1]), born at Shellsburg, Iowa, 26 July 1870, died there 5 April 1942. He married DELLA MURRAY who was living in 1961.

Children:

i. MARY GLADYS,[14] b. 11 Nov. 1900; m. 10 June 1932 JEROME GEISMAR; no issue; reside in Cedar Rapids, Iowa.
ii. VIRGIL CLARE, b. 7 Sept. 1902; resides in Cherry Valley, Calif.
iii. HARRIET LUCILE, b. 28 May 1912; m. 9 Dec. 1930 JOHN OWENS of Palo, Iowa.
iv. DONALD LEROY, b. 22 Feb. 1917; unm.

108. HARRY JEFFERSON[13] PENROSE (*Lewis*,[12] *Steadman*,[11] *Everard*,[10] *Samuel*,[9] *Robert*,[8] *Robert*,[7] *Robert*,[6] *Robert*,[5] *Thomas*,[4] *John*,[3] *Nicholas*,[2] *Thomas*[1]), born in Linn County, Iowa, 17 June 1872, died in Shellsburg, Iowa, 31 Aug. 1948. He was a farmer but was admitted to the bar in 1898. He married in Cedar Rapids, Iowa, 9 Aug. 1905, BESSIE HOLLY BOYD, born 26 Aug. 1880, died in Vinton, Iowa, 20 June 1950, daughter of Willoughby Watson Boyd by his wife Nellie M. Richey.

Children:

i. RICHARD LEWIS,[14] b. 14 Aug. 1906; m. 29 Aug. 1929 BETH LENORE LITTRELL, b. 14 Oct. 1908.
Child: 1. *William Dennis*.[15]
ii. WESTON BOYD, b. 4 Nov. 1907; m. at the Little Brown Church in the Vale, Nashua, Iowa, 6 June 1940, INEZ MAXINE WHITNEY, b. 23 Nov. 1903, daughter of Harley J. and Lena Theresa (LeClerc) Whitney; now reside in Siloam Springs, Ark.
Child: 1. *Harry Whitney*,[15] b. in Vinton, Iowa, 23 April 1941.
iii. HELEN RAE, b. 16 Aug. 1910; m. in Shellsburg, 27 May 1933, DUDLEY WATSON DAY III, b. 18 May 1907, son of Dudley Watson Day II by his wife Lula M. Dow; reside now in Libertyville, Ill. Mrs. Day has been very helpful in gathering information on the Iowa Penroses.
Children (surname *Day*), b. in Flushing, N. Y.: 1. *Barbara Helen*, b. 7 April 1936. 2. *Dudley Watson*, b. 13 Jan. 1939; d. 23 Jan. 1939.

109. ALEXANDER PECKOVER DOYLE[14] PENROSE (*James Doyle*,[13] *James Doyle*,[12] *George*,[11] *Daniel*,[10] *Richard*,[9] *Daniel*,[8] *John*,[7] *Richard*,[6] *Robert*,[5] *Thomas*,[4] *John*,[3] *Nicholas*,[2] *Thomas*[1]), of West Bradenham Hall and Thiberton Grange, co. Norfolk, born 12 Aug. 1896, died 23 Aug. 1950. He married first, 8 April 1919, BERTHA GWENDOLEN BAKER, daughter of Philip B. Baker; and secondly, in 1929, FRANCES CONSTANCE SMYTH, daughter of the Rev. Arthur Worsley Smyth, and widow of ———— Saxon. See Burke's *Landed Gentry*, 1939, p. 1788.

Children by first wife:

i. SHEILA MARGARET,[15] b. in Golders Green 30 Oct. 1920; m. 7 Jan. 1949 GEOFFREY HUGO DAW, son of Dr. Samuel W. P. Daw of Leeds.
ii. ANGELA PRISCILLA ELIZABETH, b. at 32 Queens Road, St. John's, 3 May 1924; m. 1 Aug. 1950 JOSEPH PIERRE DERVILLE, son of Joseph Derville, of Paris.

Children by second wife:

iii. ALEXANDER JEREMY PECKOVER, b. 16 Dec. 1929.
iv. SAMUEL, b. 18 Sept. 1933.

110. LIONEL SHARPLES[14] PENROSE (*James Doyle,*[13] *James Doyle,*[12] *George,*[11] *Daniel,*[10] *Richard,*[9] *Daniel,*[8] *John,*[7] *Richard,*[6] *Robert,*[5] *Thomas,*[4] *John,*[3] *Nicholas,*[2] *Thomas*[1]), of Colchester in 1939, was born 11 June 1898. He married MARGARET LEATHES, only daughter of Professor J. B. Leathes, F.R.S. He and his wife are both physicians.

Children:

i. OLIVER,[15] b. 6 June 1929.
ii. ROGER JOHN, b. 8 Aug. 1931.
iii. JONATHAN, b. 7 Oct. 1933.
iv. SHIRLEY VICTORIA, b. 22 Feb. 1945.

111. ROLAND ALGERNON[14] PENROSE (*James Doyle,*[13] *James Doyle,*[12] *George,*[11] *Daniel,*[10] *Richard,*[9] *Daniel,*[8] *John,*[7] *Richard,*[6] *Robert,*[5] *Thomas,*[4] *John,*[3] *Nicholas,*[2] *Thomas*[1]) was born 14 Oct. 1900. He married first, 21 Dec. 1925, VALENTINE ANDREE BOUÉ, daughter of Lieutenant Colonel Boué of Condom, Gers, France, from whom he was divorced in 1939; and secondly, 3 May 1947, ELIZABETH LEE MILLER, daughter of Theodore Miller of Poughkeepsie, N. Y.

Child by second wife:

i. ANTHONY WILLIAM ROLAND,[15] b. 9 Sept. 1947.

112. BERNARD EDMUND[14] PENROSE (*James Doyle,*[13] *James Doyle,*[12] *George,*[11] *Daniel,*[10] *Richard,*[9] *Daniel,*[8] *John,*[7] *Richard,*[6] *Robert,*[5] *Thomas,*[4] *John,*[3] *Nicholas,*[2] *Thomas*[1]) was born 20 Sept. 1903. He married 21 May 1948 ANN ISOBEL NOEL, daughter of Sir Robert McLean of Laidlawsted, Selkirkshire.

Child:

i. JAMES BERNARD KILLIGREW,[15] b. 5 May 1951.

UNPLACED ITEMS

From the marriage register of the Parish of Wheldrake, Yorkshire, the Rev. Canon Arnold Speak, Rector of Wheldrake and Rural Dean of Escrick, has supplied the following items which certainly pertain to the Wheldrake family of Penroses but cannot be placed.

23 April 1610	Matthew Penrose and Isabel Byarley
12 Nov. 1615	Robert Clarkson and Mary Penrose
13 July 1619	William Tate and Elizabeth Penrose
9 Nov. 1623	John Raimes and Elizabeth Penrose
22 June 1624	Henry Lazenby and Ellen Penrose

NOTES ON THE PERKINS PEDIGREE.

S. G. DRAKE, ESQ.,

Dear, Sir: In the Perkins Pedigree published in your   No. 185, it is stated that John Perkins of Ipswich, was born at Newent, Co. Gloucester. Searches at that place have failed to confirm that statement; but the following families of Perkins were living in that vicinity: —

Hasfield is about four miles due East from Newent. Minstersworth the same distance South; inhabitants from either place might be called of Newent, which is the larger town. Gloucester is about five miles South-east of Newent. Tewksbury eight miles to the North-east. Kimmerton within three miles of Tewksbury; Barnwood is close by Gloucester; Hartbury, perhaps the same as Harpery, is very near Hasfield and Newent. There is also a Parkins Grove in the vicinity.

I think that these will warrant us in giving more credit to the common report about John Perkins's place of birth, than such reports usually receive.

Thomas Perkins of Minsterworth, will proved May 7, 1552, mentions Wife Jane, son John, daughter Mary, brother William Hassard, and Kinsman William Wymon.

William Perkins of Minsterworth, will proved Dec. 19, 1551, wife Anne, son John and other children, son-in-law William Brether.

Thomas Perkins of Tewksbury, will proved July 5, 1553, mentions wife Elizabeth, sister Sybil, daughter Margaret, sons Robert and Thomas. — Robert Perkins living at Cogdon.

Elizabeth Perkins of Tewksbury, will proved May 27, 1556, mentions late husband Thomas P., son Thomas and his daughter Elizabeth, son Richard and his daughter Alia. Daughter Margaret. Kinsman John Tyrvell.

Thomas Perkins of Tewksbury, will proved Nov. 3, 1580, mentions wife Elizabeth, son Thomas, daughter Anne, wife of Richard Butler, son-in-law Thomas Leaper, daughter-in-law Margery Leaper. Mentions Mary Roberts.

Thomas Perkins, of Hacelfield, will proved 1558, mentions wife Elizabeth, gives son John the younger a house in the Parish of Elderfield. Elizabeth his widow died same year. Her will mentions daughters Joan the elder and Joan the younger; son John the younger.

Joan Perkins of Haffield, will proved Feb. 4, 1563, mentions sister Joan, Brothers John and Thomas who had children, Sybil and Margaret.

Walter Perkyns of Harpery, will proved 1558, mentions wife Elizabeth, children, Richard, John, Margery, Isabel and Margaret, all under 21.— Overseers, Thomas Perkyns and John Barston.

Hugh Perkins of Barnewood, will proved 1588. Wife Eleanor, children Richard, William, George, Walter, John, Margaret and Elizabeth.

Richard Perkins of Kemerton, will proved Sept. 28, 1583, mentions wife Anne, son Richard, Francis, Edward and Thomas.

Perhaps some of the name here may find herein sufficient encouragement to pursue the investigation.

Yours truly,

W. H. WHITMORE.

THE IDENTITY OF JOHN PERS OF WATERTOWN.—1. John Pers of Norwich, co. Norfolk, England [the founder of one branch of the Peirce or Pierce family in this country], emigrated to New England in 1637 with his wife Elizabeth and their four youngest children, and settled at Watertown ("Peirce Genealogy" by Frederick C. Peirce, published 1880, p. 17; Banks' "Topographical Dictionary of English Emigrants to New England, 1620-1650", pp. 231, 119). He was admitted freeman in 1638 (Savage's Geneal. Dict., vol. 3, p. 428; Bond's Watertown, p. 393; Farmer's Register, p. 228). He may have been in New England prior to 1637 (see the extract from the Mayor's Court Books, Norwich, 1634-1646, fo. 137, quoted in THE REGISTER, vol. 86, p. 258). His eldest son, Anthony[2] of Watertown, was admitted freeman in 1634 ("Peirce Genealogy", p. 21).

According to a register of certain emigrants to New England, preserved in the English Exchequer, John[1] Pers was 49 years old on 8 April 1637 (*ibid.*, p. 17). He died testate at Watertown 19 Aug. 1661. Both Savage and Marvin refer to him as "a man of good estate" (Savage, *op. cit.*, vol. 3, p. 428; Marvin, "History of Lancaster", p. 61; see also "Peirce Genealogy", p. xii). He is stated to have been one of the original proprietors of Lancaster, Mass. (Marvin, *op. cit.*, p. 61; see also "Early Records of Lancaster", by H. S. Nourse, pp. 30-31; Farmer's Register, p. 228). However, he probably never resided there.

2. John[1] Pers of Norwich and Watertown was a weaver. Francis Bloomfield says in his "History of Norwich" (published London, 1745) that in the reign of King Edward III, Norwich became "the most flourishing city of all England by means of its great trade in worsteds, fustian, and all other woolen manufacturers". The "Register of the Freemen of Norwich, 1548-1713", by Percy Millican (published Norwich, 1934), contains two entries, under the heading of "Worsted Weavers", which would appear to be of interest in connection with John[1] Pers, the Watertown emigrant, viz:

P. 158—"Johes Perss, app [apprentice], (Tho. Bassingthwayt), 10 Dec. 11 Jac., f. 37a."

[Note. James I became King of England on 24 March 1603.]
P. 165—"Willus Springall, app. (John Pers), 20 June 1636, f. 40c."

3. The "Society of Colonial Wars—Index of Ancestors" (published 1922) includes the following (p. 373):

"Pierce, John,—1661, Watertown, Mass., Deputy, 1638-39". The implication would appear to be that John[1] Pers (Pierce) of Watertown (who died in 1661) was a Deputy. However, no mention of any such service is made either in the "Peirce Genealogy", above referred to, or in the "Seven Pierce Families" (1936), by H. C. Pierce. Reference should also be made to Bond's Watertown for the list of the deputies from Watertown to the General Court, with the dates of their election. It would seem clear that "Pierce, John, 1661, Watertown, Mass., Deputy 1638-39" should read "Pierce, John,

1661, Dorchester, Mass., Deputy 1638-39" (see Savage's Geneal. Dict., vol. 3, p. 427; see also "Peirce Genealogy" (1880) above referred to, p. xi).

4. So far as the present writer is aware no adequate report has been published concerning the English ancestry of John[1] Pers of Watertown. It would seem probable, however, that the John Pers family lived for many years in or near Norwich in co. Norfolk, England. The "Calendar of The Freemen of Norwich—From 1317 to 1603 (Edward II to Elizabeth, inclusive)", compiled by John L'Estrange (London, 1888), lists a Henry Pers, Glazier, 5 Henry VI.

In his "Genealogy of Thomas[1] Pierce of Charlestown, Mass.", published 1882, Frederic Beech Pierce says—

> "As yet the ancestry in England of the Peirce family has not been followed out in an authentic manner; but in the History of Norwich, Norfolk County, England, under the head of St. Peter's Church, in that town, we find the following in relation to the family living there then—'Sparks Chantry, in this church, was granted, July 23rd, in the 4th of Edward VI, with all its land and rents, etc., in the tenure of Robermore, to Nicholas Le Strange. And in the 23rd of Elizabeth, Peter Perse, cousin and heir of Humphrey Cony, late of this town, held part of these lands, being son of Thomas Perse, son of Margaret Perse, sister of John Cony, father of Humphrey' ".

There is an account by Francis Bloomfield of a Stephen Perse, Senior Fellow of Caius College, Cambridge University, who died the 30th of September 1615 ("History of Norwich", vol. II, p. 215). No attempt has been made, however, to connect this Stephen with the John Pers family of Norwich and Watertown. And the same comment applies to the Peter Perse and Henry Pers previously referred to.

Attention is called to the Index (compiled by Miss M. A. Farrow) of Wills proved in the Consistory Court of Norwich, 1550-1603, "and now preserved in the District Probate Registry at Norwich". This Index contains the following Pierce names:

1550-1603	Register Book
1552—Pierce, Persse, John, Wigenhall, Magdalen	48 Lincolne
1587—Pierce, Perse, John, Swaffham, Norfolk, Yeoman	103 Homes
1597—Pierce, Pearse, John, Hickling, Norfolk	160 Eade
1591—Pierce, Pers, Richard, Cantley, husbandman	19 Appleyard
1592—Pierce, Pers, Richard, junior, Cantley, Norfolk, yeoman	78 Andrews
1592—Pierce, Pierse, Thomas, Mattishall Burgh, Norfolk	168 Bircham
1584—Pierce, Peyrs, William, Wigenhall Peter, Norfolk, yeoman	366 Bate

5. Apparently no real investigation has been made of the connection (if any) of John[1] Pers of Watertown with other families bearing the name of Pierce (in whatever way it has been spelled) that came to New England in the 17th century. In 1882 Frederic Beech Pierce (the compiler of the record of the posterity of Thomas[1] Pierce, 1583-1666, of Charlestown, Mass., hereinabove referred to) suggested that this Thomas[1] Pierce was a brother of John[1] Pers of Watertown "and also of Robert of Dorchester, as the same coat of arms is found in that family". There would appear, however, to be no satisfactory evidence establishing such a relationship ("The Locke Family" (1853), by John G. Locke, p. 317; "The Peirce family of the Old Colony" (1870), by Ebenezer W. Peirce, p. 5). The most recent compiler of genealogies of these families makes no reference to the suggestion (see "Seven Pierce Families", by Harvey Cushman Pierce). The present writer is unable to say whether Robert[1] Pierce, of Dorchester, came from Norwich, co. Norfolk, England. And the same uncertainty exists with respect to Thomas[1] Pierce of Charlestown. It has been stated that Thomas[1] Pierce, the founder of the Charlestown family, came from Stepney, co. [Middlesex], England (see Burke's "Landed Gentry", published London, 1939, p. 2866).

THE PIERCE-FESSENDEN CONNECTIONS.—Elizabeth[6] Pierce or Peirce (Jonas,[5] John,[4] Daniel,[3] Anthony,[2] John[1]), born in Lexington, Mass., 31 May 1735; married

15 Nov. 1753 Timothy[3] Fessenden, 1731-1805, of Lexington and Westminster, Mass. ("Peirce Genealogy", by Frederick C. Peirce, 1880, p. 49). Capt. Solomon[6] Pierce, born 15 June 1742, brother of Elizabeth[6], married 15 Dec. 1763 Amity[4] Fessenden (*ibid.*, p. 50). Sarah[7] Pierce, born 28 Oct. 1754, niece of Elizabeth[6] Pierce, married 21 Nov. 1771 Samuel[4] Fessenden (*ibid.*, p. 69).

Timothy[3] Fessenden (Thomas,[2] Nicholas[1]) was a son of Thomas[2] Fessenden, born in 1684, by his second wife, Abigail[3] Locke (Joseph,[2] Dea. William[1]), a first cousin once removed of the Rev. Dr. Samuel[4] Locke (Samuel,[3] Ebenezer,[2] Dea. William[1]), President of Harvard College, 1770-1773 (see "The Locke Family", by John G. Locke, pp. 27, 45, 51). Timothy[3] Fessenden was probably a great-nephew of Mrs. John[3] Sewall (Hannah[1] Fessenden), a sister-in-law of the eminent Chief Justice Samuel[3] Sewall and of Stephen[3] Sewall from whom Chief Justice Stephen Sewall (Harvard, 1721), derived his descent (*ibid.*, p. 313; Paige's Cambridge, p. 542; Farmer's Register, p. 259).

Timothy[3] Fessenden was a nephew of Nicholas[2] Fessenden (Harvard, 1701), and of the Rev. Benjamin[2] Fessenden (Harvard, 1718) (Paige's Cambridge, p. 542). He was a first cousin of Stephen[3] Fessenden (Nicholas[2]) Harvard, 1737; William[3] Fessenden (William[2]), Harvard, 1737; and Rev. Thomas[3] Fessenden (William[2]), Harvard, 1758. His full brother, John[3] Fessenden, born in 1729, "was for many years one of the most active, prominent, and highly honored men in Worcester County", Mass. (Heywood's "History of Westminister", p. 645). His sister, Elizabeth[3] Fessenden, born in 1721; married 10 Nov. 1741 John[4] Pierce (John,[3] Thomas,[2] Robert[1]) of the "Robert Pierce Family" of Dorchester, Mass. (Peirce genealogy above referred to, p. 250; "The Locke Family", p. 318).

Amity[4] Fessenden, born in 1743, the wife of Capt. Solomon[6] Pierce, was a sister of Samuel[4] Fessenden (Samuel,[3] Thomas,[2] Nicholas[1]) of Lexington, who married Sarah[7] Pierce, niece of Elizabeth[6] Pierce above referred to (Peirce genealogy, p. 69). She was a daughter of Samuel[3] Fessenden and a granddaughter of Thomas[2] Fessenden by his first wife, Abigail Poulter ("The Locke Family", p. 314).

Abigail[4] (Poulter) Fessenden was a daughter of Jonathan[3] Poulter (John,[2] John[1]), born in Billerica, Mass., 25 Jan. 1668/9 (Hudson's Lexington (2nd edition), vol. 2, p. 545). She was a grand-daughter of John[2] Poulter, born in Raleigh, England, in 1635 (*ibid.*). John[2] Poulter married 29 Dec. 1662 Rachel[2] Eliot of Braintree, Mass., born in 1643, "daughter of Francis and Mary (Saunders) and niece of Rev. John Eliot, the Apostle of the Indians" (*ibid.*).

Elizabeth[2] Poulter, born in Raleigh, England, in 1633, a sister of John[2] Poulter; married 22 Nov. 1654, as his first wife, Jonathan[2] Danforth of Billerica. He was a brother of Deputy Governor Thomas[2] Danforth of the Massachusetts Bay Colony, and of the Rev. Samuel[2] Danforth, pastor in Roxbury and Fellow of Harvard College. The Rev. Samuel[2] Danforth married Mary[2] Wilson, daughter of the noted Rev. John[1] Wilson, a graduate of Eton and Cambridge University, and Boston's first pastor (Hazen's "History of Billerica, Genealogical Register", pp. 34, 114; THE REGISTER, * vol. 61, p. 39).

The Rev. John[1] Wilson was a son of the Rev. Dr. William Wilson, D.D., 1542-1615, Canon of Windsor, England, and an Oxford graduate, by his wife, Isabel Woodhall, a niece of Edmund Grindall, the celebrated Archbishop of Canterbury, described by ** Lord Bacon as the "gravest and greatest prelate of the land" (THE REGISTER, vol. 61, p. 37). Mary[2] Wilson, daughter of the Rev. John[1] Wilson and the wife of the Rev. Samuel[2] Danforth, is a direct ancestor through the Bromfields, Powells, and Masons of Patrick[5] Grant (Alexander Galt,[4] Judge Robert,[3] Patrick,[2] Patrick[1]), Harvard, 1945, who married Rosamond Williams[12] Pierce, a great-great-great-great-granddaughter of John[6] Pierce, brother of the Solomon[6] and Elizabeth[6] Pierce referred to above.

Dedham, Mass.   JOHN B. PIERCE.

*P. 832, the third volume of this series.
**P. 830, the third volume of this series.

SOME ACCOUNT OF THE PETERS FAMILY.

The following letter of the Rev. Thomas Peters may throw some light on the early beginnings of our country. It has never been printed (to our knowledge) before. Concerning its author we know very little, as he continued but a short time in New England, or, about six years. It would however be inferred from Farmer's Register, that he did not arrive in the country till 1646, which inference would be incorrect, as will appear by this article. The passage of Mr. Farmer concerning him was probably drawn from that book of Samuel Peters, "a work," in that careful author's language, "which it is hazardous to quote," and is as follows. "Thomas was a brother of Hugh Peters, was a minister in Cornwall, England, from whence he was driven by *Sir Ralph Hopton* in the time of the civil wars. He came to New England and commenced a settlement at Pequot River with John Winthrop [jr.] in 1646. He remained here but a short time, being called back to his people, to which he returned in 1647."

When an individual has become a memorable point in history, whether from his good or bad fortune, or good or bad qualities, (by the present standard of men's judgments,) there is a natural desire to know some-

925

thing of his kindred or family. The course pursued by the *Rev. Hugh Peters* in aid of those opposed to the arbitrary rule of *Charles the First*, and the fate he met with at the restoration, place him among those conspicuous points in history. He came earlier to America than his brother, but continued here nearly an equal length of time. The family seat of the Peters appears to have been at Fowey, in Cornwall, and here *Hugh* was born, as probably were his brothers, if he had more than one. The family had long been of considerable note when *Hugh* came upon the stage, and as late as the time of *Warburton*, one of the family attracted his attention by his literary productions. This was the *Rev. Charles Peters*, A. M., rector of Bratton-Clovelly, in Devon, and afterwards of St. Maybin, in Cornwall. To form an estimate of the literary abilities of this gentleman, we must look elsewhere than in the "Divine Legation." A historian of Cornwall, Dr. Polwhele, gives him a fine character, as well literary as moral. He was born in 1691, and died in 1775, a. 84.

Under 1646, Governor Winthrop mentions that "a plantation was begun at Pequod river, by *Mr. John Winthrop, jr.*, *Mr. Thomas Peter*, a minister, (brother to Mr. [*Hugh*] *Peter*, of Salem.") And in a letter which Winthrop wrote to his son, dated, "Boston, 16(9)46," he says, The Rainbow went hence the 10th of this present with 80 passengers, but Mr. Peters is resolved to go by Malago with Captain Hawkins. (The same Capt. Thomas Hawkins, probably, who arrived at Boston in October, 1646.) Hence it is fair to infer that Mr. Peters sailed for England towards the close of 1646, and from a passage in Dr. Trumbull's History of Connecticut there can be little or no doubt that he came over in 1639. The interesting passage from Trumbull is as follows. "About midsummer [1639,] Mr. *George Fenwick*, with his lady and family, arrived in a ship of 250 tons. Another ship came in company with him. They were both for Quinnipiack. Mr. Fenwick and others came over with a view to take possession of a large tract upon the river, in behalf of their lordships, the original patentees, and to plant a town at the mouth of the river. A settlement was soon made and named Saybrook, in honor to their lordships, Say and Seal and Brook. *Mr. Fenwick, Mr. Thomas Peters*, who was the first minister in the plantation, Capt. *Gardiner*, *Thomas Leffingwell*, *Thomas Tracy*, and Capt. *John Mason*, were some of the principal planters. Indeed the *Huntingtons, Baldwins, Raynolds's, Backus's, Bliss's, Watermans, Hides, Posts, Smiths*, and almost all the names afterwards to be found at Norwich were among the first inhabitants of Saybrook."

Thomas Peters was probably influenced to return to England from the circumstance of the conspicuousness of his brother *Hugh*, who was now or about this time at the zenith of his popularity. Probably Capt. Hawkins brought over the great and important news of the "deathblow given to royalty in the west of England," in the signal defeat at Torrington in Devonshire. It was there that *Hugh*, then chaplain to the Parliament's forces, exhorted them to exertion in the cause with great effect. Torrington surrendered to Gen. Fairfax on the 17th of

February, 1646, and only one month previous Dartmouth had surrendered under similar circumstances. Here too " the celebrated *Hugh Peters*" was equally conspicuous. *Sir Thomas Fairfax* having prepared to storm the place, Peters exhorted the soldiers in a manner and tone which ensured them to do their duty, and success crowned their arms at every point.

We have given a much longer preface to our short letter than we had any idea of when we commenced it. There is no date to the letter, but it is pretty certain that it was written in 1646, and perhaps early in that year. A war was kept up between the Mohegans and Narragansets, and messengers were often passing from Boston to the Indians in Connecticut, and it is probable that this letter was brought to Boston by a messenger of that kind.

It may be proper to add, that there seems to have been a relationship between the *Peters* and Winthrop families, other than that formed by the marriage of John Winthrop, jr. to *Elizabeth*, the daughter of *Hugh Peters*. Gov. Winthrop of Boston, writing to his son John of Connecticut, 26(8)46, mentions the arrival of Capt. Hawkins, " upon the last day of the week at evening, in a ship of 220 tons," and that, " there came no more in her but my sister, *Peter*." Again, he writes, 7(9)48, (to his son,) " we have now received full and certain intelligence from England by Capt. Hawkin's ship, (God was pleased to change his voyage and send him to heaven by the way.)" In this letter he speaks of the news from the contending armies, and adds, in a sort of postscript, " My brother *Peter* took the Duke of Hamilton prisoner."

No attempt at explanation appears in Winthrop's history, where these letters first appeared in print, under the editorship of Mr. Savage. Perhaps he did not wish to commit himself by any conjecture ; but we plead ignorance and ask for information. Did *Hugh Peters* marry a sister of Gov. Winthrop ? Hugh Peters *was at* the taking of the Duke of Hamilton in Preston fight, and if Winthrop means *him*, the rumor that Peters " took the duke prisoner," proved unfounded ; and if he did not mean *him*, who did he mean ? That Peters was in the bloody battle at Preston there can be no question, and we are told by some, that he encouraged the men by his presence, mounted, and, with a drawn sword, inspired the soldiers to firmness.

There is among the English Pedigrees, one of *Peters*, from which we take the following :

The Lady Alice Pole, in the reign of Henry III., (1216—1272,) gave the manor and castle of Compton, in Devonshire, to one of the family of Peter, whose posterity afterwards took the name of the place. Another branch settled at Torr-Newton, in the adjacent parish of Torr-Brian, of which was

JOHN PETER, who lived in the reigns of Richard II. (1377, &c.) and Henry IV. (1399, &c.,) and who by his wife Alice, left issue, two sons,

I.   JOHN, his successor.

II. NICHOLAS, who succeeded to his mother's estates at Bakebeare, in Dorsetshire, and Milton, in Hants, and was M. P. for Shaftesbury, 28 Henry IV. (1450 ;) he d. *s. p.*

JOHN (I.,) the elder brother, inherited his father's estates in Devonshire, and left issue

WILLIAM, who it appears was 24 years of age in 1475, (14 Edward IV.). At which time he came into possession of his father's estates, and also those of his uncle, who d., as before mentioned, *s. p.* He had issue

I. JOHN of Torr-Newton, who m. Alice, dau. of John Collins, Esq., of Woodlands, and was father of Sir William Peter, or Petre, principal Secretary of State in the reigns of Henry VIII.,* Edward VI., Mary, and Elizabeth, and ancestor of the Lords Petre of Writtle, in the co. of Essex.

II. WILLIAM, who succeeded to his father's estates in Dorsetshire and Hants, and further increased his patrimony by his marriage with Joan, only dau. and heiress of Sir Roger Arundel of Calwoodly, co. Devon, by whom he had issue, three sons,

I. ROGER, who d. young.

II. WILLIAM, who succeeded his father, and d. *s. p.*, 37 Henry VII., (1522.)

III. JOHN, of Bowlay, near Exeter, and was M. P. from that city, time Philip and Mary. He m. Wilmot. dau. of John Peter, Esq., his cousin, of Torr-Newton, and sister of Sir William Peter, Secretary of State, and d. 1579, leaving a large family, among whom were

I. JOHN, who was a member of the first Parliament of Philip and Mary for Dartmouth, (the same Parliament in which his father was a member for Exeter,) but d. *s. p.* in the lifetime of his father.

II. OTHO, who succeeded to the estates of his father in Devonshire, as well as to those of his mother's brother, John Peter, custumar of Exeter, in other lands possessed by him in the same county, and was seated at Bowhay. Of this branch of the Peters family, is the present Earl Bathurst of Bowhay. There is in Exminster church near Exeter, a long latin inscription, commemorative of OTHO PETER, ESQ., which OTHO was father of the last male heir, who m. Frances, dau. of *Thomas Southcote, Esq.*

III. THOMAS, to whom his father gave divers lands in Cornwall, (which lands had been acquired of William Peter, his grandfather, by marriage with Joan Arundel,) m. Agnes, dau. of Thomas Godolphin, of Godolphin, Esq., (by his 2d wife. dau. of the noble house of Granville,) and was succeeded by his eldest son,

ROBERT, who was bred a soldier, and served with distinction under Sir Edward Poynings at Havre, and in the Low Countries. In

---

* This king appointed Sir William Peter one of the overseers of his will, 1546. There is, in Prince's *Worthies of Devonshire*, a long and exceedingly interesting life of Sir William Peter, knight, and a pedigree of the family, not much differing in import from this we give from Burkes.

the 13th Elizabeth he was M. P. for Fowey, in the 14th for Penryn, and in the 28th of the same reign, for Dartmouth. He m. Thomasine, dau. of John Kestell of Kestell, co. Cornwall, Esq., and left issue two sons,

I.   HENRY, his heir,
II. JOHN, of Treverran, who m. Elizabeth, dau. of William Thoms, of Devonshire,

HENRY (the heir,) M. P. for Fowey, in the 1st Parliament of James I., m. in 1609, Deborah, dau. of John Treffrey, Esq. of Place, a lineal descendant of Sir John Treffrey, who for his gallant services in France, particularly at Crecy and Poictiers, was created Knt. Banneret by the Black Prince, and permitted by Edward III. to quarter the royal lilies of France alternately with the arms of his own family. This HENRY PETER d. in 1619, leaving issue by his wife Deborah,

THOMAS, b. 1610, who m. in 1632, Elizabeth, only daughter and heiress of Henry Michell, Esq., of Harlyn, co. of Cornwall. Having been an active royalist in the civil wars between *Charles* and his Parliament, THOMAS PETER was for a long time imprisoned by Cromwell, but obtained his release on the 2d Feb., 1653, through the influence of his maternal kinsman, the celebrated HUGH PETERS. He d. in 1675, leaving three sons and a dau., m. to Henry Vincent, Esq. The successor of THOMAS PETER was his son GREGORY, Esq., of Harlyn.

The English genealogist here makes the following mystifying note, and in a confused manner, without intention probably, gives us the clue to the genealogy of HUGH PETERS.

" HUGH PETERS was of a family which had been driven from Antwerp on account of its religion. He was the s. of Thomas Dikewood Peters, a merchant of Fowey, by Martha, dau. of John Treffry, Esq., of Place. The name of Peters was first assumed by Thomas Dykewood, the grandfather of Hugh."

We will close our present account by a brief extract from the Life of HUGH PETERS, by the Rev. Samuel Peters, LL. D., on the genealogy of the family, although it may be less satisfactory even than that we have already given; but as he claims kindred to HUGH, and consequently to Thomas, we ought certainly to let him be heard. This is his account:

" Mr. Hugh Peters was born of a rich family, but was made poor by Archbishop Laud by fines in the star chamber court, for his nonconformity to the ceremonies of the Church of England; and he gloried in his poverty, in his stripes, and imprisonment. The family of which he had his descent came from Normandy, with William the Conqueror, in 1066, and John Peters was knighted by Henry VIII., and his grandson, John, was created baron by James I., in 1603.

" The genealogy of Lord Peters in the Herald's office, points out a curious circumstance respecting the mode of spelling the name. The name of the oldest son is wrote *Petre;* the name of the second son,

Petres; that of the third, *Peter,* that of the fourth, Peters, and the fifth is *Petrie.* William Peters was the fourth son of Sir John Petre, Knt., of Exeter, in Devonshire. He m. Miss Elizabeth Treffry of Fowey, in Cornwall, a family of great antiquity, which yields not in gentility to any in Cornwall, and which resides in the same place and house to this day [1807]. Said William Peters was a merchant at Fowey, and had many sons and daughters by Elizabeth his wife. At present only three of these sons will be named. They became eminent puritan characters in Old and New England. WILLIAM was the oldest son. THOMAS, [the author of our letter,] and Hugh."

It is said,* that while at Saybrook, Thomas Peters established a school, which eventually became the foundation of Yale College. The Rev. Samuel Peters, LL. D., from whose Life of Hugh we have here extracted, was descended from WILLIAM, who settled near Boston in 1634, and whose posterity have now become quite numerous in Connecticut. There are no descendants of Thomas in this country, but of Hugh there are, in the female line. We may hereafter give a regular genealogy of the descendants of WILLIAM PETERS.

SIR,

Y^r letter to so vnworthy a creatur gaue no small refreshment, let these of mine testifie my reall and cordiall thanks. No man icyes [rejoices?] mo^r at ye iron mines* successe than myselfe who publish it as [a] very mercy of God in this nicke of times and help ō [on] wth my prayers y^t still it may psp [prosper] and answer y^r and our desires. Sir, M^r· ffen-wicke and his Lady present their due respects vnto you, giving thanks for the shoot instruments ; but her rabbets are most ded — not past two alive. Some vermine having devoured them. Neithr can I heare of any in these pts as yet. Nor will I cease to inquir. I humbly beseech you to inclose this to my brother to be sent safely to him by some friend of yors. For til this 18th letter I haue sent him, and so to my wife, yet neuer could re-ceiue one sellable frō either. We heare of 2 Bristoll ships wth you. I feare their cōing [coming] is not for good. The Lord guide y^r counsells and give yor hands full of zeale for his hono^r· Wee haue death of our Indian friends in Neanticot on oure side, slaine by the Naragantzets, and the death of English on tother side at Stamford, that calle for action ; for vp and be doing frō such as a^r in the Lords stead heare. Thee parlia-ments dilections‡ braught most of Englands miseries on y^ee saints. Y^ee Lord help y^r spirits to be stirring betims. And with his owne spirit of power and wisdō. Let my due service be tendred to y^r godly yoakfellow, y^r son and his and all y^rs· To Mr. Cotton, Mr. Wilson and all theirs, and

---

* Preface to a new edition of a History of Connecticut, by Rev. Samuel Peters, LL. D.

† The " iron mines " here referred to were at Lynn ; they were not wrought at Brain-tree until the early part of 1652, though the same company seems to have been interested in both. Mr. Lewis has, in his *History of Lynn,* cleared up this important and neglected matter, as to Lynn ; and we hope ere long an historian of Braintree will do as much for the Iron Works of that place. We will engage to help him, whoever he may be.

‡ This word seems to be used here more according to its old Latin signification, than to any meaning attached to it by either early or late English lexicographers. It is pretty evident the writer thought too much *charity* had been extended towards the king and his party.

all my good friends in Boston.   Begging y^r and all their helping prayers
to the throne of mercy. *

Frō y^r unworthy servant
THO: PETERS.

[Superscribed.]
To the wor^ll his much honored
freind John Winthrop
Esquire at his house
in Boston these
present.

SOME ACCOUNT OF THE PETERS FAMILY: ADDITION.—The identity of Rev. Thoma-
Peters who came to Connecticut in 1639 with George Fenwick, but returned to England appeared in THE REGISTER, volume II. As shown in *D.N.B.* this man was brother
to the famous Hugh Peters.

The will of Thomas Peters, "twenty years at Mylor in Cornwall as preacher of the
Gospel of Jesus Christ, though with little success", is dated 26 Oct. 1654 and was
proved 19 January following. It names the testator's children, John (to receive lands
in Fowey and schooling at Oxford), Mary, Sarah, Ann and Elizabeth. The testator
names his wife Ann and his brother-in-law Robert Hancocke, gent.

The will of the son, John Peters, is also at P.C.C., dated 27 Dec. 1672 and proved
30 Dec. 1673. It names his wife Jane and her children Richard Mildren and Mary
Mildren, from which it would seem that John left no issue. His will, which styles
him of Mylor in Cornwall, gent., together with the will of his father, have been forwarded (in abstract form) to the Library of the Society for retention.

Arlington, Va.   JOHN G. HUNT.

* We may possibly have mistaken some words in this letter, as it is altogether the most
difficult specimen of old chirography we ever undertook to decipher, though our *trials* in
this way have not been small.   Not but that we have had worse MSS. to deal with, owing
to their having been so long exposed to dampness, and become obscure in that way, but
this letter of *Peters* is as fair and legible as it was *the day he had his hand upon it.*

931

NOTES ON THE PITKIN ANCESTRY IN ENGLAND

Communicated by Miss MARY KINGSBURY TALCOTT of Hartford, Conn.

THESE Pitkin notes were gathered by the compiler in England during the past summer, and, while not giving a complete family record, they furnish interesting particulars regarding the English origin of a family which has been a prominent one in Connecticut, having furnished a Governor, a United States Senator, several Judges of the Superior Court and other eminent lawyers, a number of military officers who served in the French and Indian Wars and in the Revolution, and also several clergymen.

William Pitkin, who came to Hartford in 1659, and was, at once, engaged to fill the position of Master of the Grammar School, had received an excellent legal education, and, judging from the contents of a number of note-books in his handwriting which have been preserved, he was well taught in theological lore. About two years later he was appointed King's Attorney for the Colony, and he was considered one of the ablest lawyers in Connecticut. He was Deputy from Hartford to the General Court from 1675 to 1684, 1689, 1690, Treasurer of the Colony, 1676–1678, Assistant, 1690–1694, holding this office at the time of his death, Commissioner of the United Colonies, for Connecticut, in 1678, Commissioner in 1683 to treat with Governor Dongan about the New York Boundary, and in 1693 one of the Commissioners to adjust the New York Boundary Line. He died Dec. 16, 1694, aged 58, according to his gravestone in the Centre Church burying-ground in Hartford. He married, about 1661, Hannah, daughter of Ozias Goodwin of Hartford. In his will, dated Sept. 27, 1694, he mentions his "dear Brother Roger," and his "Sister Woolcott." The latter was the brilliant and attractive Martha Pitkin, who came to New England in

1661 to visit her brother, hoping, according to tradition, to take him back to England with her. So great was the admiration aroused by her talents and brilliancy it was decided by some of the elders of the Colony that such a desirable personality should not be allowed to leave the Colony, and that she should be induced to remain. It is also said that some of the younger men drew lots to decide which of them should be fortunate enough to pay his addresses to her. Simon Wolcott, of Windsor, was the lucky man, and she married him and became the ancestress of a distinguished race—governors, judges, etc. After Mr. Wolcott's death she married a second husband, Hon. Daniel Clark. She died in East Windsor, Oct. 13, 1719, " in her 80th year," which corresponds exactly to the date of her baptism in Berkhamsted, Co. Herts, in 1639.

It will be seen that all the particulars the compiler has found in England agree with such traditional knowledge as we had of the early history of the Pitkins, and it is interesting to know that the father of William, Roger, and Martha was an Oxford graduate, and Master of the famous old school at Berkhamstead, originally founded by King Henry VIII, but re-organized and endowed by Edward VI, and known as the Free School of King Edward VI. Some Pitkin wills of an earlier date were found, and as the testators lived in the vicinity of Berkhamstead they were probably related to William, the burgess of Berkhamstead. The will of Robert Pytkyne of Ivinghoe, Co. Bucks, dated Feb. 27, 1579, mentions two sons named William, William the elder, and William the younger, and a further search may reveal a relationship.

In Vol. 34, pp. 194–5, of the REGISTER is printed a letter from Walter Barnesley, of London, to William Pitkin in Hartford, written in 1667, which confirms the foregoing statements. See also the *Pitkin Genealogy, by A. P. Pitkin, Hartford, 1887,* and *Mrs. Salisbury's Family Histories, 1892, Vol. 2.*

ABSTRACTS OF PITKIN WILLS

The will of WILLIAM PITKIN of Berkhamstead St. Peter in ye County of Hertford, 12 June 1644. To son John Pitkin £300; to daur Martha Pitkin £300; to daur Joane Pitkin £200; to daur Jane Pitkin £200; to daur Elizabeth Lawson, wife of Willm Lawson, £20. To my grande childe Willm Pitkin all those my six tenements situated at Wadnam Greene in ye phe of Fullame in ye County of Midd to him and his heyers forever, and untill he shall attayne to the age of one and twentye yeares, the rents thereof to be received by my Executor and imployed for and towardes his maintenance and educacion. To my granchilde Roger Pitkin £150 to be payed unto him when he attaines the age of one and twentye yeares, and in ye meantime ye interest to be imployed for his maintenance and educacion. Unto my granchilde Martha Pitkin £150 of current English money to be payed to her or to her Assines att hir age of one and twentye yeares, and in ye meantime ye interest thereof to go for and towardes her maintenance or other preferment. If any or either of my children, John Pitkin, Martha Pitkin, Joane Pitkin, or Jane Pitkin, shall die before their Legacies be payed to them, the amount of the said Legacy to be divided among the survivors of them. If any of my said granchildren, Willm Pitkin, Roger Pitkin, or Martha Pitkin, shall die before receiving their Legacy, ye said Legacy shall remaine to ye Executor. All ye rest of my goods and chattells and Freehold Lands, subsequentyed my Debts and Legacyes being pay^d, I give unto my son Francis Pitkin, whom I make my Sole Executor. I desire my well beloved Coosen Mr Roger Pitkin to be Overseer, and I give him twenty shillings to buy him a ringe. [Signed] Will͞m Pitkin. Witnesses: Roger Pitkin, Henry Hardinge, Edmond Geare. Proved Martii 1644[-5]. Inventory of William Pitkyn of Barkhamstead St. Peter, in ye county of Hertford, gentleman, deceased, taken by John Benninge and Willm Lake, gent., the xiiii daye of March, 1644[-5]. (P. C. C., Hitchin Division.)

The will of ROGER PITKIN of Harrold in the county of Bedford, gentleman, 13 Oct. 1651. To Kinsman Edward Allyn an annuity of £5 yearly during his life. Loving wife Anne to have her jointure out of the messuage and lands in Wootton and Kempston; also to have an annuity, or yearly rent charge, of £30 from the said lands. A Cottage and Close or pasture lying in Wymington in the County of Bedford to my Loving Kinsman John Pitkin, and to him the messuage or Inn in Bedford called the Falcon. To loving kinsman John Greene of Clement's Inn, Gent., £50. To God Sonne John Grave (?) £50. To Roger Pitkin my God Sonne, late the Sonne of William Pitkin, deceased, £50. To Jane Money, the Dau^r of my Sister Joan Money, £100 to be paid when she shall attaine the age of twentie yeares. To Kinsman Thomas Woodward 20s. to buy him a ringe. To Thomas Money, the Sonne of Joan Money my Sister, £700. To Mr [*illegible*] of the towne of Bedforde Church, £5, he to preach at my Funerall. To Loving Friend John Browne, Gentleman, £10. To God daughter Jane Chamberlain, £5 to buy her a piece of plate. To the poore of Stagden £6; to the poore of Kempston £5; to the poore of Wootton £5. If it please God I depart this Life att Harrold where I now live, then I give to the poore of Harrold £5. All the remainder of my estate to Kinsman John Pitkin, and he the sole Executor, on condition that he enter into a bond of £2000 unto the aforesaid Thomas Money, and if the said John Pitkin shall refuse to do this, then Thomas Money shall become Executor. Kinsman John Greene, Gentleman, Friend John Browne, Gentleman, Overseers. Witnesses: John Browne, John Greene, Francis Pitkin. Proved 9 Feb. 1651[-2] by John Pitkin, Executor. (P. C. C., Bowyer, 39.)

"John Pitkin ye elder, gent.," was buried at Kempston, Dec. 27, 1692. Very possibly he was the John Pitkin mentioned in the above will. There are many Pitkin entries in the Kempston Register between 1670 and 1700.

EXTRACTS FROM THE PARISH REGISTER
OF BERKHAMSTEAD ST. PETER

Baptisms

1607[-8], Jan. 3, George, sonne of Wyllyam Pitkyn
1608, Dec. 11, Wyllyam ye sonne of Wyllyam Pitkyn
1612, Oct. 17, Martha, ye daughter of Will͞m Pitkyn
1613, Frauncys ye sonne of Willia Pitkyn
1616, Nov. 10, George ye sonne of Wm Pitkyn, gent.
1618, March 14, Martha, ye daughter of Willm Pitkyn, gent.

1621, July 1, Elizabeth ye daughter of Willm Pitkyn, gent.
1623, Octob. 19, John, sonne of Willm Pitkyn, gent.
1626, Sept. 26, Jhone, ye daughter of William Pitkyn, gent.
1628, April 8, Jane, ye daughter of Willyam Pitkyn, gent.
1638, Novr 28, Roger, sonne of William Pitkyn, Scholemaster.
1639, Dec. 12, Martha, daughter of Willy^m Pitkyn, Scholemaster.
1646/7, Sarah ye daughter of Mr Fra: Pitkin, baptized 21 Jan.
1649, Joan, ye daughter of Mr Pitkin bap. 25 May

Burials

1640, Nov. 4, Jane, daughter of Willm Pitkyn Scholemaster, buried.
1641, Dec. 28. The wife of Willm Pitkyn, Scholem^r buried.

Another copy of the parish register gives the following:

1644[–5], Willyam Pitkin gent^l. was buried the 6 day of January.
1638, Rogger the Sonne of William & Elizabeth Pitkin, Scolemaster, was baptized 28 November.
1639, Martha the Daughter of William Pitkin, Scolemaster And Elizabeth his wife was baptized the XII of December.

Rev. William Pitkin was Master of the Grammar School of Berkhamstead in 1636, and later. He was buried at St. Dunstan's, Fleet Street, London. *Lectures on the History and Antiquities of Berkhamstead, by Rev. John W. Cobb, M.A., p. 116.*

Chauncy's Historical Antiquities of Hertfordshire also mentions him as Master of the School, and says he died before 1648. *II, 534, 547.*

In Cussans's County History of Hertfordshire it is stated that Willm Pitkyn was one of the jurors of the Honour of Barkhamstead in the County of Hertford. He was also a freeholder. In 1619 William Pitkin, Gent., was named as one of the Burgesses—one of the twelve men in the Borough "of the best and most honest Burgesses who shall be called Capital Burgesses of the Burrough, and shall be the Common Council of the Burrough,"—and a Charter was granted to them by King James.

He is mentioned in this charter as "Willelmus Pitkin, generosus." William Pitkin was Bailiff in 1638; Francis Pitkin was Bailiff in 1650; William Pitkin was one of the Chief Burgesses in 1628 and in 1645, and represented Berkhamstead in Parliament.

William Pitkin, son of William of Berkhamstead, Herts, pleb., Pembroke College, Oxford, matriculated Feb. 6, 1628/9, aged 20; B.A. next day; M.A. Oct. 17, 1631.

Burials

July 24, 1643, ——— Pitkin, A minister was buryed from Mr Sturmey's in Chancery Lane.
Sept. 12, 1643, Mr George Pittkin, gent., was buryed from Mr Sturmies' Chancery Lane.

DEPOSITION OF MRS. MARY OSGOOD.—"The deposition of Mrs. Mary Osgood (alias Clemence), now of Andover, in the County of Essex in New England, formerly of the City of Coventry in Warwickshire, Old England, aged 58 years, who testifieth & saith that before the year Anno Dom°. 1652, I lived in the City of Coventry abovesaid, and boarded at the house of Mr. Biddle in Hog Lane, & was then well acquainted with Mrs. Ann Potter, grand-daughter to Thomas Potter, Esqr. who had been Mayor of the City; the said Mrs. Ann Potter her father's name was as I have been informed, Humphrey Potter, the only son of said Thomas Potter, Esqr; the abovesaid Ann Potter (whose parents as I have heard were murdered in Ireland) is now living in Salem in New England & wife to Mr. Anthony Neadham; and also said Mary Osgood does further testify that Mrs. Rebeccah Bacon, aunt to the abovesaid Ann Potter, sent to England for her, which invitation she accepted. Mrs. Mary Osgood made oath to what is abovewritten this 19 July, 1695, before me, Dudley Bradstreet, Jus. Peace. Examined, S. Sewall, Register." [*Copied by C. M. Endicott, from Essex Registry of Deeds,* Bk. X. Folio 190.

PRATT.—In looking over a bundle of family papers, recently, I came upon a small parchment which may prove to be of interest to some reader of the REGISTER. Through the kindness of Ernest Cheyne, Esq., of the Probate Registry, Somerset House, London, a few words which could not be deciphered, owing to an ancient fold in the document, have been recovered so that it is possible to print the full text of this Letter of Administration. It bears two five-shilling stamps.

THOMAS by divine providence Archbishop of Canterbury primate of all England and Metropolitan

To our well beloved in Christ JAMES PRATT the natural and lawful Brother and next of kin of SAMUEL PRATT late of Boston in New England a Batchelor deceased.

Greeting whereas the said SAMUEL PRATT as is alledged lately died intestate having whilst living and at the time of his death Goods Chattels or Credits in divers dioceses or Jurisdictions by reason whereof the sole ordering and granting administration of all and singular the said Goods Chattels and Credits and also the auditing allowing and final discharging the accompt thereof are well known to appertain only and wholly to us and not to any inferior Judge. We being desirous that the said Goods Chattels and Credits may be well and faithfully Administered applied and disposed of according to Law Do therefore by these presents grant full power and Authority to you in whose fidelity we confide to administer and faithfully dispose of the Goods Chattels and Credits of the said deceased and to ask demand recover and receive whatever Debts and Credits which whilst living and at the time of his death did any way belong to his Estate and to pay whatever Debts the said deceased at the time of his death did owe so far as such Goods Chattels and Credits will thereto Extend and the Law requires you having been already sworn well and faithfully to Administer the same and to make a true and perfect Inventory of all and Singular the said Goods Chattels and Credits and to Exhibit the same into the Registry of our prerogative Court of Canterbury on or before the last day of January next ensuing and also to render a Just and true accompt thereof on or before the last day of July which shall be in the year of our Lord One Thousand Seven hundred and Sixty eight and We do by these presents ordain depute and constitute you Administrator of all and Singular the Goods Chattels and Credits of the said

deceased Given at London the third Day of July in the Year of Our Lord one
thousand seven hundred and sixty seven and in the tenth Year of Our Translation.

$$\left. \begin{array}{l} \text{W}^{\text{m}}.\ \text{Legard} \\ \text{Hen : Stevens} \\ \text{John Stevens} \end{array} \right\} \begin{array}{l} \textit{Deputy} \\ \textit{Registers.} \end{array}$$

Extracted by Robt Longdon proctor in Drs Commons

(*on seal*) Longdon
Search
1^{s} 6

I am unable to identify these brothers, but a thorough examination of our
public records may establish their identity. It is possible that James Pratt never
came to America, and that his brother was here for only a brief period.
Cambridge, Mass.   HENRY H. EDES.

PARENTAGE OF JOHN PRESCOTT, WHO SETTLED IN 1645 AT LANCASTER, MASS.—
At page 238 of the July 1958 REGISTER, the Society records receipt of a Prescott
genealogy dated 1957, wherein Frederick Lewis Weis presents "eight lines of descent
of John Prescott, founder of Lancaster, Mass., 1645, from Alfred the Great, King of
England, 871-901."
The aforesaid eight lines record some of the ancestors of Ralph Prescott of Shevington, parish of Standish, Lancashire, who died testate in 1608/9; in his will he named
his wife Elene, daughters Elene, Alice, and Cecilie, and son John.
Dr. Weis has identified the aforesaid legatee, John, with John Prescott, settler in
1645 of Lancaster, Mass., for the following reasons:

  i. Prescott is claimed to have founded Lancaster (in which case, he or his father
       probably came from Lancashire).
  ii. His wife in 1678 identified him with Halifax, Yorkshire, where their children
       were baptized.
  iii. His father's will is claimed to identify him with the Prescott family of Standish
        Parish, Lancashire.

While Prescott was a founder, he should not be called "the founder" of Lancaster,
for others were associated with him in the purchase and settlement of that town.
An identification by his wife, showing that Prescott had lived in Halifax, cannot be
held to prove association with Standish parish, some forty miles away from Halifax.
A will of a testator who died in 1608/9 can hardly be held to prove any connection

with an emigrant who left England several decades afterwards, in the absence of other factors.

The published Parish Register of Standish Parish, in Lancashire, fails to record the baptism of a John Prescott of Shevington. However, that register includes the following entry:

"Buried, 28 Oct. 1616, John Prescott of Shevington". In the absence of contrary proof, the preceding entry must be held to record the interment of the legatee, John Prescott, son of Ralph Prescott, of Shevington, the above testator.

In the light of this evidence, it would seem that we who descend from Prescott of Lancaster, Mass.,must reject the parentage of Prescott, advanced by Dr. Weis.

It is significant, that there were several persons named John Prescott in Standish parish, as indicated by the following entries from the printed registers:

John Prescott of Shevington, buried 20 July 1579
John Prescott buried 1563/4; John Prescott buried 1570
    "   "   '   1585 ;   "   "   "   1611
    "   "   "   1614 ;   "   "   "   1615.
John Prescott baptized in 1612, son of John.
    "   "   "   " 1613, son of Thomas.
John Prescott had wife Margaret in July, 1628.
    "   "   "   " Grace, 26 Nov. 1637.

Cecilie, bap. 1602, and Ellen, bapt. 1607, daughters of John Prescott.
Cecilie Prescott was buried in 1628.

Further, it would seem to be highly significant that John Prescott of Lancaster had no known issue named Ralph, Roger, Alexander, Ellen, Helen, Cecile or Alice, which are the names one would expect to be commemorated in the family of a descendant of the armigerous Prescotts of Shevington. Moreover, the only son of that gentle English family would probably not have been a blacksmith, as was our John Prescott of Lancaster.

Since the foregoing was prepared, the following records have come to my attention: In Errington (adjoining Sowerby, Halifax Parish) one Bridget Prescot was buried 12 July 1624 ("Heptonstall Parish Registers", printed). Chances are that she was sister or mother of John Prescott who settled in Lancaster in 1645.

The following records are from printed Lancashire Parish registers:
Christened 27 Nov. 1606, John, son of Henry Prescot (at Prescot).
    "   20 Apr. 1606, John Preskot, son of James (at Ornskirk).

Further, wills at Chester indicate that the Prescotts were living in the early seventeenth century in Halsall, Heskin, Ince in Makerfield, Standish, Newlon, Upholland, Wigan, Gorton, Coppul and Sefton. The will of Robert Orrell the elder of Wigan, dated 1623, names his cousin William Molyneux, gent, and leaves legacies to Cicely, Jane, Agnes and Elizabeth, daughters of John Prescot (Chetham Soc., vol. 37 (1897), pp. 22 through 25).

In my opinion, one would have to search the registers of all the parishes named above as well as of the parishes in Lancs. that adjoin Yorkshire, before he could venture an opinion as to who was the father of John Prescott, in 1645 of Lancaster. My own thought is that the latter John, a blacksmith, may have been son or nephew of Richard Prescott of Ince, Lancs., blacksmith, whose will, dated 1633, is at Chester.

There is reason to suppose that this blacksmith, Richard, lived at Ince in Makerfield, not Ince-Blundell. Ince in Makerfield is (or was) a hamlet adjoining Wigan lying toward Halifax from Wigan, according to an old map of Lancashire (in the front part of Gregson's "Portfolio of Fragments" concerning Lancashire.

Arlington, Va.   JOHN G. HUNT.

NOTES

ORIGIN OF GENERAL U. S. GRANT.—Almost every writer who has occasion to allude to the subject, assumes that he was of Scotch ancestry; but of this I have seen no evidence, though I have carefully studied the history of the Grant family since 1859; years before the General had made himself famous. There is no doubt of his descent from Mathew Graunt of Windsor, Conn., an Englishman of good education, in whose writings I do not remember to have seen a single Scotch expression. Dr. J. H. Trumbull, of Hartford, Conn., many years ago, made public the principal dates in his life from a record made by himself, but I have seen no hint of his probable origin till the New York Gen. and Biog. Record of January, 1887, p. 40, published the marriage at St. Mary's Le Strand, London, 25 March, 1609, of "Mathew Graunt and Susan Shewers, by licence from the faculties."

The coincidence of names would suggest that this may have been a second marriage of our Mathew Graunt's father; and London, as the place in which to look for his ancestry.   D. WILLIAMS PATTERSON.
Newark Valley, N. Y.

MATTHEW GRANT-GREY, EARL OF KENT: CORRECTION: — The statement that Priscilla, wife of Matthew Grant (Emi.) of Windsor, Conn., was the daughter of Rev. Anthony Grey has been repeated again and again in various publications. I offer the following correction as the error is being included in Grant records. In view of the fact that Matthew specifically stated that his first wife, Priscilla, was born Monday, February 27, 1601 and died April 1644 age 43, the following is quite convincing:

"Parish records of the Church at Burbeck, where Rev. Anthony Grey was Rector, according to Leicester Coll. by Nichols —

1 — Monument and Arms of Anthony Grey, who died Nov. 9, 1643 AND OF HIS WIFE, MAGDALEINE (PUREFOY) WHO DIED APRIL 16, 1653, ae 81. Their children were Priscilla b. March 14, 1609, died young. Priscilla, again, born May 7, 1615, married John St. Nicholas, Esq.

2 — The Inscription on the Monument of Priscilla reads: — "The noble and virtuous Priscilla Grey, youngest daughter of Rt. Hon. Anthony Gray, Earl of Kent; a singular pattern of purity and virtue in her single and married state; deceased September 16, 1665 in the 51st year of her age, and lyeth here interred, resting in hope." Buried Sept. 20, 1665.

"Here lyeth the body of John St. Nicholas, husband of Lady Priscilla, died May 21, 1698."

These items prove conclusively that Priscilla, wife of Matthew Grant, was not the daughter of Anthony Gray, Earl of Kent.

Chicago, Ill.   MRS. MARIE TYLEE McHUGH.

REBECCA, WIFE, FIRST, OF SAMUEL GREENHILL; AND, SECONDLY, OF JEREMY ADAMS. — During the summer of 1955, the contributor discovered the record of the marriage of Samuel Greenhill (Grinnell) in the copy of the Register of Cranbrook, Kent, in the Library of the Society of Genealogists, London:

24 June 1628, Samuel Grinnel and Rebecca Baseden.

There are a number of Baseden entries in the Cranbrook Register, but the parentage of Rebecca has not been determined.

The baptisms of Rebecca and Thomas, children of Samuel and Rebecca Greenhill, appear in the Register of the nearby Parish of Staplehurst:

Rebecca was baptised 24 Feb. 1630, married John Shepard of Cambridge and Hartford; Thomas was baptised 20 Jan. 1632/3. He died in Hartford unmarried in 1653.

Samuel Greenhill came to Cambridge, Mass., in 1634 in the same ship with Simon Willard.

Boston, Mass.   ARTHUR ADAMS.

HASKITT. [Copied from Notarial Records of co. Essex, by H. F. WATERS.]
Elizabeth Haskitt's Oath & Certificate Entred May 30th, '98.

Mrs. Elizabeth Haskitt widow formerly the wife of Stephen Haskitt of Salem personaly appeared (before me) ye subscriber & made Oath that she hath six children liuing (viz) one sonne whose name is Elias Haskitt aged about Twenty Eight yeares & fiue Daughters Elizabeth* Mary Sarah Hannah & Martha all which she had by her husband ye abouesaid mr Stephen Haskitt & Were his Children by him begotten of her body in Lawfull Wedlock being married to him by Doctor Ceauell in Exiter in ye Kingdome of England & whose sd husband serued his time with one mr Thomas Oburne a chandler and sope boyler in sd place & was ye reputed Sonne of —— Haskit of Henstredge (so called) in Summersetshire in sd Kingdome of England & haue often heard my sd husband say that he had but one brother whose name was Elias Hasket & that he liued in said Towne of Henstredge.   ELIZABETH HASKITT.

Sworne Salem May ye 30th 1698 before me John Hathorne One of ye Councill & Justice pe & Q. in ye County of Essex in his Majties province of ye Massachusets Bay in New England.

HATHORNE-WHISTLER.—In Mr. Waters's *Gleanings*, Vol. I., page 45, is given an abstract of the will of Nath. Hathorne, 1654, wherein is an allusion to the testator's brothers-in-law John Whistler, Ralphe Whistler and Thomas Whistler. There is a genealogical pitfall here, for although John and Thomas Whistler were brothers of the testator's wife Martha, Ralphe Whistler was "brother-in-law" in an entirely different way, viz., by his having married his second cousin Frances Whistler, who was a sister of Mrs. Hathorne. The said John, Thomas, Frances and Martha were children of John Whistler, of New Windsor, esquire, whose will was made Feb. 10, 1641, and was proved March 21, 1644-5.

Dr. Daniel Whistler, who also is mentioned in Nath. Hathorne's will, was a man of some note, and is mentioned in the Diaries of both Evelyn and Pepys. He was a most unworthy President of the College of Physicians (see Munk's Roll of the Coll. of Physicians, i, 230). He, too, was a second cousin of Martha Hathorne, and also second cousin to Ralphe Whistler. The "rich widow" whom he married was Elizabeth, daughter of William Holcroft of co. Lanc., and sister of Sir William Holcroft. Her first husband was Robert Lowther, by whom she had a son Anthony Lowther, which Anthony married William Penn's sister Margaret (cf. *Gleanings*, 1435).   J. C. C. SMITH.
London, England.

HAYES.—In the Wentworth Genealogy the Rev. Alonzo H. Quint stated that tradition attributed the origin of the John Hayes who appeared in Dover, N. H., about 1680, to Scotland. The following comments seem to point to a different conclusion. John Hayes settled in that part of Oyster River known as "Barbadoes," presumably because he had friends or relations there. It is well known that there were close trade relations between Portsmouth and Dover and the Island of Barbadoes; that some early settlers of that region migrated from Barbadoes; and that others went to this island and remained several years, returning later to New Hampshire. A family by the name of Hayes was among the prominent Barbadoan planters, and like the Youngs—a name likewise common in both localities—had trade relations with New England. Moreover, Waters's Genealogical Gleanings proved that the Hayes family in Barbadoes sprang from a family living on the Surrey side of London. These statements are based on scattered entries in early colonial papers, already in print.
          A. E. H. S.

---

* This Elizabeth Haskett m. 1st, William Dynn, June 6, 1684, and m. 2d, Roger Derby, as his second wife; as has been ascertained by Mr. E. S. Waters, now of Chicago.   w.

HAYFIELD, HAFFIELD, HAFFELL. [Abstract from Mass. Archives and co. Essex Court Papers, by H. F. WATERS.]

Richard Hayfield of "Sudbury, Old England," married, it seems, first, Judith, secondly, Martha, by each of whom he had issue. He came over to Ipswich with his second wife and her children and with the two surviving children of his first wife, viz. :—Mary and Sarah, of whom the former m. *Josiah Cobbet* and the latter m. John Ilsley. Of the issue of his second wife, Ruth m. Thomas White (son of John White of Lancaster), Martha m. Richard Coye, who, with his bro: Matthew and, I think, his sister Mary, was brought over in 1638 from Boston, Lincolnshire, England, by Mr. Whittingham. From evidence on file I am led to suspect that the old home of the Coyes was not very far from Boston. Rachel Haffield m. Laurence Clinton, who won his way into her good graces by his physical beauty and his boasting professions of riches and high connections.

WILL OF ALICE HAYNE, 1620, OF SEMLEY, ENG.

Communicated by D. F. HAYNES, Esq., Baltimore, Md.

THE following is a copy of the will of Alice Hayne, widow, of Semley, co. Wilts, England, the mother of Walter Haynes, born 1583, who with wife Elizabeth, five children and three servants, came from Sutton Mandeville, Wiltshire, England, in 1638, in the ship "Confidence," to Boston, and settled at Sudbury, Mass., where he died 14 February, 1664–5. This will is written on one page of one leaf folio paper, not signed. It is preserved among the Salisbury Wills, P. P. C. London (Archdeaconry of Sarum). Dated 2d March, 1620–1; proved by Walter Hayne the Ex^r, 2d March, 1623–4.

" In the name of God Amen, the 2^d daye of March in the xviijth yere of the reigne of our Sovraigne Lord King James and the yere of our Lord God One thousand Sixe hundred and twentie. I Alce Hayme of p^{r}fecte memorie praising God doe make this my laste Will and testament in maner and forme following. ffirst I bequethe my Soule to our Lorde Jesus Christ my only Savior and redemer and my bodie to be buried in the Church yeard of Semblie,—It: I geve to the same Church vj^d. It: I geve to my daughter Elizabeth Read my great brass pot or Croke my best cov^{r}led and blanket one bolster one pillow and pillowber and my best gowne two wastcoates: ij aperons j smock j Coffer j barrell j tubbe. It: I bequethe to hir sonne Christopher Read v^s: It: I bequethe to Thomas, John and William her sonnes each of them a Pewter dishe. It: to hir sonn Marmaduke xijd.

It: I bequethe to hir daughter Elizabeth Reade one brass pann of a gallon and one double Kershew of Hollon.

It: I geve to my said daughter Elizabeth one paire of sheetes iij Kershawes iij Partletts and ij table napkins.

It: I bequeth to Marmaduke Maning xii^d.

It: I geve Susan Hayme my best Pewter dishe.

It: I bequeth to my daughter Roose my bedstedd and fetherbedd wch I lie in as it is furnished and my bigest brass pann except one and a gowne or gowne cloth and my ij best Petticoates. And whereas I have lent my Son in law Andrew Ivie xx^s I do geve it to his sonn Andrew.

It: I geve John Ivie thelder and John Ivie the yonger my daughters sonnes xij^d a Peece. It: I geve Grace Ivie my little brass pann wch I have formerly deliv'd to my daughter Rose and one hollon aperon. It: I geve my said daughter Roose ij Kershewes and iiij aperons and ij smokes and the rest of my wearing ape'll ungiven wth my Cloke and a little Coffer by my bed but the bigest brass pann save one wch I appointed to my daughter Roose my will is shall remaine to John Ivie thelder hir sonn. It: I geve my sonn Walter Haymes daughter Elizabeth my next best cov^{r}led and one best shet.

941

It: I geve to Suffraine Hayme my best bore Cloth and an apon, and Marie Hayme a pillowber and one Pewter dishe and Elizabeth Hayme a Pewter dishe and Suffraine a Pewter dishe: It: my Sonn Walter Hayme shall have the use of my bigest brass pann during his life wch pann I give to Thomas Hayme his sonn and my Silver spoone. It: I bequeth to Walter Hayme my sonn the half yeres p'fitt of my tenement after my decease whome 1 make and ordaine to be my whole Executor to whome I bequethe all the rest of my goods.

In wittnes whereof I have Sette my hande the day and yere abov written. In the p'sence of Marmaduke Read and Walter Hayme and John Blanford.''

Then follows

'' An Inventorie of all the Goodes of Alce Hayme widow lat deseased in Semlie taken the xxiiij of feburarie 1623. S͞m totall xxiij^{li} xij^s iiij^d,'' written on one page foolscap paper and annexed to will.

NOTES.

Semley is a parish in Wiltshire, four and three-fourths miles from Hindon (S. by W.), and about the same distance E. N. E. from Shaftsbury or Shaston in Dorsetshire, and in the vicinity of Sutton Mandeville and Wardour Castle.

Elizabeth, the daughter of Walter Hayme named in the will, probably was the daughter that married Roger Goard, and remained in England, named in her father's will made 25 May, 1659, proved 4 April, 1665.

Thomas, Suffraine and Mary, the only other children of Walter born at the date of his mother's will, came to New England with their parents in 1638.

Semley church has been restored, and a recent visit at Semley and at Sutton Mandeville developed n‧ footprints of the Hayne family of 1620.

The marriage of John Hayne and Alice Lambert, 23d October, 1575, is found on the Sherburne, Dorset, register, and which may be the marriage of Walter Hayne's parents.

Walter Hayne's family in England seem to have belonged to the one writing themselves Hayne and Haine. The name being written Hayme in this will proves little as to its correct spelling, the scribes of that day being frequently in error. In the Sudbury Records and by the descendants of Walter, the founder of the Sudbury family, the name is invariably spelled Haynes, and was so written by Walter himself when signing his will.

The Maternal Ancestry of Capt. William Hedge, Pioneer Settler of Lynn, Sandwich, and Yarmouth, Mass.—The Register, vol. 53, shows that Capt. William Hedge's father, Elisha, was a son of Thomas Hedge of Adston, Northants, and London, whose will, dated 1621, was proved in 1623. The will of Captain Hedge's uncle, Richard Ward, of Canons Ashby, Northants, mentions his (Richard's) mother, Frances Ward, of Middleton Cheney, Northants.

The rare monograph "Notes to Accompany a Pedigree of the Family of Ward of Middleton Cheney, &c., Northants", by J. T. H. du Boulay, 1890,* indicates that Wm. Hedge, supra, was a son of Ann Ward and her husband, Elisha Hedge, whom she married 12 July 1610 in Middleton Cheney. Ann had died by 1633. Savage shows that in 1634 Captain Hedge was a freeman in Lynn.

Elisha Hedge, supra, had a brother Abraham. It is significant that Captain Hedge of New England had sons Abraham and Elisha.

Du Boulay shows that Ann Ward's mother Frances's will was dated 1633 and proved in 1635. Frances was the widow of Thomas Ward, baptized in Middleton Cheney in 1561, buried there in 1613, "Thomas Ward, gent." Thomas was the son of Richard Ward, buried in Middleton Cheney in 1585, by his wife Agnes. Richard was the son of Thomas Ward (will dated 1564, proved in 1566) by his wife Emma.

Arlington, Va.   John G. Hunt.

---

*This monograph is not at the Bodleian or at the British Museum. Mr. J. B. Whitmore, continuator of Marshall's "Index to British Pedigrees", kindly furnished a copy, which is now preserved at the Library of the New England Historic Genealogical Society, together with copies of the wills of the widow Frances Ward, and of the earliest Thomas Ward, supra. A copy of the pedigree is now at the Library of Congress.

Thomas Hedge.—Thomas Hedge, named in the October 1957 number of The *
Register, p. 319, in his will left legacies at Daventry, Northants. He may well have
been related to William Hedge, 1410-1451, Northants., a member of Parliament, who
died Mon., 10 May 1451 (Cal. Pat. Rolls, 1451). Also he may have been related to
Henry Hodges of Daventry, whose will, 1558/9, was at Peterboro (fo. 11, Bk. Q,
North't'n & Rutl. Wills), when those wills were indexed in the Record Society Publications.

Arlington, Va.   JOHN G. HUNT.

*The preceding article.

Hibbins and Bellingham.—Mrs. Ann Hibbins, whose will is printed in the
Register, vi., 283, was the widow of William Hibbins, a merchant of Boston.
As is well known she was executed for witchcraft in June, 1656. Previous to
her marriage to Mr. Hibbins she had a husband by the name of Moore, and her
sons John, Joseph and Jonathan are named in her will. It has been often stated
that she was a sister of Governor Richard Bellingham.

Capt. Charles Hervey Townshend, of New Haven, Ct., has sent us some
entries from the Boston, Lincolnshire register, which he copied some years
ago from Col. Joseph L. Chester's transcript. From them we infer that it was
Mr. Hibbins's first wife (Hester) and not his last wife (Ann) who was a sister
of Gov. Bellingham. The entries are:

" William Hibbin and Hester Bellingham married March 4th, 1632-3."
" Child of Mr. Richard Bellingham Recorder bur. April 7, 1626."
Another child Mar. 27, 1628.

WILL OF NOWELL HILTON,

Probated 17 Sept. 1689, at Doctors Commons, London.

Communicated by John T. Hassam, A.M., of Boston.

KNOW ALL MEN BY THESE presents that I Nowell Hilton of Charles-
towne in the County of midd̃x in New England Marriner for divers
good causes and valluable considerations me thereunto especially moving
Have made Ordained constituted and in my stead and place putt and deputed and by these p'sents doe make Ordaine Constitute and in my stead
and place putt and depute my Trusty and loving Kinsman Nathaniell Cutler of the Parish of Stepney in the County of Middlesex Sawyer my true
and lawfull Attorney (irrevocable) for me and in my name and to my use
to ask demand sue for recover and receive of and from all and singuler
such person or persons whom it doth shall or may concerne all and singuler such wages debts dues sum or sums of money Legacies Merchandizes

goods Chattells and all other demands whatsoever now due unto me or which shall become at any time or times hereafter due owing belonging or in any wise appertaining unto by or from any person or persons whatsoever Be it due for my Service done or to be done on Board of any his Ma^tie^s Ships Vessells or ffrigotts or on Board of any other Ship Vessell or ffriggott whatsoever or be it due or which shall become due unto me upon Bonds Bills Specialties Bookes accounts or for and by reason of any other matter cause or thing whatsoever or otherwise howsoever Giveing and by these presents granting unto my said attorney my full power and lawfull authority in and about the Recovery and Receipt of the premisses every or any part thereof as fully largely and amply in every respect to all intents constructions and purposes as I my selfe might or could doe were I then and there personally present and upon the Receipt of the premisses or any part thereof acquittances or other sufficient discharges for me and in my name to make Seale and deliver and one attorney or more to make and againe at his pleasure to Revoke Ratifieing and allowing all that and whatsoever else my said attorney shall Lawfully doe or cause to be done in my name or otherwise in and about the Recovery and receipt of the premisses by virtue of these presents And in case of death then I the said Nowell Hilton doe hereby give and bequeath unto my said loving friend Nathaniell Cutler all and singuler my wages debts dues duties sum or sums of monie Legacies Merchandizes Cloaths goods Chattells whatsoever and all other my Estate as well reall as personall of what nature kind or quallity soever that shall any waies be due oweing belonging or appertaining unto me at the time of my decease unto my said Attorney Nathaniell Cutler his Executors administrators and assignes To have and to hold the same unto my loving friend Nathaniell Cutler his Executors administrators or assignes forever Revoakeing all former and other Wills deeds of Guifts and Letters of Attorney by me at any time heretofore made declareing this to be my last will and Testament and none other In Witnesse whereof I have hereunto sett my hand and Seale the Sixth day of October Anno domini one Thousand Six Hundred Eighty Seaven annoq Regni Regis Jacobi Secundi ang^l &c. tert Nowell Hilton

Sealed Signed delivered Published and declared by the above named Nowell Hilton for and as his last and Will and Testament in the presence of us Mary Story her marke Cuthbert Stoy [Story?] Saml Sapp at the two Anchors and Three Starrs on Wapping wall.

Decimo *Septimo die Mensis Septembris Anno domini Millesimo Sexcentesimo Octogesimo Nono Em^t Com^o Nathanieli Cutler universali Legatar^) nominato in Testamento sive ultima voluntate Nowell Hilton nuper de Charles Towne in Com Middlese^s in Nova Anglia Nautæ defuncti haben^) &c ad administrand bona Jura et Cred dicti defuncti juxta tenorem et effectum Testi ipsius def^ti (Eo quod nullus Executor in eodem Testamento nominatur) De bene et fideliter administrand eadem ad Sancta dei Evangelia Jurat.*

944

HOBBS, PAGE.—The following memoranda from the Register of St. Bartholomew's Parish Church, Crewkerne, co. Somerset, may be worth preserving. They were sent me by my friend, Sir Robert White-Thomson, of Broomford Manor, in Devon, who had the Crewkerne register examined for me; and, though not legally attested, are signed by John England, Parish Clerk. A comparison of them with the will of Col. Nicholas Paige of Rumney Marsh will show that beyond reasonable doubt, Richard and Elizabeth Hobbes of Crewkerne were the parents of Sarah Hobbes, second wife of Capt. John Gerrish of Boston, and of Martha Hobbes, wife of Nathaniel Oliver.

"Richard Hobbes & Elizabeth Page were married in the Parish Church, June 13th, 1671.

"The following children of above Richard and Elizabeth Hobbes were Baptized:

John July 11th 1673
Margaret Oct 20 1674 [The Margaret Ferguson of Col. Paige's will. B. W.]
Sarah Nov. 14th 1676 [Mrs. John Jerrish, of Boston. Married, I think, at Rumney Marsh. The record of date is lost. B.W.]
Elizabeth Oct 4th, 1683."

▴ A subsequent note from Crewkerne, in the handwriting of the clerk, reads: "Have found the following entry: James Hatter and Late wife of Nicholas Paige married Sept 20 1567"

This clearly shows that the ancestors of Colonel Nicholas Paige of Rumney Marsh were resident in Crewkerne, Somerset, in the time of Queen Elizabeth.

358 Marlborough Street, Boston, Mass.   BARRETT WENDELL.

HOLMES-HOLBROOK:—Mr. Philip H. Blake of Mystole House, Chartham, Kent, England, has sent me the following marriage record from the parish register of St. Mary Bredman, Canterbury.

10 April 1743 Robert Holmes of Boston in New England and Frances Holbrook of this parish.

Portland, Maine.   WALTER G. DAVIS.

HUBBARD. — According to Austin's Genealogical Dictionary of Rhode Island, p. 106, Samuel Hubbard was born in 1610, son of James and grandson of Thomas, and says of himself: "I was born of good parents, my mother brought me up in the fear of the Lord, in Mendelsham," etc. From Rev. A. W. Darwin, M.A., of Stonham Aspal Rectory, Stowmarket, co. Suffolk, Eng., Honorary Secretary of the Suffolk Institute of Archæology, I have received the following records of Hubbard baptisms taken from the parish registers of Mendlesham, co. Suffolk. Although they do not include the baptismal record of Samuel Hubbard, they give the baptisms of a daughter and two sons of James, the sons being probably brothers of Samuel, and of two children of Thomas, who was probably the grandfather of Samuel. No further Hubbard baptisms were found in the Mendlesham registers of that period.

Baptisms

1562 Richard son of Thomas Hubberde 13 September.
1562 Elizabeth daughter of Thomas Hubberde 13 September.
1569 Elizabeth daughter of Jeremy Hubberd 10 October.
1571 John son of Jeremy Hubberd 5 February [? 1571/2].
1575 Faith daughter of Roger Hubberd 21 May.
1592 Robert son of Robert Hubberd 6 June.
1595 Rebecca daughter of James Hubberd, at Little Stonham, 21 March [? 1595/6].
1601 Thomas son of James Hubberd 21 April.
1601 Eme daughter of Robert Hubberd 2 November.
1603 James son of James Hubberd 14 August

Newport, R. I.   G. ANDREWS MORIARTY, JR.

945

LETTER FROM JOHN HULOTT OF BARBADOS TO GEORGE LITTLE OF NEWBURY, MASS., 1659.

[Communicated.]

THE original of the following letter is in the possession of Mr. Joseph Little, Jr., of Newbury, Mass., now living on the old George Little homestead. George Little, to whom the letter is addressed, came from Unicorn Street, London, to Newbury, Mass., in 1640. He made numerous purchases of land both in Newbury and other places. Several years after his arrival in Newbury, he married Alice Poor, who sailed for New England in the Bevis in 1638. He had five children. Joseph was nearly six years old, and John nearly four, when this letter was written.

There is a tradition in the family of lands in Barbadoes deeded to ancestors, and that two young men living in the neighborhood and the deeds disappeared together, and the supposition was that they represented themselves as being of the name of Little and took possession accordingly. About twenty-five families of Geo. Little's descendants, of the same name, are residents of Newbury, a number of them living on land owned by him. The family living on the homestead have members of the fifth, sixth, seventh and eighth generations. For a fuller account of George Little and sixty-five hundred of his posterity, see "The Descendents of George Little," by George Thomas Little, A.M., published at Auburn, Me., 1882.

BARBADOE.

Loueing Brother my kind love with my wife remembered and wishing you health as wee are all here at present thanks bee to god, These are to acquaint you that I have sent by this berer ninty yards of dimity the which I hope you will turne to A good Acct. I am advised it is farr better than sugar wherefore was wished to send it rather than sugar it being for yᵉ Acct. of yourselfe & Mr. Hen: Jefferson, I shall desire you to make up the Account with Mr. Jefferson: I send you —— —— 7 baggs of cotton by via Hester. I hope they will turn to A good Acct. you will receive I hope—same man those things by whome I intend to send by pray send mee word of the receipt of the same. I shall desire you to Acquaint Mr. John Biship that his goods which came from Boston the Last yeere turned to a very bad Acct. wherefore shall desire you to make up Accounts with him there, & so send mee word what ye doo in the business. Brother I recd A barrill of beefe & i firkin of butter from you but it was here in the Land 6 or 7 weekes before I heard of it which beeing tumbled up & downe here when ye fire was spoyled it & was turned upon my hands againe after I had sold it, pray make up the Acct.

(A fold and torn open here)

send me word what you make of these goods . . . . . for if dimity bee A Comodity I can send you a good quantity every yeere & shall desire you to send mee provisions for it hither againe. Thus remembering my Loue & my wifes to you & your wife & Children doo for present Comit you all to god, & rest   Your ever Loueing

May the 17th of   BROTHER JOHN HULOTT.
 1659.   946

I could wish that one of my Cousins were here to see if he did like this place & live with me if you thinke so . . . . . for Awhile & if hee did not Like here, it shall not Cost him anything for his being nor his passage back again.   J. H.

Loueing Brother it may be you are unwilling to send youre sonne now by reason he is young, if you will keepe him to scoule three or foure years more I doe heare ingage to pay for his scoulling and Clothing for it is my will with my wife's consent that after my decease and wifes that you and yours shall have all my estate witness my hand.

[Superscriptione]
To his Loueing Brother
Mr. Gorg Littell
dwelling in Newbery.

Yˢ Mr Jam (*torn*) ading.

HUMFREY.—In a study of the life of John Humfrey, one of the founders of the Massachusetts Bay Colony, I have been led to the conclusion that he was the John Humfrey who signed the pedigree in Harleian MS. 1166, fo. 9ᵇ, as published in the Visitation of Dorset, 1623, p. 57. He is recorded there as son and heir of "Michael Humfrey of Chaldon in com. Dorset," and aged 26 years in 1623, with wife Elizabeth, daughter of "Herbert Pelham of Compton in com. Dorset," and John Humfrey, son and heir, aged *one year*.

On page 105 of the History of the Ancient and Honorable Artillery Company is the statement that John Humfrey's eldest son John joined the company in 1641, which would make him about 19 or 20 at that time.

But the best evidence of identity is a comparison of the pedigree signature with the signature of John Humfrey in his letter to his brother-in-law, Isaac Johnson, in 1630, as shown in 4 Mass. Historical Society Collections, vol. 6, pl. 1.[*] Though written seven years apart, and the signature attached to the pedigree a formal one, while the other was a careless one closing a familiar letter to his brother-in-law, I believe any expert in hand writing would pronounce them belonging to the same hand.

It would be interesting to obtain, if possible, the will of Michael Humfrey. He is mentioned in the list of adventurers at Cape Ann by John White of Dorchester in 1634, but among those "all sithence deceased" (REGISTER, vol. 61, p. 279). Further along in the list we find "John Humfrey, gent., living in New England."

I think investigation will prove that Michael Humfrey of Windsor, Conn., was a grandson of the Michael of the Dorset pedigree and nephew of John Humfrey of the Massachusetts Bay Colony.

[*] The arms in the seal following the signature appear to be the same as those accompanying the Humfrey pedigree in the Visitation of Dorset, p. 57, viz. "Gules, a crosscroslet botonné argent, charged on each end with three escallops sable," and marked "Respited for proof of his right to this coate."—EDITOR.

From Visitation of Dorset, 1623.

From 4 Mass. Hist. Soc. Coll. vi.

947

If the foregoing descent be correct, it is evident that the Lady Susan, sister of the Earl of Lincoln, was his *second* wife and not the mother of John the eldest son. It is also probable that he was a brother-in-law of Herbert Pelham, another of the founders of the Massachusetts Bay Colony.

Geneva, Ill.   H. B. ALEXANDER.

HUMPHREY-OTLEY. — It is known that Adam Otley of Lynn, Mass., married a daughter of John Humphrey, and the following record shows that this daughter was Elizabeth:

1 August 1648. Administration on the goods of Adam Otley, late in parts beyond the sea, was granted to Elizabeth, his relict. (P.C.C., Administration Act Book, 1648, fo. 92.)

RICHARD INGERSOLL OF SALEM, MASS.: HIS MARRIAGE AND FAMILY.—It has often been published that Richard Ingersoll of Salem, Mass., was married at Sandy, Bedfordshire, England, 20 October 1616, to Agnes, or Ann, Langley. That he was certainly of that shire when he came to New England in 1629 is proved by contemporary accounts.

But the date of the marriage as published is not correct. According to the Registers of St. Swithin's at Sandy, abstracts of which were made by the rector in September 1935, Richard Inkersall married Agnes Langlye on 10. October 1611. Their first child, Alice, was baptized there 21 December 1612.

It seems probable that Richard's children were born in this order: Alice, George, Joanna, Sarah, John, Bathsheba, and Nathaniel, and possibly two of their children died in infancy. Ingersoll data now in print are disappointingly inaccurate.

Watertown, Mass.   WINIFRED LOVERING HOLMAN.

JACKSON.—The ancestry of the first two settlers of Cambridge and Newton, John and Edward Jackson, has been courteously supplied by a lineal descendant, Mr. Edward G. Jackson of St. Louis, Mo.

Christopher Jackson of Mile End, London, married Susan Johnson of Mile End, 5 Oct. 1602 (London Marriages). He was bur. 5 Dec. 1633. Children: I. John, bapt. 6 June 1603; m. (1) Abigail; m. (2) Margaret; d. 30 Jan. 1675. II. Edward, bapt. 3 Feb. 1605: m. (1) Frances; m. (2) Elizabeth Oliver, 14 Jan. 1649; d. 17 June 1681. III. Miles, bapt. 28 June 1607. This list of Christopher's sons is copied from the " Register of St. Dunstan's Church, Stepney." His residence is first given as Mile End, afterwards as Bednall Green, and his occupation as merchant tailor. The date of John's baptism is evidently 1603, instead of 1602 as recorded in the " Register." There is a good account of St. Dunstan's, Stepney, in Hare's " Walks in London."

Los Angeles, Calif.   ORRA EUGENE MONNETTE.

948

ORIGIN OF THE KELLOGG FAMILY.—The following extract from the will of Nathaniel Kellogg of Farmington, Conn., is evidence that the family came from England, rather than from Scotland, as was supposed by the writer of the article in the Register, vol. xii., p. 201. The will is dated, "Junn the 4th, 1657," and is signed by "Nathanell Kellog." The will is on file, only, at Hartford, the records for a few years about 1660 being lost.

"*Item.* I giue and bequeaue my whol estat, Reall and personall, unto my deere and Louing wife, Elisebeth Kelodg, duerin the tyme of her Natterall life, and at the eand theare of I giue all my houses and Landes in fermingtunun to my Brother John Kelodg, and to my Sister Janne Aallisun, and to my Sister Rachell Caue, all dwelling in olld engiland. * * And my will is that these three, my brother and sisters, shall pay to my Cosen Joseph's [Kelodg] three children, six pounds starling; &c."

In the original, the word here printed in brackets is interlined. This "Cosen Joseph" was undoubtedly Lieut. Joseph Kellogg, then of Farmington, and afterwards of Hadley, Mass. As appears on page 125 of this volume, this Lieut. Joseph had four children born previous to the date of the will just quoted, of whom three are said to have "died young." Probably but one of them died previous to this date.

(174) Daniel Kellogg, of Norwalk, Conn., (page 129,) may have been a brother, or cousin-german of (82) Joseph[a]. There is a tradition among the descendants of this Daniel, that the family came from the Isle of Wight; but it is not known that there is any evidence supporting the tradition.

Joseph Kellogg, said to be the grandfather of (202) Capt. Joseph, was almost certainly the Deerfield captive of that name, and grandson of (82) Joseph. See the Introduction to the Foote Genealogy, p. xxvii; also, Documentary History of N. Y., vol. 3, p. 629, (4to ed.)   ALLYN S. KELLOGG.

Vernon, Conn., Aug. 11, 1860.   ————

THE KELLOGG FAMILY IN ENGLAND.—(Extracts from the Parish Register of St. Michael's Church in Braintree, Essex, England.)

I send you the above for publication, thinking that it may interest friends in America. The Registers of the Parish Church of Braintree prior to 1660 have been lost.

Baptisms.

Nathaniel the sonne of Nathaniel Kaloge was baptized on the 1st day of December 1669.

Ann Kelough daughter of Nathaniel and Ann Kelough was baptized 1749 O. S., 1750 N. S.

Married.

23 December 1718 William Wood of Hatfield singleman married Mary Kellock singlewoman of this Parish.

Deaths.

Ann Kellog died 1661.

Robert Kelluck buried on the 18 January 1666 O. S., 1667 N. S.

Elizabeth daughter of Martin Kelog was buried 7 Sept 1679.

Henry Kellog son of Martin was buried 8 October 1680.

Richard Callog was buried on the 7 January 1682.

Martin Callogg, an honest man, was buried 29 January 1685 O. S.

8 Rue Eanard, Geneva, Switzerland.   JUSTIN P. KELLOGG.

KING, BROWNE.—In Phillimore and Gurney's Buckinghamshire Parish Registers, vol. 6, pp. 10, 11, occur the following marriages at High Wycombe:

   Daniel King & Eliz. Guy   4 Oct. 1624

   Chaddus Browne & Eliz. Sharparowe 11 Sept 1626

It was surmised by Mr. Henry F. Waters, who furnished the information to Mr. Rufus King for his "Pedigree of King of Lynn, Mass.," that Daniel King, Sr.,'s wife's family name was Guy. Her first name was known to be Elizabeth. The correctness of the surmise is borne out by the marriage mentioned above, to which Mr. Waters has called attention. High Wycombe is not far from Beaconsfield, in the same county, of which place Daniel King, Jr., was in May 1653, being bound for New England. (Cf. REGISTER, vol. 33, pp. 375-6.)

The date of Chaddus Browne's marriage, as above, and the first name of his wife, are right for Chad Browne of Rhode Island. The locality seems likely, judging by the names of his associates as shown by Sylvester Baldwin's nuncupative will. (*Ex inform.* William P. Greenlaw; cf. Chad Browne Memorial, pp. 7-8, and Waters's Genealogical Gleanings, vol. 1, p. 708.)

THE EDITOR.

LAKE FAMILY.

[Communicated by WILLIAM H. WHITMORE.]

In the *Register*, xiii, 116, will be found a brief notice of the family of Thomas Lake of Boston. The following abstract of the will of Sir Edward Lake, the first baronet, is taken from a contemporaneous copy, formerly owned by Capt. Thomas Lake, and now in the possession of J. Wingate Thornton, Esq.

He desires (1) that his body shall be buried in Lincoln Minster, with some decent monumental rememberance to be erected by his executors, and that his wife Anne's body shall also be placed there. (2) "I give to the church or Chappell of Normanton near Pontefract in Yorkshire (if there be a church or chappell there, which I know not) where my paternall Ancestors have lived for many ages," £5 for a clock. (3) "To my deare friend and loving kinsman, Henry Bigland of Wormingburst in the county of Sussex," a ring, and the same to "his brother, Mr. Edward Bigland of Graies' Inn." (4) "To my servant and kinsman Christopher Lake, £10." (5) Furniture, &c., to wife Ann, except "my watch, my carabin, with the barrill staffe, belonging to it, made by Harman Barne, my great faire chess board with the case with my crest on it, and all my horse armes and other armes, and my best sword and and seal at armes, the picture of the late blessed King and Martir, my most deare master King Charles the first, as it is in a frame, in the shape of a Martir, in a white robe with a psalm in his right hand and a Crown of stars upon his head, with an inscription in a table hanging under it, — as also the picture of my most noble Lord, Thomas, late Earl of Strafford, Lord Lieutenant of Ireland. Item, my patent of Baronett and Mr. Dugdale, Norroy King at Armes, his Testimoniall under his hand and the seale of his office of Herauld of the Coate of arms and crest of augmentation given me by the said King Charles the first to be borne for ever before my owne Coat of Armes." — all which were to go to his heirs for transmission.

(6) He requests his executor and his heirs, that as far as possible they may have "for their Christian name, the name of Biby in remembrance of and for the preservation of the paternal name of my said dear wife," and that the other children may "have no other Christian names than that of Biby as aforesaid, or else Seaman, in rememberance of my dear wife's mother's sirname, or of Caley in rememberance of Sir Hugh Caley, whose coheir my Ancestor in the time of King Edward the third, married, or Wardall in remembrance of my mother's daughter and co-heir of Edward Wardall." The heir was to have the name of Biby "in remembrance of my wife's father, Simon Bibye of Burkden in the county of Huntingdom."

950

(7) A ring to "cousin Francis Lake of Hatcliffe; one to my brother John Lake; and £5 to "the eldest son of my brother Luke Lake." (8) "I make my most deare and Loving Brother, Thomas Lake, full and sole Executor."
Signed   8 April, 1665.

A codicil of 6 Oct., 1670, explains that these names of Biby, &c., are only for children born after seven years after his death. It mentions also "Christopher Lake of Harpswell, and such of my name and kindred as live at (Petney, the capital letter is. doubtful.—Ed.) or elsewhere,"—"cousin Henry Bigland of Long Whitton in the County of Leicester," makes Stephen Lake of Graies' Inn, eldest son of my brother, Thomas Lake, executor.

Codicil—17 Jany 1671, as Stephen Lake is dead he makes Thomas Lake, his brother, Executor, and "failing him the next heir male of my brother Thomas Lake."

The son Thomas Lake, Jr., succeeded to his uncle's property, and dying 22 May, 1711, was the father of Bybye, 3d bart., and thence through Atwell,[4] James-Winter,[5] James-Samuel-William,[6] and James-Samuel,[7] ancestor of Sir Atwell-King Lake, eighth and present baronet.

I believe that Mr. Savage has not recorded this connection though it is indisputable. Mr. Thornton has a fine impression of the seal of Capt. Thomas Lake of Boston, brother of Sir Edward. The services for which the title was conferred on Edward Lake, are recited "more particularly that at the battle at Edge Hill, where he received sixteen wounds to the extreme danger of his life, and his left arm being then disabled by a shot, he held his bridle in his teeth," in the patent printed in *Collier's Dictionary*.

LAKIN.—Butler informs us in the History of Groton, that the "*Larkins*" of that place came from Redington, Eng. Savage (under "Lakin") says there is no such place, and suggests *Rid*lington,—nay, two Ridlingtons. But if you turn to his "additions and corrections" (vol. i. p. 507) you observe that Robert and John Blood, of Concord, Mass., sold an estate at Ruddington, Nottinghamshire, in 1649. Now it seems to me that as Richard Blood was one of the first settlers of Groton, and was a brother of Robert, the Bloods and the Lakins may have come from the same place. This Ruddington is only about ten miles from Duffield in Derbyshire, whence the Bloods of County Clare, Ireland, and Birmingham, England, came about 1595.

In this connection I may say that I have a genealogy of the County Clare family of Bloods, brought down from the *Edmund* Blood who went to Ireland, 1595, an officer in Lord Inchiquin's army, and was afterwards M. P. for Ennis. It was sent me by Lt. Col. Bindon Blood, R. E.

It appears from this that the famous Colonel Thomas Blood was of that branch; also, the Miss Gertrude Blood, who married recently Lord Colin Campbell.

My Birmingham correspondent has sent me a pedigree of the two European branches of Blood, a copy of which I have deposited with the New England Historic Genealogical Society.   HENRY AMES BLOOD.

1449 *Mass. Avenue, Washington, D. C.*

LATHAM.—Some of your readers will remember that in the "Ancestry of Thirty-Three Rhode Islanders, &c.," there was an account given of Lewis Latham, Gent., Falconer to King Charles I., with a conjecture that he was related to Symon Latham, author of a work on Falconry. (A portrait of Lewis Latham appears in a recent work, "The Ancestral Dictionary.") It has just come to the knowledge of the undersigned through "Bedfordshire Notes and Queries"—vol. ii., part xx., pages 231, 232—that Lewis Latham had not only this brother Symon, but another brother William, a sister Ursula, wife of William Carter, and a sister Elizabeth, wife of Thomas ————. J. O. AUSTIN.
P. O. Box 81, Providence, R. I.

LAWRENCE.—Rev. Lawrence B. Thomas, on page 129 of his Pedigrees of Thomas, Chew and Lawrance (New York, 1883), quotes a MS. letter received from the late Mr. G. D. Scull, the editor and author, who was a frequent and valued contributor to the REGISTER, announcing the discovery, on the Register of St. Stephen's Church, just outside of St Albans, Hertfordshire, of a record of the marriage, 16 Feb. 1617-8, of William Lawrence and Joan Brooke; and Mr. Thomas entertains "no reasonable doubt they were the ancestors of the American family."

As applicable to the above, attention should be given to the age of Jane, wife of George Giddings, of Ipswich, a daughter of Joan Tuttle, which is entered on the list of passengers by the Planter (REGISTER, vol. 14, pp. 303-4) as 20 years, on 2d April, 1635. GEO. A. GORDON.

LAWRENCE—John Lawrence married Elizabeth Kettleborough, both single, at Fokenham Magna, co. Suffolk, 12 Oct. 1630 ("East Anglian Marriages" mss. of E. A. Hutchinson, *ex penes* Society of Genealogists, London).

The first wife of John Lawrence of Watertown, 1636, and later of Groton, who died in 1667, was named Elizabeth.

Wells, Maine. G. ANDREWS MORIARTY.

LECHMERE.—The following memoranda concerning the New-England Lechmeres of Lechmere's Point, Cambridge, and Sir E. Lechmere of the Ryd and Severn End, Worcestershire, both of whom are mentioned by Dr. Oliver Wendell Holmes in his "Hundred Days in Europe," were sent to Mrs. Dr. Francis P. Sprague, 229 Commonwealth Avenue, Boston, by one of her Russell connections in England.

The Lechmeres of Lechmere's Point descended from Thomas Lechmere, son of Edmund Lechmere, of Severn End, Hanley, Worcestershire, by Lucy Hungerford. His birth is noted in his grandfather, Judge Lechmere's diary, thus: "June 18 1683 My daughter Lechmere was delivered of a sone named Thomas Benedicat Deus Amen." This diary is contained in the history of the House of Lechmere, published by E. P. Shirley. A note is appended to this entry, "Mr Thos Lechmere died at Boston New Engld 4th June 1765. He was Surveyor General of the Kings Customs & ancestor of the American branch. A piece of land at Hanley is called New England & is planted with oaks the seeds of which were sent from America by Thomas Lechmere." "in Jany 1733 he married Ann Winthrop."

In Colonel Lechmere Russell's possession is Ann Winthrop's bible, with, in her son Richard Lechmere's writing, the statement it was his mother's bible. He returned on war of Independence to Engld & has *now* no male representatives his daughters are represented by Coores of Scrunten Hall Yorkshire, Russells (Sir Edward) of Ashford Hall Ludlow, & Worralls whose representatives now are Sir H. Lechmere Stuart Bart. & Eyre Coote of West Park Eyre.

LOTHROP-LATHROP-LOWTHORP.—In THE REGISTER, October 1930, pp.437-9, Mr. G. Andrews Moriarty contributed further information on the ancestry of Rev. John Lothrop, early settler of Barnstable, New England.

The following extracts, from "Yorkshire Fines", may be of added interest to Lowthorp descendants:

"Easter, 1596—William Dixon, Thomas Pattenson, Lawrence Lowthropp, John Constable, and Thomas Lowthropp, *versus* Brian Pattenson and Alice, his wife, re property in Etton".

"Hilary, 1557/8—Robert Lowthorpe *versus* Marmaduke Whytyng and Alice, his wife, re lands in Wolkyngton".

Many data concerning the early Lowthrops may be obtained from the "Bridlington Chartulary" and from "Transactions, East Riding Antiquarian Society", vol. 21. These pertain to the period prior to 1400.

Arlington, Va.   JOHN G. HUNT.

THE EARLY LYONS OF SALEM, MASS.—As shown by Savage and Pope in their works concerning early settlers of New England, John Lyon was identified with Salem in 1638 and 1648. The vital records of Salem show that one James Lyon of Salem died in 1661. Was he related to the aforesaid John Lyon? The latter appears to be testator of this name whose will, dated 29 Oct. 1657, was proved in P.C.C., London, 13 Oct. 1658 (ref. 559 Wootton), as follows:

"John Lyon, late of New England beyond the seas, but now belonging unto the Elizabeth, Frigate in the States Service of the Commonwealth of England—mariner, under the command of Captayne Coleman . . . to Alice Linsey my loved and loving landlady and her Exor's. assigns and administrators for ever, on condition that she pays my debts and sees that I am decently buried, provided alsoe that I live from this sickness during which she has nursed me so lovingly, I bequeath all my goods and wages, but if I should recover my health then this deed of gift to be voyd and of non effect.

John Lyon, his mark

Witnesses: William Sheare, his marke; Thomas Raistone

Francis Hodgson; George Wyatt servant"

On 13 Oct. 1658 administration was granted to Alice Linsey, the principal and sole legatee in the will.

Arlington, Va.   JOHN G. HUNT.

CHRISTOPHER MARTIN, AND HIS SERVANT SOLOMON PROWER, came in the Mayflower. The former is said by Bradford to have come from Billericay, in Essex. See *History of New Plymouth Plantation*, pp. 56, 448 and 452.

Rev. Thomas W. Davids, of Colchester, Eng., furnishes the following extracts from the old Archidiaconal Registry at Chelmsford, which will be interesting in this connection :—

1619-20, March 3. Solomon Prower (of Billericay) cited for refusing to answer me¶ at all (at Catechising), unless I would ask him some questions in some Catechisme.

Same day. Christopher Martin (of Billericay) for suffering his sonne to answer me . . . . that his father gave him his name.

MASON AND VEREN, of New England.—Will of Jane Searle of Otterton, Devon, widow, mentions: Son Conant's oldest son and daughter. Daughters Jane Mason and Mary Veren in New England, £5 apiece. Daughter Sara Gover and little Sara her dau. and Abe her son. Daughter-in-law Mary Conant. Cousin Sarah Upham, "as a token of my love" 10 s. To the poor of Budleigh 10 s. To the poor of Sidmouth 10 s. Residue to son Richard Conant. Dated 1 May, 1665. Wit. Thos. Upham, Blanche Peale. Pvd. P. C. C. 20 June 1658 by oath of Ri. Conant the son and sole exor. (301, Wootten.)

8 Hampton Rd., Redland, Bristol, Eng.   W. U. REYNELL UPHAM.

¶ William Pease. See Annals of Evangelical Nonconformity in Essex, p. 155.

WILL OF SAMUEL MATHER.

LATELY in a search among the Irish wills in Dublin I gleaned incidentally many interesting items which fill important gaps in our early New England genealogy. I hope to communicate some of these later on to the REGISTER, but first all think the will of Richard Mather's famous eldest son is worthy of being printed in full.*

LOTHROP WITHINGTON.

9 COPTIC STREET, W. C., LONDON.

[*Dublin Diocesan Will and Grant Book*, 1672–1678, fo. 19.]

IN the name of God amen the eighteenth day of August in the year of our Lord God one thousand six hundred seaventy and one, I Samuel Mather of Oxmontowne in the suburbs of the City of Dublin, minister of the Gospell being sick in body, but of good and pfect memorie (thanks be to God for the same) doe make and ordaine this my last will and Testament in manner and form following (that is to say) first I commit my soule to the hands of God, hoping to be saved by the alone merrits of my only redeemer Jesus Christ, who through the eternal spirit offered himself without spott to God for me, and my body I leave to be

---

* Rev. Samuel Mather, M.A., the eldest son of Rev. Richard and Katharine (Hoult) Mather, was born at Much Wootton, Lincolnshire, May 13, 1626. He accompanied his parents and three brothers to Boston, Mass., where they arrived Aug. 17, 1635. His father was settled at Dorchester as pastor, Aug. 23, 1636. Samuel was graduated at Harvard College in the class of 1643. In 1655 he returned to England, and after preaching in England, Scotland and Ireland, settled in Dublin, where he died Oct. 29, 1671. See memoir by John L. Sibley, in *Harvard Graduates*, vol. i., pp. 78–87; *Mather's Magnalia*, vol. ii., pp. 39–58, bk. iv., chap. 2; Horace E. Mather's *Lineage of Rev. Richard Mather*, and other authorities cited by Mr. Sibley.

See also will of Rev. Richard Mather, REGISTER, vol. 20, pp. 248–255.—EDITOR.

decently buried in such place and in such order as to my execut^ors hereafter named shall thinke meet and convenient, firmely believing, that though it be sowne a naturall body, yet it shall be raised a spirituall body, by the power of the Lord Jesus-Christ who shall change my vile body that it may be fashioned like unto his glorious body according to the workeing whereby he is able to subdue all things to himself. AND for the settling of my temporal estate, and such goods, Chatls and debts as it hath pleased God in mercy to bistow upon me I doe hereby order, give and dispose of the same in manner and form as following,

Imp^rs. I give and bequeath to my dear wife Hanah Mather the summe of three hundred pound steg or the third part of my whole estate that I shal dye seized of, at her owne choice and election. Item I give to my sd dear wife all the furniture of the blew chamber, as it now stands furnished with all the other household goods what soever shee brought with her and all the plate of what kind soever, which hath been given me by any of her kindred, since our marriage, aloe I give unto her the ringe, that shee did weare on the day on which we were married with all other the rings, jewells that she had before our marriage. Item, I give and bequeath my double porcion of my father's manuscripts and books in New England to my nephew Samuell Mather, son of my brother Timothy Mather, he payeing ther out to my brother Increase Mather three pounds ster and three pounds ster to the widdow and children of my late brother Eliezer Mather and to be equally distributed amongst them. Item, I give and bequeath my own writings and manuscripts to my brother Nathaniel Mather, minister at Sudbury in the county of Suffolk in the Kingdom of England. Item, I give and bequeath unto my beloved sister-in-law Frances Howard widow twenty shillings ster to buy her a mourning ring withall, aloe I give and bequeath unto her foure children Francis Stephen Martha and John Howard to each of them twenty shillings ster. Item I give and bequeath unto my wel beloved sister in law Mary Christian twenty shillings ster to buy her a mourning ring withall, also I give unto her three children Minard Michael and Mary Christian to each of them twenty shillings ster. Item I give and bequeath a small legacie of seaven pounds ster to the treasury of the church (whereof I am pastor) to be employed to the use of the poore members of the said church. Item I give and bequeath unto my daughter Catherine Mather all the rings and jewells that were my former wife's excepting therout one ring which I gave to my now wife on the day of our marriage. Item, I give unto my said daughter Catherine Mather all the rest and remainder of my estate whatsoever it be and wheresoever it shall be found to be improved by my Ex^rs for the present maintenance and the future use of my s^d daughter untill such time as it shall please God to dispose of her in marriage or that she attaine to the age of one and twenty yeares. [?And if she die before said marriage or age of one and twenty years] as aforesaid, that then and in such case my will and meaning is that whatsoever of the said estate I have given to my s^d daughter by this my last will and testament as shall be then remaining shall be divided into four equall parts, and to be given one fourth part to my brother Timothy Mather, and one other fourth part to my brother Nathaniel Mather and one other fourth part to my brother Increase Mather, and one other fourth part to be given to the children of my late brother Eliazer Mather, deceased to be equally distributed amongst them. And lastly I do hereby nominate, appoint and ordaine my dear and welbeloved wife Hannah Mather, and my trusty and welbeloved friends Thomas Hooke of the Citty of Dublin m'chant and Paul Palmer of the said Citty distiller executors of this my last will and testament and my welbeloved friends Timothy Tailer of Smithfield in the suburbs of the said Dublin minister Wm Markham Jo : Brice Arthur Emerton of sd citty gent and Isaac Dobson the elder late of the sd citty apothecary overseers, and I doe hereby revoke and make null and void all former wills. In witness whereof I have hereunto put my hand and seale vnto this my present last will and Testament the day and yeare first above written   SAMUELL MATHER. [seal]

Signed sealed and declared by the said Samuell Mather to be his last will and Testament in the p'sence of vs the word (overseers) interlined over the last line but one before sealing hereof Timothy Taylor Wm Cist Edward Billings

Proved 7 March 1672 by Hannah Mather, Tho. Hooke and Paul Palmer.

Do. fol. 32—acquittance to same 13 June 1673.

Do. fol. 34, 11 Sept. 1673. Letters of tutelage of Catherine Mather, daughter and heir of Samuel Mather of Dublin clerk, deceased, during minority, to Nathaniel Mather and Richard Stephens Esq.

MICHAEL METCALF.—" In the Life of Matthew Wren, Bishop of Ely (*Parentalia*, p. 101), wherein he is defending himself against some charges of persecution, he speaks of ' Michael Metcalf and Nicholas his son, a Dornix weaver of some estate.' "—*London Notes and Queries* for 1860, Sept. 20, 2d series, vol. x, p. 250. See *Reg.*, VI, 171.

Matthew Wren, b. ab. 1586, d. 1667, æ. 81; made bishop of Hereford, 1634, afterwards translated to Norwich, and in 1638 to Ely.

MIXER.—Savage's Genealogical Dictionary says that Isaac Mixer came in 1634, aged 31, with wife Sarah, aged 33, and son Isaac, aged 4. In vol. 1, p. 103, of Phillimore and Blagg's Suffolk Marriages, is found

Isaac Mixer Jun. and Sarah Thurston married May 11, 1629.

Isaac Mixer, widower and Anna Bloss widow married 12 Feb. 1628.

These are in the registers of Capel St. Mary, and in the same volume are

Joseph Briden and Jane Mixer married June 11, 1618.

George Mixer and Doreth Chisnall married 26 Oct. 1620.

It seems possible that this is the family of Isaac Mixer of Watertown.

           MARY LOVERING HOLMAN.

255 Warren Street, Roxbury, Mass.

WILL OF REV. THOMAS MORSE, OF FOXEARTH, COUNTY OF ESSEX, ENGLAND—1596.

[Copied by Horatio G. Somerby.]

In the name of God Amen. I Thomas Morse, Minister of God his word in the Countie of Essex and in the Dyocesse of London, do make and ordeyne this my Last [sic] and Testament in manner and forme followinge, first althoughe weake in Bodye yet in good and perfecte Remembrance thancks be unto God Doe bequeathe my soule to almighty God, and my Bodye unto the earthe from whence it was taken. *Item,* I give and bequeathe to my nyne children now lyvinge, nyne score Poundes of good and lawful money of Englande, that is to saie, To John, Samuel, Daniell, Joseph, Jeremye, James, Nathaniell and Phillipp my sonnes, and to Sara my daughter, and to every of them Twentye Pounds att the age of Three and twentye yeares, Savinge my mynde is that my daughter Sara shall receive her porcon of Twenty poundes at the age of One and Twentye yeares. And yf any of them doe departe this life before theis yeares of age be expired, Then I will that his or her parte or partes be equally devyded amonge my children wch shall be then livinge. I give and bequeathe unto Richard Morse my brother, Fortie shillings of lawfull money. *Item,* I give more unto Margarett Morse my sister, Twentye shillings. *Item,* I give unto my eight youngest children Eight Bybles, every of them a Byble to be provyded at the cost and charges of my eldest sonne uppon wch Condicon I give hym all my Bookes in my Studdye. *Item,* I give and bequeathe unto the poore of the Parishe of Foxenats [Foxearth] Tenne shillings. The rest of my goods, money, plate, Bonds, morgages, cattle, household stuffe, or whatsoever else unbequeathed, my Legacyes discharged, I give unto Margaret my wife, with condicon to bringe upp my children in Learnynge with all things fitt for them untill she shall place them in some honest service, whome I make my sole Executrixe for the performance of this my last will and Testament. Also I will that yf Margarett my saide wife doe dispose herselfe to marrye, that then she and he whome she shall marrye with enter into sufficient Bondes unto my eldest sonne then livinge before her marriage for the discharge of all these things which concerne here to be discharged in this my will. Also, yf yt please God she doth marrye that she doe enter into sufficient Bondes to give unto my eight sonns before rehearsed Thirty and fyve poundes equallye to be devyded amounge them and unto my daughter Sara tenne poundes wch is all Five and Forty poundes, To be paide wth in one yeare after the marriage of the saide Margaret or att the severall yeares of their ages before menconed. And yf she shall refuse to enter into sufficient bonds for the discharge of theis Legacies before expressed or any parte of them, I then will that my eldest sonne then livinge shalbe Executour in her place, and she to resigne all over to hym. And he to enter into sufficient bonds to paye unto Margarett my Wiefe wth in one yeare after the takinge of this Office, Fourescore pounds of good and lawfull money of Englande, besydes she shall enioye all my household stuffe and cattell, Onlie my will is that she shall deliver in all my Bonds, morgages and money. And yf any be consumed, she for to make it good. And that my sonne shall enter into sufficient Bondes for the dischardinge of my will as ys before required of my Wiefe. And yf Margarett my Wife doe departe this liefe unmarryed, that then my desyre and will is that she geve unto my Foure Children which I had by my first wiye Twentye poundes of good and lawfull money, that is eche of them Fyve poundes. And this is my true mynde and will the which I doe testefye by my hande and seale this Tenth of November, and in the yeare of our Lorde 1596.

THOMAS MORSE, his mark.

In witnes whereof we have setto oᵣ names,

This will was probated at London April 28, 1597.

RICHARD CARTER,
RICHARD BLOCK,
WILLIAM DOWNES, his mark.

[The above Rev. Thomas Morse was no doubt the father of Samuel, of Dedham and Medfield, who, aged 50, in 1635, embarked at London, having in filial reverence named a son Thomas, who died at Dedham, s. p.; another, Samuel after himself, who returned to England and served as Colonel under Cromwell, and four other sons after four of his brothers; and not having enough to go round, he was probably suffered to name a grandson Nathaniel towards completing the list. Robert, Thomas, Anthony, William and Edward were the *great* family names, both in Suffolk and Wiltshire. If Rev. Thomas named a son Thomas for himself and father, (?) and another Robert for his grandfather, (?) they probably died before the date of this will. The baptismal names of the above sons were peculiar; only one of them occurring on any Morse will discovered prior to 1650. From the early adoption of surnames until 1553, both upon the continent and in England, the name was invariably spelt Mors, as it still is throughout Germany its birth place, probably in the Count de Mors about 1200–1300. German immigrants have no doubt carried the name into Russia. The geographical centre of the name in England was the co. of Suffolk, where it was not probably planted until after 1400, and then by a single family, as their peculiar Christian names in 1500–1600 in this and conterminous Counties indicate, and as references to each other in their thirty wills show. The Morses of Wiltshire were undoubtedly a colony from Suffolk, for they carried with them and transmitted the identical names peculiar to the Morses of Suffolk, and still have the same family arms. These perchance might have been the arms of the Count de Mors of Nassau, Germany, enrolled by courtesy at the English Herald Office with e final added to the name to make it English; for the arms are too simple and the emblems too ancient to have been conferred so lately as the admission of e to the name, and the family claim for them about 200 years higher antiquity than the appearance of their name in England, going back quite to the age of the German Count. But my correspondence with honoured Gent. of the race in Europe, and exploration of ancient records in England, are not completed, and more light may yet be received to modify my conclusions.

Of the early rank of the name little has been gathered. From the will of Widow Margaret Mors, probably the great grandmother or

958

aunt of the Rev. Thomas, made in 1510, it is evident that she owned the Church in which she directed her body to be interred. One, a husbandman, held a life lease of a manor ; others had many houses and freehold estates ; one owned half of 6 ships, another half of 4, and quite a number were less interested in navigation. One of their ships was probably the famous Speedwell. No mechanics are named in the wills before 1635, except one worsted weaver and three cloth workers. About half were husbandmen, and many bequeathed small sums to the poor of one, two, three, and sometimes twenty parishes. Several ranked as Gentlemen. Nicholas was Gov. of Bengal about 1750, and grandfather of Lord Bixley, Chancellor of the Exchequer. Another married Oliver Cromwell, great grandson of the Protector ! But no one is believed to have been knighted in England before Sir Robert, the East India General, about the middle of the last century, who kept and transmitted the ancient arms now held by his grandson, a baronet.

As my working days may not be prolonged to finish an improved edition of my Memorial of the Morses, I beg leave to add that no evidence has reached me of the least connection between Morse and Moss, Morris or Moors, or that any two of them have ever been used in England as convertible names, or in the United States until since 1790. Moss, with the Jews a contraction for Moses, is extremely common throughout the three kingdoms ; but Morse has never there been a very common name, and "is now rather seldom to be met with," and the London Directory confirms it. In the United States, the British Provinces and the Eastern Circles of Germany it is very common, and may ere long require weeding out, according to the German custom of compelling the subjects of an embarrassingly common name to choose and take on another.

Boston, April 12, 1865.   Abner Morse.]

[Rev. Abner Morse corrected a part of the proof of the above communication, and left in manuscript a few lines to be added, but he deceased before the type was set for the revised article. He died at Sharon, Mass., May 16, 1865, aged 71 years, 6 mos. 11 ds. An obituary notice of our esteemed friend and fellow member may be expected in a future number.—Editor.]

MORTIMORE, *alias* TANNER, AND HATHERLY. — In looking over Worthy's "Devonshire Wills" (London, 1896), I happened upon the following abstract of a will which helps to throw some light on the English ancestry of Timothy Hatherly of Scituate. On pages 253–4 I find:

"1637. The last will of Elinor Mortimore, otherwise Tanner, of Fremington, widow. She desires to be buried in the parish churchyard, just by the chancel door, near to the 'sepulchre' of her husband William Mortimore, *alias* Tanner, and leaves 10s to the poor of the parish. Mentions sons Matthew and Henry Mortimore, *alias* Tanner, and daughter Elinor Friend; also son Tymothy Hatherley and daughter Eylin Hanver."

This will was proved the 30th August, 1637. In her husband's will, proved the 12th September, 1615, I find no mention of any "Hatherley" or "Hanver," and this lends color to the surmise that the two mentioned above were her children by a former marriage. Nicholas Mortymer, in his will, proved the 11th December, 1613 (page 252), leaves "to Elizabeth Hatherleigh my second beste dublett and jerkyn, my best wastcoatt, and one canvas shirt;" and "to John Hatherleigh my best hatt." I give these last items for what they are worth.

Mr. Henry F. Waters, to whom I showed the first will, said that he had no doubt that Timothy Hatherly and his sister, Eglin Hanford, of Scituate, were the persons mentioned. Eglin Hanford came with two daughters in the *Planter*, in 1635. Another daughter, Lettice, seems to have arrived earlier, for she married Edward Foster, of Scituate, the 8th April of the same year. Timothy Hatherly, though married twice, left no children.

I hope that the above may lead to some further investigations. If not, it may still prove of some interest to the numerous descendants of Edward Foster.

15 Oxford Street, Cambridge.   F. APTHORP FOSTER.

WILLIAM MULLINS.—It has been repeatedly affirmed that William Mullins, the Mayflower passenger, was a Huguenot named Molynes. This may or may not be so, and that he was a Huguenot or of Huguenot ancestry still remains to be proved. The names of his parents are unknown, and all that is known about his origin is that he was from Dorking in Surrey. The name *Molynes* is Anglo-Norman quite as much as it is French. Until, therefore, further evidence is brought to light as to his antecedents, he should not be claimed as a Huguenot. Certain Huguenot societies in this country are said to be admitting members in right of their descent from William Mullins or Molynes. If this is so, they are quite wrong in so doing, until it can be proved that William Mullins was of Hugenot descent, a statement for which evidence is now totally lacking.

Bristol, R. I.   G. ANDREWS MORIARTY.

NOTES ON THE FIRST WIFE AND PARENTAGE OF THOMAS NELSON OF ROWLEY, MASS.:—Thomas Nelson came over from England in 1638 in the company of the Rev. Ezekial Rogers and founded the town of Rowley, Massachusetts Bay. He brought with him two sons, Philip and Thomas. Of his wife there is no mention and even her first name has been unknown. However, on page 27 of *Rowley, Massachusetts . . .* by Amos Everett Jewett and Emily Mable Adams Jewett we find an entry which Professor Hazen had copied from the Rowley, Yorkshire, record for 1637 in the Bishop's Transcripts at York, England: "Dorothie the wife of Mr. Thomas Nelson buryed Sept. 27". Now we have the given name of the mother of his sons Philip and Thomas. Paver's marriage licenses of Yorkshire provides the family name: "Thomas Nelson of Cottingham and Dorothy Stapleton of All Saints, North St., York, married 1626". We have yet to find to which branch of the Stapleton family Dorothy belonged but there was a Christopher Stapleton living in Cottingham at the time of Dorothy's marriage to Thomas Nelson, resident of that town.

The will of Thomas Nelson (see THE REGISTER, 3:267-268) provides the clue to Thomas' parentage. In it he mentions his Aunt Katherine Witham. According to the visitation by Dugdale, vol. 2, Cuthbert Witham of Garfourth in West Yorkshire married as his second wife, Katerine, widow of William Walker of Balnhall, co. Ebor, and daughter of Thomas Nelson of Thoresby, co. Lincoln. Therefore, Thomas Nelson of Rowley was the grandson of Thomas Nelson of Thoresby and son of the younger Thomas.

Little Compton, R.I.   THE LATE BENJAMIN F. WILBOUR

NEWGATE.—Lechford's Note-Book, as published by the American Antiquarian Society, requires us to make many corrections to the Genealogical Dictionary of New England, some of which are not mentioned by the Editor. Savage says that Theodore Atkinson " came, in the employment of John Newgate, from Bury in co. Lancaster," but Newgate's will, as drawn by Lechford, mentions his " Lands and Tenements lying in Horningerth in the County of Suffolk." This shows that John Newgate really came from Bury St. Edmunds in Suffolk, from which Horningerth or Horningsheath is only two miles distant.   W. S. APPLETON.

NORTHEND AND WIGGLESWORTH.—John Northend and Edward Northend were witnesses to the will of William Wiglesworth of Shipden, parish of Halifax, Yorkshire, England, which will is dated 16 October, 1590. Can the early settler of Rowley, Ezekiel Northend, be traced to either of the above persons or to that locality?

Does not this connection of the names of Wiglesworth and Northend, and the subsequent appearance of one of the latter name in the company of the Rev. Ezekiel Rogers at Rowley, lend a shade of probability to the theory broached by Mr. Dean in his *Memoir of Rev. Michael Wigglesworth* (page 18), that Wigglesworth may have come over with Rogers? The above testator, William Wigglesworth, calls Edward Northend his brother-in-law.   JOHN M. BRADBURY.
Ipswich, Mass.

ODELL.—William Odell, the founder of an American family of that name, is traced as early as 1639 at Concord, Mass., where his children James (died 1641) and Rebecca were born. He may have been the brother of Ursula Wodell (also written Odle), who married Christopher Woolly (Wollie) at Concord in 1646.

William Odell died at Fairfield, Conn., in 1676; his will proved there June 6th of that year mentions, among others, his sons William and John Odell and daughter Rebecca Moorehouse, and disposes of lands in Concord and Fairfield.

William Odell's English ancestry seems likely to be ascertained from the following interesting clue :

Cranfield, Bedfordshire, England, is a small parish about eight miles from the village of Odell in the same county. The Cranfield Church Register records nearly seventy entries of Odell baptisms, marriages and burials, between the years 1602 and 1625, the name being variously written Wodell, Odell, Odle, Woddell, Woddle, etc. (See REGISTER, vol. 45, pages 7–8.) *Among these entries are the following :—

1602, Feb. 24, William, son of William Wodell of Warleyend, baptized.

1615, July 22, William Odle of Worley, buried.

Perhaps this is the record of the baptism of William Odell who came to New England, and of the burial of his father.

The name "Warleyend" is doubtless that of a hamlet about one mile from Cranfield, which appears on an old map of Bedfordshire as "Wallerd or Wall End."

In Cranfield Parish there was, in 1632, a district, or possibly an estate, known as "Virginia." Now it is a very significant and suggestive fact, as disclosed by the local New England records, that at Concord, Mass., the original road, cut through the woods by the first settlers, has been called since 1650 "the Virginia Road," and the district through which it runs, "Virginy." It is also a fact that, at Concord, the plain just at the end of Virginia was described as "Cranefield" in the Town Records as early as 1648, and has so continued to be described almost to the present day. It would certainly seem that these names, "Virginia" and "Cranefield," were given by the early settlers of Concord in memory of their English home.

It should also be borne in mind that the first minister of Concord, the Rev. Peter Bulkeley, who came to New England in 1635, was from Odell Parish, Bedfordshire, where he had been rector for many years.

What has been related herein seems to furnish a good foundation for further research.   RUFUS KING.

Yonkers, New York.

*Pp. 806–807, this volume.

ABSTRACT OF THE WILL OF ANDREW OSBORNE, OF LONDON, 1614.

Hartford, November 19, 1857.

DEAR SIR,—I forward you an abstract of an early will ;—from the original in the collection of the Connecticut Historical Society, handsomely engrossed on parchment and in good preservation, except the fold on which were the signatures and attestation, which has been cut off. I know nothing of the history of the document or of its line of descent to the place of its present deposit : but as the names of Osborne, Plympton, and Center were all represented, at an early period, in New England, the will may possibly supply important genealogical information to some of the descendants.
                                                       Yours, &c.   J. H. T.

Andrew Osborne, "citizen and marchant taylor of London," by his will executed Nov. 20th, 1614, directs his body "to be buried within his Majesty's free Chappell Church of St. George wᵗʰin his highnes Castle of Windsor," and gives his estate as follows :—

To his wife *Margaret*, the lease of his house " called the Garter house," within the castle of Windsor ; the lease of his house called " the Bucks head" in Watling Street, parish of St. Augustine, city of London ; and

962

the lease of a house where "now dwelleth one Robert Woodward, draper," in said Watling Street, "known by the name of the signe of the Lute and Tunn,"—for her life, and at her death, the unexpired term to belong to his three sons, *John, Charles* and *Edward* Osborne. Also, to his wife, the use for five years after his decease, with the rents and profits of his "five houses in Distaffe Lane," city of London; and of his "sixteen houses scituate and being wthout Temple Barr," in parish of St. Clement Danes ; and of one house in Gutter Lane ; with remainder as before, to his sons; and from the rents of these houses an annual payment of £200 to be made to *Andrew, Henry, Richard* and *Alice Plumpton,* the children of his son-in-law, *Henry Plumpton,* citizen and salter of London, now dwelling in Fryday Streete, city ; and an annual payment of £100 to his "cozen *Joane Center.*"

Item. To *Margaret Center,* £20, in money.

Item. To his son *John* : "two houses in the Ile of Tennett," county of Kent ; 22 acres of arable land in Hallingburne parish, Kent, lately purchased of Sir Thomas Flud (?) ; 16 acres, in Newington parish, Kent, now " in tenure of John Osborne, gent."

Item. To son *Charles,* £250 in money.

Item. To son *Edward,* £250 in money.

Item. To the parish church of Hartlipp, county of Kent," where I was born," 40 marks, for the poor of the parish.

The residue of his estate to his wife, who is made sole executrix : his son-in-law, *Henry Plumpton* and *John Peerson,* notary public, named overseers.

Executed in presence of *Philip Boles, William Hale, William Newman,* and *John Peerson.*

PALMER, Roger. In Nichols's History of the county of Leicester, in the pedigree of Palmer of Osgathorpe, Edward Palmer, of Nayton, Norfolk, who died about 1630, aged 55, is said to have left four sons, of whom Roger "went to Virginia, and afterwards to New-England." Can he be identified here?　　　　　w. s. a.

ANCESTRY OF PALMES.—In Nichols's History of Leicestershire is the pedigree of one early settler of Connecticut, which I think has never yet been printed in this country. It is taken from the Visitation of the County of Leicester, and I have myself seen it at the College of Arms. It is as follows:

William[1] Palmes, of Naburn, Yorkshire, was father of Guy,[2] who was father of Bryan[3] of Ashwell, co. Rutland, who was father of Francis[4] of Ashwell, who was father of Sir Francis[5] of Ashwell, who was father of Andrew[6] of Sherborn, Hampshire, who died at Stapleford, Nottinghamshire, about 1666, aged 73, and leaving the following children:

Thomas,[7] William,[7] John,[7] Guy,[7] Stephen,[7] all died unmarried.
Edward,[7] in New-England, 1681, and married there.
Bryan,[7] born 1641, of Melton, Leicestershire, living 1681, signed pedigree.
Jane,[7] Elizabeth,[7] m. Edward Chambers, of Torksey, Lincoln's Arme.[7]

　　　　　　　　　　　　　　　　　　W. S. APPLETON.

WILL OF HERBERT PELHAM, ESQ., 1672.*

[Communicated by SAMUEL G. DRAKE, A. M.]

Among the early promoters of the settlement of New England, was Herbert Pelham, Esq., of Ferrers in Essex. He came to New England in 1639, resided at Cambridge, and was five years connected with the government of Massachusetts. Among other employments he served as a commissioner of the United Colonies, and returned to England, where he died before the 30th of March, 1676. The towns of Pelham in New England perpetuate his name.

The family is traced to a period anterior to the conquest of England by the Normans, with a degree of certainty of which few families can boast. The name is derived from the lordship of Pelham in Hertfordshire, which, in 1292, was possessed by Walter de Pelham. The arms of the family (the Pelicans) were painted in the Church of Pelham at a very early date. The estate of Swinsted, mentioned in this will was owned by this Walter de Pelham, who died 21 Edw. I, leaving sons William de Pelham and Walter de Pelham. Thomas de Pelham was son and heir of the latter, who also had a son Thomas. This Thomas was father of John de Pelham "of great fame in the reign of Edward III, and in memory of his valiant acts, his figure in armor, with the arms of the family on his breast, was painted in glass in the Chapter house at Canterbury." He accompanied Edward in his French wars and was at the battle of Poictiers, 19 Sept., 1356, and claimed to have had a principal share in taking the French king, John, prisoner.†

The wife of this John de Pelham, was Joan, daughter of Vincent Herbert; and thus was introduced the name of Herbert into the Pelham family. Vincent Herbert was the ancestor of the Earl of Winchelsea and Nottingham, flourishing about one hundred years ago. He was succeeded by his son of the same name, Sir John Pelham, knight, upon whom great honors were bestowed. He died 12 Feb., 1428, leaving an only son, John. Without noting the intermediate generations, it is sufficient for this note to observe that the immediate ancestor of our testator was named Herbert Pelham, his grandfather was Anthony Pelham of Buxstead in Sussex. His mother was Elizabeth, one of the six daughters of Thomas West, Lord de la Warr. His wife was Penelope, also daughter of the Lord de la Warr. His father died 31 July, 1625, aged 39. Herbert was born 1601, died before 31 March, 1676.

---

* Mr. Savage, in his *New Eng. Dictionary*, refers to the will of Herbert Pelham, but it does seem from his article that he never saw a copy of it.
† For minute particulars see Collins' *Peerage*, edition 1741, i, 395.

His father had three brothers, John, Thomas and William, and two sisters. John died *sine prole*, Thomas died unmarried, and William thus became the principal heir from whom was descended the Lord Thomas Pelham, of Laughton, Sussex, whose second wife was Grace Holles, daughter of the Earl of Clare, and sister to the Duke of Newcastle. Their son Thomas became Duke of Newcastle, 1715. Herbert Pelham's cousin, Sir John Pelham, named him in his will, as one of its overseers. This Sir John married Judith, daughter of the celebrated lord, Oliver St. John, of Bletsoe.

Arms.—Azure, three pelicans argent, wounding themselves in the breast, Gules.

In the name of God, amen. I Herbert Pelham of Ferrers in Bewers Hamlet, in the County of Essex, Esqr: weighing the Certainty of Death and the uncertainty of the time thereof, and being desirous to settle such temporal Estate as the Lord hath betrusted me with all, in such case as I would have it go after my Decease, to make & ordain this my last Will in manner & forme following: Imprimis I give unto my Son, Waldegrave Pelham all those lands, tenements & hereditaments, with all the rents & arrearages of rents, due which belong to me by virtue of a settlement of James Thacker, late of Paristhaws in the County of Sussex Esqr: or by virtue of any Settlement of William Thacker and John Thacker Sons of the said James Thacker or by any other ways or means Whatsoever which were Settled by him or them upon Katharine Pelham, my Grand mother, and Sister of the Said James Thacker and descend upon me as Heir of the Said Katharine Pelham, and Whereas I have Settled my Mannor at Swinstead alias Swineshead in ye County of Lincolne upon my Son Waldegrave Pelham, and the Heirs male of his Body, which Settlement according to my Deed thereof made I do hereby confirme, and whereas by my Indenture made the twelfth of December in the nineteenth year of King Charles the Second Anno Domini one thousand Six hundred Sixty Seven. I have Settled after my decease the Farme late in the Tenure of James Browning, and now in the Tenure of Thomas Larry lying and being in Swinstead Northend, in the County of Lincolne, My Will now is that the yearly Rent of the Said Farme be paid vizt to my Sister Penelope Bellingham wife to Richard Bellingham Esqr: Thirty Pounds yearly dureing the Terme of her natural life and Ten Pounds a year unto Elizabeth Pelham my Sister for and dureing the Terme of her natural life and the Residue of Said Rent, being Ten Pounds, My Will is it be paid unto Penelope Winslow my Daughter for and dureing the Terme of her Natural life and what Taxes may be laid on Said Farme to be borne by Each according to the Rents they Receive, and from and after the death of the Said Penelope Bellingham My Will is that my Sister Elizabeth Pelham (if she survive her) receive Ten Pounds a year more out of the Said Rents for and During the terme of her natural Life and my Will is that my Daughter Penelope Winslow if She Survive my Sister Bellingham receive likewise Ten Pounds a year more out of the Said Rents for and dureing the Terme of her natural life and my Will is that my Son Edward Pelham if he Survive my Sister Bellingham Receive Likewise Ten Pounds a year out of the Said Rents dureing the Terme of his natural Life, and that after the death of my Said Sisters and Daughter the Whole Rent to be paid unto Edward Pelham, my Son for and dureing the Terme of his natural life, and after his decease my Will is that the Said Lands be to my Sone Waldegrave Pelham and the Heirs Males of his Body lawfully begotten and for want of such Issue, to the Heirs Male of Edward Pelham Lawfully begotten and for want of such Issue to Henry Pelham, and the Heirs Males of his Body Lawfully begotten, and for want of Such Heirs to my Right Heirs for Ever, and Whereas, I have Settled by Deed upon my Son Edward Pelham for life my Lands at Smeeth Hall in the Tenure of M^r: Hart and others, being Four Hundred and fourscore acres of Low ground and late part of a great ffenn called the Eight Hundred ffenn with a House and Land which I Purchased of Christopher Pridgeon, Situate in Chapell Hill in the County of Lincolne, after that my Debts are paid with Power of Revocation, now my Will is he receive not any Rent till my Debts are all paid, and after my Debts be paid my Will is that the Next years Rent growing due as aforesaid be paid to my Daughter Anne Pelham, and the next year after that to my Son Henry Pelham and Jeremiah Stonnard Viz^t Twenty Pounds to my Son Stonnard, and the Residue to my Son Henry, and my Will further is that the third Years Rent after my debts be paid be unto my Son Josias Winslow in Satisfaction of a debt which he Says my Sone Nathanel Pelham ows him, and the fourth years Rent be paid to my Daughter Penelope Winslow if She be then liveing if not to Such Children as She Shall have then liveing to be divided between them, and my Will is that the next three Years Rent, which Shall grow due after those mentioned as aforesaid be paid into the hands of my Son Winslow for the use of my Son Edward Pelham to be paid unto him in New England if he Reside there upon the Conditions hereafter Expressed, That is to Say If he the Said Edward Pelham Shall so behave and Demean himself that he can procure either the hands of the Governour and four of the Majestraits or assistants of the Collony of the Massachusetts Bay or of New Plimoth Goverment that he is now grown Serious, Sober and Solid, and follows his Study and Avoids all Idle and Profuse Company, and that they Verily believe there is a real change in him for the better and not only to attain his ends thereby, then upon such Certificate under the hands of Five of either Government that then Such three years Rent so paid as aforesaid for his benefit be for his use and paid unto him by my Son Winslow, and that afterwards he Receive the Said Rents mentioned as aforesaid for and dureing the Terme of his life, as in the Said Deed is Expressed but if in all these years he will not be reclaimed, then my Will is Dureing his life the Said Rents be paid yearly as Followeth, that is to say, the First Years Rent after the three years formerly mentioned be Received by my Sone Waldegrave Pelham, the Second by my Daughter Winslow, the Third by my Daughter Clark, the fourth by my Daughter Anne, the fifth by my Son Henry and then to begin again to my Son Waldegrave and the Rest Successively Dureing the Life of the Said Edward. Item, I give all my Lands in the Realm of Ireland, Lying and being in the Parish of Owenboy in the Barrony of Kerrycurry, in the County of Cork, and now in the Tenure of Edward Goble, Robert Porter and Edward Porter or their assignees unto my Son Henry Pelham and the Heirs males of his Body Lawfully to be Begotten and for want of Such Issue male, to my Son Waldegrave Pelham and the Heirs males of his Body Lawfully to be begotten, and for want of Such Issue, to my Right Heirs forever, with all Such Rents as are Due at the time of my Death that are in the Tenants hands to be paid unto my Son Henry Pelham and for any Lands in Wigtofte in the County of Lincolne, my will is that my Daughter Katharine Clark receive Twenty Five pounds a year out of the Said Rents dureing the Terme of her Natural Life and That my Daughter Anne Pelham receive Twenty Five pounds a year Dureing the Terme of her Natural Life and the remainder of yᵉ said rent in Wigtofte to be unto my Son Henry Pelham, for and Dureing the Terme of his natural life and after the Death of them or either of them, their part so Dyeing to be paid to the use of Waldegrave Pelham and Herbert Pelham my Grand children for and dureing the Terme of their Natural lives, and the Revertion of the Said Lands to go as the other to the Heirs Male of the Family afterwards. Item, I give unto my Son Edward Pelham, all my Lands, Tennements and Hereditaments in New England in the Massachusetts Bay in America, Situate, lying and being in Cambridge, Watertown, Sudbury or else-where within the Said Collony, which are laid out unto me, also all others which are Due to me from any of the Said Towns or from the Country which are not yet laid out unto me, together with all Such Rents and arrearages of Rents as Shall be Due unto me at the Time of my Death, for any Lands letten within Said Collony. Item, I give all my Plate in New England to my Son Edward Pelham with one great Silver Tankard, wᶜʰ was given him by his Grandfather Godfry Bossevile, Esqʳ with the inlaid Cabinet and all in it that Stands in the Kitchen Chamber at Ferrers, and all other Brass, Beding and Linnin with all my Books and other Utensills and moveables which I have in the Massachusetts Bay in New England. My Will is that it be Equally Divided between my Son Edward Pelham and my Daugh-ter Penelope Winslow. Item, I give unto my Daughter, the Wife of Mʳ Cuthlach Elliot, the Great Red Cabinet which was her Mothers, and used to Stand in the Hall Chamber, and the Little Silver Cup with the cover to it, I give to her Daughter Elizabeth. Lastly I make and ordain My Son Waldegrave Pelham, Executor of this my Last Will and Testament, and Do hereby Revoke all other Wills by me formerly made. In Witness whereof I have Sett to my hand and Seal this first Day of January in the Year of our Lord God, one thou-sand Six Hundred Seventy and two and in the Reign of Our Sover-eign Lord Charles the Second yᵉ four and twentieth being four Sheets in Number,

Testes *Robert Chaplin*, *Herbert Pelham.*
      Samuel Gibson,
  & William Gibbs.

Probatum Londini &c: Coram Venti viro Hento Fauconberge Legum Doctor Surrŏ: &c. Tricesimo Die mensis martii. Anno Domⁱ. 1676. Juramento Waldegrave Pelham filii et extoûs, &c. O'ni &c: de bonis &c: Juramᵗ.

                Thomas Welham, Regʳⁱⁱ: Depᵗᵘˢ:

PERKINS FAMILY.—In the article in our last No. on the genealogy of this family, mention is made on page 212, of a written account left by the Rev. Wm. Perkins, of Topsfield. We give so much of this as relates to his English ancestry.

" The lineage of George Perkins, and Catherine, his wife, of Abbots Salford, in the county of Warwick, yeoman :—Beatrice, bp., Joanna, bp. May 14, 1571 ; Anne, bp. Feb. 28, 1573 ; Thomas, bp. Feb. 14, 1576 ; William, bp. Jan. 1, 1579 ; Frances, bp. April 23, 1583.

" The lineage of William Perkins, of London, merchant tailor, by Catherine, his first wife, married May 22, 1603, which Catherine deceased Sept. 18, 1618 :—Bathsua, b. May 24, 1605 ; William, b. Aug. 25, 1607 ; John, b. Jan. 1608 ; Toby, b. March, 1609 ; Sarah, b. Low-Sunday, April 19, 1612 ; Rebecca, b. Jan. 27, 1614 ; Harrington, b. March, 30, 1615. By Mary, his second wife, daughter of Mr. George Purchas, of Thaxstead, in the county of Essex, being married March 30, 1619 ; which Mary deceased Oct. 29, 1639, when she had been married 20 years and 7 months :—Harrington, b. Jan. 22, 1620 ; Edward, b. Jan. 18, 1622—his fathe.'s sixth son, and his mother's sixth child, ergo, Edward the sixth ; Samuel, b. June 13, 1624 ; Elizabeth, b. May 15, 1629. Ex autographo charrissimi Patris manu Edwardi ibidem nominati. February 16, 1670."

JOHN PLUMBE.—Dr. Savage says of John Plumbe, " Not kn. whence he came." Middlesex Deeds, vol. iii., page 77-9, doc. No. 5. Thomas Cox, of Waltham Magna, Co. Essex, clerke ; Wm. Cox, clothier of Coggeshall Magna and Jeremiah Garrard of Witham, clothier, Ex-rs of Sarah Tanner the Ex'x of William Tanner dec'd ; give Power of Attorney, dated London Jany. 13, 1660-1, to John Plumbe of Hartford ; son of George Plumbe of Imworth, Co. Essex in England, to Recover of John Allen of Charlestown, and others. Recorded 9 (5) 1664. Copied at E. Cambridge.   w.

POMEROY.—For many years extensive search has been made in England for the ancestry of Eltweed Pomeroy, who came to Dorchester, Mass., in 1630, but no mention of his name had been found there until recently. In Vol. 5, page 28, of Phillimore's " Somersetshire Parish Registers " is given the marriage, in Crewkerne, of Eltweed Pomery of Bemister [co. Dorset] and Margery Rocket, May 7, 1629. This I believe to be the marriage of the pioneer. It has been stated that the wife of our Eltweed Pomeroy was named Mary, but no original records give this name, and the idea that she bore it was probably derived from the fact that Eltweed Pomeroy had two daughters named Mary.

Boston, Mass.   J. GARDNER BARTLETT.

WILL OF HENRY POOLE, 1643.

Communicated by JOHN S. H. FOGG, M.D., of South Boston, Mass.

I Henry Poole Late of the Citye of London, Girdler, and now resident in Boston in New England Being willing to prouide for my departure out of this ꝑesent Liffe though weake & sicke of body yet of good and ꝑfect memory Thanckes be giuen to God for the same; doe now make ordaine & declare this my Last will and testament in manner and forme following.

IMPRIMIS, I will that all such debts and dutyes I am of right owing to any ꝑson or ꝑsons be well and truly paid and contented by my Executor heere affter named, and affter my debts are paid and funerall expences ꝑformed I will that all my goods, chattells and debts shal be Deuided into three Equall parts, Whereof I will that my deare & Loueing wiffe Elizabeth Poole shall haue one Equall part to her owne proper vse, of all my said goods Chattells and debts affter the Laudable Custome of the City of London: and the second equall part of all my said goods, chattells and debts whatsoeuer I bequeath to my three sonns to be deuided amongst them; That is to say, to my Eldest sonne Henry one hundred pounds and my second sonne Robert ffitye pounds (more) then my will is shall be giuen and bequeathed to my Yongest sonne Edmond Poole. And yf my said deare & Loueing wiffe shall happen to bee wᵗʰ child I bequeath vnto him or her an equall portion wᵗʰ my sonne Edmond, To be paid and deliuered to them and euery of them according to the proportion before mentioned when they shall accomplish and come to there Lawfull ages of one & twenty yeeres or else to bee marryed, and yf any of my said children shall decease before they accomplish said ages and before that tyme bee not married that then I bequeath his or her part (of the soe deceased) to the other of them then suruiuing to be deliuered to them as aforesaid.

And the third equall part of all my said goods Chattells and debts I reserue vnto my Executor or Executrix heereaffter expressed therew^th to pforme my Legacies and bequests, heereaffter specifyed, That is to say the residue of all my goods Chattells and debts affter my debts bee paid my funerall expences pformed and these my Legacyes contained in this my present testament fullfild I Wholy Liue and bequeath to my said Children to be deuided among them and deliu'd vnto them as I haue aboue Willed and declared.

Item, I giue and bequeath vnto my ffather Rowland Poole for a ring twenty shillings and to my Sister Martha Castle twenty shillings for the same vse.

Item, I bequeath to Robert Castle, Thomas Bendish Esquire and M^r ——— Peter each of them twenty fiue shillings for the aforesaid vse. Item, I bequeath to my Brother Randall Poole and his children the summe of ten pounds and to Anna Paullmoore forty shillings. Item, I giue and bequeath to the Colledge of Cambredg in New England ten pounds, and to William Bartholemew fforty shillings. And I will and my mynd and intent is that my wiffe or any whom she shall ordaine and appointe shall haue the keeping gouernance & bringing vp of my said Children during there non-ages, and alsoe the disposall and imployment of there and euery of there portions (bequeathed and shalbe comeing to them or any of them as aforesaid) too and for the vse beniffet and behoofe of them & euery of them as is before expresed. And of this my present testament I make and ordaine my said deare Wiffe Elizabeth Poole my sole Executrix. And of the execution of the same I make and ordaine Robert Castle and Thomas Bendish Esquires Ouerseers in England, and for the Mannaging and composing of my affaires in New England and the better obtaining and pcuring all my goods chattles & debts heere I doe alsoe constitute and ordaine Nehemiah Bourne William Dauis Robert Cooke and Thomas Dayton Over-seers of this my Last will & Testament, And do giue & grannt vnto them and euery of them full power and authority to psecute any pson or psons for euery debt or debts duty appertainnige to me by specialtie or otherwayes & to pcure and receiue the same and dispose thereof for the best aduantage of my wiffe & children according to my trust committed vnto them. And for There Labour and paynes therein I giue & bequeath to my Ouerseers twenty Nobles a peece. And I Vtterly reuoke & disanull euery other former Testaments wills Legacies bequeasts Executors & Ouerseers by mee in any wise before this tyme named willed & bequeathed. In Wittnese whereof I haue heerevnto set my hand & Seale, Dated at Boston in New England the twenty^th day of August Annoq. Dom̃. 1643.

Sealed Signed & deliu'd   HEN : POOLE.
   in ꝑesents of vs.
Richard Shearman   Jo Wakelin
Thomas Bartholmew   George Story.

[The original of the above will of Henry Poole is in the possession of Dr. Fogg, who has kindly copied it for the REGISTER. The original contains no memorandum of its being probated, and there is no entry relative to the will on the records of the Suffolk Probate Court. It is probable that Mr. Poole did not live long after the date of his will, as the Hon. Josiah Quincy in his History of Harvard University, vol. i., page 458, quotes from College Book No. III. an entry of a cash receipt by the college " as of the year 1642 " of ten pounds from "Henry Pool." If the amount was paid under the will, it must have been received later than 1642, for the will is dated 1643. What more is known of this Henry Poole?—EDITOR].

POOLE.—Since the publication of the Poole Genealogy, it has been discovered that the wife of Edward[1] Poole of Weymouth, Mass., 1635, was Sarah, daughter of John and Jane (Porthesy) Pynney, son of John and Johane (   ) Pynney, all of Broadway, co. Somerset, England. She was a niece of Humphrey Pynney, the early settler at Windsor, Conn. Her name was learned from the will of her uncle, Edmund Pynney of Broadway. Aspinwall's Notarial Records (page 12) mention a bequest to her by her said uncle. Stiles's History of Windsor mentions the will.

The only wife of Joseph[2] Poole (Edward[1]) was Elizabeth,[3] daughter of John[2] (Abraham[1]) and Alice Shaw.   MURRAY E. POOLE.
Ithaca. N. Y.

From Chancery Bills and Answers, 1758–1800:
Teale vs. Pope.—Mathew Pope died 1779, leaving Mathew Pope who now resides in York Town, Virginia, his eldest son. Defendant John Pope sworn at Cranbrook, co. Kent, 17 Jan. 1789.   GERALD FOTHERGILL.
11 Brussels Road, New Wandsworth, London, Eng.

PRATT.—In the Worcester Co. Registry is a deed of 1715, from Edward Pratt, formerly of St. Paul's, Shadwell, in the county of Middlesex, London, England, victualler, now of Sherborn, Mass.   W. S. A.
[Morse, in his History of Sherborn and Holliston, though he gives a family by the name of Pratt, mentions no Edward Pratt.--ED.]

PREBLES IN ENGLAND.—[*Extracts from wills recorded in Rochester, county Kent, England.*] — Died 1521. *John Prebyll* of Watering near Rochester — in his will he mentions his wife Alice, his sons John, Robert and Stephen—all under twenty—and a brother William.

1581. Died *John Preble* of East Barninge — Kent Yeoman. He mentions his son Richard under twenty—his son John and daughter Annys. He mentions his brothers William and Thomas, and his sisters Harling and Call, and speaks of his late father John Preble.

1617. *Thomas Preble* of Barneige leaves a wife Margaret and children John, Richard, Mary, Margaret and Ione the wife of Thomas Warley.

From the wills at Canterbury. — Died 1634. *Robert Prebble* of Denton, Kent. He had sons *Abraham*, Robert, Benjamin and Jacob. Sisters Elinor, Margaret and Frances.

Robert Prebble was *possibly* the father of Abraham, who emigrated, two years after his death, in 1636, to America.

1636. *John Prebble* of Elham, husbandman. His wife Gilliam, sons William and John, grandson John, son of his son John, daughters Johanna, Mildred, Susan Parnell and Alfra.

1659. John Prebble of Boughton under the Bleau, mentions parishes of Hearnhill, Kent, and Goodnerstone, Kent; wife Mary, sons William and John, daughter Mary.

At Doctors Commons. — 1675. Died, John Prebble of London, leaving only a widow Jane.   GEO. HENRY PREBLE.

ORIGIN OF DIGORY PRIEST, EARLY SETTLER IN PLYMOUTH, NEW ENGLAND.—According to his manuscripts, now at the Rare Book Collection, Library of Congress, the late Col. Charles E. Banks evidently felt that there was a possible connection between the above-named Digory Priest and that Digory Priest who was baptized in Poughill, Cornwall, in 1598. Willison in his "Saints and Strangers" tells us that the New England settler, Digory Priest, was born about 1579, and died in Plimouth Plantation, New England, in 1621; he had once been a hatter of London.

According to the 1620 Visitation of Devonshire (Harleian, vol. 6, pp. 225, 226) one Hugh Prust, son of Peter Prust, lived at Gorven in Hartland, Devonshire (very near Poughill, Cornwall); Hugh's first wife died in 1572/3, and he then married Agnes Wood, who was buried in Hartland 19 Jan. 1582/3. Their fifth child and fourth son was Digory *Prust*, who would evidently have been born about the same time that Digory Priest of New England was born. The published parish register of Hartland, Devonshire, includes the following entry:

"11 August 1582, baptized Digorius, son of Peter Prust."

In this connection it should be mentioned that Prust and Priest are varying forms of the same name, according to the index of "Devonshire Wills", published by the British Record Society. The cited register entry may mean that Digorius was grandson of Peter, if Hugh (*supra*) had died prior to 11 Aug. 1582.

Arlington, Va. JOHN G. HUNT.

WILLIAM PULLEN.—If William Pullen who was born at Shobrook, 6 miles from Exeter in England, and came into these parts about 30 or 40 years ago, is yet alive, and will come to William Wesson of Hopkinton in New England, he may hear of an estate in land worth Five hundred pounds sterling per annum, left him by one Mr. Pullen of Thorverton, near Exeter, and there is no heir found to enjoy it.— *Boston Evening Post*, June 11th, 1753.

Baudicour, Mr. 693
Baugh, George 660
Baxter, Charles 724
  James Phinney 620
  Rd. 733
  Richard 724, 730
  William 733
Bayley, Fran. 182
  Francis 184
  Jane 182
  Richard 553
  Sarah 833
  Thomas 833, 834
Baylie, Rev. Thomas 834
Baylies, Francis 377
Baylof, Agnes de 36
  Odo de 36
Baynard, Barbara 65, 70
  Thomas 65, 70
Baynbery, Richard 255
Baynes, John 312
  Richard 657
Bayning, Mary 71
  Vis't 71
Bayrume, Wm. 715
Beacon, Sibilla 683
  Theodore 683
Beacroft, John 907
Beagan, Richard 391
Beal, John 822
Beale, Anna 883
  Elizabeth 883
  Joseph 903
  Mary 386
  Mary Pike 883
  Thomas 883
Beaman, Charles C. 114
Beamer, Anne 418, 419
Beane, Dionis 200
  Henry 199, 200
Beard, Charles R. 510
Beare, John 671
Beasley, John 416
  Susannah 416, 418
Beauchamp, Earl of 72
  Lord 67
  Anne de 674
  Edw'd, Lord 67
  Giles de 674
  Hugh de 21
  John de 674
  Sir John de 674
  Sir Richard de 674
  Simon de 21, 22
  Walter de 673
  William, 5th Baron 673
  Sir William de 673
Beauclerc, Henry 19
Beaumont, Constance 658
  John, Lord 658
  S. 159
Beaupell, Sir Henry 667
  Margaret 667
Beavan, James 418, 419
Beaver, Mr. 682
  Michael 682
Beazley, Elizabeth 416
  William 416
Beche alias Marshall,
  Joan 657
  Roger 657
Becher, Brig. Ralph Fred-
  erick Richard 918
  Zoe Louise 918
Beck, Mary 626
  Samuel 626
  Sarah 626
  Thomas 626

Becke, Ellen 787
  Elline 781
  John 8
Becker, Julianna 594
Beckingham, (?) 839
  Margaret 839
  Thomas 839
Beconsawe, Sir White 381
Bedford, Duke of 371
  Earl of 389, 390, 393
  Rebecca 684
Bedowe, Richard 657
Beech, Ellyn 261
Beed, Thomas 465, 466
Beel, Edmond 399
Beeston, Doro. 126
Beex, John 798
Beighton, Elizabeth 162
  Thomas 162
Bekenstall, Margaret 386
Belcher, Gov. 699
  Aurelia 674
  Benjamin 674
  Benjamin Barney 674
  Deborah Hunt 674
  Gregory 674
  Dea. Gregory 674
  Jonathan 699
  Rrv. Joseph 674
  Olive 674
Belchier, William 272
Belingham, Mr. 857
Bell, Ann 67, 69, 70,
  73, 74
  Edward 70, 73
  Dr. Whitfield J. 546
Bellingham, (?) 861, 965
  Gov. 53, 368, 401, 842,
  843, 943
  Hester 943
  Penelope 861, 965
  Richard 223, 861, 943,
  965
  Gov. Richard 857, 943
Bellomont, Earl, Lord
  Coote 56
Bemis, Maria 378
  Mary 366
Bendish, Thomas 970
Benedict, Thomas 127
  Wm. 127
Benet, (?) 224
Benion, Adam 656
  Joan 656
Bennet, Anne 465
  Katherine 853
  Samuel 853, 857
  William 446, 465, 739
Bennett, Christian 446
  John 639
  Philip 51
  Robert 51
  William 446
Benninge, John 934
Bennyon, Thomas 657
Benson, Elizabeth 159
  John 159
  William 288
Benten, (?) 601
Benton, Andrew 607
  Sibell 601
  Sybil 606
Bentten, Andrew 601
  Sibell 601
Benyon, Adam 656
  Joan 656
  Robert 657
  Thomas 657

Berd, Francis 579
Berenger, Elizabeth 39
  William 39
Beresford, Mrs. 75
  John 75, 76
Beriffe, John 91
Berkeley, Lord 349
  Lord Lieutenant 350
  Elizabeth 674
  Sir John 674
  Sr. William 51
Berkley, Lord 408
Bernard, K. of Italy 673
Bernard, Sir 583
Bernard, Gov. 331,332
  Capt. Thomas 51
Bernardin, Jeanne 813
Berrie, Dr. 615
  William 616
Berriman, John 73
Berry, Dr. 614, 615, 616,
  617, 618
  Elizabeth 700
  Hester 348
  Richard 614
  Dr. Richard 614, 616
Best, Mary 418, 428, 429
Bestone, John 257
Beswicke, Mary 300
  William 300
Bethune, George 799
Beton, Thomas 632
Betterly, Wilson S. 907
Betton, Margery 632
Betts, John 100
Beuthen, F. D. 594
Bibye, Simon 950
Bickford, John 844
  Mary 844
  Richard 844
  Thomas 844
  Walter 844
Bickley, Brun 407
  Elizabeth 407
Biddle, Mr. 936
Bides, (?) 201
  Joan 201
  Joane 201
  John 201
Bidwell, Thomas 574
Bigg, Anne 683
  John 683
Bigland, Edward 950
  Henry 950, 951
Bigod, Joan 215
  Sir Roger 215
Bill, Elizabeth 330
  Richard 330, 333
  Sarah Davis 330
Billings, Edward 956
Billingsley, Daniel 184
  Daniell 182
  Grace 182
Billington, (?) 773
  John 772
Bindon, Viscount 66, 71,
  76
  Cicely 408
  Douglas 71, 76
Bingley, Francis 157
  Johane 809
Bining, Prof. Arthur Cecil
  500
Birchall, Oumffraye 715
Birche, Raphe 723
Birchshooe, Oumffraye
  715
Bird, Mrs. 263

Bird, Owen 524
  Richard 48, 524
  Willimi 231
  Sr. William 766
Birde, Mariam 48
Biscoe(e), Nathaniell
  291
Biship, John 946
Bishop, Anne 392
  Avis Abbot 392
  Edith 392
  Elinor Watkins 389
  Humphrey 392
  Joan Watkins 392
  John 300, 389
  Thomas 389, 392
Bishpam, Mr. 730
  Thos. 733
  Wm. 730
Bishpome, Thomas 730
Bixley, Lord 959
Black, Joseph 884
  Margaret 884
  William 287
Blackborne, James 739
Blackburne, William 745
Blacke, John 237
Blackleech, Catherinam 265
Blackmore, John 660
Blackwell, John 442
Blackwey, Richarde 180
Blades, Bygot 869
  Edith 205
  Richard 205
Blage, (?) 600, 606
Blake, Philip H. 945
Blakeway, (?) 766, 767,
  768
  Jacob 756, 767, 768,
  769, 770
  Jacobs 766
Blanchard, Mris. 239
Bland, Isabel 622, 623,
  624
  John 263, 623
Blanford, John 942
Blanshard, George 868
Blatchinden, Elizabeth 210
Blaton, Ann 231
Blaydes, Frederic A. 806
Blechindon, (?) 209
  Elizabeth 209
Bleddyn, (?) 630
Blemell, John 85, 86, 88
  Rev. John 85
  Thomas 85
Blemill, James 86
  Jasper 86
  John 86
  Martha 86
  Mary 86
  Thomas 86
Blennerhasset, John 94
  Kateryn 93
  Katherine 93
  Sir Thomas 93
Blennerhassett, Katherine
  92
  Samuel 105
Blicke, William 294
Blike, Willm. 279
Blinkensopp, Christopher
  260
  Elizabeth 260
Blithe, (?) 70, 73
  Elizabeth 73
Block, Richard 958
Blois, Sir F. 106
Blomefield, Francis 106

Blood, Lt. Col. Bindon
  951
  Edmund 951
  Gertrude 951
  Henry Ames 951
  John 951
  Richard 951
  Robert 951
  Col. Thomas 951
Bloomfield,Francis 922,
  923
  Henry 206
Blore, Mrs. E. M. 1
Bloss, Anna 956
Blount, Dorothy 574
  Sir Nicholas 183
  Sir Walter 183, 658
  William 183
  William, 4th Baron
  Mountjoy 574
Bluet, Anne 571, 575
  Arthur 575
  Dorothy 574, 575
  Dorothy Blount 575
  Elizabeth 575
  Elizabeth Portman 575
  John 571, 574, 575
  Mary 575
  Richard 575
  Suzanna 575
  Sir Walter 574
Blundell, Alice 22
  John 720
  William 22
Blunt, Elizabeth 533
  Sir Nicholas 183
  Ursula 181, 183
  William 533
Blwett, John 574
Blyth, Marie 841
Blythe, Alice 841
Boardman, Daniel 475,
  476
  Richard 729
Boate, Anne 562
  John 562
Bodin 171, 172
Bodrigan, Anne 667
  Sir Nicholas 667
Boissonade, P. 813
Boler, Frederick 288
  Fredericka 288
  Henry 288
Boles, Philip 963
Boleyn, Anna, Q. of
  Eng. 662
Bolles, Sir John 443
  Mary 443
Boltby, Adam de 34
  Iveta de 34
  John de 34
  Jordan de 34
  Odo de 34, 35
Boltebi, Adam de 35
Bolton, John 714
Bolyn, Sir Thos. 401
Bommer, John 825
Bond, Dr. 835
  Rev. Sampson 751
Bonde, Robert 95
Bonnels, Samuell 825
Bonner, Thomas 618
Bonython, (?) 642, 645
  Capt. 642. 643, 644
  645
  John 645
  Capt. Richard 642, 643
Boomer, Richard 263
  Robert 263

Rose 262, 263
Boote, Zachias 524
Booth, Widdow 560
  John 560
  Mary 560
  Robert 560
  William 558, 560
  Willim 559
  Willm 556
Boothe, John 559
  Marie 559
  Rich. 559
  Robert 559
  William 556, 559
Bordman, Richard 734
  Thomas 716
Borland, Mr. 698
  Francis 799
  John 799
Born, (?) 221
  John 221
Borne, John 221
Borough, Sr. John 579
Borrowes, Anne 130, 141
Bose, Mr. 686, 693
Boseveile, Elizabeth 211
  Godfrey 211, 862
Bosseveile, Godfry 967
Bosseville, Elizabeth
  211
  Godfrey 211
Bostocke, Thomas 209, 211
Bosvile, Elizabeth 859
  Godfrey 859
Bosworth, Alice 474, 475,
  475, 476
  Joseph 474
Boteler, Isabella 470
  Sir Francis 470
Botetourt, John 770
  John de 769
  Maud 770
B'thwell, Ric'd 721
Botiler, Hawis le 28
  Hawise de 24
  Hawise le 27, 28
  Hawise Gobion le 28
  John le 27
  Philip le 27
  Ralph de 24
  Ralph le 26, 27, 28
Bottrill, F. W. 567
Boue, Lieut. Col. 920
  Valentine Andree 920
Boughton, Miss 567
  Sir C. R. 567
  Edward 828
Bouker, Abraham 737
  Mary 738
Bould, John 237
Boulton, Thomas 723
Bounker, Edward 281
Bourchier, John, Earl of
  Bath 575
Bourne, (?) 221
  Elizabeth 221
  Jane Harris 221
  John 221
  Rev. Lawrence 163
  Martha 756
  Nehemiah 970
  Thomas 756
Boutcher, John 195
Bovell, Vincent 869
Bovencourt, Guidon de 171
Bovingdon, Thomas 287
Bowcher, William 717
  Wm. 717
Bowden, Joane 729

988

991

992

994

Elizabeth 221, 223, 224
Elizabeth Bourne 221, 222
Howell 416
Isabel 672
Jane 226
John 221, 222, 223, 224
Capt. John 222, 223
Katherine 299
Dr. Malachi 299
Martha Lake 597, 609
Mary 221, 226
Richard 220, 221
Robert 526
Dr. Robert 299
Samuel 220
Sarah 221, 222, 223, 224, 225
Susan 220, 222
Susanna 220
T. W. 223
Rev. Thaddeus Mason 226
Thaddeus William 225, 226
Thomas 226, 525, 610
William 220, 221, 222, 223, 224, 225, 325, 326, 524, 572
Wm. 222, 223
Harrison/Harryson (?) 139, 141, 143, 339, 530, 878
Mr. 301, 817
Alice 156
Bridget 877
Edward 181, 182, 184
Ellen 140, 141
Ellen Gregson 161
Elyn 130
Fiske Goodeve 301
George 301, 878
Henri 142
Henrie 135, 139
Henry 528, 536
Jane 130, 132, 139, 140, 141, 161
John 137, 139, 612
Rev. John 301, 306
Mary 180, 181, 182
Richard 265, 852
Robt. 485
Roger 156
Thomas 602
Rev. Thomas 590
Thos. Haynes 307
Rev. W. John 309
Willfrey 867
William 139, 141
Will'm 130, 133
Harrold, Richard 748
Harryes, William 600
Harrys, Gyles 635
Harryson. See Harrison.
Harsall, Hugh 238, 244
Harsnet, Samuell 247
Harssant, Katheren 846, 847
Thomas 847
Thome 846
Hart, Mr. 966
Richardson 647
Robert 868
Harte, Alice 733, 736
Christopher 720
Richard 101
Robert 733

Roger 733
Hartford, Dr. 891
Hartley, Prof. E. N. 487, 489
Prof. E. Neal 500
Hartlib, Samuel 368
Hartridge, (?) 385
Hartwell, Sarah 366, 378
William 757
Hartzell, Mary 892
Haruard, Anne 246
John 246
Thomas 238
Harvard(e)/Harverd(e) (?) 269
Mr. 243, 247, 270
Mrs. 249
Widow 243, 244
Ann 243, 246, 247
Annam 245
Catherine 228
Elizabeth 200, 242
Johan 256, 257
Johann 256
Johanni 243
Johe'm 245
John 228, 229, 230, 232, 238, 240, 241, 242, 243, 244, 245, 246, 247, 248, 249, 257, 261, 266, 267, 268, 269
Rev. John 228, 270
Jone 257
Katherin 233, 243
Katherinae 233
Katherine 245
Katherine Rogers 230, 248
Margaret 230, 256
Margarete 231
Margarett 231
Marye 243
Peter 228, 232, 243, 244
Richard 229, 244
Robert 228, 229, 230, 232, 233, 241, 243, 244, 245, 248, 249, 257, 258, 268, 269, 270
Tho. 230
Thomas 228, 230, 231, 232, 233, 238, 240, 242, 243, 244, 246, 256, 257, 258, 270
William 241, 243
Harvarde. See Harvard.
Harverd(e). See Harvard.
Harvey/Harvie/Harvy/Harvye
Mrs. 244
Cristiana 256
Cristianam 256
Cristinam 256
Elizabeth 51
Isabel 465
Johan 257
Johem 256
John 229, 243, 256
Katherine 244
Peter 243
Richard 244
Ricu 256
Robert 230, 243, 244, 258, 465
Robt. 243
Symon 258
Thomas 243, 244, 257

Harvie. See Harvey.
Harvy(e). See Harvey.
Harwar, Margaret 231
Harward, Alse 231
Jane 231
Joh'i 266
John 266
Jone 231
Margarete 232
Margarett 231, 232
Thomas 231, 266
Thos. 266
Harwod, Robertus 251
Harwood, (?), Elizabeth 251
Jo. 270
John 270
Hase, Elizabeth 646
Thomas 646
Haseltine, Charles F. 485
James 485
John 485
Hasket, Elias 940
Haskett, Bennett 511
Elizabeth 940
Haskit, (.) 940
Haskitt, Elias 940
Elizabeth 940
Hannah 940
Martha 940
Mary 940
Sarah 940
Stephen 940
Hasleden, Jane 730
John 723, 735
Rafe 733
Haslegreeve, Ellen 735
Hassam, Mr. 682
John T. 230, 249, 943
Hassard, William 921
Hastings, Elizabeth de 770
Sir Henry de 770
Sir John de 770
Dame Marg't 70
Hasye, Rychard 283
Hatch, Elizabeh 293, 294
Elizabeth 293, 294
John 64, 294
Will'mus 587
Hatcham, William 256
Hather, Widow 8
Hatherleigh, Elizabeth 960
John 960
Tymothy 960
Hatherly, Timothy 960
Hathorne, Mrs. 940
John 465, 940
Martha 940
Nath. 940
Hatley, (?) 273
Hatter, James 945
Richard 869
Hauck, Johannes 593
Haughton, Agnes of 177
Edward 715
Henry 300, 715
James 715, 743
John 715
Nicholas 715
Ranulf de 177
Richard 715
Richarde 713
Haukins, Richard 265
Hause, Adiell 297
Agnes 281
Anne 297

Henry 281
Hugh 281
Joan 281
John 281
Margery 281
Mary 281
Raffe 281
Rich. 297
William 281
Haux, John 298
Hawcliffe, (?) 251
Margaret 251
Hawell, John 721
Hawes/Hawis/Haws(e)/
Hawys
(?) 273, 274, 276,
288, 297
Goodman 283
A-(?) 297
Abigaill 292
Adiel 296, 297
Agnes 280,281, 282,
284, 285, 287, 288,
289, 290, 291, 292,
298
Alice 278, 282, 283,
285, 286, 290, 292,
293, 298
Alis 279
Amey 285, 290
Amye 283
An 277, 296
Ann 273, 275, 277,
296, 297, 298
Anna 277
Anne 277, 280, 284,
285, 288, 296, 297,
298
Anthony 284
Benedict 294
Benett 278, 290
Bennet 293, 297, 298
Bennett 290, 298
Catherine 273, 281
Cisley 290
Cleames 283
Constance 273, 274
Dennis 297
Edmond 271, 272, 274,
275, 276
Edmund 275, 282, 288,
298
Edward 275, 283, 288,
293, 297, 298
Elenor 297
Elinor 273, 297
Elizabeth 273, 274,
275, 279, 284, 286,
288, 291, 292, 293,
295, 295, 296, 297,
298
Elline 287, 290
Elyn 282
Elzabeth 284
Faith 298
Faythe 290
Frances 294, 296, 297,
298
Francis 271, 292, 297
Frank M. 271
Frank Mortimer 277, 295
George 278, 281, 288
Hana 278, 293
Hanna 297
Harry 286
Henery 298
Henrie 298
Henry 281, 282, 285,

287, 292, 293, 294,
296, 297
Henrye 287
Hew 287
Hugh 286
Humfrey 285, 286
Humfry 298
Isabell 281, 286, 287
James Anderson 271
James W. 271, 276
Jane 274, 275, 279,
281, 284, 296
Joan 279, 281, 298
Joane 280, 286, 292,
293, 297
John 271, 275, 278,
279, 280, 282, 283,
284, 285, 286, 287,
288, 290, 291, 292,
294, 296, 297, 298
Jonas 296
Jone 282, 283
Joseph 297
Julya 281
Katerine 291
Katherine 291, 292
Lucy 275
Margaret 273, 276,
282, 286, 288, 292,
296
Margery 282, 284, 296
Margret 286
Marie 298
Martha 296
Mary 275, 279, 283,
284, 290, 292, 293,
294, 297, 298
Mathew 295, 296
Mathewe 296
Matthew 291, 296
Maudlin 296
Michael 284
Myhyll 284
Nicholas 280, 288, 289,
290, 291, 292
Nicolas 291
Obadiah 277, 296
Obadias 278, 293
Obediah 277
Phillipe 286
Priscilla 293, 296
Rafe 284, 289
Raffe 284
Ralfe 297
Ralph 284, 285, 286,
287, 291
Ralphe 285, 286, 287,
297
Raphe 285
Rich. 296
Richard 271, 275, 277,
278, 279, 280, 281,
282, 284, 285, 288,
289, 290, 291, 293,
294, 295, 296, 297,
298
Robert 275, 282, 285,
286, 288, 295, 297,
298
Ruth 275
Rychard 284
Samuell 295, 296
Sara 297
Sarah 292
Sibbell 296
Susan 287, 296
Susanna 296, 297
Thomas 272, 273, 274,

275, 276, 279, 280,
281, 282, 284, 285,
286, 287, 288, 289,
291, 292, 293, 295,
297, 298
Thruston 284
Umphrey 283
Ursula 272, 274, 275
William 272, 273, 274,
275, 279, 280, 281,
283, 285, 286, 287,
288, 289, 290, 291,
292, 295, 296, 298
Willm 279, 285, 286
Willyam 289, 291
Wyllm 279
Hawfoote, Peter 56
Hawghton, Anne 740
James 740
Nicholas 740
Richard 740
Hawies, Alis 279
Henry 279
Mary 279
Richard 279
Robert 279
Thomas 279
Hawis. See Hawes.
Hawkes, Bridget 890
John 898
Mary 877, 890, 898
Samuel 890
William 890
Hawkins, (?) 437
Capt. 926, 927
David 406
Elizabeth 669
Capt. Thomas 926
Haws. See Hawes.
Hawse. See Hawes.
Hawtain, (?) 300
Edward 299
Hawtaine, Gerrard 300
Henrie 299, 300
Henry 299, 300
Margaret 299, 300
Mary 299, 300
Thomas 299
Hawtayne, Mrs. 299
Edward 300
George H. 299
Gerald 300
Henry 300
Margaret 299, 300
Rev. W. 299
Rev. Wm. 299
Hawten, Edward 300
Gerrard 300
Thomas 300
Hawthen, Edward 300
Gerald 300
Gerrard 300
Margaret 300
Hawys. See Hawes.
Haxby, Stabler 867
Haydock, Evan 735
Hayes, (?) 298
Benedick 298
Benjamin 298
Bennett 298
Elizabeth 646
John 940
Radulph 298
Robert 298
Thomas 646, 648
Hayfield, Judith 941
Martha 941
Mary 941

Richard 941
Ruth 941
Sarah 941
Hayler, (?) 342
Tho. 342
Hayman, John 588
Hayme, Alce 941, 942
Elizabeth 942
Marie 942
Mary 942
Roose 941
Suffraine 942
Susan 941
Thomas 942
Walter 942
Haymes, Elizabeth 941
Walter 941
Hayne, (?) 162, 587
Alice 941
John 942
Richard 586
Walter 941, 942
Haynes, Gen. 305
Gov. 308
Maj. Gen. 308
Mr. 303
Adriana Grace 310
Alice 302
Ann 305
Anne 192, 301, 306
Catherine 309
Charles 308
D. F. 941
Deborath 192
Elizabeth 192, 941
Emanuel 302, 308
Emanuell 192, 193
Hannae 308
Hannah 307
He. 305, 307
Hezekiah 192, 301, 302
  304, 305, 306, 307,
  309
Gen. Hezekiah 302, 303,
  305, 306, 307
Maj. Gen. Hezekiah 208,
  304
Jabez 418, 419
James 301, 304, 305
Jane 302
Jo. 191
John 191, 192, 193,
  208, 211, 212, 218,
  301, 302, 304, 305,
  306, 307, 308, 309,
  310
Col. John 211
Gov. John 191, 192,
  302, 303, 308, 309,
  310
Jonathan 193
Joseph 309
Rev. Joseph 309
Mabel 192
Margaret 192
Martha 192
Mary 192, 193, 301,
  302, 306, 307, 418,
  419
Nicholas 192, 302, 303
Philadelphia 192
Priscilla 192
Richard 302, 418, 419
Robert 301
Sara 192
Sarah 309
Thomas 301, 302, 303,
  304, 305, 307

Walter 941, 942
William 302, 303, 418,
  419
Hays, Jonathan 299
Haytayne, Gerrard 300
Hayward, Ann 684
Anna 188
Freda Irene Mary 916
J. F. 514
John 188
Richard 640
Sarah 188
Hazard, Elizabeth 326
Hannah 326
Mary 316
Mary Brownell 326
Robert 326
Samuel 326
Sarah 326
Stephen 326
Susanna 326
Thomas 326
Hazely, Clement 298
Hazen, Prof. 961
Tracy Elliot 547, 777
Hazilrigge, Sir Thomas 71
Hazlewood, Edward 71
Hazzard, Elizabeth 326
Heacock, Jesse 900
Jesse G. 894
Jonathan 885
Mary 885
Tacy Thompson 900
William 900
Head, Grace 818
Lawrence 818
Heard, Isaac 803
Sir Isaac 803, 804
Hearing, Dorothy 652
Elizabeth 652
John 652
Julynes 652
Margaret 653
Margeret 652
Richard 652
William 652, 654
Hearinge, Richard 654
William 654
Hearn, Ellen 541
George 541
Hearne, (?) 538
Agnes 537, 538
Alice 537, 539, 540
Ann 539
Catharine 541
Dinah 539
Eady 538
Edmond 537, 542
Edmund 538, 539
Edward 539, 540
Elizabeth 538
Ellen 493, 535, 536,
  539, 540, 541
Ellin 536
Francis 539, 542
George 537, 538, 539,
  540, 541, 542
Grace 539
Hannah 540
Herry 538
Isaac 538
Joan 537, 539, 540
Joane 537, 542
John 537, 538, 539,
  540, 541, 542
Jone 539
Margaret 539, 540
Mary 538, 539

Matthew 537, 538
Matthias 537
Merill 537
Merril 538
Phoebe 538
Robert 537
Sarah 538
Sibbel 537, 538
Silvester 538
Stephen 537
Susan 538, 539
Susanna 537
Sybell 537
Thomas 537, 538
William 537, 538, 539,
  540, 541, 542
Wm. 537
Heart, J. W. 907
Hearth, J. W. 907
Heath, J. W. 907
Hedendon, Sisbell 603
Hedge, Capt. (42
Abraham 942
Ann 942
Elisha 942
Thomas 942, 943
William 943
Capt. William 942
Wm. 942
Hedges, William 236
Hegone, Mogg 582
Heire, Gregorie 138, 144
Hellier, (?) 407
George 408. 572
Humphrey 572
Sarah 407
Sarah Hooke 572
Helme, (?) 326
Mrs. 323
Benedict 327
Chri. 323
Christopher 311, 312,
  314, 315, 316, 317,
  318, 300, 321, 322,
  323, 324, 325, 326
Dorcas 326
Elizabeth 326
James 327
John 321, 326
Jonathan 327
Margaret 321, 324,
  326
Margarett 324
Marget 324
Mary 325, 326
Mercy 326
Nathaniel 327
Oliver 327
Rouse 321, 325, 326
  327
Rowland 635
Samuel 325, 326, 327
Sands, 327
Sarah 327
Silas 327
Simeon 327
Thomas 326
William 314, 316, 317,
  320, 321, 325, 326,
  327
Helmes, Mr. 322, 324
Chri. 322
Christo. 324
Christopfer 325
Christopher 321, 322,
  324
Margaret 321, 325
Margarett 325

Man, Johan 245
Johannam 245
Johe'm 245
John 245, 246
Mary 246
Oliver 713
Olyve 713
Rich. 745
Richard 746
Thomas 601
William 713
Manbuy, William 236
Manchester, Richard 736
Richarde 717
Mandeville, Arnulf de
169
Sir John 813
William de 36
Manfeld, Lancelot 675,
676
Manfield, Richard 216
Maning, Marmaduke 941
Manis, (?) 698
Manly, J. M. 99
Mann, Conklin 675
George 734
James 748
Jas. 715
Nathaniel 224
Manne, Christopher 740
Elizabethe 740
Ellin 740
James 740
Willm. 740, 741
Manning, Thomas 632
Manninge, Jacob 259
Percival 259
William 638
Mannington, (?) 70
Mannsfielde, William 678
Manou, M. 704
Mansell, Robert 408
Mansfield, Col. 477
Manton, Dr. 375
Manwaring, John 158
Love 677
Oliver 677
Prudence 677
Many, Walter of 64
Mapcrofte, Richard 262
Maplet, (?) 681
Anne 681
Edward 78
Elizabeth 680, 681
Ellen 78, 678, 679,
680, 681
Ellen (?) 680
Henry 78
John 78, 678, 680,681
Rev. John 78, 678,
680
Margaret 78, 681
Mary 78, 680, 681
Mary (?) 681
Sara 680, 681
Thomas 78, 680, 681
Maplett, Dr. 78
Mr. 680
Anne 679
Elizabeth 679
Ellen 680, 682
Ellenn 678
Hellen 680
John 678, 679, 680,
682
Dr. John 77, 78, 678,
681
Margaret 678
Marie 679

Mary 78, 678, 679, 682
Thomas 678, 682
Marbury, Mr. 459, 461
Mrs. 461
Parson 461
Ann 459
Anne 315, 319, 455,
456, 457, 458, 462
Anthony 456, 457, 458,
461
Bridget 456, 458, 461
Catharine 457, 461,
462
Daniel 456, 458
Edward 455, 457
Elizabeth 456, 458,
461
Emma 456, 458
Erasmus 456, 458
Francis 456, 457, 458,
461
Rev. Francis 316, 317
318, 319, 461, 462
George 457
Jeremiah 456
Jeremuth 456, 458
Jerimoth 456
Jerimuth 458
John 456, 458
Katharine 458, 459,
460
Katherine 316, 318,
319
Leonard 487
Mary 456, 457, 461
Stephen 461
Susan 458, 461
Susanna 456
Thomas 461
William 318, 319, 457
Marchante, Elizabeth 194
Margaret 194
Thomas 194
Marcy, Anne 188
John 188
Sarah Hadlock 188
Maret, Richard 524
Marete, Richard 524
Marhsll, Catherine 660
Marion, John 670
Samuel 670
Markham, Sir Clements 45
Wm. 956
Markland, Elizabeth 726
Jas. 720
Matt 726
Marks, Robert 94
Varlborough, (?) 360
Varney, Wm. de 191
Marrage, Widow 599
Marris, Elizabeth 612
Marrow, Samuel 214
Marsh, Eleanor 622
Elizabeth 726
Margaret 562
Peter 725, 726
Thos. 562
Walter 662
Marshall, (?) 628, 657,
658, 772
Dr. 795
Anne 684
Benjamin 684, 685
Beulah 683
Charles 683
Edward 326
Eleanor 684
Elinor 684
Elizabeth 627, 641,

649, 656, 659, 660,
684
George 471
George W. 682, 685,
793
Dr. George William 313
Hannah 683
Henry 685
Jane 258
Joan 657
Johannem 656
Johannes 656
John 559, 655, 656,
682, 683
Joseph 683
Judith 656, 659, 660
Katherine 659
Katherine Mitton 659
Katherine Mytton 658
Marian 916
Marie 682, 683
Martha 266
Mary 326, 656, 659,
660, 683, 684
Ralph 655
Ricardus 656
Richard 655, 656, 657,
659, 660, 683, 685
Robert 684
Roger 656, 657, 658,
659
Sybill 682, 683
Sybilla 683
Thomas 326, 655,656,
659, 660
Willelmi 656
William 655, 656, 657
Will'm 559
Marshall als Baker, Rich-
ard 655
Marsham, Sir John, Bart.
664
Thomas 664
Marshe, Dr. 725
John 720
Thomas 732
Marson, Thomas 503
Wyllam 503
Marston, Richard 524
Martaine, Thomas 841,
844
Marteine, John 844
Martel, Geoffrey 33
Marten, Bridget 527
Elizabeth 527
Henrici 232, 233, 239,
243
Henrico 246
Martin, Abigail 833, 844
Alice 869, 871
Anne 841, 869, 871
Christopher 953
Elizabeth 527
Joanna 227
John 844
Rev. John 812
Joseph 844
Mary 8ᵉ8
Richard 844
Robert 227, 869, 871
Susan 812
Susan T. 677
Susannah 812
Thomas 841, 844, 845
William 844
Rev. William 812
Wilmote 844
Wilmott 844

1016

Moor, Anne 116
Bridget 116
Catherine 115, 116
Rev. Charles 788
Edward 115, 116
Elizabeth 116
Enoch 115, 116
Felice 116
Francis 116
Nicholas 116
Phillip 115
Samuel 116
Sar. 114
Sara 116
Thomas 114, 115, 116
Williamin 116
Moore, (?) 943
Mr. 253
Alice 418, 419
Anna 115
Anne 116, 118, 121
Bridget 116
Catherine 115, 116
Edward 115, 116, 117,
118, 119, 121, 137,
162, 563
Elizabeth 116, 119,
120, 121, 457
Ellinora 764
Enoch 115, 116, 117,
118, 119, 120, 121
Enoche 120
Felice 116
Francis 116, 120, 121,
122
George 898
Hercules 852
Jane 116
Jasperus 764
John 65, 110, 112, 121,
943
Jonathan 943
Joseph 943
Judith 116
Katherine 121, 122
Margaret 121
Maria 764
Mary 116, 137
Maurice Peter 563
Merry 116
Nicholas 115, 116, 117,
118, 120, 121
Phillip 115, 118, 120
Richard 763
Richarde 780
Richardus 764
Roy 910
Samueila 118
Samuel 115, 116, 117,
118, 119, 121, 122
Samuelis 764
Sara 116, 118, 119,
121
Sarah 122
Thomas 115, 116, 118,
119, 120, 121, 122
Willamin 116, 117, 118,
119
William 115
Moorehouse, Rebecca 962
Mooreton, Mr. 239
Moorhouse, Henry P. 481
Morcar, Thegn 168
More, (?) 763
Dr. 615
Alice 103
Caterinae 764
Catherine 764, 765, 766
767, 768, 769

Elizabeth 767
Ellen 763, 769
Enoch 115
Francis 114, 115
Jasper 763, 764, 767,
769, 770
John 284
Judith 115
Katharine 765
Katherine 765, 766,
767, 769, 770
Mercy 621
Merry 115
Nicholas 115
Richard 543, 763, 764,
767, 769, 770
Robert 615, 621
Samuel 114, 117, 543,
764, 767, 768, 769,
770
Samuelis 764
Samuell 115, 765, 766,
767
Sara 115
Thomas 770
Sir Thomas 66
William 253
Morel, Arkil 174, 175
Morepeth, Peter de 30
Moreton, Mr. 239
Mris. 239
Thomas, Bishop of
Chester 741
Morgan, (?) 424
Master 252
Anne 158
John 70, 891
Sylvanus 56
W. Istlyn 420
Moriarty, Mr. 484
G. A. 487
Prof. G. Andrews 670
George Andrews 317,
320, 379, 483, 585,
753, 771, 841, 945,
Morice Baronets 751
Secretary 750
Jevan 751
Sir William 750
Morison, Samuel Eliot
792
Morley, James 617
John 613, 619
William 855
Morphy, Rev. Richard
401
Morrell, John Dorrance 1,
12
Morres, Jas. 720
Richard 716
Morrice, Jennit 726
Morris, (?) 636, 639
Mr. 629, 631
Anne 272
David 527
George 629
John 733
Joseph 629, 630, 649,
651, 654, 655
Col. Maurice Morgan
905
Rt. 762
Thomas 443
Morrison, Hannah 478
James 888
Sarah 478
Thomas 478
Morrys, Jas. 714
Mors, Count de 958

Widow Margaret 958
Morse, Abner 959
Rev. Abner 67, 959
Annas 771
Anthony 958
Daniell 957
David 379
Dea. David 379
Edward 958
Ezra 379, 380, 382
J. Howard 771
James 957
Jeremye 957
Joanna 379, 382
John 91, 379, 771,
957
Rev. John 379
Joseph 957
Lyonell 95
Margaret 957
Margarett 957, 958
Nathaniel 379, 958
Nathaniell 957
Nicholas 959
Peter 379
Phillip 957
Richard 957
Robert 958
Sir Robert 959
Samuel 379, 771, 957,
958
Sara 957
Dea. Seth 379
Tho. 728
Thomas 957, 958
Rev. Thomas 957, 958
959
William 958
Morswood, John 832
Morteine, Johis de 28
Morteyn, Catherine de 25
Constance de Merston
de 25
Edmund de 25
Magister Edmund de 25
Elizabeth 27
Elizabeth de 25, 27,
28
Joan de 25, 28, 38
John 27
John de 25, 26, 27,
28
Sir John de 27, 28,
29, 38
Lucy de 19, 38
Thomas de 25
Morteyne, Johi de 28
Mortifield, Ione 844
Mortimer, Joan 771
John 559
Sir Walter 771
Mortimore, Elinor 960
Mortimore als Tanner,
Henry 960
Matthew 960
William 960
Mortmer, Ellen 297
Morton, Mr. 237, 243
Nicholai 243
Nicholas 247
Rev. Nicholas 243
Nichollas 241, 242
Thos. 64
Mortymer, Nicholas 960
Morville, Hugh de 169,
170
Thomas 169
Morvois, Bertha de 673
Mosely, Capt. 360

1021

Richard 866, 867, 868,
870, 872, 873, 874,
875, 876, 878, 879,
881, 883, 885, 887,
888, 889, 890, 891,
895, 896, 897, 898,
899, 901, 902, 903,
904, 905, 906, 910,
911, 912, 913, 914,
915, 916, 917, 918,
919, 920
Richard Lewis 919
Robert 867, 868, 870,
872, 873, 874, 875,
876, 878, 879, 880,
881, 883, 884, 885,
886, 887, 888, 889,
890, 891, 892, 893,
894, 895, 896, 897,
898, 899, 900, 901,
902, 903, 904, 905,
906, 907, 908, 910,
911, 912, 913, 914,
915, 916, 917, 918,
919, 920
Robert FitzGerald 905
Robert Samuel 903
Robert Tait 906
Robert Uniacke Fitz-
Gerald 898, 904
Robert William 877,
878, 899, 906, 911,
914, 916
Robert William Edward
914
Roger John 920
Roland Algernon 916,
920
Rory Desmond Fane 918
Rosemary Ruth 918
Ruth Esme 917
Samuel 876, 877, 878,
881, 883, 885, 889,
890, 892, 893, 894,
895, 897, 898, 899,
900, 903, 905, 906,
908, 911, 914, 915,
918, 919, 920
Samuel George 899
Samuel Neale 888, 896,
897, 903, 911, 916
Sar Elizabeth 906
Sarah 883, 885, 886,
888, 889, 890, 891,
892, 893, 894, 895,
896, 897, 900, 901,
902
Sarah Ann 896
Sarah Eliza 903, 911
Sarah Elizabeth 898,
902
Sarah Josephine 917
Sheila Margaret 920
Shirley Victoria 920
Steadman 880, 900, 908,
909, 914, 915, 919
Mrs. Steadman 909
Stidman 908
Susan 918
Susan Alice 906
Susan Ann 907
Susanna 887, 894
Susannah 887
Susanne 890
Sylvia Janet 913
Tacy 900
Thomas 866, 867, 868,
869, 870, 871, 872,

874, 875, 876, 878,
881, 883, 884, 885,
886, 887, 888, 889,
890, 891, 892, 893,
894, 895, 896, 897,
898, 899, 900, 901,
902, 903, 904, 905,
906, 907, 908, 910,
911, 912, 913, 914,
915, 916, 917, 918,
919, 920
Capt. Thomas 864
Virgil Clare 919
Washington Hicks 900,
907
Weston Boyd 919
William 866, 867, 868,
870, 871, 872, 873,
874, 876, 877, 878,
880, 881, 883, 885,
886, 887, 888, 889,
890, 891, 892, 893,
894, 895, 897, 898,
899, 900, 901, 904,
905, 906, 910, 912,
913, 914, 917, 918
William C. 911
William Dennis 919
William Edward 889
William H. 901
William Henry 890,
897, 899, 905, 917
William Oscar 915
William Robert 906,
914
William W. 902
William Watherston 906
Penrose-FitzGerald, Cecil
Philippa Uniacke 917
Charles Bryan 912
Charles Cooper 904,
917
Adm. Charles Cooper
912
Edward Uniacke 912
Elizabeth Constance
917
Geraldine Frances
Louisa 904
Geraldine Patricia 917
Herbert James Cooper
912
James Henry Brabazon
904, 905
John Henry Brabazon
912
John Uniacke 912
Rear Adm. John Uniacke
917
Laura Frances 912
Mae 904
Mary Elizabeth 912
Matilda Sophia Geor-
gina 904
Maurice John 912
Michael John Robert
Uniacke 917
Nesta Fanny Harriet
912
Robert 912
Robert Francis Uniacke
912, 917
Robert Uniacke 904,
917
Sir Robert Uniacke,
Bart. 912
Romayne 917
Sarah 912

Timothy Michael 917
Penrose-Thackwell, Col.
914
Elenor Maude Charlotte
914
Geoffrey Joseph Elliott
914
Marjory Helen Florence
914
Mary Geraldine Harriet
914
William John Rawdon
914
Penrose-Welstead, Eleanor
Mary 919
Frank Philip 914
Harry Hugh 914
Iris 914
Reginald Hugh 919
Rosemary Geraldine
919
Samuel 918
Rev. Samuel 914
Samuel Quayle 914, 918
Samuel Richard 918
Penthievre, Count of
171
Alan of 172
Brian of 172
Eudes, Count of 172
Pentres, Thomas 287
Penyngt'n, Elizabeth
713
Pepin, Count of Senlis
673
Pepin, K. of Italy 673
Pepis, Mary 86
Pepper, Elizabeth 188
Pepper(r)ell, Sir Willi-
am 695, 803
Pepys, (?) 940
Elizabeth 86
Isaac 123
Judith 86
Mary Gosnold 86
Richard 86
Sir Richard 86, 88
Perch, Eleanor 660
Eleanor Sherrer 660
George 660
John 660
Katherine 660
Thomas 660
Percival, Sarah 685
Percy, George 105
Henry, D. of Northum-
berland 105
Perfect, George 919
Gertrude Eugenia 919
Perimar, Roger 278
Rychard 278
Perkin, Mr. 653
Richard 852
Perkins, Alia 921
Anna 695
Anne 921, 968
Bathsua 968
Beatrice 968
Catherine 968
Edward 921, 968
Eleanor 921
Eliza 695
Elizabeth 921, 968
Frances 968
Francis 921
George 921, 968
Harrington 968

Mary 377, 378
Ruth 377, 378
Quinsey, (?) 369, 377
  Daniel 222
Quint, Rev. Alonzo H.
  940
Quintilianus, (?) 761
Rabaud, Catherine 812
Rabenett, Thomas 234
Rabone, George 623
Rackham, Bertha 916
Radcliff, James de 748
  Ric de 748
Radcliffe, Mr. 558
  Alex. 735, 747
  Alexander 743, 747
  Heath 740
Radclyf, Ric de 748
Radclyffe, Alexander 746,
  747
Radford, Stephanus 587
Radlynne, Alice 599
Radwell, Em. 808
Raimes, John 920
Rainsborough, Judith 113
  Martha 108
  William 113
  Capt. William 108, 113
  Wm. 220
  Col. Wm. 220
Rainsford, Joan 273
Raistone, Thomas 953
Rait, Barbara 801
  John 801
  Robert 801
  Wm. 801
Raithbeck, Thomas 448
Ralegh, William 484
Raleigh, Bridget 319
  Sir Edward 319
  Sir Walter 71, 73
  William 483, 484
Ralph, son of Osmund 36
Rance, Richard 283
Randall, Barnard 855
  Ellen Maplett 679
  George 878, 889, 890
  Margaret 878, 890
  Margaret Devonsher 889,
  890
  Mary 878, 889
  Mathew 678
  Matthew 678, 679, 680,
  682
  Samuel 878
  William 679, 680
Randdole, (?) 287
Randes, Widow 8
Randoll, Jone 680
  Mathewe 680
Randolph, (?) 54, 61
Rands, James 917
Ranicar, Roger 745
Ranicker, Roger 746
Ranikares, Roger 740
Ranolds, Robert 181
Ransom, Elizabeth 916
Rapin, Mr. 687, 692
  M. de 691
Rasing, Anne 251
  John 251
  Rafe 251
  Ralphe 251
  Richard 251
  Thomas 251
  Wm. 251
Rastall, William 272
Ratcliffe, Sir Alexander
  470

Jane 470
Ratliffe, Mr. 261
Raudenbush, Rebecca 909
Raunce, Edward 286
Raven, Susan 758
Raw, Alice 872
Rawlins, Henry 256
Rawlinson, Joh'es 266
Rawson, Edw. 343
  Edward 412
  ffrances 550
  M'tine 780
  William 343
Rawsone, Ranse 781, 782
Ray, Catherine 585
  Mary 585
  Mary Thomas 585
  Simon 585
Raye, Simon 709
Raymes, George 868
  Jane 868
  Janie 868
Rayner, Richard 233
Raynolds, Henry 745
Raynsford, Edward 343
Raysing, Ralph 252
  Rose 251, 252
Read, Mr. 873, 875
  Christopher 941
  Elizabeth 941
  Ernest 918
  ffrancis 825
  Hugo 865, 873, 877,
  878, 881, 918
  Hugo Ernest Gildart
  917, 918
  John 941
  Marmaduke 941, 942
  Susan Brigid 918
  Thomas 941
  William 941
Reade, Col. 609
  Alice 262
  Edmund 598, 600, 608,
  609
  Elizabeth 941
  Elizabeth Cook 608
  Sir John 616
  Margaret 598, 608
  Col. Thomas 609
Reason, Radulphi 251
  Rose 239, 245, 248,
  251
Redding, Em. 296
Redfort, John 131
  Robert 131
  Thomas 131
Redge, Joan 520
  Johan 527
  Oliver 520, 527
Redstone, L. J. 97, 278
  Lilian J. 93, 98, 710
  785
  Lillian J. 106
  Vincent Burrough 710
Reed, Col. James 822
  Sarah 886
  Thomas 886
Reede, Richard 262
Reepham, (?) 312
Reeps, John 465
Rees, John ap 525, 531
Reeve, (?) 847
  John 726
  Thomas 847
Regester, David 884
  John 884
  Joseph 884

Robert 884
Reignolde, George 600,
  605, 606
Reignolt, Owen ap 630
Reine, Fred'k 189
Reinger, (?) 663
Remington, (?) 448
  James 448
Renalls, (?) 738
Rendle, Mr. 229, 269
  William 229, 269
Rene, John 286
Renett, Thos. 579
Repley, George 284
Rerd, Ned 727
Rett, Edward 825
Revell, Mr. 774
  John 774
Revett, Robert 93
Reymes, William 825
Reyner, Rev. Jno. 378
  Rev. John 377
  Richard 713
Reynes, John 27
  John de 27
  Richard 26, 27
  Richard de 27
  Thomas 27
  Thomas de 27
  Sir Thomas 26
Reynoldes, Anne 601, 607
  Marie 601, 607
Reynolds, Joseph 684
  Richard 110, 284, 286
Reynoulde, John 524
Rhames, George 868
  Jane 868
Rheged, Urian 426
Rhys Sais 629
  Elidir ap 631
Rice, Robert Garraway
  247
Rich, Baron 533
  Richard 533
  Robert 798
Richard I, Coeur de Lion,
  K. of Eng. 831
Richard II, K. of Eng.
  760
Richard III, K. of Eng.
  760
Richard, Duke 29
Richard, Jeffrey ap 633
Richards, (?) 892
  Alice 891, 892, 893
  Richard 524
  Roger 524
Richardson, Amos 892,
  893
  David 479
  Douglas 1
  Lieut.-Gen. Sir George
  913
  Hannah 479
  Joseph 480
  Joshua 376
  Katherine 550
  Rebecca 479
  Ruth Louisa 480
  Sarah 480
  Thos. 720
Richbell, Abraham 599
Richey, Nellie M. 919
Richmond, Earl of. See
  Alan the Red.
Richmond, Ann 78
  Christopher 78
  John 644

1037